1,001 SAT Practice Questions

for dummies®
A Wiley Brand

by Ron Woldoff

1,001 SAT Practice Questions For Dummies®

Published by: **John Wiley & Sons, Inc.**, 111 River Street, Hoboken, NJ 07030-5774, www.wiley.com

For general information on our other products and services, please contact our Customer Care Department within the U.S. at 877-762-2974, outside the U.S. at 317-572-3993, or fax 317-572-4002. For technical support, please visit www.wiley.com/techsupport.

Wiley publishes in a variety of print and electronic formats and by print-on-demand. Some material included with standard print versions of this book may not be included in e-books or in print-on-demand. If this book refers to media such as a CD or DVD that is not included in the version you purchased, you may download this material at http://booksupport.wiley.com. For more information about Wiley products, visit www.wiley.com.

Library of Congress Control Number: 2016935432

ISBN 978-1-119-21584-4 (pbk); ISBN 978-1-119-21563-9 (ebk); ISBN 978-1-119-21566-0 (ebk)

Manufactured in the United States of America

10 9 8 7 6 5 4 3 2 1

Contents at a Glance

Table of Contents

Introduction

Welcome to *1,001 SAT Practice Questions For Dummies*. Don't take the *dummies* thing literally — you're obviously smart and capable. You're getting through high school and about ready to go to college. You'll graduate to join the elite group of approximately 30 percent of U.S. citizens who hold bachelor's degrees, and some of you will even go on to graduate or doctorate school.

Between you and your goal is the SAT: a test designed to challenge your ability to remember everything you've learned how to do since freshman year. To clear this hurdle, you need some practice and pointers on how best to answer the questions. This book provides that and more: It goes beyond providing relevant practice questions by showing simple and effective ways to solve challenging SAT problems.

What You'll Find

The SAT practice problems in this book are divided into five chapters: two verbal, two math, and one writing. Questions are adjusted and repeated to give you practice and mastery. If you struggle with one question, you can find a group of similar questions to practice and hone your skills. This book serves as an effective standalone refresher of SAT basics or as an excellent companion to the latest edition of *SAT For Dummies* (Wiley). Either way, this book helps you identify subject areas you need to work on so you can practice them until you're a pro and thus prepare for test day.

If you get a problem wrong, don't just read the answer explanation and move on. Instead, come back to the problem and solve it again, this time avoiding the mistake you made the first time. This is how you improve your skills and figure out how to solve the problems correctly and easily.

Whatever you do, stay positive. The challenging problems in this book aren't meant to discourage you; they're meant to show you how to solve and master them.

How This Book Is Organized

The first half of this book gives you questions covering reading and English, math, and essay writing. All the answers and explanations are in the second half of the book.

The reading and verbal questions in this book cover the following topics:

- **Reading comprehension:** The SAT gives you five reading passages or pairs of passages along with ten or eleven questions based on each. The questions challenge your ability to discern the purpose of the passage and the significance of the details.
- **English/Writing:** The SAT also gives you four writing passages, each with eleven questions, that give you the opportunity to correct for grammar, rewrite a phrase for style and clarity, or add or move a sentence for logic and flow. These questions are designed to see how well you write clearly and effectively.

True to the actual exam, about a third of the math questions in this book should be worked without a calculator, and the rest, with a calculator. Also, about a fourth of these questions aren't multiple-choice: Instead, you fill in the answer. These questions cover the following topics:

- **Arithmetic:** These questions are based on core arithmetic concepts, including prime numbers, absolute values, decimals, fractions, and ratios. Don't be fooled by their simple nature: These questions can be as challenging as any that you find on the SAT.
- **Geometry:** Geometry covers basic shapes, such as triangles, circles, and squares. These questions also go into basic 3D solids, including cylinders, boxes, prisms, spheres, and cones.
- **Algebra:** These questions are extensions of arithmetic, going into exponents, square roots, and numeric sequences. They explore variations of solving for x and linear equations having x and y.
- **Word problems:** No set of word problems is complete without the two trains coming from Chattanooga. These questions cover those types of problems along with averages, probability, and setting up equations from a story.
- **Graphs and data interpretation:** The SAT problems feature variations of challenging tables and graphs; you're given a graph or two along with a few questions based on those graphs.

You have the option of writing a single, 50-minute essay on the SAT, and these pages provide plenty of practice. For your essay, the SAT gives you an opinion piece or call to action in the form of a reading passage. Your task is to demonstrate that you comprehend the passage by analyzing the way that the author approaches the topic. The SAT does *not* ask for your opinion, so be sure to stay objective.

Beyond the Book

Your purchase of this book gives you so much more than a thousand (and one) problems to work on to improve your skills with the SAT. It also comes with a free, one-year subscription to hundreds of practice questions online. Not only can you access this digital content anytime you want, on whichever device is available to you, but you can also track your progress and view personalized reports that show you which concepts you need to study the most.

What you'll find online

The online practice that comes free with this book offers you the same questions and answers that are available here. Of course, the real beauty of the online problems is your ability to customize your practice. In other words, you get to choose the types of problems and the number of problems you want to tackle. The online program tracks how many questions you answer correctly versus incorrectly so you can get an immediate sense of which topics need more of your attention.

This product also comes with an online Cheat Sheet that helps you increase your odds of performing well on the SAT. To get the Cheat Sheet, go to `www.dummies.com` and type this book's title in the Search box. (No access code required. You can benefit from this info before you even register.)

How to register

To gain access to practice online, all you have to do is register. Just follow these simple steps:

1. **Find your PIN access code:**
   - **Print-book users:** If you purchased a print copy of this book, turn to the inside front cover of the book to find your access code.
   - **E-book users:** If you purchased this book as an e-book, you can get your access code by registering your e-book at `www.dummies.com/go/getaccess`. Go to this website, find your book and click it, and answer the security questions to verify your purchase. You'll receive an email with your access code.
2. **Go to `Dummies.com` and click *Activate Now.***
3. **Find your product (*1,001 SAT Practice Questions For Dummies*) and then follow the on-screen prompts to activate your PIN.**

Now you're ready to go! You can come back to the program as often as you want — simply log in with the username and password you created during your initial login. No need to enter the access code a second time.

TIP

For Technical Support, please visit `http://wiley.custhelp.com` or call Wiley at: 1-800-762-2974 (U.S.) or +1-317-572-3994 (international).

Where to Go for Additional Help

The solutions to the practice problems in this book are meant to walk you through how to get the right answers; they're not meant to teach the material. If certain concepts are unfamiliar to you, you can find help at `www.dummies.com`. Just type "SAT" into the search box to turn up a wealth of SAT-related information.

If you need more detailed instruction, check out *SAT For Dummies*, 9th Edition, written by Gerri Woods and yours truly.

1 The Questions

IN THIS PART . . .

Become familiar with the ways the SAT asks you to comprehend reading passages. Answer questions about purpose, main ideas, supporting information, details, vocabulary, and more.

Correct writing mistakes in the English/Writing section. Fix grammar and punctuation, add clarity, improve style and flow, and demonstrate logic in writing.

Check your understanding of math concepts and calculations on the No-Calculator and Calculator sections of the SAT. Work on hundreds of arithmetic, algebra, geometry, data-interpretation, and word problems so you can recognize common traps and tricks.

Practice writing essays that analyze someone else's argument.

Chapter 1

Reading Comprehension

Reading comprehension questions on the SAT are grouped by passage, where a single passage has ten or eleven questions on it. The passage appears once, and the questions follow sequentially.

All Reading Comprehension questions are based directly on what's in the passage. You don't need to know anything about the subject outside the passage. If you're familiar with the topic, you may easily comprehend the passage, but be careful not to mix your own knowledge of the topic with what's in the passage.

The Problems You'll Work On

When working through the questions in this chapter, be prepared to

- Choose one answer from a multiple-choice selection.
- Select a sentence from the passage to support a previous answer.
- Answer questions based on biological and physical science topics, including physics, chemistry, and astronomy.
- Understand the impact of social science topics, including history, psychology, and business.
- Get the gist of humanities topics, including art, music, philosophy, drama, and literature.

What to Watch Out For

Trap answers include the following:

- Facts that aren't mentioned in the passage
- Things that are true but don't answer the question
- Terms that twist the facts around, such as *never* for *always*

Passage A

Questions 1–10 are based on the following information. Read the passage and answer each question based on information stated or implied in the passage.

The following passage is an excerpt from Introverts For Dummies, *by Joan Pastor, PhD (Wiley).*

Fifty percent of gifted kids are introverts. And three-quarters of "supergifted" kids — children with IQs above 160 — are innies.

You'd think these brilliant kids would flourish in school, but frequently, they don't. Instead, they may spend hours bored to tears as their teachers go over material they already know. They may also get into trouble for ignoring classroom assignments and pursuing their own interests instead. Worse yet, these children's remarkable talents often go undeveloped.

That's why smart parents often seek better options for them. If you think your introverted child is gifted, ask for a professional evaluation by a psychologist. If testing confirms your opinion, ask your school what services it offers for gifted children. Some schools have excellent programs for very bright children, while others fall far short.

If your child's current school can't fully meet her needs, explore other options. Some communities have magnet schools specifically designed for gifted children. Your child may also enjoy a math, science, or arts camp during the summer. And museums, nature centers, and recreation centers frequently offer programs that will excite your innie.

Additionally, consider supplementing your child's education with online courses on her favorite topics. Often, these courses allow students to learn at their own pace, so instead of twiddling her thumbs while she waits for her classmates to catch up, your child can go full steam ahead. The Khan Academy (`www.khanacademy.org`) and other free online educational sites can also be great resources.

If your child is far more advanced than other kids her age, her school may suggest moving her up an extra grade. But be aware that gifted innies who are way ahead of the pack intellectually may still need to be around same-age peers to learn social skills. So if this option comes up, consider your child's overall social and intellectual development and ask yourself if she's truly ready to study — and play — with older children.

Another issue to keep in mind is that the higher a child's IQ is, the greater the chances are that the child will also have a learning disability. If your child is gifted but still struggles in some areas, make sure you explore this possibility.

1. According to the passage, "supergifted" kids most likely do *not*

(A) identify as introverts

(B) have above-average IQs

(C) have advanced social skills

(D) have learning disabilities

2. Pastor claims that which of the following is the reason gifted kids struggle in school?

I. They are shy as introverts.

II. They already know the material.

III. They ignore classroom assignments.

(A) I and II

(B) II and III

(C) I and III

(D) I, II, and III

3. Pastor uses the phrase "these children's remarkable talents" (line 10) to make the point that

(A) the children are more advanced than their peers

(B) the children have a lot to learn

(C) the children should learn a trade

(D) the children could excel as performers

4. Which choice provides the best evidence for the answer to the preceding question?

(A) Lines 4–5 ("You'd think . . . they don't.")

(B) Lines 17–18 ("Some schools . . . fall far short.")

(C) Lines 36–37 ("her school . . . grade.")

(D) Lines 46–47 ("If your child . . . some areas,")

5. The main theme that Pastor describes in the passage is that gifted, introverted children

(A) could excel in the academic setting provided by almost any school

(B) should avoid online distractions from true academic discourse

(C) could benefit from advancing an extra grade to be with peers at their intellectual level

(D) could perform extremely well in the right academic setting

6. Which choice provides the best evidence for the answer to the preceding question?

(A) Lines 4–5 ("You'd think . . . they don't.")

(B) Lines 17–18 ("Some schools . . . fall far short.")

(C) Lines 20–22 ("Some communities . . . children.")

(D) Lines 36–37 ("her school . . . grade.")

7. As used in line 38, "pack" most nearly means

(A) a group of dogs

(B) a group of kids

(C) prepare for a trip

(D) worn on one's back

8. The second paragraph (lines 4–11) is primarily concerned with

(A) drawing a contrast between intellectual ability and academic performance

(B) showing a parallel between suitable surroundings and personal growth

(C) illustrating the success of exploring options outside the child's academic setting

(D) suggesting a possible correlation between high IQ and learning disability

9. Pastor suggests that parents of gifted children should

I. explore options outside the classroom

II. explore schools outside the district

III. explore resources outside the school

(A) I and II

(B) II and III

(C) I and III

(D) I, II, and III

10. Which choice provides the best evidence for the answer to the preceding question?

(A) Lines 4–5 ("You'd think . . . they don't.")

(B) Lines 12–13 ("That's why . . . for them.")

(C) Lines 17–18 ("Some schools . . . fall far short.")

(D) Lines 20–22 ("Some communities . . . children.")

Passage B

Questions 11–20 are based on the following information. Read the passage and answer each question based on information stated or implied in the passage.

The following passage is an excerpt from U.S. History For Dummies, *3rd Edition, by Steve Wiegand (Wiley).*

America's front door was wide open, and people poured in. Between 1866 and 1915, 25 million immigrants came to the United States. Most of them came from Italy and Southeastern Europe, but they also came from Scandinavia, Russia, Poland, Germany, Ireland, England, and France. By 1910, 15 percent of the country's total population was foreign-born. Most of them came to escape hard economic times at home, despotic governments, or both. Many times their expectations were unrealistically high. "America is all puddings and pies!" enthused one young man as he stepped off the ship in New York.

Despite the warning of a popular immigrant guidebook to "forget your past, your customs, and your ideals," many of the new Americans clung to their own languages, customs, and cuisines, and gravitated to communities populated by others from their country. The presence of so many immigrants in so short a time caused alarm in some "natives," who feared the newcomers would weaken their chances in the job market and pollute American culture. But it wasn't until 1921, after World War I had created millions of refugees in Europe, that Congress tightened immigration policies concerning Europeans.

In the meantime, as much as 80 percent of the immigrant wave settled in Northern cities. By the turn of the century, more than a third of Chicago's populace was foreign-born, and there were more Irish in New York City than there were in Ireland. The immigrants weren't the only newcomers in town, because there were plenty of American-born country folks moving to urban areas, as well. By 1900, 30 million Americans lived in cities, about a third of all U.S. residents. The number of cities larger than 100,000 increased from 9 to 50 between 1860 and 1910.

But many parts of the big cities were festering sores. In those areas, fire protection, street cleaning, sewage systems, garbage collection, and water treatment barely existed. The Chicago River was an open sewer. Baltimore's sewers emptied into the tidal basin and in the summer heat, journalist H. L. Mencken wrote, it "smelled like a billion polecats."

Housing was often designed to cram the most people into the least space. It wasn't uncommon for 24 four-room apartments to be built on a 2,500-square-foot lot. Tenement slums took on fitting names, such as "Hell's Kitchen," "Bone Alley," or "Poverty Gap."

Gradually, things improved in the major urban areas. No one, rich or poor, wanted to live in filth, and after the link between disease and poor sanitation was firmly established, city leaders began to develop adequate sewage and water systems. Public transit systems, based on streetcars or trolleys, were put in place. But none of it happened overnight, and more than a few farmers-turned-city-dwellers must have yearned more than once to be home on the range.

11. What is the purpose of the phrase "America is all puddings and pies!" (lines 11–12)?

(A) To demonstrate that immigrants looked forward to eating sweets

(B) To reflect the hope and excitement felt by the immigrants

(C) To show the lifestyle that the immigrants looked forward to

(D) To exemplify the dietary habits of New Yorkers

12. Which choice provides the best evidence for the answer to the preceding question?

(A) Lines 8–10 ("Most of them . . . or both.")

(B) Lines 10–11 ("Many times . . . unrealistically high.")

(C) Lines 40–42 ("In those areas . . . existed.")

(D) Lines 58–59 ("Public transit . . . in place.")

13. What is the purpose of the phrase "there were . . . in Ireland" (lines 30–31)?

(A) To exemplify the presence of immigrants

(B) To show the dwindling population in certain other countries, including Ireland

(C) To allude to the disproportionate number of Irish in New York

(D) To show the dwindling numbers of other Americans

14. Which choice does the answer to the preceding question exemplify?

(A) Lines 8–10 ("Most of them . . . or both.")

(B) Lines 19–23 ("The presence . . . culture.")

(C) Lines 28–30 ("By the turn . . . foreign-born,")

(D) Lines 58–59 ("Public transit . . . in place.")

15. The purpose of the passage is to describe

(A) the countries most immigrants came from

(B) the effects of immigration on cities such as Chicago and New York

(C) Baltimore's billion polecats

(D) the flow of immigrants and the evolution of big American cities

16. In this passage, Wiegand makes use of

(A) literary narrative

(B) metaphor

(C) emotion

(D) persuasion

17. What does Wiegand suggest was the path of many immigrants?

(A) From danger and poverty to comfort and security

(B) From danger and poverty to overcrowding and filth

(C) From comfort and security to overcrowding and filth

(D) From overcrowding and filth to comfort and security

18. According to the passage, which of the following prompted Congress to tighten immigration policies?

(A) The millions of refugees following World War I

(B) The 25 million immigrants between 1866 and 1915

(C) The 80 percent of the immigrant wave that settled in Northern cities

(D) The inner-city housing problems

19. What is the purpose of the last paragraph?

(A) It describes the squalid conditions in the cities.

(B) It suggests that circumstances were starting to improve.

(C) It showcases the farmers who traveled to the city.

(D) It describes a timeline of events.

20. If the numbers stated in the passage are true, which of the following had a 15 percent foreign-born population?

(A) New York City

(B) Chicago

(C) Northern cities

(D) America

Passage C

Questions 21–28 are based on the following information. Read the passage and answer each question based on information stated or implied in the passage.

The following passage is an excerpt from Clinical Anatomy For Dummies, *by David Terfera, PhD, and Shereen Jegtvig, DC, MS (Wiley).*

Each spinal nerve is formed from the convergence of *posterior* and *anterior nerve roots.* The cell bodies of the anterior nerve roots are located in the *anterior horns of gray matter* in the spinal cord, and the cell bodies of posterior nerve roots are located as a mass of cell bodies called the *spinal ganglia* (posterior root ganglia) outside of the cord. The anterior nerve roots contain motor fibers, and the posterior nerve roots contain sensory fibers. The spinal nerve roots merge to form spinal nerves (spinal nerves contain both sensory and motor fibers) where they leave the vertebral canal.

Just past the point where the nerve roots merge, each spinal nerve divides into a *posterior ramus* and an *anterior ramus.* The posterior ramus innervates the skin and deep back muscles, and the anterior ramus innervates the rest of the trunk and the extremities. The rami (like the spinal nerves) are mixed (contains both sensory and motor fibers). The *recurrent meningeal branch of the spinal nerves* innervates most of the vertebral column; however, the zygapophysial joints are innervated by *the medial branches of the posterior rami.*

The spinal cord tapers into a conical-shaped *conus medullaris* and actually ends around the level of the 2nd lumbar vertebra, so the nerve roots that emerge past that point become quite long because they have to extend down to exit the intervertebral foramens in the remaining lumbar and sacral levels. The collection of those spinal roots resembles a horse's tail, so it's referred to as the *cauda equina.*

The spinal nerve roots may be impinged by arthritic osteophytes or by disc herniations. Pressure on the posterior nerve roots causes pain in the back and in any extremity served by the nerve roots being affected. Pressure on anterior nerve roots results in motor weakness. A patient with nerve-root impingement of one of the lumbar spinal nerve roots due to a herniated disc may feel pain and tingling in the buttock, hip, and leg. Nerve-root impingement in the neck can cause pain and weakness in the arm and forearm.

21. According to the passage, the *cauda equine* is so named because it resembles

(A) a tingling leg

(B) a cone

(C) a horse's tail

(D) a cell body

22. A person experiencing pain in the arm and forearm without an actual cause in that area is most likely suffering from

I. arthritic osteophytes

II. disc herniations

III. innervated vertebral column

(A) I and II

(B) II and III

(C) I and III

(D) I, II, and III

23. The purpose of the passage is to

(A) describe the placement of the spinal nerves

(B) explore the issues that arise from maladies such as herniated discs

(C) discuss the naming conventions of certain features

(D) illustrate the roles of certain spinal nerves

24. The purpose of the last paragraph is to

(A) support the theory that motor weakness arises from issues with the spine

(B) explore the tapering of the spinal cord into the *cauda equina*

(C) explain the causes of pain and tingling in the extremities

(D) describe the causes and symptoms of impinged spinal nerve roots

25. According to the passage, each spinal nerve is formed by

I. posterior nerve roots

II. anterior nerve roots

III. medial branch roots

(A) I and II

(B) II and III

(C) I and III

(D) I, II, and III

26. The use of the word "actually" (line 25) suggests that

(A) most textbooks describe the spinal cord ending at the 1st lumbar vertebra

(B) there is a common misconception about the placement of the spinal cord

(C) one would expect the spinal cord to extend through all the vertebrae

(D) the nerve roots that emerge past the 2nd lumbar vertebra are typically considered part of the spinal cord

27. Past the point where the nerve roots merge, each spinal nerve divides into

(A) the posterior and anterior nerve roots

(B) the posterior and anterior rami

(C) the recurrent meningeal branch

(D) the medial branches of the posterior rami

28. Sensory motor fibers are contained within

I. posterior nerve roots

II. anterior nerve roots

III. the anterior ramus

(A) I and II

(B) II and III

(C) I and III

(D) I, II, and III

29. In context, the word "mixed" (line 19) means

(A) diverse

(B) combined

(C) assorted

(D) hybrid

30. How are the rami specifically like the spinal nerves?

(A) Both are primarily motor fibers.

(B) Both are spinal nerves.

(C) Both contain a combination of sensory fibers and motor fibers.

(D) Both innervate the trunk and extremities.

Passage D

Questions 31–40 are based on the following information. Read the passage and answer each question based on information stated or implied in the passage.

The following passage is an excerpt from Global Issues: An Introduction, *5th Edition, by Kristen A. Hite and John L. Seitz (Wiley-Blackwell).*

The population of the world is growing. No one will be startled by that sentence, but what is startling is the rate of growth, and the fact that the present growth of population is unprecedented in human history. The best historical evidence we have today indicates that there were about 5 million people in the world in about 8000 BCE. By 1 CE there were about 200 million, and by 1650 the population had grown to about 500 million. The world reached its first billion people in about 1800. While it took thousands of years for the global population to reach 1 billion, it only took a little over a century for the population to reach the next billion: the second billion came about 1930. The third billion was reached about 1960, the fourth about 1974, and the fifth about 1987. The sixth came in 1999 and the seventh in 2011. The eighth billion is expected by 2024.[1] These figures indicate how rapidly the population is increasing. Table 1.1 shows how long it took the world to add each billion of its total population. A projection is also given for the next billion.

How can we explain this dramatic increase in population growth? Development gains over the last two centuries have seen major improvements in health conditions for many and the overall lowering of the death rate, dramatically and rapidly reducing rates of early death by disease. With this great success came a population explosion, the rapid increase of the number of humans on the planet that we are facing today, with significant impacts for the Earth's resources. While population growth rates are starting to stabilize in many places, the total number of people on the planet continues to increase while natural resources continue to decline. This chapter explores the complex situation of the global population in the context of development, and later chapters explore the relationships between population, wealth, food, energy, climate, and the environment.

Table 1.1 Time taken to add each billion to the world population, 1800–2046 (projection)

Date	Estimated world population (billions)	Years to add 1 billion people
1800	1	2,000,000
1930	2	130
1960	3	30
1974	4	14
1987	5	13
1999	6	12
2011	7	12
2024 (projected)	8	13
2046 (projected)	9	22

Source: Data from UN Department of Economic and Social Affairs, Population Division, World Population Prospects: The 2012 Revision.

There is another way to look at population growth, one that helps us understand the uniqueness of our situation and its staggering possibilities for harm to life on this planet. Because most people born can have children of their own, the human population can – until certain limits are reached – grow exponentially: 1 to 2; 2 to 4; 4 to 8; 8 to 16; 16 to 32; 32 to 64; 64 to 128; and so on. When something grows exponentially, there is hardly discernible growth in the early stages and then the numbers shoot up. The French have a riddle they use to help teach the nature of exponential growth to children. It goes like this: if you have a pond with one lily in it that doubles its size every day, and which will completely cover the pond in 30 days, on what day will the lily cover half the pond? The answer is the twenty-ninth day. What this riddle tells you is that if you wait until the lily covers half the pond before cutting it back, you will have only one day to do this – the twenty-ninth day – because it will cover the whole pond the next day.

[1] *UN Department of Economic and Social Affairs (DESA), Population Division, World Population Prospects: The 2012 Revision, at* **http://esa.un.org/unpd/wpp/unpp/panel population.htm** *(accessed July 2015).*

31. According to the passage, what was a direct result of development gains?

(A) An explosion of world population

(B) Major improvements in health conditions

(C) Exponential growth of world population

(D) The diminishing of natural resources

32. Which of the following was a specific result of the answer to the preceding question?

(A) Lines 2–3 ("but what is . . . of growth")
(B) Lines 27–28 ("dramatically . . . disease")
(C) Lines 34–36 ("the total number . . . decline")
(D) Lines 58–60 ("if you . . . do this")

33. According to the passage,

(A) population growth rates are starting to stabilize in many places
(B) population growth rates are out of control in most places
(C) population health has significantly deteriorated in many places
(D) population resources have increased in many places

34. What is implied by the phrase "until . . . reached" (line 46)?

(A) Humans will cover the entire earth.
(B) Humans will run out of natural resources.
(C) Humans will lose the capacity to reproduce.
(D) Humans will run out of room.

35. According to Table 1.1, what was the approximate world population in 1945?

(A) Between 1 billion and 2 billion
(B) Between 2 billion and 3 billion
(C) Between 3 billion and 4 billion
(D) Over 4 billion

36. As the estimated world population increases, the number of years estimated to add 1 billion people

(A) decreases sharply
(B) decreases and then increases slightly
(C) increases sharply
(D) increases and then decreases slightly

37. What other factor do the authors attribute to the rapid population growth besides exponential growth?

(A) Enhancements in living conditions
(B) Improvements in health conditions
(C) Reduction of dangerous animals
(D) Mitigation of harmful weather conditions

38. What is the message of the French riddle in the last paragraph?

(A) By the time we realize population overgrowth is an issue, it will be too late.
(B) The human population will cover the earth in the same way that the lily covers the pond.
(C) The human population will cover half of the available space before we realize that it is an issue.
(D) If continued, the 29th line of Table 1.1 will show that the earth has reached half of its capacity for supporting the population.

39. Which choice supports the answer to the preceding question?

(A) Lines 2–3 ("but what is . . . of growth")
(B) Lines 23–24 ("How can . . . growth?")
(C) Lines 51–52 ("The French . . . children")
(D) Lines 58–60 ("if you . . . do this")

40. The French riddle makes use of

(A) imagery
(B) simile
(C) folklore
(D) analogy

Passage E

Questions 41–50 are based on the following information. Read the passage and answer each question based on information stated or implied in the passage.

The following passage is an excerpt from Biology For Dummies, *2nd Edition, by Rene Fester Kratz, PhD, and Donna Rae Siegfried (Wiley).*

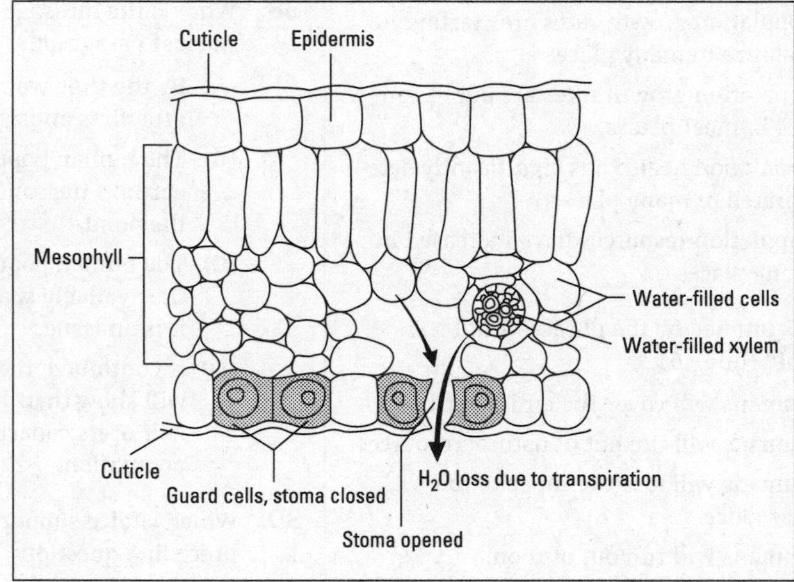

FIGURE 1-1

The cuticle is a layer of cells found on the top surfaces of a plant's leaves. It lets light pass into the leaf but protects the leaf from losing water. Many plants have cuticles that contain waxes that resist the movement of water into and out of a leaf, much like wax on your car keeps water off the paint.

Guard cells are found on the bottom of a plant's leaves, near a stomate, a tiny opening that you can't see with your naked eye. (An individual opening is called a stomate, or stoma; several penings are called stomates, or stomata.)

Plants need to keep their stomates, shown in the figure, open in order to obtain carbon dioxide for photosynthesis and release oxygen. However, if the stomates are open too long or on a really hot day, the plant can lose too much water. To prevent such water loss from happening, each stoma has two guard cells surrounding it.

Guard cells can swell and contract in order to open and close the stomates. When the Sun is shining and photosynthesis is occurring, guard cells swell up with water like full balloons, which stretches them outward and opens the stomates. At night, when photosynthesis isn't occurring, the guard cells release some water and collapse together, closing the stomates.

Some plants that live in very hot, dry environments save water by opening their stomates at night and storing carbon dioxide in their leaves. Then, during the day when it's hot and dry, they keep their stomates closed to conserve water, performing photosynthesis with the carbon dioxide they stored during the night.

41. According to the passage, the functioning of stomates is most like the functioning of

(A) the nuclei of cells
(B) the pores of skin
(C) hair follicles
(D) digestive enzymes

42. A result of the stomates being open too long is that

(A) the plant can lose too much water
(B) the plan can lose too much carbon dioxide
(C) the plant can take in extra oxygen
(D) the plant can take in too much sunlight

43. The authors of the passage make use of

(A) parables
(B) emotions
(C) analogies
(D) hyperbole

44. What is the purpose of the phrase "When the Sun . . . occurring" (lines 21–22)?

(A) To specify the source of light
(B) To create a visual outdoor image
(C) To create a silly tone
(D) To describe a process by starting with the catalyst

45. According to the passage, what is the primary purpose of the guard cells?

(A) To prevent the plant from losing too much water
(B) To protect the plant from intruders
(C) To take in carbon dioxide during photosynthesis
(D) To reflect certain rays from the Sun that may be harmful

46. Which sentence provides the best evidence for the answer to the preceding question?

(A) Lines 2–3 ("It lets . . . losing water.")
(B) Lines 4–7 ("Many plants . . . paint.")
(C) Lines 15–17 ("However, if . . . water.")
(D) Lines 17–19 ("To prevent . . . surrounding it.")

47. A suitable title for this passage would be

(A) Plant Leaves and CO_2 Processing
(B) The Stomates and Guard Cells of the Plant Cuticle
(C) Plant Control of Water Loss
(D) Desert-Climate Plants

48. Which sentence provides the best example of the answer to the preceding question?

(A) Lines 4–7 ("Many plants . . . paint.")
(B) Lines 21–24 ("When the Sun . . . stomates.")
(C) Lines 28–30 ("Some plants . . . leaves.")
(D) Lines 31–34 ("Then, during . . . night.")

49. What is the purpose of the last paragraph?

(A) To provide an example of a plant's use of stomates to conserve water
(B) To provide an example of plants that perform photosynthesis at an unusual time
(C) To provide an example of plants that struggle to survive
(D) To provide an example of plants that use less wax on their cuticles

50. According to the information presented in the passage, the xylem is contained within the

(A) cuticle
(B) epidermis
(C) mesophyll
(D) stomates

Passage F

Questions 51–60 are based on the following information. Read the passage and answer each question based on information stated or implied in the passage.

The following passage is an excerpt from World Literature in Theory, *by David Damrosch, Editor (Wiley-Blackwell).*

What are we to make of world literature today? The cultural and political realignments of the past two decades have opened the field of world literature to an unprecedented, even vertiginous variety of authors and countries. At once exhilarating and unsettling, the range and variety of literatures now in view raise serious questions of scale, of translation and comprehension, and of persisting imbalances of economic and cultural power. At the same time, the shifting landscape of world literature offers new opportunities for readers to encounter writers located well beyond the select few western European countries whose works long dominated worldwide attention. Whereas in past eras works usually spread from imperial centers to peripheral regions (from China to Vietnam, from London to Australia and Kenya, from Paris to almost everywhere), an increasingly multipolar literary landscape allows writers from smaller countries to achieve rapid worldwide fame. While still in his fifties, Orhan Pamuk became the second-youngest recipient of the Nobel Prize for Literature and was translated into 56 languages, Vietnamese included; he has many more readers abroad than in his native Turkey. Increasingly complex patterns of travel, emigration, and publication make "national" languages and literatures more and more international in character. The winner of the Nobel Prize in 2000, Gno Xingjian, has long lived in France and has become a French citizen, yet he continues to write in Chinese. Cultural hybridity is also found within the borders of China itself, as in the stories of the Sino-Tibetan writer Tashi Dawa, who has blended elements drawn from Tibetan folklore and international magical realism for his writings in Chinese; in a very real sense, his works were participating in world literature even before they began to be translated and read abroad.

51. In the context in which it appears, "vertiginous" (line 4) most nearly means

(A) conceivable
(B) dizzying
(C) enlightening
(D) edifying

52. Which of the following statements are given as examples of cross-cultural influence in literature?

I. Distributing literary works from London to Kenya
II. A French citizen writing in Chinese
III. Blending magical realism with Tibetan folklore

(A) I and II
(B) II and III
(C) I and III
(D) I, II, and III

53. According to the passage, how has the potential reach of literature changed?

(A) It may be translated into over 50 languages.
(B) It may allow authors to continue to write in their native languages.
(C) It may be discovered by readers from all over the world.
(D) It may bring the authors the Nobel Prize recognition that they deserve.

54. Which choice best describes the phenomenon described in the preceding question?

(A) Lines 1–5 ("The cultural . . . countries.")
(B) Lines 9–14 ("At the same time . . . attention.")
(C) Lines 25–28 ("Increasingly . . . character.")
(D) Lines 31–38 ("Cultural . . . abroad.")

55. What is the significance of two of the three authors mentioned in the passage having won the Nobel Prize?

(A) It exemplifies the significance of the new readers that authors may now reach.

(B) It exemplifies the cultural diversity embraced by the Nobel Committee.

(C) It exemplifies the quality of work that readers may not otherwise access.

(D) It exemplifies the opportunities for recognition that these authors may not have otherwise had.

56. According to the passage, Orhan Pamuk is from

(A) China

(B) Vietnam

(C) Turkey

(D) France

57. What is the purpose of the text "What are we . . . power" (lines 1–9)?

(A) It describes an evolution that has a result.

(B) It describes a problem that needs a solution.

(C) It describes a pattern that has emerged.

(D) It describes the result of a historical event.

58. Which of the following best summarizes the main idea of the passage?

(A) Writers from almost anywhere have better opportunities to win the Nobel Prize.

(B) Writers from almost anywhere can now achieve global recognition.

(C) The cultural and political landscape has been significantly realigned over the past two decades.

(D) An author can move to another country and continue to write in his native language.

59. Which choice provides the best evidence for the answer to the preceding question?

(A) Lines 1–5 ("The cultural . . . countries.")

(B) Lines 9–14 ("At the same time . . . attention.")

(C) Lines 18–20 ("an increasingly . . . fame")

(D) Lines 31–38 ("Cultural . . . abroad.")

60. What is the significance of the phrase "in a very real . . . abroad" (lines 36–38)?

(A) It suggests that Dawa was ahead of his time.

(B) It reminds us of the importance of international authors.

(C) It implies that Dawa should also have received the Nobel Prize.

(D) It indicates that Dawa was well-versed in many languages.

Passage G

Questions 61–70 are based on the following information. Read the passage and answer each question based on information stated or implied in the passage.

The following passage is an excerpt from GRE For Dummies, *8th Edition, by Ron Woldoff and Joe Kraynak (Wiley).*

A key study has shown that the organic matter content of a soil can be altered to a depth of 10 cm or more by intense campfire heat. As much as 90 percent of the original organic matter may be oxidized in the top 1.3 cm of soil. In the surface 10 cm, the loss of organic matter may reach 50 percent if the soil is dry and the temperature exceeds 250 degrees. The loss of organic matter reduces soil fertility and water-holding capacity and renders the soil more susceptible to compaction and erosion.

Sandy soils attain higher temperatures and retain

heat longer than clay soils under similar fuel, moisture, and weather conditions. From this standpoint, it is desirable to locate campgrounds in an area with loam or clay-loam soil. Sandy soils are less susceptible to compaction damage, however, and are more desirable for campgrounds from this standpoint.

A water-repellent layer can be created in a soil by the heat from the campfire. This condition was noted only in sandy soils where the temperature remained below 350 degrees during the campfire burn. Campfires often produce temperatures above this level. By comparison, forest fires are a shorter-duration event, and soil temperatures produced are more likely to create water repellency-inducing conditions. The greater extent of forest fires makes them a more serious threat than campfires in terms of causing soil-water repellency.

If the soil remained moist for the duration of the campfire, the increased heat capacity of the soil and heat of water vaporization kept the soil temperature below 100 degrees. At this temperature, little loss of organic matter occurred, and no water repellency was created. For areas where the soil remains very moist, campfires probably have little effect on the soil properties.

Studies show that softwood fuels burn faster and produce less heat flow into the soil than do hardwood fuels under the same conditions. Elm and mesquite were the hottest burning and longest lasting fuels tested. In areas where some choice of fuels is available, the use of softwood fuels should be encouraged in an effort to minimize the effect of campfires on soil properties.

By restricting the fire site to the same area, the effects of campfires on the soil in a campground can be lessened, even if permanent concrete fireplaces are not installed. In this manner, any harmful effects are restricted to a minimum area. If campfires are allowed to be located at random by the user, the harmful effects tend to be spread over a larger part of the campground. The placement of a stone fire ring in the chosen location is one way to accomplish the objective.

These data support the decision to install permanent fireplaces in many areas and to restrict the use of campfires elsewhere in the park. This eliminates the harmful effects of campfires on the soil and allows the campground to be located on sandy soil with low compactibility and good drainage.

61. According to the passage, what is the benefit of moisture in the soil?

(A) It facilitates the extinguishing of the fire.

(B) It mitigates fire damage to the soil by increasing the soil's heat capacity.

(C) It bolsters ambient fire heat by releasing vapor and steam.

(D) It transfers clay soil properties to sandy soil conditions.

62. Which sentence best supports the answer to the preceding question?

(A) Lines 20–21 ("A water-repellent . . . campfire.")

(B) Lines 35–37 ("At this temperature . . . created.")

(C) Lines 37–39 ("For areas . . . properties.")

(D) Lines 58–60 ("These data . . . the park.")

63. The main idea of this passage is that

(A) soil temperature affects soil fertility

(B) only certain woods allow for high-quality campfires

(C) soils must be able to absorb water to sustain organic matter

(D) steps can be taken to minimize soil damage from campfires

64. According to the passage, long-lasting campfires are more likely than short-lived ones to

(A) create water repellency-inducing conditions

(B) maintain soil fertility

(C) occur with softwood fuels

(D) produce higher soil temperatures

65. The authors would be most likely to agree with which of the following?

(A) Campfires should be banned as destructive to campground soil.

(B) Organic matter decreases soil erosion.

(C) Clay-loam soil is preferable to sandy soil for campsites.

(D) Campfires will not burn in areas with moist soil.

66. Which sentence best supports the answer to the preceding question?

(A) Lines 8–11 ("The loss . . . erosion.")

(B) Lines 20–21 ("A water-repellent . . . campfire.")

(C) Lines 35–37 ("At this temperature . . . created.")

(D) Lines 58–60 ("These data . . . the park.")

67. According to the passage, elm and mesquite are probably

(A) fast-burning softwoods

(B) fast-burning hardwoods

(C) slow-burning softwoods

(D) slow-burning hardwoods

68. The passage suggests that the best way to reduce soil damage from fire is to

I. use soft fuel

II. vary the location of the fires

III. have the fires on moist soils

(A) I and II

(B) II and III

(C) I and III

(D) I, II, and III

69. What is the purpose of mentioning "permanent concrete fireplaces" (lines 50–51)?

(A) The authors allude to an ideal solution.

(B) The authors caution against a certain decision.

(C) The authors describe a dangerous situation.

(D) The authors recommend an alternative course of action.

70. What approach does the passage take?

(A) It warns of a dangerous outcome.

(B) It advocates the restriction of a harmful activity.

(C) It offers guidance and suggestions.

(D) It suggests that an overhaul be effected.

Passage H

Questions 71–80 are based on the following information. Read the passage and answer each question based on information stated or implied in the passage.

The following passage is an excerpt from Pride and Prejudice, *by Jane Austen (public domain).*

It is a truth universally acknowledged, that a single man in possession of a good fortune, must be in want of a wife.

However little known the feelings or views of such a man may be on his first entering a neighbourhood, this truth is so well fixed in the minds of the surrounding families, that he is considered the rightful property of some one or other of their daughters.

"My dear Mr. Bennet," said his lady to him one day, "have you heard that Netherfield Park is let at last?"

Mr. Bennet replied that he had not.

"But it is," returned she; "for Mrs. Long has just been here, and she told me all about it."

Mr. Bennet made no answer.

"Do you not want to know who has taken it?" cried his wife impatiently.

"*You* want to tell me, and I have no objection to hearing it."

This was invitation enough.

"Why, my dear, you must know, Mrs. Long says that Netherfield is taken by a young man of large fortune from the north of England; that he came down on Monday in a chaise and four to see the place, and was so much delighted with it, that he agreed with Mr. Morris immediately; that he is to take possession before Michaelmas, and some of his servants are to be in the house by the end of next week."

"What is his name?"

"Bingley."

"Is he married or single?"

"Oh! Single, my dear, to be sure! A single man of large fortune; four or five thousand a year. What a fine thing for our girls!"

"How so? How can it affect them?"

"My dear Mr. Bennet," replied his wife, "how can you be so tiresome! You must know that I am thinking of his marrying one of them."

"Is that his design in settling here?"

"Design! Nonsense, how can you talk so! But it is very likely that he *may* fall in love with one of them, and therefore you must visit him as soon as he comes."

"I see no occasion for that. You and the girls may go, or you may send them by themselves, which perhaps will be still better, for as you are as handsome as any of them, Mr. Bingley may like you the best of the party."

"My dear, you flatter me. I certainly have had my share of beauty, but I do not pretend to be anything extraordinary now. When a woman has five grown-up daughters, she ought to give over thinking of her own beauty."

"In such cases, a woman has not often much beauty to think of."

"But, my dear, you must indeed go and see Mr. Bingley when he comes into the neighbourhood."

"It is more than I engage for, I assure you."

"But consider your daughters. Only think what an establishment it would be for one of them. Sir William and Lady Lucas are determined to go, merely on that account, for in general, you know, they visit no newcomers. Indeed you must go, for it will be impossible for us to visit him if you do not."

"You are over-scrupulous, surely. I dare say Mr. Bingley will be very glad to see you; and I will send a few lines by you to assure him of my hearty consent to his marrying whichever he chooses of the girls; though I must throw in a good word for my little Lizzy."

"I desire you will do no such thing. Lizzy is not a bit better than the others; and I am sure she is not half so handsome as Jane, nor half so good-humoured as Lydia. But you are always giving *her* the preference."

"They have none of them much to recommend them," replied he; "they are all silly and ignorant like other girls; but Lizzy has something more of quickness than her sisters."

"Mr. Bennet, how *can* you abuse your own children in such a way? You take delight in vexing me. You have no compassion for my poor nerves."

"You mistake me, my dear. I have a high respect for your nerves. They are my old friends. I have heard you mention them with consideration these last twenty years at least."

"Ah, you do not know what I suffer."

"But I hope you will get over it, and live to see many young men of four thousand a year come into the neighbourhood."

"It will be no use to us, if twenty such should come, since you will not visit them."

"Depend upon it, my dear, that when there are twenty, I will visit them all." Mr. Bennet was so odd a mixture of quick parts, sarcastic humour, reserve, and caprice, that the experience of three-and-twenty years had been insufficient to make his wife understand his character. *Her* mind was less difficult to develop. She was a woman of mean understanding, little information, and uncertain temper. When she was discontented, she fancied herself nervous. The business of her life was to get her daughters married; its solace was visiting and news.

71. The primary purpose of the passage is to

(A) introduce Mr. and Mrs. Bennet and the dynamic that they share

(B) suggest that the Bennet daughters meet Mr. Bingley

(C) make the case that Mr. Bingley must be in need of a wife

(D) make the case that Mr. Bennet visit Mr. Bingley

72. What is Mrs. Bennet's primary purpose?

(A) To bring friendliness and welcoming throughout the neighborhood

(B) To help her daughters overcome any shortcomings

(C) To see her daughters married to wealthy men

(D) To convince her husband that their daughters are ready for marriage

73. Which statement best supports the answer to the preceding question?

(A) Lines 6–9 ("this truth . . . daughters.")

(B) Lines 42–44 ("But it is . . . one of them,")

(C) Lines 90–92 ("But I hope . . . neighbourhood.")

(D) Lines 104–105 ("The business . . . married;")

74. What is the purpose of the opening statement "It is . . . a wife" (lines 1–3) in the first two paragraphs?

(A) To serve as a reminder of an undeniable truth

(B) To describe an inescapable fate

(C) To introduce a conviction and irony

(D) To explain insatiable needs

75. Based on the passage, what is Mrs. Bennet most likely to engage in the most?

(A) Charity

(B) Housework

(C) Nurturing and caring

(D) Gossip

76. Which statement best supports the answer to the preceding question?

(A) Lines 22–24 ("Why, my dear . . . England;")

(B) Lines 42–44 ("But it is . . . one of them,")

(C) Lines 90–92 ("But I hope . . . neighbourhood.")

(D) Lines 105–106 ("its solace . . . news.")

77. How many daughters do the Bennets have?

(A) Two

(B) Three

(C) Four

(D) Five

78. What does Mr. Bennet mean when he says, "Depend . . . them all" (lines 95–96)?

(A) He will visit the new neighbors only when there are more of them to visit.

(B) He is committing to a course of action for a scenario which will not likely happen.

(C) He is using gentle humor to assuage his wife's concerns.

(D) He wants his daughters to have a good selection of men to choose from.

79. In line 41, "design" most nearly means

(A) purpose

(B) layout

(C) schematic

(D) blueprint

80. In line 69, "a few lines" most nearly means

(A) drawings

(B) poetry

(C) message

(D) boundaries

Passage I

Questions 81–90 are based on the following information. Read the passage and answer each question based on information stated or implied in the passage.

The following passage is an excerpt from Anna Karenina, *by Leo Tolstoy (public domain).*

Happy families are all alike; every unhappy family is unhappy in its own way.

Everything was in confusion in the Oblonskys' house. The wife had discovered that the husband was carrying on an intrigue with a French girl, who had been a governess in their family, and she had announced to her husband that she could not go on living in the same house with him. This position of affairs had now lasted three days, and not only the husband and wife themselves, but all the members of their family and household, were painfully conscious of it. Every person in the house felt that there was no sense in their living together, and that the stray people brought together by chance in any inn had more in common with one another than they, the members of the family and household of the Oblonskys. The wife did not leave her own room, the husband had not been at home for three days. The children ran wild all over the house; the English governess quarreled with the housekeeper, and wrote to a friend asking her to look out for a new situation for her; the man-cook had walked off the day before just at dinner time; the kitchen-maid, and the coachman had given warning.

Three days after the quarrel, Prince Stepan Arkadyevitch Oblonsky—Stiva, as he was called in the fashionable world—woke up at his usual hour, that is, at eight o'clock in the morning, not in his wife's bedroom, but on the leather-covered sofa in his study. He turned over his stout, well-cared-for person on the springy sofa, as though he would sink into a long sleep again; he vigorously embraced the pillow on the other side and buried his face in it; but all at once he jumped up, sat up on the sofa, and opened his eyes.

"Yes, yes, how was it now?" he thought, going over his dream. "Now, how was it? To be sure! Alabin was giving a dinner at Darmstadt; no, not Darmstadt, but something American. Yes, but then, Darmstadt was in America. Yes, Alabin was giving a dinner on glass tables, and the tables sang, *Il mio tesoro*—not *Il mio tesoro* though, but something better, and there were some sort of little decanters on the table, and they were women, too," he remembered.

Stepan Arkadyevitch's eyes twinkled gaily, and he pondered with a smile. "Yes, it was nice, very nice. There was a great deal more that was delightful, only there's no putting it into words, or even expressing it in one's thoughts awake." And noticing a gleam of light peeping in beside one of the serge curtains, he cheerfully dropped his feet over the edge of the sofa, and felt about with them for his slippers, a present on his last birthday, worked for him by his wife on gold-colored morocco. And, as he had done every day for the last nine years, he stretched out his hand, without getting up, towards the place where his dressing-gown always hung in his bedroom. And thereupon he suddenly remembered that he was not sleeping in his wife's room, but in his study, and why: the smile vanished from his face, he knitted his brows.

"Ah, ah, ah! Oo!. . ." he muttered, recalling everything that had happened. And again every detail of his quarrel with his wife was present to his imagination, all the hopelessness of his position, and worst of all, his own fault.

"Yes, she won't forgive me, and she can't forgive me. And the most awful thing about it is that it's all my fault—all my fault, though I'm not to blame. That's the point of the whole situation," he reflected. "Oh, oh, oh!" he kept repeating in despair, as he remembered the acutely painful sensations caused him by this quarrel.

81. What is meant by the words "but all . . . conscious of it" (lines 10–12)?

(A) Stepan did not want the family to know.

(B) The family members were disappointed.

(C) The family members were in pain.

(D) Stepan was in pain.

82. The author probably thinks happy families are

(A) interesting
(B) boring
(C) worth writing about
(D) commonplace

83. The family is probably

(A) wealthy and happy
(B) wealthy but not happy
(C) not wealthy but happy
(D) neither wealthy nor happy

84. Which phrase best supports the answer to the happiness part of the preceding question?

(A) Lines 1–2 ("Happy . . . own way.")
(B) Lines 14–16 ("the stray . . . the family")
(C) Lines 50–53 ("And noticing . . . the sofa,")
(D) Lines 70–71 ("all my . . . blame.")

85. Stepan probably most regrets

(A) his indiscretions
(B) the family finding out
(C) his pain from being caught
(D) hurting his wife

86. The primary purpose of the passage is to

(A) introduce Stepan as a vulnerable, misunderstood figure
(B) introduce Stepan as a victim of uncontrollable circumstances
(C) introduce Stepan as an uncaring, destructive force
(D) introduce Stepan as a controlling, authoritative figure

87. The purpose of the last paragraph is to show that

(A) Stepan hopes to reconcile with his wife
(B) Stepan was driven to have the affair
(C) Stepan can't handle a quarrel
(D) Stepan can't take responsibility for his actions

88. Which phrase best supports the answer to the preceding question?

(A) Lines 46–47 ("Stepan . . . a smile.")
(B) Lines 59–62 ("And thereupon . . . brows.")
(C) Lines 66–67 ("all the hopelessness . . . fault.")
(D) Lines 70–71 ("though . . . situation,")

89. What is the purpose of the phrase "he stretched . . . his bedroom" (lines 57–59)?

(A) It shows how significantly the housing staff's discomfort affects Stepan.
(B) It shows how little of an effect the separation has had on Stepan.
(C) It shows that Stepan did not really know where he was.
(D) It shows that the bathrobe should have been in its place near the couch.

90. Stepan seems most concerned about

(A) his wife
(B) himself
(C) his marriage
(D) his household

Passage J

Questions 91–100 are based on the following information. Read the passage and answer each question based on information stated or implied in the passages.

Passage 1 is an excerpt from Networks of Outrage and Hope: Social Movements in the Internet Age, *by Manuel Castells (Wiley-Blackwell). Passage 2 is an excerpt from* Tap, Click, Read: Growing Readers in a World of Screens, *by Lisa Guernsey and Michael H. Levine (Wiley-Blackwell).*

Passage 1

Given the role of the Internet in spreading and coordinating the revolt, it is significant to point out that Tunisia has one of the highest rates of Internet and mobile phone penetration in the Arab world. In November 2010, 67 percent of the urban population had access to a mobile phone, and 37 percent were connected to the Internet. In early 2011, 20 percent of Internet users were on Facebook, a percentage that is two times higher than in Morocco, three times higher than in Egypt, five times higher than in Algeria or Libya, and twenty times higher than in Yemen. Furthermore, the proportion of Internet users among the urban population and particularly among the urban youth was much higher. Since there is a direct connection between young age, higher education and the use of the Internet, the unemployed college graduates who were the key actors in the revolution were also frequent Internet users, and some were sophisticated users who utilized the communicative potential of the Internet to build and expand their movement. The communicative autonomy provided by the Internet made possible the viral diffusion of videos, messages and songs that incited rage and gave hope. For instance, the song "Rais Lebled" by a famous rapper from Sfax, El General, denouncing the dictatorship became a hit on the social networks. Of course, El General was arrested, but this incensed the protesters even further and strengthened their determination in the struggle for "complete transition," as they put it. Thus, it seems that in Tunisia we find a significant convergence of three distinctive features:

1. The existence of an active group of unemployed college graduates, who led the revolt, bypassing any formal, traditional leadership;
2. The presence of a strong cyberactivism culture that had engaged in the open critique of the regime for over one decade;
3. A relatively high rate of diffusion of Internet use, including household connections, schools and cybercafés.

Passage 2

To cite the old Chinese proverb, "We live in interesting times." One indicator: just pause from reading this book for a moment and reflect on the recently invented digital devices you have close at hand. Open up your smartphone or tablet and observe a cornucopia of entertainment and lifestyle apps—games, photography, music, cooking, sports—as well as social ones that link you to friends, family, and colleagues across the globe, not to mention apps for messaging anyone, anytime. Most of us have instant access to the world's information via powerful, personalized search engines that fit in our pockets. Later in the book we talk to experts who now wonder about the burdens of being always connected. But how often have you wondered, How on Earth did we live without our devices?

Hard as it is to believe, a little over five years ago, there was no such thing as an iPad or touchscreen tablet computer. Similarly, smartphones as we know them, with interactive touchscreens, advanced operating systems, and anytime, anywhere access to the Internet, did not exist until the first iPhone was introduced in January 2007. In the relatively few years since their release, mobile technologies have become ubiquitous and certainly changed most Americans' lives. Today, nearly 60 percent of American adults own a smartphone. More than 50 percent have a hand-held device such as a tablet computer or dedicated e-reader like a Kindle. And the choices of content are simply dizzying. For example, as of this writing there are some 1.3 million apps available in the iPhone store alone; there were less than a hundred thousand in late 2009. Yet for those who may want to put the genie back in the bottle: there's no app for that. There's no going back to a less connected age.

91. Taken together, the passages would suggest that

(A) more revolutions are likely to come from the young and increasingly online population

(B) as more people become connected, they are likely to make more rational decisions

(C) at some point, the percentage of connected people is likely to go down

(D) as the world becomes more and more connected, arrests for dissenting artists and musicians are likely to increase

92. Which phrase best supports the answer to the preceding question?

(A) Lines 2–5 ("it is significant . . . Arab world.")

(B) Lines 22–25 ("The communicative . . . gave hope.")

(C) Lines 48–52 ("Open up . . . across the globe,")

(D) Lines 78–79 ("Yet for those . . . app for that.")

93. What is the author's purpose in mentioning "the old Chinese proverb, 'We live in interesting times'" (lines 44–45)?

(A) To place attention on how interesting the modern devices can be

(B) To show the foresight held by the ancient Chinese

(C) To remind the reader that things have always been changing

(D) To reflect on how things today are so different

94. As used in line 18, "actors" most nearly means

(A) beneficiaries

(B) supporters

(C) instigators

(D) portrayers

95. Unlike Passage 1, Passage 2 makes use of

(A) analogy

(B) imagery

(C) pedagogy

(D) theology

96. The primary message of Passage 2 is that

(A) we continue increasing reliance on our mobile devices, and there is no going back

(B) our times continue to become more interesting, and there is no going back

(C) the number of apps continues to increase, and there is no going back

(D) mobile device usage continues to increase, and there is no going back

97. Which statement best reflects the answer to the preceding question?

(A) Lines 44–45 ("We live . . . times.")

(B) Lines 59–60 ("How on . . . devices?")

(C) Lines 74–75 ("And the . . . dizzying.")

(D) Lines 78–79 ("Yet for those . . . app for that.")

98. What was the main significance of Tunisia in the Arab Spring?

(A) Sfax was a hotspot of dissent and unrest.

(B) The rapper El Général made use of social networks to denounce the dictatorship.

(C) The revolt occurred sooner because its citizens were more connected than in other Arab countries.

(D) It citizens were looking for "complete transition."

99. As used in line 49, "cornucopia" most nearly means

(A) a horn filled with good food

(B) a Thanksgiving icon

(C) a plethora

(D) a mythical source of nutrition

100. Which best describes the overall relationship between Passage 2 and Passage 1?

(A) Passage 2 describes an overall trend, while Passage 1 describes a specific aspect of it.

(B) Passage 2 describes a platform of change, while Passage 1 describes events likely to occur.

(C) Passage 2 explains a phenomenon, while Passage 1 describes a mitigating factor.

(D) Passage 2 begins a story, while Passage 1 ends it.

Passage K

Questions 101–110 are based on the following information. Read the passage and answer each question based on information stated or implied in the passage.

Passage 1 is an excerpt from The Wiley-Blackwell Companion to Sociology, *edited by George Ritzer (Wiley-Blackwell). Passage 2 is an excerpt from* The Posthuman, *by Rosi Braidotti (Wiley-Blackwell).*

Passage 1

Ritzer (2009) has recently argued that the focus on either production or consumption has always been misplaced and that all acts always involve both. That is, all acts of production and consumption are fundamentally acts of prosumption. The assembly-line worker is always consuming all sorts of things (parts, energy, tools) in the process of production, and conversely the consumer in, for example, a fast food restaurant is always producing (garnishes for a sandwich, soft drinks from the self-serve dispenser, the disposal of debris derived from the meal). This suggests a dramatic reorientation of theorizing about the economy away from production or consumption and in the direction of prosumption.

Prosumption is not only a historical reality, but it is becoming increasingly ubiquitous with the emergence on the internet of Web 2.0. Web 1.0 (e.g., AOL) typically involved sites that were created and managed by producers and used more or less passively by separable consumers. The latter not only did not produce the websites, but usually could not alter their content in any meaningful way. In contrast, Web 2.0 is defined by sites (e.g., Facebook, blogs) the contents of which are produced, wholly (blogs) or in part (Facebook), by the user. While everything about some 2.0 sites (a blog, for example) is likely produced by those who also consume them, on others (the Facebook page) the basic structure of the site is created by the producer, while all of the content comes from the consumer(s). Even though something of the distinction between producer and consumer remains in the latter case, it is clear that Web 2.0 is the paradigmatic domain of the prosumer. As the internet continues to evolve, we can expect to see more and more user-generated content and therefore an even greater role for the prosumer.

Of course, this shift to prosumption does not mean that sociological theorists should ignore production (the production end of the prosumption continuum) or consumption (the consumption end of that continuum). On the production side, there is certainly no end of issues to concern the theorist. Among others, there is David Harvey's (2005) interest in, and critique of, neoliberalism, as well as Hardt and Negri's (2000) interest in the transformation of the capitalist and proletariat into Empire and Multitude in the global age.

Passage 2

What the neo-liberal market forces are after, and what they financially invest in, is the informational power of living matter itself. The capitalization of living matter produces a new political economy, which Melinda Cooper (2008) calls 'Life as surplus'. It introduces discursive and material political techniques of population control of a very different order from the administration of demographics, which preoccupied Foucault's work on bio-political governmentality. The warnings are now global. Today, we are undertaking 'risk analyses' not only of entire social and national systems, but also of whole sections of the population in the world risk society (Beck, 1999). Data banks of bio-genetic, neural and mediatic information about individuals are the true capital today, as the success of Facebook demonstrates at a more banal level. 'Data-mining' includes profiling practices that identify different types or characteristics and highlights them as special strategic targets for capital investments. This kind of predictive analytics of the human amounts to 'Life-mining', with visibility, predictability and exportability as the key criteria.

101. What does Ritzer argue is the difference between production and consumption?

(A) Production is creating, and consuming is using.

(B) Production is recent, and consumption is historical.

(C) Production is permanent, and consumption is temporary.

(D) They are opposite sides of the same spectrum.

102. Which sentence best reflects the answer to the preceding question?

(A) Lines 1–4 ("Ritzer (2009) . . . both.")

(B) Lines 16–18 ("Prosumption . . . Web 2.0.")

(C) Lines 39–43 ("Of course . . . continuum).")

(D) Lines 45–49 ("Among others . . . global age.")

103. Unlike Web 1.0, Web 2.0 is specifically

(A) newer and therefore better

(B) fueled by content produced by the user

(C) an asset to the neo-liberal market forces

(D) a reflection of the distinction between the producer and the consumer

104. What would the author of Passage 2 attribute to a phenomenon described in Passage 1?

(A) The prosumptive shift to Web 2.0 paves the way for life-mining.

(B) The continuum of production and consumption set the stage for bio-political governmentality.

(C) The assembly-line worker who produces and consumes represents a whole section of the population in the world risk society.

(D) The sociological theorist who ignores production or consumption cannot fathom life as surplus.

105. Which sentence best reflects the answer to the preceding question?

(A) Lines 4–5 ("That is . . . prosumption.")

(B) Lines 5–12 ("The assembly-line . . . meal).")

(C) Lines 39–43 ("Of course . . . continuum).")

(D) Lines 63–67 ("Data banks . . . level.")

106. The emergence of Web 2.0 is an example of

(A) production

(B) consumption

(C) prosumption

(D) neo-liberalism

107. As used in line 71, "Life-mining" most nearly means

(A) an extent of data-mining

(B) the use of Facebook

(C) Cooper's "Life as surplus"

(D) Foucault's bio-political governmentality

108. What is the primary purpose of Passage 1?

(A) To explain the success of Web 2.0 sites such as Facebook

(B) To describe the shift to prosumption and the accompanying emergence of Web 2.0

(C) To portray the perspective of sociological theorists, such as Harvey, on neoliberalism

(D) To depict the observation of sociological theorists, such as Hardt and Negri, on the transformation of the capitalist and proletariat into Empire and Multitude

109. What is the primary purpose of Passage 2?

(A) To describe a marketing phenomenon

(B) To offer a global warning

(C) To explain profiling practices

(D) To show predictability

110. Which sentence best reflects the answer to the preceding question?

(A) Lines 50–52 ("What the . . . itself.")

(B) Lines 55–59 ("It introduces . . . governmentality.")

(C) Lines 63–67 ("Data banks . . . level.")

(D) Lines 70–73 ("This kind . . . criteria.")

Passage L

Questions 111–120 are based on the following information. Read the passage and answer each question based on information stated or implied in the passage.

The following passage is an excerpt from The Galápagos: A Natural Laboratory for the Earth Sciences, *edited by Karen S. Harpp, Eric Mittelstaedt, Noémi d'Ozouville, and David W. Graham (The American Geophysical Union and Wiley-Blackwell).*

Evidence from Volcanic History and Geomorphology

The Galápagos Islands are a hotspot-related chain that lies adjacent to the Galápagos Spreading Center (GSC). The islands lie on the Nazca plate, which moves almost directly east at about 51km/my (no-net rotation reference frame) [*Argus et al.*, 2010]. Consequently, the youngest volcanoes lie in the western part of the archipelago, and the seven shield volcanoes of Isabela and Fernandina are the focus of this paper.

Sixty-two eruptions have been observed and recorded in the western Galápagos, the first in 1797 [*Simkin and Siebert*, 1994]. The actual number of eruptions is likely to be nearly twice this number, however, as twenty-six eruptions have been witnessed since 1950 (when the islands were permanently inhabited), suggesting that prior eruptions were likely underreported (Figure 5.2). There is a pattern to the activity: Fernandina, Wolf, Cerro Azul, and Sierra Negra have each had more than ten recorded eruptions, whereas Alcedo, Darwin, and Ecuador have had only one or no observed eruptions. Alcedo and Darwin have both been carried away from the core of the Galápagos hotspot, and thus may be in a dying phase of evolution. In contrast, Ecuador is at the leading edge, lying west of Volcan Wolf, but it has undergone a sector collapse, which may have affected its recent eruption rate [*Geist et al.*, 2002].

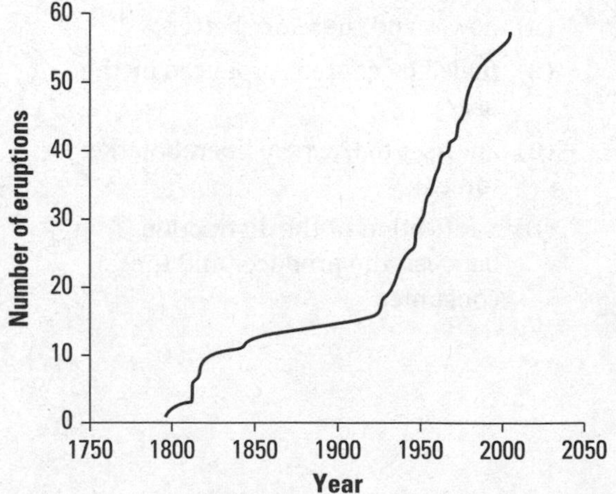

FIGURE 5-2: Cumulative number of eruptions reported from the western Galápagos. Human inhabitation and visitation increased dramatically in the mid-20th century. The eruption rate since 1950 has been approximately one eruption every two years.

The western Galápagos shields have characteristic morphologies, which in part reflect their shallow magmatic plumbing systems. In addition to their large and deep calderas, they have unusually steep upper slopes and circumferential eruptive fissures on their upper parts, and radial fissures on their lower flanks [*McBirney and Williams*, 1969; *Nordlie*, 1973; *Mouginis-Mark et al.*, 1996; *Chadwick and Howard*, 1991]. The distribution of vents is believed to result from a combination of stresses imparted by a shallow magma chamber, surface loading, and the steep slopes and caldera walls [*Chadwick and Dieterich*, 1995; *Reynolds et al.*, 1995; *Chadwick et al.*, 2011]. The steep summit carapace forms because low volume, stubby lava flows erupt from the circumferential fissures, and more voluminous lava flows erupt from the lower radial vents [*Simkin*, 1972; *Naumann and Geist*, 2000]. Both circumferential and radial eruptive vents have fed historical eruptions in about equal numbers, and mechanical modeling suggests that they may alternate in time on a given volcano in a stress feedback relationship. Circumferential dikes are fed from the upper margins of flat-topped subcaldera sill-like magma reservoirs [*Chadwick and Dieterich*, 1995; *Yun et al.*, 2006; *Chadwick et al.*, 2011]. Because radial dikes feed lower-elevation and submarine eruptions, they likely originate from a deeper part of the system.

The submarine flanks of the volcanoes differ substantially from their subaerial parts: focused rift zones characterize the submarine parts of Fernandina, Cerro Azul, Ecuador, and Wolf volcanoes [*Geist et al.*, 2006b; 2008a], whereas the subaerial volcanoes only have diffuse concentrations of radial vents in certain sectors [*Chadwick and Howard*, 1991]. The greater degree of focusing of the vents on the submarine slopes is attributed to a positive feedback between topography stubby lavas, and dike emplacement [*Geist et al.*, 2006b].

The Galápagos calderas are up to hundreds of meters deep, but evidence suggests they do not form by singular collapse events tied to individual voluminous eruptions. Instead, the calderas appear to form incrementally by repeated small co-eruption collapse events, sometimes in response to remarkably small eruptions. Wolf, Cerro Azul, Alcedo, and Fernandina each have undergone several cycles of partial refilling, followed by renewed collapse off-center from the previous collapses, exposing caldera-filling lavas in the new caldera wall [*Simkin and Howard*, 1970; *Chadwick et al.*, 1991; *Rowland and Munro*, 1992; *Munro et al.*, 1996; *Geist et al.*, 2005; *Naumann and Geist*, 2000; *Geist et al.*, 1994; *Allan and Simkin*, 2000; *Howard*, 2010]. Sierra Negra, Alcedo, and Darwin volcanoes are currently in a phase of caldera filling [*Geist et al.*, 1994; *Reynolds and Geist*, 1995; *Naumann and Geist*, 2000]. No overt change in the magmas' compositions can be tied to caldera filling versus caldera subsidence, so foundering versus filling is probably not simply tied to magma supply rate.

One of the largest caldera collapses in historical times took place at Fernandina in 1968, when the caldera collapsed 350 m over a period of twelve days, accounting for a volume of 1.5 km^3 [*Simkin and Howard*, 1970; *Filson et al.*, 1973; *Howard*, 2010]; the volume of erupted material accompanying this event was less than 1% of the volume of the caldera collapse. Either a major submarine eruption went undetected (at the same time as the small subaerial eruption), a large intrusion moved a significant volume of magma from the sub-caldera magma reservoir into the volcano flanks (but did not erupt), or the caldera collapse was driven by loading of the crust with dense, intrusive rocks [*Walker*, 1988].

111. According to the passage, where and when did one of the largest caldera collapses in historical times take place?

(A) Cerro Azul, 2006

(B) Isabela, 1950

(C) Fernandina, 1968

(D) Ecuador, 1991

112. What percent of the volume of that large caldera collapse was the volume of erupted material accompanying this event?

(A) Less than 1%

(B) More than 1%

(C) Less than 75%

(D) More than 75%

113. Which of the following is *not* a likely cause of the low percentage of erupted material in the collapse referenced in the preceding question?

(A) A major submarine eruption went undetected.

(B) A subaerial eruption occurred.

(C) A large intrusion moved a significant volume of magma from the sub-caldera magma reservoir.

(D) The crust was loaded with dense, intrusive rocks.

114. According to Figure 5.2, the number of volcanic eruptions in 2050 will probably be

(A) close to 80

(B) close to 60

(C) close to 40

(D) close to 20

115. What is a drawback of the data collected in Figure 5.2?

(A) Certain islands may not have been included each year.

(B) Earthquakes may have been counted as eruptions.

(C) The definition of an eruption has changed.

(D) Past eruptions may not have been reported.

116. Which phrase provides the best support for the answer to the preceding question?

(A) Lines 16–17 ("prior . . . underreported.")

(B) Lines 29–30 ("The western . . . morphologies,")

(C) Lines 57–58 ("The submarine . . . parts:")

(D) Lines 74–76 ("Wolf, Cerro Azul . . . refilling,")

117. According to the passage, what is likely the primary cause of the Galápagos calderas?

(A) Singular collapse events

(B) Repeated small co-eruption events

(C) Individual voluminous eruptions

(D) The magma supply rate

118. The first eruption was observed and recorded in the Galápagos in

(A) 1797

(B) 1831

(C) 1950

(D) 1968

119. As used in line 31, "plumbing systems" most nearly means

(A) the sewer and waste channels

(B) the underground channels of seawater

(C) the channels in which magma flows

(D) the channels of freshwater irrigation

120. Which of the following is *not* believed to contribute to the stresses that formed the distribution of vents of the western Galápagos shields?

(A) A shallow magma chamber

(B) The circumferential eruptive and radial fissures

(C) The surface loading

(D) The steep slopes and caldera walls

Chapter 2

English/Writing

The SAT provides four writing passages, each with 11 questions that give you the opportunity to correct for grammar, rewrite a phrase for style and clarity, or add or move a sentence for logic and flow. These questions are designed to see whether you can write clearly and effectively.

The Problems You'll Work On

When working through the questions in this chapter, be prepared to

- Correct punctuation, including commas, semicolons, and dashes.
- Rewrite sentences for logic and flow.
- Get the gist of phrases and choose the right transition words (such as *but, however,* and *therefore*).
- Add or move sentences for style and clarity.
- Create effective working titles for passages.

What to Watch Out For

The answer choices can be deceiving. Watch out for trap answer choices that

- Appear grammatically correct but don't support the logic or flow of the passage
- Seem to clarify but actually have a lot of unnecessary wording
- Work well by themselves but aren't consistent with a phrase earlier or later in the passage

Passage 1

Questions 121–131 are based on the following information.

The following passage is an excerpt from The New American High School *by Theodore Sizer (Wiley-Blackwell).*

We have long believed that every American teenager [121] deserved an education that will equip [122] them for a lifetime of constructive activity. We responded over a century ago by creating a locally controlled system of secondary schools. The word *system*, itself, is instructive; it was not imposed by federal or state authorities; instead, it largely evolved in its details if not its structure. In community after community, citizens at the grassroots—the parents of the school-age [123] children organized their schools along lines that they felt were universally endorsed and thus could be considered the "best."

[124] Things were not always as they seemed; a high school was started here but not there; one high school offered a rich program of offerings, another only the bare bones. The schools took root most quickly in the Northeast and Midwest in the latter part of the nineteenth century, as these areas of the [125] country, especially in urban areas, [126] had excess tax-raised money that could be used to erect a building and gather a principal and staff. [127] Southern states were still recovering from the dislocations and costs of the Civil War, and their populations included many African American citizens for whom schooling had to be provided from scratch. [128] The notion of a mass, universally inclusive national education system took decades to establish. This is still in motion, as witnessed by a surge in Latino populations from Mexico and elsewhere. These populations carry with them a mix of languages, customs, and expectations. There is energy in this, but the constantly differing demands challenge us—and should.

Over a century ago, our elected officials, with the citizens' blessing, decided to design the high schools on the basis of [129] student's ages. ("If you are sixteen, [130] you are most likely to be in eleventh grade.") A late-nineteenth-century nation dominated by farmers arranged for school to take place only during the nine months when teenagers were not needed in the fields. These predecessors organized the work of students and teachers into subjects, each occupying a block or two of designated time, each to be covered as prescribed by [131] common plans. By the 1920s, high school had come to be a kind of secular religion, and criticizing its basic design was therefore, in some quarters, a form of blasphemy.

121. (A) NO CHANGE
(B) deserves
(C) had deserved
(D) had been deserving

122. (A) NO CHANGE
(B) him or her
(C) one
(D) it

123. (A) NO CHANGE
(B) children,
(C) children;
(D) children—

124. Which of the following choices summarizes the patchy framework discussed in the rest of the sentence?
(A) NO CHANGE
(B) The process was at first hit or miss;
(C) Things got to a rough start;
(D) The process was slow to get going;

125. (A) NO CHANGE
(B) country;
(C) country—
(D) country

126. (A) NO CHANGE
(B) have
(C) did have
(D) having

127. At this point, the writer is considering adding the following phrase:

In the early twentieth century,

Should the writer make this addition?

(A) Yes, because it builds the timeline of the formation of the modern high school.
(B) Yes, because it sets the context of the Southern states recovering from the Civil War.
(C) No, because the time when this occurred is a separate topic and not central to the narrative.
(D) No, because it implies that things may have turned out differently had this initiative been at a different time.

128. Which choice most effectively combines the underlined sentences?

(A) A surge in Latino populations from Mexico and elsewhere carried with them a mix of languages, customs, and expectations; it was these which was attracted to the notion of a mass, universally inclusive education system which took decades to establish and is still in motion.
(B) What took decades to establish and is still in motion is the notion of a mass, universally inclusive education system that would accommodate a surge in Latino populations from Mexico and elsewhere which carried with them a mix of languages, customs, and expectations.
(C) The notion of a mass, universally inclusive national education system took decades to establish and is still in motion, as witnessed by a surge in Latino populations from Mexico and elsewhere, carrying with them a mix of languages, customs, and expectations.
(D) The notion of a mass, universally inclusive national education system took decades to establish and is still in motion and is witnessed by a surge in Latino populations from Mexico and elsewhere which carried with them a mix of languages, customs, and expectations.

129. (A) NO CHANGE
(B) students
(C) students'
(D) students's

130. (A) NO CHANGE
(B) he is
(C) they are
(D) it is

131. (A) NO CHANGE
(B) common planning
(C) commonly planned
(D) a common plan

Passage 2

Questions 132–142 are based on the following information.

The following passage is an excerpt from The Wiley-Blackwell Companion to Sociology, *edited by George Ritzer (Wiley-Blackwell).*

The future of science and technology can be summed up in one [132] word; more. We will have more scientific knowledge in the coming years, [133] not least due to the fact that the formal institution of science is now geared up to producing huge amounts of data, conference papers, and [134] writing journal articles. And [135] there will be more technology as technocapitalism seeks to invigorate existing [136] markets— and to construct new ones —markets through creating new technological products, and governments continue to seek technological solutions to societal problems. For sociology of science and technology the challenge is [137] to understand why current trends are continuing and to provide frameworks for understanding what science and technology mean in society. This is a big challenge, touching upon issues ranging from the relationship between [138] individuals and their personal technologies to the very nature of humanity itself (Fuller 2007a: ch. 6). [139] In addition, the range of theories available and the history of social analyses of science and technology should reassure us that this challenge can be surmounted, at least to some degree and in the confines of academic discourse.

The even greater challenge is to analyze and, perhaps, confront the wider context of scientism and technological determinism [140] that challenges us today. Sociologists of knowledge have long realized that escaping from the clutches of dominant thought in society [141] can be done. This explains, at least in part, the continuing tension between the natural sciences and those who apply formal scientific methods, knowledge, and theory to the production of technologies, and [142] those applying social theoretical frameworks to make sense of science and technology. This is a gap that, at least for the foreseeable future, will not be easily bridged.

132. (A) NO CHANGE
(B) word:
(C) word,
(D) word—

133. At this point the author is considering adding the following phrase:

and more evidence of such,

Should the author make this addition?

(A) Yes, because it adds emphasis.
(B) Yes, because it adds clarification.
(C) No, because it is redundant.
(D) No, because it is confusing.

134. (A) NO CHANGE
(B) journal articles
(C) composing journal articles
(D) writing of journal articles

135. (A) NO CHANGE
(B) there shall be
(C) we will have
(D) we will know

136. (A) NO CHANGE
(B) markets,
(C) markets:
(D) markets

137. At this point the author is considering adding the following phrase:

not to predict the future but

Should the author make this addition?

(A) Yes, because it offsets this point from the thesis of the passage, which is the future.
(B) Yes, because it clarifies the point that the future is predicted and not simply known.
(C) No, because it distracts from the current trends, which is the point of the passage.
(D) No, because it is redundant, as the future cannot be predicted.

138. (A) NO CHANGE
(B) the individual and
(C) individuals with
(D) DELETE the underlined portion

139. (A) NO CHANGE
(B) Furthermore,
(C) Yet
(D) On the other hand,

140. (A) NO CHANGE
(B) that confounds us today
(C) that we deal with today
(D) DELETE the underlined portion

141. Which of the following choices supports the point of the paragraph?
(A) NO CHANGE
(B) is a simple process
(C) is no easy matter
(D) takes time

142. Which of the following choices most closely matches the style of the paragraph?
(A) NO CHANGE
(B) the individuals
(C) the scientists
(D) the sociologists

Passage 3

Questions 143–153 are based on the following information.

The following passage is an excerpt from Tap, Click, Read, *by Lisa Guernsey and Michael H. Levine (Wiley-Blackwell).*

One recent day in California, a six-year-old boy named Brandon was hanging out at home, [143] and watching one of Disney's *Ice Age* movies, when he saw a scene that captivated him. On the screen were the lovable animations of *Ice Age*'s prehistoric beasts, loping along the [144] barren, icy terrain. Brandon turned to his father: "Papi, at that time, what was it like? There weren't any buses?" Smiling, his father, [145] José Rubén, saw this as a teachable moment. He went to his computer, pulled up YouTube, and searched for videos that would show his son more about what life was like [146].

"We watched videos where it is shown and everything," the father said as he [147] recast this scene for Amber Levinson, a Stanford researcher whose work informed a recent report from the Joan Ganz Cooney Center. [148] Brandon and José Rubén were soon watching a documentary about dinosaurs and other species. This was after their interests led them from one history video to another.

What does watching Disney movies and a dinosaur documentary have to do with reading and literacy? So much more than you might think. Here was a moment in which Brandon was engaged in building his knowledge base, getting an introduction to concepts and ideas that [149] not only gave him a little more understanding of the Ice Age, but also helped him put the Ice Age into context of other periods in history and start to gain a framework for thinking about how time passes and how change happens. He was hooked in enough to start [150] the reflecting upon and then store new information for recall sometime in the future when he may be asked to talk about, read about, or write about—*be literate about*—how life has changed on Planet Earth [151].

What's more, Brandon was also getting a lesson in media literacy and digital literacy. Though his father may not have even realized it, he was modeling what it looks like to use digital information to gain a deeper sense of the world. He recognized the importance of Brandon's question and addressed [152] them by spending time helping him find answers. He showed what it looks like to search for information online and make distinctions between fiction (a movie) and non-fiction [153] (a video).

143. (A) NO CHANGE
(B) watching
(C) watched
(D) was watching

144. (A) NO CHANGE
(B) barren
(C) barren and
(D) DELETE the underlined portion

145. (A) NO CHANGE
(B) José Rubén
(C) José Rubén—
(D) DELETE the underlined portion and preceding comma

146. At this point, the author is considering adding the following phrase:

during that time

Should the author add this phrase?

(A) Yes, because it adds to the conversational tone of the passage.
(B) Yes, because it clarifies the time period José Rubén wanted to show Brandon.
(C) No, because it distracts from the main point of the passage.
(D) No, because it is not consistent with the theme of the passage.

147. (A) NO CHANGE
(B) recounted
(C) recanted
(D) retracted

148. Which of the following choices most effectively combines the two underlined sentences?

(A) Brandon and José Rubén were soon watching a documentary about dinosaurs and other species, after their interests led them from one history video to another.
(B) After their interests led them from one history video to another, Brandon and José Rubén were soon watching a documentary about dinosaurs and other species.
(C) Brandon and José Rubén's interests led them from one history video to another, and soon the two of them were watching a documentary about dinosaurs and other species.
(D) Their interests led from one history video to another, and soon Brandon and José Rubén were watching a documentary about dinosaurs and other species.

149. (A) NO CHANGE
(B) for one thing
(C) for starters
(D) had the effect of

150. (A) NO CHANGE
(B) to reflect
(C) reflections
(D) the reflection

151. At this point, the author is considering adding the following phrase:

over so many years

Should the author add this phrase?

(A) Yes, because it clarifies when life has been changing.
(B) Yes, because it adds emphasis.
(C) No, because it distracts and confuses.
(D) No, because it is obvious.

152. (A) NO CHANGE
(B) it
(C) those
(D) that

153. (A) NO CHANGE
(B) (a documentary)
(C) (another movie)
(D) DELETE the underlined portion

Passage 4

Questions 154–164 are based on the following information.

The following passage is an excerpt from On the Rocketship: How Top Charter Schools Are Pushing the Envelope, *by Richard Whitmire (Wiley-Blackwell).*

August 2013: Milwaukee, Wisconsin

This Thursday morning marks day [154] number four of the opening week for Southside Prep, Rocketship Education's first school in Milwaukee and the [155] charter group's first launch outside its California base. A lot hinges on the success of this school, which may explain why founding principal Brittany Kinser is nervous as she prepares for her first morning coffee with parents. About forty parents, almost all of them Latinos who took a chance by enrolling their children in a little-known school, [156] await her arrival in the cafeteria. Southside Prep opened with 270 students, a little more than 200 students short of the goal, [157] which was 500 students. Kinser's job this morning is to keep these parents happy and convince them to recruit their friends and relatives to switch schools [158] and instead send their children here. She's about to ask the parents what they like and don't like about Rocketship's first week. It's that second question [159] that makes her nervous.

The contrast between these Latino parents and the young, nearly all-white staff at Southside Prep, all graduates of top colleges, is stark. Kinser may be thirty-six but she looks at least a decade younger. Her quick body language and trim figure suggest that she is not just a runner, [160] and a serious runner at that. Just minutes earlier at the "launch," a Rocketship tradition in which the entire school gathers each morning to chant the school's aspirational creed, hand out awards, and dance crazily to some really, really loud music, everyone gyrated to Katy Perry's "Firework," not exactly traditional school music. In tradition-bound Milwaukee, this is something different: a shot of hip California [161] arrives in, of all places, South Side Milwaukee, a neighborhood that in just a decade flipped from Polish to Latino. And now this change, a Silicon Valley startup school located in a refurbished party props warehouse. How weird is that? Would these parents accept or reject Rocketship? Getting the Milwaukee launch off [162] smooth means everything to Rocketship. Stumble here and the stumble reverberates across the county. No wonder Kinser is nervous. [163] [164]

154. (A) NO CHANGE
(B) of
(C) counting
(D) DELETE the underlined portion

155. (A) NO CHANGE
(B) the first launch of the charter school
(C) the charter school's first launching
(D) the first launching of the charter school

156. (A) NO CHANGE
(B) are waiting for
(C) await for
(D) DELETE the underlined portion

157. (A) NO CHANGE
(B) of 500 students [and delete the comma following "goal"]
(C) which was 500 students this year
(D) DELETE the underlined portion and end the sentence with a period

158. (A) NO CHANGE
(B) and send
(C) sending
(D) while sending

159. (A) NO CHANGE
(B) making
(C) while making
(D) DELETE the underlined portion

160. (A) NO CHANGE
(B) but also a serious runner
(C) but a serious runner
(D) DELETE the underlined portion

161. (A) NO CHANGE
(B) arrived
(C) arriving
(D) will be arriving

162. (A) NO CHANGE
(B) smoothly
(C) smoother
(D) DELETE the underlined portion

163. At this point, the author wants to shift focus from the school and principal to the founders. Which sentence most effectively does this?
(A) The Rocketship concept has a fascinating story, beginning with the founders.
(B) Getting to know why Kinser is nervous requires learning the Rocketship story, which means getting to know the founders.
(C) Kinser played a pivotal role in the establishment of the Rocketship school in the Milwaukee neighborhood.
(D) Katy Perry's "Firework" was an unusual but fitting song at the enrollment event.

164. How should the author best add the sentence that is the answer to the preceding question?
(A) Put it at the end of the final paragraph in the passage.
(B) Use it to begin a new paragraph that continues the passage.
(C) Use it to begin the passage.
(D) Not use the sentence.

Passage 5

Questions 165–175 are based on the following information.

The following passage is an excerpt from 35 Seasons of U.S. Antarctic Meteorites (1976–2010): A Pictorial Guide to the Collection, *edited by Kevin Righter, Catherine Corrigan, Timothy McCoy, and Ralph Harvey (Wiley-Blackwell).*

The information that would first lead U.S. teams [165] in search for meteorites in Antarctica [166] was presented at an evening session of the Meteoritical Society on 27 August 1973 in Davos, Switzerland. On that occasion, Dr. Makoto Shima of the Institute of Physical and Chemical Research of Japan described four meteorite fragments with differing mineralogical and chemical compositions that [167] were collected in 1969 from a downhill sloping patch of bare ice in the Yamato Mountains of eastern Antarctica.

In the audience [168] sat William A. Cassidy, of the University of Pittsburgh. Bill Cassidy wrote later that, on hearing that report, a comic-strip lightbulb appeared in his mind with a message reading: "Meteorites are *concentrated* on the ice!" [169] Cassidy expected the whole room to be excited, but looking around he found the audience looking as comatose and glassy-eyed [170] that audiences sometimes do. I was chairing the session that evening, but I was much too preoccupied with keeping the speakers more or less on schedule to be having any eureka experiences.

After the session, Cassidy talked with Dr. Shima and his wife, Dr. Masako [171] Shima—both of whom are chemists who were then visiting the Max-Planck-Institut für Chemie in Mainz. Dr. Shima explained to Cassidy that the team of glaciologists in the Yamato Mountains had collected five more meteorites from the same patch of ice. Of the nine meteorites, only the four they had reported on had been analyzed for their chemical compositions and rare gas contents. These had been identified as (a) an enstatite chondrite, (b) a Ca-poor achondrite, (c) a probable carbonaceous chondrite, and (d) an olivinebronzite chondrite. The remaining five also clearly were meteorites of differing types. Earlier that summer the Shimas had coauthored an article about the four analyzed meteorites [172] <u>along with</u> Dr. Heinrich Hintenberger of Mainz, in *Earth and Planetary Science Letters* [*Shima et al.*, *1973*], and the Shimas also had published a brief summary of their chemical results in the abstract volume of the meeting at Davos [*Shima and Shima, 1973*]. But Cassidy had not seen the article and [173] <u>had skimmed</u> too quickly through the abstracts.

At the meeting, Cassidy was captivated by the evidence that meteorites from different falls sometimes are concentrated by the dynamics of ice motion. Within the hour, he began planning a proposal to the National Science Foundation's Division of Polar Programs to lead an expedition to search for meteorite concentrations on patches of ice in Antarctica. He assumed that the concentration in the Yamato Mountains could not be unique in a huge continent making up 9% of the Earth's land surface, so he [174] <u>proposed</u> to work out of McMurdo Station, the U.S. base that lies near the opposite edge of Antarctica from the Yamato Mountains. [175]

165. (A) NO CHANGE
(B) with the
(C) to
(D) DELETE the underlined portion

166. (A) NO CHANGE
(B) were
(C) to be
(D) DELETE the underlined portion

167. (A) NO CHANGE
(B) was
(C) had been
(D) to be

168. (A) NO CHANGE
(B) was sitting
(C) would be sitting
(D) DELETE the underlined portion

169. Which sentence, placed here, effectively sets up William Cassidy's excitement as a contrast to the other attendees' apparent lack of interest?
(A) The ice was a natural collecting place for meteorites.
(B) To him, this was a new and electrifying idea.
(C) This made perfect logical sense.
(D) The others in the audience were as quiet as before.

170. (A) NO CHANGE
(B) as
(C) the way
(D) which

171. (A) NO CHANGE
(B) Shima,
(C) Shima;
(D) Shima

172. (A) NO CHANGE
(B) partnered with
(C) with
(D) DELETE the underlined portion

173. (A) NO CHANGE
(B) skimmed
(C) was skimming
(D) skims

174. (A) NO CHANGE
(B) shall propose
(C) would propose
(D) had to propose

175. A suitable title for this passage is

(A) The Composition Variety of Four Early Meteorite Fragments Discovered in the Yamato Mountains

(B) The Origin and Early History of the Yamato Mountains Search for Meteorites Program

(C) The Origin and Early History of the Japanese Antarctic Search for Meteorites Program

(D) The Origin and Early History of the U.S. Antarctic Search for Meteorites Program

Passage 6

Questions 176–186 are based on the following information.

The following passage is an excerpt from A Practical Guide to Scientific Data Analysis, *by David J. Livingstone (Wiley-Blackwell).*

Statistics is often concerned [176] with the treatment of a small number of samples [177] who have been drawn from a much larger population. Each of these samples may be described by one or more variables which have been measured or calculated for that sample. For each variable there [178] exist a population of samples. It is the properties of these populations of variables that allow the assignment of probabilities, for example, the likelihood that the value of a variable will fall into a particular range, and the assessment of significance (i.e. is one number significantly different from another). Probability theory and statistics [179] are, in fact, separate subjects; each may be said to be the inverse of the other, but for the purposes of this discussion, they may be regarded as doing the same job.

(1) Perhaps one of the most familiar concepts in statistics [180] are the frequency distributions. (2) A plot of a frequency distribution is shown in Figure 2.1, where the ordinate (y-axis) represents the number of occurrences of a particular value of a variable given by the scales of the abscissa (x-axis). [181]

If the data is [182] discrete—usually but not necessarily measured on nominal or ordinal scales, then the variable values can only correspond [183] for the points marked on the scale on the abscissa. If the data is continuous, [184] then a problem arises in the creation of a frequency distribution, since every value in the data set may be different and the resultant plot would be a very uninteresting straight line at $y = 1$. This may be overcome by taking ranges of the variable and counting the number of occurrences of values within each range. For the example shown in Figure 2.2 (where there are a total of 50 values in all), the ranges are 0–1, 1–2, 2–3, and so on up to 9–10.

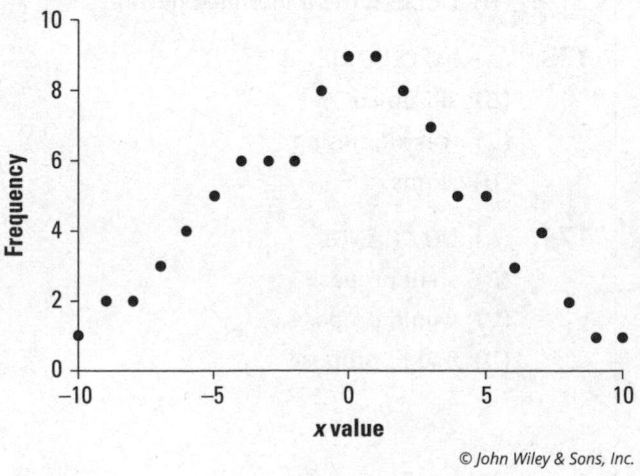

FIGURE 2-1

Frequency
x range
© John Wiley & Sons, Inc.

FIGURE 2-2

It can be seen that these points fall on a roughly bell-shaped curve with the largest number of occurrences of the variable occurring around the peak of the curve, corresponding to the mean of the set. [185] [186]

176. (A) NO CHANGE
(B) for
(C) about
(D) and worried

177. (A) NO CHANGE
(B) as they
(C) which
(D) DELETE the underlined portion

178. (A) NO CHANGE
(B) exists
(C) could be
(D) had to have been

179. (A) NO CHANGE
(B) is, in fact, a separate subject;
(C) are, in fact, separate subjects—
(D) is, in fact, a separate subject—

180. (A) NO CHANGE
(B) are frequency distributions
(C) is the frequency distribution
(D) DELETE the underlined portion

181. To initiate thought on this topic, the author is considering adding this rhetorical question:

How are the properties of the population used?

Where in this paragraph should this question be added?

(A) Before Sentence 1
(B) After Sentence 1
(C) After Sentence 2
(D) The question should not be added.

182. (A) NO CHANGE
(B) discrete,
(C) discrete:
(D) discrete and

183. (A) NO CHANGE
(B) to
(C) about
(D) in

184. (A) NO CHANGE
(B) when
(C) it follows that
(D) DELETE the underlined portion

185. A suitable title for this passage is

(A) A Plot of a Population
(B) Data Distribution
(C) The Axes x and y
(D) Separating Data

186. A suitable title for the graphs is

(A) Dots as a Triangle
(B) The Nature of Data
(C) Frequency and the x-Value
(D) The Pyramid

Passage 7

Questions 187–197 are based on the following information.

The following passage is an excerpt from Biology For Dummies, *by Rene Fester Kratz, PhD, and Donna Rae Siegfried (Wiley).*

In the inner membranes of the mitochondria in your [187] cells, hundreds of little cellular machines are busily working to transfer energy from food molecules to ATP. The cellular machines are called *electron transport chains,* and [188] their made of a team of proteins that [189] is seated in the membranes transferring energy and electrons throughout the machines.

The coenzymes NADH and $FADH_2$ carry energy and electrons from glycolysis and the Krebs cycle [190] to the electron transport chain. The coenzymes transfer the electrons to the proteins of the electron transport chain, which [191] pass the electrons down the chain. Oxygen collects the electrons at the end of the chain. [192] When oxygen accepts the electrons, it also picks up protons (H^+) and becomes water (H_2O).

The proteins of the electron transport chain are [193] as a bucket brigade that works by one person dumping a bucket full of water into the next person's bucket. The buckets are the proteins, or electron carriers, and the water inside the buckets [194] represent the electrons. The electrons get passed from protein to protein until they reach the end of the chain.

While electrons are transferred along the electron transport chain, the proteins [195] are using energy to move protons (H^+) across the inner membranes of the mitochondria. They pile the protons up like water behind the "dam" of the inner membranes. These protons then flow back across the mitochondria's membranes through a protein called *ATP synthase* that transforms the kinetic energy from the moving protons into chemical energy in ATP by capturing the energy in chemical bonds as [196] it added phosphate molecules to ADP.

The entire process of how ATP is made at the electron transport chain is called the *chemiosmotic theory of oxidative phosphorylation.* [197]

187. (A) NO CHANGE
(B) cells;
(C) cells—
(D) cells

188. (A) NO CHANGE
(B) there
(C) they're
(D) the

189. (A) NO CHANGE
(B) sits
(C) has been seated
(D) are seated

190. (A) NO CHANGE
(B) for
(C) with
(D) over to

191. (A) NO CHANGE
(B) passes
(C) are passing
(D) is passing

192. At this point, the authors are considering adding the following sentence in parentheses:
(If you didn't have oxygen around at the end of the chain to collect the electrons, no energy transfer could occur.)
Should they add this phrase?
(A) Yes, because it adds light humor to a scientific topic.
(B) Yes, because it effectively sets up the role of oxygen in the next sentence.
(C) No, because it distracts from the narrative of transferring energy to ATP.
(D) No, because oxygen is not actually part of the process.

193. (A) NO CHANGE
(B) to be
(C) as if
(D) like

194. (A) NO CHANGE
(B) represents
(C) is
(D) are

195. (A) NO CHANGE
(B) use
(C) make use of
(D) get use from

196. (A) NO CHANGE
(B) is added
(C) it adds
(D) adding

197. A suitable title for this passage would be
(A) Proteins and the Transport Chain
(B) Transferring Energy to ATP
(C) Your Inner Bucket Brigade
(D) Mitochondria and the Krebs Cycle

Passage 8

Questions 198–208 are based on the following information.

The following passage is an excerpt from Sherlock Holmes For Dummies, *by Steven Doyle and David A. Crowder (Wiley).*

The public was wildly enthusiastic about Sherlock Holmes, [198] truly one man didn't share that feeling. Incredibly, it was Arthur Conan Doyle himself. He had greater ambitions in mind as a [199] writer but he believed he'd make his mark in literature by writing historical novels. [200] Doyle began to see the detective as an impediment to his work instead of as a part of it.

Economic realities kept Doyle writing about Holmes for a while longer, [201] but he soon began to plot a way out. While vacationing in Switzerland, he found a way to make sure Sherlock never bothered him again.

[202] To add a new, interesting character, Doyle created another character who was as great a villain as Holmes was a hero: Professor Moriarty, the "Napoleon of crime," the most serious threat Holmes would ever face.

It was on that vacation in Switzerland that Doyle found the crime scene: Reichenbach Falls. With its thundering cascade plunging over 800 feet and its mist rising out of a fearful chasm far below, it seemed a perfectly [203] beautiful place for Holmes to end his career. Upon his return to England, Doyle wrote "The Final Problem," and on the night he finished it, he wrote in his diary just two words, "Killed Holmes."

(1) Doyle never realized how popular Sherlock Holmes was until he killed him. (2) "I was amazed at the concern expressed by the public," he wrote in his autobiography. (3) "They say a man is never properly appreciated until he is [204] dead, and the general protest against my summary execution of Holmes taught me how many and numerous were his friends." [205]

Over 20,000 people canceled their subscriptions to *The Strand Magazine* in protest. Young men in London took to wearing black mourning bands. Some young women wore black. The Prince of Wales expressed [206] dismay; it was rumored that Queen Victoria herself "was not amused."

In the timeline of the Sherlockian [207] cannon, Sherlock Holmes was officially dead from 1891 to 1894. In reality, ten years passed before Doyle decided to officially reverse the death sentence and bring Holmes back to life. [208]

198. (A) NO CHANGE
(B) furthermore
(C) but
(D) therefore

199. (A) NO CHANGE
(B) writer;
(C) writer,
(D) writer and

200. At this point, the authors want to add a sentence to set up the public's response to Holmes's death later in the passage. Which choice most effectively does this?

(A) The public enjoyed both Sherlock Holmes and Professor Moriarty, the supervillain who would take his life.
(B) Reichenback Falls was soon to occupy a place in Holmes's history and the public mind.
(C) The public, however, wanted more Sherlock Holmes.
(D) Though Doyle enjoyed writing about Sherlock Holmes, he wanted something more.

201. (A) NO CHANGE
(B) and
(C) furthermore
(D) DELETE the underlined portion

202. Which answer choice most effectively supports Doyle's reason for creating Professor Moriarty?

(A) NO CHANGE
(B) To break from the mundane,
(C) To keep things interesting,
(D) To kill off Sherlock Holmes,

203. Which word choice most effectively describes the role of Reichenbach Falls as Holmes's place of death?

(A) NO CHANGE
(B) orderly
(C) dramatic
(D) natural

204. (A) NO CHANGE
(B) dead—
(C) dead;
(D) dead:

205. The authors are considering adding this quote from Doyle as an example of the public's response to Holmes's death:

"'You Brute!' was the beginning of the letter which one lady sent me. . . ."

Where in this paragraph should this sentence be added?

(A) Before Sentence 1
(B) After Sentence 1
(C) After Sentence 2
(D) After Sentence 3, continuing the quote from Doyle

206. (A) NO CHANGE
(B) dismay—
(C) dismay, furthermore
(D) dismay, and

207. (A) NO CHANGE
(B) canon
(C) maxim
(D) axiom

208. A suitable title for this passage would be

(A) The Death (and Rebirth) of Sherlock Holmes
(B) Professor Moriarty: The Napoleon of Crime
(C) Sherlock Holmes and *The Strand Magazine*
(D) Sir Arthur Conan Doyle and Sherlock Holmes

Passage 9

Questions 209–219 are based on the following information.

The following passage is an excerpt from Dendroclimatic Studies: Tree Growth and Climate Change in Northern Forests, *by Rosanne D'Arrigo, Nicole Davi, Gordon Jacoby, Rob Wilson, and Greg Wiles (Wiley-Blackwell).*

The research described [209] here in adheres to the basic principles of dendrochronology, as [210] was outlined in introductory and general texts by Stokes and Smiley (1968), Fritts (1976), Schweingruber (1988), Cook and Kairiukstis (1990), Speer (2012), and others. [211] There is a method known as cross-dating. This derives the main premise of dendrochronology and is the establishment of precise, high-resolution (annually resolved) tree-ring chronologies (references above; Glossary). The cross-dating technique is based upon the observation that there is a common climatic and environmental signal in the ring-width variations of samples of wood compiled from trees (of the same species) [212]. Relatively narrow (wide) rings are used to infer more adverse [213] (favorable) environmental conditions for growth. When performed correctly, this method [214] insures that there are no dating errors resulting from anomalous growth patterns. These include, for example, false rings (Glossary); in which growth is slowed, resulting in thicker-walled cells, for a period during the growing season due to a particular adverse event, such as drought, or missing rings (in which radial growth is not laid down in a particular wood sample or tree due to an adverse event; Glossary). Although it has been [215] implied by Mann and colleagues (2012), based on tree-growth model simulations, that such missing rings can occur amongst all trees at a given site following major volcanic events (e.g., in 1258, 1815), there is no actual tree-ring evidence that this is in fact the case, as indicated in several subsequent presentations and publications (Anchukaitis et al., 2012a; Esper et al., 2013, in press; D'Arrigo et al., 2012a; D'Arrigo et al., 2001b; Journal of Geophysical Research, in press).

The science of dendroclimatology evolved from the need to understand past and present climate variability as well as the factors impacting tree growth and climate response on a range of spatial and [216] vascular scales. Determination of how climate has varied in the past is also critically important for evaluating the sensitivity of the Earth's climate system to both natural and anthropogenic forcing. [217] Yet instrumental observations are limited in length and spatial coverage, particularly in many remote far northern regions, where station records may only span a few decades. Overcoming these limitations requires high-resolution, precisely dated proxy data archives, [218] like tree rings, so that we may derive a long-term perspective for conditions during the recent anthropogenic era, during which profound and rapid changes are now taking place. [219]

209. (A) NO CHANGE
(B) herein
(C) heron
(D) heroine

210. (A) NO CHANGE
(B) were
(C) had been
(D) DELETE the underlined portion

211. Which of the following is the best way to combine these two sentences?

(A) There is a method known as cross-dating, which derives the main premise of dendrochronology and is the establishment of precise, high-resolution (annually resolved) tree-ring chronologies.

(B) A method, known as cross-dating, derives the main premise of dendrochronology and is the establishment of precise, high-resolution (annually resolved) tree-ring chronologies.

(C) The main premise of dendrochronology is the establishment of precise, high-resolution (annually resolved) tree-ring chronologies, derived using the method known as cross-dating.

(D) The main premise of dendrochronology is the establishment of precise, high-resolution (annually resolved) tree-ring chronologies, which is derived using the method known as cross-dating.

212. Which of the following phrases best completes the sentence and clarifies that the ring widths were compared with little other variation?

(A) from the same site and region

(B) from various locations at the site

(C) of various ages

(D) at different heights of the trunks

213. (A) NO CHANGE

(B) (or different)

(C) (from the forest)

(D) DELETE the underlined portion

214. (A) NO CHANGE

(B) ensures

(C) ansures

(D) unsures

215. (A) NO CHANGE

(B) alluded

(C) implicated

(D) suggested

216. (A) NO CHANGE

(B) temporal

(C) cyclical

(D) meteorological

217. (A) NO CHANGE

(B) Furthermore,

(C) On the other hand,

(D) And,

218. (A) NO CHANGE

(B) formerly

(C) such as

(D) DELETE the underlined portion

219. A suitable title for this passage would be

(A) True and False Tree Rings

(B) Correctly Dating Trees from Rings

(C) The Earth's Climate and Tree Rings

(D) Basic Tree-Ring Principles

Passage 10

Questions 220–230 are based on the following information.

The following passage is an excerpt from Robert's Rules For Dummies, *by C. Alan Jennings, P.R.P. (Wiley).*

You don't really have an organization until you define it by adopting bylaws. [220] And producing the right bylaws for your unique group requires a good deal of focus.

So when you reach the point in your organizational [221] discussion at which everyone has agreed to form an association, the time has come to authorize and appoint a committee to put together a set of bylaws for your organizing group to consider and [222] adapt.

[223] Your committee volunteers need to commit to several regular meetings, because the job can take a while.

A parliamentarian is a valuable consultant at this stage of the organizational process. You can save [224] yourself, every member of the bylaws committee, and pretty much everyone involved countless hours by getting some professional [225] help for this part of the process.

If you want to make the best decision when selecting members of your bylaws committee, [226] be sure to include on the committee all your best thinkers and writers. Just as important, make sure you include anybody [227] who will probably have a lot to say about all the rules and details that go in bylaws. Get those people to the committee meetings and put them to work. Otherwise, they'll wear you out at the meeting in which the bylaws are up for official adoption. Agreeing to build a new organization is [228] the first step; quite another is agreeing on all the details of how the group needs to operate.

Taking into account the ideas and concerns of anybody interested at the committee level can actually help you develop a good set of bylaws that doesn't tie your hands at inappropriate [229] times, [230] nor leave you open to the whims of bothersome members after you nail things down.

220. (A) NO CHANGE
(B) However
(C) Currently
(D) Be aware, however, that

221. (A) NO CHANGE
(B) survey
(C) meeting
(D) dictum

222. (A) NO CHANGE
(B) adopt
(C) adept
(D) adroit

223. At this point, Jennings wishes to add a line that states the importance of the work that the committee does. Which of the following choices does this best?
(A) The members of this committee must be carefully selected.
(B) This committee is highly visible among many organizations.
(C) The trust bestowed upon this committee is an important statement of faith.
(D) This committee does some important work that has far-reaching effects.

224. (A) NO CHANGE
(B) all the people in the bylaws committee, including yourself,
(C) yourself and every member of the bylaws committee
(D) all the people involved, including yourself and the other members of the bylaws committee

225. (A) NO CHANGE
(B) assistance
(C) attitude
(D) opinions

226. (A) NO CHANGE
(B) always
(C) make sure to
(D) DELETE the underlined portion

227. (A) NO CHANGE
(B) whom
(C) that
(D) which

228. (A) NO CHANGE
(B) a start;
(C) one thing;
(D) true;

229. (A) NO CHANGE
(B) times;
(C) times—
(D) times

230. (A) NO CHANGE
(B) or
(C) and
(D) DELETE the underlined portion

Passage 11

Questions 231–241 are based on the following information.

The following passage is an excerpt from U.S. History For Dummies, *by Steve Wiegand (Wiley).*

Hopscotching from the British Isles to the Shetland Islands to the Faroe Islands, the Vikings arrived in Iceland about AD 870. [231] Around 985, a colorful character known as Eric the Red discovered Greenland and [232] lead settlers there.

[233] Like many things in human history, the [234] Vikings first visits to the North American continent were by accident. The first sighting of the New World by a European probably occurred around 987, when a Viking named Bjarni Herjolfsson sailed from Iceland to hook up with his dad and missed Greenland. Herjolfsson wasn't impressed by what he saw from the ship, and he never actually set foot on land before heading back to Greenland. [235]

Herjolfsson was followed about 15 years later by the son of Eric the Red. His name was Leif Ericsson, also known as Leif the Lucky. Leif landed in what's now Labrador, a part of Newfoundland, Canada. [236] Amazed by his discovery, Leif called the area Vinland. He spent the winter in the new land and then left to take over the family business, which was [237] to run colonies in Greenland that his dad had founded.

His brother Thorvald visited Vinland the next year. Thorvald got into a fight with the local inhabitants, and [238] he thus gained the distinction of being the first European to be killed by the natives in North America. (Vikings called the natives *skraelings*, a [239] laudable term meaning "dwarves.") After his death, Thorvald's crew went back to Greenland.

The next Viking visit was meant to be permanent. Led by a brother-in-law of Leif's named Thorfinn Karlsefni, [240] and an expedition of three ships, some cattle, and about 160 people — including some women — created a settlement. [241]

231. At this point, Wiegand wants to add a sentence that alludes to the reason the Vikings left Iceland and went to Greenland. Which of the following choices does this?
(A) Food and comforts in Iceland were plentiful.
(B) But Iceland got crowded pretty quickly.
(C) Warmed by the Gulf Stream, Iceland is temperate most of the year round.
(D) Though warm, the summers in Iceland can be chilly.

232. (A) NO CHANGE
(B) leaded
(C) led
(D) laud

233. (A) NO CHANGE
(B) As
(C) Such as
(D) As it were

234. (A) NO CHANGE
(B) Vikings'
(C) Vikings's
(D) Vikingz

235. At this point, the author is considering adding the following sentence:

Herjolfsson was later reproached by King Eric Haakonsson for his lack of investigation.

Should the author add this sentence?

(A) Yes, because it is important information for the series of events.
(B) Yes, because it is an interesting fact that supports the narrative.
(C) No, because it contradicts the theme of the Viking discovery.
(D) No, because it is irrelevant and distracts from the flow of the narrative.

236. Which of the following best explains the name Vinland given by Leif Ericsson?

(A) NO CHANGE
(B) Wistful for unexplored business opportunities back home,
(C) Considering his options of whether to settle permanently,
(D) Mistaking seasonal berries for grapes,

237. (A) NO CHANGE
(B) running
(C) to be running
(D) setting and running

238. (A) NO CHANGE
(B) Thorvald
(C) he was
(D) DELETE the underlined portion

239. (A) NO CHANGE
(B) stoic
(C) contemptuous
(D) veracious

240. (A) NO CHANGE
(B) with
(C) along
(D) DELETE the underlined portion

241. A suitable title for this passage would be

(A) Following in Eric the Red's Footsteps
(B) North America as a Nordic Destination
(C) Visits by the Vikings
(D) Karlsefni Establishes a Permanent Settlement

Passage 12

Questions 242–252 are based on the following information.

The following passage is an excerpt from Imaging Marine Life: Macrophotography and Microscopy Approaches for Marine Biology, *edited by Emmanuel G. Reynaud (Wiley-Blackwell).*

Today, the possibilities for ocean exploration and imaging are [242] <u>close to</u> infinite. In addition to scuba diving, fast computers, remotely operated vehicles (ROVs), deep sea submersibles, reinforced diving suits, and satellites, other technologies are being developed. [243] <u>Because of</u> ongoing technological advances, it is estimated that only 5% of the oceans have been explored. [244] Many new discoveries await us as we use new instruments and deep submergence vehicles to explore the "inner space" in the twenty-first century.

In the future, oceanographers want to go beyond learning about what is down there in the ocean to learning about what is going on down there. They want to observe ocean processes that change over days, weeks, seasons, years, or decades. [245] <u>Furthermore,</u> it is difficult and expensive to send research ships back to the same site for repeat measurements. Sometimes rough seas and stormy weather make it [246] <u>easy</u> to send ships to certain parts of the oceans at certain times.

Consequently, oceanographers [247] launch a new era of ocean exploration. [248] They want to make continuous measurements of various ocean properties and events. To do this, they will establish long-term ocean floor observatories with arrays of sensors and instruments. Data from the observatories will be sent to shore-based laboratories via submerged fiber-optic cables or via cables linked to moored buoys that can transmit data via satellite. The data can then be made available [249] via the Internet.

(1) Oceanographers will, [250] in the future—use different types of ROVs and AUVs that can "fly" in the oceans or along the seafloor while collecting measurements. (2) Oceanographers are also developing instrumented buoys moored thousands of miles from shore, and free-floating drifting instruments that can transmit data to scientists in their laboratories using satellites and the Internet. [251] The data can be downloaded when the AUVs surface or dock at an underwater docking site. [252]

242. (A) NO CHANGE
(B) impossibly
(C) nearly
(D) DELETE the underlined portion

243. (A) NO CHANGE
(B) In spite of
(C) Following
(D) DELETE the underlined portion

244. At this point, Reynaud wishes to add a sentence that exemplifies how little we know about the ocean. Which of the following sentences does this?
(A) Surprisingly, we know more about the moon than we do the ocean.
(B) Scientists discover more and more about the ocean every day.
(C) The technology in use and in development will be fully utilized to explore our underwater environment.
(D) Oceanographers and marine biologists are exploring the vast blue wilderness that is our backyard.

245. (A) NO CHANGE
(B) Consequently,
(C) Nevertheless,
(D) However,

246. (A) NO CHANGE
(B) impossible
(C) palatable
(D) accessible

247. (A) NO CHANGE
(B) are launching
(C) will launch
(D) think about launching

248. Which of the following is the best way to combine the two underlined sentences?
(A) They want to establish long-term ocean floor observatories with arrays of sensors and instruments that make continuous measurements of various ocean properties and events.
(B) They want to make continuous measurements of various ocean properties and events, and to do this, they will establish long-term ocean floor observatories with arrays of sensors and instruments.
(C) They want to establish long-term ocean floor observatories, using arrays of sensors and instruments, and making continuous measurements of various ocean properties and events.
(D) Using arrays of sensors and instruments, and making continuous measurements of various ocean properties and events, they want to establish long-term ocean floor observatories.

249. (A) NO CHANGE
(B) to
(C) for observers on
(D) for use on

250. (A) NO CHANGE
(B) in the future,
(C) in the future;
(D) in the future

251. To make the most logical sense, this sentence should be placed
(A) where it is now
(B) before Sentence 1
(C) after Sentence 1
(D) DELETE this sentence

252. A suitable title for this passage would be
(A) Past Data Collection
(B) Oceanographers and Data Collection Instruments
(C) The Future of Oceanography
(D) The Limitations of Current Data Collection Methods

Passage 13

Questions 253–263 are based on the following information.

The following passage is an excerpt from Leadership Rules: How to Become the Leader You Want to Be, *by Chris Widener (Wiley-Blackwell).*

It is such a unique sound, [253] the chirp of chicks in the nest. That's the sound Mike Keller heard, and he didn't like it much.

(1) It wouldn't have been so bad except that it was his driveway. (2) The driveway to the house he wished he wasn't moving into. [254] His new driveway. (3) Born and raised in Chicago, he had no desire to live in Texas—but here he was, the newest resident of East Creek, Texas, about an hour outside of Dallas. [255]

What in the world am I doing here? he thought as he and his son Billy drove down the short driveway to the three-bedroom [256] cottage he'd rented sight unseen. The one thing he did like about the house was that it was cheap, cheap, cheap. Especially compared to [257] houses in the surrounding areas.

As the car rolled to a stop, Mike and Billy took in the scene. The paint was [258] chipping, and one of the window screens was falling out. The screen door on the front entrance was swinging back and forth in the wind. The front yard didn't have a shred of green left in the grass. *Yep, this is Texas in August, all right.*

"Well son, here we are."

"Yep. . . . Here we are."

Billy's resignation was obvious. The kid had been no more pleased than you could expect about being pulled away from his friends in high school, but he'd been a good sport about [259] it. He stuck by his choice to live with his father when his parents split up. Mike and Billy had been baching it for the last year or so, ever since Mike's wife, Kristy, [260] announced that she wanted a separation.

Maybe the distance will do us all some good, Mike thought. He and Kristy had been trying for a reconciliation but [261] not making progress, and Mike's job at Markston Machine Corporation had been going poorly on top of it. The stress had been so bad, anything might be an improvement. Mike opened the car door and stood up, feeling like [262] he'd stepped into an oven. "Let's leave the stuff in the car for now, son, and get the lay of the land in the house first." The movers would be there the next day, [263] and Mike and Billy had brought down a carload of things to make the place barely habitable.

253. Which choice most effectively illustrates the sound of arriving while setting up the start of the next paragraph?
(A) NO CHANGE
(B) the squeak of dusty brakes
(C) the crunch of gravel under tires
(D) the creak of door hinges needing oil

254. To provide emphasis, where should this sentence be placed?

(A) Before Sentence 1

(B) After Sentence 1

(C) Where it is now

(D) After Sentence 3

255. At this point, the author is considering adding the following sentence:

To him, it might as well have been an hour out of Podunk.

Should the author do so?

(A) Yes, because it adds detail regarding the remoteness of East Creek, Texas.

(B) Yes, because it adds detail about how Mike Keller feels.

(C) No, because it is unnecessary and distracting.

(D) No, because Podunk is nowhere near East Creek, Texas.

256. Which word creatively sets up the poor condition of the house described later in the passage?

(A) NO CHANGE

(B) villa

(C) rambler

(D) house

257. Which of the following specifically highlights Mike Keller's perception of the cheap rent?

(A) NO CHANGE

(B) what housing costs in Chicago.

(C) the amount he had budgeted for rent.

(D) what housing costs closer in to Dallas.

258. (A) NO CHANGE

(B) chipping;

(C) chipping—

(D) chipping

259. Which choice most effectively combines the two sentences at the underlined portion?

(A) it, sticking by

(B) it: sticking by

(C) it by sticking by

(D) it and stuck

260. (A) NO CHANGE

(B) had announced

(C) had been announcing

(D) announces

261. Which of the following emphasizes the lack of communication between Mike and Kristy?

(A) NO CHANGE

(B) it was going nowhere,

(C) were having issues doing even that,

(D) speaking different languages,

262. Which answer choice most emphasizes the uncomfortable weather?

(A) NO CHANGE

(B) he'd been sitting for hours.

(C) the toll of the road was getting to him.

(D) he had to be strong for his son, Billy.

263. (A) NO CHANGE

(B) but

(C) furthermore

(D) consequently

Passage 14

Questions 264–274 are based on the following information.

The following passage is an excerpt from No Fear of Failure: Real Stories of How Leaders Deal with Risk and Change, *by Gary Burnison (Wiley-Blackwell).*

This is an excerpt of a writing about Michael Bloomberg, former mayor of New York City and founder of Bloomberg LP.

It seemed only natural to delegate responsibility and authority in order to run a city of 8.3 million people with 300,000 employees and an infrastructure that operates [264] 24/7 . . . just as it would to run a multibillion-dollar company. [265] And, in some organizations, delegation is limited. Information, power, access, and control are held tightly within a very small circle, which is [266] not particularly effective nor empowering. In governments, power tends to be centralized, a style of management that Bloomberg [267] considered to be the sign of a "control freak." To his way of thinking, in both business and government, delegating is "a very big deal"—engendering mutual trust and igniting passion to achieve a bigger purpose.

"You only get good people if you give them authority. Why would people who are any good want to go to an organization where they are going to be a clerk? You want to be able to do new things," he [268] adds. "That doesn't mean I'm always going to accept someone's ideas, but that person has to know he's part of it; otherwise, he doesn't want to work here."

Bloomberg gave the example of recruiting three senior people to serve as [269] deputy mayors in his administration. Any of them would be welcomed—and well compensated—in the private sector, yet they chose to work for the city as part of Bloomberg's team. Instead of financial remuneration, they were motivated by a sense of [270] mission, and a desire to make a [271] difference. What they asked for in return was respect and recognition. "Why would any of these three want to come to work for me in a junior position? It's because they want to be part of a team—and I delegate. Delegation is empowering people to make decisions and then backing them," he explained.

During our discussion, it was easy to see why people want to work for Bloomberg: [272] he was clearly a role model. [273] It follows that he is mayor of one of the world's most important financial and commercial hubs, that his name has been floated occasionally as a possible presidential candidate, or that he is a successful billionaire entrepreneur, Bloomberg came across as an in-his-shirt-sleeves kind of a guy who brushed off an attempt to address him as Mr. Mayor and insisted on being called Mike. [274]

264. (A) NO CHANGE
(B) 24/7;
(C) 24/7—
(D) 24/7

265. (A) NO CHANGE
(B) Yet,
(C) This is why,
(D) Furthermore,

266. (A) NO CHANGE
(B) negatively
(C) neither
(D) DELETE the underlined portion

267. (A) NO CHANGE
(B) considers
(C) does consider
(D) has considered

268. (A) NO CHANGE
(B) added
(C) is adding
(D) DELETE the underlined portion

269. (A) NO CHANGE
(B) a deputy mayor
(C) deputies mayor
(D) deputies mayors

270. (A) NO CHANGE
(B) mission
(C) mission—
(D) mission;

271. Which of the following correctly combines the two sentences at the underlined portion?
(A) difference; what
(B) difference, what
(C) difference and what
(D) difference while what

272. Which of the following emphasizes Mayor Bloomberg's approach of considering himself part of the team?
(A) NO CHANGE
(B) he was very successful
(C) he was accessible and real
(D) he was good at his job

273. (A) NO CHANGE
(B) Because
(C) No matter that
(D) A mystery is that

274. At this point, the author is considering adding the following sentence:

As a leader, Bloomberg was clearly in the trenches with his team.

Should the author add this sentence?
(A) No, because it distracts from the flow of the narrative.
(B) No, because there are no trenches in an office.
(C) Yes, because it lends the image of Mayor Bloomberg working with his team.
(D) Yes, because it effectively concludes the discussion of Mayor Bloomberg's teamwork approach.

Passage 15

Questions 275–285 are based on the following information.

The following passage is an excerpt from Soil Science Simplified, *6th Edition, by Neal S. Eash, Thomas J. Sauer, Deb O'Dell, Evah Odoi, and Mary C. Bratz (Illustrator) (Wiley-Blackwell).*

(1)

Soil is a natural resource [275] where which people are dependent in many ways. Since the birth of the soil conservation movement in the [276] 1930s, there [277] have been an increased interest in conserving the soil. The environmental awareness and concerns that have occurred over the past several decades have focused attention on the need to conserve soil as a fundamental part of the ecosystem. There is, [278] truly, little public understanding of the soil's complexity.

(2)

Careful observers may see soil exposed in roadbanks or [279] excavations. It may be noticed that the soil does not look the same in all locations. Sometimes the differences are apparent in the few inches of surface soil that the farmers plow, but greater variations can usually be seen by looking at a cross section of the top 3 or 4 ft. (0.9 or 1.2 m) of soil.

(3)

[280] The quality and quantity of vegetative growth depends on the properties of the soil layers. Roads and structures may [281] fail if they are constructed on soils with undesirable characteristics. Special care must be taken to overcome soil limitations for specific engineering [282] usages. Satisfactory disposal of human waste and livestock manure is becoming an increasing [283] concern . . . particularly where soils are used as a disposal site.

(4)

Poor yields of agricultural crops and poor growth of trees may result from a mismatching of crops [284] with soils. This mismatching may happen because the landowner has not examined the soil horizons or understood [285] their limitations. Soil scientists study the factors necessary for proper soil management and plant growth.

275. (A) NO CHANGE
(B) on
(C) with
(D) when

276. (A) NO CHANGE
(B) 1930's
(C) 1930s'
(D) 1930s's

277. (A) NO CHANGE
(B) has been
(C) were
(D) will be

278. (A) NO CHANGE
(B) therefore
(C) however
(D) DELETE the underlined portion and surrounding commas

279. Which of the following correctly combines the two sentences at the underlined portion?
(A) excavation it
(B) excavation, it
(C) excavation and it
(D) excavation, and it

280. Where is the best place for this sentence?
(A) At the end of Paragraph 1
(B) At the end of Paragraph 2
(C) Where it is now
(D) At the end of Paragraph 3

281. (A) NO CHANGE
(B) be destroyed
(C) crumble
(D) eventually need repair

282. (A) NO CHANGE
(B) usefulness
(C) uses
(D) DELETE the underlined portion

283. (A) NO CHANGE
(B) concern;
(C) concern,
(D) concern

284. (A) NO CHANGE
(B) and
(C) among
(D) mixed with

285. (A) NO CHANGE
(B) its
(C) it's
(D) there

Passage 16

Questions 286–296 are based on the following information.

The following passage is an excerpt from Out-Executing the Competition: Building and Growing a Financial Services Company in Any Economy, *by Irving H. Rothman (Wiley-Blackwell).*

This was more than a situation where a company might pull the plug on an inefficient or money-losing department. The concept of a captive finance company within the AT&T empire was a notion that held extraordinary promise, and here it was, [286] about to fail. None of us wanted to see that happen, but what could be done to ensure that this promising idea would [287] be okay?

In early 1986, President and COO Tom Wajnert called me into his office and [288] laid it on the line. "I want you to take oversight responsibility," he said. One could take the view that he wanted to distance himself from what appeared to be an impending disaster. The two people running the operation for us at the time, Gerri Gold and Jim Tenner, were high performers trying to fix a huge [289] mess. I feared they were about to watch their extremely promising careers [290] come to an end before they'd even had a chance to succeed.

Gerri was bright, [291] energetic . . . and highly motivated. She had joined us after earning a degree in business administration from the University of Michigan and an MBA from New York University. Jim was a product [292] of Middlebury College in Vermont and held a Masters from Dartmouth's Tuck School of Business. They had worked under AT&T Treasurer S. Lawrence "Larry" Prendergast as part of the original study team that wrote the business plan for the captive finance business.

They were intelligent and already accomplished, with big futures if they could make this project work. We were struggling to devise an operating methodology that could [293] help set things right when Gerri and Jim approached me one day and suggested we meet with one of the consultants advising American Transtech. Transtech, a sister subsidiary company at AT&T, was a securities process business—in effect, a processing [294] clearinghouse, that had a unique approach to organizational design.

[295] Their idea was to organize small, autonomous teams of employees with broad responsibility to operate without the structure of a linear management style. Although common to many American businesses these days, it was a radical concept in the 1980s. In practice, it created a [296] prodigal work environment.

286. Which of the following provides the most visual representation of the disaster that may happen?

(A) NO CHANGE

(B) losing steam

(C) approaching disaster

(D) veering toward the ditch

287. Which of the following most implies a successful recovery?

(A) NO CHANGE

(B) remain on track

(C) be salvageable

(D) be cutting losses

288. Which of the following suggests a direct approach?

(A) NO CHANGE

(B) asked politely

(C) had an idea

(D) spoke confidently

289. Which of the following correctly combines the two sentences at the underlined portion?

(A) mess I

(B) mess, I

(C) mess and I

(D) mess, and I

290. Which of the following is most consistent with the writer's creative, colloquial writing style?

(A) NO CHANGE

(B) be endangered

(C) circle the drain

(D) be damaged

291. (A) NO CHANGE
(B) energetic,
(C) energetic;
(D) energetic—

292. (A) NO CHANGE
(B) from
(C) at
(D) with

293. Which of the following, with the writer's colloquial writing style, suggests that the situation can become successful?
(A) NO CHANGE
(B) still help turn a profit
(C) produce good year-end results
(D) turn this lemon into lemonade

294. (A) NO CHANGE
(B) clearinghouse
(C) clearinghouse;
(D) clearinghouse—

295. (A) NO CHANGE
(B) There
(C) It's
(D) Its

296. (A) NO CHANGE
(B) laissez-faire
(C) wistful
(D) erstwhile

Chapter 3

Math: No-Calculator Section

The first math section on the SAT doesn't allow the use of a calculator. These questions tend to be less math-heavy and more concept-based, and they cover the same topics that you cover in high school. If you're fresh out of math class, you'll probably be fine going through these quickly. However, if you haven't seen some of these topics since freshman year, you may want to work them carefully and pay close attention to the solutions.

The Problems You'll Work On

When working through the questions in this chapter, be prepared to answer questions on

- **Basic math,** including fractions, decimals, percentages, and ratios
- **Algebra,** including linear equations, coordinate geometry, and quadratic equations
- **Geometry,** which covers both basic shapes and three-dimensional solids
- **Word problems,** including rate of travel, averages, probability, and equation setup
- **Tables and graphs,** including data analysis

What to Watch Out For

Shortfalls in math are in three basic categories. See whether you're prone to one of these in particular:

- Mistakes in simple math, such as not placing the decimal point correctly
- Mistakes in working the problem, such as multiplying exponents when you should be adding them
- Not knowing how to work a certain math problem, such as a probability

Multiple Choice

Select the answer to each question. Do not use a calculator.

297. If $2x+3=5$, what is the value of $3x+5$?

(A) 2
(B) 3
(C) 5
(D) 8

298. Based on this system of equations, what is the value of $x+y$?

$$15x+25y=60$$
$$10x+20y=25$$

(A) 2
(B) 3
(C) 5
(D) 7

299. If $h<0$ and $y=5$ in the following equation, what is the value of h?

$$\sqrt{3h^2-2}-y=0$$

(A) −1
(B) −2
(C) −3
(D) −5

300. Which of the following is equivalent to this expression, where $i^2=-1$?

$$(3i+3)(5i-5)$$

(A) $-30(i+1)$
(B) $-30i$
(C) −30
(D) 0

301. If $\frac{x-2}{5}=h$ and $h=2$, what is the value of x?

(A) 8
(B) 10
(C) 12
(D) 14

302. If $(x-3)^2=25$ and x is negative, what is the value of x?

(A) −2
(B) −3
(C) −5
(D) −7

303. If $ab-c=1$ and $\frac{ab}{6}=1$, what is the value of c?

(A) 2
(B) 3
(C) 4
(D) 5

304. For $i=\sqrt{-1}$, what is the value of $(2+3i)(5-7i)$?

(A) $32-2i$
(B) $22+2i$
(C) $31+i$
(D) $-2+i$

305. For $i=\sqrt{-1}$, what is the value of $(6+5i)-(3+2i)$?

(A) $1+i$
(B) $2+2i$
(C) $3+3i$
(D) $5+5i$

306. During each of the last 3 baseball games, Joe hit d doubles and h home runs. Which of the following expressions represents the total number of doubles and home runs that Joe hit during these 3 baseball games?

(A) $d+h$
(B) $3(d+h)$
(C) $6(d+h)$
(D) $6dh$

Use the following information to answer Questions 307 and 308.

Each week, Eric collects d daisies, of which he gives s to his sister and keeps the rest for himself.

307. Which of the following expressions represents the total number of daisies that Eric gives to his sister over the course of w weeks?

(A) sw

(B) $d + sw$

(C) $w(d - s)$

(D) $w(d + s)$

3. Which of the following expressions represents the total number of daisies that Eric keeps for himself over the course of w weeks?

(A) sw

(B) $d + sw$

(C) $w(d - s)$

(D) $w(d + s)$

Use the following information to answer Questions 309 and 310.

Susan is a high school math teacher. Each week, she receives 8 quizzes to grade from each of s students. Assuming each week begins with no quizzes left over from the previous week, the number of quizzes that she has left to grade at the end of each day can be estimated with the equation $q = 8s - 10d$, where q is the number of quizzes and d is the number of days she has worked that week.

309. What is the meaning of the 10 in the equation?

(A) The number of days it will take Susan to finish the quizzes

(B) The number of quizzes Susan has left to grade

(C) The number of quizzes Susan grades per day

(D) The number of students

310. If two students were to join her class, which of the following equations would show the revised number of quizzes left to grade each day?

(A) $q = 8s + 2 - 10d$

(B) $q = 8(s + 2) - 10d$

(C) $q = 8s - (10d + 2)$

(D) $q = 10s - 10d$

311. What is the value of y in this equation?

$$(x^2 - 2xy + y^2) = (x + 2)^2$$

(A) −4

(B) −2

(C) 2

(D) 4

312. A furniture builder will build a number of identical tables. The builder's fee can be calculated by the expression $tklw$, where t is the number of tables, k is the cost of material per square foot, l is the length of each table, and w is the width of each table. If the customer asks the builder to make the tables shorter and wider, which of the factors in the expression would change?

(A) t and k

(B) k and l

(C) l and w

(D) w and t

313. If $2h = 30$, what is the value of $5h + 5$?

(A) 15

(B) 25

(C) 60

(D) 80

314. If $\frac{4}{3}b = 12$, what is the value of $2b$?

(A) 9

(B) 18

(C) 27

(D) 36

315. Which of the following is equal to $x^{\frac{a}{b}}$ for all values of x?

(A) $\sqrt[b]{x^a}$

(B) $\sqrt[a]{x^b}$

(C) $\sqrt[b]{x^{\frac{1}{a}}}$

(D) $\sqrt[a]{x^{\frac{1}{b}}}$

316. Which of the following is equal to $27^{\frac{1}{3}}$?

(A) 3

(B) $3\sqrt{3}$

(C) 9

(D) 27^3

317. Which of the following is equal to $5^{\frac{6}{3}}$?

(A) 5

(B) $3\sqrt{30}$

(C) 25

(D) 25^2

318. Which of the following is equal to $\sqrt{2^4}$?

(A) 2

(B) 4

(C) 8

(D) 16

319. The number of members of Club *X* is five times the number of members of Club *Y*. If 50 members are in Club *X* and *y* members are in Club *Y*, which of the following equations is true?

(A) $50y = 5$

(B) $\frac{y}{5} = 50$

(C) $y + 5 = 50$

(D) $5y = 50$

320. Which of the following is equivalent to this expression?

$$\left(-2x^2y + 3y^2 - 6xy^2\right) - 2\left(-x^2y - 3y^2 - 3xy^2\right)$$

(A) $9y^2$

(B) $4x^2y + 9xy$

(C) $4x^2y - 6xy^2$

(D) $6xy^2$

Use the following information to answer Questions 321 and 322.

$$A = P\frac{r(1+r)^n}{(1+r)^n - 1}$$

This formula gives you the payment amount per period for a loan, where *A* is the payment, *P* is the principal loan amount, *r* is the interest rate per period, and *n* is the total number of periods.

321. Which of the following equations gives *P* in terms of *A*, *r*, and *n*?

(A) $P = A\frac{r(1+r)^n}{(1+r)^n - 1}$

(B) $P = A\frac{(1+r)^n - 1}{r(1+r)^n}$

(C) $A = P\frac{r(1+r)^n - 1}{(1+r)^n}$

(D) $A = P\frac{(1+r)^n}{r(1+r)^n - 1}$

322. Which of the following shows the adjusted formula if the number of periods were to increase by 6?

(A) $A = P\frac{r(1+r)^{n+6}}{(1+r)^n - 1}$

(B) $A = P\frac{r(1+r)^{n+3}}{(1+r)^{n+3} - 1}$

(C) $A = P\frac{r(1+r)^{n+6}}{(1+r)^{n+3} - 1}$

(D) $A = P\frac{r(1+r)^{n+6}}{(1+r)^{n+6} - 1}$

323. If $\frac{12}{x+18}=\frac{3}{x}$, what is $\frac{x}{3}$?

(A) 2

(B) 3

(C) 4

(D) 5

324. If $\frac{x+5}{2}=\frac{x+2}{3}$, what is the value of x?

(A) −2

(B) −5

(C) −10

(D) −11

325. If $\frac{x+3}{4}=\frac{4}{x-3}$ and $x<0$, what is the value of x?

(A) −2

(B) −3

(C) −5

(D) −7

326. If $\frac{x+5}{3}=-\left(\frac{3}{x-5}\right)$ and $x>0$, what is the value of x?

(A) 2

(B) 3

(C) 4

(D) 5

327. Given this system of equations, what is the value of $2x-y$?

$$5x+3y=10$$
$$3x-2y=7$$

(A) 2

(B) 3

(C) 4

(D) 5

328. Given this system of equations, what is the value of y?

$$2x^2-6x+y=2z+3$$
$$x^2+3x=z$$

(A) 3

(B) 4

(C) 5

(D) 7

329. The function f is defined by a polynomial. Some values of x and $f(x)$ are shown in the table. What is the value of $(f(3))^2$?

x	$f(x)$
2	1
3	4
5	7

(A) 3

(B) 5

(C) 12

(D) 16

330. The function f is defined by a polynomial. Some values of x and $f(x)$ are shown in the table. If $x=3$, what is the value of $f(x+2)$?

x	$f(x)$
3	2
5	6
8	7

(A) 3

(B) 5

(C) 6

(D) 9

331. The function f is defined by a polynomial. Some values of x and $f(x)$ are shown in the table. What is the value of $\frac{2f(3)}{5}$?

x	$f(x)$
2	6
3	5
4	7
5	6

(A) 2

(B) 3

(C) 5

(D) 10

332. The line $y = mx + b$ is graphed in the xy-plane, where m is the slope. What is the slope in terms of b, x, and y?

(A) $\frac{y-b}{x}$

(B) $\frac{y-x}{b}$

(C) $\frac{x}{y-b}$

(D) $\frac{b}{y-x}$

333. In the xy-plane, at what two points does the parabola with the equation $y = x^2 - 9$ cross the x-axis?

(A) −9, 0

(B) −3, 3

(C) −3, 0

(D) 0, 3

334. In the xy-plane, at what two points does the parabola with the equation $y = x(x-1) - 6$ cross the x-axis?

(A) −2, 3

(B) −3, 3

(C) 1, 6

(D) −6, −1

335. In the xy-plane, at what two points does the parabola with the equation $y = x^2 + 1$ cross the line where $y = 5$?

(A) −5, 5

(B) −3, 3

(C) −2, 2

(D) −1, 1

336. In the following drawing, if $x° + z° = 130$, what is the value of $b°$?

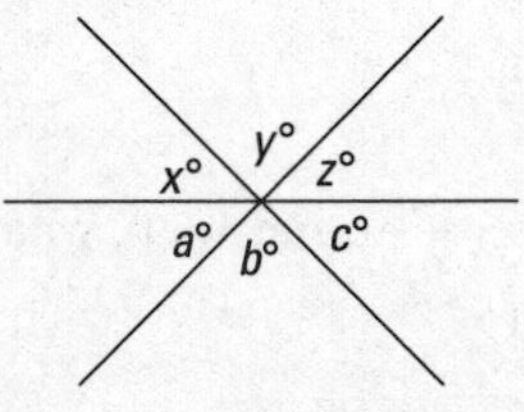

© John Wiley & Sons, Inc.

<u>Note:</u> Drawing not to scale.

(A) 40

(B) 50

(C) 60

(D) 70

337. In this drawing, if $w° + x° + y° = 120$ and $x° + y° + z° = 110$, what is the value of $x° + y°$?

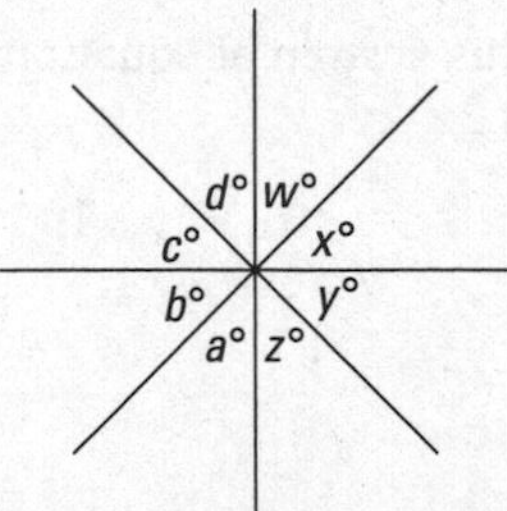

© John Wiley & Sons, Inc.

<u>Note:</u> Drawing not to scale.

(A) 30

(B) 40

(C) 50

(D) 60

338. In the quadratic equation $y = x^2 - 2x - 15$, what are the coordinates of the vertex of the parabola?

(A) $(1, 16)$
(B) $(-1, 16)$
(C) $(1, -16)$
(D) $(-1, -16)$

339. What are the solutions to the equation $3x^2 + 6x = 45$?

(A) −5, 3
(B) −3, 5
(C) 3, 5
(D) −5, −3

340. What are the solutions to the equation $2x^2 + 12x = -8$, where $i = \sqrt{-1}$?

(A) $x = 3 \pm \sqrt{5} - 2i$
(B) $x = -3 \pm \sqrt{5} + 2i$
(C) $x = 3 \pm \sqrt{5}$
(D) $x = -3 \pm \sqrt{5}$

341. If $x > 0$, what are the solutions to the equation $-x^2\left(x^2 - 13\right) = 6^2$?

(A) 2, 3
(B) 3, 5
(C) 5, 7
(D) 7, 11

342. What are the solutions to the equation $x^9 + 8x^3 = 9x^6$?

(A) 0, 1, 2
(B) 0, 2, 3
(C) −2, −1, 0
(D) −3, −2, 0

343. In this equation, where *k* is a constant, what is the value of *k*?

$$15x^2 + 20x + 25 = 3kx^2 + 4kx + 2k + 15$$

(A) 2
(B) 3
(C) 4
(D) 5

344. In a certain isosceles triangle, if one angle measures 110°, what is the measure of one of the other two angles?

(A) 25°
(B) 35°
(C) 70°
(D) 90°

345. In a certain isosceles triangle, if one angle measures 40°, which *could* be the measure of any of the other angles?

I. 40°
II. 70°
III. 100°

(A) I or II
(B) I or III
(C) II or III
(D) I, II, or III

346. In triangle *ABC*, where $C = 90°$ and the hypotenuse is 5, $\sin A = \frac{3}{5}$. What is $\cos B$?

(A) $\frac{3}{5}$
(B) $\frac{4}{5}$
(C) $\frac{3}{4}$
(D) 1

347. If $3y - 2 = 15$, what is $6y + 3$?

(A) 15
(B) 17
(C) 34
(D) 37

348. If $2x = \pi$, what is $\dfrac{(4x)^2}{\pi}$?

(A) 2π

(B) 3π

(C) 4π

(D) 5π

349. If $i^2 = -1$ and $3y = 2i$, what is the value of $9y^2$?

(A) −2

(B) −3

(C) −4

(D) −5

350. Which of the following ordered pairs (x, y) satisfies these equations?

$$x + y = 3$$
$$2x + y = 5$$

(A) $(1, 2)$

(B) $(2, 1)$

(C) $(1, -2)$

(D) $(2, -1)$

351. Which of the following sets of ordered pairs (x, y) satisfies these equations?

$$x^2 - y = 4$$
$$y = 5$$

(A) $(0, 5)$ and $(0, -5)$

(B) $(2, 5)$ and $(2, -5)$

(C) $(3, 5)$ and $(-3, 5)$

(D) $(4, 5)$ and $(-4, 5)$

352. Which of the following is equivalent to this expression?

$$\sqrt{4x^4 + 12x^2y^3 + 9y^6}$$

(A) $2x^2 + 3y^3$

(B) $(2x^2 + 2y^2)\sqrt{2y}$

(C) $(2x^3 + 2y^3)\sqrt{2}$

(D) $3x^3 + 2y^2$

353. Which of the following is equivalent to this expression?

$$x^3(x^6 - x^3)(x^6 + x^3)$$

(A) $x^6(x^3 - 1)$

(B) $x^9(x^6 - 1)$

(C) x^9

(D) x^{27}

354. What is the value of y in this equation?

$$\sqrt{3y^3 + 19} - 5 = 5$$

(A) 2

(B) 3

(C) 4

(D) 5

355. What are the solutions to this equation?

$$x = 5\sqrt{x} - 6$$

(A) 2, 3

(B) 3, 5

(C) 4, 7

(D) 4, 9

356. A certain right triangle has a hypotenuse of 2. If one of the angles is 30°, what is the area of the triangle?

(A) $\dfrac{\sqrt{3}}{2}$

(B) $\dfrac{1}{2}$

(C) $\sqrt{3}$

(D) 1

357. In this equation, what is the value of $x - y$?

$$\frac{2^x}{2^y} = 16$$

(A) 2

(B) 3

(C) 4

(D) 5

358. If $x^5(x^2-1)=2$, what is the value of $\frac{3^{x^7}}{3^{x^5}}$?

(A) 3

(B) 9

(C) 27

(D) 81

359. What is the value of a in this equation if $b^2=5$ and $a<0$?

$$\left(2^{a+b}\right)^{a-b}=16$$

(A) −1

(B) −2

(C) −3

(D) −4

360. A certain vendor at a farmers' market sells apples and pears. The prices of these fruit can be found with these equations, where a represents the price per bag of apples and p represents the price per bag of pears, in dollars:

$$a=2.5+1.5x$$
$$p=1.5+1.75x$$

What is the price of a bag of apples, in dollars, if the prices per bag of both fruit are the same?

(A) 7

(B) 7.5

(C) 8

(D) 8.5

361. A certain furniture supply store sells mahogany and cedar. The prices of these woods can be found with these equations, where m and c represent the prices per pallet of mahogany and cedar, respectively, in dollars.

$$m=16+25x$$
$$c=24+15x$$

What is the price of a pallet of cedar, in dollars, when the prices per pallet of both woods are the same?

(A) 12

(B) 24

(C) 36

(D) 48

362. If $x-4$ is a factor of x^2+x-4b, what is the value of b?

(A) 4

(B) 5

(C) 6

(D) 8

363. In this system of equations, what is the value of $x+y$?

$$2x+y=4$$
$$x+2y=5$$

(A) 3

(B) 5

(C) 7

(D) 9

364. The area of a triangle, A, can be shown in terms of its base, b, and height, h. Which equation represents h in terms of A and b?

(A) $h=\frac{2b}{A}$

(B) $h=\frac{2A}{b}$

(C) $h=\frac{A}{2b}$

(D) $h=\frac{b}{2A}$

365. The area of a trapezoid, T, can be shown in terms of its bases, b_1 and b_2, and its height, h. Which equation represents h in terms of T, b_1, and b_2?

(A) $h=\left(\dfrac{b_1+b_2}{2}\right)T$

(B) $h=\left(\dfrac{T^2}{b_1+b_2}\right)$

(C) $h=\left(\dfrac{2}{b_1+b_2}\right)T$

(D) $h=\left(\dfrac{b_1+b_2}{4}\right)$

366. What is the value of $a+b$ if $a-b=5$ and $a^2-b^2=15$?

(A) 3

(B) 5

(C) 7

(D) 9

367. In this system of equations, what is the value of $\frac{1}{15}x+\frac{1}{15}y$?

$$\frac{1}{3}x-\frac{1}{5}y=5$$
$$\frac{1}{5}x-\frac{1}{3}y=3$$

(A) 1

(B) 2

(C) 3

(D) 5

368. A certain store sells apples at $0.50 each and pears at $0.75 each. If Murray spent $12.50, with no tax, for the same number of apples and pears, how many apples did he buy?

(A) 9

(B) 10

(C) 11

(D) 12

369. What is the area of this trapezoid?

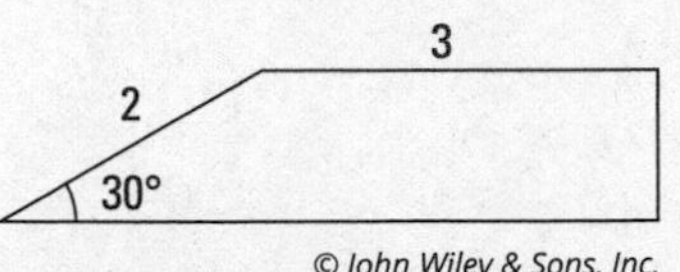

© John Wiley & Sons, Inc.

(A) $3+\sqrt{3}$

(B) $6+\sqrt{3}$

(C) $3+\dfrac{\sqrt{3}}{2}$

(D) $6+\dfrac{\sqrt{3}}{2}$

370. What is the area of this square?

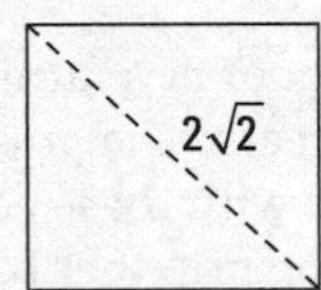

© John Wiley & Sons, Inc.

(A) 2

(B) 3

(C) 4

(D) 5

371. What is the volume of a cube having an edge length of $\sqrt[3]{5}$?

(A) 2

(B) 3

(C) 4

(D) 5

372. $f(d)=2{,}000+\left(2^{\frac{d}{3}}+\frac{d}{2}\right)1{,}000$

This equation is a model of projected cell growth in a lab, where d represents the number of days and $f(d)$ represents the approximate number of cells. According to the model, what is the projected number of cells at the end of the 12th day?

(A) 24,000

(B) 28,000

(C) 30,000

(D) 32,000

373. $\frac{3-2i}{4-3i}$

Which of the following is equivalent to this expression? Note that $i^2=-1$.

(A) $\frac{9-i}{5}$

(B) $\frac{18-i}{10}$

(C) $\frac{18+i}{25}$

(D) $\frac{18+i}{50}$

374. Which of the following equations has a graph in the xy-plane where y is always greater than or equal to 2?

(A) $y=x^2+1$

(B) $y=2x+2$

(C) $y=2x^2+2$

(D) $y=2x^2-2$

375. A line intercepts the y-axis at $(0,3)$ and crosses the point $(1,4)$. What is the equation of this line?

(A) $y=x+3$

(B) $y=2x+3$

(C) $y=x+5$

(D) $y=2x+5$

376. In this system of equations, at what point on the xy-plane do the lines cross?

$$y=2x+1$$
$$y=x+2$$

(A) $(0,3)$

(B) $(1,3)$

(C) $(1,5)$

(D) $(2,5)$

377. What is the area of this parallelogram?

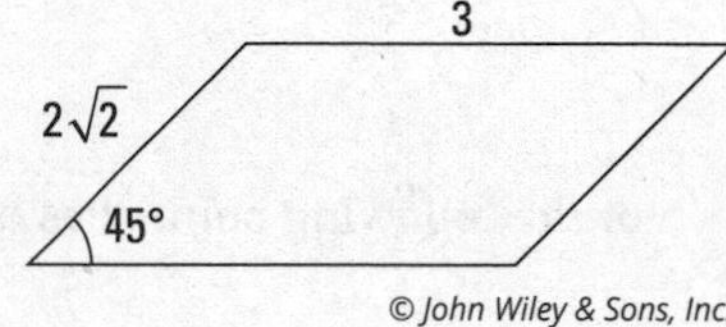

© John Wiley & Sons, Inc.

(A) 4

(B) 5

(C) 6

(D) 8

378. What is the value of $a-b$ if $3^{a^2-b^2}=9$ and $a+b=1$?

(A) 2

(B) 3

(C) 4

(D) 6

379. What is the solution (x,y) to this system of equations?

$$x+2y=3$$
$$5x+9y=12$$

(A) $(3,3)$

(B) $(-3,3)$

(C) $(3,-3)$

(D) $(-3,-3)$

Questions 380 and 381 are based on the following information.

A line in the xy-plane passes through the points $(2,3)$ and $(5,7)$.

380. What is the slope of the line?

(A) $\frac{4}{3}$

(B) $\frac{3}{4}$

(C) $-\frac{3}{4}$

(D) $-\frac{4}{3}$

381. Which of the following points lies on the line?

(A) $(1,2)$

(B) $(3,4)$

(C) $(0,0)$

(D) $(-1,-1)$

382. If $a>2$, which of the following expressions is equivalent to $\frac{1}{\frac{1}{a+2}-\frac{1}{a-2}}$?

(A) $\frac{a^2}{2}$

(B) $\frac{a^2}{4}-1$

(C) $1-\frac{a^2}{4}$

(D) $1-\frac{a^2}{2}$

383. In the following triangle, $BC = CD$ and $\overline{AB}$ is parallel to $\overline{CE}$. If $BD = 3$, what is the length of $\overline{DE}$?

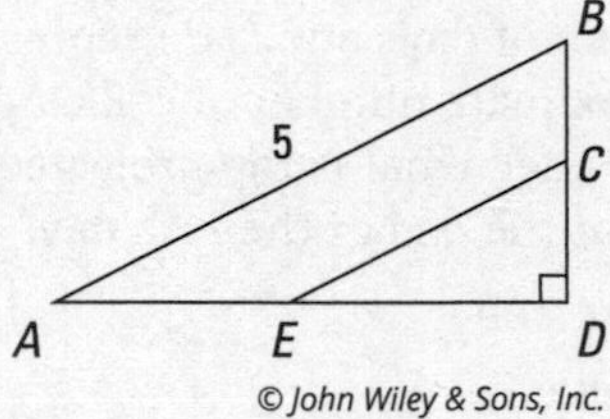

© John Wiley & Sons, Inc.

(A) 2

(B) 3

(C) 4

(D) 5

384. In the drawing, l_1 is parallel to l_2. What is the value of a?

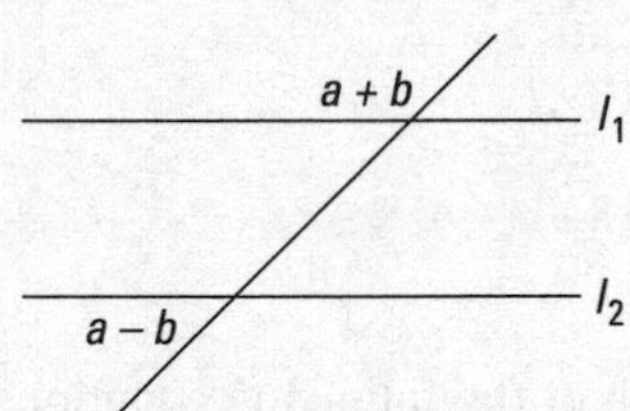

© John Wiley & Sons, Inc.

(A) 60°

(B) 70°

(C) 80°

(D) 90°

385. $P = \dfrac{A(1+i)^n - 1}{i(1+i)^n}$

The preceding equation represents the present worth of a uniform annual series where P is the present value, A is the accrual, i is the rate of interest, and n is the number of periods. Which of the following represents A in terms of P, i, and n?

(A) $A = \dfrac{P(1+i)^n - 1}{i(1+i)^n}$

(B) $A = \dfrac{Pi(1+i)^n}{(1+i)^n - 1}$

(C) $A = \dfrac{Pi(1+i)^n}{(1+i)^n + 1}$

(D) $A = \dfrac{Pi(1+i)^n}{(1+i)^n + 1}$

386. $P = G\dfrac{1-(1+ni)(1+i)^{-n}}{i^2}$

This equation represents the present worth of an arithmetic gradient series where P is the present value, G is the gradient, i is the rate of interest, and n is the number of periods. Which of the following represents G in terms of P, i, and n?

(A) $G = P\dfrac{1+(1-ni)(1-i)^n}{i^2}$

(B) $G = P\dfrac{i^2}{1+(1-ni)(1-i)^n}$

(C) $G = P\dfrac{1-(1+ni)(1+i)^{-n}}{i^2}$

(D) $G = P\dfrac{i^2}{1-(1+ni)(1+i)^{-n}}$

387. In this system of equations, b is a constant. If the system has infinite solutions, what is the value of b?

$$x + 2y = 3$$
$$2x + by = 6$$

(A) 2

(B) 4

(C) 6

(D) 8

388. In the equation $5y = 30$, what is the value of $y - 4$?

(A) 2

(B) 4

(C) 6

(D) 8

Questions 389 and 390 are based on the following information.

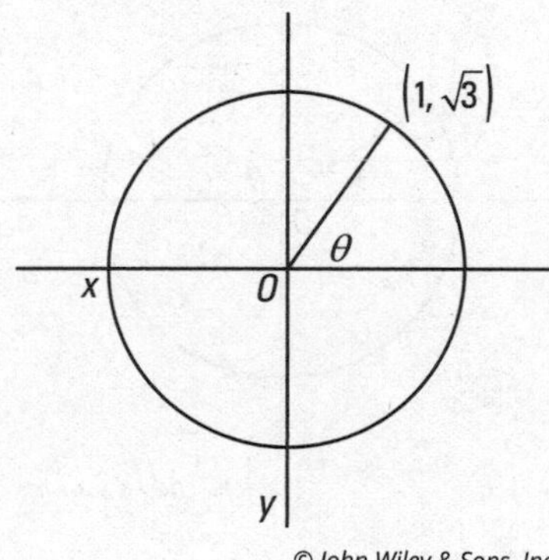

In the xy-plane, O is the center of the circle.

389. What is the degree measure of angle θ?

(A) 30°

(B) 45°

(C) 60°

(D) 75°

390. What is the radian measure of angle θ?

(A) $\frac{2\pi}{3}$

(B) π

(C) $\frac{\pi}{2}$

(D) $\frac{\pi}{3}$

391. A circle on the *xy*-plane has a radius of 9. What is the value of *x* in the following equation?

$$(x-2)^2+(y+3)^2=x^2$$

(A) 1

(B) 3

(C) 9

(D) 81

Questions 392 and 393 are based on the following information.

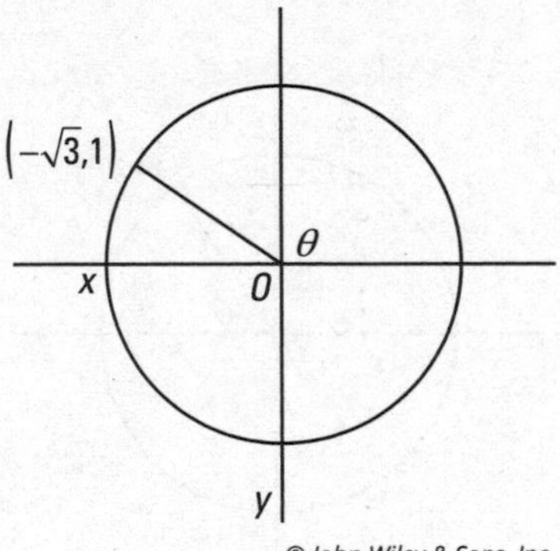

© John Wiley & Sons, Inc.

In the *xy*-plane, O is the center of the circle.

392. What is the sine of angle θ?

(A) 0.5

(B) $\sqrt{3}$

(C) 1

(D) 2

393. What is the cosecant of angle θ?

(A) 0.5

(B) $\sqrt{3}$

(C) 1

(D) 2

394. If $(x+7)^2=36$ and $x<-5$, what is the value of *x*?

(A) −5

(B) −7

(C) −9

(D) −13

395. For $i=\sqrt{-1}$, what is the value of $(5-4i)(3+2i)$?

(A) $23+2i$

(B) $23-2i$

(C) $23+i$

(D) $23-i$

396. At his job, Joe earns *d* dollars for every hour up to 40 hours and $2d+h$ dollars for every hour over 40 hours. If Joe worked 48 hours last week, which of the following represents the number of dollars he earned, without taxes?

(A) $40d+8h$

(B) $56d+8h$

(C) $60d+8h$

(D) $80d+8h$

Use the following information to answer ***Questions 397 and 398.***

Alex delivers newspapers around his neighborhood. Every Sunday, he delivers *p* papers to each of *s* streets. Assuming he delivers the same number of papers each Sunday, the number of papers that he has left to deliver after each street day can be estimated with the equation $n=ps-dp$, where *d* is the number of streets that he has delivered to and *n* is the total number of papers delivered each Sunday.

397. What is the meaning of the *pd* in the equation?

(A) The number of papers Alex has yet to deliver

(B) The number of papers Alex delivers each Sunday

(C) The number of papers Alex has delivered so far

(D) The number of papers Alex can carry at one time

398. If Alex adds *c* streets to his current route, which new equation represents the number of papers that he delivers each Sunday?

(A) $n = p(c+s)-(c+d)p$

(B) $n = p(c+s)-dp$

(C) $n = cps - dp$

(D) $n = cps - cdp$

399. Which of the following is equivalent to $5^{\frac{2}{3}}$?

(A) $\sqrt[3]{5^2}$

(B) $\sqrt[2]{5^3}$

(C) $\sqrt[3]{5^{\frac{1}{2}}}$

(D) $\sqrt[2]{5^{\frac{1}{3}}}$

400. Which of the following is equivalent to this expression?

$$3(-3a^2b+3b^2-3ab^2)-9(-a^2b+b^2-3ab^2)$$

(A) $9ab^2$

(B) $4a^2b+9ab^2$

(C) $4a^2b-9ab^2$

(D) $18ab^2$

401. What is the value of $5\sqrt{20}$?

(A) $5\sqrt{5}$

(B) $7\sqrt{5}$

(C) $10\sqrt{5}$

(D) $20\sqrt{5}$

Use the following information to answer ***Questions 402 and 403.***

$$FV = P\left(\frac{\left(1+\frac{r}{m}\right)^{m\cdot t}-1}{\frac{r}{m}}\right)$$

This formula gives you the future value of an annuity, where *FV* is the future value, *P* is the payment, *r* is the annual interest rate, *m* is the number of periods per year, and *t* is the number of years.

402. Which of the following gives P in terms of *FV*, *r*, *m*, and *t*?

(A) $P = FV\left(\frac{\left(1+\frac{r}{m}\right)^{m\cdot t}-1}{\frac{r}{m}}\right)$

(B) $P = FV\left(\frac{\frac{r}{m}}{\left(1+\frac{r}{m}\right)^{m\cdot t}-1}\right)$

(C) $P = FV\left(\frac{\left(1+\frac{m}{r}\right)^{m\cdot t}-1}{\frac{m}{r}}\right)$

(D) $P = FV\left(\frac{\frac{m}{r}}{\left(1+\frac{m}{r}\right)^{m\cdot t}-1}\right)$

403. Which of the following equations shows the adjusted formula if the interest rate were 3 percentage points more than r (where $r > 1\%$)?

(A) $FV = P\left(\frac{\left(1+\frac{r+3}{m}\right)^{m\cdot t}-1}{\frac{r+3}{m}}\right)$

(B) $FV = P\left(\frac{\left(1+\frac{3r}{m}\right)^{m\cdot t}-1}{\frac{3r}{m}}\right)$

(C) $FV = P\left(\frac{\left(1+\frac{r+0.03}{m}\right)^{m\cdot t}-1}{\frac{r+0.03}{m}}\right)$

(D) $FV = P\left(\frac{\left(1+\frac{1.03r}{m}\right)^{m\cdot t}-1}{\frac{1.03r}{m}}\right)$

404. The line $y = mx + b$ is graphed in the xy-plane, where m, as a constant, is the slope. What is the equation of the line perpendicular to $y = mx + b$?

(A) $y = \frac{1}{m}x + b$

(B) $y = -mx + b$

(C) $y = -\frac{1}{m}x + b$

(D) $y = 2mx + b$

405. In the xy-plane, at what two x-values does the parabola with the equation $y = x^2 - 100$ cross the x-axis?

(A) −10, 0

(B) −10, 10

(C) −10, 5

(D) 10, 0

406. In the xy-plane, at what two x-values does the parabola with the equation $y = x^2 - 3(x+6)$ cross the x-axis?

(A) −6, 9

(B) −3, 6

(C) −3, 9

(D) −6, 3

407. In the xy-plane, at what two x-values does the parabola with the equation $y = x^2 + 9$ cross the line $y = 18$?

(A) −5, 5

(B) −3, 3

(C) −2, 2

(D) −1, 1

408. In the drawing, if $y = 50$, what is the value of $x - b$?

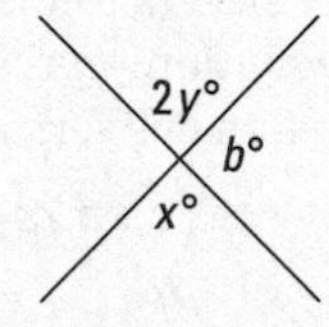

Note: Drawing not to scale.

(A) 20

(B) 40

(C) 60

(D) 80

409. In the quadratic equation $y = x^2 - 6x$, what are the coordinates of the vertex of the parabola?

(A) $(0, 0)$

(B) $(3, 0)$

(C) $(0, 9)$

(D) $(3, -9)$

410. What are the solutions to the equation $\frac{1}{x^2 - x} = \frac{1}{6}$?

(A) $\frac{1}{2}, \frac{1}{3}$

(B) $-\frac{1}{2}, \frac{1}{3}$

(C) 2, 3

(D) −2, 3

411. What are the solutions to the equation $0.5x^2 + 2x = -17$, where $i = \sqrt{-1}$?

(A) $x = -1 \pm \sqrt{30}$

(B) $x = 1 \pm \left(\sqrt{30} - i\right)$

(C) $x = -2 \pm i\sqrt{30}$

(D) $x = 2 \pm \sqrt{30}$

412. If $x < 0$, what are the solutions to the equation $x^2\left(x^2 - 5\right) = -2^2$?

(A) −5, −4

(B) −4, −3

(C) −3, −2

(D) −2, −1

413. What are the solutions to the equation $x^2(x-3) = 10x$?

(A) −2, 0, 5

(B) −5, 0, 2

(C) −2, −1, 0

(D) −3, −2, 0

414. In a certain isosceles triangle, if one angle measures 92°, which of the following could be the measure of any of the other angles?

I. 44°

II. 92°

III. 108°

(A) I only

(B) I or II

(C) II or III

(D) I, II, or III

415. In triangle *ABC* where $C = 90°$ and the hypotenuse is 5, $\csc A = \frac{5}{3}$. What is $\sec B$?

(A) $\frac{5}{3}$

(B) $\frac{5}{4}$

(C) $\frac{4}{3}$

(D) 1

416. If $i^2 = -1$ and $a + b = i$, what is the value of $a^2 - b^2$?

(A) −2

(B) −1

(C) $i(a-b)$

(D) $i(a+b)$

417. At which two points does the line with the equation $y = 9$ cross $y = (x+3)^2 + 5$?

(A) $(1, 9)$ and $(5, 9)$

(B) $(-1, 9)$ and $(5, 9)$

(C) $(-1, 9)$ and $(-5, 9)$

(D) $(1, 9)$ and $(-5, 9)$

418. Which of the following is equivalent to this expression?

$$\sqrt{a^4 - b^4}$$

(A) $\sqrt{a^2 + b^2}\sqrt{a^2 + b^2}$

(B) $\sqrt{a^2 - b^2}\sqrt{a^2 - b^2}$

(C) $\sqrt{a^2 + b^2}\sqrt{a + b}\sqrt{a - b}$

(D) $\sqrt{a^2 - b^2}\sqrt{a + b}\sqrt{a - b}$

419. If $y = 1$, what is the value of this expression?

$$y^3\left(y^6 - y^3\right)\left(y^6 + y^3\right)$$

(A) 0

(B) 1

(C) 3

(D) 9

420. What are the solutions to this equation?

$$\left(\sqrt[3]{x}\right)^2 - 3\sqrt[3]{x} + 2 = 0$$

(A) 1, 2

(B) 2, 3

(C) 1, 8

(D) 8, 9

421. The surface area of a cube, C, can be shown in terms of its edge, e. Which of the following equations represents e in terms of C?

(A) $e = \sqrt{\frac{C}{6}}$

(B) $e = \sqrt{\frac{6}{C}}$

(C) $e = \sqrt{\frac{C}{3}}$

(D) $e = \sqrt{\frac{3}{C}}$

422. The volume of a cylinder, V, can be shown in terms of its radius, r, and its height, h. Which of the following equations represents r in terms of V and h?

(A) $r = \sqrt{\frac{\pi h}{V}}$

(B) $r = \sqrt{\frac{V}{\pi h}}$

(C) $r = \sqrt{\frac{Vh}{\pi}}$

(D) $r = \sqrt{\frac{h}{\pi V}}$

423. What is the area of this trapezoid?

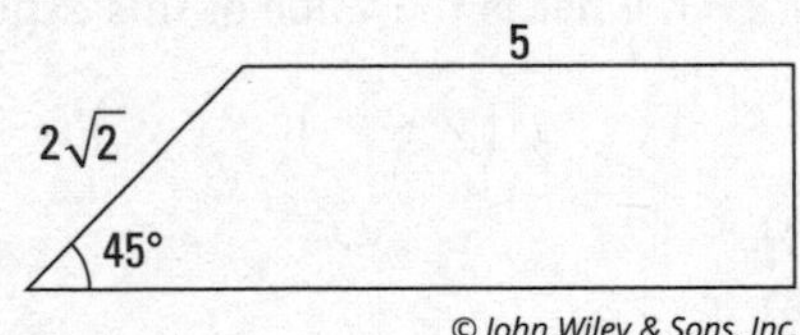

© John Wiley & Sons, Inc.

(A) 6

(B) 9

(C) 12

(D) 15

424. If $AB = BC$, what is the area of square $ACDE$?

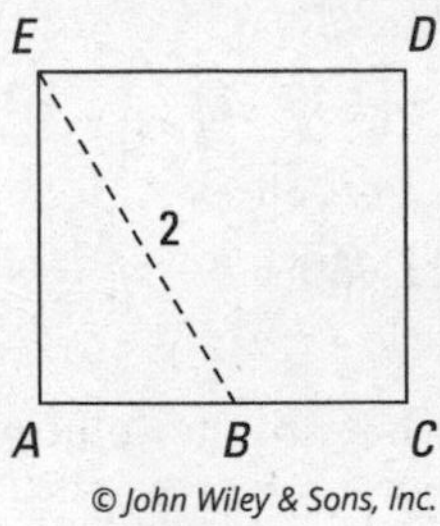

© John Wiley & Sons, Inc.

(A) $\frac{13}{9}$

(B) $\frac{16}{9}$

(C) 2

(D) $\frac{16}{7}$

425. What is the volume of a cylinder having a radius of $\sqrt{3}$ and a height of 6?

(A) 3π

(B) 9π

(C) 18π

(D) 27π

426. Which of the following is equivalent to this expression? Note that $i^2 = -1$.

$$\frac{1-i}{1+i}$$

(A) $2i$

(B) i

(C) $-i$

(D) $-2i$

427. Which of the following has a graph in the xy-plane where y is always less than or equal to -3?

(A) $y = x^2 - 3$

(B) $y = x^2 + 3$

(C) $y = -x^2 - 3$

(D) $y = -x^2 + 3$

428. A line intercepts the x-axis at $(2, 0)$ and crosses the point $(-2, -2)$. What is the equation of this line?

(A) $y = \frac{1}{2}x - 1$

(B) $y = \frac{1}{2}x + 1$

(C) $y = 2x - 1$

(D) $y = 2x + 1$

429. In the following drawing, l_1 is parallel to l_2, and $x = 3y$. What is the value of y?

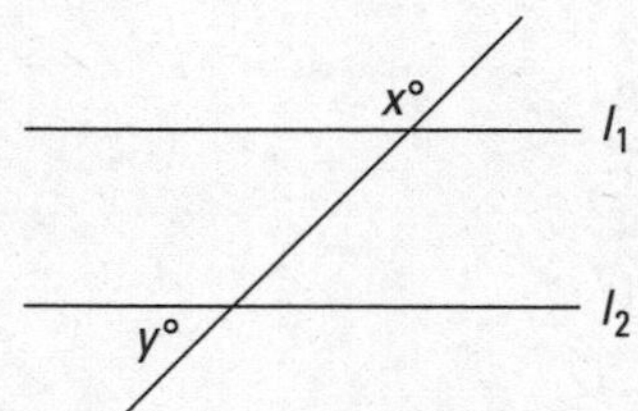

© John Wiley & Sons, Inc.

(A) 45

(B) 90

(C) 135

(D) 180

430. If $x \neq 0$, what is the value of $\dfrac{\left(x^{\frac{1}{3}}\right)^{12}}{\left(x^{\sqrt{2}}\right)^{\sqrt{2}}}$?

(A) $x^{\frac{1}{2}}$

(B) $x^{\frac{3}{\sqrt{2}}}$

(C) x

(D) x^2

431. What is the solution (x, y) to this system of equations?

$$3x + 2y = 5$$
$$x + y = 2$$

(A) $(1, 1)$

(B) $(-1, 1)$

(C) $(1, -1)$

(D) $(-1, -1)$

Questions 432 and 433 are based on the following information.

A line in the xy-plane passes through the points $(-1, -1)$ and $(0, 2)$.

432. What is the slope of the line?

(A) 3

(B) −3

(C) $\frac{1}{3}$

(D) $-\frac{1}{3}$

433. Which of the following points lies on the line?

(A) $(-2, -3)$

(B) $(-2, -4)$

(C) $(-2, -5)$

(D) $(-2, -7)$

434. The line $y = mx + b$ is graphed in the xy-plane. What is x in terms of b, m, and y?

(A) $\dfrac{y - m}{b}$

(B) $\dfrac{y - b}{m}$

(C) $\dfrac{m}{y - b}$

(D) $\dfrac{b}{y - m}$

435. In the xy-plane, at what two x-values does the parabola with the equation $y = x^2 - 100$ cross the x-axis?

(A) 5, 10

(B) −5, 10

(C) −10, 10

(D) −10, 5

436. In the *xy*-plane, at what two *x*-values does the parabola with the equation $y = x(x+2) - 15$ cross the *x*-axis?

(A) −5, 3

(B) −3, 5

(C) 2, 13

(D) −13, −2

437. In the *xy*-plane, at what two *x*-values does the parabola with the equation $y = x^2$ cross the line $y = 9$?

(A) −5, 5

(B) −3, 3

(C) −2, 2

(D) −1, 1

438. Based on this equation, if $y^6 = 4$, what is the value of x^2?

$$\left(x^2 - y^3\right)\left(x^2 + y^3\right) = 5$$

(A) 2

(B) 3

(C) 4

(D) 5

439. If $x > 0$, what is the value of *x* in this equation?

$$2\sqrt{x^4} + 4 = 12$$

(A) 2

(B) 3

(C) 4

(D) 5

440. What are the solutions to this equation?

$$x = 10\sqrt{x} - 24$$

(A) 24, 36

(B) 35, 49

(C) 16, 36

(D) 24, 48

441. What is the volume of a cylinder having a radius of $\frac{\sqrt{3}}{2\pi}$ and a height of 4π?

(A) 2

(B) 3

(C) 4

(D) 5

442. Which of the following is equivalent to this expression? Note that $i^2 = -1$.

$$\frac{2+2i}{2-2i}$$

(A) $\frac{i}{8}$

(B) $\frac{i}{4}$

(C) $\frac{i}{2}$

(D) i

443. If $\frac{8x}{3} + 1 = 17$, what is the value of 3*x*?

(A) 6

(B) 12

(C) 18

(D) 24

444. What is the value of *n* in this equation?

$$\sqrt[3]{n^3 - 19} + 7 = 10$$

(A) 2

(B) 3

(C) 4

(D) 5

445. In this equation, if $a + b = 2$, what is the value of $2(a-b)$?

$$\frac{2^{2a^2}}{4^{b^2}} = 4$$

(A) 1

(B) 2

(C) 4

(D) 8

446. If $x^3(x^2-1)=1$, what is the value of $\frac{17^{x^5}}{17^{x^3}}$?

(A) 1

(B) 17

(C) 34

(D) 51

447. What is the value of x in this equation?

$$(2^4)^2 = 4^x$$

(A) 1

(B) 2

(C) 4

(D) 8

448. In this system of equations, what is the value of $x-y$?

$$8x+3y=25$$
$$3x+8y=15$$

(A) 2

(B) 3

(C) 4

(D) 5

449. What is the value of p^2+q^2 if $p^2-q^2=7$ and $p^4-q^4=28$?

(A) 2

(B) 3

(C) 4

(D) 5

450. This equation is a model of projected fish population at a lake, where w represents the number of weeks and $f(w)$ represents the approximate number of fish. According to the model, what is the projected number of fish at the end of the 24th week?

$$f(w)=150+\left(5^{\frac{w}{12}}+\frac{w}{4}\right)$$

(A) 11

(B) 122

(C) 131

(D) 181

451. What is the value of $3^{x^2-y^2}$ if $x-y=\frac{1}{6}$ and $x+y=18$?

(A) 9

(B) 18

(C) 27

(D) 36

452. If $\frac{x+3}{3}=n$ and $n=6$, what is the value of x?

(A) 12

(B) 13

(C) 14

(D) 15

453. If $(2x-9)^3=-27$, what is the value of x?

(A) 2

(B) 3

(C) 4

(D) 5

454. If $z-xy=15$ and $\frac{xy}{5}=2$, what is the value of z?

(A) 12

(B) 13

(C) 24

(D) 25

455. For $i = \sqrt{-1}$, what is the value of $i(4+3i)(2-i)$?

(A) $6i - 2$

(B) $11i - 2$

(C) $11i - 1$

(D) $11 - 2i$

456. For $i = \sqrt{-1}$, what is the value of $(3+2i) - 2(4+i)$?

(A) −2

(B) −3

(C) −4

(D) −5

457. During each of the last 4 football games, the Tigers scored $2t$ touchdowns and $3f$ field goals. Which of the following represents the total number of touchdowns and field goals that the Tigers scored during these 4 games?

(A) $2t + 3f$

(B) $4t + 8f$

(C) $8t + 12f$

(D) $12t + 16f$

458. Based on this equation, if $b^2 = 16$, what is the value of a^2?

$$(a^2 - b)(a^2 + b) = 9$$

(A) 2

(B) 3

(C) 4

(D) 5

459. If $x > 0$, what is the value of x in this equation?

$$3\sqrt{x^3} + 6 = 30$$

(A) 2

(B) 3

(C) 4

(D) 5

460. The line $y = mx + b$ is graphed in the xy-plane. Which equation is of a line parallel to $y = mx + b$?

(A) $y = mx + 2b$

(B) $y = 2mx + b$

(C) $y = -\frac{1}{m}x + b$

(D) $2y = mx + b$

461. What are the solutions to the equation $(y^2 - 5)^3 = -1$?

(A) 2, 3

(B) −2, 2

(C) −2, 3

(D) −3, −2

462. What are the solutions to the equation $(x-3)^2 = 25$?

(A) 2, 8

(B) −8, 2

(C) −2, 8

(D) −8, −2

463. What are the solutions to the equation $x^3(x^3 + 9) = (-2)^3$?

(A) 1, 2

(B) −1, 2

(C) −2, −1

(D) −2, 1

464. If $x > 0$, what are the solutions to the equation $x^6 - 10x^4 = -9x^2$?

(A) 1, 2

(B) 2, 3

(C) 1, 3

(D) 2, 4

465. $12x^2+9x+15=8nx^2+6nx+2n+12$

In this equation, where n is a constant, what is the value of n?

(A) 1.5
(B) 3.0
(C) 4.5
(D) 6.0

466. If $x \neq 0$, what is the value of $\frac{\left(x^9\right)^{\frac{2}{3}}}{\left(x^{\sqrt{8}}\right)^{\sqrt{2}}}$?

(A) x^2
(B) x
(C) $x^{\frac{3}{\sqrt{2}}}$
(D) $x^{\frac{1}{2}}$

467. What is the solution (x, y) to this system of equations?

$$7x+5y=24$$
$$x=y$$

(A) $(1,1)$
(B) $(2,2)$
(C) $(3,3)$
(D) $(4,4)$

Questions 468 and 469 are based on the following information.

A line in the xy-plane passes through the points $(-2,-2)$ and $(1,7)$.

468. What is the slope of the line?

(A) 3
(B) −3
(C) $\frac{1}{3}$
(D) $-\frac{1}{3}$

469. Which of the following points lies on the line?

(A) $(4,22)$
(B) $(5,22)$
(C) $(6,22)$
(D) $(7,22)$

470. In the xy-plane, at what two x-values does the parabola with the equation $y=-2x^2+32$ cross the x-axis?

(A) 2, 4
(B) −2, 4
(C) −4, 4
(D) −4, 2

Grid-In

The grid gives you four boxes for writing each answer using the numerals 0–9 and a decimal point or fraction bar, if needed. Use decimals or improper fractions rather than mixed numbers. You may not use a calculator.

471. $8x^2+12x+21=2hx^2+3hx+4h+5$

In this equation, where h is a constant, what is the value of h?

472. In a certain right triangle, one angle measures 75°. What is the measure of the smallest angle, in degrees? Disregard the degree symbol when gridding your answer.

473. If $31.5x+5=4$, what is $63x+6$?

474. Based on this system of equations, what is the value of $2x+2y$?

$$8x+9y=27$$
$$2x+3y=15$$

475. If z is an integer, what is the value of z in this equation?

$$\sqrt{5z^3+60}+40=50$$

476. The height of a certain right triangle is 2. If one of the angles is 45°, what is the area of the triangle?

477. Based on this equation, if $a+b=1$, what is the value of $a-b$?

$$\frac{3^{a^2}}{3^{b^2}}=27$$

478. If $x^9(x^2-1)=3$, what is the value of $\frac{2^{x^{11}}}{2^{x^9}}$?

479. What is the value of a in this equation if $b^2=3$ and $a>0$?

$$\left(2^{2a+2b}\right)^{2a-2b}=16$$

480. Based on this system of equations, what is the value of $2x+\frac{y}{2}$?

$$7x+3y=4$$
$$3x+2y=2$$

481. What is the value of $n-p$ if $n+p=11$ and $n^2-p^2=110$?

482. Based on this system of equations, what is the value of $x+y$?

$$\frac{1}{2}x-\frac{1}{3}y=3$$
$$\frac{1}{3}x-\frac{1}{2}y=2$$

483. What is the volume of a cylinder having a radius of 2 and a height of $\frac{3}{\pi}$?

484. $c(m)=300+\left(3^{\frac{m}{6}}+\frac{m}{3}\right)10$

This equation is a model of the projected canary population on an island, where m represents the number of months and $c(m)$ represents the approximate number of birds. According to the model, what is the projected number of canaries at the end of the 18th month?

485. What is the value of $5^{a^2-b^2}$ if $a-b=\frac{1}{3}$ and $a+b=6$?

486. In this triangle, $BC=CD$ and $\overline{AB}$ is parallel to $\overline{EC}$. If triangle CDE has an area of 6, what is the area of triangle BDA?

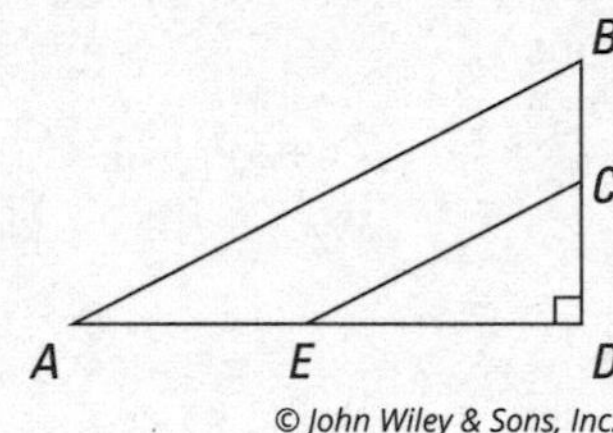

© John Wiley & Sons, Inc.

487. If $x>0$, for what value of x is $\frac{3(x^3)^2}{2(x^2)^2}=6$?

488. For what value of c is $5\sqrt{\frac{c}{5}}+5=55$?

489. If $h>0$, for what value of h is $\frac{h^2}{25}-18=18$?

490. If $\frac{5a}{b}=20$, what is the value of $\frac{3a}{2b}$?

491. For the function f defined here, k is a constant and $f(3)=15$. What is the value of $f(5)$?

$$f(x)=kx^2-3$$

492. The function f is defined by a polynomial. Some values of x and $f(x)$ are shown in the table. If $x = 3$, what is the value of $f(3x)$?

x	$f(x)$
7	2
8	5
9	10

493. The function f is defined by a polynomial. Some values of x and $f(x)$ are shown in the table. What is the value of $\frac{(f(5))^2}{6}$?

x	$f(x)$
2	6
3	5
4	7
5	6

494. If $\frac{x}{x+50} = \frac{1}{3}$, what is $\frac{x}{5}$?

495. If $\frac{3}{x-1} = \frac{4}{x+2}$, what is the value of x?

496. If $\frac{z+6}{8} = \frac{8}{z-6}$ and $z > 0$, what is the value of z?

497. If $\frac{y+10}{8} = -\left(\frac{8}{y-10}\right)$ and $y > 0$, what is the value of y?

498. Given this system of equations, what is the value of $2x - 2y$?

$$4x - 3y = 18$$
$$3x - 2y = 15$$

499. Given this system of equations, what is the value of $2x + y$?

$$8x^2 + 6x + y = 4z + 5$$
$$2x^2 + x = z$$

500. The function f is defined by a polynomial. Some values of x and $f(x)$ are shown in the table. What is the value of $2\left(\left(f(4)\right)^2\right)$?

x	$f(x)$
3	7
4	3
5	1

501. Simplify $16^{\frac{1}{4}}$.

502. Simplify $4^{\frac{12}{4}}$.

503. Simplify $\sqrt{4^3}$.

504. The number of members in Club A is 40 more than the number of members in Club B. If 80 members are in Club A, how many members are in Club B?

505. If $2n - 3p$ is a factor of the expression $4n^2 - p^2q$, what is the value of q?

506. If $x - 2$ is a factor of $x^2 + 6x - y^2$ and $y > 0$, what is the value of y?

507. If $11g = 55$, what is the value of $8g + 3$?

508. If $8n = 64$, what is the value of $\frac{n}{2}$?

509. For $i = \sqrt{-1}$, what is the value of $(5+5i)(5-5i)$?

510. If $\frac{2x+3}{7} = h$ and $h = 3$, what is the value of x?

511. If $n + pq = 12$ and $\frac{pq}{2} = 5$, what is the value of n?

512. If $x \neq 0$, what is the value of $\frac{(2x^3)^4}{(x^2)^6}$?

513. If $x \neq 0$, what is the value of $\frac{\left(8x^3\right)^2}{\left(4x^2\right)^3}$?

514. For what value of a is $\frac{a}{5}+5=10$?

515. For what value of h is $\frac{2h}{3}-5=7$?

516. In this system of equations, h is a constant. If the system has infinite solutions, what is the value of h?

$$3x+2y=4$$
$$hx+3y=6$$

517. Given this equation, what is the value of $a+b+c$?

$$x(2x+3)-2(x-3)=ax^2+bx+c$$

518. Given this equation, what is the value of $a+b+c$?

$$x(3x+4)+3(x-2)=ax^2+bx+c$$

519. If a, b, and c are integers, $6x^2+cx+6=(ax+2)(bx+3)$ for all values of x, and $1<a<b$, what is the value of c?

520. If $\frac{2c}{d}=3$, what is the value of $\frac{3d}{c}$?

521. For the function f defined here, a is a constant and $f(3)=24$. What is the value of $f(2)$?

$$f(x)=ax^2+ax$$

522. For the function g defined here, k is a constant and $g(2)=18$. What is the value of $g(4)$?

$$g(h)=\frac{kh^2}{2}+2kh$$

Questions 523 and 524 are based on the following information.

x	$f(x)$	$g(x)$
2	6	5
3	2	9
4	8	1
5	4	4

Some of the values of the functions $f(x)$ and $g(x)$ are shown in the table.

523. For which value of x shown in the table is $f(x)=g(x)$?

524. What is the value of $g(f(3))$?

525. What is the surface area of a cube having an edge length of $\sqrt{2}$?

Chapter 4

Math: Calculator Section

The second math section on the SAT does allow the use of a calculator. These questions tend to be more challenging and more math heavy than the questions in the No-Calculator Section featured in Chapter 3. They also test your ability to work with the math concepts but with more calculating thrown in.

Because the math concepts drive these questions, the questions demand careful thought and insight to recognize and sidestep common traps; otherwise, you may stumble into a lot of unnecessary math. Also, don't use your calculator for simple operations, such as 2 times 5, because you're more likely to punch a number in wrong than work it out incorrectly in your head.

The Problems You'll Work On

These questions cover the same topics as the Math: No-Calculator Section questions:

- **Basic math,** including fractions, decimals, percentages, and ratios
- **Algebra,** including linear equations, coordinate geometry, and quadratic equations
- **Geometry,** which covers both basic shapes and three-dimensional solids
- **Word problems,** including rate of travel, averages, probability, and equation setup
- **Tables and graphs,** including data analysis

What to Watch Out For

Common shortfalls include the following:

- Mistakes in using the calculator, such as punching in a number incorrectly
- Mistakes in working the problem, such as multiplying exponents when you should be adding them
- Not knowing how to work a certain math problem, such as a probability

Multiple Choice

Select the answer to each question. You may use a calculator.

526. Joe subscribes to an online movie service that charges a weekly fee of \$3 plus \$2.75 per movie watched. Which of the following functions gives Joe's cost, in dollars, for a week in which he watches m movies?

(A) $C(m) = 2.75m$

(B) $C(m) = 2.75m + 3$

(C) $C(m) = 3m + 2.75$

(D) $C(m) = 3m$

527. An office supply store sells pencils either individually or in boxes of 12. If on a certain day the store sold 215 pencils, of which 35 were sold individually, which equation shows the number of boxes, b, sold that day?

(A) $b = \frac{215-12}{35}$

(B) $b = \frac{215}{35} - 12$

(C) $b = \frac{215-35}{12}$

(D) $b = \frac{215}{12} - 35$

528. An equilateral triangle has perimeter P and side length s. Which of the following represents s in terms of P?

(A) $s = 3P$

(B) $s = 3P^2$

(C) $s = \frac{P^2}{3}$

(D) $s = \frac{P}{3}$

529. Which ordered pair (x, y) satisfies this system of equations?

$$x - 2y = 3$$
$$x - 4y = 7$$

(A) $(1, 2)$

(B) $(1, -2)$

(C) $(-1, -2)$

(D) $(-1, 2)$

530. Which ordered pair (x, y) satisfies this system of equations?

$$x + y = 5$$
$$x - y = 3$$

(A) $(4, 1)$

(B) $(4, -1)$

(C) $(-4, -1)$

(D) $(-4, 1)$

531. A delicatessen is filling cups of iced tea from a dispenser that contains 4 gallons of iced tea. How many 16-ounce cups can be filled from the dispenser? (1 gallon=128 ounces)

(A) 16

(B) 32

(C) 48

(D) 64

532. Jonathan drove at an average speed of 65 miles per hour for 4 hours. If his car gets 22 miles per gallon, approximately how many gallons did he use for this trip?

(A) Slightly under 10

(B) Slightly over 10

(C) Slightly under 12

(D) Slightly over 12

533. What is the slope of the line in the xy-plane that passes through the points $(2, 1)$ and $\left(3\frac{1}{2}, 2\right)$?

(A) $\frac{2}{3}$

(B) $\frac{3}{2}$

(C) 2

(D) 1

534. The ratio of pens to pencils in a certain box is $\frac{2}{3}$. Which of the following could *not* be the number of pencils in the box?

(A) 6

(B) 12

(C) 17

(D) 18

535. A movie theater is giving away a certain number of free tickets each week until it runs out. The following equation can be used to model the number of free tickets, t, that remain to be given away d days after the promotion began. What does it mean if $(50, 150)$ is a solution to this equation?

$$t = -5d + 400$$

(A) The theater has given out a total of 200 tickets.

(B) On the 50th day, 150 tickets remain to be given out.

(C) The theater is giving out 50 tickets a day for 150 tickets total.

(D) The theater has 50 days remaining until it runs out of tickets.

Questions 536–538 refer to the following information.

An auto dealer's lot has 50 vehicles.

	Gasoline	Electric	Hybrid	Total
Cars	6	4	11	21
Trucks	7	3	8	18
Vans	5	4	2	11
Total	18	11	21	50

536. Which of the following is the percent of vehicles that are electric?

(A) 15%

(B) 18%

(C) 22%

(D) 25%

537. Based on the table, if 25 comparable auto dealers have an approximate total of 4,000 cars, which of the following is the best estimate of the number of trucks that are hybrid?

(A) 200

(B) 450

(C) 530

(D) 640

538. If a vehicle were to be selected at random, how many times more likely is it for the vehicle to be a gasoline car than an electric truck?

(A) 1.0

(B) 1.5

(C) 2.0

(D) 2.5

539. In a certain rectangle, if the length were doubled while the width was reduced by half, how would the area of the rectangle change?

(A) The area would increase by 50 percent.

(B) The area would decrease by 50 percent.

(C) The area would stay the same.

(D) The change of area would depend on the numbers.

540. In a certain rectangle, if the length and width were both doubled, how would the area of the rectangle change?

(A) The area would increase by 50 percent.

(B) The area would double.

(C) The area would triple.

(D) The area would increase by a factor of 4.

541. Each week, Sally purchases a mixture of 5 pounds of almonds and 2 pounds of chocolates. This week, she purchased 40% more almonds and 50% more chocolates. By approximately what percentage did the total weight of her purchase increase?

(A) 21%

(B) 32%

(C) 43%

(D) 54%

542. Tommy draws a rectangle on a large sheet of construction paper. The rectangle has a length that is 2 inches longer than twice its width. If the rectangle has an area of 40 square inches, what is its width, in inches?

(A) 2

(B) 4

(C) 5

(D) 8

543. For her class assignment, Millie prints essays that use either one or two sheets of paper. If she prints 40 essays and uses 72 sheets of paper, how many essays use two sheets of paper?

(A) 32

(B) 34

(C) 35

(D) 38

544. In a certain square, if each side length were increased by 50%, how would the total area change?

(A) The area would increase by less than 50%.

(B) The area would increase by more than 50% but less than 100%.

(C) The area would increase by more than 100% but less than 200%.

(D) The area would increase by more than 200%.

545. Henry subscribes to water delivery service that charges a monthly fee of $5 plus another $8 per 5-gallon bottle delivered. Which of the following functions gives Henry's cost, in dollars, for a month with g bottle deliveries?

(A) $C(g)=8g$

(B) $C(g)=8g+3$

(C) $C(g)=8g+5$

(D) $C(g)=5g+8$

546. A snack shop sells pieces of bubble gum either individually or in packs of 8. If on a certain day the shop sold 93 pieces of bubble gum, of which 21 were sold individually, which equation shows the number of packs, p, sold that day?

(A) $p=\frac{93}{8}-21$

(B) $p=\frac{93-21}{8}$

(C) $p=93-\frac{21}{8}$

(D) $p=\frac{93-8}{21}$

547. Which ordered pair (x, y) satisfies this system of equations?

$$2x+3y=17$$
$$x-y=6$$

(A) $(7,1)$

(B) $(7,-1)$

(C) $(-7,-1)$

(D) $(-7,1)$

548. Phil is making orange juice from cans of concentrated orange juice. If each can yields 48 ounces of orange juice and he has 8 cans, how many gallons of orange juice can Phil make? (1 gallon = 128 ounces)

(A) 3.0

(B) 3.5

(C) 4.0

(D) 4.5

549. Carlton drove at an average speed of 50 miles per hour for 6 hours. If his car gets 17 miles per gallon, approximately how many gallons did he use for this trip?

(A) Just under 18

(B) Just over 18

(C) Just under 22

(D) Just over 22

550. What is the y-intercept of the line in the xy-plane that passes through the points $(18,15)$ and $(24,19)$?

(A) 8

(B) 7

(C) 3

(D) 2

551. The ratio of cats to dogs at a certain shelter is $\frac{8}{11}$. Which of the following could *not* be the number of dogs at the shelter?

(A) 33

(B) 43

(C) 121

(D) 143

Questions 552–554 refer to the following information.

A restaurant has 40 tables.

	Booth	Low Seat	High Seat	Total
Two-seater	4	5	3	12
Four-seater	6	9	5	20
Six-seater	4	2	2	8
Total	14	16	10	40

552. Assuming there are no other seats, how many seats total does the restaurant have?

(A) 48

(B) 60

(C) 152

(D) 190

553. If the restaurant is part of a franchise of 200 identical restaurants, then based on the table, how many high seat tables are there?

(A) 2,000

(B) 4,500

(C) 5,400

(D) 6,000

554. If a customer were to randomly sit at one of the tables, what is the likelihood that he would sit at a six-seater table?

(A) 0.15

(B) 0.20

(C) 0.25

(D) 0.30

555. Each week, Giuseppe Pizzeria purchases a mixture of 30 pounds of cheese and 20 pounds of flour. This week, the restaurant purchased 20% less cheese and 40% less flour. By what percentage did the total weight of the purchase decrease?

(A) 22%

(B) 28%

(C) 32%

(D) 38%

556. A farm is 30 square miles. If the length is 1 mile longer than three times the width, what is the farm's width, in miles?

(A) 3

(B) 4

(C) 5

(D) 8

557. Henry is hanging posters and using either 2 or 3 pieces of tape. If he uses a total of 47 pieces of tape to hang 19 posters, how many posters needed 3 pieces of tape?

(A) 6

(B) 7

(C) 8

(D) 9

558. In a certain rectangle, if each side length were decreased by 50%, how would the total area change?

(A) The area would decrease by 25%.

(B) The area would decrease by 50%.

(C) The area would decrease by 75%.

(D) The area would decrease by 100%.

559. If $a = bc$ (where c is a constant) and $a = 50$ when $b = 10$, what is the value of a when $b = 7$?

(A) 28

(B) 35

(C) 40

(D) 42

560. If $3x+5$ is 7 more than 19, then what is the value of $5x$?

(A) 7

(B) 14

(C) 28

(D) 35

561. A city planner draws a street with crosswalks separated by $\frac{1}{3}$ of a mile. Based on the following information, how far apart are these crosswalks, in feet?

$$1 \text{ mile} = 1{,}760 \text{ yards}$$
$$1 \text{ yard} = 3 \text{ feet}$$

(A) 1,240

(B) 1,760

(C) 2,180

(D) 2,500

562. For what value of x is $|x+3|+5=0$?

(A) 2

(B) 3

(C) 5

(D) There is no such value of x.

Questions 563 and 564 are based on the following information.

The speed of light, c, is shown in miles per second.

$$c = 186{,}000 \text{ mi/s}$$

563. Which of the following represents the amount of time needed for light to travel 5 miles?

(A) $\frac{1}{37{,}200}$ seconds

(B) $\frac{1}{74{,}400}$ seconds

(C) $\frac{1}{186{,}000}$ seconds

(D) $\frac{1}{930{,}000}$ seconds

564. What is the distance traveled by light in 1 hour?

(A) 11,160,000 miles

(B) 66,960,000 miles

(C) 111,600,000 miles

(D) 669,600,000 miles

565. Given this inequality, x has how many possible integer values?

$$-\frac{2}{5} < \frac{x}{5} - 1 < \frac{2}{5}$$

(A) Two

(B) Three

(C) Four

(D) Five

566. In the xy-plane, if $(0, 2)$ is the solution to this system of equations, which of the following is the value of b?

$$y = \frac{3}{2}x + b$$
$$y = \frac{4}{3}x + b$$

(A) 0

(B) 1

(C) 2

(D) 3

567. A hot dog cart sells hot dogs for \$2.50 each and sodas for \$1.50 each. The hot dog cart's revenue from selling a total of 400 hot dogs and sodas in one day was \$850.00. How many sodas were sold that day?

(A) 75

(B) 100

(C) 150

(D) 250

Questions 568 and 569 are based on the following information.

Joe bought a tablet at a warehouse store that gave a p percent discount off of r, its original retail price. The total amount Joe paid was d dollars, including a t percent sales tax on the discounted price.

568. Which of the following represents d, the amount Joe paid?

(A) $d = r\left(\frac{p}{100}\right)\left(1+\frac{t}{100}\right)$

(B) $d = r(p)\left(1+\frac{t}{100}\right)$

(C) $d = r\left(\frac{100-p}{100}\right)\left(\frac{t}{100}\right)$

(D) $d = r\left(\frac{100-p}{100}\right)\left(1+\frac{t}{100}\right)$

569. Which of the following represents r, the original retail price?

(A) $r = \left(\frac{100}{100-p}\right)\left(\frac{100}{100+t}\right)d$

(B) $r = \left(\frac{100-p}{100}\right)\left(1+\frac{t}{100}\right)d$

(C) $r = \left(\frac{100}{100-p}\right)\left(1+\frac{t}{100}\right)d$

(D) $r = \left(\frac{100-p}{100}\right)\left(\frac{100}{100+t}\right)d$

Questions 570–572 are based on the following information.

Grades received in Ms. Hoyt's class on the science final:

	A	B	C	D	F	Total
Boys	5	3	5	3	2	18
Girls	6	4	2	5	0	17
Total	11	7	7	8	2	35

570. If one student is randomly chosen from the class, what is the probability that the student earned either a B or a C on the final?

(A) 0.14

(B) 0.28

(C) 0.40

(D) 0.42

571. Out of the students who earned an A, if one boy and one girl are selected at random to get ice cream for the rest of the class, how many possible ways are there to choose the two students?

(A) 11

(B) 16

(C) 25

(D) 30

572. Out of the boys who earned an A, if one is selected at random to get plastic spoons, one is selected at random to get paper bowls, and a third is selected at random to get napkins, how many possible ways are there to choose the three students?

(A) 11

(B) 18

(C) 30

(D) 60

Questions 573–575 are based on the following information.

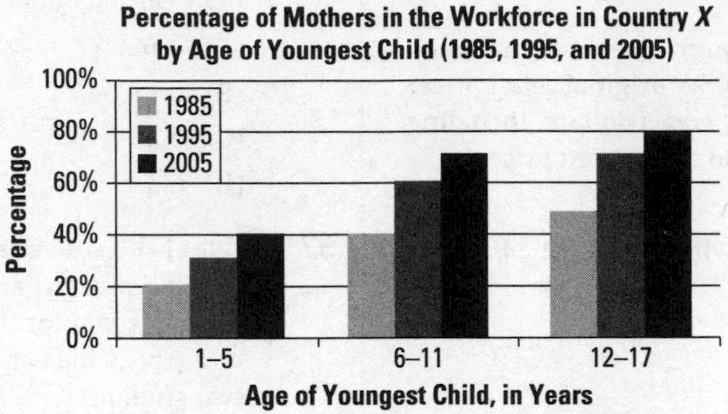

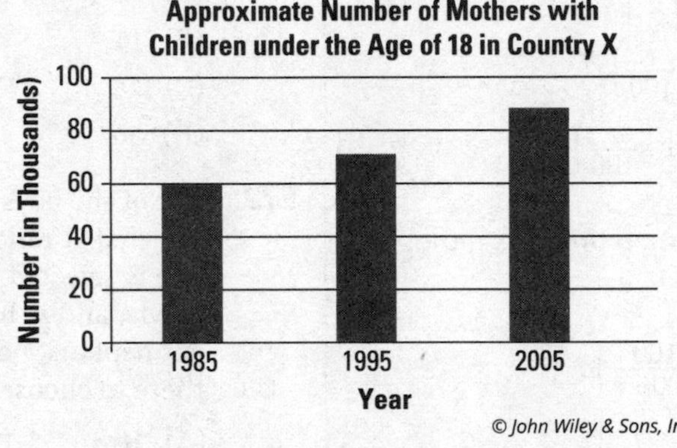

573. If the number of mothers with children under the age of 18 increased by 10% from 2005 to 2010 and the percentage of mothers in the workforce stayed about the same during that time, what was the approximate number of mothers with youngest children ages 12 to 17 in the workforce in 2010?

(A) 75,000

(B) 80,000

(C) 85,000

(D) 90,000

574. What is the approximate ratio of the percent of mothers in the workforce in 1985 with youngest children ages 1 to 5 to the percent of mothers in the workforce in 1995 with youngest children ages 12 to 17?

(A) 2 to 7

(B) 4 to 7

(C) 1 to 3

(D) 5 to 9

575. Which of the following can be inferred from the data in the graphs?

I. The population of Country *X* is steadily increasing.

II. The percentage of single mothers is steadily increasing.

III. The demand for daycare in Country *X* is steadily increasing.

(A) I and II

(B) II and III

(C) I and III

(D) I, II, and III

Questions 576–578 are based on the following information.

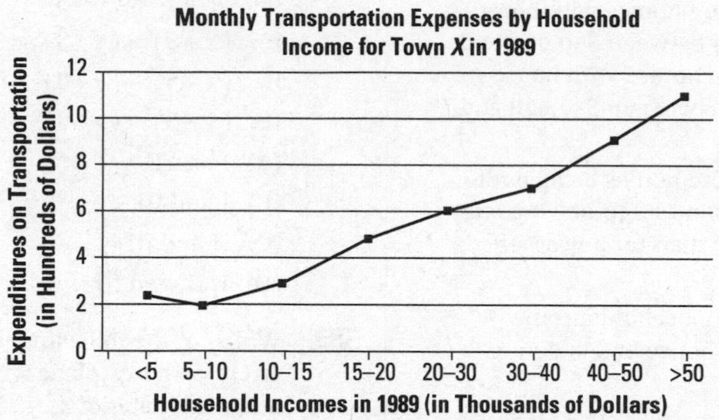

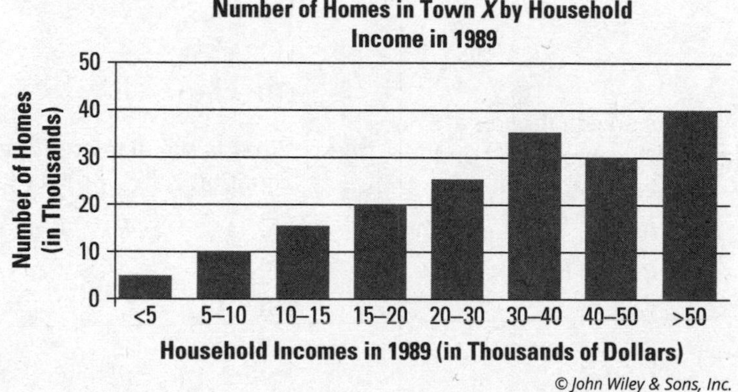

© John Wiley & Sons, Inc.

576. For the homes with household incomes of $20,000 to $30,000, what was the approximate total expenditure on transportation in 1989?

(A) $15,000,000

(B) $18,000,000

(C) $150,000,000

(D) $180,000,000

577. What is the approximate ratio of homes with household incomes between $5,000 and $10,000 to homes with household incomes between $30,000 and $40,000?

(A) 2 to 7

(B) 4 to 7

(C) 1 to 3

(D) 5 to 9

578. Which of the following *cannot* be inferred from the data in the graphs?

I. There are more homes with household incomes between \$50,000 and \$60,000 than homes with household incomes between \$30,000 and \$40,000.

II. There are more homes being built for the \$30,000 to \$40,000 income demographic than for any other demographic.

III. The median household income in Town X is between \$30,000 to \$40,000.

(A) I and II

(B) II and III

(C) I and III

(D) I, II, and III

579. Which of the following is an equation of a circle in the *xy*-plane with center $(3, 4)$ and a radius of 3?

(A) $(x-3)^2+(y-4)^2=9$

(B) $(x-3)^2+(y-4)^2=3$

(C) $(x-3)^2-(y-4)^2=\sqrt{3}$

(D) $(x-3)^2-(y-4)^2=9$

580. Which of the following is an equation of a circle in the *xy*-plane with center $(2, 1)$ and a radius endpoint of $(3, 2)$?

(A) $(x-2)^2+(y-1)^2=1$

(B) $(x-2)^2+(y-1)^2=\sqrt{2}$

(C) $(x-2)^2+(y-1)^2=2$

(D) $(x-2)^2+(y-1)^2=4$

581. Which of the following is an equation of a circle tangent to the *x*-axis at $(-4, 0)$ and to the *y*-axis at $(0, -4)$?

(A) $(x-4)^2+(y-4)^2=16$

(B) $(x-4)^2+(y+4)^2=16$

(C) $(x+4)^2+(y-4)^2=16$

(D) $(x+4)^2+(y+4)^2=16$

582. Which of the following *could* be the equation of a circle tangent to the *x*-axis at $(5, 0)$ and having a radius of 3?

I. $(x+5)^2+(y+3)^2=9$

II. $(x-5)^2+(y+3)^2=9$

III. $(x-5)^2+(y-3)^2=9$

(A) I and II

(B) I and III

(C) II and III

(D) I, II, and III

583. Which of the following is the equation of a circle in the *xy*-plane with a center at $(0, 0)$ and a diameter of 4?

(A) $x^2+y^2=\sqrt{2}$

(B) $x^2+y^2=2$

(C) $x^2+y^2=4$

(D) $x^2+y^2=16$

584. What is the diameter of a circle whose equation is $(x+64)^2+(y-48)^2=21^2$?

(A) 3

(B) 7

(C) 21

(D) 42

585. Which of the following *could* be the equation of a circle tangent to the *y*-axis at $(0, -7)$ and having a radius of 5?

I. $(x+5)^2+(y+7)^2=25$

II. $(x-5)^2+(y+7)^2=25$

III. $(x-5)^2+(y-7)^2=25$

(A) I and II

(B) I and III

(C) II and III

(D) I, II, and III

586. What is the radius of a circle whose equation is $\sqrt{(x+27)^2+(y-15)^2}=9$?

(A) $\sqrt{3}$

(B) 3

(C) 9

(D) 81

587. Joe is a biologist studying cell division. He noticed that type A cells divided at 150% of the rate of type B cells. Based on Joe's observation, if in one hour the type B cells divided 200 times, how many times did the type A cells divide?

(A) 100

(B) 200

(C) 300

(D) 400

Questions 588–590 are based on the following information.

Karen is a biologist studying cell division. She noticed that after the 3rd day, she could find the number of cells using the equation $C(d) = 1{,}000d(d-2)$, where C represents the number of cells and d is the number of days.

588. According to the equation, which of the following represents the number of cells on the 5th day?

(A) 5,000

(B) 15,000

(C) 25,000

(D) 40,000

589. According to the equation, on which day will there be 24,000 cells?

(A) 6th

(B) 7th

(C) 8th

(D) 9th

590. If on the 8th day, there are 56,000 cells, which of the following adjusted formulas is correct?

(A) $C(d) = 1{,}000d^2$

(B) $C(d) = 1{,}000d(d-1)$

(C) $C(d) = 1{,}000d(d-3)$

(D) $C(d) = 2{,}000d$

Questions 591–593 are based on the following information.

Henry is a biologist studying cell division. He noticed that starting with the 4th day, he could find the number of cells using the equation $C(d) = 100\left(2^{\frac{d}{3}}\right) + 500$, where C represents the number of cells and d is the number of days.

591. According to the equation, which of the following represents the number of cells on the 6th day?

(A) 400

(B) 900

(C) 64,000

(D) 64,500

592. According to the equation, on which day will there be 2,100 cells?

(A) 9th

(B) 10th

(C) 11th

(D) 12th

593. If on the 12th day there are actually 1,300 cells, which of the following adjusted formulas is correct?

(A) $C(d) = 100\left(2^{d}\right) + 500$

(B) $C(d) = 100\left(2^{\frac{d}{2}}\right) + 500$

(C) $C(d) = 100\left(2^{\frac{d}{4}}\right) + 500$

(D) $C(d) = 100\left(2^{\frac{2d}{3}}\right) + 500$

594. If the system of inequalities $y > x + 3$ and $y > -x + 2$ is graphed in the *xy*-plane below, which quadrants contain all the solutions to the system?

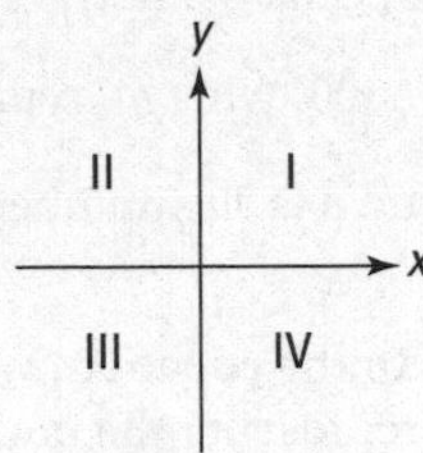

© John Wiley & Sons, Inc.

(A) Quadrants I and II

(B) Quadrants II and III

(C) Quadrants III and IV

(D) Quadrants I and IV

595. If the system of inequalities $y > x - 5$ and $y < -2x - 3$ is graphed in the *xy*-plane below, which quadrants contain all the solutions to the system?

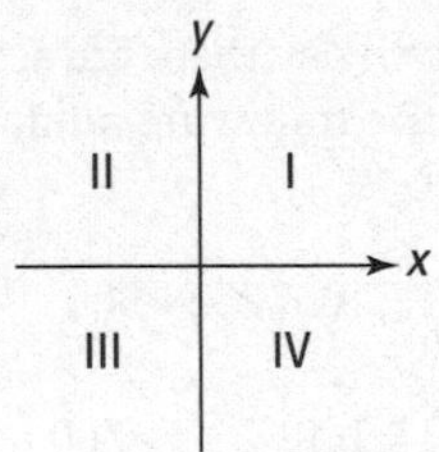

© John Wiley & Sons, Inc.

(A) Quadrants I, II, and III

(B) Quadrants II, III, and IV

(C) Quadrants I, II, and IV

(D) Quadrants I, III, and IV

596. For the function $f(x)$, the value of $f(5)$ is 0. Which of the following must be true of $f(x)$?

(A) $x + 5$ is a factor of $f(x)$

(B) $x - 5$ is a factor of $f(x)$

(C) x is a factor of $f(x)$

(D) 5 is a factor of $f(x)$

597. For the function $f(x)$, the value of $f(-3)$ is 0. Which of the following must be true of $f(x)$?

(A) $x + 3$ is a factor of $f(x)$

(B) $x - 3$ is a factor of $f(x)$

(C) x is a factor of $f(x)$

(D) 3 is a factor of $f(x)$

598. For the function $f(x)$, the value of $f(2)$ is 3. Which of the following must be true of $f(x)$?

(A) $x + 2$ is a factor of $f(x)$

(B) $x - 2$ is a factor of $f(x)$

(C) The remainder when $f(x)$ is divided by $x - 2$ is 3

(D) The remainder when $f(x)$ is divided by $x + 2$ is 3

599. For the function $f(x)$, the value of $f(-5)$ is 4. Which of the following must be true of $f(x)$?

(A) $x + 5$ is a factor of $f(x)$

(B) $x - 5$ is a factor of $f(x)$

(C) The remainder when $f(x)$ is divided by $x - 5$ is 4

(D) The remainder when $f(x)$ is divided by $x + 5$ is 4

600. Which of the following equivalent forms of the equation shows the coordinates of the vertex of the parabola as constants in the equation?

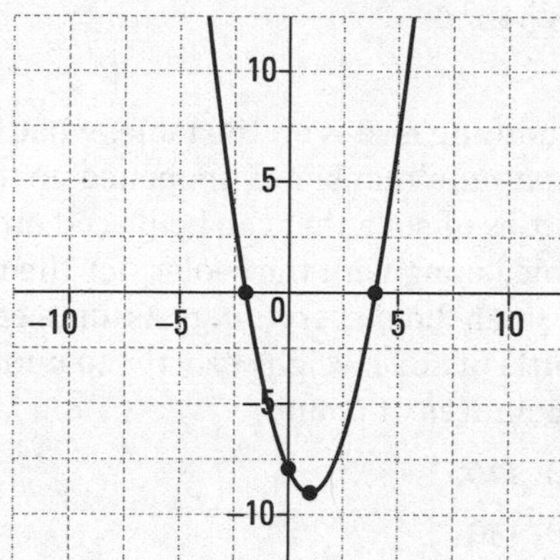

© *John Wiley & Sons, Inc.*

(A) $y = (x+2)(x-4)$
(B) $y = x^2 - 2x - 8$
(C) $y = x(x-2) - 8$
(D) $y = (x-1)^2 - 9$

601. Which of the following equivalent forms of the equation shows the coordinates of the vertex of the parabola as constants in the equation?

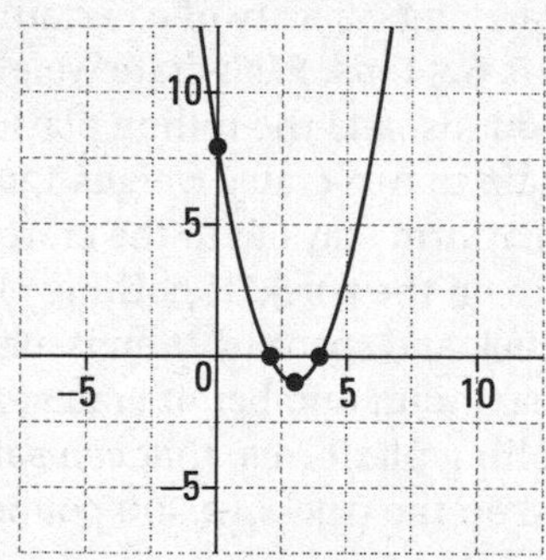

© *John Wiley & Sons, Inc.*

(A) $y = (x-2)(x-4)$
(B) $y = x^2 - 6x + 8$
(C) $y = (x-3)^2 - 1$
(D) $y = x(x-6) + 8$

602. The following drawing shows the graph of the equation $y = x^2 - 2x - 3$. Which of the following equations is equivalent to the equation of the graph?

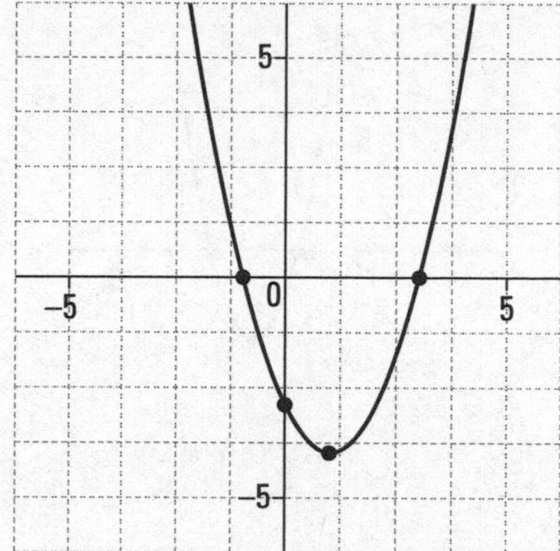

© *John Wiley & Sons, Inc.*

(A) $y = (x-1)^2 + 4$
(B) $y = (x-1)^2 - 4$
(C) $y = (x+1)^2 + 4$
(D) $y = (x+1)^2 - 4$

603. The following drawing shows the graph of the equation $y = x^2 + 4x - 5$. Which of the following equations is equivalent to the equation of the graph?

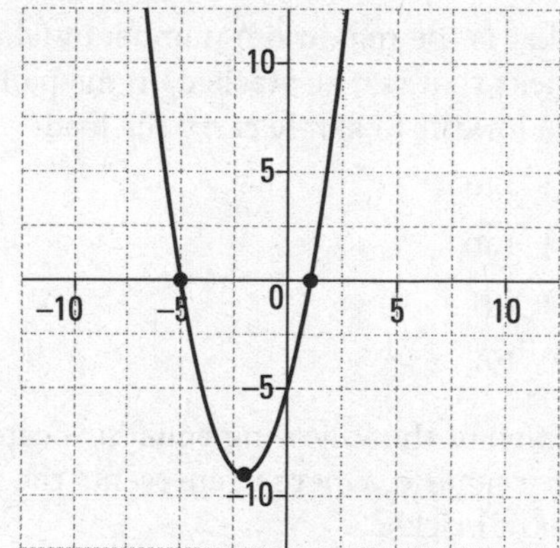

© *John Wiley & Sons, Inc.*

(A) $y = (x+2)^2 - 9$
(B) $y = (x+2)^2 + 9$
(C) $y = (x-2)^2 - 9$
(D) $y = (x-2)^2 + 9$

604. The following drawing shows the graph of the equation $y = x^2 - 8x + 12$. Which of the following equations is equivalent to the equation of the graph?

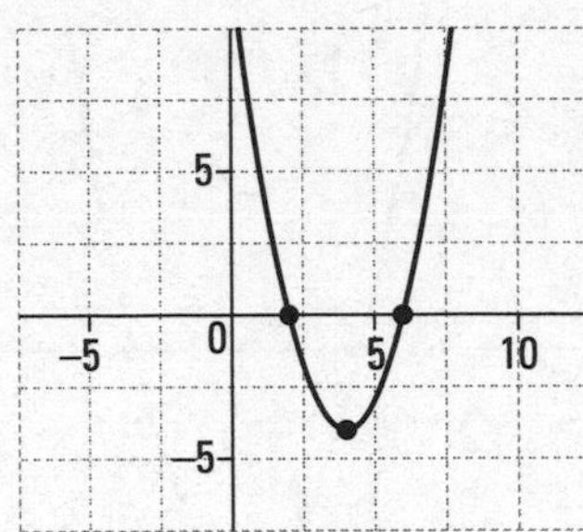

© John Wiley & Sons, Inc.

(A) $y = (x+4)^2 + 4$

(B) $y = (x+4)^2 - 4$

(C) $y = (x-4)^2 + 4$

(D) $y = (x-4)^2 - 4$

Questions 605 and 606 are based on the following information.

The weight capacity of a certain forklift is 1,000 pounds. A wooden pallet weighs 46 pounds, and red bricks weigh 5 pounds each.

605. What is the maximum number of whole bricks that can be stacked on the pallet for the forklift to safely carry the load?

(A) 189

(B) 190

(C) 191

(D) 192

606. Which of the following equations captures the scenario, where x represents the number of bricks?

(A) $1{,}000 \ge 5x - 46$

(B) $1{,}000 \ge 5x + 46$

(C) $1{,}000 \le 5x - 46$

(D) $1{,}000 \le 5x + 46$

Questions 607 and 608 are based on the following information.

The weight capacity of a certain folding picnic table is 200 pounds. A cooler loaded with ice weighs 38 pounds.

607. If nothing else is on the table, what is the maximum number of unopened 20-ounce bottles of soda that can be placed on the table, along with the cooler, for the table to safely hold everything? Assume each bottle of soda weighs exactly 20 ounces. (16 ounces = 1 pound)

(A) 129

(B) 130

(C) 131

(D) 132

608. Which of the following equations captures the scenario, where x represents the number of bottles of soda?

(A) $200 \ge \frac{4x}{5} + 38$

(B) $200 \ge \frac{4x}{3} + 38$

(C) $200 \ge \frac{5x}{4} + 38$

(D) $200 \ge \frac{5x}{3} + 38$

609. The carrying capacity of a certain flatbed truck is 6.5 tons. Each crate weighs 550 pounds, and the rolling platform that holds up to two crates weighs 120 pounds. The platform stays with the crates while they're on the truck. If nothing else is on the truck and space isn't an issue, what is the maximum number of crates, along with the rolling platforms, that can safely be placed on the truck? (2,000 pounds = 1 ton)

(A) 18

(B) 19

(C) 20

(D) 21

610. At his new job, Joe earns \$60 per day plus \$3 for each sale. If x represents the number of sales in one day, which of the following equations shows the amount he earns in one day, before taxes?

(A) $y = \frac{1}{20}x$

(B) $y = 60x + 3$

(C) $y = 3x + 60$

(D) $y = 60x - 3$

611. The bottom edge of a 15-foot banner is to have a notch clipped into it every 3 inches, starting with each end but not including the end. How many notches are to be clipped into the banner? (1 foot = 12 inches)

(A) 59

(B) 60

(C) 61

(D) 62

612. A landscaper wants to plant shrubs 6 feet apart along a fence, starting with one end of the fence and ending at the other. If the fence is 60 feet long, how many shrubs will be planted?

(A) 9

(B) 10

(C) 11

(D) 12

Questions 613 and 614 are based on the following information.

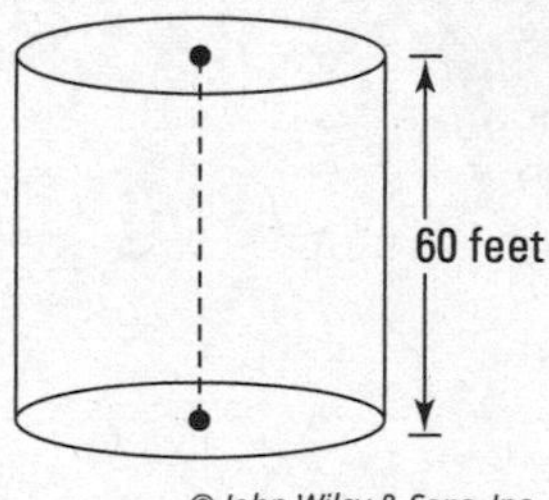

© John Wiley & Sons, Inc.

A city uses a water storage tank that's in the shape of the right circular cylinder, as shown here. The volume of the tank is $5,400\pi$ cubic feet.

613. What is the radius of the tank?

(A) 9 feet

(B) 30 feet

(C) 90 feet

(D) 900 feet

614. What is the volume of the tank in cubic yards? (1 yard = 3 feet)

(A) $1,800\pi$ cubic yards

(B) 600π cubic yards

(C) 200π cubic yards

(D) 20π cubic yards

Questions 615 and 616 are based on the following information.

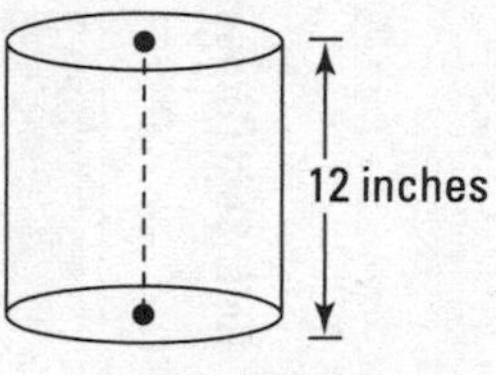

© John Wiley & Sons, Inc.

A jar of flour is in the shape of the right circular cylinder, as shown here. The volume of the jar is 432π cubic inches.

615. What is the diameter of the jar?

(A) 6 inches

(B) 12 inches

(C) 18 inches

(D) 24 inches

616. What is the volume of the jar in cubic feet? (1 foot = 12 inches)

(A) π cubic feet

(B) $\frac{\pi}{2}$ cubic feet

(C) $\frac{\pi}{3}$ cubic feet

(D) $\frac{\pi}{4}$ cubic feet

617. For what value of x is the function $f(x)$ undefined?

$$f(x)=\frac{2x}{2(x-5)^2+(2-x)}$$

(A) 2

(B) 4

(C) 5

(D) 6

618. For what value of g is the function $g(h)$ undefined?

$$g(h)=\frac{h}{2(h-7)^4-2(h-5)^3}$$

(A) 2

(B) 5

(C) 6

(D) 7

Questions 619–621 are based on the following information.

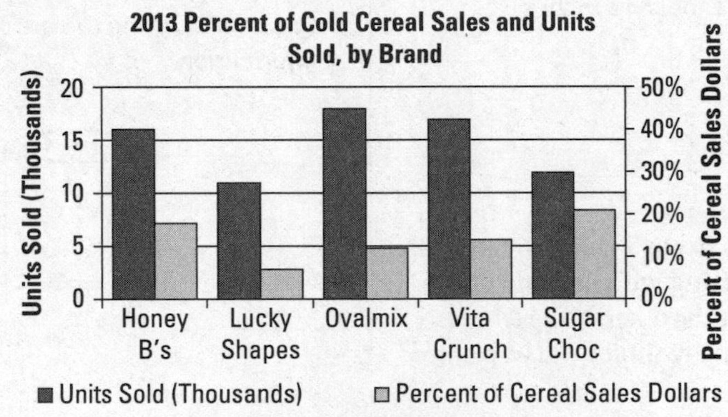

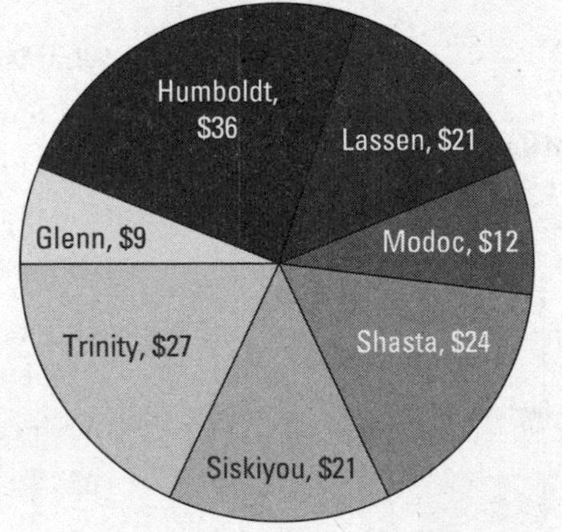

619. If the total 2013 cold cereal sales for the seven counties assessed were \$150,000, what percent of these sales was purchased by Humboldt County? Disregard the percentage symbol when choosing your answer.

(A) 22

(B) 24

(C) 26

(D) 27

620. Which brand of cereal has the highest average selling price per box?

(A) Honey B's

(B) Lucky Shapes

(C) Ovalmix

(D) Sugar Choc

621. If residents of Glenn County primarily purchase the Lucky Shapes brand cereal and residents of Trinity County primarily purchase the Sugar Choc brand cereal, what is the approximate ratio of the number of boxes sold in Glenn County to the number of boxes sold in Trinity County?

(A) 5:1

(B) 3:1

(C) 1:1

(D) 1:3

Questions 622–624 are based on the following information.

	Enrollment			
Sub-district	**6th Grade**	**7th Grade**	**8th Grade**	**Totals**
Aguilar	83	99	89	271
Bayfield	107	103	96	306
Creede	74	70	67	211
De Beque	40	36	39	115
Eaton	69	64	69	202
Totals	373	372	360	1105

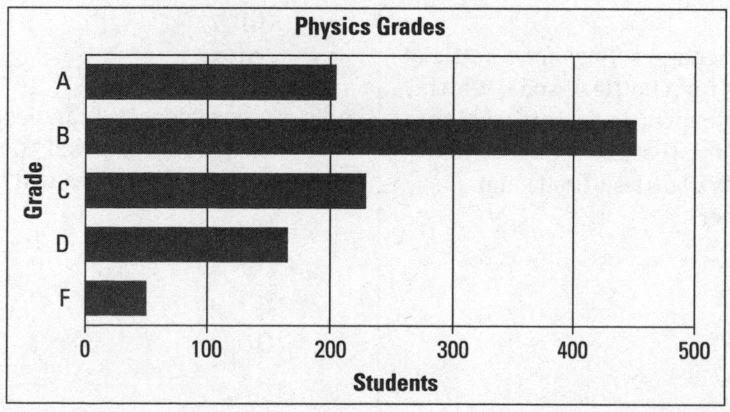

622. What is the approximate ratio of students earning a C to those earning a B?

(A) 1:2

(B) 2:1

(C) 3:2

(D) 4:3

623. If all the students from Creede, and only those students, are earning A's, and if the rest of the grades are evenly distributed among students in the other sub-districts, approximately how many students from Bayfield are earning B's?

(A) 50

(B) 75

(C) 150

(D) 225

624. If all the grades are evenly distributed throughout all sub-districts and classes, approximately how many students in De Beque are *not* earning a B?

(A) 20

(B) 40

(C) 70

(D) 100

625. $\left(\frac{1}{8}-\frac{3}{10}\right)+\left(\frac{1}{4}-\frac{1}{5}\right)+\left(\frac{5}{8}-\frac{1}{2}\right)=$

(A) 0

(B) $\frac{1}{2}$

(C) $\frac{3}{4}$

(D) $\frac{7}{8}$

626. A soda machine charges $0.75 for a bottle of water and $1.25 for a bottle of soda. Which of the following expressions represents the amount, in dollars, that the soda machine collects if it sells s bottles of soda and w bottles of water?

(A) $0.75s+1.25w$

(B) $0.75s-1.25w$

(C) $1.25s+0.75w$

(D) $1.25s-0.75w$

627. A soda machine charges $0.75 for a bottle of water and $1.25 for a bottle of soda. If in one day it sells 40 items and collects $40, how many bottles of soda did it sell?

(A) 15

(B) 20

(C) 25

(D) 30

628. A hot dog vendor charges $0.80 for a soda and $1.60 for a hot dog. Which of the following expressions represents the amount, in dollars, that the vendor collects if he sells s sodas and h hot dogs?

(A) $1.60h+0.80s$

(B) $1.60h-0.80s$

(C) $0.80h+1.60s$

(D) $0.80h-1.60s$

629. A hot dog vendor charges $0.80 for a soda and $1.60 for a hot dog. If in one day he sells 200 items and collects $319.20, how many hot dogs did he sell?

(A) 198

(B) 199

(C) 200

(D) 201

630. A machine selects exactly 11 beads from every 500 beads produced. If 4,000 beads are produced, how many beads will the machine select?

(A) 33

(B) 55

(C) 77

(D) 88

631. A boy chooses 3 candies from every 25. If his parents received 300 candies as gifts, how many candies will the boy choose?

(A) 32

(B) 35

(C) 36

(D) 38

632. A rope over a pulley is attached to a weighted lever. When an object weighing *p* pounds is attached to the other end of the rope, the lever moves a distance *d*, as shown in the equation. What is the value of *p* when *d* is 38?

$$d = 13 + 2.5p$$

(A) 9

(B) 10

(C) 11

(D) 12

633. A salesman earns a base salary plus commission. When he sells *u* units, he earns *d* dollars, as shown in the equation. What is the value of *u* when *d* is 390?

$$d = 110 + 40u$$

(A) 5

(B) 6

(C) 7

(D) 8

634. If $7x = 450 + 2x$, what is the value of 2*x*?

(A) 30

(B) 60

(C) 90

(D) 180

Questions 635 and 636 are based on the following information.

The amount of money an appliance salesman earns is directly proportional to the number of appliances he sells. The salesman earns $2,400 in a month when he sells 60 appliances.

635. How much will the salesman earn in a month when he sells 90 appliances?

(A) $3,000

(B) $3,200

(C) $3,600

(D) $4,000

636. The salesman uses 25% of the money earned to pay his assistant. The rest of the money is his profit. What is the profit the salesman makes during a month when he sells 60 appliances?

(A) $1,800

(B) $2,100

(C) $2,400

(D) $2,700

Questions 637 and 638 are based on the following information.

The amount of money a rental agent earns is directly proportional to the number of units she rents. The agent earns $6,000 in a month in which she rents 25 units.

637. How much will the agent earn in a month in which she rents 35 units?

(A) $8,000

(B) $8,400

(C) $9,200

(D) $9,600

638. The agent uses 40% of the money earned to pay for marketing. The rest of the money is her profit. What is the profit the agent makes during a month in which she rents 50 units?

(A) $7,200

(B) $8,000

(C) $8,400

(D) $8,800

639. Three times a number *x* is 5 minus 50. What number results when four times the number *x* is added to 10?

(A) 40

(B) 50

(C) 60

(D) 70

640. Six times a number y divided by 2 is 18 plus 18. What number results when 3 times the number y is subtracted from 2?

(A) 34

(B) 28

(C) −28

(D) −34

641. This equation represents a parabola in the rectangular coordinate system. Which of the equivalent forms of the equation shows the x-intercepts of the parabola as either constants or coefficients?

$$y = x^2 + 5x + 6$$

(A) $y - 6 = x^2 + 5x$

(B) $y = x(x+5)+6$

(C) $y - 6 = x(x+5)$

(D) $y = (x+2)(x+3)$

642. This equation represents a parabola in the rectangular coordinate system. Which of the equivalent forms of the equation shows the x-intercepts of the parabola as either constants or coefficients?

$$y = x^2 - 8x + 15$$

(A) $y = (x-3)(x-5)$

(B) $y - 15 = x^2 - 8x$

(C) $y = x(x-8)+15$

(D) $y - 15 = x(x-8)$

643. This equation represents a parabola in the rectangular coordinate system. Which of the equivalent forms of the equation shows the x-intercepts of the parabola as either constants or coefficients?

$$y = x(x+5) - 14$$

(A) $y + 14 = x^2 + 5x$

(B) $y + 14 = x(x+5)$

(C) $y = (x-2)(x+7)$

(D) $y = x^2 + 5x - 14$

644. This equation represents a parabola in the rectangular coordinate system. Which of the equivalent forms of the equation shows the x-intercepts of the parabola as either constants or coefficients?

$$y = x(x-1) - 110$$

(A) $y + 110 = x(x-1)$

(B) $y + 110 = x^2 - x$

(C) $y = (x-11)(x+10)$

(D) $y = x^2 - x - 110$

645. At 8:00 a.m., a certain graduated cylinder sitting on a warming plate contains exactly C milliliters of ethanol. This volume goes down exactly 3 milliliters for every minute that the cylinder sits on the warming plate. If at 9:15 a.m. the graduated cylinder contains 150 milliliters of ethanol, what is the value of C?

(A) 300

(B) 325

(C) 350

(D) 375

646. At 9:00 a.m. Tuesday, a certain rain gauge contains exactly M milliliters of water. This volume increases exactly 4 milliliters each hour. If at noon Friday the rain gauge contains 335 milliliters of water, what is the value of M?

(A) 25

(B) 30

(C) 35

(D) 40

647. A cargo ship carries containers that weigh either 200 tons or 275 tons each. The cargo ship can carry up to either 80 containers or a weight of 180,000 tons. Which of the following systems of inequalities represents this relationship, where x is the number of 200-ton containers and y is the number of 275-ton containers?

(A) $\begin{cases} 200x + 275y \leq 180{,}000 \\ x + y \leq 80 \end{cases}$

(B) $\begin{cases} \dfrac{200}{x} + \dfrac{275}{y} \leq 180{,}000 \\ x + y \leq 80 \end{cases}$

(C) $\begin{cases} 200x + 275y \leq 180 \\ x + y \leq 80{,}000 \end{cases}$

(D) $\begin{cases} 200x + 275y \leq 80{,}000 \\ x + y \leq 180 \end{cases}$

648. A tea producer produces boxes of tea that have either 60 tea bags or 85 tea bags. The tea producer can produce either 400 boxes or a total of 30,000 tea bags. Which of the following systems of inequalities represents this relationship, where x is the number of 60-bag boxes and y is the number of 85-bag boxes?

(A) $\begin{cases} \dfrac{60}{x} + \dfrac{85}{y} \leq 30{,}000 \\ x + y \leq 400 \end{cases}$

(B) $\begin{cases} 60x + 85y \leq 400 \\ x + y \leq 30{,}000 \end{cases}$

(C) $\begin{cases} 60x + 85y \leq 40{,}000 \\ x + y \leq 300 \end{cases}$

(D) $\begin{cases} 60x + 85y \leq 30{,}000 \\ x + y \leq 400 \end{cases}$

649. Bill's Hardware carries two types of paver brick: one weighing 5 pounds and the other weighing 7 pounds. If Bill's flatbed truck can carry either 5,000 pounds or 900 bricks, which of the following systems of inequalities represents this relationship, where x is the number of 5-pound bricks and y is the number of 7-pound bricks?

(A) $\begin{cases} 5x + 7y \leq 9{,}000 \\ x + y \leq 500 \end{cases}$

(B) $\begin{cases} 5x + 7y \leq 5{,}000 \\ x + y \leq 900 \end{cases}$

(C) $\begin{cases} \dfrac{x}{5} + \dfrac{y}{7} \leq 5{,}000 \\ x + y \leq 900 \end{cases}$

(D) $\begin{cases} 5x + 7y \leq 900 \\ x + y \leq 5{,}000 \end{cases}$

650. A farm produces eggs packaged in cartons containing either 12 eggs or 18 eggs. The shipping truck can carry either 18,000 eggs or 1,200 cartons. Which of the following systems of inequalities represents this relationship, where x is the number of 12-egg cartons and y is the number of 18-egg cartons?

(A) $\begin{cases} 12x + 18y \leq 18{,}000 \\ x + y \leq 1{,}200 \end{cases}$

(B) $\begin{cases} \dfrac{x}{12} + \dfrac{y}{18} \leq 12{,}000 \\ x + y \leq 1{,}200 \end{cases}$

(C) $\begin{cases} 12x + 18y \leq 12{,}000 \\ x + y \leq 1{,}800 \end{cases}$

(D) $\begin{cases} 12x + 18y \leq 12{,}000 \\ x + y \leq 1{,}200 \end{cases}$

651. A function f satisfies $f(4) = 7$ and $f(9) = 13$. A function g satisfies $g(7) = 12$ and $g(9) = 14$. What is the value of $g(f(4))$?

(A) 7

(B) 12

(C) 13

(D) 14

652. A function f satisfies $f(5)=8$ and $f(8)=2$. A function g satisfies $g(2)=3$ and $g(8)=5$. What is the value of $g(f(f(5)))$?

(A) 2

(B) 3

(C) 5

(D) 8

653. A function f satisfies $f(x)=x^2$, and a function g satisfies $g(x)=\sqrt{x}$. What is the value of $4f(3g(2))$?

(A) 9

(B) 18

(C) 36

(D) 72

654. A function f satisfies $f(x)=\frac{3x}{2}$, and a function g satisfies $g(x)=\frac{x}{6}$. What is the value of $2g(3f(2))$?

(A) 2

(B) 3

(C) 6

(D) 9

655. In a certain greenhouse, a tree grows 20% taller each month. If today the tree is 10 feet tall and the greenhouse is 40 feet tall, which of the following inequalities describes the number of months, *m*, before the tree reaches the top of the greenhouse?

(A) $(10.2)^m < 40$

(B) $10(1.2)^m < 40$

(C) $10(0.2)^m < 40$

(D) $1.2(10)^m < 40$

656. A drinking glass contains 0.5 liters of water. Each day, 10% of its water evaporates. Which of the following inequalities describes the number of days, *d*, before the glass contains only 0.2 liters of water?

(A) $0.5(0.1)^d > 0.2$

(B) $0.5(1.1)^d > 0.2$

(C) $0.5(0.9)^d > 0.2$

(D) $0.5(1.9)^d > 0.2$

657. The money in a savings account increases 0.8% each month. Which of the following equations shows the future value, *FV*, of the money in the account based on the present value, *PV*, after a period of *m* months?

(A) $FV = PV(0.08)^m$

(B) $FV = PV(1.008)^m$

(C) $FV = \frac{PV^m}{1.08}$

(D) $FV = PV(1.08)^m$

658. The money in a savings account increases 0.6% each month. Which of the following equations shows the present value, *PV*, of the money in the account based on the future value, *FV*, after a period of *m* months?

(A) $PV = \frac{(1.006)^m}{FV}$

(B) $PV = \frac{FV}{(1.006)^m}$

(C) $PV = \frac{FV}{(1.06)^m}$

(D) $PV = \frac{(1.06)^m}{FV}$

659. The money in a savings account increases by an annual interest rate of *i* percent. If the interest accrues monthly, which of the following equations shows the present value, *PV*, of the money in the account based on the future value, *FV*, after a period of *m* months?

(A) $FV = PV(1+i)^m$

(B) $FV = PV\left(1+\frac{i}{12}\right)^m$

(C) $FV = PV\left(\frac{i}{12}\right)^m$

(D) $FV = PV\left(1+\frac{i}{1,200}\right)^m$

660. The distance traveled by the moon in one full orbit around the Earth is approximately 1,500,000 miles. If the moon completes one full orbit in approximately 27 days and 8 hours, which of the following is the closest to the average speed of the moon as it orbits the Earth?

(A) 1,800 miles per hour

(B) 2,100 miles per hour

(C) 2,300 miles per hour

(D) 2,600 miles per hour

661. The time that it takes Mars to complete one orbit around the sun is 687 days. If Mars travels at an approximate speed of 54,000 miles per hour, approximately how far does it travel in one full orbit around the sun?

(A) 37,098,000

(B) 89,035,200

(C) 370,980,000

(D) 890,352,000

Questions 662 and 663 are based on the following information.

The planet Mercury is 36,000,000 miles from the sun and completes one full orbit around the sun in 88 days. Although Mercury's orbit is the most eccentric (noncircular) of all of the planets' orbits, for these problems, assume that its orbit is circular.

662. What is the approximate distance, in miles, traveled by Mercury as it completes one full orbit around the sun?

(A) 226,000,000

(B) 72,000,000

(C) 36,000,000

(D) 12,000,000

663. What is the approximate speed, in miles per hour, at which Mercury travels as it orbits the sun?

(A) 121,000

(B) 107,000

(C) 88,000

(D) 36,000

664. An auto dealer's cars have a mean value of $22,000 and a median value of $25,000. Which of the following situations could explain the difference between the mean and the median?

(A) A few cars are valued much less than the rest.

(B) Many of the cars have values between $22,000 and $25,000.

(C) The cars have values that are close to each other.

(D) A few cars are valued much more than the rest.

665. The test scores in an algebra class have a mean value of 86 and a median value of 82. Which of the following situations could explain the difference between the mean and the median?

(A) A few students scored much lower than the rest.

(B) Many of the students have scores between 82 and 86.

(C) The students have scores that are close to each other.

(D) A few students scored much higher than the rest.

666. The exam scores in a German class have a mean value of 92 and a median value of 92. Which of the following situations could explain the similarity between the mean and the median?

(A) Most students scored below 92.

(B) Most students scored above 92.

(C) The students received extra credit.

(D) The exam scores are evenly spaced out.

667. A construction manager estimates that a building will cost e dollars to complete. The goal is for the estimate to be within \$100,000 of the actual cost to complete the building. If the manager meets the goal and it costs a dollars to complete the building, which of the following inequalities represents the relationship, in dollars, between the estimated cost and the actual cost?

(A) $|e-a|<100{,}000$

(B) $|e-a|>100{,}000$

(C) $e-100{,}000<a$

(D) $a-100{,}000<e$

668. A landscaper estimates that it will cost e dollars to landscape a yard. The goal is for the estimate to be within 10% of the actual cost to complete the yard. If the landscaper meets the goal and it costs a dollars to complete the yard, which of the following inequalities represents the relationship, in dollars, between the estimated cost and the actual cost?

(A) $|e-a|<\frac{a}{10}$

(B) $|e-a|<\frac{e}{10}$

(C) $|e-a|<a-e$

(D) $|e-a|<e+10\%$

Questions 669–671 refer to the following information.

$$V=\frac{4\pi r^3}{3}$$

The volume of a sphere can be found with this formula.

669. Which of the following expresses the cube of the radius in terms of the volume and π?

(A) $r^3=\frac{3V}{4\pi}$

(B) $r^3=\frac{4\pi}{3V}$

(C) $r^3=\frac{4V}{3\pi}$

(D) $r^3=\frac{3\pi V}{4}$

670. Which of the following expresses π in terms of the volume and the radius?

(A) $\pi=\frac{3}{4r^3V}$

(B) $\pi=\frac{3r^3V}{4}$

(C) $\pi=\frac{3r^3}{4V}$

(D) $\pi=\frac{3V}{4r^3}$

671. If the radius of a certain sphere were to double from 3 to 6, what would happen to the volume?

(A) It would be multiplied by 2.

(B) It would be multiplied by 3.

(C) It would be multiplied by 4.

(D) It would be multiplied by 8.

Questions 672–674 refer to the following information.

$$A=4\pi r^2$$

The surface area of a sphere can be found with this formula.

672. Which of the following expresses the square of the radius in terms of the volume and π?

(A) $r^2=\frac{4\pi}{A}$

(B) $r^2=\frac{A}{4\pi}$

(C) $r^2=\frac{4}{A\pi}$

(D) $r^2=\frac{A\pi}{4}$

673. Which of the following expresses π in terms of the area and the radius?

(A) $\pi=\frac{4r^2}{A}$

(B) $\pi=\frac{A}{4r^2}$

(C) $\pi=\frac{4}{Ar^2}$

(D) $\pi=\frac{Ar^2}{4}$

674. If the radius of a certain sphere were to increase from 5 to 10, what would happen to the surface area?

(A) It would double.
(B) It would triple.
(C) It would quadruple.
(D) It would quintuple.

Questions 675 and 676 are based on the following information.

$$x^2 + y^2 + 6x - 4y = -9$$

The equation of a circle in the *xy*-plane is shown here.

675. What is the radius of the circle?

(A) 1
(B) 2
(C) 3
(D) 4

676. What are the (x, y) coordinates of the center?

(A) $(-3, 2)$
(B) $(-2, 3)$
(C) $(3, -2)$
(D) $(2, -3)$

Questions 677 and 678 are based on the following information.

$$x^2 + y^2 - 6x - 8y = 0$$

The equation of a circle in the *xy*-plane is shown here.

677. What is the radius of the circle?

(A) 2
(B) 3
(C) 4
(D) 5

678. What are the (x, y) coordinates of the center?

(A) $(-3, -4)$
(B) $(-4, 3)$
(C) $(3, 4)$
(D) $(4, -3)$

Questions 679 and 680 are based on the following information.

$$x^2 + y^2 + 2x + 2y = 7$$

The equation of a circle in the *xy*-plane is shown here.

679. What is the radius of the circle?

(A) 1
(B) 2
(C) 3
(D) 4

680. What are the (x, y) coordinates of the center?

(A) $(2, 2)$
(B) $(1, 1)$
(C) $(-1, -1)$
(D) $(-2, -2)$

Questions 681 and 682 are based on the following information.

$$x^2 + y^2 - 4y = 0$$

The equation of a circle in the *xy*-plane is shown here.

681. What is the radius of the circle?

(A) 1
(B) 2
(C) 3
(D) 4

682. What are the (x, y) coordinates of the center?

(A) $(0,2)$

(B) $(2,0)$

(C) $(0,0)$

(D) $(2,2)$

Questions 683 and 684 are based on the following information.

$$x^2 + y^2 - 20x = -75$$

The equation of a circle in the xy-plane is shown here.

683. What is the radius of the circle?

(A) 4

(B) 5

(C) 6

(D) 7

684. What are the (x, y) coordinates of the center?

(A) $(0,10)$

(B) $(10,0)$

(C) $(0,0)$

(D) $(10,10)$

685. The graph of a certain line ℓ in the xy-plane has intercepts at $(a,0)$ and $(0,b)$. If $a = b$, what is the slope of line ℓ?

(A) 1

(B) 0

(C) −1

(D) Undefined

686. The graph of a certain line ℓ in the xy-plane has intercepts at $(a,0)$ and $(0,b)$. If $a < 0$ and $b < 0$, which of the following quadrants does line ℓ *not* cross into?

(A) Quadrant I

(B) Quadrant II

(C) Quadrant III

(D) Quadrant IV

687. The graph of a certain line ℓ in the xy-plane has intercepts at $(a,0)$ and $(0,b)$. If $a = -b$, what is the slope of line ℓ?

(A) 1

(B) 0

(C) −1

(D) Undefined

688. The graph of a certain line ℓ in the xy-plane has intercepts at $(a,0)$ and $(0,b)$. If $|a| = |b|$, which of the following *could* be the slope of line ℓ?

(A) 1 or 0

(B) 0 or −1

(C) −1 or 1

(D) There are too many possibilities.

689. The graph of a certain line ℓ in the xy-plane has a positive slope and a negative y-intercept. Which of the following quadrants does line ℓ *not* cross into?

(A) Quadrant I

(B) Quadrant II

(C) Quadrant III

(D) Quadrant IV

690. The graph of a certain line ℓ in the xy-plane has a negative slope and a positive y-intercept. Which of the following quadrants does line ℓ *not* cross into?

(A) Quadrant I

(B) Quadrant II

(C) Quadrant III

(D) Quadrant IV

691. The graph of a certain line ℓ in the xy-plane has intercepts at $(a, 0)$ and $(0, b)$. If $b = 2a$ and $b > a > 0$, what is the slope of line ℓ?

(A) 0

(B) $-\frac{1}{8}$

(C) $-\frac{1}{4}$

(D) $-\frac{1}{2}$

692. The graph of a certain line ℓ in the xy-plane has intercepts at $(a, 0)$ and $(0, b)$. If $|a| = |2b|$ and $0 > a > b$, what is the slope of line ℓ?

(A) −2

(B) 1

(C) 0

(D) 2

693. If f feet, 9 inches is equal to 45 inches, what is the value of f? (1 foot = 12 inches)

(A) 3

(B) 5

(C) 36

(D) 41

694. If y yards, 6 inches is equal to 114 inches, what is the value of y? (1 yard = 36 inches)

(A) 2

(B) 3

(C) 5

(D) 8

695. In one week, Dan earned $30 more than Todd. If together they earned $250, how much did Dan earn?

(A) $120

(B) $140

(C) $150

(D) $280

696. In one month, Juliet collected 15 more gold coins than Karen. If together they collected 65 coins, how many did Juliet collect?

(A) 30

(B) 35

(C) 40

(D) 45

697. A botanist estimates that a certain tree grows at a rate of 3 feet per year. If today the tree is 11 feet tall, how many years will it take for the tree to reach 32 feet?

(A) 4

(B) 5

(C) 6

(D) 7

698. A geologist estimates that a certain mountain rises at a rate of 1.5 inches per year. At this rate, how many years will it take the mountain to rise 12 feet? (1 foot = 12 inches)

(A) 96

(B) 144

(C) 216

(D) 288

Questions 699 and 700 are based on the following information.

A zoologist estimates that a certain fish, which today is 10 inches, grows at a rate of 20% per month.

699. Approximately how many months will it take the fish to surpass 20 inches?

(A) 4

(B) 5

(C) 6

(D) 7

700. Which of the following formulas captures the fish's rate of growth, where m is the number of months and L is its length in inches?

(A) $L = 1.2(10)^m$

(B) $L = 10(1.2)^m$

(C) $L = 10(1.2)m$

(D) $L = \frac{10(1.2)}{m}$

Questions 701–703 are based on the following information.

John planted a tree in his garden. Each month thereafter, the tree grew by the same amount. This equation models the height, h, in feet that the tree has grown after m months:

$$h = 1.2m + 12$$

701. According to the model, how tall, in feet, was the tree when John first planted it?

(A) 12

(B) 15

(C) 18

(D) 21

702. According to the model, how tall, in feet, does the tree grow each month?

(A) 0.6

(B) 1.2

(C) 1.8

(D) 2.4

703. According to the model, how tall, in feet, will the tree be after 5 months?

(A) 12

(B) 15

(C) 18

(D) 20

Questions 704–706 are based on the following information.

George planted a palm tree in his backyard. Each month thereafter, the palm tree grew by a certain percent. This equation models the height, h, in feet that the tree has grown after m months:

$$h = 10(1.2)^m$$

704. According to the model, how tall, in feet, was the palm tree when George first planted it?

(A) 10

(B) 12

(C) 15

(D) 18

705. According to the model, by what percent does the palm tree grow each month?

(A) 10%

(B) 20%

(C) 110%

(D) 120%

706. According to the model, about how tall, in feet, will the palm tree be after 3 months?

(A) 12.0

(B) 14.4

(C) 17.3

(D) 20.7

Questions 707–709 are based on the following information.

Gerry places a bird feeder filled with 10 pounds of birdseed in her front yard. Each week, the birds eat 20% of the seed from the feeder.

707. Which of the following equations models the amount of birdseed, s, in pounds, remaining in the feeder after w weeks?

(A) $s = 10(0.2)^w$

(B) $s = 10(0.8)^w$

(C) $s = 10(1.2)^w$

(D) $s = 10(1.8)^w$

708. At this rate, how many pounds of seed will remain after the second week?

(A) 8.0

(B) 6.4

(C) 5.1

(D) 4.1

709. Based on the information presented, which of the following statements is true?

(A) The birds will finish the birdseed after 5 weeks.

(B) The birds will finish the birdseed after 8 weeks.

(C) The birds will finish the birdseed after 16 weeks.

(D) The birds will never finish the birdseed.

Questions 710–712 are based on the following information.

Jeffrey received a \$50 gift from his relatives. Each week, he spends exactly half of the remaining gift.

710. Which of the following equations models the number of dollars, d, remaining after w weeks?

(A) $d = 50(1.5)^w$

(B) $d = \dfrac{50(0.5)}{w}$

(C) $d = 50(0.5)^w$

(D) $d = \dfrac{50(1.5)}{w}$

711. At this rate, how much money will remain after the third week?

(A) \$50.00

(B) \$25.00

(C) \$12.50

(D) \$6.25

712. Based on the information presented, which of the following statements is true?

(A) Jeffrey will have spent all his money after 2 weeks.

(B) Jeffrey will have spent all his money after 4 weeks.

(C) Jeffrey will have spent all his money after 8 weeks.

(D) Jeffrey will never spend all his money.

Questions 713 and 714 are based on the following information.

In the following figure, point O is the center of the circle.

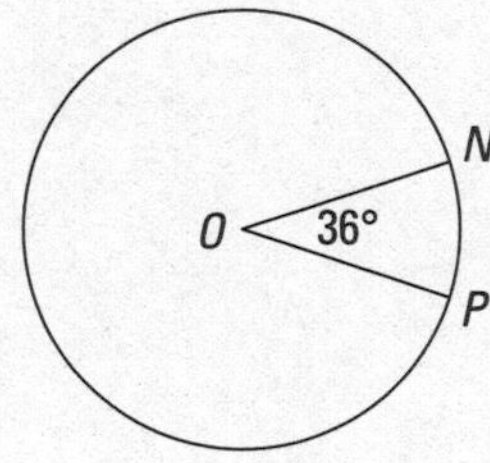

© John Wiley & Sons, Inc.

713. What fraction of the circle is minor arc NOP?

(A) $\frac{1}{6}$

(B) $\frac{1}{10}$

(C) $\frac{1}{12}$

(D) $\frac{3}{10}$

714. If the radius of the circle is 5, what is the length of minor arc *NOP*?

(A) π

(B) 2π

(C) 5π

(D) 10π

Questions 715 and 716 are based on the following information.

In the following figure, point *O* is the center of the circle.

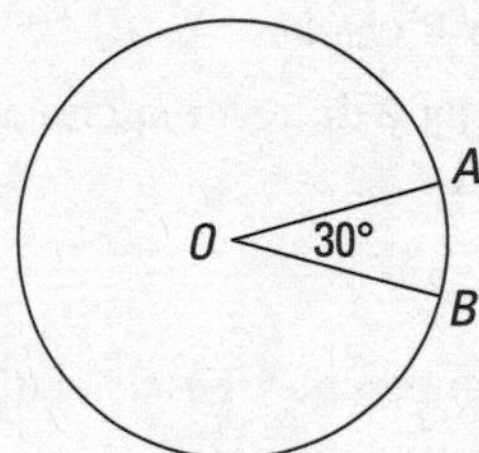

© John Wiley & Sons, Inc.

715. What fraction of the circle is minor arc *AOB*?

(A) $\frac{1}{6}$

(B) $\frac{1}{10}$

(C) $\frac{1}{12}$

(D) $\frac{3}{10}$

716. If the length of minor arc *AOB* is 5π, what is the circumference of the circle?

(A) $\frac{5\pi}{12}$

(B) 10π

(C) 20π

(D) 60π

Questions 717 and 718 are based on the following information.

In the following figure, point *O* is the center of the circle.

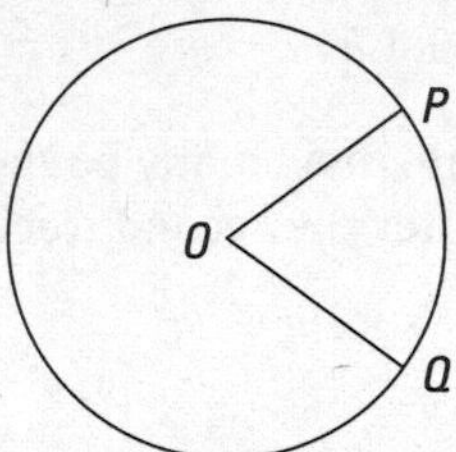

© John Wiley & Sons, Inc.

717. If minor arc *POQ* is $\frac{1}{6}$ of the circle, what is the measure of angle *POQ*?

(A) 30°

(B) 60°

(C) 90°

(D) 120°

718. If minor arc *POQ* is $\frac{1}{6}$ of the circle and the radius of the circle is 6, what is the length of minor arc *POQ*?

(A) π

(B) 2π

(C) 5π

(D) 10π

Questions 719 and 720 are based on the following information.

In the following figure, point *O* is the center of the circle.

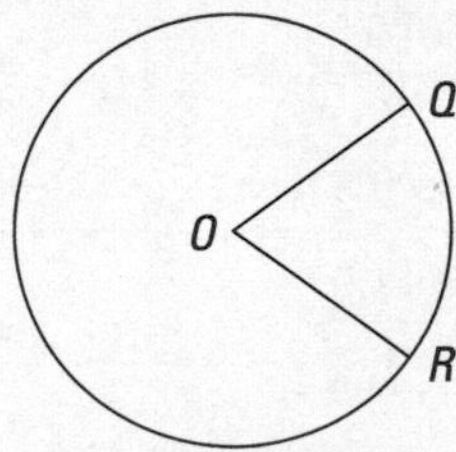

© John Wiley & Sons, Inc.

719. If minor arc QOR is $\frac{1}{5}$ of the circle, what is the measure of angle QOR?

(A) 36°

(B) 54°

(C) 72°

(D) 90°

720. If minor arc QOR is $\frac{1}{5}$ of the circle and its length is 10π, what is the circumference of the circle?

(A) $\frac{\pi}{2}$

(B) 20π

(C) 36π

(D) 50π

721. The table shows some values of the function f. Which of the following defines f?

x	1	2	3
$f(x)$	2	5	10

(A) $f(x) = x^2 + 2$

(B) $f(x) = x^3 - 2$

(C) $f(x) = x^2 + 1$

(D) $f(x) = x^3 - 1$

722. The table shows some values of the function f. Which of the following defines f?

x	1	2	3
$f(x)$	-1	6	25

(A) $f(x) = x^2 + 2$

(B) $f(x) = x^3 - 2$

(C) $f(x) = x^2 + 1$

(D) $f(x) = x^3 - 1$

723. The table shows some values of the function f. Which of the following defines f?

x	2	4	6
$f(x)$	200	400	800

(A) $f(x) = 100x$

(B) $f(x) = 100(1)^x$

(C) $f(x) = 100(2)^{x/2}$

(D) $f(x) = 100(4)^{x/4}$

724. The table shows some values of the function f.

x	2	4	8
$f(x)$	200	400	1,600

Which two of the following *could* be f?

I. $f(x) = 100x$

II. $f(x) = 100(2)^{x/2}$

III. $f(x) = 100(4)^{x/4}$

(A) I and II

(B) II and III

(C) I and III

(D) I, II, and III

725. At a certain high school club, approximately 10% of the boys and 15% of the girls are earning scholarships. If there are 139 boys and 202 girls, which of the following is closest to the number of students who are earning scholarships?

(A) 25

(B) 30

(C) 33

(D) 44

726. At a certain sporting event, approximately 42% of the boys and 57% of the girls are rooting for Team B. If there are 245 boys and 318 girls, which of the following is closest to the number of students who are rooting for Team B?

(A) 99

(B) 284

(C) 285

(D) 563

727. Which of the following is the sum of these two polynomials?

$$2x^2 + 3x - 5$$
$$3x^2 - 5x + 6$$

(A) $5x^2 + 8x + 11$

(B) $5x^2 + 8x + 1$

(C) $5x^2 - 2x + 1$

(D) $5x^2 - 2x - 1$

728. Which of the following is the difference of these two polynomials?

$$4x^2 + 3x - 2$$
$$3x^2 - 2x - 1$$

(A) $x^2 + 5x - 1$
(B) $x^2 + x - 1$
(C) $7x^2 + x - 1$
(D) $7x^2 - x - 3$

729. Which of the following is the product of these two binomials?

$$x + 2$$
$$x - 5$$

(A) $x^2 - 10$
(B) $x^2 + 10$
(C) $x^2 - 3x - 10$
(D) $x^2 + 3x - 10$

730. Which of the following is a factor of both of these polynomials?

$$x^2 - 2x - 3$$
$$x^2 - x - 6$$

(A) $x - 2$
(B) $x - 3$
(C) $x + 2$
(D) $x + 3$

731. Which of the following is a factor of both of these polynomials?

$$x^2 + 6x + 9$$
$$x^2 - 9$$

(A) $x - 2$
(B) $x - 3$
(C) $x + 2$
(D) $x + 3$

732. Given that this system of equations is true, what is the value of x?

$$x^2 + 5x + 6 = 0$$
$$x^2 - x - 6 = 0$$

(A) 3
(B) 2
(C) −2
(D) −3

733. Given that this system of equations is true, what is the value of x?

$$x^2 - 2x - 8 = 0$$
$$x^2 - 16 = 0$$

(A) 4
(B) 2
(C) −2
(D) −4

734. If $\frac{2}{3}x = \frac{3}{4}$, what is the value of x?

(A) $\frac{8}{9}$
(B) $\frac{9}{8}$
(C) $\frac{4}{3}$
(D) $\frac{3}{2}$

735. If $\frac{6}{5}x = \frac{4}{3}$, what is the value of x?

(A) $\frac{10}{9}$
(B) $\frac{9}{10}$
(C) $\frac{5}{6}$
(D) $\frac{3}{4}$

736. On her skateboard, Sally travels 85 feet in 10 seconds. At this rate, which of the following is closest to the distance, in feet, she will travel in 3 minutes?

(A) 900
(B) 1,200
(C) 1,500
(D) 1,800

737. On his bicycle, Scott travels 60 feet in 5 seconds. At this rate, which of the following is closest to the distance he will travel in 20 minutes?

(A) Fifteen thousand feet

(B) Eighteen thousand feet

(C) Twenty thousand feet

(D) Twenty-two thousand feet

738. On her inline skates, Kate travels 170 feet in 20 seconds. At this rate, which of the following is closest to the distance she will travel in 30 minutes? (1 mile = 5,280 feet)

(A) Slightly less than one mile

(B) Slightly more than one mile

(C) Slightly less than two miles

(D) Slightly more than two miles

739. The cost of a car rental is \$20 per day plus \$0.35 per mile driven. Which of the following equations gives the cost, *c*, in dollars, for *m* miles driven over *d* days?

(A) $c = 20.35d + m$

(B) $c = 2d + 35m$

(C) $c = 20d + 35m$

(D) $c = 20d + 0.35m$

740. The cost of a bike rental is \$6 per hour plus \$0.15 per mile ridden. Which of the following equations gives the cost, *c*, in dollars, for *m* miles ridden over *m* hours?

(A) $c = 6h + 0.15m$

(B) $c = 6h + 15m$

(C) $c = 0.6h + 15m$

(D) $c = 6.15h + m$

741. In the following image, the angles are supplementary. What is the value of *k*?

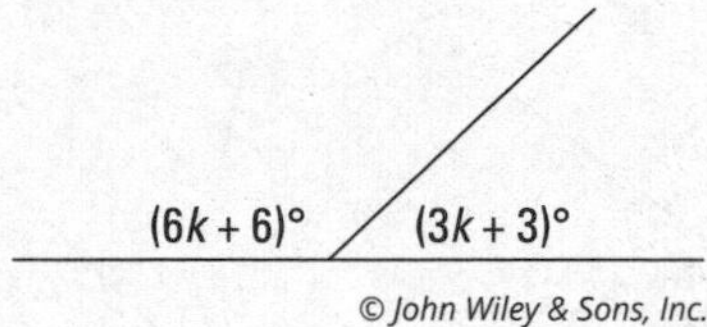

(A) 17

(B) 18

(C) 19

(D) 20

742. In the following image, the angles are supplementary. What is the value of *p*?

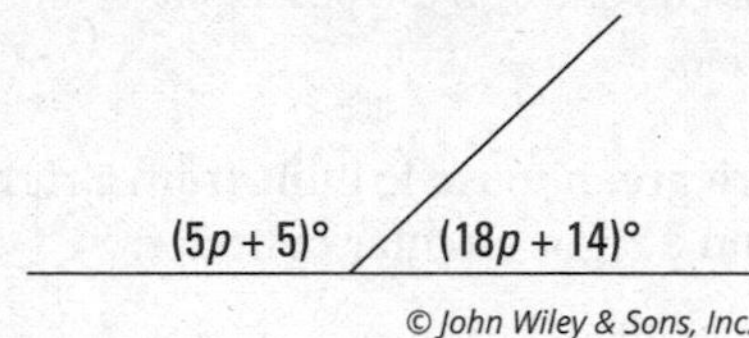

(A) 7

(B) 8

(C) 9

(D) 10

743. In the following image, angles *n* and *p* are acute, and $\cos(n°) = \sin(p°)$. If $n = 5x$ and $p = 4x$, what is the value of *x*?

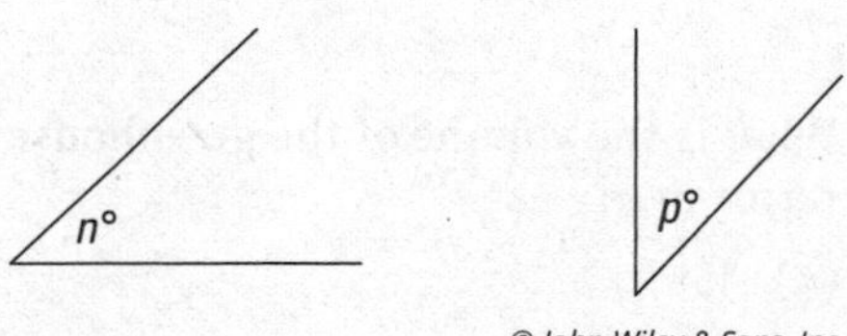

(A) 7

(B) 8

(C) 9

(D) 10

744. In the following image, angles q and r are acute and $\sin(q°) = \cos(r°)$. If $q = 8x + 3$ and $r = 13x + 3$, what is the value of x?

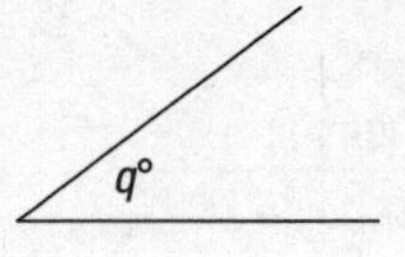

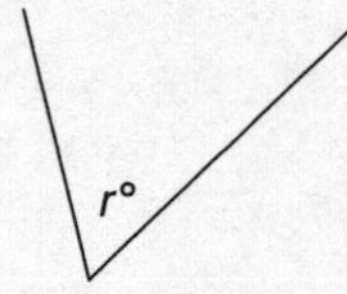

(A) 4

(B) 5

(C) 6

(D) 7

Questions 745 and 746 are based on the following information.

A miniature greenhouse is built from a right circular cone and a right circular cylinder:

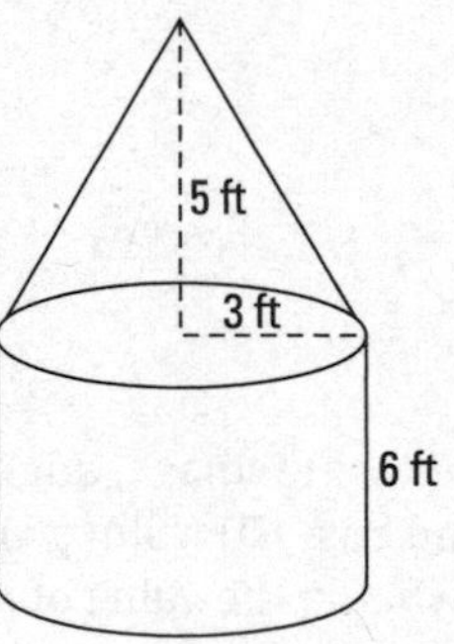

745. What is the volume of the greenhouse in terms of π?

(A) 45π

(B) 54π

(C) 69π

(D) 99π

746. Which is closest to the volume of the greenhouse in cubic feet?

(A) 180

(B) 200

(C) 220

(D) 250

Questions 747 and 748 are based on the following information.

A cotton candy machine is built from a right circular cone and a right circular cylinder:

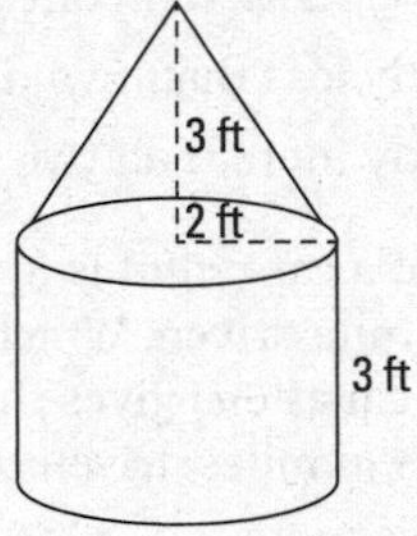

747. What is the volume of the cotton candy machine in terms of π?

(A) 16π

(B) 18π

(C) 21π

(D) 24π

748. Which is closest to the volume of the cotton candy machine in cubic feet?

(A) 20

(B) 30

(C) 40

(D) 50

749. The sum of three numbers is 985. The first number is 50% more than the sum of the other two numbers. What is this first number?

(A) 420

(B) 530

(C) 591

(D) 640

750. The sum of five numbers is 300. The first number is equal to five times the sum of the other four numbers. What is this first number?

(A) 220

(B) 230

(C) 250

(D) 260

751. The sum of four numbers is 390. The first number is equal to half the sum of the other three numbers. What is this first number?

(A) 120

(B) 130

(C) 150

(D) 160

752. The sum of 25 numbers is 100. The sum of the first five numbers is equal to one-third of the sum of the other 20 numbers. What is the average of these first five numbers?

(A) 2

(B) 3

(C) 5

(D) 6

753. The sum of six numbers is 39. The sum of the first two numbers is equal to twice the sum of the other four numbers. What is the average of these first two numbers?

(A) 2

(B) 3

(C) 13

(D) 16

Questions 754–756 are based on the following information.

In surveying a beach, a geologist estimates that, starting from the present, the tons of sand on the beach will wash away at a rate of 5 percent every 5 years. The beach presently has 40,000 tons of sand.

754. Which of the following expressions represents the geologist's estimate of the remaining tons of sand on the beach *y* years from now?

(A) $40,000(0.95)^{5y}$

(B) $40,000(0.95)^{0.5y}$

(C) $40,000(0.95)^{y}$

(D) $40,000(0.95)^{y/5}$

755. According to the geologist's estimate, approximately how many tons of sand will remain after 15 years?

(A) 32,000

(B) 35,000

(C) 35,000

(D) 40,000

756. If the geologist is correct, how much time will elapse before the sand is completely washed from the beach?

(A) 30 years

(B) 50 years

(C) 70 years

(D) The sand will never be completely washed away from the beach.

Questions 757–759 are based on the following information.

A city police commissioner intends to reduce the number of street crimes by a rate of 20 percent every three years. The number of street crimes is presently 12,000 per year.

757. Which of the following expressions represents the police commissioner's goal of reduced street crimes *y* years from now?

(A) $12{,}000(0.80)^{y/3}$

(B) $12{,}000(0.80)^{3y}$

(C) $12{,}000(0.80)^{0.3y}$

(D) $12{,}000(0.80)^{y}$

758. If the police commissioner is successful, which is the closest to the number of street crimes after 6 years?

(A) 7,200

(B) 7,500

(C) 7,700

(D) 9,600

759. If the police commissioner is successful in his goal, how much time will elapse before street crimes are gone from the city?

(A) 5 years

(B) 15 years

(C) 30 years

(D) The street crimes will never be completely gone from the city.

Questions 760–762 are based on the following information.

A sociologist estimates that the population of a certain city increases by a rate of 20 percent every five years. The city currently has a population of 60,000.

760. Which of the following expressions represents the sociologist's estimate of population growth *y* years from now?

(A) $60{,}000(1.20)^{0.5y}$

(B) $60{,}000(1.20)^{y/5}$

(C) $60{,}000(1.20)^{5y}$

(D) $60{,}000(1.20)^{y}$

761. If the sociologist is correct, which is the closest to the city's population after 10 years?

(A) 82,000

(B) 84,000

(C) 86,000

(D) 88,000

762. If the sociologist is correct, which is closest to the number of years that will elapse before the population of the city doubles?

(A) 5 years

(B) 15 years

(C) 20 years

(D) The population of the city will never double.

Questions 763–765 are based on the following information.

Books	Hardcover	Paperback
Fiction	—	—
Nonfiction	—	—
Total	36	102

This incomplete table summarizes the number of hardcover and paperback books by genre at the Printed Book store. There are twice as many paperback as hardcover fiction books, and there are four times as many paperback as hardcover nonfiction books.

763. How many hardcover nonfiction books does the store have?

(A) 12

(B) 15

(C) 18

(D) 21

764. Which of the following is closest to the probability that a book selected at random is a paperback nonfiction book?

(A) $\frac{5}{23}$

(B) $\frac{8}{23}$

(C) $\frac{10}{23}$

(D) $\frac{12}{23}$

765. Which of the following is closest to the probability that a hardcover book selected at random is fiction?

(A) $\frac{1}{3}$

(B) $\frac{5}{12}$

(C) $\frac{1}{2}$

(D) $\frac{7}{12}$

Questions 766–768 are based on the following information.

Guitars	Acoustic	Electric
Cedar	—	—
Mahogany	—	—
Total	10	40

This incomplete table summarizes the number of cedar and mahogany guitars by type at Guitar City. There are three times as many electric as acoustic cedar guitars, and there are five times as many electric as acoustic mahogany guitars.

766. How many mahogany acoustic guitars does the store have?

(A) 3

(B) 5

(C) 8

(D) 10

767. Which of the following is closest to the probability that a guitar selected at random is a mahogany electric guitar?

(A) 25%

(B) 40%

(C) 50%

(D) 80%

768. Which of the following is closest to the probability that an acoustic guitar selected at random is cedar?

(A) One out of two

(B) One out of three

(C) Two out of three

(D) Three out of five

769. In these equations, a and b are constants. If a minus b is 6, which of the following is true?

$$8x + a = 11x + 3$$
$$7y + b = 10y + 3$$

(A) x is 2 more than y.

(B) x is 2 less than y.

(C) x is 1 more than y.

(D) x is equal to y.

770. In these equations, a and b are constants. If a minus b is 2, which of the following is true?

$$7x + a = 11x + 3$$
$$4y + b = 6y + 1$$

(A) x is twice the value of y.

(B) x is half the value of y.

(C) x is a third of the value of y.

(D) x is equal to y.

771. If the following expression is rewritten in the form $ax^2 + bx + c$, where a, b, and c are constants, what is the value of c?

$$\left(2x^2 + 3x - 5\right) - 5\left(x^2 + 2x - 1\right)$$

(A) 0

(B) 1

(C) 2

(D) c is undefined

772. If the following expression is rewritten in the form $ax^2 + bx + c$, where a, b, and c are constants, what is the value of c?

$$\left(3x^2 - 5x - 2\right) + 2\left(-2x^2 + 4x - 1\right)$$

(A) 0

(B) −2

(C) −4

(D) c is undefined

Questions 773–776 are based on the following information.

In a circle with center O, points N and P lie on the circle, and angle NOP has a measure of $\frac{\pi}{2}$ radians.

773. The length of the circumference contained by angle NOP is what fraction of the circle?

(A) $\frac{2}{3}$

(B) $\frac{1}{2}$

(C) $\frac{1}{3}$

(D) $\frac{1}{4}$

774. What is the degree measure of angle NOP?

(A) 90°

(B) 135°

(C) 180°

(D) 215°

775. If the circle has a radius of 4, what is the length of minor arc NP?

(A) 2π

(B) 3π

(C) 4π

(D) 5π

776. If the circle has a radius of 4, what is the area of the sector formed by angle NOP?

(A) 2π

(B) 3π

(C) 4π

(D) 5π

Questions 777–780 are based on the following information.

In a circle with center O, points Q and R lie on the circle, and angle QOR has a measure of $\frac{3\pi}{4}$ radians.

777. The length of the circumference contained by angle QOR is what fraction of the circle?

(A) $\frac{2}{3}$

(B) $\frac{1}{2}$

(C) $\frac{1}{3}$

(D) $\frac{3}{8}$

778. What is the degree measure of angle QOR?

(A) 90°

(B) 135°

(C) 180°

(D) 215°

779. If the circle has a radius of 8, what is the length of minor arc QR?

(A) 2π

(B) 3π

(C) 4π

(D) 6π

780. If the circle has a radius of 8, what is the area of the sector formed by angle *QOR*?

(A) 6π

(B) 18π

(C) 24π

(D) 32π

Questions 781–784 are based on the following information.

In a circle with center *O*, points *K* and *L* lie on the circle, and angle *KOL* has a measure of 45°.

781. The length of the circumference contained by angle *KOL* is what fraction of the circle?

(A) $\frac{1}{4}$

(B) $\frac{1}{5}$

(C) $\frac{1}{6}$

(D) $\frac{1}{8}$

782. What is the radian measure of angle *KOL*?

(A) $\frac{\pi}{2}$

(B) $\frac{\pi}{4}$

(C) $\frac{\pi}{6}$

(D) $\frac{\pi}{8}$

783. If the circle has a radius of 4, what is the length of minor arc *KL*?

(A) π

(B) 2π

(C) 3π

(D) 4π

784. If the circle has a radius of 4, what is the area of the sector formed by angle *KOL*?

(A) 2π

(B) 3π

(C) 4π

(D) 6π

785. On the four exams in pre-calc, Jane earned an 84, 87, 91, and 93. If all exams are weighted equally, nothing else determines her grade, and 100 is the highest she can score on an exam, what minimum score does Jane have to get on her fifth exam to bring her mean score to 90?

(A) 90

(B) 95

(C) 99

(D) Jane cannot reach her goal.

786. At the swim meet, Carly scored 6.8, 7.1, and 8.1 on her three dives. If 10.0 is the highest she can score and all the dives are weighted equally, what is the minimum that she needs to score on her fourth dive for an average score of 8.0?

(A) 9.1

(B) 9.9

(C) 10.0

(D) Carly cannot reach her goal.

787. On the five exams in physics, Tommy earned an 80, 83, 87, 91, and 93. If all exams are weighted equally, nothing else determines his grade, and 100 is the highest he can score on an exam, what minimum score does Tommy have to get on his sixth exam to bring his mean score to 90?

(A) 90

(B) 95

(C) 99

(D) Tommy cannot reach his goal.

788. If the trapezoid has an area of $(a-5)^2$, what is the height of the trapezoid?

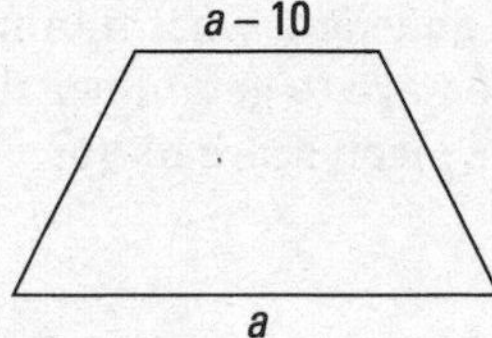

© John Wiley & Sons, Inc.

(A) $\frac{a-5}{2}$

(B) $a-5$

(C) $(a-5)^2$

(D) $a-10$

789. If the trapezoid has a height of $b-3$, what is the area of the trapezoid?

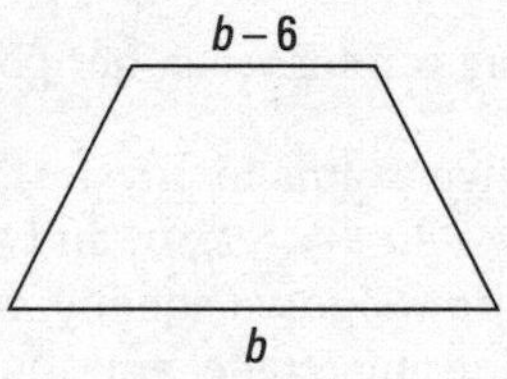

© John Wiley & Sons, Inc.

(A) $\frac{b-3}{2}$

(B) $b-3$

(C) $(b-3)^2$

(D) $b-6$

790. The sum of 3*x* and 4*y* is 50. If $y=5$, what is the value of *x*?

(A) 5

(B) 10

(C) 12

(D) 15

791. If *n* is a positive integer, which of the following represents the product of *n* and the integer following *n*?

(A) n^2+1

(B) n^2+2

(C) $(n+1)^2$

(D) n^2+n

792. If a boy on a snow sled travels downhill at a constant rate of 25 kilometers per hour, how many meters does he travel in 18 seconds? (1 kilometer = 1,000 meters)

(A) 5

(B) 25

(C) 75

(D) 125

793. If $x>0$, what is the value of *x* when $f(x)=13$.

$$f(x)=x^2+2x-2$$

(A) 3

(B) 5

(C) −3

(D) −5

794. The square is inscribed within the circle and has a side length of $\sqrt{2}$. What is the area of the shaded portion of the drawing?

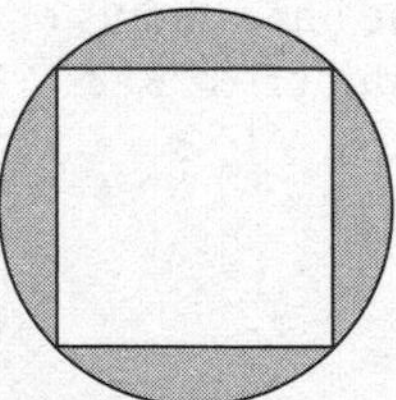
© John Wiley & Sons, Inc.

(A) $2-\pi$

(B) $\pi-2$

(C) $\pi-\sqrt{2}$

(D) $\pi-4$

795. What is the area of the shaded triangle?

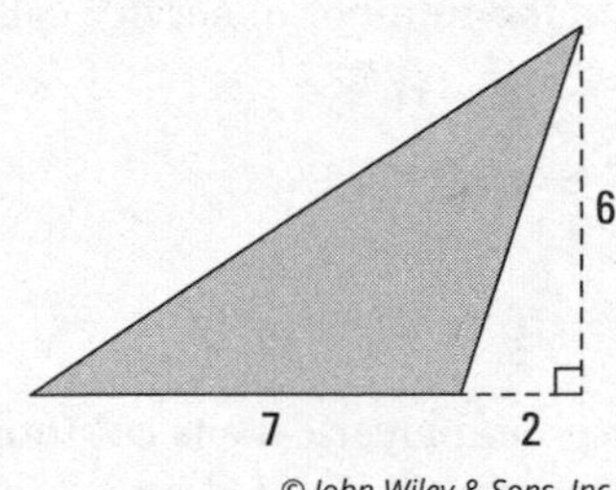

© John Wiley & Sons, Inc.

(A) 54

(B) 42

(C) 27

(D) 21

796. If n is the units digit of 5^{40}, what is the value of n?

(A) 1

(B) 5

(C) 8

(D) 10

797. A cart carries 5 parcels weighing 3 pounds each and 10 parcels weighing 9 pounds each. What is the average parcel weight, in pounds?

(A) 5

(B) 7

(C) 9

(D) 10

798. If the circle shown has a radius of 5 and angle *CAB* originates in the center of the circle and measures $36°$, what is the length of minor arc *BC*?

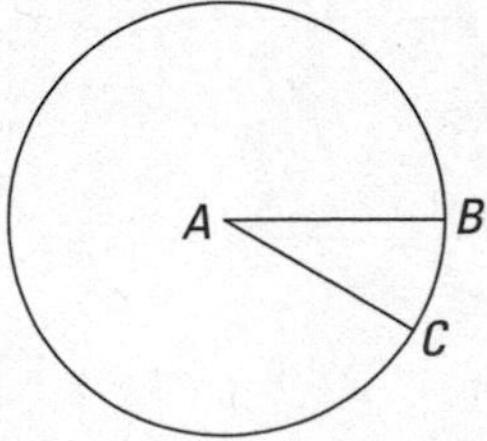

© John Wiley & Sons, Inc.

(A) π

(B) 2π

(C) 3π

(D) 4π

799. x, y, and z are integers, and $7 > x > y > z > 1$. If the sum of z^2 and y^2 is x^2, what is the value of x?

(A) 2

(B) 3

(C) 5

(D) 7

800. The sum of $10x$ and $12y$ is 100. If $x = 4$, what is the value of y?

(A) 5

(B) 10

(C) 12

(D) 15

801. In the xy-plane, if a point with the coordinates (c, d) lies in the solution set of this system of inequalities, what is the minimum possible value of d?

$$y > -4x + 540$$
$$y > 2x$$

(A) Slightly below 90

(B) Slightly above 90

(C) Slightly below 180

(D) Slightly above 180

802. In the xy-plane, if a point with the coordinates (e, f) lies in the solution set of this system of inequalities, what is the maximum possible value of f?

$$y < -x + 1{,}000$$
$$y < 2x + 100$$

(A) Slightly below 300

(B) Slightly above 300

(C) Slightly below 700

(D) Slightly above 700

Questions 803 and 804 are based on the following information.

The rental for a boat, not including fees and taxes, is $22 per hour plus $0.60 per minute that the motor runs.

803. If Johnny had the boat for 2 hours and paid $98.00, not including fees and taxes, for how long did he run the motor?

(A) 90 minutes

(B) 110 minutes

(C) Just under 127 minutes

(D) Just over 128 minutes

804. Which of the following equations represents the cost, c, in dollars, of renting the boat, where h represents the hours rented and m represents the minutes that the motor ran?

(A) $c=\frac{22}{3}h+6m$

(B) $c=22h+\frac{3m}{5}$

(C) $c=22h+\frac{3m}{10}$

(D) $c=\frac{22}{6}h+6m$

Questions 805 and 806 are based on the following information.

An auto club membership costs $58 per year plus $16 per service call, before fees and taxes.

805. If Annie had five service calls last year, how much did she pay in full for the membership, before fees and taxes?

(A) $128

(B) $138

(C) $148

(D) $158

806. Which of the following equations represents the cost, c, of the membership, where s represents the number of service calls?

(A) $c=58s+16$

(B) $c=32s+58$

(C) $c=16s+58$

(D) $c=16s+48$

807. If a 5-pound layer cake is cut into 8 slices and each slice is divided into 5 equal pieces, how much does each piece weigh? (1 pound = 16 ounces)

(A) 1 ounce

(B) 2 ounces

(C) 3 ounces

(D) 4 ounces

808. If a gallon of orange juice is divided into 4 quarts and each quart is poured evenly into 5 glasses, how much orange juice is in each glass? (1 gallon = 128 ounces)

(A) 5.2 ounces

(B) 5.6 ounces

(C) 6.4 ounces

(D) 6.8 ounces

809. In Town X, Tom surveyed 650 random citizens to determine whether they will vote for Candidate A or Candidate B. Of those surveyed, 400 said they would vote for Candidate B. Based on this survey, about how many of Town X's 9,000 voting-eligible citizens are expected to vote for Candidate B?

(A) 4,500

(B) 5,000

(C) 5,500

(D) 6,000

810. Of the 70 employees surveyed on whether they prefer a holiday party or dinner, 25 indicated they prefer a holiday party. If there are 400 employees total, how many are expected to prefer a holiday party?

(A) 143

(B) 144

(C) 145

(D) 148

811. Of the 720 citizens surveyed on whether they support a new law, 305 indicated they oppose the law. If there are 60,000 citizens in the city, about how many citizens probably oppose the law?

(A) 25,240

(B) 25,440

(C) 25,640

(D) 25,740

812. On Tuesday, Sean collected 7 more donations than Emily. On Wednesday, Emily collected 11 more donations than Sean. If together on both days, they collected 58 donations, how many donations did Emily collect?

(A) 31

(B) 33

(C) 35

(D) 37

813. If Sam earned 10% more than Robin and together they earned $1,050, how much did Robin earn?

(A) $400

(B) $450

(C) $500

(D) $550

814. In the *xy*-plane, the graph of function *f* has *x*-intercepts at −2, 2, and 3. Which of the following could define *f*?

(A) $f(x)=(x^2-4)(x-3)$

(B) $f(x)=(x^2-2)(x+3)$

(C) $f(x)=(x^2+2)(x-3)$

(D) $f(x)=(x^2+2)(x+3)$

815. In the *xy*-plane, the graph of the function shown below has how many *x*-intercepts?

$$f(x)=(x^2-x-6)(x^2-9)$$

(A) One

(B) Two

(C) Three

(D) Four

816. In the *xy*-plane, at what points does the graph of the function shown below cross the *x*-axis?

$$f(x)=(x^2-x-6)(x^2-9)$$

(A) −2, 2, 3

(B) −3, −2, 3

(C) −3, 2, 3

(D) The graph of the function does not cross the *x*-axis.

817. In the *xy*-plane, the graph of function *f* has *x*-intercepts at −5, −3, and 5. Which of the following could define *f*?

(A) $f(x)=(x+3)(x^2+5)$

(B) $f(x)=(x-3)(x^2-5)$

(C) $f(x)=(x-3)(x^2+25)$

(D) $f(x)=(x+3)(x^2-25)$

818. In the *xy*-plane, the graph of the function shown below has how many *x*-intercepts?

$$f(x)=(x^2-11x+28)(x^2-49)$$

(A) One

(B) Two

(C) Three

(D) Four

819. In the xy-plane, at what points does the graph of the function shown below cross the x-axis?

$$f(x)=(x^2-11x+28)(x^2-49)$$

(A) −7, 4, 7
(B) −7, −4, 7
(C) −4, 4, 7
(D) The graph of the function does not cross the x-axis.

820. In the xy-plane, at what points does the graph of the function shown below cross the x-axis?

$$f(x)=x^2+4$$

(A) −4, 0, 4
(B) −3, 0, 3
(C) −2, 0, 2
(D) The graph of the function does not cross the x-axis.

Questions 821 and 822 are based on the following information.

This equation is drawn on the standard xy-plane.

$$y=(\sqrt{x}-2)(\sqrt{x}+2)$$

821. Based on the equation, what is the least possible value of y?

(A) −4
(B) 0
(C) 2
(D) There is no least value of y.

822. Into which quadrants does the graph of the equation cross?

(A) I and II only
(B) I, II, and III
(C) II, III, and IV
(D) I and IV only

Questions 823 and 824 are based on the following information.

This equation is drawn on the standard xy-plane.

$$y=-(\sqrt{x}-\sqrt{3})(\sqrt{x}+\sqrt{3})^2$$

823. Based on the equation, what is the greatest possible value of y?

(A) −3
(B) 0
(C) 3
(D) There is no greatest value of y.

824. Into which quadrants does the graph of the equation cross?

(A) I and III only
(B) I, II, and III
(C) II, III, and IV
(D) II and III only

Questions 825–829 are based on the following information.

This equation is drawn on the standard xy-plane.

$$y=((\sqrt{x}-\sqrt{2})(\sqrt{x}+\sqrt{2}))^2$$

825. Based on the equation, what is the greatest possible value of y?

(A) 0
(B) $\sqrt{2}$
(C) 2
(D) There is no greatest value of y.

826. How many quadrants does the graph cross into?

(A) One
(B) Two
(C) Three
(D) Four

827. Where does the graph intercept the x-axis?

(A) 1

(B) 2

(C) 3

(D) 4

828. Where does the graph intercept the y-axis?

(A) 1

(B) 2

(C) 3

(D) 4

829. Which of the following equations is equivalent to the given equation?

(A) $y=-\left(\left(\sqrt{x}-\sqrt{2}\right)\left(\sqrt{x}+\sqrt{2}\right)\right)^2$

(B) $y=\left(-\left(\sqrt{x}-\sqrt{2}\right)\left(\sqrt{x}+\sqrt{2}\right)\right)^2$

(C) $y=\left(\left(-\sqrt{x}-\sqrt{2}\right)\left(\sqrt{x}+\sqrt{2}\right)\right)^2$

(D) $y=\left(\left(\sqrt{x}-\sqrt{2}\right)\left(\sqrt{x}-\sqrt{2}\right)\right)^2$

Questions 830–834 are based on the following information.

This equation is drawn on the standard xy-plane.

$$y=\left(\left(\sqrt{x}-\sqrt{3}\right)\left(\sqrt{x}+\sqrt{5}\right)\right)^2$$

830. Based on the equation, what is the greatest possible value of y?

(A) 0

(B) $\sqrt{3}$

(C) $-\sqrt{5}$

(D) There is no greatest value of y.

831. Which quadrant does the graph cross into?

(A) Quadrant I

(B) Quadrant II

(C) Quadrant III

(D) Quadrant IV

832. Where does the graph intercept the x-axis?

(A) 1

(B) 2

(C) 3

(D) 4

833. Where does the graph intercept the y-axis?

(A) 0

(B) 3

(C) 5

(D) 15

834. Which of the following equations is equivalent to the given equation?

(A) $y=\left(\left(\sqrt{x}-\sqrt{3}\right)\left(\sqrt{x}-\sqrt{5}\right)\right)^2$

(B) $y=\left(\left(\sqrt{x}-\sqrt{3}\right)\left(-\sqrt{x}+\sqrt{5}\right)\right)^2$

(C) $y=\left(-\left(\sqrt{x}-\sqrt{3}\right)\left(\sqrt{x}+\sqrt{5}\right)\right)^2$

(D) $y=-\left(\left(\sqrt{x}-\sqrt{3}\right)\left(\sqrt{x}+\sqrt{5}\right)\right)^2$

Questions 835 and 836 are based on the following information.

In the following drawing, O is the center of the circle, $\overline{BC}$ passes through the center of the circle, the radius of the circle is 1, and $AB = 1$.

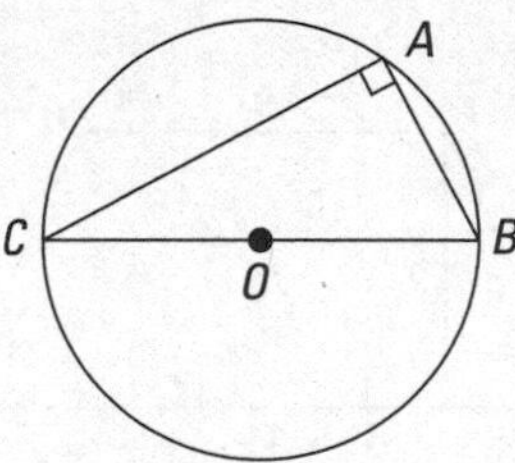

835. What is the area of triangle CAB?

(A) $\frac{1}{2}$

(B) $\frac{\sqrt{3}}{2}$

(C) $\sqrt{3}$

(D) 2

836. What is the length of minor arc AB?

(A) $\frac{\pi}{6}$

(B) $\frac{\pi}{3}$

(C) $\frac{\pi}{2}$

(D) π

837. In the following drawing, if $AD = DC$, which of the following is true?

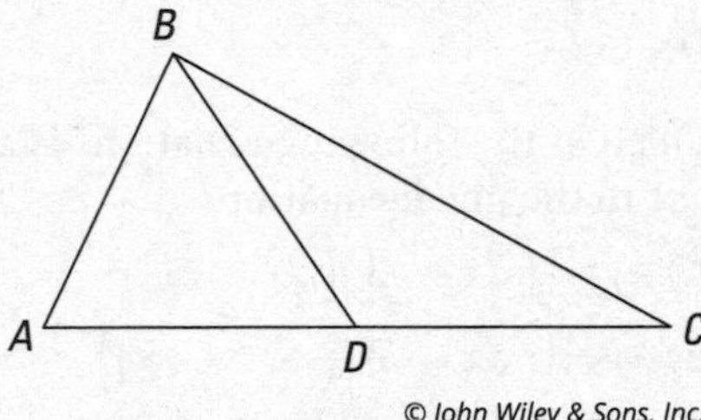

© John Wiley & Sons, Inc.

(A) Triangle ABD has a greater area than triangle BCD.

(B) Triangle BCD has a greater area than triangle ABD.

(C) The triangles have equal areas.

(D) The areas cannot be compared without more information.

838. What is the area of the trapezoid?

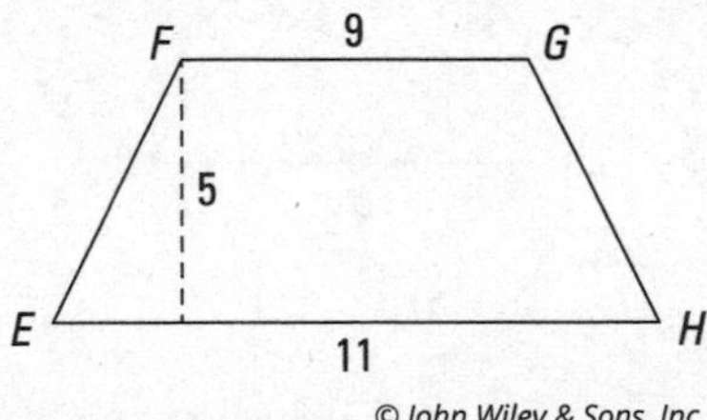

© John Wiley & Sons, Inc.

(A) 45

(B) 50

(C) 55

(D) 60

839. In the following drawing, which of the following is true?

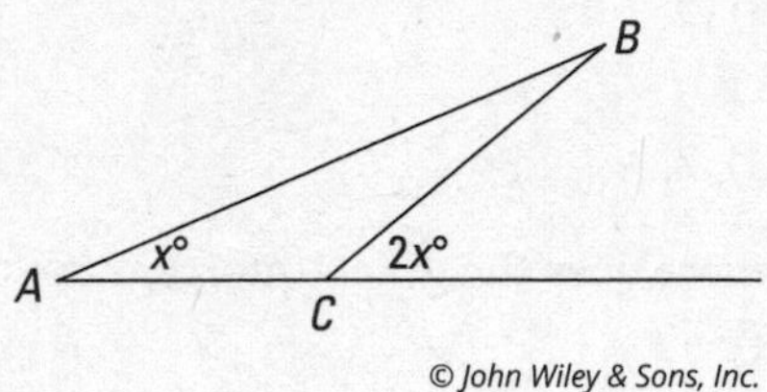

© John Wiley & Sons, Inc.

(A) $AC > BC$

(B) $AC < BC$

(C) $AC = BC$

(D) The segments cannot be compared without more information.

840. In the following equation, what is the sum of the possible values of x?

$$x^2 - x - 6 = 0$$

(A) 1

(B) 0

(C) −1

(D) −6

841. In the xy plane, what is the slope of the line whose equation is $2x + 3y = 5$?

(A) $-\frac{3}{2}$

(B) $-\frac{2}{3}$

(C) $\frac{2}{3}$

(D) $\frac{3}{2}$

842. If the average of x, y, and z is 5, what is the average of $4x + y$, $2y - x$, and $3z + 27$?

(A) 18

(B) 24

(C) 27

(D) 31

Questions 843 and 844 are based on the following information.

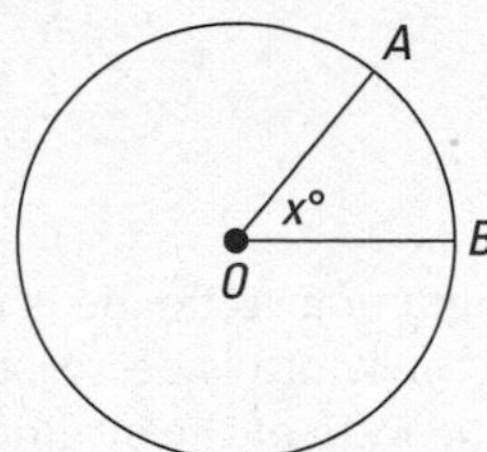

© John Wiley & Sons, Inc.

The circle shown has the center O and a radius of 8; $x = 45$.

843. What is the length of minor arc $\widehat{AB}$?

(A) $\frac{\pi}{2}$

(B) π

(C) $\frac{3\pi}{2}$

(D) 2π

844. What is the area of minor sector *AOB*?

(A) 2π

(B) 4π

(C) 8π

(D) 16π

845. If the radius *r* of a circle increases by 50%, what is the area of the larger circle in terms of *r*?

(A) $\frac{3\pi r^2}{2}$

(B) $2\pi r^2$

(C) $\frac{4\pi r^2}{3}$

(D) $\frac{9\pi r^2}{4}$

846. In this drawing, if the circle is inscribed within the square, what fraction of the square is occupied by the circle?

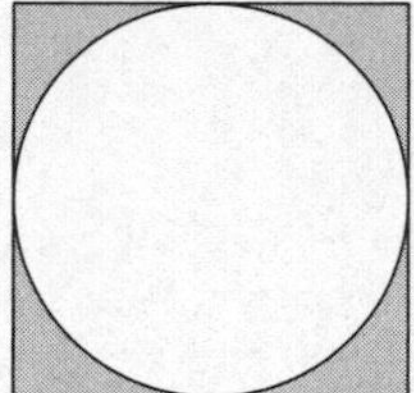
© John Wiley & Sons, Inc.

(A) $\frac{\pi}{4}$

(B) $\frac{\pi}{5}$

(C) $\frac{\pi}{6}$

(D) $\frac{\pi}{8}$

847. What is the radius of a right circular cylinder with a volume of 50π and a height of 2?

(A) 2

(B) 3

(C) 4

(D) 5

848. If *n* is a positive integer between 200 and 500, how many possible values of *n* have a units digit of 5?

(A) 28

(B) 29

(C) 30

(D) 31

849. Square *ABCD* is in the *xy*-coordinate plane, and each side of the square is parallel to either the *x*-axis or the *y*-axis. If points *A* and *C* have coordinates of $(-2, -1)$ and $(3, 4)$, respectively, what is the area of the square?

(A) 24

(B) 25

(C) 36

(D) 49

850. A car travels at a constant rate of 20 meters per second. How many kilometers does it travel in 10 minutes? (1 kilometer = 1,000 meters)

(A) 5

(B) 12

(C) 15

(D) 20

851. If $(x-5)^2 = 900$ and $x > 0$, what is the value of x?

(A) 25

(B) 35

(C) 45

(D) 50

852. A circular pool of radius r feet is surrounded by a circular sidewalk of width $\frac{r}{2}$ feet. In terms of r, what is the area of the sidewalk?

(A) $2\pi r^2$

(B) $\frac{5\pi r^2}{4}$

(C) $\frac{9\pi r^2}{4}$

(D) πr^2

853. The following drawing shows a regular hexagon. What is the value of x?

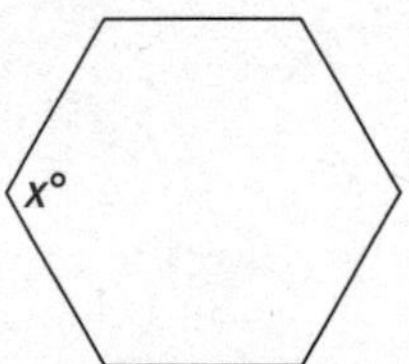

© John Wiley & Sons, Inc.

(A) 120

(B) 150

(C) 180

(D) 270

854. If n divided by 35 has a remainder of 3, what is the remainder when n is divided by 7?

(A) 0

(B) 1

(C) 2

(D) 3

855. If the length of a rectangle is increased by 20% and the width is decreased by 20%, what is the ratio of the original area to the new area?

(A) $4:3$

(B) $5:4$

(C) $10:9$

(D) $25:24$

856. What is the area of an equilateral triangle with a base of 4?

(A) $4\sqrt{3}$

(B) $8\sqrt{3}$

(C) $12\sqrt{3}$

(D) $15\sqrt{3}$

857. What is the area of an equilateral triangle with a base of 6?

(A) $6\sqrt{3}$

(B) $9\sqrt{3}$

(C) $15\sqrt{3}$

(D) $18\sqrt{3}$

858. Two lines represented by the equations $y = x + 1$ and $y = 2x + 3$ intersect at point P. What are the coordinates of P?

(A) $(-2, -1)$

(B) $(-1, 2)$

(C) $(1, -2)$

(D) $(2, -1)$

859. If the square shown below has a side length of 5, what is the distance between points *A* and *C*?

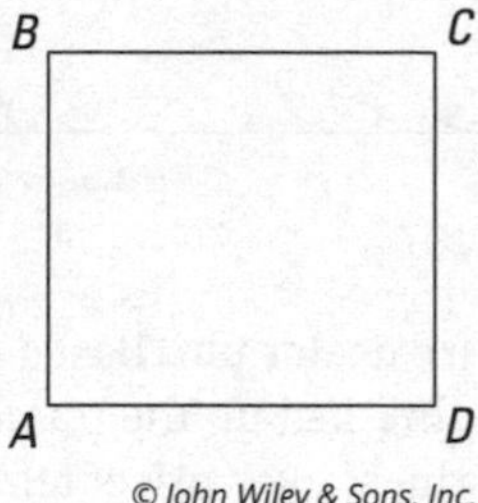

© John Wiley & Sons, Inc.

(A) $5\sqrt{2}$
(B) $5\sqrt{3}$
(C) 8
(D) 10

860. In the following equation, what is the sum of the possible values of *x*?

$$\frac{x^2}{50} - 3 = 5$$

(A) 1
(B) 0
(C) −1
(D) −5

Grid-In

The grid gives you four boxes for writing each answer using the numerals 0–9 and a decimal point or fraction bar, if needed. Use decimals or improper fractions rather than mixed numbers. You may use a calculator.

861. An administrative assistant can type at least 35 words per minute and at most 55 words per minute. Given 20 minutes to work, how many words could she type? Round your answer to the nearest 100.

862. Joanne is looking to purchase a new headset priced between $10 and $11, inclusive. If sales tax is 10% and there are no other fees, what is the total number of dollars that Joanne could spend on her new headset, to the nearest tenth of a dollar? Disregard the dollar sign when gridding your answer.

863. Henry spends between $\frac{1}{4}$ and $\frac{1}{3}$, inclusive, of his weekly paycheck on groceries. If he spent $120 last week, how much could last week's paycheck have been? Round your answer to the nearest 10 dollars.

864. A machine can produce at least 50 and at most 60 plastic parts per minute. If the machine runs for exactly 2 hours, how many plastic parts could it produce? Round your answer to the nearest 100 parts.

865. A box of paperclips contains at least 70 and at most 80 paperclips. If 20 boxes are in a carton, how many paperclips could be contained in a shipment of 5 cartons? Round your answer to the nearest 100 paperclips.

866. Based on this equation, if $x > 0$, what is the value of *x*?

$$x(x-10) = 600$$

867. Based on this equation, what is one possible value of *x*?

$$x - \frac{x^2}{500} = 120$$

868. Based on this equation, if $x > 0$, what is the value of *x*?

$$x^2 = 90,000$$

869. Based on this equation, what is the value of *x*?

$$(\sqrt{x}-2)(\sqrt{x}+2) = 0$$

870. Based on this equation, what is one possible value of *x*?

$$x^2(x^2-13) = -36$$

871. If n is an integer between 2 and 50 and $\frac{55}{n}$ is an integer, what could be the value of n?

872. If a right circular cylinder has a volume of 36π and the base and height are both integers greater than 1, what is a possible sum of the radius and height?

Questions 873 and 874 are based on the following information.

Bobby currently has eight more toy cars than Jackie. If Bobby were to give two of his cars to Jackie, Bobby would have twice the cars that Jackie would have.

873. How many toy cars does Bobby have before the gift?

874. How many toy cars does Jackie have after Bobby's gift?

875. In the xy-coordinate plane shown below, line ℓ passes through the origin, point P lies on line ℓ, and the (x, y) coordinates of point P are $(2, 1)$.

What is the slope of line ℓ?

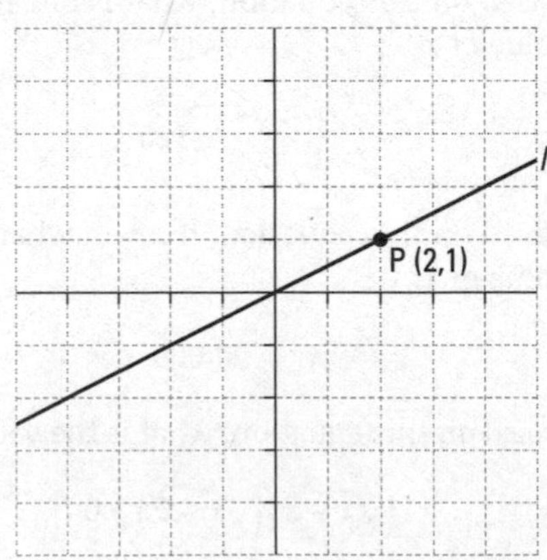

© John Wiley & Sons, Inc.

876. In the triangle shown below, if $x = 42$, what is the value of y?

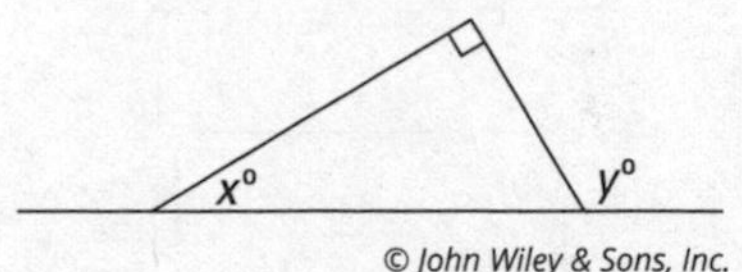

© John Wiley & Sons, Inc.

877. A furniture dealer purchased an end table for \$100, marked up the purchase price by 20% for the sticker price, and then sold the end table at a 20% discount from the sticker price. What was the selling price of the end table? Disregard the dollar sign when gridding your answer.

878. If a sprinter runs 10 kilometers per hour, how many meters does he run in 30 seconds? (1 kilometer = 1,000 meters)

879. If the average of x, y, and z is 1, what is the average of $8x + 2z$, $z - 2x + 3y$, $y - x + z$, and $4 - x$?

880. If $x^2 - 4x = 0$, what is one possible value of x?

881. If an electronics dealer discounts the price of a \$2,000 TV by 10% and then reduces the amount of the discount by 25%, what is the final asking price of the TV, before taxes and fees? Disregard the dollar sign when gridding your answer.

882. In the xy-coordinate plane, line ℓ passes through both the origin and point P. If the (x, y) coordinates of point P are $(1, \sqrt{3})$ respectively, how far is point P from the origin?

Questions 883 and 884 are based on the following information.

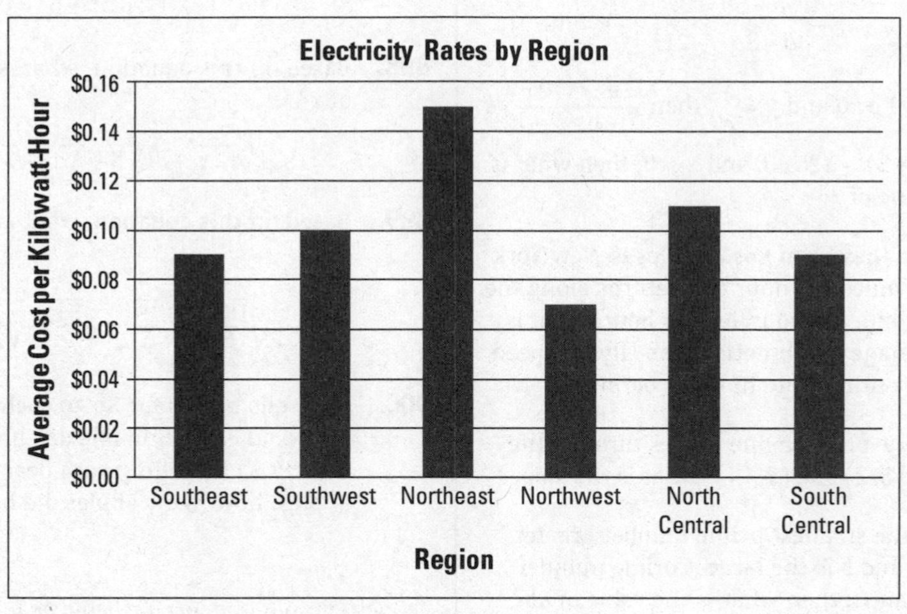

© John Wiley & Sons, Inc.

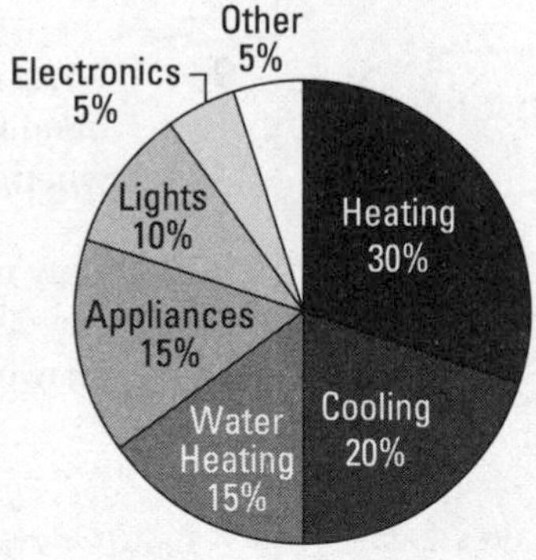

© John Wiley & Sons, Inc.

Note: Graphs drawn to scale.

883. Assuming the average household uses 15 kilowatt-hours (kWh) of electricity per day to heat its home, how much would the average household pay for electricity per year if located in the northeast region? Round your answer to the nearest hundred and disregard the dollar sign when gridding your answer.

884. The Joneses live in the north central region. After paying $4,500 for electricity last year, they installed a new geothermal furnace and extra insulation at a cost of $4,725, which cut their heating bill by 35%. At this rate, how many years will it take them to recoup their investment? Round your answer to the nearest whole year.

885. Based on this system of equations, what is the value of $a+b$?

$$16a+5b=37$$
$$3b-8a=-21$$

886. If $x \neq -1$ or 0 and $y=\frac{1}{x}$, then $\frac{1}{x+1}+\frac{1}{y+1}=$?

887. If $5(x+2)^2-125=0$ and $x>0$, then what is the value of x?

888. A plane flies from Los Angeles to New York at 600 miles per hour and returns along the same route at 400 miles per hour. What is the average (arithmetic mean) flying speed for the entire route in miles per hour?

889. In the *xy*-plane, a line passes through the points $(3, 2)$ and $(8, 14)$. What is the slope?

890. If a is the smallest prime number greater than 3 and b is the largest prime number less than 11, then what is the value of ab?

891. In the system of equations that follows, what is the value of xy?

$$7x+4y=53$$
$$9x-4y=-5$$

892. Given the system of equations that follows, what is the value of $a+b$?

$$3a+5b=12$$
$$3b+5a=28$$

893. If x is an integer and $10<\sqrt{x}<12$, what is the value of x?

894. If 16 ounces of lemonade mix makes 2 gallons of lemonade, how much mix is needed to make 3 quarts of lemonade? (1 gallon = 4 quarts)

895. If x is an integer and $5<\sqrt{x}<9$, what is one possible value of x?

896. Based on this equation, what is the value of x?

$$\left(\sqrt{x}-\sqrt{5}\right)\left(\sqrt{x}+\sqrt{5}\right)=0$$

897. Based on this equation, if $x>0$, what is the value of x?

$$(2x+2)(5x-5)=0$$

898. Based on this equation, what is the value of x?

$$\left(\sqrt{12x}-\sqrt{12}\right)\left(\sqrt{3x}+\sqrt{3}\right)=0$$

899. Based on this equation, what is the value of x?

$$\left(\sqrt{\frac{18x}{5}}-\sqrt{\frac{18}{5}}\right)\left(\sqrt{\frac{5x}{2}}+\sqrt{\frac{5}{2}}\right)=0$$

900. Colt sells apples for \$0.30 each and peaches for \$0.50 each. If in one day he earns exactly \$3.00 selling both peaches and apples, how many apples did he sell?

Questions 901 and 902 are based on the following information.

The minute hand of a standard clock traveled from 12:15 p.m. to 1:00 p.m.

901. What is the degree measure that the minute hand traveled? Disregard the degree symbol when gridding your answer.

902. How many π radians did the minute hand travel? Disregard the π when gridding your answer.

Questions 903 and 904 are based on the following information.

The minute hand of a standard clock traveled from 2:00 p.m. to 6:00 p.m.

903. What is the degree measure that the minute hand traveled? Disregard the degree symbol when gridding your answer.

904. How many π radians did the minute hand travel? Disregard the π when gridding your answer.

Questions 905 and 906 are based on the following information.

The Earth orbits the sun in 365.256 days (1 sidereal year). Assume the Earth's orbit is circular with the sun at the center.

905. What is the degree measure that the Earth travels in 60.876 days? Round your answer to the nearest 10 degrees, and disregard the degree symbol when gridding your answer.

906. How many π radians does the Earth travel in 90 days? For your answer, round the decimal to one decimal place or write the fraction with a single-digit denominator, and disregard the π.

Questions 907 and 908 are based on the following information.

The Earth travels about 940,000,000 kilometers in a single, full orbit around the sun. Assume the Earth's orbit is circular with the sun at the center.

907. What is the degree measure that the Earth travels in 18,800,000 kilometers? Disregard the degree symbol when entering your answer.

908. How many π radians does the Earth travel in 117,500,000 kilometers? Disregard the π when gridding your answer.

909. A certain truck engine is tuned to idle at 1,200 revolutions per minute. How many degrees does it turn in half of a second? Disregard the degree symbol when gridding your answer.

910. A certain truck engine is tuned to idle at exactly 1,200 revolutions per minute. How many π radians does it turn in exactly 10 seconds? Disregard the π when gridding your answer.

Questions 911 and 912 are based on the following information.

Henry opened a bank account that earns 6 percent annual interest, compounded monthly. His initial deposit was $500, and he uses the expression $\$500(1+i)^m$ to find the value of the account after m months.

911. What is the value of i in the expression?

912. If no other transactions take place within the account, what would be the value of the account after 24 months? Disregard the dollar sign when gridding your answer, and round your answer to the nearest whole dollar. For example, 1.5 rounds up to 2.

Questions 913 and 914 are based on the following information.

Janice opened a bank account that earns 4 percent annual interest, compounded quarterly. Her initial deposit was $1,000, and she uses the expression $\$1{,}000(1+i)^q$ to find the value of the account after q quarters. (1 quarter = 3 months)

913. What is the value of i in the expression?

914. If no other transactions take place within the account, what would be the value of the account after 18 months? Disregard the dollar sign when gridding your answer, and round your answer to the nearest whole dollar. For example, 1.5 rounds up to 2.

Questions 915 and 916 are based on the following information.

Carlos opened a bank account that earns 5.2 percent annual interest, compounded weekly. His initial deposit was $800, and he uses the expression $\$800(1+i)^w$ to find the value of the account after w weeks. Assume the year has exactly 52 weeks.

915. What is the value of i in the expression?

916. If no other transactions take place within the account, what would be the value of the account after 8 weeks? Disregard the dollar sign when gridding your answer, and round your answer to the nearest whole dollar. For example, 1.5 rounds up to 2.

Questions 917 and 918 are based on the following information.

An ether mixture in a jar evaporates at a rate of 15% per week. The volume of ether begins at 800 milliliters, and the remaining amount can be found with the expression $800(m)^w$ after w weeks.

917. What is the value of m in the expression?

918. If no other liquid is added or removed from the jar, how many milliliters of ether mixture would remain after 5 weeks? Round your answer to the nearest whole milliliter. For example, 1.5 rounds up to 2.

Questions 919 and 920 are based on the following information.

A plant that is exactly 48 inches tall grows at a rate of 22% per month. Its height, in inches, can be found with the expression $48(g)^m$ after m months.

919. What is the value of g in the expression?

920. Based on the expression, how tall will the plant be (in inches) after 5 months? Round your answer to the nearest whole inch. For example, 1.5 rounds up to 2.

921. A school rally has 800 boys and 600 girls. If 300 more boys sign up, how many girls need to be added so that the ratio of boys to girls is $2:3$?

922. A ranch has 25 colts and 25 fillies. If 5 more colts are brought in, how many fillies should be added so that the ratio of colts to fillies is $3:4$?

923. A landscaper has procured 360 red, 150 green, and 600 blue tiles for a public park. If 220 additional red and 140 additional green tiles are brought in, how many red tiles should be added so that half of the tiles are red?

924. A city water reservoir contains 42,000 gallons of water. New water flows in at a rate of 2,400 gallons per hour. At this rate, how many gallons are added to the reservoir in 25 minutes?

Questions 925 and 926 are based on the following information.

A city water reservoir contains 36,000 gallons of water. The water is consumed at a rate of 780 gallons per hour.

925. At this rate, how many gallons will be consumed after 42 minutes?

926. At this rate, how much time, in minutes, will it take the reservoir to reach 23,000 gallons?

Questions 927 and 928 are based on the following information.

The fuel tank of a certain car holds 18.6 gallons. The car uses between 0.03 and 0.06 gallons per mile.

927. At this rate, how many gallons could the car use to travel 25 miles? Round your answer to the nearest quarter gallon.

928. At this rate, how many miles could the car travel before the fuel level in its tank reaches 15.0 gallons? Round your answer to the nearest 10 miles.

Questions 929 and 930 are based on the following information.

The fuel tank of a certain motorcycle holds 4.5 gallons. The motorcycle uses between 0.025 and 0.035 gallons per mile.

929. At this rate, how many gallons could the motorcycle use to travel 20 miles? Round your answer to the nearest tenth of a gallon.

930. At this rate, how many miles could the motorcycle travel before the fuel level in its tank reached 3.5 gallons? Round your answer to the nearest whole mile.

931. In the system of equations that follows, what is the value of $a+b$?

$$a+b+2c=650$$
$$a+b+c=505$$

932. In the system of equations that follows, what is the value of $2(e+f)$?

$$e+f+2g=280$$
$$e+f+g=160$$

933. The average of g and h is 21, and the average of j and k is 51. What is the average of g, h, j, and k?

934. If $\frac{a}{b}=12$ and $b=48$, what is $\frac{1}{2}a$?

935. If a and b are positive integers and $\left(a^b\right)^3=729$, what could be the value of $a+b$?

936. If $x>0$, x and y are integers, and $x^y=16$, what is the sum of all the possible values of x?

937. If $x>0$, x and y are integers, and $x^{2y}=64$, what is the sum of all the possible values of y?

938. If $x>0$, x and y are integers, and $x^y=81$, what is the sum of all the possible values of y?

939. Two circles, one having a radius of 5 and the other a radius of 9, are tangent. If point A is on one circle and point B is on the other, what is the maximum length of segment $\overline{AB}$?

940. What is the ratio of the area of a circle having a radius of 3 to the area of a circle having a radius of 9?

Questions 941–945 are based on the following information.

In this drawing, the horizontal line divides the shape in half, the five top blocks are exactly the same, and the bottom three blocks are exactly the same.

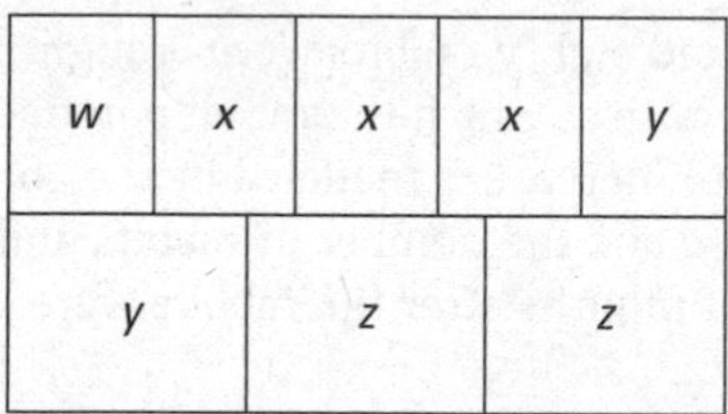

941. What fraction of the drawing is labeled x?

942. What fraction of the drawing is labeled y?

943. What fraction of the drawing is labeled z?

944. What is the ratio of one block x to one block z?

945. What is the ratio of all the blocks labeled x to all the blocks labeled z?

Questions 946 and 947 are based on the following information.

$$D = 100\left(2^{\frac{y+2}{4}}\right)$$

One hundred deer were placed on an island. The rate at which the deer population is expected to increase is modeled by the above equation, where D is the number of deer and y is the number of years after the deer were placed on the island.

946. Based on this model, how many deer are expected to be on the island after 10 years?

947. If the number of deer originally placed was actually 120, then based on this model, how many deer are expected to be on the island after 10 years?

Questions 948 and 949 are based on the following information.

$$R = 180\left(3^{\frac{m-2}{3}}\right)$$

One hundred eighty rabbits were brought to a farm. The rate at which the rabbit population is expected to increase is modeled by the above equation, where R is the number of rabbits and m is the number of months after the rabbits were brought to the farm.

948. Based on this model, how many rabbits are expected to be at the farm after 11 months?

949. If the number of rabbits originally brought in was actually 240, then based on this model, how many rabbits are expected to be at the farm after 11 months?

Questions 950 and 951 are based on the following information.

$$S = 25\left(2^{\frac{m-1}{4}}\right)$$

Twenty-five starfish were brought to a marine habitat. The rate at which the starfish population is expected to increase is modeled by the above equation, where S is the number of starfish and m is the number of months after the starfish were brought to the habitat.

950. Based on this model, how many starfish are expected to be at the habitat after 25 months?

951. If the number of starfish originally brought in was actually 75, then based on this model, how many starfish are expected to be at the habitat after 13 months?

Questions 952 and 953 are based on the following information.

Loretta buys a gift box that is 10 inches by 8 inches by 6 inches.

952. What is the very minimum amount of wrapping paper, in square inches, that Loretta needs to wrap the gift?

953. What is the minimum amount of wrapping paper, in square feet, that Loretta needs to wrap the gift? (1 foot = 12 inches)

Questions 954 and 955 are based on the following information.

Johnny has a rectangular swimming pool that is 45 feet long by 20 feet wide.

954. What is the minimum amount of tarp, in square feet, that Johnny needs to cover the pool?

955. What is the minimum amount of tarp, in square yards, that Johnny needs to cover the pool? (1 yard = 3 feet)

956. Given the following equation, if $x > 0$, what is the value of x?

$$\frac{x^{18} - 19}{18} = -1$$

957. Given the following equation, if $a = b$, what is the value of $a + b$?

$$\frac{a^b}{5} - 3.4 = 2$$

958. Eighty marbles are in a box; 40% of these are cat's eyes, and 25% of the cat's eyes are blue. How many blue cat's eye marbles are there?

959. An electronics dealer raised the price of a TV by 20% to $1,800. What was the original price? Disregard the dollar sign when gridding your answer.

Questions 960–962 are based on the following information.

A mosaic of identically sized square tiles has 80 columns and 60 rows.

960. If 3 of the rows are only indigo tiles and there are no other indigo tiles, how many tiles are indigo?

961. From 80 columns and 60 rows, if 12 rows and 18 columns are removed, how many tiles remain?

962. From 80 columns and 60 rows, if 10% of the rows and 10% of the columns are removed, and half of the 9-tile squares are replaced with 1 larger tile, how many tiles are there total?

963. Alison is looking to purchase a car priced between $30,000 and $42,000. Sales tax is 7.8%, and the dealer's fee is $600, included in the amount being taxed. If there are no other fees and charges, how much in taxes could she pay for her new car? Round your answer to the nearest hundred dollars, and disregard the dollar sign when gridding your answer.

964. A copier can produce at least 15 and at most 25 copies per minute. If the copier runs for exactly 5 hours, how many copies could it produce? Round your answer to the nearest 500 copies.

965. A box of rubber bands contains at least 200 and at most 220 rubber bands. If 6 boxes are in a case, how many rubber bands could be contained in a shipment of 4 cases? Round your answer to the nearest 100 rubber bands.

966. Based on the following equation, if $x > 0$, what is the value of x?

$$x(x+1) = 420$$

967. Based on the following equation, what is the value of x?

$$x - \frac{x^2}{1,200} = 300$$

968. Based on the following equation, if $y = 4$, what is the value of x?

$$x^3 = x^2 y$$

969. Based on the following equation, what is the value of x?

$$\left(\sqrt{x} - \sqrt{17}\right)\left(\sqrt{x} + \sqrt{17}\right) = 0$$

970. Based on the following equation, what is one possible value of x?

$$x^3\left(x^3 - 28\right) = -27$$

971. If n is a prime number between 2 and 700 and $\frac{770}{n}$ is an integer, what could be the value of n?

972. Given the following equation, where $i = \sqrt{-1}$, what is the value of x?

$$\left(\sqrt{x} - 3i\right)\left(\sqrt{x} + 3i\right) = 18$$

973. Given the following equation, where $i = \sqrt{-1}$ and $x > 0$, what is the value of x?

$$\frac{x}{i} = -i$$

974. Given the following equation, where $i = \sqrt{-1}$ and $x > 0$, what is the value of x?

$$i\left(x^2 - 5\right) = i^3$$

975. You can find the surface area of a sphere with the formula $A = 4\pi r^2$. What is the radius of a sphere having a surface area of 144π?

976. You can find the surface area of a sphere with the formula $A = 4\pi r^2$. What is the diameter of a sphere having a surface area of 100π?

977. You can find the volume of a sphere with the formula $V = \frac{4}{3}\pi r^3$. What is the radius of a sphere having a volume of $36{,}000\pi$?

978. You can find the volume of a sphere with the formula $V = \frac{4}{3}\pi r^3$. What is the diameter of a sphere having a volume of 288π?

979. You can find the surface area of a cone with the formula $A = \pi r\left(r + \sqrt{h^2 + r^2}\right)$. What is the height of a cone having a radius of 3 and a surface area of 24π?

980. You can find the surface area of a cone with the formula $A = \pi r\left(r + \sqrt{h^2 + r^2}\right)$. What is the height of a cone having a radius of 6 and a surface area of 96π?

981. If $2(x-7)^2 - 72 = 0$, what is one possible value of x?

Questions 982–984 are based on the following information.

A circle in the xy-plane is represented by the equation $(x-4)^2 + (y-9)^2 = 36$.

982. What is the x-value of the (x, y) coordinates of the center of the circle?

983. What is the y-value of the (x, y) coordinates of the center of the circle?

984. What is the radius of the circle?

985. Henry skates uphill on a paved path at an average speed of 10 miles per hour and downhill on the same path at an average speed of 15 miles per hour. What is his average (arithmetic mean) skating speed for the entire route, in miles per hour?

986. Yan swims upstream at an average speed of 3 knots (nautical miles per hour) and downstream on the same route at an average speed of 5 knots. What is her average (arithmetic mean) swimming speed for the entire route, in knots?

987. If $2\sqrt{3}(x-4)^2 - 8\sqrt{3} = 0$, what is one possible value of x?

988. The radius of circle A is three times the radius of circle B. How many times greater than the area of circle B is the area of circle A?

989. The radius of circle C is four times the radius of circle D. How many times greater than the area of circle D is the area of circle C?

990. If $\frac{3\sqrt{5}(x-11)^2}{24\sqrt{20}} = 1$, what is one possible value of x?

991. If $\frac{4\sqrt{2}(x-7.5)^2}{9\sqrt{32}}=1$, what is one possible value of x?

992. If $(x-6)^{18}=1$, what is one possible value of x?

993. If $\left(x-\frac{5}{2}\right)^2\sqrt{2i}=\frac{1}{4}\sqrt{2i}$, what is one possible value of x?

994. If $\left(x-\frac{1}{2}\right)^4\sqrt{11}=\frac{1}{16}\sqrt{11}$, what is one possible value of x?

995. If $\frac{(x-11)^2}{3^4}=1$, what is one possible value of x?

996. If f feet, 6 inches is equal to 102 inches, what is the value of f? (1 foot = 12 inches)

997. The equation of a circle in the xy-plane is shown here. What is the radius of the circle?

$$(x+2)^2+(y-3)^2=9$$

998. The equation of a circle in the xy-plane is shown here. At what x-value is the circle tangent to the x-axis?

$$(x+2)^2+(y-3)^2=9$$

Chapter 5

Essays

If you choose to take the essay portion of the SAT, you have 50 minutes to read a passage and write one essay. Be sure to present a clear and logical analysis and use language precisely. Write your essay by hand and be sure it's legible.

REMEMBER

Your essay is *not* about whether you agree with the author. It's on how well the author has written the passage.

The Problems You'll Work On

When working through the practice essays based on the sample topics in this chapter, be prepared to

» Declare your position and support it with sound reasoning and examples.

» Communicate clearly so your point can be understood by someone who doesn't know the topic.

» Critically think about how a topic fits in the big picture.

» Analyze an argument that hinges on flawed assumptions or missing information.

» Clearly describe how the flawed assumption and missing information affect the validity of the argument.

What to Watch Out For

Your challenge is to complete one quality essay in 50 minutes. Avoid these common pitfalls:

» Assuming the essay graders can read your mind and therefore not clearly describing your reasoning or point of view

» Taking too long to think about your topic and then rushing through the writing process and making all kinds of grammatical and spelling errors

» Getting stuck on the essays and panicking, thus using up all the energy that you need for the rest of the SAT

Essay Prompts

You have 50 minutes to read a passage and handwrite an essay.

999. Read the following passage and write an essay analyzing the author's argument. Consider how the author

- supports the claims using facts or examples as evidence
- uses reasoning to connect claims and evidence to develop ideas
- adds power to his/her ideas with stylistic or persuasive elements, including emotional appeals and word choice
- strengthens the logic and persuasiveness of the argument

Excerpted from Martin Luther King Jr.'s "I have a dream" speech, delivered August 28, 1963 at the Lincoln Memorial in Washington, D.C.

1

Five score years ago, a great American, in whose symbolic shadow we stand today, signed the Emancipation Proclamation. This momentous decree came as a great beacon light of hope to millions of Negro slaves who had been seared in the flames of withering injustice. It came as a joyous daybreak to end the long night of captivity.

2

But one hundred years later, the Negro still is not free. One hundred years later, the life of the Negro is still sadly crippled by the manacles of segregation and the chains of discrimination. One hundred years later, the Negro lives on a lonely island of poverty in the midst of a vast ocean of material prosperity. One hundred years later, the Negro is still languished in the corners of American society and finds himself in exile in his own land. So we have come here today to dramatize a shameful condition.

3

In a sense we've come to our nation's Capital to cash a check. When the architects of our republic wrote the magnificent words of the Constitution and the Declaration of Independence, they were signing a promissory note to which every American was to fall heir.

4

This note was a promise that all men, yes, black men as well as white men, would be guaranteed the unalienable rights of life, liberty, and the pursuit of happiness.

5

It is obvious today that America has defaulted on this promissory note insofar as her citizens of color are concerned. Instead of honoring this sacred obligation, America has given the Negro people a bad check; a check which has come back marked "insufficient funds."

6

But we refuse to believe that the bank of justice is bankrupt. We refuse to believe that there are insufficient funds in the great vaults of opportunity of this nation. So we have come to cash this check—a check that will give us upon demand the riches of freedom and the security of justice.

7

We have also come to this hallowed spot to remind America of the fierce urgency of now. This is no time to engage in the luxury of cooling off or to take the tranquilizing drug of gradualism.

8

Now is the time to make real the promises of democracy. Now is the time to rise from the dark and desolate valley of segregation to the sunlit path of racial justice. Now is the time to lift our nation from the quicksands of racial injustice to the solid rock of brotherhood. Now is the time to make justice a reality for all of God's children.

9

It would be fatal for the nation to overlook the urgency of the moment. This sweltering summer of the Negro's legitimate discontent will not pass until there is an invigorating autumn of freedom and equality. Nineteen sixty-three is not an end, but a beginning. Those who hope that the Negro needed to blow off steam and will now be content will have a rude awakening if the nation returns to business as usual. There will be neither rest nor tranquility in America until the Negro is granted his citizenship rights. The whirlwinds of revolt will continue to shake the foundations of our nation until the bright day of justice emerges.

10

But there is something that I must say to my people who stand on the warm threshold which leads into the palace of justice. In the process of gaining our rightful place we must not be guilty of wrongful deeds. Let us not seek to satisfy our thirst for freedom by drinking from the cup of bitterness and hatred. We must forever conduct our struggle on the high plane of dignity and discipline. We must not allow our creative protest to degenerate into physical violence. Again and again we must rise to the majestic heights of meeting physical force with soul force.

11

The marvelous new militancy which has engulfed the Negro community must not lead us to a distrust of all white people, for many of our white brothers, as evidenced by their presence here today, have come to realize that their destiny is tied up with our destiny. And they have come to realize that their freedom is inextricably bound to our freedom. We cannot walk alone.

1,000. Read the following passage and write an essay analyzing the author's argument. Consider how the author

- supports the claims using facts or examples as evidence
- uses reasoning to connect claims and evidence to develop ideas
- adds power to his/her ideas with stylistic or persuasive elements, including emotional appeals and word choice
- strengthens the logic and persuasiveness of the argument

The following passage is an excerpt from the introduction to Building School 2.0: How to Create the Schools We Need, *by Chris Lehmann and Zac Chase (Jossey-Bass).*

1

This book is borne of a spirit of hope that we can build healthier, more relevant, more caring schools that, in turn and in time, will help to build a healthier world.

2

According to Wolfram Alpha, there are fifty-nine million K–12 students in the United States. That's fifty-nine million families' dreams, fifty-nine million young people whose lives are still loaded with potential, fifty-nine million young people whose stories have yet to be written, fifty-nine million students who deserve to be encouraged to believe, "You can," before having someone tell them, "You can't." For that matter, the over three million teachers all over this country also deserve someone to tell them "You can," before having someone tell them, "You can't."

3

And yet, so much of what happens in school happens because we believe that we must prepare children for the world as it used to exist. Never mind that we have no idea what the world will look like for kids in kindergarten right now—and we might not even know what it will look like for the kids in ninth grade—we continue to replicate the factory-age structures and compliance-based codes of conduct that have governed school for decades because it "feels like school" to parents and politicians and school administrators all over the world.

4

Worse, in the twenty-first century the massive technological changes that have vastly changed our society have had little effect on our schools; in too many places, the technology is merely being used as the next, best filmstrip, or worse, a better way to quiz and test our students, rather than as a way to open up our classroom windows and doors so that students can learn what they need to, create what they want, and expand the reach of their ideas to almost limitless bounds.

5

In 1518, Martin Luther nailed ninety-five theses to the door of the church. He envisioned a world where the church did not act as a go-between—and in his mind, a barrier—between God and man. We need to understand now that school does not need to be a go-between—and, too often, it is a barrier—between students and learning. We can remake school so that students can feel more directly empowered to learn deeply alongside teachers who share a vision of the sense of joy that learning can unlock.

6

For our ninety-five theses, we ask you to suspend your disbelief that schools can be better than they are now. In fact, we ask you to suspend your disbelief that the world can be a better place. Each thesis in the text could lead to more questions, deeper discussion, more research, and, we hope, positive action. It is our hope that, individually, each thesis could help students and parents and educators to examine specific practices in their schools as they exist, and taken collectively, they can help communities create a new vision of school, built on the best of what has come before us, steeped in the traditions of progressive educators of the past hundred years, but with an eye toward a future we cannot fully imagine.

1,001. Read the following passage and write an essay analyzing the author's argument. Consider how the author

- supports the claims using facts or examples as evidence
- uses reasoning to connect claims and evidence to develop ideas
- adds power to his/her ideas with stylistic or persuasive elements, including emotional appeals and word choice
- strengthens the logic and persuasiveness of the argument

The following passage is an excerpt from Overloaded and Underprepared: Strategies for Stronger Schools and Healthy, Successful Kids, *by Denise Pope, Maureen Brown, and Sarah Miles (Jossey-Bass).*

HOW DOES THIS WORK? PRINCIPLES FOR CHANGE

1

Our concept is straightforward: we believe that effective school change happens when all stakeholders—administrators, faculty, parents, counselors, and students—come together to identify problems and work on solutions. This is not a revolutionary concept, but how often have we seen reform efforts superimposed on schools with little student or teacher voice or input, and how often have we watched them fail? School reform experts agree: When schools work with a team of stakeholders in a focused way, they can make real progress toward improving policies and practice (Barth, 1991; for review, see Desimone, 2002).

2

At Challenge Success, we partner with suburban and urban public, charter, parochial, and independent schools. Schools involved in our program send full teams to attend an intensive conference in the fall, where they identify problems to be addressed at their school sites. In some cases, teams have a pretty good sense of what needs to be worked on when they arrive; in others, predetermined ideas are turned on their heads based on discussions and workshops at the conference. Our process allows schools to take the time to determine the root causes of student stress and disengagement at their particular site, and then we help the school design an individualized school plan for changes during the year to increase student engagement and well-being. We provide each school with a coach, who guides the team through this process every step of the way. This team-based, site-specific approach is key, and the coach helps to make sure schools stay on track and don't lose focus throughout the year. The coach serves as a primary facilitator and liaison who shares research-based approaches and best practices and helps schools to select and implement these at their sites. Finally, teams reconvene each spring to problem-solve challenges with other schools and to celebrate success stories. Many schools admit that without the helpful prodding from an experienced coach and without the built-in accountability that comes with attending the spring conference, they might not have made as much progress throughout the year.

3

We don't want "flash in the pan" results at Challenge Success schools; we want changes to stick. Too often schools enact the newest policies or practices du jour without thinking through how these changes fit with long-term goals and other initiatives going on at the school or district level. We know that in order to effect lasting change, several things need to happen: Everyone on the team needs to feel like he or she is a part of the process, and all voices need to be heard. You'd be surprised by how wise a sixth grader can be if you give her a chance to speak her mind. Our successful teams have a common vision for the long term, and they work with us to develop a roadmap to get to where they want to go. Team leaders take what they learn at our conferences back to their broader community to educate more students, teachers, and parents in order to earn their buy-in. When all of this work has been done thoughtfully, we see a culture of collaboration and trust form alongside a willingness to change that frequently doesn't develop with a top-down approach.

2 The Answers

IN THIS PART . . .

Here's where you can find the answers and explanations for all the problems in this book. As you read through the explanations, if you find that you need a little more help with certain concepts, *For Dummies* has your back. Check out this title if you need more help with the concepts and material covered on the SAT:

SAT For Dummies, 9th Edition, by Geraldine Woods and Ron Woldoff (Wiley)

Visit www.dummies.com for more information.

Chapter 6

The Answers

Chapter 1

1. **C. have advanced social skills**

The passage states that "supergifted" kids have high IQs, are likely introverted, and are possibly learning disabled, but they need to be with kids their own age for social development.

2. **B. II and III: They already know the material, and they ignore classroom assignments.**

The passage states that the children know the material and ignore classroom assignments. It may be true that the children are shy as introverts, but the passage doesn't say that.

3. **A. the children are more advanced than their peers**

The point is that the children are gifted and could do extremely well in the right circumstances. The other answer choices may be true, but those points aren't made in the passage.

4. **C. "her school may suggest moving her up an extra grade"**

If the child is more advanced than her peers, the school would suggest moving her up an extra grade to accommodate her remarkable talents.

5. **D. could perform extremely well in the right academic setting**

The passage recommends seeking schools that have programs for gifted children. Choice (A) is wrong because some schools fall short. Choice (B) is wrong because the passage recommends Khan Academy. Choice (C) is wrong because the passage recommends children stay with their own age group and avoid advancing a grade unless they're emotionally ready.

6. **C. "Some communities have magnet schools specifically designed for gifted children."**

You're looking for a sentence that supports the idea that gifted children could perform extremely well in the right academic setting. The correct answer tells you that some schools are specifically designed for gifted children.

7. **B. a group of kids**

The child is "ahead of the pack" intellectually because she's more gifted than the other kids.

8. **A. drawing a contrast between intellectual ability and academic performance**

Choice (B) is wrong because it describes the point of the second and third paragraphs. Choice (C) is the point of the entire passage. Choice (D) is the point of the final paragraph.

9. **D. I, II, and III: Explore options outside the classroom, explore schools outside the district, and explore resources outside the school.**

The passage specifically mentions all three of these options for parents.

10. **B. "That's why smart parents often seek better options for them."**

"Them," of course, refers to the children. Parents seeking better options for their children will look outside the classroom, district, and school.

11. **B. To reflect the hope and excitement felt by the immigrants**

The passage explains that the immigrants had unrealistic expectations. Choice (A) is wrong because the immigrants did not perceive America to be full of desserts. Choice (C) is wrong because though the immigrants may have expected a certain lifestyle, the sentence is clearly an example of their excitement. Choice (D) is wrong because, of course, the puddings and pies are metaphors.

12. **B. "Many times their expectations were unrealistically high."**

The "puddings and pies" statement in the preceding question is an example of the hope and excitement that the immigrants felt.

13. **A. To exemplify the presence of immigrants**

The passage mentions the influx of immigrants. Choice (B) is wrong because the passage doesn't mention other countries. Choices (C) and (D) are wrong because there's no comparison between the numbers of Irish and other Americans.

14. **C. "By the turn of the century, more than a third of Chicago's populace was foreign-born"**

The fact that there were more Irish in New York than in Ireland is an example of the influx of immigrants.

15. **D. the flow of immigrants and the evolution of big American cities**

Though all the answer choices are true and in the passage, the purpose of the passage is to describe the flow of immigrants and the evolution of big American cities.

16. **B. metaphor**

"America's front door," "festering sores," and "home on the range" are examples of metaphors in this passage. Choice (A) is wrong because there's no literary narrative (fictional storytelling). Choice (C) is wrong because there's no use of emotion, and Choice (D) is wrong because the passage isn't encouraging any course of action.

17. **B. From danger and poverty to overcrowding and filth**

Wiegand describes the migration from hard economic times and despotic governments to cities that were overly crowded and filthy.

18. **A. The millions of refugees following World War I**

Congress tightened immigration policies in response to these European refugees in 1921. None of the other events, though true in the passage, directly prompted Congress to take any action.

19. **B. It suggests that circumstances were starting to improve.**

The passage describes the influx of immigrants and the movement of both immigrants and native-born Americans to the cities. Then it describes the squalid conditions of those cities. The last paragraph describes the implementation of sewage, water, and transportation systems. Choice (A) is wrong because the two preceding paragraphs describe the squalid conditions, but the last one doesn't. Choice (C) is wrong because though the farmers are mentioned, they aren't the purpose of the paragraph. Choice (D) is wrong because the only reference to time is that "none of it happened overnight," which is not a timeline.

20. **D. America**

In the first paragraph, the passage states that by 1910, 15 percent of the country's population was foreign-born.

21. **C. a horse's tail**

The last line of the third paragraph declares that the collection of spinal roots was named for its resemblance of a horse's tail.

22. **A. I and II: Arthritic osteophytes and disc herniations**

The last paragraph states that arthritic osteophytes and disc herniations cause pain in the extremities. An innervated vertebral column is a normal part of the spinal construction, per the first paragraph.

23. **A. describe the placement of the spinal nerves**

The passage provides a high-level description of the placement of the spinal nerves. Choice (B) is wrong because it isn't the purpose of the entire passage. Choice (C) is wrong because the naming convention is only briefly mentioned. Choice (D) is wrong because the passage only alludes to the roles of the nerves by describing the issues that arise when certain nerves are compromised.

24. **D. describe the causes and symptoms of impinged spinal nerve roots**

The last paragraph starts and ends with nerve-root impingement, and the paragraph itself describes the causes and symptoms of these impingements.

25. **A. I and II: Posterior nerve roots and anterior nerve roots**

The first sentence states that each spinal nerve is formed by the convergence of the posterior and anterior nerve roots. The medial branch, Statement III, is not part of this.

26. C. one would expect the spinal cord to extend through all the vertebrae

The authors declare that the spinal cord "actually ends around" the 2nd vertebra, as if to suggest that most people think otherwise. Choice (A) is wrong because there's no indication that most textbooks misplace the end of the spinal cord. Choice (B) is wrong because the statement is about where the spinal cord ends, not where it's placed. Choice (D) is wrong because the word *actually* concerns the end of the spinal cord; the note on nerve roots follows that point.

27. B. the posterior and anterior rami

The first sentence of the second paragraph describes that past the point where the nerve roots merge, each spinal nerve divides into the posterior ramus and the anterior ramus.

28. C. I and III: Posterior nerve roots and the anterior ramus

The first paragraph explains that posterior nerve roots have sensory fibers and that anterior nerve roots have motor fibers. The paragraph goes on to state that the spinal nerves themselves are mixed. The second paragraph explains that, like the spinal nerves, the rami are mixed, whether posterior or anterior.

29. B. combined

The word refers to the rami containing both (a combination of) sensory and motor fibers. Choice (A) is wrong because *diverse* refers to the inclusion of all facets. Choice (C) is wrong because *assorted* refers to a variety. Choice (D) is wrong because *hybrid* refers to a single item that is a result of two.

30. C. Both contain a combination of sensory fibers and motor fibers.

This is stated halfway through the second paragraph. Choice (B), although true, is not specific enough.

31. B. Major improvements in health conditions

The passage states that development gains over the last two centuries led to major improvements in health conditions.

32. **B. "dramatically and rapidly reducing rates of early death by disease"**

Major improvements in health conditions would dramatically and rapidly reduce rates of early death by disease. No other answer choice is a specific result of improved health conditions.

33. **A. population growth rates are starting to stabilize in many places**

The passage states that although the total number of people continues to increase, population growth rates have stabilized in many places. This makes Choice (B) wrong. Choice (C) is wrong because population health has greatly improved. Choice (D) is wrong because resources are running out.

34. **B. Humans will run out of natural resources.**

The passage states that natural resources are decreasing, but it doesn't mention room to live, Choices (A) and (D), or reproductive capacity, Choice (C).

35. **B. Between 2 billion and 3 billion**

The graph shows the 1930 population and 1960 population as 2 billion and 3 billion, respectively. This places the 1945 population between those two counts.

36. **B. decreases and then increases slightly**

The number of years estimated to add 1 billion starts at 2,000,000, drops down to 12, then increases slightly to 22.

37. **B. Improvements in health conditions**

The second paragraph explains that the death rate is lowered by the reduction of disease. None of the other answer choices (living conditions, animals, or weather) are mentioned in the passage.

38. **A. By the time we realize population overgrowth is an issue, it will be too late.**

The French riddle suggests that the lily coverage becomes significant — covering half the pond, prompting action — only one day before the lily covers the whole pond. Before this (while the lily is covering one-eighth, one-fourth, and so on), no one takes notice.

39. **D. "if you wait until the lily covers half the pond before cutting it back, you will have only one day to do this"**

This suggests that by the time the lily growth is significant, covering half the pond, it's too late to act upon it.

40. **D. analogy**

An *analogy* compares the common logic between two things — here, the population growth and lily growth. Choice (A) is wrong because imagery involves visual detail; for example, the authors might suggest that you visualize a lily pad growing across a pond. Choice (B) is wrong because a *simile* is a comparison using *like* or *as*: "Like a lily growing across a pond" is a simile. Choice (C) is wrong because folklore involves a group's traditional beliefs and stories, like fairy tales.

41. **B. the pores of skin**

The stomates open and close much like the pores of skin. Though the purpose is different, the question asks about the functioning.

42. **A. the plant can lose too much water**

Line 17 indicates that the plant can lose too much water if the stomates are open too long.

43. **C. analogies**

Comparing cuticle wax to car wax and comparing guard cells to balloons are examples of analogies. The authors don't use any of the other literary devices in this passage.

44. **D. To describe a process by starting with the catalyst**

The process is photosynthesis, and the catalyst is the Sun shining. Choice (A) is wrong because the light source doesn't have any bearing on the point of the passage. Choice (B) is wrong because you can't see the stomates, guard cells, or photosynthesis without magnification. Choice (C) is wrong because it's not really silly.

45. **A. To prevent the plant from losing too much water**

The guard cells control the opening of the stomate. If the stomate is open for too long, the plant loses too much water. The guard cells have little to do with protecting from intruders or reflecting the Sun's rays. Though the guard cells may affect taking in carbon dioxide, the passage describes them as guarding against the loss of water.

46. **D. "To prevent such water loss from happening, each stoma has two guard cells surrounding it."**

This sentence clearly describes the purpose of the guard cells.

47. **C. Plant Control of Water Loss**

The passage is specifically about how plants, especially in hot or dry climates, control for water loss using mechanisms in their leaves.

48. **C. "Some plants that live in very hot, dry environments save water by opening their stomates at night and storing carbon dioxide in their leaves."**

This sentence gives an example of how a plant saves water. Choice (A) is wrong because it discusses the plant cuticles and wax. Choice (B) is wrong because it discusses the way the guard cells open the stomates. Choice (D) is wrong because it focuses on the carbon dioxide used for photosynthesis.

49. **A. To provide an example of a plant's use of stomates to conserve water**

The paragraph explains what some plants do in hot and dry climates. Even though Choice (B) is true, it's the wrong answer because the timing of the photosynthesis is not the purpose of the paragraph. Choices (C) and (D) are wrong because the paragraph doesn't indicate that the plant struggles, nor does it indicate that any different amount of wax exists on the plant's cuticles.

50. **C. mesophyll**

According to the drawing, the xylem is within the mesophyll, and the cuticle, epidermis, and stomates are outside the mesophyll.

51. **B. dizzying**

Vertiginous means spinning, whirling — movement that would cause someone to become dizzy. You may have heard the word *vertigo,* which means "dizziness." Because this passage describes the variety of literature as overwhelming, in both positive and negative ways, the variety of authors and countries is considered vertiginous.

You can immediately rule out *conceivable,* which means believable. Although literature may be *enlightening* (informative) and *edifying* (intellectually enriching), the *variety* of authors and countries would probably not be considered enlightening or edifying in this context.

52. **B. II and III: A French citizen writing in Chinese; blending magical realism with Tibetan folklore**

Gno Xingjian is mentioned as a French citizen who continues to write in Chinese, and Tashi Dawa blends elements drawn from Tibetan folklore and international magical realism for his writings in Chinese. This question is a little tricky, because cultural hybridity isn't mentioned until the second example of it is presented. Statement I is wrong because in this passage, *cultural hybridity* refers to the blending of cultures within a literary work, not the exchange of literary works between countries or cultures, although such exchanges no doubt promote cultural hybridity in literature.

53. **C. It may be discovered by readers from all over the world.**

Instead of European authors dominating worldwide attention, now authors from almost anywhere can reach readers almost anywhere. Choice (A) is wrong because although the passage mentions that Pamuk's work was translated into 56 languages, this isn't necessarily a new development. Choice (B) is wrong because most authors have always written in their native languages. Choice (D) is wrong because changes in reach don't necessarily bring Nobel recognition.

54. **B. "At the same time, the shifting landscape of world literature offers new opportunities for readers to encounter writers located well beyond the select few western European countries whose works long dominated worldwide attention."**

This sentence clearly describes the way that readers can encounter writers beyond the select few western European countries. Choice (A) is wrong because though it sets the stage for the phenomenon to occur, it doesn't describe the actual phenomenon. Choice (C) is wrong because the globalization of language is a result of the phenomenon, not the phenomenon itself. Choice (D) is wrong because it focuses on the example of Tashi Dawa.

55. D. It exemplifies the opportunities for recognition that these authors may not have otherwise had.

Had these authors not so effectively reached the global market, they may never have been recognized by the Nobel Committee. Choice (A) is wrong because the purpose of writing is not to reach significant readers. Choice (B) is wrong because the examples are about the authors, not the Nobel Committee. Choice (C) is wrong because a significant amount of quality work does not get Nobel recognition.

56. C. Turkey

The passage describes more of Pamuk's readership as being outside his "native Turkey."

57. A. It describes an evolution that has a result.

The evolution is the cultural and political realignments of the past two decades, and the result is the increased global reach of authors.

58. B. Writers from almost anywhere can now achieve global recognition.

The passage describes authors reaching increasingly global audiences. Choices (A), (C), and (D) are certainly true but not the main point of the passage.

59. C. "an increasingly multipolar literary landscape allows writers from smaller countries to achieve rapid worldwide fame"

Writers from smaller countries can now achieve worldwide fame. Choices (A) and (B) are wrong because they describe how writers can reach global readers but not specifically how they can achieve fame. Choice (D) is wrong because it focuses on the example of Tashi Dawa.

60. A. It suggests that Dawa was ahead of his time.

Dawa was participating in world literature even before the globalization events described in the passage. Choice (B) is wrong because the passage describes the authors' global access, not importance. Choice (C) is wrong because the passage doesn't discuss the merits of earning a Nobel Prize. Choice (D) is wrong because the passage mentions Dawa's works being translated, not that Dawa himself spoke other languages.

61. **B. It mitigates fire damage to the soil by increasing the soil's heat capacity.**

The passage states that areas where the soil remains moist have the least damage from the fire. None of the other answer choices is supported by the passage.

62. **C. "For areas where the soil remains very moist, campfires probably have little effect on the soil properties."**

This sentence explains the effect of soil moisture on the potential damage that campfires can cause to the soil.

63. **D. steps can be taken to minimize soil damage from campfires**

This passage contains a lot of dry detail (so to speak) about how campfires damage soil and impact its ability to support life, and the authors use these details to recommend a certain action. Choice (D) fits perfectly with the authors' concern that campfires cause soil damage, which must be minimized. Choices (A) and (C) are true statements, but they're only two of several factors that the authors mention. Choice (B) is also a detail, but that choice is wrong primarily because the authors are concerned that certain woods lead to soil damage, not with how well the woods work for the campfire per se.

Remember: Just because a statement is true doesn't mean it's the main idea.

64. **D. produce higher soil temperatures**

Common sense suggests that Choice (D) is the right answer — a notion that's confirmed by the third paragraph, which mentions that short-lived forest fires are more likely than campfires to create water repellency-inducing conditions, knocking out Choice (A). This information implies that campfires last longer. Combine this reasoning with the explicit mention that campfires typically exceed 350 degrees, and you've got your answer. Choice (C) is directly contradicted by the fourth paragraph, and the Choice (B) doesn't make sense. The passage often mentions that heat flow into the soil damages it. A long-lasting campfire produces more heat flow than a short-lived one.

Tip: Although you certainly don't need to have any background knowledge to answer Reading questions (all the necessary info is given or implied in the passage), don't hesitate to use your common sense, especially with biological and physical science passages. Common sense is a good place to start, but do be sure to check your *obvious* answer with the facts given in the passage.

65. B. Organic matter decreases soil erosion.

The last sentence of the first paragraph states that the loss of organic matter reduces water-holding capacity and renders the soil more susceptible to erosion. Choice (A) is wrong because the authors support controlling campfires, not banning them. Choice (C) is wrong because the discussion is on the campfires, not the campsites. Choice (D) is wrong because campfires do burn on moist soils.

66. A. "The loss of organic matter reduces soil fertility and water-holding capacity and renders the soil more susceptible to compaction and erosion."

This sentence states that the loss of organic matter makes the soil more susceptible to erosion.

67. D. slow-burning hardwoods

The passage states that softwoods burn faster and that elm and mesquite are the slowest burning, so they're probably hardwoods.

68. C. I and III: use soft fuel and have the fires on moist soils

The passage states that faster-burning soft fuel is less harmful and that moisture in the soil helps protect against damage, making Statements I and III true. It also states that fires should be in a few designated areas, making Statement II false.

69. A. The authors allude to an ideal solution.

The passage is about soil damaged by campfires. If the fire is on a permanent concrete fireplace, it will not affect the soil. This, however, isn't mentioned in the passage. Though the other choices are certainly true, only Choice (A) identifies the purpose of the phrase.

70. C. It offers guidance and suggestions.

The passage suggests continuing to use campfires but in a less harmful way. Choice (A) is wrong because the only harm mentioned is the altering of soil, which isn't necessarily dangerous. Choice (B) is wrong because the passage doesn't advocate the restriction of campfires. Choice (D) is wrong because the passage suggests only a slight change, not an overhaul of the way campfires are used.

71. A. introduce Mr. and Mrs. Bennet and the dynamic that they share

The couple's dynamic, Mr. Bennet's nonchalance, and Mrs. Bennet's materialistic goals set the stage for the entire story. Choice (B) is wrong because it states Mrs. Bennet's goal, not the purpose of the entire passage. Choice (C) is wrong because there's no specific discussion of Mr. Bingley. Choice (D) is wrong because the passage describes Mrs. Bennet's persuading Mr. Bennet to visit Mr. Bingley.

72. C. To see her daughters married to wealthy men

The entire passage describes Mrs. Bennet's attempts to introduce her daughters to Mr. Bingley, who you know from the passage is wealthy. Choice (A) is wrong because she's planning a welcoming party with the ulterior motive of pairing Mr. Bingley with one of her daughters. Choice (B) is wrong because there's no discussion of the daughters overcoming any shortcomings. Choice (D) is wrong because the topic of discussion is not the readiness for marriage but rather the person of marriage.

73. D. "The business of her life was to get her daughters married;"

This statement clearly describes Mrs. Bennet's drive to see her daughters wed.

74. C. To introduce a conviction and irony

The first two paragraphs show the perspective of Mrs. Bennet, who is convinced both that Mr. Bingley needs a wife and that it is her place to offer him the selection of her daughters.

75. D. Gossip

The passage describes Mrs. Bennet's obsession with her neighbors, her daughters, her vanity, and the "news" of the neighborhood.

76. D. "its solace was visiting and news"

Mrs. Bennet takes solace in "visiting and news," meaning she visits her friends and shares gossip.

77. D. Five

The passage quotes Mrs. Bennet as saying, "When a woman has five grown-up daughters . . ."

78. **C. He is using gentle humor to assuage his wife's concerns.**

Mr. Bennet supports his wife but doesn't see the urgency of chasing down Mr. Bingley. His attitude toward his wife is further evidenced when he says, "I have a high respect for your nerves. They are my old friends. I have heard you mention them with consideration these last twenty years at least."

79. **A. purpose**

In response to Mrs. Bennet's declaration that Mr. Bingley is to marry one of their daughters, Mr. Bennet asks, "Is that his design in coming here?" meaning, "Is that his purpose in coming here?"

80. **C. message**

Mrs. Bennet is to bring Mr. Bingley "lines" noting Mr. Bennet's "hearty consent to his marrying whichever [daughter] he chooses."

81. **A. Stepan did not want the family to know.**

Stepan doesn't seem to feel regret for his actions, but he feels awkward because of the disruption that he caused.

82. **B. boring**

The first phrase, "happy families are all alike," suggests that happy families are neither interesting nor worth writing about. There's nothing in the passage that suggests they're commonplace.

83. **B. wealthy but not happy**

The family has servants, cooks, and maids, suggesting that it's wealthy; and it's clearly not happy, with the cook walking away and the English governess looking for a new job. (A governess is a woman hired to teach children in a private household.)

84. **B. "The stray people brought together by chance in any inn had more in common with one another than they, the members of the family"**

A happy family has members who bond; this unhappy family has members with nothing in common.

85. **C. his pain from being caught**

Besides the family falling apart, the passage discusses Stepan's longing for more women (based on his dream) and his pain caused by the quarrel — but it says nothing on the pain he caused his wife.

86. **C. introduce Stepan as an uncaring, destructive force**

The passage is all about Stepan cheating on his wife, not caring, and wreaking havoc not only on his marriage but also on the household.

87. **D. Stepan can't take responsibility for his actions**

The fact he deflects blame makes Choice (D) correct. Choice (A) is wrong because the paragraph mentions neither hope nor regret. Choice (B) is wrong because there's no indication that anything caused him to have his affair. Choice (C) is wrong because the pain of the quarrel isn't the point of the paragraph.

88. **D. "though I'm not to blame. That's the point of the whole situation,"**

These are Stepan's words, that the affair is not his fault. This indicates that Stepan can't take responsibility for his actions.

89. **B. It shows how little of an effect the separation has had on Stepan.**

The passage mentions that the quarrel happened three days earlier, yet Stepan isn't affected enough to remember that he isn't sleeping in his own room.

90. **B. himself**

Stepan's only concern is about the anger that his wife directs at him. He doesn't seem concerned that he hurt her.

91. **A. more revolutions are likely to come from the young and increasingly online population**

The passages state that along with increasing connectivity, there's an increasing awareness of the plight of others. Choice (B) is wrong because nothing is mentioned about making rational decisions. Choice (C) is wrong because the connectivity trend is only increasing. Choice (D) is wrong because the rapper El Général is just an example of an online-driven event, not a trend.

92. **B. "The communicative autonomy provided by the Internet made possible the viral diffusion of videos, messages and songs that incited rage and gave hope."**

The number of individuals online is increasing, and people find strength in numbers, even if those numbers of supporters are online.

93. **C. To remind the reader that things have always been changing**

Though the phrase introduces the topic of modern touchscreen devices and connectivity, the author's claim that this is an old proverb suggests that things have always been changing. Choices (A) and (D) are wrong because the proverb has little to do with modern times. Choice (B) is wrong because the passage doesn't mention the Chinese themselves — simply the proverb.

94. **C. instigators**

The passage mentions that these "actors" used the Internet to "build and expand their movement." This suggests that the actors are the instigators of the revolution.

95. **A. analogy**

The "cornucopia" and "genie back in the bottle" are examples of analogies.

96. **D. mobile device usage continues to increase, and there is no going back**

Though the other statements are true, only Choice (D) is the primary message: that more and more devices are in our hands, with more and more apps to go with them.

97. **D. "Yet for those who may want to put the genie back in the bottle: there's no app for that."**

Things have changed for good, as reflected in this figure of speech.

98. **C. The revolt occurred sooner because its citizens were more connected than in other Arab countries.**

The passage uses Tunisia as an example of how the Internet and social networks brought fuel to the revolution. Though the other answer choices may be true, none was the main significance of Tunisia in the Arab Spring.

99. **C. a plethora**

A *plethora* means "an abundance," which is how the passage refers to the number of entertainment and lifestyle apps available.

100. **A. Passage 2 describes an overall trend, while Passage 1 describes a specific aspect of it.**

Passage 2 describes the prevalence of social network devices, and Passage 1 describes how these devices fueled the Arab Spring, starting with Tunisia. Choice (B) is wrong because Passage 1 doesn't describe events likely to occur. Choice (C) is wrong because Passage 1 doesn't describe a mitigating factor. Choice (D) is wrong because Passage 2 doesn't begin a story, nor does Passage 1 end one.

101. **D. They are opposite sides of the same spectrum.**

In the first paragraph, Ritzer declares that "all acts always involve both" and that "all acts of production and consumption are fundamentally part of presumption." Therefore, to Ritzer, they're part of the same spectrum.

102. **C. "Of course, this shift to prosumption does not mean that sociological theorists should ignore production (the production end of the prosumption continuum) or consumption (the consumption end of that continuum)."**

Describing production and consumption as part of the same continuum suggests that they're in the same spectrum.

103. **B. fueled by content produced by the user**

The second paragraph of Passage 1 states that "Web 2.0 is defined by sites (e.g., Facebook, blogs) the contents of which are produced, wholly (blogs) or in part (Facebook), by the user."

104. **A. The prosumptive shift to Web 2.0 paves the way for life-mining.**

Passage 1 describes the prosumptive shift — that is, the shift to prosumption — from Web 1.0 to 2.0 as the shift from professionally produced content to user-created content. Users creating their own content will create demographic data, which will then be "life-mined."

105. **D. "Data banks of bio-genetic, neural and mediatic information about individuals are the true capital today, as the success of Facebook demonstrates at a more banal level."**

The sentence explains how users, by creating profiles and updates, produce the copious, valuable life-mining resources that are harvested by portals such as Facebook.

106. **C. prosumption**

The second paragraph of Passage 1 states that "prosumption is becoming increasingly ubiquitous with the emergence [. . .] of Web 2.0."

107. **A. an extent of data-mining**

The last two sentences describe life-mining as a kind of predicitive analysis and profiling based on data-mining. (Data-mining refers to using electronic databases to extract demographic data and other information, usually for marketing purposes.)

108. **B. To describe the shift to prosumption and the accompanying emergence of Web 2.0**

The passage opens with the description of prosumption, then exemplifies it with Web 2.0, and then closes with the effects of prosumption. Though the passage mentions the topics of the other answer choices, none of these is the primary purpose of the passage.

109. **B. To offer a global warning**

The passage describes the data being collected for the purpose of "risk analysis" and "population control." Choice (A) is wrong because though the data has a marketing value, that isn't the primary purpose of the passage. Choice (C) is wrong because the profiling practices aren't explained. Choice (D) is wrong because nothing is shown to be predictable.

110. **B. "It introduces discursive and material political techniques of population control of a very different order from the administration of demographics, which preoccupied Foucault's work on bio-political governmentality."**

A new kind of population control in the sphere of government presence and control indicates a warning.

ANSWERS 101–200

111. **C. Fernandina, 1968**

The first sentence of the last paragraph states this.

112. **A. Less than 1%**

The first sentence of the last paragraph states this.

113. **B. A subaerial eruption occurred.**

The *subaerial eruption* is the erupted material referenced in this question, and it's not likely that the eruption caused itself. Choices (A), (C), and (D) are stated in the last paragraph as likely causes.

114. **A. Close to 80**

Continue the line upward and to the right. The point that is above 2050 is to the right of where the number of eruptions would show 80.

115. **D. Past eruptions may not have been reported.**

Although it's possible that the number of eruptions has increased almost each year, it's not likely that the number of eruptions was close to zero before 1800.

116. **A. "prior eruptions were likely underreported."**

This quote from the passage almost perfectly matches the answer to the preceding question.

117. **B. Repeated small co-eruption events**

The fifth paragraph states that this is the primary cause of the calderas and that it wasn't from the other answer choices.

118. **A. 1797**

The first sentence of the second paragraph states this fact.

119. **C. the channels in which magma flows**

The sentence describes the channels as "magmatic" plumbing systems, which clarifies that the channels carry magma.

120. B. The circumferential eruptive and radial fissures

The third paragraph states that the other three answer choices are believed to contribute to the distribution of vents. Choice (B) describes the vents themselves, not the cause of the vents.

Chapter 2

121. B. deserves

"Have . . . believed" is present perfect tense, so "deserves" is in present tense.

122. B. him or her

"Every American teenager" is singular, so the pronoun that refers to it must also be singular. Choice (C) is wrong because "one" does not go with "every American teenager," and Choice (D) is wrong because "it" isn't used to refer to a person.

123. D. children—

The modifier opens with a dash, so it should be closed with a dash.

124. B. The process was at first hit or miss;

"Hit or miss" summarizes the patchy start described in the rest of the sentence. "Not as they seemed," "rough start," and "slow going" are general statements suggesting the early schools were all the same and not patchy.

125. A. NO CHANGE

The modifier ends with a comma (after "areas,") so it has to begin with a comma.

126. A. NO CHANGE

The noun is "areas," so "had" is the correct verb. "Did have" and "having" don't make sense in this context.

127. B. Yes, because it sets the context of the Southern states recovering from the Civil War.

The fact that the Southern states were recovering contributes to the high school success in the North but stagnation in the South.

128. C. The notion of a mass, universally inclusive national education system took decades to establish and is still in motion, as witnessed by a surge in Latino populations from Mexico and elsewhere, carrying with them a mix of languages, customs, and expectations.

The correct answer places emphasis on the need for such a school system and supports this emphasis by describing a new population that could benefit from it. Choice (A) is wrong because it emphasizes the Latino population, which is not the point of the sentence. Choice (B) is wrong because it emphasizes the time spent, not the promise of a new school system. Choice (D) is simply a run-on sentence.

129. C. students'

The possessive of a plural noun ending in *s* simply has the apostrophe after the *s*.

130. A. NO CHANGE

This matches the opening of the phrase, "if you are sixteen."

131. D. a common plan

In the sentence, "each" is singular, so it has to refer to "a common plan," also singular. You know there's one plan from the context of the passage, which describes the high school plan as a single plan.

132. B. word:

The colon is used to offset an example.

133. C. No, because it is redundant.

Science is based on attempts to prove ideas, so scientific knowledge is redundant to scientific evidence.

134. **B. journal articles**

The other two items in the list, "data" and "conference papers," are nouns, so this item must also be a noun.

135. **C. we will have**

This phrase matches the beginning of the preceding sentence, "We will have more scientific knowledge," and this repetition is an effective way to add emphasis and flow.

136. **A. NO CHANGE**

The phrase "and to construct new ones" ends with a dash, so it has to begin with a dash.

137. **A. Yes, because it offsets this point from the thesis of the passage, which is the future.**

The point of the passage is the future, and this sentence is a subtopic that focuses on the present. It therefore needs a transitional phrase from the future to the present.

138. **A. NO CHANGE**

"The individuals" has to be plural to have a relationship between "their personal technologies." The word "between" needs the word "and."

139. **C. Yet**

The previous sentence talks about the big challenge ahead, and the current sentence talks about overcoming the challenge, so a contrasting transition is needed. The transition "on the other hand" would work, but it needs "on one hand" to precede it in the passage.

140. **D. DELETE the underlined portion**

It's already understood that these issues challenge us today, so this phrase is redundant.

141. **C. is no easy matter**

The point of the paragraph is that a challenge is ahead, and this phrase contributes to the tension. Also, the last sentence reads that "this gap cannot be easily bridged."

142. A. NO CHANGE

The tension in question is between "the natural sciences," "those who apply formal scientific methods," and "those applying social theoretical frameworks to make sense of science and technology" (the correct answer here).

143. B. watching

"Watching" is parallel to the other verb, "hanging." The "when" later in the sentence serves the purpose of "and," so the "and" isn't needed here.

144. A. NO CHANGE

Two unrelated adjectives are separated by a comma. The adjective "barren" is needed because it helps with the imagery and is not redundant to "icy."

145. A. NO CHANGE

There is a comma before the name, so there needs to be one afterward. Deleting the father's name is not consistent with the writing style because the boy and the Stanford researcher are also named in the passage.

146. B. Yes, because it clarifies the time period José Rubén wanted to show Brandon.

The phrase clarifies that José Rubén wanted to show Brandon videos about the dinosaur era.

147. B. recounted

The correct answer means told what happened. *Recast* means to change the story, and *recant* and *retract* mean to withdraw, as in a contract or offer.

148. C. Brandon and José Rubén's interests led them from one history video to another, and soon the two of them were watching a documentary about dinosaurs and other species.

This arrangement correctly begins with the subjects, not the pronoun, and places the events in order: from history videos to a dinosaur documentary.

149. **A. NO CHANGE**

This phrase connects to the idiom "but also" later in the sentence.

ANSWERS 101–200

150. **B. to reflect**

This verb form is parallel to the following verb "store."

151. **D. No, because it is obvious.**

Discussion of how life changes on Planet Earth clearly covers a period of many years, so that doesn't need to be stated.

152. **B. it**

The pronoun refers to the singular noun "question."

153. **B. (a documentary)**

The passage describes the transition from a movie to a documentary. Including those words here is appropriate for concluding the passage.

154. **D. DELETE the underlined portion**

"Day four" is clear and acceptable.

155. **A. NO CHANGE**

This phrase is parallel to the preceding phrase, "Rocketship Education's first school."

156. **A. NO CHANGE**

"Await her arrival" is complete and correct.

157. **D. DELETE the underlined portion and end the sentence with a period**

Stating that the enrollment of 270 was more than 200 short of the goal implies the goal was close to 500. This point does not have to be exact to support the purpose of the passage.

158. B. and send

"Switch schools and send" is clear and concise.

159. A. NO CHANGE

"Second question that makes" is clear and concise.

160. C. but a serious runner

The idiom "not just" is followed by the word "but": "Not just A but B." The word "also" isn't needed.

161. B. arrived

Though the passage is in the present tense, the "shot of hip California" arrived before the telling of the events.

162. B. smoothly

This is an adverb modifying the verb "getting."

163. B. Getting to know why Kinser is nervous requires learning the Rocketship story, which means getting to know the founders.

This sentence effectively transitions from Kinser herself to the founders of the school.

164. B. Use it to begin a new paragraph that continues the passage.

The sentence begins a new point, which is the discussion of the founders. For this reason, it should begin a new paragraph.

165. C. to

"Lead to search" is clear and concise.

166. A. NO CHANGE

"The information was presented" is clear and concise.

ANSWERS 101–200

167. **C. had been**

The fragments were collected before the conference, which is also described in the past tense.

168. **A. NO CHANGE**

"In the audience sat William" is clear and concise.

169. **B. To him, this was a new and electrifying idea.**

Cassidy was excited by the new and electrifying idea, while others in the audience appeared uninterested.

170. **B. as**

"Looking as glassy-eyed as audiences sometimes do" is correct.

171. **B. Shima,**

The phrase following is a modifier, so it's offset by a comma.

172. **C. with**

"The Shimas had coauthored an article with Dr. H." is clear and concise.

173. **A. NO CHANGE**

This is parallel to the other verb in the sentence, "had not seen."

174. **C. would propose**

At this point of the story, Cassidy was planning the proposal to the National Science Foundation.

175. **D. The Origin and Early History of the U.S. Antarctic Search for Meteorites Program**

The passage describes the U.S. teams preparing to explore patches of ice in Antarctica. The Yamato Mountains and early meteorite fragments are details to the story.

176. **A. NO CHANGE**

"Concerned with" means area of focus. "Concerned for" or "about" means worried about the well-being.

177. **C. which**

"Samples which have been drawn" is correct. The pronoun "who" is only used to refer to a person or persons.

178. **B. exists**

"Each" is singular, and the population of samples definitely exists.

179. **A. NO CHANGE**

Theory and statistics are two separate subjects. The semicolon correctly joins the two independent sentences.

180. **C. is the frequency distribution**

"One . . . is" is correct.

181. **A. Before Sentence 1**

The word "perhaps" is intended to follow a rhetorical question in the passage.

182. **B. discrete,**

The modifier ends with a comma, so it also should begin with one.

183. **B. to**

"Correspond to" is correct.

184. **D. DELETE the underlined portion**

"If" does not need to be followed by "then."

185. **B. Data Distribution**

The passage describes the natural ways in which data is distributed on a graph.

186. **B. The Nature of Data**

The graphs show the nature, or arrangement, of generic sets of data.

187. **A. NO CHANGE**

The opening prepositional phrase needs to be offset by a comma.

188. **C. they're**

This is the correct contraction of *they* and *are.*

189. **B. sits**

"A team . . . sits" is correct and more concise than "A team . . . that is seated.".

190. **A. NO CHANGE**

"Carry energy . . . to" is correct.

191. **A. NO CHANGE**

"Coenzymes . . . pass" is correct.

192. **B. Yes, because it effectively sets up the role of oxygen in the next sentence.**

The next sentence describes what happens when oxygen accepts the electrons mentioned in the preceding sentence.

193. **D. like**

The sentence compares the transport chain to a bucket brigade, and "like" is the correct word for a comparison.

194. **B. represents**

"The water . . . represents" is correct for this analogy.

195. **B. use**

"The proteins use energy" is correct.

196. **C. it adds**

"A protein . . . that transforms . . . as it adds" is correct; the verbs have the same form.

197. **B. Transferring Energy to ATP**

The opening sentence introduces the transfer of energy from food molecules to ATP. The passage continues to explore this process and concludes with the name of the ATP energy transfer process.

198. **C. but**

That Sir Doyle didn't share the feeling is a contradiction to the public's enthusiasm, so a contrast transition is needed.

199. **B. writer;**

The semicolon correctly joins the two complete sentences.

200. **C. The public, however, wanted more Sherlock Holmes.**

This sentence clearly describes what the public wants, which sets up the public's reaction later in the passage. Choice (A) is wrong because it doesn't state that the public wanted more, simply that they enjoyed the character. It's the wanting more that caused the public reaction.

201. **A. NO CHANGE**

The second half of the sentence, where Doyle plots to kill Holmes, contradicts the first part of the sentence, where Doyle writes about Holmes. The contrast transition is needed here.

202. **D. To kill off Sherlock Holmes,**

The professor was created specifically to kill Holmes so that Doyle could pursue other forms of writing.

203. **C. dramatic**

The thundering cascade plunging 800 feet and the fearful chasm far below are far more than beautiful, orderly, or natural.

204. **A. NO CHANGE**

The comma correctly combines with the following "and" to join the two complete sentences.

205. **D. After Sentence 3, continuing the quote from Doyle**

The specific example properly follows Doyle's description of the general protest.

206. **D. dismay, and**

The comma and conjunction correctly join the two complete sentences. The sentences are not directly related, so the "and" is a sufficient conjunction.

207. **B. canon**

The definition of *canon* is "a collection of sacred books." The other words have meanings that don't fit: *cannon* is a weapon, and *maxim* and *axiom* both refer to a truth that is self-evident.

208. **A. The Death (and Rebirth) of Sherlock Holmes**

The passage describes the effects and reversal of Holmes's death.

209. **B. herein**

As used, *herein* is one word meaning "here in this writing." The other answer choices don't fit: *here in* isn't the proper use of words in this context, *heron* is a large bird, and *heroine* is a female hero.

210. D. DELETE the underlined portion

"As outlined" is correct and concise.

211. C. The main premise of dendrochronology is the establishment of precise, high-resolution (annually resolved) tree-ring chronologies, derived using the method known as cross-dating.

Placing "the main premise of dendrochronology" first places emphasis on the point of the sentence, and the words "which is" are not necessary.

212. A. from the same site and region

If the trees were sampled from the same site and region, there was little other variation.

213. A. NO CHANGE

This contrast to "adverse" is parallel to the beginning of the sentence, which says "relatively narrow (wide)."

214. B. ensures

Ensures means to make sure. The other answers don't fit: *Insures* means to provide insurance, and *ansures* and *unsures* aren't actual words.

215. D. suggested

Suggested means that the scientific idea is proposed but not confirmed. The other answer choices mean the idea is confirmed but not directly stated.

216. B. temporal

Temporal means time-based, which is the correct answer because both the preceding and following sentences talk about the Earth's past leading up to today.

217. A. NO CHANGE

A contrast transition is correct because the preceding sentence discusses the critical nature of observations, and this sentence discusses the limitations of observations. "On the other hand" would need "on the one hand" to precede it.

218. **C. such as**

This correctly sets up the example that follows.

219. **D. Basic Tree-Ring Principles**

This title correctly highlights the overall discussion of the passage. The other answer choices highlight details.

220. **A. NO CHANGE**

This conjunction correctly complements the thought of adopting bylaws by producing them. The rule about not starting a sentence with a conjunction isn't a real rule.

221. **C. meeting**

This answer correctly describes a group of people who come together to form an association.

222. **B. adopt**

Adopt correctly means to use and integrate. The other answer choices have different meanings: *adapt* means to change, *adept* means skilled, and *adroit* means clever.

223. **D. This committee does some important work that has far-reaching effects.**

The other choices don't mention the importance of the work that this committee does.

224. **C. yourself and every member of the bylaws committee**

This answer is the most concise and omits the redundant "everyone/all the people involved."

225. **B. assistance**

"Getting professional assistance" correctly refers to hiring a professional. "Professional help" is a polite term for psychological help.

226. **D. DELETE the underlined portion**

The other answer choices are grammatically correct but redundant. "If you need help, hire someone" doesn't need further emphasis.

227. **A. NO CHANGE**

"Include anybody who will" is correct.

228. **C. one thing;**

This phrase correctly sets up "quite another," which follows.

229. **D. times**

The set of bylaws "doesn't A or B." No punctuation is needed.

230. **B. or**

"Doesn't A or B" is correct. "Nor" would need to be preceded by "neither."

231. **B. But Iceland got crowded pretty quickly.**

This is the only answer choice that provides a reason for the Vikings to proceed to another country.

232. **C. led**

This is the past tense of "lead." The other answer choices have different meanings.

233. **A. NO CHANGE**

This word is used for comparisons: The Vikings' first visits are being compared to "many things in human history."

234. **B. Vikings'**

The plural possessive has an *s* apostrophe without a following *s*.

235. **D. No, because it is irrelevant and distracts from the flow of the narrative.**

The passage is specifically about the Viking forays into North America. The specific fate of a certain explorer returning to Norway is out of scope.

236. **D. Mistaking seasonal berries for grapes,**

The "grapes" led Leif Ericsson to call the land "Vinland."

ANSWERS 201–300

237. **B. running**

"Which was running colonies" is correct and flows better than "which was to run colonies."

238. **A. NO CHANGE**

The comma and conjunction "and" require a noun or pronoun ("he") to follow.

239. **C. contemptuous**

The new SAT still uses vocab questions, though not many. The correct answer means "full of contempt." *Laudable* means "praiseworthy," *stoic* means "of few words," and *veracious* means "truthful."

240. **D. DELETE the underlined portion**

The first part of the sentence, "Led . . . Karlsefni," modifies "an expedition," so no conjunction is needed.

241. **C. Visits by the Vikings**

The passage describes several visits to different continents by the Vikings.

242. **C. nearly**

The possibilities are not quite infinite, and this answer is more concise than "close to."

243. **B. In spite of**

The sentence reads, "Only 5% of the oceans have been explored." A contradictory transition is needed to counter all the ongoing technological advances.

244. **A. Surprisingly, we know more about the moon than we do the ocean.**

This sentence illustrates how little we know about the ocean by comparing our knowledge of this to something not even on our planet.

245. **D. However,**

A contrast transition is needed to connect the oceanographers' desires and their limitations. Choice (C) is wrong because *nevertheless* is used for an argument, not a situation.

246. **B. impossible**

Rough conditions would prevent ships from traveling. The other answer choices have different meanings and either don't make logical sense or don't fit the narrative of the passage.

247. **B. are launching**

The verb is correctly present tense, as the actions that follow are the actions of launching. In the sentence as-is, "launch" reads like a tendency, not an action.

248. **A. They want to establish long-term ocean floor observatories with arrays of sensors and instruments that make continuous measurements of various ocean properties and events.**

Not only is this answer concise and parallel, but it also establishes the result of their efforts (the long-term ocean floor observatories) as the point of the sentence.

249. **A. NO CHANGE**

The Internet is a portal for accessing information. "Via" is parallel to the other parts of the data path in the previous sentence: "via fiber optics or via cable." Also, it's more concise than Choices (C) and (D). Choice (B), "to," doesn't fit the meaning of the sentence.

250. **B. in the future,**

The modifier "in the future" opens with a comma, so it also has to close with one.

ANSWERS 201–300

251. C. After Sentence 1

Sentence 1 describes the collection of data, so the underlined sentence, describing the harvesting of data, should follow.

252. C. The Future of Oceanography

The passage describes oceanographic data collection methods that are under development.

253. C. the crunch of gravel under tires

This both illustrates the sound of a car arriving and sets up the discussion of the driveway in the following paragraph.

254. B. After Sentence 1.

Sentence 1 introduces the driveway, and the underlined sentence brings home the fact that it's Mike's new driveway. Sentence 2 then transitions into discussion of the town.

255. B. Yes, because it adds detail about how Mike Keller feels.

The purpose of the passage is to describe the despair that Mike feels when moving into his new home in a remote town.

256. C. rambler

This word creatively sets up the poor condition of the house. The other answer choices are either neutral or flattering.

257. B. what housing costs in Chicago.

Mike's perception is based on what he's used to, which is founded on where he's from. In this case, it's the housing prices in Chicago.

258. A. NO CHANGE

The comma and the word "and" correctly join the two complete sentences.

259. **A. it, sticking by**

This correctly makes the part after the comma a modifier.

260. **B. had announced**

The event precedes another event in the past, so this verb form gets the word "had."

261. **D. speaking different languages,**

This answer specifically focuses on the lack of communication.

262. **A. NO CHANGE**

This answer choice emphasizes the uncomfortable heat.

263. **B. but**

A contrast transition is needed here. The movers are bringing all of Mike and Billy's belongings, and the contrast is that Mike and Billy brought a few things on their own.

264. **C. 24/7—**

The dash correctly emphasizes the abrupt change in thought from a city to a company.

265. **B. Yet,**

The contrast transition correctly joins the contradicting ideas that delegation is useful but some companies don't use it.

266. **C. neither**

This correctly sets up the idiomatic "nor" later in the sentence.

267. **A. NO CHANGE**

This correctly goes with the entire passage, which places Bloomberg's words and actions in the past tense.

268. B. added

The entire passage is in the past tense, so this verb should also be in the past.

269. A. NO CHANGE

The adjective "deputy" does not change when the noun "mayor" becomes plural.

ANSWERS 201–300

270. B. mission

"They were motivated by A and B" is correct, with no punctuation.

271. A. difference; what

The semicolon correctly joins the two complete sentences. A conjunction ("and" or "while") would have to be used with a comma.

272. C. he was accessible and real

Mayor Bloomberg is part of the team by being accessible and real, not remote and standoffish like other managers.

273. C. No matter that

The point is that despite his success, Mayor Bloomberg treats his team members as equals.

274. D. Yes, because it effectively concludes the discussion of Mayor Bloomberg's teamwork approach.

The paragraph describes Mayor Bloomberg's approach to teamwork, and this sentence concludes the paragraph.

275. B. on

Move the sentence around so it reads, "People are dependent on," which is idiomatically correct.

276. A. NO CHANGE

The plural of 1930 does not get an apostrophe.

277. **B. has been**

"There has been an increased interest" is correct.

278. **C. however**

The importance of soil conservation contrasts with the little public knowledge of the soil's complexity.

279. **D. excavation, and it**

The comma and conjunction are both needed to join the two complete sentences.

280. **B. At the end of Paragraph 2**

The sentence describes the effect of soil on vegetation growth, which goes along with the end of Paragraph 2, which describes farming applications. It does not go with Paragraph 3, which describes engineering and construction applications.

281. **A. NO CHANGE**

This answer is concise, and "crumble" is too specific.

282. **C. uses**

"Specific engineering uses" is correct.

283. **C. concern,**

The comma correctly connects the modifier "particularly where . . ."

284. **B. and**

"Mismatching of A and B" is idiomatically correct.

285. **A. NO CHANGE**

This is the correct possessive pronoun for "soil horizons," which is plural.

286. D. veering toward the ditch

This answer provides a specific visual of the impending disaster.

287. B. remain on track

This answer suggests that, like a train on a track, the project would stay true and reach its goal.

288. A. NO CHANGE

This answer suggests that the speaker got right to the point and made a clear, direct decision.

289. D. mess, and I

The comma and conjunction are both needed to join the two complete sentences.

290. C. circle the drain

This matches colloquial phrases such as "pull the plug" and "remain on track."

291. B. energetic,

"A, B, and C" is correct, with a comma after "B." A comma doesn't have to follow the "B," but the series can't have an ellipse, semicolon, or hyphen instead.

292. A. NO CHANGE

"Product of" is idiomatically correct.

293. D. turn this lemon into lemonade

This phrase uses the writer's colloquial style to describe a situation of recovery.

294. **D. clearinghouse—**

The modifier opens with a dash, so it needs to close with one. The last part of the sentence, "that had a unique approach," continues the sentence from "was a securities process business."

295. **D. Its**

The idea belongs to the company, which is singular. A possessive pronoun never has an apostrophe — "it's" is short for "it is."

296. **B. laissez-faire**

More SAT vocab. The correct answer means free and unrestricted. *Prodigal* means lavish and wasteful. *Wistful* means regretful, and *erstwhile* means former.

Chapter 3

297. **D. 8**

Solve for x and plug that into $3x+5$:

$$\begin{aligned} 2x+3&=5\\ 2x&=2\\ x&=1 \end{aligned}$$

$$3x+1=3(1)+1=8$$

298. **D. 7**

Subtract the equations and isolate the $x+y$:

$$\begin{aligned} 15x+25y&=60\\ \underline{-(10x+20y}&\underline{=25)}\\ 5x+\ \ 5y&=35\\ x+\ \ \ \ y&=\ 7 \end{aligned}$$

299. C. −3

Plug in 5 for y and simplify the equation:

$$\begin{aligned}\sqrt{3h^2-2}-y&=0\\ \sqrt{3h^2-2}-5&=0\\ \sqrt{3h^2-2}&=5\\ 3h^2-2&=25\\ 3h^2&=27\\ h^2&=9\\ h&=3,-3\end{aligned}$$

Because $h<0$, it must equal −3.

300. C. −30

FOIL the expression:

$$\begin{aligned}(3i+3)(5i-5)&=15i^2-15i+15i-15\\ &=15i^2-15\\ &=15(-1)-15\\ &=-15-15\\ &=-30\end{aligned}$$

301. C. 12

Substitute 2 for h, and the equation looks like this:

$$\frac{x-2}{5}=2$$

Multiply both sides by 5 to solve:

$$\begin{aligned}x-2&=10\\ x&=12\end{aligned}$$

302. A. −2

If $(x-3)^2$ equals 25, then $(x-3)$ equals either 5 or −5. Set this up as two separate equations:

$$\begin{aligned}x-3&=5 \quad\text{or}\quad x-3=-5\\ x&=8 \qquad\qquad\quad x=-2\end{aligned}$$

Because x is negative, it equals −2.

303. D. 5

First solve for ab. Start with $\frac{ab}{6} = 1$ and multiply both sides by 6 so $ab = 6$. Plug this value into the first equation:

$$\begin{aligned} ab - c &= 1 \\ 6 - c &= 1 \\ -c &= -5 \\ c &= 5 \end{aligned}$$

304. C. $31 + i$

Start by FOILing the expression:

$$\begin{aligned} &(2+3i)(5-7i) \\ &= 10 - 14i + 15i - 21i^2 \end{aligned}$$

$i^2 = -1$, so plug that in:

$$10 - 14i + 15i - 21(-1)$$

And simplify the expression:

$$10 - 14i + 15i + 21 = 31 + i$$

305. C. $3 + 3i$

Starting with the given expression, distribute the negative and then drop the parentheses:

$$\begin{aligned} &(6+5i)-(3+2i) \\ &= (6+5i)+(-3-2i) \\ &= 6+5i-3-2i \end{aligned}$$

Then combine like terms:

$$\begin{aligned} &6+5i-3-2i \\ &= 3+3i \end{aligned}$$

306. B. $3(d + h)$

If Joe hit d doubles and h home runs in each game, then over 3 games, he hit $3d$ doubles and $3h$ home runs, for a total of $3d + 3h$ or $3(d + h)$.

ANSWERS 301–400

307. **A.** sw

Each week, Eric's sister gets s daisies. Multiply s by the number of weeks, w, for an answer of sw.

308. **C.** $w(d-s)$

Each week, Eric collects d daisies and gives s to his sister, so he keeps $(d-s)$. Multiply this by the number of weeks, w, for an answer of $w(d-s)$.

309. **C. The number of quizzes Susan grades per day**

If Susan receives 8 quizzes from s students, then you can estimate the number of quizzes she receives with $8s$. Subtract the number of quizzes she has graded, represented by $10d$, for the number of quizzes left over. If d is the number of days Susan has worked that week, then she grades 10 quizzes per day.

310. **B.** $q = 8(s+2) - 10d$

If the number of students, s, increases by 2, the new number of students is $(s+2)$. The rest of the equation remains unchanged.

311. **B.** -2

Factor the first expression into

$$(x-y)(x-y)$$

which is the same as

$$(x-y)^2$$

Because $(x-y)^2 = (x+2)^2$, $-y = 2$, or $y = -2$.

312. **C.** l **and** w

If the customer asks the builder to make the tables shorter and wider, the length and width will change; l represents the length, and w represents the width.

313. **D. 80**

If $2h = 30$, $h = 15$. Plug this value into the expression and simplify:

$$\begin{aligned}&5h+5\\&=5(15)+5\\&=75+5\\&=80\end{aligned}$$

314. **B. 18**

The trap is giving the value of b rather than the value of $2b$. Start with the given equation and simplify it:

$$\begin{aligned}\frac{4}{3}b&=12\\4b&=36\\2b&=18\end{aligned}$$

315. **A.** $\sqrt[b]{x^a}$

When an exponent appears as a fraction, the numerator of the fraction remains the exponent, and the denominator becomes the radical. In the expression $x^{\frac{a}{b}}$, the numerator a remains the exponent, and the denominator b becomes the radical.

316. **A. 3**

An exponent of $\frac{1}{3}$ is equivalent to a cube root. Therefore, $27^{\frac{1}{3}} = \sqrt[3]{27} = 3$.

317. **C. 25**

Reduce the fraction $\frac{6}{3}$ to 2. Now you're looking for 5^2, which equals 25.

318. **B. 4**

The simplest way to solve this problem is to take the 4th root of 2, which is 16, and then square-root that for an answer of 4.

319. **D.** $5y = 50$

Club X has five times the members of Club Y, so set up the equation:

$$X = 5Y$$

ANSWERS 301–400

Club X has 50 members and Club Y has y members, so substitute 50 for X and y for Y in the equation: $50 = 5y$. Reverse the order for the correct answer.

320. **A.** $9y^2$

Distribute the –2 in the second expression:

$$\left(2x^2y+6y^2+6xy^2\right)$$

Add this to the first expression:

$$\left(-2x^2y+3y^2-6xy^2\right)+\left(2x^2y+6y^2+6xy^2\right)$$

Drop the brackets:

$$-2x^2y+3y^2-6xy^2+2x^2y+6y^2+6xy^2$$

And cancel out the like terms to get $9y^2$.

321. **B.** $P=A\frac{(1+r)^n-1}{r(1+r)^n}$

To solve for P, multiply both sides of the equation by the reciprocal of the fraction. Multiplying both sides by $\frac{(1+r)^n-1}{r(1+r)^n}$ cancels the fraction from the P side and ties it to the A side.

$$A\left((1+r)^n-1\right)=P\left(r(1+r)^n\right)$$

$$A\frac{(1+r)^n-1}{r(1+r)^n}=P$$

322. **D.** $A=P\frac{r(1+r)^{n+6}}{(1+r)^{n+6}-1}$

You know that n represents the number of periods. If the number of periods were to increase by 6, n becomes $n+6$ in both places where n appears in the original formula.

323. **A.** 2

Cross-multiply the equation and solve for x:

$$\frac{12}{x+18}=\frac{3}{x}$$

$$12x=3x+54$$

$$9x=54$$

$$x=6$$

Place x over 3 for the answer.

324. **D. −11**

Cross-multiply the equation and solve for x:

$$\frac{x+5}{2}=\frac{x+2}{3}$$
$$3x+15=2x+4$$
$$x=-11$$

325. **C. −5**

Cross-multiply the equation and solve for x:

$$\frac{x+3}{4}=\frac{4}{x-3}$$
$$x^2-9=16$$
$$x^2=25$$
$$x=5,-5$$

Because $x<0$, x has to be −5.

326. **C. 4**

Transfer the negative sign to the 3 in the numerator, and then cross-multiply the equation and solve for x:

$$\frac{x+5}{3}=\frac{-3}{x-5}$$
$$x^2-25=-9$$
$$x^2=16$$
$$x=4,-4$$

Because $x>0$, x has to be 4.

327. **B. 3**

Subtract the second equation from the first equation:

$$\begin{array}{r} 5x+3y=10 \\ -(3x-2y=\ 7) \\ \hline 2x-\ \ y=\ 3 \end{array}$$

ANSWERS 301–400

328. A. 3

Multiply the second equation by 2 and subtract it from the first equation:

$$\begin{array}{rl} 2x^2 - 6x + y = 2z & +3 \\ -\left(2x^2 - 6x \quad = 2z\right) & \\ \hline y = & 3 \end{array}$$

329. D. 16

According to the table, $f(3) = 4$. Therefore, $\left(f(3)\right)^2 = (4)^2 = 16$.

330. C. 6

If $x = 3$, then $x + 2 = 5$. According to the table, $f(5) = 6$.

ANSWERS 301–400

331. A. 2

According to the table, $f(3) = 5$. Therefore, $\frac{2f(3)}{5} = \frac{2(5)}{5} = 2$.

332. A. $\frac{y-b}{x}$

Start with the given equation and solve for m:

$$y = mx + b$$
$$y - b = mx$$
$$\frac{y-b}{x} = m$$

333. B. −3, 3

The parabola crosses the x-axis where the values for x make y equal to 0. To find these x-values, set y equal to 0 and find the roots of the quadratic:

$$0 = x^2 - 9$$
$$0 = (x+3)(x-3)$$
$$x = -3, 3$$

334. **A. −2, 3**

The parabola crosses the *x*-axis where the values for *x* make *y* equal to 0. To find these *x*-values, set *y* equal to 0, distribute the *x*, and find the roots of the quadratic:

$$y = x(x-1)-6$$
$$0 = x^2 - x - 6$$
$$0 = (x-3)(x+2)$$
$$x = 3, -2$$

335. **C. −2, 2**

The parabola crosses $y = 5$ where the values for *x* make *y* equal to 5. To find these *x*-values, set *y* equal to 5 and find the roots of the quadratic:

$$5 = x^2 + 1$$
$$0 = x^2 - 4$$
$$0 = (x+2)(x-2)$$
$$x = -2, 2$$

336. **B. 50**

As supplementary angles, $x° + y° + z° = 180$. If $x° + z° = 130$, $y° = 50$. Because $y°$ and $b°$ are opposite angles, $y° = b°$.

337. **C. 50**

As supplementary angles, $w° + x° + y° + z° = 180$. If $w° + x° + y° = 120$, $z° = 60$; and if $x° + y° + z° = 110$, $w° = 70$. If $z° + w° = 130$, $x° + y° = 50$.

338. **C. (1, −16)**

To find the coordinates of the vertex of a parabola, factor the equation to find the roots:

$$y = x^2 - 2x - 15$$
$$y = (x-5)(x+3)$$

This tells you that when $y = 0$, the parabola crosses the x-axis at $(5, 0)$ and $(-3, 0)$. Thus, the x-coordinate is halfway between 5 and −3, which is 1. To find the y-coordinate of the vertex, substitute 1 for x in the equation:

$$\begin{aligned} y &= x^2 - 2x - 15 \\ &= (1)^2 - 2(1) - 15 \\ &= 1 - 2 - 15 \\ &= -16 \end{aligned}$$

339. A. −5, 3

Simplify the equation, set it equal to 0, and factor it out:

$$\begin{aligned} 3x^2 + 6x &= 45 \\ x^2 + 2x &= 15 \\ x^2 + 2x - 15 &= 0 \\ (x-3)(x+5) &= 0 \\ x &= 3, -5 \end{aligned}$$

340. D. $x = -3 \pm \sqrt{5}$

First simplify the equation and set it equal to 0:

$$\begin{aligned} 2x^2 + 12x &= -8 \\ x^2 + 6x &= -4 \\ x^2 + 6x + 4 &= 0 \end{aligned}$$

Next, use the quadratic formula, where $a = 1$, $b = 6$, and $c = 4$:

$$\begin{aligned} x &= \frac{-b \pm \sqrt{b^2 - 4ac}}{2a} \\ &= \frac{-6 \pm \sqrt{6^2 - 4(1)(4)}}{2(1)} \\ &= \frac{-6 \pm \sqrt{36 - 16}}{2} \\ &= \frac{-6 \pm \sqrt{20}}{2} \\ &= \frac{-6 \pm 2\sqrt{5}}{2} \\ &= -3 \pm \sqrt{5} \end{aligned}$$

ANSWERS 301–400

341. **A. 2, 3**

Distribute the x^2 and set the equation equal to 0:

$$-x^2(x^2-13)=6^2$$
$$-x^4+13x^2=36$$
$$-x^4+13x^2-36=0$$
$$x^4-13x^2+36=0$$

Next, factor the equation to find the roots:

$$x^4-13x^2+36=0$$
$$(x^2-4)(x^2-9)=0$$
$$x^2=4,9$$
$$x=2,-2,3,-3$$

Because $x>0$, x can be only 2 or 3.

342. **A. 0, 1, 2**

Set the equation equal to 0 and factor out an x^3:

$$x^9+8x^3=9x^6$$
$$x^9-9x^6+8x^3=0$$
$$x^3(x^6-9x^3+8)=0$$

Next, factor the expression to find the roots:

$$x^3(x^6-9x^3+8)=0$$
$$x^3(x^3-8)(x^3-1)=0$$
$$x=0,2,1$$

For the equation to equal 0, x has to equal 0, 1, or 2.

343. **D. 5**

Compare parts of the two sides of the equation, pairing up the terms based on the exponents of x:

$$15x^2=3kx^2$$
$$20x=4kx$$
$$25=2k+15$$

Regardless of which portion of the equation you use, $k=5$.

ANSWERS 301–400

344. **B. 35°**

If one angle measures 110°, the other two angles total 70°. Because an isosceles triangle has two identical angles, the two other angles are each 35°.

345. **D. I, II, or III: 40°, 70°, or 100°**

An isosceles triangle has two identical angles. If one of those angles is 40°, then the other angle is also 40°, and the third angle is 100° (because the three angles always total 180°). If the unique angle is 40°, then the other two angles are each 70°.

346. **A.** $\frac{3}{5}$

Using SOH CAH TOA, $\sin A$ is opposite over hypotenuse; these sides are in the ratio of 3 to 5, respectively.

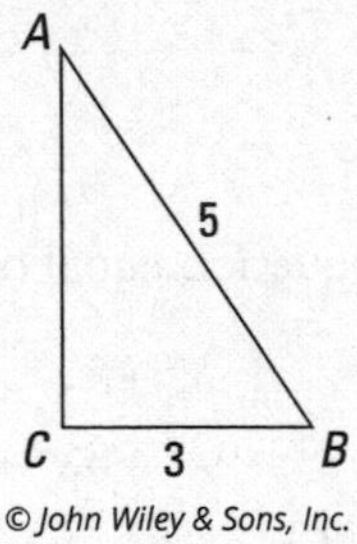

© John Wiley & Sons, Inc.

Next, $\cos B$ is adjacent over hypotenuse. The side opposite angle A is the same side adjacent to angle B, making the answer 3 over 5.

347. **D. 37**

You don't actually have to solve for y. Just figure out what $3y$ is, and then double that and add 3:

$$\begin{aligned} 3y - 2 &= 15 \\ 3y &= 17 \\ 6y &= 34 \\ 6y + 3 &= 37 \end{aligned}$$

348. **C. 4π**

Plug in π for $2x$ and simplify the expression:

$$\frac{(4x)^2}{\pi} = \frac{(2\pi)^2}{\pi} = \frac{4\pi^2}{\pi} = 4\pi$$

349. **C. −4**

Factor out 3*y* and replace it with 2*i*:

$$\begin{aligned} 9y^2 &= (3y)(3y) \\ &= (2i)(2i) \\ &= 4i^2 \\ &= 4(-1) \\ &= -4 \end{aligned}$$

350. **B. (2, 1)**

Subtract the first equation from the second equation:

$$\begin{array}{r} 2x + y = 5 \\ -(x + y = 3) \\ \hline x \quad\quad = 2 \end{array}$$

Plug 2 in for *x* in the first equation, and $y = 1$.

351. **C. (3, 5) and (−3, 5)**

Plug in 5 for *y*:

$$\begin{aligned} x^2 - 5 &= 4 \\ x^2 &= 9 \\ x &= 3, -3 \end{aligned}$$

352. **A. $2x^2 + 3y^3$**

Factor the given expression into two identical expressions:

$$\begin{aligned} &\sqrt{4x^4 + 12x^2y^3 + 9y^6} \\ &= \sqrt{(2x^2 + 3y^3)(2x^2 + 3y^3)} \\ &= 2x^2 + 3y^3 \end{aligned}$$

ANSWERS 301–400

353. **B.** $x^9\left(x^6-1\right)$

First FOIL the binomials and distribute the x^3:

$$\begin{aligned} &x^3\left(x^6-x^3\right)\left(x^6+x^3\right)\\ &=x^3\left(x^{12}+x^9-x^9-x^6\right)\\ &=x^3\left(x^{12}-x^6\right)\\ &=x^{15}-x^9 \end{aligned}$$

Next, factor out x^9:

$$x^9\left(x^6-1\right)$$

354. **B.** 3

Simplify and solve for y:

$$\begin{aligned} \sqrt{3y^3+19}-5&=5\\ \sqrt{3y^3+19}&=10\\ 3y^3+19&=100\\ 3y^3&=81\\ y^3&=27\\ y&=3 \end{aligned}$$

355. **D.** 4, 9

Set the equation equal to 0 and factor it like a quadratic:

$$\begin{aligned} x&=5\sqrt{x}-6\\ x-5\sqrt{x}+6&=0\\ \left(\sqrt{x}-2\right)\left(\sqrt{x}-3\right)&=0\\ \sqrt{x}&=2,3\\ x&=4,9 \end{aligned}$$

356. **A.** $\frac{\sqrt{3}}{2}$

If one of the angles is 30°, the other angle is 60°, making this a 30-60-90 triangle, with a side ratio of $1:\sqrt{3}:2$. The 2 is the hypotenuse, making the other two sides 1 and $\sqrt{3}$. These numbers are also the base and height, so plug them into the formula for the area of a triangle:

$$A=\frac{1}{2}bh=\frac{1}{2}(1)\sqrt{3}=\frac{\sqrt{3}}{2}$$

357. **C. 4**

Start with the fraction and subtract the exponents, just as you'd do to divide any other terms with like bases:

$$\frac{2^x}{2^y} = 2^{x-y}$$

You know that 16 equals 2^4, so set 2^4 equal to the 2 with the subtracted exponents:

$$2^{x-y} = 2^4$$

Therefore $x - y = 4$.

358. **B. 9**

Simplify by distributing the x^5:

$$x^5\left(x^2 - 1\right) = 2$$
$$x^7 - x^5 = 2$$

In the fraction, subtract the exponents just as you'd do to divide any other terms with like bases:

$$\frac{3^{x^7}}{3^{x^5}} = 3^{x^7 - x^5}$$

Substitute 2 for $x^7 - x^5$:

$$3^{x^7 - x^5} = 3^2 = 9$$

359. **C. –3**

Simplify the exponential expression by multiplying the exponents, just as you'd do for any other base with an exponent of an exponent:

$$\left(2^{a+b}\right)^{a-b} = 16$$
$$2^{(a+b)(a-b)} = 16$$
$$2^{a^2-b^2} = 16$$

You know that 16 equals 2^4, so set 2^4 equal to the 2 with the subtracted exponents:

$$2^{a^2-b^2} = 2^4$$

ANSWERS 301–400

Therefore, $a^2 - b^2 = 4$. You know that $b^2 = 5$, so plug in the value of b^2:

$$\begin{aligned} a^2 - b^2 &= 4 \\ a^2 - 5 &= 4 \\ a^2 &= 9 \\ a &= 3, -3 \end{aligned}$$

You also know that $a < 0$, so a has to be -3.

---

360. D. 8.5

When the prices per bag of both fruit are the same, the equations have the same value. Set them equal to each other and solve for x:

$$\begin{aligned} 2.5 + 1.5x &= 1.5 + 1.75x \\ 1 + 1.5x &= 1.75x \\ 1 &= 0.25x \\ x &= 4 \end{aligned}$$

Plug this value of x back into the apples equation to solve for a:

$$\begin{aligned} a &= 2.5 + 1.5x \\ &= 2.5 + 1.5(4) \\ &= 2.5 + 6 \\ &= 8.5 \end{aligned}$$

---

361. C. 36

When the prices per pallet of both woods are the same, the equations have the same value. Set them equal to each other and solve for $5x$:

$$\begin{aligned} 16 + 25x &= 24 + 15x \\ 25x &= 8 + 15x \\ 10x &= 8 \\ 5x &= 4 \end{aligned}$$

If $5x = 4$, then $15x = 12$. Plug 12 in for $15x$ in the cedar equation and solve for c:

$$\begin{aligned} c &= 24 + 15x \\ &= 24 + 12 \\ &= 36 \end{aligned}$$

362. B. 5

Factor the quadratic with $(x-4)$ as one of the factors:

$$x^2 + x - 4b$$
$$= (x-4)(x+b)$$

Now FOIL it out:

$$x^2 + bx - 4x - 4b$$

The middle value of the given quadratic is x, so

$$\begin{aligned} bx - 4x &= x \\ bx &= 5x \\ b &= 5 \end{aligned}$$

363. A. 3

You don't need separate values of x or y, so don't bother substituting. Simply add the equations together and divide by 3:

$$\begin{aligned} 2x + \ \ y &= 4 \\ +(x + 2y &= 5) \\ \hline 3x + 3y &= 9 \\ x + \ \ y &= 3 \end{aligned}$$

364. B. $h = \frac{2A}{b}$

Set up the equation and solve for h:

$$\begin{aligned} A &= \frac{bh}{2} \\ 2A &= bh \\ \frac{2A}{b} &= h \end{aligned}$$

365. C. $h = \left(\frac{2}{b_1 + b_2}\right)T$

Set up the equation and solve for h:

$$T = \left(\frac{b_1 + b_2}{2}\right)h$$

$$\left(\frac{2}{b_1 + b_2}\right)T = h$$

ANSWERS 301–400

366. A. 3

Start by factoring a^2-b^2:

$$a^2-b^2=(a-b)(a+b)$$

Now plug in the values that the question gives you:

$$\begin{aligned}a^2-b^2&=(a-b)(a+b)\\15&=(a+b)(5)\\3&=(a+b)\end{aligned}$$

367. A. 1

Subtract the equations:

$$\begin{array}{r}\frac{1}{3}x-\frac{1}{5}y=5\\-\left(\frac{1}{5}x-\frac{1}{3}y=3\right)\\\hline\end{array}$$

Do this by giving them a common denominator:

$$\begin{array}{r}\frac{5}{15}x-\frac{3}{15}y=5\\-\left(\frac{3}{15}x-\frac{5}{15}y=3\right)\\\hline\frac{2}{15}x+\frac{2}{15}y=2\end{array}$$

Now divide everything by 2 to match the question:

$$\frac{1}{15}x+\frac{1}{15}y=1$$

368. B. 10

If Murray bought the same number of apples and pears, he spent $1.25 on one pair of apples and pears (because $0.50 + $0.75 = $1.25). Divide the total amount he spent by this:

$$\$12.50\div1.25=10$$

Murray bought 10 apples and 10 pears.

369. C. $3+\frac{\sqrt{3}}{2}$

The left-hand side of the trapezoid is a 30-60-90 triangle, with a side ratio of $1:\sqrt{3}:2$, where 1 is the short leg, $\sqrt{3}$ is the long leg, and 2 is the hypotenuse. This means that the height of the trapezoid is 1 and the bottom base is $2+\sqrt{3}$. Plug these values into the formula for the area of the trapezoid and simplify:

$$\begin{aligned} A &= \left(\frac{b_1+b_2}{2}\right)h \\ &= \left(\frac{3+\left(3+\sqrt{3}\right)}{2}\right)(1) \\ &= \left(\frac{6+\sqrt{3}}{2}\right) \\ &= 3+\frac{\sqrt{3}}{2} \end{aligned}$$

370. **C. 4**

The dashed line divides the square into two 45-45-90 triangles, each of which has a side-length ratio of $1:1:\sqrt{2}$, where 1 is the leg and $\sqrt{2}$ is the hypotenuse. Here, if the diagonal of the square (and the hypotenuse of the triangle) is $2\sqrt{2}$, the side length is 2, making the area of the square 4.

371. **D. 5**

The volume of a cube is $V=e^3$, where *e* is the edge length. Plug the length of the edge into the equation for your answer:

$$\begin{aligned} V &= e^3 \\ &= \left(\sqrt[3]{5}\right)^3 \\ &= 5 \end{aligned}$$

372. **A. 24,000**

Plug 12 in for *d* and simplify the equation:

$$\begin{aligned} f(12) &= 2{,}000+\left(2^{\frac{12}{3}}+\frac{12}{2}\right)1{,}000 \\ &= 2{,}000+\left(2^4+6\right)1{,}000 \\ &= 2{,}000+(16+6)1{,}000 \\ &= 2{,}000+(22)1{,}000 \\ &= 2{,}000+22{,}000 \\ &= 24{,}000 \end{aligned}$$

ANSWERS 301–400

373. **C.** $\frac{18+i}{25}$

Simplify the denominator by multiplying top and bottom by the denominator's conjugate, $4+3i$:

$$\frac{(3-2i)(4+3i)}{(4-3i)(4+3i)}$$
$$=\frac{12+9i-8i-6(i^2)}{16-9(i^2)}$$
$$=\frac{12+9i-8i-6(-1)}{16-9(-1)}$$
$$=\frac{12+9i-8i+6}{16+9}$$
$$=\frac{18+i}{25}$$

374. **C.** $y=2x^2+2$

The x^2 ensures that whichever value is used for x, $2x^2$ is always positive, because any number squared becomes positive. The lowest possible value for $2x^2$ occurs when $x=0$, in which case $2x^2=0$ and $2x^2+2=2$.

375. **A.** $y=x+3$

Start with the equation $y=mx+b$. The b is the y-intercept, 3, and the m is the slope, or rise over run; here, the line rises 1 $(4-3=1)$ and runs 1 $(1-0=1)$ for 1 over 1, which equals 1. Plug these values into the equation for a line:

$$y=mx+b$$
$$y=(1)x+(3)$$
$$y=x+3$$

376. **B.** $(1,3)$

Start by subtracting one equation from the other to get the value of x:

$$\begin{aligned} y &= 2x+1 \\ -(y &= x+2) \\ \hline 0 &= x-1 \\ x &= 1 \end{aligned}$$

Plug this value of x into one of the equations to get the value of y:

$$y = x + 2$$
$$y = (1) + 2$$
$$y = 3$$

377. C. 6

The area of a parallelogram comes from the base times the height. The height is the perpendicular distance between the top and the bottom, not the length of the slanted side.

The base is 3. To find the height, look at the 45° angle. This tells you that the left-hand side of the parallelogram is a 45-45-90 triangle, which has a side-length ratio of $1:1:\sqrt{2}$, where 1 is the leg and $\sqrt{2}$ is the hypotenuse.

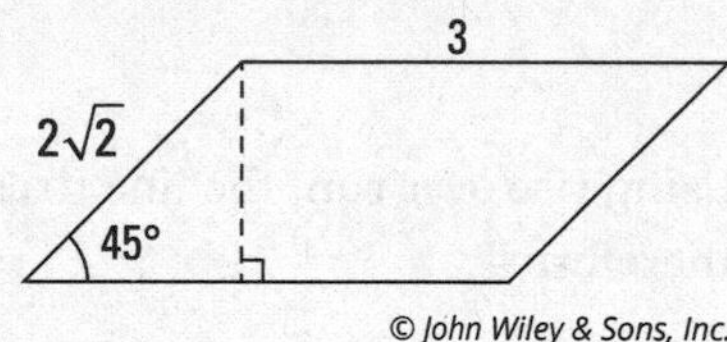

© John Wiley & Sons, Inc.

If the hypotenuse of the triangle is $2\sqrt{2}$, each side of the triangle is 2, making the height of the parallelogram 2 and the area 6:

$$A = bh = 3(2) = 6$$

378. A. 2

Factor the $a^2 - b^2$ into $(a+b)(a-b)$. Because $a + b = 1$,

$$a^2 - b^2 = (a+b)(a-b)$$
$$a^2 - b^2 = (1)(a-b)$$
$$a^2 - b^2 = (a-b)$$

Plug this value into the given equation:

$$3^{a^2-b^2} = 9$$
$$3^{(a-b)} = 9$$

And turn the 9 into 3^2 so the bases match:

$$3^{(a-b)} = 3^2$$
$$(a-b) = 2$$

ANSWERS 301–400

379. B. $(-3, 3)$

Start by isolating the *y*. Multiply the first equation by 5 and then subtract the second equation:

$$\begin{array}{r} 5x+10y=15 \\ -(5x+\ 9y=12) \\ \hline y=\ 3 \end{array}$$

Now plug 3 in for *y* in the first equation:

$$\begin{aligned} x+2(3)&=3 \\ x+6&=3 \\ x&=-3 \end{aligned}$$

380. A. $\frac{4}{3}$

Using rise over run, the line rises $4\ (7-3)$ and runs $3\ (5-2)$. The slope is therefore $\frac{4}{3}$.

381. D. $(-1, -1)$

The line rises $4\ (7-3)$ and runs $3\ (5-2)$. Take this slope in the other direction from the point $(2, 3)$: The line goes left 3 and down 4, bringing you to $(-1, -1)$.

382. C. $1-\frac{a^2}{4}$

Simplify the fraction by adding the two fractions on the bottom. Start by giving them a common denominator:

$$\begin{aligned} \frac{1}{\frac{1}{a+2}-\frac{1}{a-2}} &= \frac{1}{\frac{1(a-2)}{(a+2)(a-2)}-\frac{1(a+2)}{(a-2)(a+2)}} \\ &= \frac{1}{\frac{a-2}{a^2-4}-\frac{a+2}{a^2-4}} \\ &= \frac{1}{\frac{-4}{a^2-4}} \end{aligned}$$

Then continue to simplify:

$$\frac{a^2-4}{-4}=\frac{a^2}{-4}+\frac{-4}{-4}=1-\frac{a^2}{4}$$

383. **A. 2**

If $BD = 3$, then $AD = 4$, because the triangle is a 3-4-5 triangle. If $\overline{AB}$ is parallel to $\overline{CE}$, the small triangle is similar to the large triangle. Shapes that are *similar* have the same side-length ratio but are different sizes. This means that the length of $\overline{DE}$ is half the length of $\overline{AD}$, or 2.

384. **D. 90°**

If l_1 is parallel to l_2, all the acute angles are equivalent and all the obtuse angles are equivalent. This makes the angles marked $a+b$ and $a-b$ supplementary, meaning they total 180°. Set up the equation and solve for *a*:

$$\begin{aligned}(a+b)+(a-b)&=180^\circ\\ a+b+a-b&=180^\circ\\ 2a&=180^\circ\\ a&=90^\circ\end{aligned}$$

385. **B.** $A=\frac{Pi(1+i)^n}{(1+i)^n-1}$

To isolate *A* and transfer the fraction to *P*, simply multiply the fraction (and the other side of the equation) by its reciprocal, $\left[\frac{i(1+i)^n}{(1+i)^n-1}\right]$. Doing so cancels the fraction from the *A* and attaches it to the *P*.

386. **D.** $G=P\frac{i^2}{1-(1+ni)(1+i)^{-n}}$

To isolate *G* and transfer the fraction to *P*, simply multiply the fraction by its reciprocal: $\frac{i^2}{1-(1+ni)(1+i)^{-n}}$. It cancels from the *G* and attaches to the *P*.

387. **B. 4**

For the system to have infinite solutions, both variables (*x* and *y*) have to cancel out when you subtract one equation from the other. Multiply the first equation by 2 so that the *x* cancels, and you see what *b* has to be for *y* to cancel:

$$\begin{aligned}x+2y&=3\\ 2x+by&=6\end{aligned}$$

$$\begin{aligned}2x+4y&=6\\ 2x+by&=6\end{aligned}$$

For *y* to cancel, you need $b = 4$.

ANSWERS 301–400

388. A. 2

Simplify the equation and isolate $y-4$:

$$5y=30$$
$$y=6$$
$$y-4=2$$

389. C. 60°

Draw a line from the labeled point to the x-axis, making a right triangle. If two of the sides are 1 and $\sqrt{3}$, the third side is 2, and this is a 30-60-90 triangle, with angles measuring 30°, 60°, and 90°. Angle θ, being the larger acute angle, is 60°.

ANSWERS 301–400

390. D. $\frac{\pi}{3}$

Draw a line from the labeled point to the x-axis, making a right triangle. If two of the sides are 1 and $\sqrt{3}$, the third side is 2, and this is a 30-60-90 triangle, with angles measuring 30°, 60°, and 90°. Angle θ, being the larger acute angle, is 60°. In radians, 180° = π, making 60° = $\frac{\pi}{3}$.

391. C. 9

The formula for a circle is $(x-h)^2+(y-k)^2=r^2$, where r is the radius of the circle. In the given equation, $x^2=r^2$ and the radius is 9, so $x=9$.

392. A. 0.5

Draw a line from the labeled point to the x-axis, making a right triangle. If two of the sides are 1 and $\sqrt{3}$, the third side is 2, and this is a 30-60-90 triangle, with angles measuring 30°, 60°, and 90°. The smaller acute angle is 30°, and angle θ, which is supplementary, is 150°.

Supplementary angles have the same sine, so you can measure the sine of the 30° angle. Using SOH CAH TOA, *sine* is opposite over hypotenuse. From the 30° angle, the side opposite is 1 and the hypotenuse is 2, so the answer is 0.5.

393. D. 2

Draw a line from the labeled point to the x-axis, making a right triangle. If two of the sides are 1 and $\sqrt{3}$, the third side is 2, and this is a 30-60-90 triangle, with angles measuring 30°, 60°, and 90°. The smaller acute angle is 30°, and angle θ, which is supplementary, is 150°.

Cosecant is the reciprocal of sine, so start by finding the sine. Supplementary angles have the same sine, so you can measure the sine of the 30° angle. Using SOH CAH TOA, *sine* is opposite over hypotenuse. From the 30° angle, the side opposite is 1 and the hypotenuse is 2, for a sine of $\frac{1}{2}$. Take the reciprocal for a cosecant of 2.

394. **D. –13**

If $(x+7)^2$ equals 36, then $(x+7)$ equals either 6 or –6. Set this up as two separate equations:

$$x+7=6 \quad \text{or} \quad x+7=-6$$
$$x=-1 \qquad\qquad x=-13$$

Because $x<-5$, x equals –13.

395. **B. $23-2i$**

Start by FOILing the expression:

$$(5-4i)(3+2i)$$
$$=15+10i-12i-8i^2$$

You know that $i^2=-1$, so plug that in:

$$15+10i-12i-8(-1)$$

And simplify the expression:

$$15+10i-12i+8$$
$$=23-2i$$

396. **B. $56d+8h$**

Joe earned d dollars for 40 hours and $2d+h$ dollars for 8 hours. Multiply these values and add them together:

$$40(d)+8(2d+h)$$
$$=40d+16d+8h$$
$$=56d+8h$$

397. **C. The number of papers Alex has delivered so far**

If Alex delivers p papers to each street and d represents the streets he has delivered to, pd represents the number of papers already delivered.

398. **B.** $\boldsymbol{n = p(c+s) - dp}$

If the number of streets increases by c, the new number of streets is $(c+s)$. The rest of the equation remains unchanged.

399. **A.** $\boldsymbol{\sqrt[3]{5^2}}$

When an exponent appears as a fraction, the numerator of the fraction remains the exponent, and the denominator becomes the radical. In the expression $5^{\frac{2}{3}}$, the numerator 2 remains as the exponent, and the denominator 3 becomes the radical.

400. **D.** $\boldsymbol{18ab^2}$

Distribute the 3 in the first expression and the −9 in the second expression:

$$\left(-9a^2b + 9b^2 - 9ab^2\right) + \left(9a^2b - 9b^2 + 27ab^2\right)$$

Drop the brackets:

$$-9a^2b + 9b^2 - 9ab^2 + 9a^2b - 9b^2 + 27ab^2.$$

And cancel out the like terms to get $18ab^2$.

401. **C.** $\boldsymbol{10\sqrt{5}}$

Factor the $\sqrt{20}$ into $\sqrt{4} \times \sqrt{5}$ and convert the $\sqrt{4}$ into 2:

$$\begin{aligned} 5\sqrt{20} &= 5 \times \sqrt{20} \\ &= 5 \times \sqrt{4} \times \sqrt{5} \\ &= 5 \times 2 \times \sqrt{5} \\ &= 10 \times \sqrt{5} \\ &= 10\sqrt{5} \end{aligned}$$

402. **B.** $\boldsymbol{P = FV\left(\dfrac{\frac{r}{m}}{\left(1+\frac{r}{m}\right)^{m \cdot t} - 1}\right)}$

To solve for P, multiply both sides of the equation by the reciprocal of the fraction. Multiplying both sides by $\left(\dfrac{\frac{r}{m}}{\left(1+\frac{r}{m}\right)^{m \cdot t} - 1}\right)$ cancels the fraction from the P side and ties it to the FV side.

403. **C.** $FV = P\left(\frac{\left(1+\frac{r+0.03}{m}\right)^{m\cdot t}-1}{\frac{r+0.03}{m}}\right)$

Here, r represents the interest rate. If this were to increase by 3 percentage points, the new rate would be $r+0.03$, because $3\% = 0.03$.

404. **C.** $y = -\frac{1}{m}x + b$

The slope of any line is the negative reciprocal of the slope of its perpendicular line. The negative reciprocal of m is $-\frac{1}{m}$. Replace m with $-\frac{1}{m}$ in the linear equation to get $y = -\frac{1}{m}x + b$.

405. **B.** −10, 10

The parabola crosses the x-axis where the values for x make y equal to 0. To find these x-values, set y equal to 0 and find the roots of the quadratic:

$$0 = x^2 - 100$$
$$0 = (x+10)(x-10)$$
$$x = -10, 10$$

406. **B.** −3, 6

The parabola crosses the x-axis where the values for x make y equal to 0. To find these x-values, set y equal to 0, distribute the −3, and find the roots of the quadratic:

$$y = x^2 - 3(x+6)$$
$$0 = x^2 - 3x - 18$$
$$0 = (x+3)(x-6)$$
$$x = -3, 6$$

407. **B.** −3, 3

The parabola crosses $y = 5$ where the values for x make y equal to 18. To find these x-values, set y equal to 18 and find the roots of the quadratic:

$$18 = x^2 + 9$$
$$0 = x^2 - 9$$
$$0 = (x+3)(x-3)$$
$$x = -3, 3$$

ANSWERS 401–500

408. A. 20

If $y = 50$, then $2y = 100$, making $b = 80$ and $x = 100$. You want $x - b$, which is $100 - 80 = 20$.

409. D. (3, –9)

To find the coordinates of the vertex of a parabola, factor the equation to find the roots:

$$y = x^2 - 6x$$
$$y = x(x - 6)$$

This tells you that the parabola crosses the x-axis at $(0, 0)$ and $(6, 0)$. Thus, the x-coordinate of the vertex is halfway between 0 and 6, which is 3. To find the y-coordinate of the vertex, substitute 3 for x in the equation:

$$y = x^2 - 6x$$
$$y = (3)^2 - 6(3)$$
$$y = 9 - 18$$
$$y = -9$$

ANSWERS 401–500

410. D. –2, 3

Cross-multiply, set the equation equal to 0, and factor it out:

$$\frac{1}{x^2 - x} = \frac{1}{6}$$
$$x^2 - x = 6$$
$$x^2 - x - 6 = 0$$
$$(x + 2)(x - 3) = 0$$
$$x = -2, 3$$

411. C. $x = -2 \pm i\sqrt{30}$

First, set the equation equal to 0:

$$0.5x^2 + 2x + 17 = 0$$

Next, use the quadratic formula, where $a = 0.5$, $b = 2$, and $c = 17$:

$$\begin{aligned} x &= \frac{-b \pm \sqrt{b^2 - 4ac}}{2a} \\ &= \frac{-2 \pm \sqrt{2^2 - 4(0.5)(17)}}{2(0.5)} \\ &= \frac{-2 \pm \sqrt{4 - 34}}{1} \\ &= -2 \pm \sqrt{-30} \\ &= -2 \pm \left(\sqrt{-1}\right)\left(\sqrt{30}\right) \\ &= -2 \pm i\sqrt{30} \end{aligned}$$

412. **D. −2, −1**

Distribute the x^2 and set the equation equal to 0:

$$\begin{aligned} x^2\left(x^2 - 5\right) &= -2^2 \\ x^4 - 5x^2 &= -2^2 \\ x^4 - 5x^2 &= -4 \\ x^4 - 5x^2 + 4 &= 0 \end{aligned}$$

Next, factor the equation to find the roots:

$$\begin{aligned} x^4 - 5x^2 + 4 &= 0 \\ \left(x^2 - 1\right)\left(x^2 - 4\right) &= 0 \\ x^2 &= 1, 4 \\ x &= 1, -1, 2, -2 \end{aligned}$$

Because $x < 0$, x can only be −2 or −1.

413. **A. −2, 0, −5**

Distribute the x^2, set the equation equal to 0, and factor out an x:

$$\begin{aligned} x^2(x - 3) &= 10x \\ x^3 - 3x^2 &= 10x \\ x^3 - 3x^2 - 10x &= 0 \\ x\left(x^2 - 3x - 10\right) &= 0 \end{aligned}$$

Next, factor the expression to find the roots:

$$\begin{aligned} x\left(x^2 - 3x - 10\right) &= 0 \\ x(x - 5)(x + 2) &= 0 \\ x &= 0, 5, -2 \end{aligned}$$

For the equation to equal 0, x has to equal −2, 0, or 5.

ANSWERS 401–500

414. A. I only: 44°

An isosceles triangle has two identical angles and one unique angle. If one angle measures 92°, that has to be the unique angle, because if two angles measured 92°, the total would be greater than 180°. Because 92° is the unique angle, the other two angles evenly divide the remaining 88° for an answer of 44°.

415. A. $\frac{5}{3}$

Using SOH CAH TOA, $\sin A$ is opposite over hypotenuse; these sides are in the ratio of 3 to 5, respectively. Cosecant is the inverse of sine, so $\frac{3}{5}$ becomes $\frac{5}{3}$.

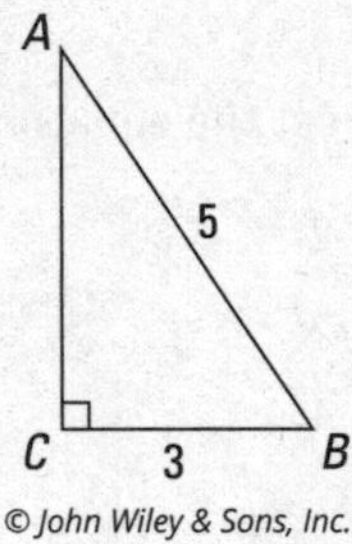

© John Wiley & Sons, Inc.

Next, $\cos B$ is adjacent over hypotenuse, which is $\frac{3}{5}$. Secant is the inverse of cosine, so $\sec B = \frac{5}{3}$.

416. C. $i(a-b)$

Start by factoring out $a^2 - b^2$ into $(a+b)(a-b)$. Because $a+b=i$, plug that in:

$$\begin{aligned}&(a+b)(a-b)\\&= i(a-b)\end{aligned}$$

417. C. $(-1, 9)$ and $(-5, 9)$

Plug in 9 for *y*:

$$\begin{aligned}9 &= (x+3)^2 + 5\\4 &= (x+3)^2\\2, -2 &= x+3\\-1, -5 &= x\end{aligned}$$

ANSWERS 401–500

418. **C.** $\sqrt{a^2+b^2}\sqrt{a+b}\sqrt{a-b}$

With a perfect square minus a perfect square, factor out the conjugates:

$$\sqrt{a^4-b^4}$$
$$=\sqrt{a^2+b^2}\sqrt{a^2-b^2}$$
$$=\sqrt{a^2+b^2}\sqrt{a+b}\sqrt{a-b}$$

419. **A.** 0

Plug in 1 for y in the expression:

$$(1)\left((1)^6-(1)^3\right)\left((1)^6+(1)^3\right)$$
$$=1(1-1)(1+1)$$
$$=1(0)(2)$$
$$=0$$

420. **C.** 1, 8

Factor the equation like any quadratic:

$$\left(\sqrt[3]{x}\right)^2-3\sqrt[3]{x}+2=0$$
$$\left(\sqrt[3]{x}-1\right)\left(\sqrt[3]{x}-2\right)=0$$
$$\sqrt[3]{x}=1,2$$
$$x=1,8$$

421. **A.** $e=\sqrt{\frac{C}{6}}$

Set up the equation and solve for e:

$$C=6e^2$$
$$\frac{C}{6}=e^2$$
$$\sqrt{\frac{C}{6}}=e$$

ANSWERS 401–500

422. B. $r = \sqrt{\frac{V}{\pi h}}$

Set up the equation and solve for *r*:

$$V = \pi r^2 h$$
$$\frac{V}{\pi h} = r^2$$
$$\sqrt{\frac{V}{\pi h}} = r$$

423. C. 12

The left-hand side of the trapezoid is a 45-45-90 triangle, with a side ratio of $1:1:\sqrt{2}$, where 1 is each short side and $\sqrt{2}$ is the hypotenuse. This means that the height of the trapezoid is 2 and the bottom base is 7. Plug these into the formula for the area of the trapezoid and simplify:

$$A = \left(\frac{b_1 + b_2}{2}\right)h$$
$$= \left(\frac{5+7}{2}\right)2$$
$$= \left(\frac{12}{2}\right)2$$
$$= 12$$

424. B. $\frac{16}{9}$

Because *AB* is half of *AE*, set the two sides of the triangle as $AE = 2AB$. Now use the Pythagorean Theorem, but substitute 2*AB* for *AE*:

$$(AB)^2 + (AE)^2 = 2^2$$
$$(AB)^2 + 2(AB^2) = 2^2$$
$$3(AB)^2 = 2^2$$
$$3(AB)^2 = 4$$
$$(AB)^2 = \frac{4}{3}$$
$$AB = \sqrt{\frac{4}{3}}$$
$$AB = \frac{2}{\sqrt{3}}$$

If $AB = \frac{2}{\sqrt{3}}$ and $AE = 2AB$, then the side of the square, *AE*, equals $\frac{4}{\sqrt{3}}$. Square this for an area of $\frac{16}{9}$

425. C. 18π

The volume of a cylinder is $V = \pi r^2 h$. Plug the values from the question into the equation:

$$\begin{aligned} V &= \pi r^2 h \\ &= \pi\left(\sqrt{3}\right)^2 6 \\ &= \pi(3)6 \\ &= 18\pi \end{aligned}$$

426. C. $-i$

Simplify the denominator by multiplying top and bottom by the denominator's conjugate:

$$\begin{aligned} &\frac{1-i(1-i)}{1+i(1-i)} \\ &= \frac{1-2i+\left(i^2\right)}{1-\left(i^2\right)} \\ &= \frac{1-2i+(-1)}{1-(-1)} \\ &= \frac{1-2i-1}{1+1} \\ &= \frac{-2i}{2} \\ &= -i \end{aligned}$$

427. C. $y = -x^2 - 3$

The x^2 ensures that whichever value is used for x, x^2 is always positive, meaning $-x^2$ is always negative. The lowest possible value for $-x^2$ occurs when $x = 0$, in which case $-x^2 = 0$ and $-x^2 - 3 = -3$.

Another method is to plug in 2, 0, and −2 for x in each answer choice to see which always has a resulting y less than 3.

ANSWERS 401–500

428. A. $y = \frac{1}{2}x - 1$

Start with the equation $y = mx + b$. The m is the slope, which you find using rise over run. From −2 to 0, the line rises 2, and from −2 to 2, the line runs 4, for a slope of $\frac{2}{4}$, or $\frac{1}{2}$.

Use the slope and the coordinates of one of the points to find the y-intercept, which is b. From the coordinates $(-2, -2)$, travel up 1 (the rise) and over 2 (the run); the line crosses the y-axis at $(0, -1)$, for a b value of 1. Plug these into the equation:

$$\begin{aligned} y &= mx + b \\ &= \frac{1}{2}x - 1 \end{aligned}$$

429. A. 45

If l_1 is parallel to l_2, all the acute angles are equivalent and all the obtuse angles are equivalent. This makes the angles marked x and y supplementary, meaning they total 180. Set up the equation and solve for y:

$$\begin{aligned} x + y &= 180 \\ 3y + y &= 180 \\ 4y &= 180 \\ y &= 45 \end{aligned}$$

430. D. x^2

An exponent raised to an exponent equals the exponents multiplied. With this info, simplify the fraction:

$$\frac{\left(x^{\frac{1}{3}}\right)^{12}}{\left(x^{\sqrt{2}}\right)^{\sqrt{2}}} = \frac{x^{\frac{1}{3} \cdot 12}}{x^{\sqrt{2} \cdot \sqrt{2}}} = \frac{x^4}{x^2} = x^2$$

ANSWERS 401–500

431. **A. $(1, 1)$**

Start by isolating the *x*. Multiply the second equation by 2 and then subtract it from the first equation:

$$\begin{array}{r} 3x+2y=5 \\ -(2x+2y=4) \\ \hline x=1 \end{array}$$

Now plug 1 in for *x* in the original second equation:

$$\begin{aligned} x+y&=2 \\ (1)+y&=2 \\ y&=1 \end{aligned}$$

432. **A. 3**

Using rise over run, the line rises 3 (from −1 to 2) and runs 1 (from −1 to 0). The slope is therefore $\frac{3}{1}$, or 3.

433. **B. $(-2, -4)$**

The line rises 3 (from −1 to 2) and runs 1 (from −1 to 0). Take this in the other direction from the point $(-1, -1)$: The line goes left 1 and down 3.

434. **B. $\frac{y-b}{m}$**

Start with the equation and solve for *x*:

$$\begin{aligned} y&=mx+b \\ y-b&=mx \\ x&=\frac{y-b}{m} \end{aligned}$$

435. **C. −10, 10**

The parabola crosses the *x*-axis where the values for *x* make *y* equal to 0. To find these *x*-values, set *y* equal to 0 and find the roots of the quadratic:

$$\begin{aligned} 0&=x^2-100 \\ 0&=(x+10)(x-10) \\ x&=-10, 10 \end{aligned}$$

ANSWERS 401–500

436. A. −5, 3

The parabola crosses the x-axis where the values for x make y equal to 0. To find these x-values, set y equal to 0, distribute the x, and find the roots of the quadratic:

$$\begin{aligned} y &= x(x+2)-15 \\ 0 &= x^2+2x-15 \\ 0 &= (x+5)(x-3) \\ x &= -5, 3 \end{aligned}$$

437. B. −3, 3

The parabola crosses $y = 9$ where the values for x make y equal to 9. To find these x-values, set y equal to 9 and find the roots of the quadratic:

$$\begin{aligned} 9 &= x^2 \\ 0 &= x^2-9 \\ 0 &= (x+3)(x-3) \\ x &= -3, 3 \end{aligned}$$

ANSWERS 401–500

438. B. 3

First FOIL the binomials:

$$\begin{aligned} (x^2-y^3)(x^2+y^3) &= 5 \\ x^4-y^6 &= 5 \end{aligned}$$

Next, plug in 4 for y^6:

$$\begin{aligned} x^4-y^6 &= 5 \\ x^4-4 &= 5 \\ x^4 &= 9 \\ x^2 &= 3 \end{aligned}$$

You know that x^2 is positive (and not equal to −3) because any number squared is positive.

439. A. 2

Simplify:

$$\begin{aligned} 2\sqrt{x^4} + 4 &= 12 \\ 2\sqrt{x^4} &= 8 \\ \sqrt{x^4} &= 4 \\ x^4 &= 16 \\ x &= 2 \end{aligned}$$

440. C. 16, 36

Set the equation equal to 0 and factor it like a quadratic:

$$\begin{aligned} x &= 10\sqrt{x} - 24 \\ x - 10\sqrt{x} + 24 &= 0 \\ \left(\sqrt{x} - 4\right)\left(\sqrt{x} - 6\right) &= 0 \\ \sqrt{x} &= 4, 6 \\ x &= 16, 36 \end{aligned}$$

ANSWERS 401–500

441. B. 3

The volume of a cylinder is $V = \pi r^2 h$. Plug the values from the question into the equation:

$$\begin{aligned} V &= \pi r^2 h \\ &= \pi\left(\frac{\sqrt{3}}{2\pi}\right)^2 4\pi \\ &= \pi\left(\frac{\sqrt{3}}{2\pi}\right)\left(\frac{\sqrt{3}}{2\pi}\right) 4\pi \\ &= \pi\frac{3}{4\pi^2}4\pi \\ &= 3 \end{aligned}$$

442. **D.** i

Simplify the denominator by multiplying the top and the bottom by the denominator's conjugate, $2+2i$:

$$\frac{(2+2i)(2+2i)}{(2-2i)(2+2i)}$$
$$=\frac{4+8i+4i^2}{4-4i^2}$$
$$=\frac{4+8i+4(-1)}{4-4(-1)}$$
$$=\frac{4+8i-4}{4+4}$$
$$=\frac{8i}{8}$$
$$=i$$

443. **C.** 18

Solve for x and then multiply by 3 to get $3x$:

$$\frac{8x}{3}+1=17$$
$$\frac{8x}{3}=16$$
$$8x=48$$
$$x=6$$
$$3x=18$$

444. **A.** 2

Simplify and solve for n:

$$\sqrt[3]{n^3-19}+7=10$$
$$\sqrt[3]{n^3+19}=3$$
$$n^3+19=27$$
$$n^3=8$$
$$n=2$$

ANSWERS 401–500

445. A. 1

First make the bases match by converting the 2^2 into 4, like this:

$$2^{2a^2} = \left(2^2\right)^{a^2} = 4^{a^2}$$

Next, simplify the fraction by subtracting the exponents, as you would to divide any other terms with like bases:

$$\frac{4^{a^2}}{4^{b^2}} = 4^{a^2-b^2}$$

Because the given fraction equals 4, $4^{a^2-b^2} = 4^1$, so $a^2 - b^2 = 1$.

Now factor the $a^2 - b^2$ and plug in 2 for $a+b$:

$$\begin{aligned} a^2 - b^2 &= 1 \\ (a+b)(a-b) &= 1 \\ 2(a-b) &= 1 \end{aligned}$$

446. B. 17

Simplify the expression by distributing the x^3:

$$\begin{aligned} x^3\left(x^2-1\right) &= 1 \\ x^5 - x^3 &= 1 \end{aligned}$$

In the fraction, subtract the exponents just as you would to divide any other terms with like bases:

$$\frac{17^{x^5}}{17^{x^3}} = 17^{x^5-x^3}$$

Substitute 1 for $x^5 - x^3$:

$$17^{x^5-x^3} = 17^1 = 17$$

ANSWERS 401–500

447. C. 4

Simplify the exponential expression by multiplying the exponents as you would for any other base with an exponent of an exponent:

$$\left(2^4\right)^2 = 4^x$$
$$2^8 = 4^x$$

You know that 4 equals 2^2, so rewrite the 4 accordingly. This way, the bases match:

$$(4)^x = \left(2^2\right)^x = 2^{2x}$$

Therefore, $2^8 = 2^{2x}$, making $8 = 2x$ and $x = 4$.

448. A. 2

Subtract the equations and divide by 5:

$$\begin{array}{r} 8x + 3y = 25 \\ -(3x + 8y = 15) \\ \hline 5x - 5y = 10 \\ x - y = 2 \end{array}$$

ANSWERS 401–500

449. C. 4

Start by factoring $p^4 - q^4$:

$$p^4 - q^4 = \left(p^2 - q^2\right)\left(p^2 + q^2\right)$$

Now plug in the values that the question gives you:

$$p^4 - q^4 = \left(p^2 - q^2\right)\left(p^2 + q^2\right)$$
$$28 = 7\left(p^2 + q^2\right)$$
$$4 = p^2 + q^2$$

450. D. 181

Plug 24 in for *w* and simplify the equation:

$$\begin{aligned} f(w) &= 150+\left(5^{\frac{w}{12}}+\frac{w}{4}\right) \\ f(24) &= 150+\left(5^{\frac{24}{12}}+\frac{24}{4}\right) \\ &= 150+\left(5^2+6\right) \\ &= 150+(25+6) \\ &= 150+(31) \\ &= 181 \end{aligned}$$

451. C. 27

Remember that $x^2-y^2=(x+y)(x-y)$. Plug in the values of $x+y$ and $x-y$ to solve for x^2-y^2:

$$x^2-y^2=(18)\left(\frac{1}{6}\right)$$

$$x^2-y^2=3$$

Now plug 3 in for x^2-y^2:

$$3^{x^2-y^2}=3^3=27$$

452. D. 15

Substitute 6 for *n*, and the equation looks like this:

$$\frac{x+3}{3}=6$$

Multiply both sides by 3 to solve:

$$\begin{aligned} x+3 &= 18 \\ x &= 15 \end{aligned}$$

453. B. 3

Simplify the equation and solve for *x*:

$$\begin{aligned} (2x-9)^3 &= -27 \\ 2x-9 &= -3 \\ 2x &= 6 \\ x &= 3 \end{aligned}$$

ANSWERS 401–500

454. D. 25

First solve for xy. Start with $\frac{xy}{5} = 2$ and multiply both sides by 2, so $xy = 10$. Plug this value into the first equation:

$$\begin{aligned} z - xy &= 15 \\ z - 10 &= 15 \\ z &= 25 \end{aligned}$$

455. B. $11i - 2$

Start by FOILing the expression and distributing the i. Remember that $i^2 = -1$.

$$\begin{aligned} &i(4+3i)(2-i) \\ &= i(8 - 4i + 6i - 3i^2) \\ &= i(8 + 2i + 3) \\ &= i(11 + 2i) \\ &= 11i + 2i^2 \\ &= 11i - 2 \end{aligned}$$

456. D. –5

Starting with the given expression, distribute the –2 and then drop the parentheses:

$$\begin{aligned} &(3+2i) - 2(4+i) \\ &= (3+2i) - 8 - 2i \\ &= 3 + 2i - 8 - 2i \\ &= -5 \end{aligned}$$

457. C. $8t + 12f$

In each game, the Tigers scored $2t$ touchdowns and $3f$ field goals; multiply these values by 4, the number of games:

$$\begin{aligned} &4(2t + 3f) \\ &= 8t + 12f \end{aligned}$$

458. D. 5

You can't start by square-rooting $b^2 = 16$, because you don't know whether b is positive or negative. Instead, FOIL the binomials:

$$\left(a^2 - b\right)\left(a^2 + b\right) = 9$$
$$a^4 - b^2 = 9$$

Next, plug in 16 for b^2:

$$a^4 - b^2 = 9$$
$$a^4 - 16 = 9$$
$$a^4 = 25$$
$$a^2 = 5$$

You know that a^2 is positive (and not equal to −5) because any number squared is positive.

459. C. 4

Simplify and solve for x:

$$3\sqrt{x^3} + 6 = 30$$
$$3\sqrt{x^3} = 24$$
$$\sqrt{x^3} = 8$$
$$x^3 = 64$$
$$x = 4$$

460. A. $y = mx + 2b$

Lines are parallel when they have the same slope. Because m represents the slope, find a line where m is unchanged in terms of y. Each answer choice, except Choice (A), multiplies or divides m, including Choice (D), where the entire equation, including m, would have to be divided by 2 to isolate the y.

461. B. −2, 2

Cube-root both sides and simplify the equation:

$$\left(y^2 - 5\right)^3 = -1$$
$$y^2 - 5 = -1$$
$$y^2 = 4$$
$$y = 2, -2$$

462. C. −2, 8

Square-root both sides. Don't forget that the square root can also be negative:

$$\begin{aligned}(x-3)^2 &= 25\\ x-3 &= 5, -5\\ x &= 8, -2\end{aligned}$$

463. C. −2, −1

Distribute the x^3 and set the equation equal to 0:

$$\begin{aligned}x^3(x^3+9) &= (-2)^3\\ x^6+9x^3 &= (-2)^3\\ x^6+9x^3 &= -8\\ x^6+9x^3+8 &= 0\end{aligned}$$

Next, factor the equation to find the roots:

$$\begin{aligned}x^6+9x^3+8 &= 0\\ (x^3+1)(x^3+8) &= 0\\ x^3 &= -1, -8\\ x &= -1, -2\end{aligned}$$

464. C. 1, 3

Set the equation equal to 0 and factor out an x^2:

$$\begin{aligned}x^6-10x^4 &= -9x^2\\ x^6-10x^4+9x^2 &= 0\\ x^2(x^4-10x^2+9) &= 0\end{aligned}$$

Next, factor the expression to find the roots:

$$\begin{aligned}x^2(x^4-10x^2+9) &= 0\\ x^2(x^2-1)(x^2-9) &= 0\\ x &= 0, 1, -1, 3, -3\end{aligned}$$

For the equation to equal 0, x^2 would have to equal 0, 1, or 9. Because $x > 0$, x can only be 1 or 3.

ANSWERS 401–500

465. **A. 1.5**

Compare parts of the two sides of the equation, pairing up terms based on the exponents of *x*:

$$12x^2 = 8nx^2$$
$$9x = 6nx$$
$$15 = 2n + 12$$

Regardless of which portion of the equation you use, $n = 1.5$.

466. **A. x^2**

An exponent raised to an exponent equals the exponents multiplied. With this info, simplify the fraction:

$$\frac{\left(x^9\right)^{\frac{2}{3}}}{\left(x^{\sqrt{8}}\right)^{\sqrt{2}}} = \frac{x^{9\cdot\frac{2}{3}}}{x^{\sqrt{8}\cdot\sqrt{2}}} = \frac{x^{\frac{18}{3}}}{x^{\sqrt{16}}} = \frac{x^6}{x^4} = x^2$$

467. **B. (2, 2)**

Because $x = y$, plug in *x* for *y* and solve for *x*:

$$7x + 5x = 24$$
$$12x = 24$$
$$x = 2$$

This means $y = 2$.

468. **A. 3**

Using rise over run, the line rises 9 (from −2 to 7) and runs 3 (from −1 to 3). The slope is therefore $\frac{9}{3}$, or 3.

469. **C. (6, 22)**

The line rises 9 (from −2 to 7) and runs 3 (from −1 to 3), for a slope of 3. To reach a *y*-value of 22 from 7, it rises 15, which means it runs 5 (because $\frac{15}{5} = \frac{3}{1}$). A run of 5 from an *x*-value of 1 brings the new *x*-value to 6.

ANSWERS 401–500

470. C. −4, 4

The parabola crosses the x-axis where the values for x make y equal to 0. To find these x-values, set y equal to 0 and find the roots of the quadratic:

$$0 = -2x^2 + 32$$
$$0 = -x^2 + 16$$
$$0 = x^2 - 16$$
$$0 = (x+4)(x-4)$$
$$x = -4, 4$$

471. 4

Compare parts of the two sides of the equation, separating the terms based on the exponents of x:

$$8x^2 = 2hx^2$$
$$12x = 3hx$$
$$21 = 4h + 5$$

Regardless of which portion of the equation you use, $h = 4$.

472. 15

If one angle measures 75° and the triangle is a right triangle, then the second angle measures 90°, and the third, smallest angle measures 15°, because $75° + 90° + 15° = 180°$.

473. 4

You don't actually have to solve for x. Just figure out what 31.5x is, and then double that and add 6.

$$31.5x + 5 = 4$$
$$31.5x = -1$$
$$63x = -2$$
$$63x + 6 = 4$$

474. 4

Subtract the second equation from the first equation and then divide everything by 3:

$$\begin{array}{r} 8x + 9y = 27 \\ -(2x + 3y = 15) \\ \hline 6x + 6y = 12 \\ 2x + 2y = 4 \end{array}$$

ANSWERS 401–500

475. 2

Simplify the expression:

$$\begin{aligned}\sqrt{5z^3+60}+40&=50\\ \sqrt{5z^3+60}&=10\\ 5z^3+60&=100\\ 5z^3&=40\\ z^3&=8\\ z&=2\end{aligned}$$

476. 2

If one of the angles is 45°, the other angle is also 45°, making this an isosceles right triangle, where the base and height are the same. That's all you need in order to find the area:

$$A=\frac{1}{2}bh=\frac{1}{2}(2)(2)=2$$

477. 3

Start with the fraction and subtract the exponents, just as you would to divide any other terms with like bases:

$$\frac{3^{a^2}}{3^{b^2}}=3^{a^2-b^2}$$

You know that 27 equals 3^3, so set 3^3 equal to the 3 with the subtracted exponents:

$$3^{a^2-b^2}=3^3$$

Therefore, $a^2-b^2=3$. To find $a-b$, factor out $a+b$ and plug in 1:

$$\begin{aligned}a^2-b^2&=3\\ (a+b)(a-b)&=3\\ (1)(a-b)&=3\\ (a-b)&=3\end{aligned}$$

478. 8

Simplify the expression by distributing the x^9:

$$x^9\left(x^2-1\right)=3$$
$$x^{11}-x^9=3$$

In the fraction, subtract the exponents just as you would to divide any other terms with like bases:

$$\frac{2^{x^{11}}}{2^{x^9}}=2^{x^{11}-x^9}$$

Substitute 3 for $x^{11}-x^9$:

$$2^{x^{11}-x^9}=2^3=8$$

479. 2

Simplify the exponential expression by multiplying the exponents, as you would with any other base with an exponent of an exponent:

$$\left(2^{2a+2b}\right)^{2a-2b}=16$$
$$2^{(2a+2b)(2a-2b)}=16$$
$$2^{4a^2-4b^2}=16$$

You know that 16 equals 2^4, so set 16 equal to the 2 with the subtracted exponents:

$$2^{4a^2-4b^2}=2^4$$

Therefore, $4a^2-4b^2=4$, making $a^2-b^2=1$. You know that $b^2=3$, so plug that in:

$$a^2-b^2=1$$
$$a^2-3=1$$
$$a^2=4$$
$$a=2,-2$$

You also know that $a>0$, so a has to be 2.

480. **1**

You don't need separate values of *x* or *y*, so don't bother substituting. Simply subtract the equations and divide by 2:

$$\begin{aligned} 7x+3y&=4 \\ -(3x+2y&=2) \\ \hline 4x+\ y&=2 \\ 2x+\frac{y}{2}&=1 \end{aligned}$$

481. **10**

Start by factoring n^2-p^2:

$$n^2-p^2=(n-p)(n+p)$$

Now plug in the values that the question gives you:

$$\begin{aligned} n^2-p^2&=(n-p)(n+p) \\ 110&=(n-p)(11) \\ 10&=n-p \end{aligned}$$

482. **6**

Subtract the equations:

$$\begin{aligned} \frac{1}{2}x-\frac{1}{3}y&=3 \\ -\left(\frac{1}{3}x-\frac{1}{2}y\right.&\left.=2\right) \\ \hline \end{aligned}$$

A common denominator works, but you could also multiply everything by 6:

$$\begin{aligned} 3x-2y&=18 \\ -(2x-3y&=12) \\ \hline x+\ y&=\ 6 \end{aligned}$$

483. **12**

The volume of a cylinder is $V=\pi r^2h$. Plug the values from the question into the equation:

$$\begin{aligned} V&=\pi r^2h \\ &=\pi(2)^2\frac{3}{\pi} \\ &=\pi(4)\frac{3}{\pi} \\ &=(4)3 \\ &=12 \end{aligned}$$

ANSWERS 401-500

484. 630

Plug 18 in for *m* and simplify the equation:

$$c(m) = 300 + \left(3^{\frac{m}{6}} + \frac{m}{3}\right)10$$

$$c(18) = 300 + \left(3^{\frac{18}{6}} + \frac{18}{3}\right)10$$

$$= 300 + (3^3 + 6)10$$

$$= 300 + (27 + 6)10$$

$$= 300 + (33)10$$

$$= 300 + 330$$

$$= 630$$

485. 25

Remember that $a^2 - b^2 = (a+b)(a-b)$. Plug in the values of $a+b$ and $a-b$ to solve for $a^2 - b^2$:

$$a^2 - b^2 = (6)\left(\frac{1}{3}\right)$$

$$a^2 - b^2 = 2$$

Now plug 2 in for $a^2 - b^2$:

$$5^{a^2 - b^2} = 5^2 = 25$$

486. 24

If $\overline{AB}$ is parallel to $\overline{EC}$, the small triangle is similar to the large triangle. Shapes that are *similar* have the same side-length ratio but are different sizes. If $BC = CD$, then *DE* is half the length of *DA*, meaning the large triangle has twice the base and twice the height as the small triangle.

The area of the small triangle is $6 = \frac{bh}{2}$, meaning $bh = 12$. Double *b* and *h* for the large triangle:

$$(2)b(2)h = (2)(2)12$$

$$4bh = 48$$

Divide this in half for an area of 24.

ANSWERS 401-500

487. **2**

An exponent of an exponent equals the exponents multiplied. With this info, simplify the fraction:

$$\frac{3\left(x^3\right)^2}{2\left(x^2\right)^2} = 6$$

$$\frac{3x^6}{2x^4} = 6$$

$$\frac{3x^2}{2} = 6$$

$$3x^2 = 12$$

$$x^2 = 4$$

$$x = 2$$

488. **500**

Simplify the equation:

$$5\sqrt{\frac{c}{5}} + 5 = 55$$

$$5\sqrt{\frac{c}{5}} = 50$$

$$\sqrt{\frac{c}{5}} = 10$$

$$\frac{c}{5} = 100$$

$$c = 500$$

489. **30**

Simplify the equation:

$$\frac{h^2}{25} - 18 = 18$$

$$\frac{h^2}{25} = 36$$

$$\sqrt{\frac{h^2}{25}} = \sqrt{36}$$

$$\frac{h}{5} = 6$$

$$h = 30$$

ANSWERS 401–500

490. **6**

Solve for the ratio $\frac{a}{b}$:

$$\frac{5a}{b} = 20$$
$$\frac{a}{b} = \frac{20}{5}$$
$$\frac{a}{b} = 4$$

Now multiply this by $\frac{3}{2}$:

$$\left(\frac{3}{2}\right)\frac{a}{b} = 4\left(\frac{3}{2}\right)$$
$$\frac{3a}{2b} = 6$$

491. **47**

$kx^2 - 3 = 15$ when $x = 3$, so plug in 3 for x and solve for k:

$$k(3)^2 - 3 = 15$$
$$k(9) - 3 = 15$$
$$9k = 18$$
$$k = 2$$

Plug in 2 for k in the equation and solve for $f(5)$:

$$f(x) = kx^2 - 3$$
$$f(5) = (2)(5)^2 - 3$$
$$= 50 - 3$$
$$= 47$$

492. **10**

If $x = 3$, then $3x = 9$. According to the table, $f(9) = 10$.

493. **6**

According to the table, $f(5) = 6$. Therefore, $\frac{(f(5))^2}{6} = \frac{(6)^2}{6} = \frac{36}{6} = 6$.

ANSWERS 401–500

494. **5**

Cross-multiply the equation and solve for *x*:

$$\frac{x}{x+50}=\frac{1}{3}$$
$$3x=x+50$$
$$2x=50$$
$$x=25$$

Place *x* over 5 for the answer.

495. **10**

Cross-multiply the equation and solve for *x*:

$$\frac{3}{x-1}=\frac{4}{x+2}$$
$$3x+6=4x-4$$
$$10=x$$

496. **10**

Cross-multiply the equation and solve for *z*:

$$\frac{z+6}{8}=\frac{8}{z-6}$$
$$z^2-36=64$$
$$z^2=100$$
$$z=-10,\ 10$$

Because $z>0$, z has to be 10.

497. **6**

Transfer the negative sign to the 8, and then cross-multiply the equation and solve for *x*:

$$\frac{y+10}{8}=\frac{-8}{y-10}$$
$$y^2-100=-64$$
$$y^2=36$$

Because $y>0$, y has to be 6.

ANSWERS 401-500

498. 6

Subtract the second equation from the first equation:

$$\begin{array}{r} 4x-3y=18 \\ -(3x-2y=15) \\ \hline x-\ \ y=\ 3 \end{array}$$

Multiply this equation by 2 for the value of $2x-2y$.

499. 5

Multiply the second equation by 4 and subtract it from the first equation:

$$\begin{array}{r} 8x^2+6x+y=4z+5 \\ -(8x^2+4x\qquad =4z) \\ \hline 2x+y=\qquad 5 \end{array}$$

500. 18

According to the table, $f(4)=3$. Therefore, $2\left(\left(f(4)\right)^2\right)=2\left((3)^2\right)=2(9)=18$.

ANSWERS 501–600

501. 2

An exponent of $\frac{1}{4}$ is equivalent to a 4th root. Therefore, $16^{\frac{1}{4}}=\sqrt[4]{16}=2$.

502. 64

Reduce the fraction $\frac{12}{4}$ to 3. Now you're looking for 4^3, which equals 64.

503. 8

The simplest way to solve this problem is to take the 3rd root of 4, which is 64, and square-root that for an answer of 8.

504. 40

If 80 members are in Club *A* and that is 40 more than in Club *B*, you can set up the following equation and solve for *B*:

$$A=40+B$$
$$80=40+B$$
$$40=B$$

505. 9

If $2n-3p$ is a factor of $4n^2-p^2q$, multiply $2n-3p$ by its conjugate, $2n+3p$, to find q:

$$(2n-3p)(2n+3p)$$
$$=4n^2-6pn+6pn-9p^2$$
$$=4n^2-9p^2$$

Because $4n^2-p^2q$, $q=9$.

506. 4

If $x-2$ is a factor of the polynomial, then for the middle part of the polynomial to be $6x$, the other factor must be $(x+8)$. Write out these factors and FOIL the expression:

$$(x-2)(x+8)$$
$$=(x^2+6x-16)$$

The given polynomial is x^2+6x-y^2, so this means that $y^2=16$, and because y is positive, it must equal 4.

507. 43

If $11g=55$, then $g=5$. Plug this value into the expression and simplify:

$$8g+3=8(5)+3=40+3=43$$

508. 4

The trap in this problem is giving the value of n rather than the value of $\frac{n}{2}$. Start with the given expression and simplify it:

$$8n=64$$
$$n=8$$
$$\frac{n}{2}=4$$

ANSWERS 501–600

509. 50

Start by FOILing the expression:

$$\begin{aligned}&(5+5i)(5-5i)\\&=25-25i+25i-25i^2\end{aligned}$$

You know that $i^2=-1$, so plug that in:

$$25-25i+25i-25(-1)$$

And simplify the expression:

$$25+25=50$$

510. 9

Substitute 3 for h, and the equation looks like this:

$$\frac{2x+3}{7}=3$$

Multiply both sides by 7 and solve:

$$\begin{aligned}2x+3&=21\\2x&=18\\x&=9\end{aligned}$$

ANSWERS 501–600

511. 2

First solve for pq. Start with $\frac{pq}{2}=5$ and multiply both sides by 2, so $pq=10$. Plug this value into the first equation and solve for n:

$$\begin{aligned}n+pq&=12\\n+10&=12\\n&=2\end{aligned}$$

512. 16

An exponent raised to an exponent equals the exponents multiplied. With this, simplify the fraction:

$$\frac{(2x^3)^4}{(x^2)^6}=\frac{(2)^4(x^3)^4}{(x^2)^6}=\frac{(16)(x^{12})}{(x^{12})}=16$$

513. **1**

An exponent of an exponent equals the exponents multiplied. With this info, simplify the fraction:

$$\frac{\left(8x^3\right)^2}{\left(4x^2\right)^3}=\frac{(8)^2\left(x^3\right)^2}{(4)^3\left(x^2\right)^3}=\frac{(64)\left(x^6\right)}{(64)\left(x^6\right)}=1$$

514. **25**

Simplify the equation and solve for *a*:

$$\frac{a}{5}+5=10$$
$$\frac{a}{5}=5$$
$$a=25$$

515. **18**

Simplify the equation and solve for *h*:

$$\frac{2h}{3}-5=7$$
$$\frac{2h}{3}=12$$
$$2h=36$$
$$h=18$$

516. **4.5**

For the system to have infinite solutions, both variables (x and y) have to cancel out. Multiply the first equation by 3 and the second equation by 2 so that the y terms will cancel:

$$3x+2y=4$$
$$hx+3y=6$$

$$9x+6y=12$$
$$2hx+6y=12$$

Because $9x$ needs to equal $2hx$ for the x terms to cancel, you can solve for h:

$$2h=9$$
$$h=4.5$$

ANSWERS 501–600

517. 9

Distribute and simplify the expressions on the left to match the quadratic on the right:

$$x(2x+3)-2(x-3)=ax^2+bx+c$$
$$2x^2+3x-2x+6=ax^2+bx+c$$
$$2x^2+x+6=ax^2+bx+c$$

From this, you know that $a=2$, $b=1$, and $c=6$, which add up to 9.

518. 4

Distribute and simplify the expressions on the left to match the quadratic on the right:

$$x(3x+4)+3(x-2)=ax^2+bx+c$$
$$3x^2+4x+3x-6=ax^2+bx+c$$
$$3x^2+7x-6=ax^2+bx+c$$

From this, you know that $a=3$, $b=7$, and $c=-6$, which add up to 4.

519. 12

Multiply the binomials to match the quadratic, and then simplify by subtracting 6 from both sides:

$$6x^2+cx+6=(ax+2)(bx+3)$$
$$6x^2+cx+6=abx^2+3ax+2bx+6$$
$$6x^2+cx=abx^2+3ax+2bx$$
$$6x^2+cx=abx^2+(3a+2b)x$$

Because $6x^2=abx^2$, $ab=6$. And because a and b are integers and $1<a<b$, you know that $a=2$ and $b=3$. Now, using $cx=(3a+2b)x$, you can plug in 2 for a and 3 for b and then solve for c:

$$cx=(3(2)+2(3))x$$
$$cx=(6+6)x$$
$$cx=12x$$
$$c=12$$

520. 2

Solve for the ratio $\frac{c}{d}$:

$$\frac{2c}{d} = 3$$
$$\frac{c}{d} = \frac{3}{2}$$

Now invert the fractions and multiply d by 3:

$$\frac{d}{c} = \frac{2}{3}$$
$$\frac{3d}{c} = \frac{6}{3}$$
$$\frac{3d}{c} = 2$$

521. 12

$ax^2 + ax = 24$ when $x = 3$, so plug in 3 for x and solve for a:

$$a(3)^2 + a(3) = 24$$
$$9a + 3a = 24$$
$$12a = 24$$
$$a = 2$$

Plug in 2 for a in the function and solve for $f(2)$:

$$f(x) = ax^2 + ax$$
$$f(2) = (2)(2)^2 + (2)(2)$$
$$= 8 + 4$$
$$= 12$$

522. 48

$\frac{kh^2}{2} + 2kh = 18$ when $h = 2$, so plug in 2 for h and solve for k:

$$\frac{kh^2}{2} + 2kh = 18$$
$$\frac{k(2)^2}{2} + 2k(2) = 18$$
$$\frac{4k}{2} + 4k = 18$$
$$2k + 4k = 18$$
$$6k = 18$$
$$k = 3$$

ANSWERS 501–600

Plug in 3 for k in the function and solve for $g(4)$:

$$g(h) = \frac{kh^2}{2} + 2kh$$

$$g(4) = \frac{(3)(4)^2}{2} + 2(3)(4)$$

$$= \frac{48}{2} + 24$$

$$= 24 + 24$$

$$= 48$$

523. **5**

According to the table, $f(5) = 4$ and $g(5) = 4$; 5 is the only value of x shown in the table where $f(x) = g(x)$.

524. **5**

According to the table, $f(3) = 2$. Plug 2 in for $f(3)$ in $g(f(3))$, and $g(2) = 5$.

525. **12**

To find the surface area of a cube, find the area of one face, and multiply that by 6. This is represented by the formula $SA = 6e^2$, where e is the edge length. Plug the length of the edge into the equation for your answer:

$$SA = 6e^2$$

$$= 6(\sqrt{2})^2$$

$$= 6(2)$$

$$= 12$$

Chapter 4

526. **B.** $C(m) = 2.75m + 3$

Each week, Joe pays \$3 for the service along with \$2.75 for each movie.

527. **C.** $b = \frac{215 - 35}{12}$

Of 215 pencils, 35 were sold individually, so $215 - 35 = 180$ were sold in boxes. Divide 180 by 12 to get b, the boxes sold that day.

528. **D.** $s = \frac{P}{3}$

If the perimeter is the sum of the three equal sides, the equation $P = 3s$ represents the perimeter. Divide both sides by 3 for the answer.

529. **C.** $(-1, -2)$

Subtract the second equation from the first equation to isolate the y:

$$\begin{aligned} x - 2y &= 3 \\ -(x - 4y &= 7) \\ \hline 2y &= -4 \\ y &= -2 \end{aligned}$$

Now plug the value for y into the first equation:

$$\begin{aligned} x - 2y &= 3 \\ x - 2(-2) &= 3 \\ x + 4 &= 3 \\ x &= -1 \end{aligned}$$

530. **A.** $(4, 1)$

Add the second equation to the first equation to isolate the x:

$$\begin{aligned} x + y &= 5 \\ +(x - y &= 3) \\ \hline 2x &= 8 \\ x &= 4 \end{aligned}$$

Now plug the value for x into the first equation:

$$\begin{aligned} x + y &= 5 \\ (4) + y &= 5 \\ y &= 1 \end{aligned}$$

531. **B. 32**

If the dispenser holds 4 gallons, it holds 512 ounces (because $4 \times 128 = 512$). Divide this by 16 for the number of cups: $512 \div 16 = 32$.

532. **C. Slightly under 12**

If Jonathan drove 65 miles per hour for 4 hours, he drove 260 miles (because $65 \times 4 = 260$). Divide this by 22 for the gallons used: $260 \div 22 = 11.82$.

533. **A. $\frac{2}{3}$**

Using rise over run, the line rises 1 (because $2 - 1 = 1$) and runs $1\frac{1}{2}$ (because $3\frac{1}{2} - 2 = 1\frac{1}{2}$). To get rid of the fraction, double these for a rise and run of 2 and 3, respectively, and a slope of $\frac{2}{3}$.

534. **C. 17**

If the ratio of pens to pencils is $\frac{2}{3}$, then for every 2 pens, there are 3 pencils. The number of pencils must be a multiple of 3, making 17 the only answer that doesn't work.

535. **B. On the 50th day, 150 tickets remain to be given out.**

If d is the number of days, then when $d = 50$, $-5d = -250$; 400 is the number of free tickets that the theater started with, and $400 - 250 = 150$.

536. **C. 22%**

Eleven of the 50 vehicles are electric. Plug these into the calculator for 22%.

537. **D. 640**

Eight of the 50 vehicles are hybrid, which is 16%; 16% of 4,000 is 640.

538. **C. 2.0**

The likelihood of the vehicle being a gasoline car is 12% ($\frac{6}{50} = 0.12 = 12\%$), and the vehicle's likelihood of being an electric truck is 6% ($\frac{3}{50} = 0.06 = 6\%$).

539. **C. The area would stay the same.**

Suppose the rectangle has a width of 10 and a length of 20, for an area of $10 \times 20 = 200$. Double the length and halve the width for new measurements of 40 and 5, respectively. The area doesn't change: $5 \times 40 = 200$.

540. **D. The area would increase by a factor of 4.**

Suppose the rectangle has a width of 10 and a length of 20, for an area of $10 \times 20 = 200$. Doubling each gives you new measurements of 20 and 40, respectively. The area increases by a factor of 4: $20 \times 40 = 800$.

541. **C. 43%**

Before the increase, Sally purchased 7 pounds of mixture, of which 5 pounds was almonds and 2 pounds was chocolates. The 40% increase in almonds adds 2 pounds ($5 \times 40\% = 2$), and the 50% increase in chocolates adds 1 pound ($2 \times 50\% = 1$). Divide the total increase of 3 pounds by the original 7 pounds for an approximate increase of 43%.

542. **B. 4**

If the area is 40 inches, then $l \times w = 40$. If the length is 2 inches longer than twice the width, then $l = 2w + 2$. Combine the equations by plugging in the value l and solve for w:

$$\begin{aligned} l \times w &= 40 \\ (2w+2) \times w &= 40 \\ 2w^2 + 2w &= 40 \\ w^2 + w &= 20 \end{aligned}$$

Now solve the equation as a quadratic:

$$\begin{aligned} w^2 + w &= 20 \\ w^2 + w - 20 &= 0 \\ (w+5)(w-4) &= 0 \\ w &= 4, -5 \end{aligned}$$

The width is positive, so it equals 4.

ANSWERS 501–600

543. A. 32

If Millie prints 40 essays, each essay gets 40 Page Ones. This leaves 32 sheets to serve as Page Twos for the essays requiring two sheets of paper.

544. C. The area would increase by more than 100% but less than 200%.

Suppose the square has a side length of 10 for an area of $10 \times 10 = 100$. Increase the side length by 50% to 15 for a new area of $15 \times 15 = 225$. The increase from 100 to 225 is more than 100% but less than 200%.

545. C. $C(g) = 8g + 5$

Each month, Henry pays $5 for the service along with $8 for each bottle.

546. B. $p = \frac{93 - 21}{8}$

Of 93 pieces of gum, 21 were sold individually, so $93 - 21 = 72$ were sold in packs. Divide 72 by 8 for p, the packs sold that day.

547. A. $(7, 1)$

Multiply the second equation by 2 and subtract it from the first equation to isolate the y:

$$\begin{aligned} 2x + 3y &= 17 \\ -(2x - 2y &= 12) \\ \hline 5y &= 5 \\ y &= 1 \end{aligned}$$

Now plug the value for y into the second equation:

$$\begin{aligned} x - y &= 6 \\ x - (1) &= 6 \\ x &= 7 \end{aligned}$$

548. A. 3.0

From 8 cans, Phil can make $8 \times 48 = 384$ ounces of juice. Divide this by 128 for the number of gallons: $384 \div 128 = 3$.

ANSWERS 501–600

549. **A. Just under 18**

If Carlton drove 50 miles per hour for 6 hours, he drove $50 \times 6 = 300$ miles. Divide this by 17 for the gallons used: $300 \div 17 = 17.65$.

550. **C. 3**

From the first point to the second point, the line travels right 6 (because $24 - 18 = 6$) and up 4 (because $19 - 15 = 4$). The y-intercept is the point at which the line crosses the y-axis, so bring the line left 6 and down 4 until the y-value is 0 and the x-value is 3.

551. **B. 43**

If the ratio of cats to dogs is $\frac{8}{11}$, then for every 8 cats, there are 11 dogs. The number of dogs must be a multiple of 11, making 43 the only answer that doesn't work.

552. **C. 152**

With 12 two-seaters, 20 four-seaters, and 8 six-seaters, the restaurant has $(12 \times 2) + (20 \times 4) + (8 \times 6) = 24 + 80 + 48 = 152$ seats.

553. **A. 2,000**

Each of 200 restaurants has 10 high seat tables, and $200 \times 10 = 2{,}000$.

554. **B. 0.20**

The likelihood of the table being six-seater is $\frac{8}{40} = 0.20$.

555. **B. 28%**

Before the decrease, Giuseppe Pizzeria purchased 50 pounds of mixture, of which 30 was cheese and 20 was flour. The 20% decrease in cheese reduced the purchase by 6 pounds (as $30 \times 20\% = 6$), and the 40% decrease in flour reduced the purchase by 8 pounds (as $20 \times 40\% = 8$). Divide the total decrease of 14 pounds by the original 50 pounds for a percent decrease of 28%.

556. **A. 3**

If the area is 30 square miles, then $l \times w = 30$. If the length is 1 mile longer than three times the width, then $l = 3w + 1$. Combine the equations by plugging in the value of l and solve for w:

$$l \times w = 30$$
$$(3w+1) \times w = 30$$
$$3w^2 + w = 30$$

At this point, you could solve the problem as a quadratic, but it may be easier to try the answer choices. Here's 3, which is the correct answer:

$$3w^2 + w = 30$$
$$3(3)^2 + 3 = 30$$
$$3(9) + 3 = 30$$
$$27 + 3 = 30$$

557. **D. 9**

If Henry hangs 19 posters, each poster gets at least 2 pieces of tape, for 38 pieces used. This leaves 9 pieces of tape to go back to the 9 posters needing 3 pieces each.

ANSWERS 501–600

558. **C. The area would decrease by 75%.**

Suppose the rectangle has a width of 6 and a length of 8 for an area of $6 \times 8 = 48$. Decrease the length and width by 50% to get 3 and 4, respectively, for a new area of $3 \times 4 = 12$. The change from 48 to 12 is 36, which, divided by the original 48, is 75%.

559. **B. 35**

If $a = 50$ when $b = 10$, then $c = 5$, because

$$a = bc$$
$$50 = 10c$$
$$5 = c$$

Now plug in 5 for c and 7 for b:

$$a = bc = (7)(5) = 35$$

560. D. 35

If $3x+5$ is 7 more than 19, then set up the following equation:

$$\begin{aligned} 3x+5 &= 7+19 \\ 3x+5 &= 26 \\ 3x &= 21 \\ x &= 7 \\ 5x &= 35 \end{aligned}$$

561. B. 1,760

From the given information, 1 mile $= 1{,}760 \text{ yards} \times 3 \text{ feet} = 5{,}280$ feet; $\frac{1}{3}$ of a mile, in feet, is thus $5{,}280 \div 3 = 1{,}760$ feet.

562. D. There is no such value of *x*.

For $|x+3|+5$ to equal 0, $|x+3|$ would have to equal −5, which it cannot; an absolute value is always positive.

563. A. $\frac{1}{37{,}200}$ seconds

First find the time needed to travel 1 mile:

$$\begin{aligned} 186{,}000 \text{ miles} &= 1 \text{ second} \\ 1 \text{ mile} &= \frac{1}{186{,}000} \text{ seconds} \end{aligned}$$

Then multiply this by 5:

$$\frac{1}{186{,}000} \times 5 = \frac{1}{37{,}200}$$

564. D. 669,600,000 miles

One hour has 60 minutes, and 1 minute has 60 seconds, so 1 hour has $60 \times 60 = 3{,}600$ seconds. Multiply this by the distance traveled in 1 second: $3{,}600 \times 186{,}000 \text{ miles} = 669{,}600{,}000$ miles.

565. B. Three

Simplify the equation, starting by multiplying everything by 5:

$$\begin{aligned} -\frac{2}{5} < \frac{x}{5} - 1 < \frac{2}{5} \\ -2 < x - 5 < 2 \\ 3 < x < 7 \end{aligned}$$

Therefore, *x* could equal 4, 5, or 6, which is three possible integer values.

ANSWERS 501–600

566. **C. 2**

The value of b is where the line crosses the y-axis, which is also the value of y when $x = 0$. If $(0, 2)$ is the solution to both equations, then for both equations, $y = 2$ when $x = 0$, meaning $b = 2$.

567. **C. 150**

Let h be the number of hot dogs and s be the number of sodas. From this, you can set up two equations: $s + h = 400$ and $1.5s + 2.5h = 850$. Because you're solving for s, use substitution to eliminate the h:

$$s + h = 400$$
$$h = 400 - s$$

$$1.5s + 2.5h = 850$$
$$1.5s + 2.5(400 - s) = 850$$
$$1.5s + 1{,}000 - 2.5s = 850$$
$$-s = -150$$
$$s = 150$$

568. **D.** $d = r\left(\frac{100 - p}{100}\right)\left(1 + \frac{t}{100}\right)$

Because p represents a percent, place it over 100 (the same way that 5% is $\frac{5}{100}$). If the discount was p percent, then Joe paid $100 - p$ percent. Multiply this by r for the pre-tax amount, and then multiply this by $1 + \frac{t}{100}$ for the taxed amount:

$$r\left(\frac{100 - p}{100}\right)\left(1 + \frac{t}{100}\right)$$

569. **A.** $r = \left(\frac{100}{100 - p}\right)\left(\frac{100}{100 + t}\right)d$

Because p represents a percent, place it over 100 (the same way that 5% is $\frac{5}{100}$). If the discount was p percent, then Joe paid $100 - p$ percent. Multiply this by r for the pre-tax amount, and then multiply this by $1 + \frac{t}{100}$ for the taxed amount:

$$d = r\left(\frac{100 - p}{100}\right)\left(1 + \frac{t}{100}\right)$$

Then solve for r. First simplify the t fraction on the right:

$$d = r\left(\frac{100 - p}{100}\right)\left(1 + \frac{t}{100}\right)$$
$$d = r\left(\frac{100 - p}{100}\right)\left(\frac{100}{100} + \frac{t}{100}\right)$$
$$d = r\left(\frac{100 - p}{100}\right)\left(\frac{100 + t}{100}\right)$$

ANSWERS 501–600

Next, divide both sides by the fractions. This flips the fractions and places them on the other side:

$$d = r\left(\frac{100-p}{100}\right)\left(\frac{100+t}{100}\right)$$

$$\left(\frac{100}{100-p}\right)\left(\frac{100}{100+t}\right)d = r$$

570. C. 0.40

Probability is the number desired over the total number; 14 students earned either a B or a C, and this number over 35 is 0.40.

571. D. 30

There are 5 possible boys and 6 possible girls. Multiply these for 30 possible combinations.

572. D. 60

Five boys earned an A, making five possibilities for one to be selected to get spoons. Four boys remain, making four possibilities to get bowls. Then three boys remain, making three possibilities to get napkins. Multiply these for the answer: $5 \times 4 \times 3 = 60$.

573. B. 80,000

The number of mothers with children under the age of 18 in 2005 is about 90,000. A 10% increase in 2010 brings the number to about 100,000. The percentage of mothers in the workforce with youngest children ages 12 to 17 in 2005 is 80%. The percentage stays about the same in 2010, and 80% of 100,000 is 80,000.

574. A. 2 to 7

The first number is 20%, and the second number is 70%. This produces a ratio of 2 to 7.

575. C. I and III: The population of Country *X* is steadily increasing, and the demand for daycare in Country *X* is steadily increasing.

Option I is correct because more mothers are having children, so the population is increasing. Option II is wrong because mothers in the workforce aren't necessarily single. Option III is correct because with both more mothers working and more babies in Country *X*, the demand for daycare increases.

ANSWERS 501–600

576. **D. $180,000,000**

Check both graphs at the 20–30 points. The first graph shows $600 per month. The second graph shows 25,000 homes. Multiply these together for a monthly expenditure of $15,000,000. Multiply this by 12 for an annual expenditure of $180,000,000.

577. **A. 2 to 7**

The graph shows approximately 10,000 homes with household incomes between $5,000 and $10,000 and approximately 35,000 homes with household incomes between $30,000 and $40,000. The ratio of 10,000 to 35,000 reduces to 2 to 7.

578. **A. I and II: There are more homes with household incomes between $50,000 and $60,000 than homes with household incomes between $30,000 and $40,000; there are more homes being built for the $30,000 to $40,000 income demographic than for any other demographic.**

This question asks you to choose the answer choices that *cannot* be inferred. For Option I, you can't make the inference because you don't know how many of those homes have incomes between $50,000 and $60,000. For Option II, you can't make the inference because you don't know how many homes are being built and for what demographic. Finally, for Option III, 75,000 homes have incomes lower than $30,000 to $40,000, and 70,000 homes have higher incomes. Because 35,000 homes are within the $30,000 to $40,000 bracket, you can infer that the median income is also in that bracket.

579. **A.** $(x-3)^2+(y-4)^2=9$

The formula for a circle is $(x-h)^2+(y-k)^2=(\text{radius})^2$, where h and k are the center of the circle.

Plug in the center and radius values from the question to get the answer.

580. **C.** $(x-2)^2+(y-1)^2=2$

The formula for a circle is $(x-h)^2+(y-k)^2=(\text{radius})^2$, where h and k are the center of the circle. To find the radius, use the center of the circle, $(2,1)$, and radius endpoint, $(3,2)$. This gives you a small 45-45-90 triangle with side lengths of 1 and thus a hypotenuse (radius) of $\sqrt{2}$. Plug the center and radius values into the formula to get the answer.

581. **D.** $(x+4)^2 + (y+4)^2 = 16$

The formula for a circle is $(x-h)^2 + (y-k)^2 = (\text{radius})^2$, where h and k are the center of the circle. If the circle is tangent to the x-axis at $(-4, 0)$ and to the y-axis at $(0, -4)$, the circle's center is $(-4, -4)$, and its radius is 16. Plug these values into the formula to get the answer.

582. **C. II and III:** $(x-5)^2 + (y+3)^2 = 9$ **and** $(x-5)^2 + (y-3)^2 = 9$

The formula for a circle is $(x-h)^2 + (y-k)^2 = (\text{radius})^2$, where h and k are the center of the circle. The circle is tangent to the x-axis at $(5, 0)$ and has a radius of 3. However, the center could be either $(5, 3)$ or $(5, -3)$. Plug these two centers into the formula, along with the radius, for the two possible equations of the circle.

583. **C.** $x^2 + y^2 = 4$

The formula for a circle is $(x-h)^2 + (y-k)^2 = (\text{radius})^2$, where h and k are the center of the circle. If the diameter is 4, then the radius is 2. Plug the center and the radius into the formula to get the answer.

584. **D. 42**

The formula for a circle is $(x-h)^2 + (y-k)^2 = (\text{radius})^2$, where h and k are the center of the circle. The circle in the question thus has a radius of 21, for a diameter of 42.

585. **A. I and II:** $(x+5)^2 + (y+7)^2 = 25$ **and** $(x-5)^2 + (y+7)^2 = 25$

The formula for a circle is $(x-h)^2 + (y-k)^2 = (\text{radius})^2$, where h and k are the center of the circle. The circle is tangent to the y-axis at $(0, -7)$ and has a radius of 5. However, the center could be either $(-5, -7)$ or $(5, -7)$. Plug these two centers into the formula, along with the radius, for the two possible equations of the circle.

586. **C. 9**

The formula for a circle is $(x-h)^2 + (y-k)^2 = (\text{radius})^2$, where h and k are the center of the circle. However, square-root both sides, and the formula looks like this:

$$\sqrt{(x-k)^2 + (y-k)^2} = \text{radius}$$

Therefore, the radius is 9.

587. C. 300

Type A cells divide at 150% of the rate of type B cells. If type B cells divided 200 times, then type A cells divided $200 \times 150\% = 300$ times.

588. B. 15,000

Plug 5 in for d and solve the equation:

$$\begin{aligned} C(d) &= 1{,}000d(d-2) \\ &= 1{,}000(5)(5-2) \\ &= 1{,}000(5)(3) \\ &= 1{,}000(15) \\ &= 15{,}000 \end{aligned}$$

589. A. 6th

It's probably easiest to plug in numbers for d and see which results in 24,000. Start with 6:

$$\begin{aligned} C(d) &= 1{,}000d(d-2) \\ C(6) &= 1{,}000(6)(6-2) \\ &= 1{,}000(6)(4) \\ &= 1{,}000(24) \\ &= 24{,}000 \end{aligned}$$

590. B. $C(d) = 1{,}000d(d-1)$

Plug 8 in for d and see which formula results in 56,000; $C(d) = 1{,}000d(d-1)$ is the only one that works:

$$\begin{aligned} C(d) &= 1{,}000d(d-1) \\ C(8) &= 1{,}000(8)(8-1) \\ &= 1{,}000(8)(7) \\ &= 1{,}000(56) \\ &= 56{,}000 \end{aligned}$$

For simplicity's sake, you can drop the 1,000 and see which formula gives you 56.

591. B. 900

Plug 6 in for d and solve the equation:

$$C(d) = 100\left(2^{\frac{d}{3}}\right) + 500$$
$$C(6) = 100\left(2^{\frac{6}{3}}\right) + 500$$
$$= 100\left(2^2\right) + 500$$
$$= 100(4) + 500$$
$$= 400 + 500$$
$$= 900$$

592. D. 12th

It's probably easiest to plug in numbers for d and see which choice results in 2,100. Here's what you get when you use 12:

$$C(d) = 100\left(2^{\frac{d}{3}}\right) + 500$$
$$C(12) = 100\left(2^{\frac{12}{3}}\right) + 500$$
$$= 100\left(2^4\right) + 500$$
$$= 100(16) + 500$$
$$= 1{,}600 + 500$$
$$= 2{,}100$$

For simplicity's sake, you can drop the 100 and see which answer gives you 21.

593. C. $C(d) = 100\left(2^{\frac{d}{4}}\right) + 500$

Plug 12 in for d and see which formula results in 1,300. $C(d) = 100\left(2^{\frac{d}{4}}\right) + 500$ is the only one that works:

$$C(d) = 100\left(2^{\frac{d}{4}}\right) + 500$$
$$C(12) = 100\left(2^{\frac{12}{4}}\right) + 500$$
$$= 100\left(2^3\right) + 500$$
$$= 100(8) + 500$$
$$= 800 + 500$$
$$= 1{,}300$$

For simplicity's sake, you can drop the 100 and see which choice gives you 13.

594. **A. Quadrants I and II**

To graph $y > x+3$, draw a line going upward and crossing the y-axis at 3; the inequality includes all the solutions above that line. To graph $y > -x+2$, draw a line going downward and crossing the y-axis at 2; the inequality includes all the solutions above that line. The result is that all the solutions are contained within a *V* shape with the vertex at right about $(0, 3)$. This *V* extends upward into Quadrants I and II.

595. **B. Quadrants II, III, and IV**

To graph $y > x-5$, draw a line going upward and crossing the y-axis at -5; the inequality includes all the solutions above that line. To graph $y < -2x-3$, draw a line going downward and crossing the y-axis at -3; the inequality includes all the solutions below that line. The result is that all the solutions are contained within a *V* shape pointing left, with the vertex slightly right of $(0, -4)$. This vertex is contained within Quadrant IV, and the *V* extends leftward into Quadrants II and III.

596. **B. $x-5$ is a factor of $f(x)$**

Think of a simple function where the value of $f(5)$ is 0, such as

$$f(x) = x-5$$

Because $x-5$ is a factor of itself, $x-5$ is a factor of $f(x)$. Now think of some complex functions where the value of $f(5)$ is 0, such as

$$f_1(x) = 2(x-5)$$
$$f_2(x) = (x-5)(x+3)$$
$$f_3(x) = (x-5)^2$$

For all these, $x-5$ is a factor of $f(x)$.

597. **A. $x+3$ is a factor of $f(x)$**

Think of a simple function where the value of $f(-3)$ is 0, such as

$$f(x) = x+3$$

Because $x+3$ is a factor of itself, $x+3$ is a factor of $f(x)$. Now think of some complex functions where the value of $f(-3)$ is 0, such as

$$f_1(x) = 3(x+3)$$
$$f_2(x) = (x+3)(x-5)$$
$$f_3(x) = (x+3)^3$$

For all these, $x+3$ is a factor of $f(x)$.

598. **C. The remainder when $f(x)$ is divided by $x-2$ is 3**

Think of a function where the value of $f(2)$ is 3, such as

$$f(x)=x+1$$

If you divide $x+1$ by $x-2$, the remainder is 3:

$$\begin{array}{r} 1 \\ (x-2)\overline{)(x+1)} \\ \underline{-(x-2)} \\ 3 \end{array}$$

599. **D. The remainder when $f(x)$ is divided by $x+5$ is 4**

Think of a function where the value of $f(-5)$ is 4, such as

$$f(x)=x+9$$

If you divide $x+9$ by $x+5$, the remainder is 4:

$$\begin{array}{r} 1 \\ (x+5)\overline{)(x+9)} \\ \underline{-(x+5)} \\ 4 \end{array}$$

600. **D. $y=(x-1)^2-9$**

Per the drawing, the coordinates of the vertex of the parabola are $(1,-9)$. Look for an equation containing 1 and −9. (In the answer, −1 contains a 1.)

601. **C. $y=(x-3)^2-1$**

Per the drawing, the coordinates of the vertex of the parabola are $(3,-1)$. Look for an equation containing 3 and −1. (In the answer, −3 contains a 3.)

602. **B. $y=(x-1)^2-4$**

The answer is a perfect square minus an integer. For the perfect square to produce $x-2x$ (in the equation), it has to contain $(x-1)^2$. FOIL out the $(x-1)^2$ to see what the integer has to be:

$$\begin{aligned} &(x-1)^2 \\ &=(x-1)(x-1) \\ &=x^2-2x+1 \end{aligned}$$

The given equation ends with −3, not 1, so subtract 4: $y=(x-1)^2-4$.

ANSWERS 601–700

603. **A.** $y = (x+2)^2 - 9$

The answer is a perfect square minus an integer. For the perfect square to produce $x^2 + 4x$ (in the equation), it has to contain $(x+2)^2$. FOIL out the $(x+2)^2$ to see what the integer has to be:

$$\begin{aligned} &(x+2)^2 \\ &= (x+2)(x+2) \\ &= x^2 + 4x + 4 \end{aligned}$$

The given equation ends with −5, not 4, so subtract 9: $y = (x+2)^2 - 9$.

604. **D.** $y = (x-4)^2 - 4$

The answer is a perfect square minus an integer. For the perfect square to produce $x^2 - 8x$ (in the equation), it has to contain $(x-4)^2$. FOIL out the $(x-4)^2$ to see what the integer has to be:

$$\begin{aligned} &(x-4)^2 \\ &= (x-4)(x-4) \\ &= x^2 - 8x + 16 \end{aligned}$$

The given equation ends with 12, not 16, so subtract 4: $y = (x-4)^2 - 4$.

605. **B. 190**

If the pallet weighs 46 pounds, the remaining forklift capacity is 954 pounds. Divide 954 by 5, the weight of each brick, for the number of bricks: $954 \div 5 = 190.8$. The question asks for the number of whole bricks, so drop the 0.8 for an answer of 190. Rounding up to 191 would exceed the capacity of the forklift.

606. **B.** $1{,}000 \geq 5x + 46$

The total weight of the load has to be *less than or equal to* 1,000, so the inequality is ≥. The forklift carries the weight of the bricks plus 46 for the pallet, so add the weight of the bricks, 5*x*, to 46.

607. **A. 129**

If the cooler with ice weighs 38 pounds, the remaining table capacity is 162 pounds. The sodas are weighed in ounces, so the table has $162 \times 16 = 2{,}592$ ounces remaining to hold sodas. Divide 2,592 by 20, the weight of each soda, for the number of bottles: $2{,}592 \div 20 = 129.6$. The question asks for the number of unopened bottles, so drop the 0.6 for an answer of 129. Rounding up to 130 would exceed the capacity of the table.

Technical Stuff: Soda is usually measured in fluid ounces, a unit of volume, and a fluid ounce doesn't necessarily weigh 1 ounce. A 20-fluid ounce bottle of soda actually weighs a little over 21 ounces, so the real-world answer is a few bottles less. On the other hand, the table's weight capacity isn't exact.

608. **C.** $200 \ge \frac{5x}{4} + 38$

Each soda weighs 20 ounces, so multiply x by 20 for the total number of ounces. Then divide this by 16 to convert it to pounds, and reduce the fraction:

$$\frac{20x}{16} = \frac{5x}{4}$$

Add 38 to account for the weight of the cooler.

609. **D. 21**

If the truck safely carries 6.5 tons, it carries $6.5 \times 2{,}000 = 13{,}000$ pounds. A platform carrying two crates weighs $(550 \times 2) + 120 = 1{,}220$ pounds. Divide 13,000 by 1,220 for 10 with a remainder of 800. This 10 represents 20 crates with 10 platforms, and the remaining 800 pounds will support one crate with one platform: $550 + 120 = 670$. That gives you a total of 21 crates.

610. **C.** $y = 3x + 60$

Each sale is worth $3, so multiply the number of sales by 3 to get the total number earned in sales. Add this to 60, his daily flat fee, for the total amount he earns in one day.

611. **A. 59**

A 15-foot banner is $15 \times 12 = 180$ inches long. Divide this by 3 for 60 notches; however, the end of the banner does not get a notch, for a total of 59 notches.

612. **C. 11**

A 60-foot fence with a shrub every 6 feet is $60 \div 6 = 10$ shrubs. Add one more shrub at the beginning for a total of 11.

613. B. 30 feet

The volume of a right circular cylinder is $V = \pi r^2 h$. Plug in the values from the question and solve for r:

$$\begin{aligned} V &= \pi r^2 h \\ 5{,}400\pi &= \pi r^2 60 \\ 5{,}400 &= 60r^2 \\ 900 &= r^2 \\ 30 &= r \end{aligned}$$

614. C. 200π cubic yards

The volume of a cube is equal to its edge length cubed. A cubic yard has an edge of 3 feet and thus a volume of 27 cubic feet. Divide the volume of the tank, $5{,}400\pi$ cubic feet, by 27 to get 200π cubic yards.

615. B. 12 inches

The volume of a right circular cylinder is $V = \pi r^2 h$. Plug in the values from the question and solve for r, and then multiply this by 2 for the diameter:

$$\begin{aligned} V &= \pi r^2 h \\ 432\pi &= \pi r^2 12 \\ 432 &= 12r^2 \\ 36 &= r^2 \\ 6 &= r \\ 12 &= d \end{aligned}$$

616. D. $\frac{\pi}{4}$ cubic feet

The volume of a cube is equal to its edge length cubed. A cubic foot has an edge of 12 inches and thus a volume of 1,728 cubic inches. Divide the volume of the jar, 432π cubic feet, by 1,728 to get $\frac{\pi}{4}$ cubic feet.

617. B. 4

For the function to be undefined, the bottom of the fraction has to equal 0. (The top of the fraction doesn't matter.) Set the bottom of the fraction equal to 0 and solve for x:

$$2(x-5)^2 + (2-x) = 0$$

There are ways to solve for *x* algebraically, such as using the quadratic formula, but it may be easier to try the answers. Here's what you get when you try 4:

$$\begin{aligned} 2(x-5)^2+(2-x)&=0\\ 2((4)-5)^2+(2-(4))&=0\\ 2(-1)^2+(-2)&=0\\ 2(1)-2&=0\\ 0&=0 \end{aligned}$$

618. **C. 6**

For the function to be undefined, the bottom of the fraction has to equal 0. (The top of the fraction doesn't matter.) Set the bottom of the fraction equal to 0 and solve for *h*:

$$2(h-7)^4-2(h-5)^3=0$$

There are ways to solve for *h* algebraically, such as using the quadratic formula, but it may be easier to try the answers. Here's what you get when you plug in 6:

$$\begin{aligned} 2(h-7)^4-2(h-5)^3&=0\\ 2((6)-7)^4-2((6)-5)^3&=0\\ 2(-1)^4-2(1)^3&=0\\ 2(1)-2(1)&=0\\ 0&=0 \end{aligned}$$

619. **B. 24**

If total sales were $150,000 and Humboldt County spent $36,000, you can find the percent by placing the Humboldt County sales over the total sales:

$$\frac{36{,}000}{150{,}000}=\frac{24}{100}=24\%$$

620. **D. Sugar Choc**

You can compare the box prices of each brand by estimating the ratio of sales dollars to units sold. The higher the ratio, the higher the brand's average selling price. Sugar Choc has the highest ratio of dollar sales to units sold, making it the highest-priced brand of cereal.

621. C. 1:1

Though actual numbers aren't provided, you can use the column graph to approximate the ratios. Because the question asks for an "approximate" answer and the answer choices are far apart, you can eyeball your numbers from the graphs.

Lucky Shapes and Sugar Choc show similar numbers of units sold, but the Sugar Choc sales dollars is about three times that of Lucky Shapes. This means, box for box, Sugar Choc costs approximately three times as much as Lucky Shapes.

If the Trinity County spending (at $27,000) is three times that of Glenn County (at $9,000), and if the Trinity cereal box costs three times the Glenn cereal box, then the two counties are purchasing approximately the same number of cereal boxes.

622. A. 1:2

The question asks for an "approximate" ratio, so eyeball the graph and compare the bars. The C bar is half the B bar, making the ratio 1:2.

623. C. 150

If the 211 Creede students are earning A's, the remaining 894 students are earning all the other grades. Looking at the bar chart, you see that the B bar is the length of the C, D, and F bars placed together. This means that about half the remaining students are earning B's. Bayfield has 306 students, and approximately half that is 150.

624. C. 70

From the bar chart, you see that about $\frac{2}{5}$ of the grades are B grades, so about $\frac{3}{5}$ are the other grades. De Beque has 115 students, and the only answer choice that's about $\frac{3}{5}$ of that is 70.

An approximate estimate is usually good enough for these questions. The answer of 70 isn't really close to the other answers, so if you eyeball the graph differently, you'll still get the right answer.

625. A. 0

The trap here is doing a lot of extra math work. Drop the parentheses to avoid this trap:

$$\frac{1}{8}-\frac{3}{10}+\frac{1}{4}-\frac{1}{5}+\frac{5}{8}-\frac{1}{2}$$

ANSWERS 601–700

Now give the fractions common denominators of either 8 or 10:

$$\frac{1}{8}-\frac{3}{10}+\frac{2}{8}-\frac{2}{10}+\frac{5}{8}-\frac{5}{10}$$

The $\frac{1}{8}, \frac{2}{8}$, and $\frac{5}{8}$ add up to 1, and the $-\frac{3}{10}, -\frac{2}{10}$, and $-\frac{5}{10}$ add up to −1. The expression, therefore, equals 0.

Note that there are other ways to simplify the fractions. On the SAT, especially with fractions, you're looking for ways to cancel and simplify.

626. **C. $1.25s + 0.75w$**

Multiply 1.25 by *s*, the bottles of soda, and add that to 0.75 times *w*, the bottles of water.

627. **B. 20**

If the machine sells *s* bottles of soda and *w* bottles of water, you can set up two equations:

$$1.25s + 0.75w = 40.00$$
$$s + w = 40$$

Multiply the second equation by 0.75 and subtract it from the first equation:

$$\begin{array}{l} 1.25s + 0.75w = 40.00 \\ \underline{-(0.75s + 0.75w = 30 \quad)} \\ 0.50s \qquad\qquad = 10 \\ \qquad\qquad s = 20 \end{array}$$

628. **A. $1.60h + 0.80s$**

Multiply 1.60 by *h*, the hot dogs, and add that to 0.80 times *s*, the number of sodas.

629. **B. 199**

If he sells *s* sodas and *h* hot dogs, you can set up two equations:

$$1.60h + 0.80s = 319.20$$
$$h + s = 200$$

Multiply the second equation by 0.80 and subtract it from the first:

$$\begin{array}{l} 1.60h + 0.80s = 319.20 \\ \underline{-(0.80h + 0.80s = 160 \quad)} \\ 0.80h \qquad\qquad = 159.20 \\ \qquad\qquad h = 199 \end{array}$$

630. D. 88

There are $4,000 \div 500 = 8$ groups of 500 beads, and $8 \times 11 = 88$.

631. C. 36

There are $300 \div 25 = 12$ groups of 25 candies, and $12 \times 3 = 36$.

632. B. 10

Start with the given equation and plug in the value of *d:*

$$d = 13 + 2.5p$$
$$38 = 13 + 2.5p$$
$$25 = 2.5p$$
$$10 = p$$

633. C. 7

Start with the given equation and plug in the value of *d:*

$$d = 110 + 40u$$
$$390 = 110 + 40u$$
$$280 = 40u$$
$$7 = u$$

634. D. 180

Solve for *x* and double the answer:

$$7x = 450 + 2x$$
$$5x = 450$$
$$x = 90$$
$$2x = 180$$

635. C. $3,600

The salesman earns $2,400 \div 60 = 40$ dollars per timeshare sold. Multiply this amount by the new number of timeshares: $40 \times 90 = 3,600$.

636. A. $1,800

You know from the question that he earns $2,400 from selling 60 timeshares. He keeps 75%; therefore, his profit is $2,400 \times 0.75 = 1,800$.

637. **B. $8,400**

The agent earns $6,000 \div 25 = 240$ dollars per unit rented. Multiply this amount by the new number of units: $240 \times 35 = 8,400$.

638. **A. $7,200**

You know from the question that she earns $6,000 from renting 25 units. This means that she earns $12,000 from renting 50 units and keeps 60%; therefore, her profit is $12,000 \times 0.60 = 7,200$.

639. **D. 70**

Set up the equation, remembering *is* means an equal sign:

$$3x = 50 - 5$$
$$3x = 45$$
$$x = 15$$

Now set up the second equation and plug in 15 for x:

$$4x + 10 = 4(15) + 10 = 60 + 10 = 70$$

640. **D. −34**

Set up the equation, remembering *is* means an equal sign:

$$6\left(\frac{y}{2}\right) = 18 + 18$$
$$3y = 36$$
$$y = 12$$

Now set up the second equation and plug in 12 for y:

$$2 - 3y = 2 - 3(12) = 2 - 36 = -34$$

641. **D. $y = (x + 2)(x + 3)$**

Find the x-intercepts of the parabola by factoring the polynomial. The x-intercepts are where $y = 0$:

$$y = x^2 + 5x + 6$$
$$y = (x + 2)(x + 3)$$

The x-intercepts are thus −2 and −3, and this factored form of the equation displays these intercepts as constants.

ANSWERS 601–700

642. **A.** $y = (x-3)(x-5)$

Find the x-intercepts of the parabola by factoring the polynomial. The x-intercepts are where $y = 0$.

$$y = x^2 - 8x + 15$$
$$y = (x-3)(x-5)$$

The x-intercepts are thus 3 and 5, and this factored form of the equation displays these intercepts as constants.

643. **C.** $y = (x-2)(x+7)$

First distribute the x to get the equation in the form of a quadratic:

$$y = x(x+5) - 14$$
$$y = x^2 + 5x - 14$$

Then find the x-intercepts of the parabola by factoring the polynomial. The x-intercepts are where $y = 0$.

$$y = (x-2)(x+7)$$

The x-intercepts are thus 2 and −7, and this factored form of the equation displays these intercepts as constants.

644. **C.** $y = (x-11)(x+10)$

First distribute the x to get the equation in the form of a quadratic:

$$y = x(x-1) - 110$$
$$y = x^2 - x - 110$$

Then find the x-intercepts of the parabola by factoring the polynomial. The x-intercepts are where $y = 0$.

$$y = (x-11)(x+10)$$

The x-intercepts are thus −10 and 11, and this factored form of the equation displays these intercepts as constants.

645. **D.** 375

From 8:00 to 9:15 a.m., the cylinder loses 3 milliliters per minute over 75 minutes for a total of 225 milliliters. If the cylinder then has 150 milliliters, it began with 375 milliliters, which is the value of C.

ANSWERS 601–700

646. C. 35

From 9:00 a.m. Tuesday to noon Friday is 75 hours, so the rain gauge gains $75 \times 4 = 300$ milliliters. Subtract this from 335 for 35, which is the value of *M*.

647. A. $\begin{cases} 200x + 275y \le 180{,}000 \\ x + y \le 80 \end{cases}$

Note that 200*x* is the weight of *x* 200-pound containers and that 275*y* is the weight of *y* 275-pound containers. This sum has to be less than or equal to 180,000, which creates the first inequality. Next, *x* is the number of 200-ton containers and *y* is the number of 275-ton containers. This sum has to be less than 80, which creates the second inequality.

648. D. $\begin{cases} 60x + 85y \le 30{,}000 \\ x + y \le 400 \end{cases}$

Note that 60*x* is the number of bags in *x* 60-bag boxes and that 85*y* is the number of bags in *y* 85-bag boxes. This sum has to be less than or equal to 30,000, which creates the first inequality. Next, *x* is the number of 60-bag boxes and *y* is the number of 85-bag boxes. This sum has to be less than or equal to 400, which creates the second inequality.

649. B. $\begin{cases} 5x + 7y \le 5{,}000 \\ x + y \le 900 \end{cases}$

Note that 5*x* is the weight of *x* 5-pound bricks and that 7*y* is the weight of *y* 7-pound bricks. This sum has to be less than or equal to 5,000, which creates the first inequality. Next, *x* is the number of 5-pound bricks and *y* is the number of 7-pound bricks. This sum has to be less than or equal to 900, which creates the second inequality.

650. A. $\begin{cases} 12x + 18y \le 18{,}000 \\ x + y \le 1{,}200 \end{cases}$

Note that 12*x* is the number of eggs in *x* 12-egg cartons and that 18*y* is the number of eggs in *y* 18-egg cartons. This sum has to be less than or equal to 18,000, which creates the first inequality. Next, *x* is the number of 12-egg cartons and *y* is the number of 18-egg cartons. This sum has to be less than or equal to 1,200, which creates the second inequality.

651. B. 12

Start with the innermost function. The problem tells you that $f(4) = 7$, so plug in 7 for $f(4)$. Now the question asks for the value of $g(7)$, which is 12.

652. **B. 3**

Start with the innermost function. The problem tells you that $f(5)=8$, so plug in 8 for $f(5)$. Now the question asks for the value of $g(f(8))$. Because $f(8)=2$, plug in 2 for $f(8)$. Now solve for $g(2)$, which is 3.

653. **D. 72**

Start with the innermost function. If $g(x)=\sqrt{x}$, then $g(2)=\sqrt{2}$, and $3g(2)=3\sqrt{2}$. If $f(x)=x^2$, $f(3\sqrt{2})=(3\sqrt{2})^2=9\times 2=18$, and 18 times 4 is 72.

654. **B. 3**

Start with the innermost function. If $f(x)=\frac{3x}{2}$, then $f(2)=\frac{3(2)}{2}=3$. Plug 3 in for $f(2)$:

$$2g(3f(2))=2g(3(3))=2g(9)$$

If $g(x)=\frac{x}{6}$, then $g(9)=\frac{9}{6}=\frac{3}{2}$, and $\frac{3}{2}$ times 2 is 3.

655. **B. $10(1.2)^m<40$**

For each month, multiply the height of the tree by 1.2 for its new height (because $100\%+20\%=120\%$). In the equation, m represents the number of times that the tree's height is multiplied by 1.2.

656. **C. $0.5(0.9)^d>0.2$**

For each day, multiply the amount of water by 0.9 for its new amount (because $100\%-10\%=90\%$). In the equation, d represents the number of times that the amount of water is multiplied by 0.9.

657. **B. $FV=PV(1.008)^m$**

Each month, the present value *PV* increases 0.8%, meaning that it's multiplied by 1.008 (because $100\%+0.8\%=100.8\%$). In the equation, m represents the number of times that the present value is multiplied by 1.008.

658. **B. $PV=\frac{FV}{(1.006)^m}$**

Each month, the present value, *PV*, increases 0.6%, meaning that it's multiplied by 1.006 (because $100\%+0.6\%=100.6\%$). In the equation, m represents the number of times that the present value is multiplied by 1.006. This gives you the following equation:

$$FV=PV(1.006)^m$$

Divide both sides by $(1.006)^m$ to get the value of *PV*.

ANSWERS 601–700

659. **D.** $FV = PV\left(1+\frac{i}{1,200}\right)^m$

If the annual interest rate is *i* percent, then it's $\frac{i}{100}$. Divide this by 12 for a monthly interest rate of $\frac{i}{1,200}$.

Each month, the present value, *PV*, increases by $\frac{i}{1,200}$, meaning that it's multiplied by $1+\frac{i}{1,200}$. In the equation, *m* represents the number of times that the present value is multiplied by $1+\frac{i}{1,200}$.

660. **C. 2,300 miles per hour**

To calculate miles per hour, start with the number of hours that it takes the moon to orbit the Earth: $(27\times 24)+8 = 656$. Divide the number of miles by this time for the average speed of the moon in miles per hour: $1,500,000 \div 656 \approx 2,287$. The closest choice is 2,300 miles per hour.

661. **D. 890,352,000**

Start with the number of hours that it takes Mars to orbit the sun: $687\times 24 = 16,488$. Multiply this time by the distance covered in one hour: $16,488\times 54,000 = 890,352,000$. (Note that some calculators don't carry that many digits. If your calculator is one of those, simply multiply 16,488 by 54 and then add three zeros to your answer.)

662. **A. 226,000,000**

The orbit of Mercury is a circle with a radius of 36,000,000. To find the circumference, use $C = 2\pi r$ with 36,000,000 as the radius, and then multiply the numbers by 3.14 for π:

$$\begin{aligned} C &= 2\pi r \\ &= 2\pi(36,000,000) \\ &= 72,000,000\pi \\ &\approx 72,000,000\times 3.14 \\ &= 226,080,000 \end{aligned}$$

The question asks for the approximate distance, so round the answer to the nearest million. (Note that some calculators don't carry that many digits. If your calculator is one of those, simply use 36 for the radius and then add six zeros to your answer.)

663. B. 107,000

The orbit of Mercury is a circle with a radius of 36,000,000. To find the circumference, use $C = 2\pi r$ with 36,000,000 as the radius, and then multiply the numbers by 3.14 for π:

$$\begin{aligned} C &= 2\pi r \\ &= 2\pi(36,000,000) \\ &= 72,000,000\pi \\ &\approx 72,000,000 \times 3.14 \\ &= 226,080,000 \end{aligned}$$

You can round the answer to the nearest million.

To find the miles per day, divide by 88:

$$226,000,000 \div 88 \approx 2,568,182$$

Now divide this by 24 for the miles traveled in one hour:

$$2,568,182 \div 24 \approx 107,008$$

Round this answer down to the nearest thousand.

664. A. A few cars are valued much less than the rest.

If the car values were evenly spaced apart, the mean and median would be the same. However, if a few cars were valued much lower than the others, these few cars would bring the mean down to a value less than the median.

665. D. A few students scored much higher than the rest.

If the test scores were evenly spaced apart, the mean and median would be the same. However, if a few students scored much higher than the rest, these few students would bring the mean up to a value greater than the median.

666. D. The exam scores are evenly spaced out.

Evenly spaced scores would explain why the mean and the median are the same. If most students scored below 92, that would bring both the mean and the median below 92. If most scored above 92, that would bring them above 92. And if the scores were randomly spread out, the mean and median would be different. Extra credit has no bearing on the similarity between the mean and the median.

667. **A.** $|e - a| < 100{,}000$

The difference between the estimated cost and the actual cost has to be less than 100,000. Placing a and e inside the absolute value bars means that it doesn't matter whether a or e is greater; the difference has to be less than 100,000.

668. **B.** $|e - a| < \frac{e}{10}$

The difference between the estimated cost and the actual cost has to be less than 10%, or $\frac{1}{10}$, of the estimated cost. Placing a and e inside the absolute value means that it doesn't matter whether a or e is greater; the difference has to be less than $\frac{e}{10}$. Choice (A), $|e - a| < \frac{a}{10}$, incorrectly compares the difference to 10% of the actual cost, not the estimated cost.

669. **A.** $r^3 = \frac{3V}{4\pi}$

To isolate r^3, multiply both sides by $\frac{3}{4\pi}$, which cancels the fraction from r^3 and ties it to V.

670. **D.** $\pi = \frac{3V}{4r^3}$

To isolate π, multiply both sides by $\frac{3}{4r^3}$, which cancels the fraction from π and ties it to V.

671. **D. It would be multiplied by 8.**

Plug in 3 as the radius and solve for the volume:

$$V = \frac{4\pi r^3}{3} = \frac{4\pi(3)^3}{3} = \frac{4\pi(27)}{3} = 4\pi(9) = 36\pi$$

Now double the radius to 6, and solve for the volume:

$$V = \frac{4\pi r^3}{3} = \frac{4\pi(6)^3}{3} = \frac{4\pi(216)}{3} = 4\pi(72) = 288\pi$$

To find the factor of increase, divide the new volume by the old volume:

$$\frac{288\pi}{36\pi} = \frac{288}{36} = 8$$

672. **B.** $r^2 = \frac{A}{4\pi}$

To isolate r^2, divide both sides by 4π.

673. **B.** $\pi = \frac{A}{4r^2}$

To isolate π, divide both sides by $4r^2$.

674. **C. It would quadruple.**

Plug in 5 for the radius and solve for the surface area:

$$A = 4\pi r^2 = 4\pi(5)^2 = 4\pi(25) = 100\pi$$

Now increase the radius to 10 and solve for the surface area:

$$A = 4\pi r^2 = 4\pi(10)^2 = 4\pi(100) = 400\pi$$

To find the factor of increase, divide the new surface area by the old one:

$$\frac{400\pi}{100\pi} = \frac{400}{100} = 4$$

675. **B.** 2

First convert the equation to the standard circle equation:

$$(x-h)^2 + (y-k)^2 = r^2$$

where *r* is the radius of the circle. From the original equation, start by moving the *x*'s and *y*'s together:

$$x^2 + y^2 + 6x - 4y = -9$$
$$x^2 + 6x + y^2 - 4y = -9$$

The $x^2 + 6x$ tells you that $(x+3)^2$ is part of the equation. FOIL this out to $x^2 + 6x + 9$. However, the $x^2 + 6x$ is by itself on the left, so add 9 to both sides of the equation:

$$x^2 + 6x + y^2 - 4y = -9$$
$$x^2 + 6x + 9 + y^2 - 4y = 0$$

Also, $y^2 - 4y$ tells you that $(y-2)^2$ is part of the equation, which FOILs out to $y^2 - 4y + 4$. However, the $y^2 - 4y$ is by itself on the left, so add 4 to both sides, like this:

$$x^2 + 6x + 9 + y^2 - 4y = 0$$
$$x^2 + 6x + 9 + y^2 - 4y + 4 = 4$$

To convert the circle to its standard form, factor x^2+6x+9 into $(x+3)^2$ and y^2-4y+4 into $(y-2)^2$, like this:

$$x^2+6x+9+y^2-4y+4=4$$
$$(x+3)^2+(y-2)^2=4$$

Now the circle is in its familiar form, and $r^2=4$, so $r=2$.

676. **A.** $(-3,2)$

First convert the equation to the standard circle equation:

$$(x-h)^2+(y-k)^2=r^2$$

where h is the x-coordinate and k is the y-coordinate of the center of the circle. From the original equation, start by moving the x's and y's together:

$$x^2+y^2+6x-4y=-9$$
$$x^2+6x+y^2-4y=-9$$

The x^2+6x tells you that $(x+3)^2$ is part of the equation. FOIL this out to x^2+6x+9. However, the x^2+6x is by itself on the left, so add 9 to both sides of the equation:

$$x^2+6x+y^2-4y=-9$$
$$x^2+6x+9+y^2-4y=0$$

Also, y^2-4y tells you that $(y-2)^2$ is part of the equation, which FOILs out to y^2-4y+4. However, the y^2-4y is by itself on the left, so add 4 to both sides, like this:

$$x^2+6x+9+y^2-4y=0$$
$$x^2+6x+9+y^2-4y+4=4$$

To convert the circle to its standard form, factor x^2+6x+9 into $(x+3)^2$ and y^2-4y+4 into $(y-2)^2$, like this:

$$x^2+6x+9+y^2-4y+4=4$$
$$(x+3)^2+(y-2)^2=4$$

Now the circle is in its familiar form, where $h=-3$ and $k=2$.

677. D. 5

First convert the equation to the standard circle equation:

$$(x-h)^2+(y-k)^2=r^2$$

where r is the radius of the circle. From the original equation, start by moving the x's and y's together:

$$x^2+y^2-6x-8y=0$$
$$x^2-6x+y^2-8y=0$$

The x^2-6x tells you that $(x-3)^2$ is part of the equation. FOIL this out to x^2-6x+9. However, the x^2-6x is by itself on the left, so add 9 to both sides of the equation:

$$x^2-6x+y^2-8y=0$$
$$x^2-6x+9+y^2-8y=9$$

Also, y^2-8y tells you that $(y-4)^2$ is part of the equation, which FOILs out to $y^2-8y+16$. However, the y^2-8y is by itself on the left, so add 16 to both sides, like this:

$$x^2-6x+9+y^2-8y=9$$
$$x^2-6x+9+y^2-8y+16=25$$

To convert the circle to its standard form, factor x^2-6x+9 into $(x-3)^2$ and $y^2-8y+16$ into $(y-4)^2$, like this:

$$x^2-6x+9+y^2-8y+16=25$$
$$(x-3)^2+(y-4)^2=25$$

Now the circle is in its familiar form, and $r^2=25$, so $r=5$.

678. C. (3, 4)

First convert the equation to the standard circle equation:

$$(x-h)^2+(y-k)^2=r^2$$

where h is the x-coordinate and k is the y-coordinate of the center of the circle. From the original equation, start by moving the x's and y's together:

$$x^2+y^2-6x-8y=0$$
$$x^2-6x+y^2-8y=0$$

The x^2-6x tells you that $(x-3)^2$ is part of the equation. FOIL this out to x^2-6x+9. However, the x^2-6x is by itself on the left, so add 9 to both sides of the equation:

$$x^2-6x+y^2-8y=0$$
$$x^2-6x+9+y^2-8y=9$$

Also, $y^2 - 8y$ tells you that $(y-4)^2$ is part of the equation, which FOILs out to $y^2 - 8y + 16$. However, the $y^2 - 8y$ is by itself on the left, so add 16 to both sides, like this:

$$x^2 - 6x + 9 + y^2 - 8y = 9$$
$$x^2 - 6x + 9 + y^2 - 8y + 16 = 25$$

To convert the circle to its standard form, factor $x^2 - 6x + 9$ into $(x-3)^2$ and $y^2 - 8y + 16$ into $(y-4)^2$, like this:

$$x^2 - 6x + 9 + y^2 - 8y + 16 = 25$$
$$(x-3)^2 + (y-4)^2 = 25$$

Now the circle is in its familiar form, where $h = 3$ and $k = 4$.

---

679. **C. 3**

First convert the equation to the standard circle equation:

$$(x-h)^2 + (y-k)^2 = r^2$$

where r is the radius of the circle.

From the original equation, start by moving the x's and y's together:

$$x^2 + y^2 + 2x + 2y = 7$$
$$x^2 + 2x + y^2 + 2y = 7$$

The $x^2 + 2x$ tells you that $(x+1)^2$ is part of the equation. FOIL this out to $x^2 + 2x + 1$. However, the $x^2 + 2x$ is by itself on the left, so add 1 to both sides of the equation:

$$x^2 + y^2 + 2x + 2y = 7$$
$$x^2 + 2x + 1 + y^2 + 2y = 8$$

Also, $y^2 + 2y$ tells you that $(y+1)^2$ is part of the equation, which FOILs out to $y^2 + 2y + 1$. However, the $y^2 + 2y$ is by itself on the left, so add 1 to both sides, like this:

$$x^2 + 2x + 1 + y^2 + 2y = 8$$
$$x^2 + 2x + 1 + y^2 + 2y + 1 = 9$$

To convert the circle to its standard form, factor $x^2 + 2x + 1$ into $(x+1)^2$ and $y^2 + 2y + 1$ into $(y+1)^2$, like this:

$$x^2 + 2x + 1 + y^2 + 2y = 8$$
$$(x+1)^2 + (y+1)^2 = 9$$

Now the circle is in its familiar form, and $r^2 = 9$, so $r = 3$.

680. **C. (−1, −1)**

First convert the equation to the standard circle equation:

$$(x-h)^2+(y-k)^2=r^2$$

where h is the x-coordinate and k is the y-coordinate of the center of the circle. From the original equation, start by moving the x's and y's together:

$$x^2+y^2+2x+2y=7$$
$$x^2+2x+y^2+2y=7$$

The x^2+2x tells you that $(x+1)^2$ is part of the equation. FOIL this out to x^2+2x+1. However, the x^2+2x is by itself on the left, so add 1 to both sides of the equation:

$$x^2+y^2+2x+2y=7$$
$$x^2+2x+1+y^2+2y=8$$

Also, y^2+2y tells you that $(y+1)^2$ is part of the equation, which FOILs out to y^2+2y+1. However, the y^2+2y is by itself on the left, so add 1 to both sides, like this:

$$x^2+2x+1+y^2+2y=8$$
$$x^2+2x+1+y^2+2y+1=9$$

To convert the circle to its standard form, factor x^2+2x+1 into $(x+1)^2$ and y^2+2y+1 into $(y+1)^2$, like this:

$$x^2+2x+1+y^2+2y=8$$
$$(x+1)^2+(y+1)^2=9$$

Now the circle is in its familiar form, where $h=-1$ and $k=-1$.

ANSWERS 601–700

681. **B. 2**

First convert the equation to the standard circle equation:

$$(x-h)^2+(y-k)^2=r^2$$

where r is the radius of the circle. From the original equation, $x^2+y^2-4y=0$, the y^2-4y tells you that $(y-2)^2$ is part of the equation. FOIL this out to y^2-4y+4. However, the y^2-4y is by itself on the left, so add 4 to both sides of the equation:

$$x^2+y^2-4y=0$$
$$x^2+y^2-4y+4=4$$

To convert the circle to its standard form, factor $y^2 - 4y + 4$ into $(y-2)^2$, like this:

$$x^2 + y^2 - 4y + 4 = 4$$
$$x^2 + (y-2)^2 = 4$$

Now the circle is in its familiar form, and $r^2 = 4$, so $r = 2$.

682. **A. (0, 2)**

First convert the equation to the standard circle equation:

$$(x-h)^2 + (y-k)^2 = r^2$$

where h is the x-coordinate and k is the y-coordinate of the center of the circle. From the original equation, $x^2 + y^2 - 4y = 0$, the $y^2 - 4y$ tells you that $(y-2)^2$ is part of the equation. FOIL this out to $y^2 - 4y + 4$. However, the $y^2 - 4y$ is by itself on the left, so add 4 to both sides of the equation:

$$x^2 + y^2 - 4y = 0$$
$$x^2 + y^2 - 4y + 4 = 4$$

To convert the circle to its standard form, factor $y^2 - 4y + 4$ into $(y-2)^2$, like this:

$$x^2 + y^2 - 4y + 4 = 4$$
$$x^2 + (y-2)^2 = 4$$

Now the circle is in its familiar form, where $h = 0$ and $k = 2$.

683. **B. 5**

First convert the equation to the standard circle equation:

$$(x-h)^2 + (y-k)^2 = r^2$$

where r is the radius of the circle.

From the original equation, start by moving the x's and y's together:

$$x^2 + y^2 - 20x = -75$$
$$x^2 - 20x + y^2 = -75$$

The $x^2 - 20x$ tells you that $(x-10)^2$ is part of the equation. FOIL this out to $x^2 - 20x + 100$. However, the $x^2 - 20x$ is by itself on the left, so add 100 to both sides of the equation:

$$x^2 - 20x + y^2 = -75$$
$$x^2 - 20x + 100 + y^2 = 25$$

ANSWERS 601–700

To convert the circle to its standard form, factor $x^2 - 20x + 100$ into $(x-10)^2$, like this:

$$x^2 - 20x + 100 + y^2 = 25$$
$$(x-10)^2 + y^2 = 25$$

Now the circle is in its familiar form, and $r^2 = 25$, so $r = 5$.

684. **B. $(10, 0)$**

First convert the equation to the standard circle equation:

$$(x-h)^2 + (y-k)^2 = r^2$$

where h is the x-coordinate and k is the y-coordinate of the center of the circle. From the original equation, start by moving the x's and y's together:

$$x^2 + y^2 - 20x = -75$$
$$x^2 - 20x + y^2 = -75$$

The $x^2 - 20x$ tells you that $(x-10)^2$ is part of the equation. FOIL this out to $x^2 - 20x + 100$. However, the $x^2 - 20x$ is by itself on the left, so add 100 to both sides of the equation:

$$x^2 - 20x + y^2 = -75$$
$$x^2 - 20x + 100 + y^2 = 25$$

To convert the circle to its standard form, factor $x^2 - 20x + 100$ into $(x-10)^2$, like this:

$$x^2 - 20x + 100 + y^2 = 25$$
$$(x-10)^2 + y^2 = 25$$

Now the circle is in its familiar form, where $h = 10$ and $k = 0$.

ANSWERS 601–700

685. **C. –1**

If the line has equal x- and y-intercepts, then pick a number for the intercepts, such as 3: The line crosses at $(3, 0)$ and $(0, 3)$. Using rise over run, the line rises 3 and runs -3, for a slope of -1.

686. **A. Quadrant I**

If the line has negative x- and y-intercepts, then suppose, for example, it crosses at $(-3, 0)$ and $(0, -3)$. It thus crosses into Quadrants II, III, and IV.

687. **A. 1**

If the x-intercept is the negative of the y-intercept, then pick numbers for the intercepts, such as 3 and −3: The line crosses at $(3, 0)$ and $(0, -3)$. Using rise over run, the line rises 3 and runs 3, for a slope of 1.

688. **C. −1 or 1**

If the line has equal x- and y-intercepts, then pick a number for the intercepts, such as 3: The line crosses at $(3, 0)$ and $(0, 3)$. Using rise over run, the line rises 3 and runs −3, for a slope of −1.

Or, if the x-intercept is the negative of the y-intercept, then pick numbers such as 3 and −3 for the intercepts: The line crosses at $(3, 0)$ and $(0, -3)$. Using rise over run, the line rises 3 and runs 3, for a slope of 1.

689. **B. Quadrant II**

If the line has a negative y-intercept, then it's automatically in Quadrants III and IV. The positive slope carries it upward, to the right, into Quadrant I.

690. **C. Quadrant III**

If the line has a positive y-intercept, then it's automatically in Quadrants I and II. The negative slope carries it downward, to the right, into Quadrant IV.

691. **D.** $-\frac{1}{2}$

If the y-intercept is twice the x-intercept, then pick numbers for the intercepts, such as 3 and 6: The line crosses at $(3, 0)$ and $(0, 6)$.

Using rise over run, the line rises 3 and runs −6, for a slope of $-\frac{1}{2}$.

692. **D. 2**

If $|b| = |2a|$ and $0 > a > b$, the intercepts are both negative.

If the x-intercept is twice the y-intercept, then pick numbers for the intercepts, such as −2 and −4, respectively: The line crosses at $(-2, 0)$ and $(0, -4)$. Using rise over run, the line rises −4 and runs −2, for a slope of 2.

693. **A. 3**

If f is the number of feet, $12f$ is the number of inches in f feet. Set up the equation:

$$\begin{aligned} 12f + 9 &= 45 \\ 12f &= 36 \\ f &= 3 \end{aligned}$$

694. B. 3

If y is the number of yards, $36y$ is the number of inches in y yards. Set up the equation:

$$\begin{aligned} 36y+6&=114 \\ 36y&=108 \\ y&=3 \end{aligned}$$

695. B. $140

If Todd and Dan earned $250, then $D+T=250$. If Dan earned $30 more than Todd, then $D-T=30$. Add the two equations to eliminate T and solve for D:

$$\begin{array}{r} D+T=250 \\ +(D-T=\ \ 30) \\ \hline 2D\quad =280 \\ D=140 \end{array}$$

696. C. 40

If Juliet and Karen collected 65 coins, then $J+K=65$. If Juliet collected 15 more coins than Karen, then $J-K=15$. Add the two equations to eliminate K and solve for J:

$$\begin{array}{r} J+K=65 \\ +(J-K=15) \\ \hline 2J\quad =80 \\ J=40 \end{array}$$

697. D. 7

Set up the equation with x as the number of years:

$$\begin{aligned} 11+3x&=32 \\ 3x&=21 \\ x&=7 \end{aligned}$$

698. A. 96

A rise of 12 feet is 144 inches, because $12\times 12=144$. Set up the equation with x as the number of years:

$$\begin{aligned} 1.5x&=144 \\ x&=96 \end{aligned}$$

699. **A. 4**

Each month, the fish's length is multiplied by 1.2 for a 20% growth. The simplest way to find the answer is to multiply 10 by 1.2 until the length surpasses 20 inches:

$$\begin{array}{l} 10.0 \\ \underline{\times 1.2} \\ 12.0 \\ \underline{\times 1.2} \\ 14.4 \\ \underline{\times 1.2} \\ 17.3 \\ \underline{\times 1.2} \\ 20.8 \end{array}$$

You multiply by 1.2 four times, so the fish surpasses 20 inches in 4 months.

700. **B.** $L = 10(1.2)^m$

Each month, the fish's length is multiplied by 1.2 for a 20% growth. The exponent m multiplies the fish's length by 1.2 m times.

701. **A. 12**

The equation shows an initial value of 12 with an additional 1.2 for each month.

Another way to find the answer is to plug 0 in for m, because 0 months had passed when John first planted the tree:

$$\begin{aligned} h &= 1.2m + 12 \\ &= 1.2(0) + 12 \\ &= 12 \end{aligned}$$

702. **B. 1.2**

The m is the number of months, so each increase of m increments increases the height, h, by 1.2 feet.

703. **C. 18**

Plug 5 in for m, because 5 months have passed since John first planted the tree:

$$\begin{aligned} h &= 1.2m + 12 \\ &= 1.2(5) + 12 \\ &= 6 + 12 \\ &= 18 \end{aligned}$$

704. A. 10

Plug 0 in for *m*, because 0 months had passed when George first planted the palm tree. Remember that any number raised to the 0 power equals 1.

$$\begin{aligned} h &= 10(1.2)^m \\ &= 10(1.2)^0 \\ &= 10(1) \\ &= 10 \end{aligned}$$

705. B. 20%

To increase a value by a certain percent, convert the percent to a decimal and add 1. The 1.2 times *m* in the model suggests a growth factor of 0.2, which is 20%.

706. C. 17.3

Plug 3 in for *m*, because 3 months have passed since George first planted the palm tree:

$$\begin{aligned} h &= 10(1.2)^m \\ &= 10(1.2)^3 \\ &= 10(1.728) \\ &= 17.28 \\ &\approx 17.3 \end{aligned}$$

707. B. $s = 10(0.8)^w$

If the birds eat 20%, then 80% remains. This means that each week, *w*, you multiply the quantity of seed by 80%, or 0.8.

708. B. 6.4

Each week, decrease the amount of seed by 20% by multiplying it by 80%, or 0.8.

Or use the equation $s = 10(0.8)^w$. Plug 2 in for *w*, because 2 weeks have passed since Gerry first placed the feeder:

$$\begin{aligned} s &= 10(0.8)^w \\ &= 10(0.8)^2 \\ &= 10(0.64) \\ &= 6.4 \end{aligned}$$

709. **D. The birds will never finish the birdseed.**

If each week the remaining birdseed decreases by 20%, then the amount becomes smaller but never reaches 0.

710. **C.** $d = 50(0.5)^w$

If Jeffrey spends 50%, then 50% remains. This means that for each week, *w*, you multiply the remaining dollars by 50%, or 0.5.

711. **D. $6.25**

Each week, decrease the number of dollars by 50% by multiplying it by 50%, or 0.5.

Or use the equation $d = 50(0.5)^w$. Plug 3 in for *w*, because 3 weeks have passed:

$$\begin{aligned} d &= 50(0.5)^w \\ &= 50(0.5)^3 \\ &= 50(0.125) \\ &= 6.25 \end{aligned}$$

712. **D. Jeffrey will never spend all his money.**

If each week the remaining dollars decrease by 50%, then the amount becomes smaller but never reaches 0. (Though practically speaking, he'll be down to a penny after 12 weeks!)

713. **B.** $\frac{1}{10}$

The entire circle is 360°. Place the 36° angle over 360° and reduce it to $\frac{1}{10}$.

714. **A.** π

First find the circumference of the circle:

$$\begin{aligned} C &= 2\pi r \\ &= 2\pi(5) \\ &= 10\pi \end{aligned}$$

Then multiply the circumference by the fraction of the circle that is minor arc *NOP* $\left(\frac{36°}{360°} = \frac{1}{10}\right)$:

$$10\pi \times \frac{1}{10} = \pi$$

ANSWERS 701–800

715. **C.** $\frac{1}{12}$

The entire circle is 360°. Place the 30° angle over 360° and reduce it to $\frac{1}{12}$.

716. **D.** 60π

If minor arc *AOB* is $\frac{1}{12}$ of the circle $\left(\frac{30°}{360°}=\frac{1}{12}\right)$, then $\frac{1}{12}$ of the circle is 5π. Multiply 5π by 12 for the circumference.

717. **B.** 60°

The entire circle is 360°. Multiply this by $\frac{1}{6}$ for the answer.

718. **B.** 2π

First find the circumference of the circle:

$$\begin{aligned} C &= 2\pi r \\ &= 2\pi(6) \\ &= 12\pi \end{aligned}$$

Then multiply this by the fraction of the circle that is minor arc *POQ*:

$$12\pi \times \frac{1}{6} = 2\pi$$

719. **C.** 72°

The entire circle is 360°. Multiply this by $\frac{1}{5}$ for the answer.

720. **D.** 50π

If minor arc *QOR* is $\frac{1}{5}$ of the circle, then $\frac{1}{5}$ of the circle is 10π. Multiply 10π by 5 for the answer.

721. **C.** $f(x) = x^2 + 1$

In each answer choice, plug in one of the numbers, such as 3, for x and see which gives you the corresponding value, such as 10, for $f(x)$.

722. **B.** $f(x) = x^3 - 2$

In each answer choice, plug in one of the numbers, such as 3, for x and see which gives you the corresponding value, such as 25, for $f(x)$.

723. **C.** $f(x)=100(2)^{x/2}$

In each answer choice, plug in one of the numbers, such as 6, for x and see which results in the corresponding value, such as 800, for $f(x)$.

724. **B. II and III:** $f(x)=100(2)^{x/2}$ **and** $f(x)=100(4)^{x/4}$

In each function, plug in one of the numbers, such as 8, for x and see which results in the corresponding value, such as 1,600, for $f(x)$.

725. **D. 44**

The key phrase in this question is *closest to;* 10% of 139 boys is $0.10\times139=13.9\approx14$, and 15% of 202 girls is $0.15\times202=30.3\approx30$. Add these together for a total of 44.

726. **B. 284**

The key phrase in this question is *closest to;* 42% of 245 boys is $0.42\times245=102.9\approx103$, and 57% of 318 girls is $0.57\times318=181.26\approx181$. Add these together for a total of 284.

727. **C.** $5x^2-2x+1$

Add each term of the two polynomials:

$$\begin{array}{r} 2x^2+3x-5 \\ +\left(3x^2-5x+6\right) \\ \hline 5x^2-2x+1 \end{array}$$

728. **A.** x^2+5x-1

Subtract each term of the second polynomial from each term of the first one:

$$\begin{array}{r} 4x^2+3x-2 \\ -\left(3x^2-2x-1\right) \\ \hline x^2+5x-1 \end{array}$$

729. **C.** $x^2-3x-10$

Product means "multiply." This is a simple FOIL operation:

$$(x+2)(x-5)=x^2-3x-10$$

ANSWERS 701–800

730. **B.** $x-3$

Factor each polynomial to its two binomials:

$$x^2-2x-3=(x+1)(x-3)$$
$$x^2-x-6=(x+2)(x-3)$$

Only $x-3$ is a factor of both.

731. **D.** $x+3$

Factor each polynomial to its two binomials:

$$x^2+6x+9=(x+3)(x+3)$$
$$x^2-9=(x+3)(x-3)$$

Only $x+3$ is a factor of both.

732. **C.** −2

Both equations are equal to 0, so set them equal to each other and solve for *x*:

$$x^2+5x+6=x^2-x-6$$
$$5x+6=-x-6$$
$$6x=-12$$
$$x=-2$$

733. **A.** 4

Both equations are equal to 0, so set them equal to each other and solve for *x*:

$$x^2-2x-8=x^2-16$$
$$-2x-8=-16$$
$$-2x=-8$$
$$x=4$$

734. **B.** $\frac{9}{8}$

Multiply both sides by the reciprocal of $\frac{2}{3}$, which is $\frac{3}{2}$, to isolate the *x*:

$$\frac{2}{3}x=\frac{3}{4}$$
$$x=\frac{3}{4}\left(\frac{3}{2}\right)$$
$$x=\frac{9}{8}$$

ANSWERS 701–800

735. **A.** $\frac{10}{9}$

Multiply both sides by the reciprocal of $\frac{6}{5}$, which is $\frac{5}{6}$, to isolate the *x*. Don't forget to cross-cancel as you simplify the fractions:

$$\frac{6}{5}x = \frac{4}{3}$$
$$x = \frac{4}{3}\left(\frac{5}{6}\right)$$
$$x = \frac{{}^{2}\not{4}}{3}\left(\frac{5}{\not{6}_{3}}\right)$$
$$x = \frac{10}{9}$$

736. **C. 1,500**

Sally travels 85 feet in 10 seconds; set this up as an equation. Find the distance traveled in one minute by multiplying both sides by 6:

$$(85\text{ feet})\times 6 = (10\text{ seconds})\times 6$$
$$510\text{ feet} = 60\text{ seconds}$$

To find the distance traveled in 3 minutes, multiply 510 by 3:

$$510\times 3 = 1,530 \approx 1,500$$

737. **A. Fifteen thousand feet**

Scott travels 60 feet in 5 seconds; set this up as an equation. Find the distance traveled in one minute by multiplying both sides by 12:

$$(60\text{ feet})\times 12 = (5\text{ seconds})\times 12$$
$$720\text{ feet} = 60\text{ seconds}$$

To find the distance traveled in 20 minutes, multiply 720 by 20:

$$720\times 20 = 14,400 \approx 15,000$$

738. **C. Slightly less than two miles**

Kate rolls 170 feet in 20 seconds; set this up as an equation. Find the distance traveled in one minute by multiplying both sides by 3:

$$(170\text{ feet})\times 3 = (20\text{ seconds})\times 3$$
$$510\text{ feet} = 60\text{ seconds}$$

To find the number of feet traveled in 20 minutes, multiply 510 by 20:

$$510\times 20 = 10,200$$

Divide this number of feet by the feet in a mile to see how many miles she traveled: $10,200 \div 5,280 = 1.93$, so Kate travels slightly less than 2 miles.

739. **D.** $c = 20d + 0.35m$

The cost is equal to 20 times the number of days, *d*, plus 0.35 times the number of miles, *m*.

740. **A.** $c = 6h + 0.15m$

The cost is equal to 6 times the number of hours, *h*, plus 0.15 times the number of miles, *m*.

741. **C. 19**

Supplementary angles total 180°. Add the angles and set them equal to 180:

$$\begin{aligned} 6k + 6 + 3k + 3 &= 180 \\ 9k + 9 &= 180 \\ 9k &= 171 \\ k &= 19 \end{aligned}$$

742. **A. 7**

Supplementary angles total 180°. Add the angles and set them equal to 180:

$$\begin{aligned} 5p + 5 + 18p + 14 &= 180 \\ 23p + 19 &= 180 \\ 23p &= 161 \\ p &= 7 \end{aligned}$$

743. **D. 10**

Because the angles are acute and $\cos(n°) = \sin(p°)$, the complementary-angle property of sines and cosines applies; it states that $n + p = 90$. Plug in 5*x* for *n* and 4*x* for *p*, and solve for *x*:

$$\begin{aligned} n + p &= 90 \\ (5x) + (4x) &= 90 \\ 9x &= 90 \\ x &= 10 \end{aligned}$$

744. **A. 4**

Because the angles are acute and $\sin(q°) = \cos(r°)$, the complementary-angle property of sines and cosines applies; it states that $q + r = 90$. Plug in $8x + 3$ for q and $13x + 3$ for r, and solve for x:

$$\begin{aligned} q + r &= 90 \\ (8x+3)+(13x+3) &= 90 \\ 21x + 6 &= 90 \\ 21x &= 84 \\ x &= 4 \end{aligned}$$

745. **C. 69π**

Per the formula bar at the beginning of the SAT's Math section, you can find the volumes of a right circular cone and cylinder with $V = \frac{1}{3}\pi r^2 h$ and $V = \pi r^2 h$, respectively.

The radius of each is 3, and the heights of the cone and cylinder are 5 and 6, respectively. Plug the numbers into the formulas and add the results together. First the cone:

$$\begin{aligned} V &= \frac{1}{3}\pi r^2 h \\ &= \frac{1}{3}\pi(3)^2 5 \\ &= \frac{1}{3}\pi(9)5 \\ &= (3)\pi 5 \\ &= 15\pi \end{aligned}$$

Then the cylinder:

$$\begin{aligned} V &= \pi r^2 h \\ &= \pi(3)^2 6 \\ &= \pi(9)6 \\ &= 54\pi \end{aligned}$$

Now add the volumes together:

$$15\pi + 54\pi = 69\pi$$

746. **C. 220**

Per the formula bar at the beginning of the SAT's Math section, you can find the volumes of a right circular cone and cylinder with $V = \frac{1}{3}\pi r^2 h$ and $V = \pi r^2 h$, respectively.

ANSWERS 701–800

The radius of each is 3, and the heights of the cone and cylinder are 5 and 6, respectively. Plug the numbers into the formulas and add the results together. First the cone:

$$\begin{aligned} V &= \frac{1}{3}\pi r^2 h \\ &= \frac{1}{3}\pi(3)^2 5 \\ &= \frac{1}{3}\pi(9)5 \\ &= (3)\pi 5 \\ &= 15\pi \end{aligned}$$

Then the cylinder:

$$\begin{aligned} V &= \pi r^2 h \\ &= \pi(3)^2 6 \\ &= \pi(9)6 \\ &= 54\pi \end{aligned}$$

Now add them together and multiply by 3.14 for π:

$$\begin{aligned} 15\pi + 54\pi &= 69\pi \\ &\approx 69 \times 3.14 = 216.66 \approx 220 \end{aligned}$$

---

747. **A.** 16π

Per the formula bar at the beginning of the SAT's Math section, you can find the volumes of a right circular cone and cylinder with $V = \frac{1}{3}\pi r^2 h$ and $V = \pi r^2 h$, respectively.

The radius of each is 2, and the height of each is 3. Plug the numbers into the formulas and add the results together. First the cone:

$$\begin{aligned} V &= \frac{1}{3}\pi r^2 h \\ &= \frac{1}{3}\pi(2)^2 3 \\ &= \frac{1}{3}\pi(4)3 \\ &= 4\pi \end{aligned}$$

Then the cylinder:

$$\begin{aligned} V &= \pi r^2 h \\ &= \pi(2)^2 3 \\ &= \pi(4)3 \\ &= 12\pi \end{aligned}$$

Now add the volumes together:

$$4\pi + 12\pi = 16\pi$$

748. D. 50

Per the formula bar at the beginning of the SAT's Math section, you can find the volumes of a right circular cone and cylinder with $V = \frac{1}{3}\pi r^2 h$ and $V = \pi r^2 h$' respectively.

The radius of each is 2, and the height of each is 3. Plug the numbers into the formulas and add the results together. First the cone:

$$\begin{aligned} V &= \frac{1}{3}\pi r^2 h \\ &= \frac{1}{3}\pi(2)^2 3 \\ &= \frac{1}{3}\pi(4)3 \\ &= 4\pi \end{aligned}$$

Then the cylinder:

$$\begin{aligned} V &= \pi r^2 h \\ &= \pi(2)^2 3 \\ &= \pi(4)3 \\ &= 12\pi \end{aligned}$$

Now add them together and multiply by 3.14 for π:

$$\begin{aligned} 4\pi + 12\pi &= 16\pi \\ &\approx 16 \times 3.14 = 50.24 \approx 50 \end{aligned}$$

749. C. 591

Call the first number x. If x is 50% more than the sum of the other two numbers, then those two numbers together equal $\frac{2}{3}x$. All three numbers then equal $\frac{2}{3}x + x$, which equals 985. Set up the equation and solve for x:

$$\begin{aligned} \frac{2}{3}x + x &= 985 \\ \frac{5}{3}x &= 985 \\ 5x &= 2{,}955 \\ x &= 591 \end{aligned}$$

ANSWERS 701–800

750. C. 250

Call the first number x. If x is equal to five times the sum of the other four numbers, then those four numbers together equal $\frac{1}{5}x$. All five numbers then equal $\frac{1}{5}x + x$, which equals 300. Set up the equation and solve for x:

$$\begin{aligned}\frac{1}{5}x + x &= 300\\ \frac{6}{5}x &= 300\\ 6x &= 1{,}500\\ x &= 250\end{aligned}$$

751. B. 130

Call the first number x. If x is equal to half the sum of the other three numbers, then those three numbers together equal $2x$. All four numbers then equal $2x + x$, which equals 390. Set up the equation and solve for x:

$$\begin{aligned}2x + x &= 390\\ 3x &= 390\\ x &= 130\end{aligned}$$

752. C. 5

Call the average of these first five numbers x; the sum of these first five numbers is $5x$. If $5x$ is equal to one-third of the sum of the other 20 numbers, then those 20 numbers together equal $(3)5x = 15x$. All 25 numbers then equal $5x + 15x$, which equals 100. Set up the equation and solve for x:

$$\begin{aligned}5x + 15x &= 100\\ 20x &= 100\\ x &= 5\end{aligned}$$

753. C. 13

Call the average of these first two numbers x; the sum of these first two numbers is $2x$. If $2x$ is equal to twice the sum of the other four numbers, then those four numbers together equal $\frac{2x}{2} = x$. All six numbers then equal $2x + x$, which equals 39. Set up the equation and solve for x:

$$\begin{aligned}2x + x &= 39\\ 3x &= 39\\ x &= 13\end{aligned}$$

754. **D.** $40,000(0.95)^{y/5}$

Each time the sand reduces by 5%, multiply the amount of sand by 95% for the remaining amount. Because this cycle occurs every five years, divide y by 5 to get the number of cycles.

755. **B. 35,000**

Each time the sand reduces by 5%, multiply the amount of sand by 95% for the remaining amount. Because this cycle occurs every five years, divide y by 5 to get the number of cycles. The model looks like this:

$$40,000(0.95)^{\frac{y}{5}}$$

Plug 15 in for y to get the answer. The key word from the question is *approximately*.

$$\begin{aligned} 40,000(0.95)^{\frac{y}{5}} &= 40,000(0.95)^{\frac{15}{5}} \\ &= 40,000(0.95)^3 \\ &= 40,000(0.86) \\ &= 34,400 \approx 35,000 \end{aligned}$$

756. **D. The sand will never be completely washed away from the beach.**

If the number of tons of sand on the beach is incrementally reduced by 5%, then the number will continuously get smaller, but it will never reach 0.

757. **A.** $12,000(0.80)^{y/3}$

Each time the number decreases by 20%, multiply the number of crimes by 80% for the remaining amount. Because this cycle occurs every three years, divide y by 3 to get the number of cycles.

758. **C. 7,700**

Each time the number decreases by 20%, multiply the number of crimes by 80% for the remaining amount. Because this cycle occurs every three years, divide y by 3 to get the number of cycles. The model looks like this:

$$12,000(0.80)^{y/3}$$

Plug 6 in for y to get the answer. The key words from the question are *closest to.*

$$\begin{aligned}12{,}000(0.80)^{y/3} &= 12{,}000(0.80)^{6/3}\\ &= 12{,}000(0.80)^2\\ &= 12{,}000(0.64)\\ &= 7{,}680 \approx 7{,}700\end{aligned}$$

759. D. The street crimes will never be completely gone from the city.

If the number of street crimes is incrementally reduced by 20%, then the number will continuously get smaller, but it will never reach 0.

760. B. $60{,}000(1.20)^{y/5}$

Each time the population increases by 20%, multiply the number by 1.20 for the increased amount. Because this cycle occurs every five years, divide y by 5 to get the number of cycles.

761. C. 86,000

Each time the population increases by 20%, multiply the number by 1.20 for the increased amount. Because this cycle occurs every five years, divide y by 5 to get the number of cycles. The model looks like this:

$$60{,}000(1.20)^{y/5}$$

Plug 10 in for y to get the answer. The key words from the question are *closest to.*

$$\begin{aligned}60{,}000(1.20)^{y/5} &= 60{,}000(1.20)^{10/5}\\ &= 60{,}000(1.20)^2\\ &= 60{,}000(1.44)\\ &= 86{,}400 \approx 86{,}000\end{aligned}$$

762. C. 20 years

Each time the population increases by 20%, multiply the number by 1.20 for the increased amount. Because this cycle occurs every five years, divide y by 5 to get the number of cycles. The model looks like this:

$$60{,}000(1.20)^{y/5}$$

Plug 20 in for y to try out the answer. The key words from the question are *closest to.*

$$\begin{aligned}60{,}000(1.20)^{y/5} &= 60{,}000(1.20)^{20/5}\\ &= 60{,}000(1.20)^4\\ &= 60{,}000(2.07)\\ &= 124{,}200 \approx 120{,}000\end{aligned}$$

763. **B. 15**

Let x be the number of hardcover fiction books and y be the number of hardcover nonfiction books (y is the number you're after). Thus, the number of paperback fiction books is $2x$, and the number of paperback nonfiction books is $4y$. From this, you can make these two equations:

$$\begin{aligned}x + y &= 36\\ 2x + 4y &= 102\end{aligned}$$

Multiply the second equation by 2 and subtract it from the first equation to isolate the y:

$$\begin{aligned}&2x + 4y = 102\\ &2(x + y = 36)\end{aligned}$$

$$\begin{array}{r}2x + 4y = 102\\ -(2x + 2y = \ \ 72)\\ \hline 2y = \ \ 30\\ y = \ \ 15\end{array}$$

764. **C.** $\frac{10}{23}$

Let x be the number of hardcover fiction books and y be the number of hardcover nonfiction books ($4y$ is the number you're after). Thus, the number of paperback fiction books is $2x$, and the number of paperback nonfiction books is $4y$. From this, you can make these two equations:

$$\begin{aligned}x + y &= 36\\ 2x + 4y &= 102\end{aligned}$$

Divide the second equation by 2 and subtract it from the first equation to isolate the y:

$$\begin{array}{r}x + \ \ y = \ \ 36\\ -(x + 2y = \ \ 51)\\ \hline -y = -15\\ y = \ \ 15\end{array}$$

ANSWERS 701–800

Now multiply this by 4 to find the number of paperback nonfiction books: $15 \times 4 = 60$.

There are $36 + 102 = 138$ books total, so the probability of selecting one of the 60 paperback nonfiction books is $\frac{60}{138} = \frac{10}{23}$.

765. **D.** $\frac{7}{12}$

Let x be the number of hardcover fiction books and y be the number of hardcover nonfiction books (x and y are the numbers you're after). Thus, the number of paperback fiction books is $2x$, and the number of paperback nonfiction books is $4y$. From this, you can make these two equations:

$$x + y = 36$$
$$2x + 4y = 102$$

Divide the second equation by 2 and subtract it from the first equation to isolate the y:

$$\begin{aligned} x + \ y &= \ 36 \\ -(x + 2y &= \ 51) \\ \hline -y &= -15 \\ y &= \ 15 \end{aligned}$$

$$\begin{aligned} x + y &= 36 \\ x + (15) &= 36 \\ x &= 21 \end{aligned}$$

There are 36 hardcover books total, so the probability of selecting one that is fiction is $\frac{21}{36} = \frac{7}{12}$.

766. **B.** 5

Let x be the number of cedar acoustic guitars and y be the number of mahogany acoustic guitars (y is the number you're after). Thus, the number of cedar electric guitars is $3x$, and the number of mahogany electric guitars is $5y$. From this, you can make these two equations:

$$x + y = 10$$
$$3x + 5y = 40$$

Multiply the first equation by 3 and subtract it from the second equation to isolate the y:

$$3x + 5y = 40$$
$$3(x + y = 10)$$

$$\begin{aligned} 3x + 5y &= 40 \\ -(3x + 3y &= 30) \\ \hline 2y &= 10 \\ y &= \ 5 \end{aligned}$$

ANSWERS 701–800

767. C. 50%

Let x be the number of cedar acoustic guitars and y be the number of mahogany acoustic guitars. Thus, the number of cedar electric guitars is $3x$, and the number of mahogany electric guitars is $5y$ ($5y$ is the number you're after). From this, you can make these two equations:

$$x + y = 10$$
$$3x + 5y = 40$$

Multiply the first equation by 3 and subtract it from the second equation; then find $5y$:

$$3x + 5y = 40$$
$$3(x + y = 10)$$

$$\begin{aligned} 3x + 5y &= 40 \\ -(3x + 3y &= 30) \\ \hline 2y &= 10 \\ 5y &= 25 \end{aligned}$$

There are $10 + 40 = 50$ guitars total, so the probability of selecting one of the 25 mahogany electric guitars is $\frac{25}{50} = 50\%$.

768. A. One out of two

Let x be the number of cedar acoustic guitars and y be the number of mahogany acoustic guitars. Thus, the number of cedar electric guitars is $3x$, and the number of mahogany electric guitars is $5y$ (x and y are the numbers you're after). From this, you can make these two equations:

$$x + y = 10$$
$$3x + 5y = 40$$

Multiply the first equation by 3 and subtract it from the second equation to isolate the y:

$$3x + 5y = 40$$
$$3(x + y = 10)$$

$$\begin{aligned} 3x + 5y &= 40 \\ -(3x + 3y &= 30) \\ \hline 2y &= 10 \\ y &= 5 \end{aligned}$$

ANSWERS 701–800

Now plug in 5 for y in the first equation to find x:

$$x+y=10$$
$$x+(5)=10$$
$$x=5$$

There are 10 acoustic guitars total, so the probability of selecting one that is cedar is $\frac{5}{10}=\frac{1}{2}$.

769. **A. x is 2 more than y.**

First simplify the equations and set them equal to a and b, respectively:

$$8x+a=11x+3$$
$$a=3x+3$$

$$7y+b=10y+3$$
$$b=3y+3$$

Because a minus b is 6, $a-b=6$ and $a=b+6$. If $a=(3x+3)$ and $b=(3y+3)$, then $(3x+3)=(3y+3)+6$.

Now simplify the equation until it matches an answer choice:

$$(3x+3)=(3y+3)+6$$
$$3x+3=3y+3+6$$
$$3x=3y+6$$
$$x=y+2$$

770. **B. x is half the value of y.**

First simplify the equations and set them equal to a and b, respectively:

$$7x+a=11x+3$$
$$a=4x+3$$

$$4y+b=6y+1$$
$$b=2y+1$$

Because a minus b is 2, $a-b=2$ and $a=b+2$. If $a=(4x+3)$ and $b=(2y+1)$, then $(4x+3)=(2y+1)+2$.

Now simplify the equation until it matches an answer choice:

$$(4x+3)=(2y+1)+2$$
$$4x+3=2y+3$$
$$4x=2y$$
$$2x=y$$

771. **A. 0**

Simplify the expression, starting with the distribution of –5 in the second half:

$$
\begin{aligned}
&(2x^2+3x-5)-5(x^2+2x-1)\\
&=(2x^2+3x-5)-5x^2-10x+5\\
&=2x^2+3x-5-5x^2-10x+5\\
&=-3x^2-7x
\end{aligned}
$$

Because there's no constant c, $-3x^2-7x$ is the same as $-3x^2-7x+0$, making $c=0$.

772. **C. –4**

Simplify the expression, starting with the distribution of 2 in the second half:

$$
\begin{aligned}
&(3x^2-5x-2)+2(-2x^2+4x-1)\\
&=(3x^2-5x-2)-4x^2+8x-2\\
&=3x^2-5x-2-4x^2+8x-2\\
&=-x^2+3x-4
\end{aligned}
$$

Therefore, $c=-4$.

773. **D. $\frac{1}{4}$**

A circle is 2π radians, and $\frac{\pi}{2}$ radians is a fourth of 2π radians, so $\frac{\pi}{2}$ radians is a fourth of the circle.

774. **A. 90°**

You know that π radians is 180°, making $\frac{\pi}{2}$ radians 90°.

775. **A. 2π**

First find the circumference:

$$
\begin{aligned}
C&=2\pi r\\
&=2\pi(4)\\
&=8\pi
\end{aligned}
$$

Now multiply this by the fraction of the circle. A circle is 2π radians, and $\frac{\pi}{2}$ radians is a fourth of 2π radians, so $\frac{\pi}{2}$ radians is a fourth of the circle:

$$8\pi\left(\frac{1}{4}\right)=2\pi$$

776. C. 4π

First find the area:

$$\begin{aligned} A &= \pi r^2 \\ &= \pi(4)^2 \\ &= 16\pi \end{aligned}$$

Now multiply this by the fraction of the circle. A circle is 2π radians, and $\frac{\pi}{2}$ radians is a fourth of 2π radians, so $\frac{\pi}{2}$ radians is a fourth of the circle:

$$16\pi\left(\frac{1}{4}\right) = 4\pi$$

777. D. $\frac{3}{8}$

A circle is 2π radians, so π radians is half the circle:

$$\frac{3\pi}{4} = \frac{3}{4}\left(\frac{1}{2}\right) = \frac{3}{8}$$

Therefore, $\frac{3\pi}{4}$ radians is $\frac{3}{8}$ of the circle.

778. B. 135°

You know π radians is 180°, making $\frac{3\pi}{4}$ radians $\frac{3}{4} \times 180° = 135°$.

779. D. 6π

First find the circumference:

$$\begin{aligned} C &= 2\pi r \\ &= 2\pi(8) \\ &= 16\pi \end{aligned}$$

Now multiply the circumference by the fraction of the circle. A circle is 2π radians, so π radians is half the circle, and $\frac{3\pi}{4}$ radians is $\frac{3}{8}$ of the circle.

$$16\pi \times \frac{3}{8} = \frac{48\pi}{8} = 6\pi$$

ANSWERS 701–800

780. C. 24π

First find the area:

$$\begin{aligned} A &= \pi r^2 \\ &= \pi(8)^2 \\ &= 64\pi \end{aligned}$$

Now multiply the area by the fraction of the circle. A circle is 2π radians, so π radians is half the circle, and $\frac{3\pi}{4}$ radians is $\frac{3}{8}$ of the circle.

$$64\pi \times \frac{3}{8} = 8\pi \times 3 = 24\pi$$

781. **D.** $\frac{1}{8}$

A circle is 360°. Divide the measure of angle *KOL* by 360° for the fraction of the circle:

$$\frac{45°}{360°} = \frac{1}{8}$$

782. **B.** $\frac{\pi}{4}$

You know that π radians is 180°. Angle *KOL* is $\frac{45°}{180°} = \frac{1}{4}$ of this, making the angle $\frac{\pi}{4}$ radians.

783. **A.** π

First find the circumference:

$$\begin{aligned} C &= 2\pi r \\ &= 2\pi(4) \\ &= 8\pi \end{aligned}$$

Now multiply the circumference by the fraction of the circle. A circle is 360°. Divide the measure of angle *KOL* by 360° for the fraction of the circle:

$$\frac{45°}{360°} = \frac{1}{8}$$

Then multiply by the circumference:

$$8\pi \times \frac{1}{8} = \pi$$

784. **A.** 2π

First find the area:

$$\begin{aligned} A &= \pi r^2 \\ &= \pi(4)^2 \\ &= 16\pi \end{aligned}$$

Now multiply this by the fraction of the circle. A circle is 360°. Divide the measure of angle *KOL* by 360° for the fraction of the circle:

$$\frac{45°}{360°} = \frac{1}{8}$$

Then multiply by the circumference:

$$16\pi \times \frac{1}{8} = 2\pi$$

785. **B. 95**

Set up the averages equation with 90 as the average and *x* as the fifth exam, and solve for *x*:

$$\begin{aligned}\frac{84+87+91+93+x}{5} &= 90\\ 84+87+91+93+x &= 450\\ 355+x &= 450\\ x &= 95\end{aligned}$$

786. **C. 10.0**

Set up the averages equation with 8.0 as the average and *x* as the fourth dive, and solve for *x*:

$$\begin{aligned}\frac{6.8+7.1+8.1+x}{4} &= 8.0\\ 6.8+7.1+8.1+x &= 32.0\\ 22.0+x &= 32.0\\ x &= 10.0\end{aligned}$$

787. **D. Tommy cannot reach his goal.**

Set up the averages equation with 90 as the average and *x* as the sixth exam, and solve for *x*:

$$\begin{aligned}\frac{80+83+87+91+93+x}{6} &= 90\\ 80+83+87+91+93+x &= 540\\ 434+x &= 540\\ x &= 106\end{aligned}$$

Because 100 is the highest he can score on an exam, Tommy cannot score the 106 needed to bring his mean score to 90.

788. **B. $a-5$**

You can find the area of a trapezoid with the formula

$$A = \left(\frac{b_1+b_2}{2}\right)h$$

where b_1 represents one base, b_2 represents the other base, and h represents the height. To find the height, set the formula equal to the area and simplify it:

$$\begin{aligned} A &= \left(\frac{b_1+b_2}{2}\right)h \\ (a-5)^2 &= \left(\frac{a-10+a}{2}\right)h \\ (a-5)^2 &= \left(\frac{2a-10}{2}\right)h \\ (a-5)^2 &= (a-5)h \\ a-5 &= h \end{aligned}$$

789. **C.** $(b-3)^2$

You can find the area of a trapezoid with the formula

$$A=\left(\frac{b_1+b_2}{2}\right)h$$

where b_1 represents one base, b_2 represents the other base, and h represents the height. To find the area, plug in the bases and the height:

$$\begin{aligned} A &= \left(\frac{b_1+b_2}{2}\right)h \\ &= \left(\frac{b-6+b}{2}\right)(b-3) \\ &= \left(\frac{2b-6}{2}\right)(b-3) \\ &= (b-3)(b-3) \\ &= (b-3)^2 \end{aligned}$$

790. **B. 10**

Set up the equation and substitute 5 for y:

$$\begin{aligned} 3x+4y &= 50 \\ 3x+4(5) &= 50 \\ 3x+20 &= 50 \\ 3x &= 30 \\ x &= 10 \end{aligned}$$

791. **D.** n^2+n

The integer following n is $n+1$. Multiply this by n for $n(n+1)=n^2+n$.

ANSWERS 701–800

792. **D. 125**

You're given the number of kilometers per hour, and you need to determine the number of meters per second, so focus on the units of measure; 25 kilometers is 25,000 meters. One hour is 60 minutes times 60 seconds, or 3,600 seconds. You know that the sled is traveling 25,000 kilometers per 3,600 seconds for 18 seconds. Now do the math:

$$\frac{25{,}000\text{ m}}{3{,}600\text{ s}}\times 18\text{ s}=\frac{250}{36}\times 18=\frac{250}{2}=125$$

793. **A. 3**

Given that $f(x)=x^2+2x-2$ and $f(x)=13$, set up and simplify the equation without the $f(x)$:

$$\begin{aligned}f(x)&=x^2+2x-2\\13&=x^2+2x-2\\0&=x^2+2x-15\\0&=(x-3)(x+5)\end{aligned}$$

This means that x equals 3 or –5. Because $x>0$, it must equal 3.

794. **B. $\pi-2$**

First find the area of the square:

$$A_{\text{Square}}=s^2=\left(\sqrt{2}\right)^2=2$$

For the area of the circle, you need its radius. Cut the square in half, corner to corner, to form two 45-45-90 triangles, where each hypotenuse is the diameter of the circle. If the side of this triangle is $\sqrt{2}$, the hypotenuse is 2, because in a right triangle, the square of the hypotenuse is the sum of the squares of the other two sides:

$$\begin{aligned}c^2&=a^2+b^2\\&=\sqrt{2}^2+\sqrt{2}^2\\&=2+2\\&=4\end{aligned}$$

$c^2=4$, so $c=\sqrt{4}=2$ is the diameter of the circle, and the radius of the circle is half the diameter, or 1. Now for the area of the circle:

$$A_{\text{Circle}}=\pi r^2=\pi(1)^2=\pi$$

Subtract the area of the square from the area of the circle for your answer:

$$A_{\text{Total}}=\pi-2$$

795. D. 21

For the area of a triangle, multiply the base by the height and divide by 2. The base of this triangle is 7, and the height is 6, for an area of 21. The 2 in the drawing has no bearing.

796. B. 5

The *units digit* is the digit in the ones place, just before where the decimal point would be. For example, in the number 123, the units digit is 3. When you're multiplying two whole numbers, the units digits of the multipliers produce the units digit of the product. So when you multiply 12×13, for example, the 2 in 12 times the 3 in 13 produces the 6 in the product, 156.

In this question, 5 times itself any number of times results in a product with a units digit of 5:

$$5 \times 5 = 25$$

$$5 \times 5 \times 5 = 125$$

and so on.

797. B. 7

Calculate the average parcel weight by totaling the weight of the parcels and then dividing the total weight by the number of parcels. You can use the following equation for weighted average:

$$\begin{aligned} \text{Weighted average} &= \frac{(5 \times 3) + (10 \times 9)}{5 + 10} \\ &= \frac{15 + 90}{15} \\ &= \frac{105}{15} \\ &= 7 \end{aligned}$$

798. A. π

If the angle *CAB* measures 36°, minor arc *BC* also measures 36°, making it a tenth of the circle:

$$\frac{36°}{360°} = \frac{1}{10}$$

A circle with a radius of 5 has a circumference of $2\pi r = 2 \times \pi \times 5 = 10\pi$. Multiply this circumference by the fraction of the circle for a minor arc length of $10\pi \times \frac{1}{10} = \pi$.

ANSWERS 701–800

799. C. 5

The only numbers less than 7 that, when squared, add up to another number squared are 3, 4, and 5, which square into $9+16=25$, respectively. Because x is the greatest of these, $x=5$.

800. A. 5

Set up the equation and substitute 5 for x:

$$\begin{aligned}10x+12y&=100\\10(4)+12y&=100\\40+12y&=100\\12y&=60\\y&=5\end{aligned}$$

801. D. Slightly above 180

Combine the inequalities to find the (x, y) values of where the lines cross. First subtract the second inequality from the first inequality; then solve for x:

$$\begin{array}{r}y>-4x+540\\ \underline{-(y>\ \ 2x\qquad\ )}\\ 0>-6x+540\end{array}$$

$$6x>540$$

$$x>90$$

Now plug in 90 for x in the second inequality to solve for y:

$$\begin{aligned}y&>2x\\y&>2(90)\\y&>180\end{aligned}$$

The (x, y) values of where the lines cross are $(90, 180)$.

Because each inequality has a y that's *greater than* the expression with the x, anything *above* the lines is within the solution set; d represents the y-value of where the lines cross, so the answer is slightly above 180.

802. C. Slightly below 700

Combine the inequalities to find the (x, y) values of where the lines cross. First subtract the second inequality from the first inequality; then solve for x:

$$\begin{array}{r}y<\ -x+1{,}000\\ \underline{-(y<\ \ 2x+\ \ 100)}\\ 0<-3x+\ \ 900\end{array}$$

$$3x<900$$

$$x<300$$

Now plug in 300 for *x* in the second inequality to solve for *y*:

$$y < 2x + 100$$
$$y < 2(300) + 100$$
$$y < 600 + 100$$
$$y < 700$$

The (x, y) values of where the lines cross are $(300, 700)$.

Because each inequality has a *y* that's *less than* the expression with the *x*, anything *below* the lines is within the solution set; *f* represents the *y*-value of where the lines cross, so the answer is slightly below 700.

803. **A. 90 minutes**

The two hours' flat fee is $22 \times 2 = 44$ dollars, leaving $98 - 44 = 54$ dollars remaining for motor charges. Divide this by $0.60 for the answer.

804. **B.** $c = 22h + \frac{3m}{5}$

Multiply 22 by *h* and add that to 0.6 times *m*. The 0.6 converts to the fraction $\frac{3}{5}$.

805. **B. $138**

The service calls cost $16 \times 5 = \$80$, and she paid $58 for the annual membership. Add these together for the answer.

806. **C.** $c = 16s + 58$

Multiply 16 by *s* and add that to 58 for the annual membership.

807. **B. 2 ounces**

The 5-pound cake is $5 \times 16 = 80$ ounces. Cut this into 8 slices for 10 ounces per slice. Divide each 10-ounce slice into 5 equal pieces to get 2 ounces per piece.

808. **C. 6.4 ounces**

The gallon of juice is 128 ounces, making each quart $128 \div 4 = 32$ ounces. Pour this evenly into 5 glasses for $32 \div 5 = 6.4$ ounces per glass.

809. **C. 5,500**

Four hundred of 650 citizens declared they will vote for Candidate B. This is $400 \div 650 = 61.5\%$ of the citizens; 61.5% of 9,000 is 5,535, which is closest to 5,500.

810. **A. 143**

Twenty-five of 70 employees declared they prefer a holiday party. This is $25 \div 70 = 35.7\%$ of the employees; 35.7% of 400 employees is 142.8, or closest to 143.

811. **D. 25,740**

Note that 305 of 720 citizens is $309 \div 720 = 42.9\%$; 42.9% of 60,000 citizens is 25,740.

812. **A. 31**

Set up two equations, where s is Sean's donations and e is Emily's:

$$\begin{aligned} s + e &= 58 \\ s + 11 &= e + 7 \end{aligned}$$

Now simplify the second equation and subtract it from the first to isolate the e:

$$\begin{array}{r} s + \ e = 58 \\ -(s - \ e = -4) \\ \hline 2e = 62 \\ e = 31 \end{array}$$

813. **C. $500**

Set up two equations, where s is Sam's earnings and r is Robin's:

$$\begin{aligned} s + r &= 1{,}050 \\ s &= 1.1r \end{aligned}$$

Plug in $1.1r$ for s in the first equation:

$$\begin{aligned} s + r &= 1{,}050 \\ 1.1r + r &= 1{,}050 \\ 2.1r &= 1{,}050 \\ r &= 500 \end{aligned}$$

814. **A. $f(x) = (x^2 - 4)(x - 3)$**

The x-intercepts occur where the value of x causes $f(x)$ to equal 0. First factor the equation:

$$\begin{aligned} f(x) &= (x^2 - 4)(x - 3) \\ &= (x - 2)(x + 2)(x - 3) \end{aligned}$$

$f(x)$ equals 0 when x equals −2, 2, or 3.

815. **C. Three**

Factor the equation:

$$\begin{aligned} f(x) &= (x^2 - x - 6)(x^2 - 9) \\ &= (x+2)(x-3)(x-3)(x+3) \end{aligned}$$

The function would touch or cross the x-axis at −2, 3, 3, and −3; however, it touches at 3 only once, for a total of three times.

816. **B. −3, −2, 3**

Factor the equation:

$$f(x) = (x^2 - x - 6)(x^2 - 9)$$
$$f(x) = ((x+2)(x-3))((x-3)(x+3))$$

The function would touch or cross the x-axis at −2, 3, 3, and −3; however, it touches at 3 only once.

817. **D. $f(x) = (x+3)(x^2 - 25)$**

The x-intercepts occur where the value of x causes $f(x)$ to equal 0. First factor the equation:

$$f(x) = (x+3)(x^2 - 25)$$
$$f(x) = (x+3)((x-5)(x+5))$$

$f(x)$ equals 0 when x equals −3, 5, or −5.

818. **C. Three**

Factor the equation:

$$f(x) = (x^2 - 11x + 28)(x^2 - 49)$$
$$f(x) = ((x-4)(x-7))((x-7)(x+7))$$

The function would touch or cross the x-axis at 4, 7, 7, and −7. However, it touches at 7 only once, for a total of three times.

819. **A. −7, 4, 7**

Factor the equation:

$$f(x) = (x^2 - 11x + 28)(x^2 - 49)$$
$$f(x) = ((x-4)(x-7))((x-7)(x+7))$$

The function would touch or cross the x-axis at 4, 7, 7, and −7. However, it touches at 7 only once.

820. **D. The graph of the function does not cross the x-axis.**

The graph crosses the x-axis where $f(x)=0$. However, $f(x)$ can never equal 0 because x^2 is always positive, and the +4 keeps the graph 4 units above the x-axis.

821. **A. −4**

FOIL the equation into $y = x-4$; this suggests that the equation represents a line with a slope of 1 and a y-intercept of −4. However, because the original equation contains $\sqrt{x}$, x can never be less than 0. Therefore, the lowest possible value of y is −4.

822. **D. I and IV only**

FOIL the equation into $y = x-4$; this suggests that the equation represents a line with a slope of 1 and a y-intercept of −4. However, because the original equation contains $\sqrt{x}$, x can never be less than 0. Therefore, the equation is not of a line; it's of a ray that begins at $y = -4$ and travels upward to the right, through Quadrant IV and into Quadrant I.

823. **C. 3**

FOIL the equation and distribute the negative:

$$y=-(x-3)$$
$$y=-x+3$$

The equation appears to represent a line with a slope of −1 and a y-intercept of 3. However, because the original equation contains $\sqrt{x}$, x can never be less than 0, meaning $-x$ can never be greater than 0. Therefore, the greatest possible value of y is 3.

824. **D. II and III only**

FOIL the equation and distribute the negative:

$$y=-(x-3)$$
$$y=-x+3$$

The equation appears to represent a line with a slope of −1 and a y-intercept of 3. However, because the original equation contains $\sqrt{x}$, x can never be less than 0, meaning $-x$ can never be greater than 0. Therefore, the equation is not of a line; it's of a ray that begins at $y = 3$ and travels downward to the left, through Quadrant II and into Quadrant III.

825. D. There is no greatest value of *y*.

FOIL the binomials:

$$y=\left(\left(\sqrt{x}-\sqrt{2}\right)\left(\sqrt{x}+\sqrt{2}\right)\right)^2$$
$$y=(x-2)^2$$

The equation represents a parabola with a vertex of coordinates $(2,0)$. However, because the original equation contains $\sqrt{x}$, x can never be less than 0, meaning the graph contains part of a parabola: the right half and a small part of the left half. The right half continues forever, so there's no greatest value of *y*.

826. A. One

FOIL the binomials:

$$y=\left(\left(\sqrt{x}-\sqrt{2}\right)\left(\sqrt{x}+\sqrt{2}\right)\right)^2$$
$$y=(x-2)^2$$

The equation appears to represent a parabola with a vertex of coordinates $(2,0)$. However, because the original equation contains $\sqrt{x}$, x can never be less than 0, meaning the graph doesn't enter Quadrants II and III. Because *y* equals a value squared, *y* can also never be less than 0, meaning the graph doesn't enter Quadrants III and IV. The graph therefore enters only Quadrant I.

827. B. 2

FOIL the binomials:

$$y=\left(\left(\sqrt{x}-\sqrt{2}\right)\left(\sqrt{x}+\sqrt{2}\right)\right)^2$$
$$y=(x-2)^2$$

The graph intercepts the *x*-axis where $y=0$. This occurs when $x=2$.

828. D. 4

FOIL the binomials:

$$y=\left(\left(\sqrt{x}-\sqrt{2}\right)\left(\sqrt{x}+\sqrt{2}\right)\right)^2$$
$$y=(x-2)^2$$

To find the *y*-intercept, set $x=0$; *y* becomes 4.

829. **B.** $y = \left(-\left(\sqrt{x}-\sqrt{2}\right)\left(\sqrt{x}+\sqrt{2}\right)\right)^2$

The additional negative inside the outer bracket becomes positive — and superfluous — when the equation is squared, much the same way that $(-2)^2 = (2)^2$. All the other variations change the value of the equation.

830. **D. There is no greatest value of *y*.**

FOIL the binomials:

$$y = \left(\left(\sqrt{x}-\sqrt{3}\right)\left(\sqrt{x}+\sqrt{5}\right)\right)^2$$
$$y = \left(x-\sqrt{3x}+\sqrt{5x}-\sqrt{15}\right)^2$$

The equation represents a parabola. However, because the original equation contains $\sqrt{x}$, x can never be less than 0, meaning the graph contains part of a parabola: the right half and a small part of the left half. The right half continues forever, so there is no greatest value of y.

831. **A. Quadrant I**

Look at the graph of $y = \left(\left(\sqrt{x}-\sqrt{3}\right)\left(\sqrt{x}+\sqrt{5}\right)\right)^2$. Because the original equation contains $\sqrt{x}$, x can never be less than 0, meaning the graph doesn't enter Quadrants II and III. Because y equals a value squared, y can also never be less than 0, meaning the graph doesn't enter Quadrants III and IV. The graph therefore enters only Quadrant I.

832. **C. 3**

The graph intercepts the x-axis where $y = 0$. To make $y = 0$, $\left(\left(\sqrt{x}-\sqrt{3}\right)\left(\sqrt{x}+\sqrt{5}\right)\right)^2$ also has to equal 0. $\left(\sqrt{x}-\sqrt{3}\right)$ tells you that if $x = 3$, $\left(\sqrt{x}-\sqrt{3}\right) = 0$, making $y = \left(\left(\sqrt{x}-\sqrt{3}\right)\left(\sqrt{x}+\sqrt{5}\right)\right)^2 = 0$. The graph, therefore, intercepts the y-axis where $x = 3$.

833. **D. 15**

FOIL the binomials:

$$y = \left(\left(\sqrt{x}-\sqrt{3}\right)\left(\sqrt{x}+\sqrt{5}\right)\right)^2$$
$$y = \left(x-\sqrt{3x}+\sqrt{5x}-\sqrt{15}\right)^2$$

ANSWERS 801–900

To find the y-intercept, set $x = 0$; y becomes 15:

$$\begin{aligned} y &= \left(x - \sqrt{3x} + \sqrt{5x} - \sqrt{15}\right)^2 \\ &= \left(0 - \sqrt{3(0)} + \sqrt{5(0)} - \sqrt{15}\right)^2 \\ &= \left(-\sqrt{15}\right)^2 \\ &= 15 \end{aligned}$$

834. **C.** $y = \left(-\left(\sqrt{x} - \sqrt{3}\right)\left(\sqrt{x} + \sqrt{5}\right)\right)^2$

The additional negative inside the outer bracket becomes positive — and superfluous — when the equation is squared, much the same way that $(-2)^2 = (2)^2$. All the other variations change the value of the equation.

835. **B.** $\frac{\sqrt{3}}{2}$

If the radius of the circle is 1, then $BC = 2$ and $AB = 1$, making this a 30-60-90 triangle with a side-length ratio of $1 : \sqrt{3} : 2$. The sides adjacent to the right angle are the base and height, which are 1 and $\sqrt{3}$. The area of a triangle is $\frac{\text{base} \times \text{height}}{2}$. Plug the base and height into the equation for the answer.

836. **B.** $\frac{\pi}{3}$

If $AB = 1$ and the radius $BO = 1$, then the radius (not shown) $AO = 1$, making triangle AOB an equilateral triangle and angle $AOB = 60°$. This means that minor arc AB represents $\frac{60°}{360°} = \frac{1}{6}$ of the circle.

The radius of 1 gives the circle a circumference of $2\pi r = 2\pi(1) = 2\pi$. Multiply this circumference by the fraction of the circle for a minor arc length of $2\pi \times \frac{1}{6} = \frac{2\pi}{6} = \frac{\pi}{3}$.

837. **C. The triangles have equal areas.**

The area of a triangle is half its base times height. The triangles have equal bases (as $AD = DC$), and they share the height, shown as a dashed line in the following drawing.

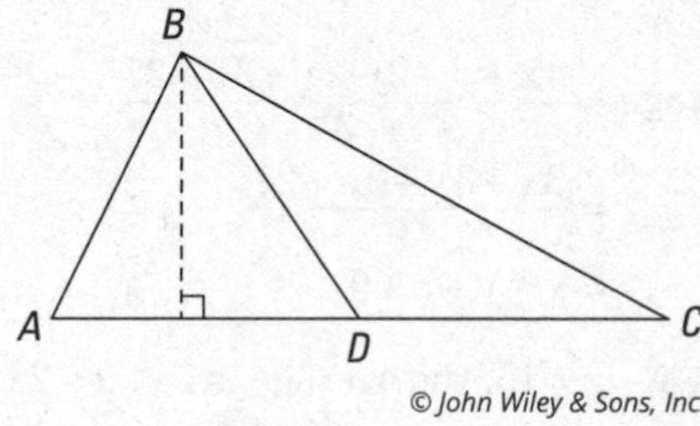

ANSWERS 801–900

838. **B. 50**

The area of a trapezoid is $\left(\frac{b_1+b_2}{2}\right)h$. Plug in the numbers from the drawing:

$$\begin{aligned} A &= \left(\frac{b_1+b_2}{2}\right)h \\ &= \left(\frac{9+11}{2}\right)5 \\ &= (10)5 \\ &= 50 \end{aligned}$$

839. **C. $AC = BC$**

Call the interior angles of the triangle *A*, *B*, and *C*, according to the labels in the drawing. Because the angle supplementary to angle *C* is 2*x*, angle *C* equals $180-2x$. The three angles of any triangle total 180, making angle *B* equal to 180 minus the other two angles, or $180-x-(180-2x)$, which can also be written as $180-x-180+2x$. The 180s cancel, and $-x+2x$ becomes *x*. Now you know two of the angles are equal, making the triangle isosceles; therefore, $AC = BC$.

840. **A. 1**

The equation $x^2-x-6=0$ becomes $(x-3)(x+2)=0$, so possible values of *x* are 3 and –2, which add up to 1.

841. **B. $-\frac{2}{3}$**

To find the slope of the line, convert the equation to slope-intercept form, which is $y = mx+b$. Solve for *y*, and *m* is the slope:

$$\begin{aligned} 2x+3y &= 5 \\ 3y &= -2x+5 \\ y &= -\frac{2}{3}x+\frac{5}{3} \end{aligned}$$

842. **B. 24**

Set up the average by dividing everything by 3 and simplifying:

$$\begin{aligned} \text{Average} &= \frac{4x+y+2y-x+3z+27}{3} \\ &= \frac{3x+3y+3z+27}{3} \\ &= x+y+z+9 \end{aligned}$$

Because $x+y+z=15$, the average is $15+9=24$.

843. **D. 2π**

If the central angle is 45 degrees, then the resulting arc is also 45 degrees, which is $\frac{45°}{360°} = \frac{1}{8}$ of the circle. If the radius of the circle is 8, then the circumference is 16π. To find the length of the arc, take $\frac{1}{8}$ of 16π, which is 2π.

844. **C. 8π**

If the central angle is 45 degrees, then the resulting arc is also 45 degrees, which is $\frac{45°}{360°} = \frac{1}{8}$ of the circle. If the radius of the circle is 8, then the area is $\pi r^2 = \pi(8)^2 = 64\pi$. To find the area of the sector, take $\frac{1}{8}$ of 64π, which is 8π.

845. **D. $\frac{9\pi r^2}{4}$**

The area of any circle is πr^2. Because the radius of the original circle increased by 50 percent, the new radius is $\frac{3r}{2}$. Plug the new radius into the area formula, or square it and multiply by π for $\frac{9\pi r^2}{4}$.

846. **A. $\frac{\pi}{4}$**

If the circle is inscribed within the square, then the diameter of the circle is equal to one side of the square. Pick a number for a side of the square, such as 6. This makes the radius of the circle 3 and the circle's area 9π, while the area of the square is $6^2 = 36$. The circle occupies $\frac{9\pi}{36}$ of the square, which reduces to $\frac{\pi}{4}$.

847. **D. 5**

You can find the volume of a cylinder with $\pi r^2 h$. You're given the volume and height, so back-solve to find the radius. Begin with $50\pi = \pi r^2 2$ (because the height is 2). Divide both sides by 2π to get $25 = r^2$; the radius is 5.

848. **C. 30**

The *units* digit is the last number before the decimal. For example, in the number 123, the units digit is 3. The numbers between 200 and 500 having a units digit of 5 are 205, 215, 225, and so on. There are ten such numbers for 200 through 300, ten for 300 through 400, and ten for 400 through 500.

849. B. 25

Draw the xy-coordinate plane and place the points A and C as directed. These are two points of the square, and you know they're the opposite corners because the question tells you the sides of the square are parallel to the axes. Find the width and height and multiply for an area of 25.

850. B. 12

Set up the conversions as fractions and do the math:

$$\left(\frac{2\not{0}\ \cancel{\text{meters}}}{1\ \cancel{\text{sec}}}\right)\left(\frac{1\ \text{km}}{1{,}\not{0}\not{0}\not{0}\ \cancel{\text{meters}}}\right)\left(\frac{6\not{0}\ \cancel{\text{sec}}}{1\ \cancel{\text{min}}}\right)\left(\frac{1\not{0}\ \cancel{\text{min}}}{1}\right)=12\ \text{km}$$

Note that the three zeros in the numerators cancel the three zeros in the denominator of the second fraction.

851. B. 35

If $(x-5)^2=900$, then take the square root of both sides to get $x-5=30$ and $x-5=-30$. Add 5s all around, and x equals either 35 or −25. Because $x>0$, it equals 35.

852. B. $\frac{5\pi r^2}{4}$

If the radius of the pool is r, then the radius from the center of the pool to the outer edge of the sidewalk is $r+\frac{r}{2}$. First, calculate the area of the combined pool and sidewalk (the larger circle) by substituting $\left(r+\frac{r}{2}\right)$ in for r in the equation for the area of a circle:

$$\begin{aligned}A&=\pi\left(r+\frac{r}{2}\right)^2\\&=\pi\left(r+\frac{r}{2}\right)\left(r+\frac{r}{2}\right)\\&=\pi\left(r^2+\frac{r^2}{4}+\frac{r^2}{2}+\frac{r^2}{2}\right)\\&=\pi\left(\frac{4r^2}{4}+\frac{r^2}{4}+\frac{2r^2}{4}+\frac{2r^2}{4}\right)\\&=\frac{9\pi r^2}{4}\end{aligned}$$

Next, calculate the area of the pool alone, which is easy: $A=\pi r^2$. Finally, subtract the area of the pool from the total area of the pool plus the sidewalk, remembering that you need a common denominator to subtract:

$$\frac{9\pi r^2}{4}-\pi r^2=\frac{9\pi r^2}{4}-\frac{4\pi r^2}{4}=\frac{5\pi r^2}{4}$$

853. A. 120

You can find the sum of the interior angles of any polygon with the formula $(n-2)(180°)$, making the sum of the hexagon's angles $(6-2)180° = (4)180° = 720°$. Because the hexagon is a regular hexagon, meaning all sides and angles are the same, each angle is 120°.

854. D. 3

Pick a number that has a remainder of 3 when divided by 35, such as 38 or 73. Divide the number by 7, and it has the same remainder.

$$\begin{array}{r} 5 \\ 7\overline{)38} \\ \underline{35} \\ 3 \end{array}$$

855. D. 25 : 24

Pick simple numbers for the length and width of the rectangle, such as 5 and 5, for an area of 25. Increase one by 20 percent and decrease the other by 20 percent, for new sides of 6 and 4 and a new area of 24. Regardless of the numbers you pick for the original rectangle, the ratio of the area of that to the new rectangle is the same.

856. A. $4\sqrt{3}$

You can find the area of an equilateral triangle by using the formula $\frac{s^2\sqrt{3}}{4}$, where s is any of the sides, including the base:

$$A = \frac{s^2\sqrt{3}}{4} = \frac{4^2\sqrt{3}}{4} = 4\sqrt{3}$$

You can also consider the equilateral triangle to be two 30-60-90 triangles, giving the triangle a height of $2\sqrt{3}$; then use the $A = \frac{1}{2}\text{base} \times \text{height}$ formula:

$$A = \left(\frac{1}{2}\right)(4)\left(2\sqrt{3}\right) = 4\sqrt{3}$$

857. B. $9\sqrt{3}$

You can find the area of an equilateral triangle by using the formula $\frac{s^2\sqrt{3}}{4}$, where s is any of the sides, including the base:

$$A = \frac{s^2\sqrt{3}}{4} = \frac{6^2\sqrt{3}}{4} = \frac{36\sqrt{3}}{4} = 9\sqrt{3}$$

You can also consider the equilateral triangle to be two 30-60-90 triangles, giving the triangle a height of $3\sqrt{3}$; then use the $A = \frac{1}{2}\text{base} \times \text{height}$ formula:

$$A = \left(\frac{1}{2}\right)(6)\left(3\sqrt{3}\right) = 9\sqrt{3}$$

858. **A. $(-2, -1)$**

With the two equations, solve for x by eliminating y. Because $y = x + 1$ and $y = 2x + 3$, replace the y in one equation with its value from the other equation:

$$\begin{aligned} y &= 2x + 3 \\ (x+1) &= 2x + 3 \\ x &= 2x + 2 \\ -x &= 2 \\ x &= -2 \end{aligned}$$

Substitute -2 for x in either original equation to get the value of y as -1.

859. **A. $5\sqrt{2}$**

Drawing a line from point A to point C splits the square into two 45-45-90 triangles. The side ratio of this triangle is $x : x : x\sqrt{2}$, so if two of the sides are 5, then the hypotenuse is $5\sqrt{2}$.

860. **B. 0**

First multiply everything by 50 to get rid of the fraction; then solve for x:

$$\begin{aligned} \frac{x^2}{50} - 3 &= 5 \\ x^2 - 150 &= 250 \\ x^2 &= 400 \\ x &= 20, -20 \end{aligned}$$

The sum of 20 and -20 is 0.

861. **700, 800, 900, 1000, or 1100**

At her slowest pace, she can type $35 \times 20 = 700$ words per minute. At her fastest pace, she can type $55 \times 20 = 1{,}100$ words per minute. Any number from 700 to 1,100 rounded to the nearest hundred is correct.

862. **11, 11.0, 11.1, 11.2, 11.3, 11.4, 11.5, 11.6, 11.7, 11.8, 11.9, 12, 12.0, or 12.1**

The lowest-priced headset would cost Joanne $\$10 \times 1.10 = \$11.00$, which you can write as 11.0 or 11, and the highest-priced headset would cost $\$11 \times 1.10 = \$12.10$, or 12.1. Any number from 11 to 12.1 rounded to the nearest tenth is correct.

863. **360, 370, 380, 390, 400, 410, 420, 430, 440, 450, 460, 470, or 480**

Suppose x is the amount of his paycheck. If Henry spent $\frac{1}{4}$ of his paycheck, then the check was

$$\begin{aligned}\frac{1}{4}x &= 120\\ x &= 480\end{aligned}$$

If he spent $\frac{1}{3}$ of his paycheck, then the check was

$$\begin{aligned}\frac{1}{3}x &= 120\\ x &= 360\end{aligned}$$

Any number from 360 to 480 rounded to the tens place is correct.

864. **6000, 6100, 6200, 6300, 6400, 6500, 6600, 6700, 6800, 6900, 7000, 7100, or 7200**

At its slowest pace, the machine produces $50 \times 2 \times 60 = 6{,}000$ plastic parts. At its fastest pace, it produces $60 \times 2 \times 60 = 7{,}200$ plastic parts. Any number from 6,000 to 7,200 rounded to the nearest hundred is correct.

865. **7000, 7100, 7200, 7300, 7400, 7500, 7600, 7700, 7800, 7900, or 8000**

At 70 paperclips per box, the shipment contains $70 \times 20 \times 5 = 7{,}000$ paperclips. At 80 paperclips per box, the shipment contains $80 \times 20 \times 5 = 8{,}000$ paperclips. Any number from 7,000 to 8,000 rounded to the nearest hundred is correct.

866. **30**

Simplify and factor the equation:

$$\begin{aligned}x(x-10) &= 600\\ x^2 - 10x &= 600\\ x^2 - 10x - 600 &= 0\\ (x-30)(x+20) &= 0\\ x &= -20 \text{ or } 30\end{aligned}$$

Because $x > 0$, the answer is 30.

ANSWERS 801–900

867. **200 or 300**

Simplify and factor the equation:

$$x - \frac{x^2}{500} = 120$$
$$500x - x^2 = 60{,}000$$
$$500x - x^2 - 60{,}000 = 0$$
$$x^2 - 500x + 60{,}000 = 0$$
$$(x-200)(x-300) = 0$$
$$x = 200 \text{ or } 300$$

868. **300**

Take the square root of both sides:

$$x^2 = 90{,}000$$
$$x = 300 \text{ or } -300$$

Because $x > 0$, the answer is 300.

869. **4**

FOIL the expression:

$$(\sqrt{x}-2)(\sqrt{x}+2) = 0$$
$$x - 4 = 0$$
$$x = 4$$

870. **2 or 3**

Simplify and factor the equation:

$$x^2(x^2-13) = -36$$
$$x^4 - 13x^2 = -36$$
$$x^4 - 13x^2 + 36 = 0$$
$$(x^2-4)(x^2-9) = 0$$
$$x^2 = 4 \text{ or } 9$$
$$x = 2 \text{ or } 3$$

871. **5 or 11**

$55 = 5 \times 11$, so n could be 5 or 11; 55 is also 1×55, but the question states that n is between 2 and 50.

872. **7 or 11**

You can find the volume of a right circular cylinder with $\pi r^2 h$, where r is the radius and h is the height. If r and h are integers, find two numbers where one squared, r, plus the other, h, equals 36, for a volume of 36π. Possible numbers are either r as 3 and h as 4, with a sum of 7, or r as 2 and h as 9, with a sum of 11.

873. **10**

Let b be the number of cars Bobby currently has, and let j be the number of cars Jackie currently has. Then set up two different equations:

$$b-8=j$$
$$b-2=2(j+2)$$

Solve for b by substituting $(b-8)$ for j in the second equation:

$$b-2=2((b-8)+2)$$
$$b-2=2(b-8+2)$$
$$b-2=2(b-6)$$
$$b-2=2b-12$$
$$10=b$$

874. **4**

Let b be the number of cars Bobby currently has, and let j be the number of cars Jackie currently has. Then set up two different equations:

$$b-8=j$$
$$b-2=2(j+2)$$

Solve for b by substituting $(b-8)$ for j in the second equation, as you did in Question 873: $b-2=2((b-8)+2)$; $b=10$.

Plug in 10 for b in the other equation:

$$b-2=2(j+2)$$
$$10-2=2(j+2)$$
$$8=2j+4$$
$$4=2j$$
$$2=j$$

Jackie had 2 cars before the gift, and now she has 4.

875. **1/2 or .5 or 0.5**

Using rise over run, the line rises one unit (from 0 to 1) and runs two units (from 0 to 2). This give the line a slope of $\frac{1}{2}$.

ANSWERS 801–900

876. 132

If $x = 42$, then the rightmost angle is $180 - 90 - 42 = 48$. This makes y supplementary to x, so y is equal to $180 - 48 = 132$.

877. 96

$100 marked up 20 percent is $\$100 \times 1.2 = \$120$, and the 20 percent discount from $120 is $\$120 \times 0.8 = \$96$.

878. 83.3

Set up the conversion steps as a series of fractions and cancel out as much as you can:

$$\begin{aligned}
&\frac{10 \text{ km}}{1 \text{ hr}} \times \frac{1{,}000 \text{ m}}{1 \text{ km}} \times \frac{1 \text{ hr}}{60 \text{ min}} \times \frac{1 \text{ min}}{2 \text{ units}} \\
&= \frac{\overset{1\ \cancel{5}}{\cancel{10}} \text{ km}}{1 \text{ hr}} \times \frac{\overset{250}{\cancel{1{,}000}} \text{ m}}{1 \text{ km}} \times \frac{1 \text{ hr}}{_{3\ \cancel{15}}\cancel{60} \text{ min}} \times \frac{1 \text{ min}}{_{1}\cancel{2} \text{ units}} \\
&= \frac{250}{3} \approx 83.3
\end{aligned}$$

The *unit* in the denominator represents the 30-second interval that the question asks for. Note that you don't have enough boxes to write the answer as a fraction, so you have to give the answer as a decimal.

879. 4

Because the average of x, y, and z is 1, write out the equation as an averages formula: $\frac{x+y+z}{3} = 1$, which tells you that $x + y + z = 3$. Now find the average of the four expressions:

$$\begin{aligned}
&\frac{(8x+2z)+(z-2x+3y)+(y-x+z)+(4-x)}{4} \\
&= \frac{8x+2z+z-2x+3y+y-x+z+4-x}{4} \\
&= \frac{4x+4y+4z+4}{4} \\
&= x+y+z+1
\end{aligned}$$

Then because $x + y + z = 3$, the answer is 4.

880. 0 or 4

Factor $x^2 - 4x = 0$ into $x(x-4) = 0$, making both 0 and 4 possible answers for x.

881. **1850**

A 10 percent discount of a \$2,000 price is $\$2{,}000 \times 0.1 = \$200$. A 25 percent reduction of the \$200 discount brings the new discount to $\$200 \times 0.75 = \$150$, for a final asking price of \$1,850.

882. **2**

Draw the coordinate plane and the line with point *P*. Then draw a line straight down from point *P* to the *x*-axis. Now you have a right triangle. Because the (x, y) coordinates of point *P* are $(1, \sqrt{3})$, these coordinates are also the base and height of the triangle. This is a 30-60-90 triangle with side ratios of $1:2:\sqrt{3}$, making the hypotenuse, and the distance between point *P* and the origin, 2.

You can also use the Pythagorean Theorem to calculate the length of the hypotenuse:

$$\begin{aligned} a^2 + b^2 &= c^2 \\ 1^2 + \sqrt{3}^2 &= c^2 \\ 1 + 3 &= c^2 \\ 4 &= c^2 \\ c &= 2 \end{aligned}$$

883. **2700**

If 15 kWh represents 30% of the family's total daily electricity usage, *x*, the total daily usage would be

$$\begin{aligned} 0.30x &= 15 \\ x &= 50 \end{aligned}$$

for 50 kWh per day. At \$0.15 per kWh in the northeast, that's a daily cost of \$7.50. Multiply \$7.50 by 365 days for an annual electricity cost of \$2,737.50; to the nearest hundred dollars, that's \$2,700.

884. **10**

In this problem, \$4,500 represents the family's total electric bill. Heating alone represents 30%, or $4{,}500 \times 0.30 = 1{,}350$. Cutting the heating bill by 35 percent saves the Joneses $1{,}350 \times 0.35 = 472.50$ annually. The \$4,725 investment pays for itself after $4{,}725 \div 472.50 = 10$ years.

885. **2**

Add the equations to get $8a + 8b = 16$ (make sure you align the *a*'s and *b*'s). Divide both sides by 8 to get $a + b = 2$.

886. 1

Substitute $\frac{1}{x}$ for y in the equation:

$$\frac{1}{x+1}+\frac{1}{\left(\frac{1}{x}+1\right)}$$

Simplify the second fraction by adding the fractions in the denominator:

$$\frac{1}{\left(\frac{1}{x}+1\right)}=\frac{1}{\left(\frac{1}{x}+\frac{1}{1}\right)}=\frac{1}{\left(\frac{1+x}{x}\right)}$$

The 1 on top of the denominator fraction flips that fraction:

$$\frac{1}{\left(\frac{1+x}{x}\right)}=\frac{x}{(1+x)}$$

Now substitute $\frac{x}{x+1}$ for the second fraction in the original equation:

$$\frac{1}{x+1}+\frac{x}{x+1}=\frac{x+1}{x+1}=1$$

887. 3

Simplify and solve:

$$\begin{aligned}5(x+2)^2-125&=0\\5(x+2)^2&=125\\(x+2)^2&=25\\x+2&=5\text{ or }-5\\x&=3\text{ or }-7\end{aligned}$$

Because $x>0$, it has to equal 3.

888. 480

To find the average speed of a trip, place the total distance over the total time.

Pick a number for the distance. To simplify the math, use the lowest common multiple of the two speeds, 600 and 400, which is 1,200.

If the plane flew to New York, a distance of 1,200 miles at 400 mph, it flew for 3 hours. If it flew back at 600 mph, it covered the 1,200 miles in 2 hours. Now you have the total distance and total time, which is 2,400 miles over 5 hours. Set it up as a fraction:

$$\frac{2{,}400\text{ mi}}{5\text{ hr}}$$

Reduce to $\frac{480\text{ mi}}{1\text{ hr}}$, or 480 mph.

889. **12/5 or 2.4**

Using rise over run, the line rises $14-2=12$ and runs $8-3=5$, for a slope of $\frac{12}{5}$.

890. **35**

The smallest prime number greater than 3 is 5, and the largest prime number less than 11 is 7, making *a* and *b* 5 and 7, respectively. Multiply these for an answer of 35.

891. **24**

Add the equations, and $4y$ and $-4y$ cancel, leaving $16x=48$, so $x=3$. Plug 3 into the second equation to find *y*: $9(3)-4y=-5$, so $y=8$. The product of *x* and *y* is 24.

892. **5**

Start by adding the equations together, making sure you align the *a* and *b* terms correctly:

$$\begin{array}{r} 3a+5b=12 \\ +(5a+3b=28) \\ \hline 8a+8b=40 \end{array}$$

Now divide everything by 8 to get $a+b=5$.

893. **121**

The only integer between 10 and 12 is 11. Square this for 121, making $\sqrt{x}=\sqrt{121}=11$ and $10<11<12$.

894. **6**

Because a gallon is 4 quarts, 2 gallons is 8 quarts. If 16 ounces of mix makes 8 quarts, then each quart requires $16\div 8=2$ ounces of mix. To make 3 quarts, you'd need $3\times 2=6$ ounces of mix.

895. **36, 49, or 64**

The integers between 5 and 9 are 6, 7, and 8. Square these for 36, 49, and 64, respectively.

896. 5

FOIL the expression and solve for x:

$$\left(\sqrt{x}-\sqrt{5}\right)\left(\sqrt{x}+\sqrt{5}\right)=0$$
$$x-5=0$$
$$x=5$$

897. 1

FOIL the expression and solve for x:

$$(2x+2)(5x-5)=0$$
$$10x^2-7x+7x-10=0$$
$$10x^2-10=0$$
$$10x^2=10$$
$$x^2=1$$
$$x=1 \text{ or } -1$$

Because $x>0$, it has to equal 1.

898. 1

FOIL the expression and solve for x:

$$\left(\sqrt{12x}-\sqrt{12}\right)\left(\sqrt{3x}+\sqrt{3}\right)=0$$
$$\sqrt{36x^2}+\sqrt{36x}-\sqrt{36x}-\sqrt{36}=0$$
$$\sqrt{36x^2}-\sqrt{36}=0$$
$$6x-6=0$$
$$6x=6$$
$$x=1$$

899. 1

FOIL the expression. Note that $\frac{18}{5}\times\frac{5}{2}=\frac{90}{10}=9$:

$$\left(\sqrt{\frac{18x}{5}}-\sqrt{\frac{18}{5}}\right)\left(\sqrt{\frac{5x}{2}}+\sqrt{\frac{5}{2}}\right)=0$$
$$\sqrt{9x^2}+\sqrt{9x}-\sqrt{9x}-\sqrt{9}=0$$
$$\sqrt{9x^2}-\sqrt{9}=0$$
$$3x-3=0$$
$$3x=3$$
$$x=1$$

900. **5**

The only ways that the sales total \$3.00 are if Colt sold 0 apples and $6 \times \$0.50 = \$3.00$ in peaches, 0 peaches and $10 \times \$0.30 = \$3.00$ in apples, or $3 \times \$0.50 = \$1.50$ in peaches plus $5 \times \$0.30 = \$1.50$ in apples. You know that it is the latter case, because he sold both peaches and apples.

901. **270**

From 12:15 p.m. to 1:00 p.m. is $\frac{3}{4}$ of the way around the clock (which totals 360°): $360° \times \frac{3}{4} = 270°$.

902. **3/2 or 1.5**

From 12:15 p.m. to 1:00 is $\frac{3}{4}$ of the way around the clock (which totals 2π): $2\pi \times \frac{3}{4} = \frac{3\pi}{2}$.

903. **1440**

From 2:00 p.m. to 6:00 p.m. is 4 times around the clock (which totals 360°): $360° \times 4 = 1{,}440°$.

904. **8**

From 2:00 p.m. to 6:00 p.m. is 4 times around the clock (which totals 2π): $2\pi \times 4 = 8\pi$.

905. **60**

To round your answer to the nearest 10 degrees, start by rounding 365.256 to 360; 60 days then is 60 degrees.

906. **1/2 or .5 or 0.5**

Ninety days is just about one-quarter of the year, or one-quarter of the Earth's orbit around the sun. A full circle (or orbit, in this case) is 2π:

$$2\pi \times \frac{1}{4} = \frac{1}{2}\pi$$

907. **7.2 or 36/5**

$\frac{18{,}800{,}000}{940{,}000{,}000} = \frac{1}{50}$, so the Earth travels $\frac{1}{50}$ of the way around the sun. A circle is 360°, so the answer is $\frac{1}{50} \times 360° = 7.2°$.

Note that if your calculator doesn't handle a number with nine digits (such as 940,000,000), you can simply remove five zeros from the numbers before dividing in the calculator:

$$\frac{18,800,000}{940,000,000} \rightarrow \frac{188}{9,400}$$

908. **1/4 or .25 or 0.25**

$\frac{117,500,000}{940,000,000} = \frac{1}{8}$, so the Earth travels $\frac{1}{8}$ of the way around the sun. A circle is 2π, so the answer is $\frac{1}{8} \times 2\pi = \frac{\pi}{4}$.

909. **3600**

Half of a second is $\frac{0.5}{60} = \frac{1}{120}$ of a minute. If the engine turns 1,200 revolutions per minute, then in half of a second, it turns $\frac{1}{120} \times 1,200 = 10$ revolutions. Each revolution is 360 degrees, so in 10 revolutions, it turns 3,600 degrees.

910. **400**

Ten seconds is $\frac{10}{60} = \frac{1}{6}$ of a minute. If the engine turns 1,200 revolutions per minute, then in 10 seconds, it turns $\frac{1}{6} \times 1,200 = 200$ revolutions. Each revolution is 2π radians, so in 200 revolutions, it turns 400π radians.

911. **.005**

For 6% annual interest, you multiply the principal by 1.06. However, because the account is compounded monthly, the 0.06 is divided by 12, for a monthly interest rate of 0.5%, or 0.005. The principal is therefore multiplied by 1.005 for the monthly accrual. The 1 is already in the formula, so simply add 0.005.

912. **564**

Use the expression with 24 as *m* and 0.005 as *i* (because the 6% annual interest is compounded monthly, and $0.06 \div 12 = 0.005$):

$$\$500(1.005)^{24} = \$500(1.127) = \$563.50$$

Round this up to 564.

913. **.01 or 0.01**

For 4% annual interest, you multiply the principal by 1.04. However, because the account is compounded quarterly, the 0.04 is divided by 4, for a monthly interest rate of 1%, or 0.01. The principal is therefore multiplied by 1.01 for the quarterly accrual. The whole number 1 is already in the formula, so simply add 0.01.

914. **1062**

Eighteen months is 6 quarters. Use the expression with 6 as q and 0.01 as i (because the 4% annual interest is compounded quarterly, and $0.04 \div 4 = 0.01$):

$$\$1{,}000(1.01)^6 = \$1{,}000(1.0615) = \$1{,}061.5$$

Round this up to 1062.

915. **.001**

At 5.2% annual interest, multiply the principal by 1.052. However, because the account is compounded weekly, the 0.052 is divided by 52, for a monthly interest rate of 0.1%, or 0.001. The principal is therefore multiplied by 1.001 for the weekly accrual. The whole number 1 is already in the formula, so simply add 0.001.

916. **806**

Use the expression with 8 as w and 0.001 as i (because the 5.2% annual interest is compounded weekly, and $0.052 \div 52 = 0.001$).

$$\$800(1.001)^8 \approx \$800(1.008) = \$806.4$$

Round this to $806, which grids as 806.

917. **.85 or 0.85**

If 15% evaporates, 85% remains. Each week, w, multiply the remaining amount of ether mixture by 0.85 for the new amount.

918. **355**

Use the expression with 5 as w and 0.85 as m:

$$800(0.85)^5 = 800(0.4437) = 354.96$$

Round this to 355.

ANSWERS 901–1001

919. **1.22**

If the plant grows 22% per month, multiply its height by 1.22 each month.

920. **130**

Use the expression with 5 as *m* and 1.22 as *g*:

$$48(1.22)^5 = 48(2.7) = 129.6$$

Round this to 130.

921. **1050**

The desired proportion of boys to girls is $2:3$. With $800 + 300 = 1{,}100$ boys, set this up as a ratio and solve for *x* to find the total number of girls needed:

$$\frac{2}{3} = \frac{1{,}100}{x}$$
$$2x = 3{,}300$$
$$x = 1{,}650$$

Because there are already 600 girls, the number to be added is $1{,}650 - 600 = 1{,}050$.

922. **15**

If 25 colts are already there and 5 are added, then there are 30 colts. For a ratio of $3:4$, the ranch needs a total of 3 colts : 4 fillies = 30 colts : 40 fillies. There are already 25 fillies, so 15 need to be added.

923. **310**

With 150 green and 600 blue existing tiles plus 140 additional green tiles, that's 890 blue and green tiles, so the landscaper needs 890 red tiles. There are only $360 + 220 = 580$ red tiles so far, so $890 - 580 = 310$ additional red tiles are needed.

924. **1000**

The water flows in at a rate of $\frac{2{,}400}{60} = 40$ gallons per minute. In 25 minutes, $25 \times 40 = 1{,}000$ gallons is added.

925. **546**

The water is consumed at a rate of $\frac{780}{60} = 13$ gallons per minute. In 42 minutes, $13 \times 42 = 546$ gallons is used.

926. **1000**

The water is consumed at a rate of $\frac{780}{60} = 13$ gallons per minute. To consume 13,000 gallons, it will take $\frac{13,000}{13} = 1,000$ minutes.

927. **1, 1.0, 1.00, 1.25, 5/4, or 10/8**

At its lowest rate, the car will use $25 \times 0.03 = 0.75$ gallons. At its highest rate, the car will use $25 \times 0.06 = 1.5$ gallons. Anything between 0.75 and 1.5, not inclusive, is considered correct, because the car uses *between* 0.03 and 0.06 gallons per mile.

928. **70, 80, 90, 100, or 110**

At its lowest rate, to consume 3.6 gallons, the car will travel $\frac{3.6}{0.03} = 120$ miles. At its highest rate, to consume 3.6 gallons, the car will travel $\frac{3.6}{0.06} = 60$ miles. Anything between 60 and 120, not inclusive, is considered correct, because the car uses *between* 0.03 and 0.06 gallons per mile.

929. **.6, 0.6, 6/10, or 3/5**

At its lowest rate, the motorcycle will use $20 \times 0.025 = 0.5$ gallons. At its highest rate, the motorcycle will use $20 \times 0.035 = 0.7$ gallons. Anything between 0.5 and 0.7, not inclusive, is considered correct, because the motorcycle uses *between* 0.025 and 0.035 gallons per mile.

930. **29, 30, 31, 32, 33, 34, 35, 36, 37, 38, or 39**

At its lowest rate, to consume 1.0 gallons, the motorcycle will travel $\frac{1.0}{0.025} = 40$ miles. At its highest rate, to consume 2.0 gallons, the motorcycle will travel $\frac{1.0}{0.035} = 28.6$ miles. Anything between 28.6 and 40, not inclusive, is considered correct because the motorcycle uses *between* 0.025 and 0.035 gallons per mile.

931. **360**

Start by subtracting the second equation from the first:

$$\begin{array}{r} a+b+2c=650 \\ -(a+b+\ \ c=505) \\ \hline c=145 \end{array}$$

Now plug 145 in for c in the second equation to solve for $a+b$:

$$a+b+c=505$$
$$a+b+145=505$$
$$a+b=360$$

932. 80

Start by subtracting the second equation from the first:

$$\begin{array}{r} e+f+2g=280 \\ -(e+f+\ \ g=160) \\ \hline g=120 \end{array}$$

Now plug 120 in for g in the second equation to solve for $2(e+f)$:

$$e+f+g=160$$
$$e+f+120=160$$
$$e+f=40$$
$$2(e+f)=80$$

933. 36

To find the average, add up all the numbers and divide by the number of numbers.

$$\frac{(g+h)+(j+k)}{4}=\frac{2(21)+2(51)}{4}$$
$$=\frac{21+51}{2}$$
$$=\frac{72}{2}$$
$$=36$$

934. 288

Plug in 48 for b and solve for a; then find half of a:

$$\frac{a}{b}=12$$
$$\frac{a}{48}=12$$
$$a=576$$
$$\frac{1}{2}a=288$$

ANSWERS 901–1001

935. **5 or 10**

Simplify the expression:

$$\left(a^b\right)^3 = 729$$
$$\sqrt[3]{\left(a^b\right)^3} = \sqrt[3]{729}$$
$$a^b = 9$$
$$a^b = 3^2 \text{ or } 9^1$$

Therefore, $a+b$ is either $3+2=5$ or $9+1=10$.

936. **22**

If $x^y = 16$, x^y could be any of these:

$$2^4 = 16$$
$$4^2 = 16$$
$$16^1 = 16$$

Therefore, x could equal 2, 4, or 16, which total 22.

937. **4**

If $x^{2y} = 64$, x^{2y} could be any of these:

$$2^6 = 64$$
$$4^3 = 64$$
$$8^2 = 64$$
$$64^1 = 64$$

Therefore, $2y$ could equal 6, 3, 2, or 1, making y equal 3, 1.5, 1, or 0.5. Because y is an integer, the sum of possible values of y is $3+1=4$.

938. **7**

If $x^y = 81$, x^y could be any of these:

$$3^4 = 81$$
$$9^2 = 81$$
$$81^1 = 81$$

Therefore, y could equal 4, 2, or 1, which total 7.

939. **28**

If the circles have radii of 5 and 9, then the diameters are 10 and 18, respectively. If the circles are touching, then the longest segment going across (segment $\overline{AB}$) has a length of 28.

940. **1/9, or .111**

Using πr^2, the area of the 3-radius circle is 9π, and the 9-radius circle has an area of 81π. Write the areas as a fraction and reduce:

$$\frac{9\pi}{81\pi}=\frac{9}{81}=\frac{1}{9}$$

941. **3/10 or .3 or 0.3**

Each of the small blocks is $\frac{1}{10}$ of the drawing, and each of the large blocks is $\frac{1}{6}$ of the drawing. Three of the small blocks are labeled *x*, which total $3\times\frac{1}{10}=\frac{3}{10}$.

942. **4/15 or .266 or .267**

The small *y* block is $\frac{1}{10}$ of the drawing, and the large *y* block is $\frac{1}{6}$ of the drawing. Add these together: $\frac{1}{10}+\frac{1}{6}=\frac{8}{30}=\frac{4}{15}$.

943. **1/3 or .333**

Each of the small blocks is $\frac{1}{10}$ of the drawing, and each of the large blocks is $\frac{1}{6}$ of the drawing. Two of the large blocks are labeled *z*, which total $2\times\frac{1}{6}=\frac{1}{3}$.

944. **3/5 or .6 or 0.6**

Each *x* block is $\frac{1}{10}$ of the drawing, and each *z* block is $\frac{1}{6}$ of the drawing. To find the ratio, divide the fractions:

$$\frac{\frac{1}{10}}{\frac{1}{6}}=\frac{1}{10}\times\frac{6}{1}=\frac{6}{10}=\frac{3}{5}$$

945. **9/10 or .9 or 0.9**

Each block x is $\frac{1}{10}$ of the drawing, making the three x blocks $\frac{3}{10}$; each block z is $\frac{1}{6}$ of the drawing, making the two z blocks $\frac{2}{6}$, or $\frac{1}{3}$. To find the ratio, divide the fractions:

$$\frac{\frac{3}{10}}{\frac{1}{3}} = \frac{3}{10} \times \frac{3}{1} = \frac{9}{10}$$

946. **800**

Plug in 10 for y and simplify the equation:

$$\begin{aligned} D &= 100\left(2^{\frac{y+2}{4}}\right) \\ &= 100\left(2^{\frac{10+2}{4}}\right) \\ &= 100\left(2^{\frac{12}{4}}\right) \\ &= 100\left(2^3\right) \\ &= 100(8) \\ &= 800 \end{aligned}$$

947. **960**

Replace the 100 with 120, plug in 10 for y, and simplify the equation:

$$\begin{aligned} D &= 120\left(2^{\frac{y+2}{4}}\right) \\ &= 120\left(2^{\frac{10+2}{4}}\right) \\ &= 120\left(2^{\frac{12}{4}}\right) \\ &= 120\left(2^3\right) \\ &= 120(8) \\ &= 960 \end{aligned}$$

948. **4860**

Plug in 11 for *m* and simplify the equation:

$$\begin{aligned} R &= 180\left(3^{\frac{m-2}{3}}\right) \\ &= 180\left(3^{\frac{11-2}{3}}\right) \\ &= 180\left(3^{\frac{9}{3}}\right) \\ &= 180\left(3^3\right) \\ &= 180(27) \\ &= 4,860 \end{aligned}$$

949. **6480**

Replace 180 with 240; then plug in 11 for *m* and simplify the equation:

$$\begin{aligned} R &= 240\left(3^{\frac{m-2}{3}}\right) \\ &= 240\left(3^{\frac{11-2}{3}}\right) \\ &= 240\left(3^{\frac{9}{3}}\right) \\ &= 240\left(3^3\right) \\ &= 240(27) \\ &= 6,480 \end{aligned}$$

950. **1600**

Plug in 25 for *m* and simplify the equation:

$$\begin{aligned} S &= 25\left(2^{\frac{m-1}{4}}\right) \\ &= 25\left(2^{\frac{25-1}{4}}\right) \\ &= 25\left(2^{\frac{24}{4}}\right) \\ &= 25\left(2^6\right) \\ &= 25(64) \\ &= 1,600 \end{aligned}$$

951. **600**

Replace 25 with 75; then plug in 13 for *m* and simplify the equation:

$$\begin{aligned}&=75\left(2^{\frac{m-1}{4}}\right)\\&=75\left(2^{\frac{13-1}{4}}\right)\\&=75\left(2^{\frac{12}{4}}\right)\\&=75\left(2^3\right)\\&=75(8)\\&=600\end{aligned}$$

952. **376**

The box has six sides. In square inches, two sides are $6\times 8=48$, two are $8\times 10=80$, and two are $6\times 10=60$. Add these up:

$$2(48+60+80)=376$$

953. **2.61**

The box has six sides. In square inches, two sides are $6\times 8=48$, two are $8\times 10=80$, and two are $6\times 10=60$. Add these up: $2(48+60+80)=376$.

A square foot is $12\times 12=144$ square inches. To find the square feet, divide 376 by 144.

954. **900**

The tarp needs to be $45\times 20=900$ square feet.

955. **100**

The tarp needs to be $45\times 20=900$ square feet. A square yard is $3\times 3=9$ square feet. To find the square yards, divide 900 by 9.

956. **1**

Simplify the equation:

$$\begin{aligned}\frac{x^{18}-19}{18}&=-1\\x^{18}-19&=-18\\x^{18}&=1\\x&=1\end{aligned}$$

ANSWERS 901–1001

957. **6**

Simplify the equation:

$$\frac{a^b}{5} - 3.4 = 2$$
$$\frac{a^b}{5} = 5.4$$
$$a^b = 27$$

$27 = 3 \times 3 \times 3 = 3^3$, making $a = b = 3$. Therefore, $a + b = 3 + 3 = 6$.

958. **8**

Multiply the two percentages by the number of marbles:

$$80 \times 40\% \times 25\% = 80 \times 0.4 \times 0.25 = 8$$

959. **1500**

The 20% is part of the original price, not the new price. To find the original price, let x equal the original price and multiply it by 1.2:

$$1.2x = 1{,}800$$
$$x = 1{,}500$$

960. **180**

Each row has 60 tiles. Multiply 60 by 3 for the answer.

961. **2976**

The new number of rows is $60 - 12 = 48$, and the new number of columns is $80 - 18 = 62$. Multiply these for the answer.

962. **2160**

The new number of rows is $60 \times 0.9 = 54$, and the new number of columns is $80 \times 0.9 = 72$. This creates a grid of $54 \times 72 = 3{,}888$ tiles. If half of these are converted to larger tiles, then $3{,}888 \div 2 = 1{,}944$ tiles remain, and 1,944 are converted to $1{,}944 \div 9 = 216$ larger tiles. The new number of tiles is $1{,}944 + 216 = 2{,}160$.

963. **2400, 2500, 2600, 2700, 2800, 2900, 3000, 3100, 3200, or 3300**

The lowest priced car would cost $30,000 plus the $600 dealer's fee. The tax on this is $30,600 \times 0.078 = 2,386.80$. The highest priced car would cost $42,000 plus the $600 dealer's fee. The tax on this is $42,600 \times 0.078 = 3,322.80$. Any number from 2,400 to 3,300 rounded to the nearest hundred is correct.

964. **4500, 5000, 5500, 6000, 6500, 7000, or 7500**

At its slowest pace, the copier produces $15 \times 5 \times 60 = 4,500$ copies. At its fastest pace, it produces $25 \times 5 \times 60 = 7,500$ copies. Any number from 4,500 to 7,500 rounded to the nearest 500 is correct.

965. **4800, 4900, 5000, 5100, 5200, or 5300**

At 200 rubber bands per box, the shipment contains $200 \times 6 \times 4 = 4,800$ rubber bands. At 220 rubber bands per box, the shipment contains $220 \times 6 \times 4 = 5,280$ rubber bands. Any number from 4,800 to 5,300 rounded to the nearest hundred is correct.

966. **20**

Simplify and factor the equation:

$$\begin{aligned} x(x+1) &= 420 \\ x^2 + x &= 420 \\ x^2 + x - 420 &= 0 \\ (x-20)(x+21) &= 0 \\ x &= -21 \text{ or } 20 \end{aligned}$$

Because $x > 0$, the answer is 20.

967. **600**

Simplify and factor the equation:

$$\begin{aligned} x - \frac{x^2}{1,200} &= 300 \\ 1,200x - x^2 &= 360,000 \\ x^2 - 1,200x &= -360,000 \\ x^2 - 1,200x + 360,000 &= 0 \\ (x-600)(x-600) &= 0 \\ x &= 600 \end{aligned}$$

968. 4

Plug in 4 for y and solve for x:

$$x^3 = x^2 y$$
$$x^3 = x^2(4)$$
$$x = 4$$

969. 17

FOIL the expression:

$$\left(\sqrt{x}-\sqrt{17}\right)\left(\sqrt{x}+\sqrt{17}\right)=0$$
$$x-17=0$$
$$x=17$$

970. 1 or 3

Simplify and factor the equation:

$$x^3\left(x^3-28\right)=-27$$
$$x^6-28x^3=-27$$
$$x^6-28x^3+27=0$$
$$\left(x^3-1\right)\left(x^3-27\right)=0$$
$$x^3=1 \text{ or } 27$$
$$x=1 \text{ or } 3$$

971. 5, 7, or 11

Factor 770 to its primes: $770 = 2\times5\times7\times11$, so n could be 5, 7, or 11.

972. 9

FOIL the equation and simplify, remembering that $i^2=-1$:

$$\left(\sqrt{x}-3i\right)\left(\sqrt{x}+3i\right)=18$$
$$x+3i\sqrt{x}-3i\sqrt{x}-(3i)(3i)=18$$
$$x-9i^2=18$$
$$x-9(-1)=18$$
$$x+9=18$$
$$x=9$$

973. 1

Multiply both sides by i to get rid of the fraction. Then solve for x, remembering that $i^2 = -1$:

$$\frac{x}{i} = -i$$
$$x = -i(i)$$
$$x = -i^2$$
$$x = -(-1)$$
$$x = 1$$

974. 2

Divide both sides by i and solve for x, remembering that $i^2 = -1$:

$$i(x^2 - 5) = i^3$$
$$(x^2 - 5) = i^2$$
$$x^2 - 5 = -1$$
$$x^2 = 4$$
$$x = 2 \text{ or } -2$$

Because $x > 0$, x equals 2.

975. 6

Set the area equal to 144π and solve for r:

$$A = 4\pi r^2$$
$$144\pi = 4\pi r^2$$
$$144 = 4r^2$$
$$36 = r^2$$
$$6 = r$$

976. 10

Set the area equal to 100π, solve for r, and double that for the diameter:

$$A = 4\pi r^2$$
$$100\pi = 4\pi r^2$$
$$100 = 4r^2$$
$$25 = r^2$$
$$5 = r$$

Therefore, $d = 10$.

977. **30**

Set the volume equal to $36,000\pi$ and solve for *r*:

$$\begin{aligned} V &= \frac{4}{3}\pi r^3 \\ 36,000\pi &= \frac{4}{3}\pi r^3 \\ 36,000 &= \frac{4}{3}r^3 \\ 27,000 &= r^3 \\ 30 &= r \end{aligned}$$

978. **12**

Set the volume equal to 288π, solve for *r*, and double that for the diameter:

$$\begin{aligned} V &= \frac{4}{3}\pi r^3 \\ 288\pi &= \frac{4}{3}\pi r^3 \\ 288 &= \frac{4}{3}r^3 \\ 216 &= r^3 \\ 6 &= r \end{aligned}$$

Therefore, $d = 12$.

979. **4**

Set the surface area equal to 24π, plug in 3 for *r*, and solve for *h*:

$$\begin{aligned} A &= \pi r\left(r + \sqrt{h^2 + r^2}\right) \\ 24\pi &= \pi(3)\left(3 + \sqrt{h^2 + 3^2}\right) \\ 24 &= 3\left(3 + \sqrt{h^2 + 3^2}\right) \\ 24 &= 9 + 3\sqrt{h^2 + 9} \\ 15 &= 3\sqrt{h^2 + 9} \\ 5 &= \sqrt{h^2 + 9} \\ 25 &= h^2 + 9 \\ 16 &= h^2 \\ 4 &= h \end{aligned}$$

980. **8**

Set the surface area equal to 96π, plug in 6 for r, and solve for h:

$$\begin{aligned} A &= \pi r\left(r+\sqrt{h^2+r^2}\right) \\ 96\pi &= \pi(6)\left(6+\sqrt{h^2+6^2}\right) \\ 96 &= 6\left(6+\sqrt{h^2+6^2}\right) \\ 96 &= 36+6\sqrt{h^2+36} \\ 60 &= 6\sqrt{h^2+36} \\ 10 &= \sqrt{h^2+36} \\ 100 &= h^2+36 \\ 64 &= h^2 \\ 8 &= h \end{aligned}$$

981. **1 or 13**

Simplify and solve:

$$\begin{aligned} 2(x-7)^2-72&=0 \\ 2(x-7)^2&=72 \\ (x-7)^2&=36 \\ x-7&=-6 \text{ or } 6 \\ x&=1 \text{ or } 13 \end{aligned}$$

982. **4**

The equation of a circle is

$$(x-h)^2+(y-k)^2=r^2$$

where (h, k) is the center of the circle and r is the radius. In this case, $h=4$.

983. **9**

The equation of a circle is

$$(x-h)^2+(y-k)^2=r^2$$

where (h, k) is the center of the circle and r is the radius. In this case, $k=9$.

984. 6

The equation of a circle is

$$(x-h)^2+(y-k)^2=r^2$$

where (h, k) is the center of the circle and r is the radius. In this case, $r^2=36$, making $r=6$.

985. 12 or 60/5

To find the average speed of a trip, place the total distance over the total time.

Pick a number for the distance. To simplify the math, use the lowest common multiple of the two speeds, 10 and 15, which is 30. If Henry skated 30 miles uphill at 10 miles per hour, he skated for 3 hours. If he skated 30 miles back at 15 miles per hour, he skated for 2 hours. Now you have the total distance and total time, which is 60 miles over 5 hours. Set it up as a fraction:

$$\frac{60\text{ mi}}{5\text{ hr}}$$

You can reduce the fraction to $\frac{12\text{ mi}}{1\text{ hr}}$, or 12 mph.

986. 3.75 or 30/8 or 15/4

To find the average speed of a trip, place the total distance over the total time.

Pick a number for the distance. To simplify the math, use the lowest common multiple of the two speeds, 3 and 5, which is 15. If Yan swam uphill, a distance of 15 nautical miles at 3 knots, she swam for 5 hours. If she swam back at 5 knots, she swam for 3 hours. Now you have the total distance and total time, which is 30 nautical miles over 8 hours. Set it up as a fraction:

$$\frac{30\text{ mi}}{8\text{ hr}}$$

This equals 15/4 or 3.75 knots.

987. 2 or 6

Simplify and solve:

$$2\sqrt{3}(x-4)^2-8\sqrt{3}=0$$
$$2\sqrt{3}(x-4)^2=8\sqrt{3}$$
$$(x-4)^2=4$$
$$x-4=-2\text{ or }2$$
$$x=2\text{ or }6$$

988. **9**

Pick a radius for circle *A*, such as 3. Circle *B* then has a radius of 9. Compare the areas:

$$\begin{aligned} \pi r^2 &: \pi r^2 \\ \pi(9)^2 &: \pi(3)^2 \\ \pi 81 &: \pi 9 \\ 81 &: 9 \\ 9 &: 1 \end{aligned}$$

989. **16**

Pick a radius for circle *C*, such as 2. Circle *D* then has a radius of 8. Compare the areas:

$$\begin{aligned} \pi r^2 &: \pi r^2 \\ \pi(8)^2 &: \pi(2)^2 \\ \pi 64 &: \pi 4 \\ 64 &: 4 \\ 16 &: 1 \end{aligned}$$

990. **7 or 15**

Simplify and solve:

$$\begin{aligned} \frac{3\sqrt{5}(x-11)^2}{24\sqrt{20}} &= 1 \\ 3\sqrt{5}(x-11)^2 &= 24\sqrt{20} \\ 3\sqrt{5}(x-11)^2 &= 24\sqrt{4\times 5} \\ 3\sqrt{5}(x-11)^2 &= (24\times 2)\sqrt{5} \\ 3\sqrt{5}(x-11)^2 &= 48\sqrt{5} \\ (x-11)^2 &= 16 \\ x-11 &= -4 \text{ or } 4 \\ x &= 7 \text{ or } 15 \end{aligned}$$

991. **4.5, 10.5, 9/2, or 21/2**

Simplify and solve:

$$\frac{4\sqrt{2}\left(x-7.5\right)^2}{9\sqrt{32}}=1$$
$$4\sqrt{2}\left(x-7.5\right)^2=9\sqrt{32}$$
$$4\sqrt{2}\left(x-7.5\right)^2=9\sqrt{16\times 2}$$
$$4\sqrt{2}\left(x-7.5\right)^2=9\times 4\sqrt{2}$$
$$\left(x-7.5\right)^2=9$$
$$x-7.5=-3 \text{ or } 3$$
$$x=4.5 \text{ or } 10.5$$

992. **5 or 7**

Simplify and solve:

$$\left(x-6\right)^{18}=1$$
$$x-6=-1 \text{ or } 1$$
$$x=5 \text{ or } 7$$

993. **2 or 3**

Simplify and solve:

$$\left(x-\frac{5}{2}\right)^2\sqrt{2i}=\frac{1}{4}\sqrt{2i}$$
$$\left(x-\frac{5}{2}\right)^2=\frac{1}{4}$$
$$x-\frac{5}{2}=-\frac{1}{2} \text{ or } \frac{1}{2}$$
$$x=2 \text{ or } 3$$

994. **0 or 1**

Simplify and solve:

$$\left(x-\frac{1}{2}\right)^4\sqrt{11}=\frac{1}{16}\sqrt{11}$$
$$\left(x-\frac{1}{2}\right)^4=\frac{1}{16}$$
$$x-\frac{1}{2}=-\frac{1}{2} \text{ or } \frac{1}{2}$$
$$x=0 \text{ or } 1$$

995. **2 or 20**

Simplify and solve:

$$\frac{(x-11)^2}{3^4}=1$$
$$(x-11)^2=3^4$$
$$x-11=-9 \text{ or } 9$$
$$x=2 \text{ or } 20$$

996. **8**

Set up the equation and solve for f:

$$12f+6=102$$
$$12f=96$$
$$f=8$$

997. **3**

The equation of a circle is $(x-h)^2+(y-k)^2=r^2$, where r is the radius. In this case, $r^2=9$, so $r=3$.

998. **3**

The equation of a circle is $(x-h)^2+(y-k)^2=r^2$, where h and k are the x- and y-values of the center, respectively, and r is the radius. In this case, $h=-2$, $k=3$, and $r^2=9$, meaning the center of the circle is $(-2, 3)$ and the circle has a radius of 3. Therefore, the circle is tangent to the x-axis at $(0, 3)$.

Chapter 5

999.

Student Essay

In response to the prevalence of racism at the time, in his famous "I Have a Dream" speech, Martin Luther King, Jr., delivers a powerful, persuasive argument that the fate and prosperity of the black man and white man are tied together and that only through peace and brotherhood can the black man achieve the equality and justice that he so rightly deserves. Dr. King effectively uses historical reference, analogy, and moral appeal to invoke emotion and persuade the audience to take action but also embrace dignity by rising above violence to a level of decency that befits all men.

Dr. King starts by painting a picture of the situation today (in 1963). He reminds his audience of the Emancipation Proclamation signed 100 years earlier and the purpose of the Proclamation and the hope that it gave to millions of enslaved people. Not only does Dr. King tell us that the Proclamation has not had its intended effect of true freedom, but he also uses metaphor to give his speech the effect of a story, not a lecture. These metaphoric words early in his speech include "manacles of segregation," "chains of discrimination," and "island of poverty in . . . a vast ocean of prosperity." With these words and historical reminders, he paints a powerful picture of the situation and prepares the audience for the analogy of the broken promise that follows.

Dr. King describes the Emancipation Proclamation as a bad check: something that makes a promise but fails to follow through. The promise of the Emancipation Proclamation is the freedom, equality, and opportunity that is entitled to all men, black and white. Dr. King further uses the analogy to describe the "insufficient funds in the great vaults . . . of this nation." By saying that we should refuse to believe this is so, Dr. King places the situation into the context of a problem that can be solved and, in doing so, gives hope to the people.

Dr. King continues by describing the sense of urgency to take peaceful action. He further uses metaphor to avoid "the tranquilizing drug of gradualism" and "rise from the dark and desolate valley . . . to the sunlit path." His message here is that action needs to happen now and that this is the time for change "until the bright day of justice emerges." The use of the analogy invokes the powerful images of desolation vs. hope to not only empathize with the despairing audience but also show the other side of the coin, that there is something that can be done and a goal that can be achieved.

Action is important, but Dr. King wants to see peaceful protest, not violence. Dr. King further appeals to emotion by reminding the audience not to be guilty of wrongful deeds. He declares that bitterness and hatred are wrong and that the struggle must be conducted on the "high plane of dignity and discipline." He is connecting with the audience's sense of right and wrong, with the message that only through decency and integrity can any man, black or white, hope to achieve equality. In the last paragraph of this excerpt, Dr. King further appeals for peace by reminding the audience that there are friends on both sides. He describes the community militancy as not a means to an end and explains that every man's freedom has the same fate. In this way, he neatly ties together the problem, solution, and means to an end while providing moral guidance.

Dr. King tells the story of the failed promise of the Emancipation Proclamation, uses emotional appeal to describe the depth of the injustice, and uses analogy to persuade a better and more promising course of action. He not only provides hope to an audience that needs it but also provides guidance on peacefully achieving the goal through brotherhood, not antagonism.

Explanation and Score

The opening paragraph effectively summarizes Dr. King's message, methods, and intended effect. In this way, the writer sets up the detailed discussion that follows.

The second paragraph analyzes Dr. King's historical references and use of analogy. Note that the essay focuses on how well the passage is composed, not the writer's opinion.

The third paragraph describes Dr. King's use of analogy and its intended effect on the audience.

The fourth paragraph continues to support the writer's point that Dr. King uses analogy to invoke emotions and encourage action.

The fifth paragraph continues to describe Dr. King's method of persuasion through analogy, word choice, and emotional appeal. It further explores Dr. King's reasoning that peace, not violence, will lead to success.

In the conclusion, the writer recaps the introduction and touches upon the points mentioned in the essay.

This essay earns a total score of 12 (out of 12) points. It gets 4 (out of 4) points for Reading, as it demonstrates a thorough understanding of the passage. It earns 4 (out of 4) points for Analysis, as it offers an insightful analysis of Dr. King's methods of persuasion and analogy. It furthermore earns 4 (out of 4) points for Writing, as it is consistent, well organized, and written with good grammar.

1,000.

Student Essay

Probably in response to the tarnished image of our nation's schools, the authors introduce a message of hope and allude to the course of action that comes later in the book. Using statistics and historical references, the authors describe a desolate but easily overcome academic mindset that, according to the authors, holds our schools back from what they could be.

The authors open with a statement of hope that things can improve. They follow this, in the second paragraph, with a picture of the importance of their message and statistics to back up the need for results. The number of K–12 students — fifty-nine million in the United States — is staggering, and according to the authors, these students are headed for disaster. The authors continue to describe the school system as an outdated and irrelevant process that forces students through a faded carbon-copy curriculum of obsolete ideas and compliance-based codes of conduct.

The problem with this perspective is that it offers a blanket statement of doom and gloom. Though the sociologist's job is to focus on societal shortcomings while ignoring successes, these authors seem to ignore the benefits that may come from a standardized, socially planned, evolving education, including the skills that students pick up and the advances in the educational system, such as earning college credits while in high school. The authors make valid points, but they ignore an important part of the picture. The result of this approach is that it offers as a solution only a complete overhaul rather than a simple repair.

The authors use certain writing techniques to hone their point. For example, the repetition of the statistic "fifty-nine million young people" in the second paragraph serves to exemplify the impact of the situation. They cleverly bring a part of history to the passage, with the actions of Martin Luther in 1518. They offer an analogy of Martin Luther's dissent and action within the church to their dissent and proposed action in today's schools. Hopefully the authors expand upon this analogy in this book, because the connection is not readily apparent: it's like comparing NASCAR to a roulette wheel to talk about probability.

The passage ends with more doom-and-gloom and offers a shimmering ray of hope (from the cloudy skies that the passage itself brings). The authors suggest that positive action makes a difference and things can improve. This is consistent with the opening paragraph.

The redeeming value of this passage is that whether today's schools are totally lame (as stated in the passage) or simply in need of improvement, the authors offer a positive, proactive message of improvement. Whether in great shape or hurting badly, everything has room for improvement, and schools can perhaps benefit from the authors' suggestions that are forthcoming in the book.

Explanation and Score

The opening paragraph captures the authors' attitude and hope for change. In this way, the writer effectively sets up the detailed discussion that follows.

The second paragraph explores the methods that the authors use — statistics and the threat of disaster — to set up the situation that needs a solution.

The third, fourth, and fifth paragraphs are where the writer further explores the passage. Remember that the SAT essay is not on whether you agree with the passage but rather on how well you think it's written. Here, the writer offers a sound critique without a personal opinion. Though it's clear that the writer doesn't agree with the authors, the writer carefully maintains an objective tone.

The conclusion reflects the introduction and recaps the essay. The writer effectively disagrees with the authors by pointing out shortcomings of the essay.

This essay earns a total score of 12 (out of 12) points. It gets 4 (out of 4) points for Reading, as it demonstrates a sound understanding of the passage. It earns 4 (out of 4) points for Analysis, as it offers an insightful analysis of the authors' use of statistics, metaphor, and bias. It furthermore earns 4 (out of 4) points for Writing, for its organization and consistency along with its use of analogy and good grammar.

1,001.

Student Essay

This passage is a sales pitch for Challenge Success schools, albeit a seemingly objective and very informative one. The authors don't claim that their school is the "best" or "all the student needs" but rather rely on straight facts and a problem-solving approach.

The passage opens right up at the heart of the issue: School reform can be effective, or it can fail, and the authors cite sources for credibility. This should get the attention of many a parent — who wants their kids in a failed reform environment, especially as described by experts cited by the authors?

The passage continues by describing the steps that their school, Challenge Success, takes to ensure landing in the camp of effective reform. The passage reads confidently but seems stuffy and scientific, describing an endless run of discussion and analysis as the key to solving the problem. The writing is dry and almost esoteric, describing the "teams to attend intensive conferences" and "research-based approaches and best practices." The passage alludes to success stories and good progress, so these methods could be effective, but the second paragraph would be more persuasive from the mention of engaging the students as kids who learn than a set of statistics and observations.

The passage redeems itself in the third and final paragraph. The problem solvers are looking for effective, long-term solutions, not the latest trend or "flash in the pan." They are eliciting the cooperation and buy-in of everyone involved by listening, not simply dictating. A problem solver is more trustworthy if he listens to the people with problems more than simply dictates. Furthermore, the authors finally portray the students as people, not case studies, by mentioning "how wise a sixth grader can be if you give her a chance." This token connection to the client base is appreciated.

This third paragraph continues to redeem the passage by describing goal setting, cooperation, and working closely to build trust with students, teachers, and parents. Ironically, the passage describes disseminating ideas from a central conference, through coaches and teams, to the schools and finally to the families, then mentions that it avoids a top-down approach.

All in all, the passage is dry, but it describes a probably effective approach to bringing fresh ideas to an old model. The mention of "best practices" and "success stories" is good, but the heart and passion of the teacher may be desiccated by the academic, statistical approach. The authors and approach are clearly well intentioned, and hopefully the studies carry the warmth and individual stories of the students, even though the passage does not really say so.

Explanation and Score

This writer takes a critical approach to the passage. She describes the writing as stuffy but reaching for warmth, and she backs this up with specific examples from the passage. Her use of classic SAT vocab words, such as *esoteric* (hard to understand) and *desiccated* (dried out completely) are a plus, and her analytic discussion of the passage's attempt at conveying warmth but losing ground to cold scientific description is dead on.

This writer also interjects her personal response to the passage ("I always trust . . ." and "I wonder if . . .") while staying objective and avoiding her opinion. That is an important skill for an effective SAT essay: Give your response and analysis without giving your opinion.

The introduction sets up what the essay is about, the body follows through, and the conclusion recaps the body and restates the intro without being repetitive. The essay is intelligent and engaging.

This essay earns a total score of 12 (out of 12) points. It gets 4 (out of 4) points for Reading, as it demonstrates a thorough understanding of the passage. It earns 4 (out of 4) points for Analysis, as it offers an insightful analysis of Challenge Success's pitch of the revised approach to primary education. It furthermore earns 4 (out of 4) points for Writing, as it uses good grammar, advanced vocabulary, and a consistent, well-organized writing style.

ANSWERS 901–1001

Index

C

F

G

H

M

N

O

P

Q

R

S

T

U

V

W

X

Y

About the Author

Ron Woldoff completed his dual master's degrees at Arizona State University and San Diego State University, where he studied the culmination of business and technology. After several years as a corporate consultant, Ron opened his own company, National Test Prep, where he helps students prepare for the GMAT, GRE, ACT, SAT, and PSAT. He created the programs and curricula from scratch, using his own observations of the tests and feedback from students. Ron has also taught his own GMAT and GRE programs as an instructor at both Northern Arizona University and the internationally acclaimed Thunderbird School of Global Management, as well as his SAT, ACT, and PSAT programs at various high schools. Ron lives in Phoenix with his lovely wife, Leisah, and their three amazing boys, Zachary, Jadon, and Adam. Find Ron on the web at `testprepaz.com`.

Dedication

This book is humbly dedicated to the thousands of students whom I have helped reach their goals. You have taught me as much as I have taught you.

Author's Acknowledgments

I would like to thank my friends Ken Krueger, Lionel Hummel, and Jaime Abromovitz, who helped me get things started when I had this wild notion of helping students prepare for the standardized tests. I would like to thank my friend Elleyne Kase, who first connected me with the *For Dummies* folks and helped make this book happen. At *Dummies*, I would like to thank Lindsay Lefevere and Tracy Boggier for setting this book in motion, along with Tim Gallan, Danielle Voirol, Penny Stuart, and Cindy Kaplan for making sure I got things right. And more than anyone else, I would like to thank my wife, Leisah, for her continuing support and always being there for me.

Publisher's Acknowledgments

Executive Editor: Lindsay Sandman Lefevere
Project Editor: Tim Gallan
Copy Editor: Danielle Voirol
Technical Editor: Cindy Kaplan
Art Coordinator: Alicia B. South

Production Editor: Tamilmani Varadharaj
Cover Image: sezeryadigar/iStockphoto

ELECTRONIC COMMERCE

Ninth Edition

Gary P. Schneider, Ph.D., CPA
Quinnipiac University

COURSE TECHNOLOGY
CENGAGE Learning™

Australia • Brazil • Japan • Korea • Mexico • Singapore • Spain • United Kingdom • United States

Electronic Commerce, Ninth Edition
Gary P. Schneider, Ph.D., CPA

VP/Editorial Director: Jack Calhoun

Publisher: Joe Sabatino

Senior Acquisitions Editor: Charles McCormick, Jr.

Senior Product Manager: Kate Mason

Editorial Assistant: Nora Heink

Development Editor: Amanda Brodkin

Content Project Manager: Jennifer Feltri

Production Project Manager: Karunakaran Gunasekaran

Manufacturing Coordinator: Julio Esperas

Marketing Manager: Adam Marsh

Senior Marketing Communication Manager: Libby Shipp

Marketing Coordinator: Suellen Ruttkay

Senior Art Director: Stacy Jenkins Shirley

Cover Designer: Craig Ramsdell

Cover Image: iStock Photo

Compositor: Pre-Press PMG

Library of Congress Control Number: 2009939853

Student Edition
ISBN-13: 978-0-538-46924-1
ISBN-10: 0-538-46924-2

Instructor Edition
ISBN-13: 978-0-538-47194-7
ISBN-10: 0-538-47194-8

Course Technology
20 Channel Center Street
Boston, Massachusetts 02210
USA

Printed in the United States of America
1 2 3 4 5 6 7 16 15 14 13 12 11 10

BRIEF CONTENTS

Part 3: Technologies for Electronic Commerce

Part 4: Integration

TABLE OF CONTENTS

Part 2: Business Strategies for Electronic Commerce

Part 3: Technologies for Electronic Commerce

Part 4: Integration

PREFACE

Electronic Commerce, Ninth Edition provides complete coverage of the key business and technology elements of electronic commerce. The book does not assume that readers have any previous electronic commerce knowledge or experience.

In 1998, having spent several years doing electronic commerce research, consulting, and corporate training, I began developing undergraduate and graduate business school courses in electronic commerce. Although I had used a variety of books and other materials in my corporate training work, I was concerned that those materials would not work well in university courses because they were written at widely varying levels and did not have the organization and pedagogic features, such as review questions, that are so important to students.

After searching for a textbook that offered balanced coverage of both the business and technology elements of electronic commerce, I concluded that no such book existed. The first edition of *Electronic Commerce* was written to fill that void. Since that first edition, I have worked to improve the book and keep it current with the rapid changes in this dynamic field.

New to this Edition

This edition includes the usual updates to keep the content current with the rapidly occurring changes in electronic commerce. The ninth edition also includes new material on the following topics:

- Expanded discussion of first-mover advantage (Chapter 1)
- Multiple marketing channels (Chapter 3)
- Revenue models for specialized information Web sites (Chapter 3)
- The future of electronic books and newspaper Web sites (Chapter 3)
- Free for many, fee for a few revenue models (Chapter 3)
- Online delivery of television shows and movies (Chapter 3)
- E-procurement software for smaller companies (Chapter 5)
- Social networking business opportunities (Chapter 6)
- Growth of mobile commerce applications on smart phones (Chapters 3, 6)
- Re-emergence of group shopping Web sites (Chapter 6)
- Click-wrap and Web-wrap contract acceptances (Chapter 7)
- Emergence of Chinese Web server software (Chapter 8)
- Growing use of Web services and other Web 2.0 technologies in electronic commerce (Chapters 6, 9)
- Expanded coverage of database management software (Chapter 9)
- Specialized customer relationship management software (Chapter 9)
- New major viruses and security threats (Chapter 10)

- Secure Sockets Layer-Extended Validation digital certificates (Chapter 10)
- Mobile banking and mobile payment services (Chapter 11)
- Use of credit card verification numbers in electronic commerce (Chapter 11)
- Expanded coverage of jobs in electronic commerce (Chapter 12)

ORGANIZATION AND COVERAGE

Electronic Commerce: Ninth Edition introduces readers to both the theory and practice of conducting business over the Internet and World Wide Web. The book is organized into four sections: an introduction, business strategies, technologies, and integration.

Introduction

The book's first section includes two chapters. Chapter 1, "Introduction to Electronic Commerce," defines electronic commerce and describes how companies use it to create new products and services, reduce the cost of existing business processes, and improve the efficiency and effectiveness of their operations. The concept of the second wave of electronic commerce is presented and developed in this chapter. Chapter 1 also describes the history of the Internet and the Web, explains the international environment in which electronic commerce exists, provides an overview of the economic structures in which businesses operate, and describes how electronic commerce fits into those structures. Two themes are introduced in this chapter and recur throughout later chapters: examining a firm's value chain can suggest opportunities for electronic commerce initiatives, and reductions in transaction costs are important elements of many electronic commerce initiatives.

Chapter 2, "Technology Infrastructure: The Internet and the World Wide Web," introduces the technologies used to conduct business online, including topics such as Internet infrastructure, protocols, and packet-switched networks. Chapter 2 also describes the markup languages used on the Web (HTML and XML) and discusses Internet connection options and tradeoffs, including wireless technologies.

Business Strategies for Electronic Commerce

The second section of the book includes five chapters that describe the business strategies that companies and other organizations are using to do business online. Chapter 3, "Selling on the Web: Revenue Models and Building a Web Presence," describes revenue models that companies are using on the Web and explains how some companies have changed their revenue models as the Web has matured. The chapter explains important concepts related to revenue models, such as cannibalization and coordinating multiple marketing channels. The chapter also describes how firms that understand the nature of communication on the Web can identify and reach the largest possible number of qualified customers.

Chapter 4, "Marketing on the Web," provides an introduction to Internet marketing and online advertising. It includes coverage of market segmentation, technology-enabled customer relationship management, rational branding, contextual advertising, localized advertising, viral marketing, and permission marketing. The chapter also explains how online businesses can share and transfer brand benefits through affiliate marketing and cooperative efforts among brand owners.

Chapter 5, "Business-to-Business Activities: Improving Efficiency and Reducing Costs" explores the variety of methods that companies are using to improve their purchasing and logistics primary activities with Internet and Web technologies. Chapter 5 also provides an overview of EDI and explores how the Internet provides an inexpensive EDI communications channel that allows smaller businesses to reap EDI's benefits. Chapter 5 describes how businesses are using technologies such as e-procurement, radio-frequency identification, and reverse auctions in the practice of supply chain management online.

Chapter 6, "Social Networking, Mobile Commerce, and Online Auctions," outlines how companies now use the Web to do things that they have never done before, such as creating social networks, engaging in mobile commerce, and operating auction sites. The chapter describes how businesses are developing social networks and using existing social networking Web sites to increase sales and do market research. The emergence of mobile commerce in meaningful volumes after many years of anticipation is outlined. The chapter also explains how companies are using Web auction sites to sell goods to their customers and generate advertising revenue.

Chapter 7, "The Environment of Electronic Commerce: Legal, Ethical, and Tax Issues," discusses the legal and ethical aspects of intellectual property usage and the privacy rights of customers. Online crime, terrorism, and warfare are covered as well. The chapter also explains that the large number of government units that have jurisdiction and power to tax makes it essential that companies doing business on the Web understand the potential liabilities of doing business with customers in those jurisdictions.

Technologies for Electronic Commerce

The third section of the book includes four chapters that describe the technologies of electronic commerce and explains how they work. Chapter 8, "Web Server Hardware and Software," describes the computers, operating systems, e-mail systems, utility programs, and Web server software that organizations use in the operation of their electronic commerce Web sites. The chapter describes the problem of unsolicited commercial e-mail (UCE, or spam) and outlines both technical and legal solutions to the problem.

Chapter 9, "Electronic Commerce Software," describes the basic functions that all electronic commerce Web sites must accomplish and explains the various software options used to perform those functions by companies of various sizes. This chapter includes an overview of Web services (Web 2.0 technologies), database management, shopping cart, and other types of software used in electronic commerce. The chapter also includes a discussion of Web hosting options for online businesses of various sizes.

Chapter 10, "Electronic Commerce Security," discusses security threats and countermeasures that organizations can use to ensure the security of client computers, communications channels, and Web servers. The chapter emphasizes the importance of a written security policy and explains how encryption and digital certificates work. The role of industry organizations in promoting computer, network, and Internet security is also outlined.

Chapter 11, "Payment Systems for Electronic Commerce," presents a discussion of electronic payment systems, including mobile banking, electronic cash, electronic wallets, and the technologies used to make stored-value cards, credit cards, debit cards, and charge cards work. The chapter describes how payment systems operate, including approval of transactions and disbursements to merchants, and describes how banks are using Internet technologies to improve check clearing and payment-processing operations. The use of mobile technologies for making small payments today and in the future is outlined. The chapter also includes a discussion of the threats that phishing attacks and identity theft crimes pose for individuals and online businesses.

Integration

The fourth and final section of the book includes one chapter that integrates the business and technology strategies used in electronic commerce. Chapter 12, "Planning for Electronic Commerce," presents an overview of key elements that are typically included in business plans for electronic commerce implementations, such as the setting of objectives and estimating project costs and benefits. The chapter describes outsourcing strategies used in electronic commerce and covers the use of project management and project portfolio management as formal ways to plan and control tasks and resources used in electronic commerce implementations. This chapter includes a discussion of change management and outlines specific jobs available in organizations that conduct electronic commerce.

FEATURES

The ninth edition of *Electronic Commerce* includes a number of features and offers additional resources designed to help readers understand electronic commerce. These features and resources include:

- **Business Case Approach** The introduction to each chapter includes a real business case that provides a unifying theme for the chapter. The case provides a backdrop for the material described in the chapter. Each case illustrates an important topic from the chapter and demonstrates its relevance to the current practice of electronic commerce.
- **Learning From Failures** Not all electronic commerce initiatives have been successful. Each chapter in the book includes a short summary of an electronic commerce failure related to the content of that chapter. We all learn from our mistakes—this feature is designed to help readers understand the missteps of electronic commerce pioneers who learned their lessons the hard way.
- **Summaries** Each chapter concludes with a Summary that concisely recaps the most important concepts in the chapter.
- **Online Companion** The Online Companion is a set of Web pages maintained by the publisher for readers of this book. The Online Companion complements the book and contains links to Web sites referred to in the book and to other online resources that further illustrate the concepts presented. The Web is constantly changing and the Online Companion is continually monitored and updated for those changes so that its links continue to lead to useful Web resources for each chapter. You can find the Online Companion for this book by visiting Course Technology's Web site at *www.cengage.com/mis* and searching for Electronic Commerce.
- **Online Companion References in Text** Throughout each chapter, there are Online Companion References that indicate the name of a link included in the Online Companion. Text set in bold, green, sans-serif letters (**Metabot Pro**) indicates a like-named link in the Online Companion. The links in the Online

Companion are organized under chapter and subchapter headings that correspond to those in the book. The Online Companion also contains many supplemental links to help students explore beyond the book's content.

- **Review Questions and Exercises** Each chapter concludes with meaningful review materials including both conceptual discussion questions and hands-on exercises. The review questions are ideal for use as the basis for class discussions or as written homework assignments. The exercises give students hands-on experiences that yield computer output or a written report.
- **Cases** Each chapter concludes with two comprehensive cases. One case uses a fictitious setting to illustrate key learning objectives from that chapter. The other case gives students an opportunity to apply what they have learned from the chapter to an actual situation that a real company or organization has faced. The cases offer students a rich environment in which they can apply what they have learned and provide motivation for doing further research on the topics.
- **For Further Study and Research** Each chapter concludes with a comprehensive list of the resources that were consulted during the writing of the chapter. These references to publications in academic journals, books, and the IT industry and business press provide a sound starting point for readers who want to learn more about the topics contained in the chapter.
- **Key Terms and Glossary** Terms within each chapter that may be new to the student or have specific subject-related meaning are highlighted by boldface type. The end of each chapter includes a list of the chapter's key terms. All of the book's key terms are compiled, along with definitions, in a Glossary at the end of the book.

TEACHING TOOLS

When this book is used in an academic setting, instructors may obtain the following teaching tools from Course Technology:

- **Instructor's Manual** The Instructor's Manual has been carefully prepared and tested to ensure its accuracy and dependability. The Instructor's Manual is available through the Course Technology Instructor Downloads. (Call your customer service representative to obtain your username and password.)
- **ExamView©** This textbook is accompanied by ExamView, a powerful testing software package that allows instructors to create and administer printed, computer (LAN-based), and Internet exams. ExamView includes hundreds of questions that correspond to the topics covered in this text, enabling students to generate detailed study guides that include page references for further review. The computer-based and Internet testing components allow students to take exams at their computers, and also save the instructor time by grading each exam automatically.
- **PowerPoint Presentations** Microsoft PowerPoint slides are included for each chapter as a teaching aid for classroom presentations, to make available to students on a network for chapter review, or to be printed for classroom

distribution. Instructors can add their own slides for additional topics they introduce to the class. The presentations are included on the Instructor's CD.

- **WebTutor** Whether you want Web-enable your class or teach entirely online, WebTutor provides customizable, rich, text-specific content that can be used with both WebCT and Blackboard. WebTutor allows instructors to easily blend, add, edit, reorganize, or delete content. Each WebTutor product provides media assets, quizzing, Web links, discussion topics, and more.

ACKNOWLEDGMENTS

I owe a great debt of gratitude to my good friends at Course Technology who made this book possible. Course Technology remains the best publisher with which I have ever worked. Everyone at Course Technology put forth tremendous effort to publish this edition on a very tight schedule. My heartfelt thanks go to Charles McCormick, Jr., Senior Acquisitions Editor; Kate Mason, Product Manager; and Karunakaran Gunasekaran, Production Project Manager, for their tireless work and dedication. I am deeply indebted to Amanda Brodkin, Development Editor extraordinaire, for her outstanding contributions to all nine editions of this book. Amanda performed the magic of turning my manuscript drafts into a high-quality textbook and was always ready with encouragement and fresh ideas when I was running low on them. Many of the best elements of this book resulted from Amanda's ideas and inspirations. In particular, I want to thank Amanda for contributing the Dutch auction example in Chapter 6 and the ideas for the cases in Chapters 7 and 8.

I want to thank the following reviewers for their insightful comments and suggestions on current and previous editions:

Paul Ambrose	University of Wisconsin, Milwaukee
Kirk Arnett	Mississippi State University
Tina Ashford	Macon State College
Rafael Azuaje	Sul Ross State University
Robert Chi	California State University-Long Beach
Chet Cunningham	Madisonville Community College
Roland Eichelberger	Baylor University
Mary Garrett	Michigan Virtual High School
Barbara Grabowski	Benedictine University
Milena Head	McMaster University
Perry M. Hidalgo	Gwinnett Technical Institute
Brent Hussin	University of Wisconsin, Green Bay
Cheri L. Kase	Legg Mason Corporate Technology
Joanne Kuzma	St. Petersburg College
Rick Lindgren	Graceland University
Victor Lipe	Trident Technical College
William Lisenby	Alamo Community College
Diane Lockwood	Albers School of Business and Economics, Seattle University
Jane Mackay	Texas Christian University
Michael P. Martel	Culverhouse School of Accountancy, University of Alabama
William E. McTammany	Florida Community College at Jacksonville

Leslie Moore	Jackson State Community College
Martha Myers	Kennesaw State University
Pete Partin	Forethought Financial Services
Andy Pickering	University of Maryland University College
David Reavis	Texas A&M University
George Reynolds	Strayer University
Barbara Warner	University of South Florida
Gene Yelle	Megacom Services

Special thanks go to reviewer A. Lee Gilbert of Nanyang Technological University in Singapore, who provided extremely detailed comments and many useful suggestions for improving Chapter 12. My thanks also go to the many professors who have used the previous editions in their classes and who have sent me suggestions for improving the text. In particular, I want to acknowledge the detailed recommendations made by David Bell of Pacific Union College regarding the coverage of IP addresses in Chapter 2.

The University of San Diego provided research funding that allowed me to work on the first edition of this book and gave me fellow faculty members who were always happy to discuss and critically evaluate ideas for the book. Of these faculty members, my thanks go first to Jim Perry for his contributions as co-author on the first two editions of this book. Tom Buckles, now a professor of marketing at Biola University, provided many useful suggestions, pointed out a number of valuable research resources, and was willing to sit and discuss ideas for this book long after everyone else had left the building. Rahul Singh, now teaching at the University of North Carolina-Greensboro, provided suggestions regarding the book's coverage of electronic commerce infrastructure. Carl Rebman made recommendations on a number of networking, telecommunications, and security topics. The University of San Diego School of Business Administration also provided the research assistance of many graduate students who helped me with work on the first seven editions of this book. Among those research assistants were Sebastian Ailioaie, a Fulbright Fellow who did substantial work on the Online Companion, and Anthony Coury, who applied his considerable legal knowledge to reviewing Chapter 7 and suggesting many improvements.

Many of my graduate students provided helpful suggestions and ideas. My special thanks go to two of those students, Dima Ghawi and Dan Gordon. Dima shared her significant background research on reverse auctions and helped me develop many of the ideas presented in Chapters 5 and 6. Dan gave me the benefit of his experiences as manager of global EDI operations for a major international firm and provided an in-depth review of Chapter 5. I am also grateful to Robin Lloyd for her help with the Lonely Planet case (in Chapter 3) and to Zu-yo Wang for his help with the Alibaba.com case (Chapter 6). Other students who provided valuable suggestions include Maximiliano Altieri, Adrian Boyce, Karl Flaig, Kathy Glaser, Emilie Johnson Hersh, Chad McManamy, Dan Mulligan, Firat Ozkan, Suzanne Phillips, Susan Soelaiman, Carolyn Sturz, and Leila Worthy.

Finally, I want to express my deep appreciation for the support and encouragement of my wife, Cathy Cosby. Without her support and patience, writing this book would not have been possible.

DEDICATION

To the memory of my father, Anthony J. Schneider.

ABOUT THE AUTHOR

Gary Schneider is the William S. Perlroth Professor of Accounting at Quinnipiac University. His prior teaching appointments include the University of San Diego, the University of Tennessee, and Xavier University. He has won several teaching awards and has served as academic director of the University of San Diego's graduate programs in electronic commerce and information systems. Gary has published more than 50 books and 100 research papers on a variety of accounting, information systems, and management topics. His books have been translated into Chinese, French, Italian, Korean, and Spanish. Gary's research has been funded by the Irvine Foundation and the U.S. Office of Naval Research. His work has appeared in the *Journal of Information Systems*, *Interfaces*, *Issues in Accounting Education*, and the *Information Systems Audit & Control Journal*. He has served as editor of the *Business Studies Journal* and the *Accounting Systems and Technology Reporter,* as accounting discipline editor of *Advances in Accounting, Finance and Economics*, as associate editor of the *Journal of Global Information Management*, and on the editorial boards of the *Journal of Information Systems*, the *Journal of Electronic Commerce in Organizations*, the *Journal of Database Management*, and the *Information Systems Audit & Control Journal*. Gary has lectured on electronic commerce topics at universities and businesses in the United States, Europe, South America, and Asia. He has provided consulting and training services to a number of major clients, including Gartner, Gateway, Honeywell, the National Science Foundation, Qualcomm, and the U.S. Department of Commerce. In 1999, he was named a Fellow of the Gartner Institute. In 2003, he was awarded the Clarence L. Steber professorship by the University of San Diego. Gary is a licensed CPA in Ohio, where he practiced public accounting for 14 years. He holds a Ph.D. in accounting information systems from the University of Tennessee, an M.B.A. in accounting from Xavier University, and a B.A. in economics from the University of Cincinnati.

PART 1

INTRODUCTION

CHAPTER 1

INTRODUCTION TO ELECTRONIC COMMERCE

LEARNING OBJECTIVES

In this chapter, you will learn about:

- What electronic commerce is and how it has evolved into a second wave of growth
- Why companies concentrate on revenue models and the analysis of business processes instead of business models when they undertake electronic commerce initiatives
- How economic forces have created a business environment that is fostering the second wave of electronic commerce
- How businesses use value chains and SWOT analysis to identify electronic commerce opportunities
- The international nature of electronic commerce and the challenges that arise in engaging in electronic commerce on a global scale

INTRODUCTION

In the late 1990s, electronic commerce was still emerging as a new way to do business; however, some companies had established solid footholds online. Amazon.com was a rapidly growing bookseller, eBay had taken the lead as a profitable auction site, and the business of providing Internet search was populated by a few well-established sites, including AltaVista, HotBot, Lycos, and Yahoo!. Most industry observers at that time believed that any new search engine Web site would find it very difficult to compete against these established operations.

Search engines at that time provided results based on the number of times a search term appeared on Web pages. Pages that included the user's search term more often would be more highly ranked and would thus appear near the top of the search results list. By 1998, two Stanford University students, Lawrence Page and Sergey Brin, had been working on a search engine research project for two years. Page and Brin believed that a search ranking based on the relationships between Web sites would give users better and more useful results. They developed search algorithms based on the number of links a particular Web page had to and from other highly relevant pages. In 1998, they started **Google** (Note: This typeface indicates a corresponding link to a related Web page in the book's Online Companion; Google's URL is http://www.google.com) in a friend's garage with about $1.1 million of seed money invested by a group of Stanford graduates and local businesspersons.

Google's page ranking system, which has been continually improved, turned out to be much better at providing users with relevant results than other search engines. Internet users flocked to Google, which became one of the most popular sites on the Internet. The site's popularity allowed Google to charge increasingly higher rates for advertising space on its Web pages. Marketing staff at Google noticed that another search engine, Goto.com (now owned by Yahoo! and operated as Yahoo! Search Marketing), was selling ad space on Web sites by allowing advertisers to bid on the price of keywords and then charging based on the number of users that clicked on the ads. For example, a car dealer could bid on the price of the keyword "car." If the car dealer were the high bidder at 12 cents, then the car dealer would pay for the ad at a rate of 12 cents times the number of site visitors that clicked the ad. Google adopted this keyword bidding model in 2000 and used it to sell small text ads that appear on search results pages.

This approach to selling advertising was extremely successful and led to Google's continued growth. When the company went public in 2004 (raising $1.67 billion), its market valuation was nearly $23 billion. Today, Google is one of the most successful online companies in the world. The Web provides a quick path to potential customers for any businessperson with a unique product or service. Google's improved page ranking system was available to anyone in the world the day it was introduced online.

ELECTRONIC COMMERCE: THE SECOND WAVE

The business phenomenon that we now call electronic commerce has had an interesting history. From humble beginnings in the mid-1990s, electronic commerce grew rapidly until 2000, when a major downturn occurred. The popular media published endless news stories describing how the "dot-com boom" had turned into the "dot-com bust." Between 2000 and 2003, many industry observers were writing obituaries for electronic commerce. Just as the unreasonable expectations for immediate success had fueled unwarranted high expectations during the boom years, overly gloomy news reports colored perceptions during this time. Beginning in 2003, electronic commerce began to show signs of new life. Companies that had survived the downturn were not only seeing growth in sales again, but many of them were showing profits. As the economy grew, electronic commerce grew also, but at a more rapid pace. Thus, electronic commerce gradually became a larger part of the total economy. In the general economic recession that started in 2008, electronic commerce was hurt less than most of the economy. Even in the face of recession, the second wave of electronic commerce is well under way. This section defines electronic commerce and describes its evolution from first wave to second wave.

Electronic Commerce and Electronic Business

To many people, the term "electronic commerce" means shopping on the part of the Internet called the World Wide Web (the Web). However, **electronic commerce** (or **e-commerce)** also includes many other activities, such as businesses trading with other businesses and internal processes that companies use to support their buying, selling, hiring, planning, and other activities. Some people use the term **electronic business** (or **e-business)** when they are talking about electronic commerce in this broader sense. For example, IBM defines electronic business as "the transformation of key business processes through the use of Internet technologies." Most people use the terms "electronic commerce" and "electronic business" interchangeably. In this book, the term electronic commerce (or e-commerce) is used in its broadest sense and includes all business activities that use Internet technologies. Internet technologies include the Internet, the World Wide Web, and other technologies such as wireless transmissions on mobile telephone networks. Companies that operate only online are often called **dot-com** or **pure dot-com** businesses to distinguish them from companies that operate in physical locations (solely or together with online operations).

Categories of Electronic Commerce

Some people find it useful to categorize electronic commerce by the types of entities participating in the transactions or business processes. The five general electronic commerce categories are business-to-consumer, business-to-business, business processes, consumer-to-consumer, and business-to-government. The three categories that are most commonly used are:

- Consumer shopping on the Web, often called **business-to-consumer** (or **B2C)**
- Transactions conducted between businesses on the Web, often called **business-to-business** (or **B2B)**
- Transactions and business processes in which companies, governments, and other organizations use Internet technologies to support selling and purchasing activities

To understand these categories better, consider a company that manufactures stereo speakers. The company might sell its finished product to consumers on the Web, which would be B2C electronic commerce. It might also purchase the materials it uses to make the speakers from other companies on the Web, which would be B2B electronic commerce. Businesses often have entire departments devoted to negotiating purchase transactions with their suppliers. These departments are usually named **supply management** or **procurement**. Thus, B2B electronic commerce is sometimes called **e-procurement**.

In addition to buying materials and selling speakers, the company must also undertake many other activities to convert the purchased materials into speakers. These activities might include hiring and managing the people who make the speakers, renting or buying the facilities in which the speakers are made and stored, shipping the speakers, maintaining accounting records, obtaining customer feedback, purchasing insurance, developing advertising campaigns, and designing new versions of the speakers. An increasing number of these transactions and business processes can be done on the Web. Manufacturing processes (such as the fabrication of the speakers) can be controlled using Internet technologies within the business. All of these communication, control, and transaction-related activities have become an important part of electronic commerce. Some people include these activities in the B2B category; others refer to them as underlying or supporting business processes.

Figure 1-1 shows the three main elements of electronic commerce. The figure presents a rough approximation of the relative sizes of these elements. In terms of dollar volume and number of transactions, B2B electronic commerce is much greater than B2C electronic commerce. However, the number of supporting business processes is greater than the number of all B2C and B2B transactions combined.

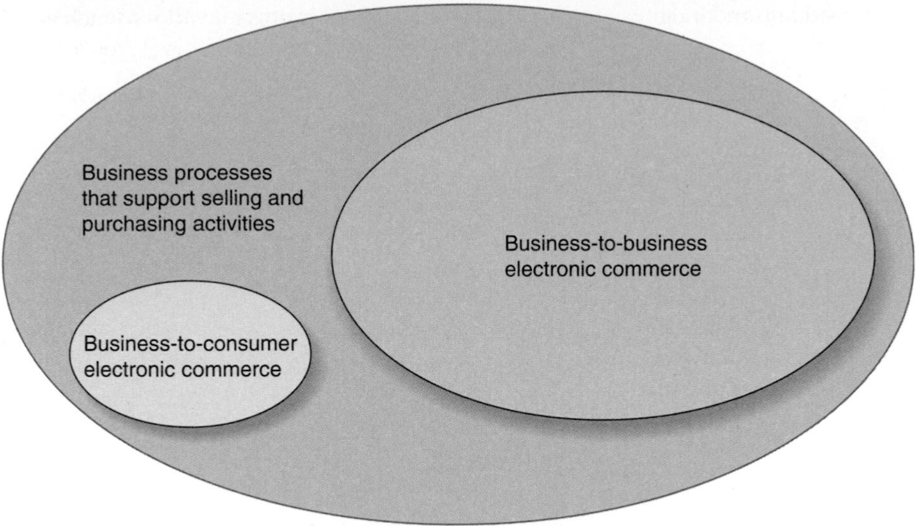

FIGURE 1-1 Elements of electronic commerce

The large oval in Figure 1-1 that represents the business processes that support selling and purchasing activities is the largest element of electronic commerce. This section provides some background and explains how business processes are built from their component parts, activities, and transactions.

For more than 70 years, business researchers have been studying the ways people behave in businesses. This research has helped managers better understand how workers do their jobs. The research results have also helped managers, and, increasingly, the workers themselves, improve job performance. By changing the nature of jobs, managers and workers can, as the saying goes, "work smarter, not harder." An important part of doing these job studies is to learn what activities each worker performs. In this setting, an **activity** is a task performed by a worker in the course of doing his or her job.

For a much longer time—centuries, in fact—business owners have kept records of how well their businesses are performing. The formal practice of accounting, or recording transactions, dates back to the 1400s. A **transaction** is an exchange of value, such as a purchase, a sale, or the conversion of raw materials into a finished product. By recording transactions, accountants help business owners keep score and measure how well they are doing. All transactions involve at least one activity, and some transactions involve many activities. Not all activities result in measurable (and therefore recordable) transactions. Thus, a transaction always has one or more activities associated with it, but an activity might not be related to a transaction.

The group of logical, related, and sequential activities and transactions in which businesses engage are often collectively referred to as **business processes**. Transferring funds, placing orders, sending invoices, and shipping goods to customers are all types of activities or transactions. For example, the business process of shipping goods to customers might include a number of activities (or tasks, or transactions), such as inspecting the goods, packing the goods, negotiating with a freight company to deliver the goods, creating and printing the shipping documents, loading the goods onto the truck, and sending a check to the freight company. One important way that the Web is helping people work more effectively is by enabling employees of many different kinds of companies to work at home or other locations (such as while traveling). In this arrangement, called **telecommuting** or **telework**, the employee logs in to the company network through the Internet instead of traveling to an office.

Some researchers define a fourth category of electronic commerce, called **consumer-to-consumer** (or **C2C**), which includes individuals who buy and sell items among themselves. For example, C2C electronic commerce occurs when a person sells an item through a Web auction site to another person. In this book, C2C sales are included in the B2C category because the person selling the item acts much as a business would for purposes of the transaction.

Finally, some researchers also define a category of electronic commerce called **business-to-government** (or **B2G**); this category includes business transactions with government agencies, such as paying taxes and filing required reports. An increasing number of states have Web sites that help companies do business with state government agencies. For example, the **CA.gov Procurement** site makes it easy for businesses to conduct online transactions with the state of California. In this book, B2G transactions are included in the discussions of B2B electronic commerce. Figure 1-2 summarizes these five categories of electronic commerce.

Category	Description	Example
Business-to-consumer (B2C)	Businesses sell products or services to individual consumers.	Walmart.com sells merchandise to consumers through its Web site.
Business-to-business (B2B)	Businesses sell products or services to other businesses.	Grainger.com sells industrial supplies to large and small businesses through its Web site.
Business processes that support buying and selling activities	Businesses and other organizations maintain and use information to identify and evaluate customers, suppliers, and employees. Increasingly, businesses share this information in carefully managed ways with their customers, suppliers, employees, and business partners.	Dell Computer uses secure Internet connections to share current sales and sales forecast information with suppliers. The suppliers can use this information to plan their own production and deliver component parts to Dell in the right quantities at the right time.
Consumer-to-consumer (C2C)	Participants in an online marketplace can buy and sell goods to each other. Because one party is selling, and thus acting as a business, this book treats C2C transactions as part of B2C electronic commerce.	Consumers and businesses trade with each other in the eBay.com online marketplace.
Business-to-government (B2G)	Businesses sell goods or services to governments and government agencies. This book treats B2G transactions as part of B2C electronic commerce.	CA.gov procurement site allows businesses to sell online to the state of California.

FIGURE 1-2 Electronic commerce categories

The Development and Growth of Electronic Commerce

Over the thousands of years that people have engaged in commerce with one another, they have adopted the tools and technologies that became available. For example, the advent of sailing ships in ancient times opened new avenues of trade to buyers and sellers. Later innovations, such as the printing press, steam engine, and telephone, have changed the way in which people conduct commerce activities. The Internet has changed the way people buy, sell, hire, and organize business activities in more ways and more rapidly than any other technology in the history of business.

Electronic Funds Transfers (EFTs)

Although the Web has made online shopping possible for many businesses and individuals, in a broader sense, electronic commerce has existed for many years. For more than 30 years, banks have been using **electronic funds transfers** (**EFTs**, also called **wire transfers**), which are electronic transmissions of account exchange information over private communications' networks.

Electronic Data Interchange (EDI)

Businesses have also been engaging in a type of electronic commerce, known as electronic data interchange, for many years. **Electronic data interchange** (**EDI**) occurs when one business transmits computer-readable data in a standard format to another business. In the 1960s, businesses realized that many of the documents they exchanged were related to the shipping of goods, for example, invoices, purchase orders, and bills of lading. These documents included the same set of information for almost every transaction. Businesses also realized that they were spending a good deal of time and money entering this data into their computers, printing paper forms, and then reentering the data on the other side of the transaction. Although the purchase order, invoice, and bill of lading for each transaction contained much of the same information—such as item numbers, descriptions, prices, and quantities—each paper form usually had its own unique format for presenting the information. By creating a set of standard formats for transmitting the information electronically, businesses were able to reduce errors, avoid printing and mailing costs, and eliminate the need to reenter the data.

Businesses that engage in EDI with each other are called **trading partners**. The standard formats used in EDI contain the same information that businesses have always included in their standard paper invoices, purchase orders, and shipping documents. Firms such as General Electric, Sears, and Wal-Mart have been pioneers in using EDI to improve their purchasing processes and their relationships with suppliers. The U.S. government, which is one of the largest EDI trading partners in the world, was also instrumental in bringing businesses into EDI.

One problem that EDI pioneers faced was the high cost of implementation. Until the late 1990s, doing EDI meant buying expensive computer hardware and software and then either establishing direct network connections (using leased telephone lines) to all trading partners or subscribing to a value-added network. A **value-added network** (**VAN**) is an independent firm that offers connection and transaction-forwarding services to buyers and sellers engaged in EDI. Before the Internet came into existence as we know it today, VANs provided the connections between most trading partners and were responsible for ensuring the security of the data transmitted. VANs usually charged a fixed monthly fee plus a per-transaction charge, adding to the already significant expense of implementing EDI. Many smaller firms could not afford to participate in EDI and lost important customers to their larger competitors who could afford EDI.

In the late 1990s, many industry observers believed that the Internet would provide smaller companies with an alternative to EDI. Many articles in the trade press announced that the death of EDI was imminent. However, EDI was well entrenched in large companies. They had invested large amounts of money in their EDI systems and had built many of their sales, purchasing, and accounting systems around EDI. And the Internet, as an inexpensive communications medium, gave smaller companies a way to participate in EDI. The companies that operated VANs gradually moved EDI traffic to the Internet, and new companies developed other ways to help smaller businesses conduct EDI transactions on the Internet. These movements of EDI traffic to the Internet have dramatically reduced the cost of participating in EDI and have made it possible for even the smallest suppliers to do business with large customers who require its use. You will learn more about EDI, VANs, and new B2B transaction technologies in Chapter 5.

The Dot-Com Boom, Bust, and Rebirth

Between 1997 and 2000, more than 12,000 Internet-related businesses were started with more than $100 billion of investors' money. In an extended burst of optimism, and what many later described as irrational exuberance, investors feared that they might miss the money-making opportunity of a lifetime. As more investors competed for a fixed number of good ideas, the price of those ideas increased. Many good ideas suffered from poor implementation. Worse, a number of bad ideas were proposed and funded. More than 5,000 of these companies went out of business or were acquired in the downturn that began in 2000. The media coverage of the "dot-com bust" was extensive. However, between 2000 and 2003, more than $200 billion was invested in purchasing electronic commerce businesses that were in trouble and starting new online ventures, according to the industry research firm WebMergers. This second wave of financial investment was not reported extensively in either the general or business media, but these investments quietly fueled a rebirth of growth in online business activity. This second wave has given many online business ideas that were poorly implemented in the early days of the Internet another chance at success.

Despite the many news stories that appeared between 2000 and 2002 proclaiming the death of electronic commerce, the growth in online B2C sales actually had continued through that period, although at a slower pace than during the boom years of the late 1990s. Thus, the "bust" that was so widely reported in the media was really more of a slowdown than a collapse. After four years of doubling or tripling every year, growth in online sales slowed to an annual rate of 20 to 30 percent starting in 2001. This growth rate continued through the recession of 2008–2009. Although the recession devastated many traditional retailers, online sales continued to grow during that period. Most experts expect to see a sustained growth rate of 10 to 20 percent through the next three years.

One force driving the growth in online sales to consumers is the ever-increasing number of people who have access to the Internet. Today, billions of people around the world do not have computers and, therefore, do not have access to the Internet. As computers become less expensive (and as devices such as mobile phones become more commonly used to access the Internet), electronic commerce could expand dramatically.

The Pew Internet & American Life Project (funded by the Pew Charitable Trusts) began conducting several long-term research projects in 2000 to study the growth of the Internet and its effects on society. You can consult its Web site for the latest reports on these and other projects that examine Internet use.

In addition to the renewed growth in the B2C sector, B2B sales online have been increasing steadily. The dollar total of B2B online sales has been greater than B2C sales because B2B incorporates EDI, which was already accounting for more than $400 billion per year in transactions in 1995, when Internet-based electronic commerce was just beginning. This book includes business processes in the B2B category, so companies' transactions with other businesses, with their employees, and with governmental agencies (for example, when they pay their taxes) are all candidates for the application of Internet technologies. The dollar amount of these transactions, even for individual businesses, is substantial. Intel is a good example of a company that sells its products to other businesses rather than to consumers. Intel accepts more than 98 percent of its orders (more than $38 billion per year) through the Internet. Intel also purchases billions of dollars' worth of supplies and raw materials on the Web each year. The total volume of all worldwide business activities on the Web is expected to exceed $9.8 trillion by 2011. Figure 1-3 summarizes the growth of actual and estimated online sales for the B2C and B2B categories.

Year	B2C Sales: Actual and Estimated $ Billions	B2B Sales (including EDI): Actual and Estimated $ Billions
2011	360	9500
2010	330	8600
2009	300	7500
2008	270	6500
2007	230	5600
2006	200	4800
2005	170	4100
2004	130	2800
2003	100	1600
2002	80	900
2001	70	730
2000	50	600
1999	25	550
1998	10	520
1997	5	490
1996	Less than 1	460

Adapted from reports by ClickZ Network (http://www.clickz.com/stats/stats_toolbox/); eMarketer (http://www.emarketer.com/); Forrester Research (http://www.forrester.com); and the *Statistical Abstract of the United States*, 2008, Washington: U.S. Census Bureau.

FIGURE 1-3 Actual and estimated online sales in B2C and B2B categories

The Second Wave of Electronic Commerce

Many researchers have noted that electronic commerce is a major change in the way business is conducted and compare it to other historic changes in economic organization such as the Industrial Revolution. However, the Industrial Revolution was not a single event, but a series of developments that took place over a 50- to 100-year period. Economists Chris Freeman and Francisco Louçã describe four distinct waves (or phases) that occurred in the Industrial Revolution in their book *As Time Goes By* (see the For Further Study and

Research section at the end of this chapter). In each wave, different business strategies were successful. Electronic commerce and the information revolution brought about by the Internet will likely go through a series of waves, too. Researchers agree that the second wave of electronic commerce is well under way. This section outlines the defining characteristics of the first wave of electronic commerce and describes how the second wave is different.

The first wave of electronic commerce was predominantly a U.S. phenomenon. Web pages were primarily in English, particularly on commerce sites. The second wave is characterized by its international scope, with sellers doing business in many countries and in many languages. Language translation and currency conversion are two impediments to the efficient conduct of global business in the second wave. You will learn more about the issues that arise in global electronic commerce later in this chapter, in Chapter 7, which concerns legal issues, and in Chapter 11, which concerns online payment systems.

In the first wave, easy access to start-up capital led to an overemphasis on creating new large enterprises to exploit electronic commerce opportunities. Investors were excited about electronic commerce and wanted to participate, no matter how much it cost or how weak the underlying ideas were. In the second wave, established companies are using their own internal funds to finance gradual expansion of electronic commerce opportunities. These measured and carefully considered investments are helping electronic commerce grow more steadily, though more slowly.

The Internet technologies used in the first wave, especially in B2C commerce, were slow and inexpensive. Most consumers connected to the Internet using dial-up modems. The increase in broadband connections in homes is a key element in the B2C component of the second wave. In 2004, the number of U.S. homes with broadband connections began to increase rapidly. Most industry estimates showed that about 12 percent of U.S. homes had broadband connections in early 2004. By late 2009, those estimates were ranging between 50 and 60 percent. Other countries, such as South Korea, subsidize their citizens' Internet access and have an even higher rate of broadband usage. Many experts believe that increased use of home Internet connections to transfer large audio and video files prompted the surge in broadband connections. Although these connections are more expensive, they are more than 10 times faster than dial-up. This increased speed not only makes Internet use more efficient, it can alter the way people use the Web. For example, a broadband connection allows a user to watch movies and television programs online—something that is impossible to do with a dial-up connection. You will learn more about different types of connections in Chapter 2 and how connection speed can affect consumers' online shopping experiences in Chapters 3 and 4.

In the first wave, Internet technologies were integrated into B2B transactions and internal business processes by using bar codes and scanners to track parts, assemblies, inventories, and production status. These tracking technologies were not well integrated. Also, companies sent transaction information to each other using a patchwork of communication methods, including fax, e-mail, and EDI. In the second wave, Radio Frequency Identification (RFID) devices and smart cards are being combined with biometric technologies, such as fingerprint readers and retina scanners, to control more items and people in a wider variety of situations. These technologies are increasingly integrated with each other and with communication systems that allow companies to communicate with each other and share transaction, inventory level, and customer demand information effectively. You will learn more about how these technologies are integrated with B2B electronic commerce in Chapter 5.

Electronic mail (or e-mail) was used in the first wave as a tool for relatively unstructured communication. In the second wave, sellers are using e-mail as an integral part of their marketing and customer contact strategies. You will learn about e-mail technologies in Chapter 2 and e-mail marketing in Chapter 4.

Online advertising was the main intended revenue source of many failed dot-com businesses in the first wave. After a two-year dip in online advertising activity and revenues, companies began the second wave with a renewed interest in making the Internet work as an effective advertising medium. Some categories of online advertising, such as employment services (job wanted ads) are growing rapidly and are replacing traditional advertising outlets. Companies such as Google have devised ways of delivering specific ads to Internet users who are most likely to be interested in the products or services offered by those ads. You will learn about second-wave advertising strategies in Chapter 4.

The sale of digital products was fraught with difficulties during the first wave of electronic commerce. The music recording industry was unable (or, some would say, unwilling) to devise a way to distribute digital music on the Web. This created an environment in which digital piracy—the theft of musical artists' intellectual property—became rampant. The promise of electronic books was also unfulfilled. The second wave is fulfilling the promise of available technology by supporting the legal distribution of music, video, and other digital products on the Web. Apple Computer's iTunes Web site is an example of a second-wave digital product distribution business that is meeting the needs of consumers and its industry. You will learn more about digital product distribution strategies in Chapter 3 and about the related legal issues in Chapter 7.

Since about 2001, industry analysts have been predicting the emergence of mobile telephone based commerce (often called **mobile commerce** or **m-commerce**) every year. And year after year, they have been surprised that the expected development of mobile commerce has not occurred. The limited capabilities of mobile telephones were a major impediment until very recently. This has changed with the increasingly widespread use of mobile phones that allow Internet access and smart phones. **Smart phones** are mobile phones that include a Web browser, a full keyboard, and an identifiable operating system that allows users to run various software packages. These phones are available with usage plans that include unlimited data transfers at a fixed monthly rate. The availability of these devices and the low cost of Internet connectivity have made mobile commerce possible on a large scale for the first time. You will learn more about the emergence and future potential of mobile commerce, which could become the basis for the third wave of electronic commerce, in Chapter 6.

Another group of technologies have emerged that have combined to make new businesses possible on the Web. The general term for these technologies is **Web 2.0** and they include software that allow users of Web sites to participate in the creation, editing, and distribution of content on a Web site owned and operated by a third party. Sites such as Wikipedia, YouTube, and MySpace are sites that use Web 2.0 technologies. You will learn about Web 2.0 business opportunities throughout this book and will learn about the technologies used to implement them in Chapter 9.

In the first wave of electronic commerce, many companies and investors believed that being the first Web site to offer a particular type of product or service would give them an opportunity to be successful. This strategy is called the **first-mover advantage**. As business researchers studied companies who had tried to gain a first-mover advantage, they learned that being first did not always lead to success (see the Suarez and Lanzolla article reference in the For Further Study and Research section at the end of this chapter). First movers must invest large amounts of money in new technologies and make guesses about what customers will want when those technologies are functioning. The combination of high uncertainty and the need for large investments makes being a first mover very risky. As many business strategists have noted, "It is the second mouse that gets the cheese."

First movers that were successful tended to be large companies that had an established reputation (or brand) and that also had marketing, distribution, and production expertise. First movers that were smaller or that lacked the expertise in these areas tended to be unsuccessful. Also, first movers that entered highly volatile markets or in those industries with high rates of technological change often did not do well. In the second wave, fewer businesses rely on a first-mover advantage when they take their businesses online. A good example of a company that was successful in the second wave by not being a first mover is illustrated in the opening case for this chapter about Google.

Figure 1-4 shows a summary of some key characteristics of the first and second wave of electronic commerce. This list is not complete because every day brings new technologies and combinations of existing technologies that make additional second-wave opportunities possible.

Electronic Commerce Characteristic	First Wave	Second Wave
International character of electronic commerce	Dominated by U.S. companies	Global enterprises in many countries participating in electronic commerce
Languages	Most electronic commerce Web sites in English	Many electronic commerce Web sites available in multiple languages
Funding	Many new companies started with outside investor money	Established companies funding electronic commerce initiatives with their own capital
Connection technologies	Many electronic commerce participants used slow Internet connections	Rapidly increasing use of broadband technologies for Internet connections
B2B technologies	B2B electronic commerce relied on a patchwork of disparate communication and inventory management technologies	B2B electronic commerce increasingly is integrated with Radio Frequency Identification and biometric devices to manage information and product flows effectively
E-mail contact with customers	Unstructured e-mail communication with customers	Customized e-mail strategies now integral to customer contact
Advertising and electronic commerce integration	Overreliance on simple forms of online advertising as main revenue source	Use of multiple sophisticated advertising approaches and better integration of electronic commerce with existing business processes and strategies
Distribution of digital products	Widespread piracy due to ineffective distribution of digital products	New approaches to the sale and distribution of digital products
First-mover advantage	Rely on first-mover advantage to ensure success in all types of markets and industries	Realize that first-mover advantage leads to success only for some companies in certain specific markets and industries

FIGURE 1-4 Key characteristics of the first two waves of electronic commerce

Large businesses, both existing businesses and new businesses that had obtained large amounts of capital early on, dominated the first wave. As the second wave gains momentum, more than 50 percent of small U.S. businesses (those with fewer than 200 employees) do not have Web sites. The second wave of electronic commerce will include a larger proportion of these smaller businesses. Providing services that help smaller companies use electronic commerce will also be a substantial area of online business.

Not all of the future of electronic commerce is based in its second wave. Some of the most successful first-wave companies, such as Amazon.com, eBay, and Yahoo!, continue to thrive by offering increasingly innovative products and services. The second wave of electronic commerce will provide new opportunities for these businesses, too.

BUSINESS MODELS, REVENUE MODELS, AND BUSINESS PROCESSES

A **business model** is a set of processes that combine to achieve a company's primary goal, which is to yield a profit. In the first wave of electronic commerce, many investors tried to find start-up companies that had new, Internet-driven business models. These investors expected that the right business model would lead to rapid sales growth and market dominance. If a company was successful using a new "dot-com" business model, investors would clamor to copy that model or find a start-up company that planned to use a similar business model. This strategy led the way to many business failures, some of them quite dramatic.

In the wake of the dot-com debacle that ended the first wave of electronic commerce, many business researchers analyzed the efficacy of this "copy a successful business model" approach and began to question the advisability of focusing great attention on a company's business model. One of the main critics, Harvard Business School professor Michael Porter, argued that business models not only did not matter, they probably did not exist. (You can read more about Porter's criticisms of the business model approach in the articles cited in the For Further Study and Research section at the end of this chapter.)

Today, most companies realize that copying or adapting someone else's business model is neither an easy nor wise road map to success. Instead, companies should examine the elements of their business; that is, they should identify business processes that they can streamline, enhance, or replace with processes driven by Internet technologies.

Companies and investors do use the idea of a **revenue model**, which is a specific collection of business processes used to identify customers, market to those customers, and generate sales to those customers. The revenue model idea is helpful for classifying revenue-generating activities for communication and analysis purposes. The details of revenue models that are used on the Web are presented in Chapter 3.

Focus on Specific Business Processes

In addition to the revenue model grouping of business processes, companies think of the rest of their operations as specific business processes. Those processes include purchasing raw materials or goods for resale, converting materials and labor into finished goods, managing transportation and logistics, hiring and training employees, managing the finances of the business, and many other activities.

An important function of this book is to help you learn how to identify those business processes that firms can accomplish more effectively by using electronic commerce technologies. In some cases, business processes use traditional commerce activities very effectively, and technology cannot improve them. Products that buyers prefer to touch, smell, or examine closely can be difficult to sell using electronic commerce. For example, customers might be reluctant to buy items that have an important element of tactile feel or condition such as high-fashion clothing (you cannot touch it online and subtle color variations that are hard to distinguish on a computer monitor can make a large difference) or antique jewelry (for which elements of condition that require close inspection can be critical to value) if they cannot closely examine the products before agreeing to purchase them.

This book will help you learn how to use Internet technologies to improve existing business processes and identify new business opportunities. An important aspect of electronic commerce is that firms can use it to help them adapt to change. The business world is changing more rapidly than ever before. Although much of this book is devoted to explaining technologies, the book's focus is on the business of electronic commerce; the technologies only enable the business processes.

Role of Merchandising

Retail merchants have years of traditional commerce experience in creating store environments that help convince customers to buy. This combination of store design, layout, and product display knowledge is called **merchandising**. In addition, many salespeople have developed skills that allow them to identify customer needs and find products or services that meet those needs.

The skills of merchandising and personal selling can be difficult to practice remotely. However, companies must be able to transfer their merchandising skills to the Web for their Web sites to be successful. Some products are easier to sell on the Internet than others because the merchandising skills related to those products are easier to transfer to the Web.

Product/Process Suitability to Electronic Commerce

Some products, such as books or CDs, are good candidates for electronic commerce because customers do not need to experience the physical characteristics of the particular item before they buy it. Because one copy of a new book is identical to other copies, and because the customer is not concerned about fit, freshness, or other such qualities, customers are usually willing to order a title without examining the specific copy they will receive. The advantages of electronic commerce, including the ability of one site to offer a wider selection of titles than even the largest physical bookstore, can outweigh the advantages of a traditional bookstore—for example, the customer's ability to browse the pages of the books. In later chapters, you will learn how to evaluate the advantages and disadvantages of using electronic commerce for specific business processes. Figure 1-5 lists examples of business processes categorized as to how well suited they are to electronic commerce and traditional commerce.

Well Suited to Electronic Commerce	Suited to a Combination of Electronic and Traditional Commerce Strategies	Well Suited to Traditional Commerce
Sale/purchase of books and CDs	Sale/purchase of automobiles	Sale/purchase of impulse items for immediate use
Sale/purchase of goods that have strong brand reputations	Banking and financial services	Low-value transactions (total sale/purchase under $10)
Online delivery of software and digital content, such as music and movies	Roommate-matching services	Sale/purchase of used, unbranded goods
Sale/purchase of travel services	Sale/purchase of residential real estate	
Online shipment tracking	Sale/purchase of high-value jewelry and antiques	
Sale/purchase of investment and insurance products		

FIGURE 1-5 Business process suitability to type of commerce

The classifications shown in the figure depend on the current state of available technologies, and thus will change as new tools emerge for implementing electronic commerce. For example, low-denomination transactions are not well suited to electronic commerce because no standard method for transferring small amounts of money on the Web has become generally accepted (although such standards are taking shape; Chapter 11 contains a more detailed discussion of this issue). If a company or group of companies could develop a standard that gains general acceptance among buyers and sellers, low-denomination transactions could move from the traditional commerce column to the electronic commerce column.

One business process that is especially well suited to electronic commerce is the selling of commodity items. A **commodity item** is a product or service that is hard to distinguish from the same products or services provided by other sellers; its features have become standardized and well known. The only difference a buyer perceives when shopping for a commodity item is its price. Gasoline, office supplies, soap, computers, and airline transportation are all examples of commodity products or services, as are the books and CDs sold by Amazon.com.

Not all commodity items are good candidates for electronic commerce. They must have an attractive shipping profile to be sold online. A product's **shipping profile** is the collection of attributes that affect how easily that product can be packaged and delivered. A high value-to-weight ratio can help by making the overall shipping cost a small fraction of the selling price. A DVD is an excellent example of an item that has a high value-to-weight ratio. Products that are consistent in size, shape, and weight can make warehousing and shipping much simpler and less costly. Commodity items that have an attractive shipping profile include books, clothing, shoes, kitchen accessories, and many other small household items.

A product that has a strong brand reputation—such as a Kodak camera—is easier to sell on the Web than an unbranded item, because the brand's reputation reduces the buyer's concerns about quality when buying that item sight unseen. Expensive jewelry has a high value-to-weight ratio, but many people are reluctant to buy it without examining it in person unless the jewelry is sold under a well-known brand name and with a generous return policy.

Other items that are well-suited to electronic commerce are those that appeal to small, but geographically dispersed, groups of customers. Collectible comic books are an example of this kind of product.

Traditional commerce, rather than electronic commerce, can be a better way to sell items that rely on personal selling skills. For example, sales of commercial real estate involve large amounts of money and a high degree of interpersonal trust. Even if commercial real estate is listed online, it will usually require personal contact to negotiate the deal. Many businesses are using a combination of personal contact enhanced by an online presence to sell items such as high-fashion clothing, antiques, or specialized food items.

A combination of electronic and traditional commerce strategies works best when the business process includes both commodity and personal inspection elements. For example, most people find information on the Web about new and used automobiles and do considerable research on specific makes and models before they visit a dealership to buy. In the case of used cars, electronic commerce provides a good way for buyers to obtain information about available models, features, reliability, prices, and dealerships, and also helps buyers find specific vehicles that meet their exact requirements. The range of conditions of used cars makes the traditional commerce component of personal inspection a key part of the transaction negotiation. The next section summarizes some advantages and disadvantages of electronic commerce.

ADVANTAGES AND DISADVANTAGES OF ELECTRONIC COMMERCE

Electronic commerce is a major development in the way business is conducted. However, it is not something that every business can or should do. Like any business strategy, electronic commerce has advantages and disadvantages.

Advantages of Electronic Commerce

Firms are interested in electronic commerce because, quite simply, it can help increase profits. All the advantages of electronic commerce for businesses can be summarized in one statement: electronic commerce can increase sales and decrease costs. Advertising done well on the Web can get even a small firm's promotional message out to potential customers in every country in the world. A firm can use electronic commerce to reach small groups of customers that are geographically scattered. The Web is particularly useful in creating virtual communities that become ideal target markets for specific types of products or services. A **virtual community** is a gathering of people who share a common interest, but instead of this gathering occurring in the physical world, it takes place on the Internet. In recent years, virtual communities have taken advantage of Web 2.0 technologies to make their activities more accessible and interesting to community members.

You will learn more about virtual communities and the business opportunities they present in Chapter 6.

Just as electronic commerce increases sales opportunities for the seller, it increases purchasing opportunities for the buyer. Businesses can use electronic commerce to identify new suppliers and business partners. Negotiating price and delivery terms is easier in electronic commerce because the Internet can help companies efficiently obtain competitive bid information. Electronic commerce increases the speed and accuracy with which businesses can exchange information, which reduces costs on both sides of transactions. Many companies are reducing their costs of handling sales inquiries, providing price quotes, and determining product availability by using electronic commerce in their sales support and order-taking processes.

Cisco Systems, a leading manufacturer of computer networking equipment, currently sells almost all its products online. Because no customer service representatives are involved in making these sales, Cisco operates very efficiently. In 1998, the first year in which its online sales initiative was operational, Cisco made 72 percent of its sales on the Web. Cisco avoided handling 500,000 calls per month and saved $500 million in that first year. Today, Cisco conducts more than 99 percent of its purchase and sales transactions online.

Electronic commerce provides buyers with a wider range of choices than traditional commerce because buyers can consider many different products and services from a wider variety of sellers. This wide variety is available for consumers to evaluate 24 hours a day, every day. Some buyers prefer a great deal of information in deciding on a purchase; others prefer less. Electronic commerce provides buyers with an easy way to customize the level of detail in the information they obtain about a prospective purchase. Instead of waiting days for the mail to bring a catalog or product specification sheet, or even minutes for a fax transmission, buyers can have instant access to detailed information on the Web.

Most digital products, such as software, music and video files, or images, can be delivered through the Internet, which reduces the time buyers must wait to begin enjoying their purchases. The ability to deliver digital products online is not just a cost-reduction opportunity; it can increase sales, too. Intuit sells its TurboTax income tax preparation software online and lets customers download the software immediately if they wish. Intuit sells a considerable amount of TurboTax software late in the evening on April 14 each year. (April 15 is the deadline for filing personal income tax returns in the United States.)

The benefits of electronic commerce extend to the general welfare of society. Electronic payments of tax refunds, public retirement, and welfare support cost less to issue and arrive securely and quickly when transmitted over the Internet. Furthermore, electronic payments can be easier to audit and monitor than payments made by check, providing protection against fraud and theft losses. To the extent that electronic commerce enables people to telecommute, everyone benefits from the reduction in commuter-caused traffic and pollution. Electronic commerce can also make products and services available in remote areas. For example, distance learning makes it possible for people to learn skills and earn degrees no matter where they live or which hours they have available for study.

Disadvantages of Electronic Commerce

Some business processes might never lend themselves to electronic commerce. For example, perishable foods and high-cost, unique items such as custom-designed jewelry can be impossible to inspect adequately from a remote location, regardless of any technologies that might be devised in the future. Most of the disadvantages of electronic commerce today, however, stem from the newness and rapidly developing pace of the underlying technologies. These disadvantages will disappear as electronic commerce matures and becomes more available to and accepted by the general population.

Many products and services require that a critical mass of potential buyers be equipped and willing to buy through the Internet. For example, online grocers such as **Peapod** initially offered their delivery services only in a few cities. As more of Peapod's potential customers became connected to the Internet and felt comfortable with purchasing online, the company was able to expand slowly and carefully into more geographic areas. After more than 10 years of operation, Peapod operates in fewer than 20 U.S. metropolitan areas. Most online grocers focus their sales efforts on packaged goods and branded items. Perishable grocery products, such as fruit and vegetables, are much harder to sell online because customers want to examine and select specific items for freshness and quality.

Peapod is a good example of how challenging it can be to build a business in an industry that requires this kind of critical mass. Although it was one of the first online grocery stores, Peapod has had a difficult time staying in business, and was even offline for a few weeks in mid-2000. Peapod was then acquired by Royal Ahold, a European firm that was willing to invest additional cash to keep it in operation. Two of Peapod's major competitors, WebVan and HomeGrocer, were unable to stay in business long enough to attract a sufficient customer base.

Established traditional grocery chains in the United States such as **Albertsons** and **Safeway** also offer online ordering and delivery services in a second wave of using Internet technologies in the grocery business. By using their existing infrastructure (including warehouses, purchasing systems, and physical stores in multiple locations), they are able to avoid having to make the large capital investment in facilities that led to the demise of first-wave dot-com grocers such as WebVan and HomeGrocer.

One online grocer that has successfully implemented an updated version of the WebVan and HomeGrocer operational approach is **FreshDirect**. By limiting its service area to the densely populated region in and around New York City, FreshDirect has found the right combination of operating scale and market. The company started in 2002 and achieved profitability in 2004 with sales of $90 million. This is a much smaller sales volume than either WebVan or HomeGrocer would have needed to be profitable.

Outside the United States, online grocers have done quite well. Three of the most successful online grocery efforts in the world are **Grocery Gateway** in Toronto, **Disco Virtual** in Buenos Aires, and **Tesco** in the United Kingdom. Grocery Gateway and Disco Virtual operate in densely populated urban environments that offer sufficiently large numbers of customers within relatively small geographic areas, which make their delivery routes profitable. Tesco started its operations in London, which offers a similar densely populated urban area. However, Tesco has also expanded its operations to selected rural areas that are near a Tesco supermarket.

Businesses often calculate return-on-investment numbers before committing to any new technology. This has been difficult to do for investments in electronic commerce because the costs and benefits have been hard to quantify. Costs, which are a function of technology, can change dramatically even during short-lived electronic commerce implementation projects because the underlying technologies are changing so rapidly. Many firms have had trouble recruiting and retaining employees with the technological, design, and business process skills needed to create an effective electronic commerce presence. You will learn more about return-on-investment calculations and employee recruitment and retention issues in Chapter 12.

Another problem facing firms that want to do business on the Internet is the difficulty of integrating existing databases and transaction-processing software designed for traditional commerce into the software that enables electronic commerce. Although a number of companies offer software design and consulting services that promise to tie existing systems into new online business systems, these services can be expensive. You will learn more about how companies deal with these software issues in Chapter 9.

In addition to technology and software issues, many businesses face cultural and legal obstacles to conducting electronic commerce. Some consumers are still fearful of sending their credit card numbers over the Internet and having online merchants—merchants they have never met—know so much about them. You will learn more about electronic commerce security, privacy issues, and payment systems later in this book. Other consumers are simply resistant to change and are uncomfortable viewing merchandise on a computer screen rather than in person. The legal environment in which electronic commerce is conducted is full of unclear and conflicting laws. In many cases, government regulators have not kept up with technologies. As you will learn in Chapter 7, laws that govern commerce were written when signed documents were a reasonable expectation in any business transaction. However, as more businesses and individuals find the benefits of electronic commerce to be compelling, many of these technology- and culture-related disadvantages will be resolved or seem less problematic.

LEARNING FROM FAILURES

PETS.COM

In February 1999, Pets.com launched its Web site with the hopes of making substantial sales to the 60 percent of U.S. households that own pets and spend more than $20 billion each year feeding, entertaining, and caring for them. More than 10,000 stores sold pet supplies. These stores included small retail outlets, grocery stores, discount retailers (such as Wal-Mart and Costco), and a new generation of pet superstores. Pets.com had acquired an excellent domain name and intended to exploit the opportunities presented by high levels of investor interest in funding electronic commerce companies. The plan for Pets.com was to spend heavily to develop a brand and a Web presence that would rapidly make the company the premier online source for pet-related products.

After launching the site, Pets.com raised $110 million from private investors in 1999, and another $80 million in a public sale of stock in early 2000. Pets.com spent more than $100 million of the money on advertising during its short life. It also spent significant sums

Continued

to create a Web store that offered more than 12,000 different products. In November 2000—less than two years after launching its Web site—Pets.com went out of business.

Pets.com had created an electronic commerce initiative in an industry in which online business offered few advantages over traditional commerce. The products had a very low value-to-weight ratio. The shipping costs for pet food, one of the company's best-selling product categories, caused it to lose money on every sale. Pet products come in all shapes, sizes, and weights, and are, therefore, difficult to pack and ship efficiently. Pets.com was also spending money rapidly at a time when investors were beginning to question the long-run viability of all electronic commerce businesses. The lesson here is that Pets.com could not develop any sustainable advantage over traditional pet stores. Without such an advantage, the business was doomed.

In the years following the Pets.com failure, a number of companies such as PETCO and PetFoodDirect.com began selling pet food and related items online. These companies were more careful than Pets.com was about what they offered for sale. By selling only items that had an appropriate shipping profile, many of these companies have now become successful. For example, veterinarians who formulate foods that meet the needs of specific pet diets are finding they can charge enough for those products to make online sales profitable.

ECONOMIC FORCES AND ELECTRONIC COMMERCE

Economics is the study of how people allocate scarce resources. One important way that people allocate resources is through commerce (the other major way is through government actions, such as taxes or subsidies). Many economists are interested in how people organize their commerce activities. One way people do this is to participate in markets. Economists use a formal definition of **market** that includes two conditions: first, that the potential sellers of a good come into contact with potential buyers, and second, that a medium of exchange is available. This medium of exchange can be currency or barter. Most economists agree that markets are strong and effective mechanisms for allocating scarce resources. Thus, one would expect most business transactions to occur within markets. However, much business activity today occurs within large **hierarchical business organizations**, which economists generally refer to as **firms**, or **companies**.

Most hierarchical organizations are headed by a top-level president or chief operating officer. Reporting to the president are a number of executives who, in turn, have a larger number of middle managers who report to them, and so on. An organization can have a relatively flat hierarchy, in which there are only a few levels of management, or it can have many reporting levels. In either case, the bottom level includes the largest number of employees and is usually made up of production workers or service providers. Thus, the hierarchical organization always has a pyramid-shaped structure.

These large firms often conduct many different business activities entirely within the organizational structure of the firm and participate in markets only for purchasing raw materials and selling finished products. If markets are indeed highly effective mechanisms for allocating scarce resources, these large corporations should participate in markets at every stage of their production and value-generation processes. Nobel laureate Ronald Coase wrote an essay in 1937 in which he questioned why individuals who engaged in commerce often created firms to organize their activities. He was particularly interested in the hierarchical structure of these business organizations. Coase concluded that transaction costs were the main motivation for moving economic activity from markets to hierarchically structured firms.

Transaction Costs

Transaction costs are the total of all costs that a buyer and seller incur as they gather information and negotiate a purchase-and-sale transaction. Although brokerage fees and sales commissions can be a part of transaction costs, the cost of information search and acquisition is often far larger. Another significant component of transaction costs can be the investment a seller makes in equipment or in the hiring of skilled employees to supply the product or service to the buyer.

To understand better how transaction costs occur in markets, consider the following example: A sweater dealer could obtain sweaters by engaging in market transactions with a number of independent sweater knitters. Each knitter could sell sweaters to one or several dealers. Transaction costs incurred by the dealer would include the costs of identifying the independent knitters, visiting them to negotiate the purchase price, arranging for delivery of the sweaters, and inspecting the sweaters on arrival. The knitters would also incur costs, such as the purchase of knitting supplies. Since individual knitters could not know whether any sweater dealer would ever buy sweaters from them, the investments they make to enter the sweater-knitting business have an uncertain yield. This risk is a significant transaction cost for the knitters.

After purchasing the sweaters, sweater dealers take them to a different market in which sweater dealers meet and do business with the retail shops that sell sweaters to the consumer. The dealers can learn which colors, patterns, and styles are in demand from price and quantity negotiations with the retail shops in this market. The sweater dealers can then use that information to negotiate price and other terms in the knitters' market. A diagram of this set of markets appears in Figure 1-6.

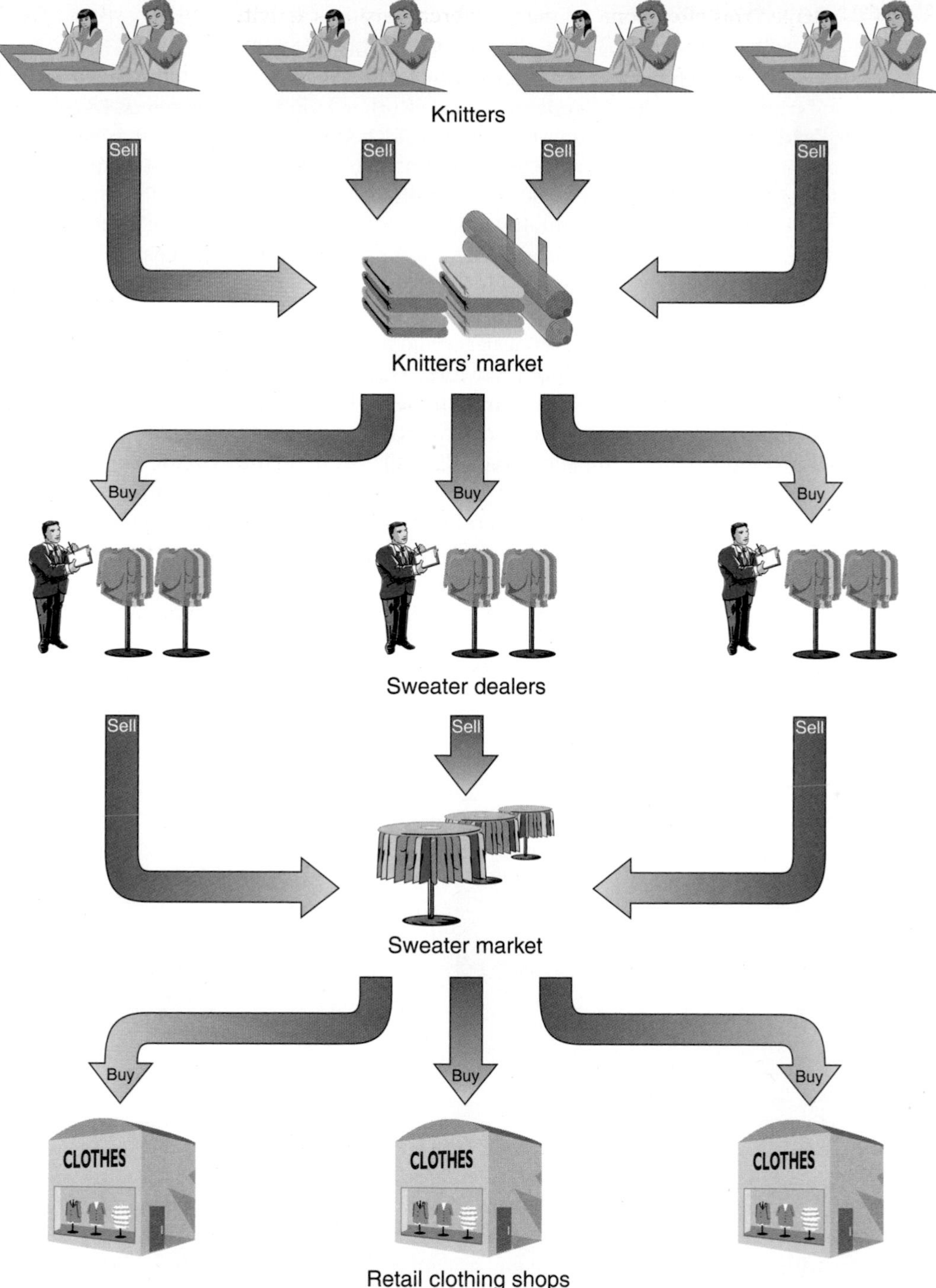

FIGURE 1-6 Market form of economic organization

Markets and Hierarchies

Coase reasoned that when transaction costs were high, businesspeople would form organizations to replace market-negotiated transactions. These organizations would be hierarchical and would include strong supervision and worker-monitoring elements. Instead of negotiating with individuals to purchase sweaters they had knit, a hierarchical organization would hire knitters, and then supervise and monitor their work activities. This supervision and monitoring system would include flows of monitoring information from the lower levels to the higher levels of the organization. It would also have control of information flowing from the upper levels of the organization to the lower levels. Although the costs of creating and maintaining a supervision and monitoring system are high, they can be lower than transaction costs in many instances.

In the sweater example, the sweater dealer would hire knitters, supply them with yarn and knitting tools, and supervise their knitting activities. This supervision could be done mainly by first-line supervisors, who might be drawn from the ranks of the more skilled knitters. The practice of an existing firm replacing one or more of its supplier markets with its own hierarchical structure for creating the supplied product is called **vertical integration**. Figure 1-7 shows how the wool sweater example would look after the knitters and the individual sweater dealers were vertically integrated into the hierarchical structure of a single sweater dealer.

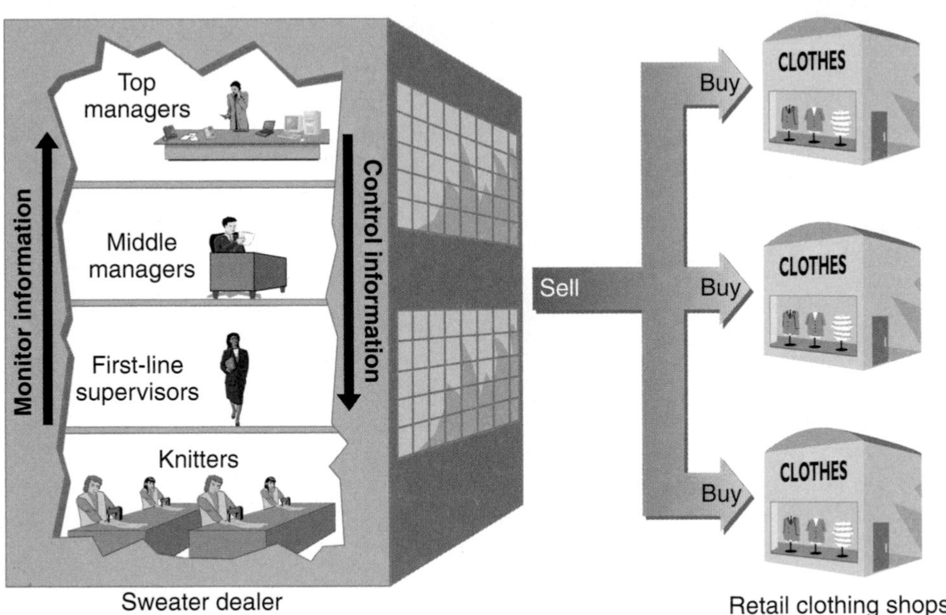

FIGURE 1-7 Hierarchical form of economic organization

Oliver Williamson, an economist who extended Coase's analysis, noted that firms in industries with complex manufacturing and assembly operations tended to be hierarchically organized and vertically integrated. Many of the manufacturing and administrative innovations that occurred in businesses during the twentieth century increased the efficiency and effectiveness of hierarchical monitoring activities. Assembly lines and other mass production technologies allowed work to be broken down into small, easily supervised procedures. The advent of computers brought tremendous increases in the ability of upper-level managers to monitor and control the detailed activities of their subordinates. Some of these direct measurement techniques are even more effective than the first-line supervisors on the shop floor.

During the years from the Industrial Revolution through the present, improvements in monitoring became commonplace and the size and level of vertical integration of firms have increased. In some very large organizations, however, monitoring systems have not kept pace with the organization's increase in size. This has created problems because the economic viability of a firm depends on its ability to track operational activities effectively at the lowest levels of the firm. These firms have instituted decentralization programs that allow business units to function as separate organizations, negotiating transactions with other business units as if they were operating in a market rather than as part of the same firm. Economists argue that large companies decentralize because they have grown too large to be managed effectively as hierarchical structures, so their managers need the information provided by market mechanisms.

To expose their decentralized operations to market mechanisms, these companies allow their divisions to operate as independent business units. A **strategic business unit (SBU)**, or simply **business unit**, is an autonomous part of a company that is large enough to manage itself but small enough to respond quickly to changes in its business environment. SBUs have their own mission and objectives; therefore, they have their own strategies for marketing, product development, purchasing, and long term growth. General Electric, one of the largest companies in the world, has used SBUs to handle its diverse business operations since the 1960s. For example, General Electric makes both jet engines and lightbulbs. These two businesses have different products, distribution channels, and customer types; therefore, they require different objectives, product development strategies, marketing plans, and manufacturing operations. General Electric's Jet Engine Division and Light Bulb Division operate as separate SBUs. Although an SBU operates as a participant in a market (rather than as part of the hierarchical structure of the owning company), the SBU itself is organized internally as a hierarchy.

Exceptions to the general trend toward hierarchies do exist. Many commodities, such as wheat, sugar, and crude oil, are still traded in markets. The commodity nature of the products traded in these markets significantly reduces transaction costs. There are a large number of potential buyers for an agricultural commodity such as wheat, and farmers do not make any special investment in customizing or modifying the product for particular customers. Thus, neither buyers nor sellers in commodity markets experience significant transaction costs.

Using Electronic Commerce to Reduce Transaction Costs

Businesses and individuals can use electronic commerce to reduce transaction costs by improving the flow of information and increasing the coordination of actions. By reducing the cost of searching for potential buyers and sellers and increasing the number of potential market participants, electronic commerce can change the attractiveness of vertical integration for many firms.

To see how electronic commerce can change the level and nature of transaction costs, consider an employment transaction. The agreement to employ a person has high transaction costs for the seller—the employee who sells his or her services. These transaction costs include a commitment to forego other employment and career development opportunities. Individuals make a high investment in learning and adapting to the culture of their employers. If accepting the job involves a move, the employee can incur very high costs, including actual costs of the move and related costs, such as the loss of a spouse's job. Much of the employee's investment is specific to a particular job and location; the employee cannot transfer the investment to a new job.

If a sufficient number of employees throughout the world can telecommute, then many of these transaction costs could be reduced or eliminated. Instead of uprooting a spouse and family to move, a worker could accept a new job by simply logging on to a different company server!

Network Economic Structures

Some researchers argue that many companies and strategic business units operate today in an economic structure that is neither a market nor a hierarchy. In this **network economic structure**, companies coordinate their strategies, resources, and skill sets by forming long-term, stable relationships with other companies and individuals based on shared purposes. These relationships are often called **strategic alliances** or **strategic partnerships**, and when they occur between or among companies operating on the Internet, these relationships are also called **virtual companies**.

In some cases, these entities, called **strategic partners**, come together as a team for a specific project or activity. The team dissolves when the project is complete; however, the partners maintain contact with each other through the ensuing period of inactivity. When the need for a similar project or activity arises, the same organizations and individuals build teams from their combined resources. In other cases, the strategic partners form many intercompany teams to undertake a variety of ongoing activities. Later in this book, you will see many examples of strategic partners creating alliances of this sort on the Web. In a hierarchically structured business environment, these types of strategic alliances would not last very long because the larger strategic partners would buy out the smaller partners and form a larger single company.

Network organizations are particularly well suited to technology industries that are information intensive. In our sweater example, the knitters might organize into networks of smaller organizations that specialize in certain styles or designs. Some of the particularly skilled knitters might leave the sweater dealer to form their own company to produce custom-knit sweaters. Some of the sweater dealer's marketing employees might form an independent firm that conducts market research on what the retail shops plan to buy in the upcoming months. This firm could sell its research reports to both the sweater dealer and the custom-knitting firm. As market conditions change, these smaller and more nimble organizations could continually reinvent themselves and take advantage of new opportunities that arise in the sweater markets. An illustration of such a network organization appears in Figure 1-8.

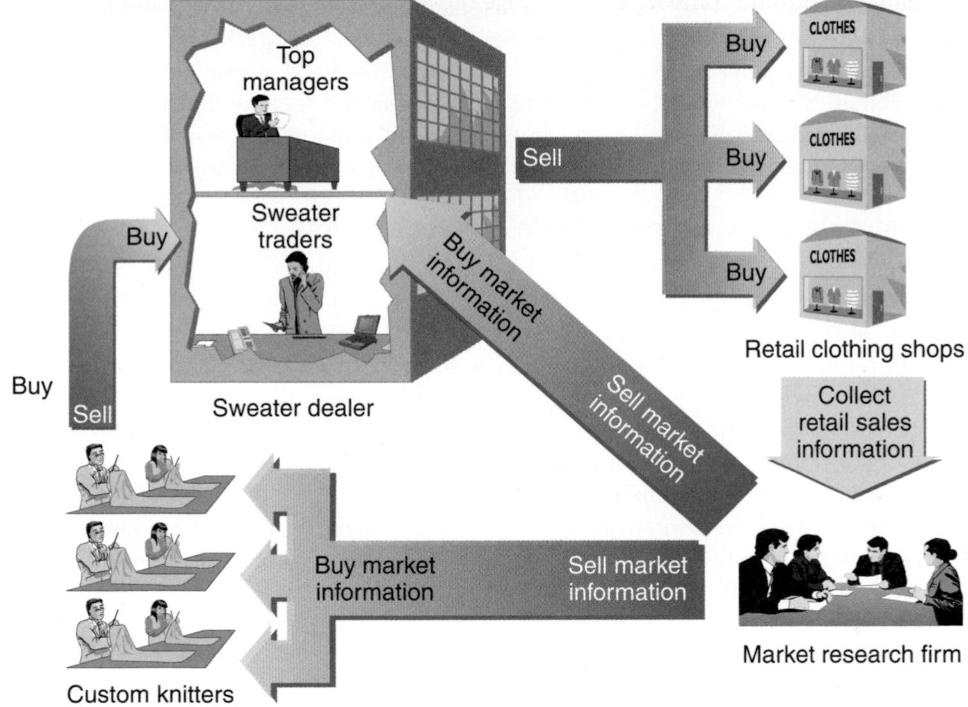

FIGURE 1-8 Network form of economic organization

Electronic commerce can make such networks, which rely extensively on information sharing, much easier to construct and maintain. Some researchers believe that these network forms of organizing commerce will become predominant in the near future. One of these researchers, Manuel Castells, even predicts that economic networks will become the organizing structure for all social interactions among people. Thomas Petzinger, a columnist for *The Wall Street Journal*, has written extensively about these new patterns of work and commerce in his newspaper columns and in his book, *The New Pioneers*. In Chapter 6, you will learn about businesses that have created Web sites (called **social networking sites**) that individuals and businesses can use to conduct social interactions online.

Network Effects

Economists have found that most activities yield less value as the amount of consumption increases. For example, a person who consumes one hamburger obtains a certain amount of value from that consumption. As the person consumes more hamburgers, the value provided by each hamburger decreases. Few people find the fifth hamburger as enjoyable as the first. This characteristic of economic activity is called the **law of diminishing returns**. In networks, an interesting exception to the law of diminishing returns occurs. As more people or organizations participate in a network, the value of the network to each participant increases. This increase in value is called a **network effect**.

To understand how network effects work, consider an early user of the telephone in the 1800s. When telephones were first introduced, few people had them. The value of each telephone increased as more people had them installed. As the network of telephones grew, the capability of each individual telephone increased because it could be used to communicate with more people. This increase in the value of each telephone as more and more telephones are able to connect to each other is the result of a network effect. Imagine how much less useful (and therefore, less valuable) your mobile phone today would be if you could only use it to talk with other people who had the same mobile phone carrier.

Using Electronic Commerce to Create Network Effects

Your e-mail account, which gives you access to a network of other people with e-mail accounts, is another example of a network effect. If your e-mail account were part of a small network, it would be less valuable than it is. Most people today have e-mail accounts that are part of the Internet (a global network of computers, about which you will learn more in Chapter 2). In the early days of e-mail, most e-mail accounts only connected people in the same company or organization to each other. Internet e-mail accounts are far more valuable than single-organization e-mail accounts because of the network effect.

Regardless of how businesses in a particular industry organize themselves—as markets, hierarchies, or networks—you will need a way to identify business processes and evaluate whether electronic commerce is suitable for each process. The next section presents one useful structure for examining business processes.

IDENTIFYING ELECTRONIC COMMERCE OPPORTUNITIES

Internet technologies can be used to improve so many business processes that it can be difficult for managers to decide where and how to use them. One way to focus on specific business processes as candidates for electronic commerce is to break the business down into a series of value-adding activities that combine to generate profits and meet other goals of the firm. In this section, you will learn one popular way to analyze business activities as a sequence of activities that create value for the firm.

Commerce is conducted by firms of all sizes. Smaller firms can focus on one product, distribution channel, or type of customer. Larger firms often sell many different products and services through a variety of distribution channels to several types of customers. In these larger firms, managers organize their work around the activities of strategic business units. Multiple business units owned by a common set of shareholders make up a firm, or company, and multiple firms that sell similar products to similar customers make up an **industry**.

Strategic Business Unit Value Chains

In his 1985 book, *Competitive Advantage*, Michael Porter introduced the idea of value chains. A **value chain** is a way of organizing the activities that each strategic business unit undertakes to design, produce, promote, market, deliver, and support the products or services it sells. In addition to these **primary activities**, Porter also includes **supporting activities**, such as human resource management and purchasing, in the value chain model. Figure 1-9 shows a value chain for a strategic business unit, including both primary and supporting activities. These value chain activities will occur in some form in any strategic business unit.

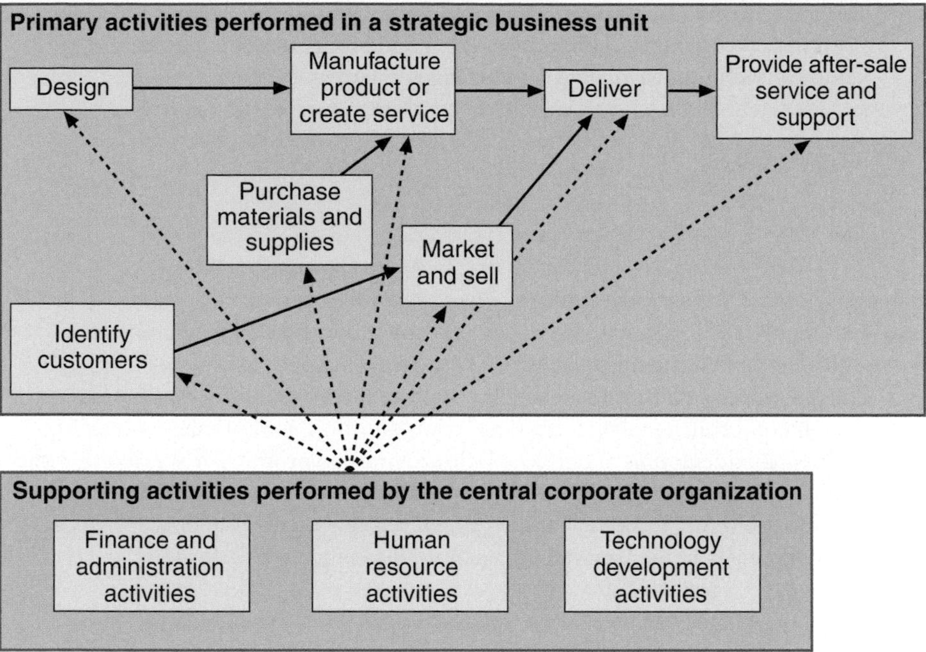

FIGURE 1-9 Value chain for a strategic business unit

The left-to-right flow in Figure 1-9 does not imply a strict time sequence for these processes. For example, a business unit may engage in marketing activities before purchasing materials and supplies. Each strategic business unit conducts the following primary activities:

- *Identify customers*: activities that help the firm find new customers and new ways to serve existing customers, including market research and customer satisfaction surveys
- *Design*: activities that take a product from concept to manufacturing, including concept research, engineering, and test marketing
- *Purchase materials and supplies*: procurement activities, including vendor selection, vendor qualification, negotiating long-term supply contracts, and monitoring quality and timeliness of delivery
- *Manufacture product or create service*: activities that transform materials and labor into finished products, including fabricating, assembling, finishing, testing, and packaging
- *Market and sell*: activities that give buyers a way to purchase and that provide inducements for them to do so, including advertising, promoting, managing salespeople, pricing, and identifying and monitoring sales and distribution channels
- *Deliver*: activities that store, distribute, and ship the final product or provide the service, including warehousing, handling materials, consolidating freight, selecting shippers, and monitoring timeliness of delivery

- *Provide after-sale service and support*: activities that promote a continuing relationship with the customer, including installing, testing, maintaining, repairing, fulfilling warranties, and replacing parts

The importance of each primary activity depends on the product or service the business unit provides and to which customers it sells. Each business unit must also have support activities that provide the infrastructure for the unit's primary activities. The central corporate organization typically provides the support activities that appear in Figure 1-9. These activities include the following:

- *Finance and administration activities*: providing the firm's basic infrastructure, including accounting, paying bills, borrowing funds, reporting to government regulators, and ensuring compliance with relevant laws
- *Human resource activities*: coordinating the management of employees, including recruiting, hiring, training, compensation, and managing benefits
- *Technology development activities*: improving the product or service that the firm is selling and that help improve the business processes in every primary activity, including basic research, applied research and development, process improvement studies, and field tests of maintenance procedures

Industry Value Chains

Porter's book also identifies the importance of examining where the strategic business unit fits within its industry. Porter uses the term **value system** to describe the larger stream of activities into which a particular business unit's value chain is embedded. However, many subsequent researchers and business consultants have used the term **industry value chain** when referring to value systems. When a business unit delivers a product to its customer, that customer may, for example, use the product as purchased materials in its value chain. By becoming aware of how other business units in the industry value chain conduct their activities, managers can identify new opportunities for cost reduction, product improvement, or channel reconfiguration.

Every product or service has an industry value chain that can be identified and analyzed for these opportunities. To create an industry value chain, start with the inputs to your SBU and work backward to identify your suppliers' suppliers, then the suppliers of those suppliers, and so on. Then start with your customers and work forward to identify your customers' customers, then the customers of those customers, and so on.

An example of an industry value chain appears in Figure 1-10. This value chain is for a wooden chair and traces the life of the product from its inception as trees in a forest to its grave in a landfill or at a sawdust recycler.

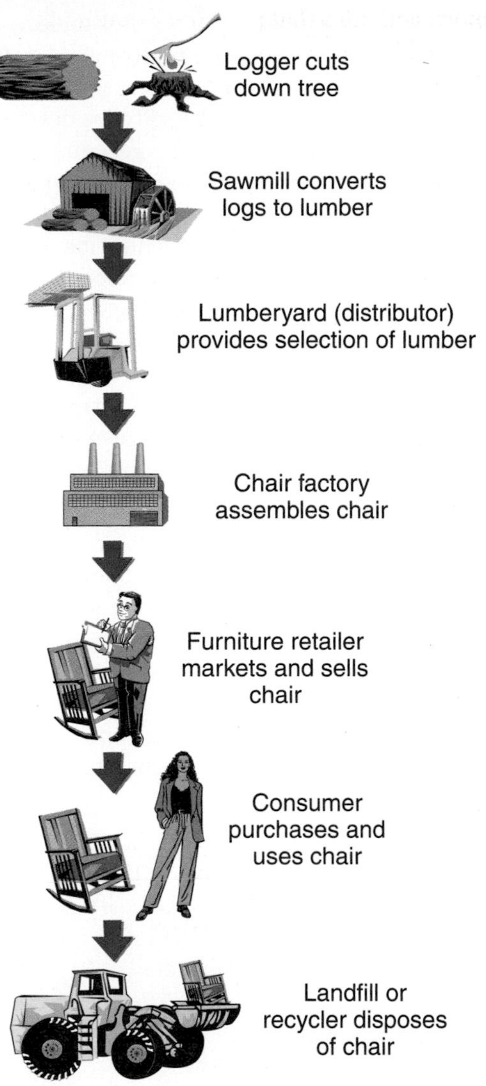

FIGURE 1-10 Industry value chain for a wooden chair

Each business unit (logger, sawmill, lumberyard, chair factory, retailer, consumer, and recycler) shown in Figure 1-10 has its own value chain. For example, the sawmill purchases logs from the tree harvester and combines them in its manufacturing process with inputs, such as labor and saw blades, from other sources. Among the sawmill customers are the chair factory, shown in Figure 1-10, and other users of cut lumber. Examining this industry value chain could be useful for the sawmill that is considering entering the tree-harvesting business or the furniture retailer who is thinking about partnering with a trucking line. The industry value chain identifies opportunities up and down the product's life cycle for increasing the efficiency or quality of the product.

As they examine their industry value chains, many managers are finding that they can use electronic commerce and Internet technologies to reduce costs, improve product quality, reach new customers or suppliers, and create new ways of selling existing products. For example, a software developer who releases annual updates to programs might consider removing the software retailer from the distribution channel for software updates by offering to send the updates through the Internet directly to the consumer. This change would modify the software developer's industry value chain and would provide an opportunity for increasing sales revenue (the software developer could retain the margin a retailer would have added to the price of the update), but it would not appear as part of the software developer business unit value chain. By examining elements of the value chain outside the individual business unit, managers can identify many business opportunities, including those that can be exploited using electronic commerce.

The value chain concept is a useful way to think about business strategy in general. When firms are considering electronic commerce, the value chain can be an excellent way to organize the examination of business processes within their business units and in other parts of the product's life cycle. Using the value chain reinforces the idea that electronic commerce should be a business solution, not a technology implemented for its own sake.

SWOT Analysis: Evaluating Business Unit Opportunities

Now that you have learned about industry value chains and SBUs, you can learn one popular technique for analyzing and evaluating business opportunities. Most electronic commerce initiatives add value by either reducing transaction costs, creating some type of network effect, or a combination of both. In **SWOT analysis** (the acronym is short for strengths, weaknesses, opportunities, and threats), the analyst first looks into the business unit to identify its strengths and weaknesses. The analyst then reviews the environment in which the business unit operates and identifies opportunities presented by that environment and the threats posed by that environment. Figure 1-11 shows questions that an analyst would ask in conducting a SWOT analysis for any company or SBU.

Strengths

- What does the company do well?
- Is the company strong in its market?
- Does the company have a strong sense of purpose and the culture to support that purpose?

Weaknesses

- What does the company do poorly?
- What problems could be avoided?
- Does the company have serious financial liabilities?

Opportunities

- Are industry trends moving upward?
- Do new markets exist for the company's products/services?
- Are there new technologies that the company can exploit?

Threats

- What are competitors doing well?
- What obstacles does the company face?
- Are there troubling changes in the company's business environment (technologies, laws, and regulations)?

FIGURE 1-11 SWOT analysis questions

By considering all of the issues that it faces in a systematic way, a business unit can formulate strategies to take advantage of its opportunities by building on its strengths, avoiding any threats, and compensating for its weaknesses.

In the mid-1990s, **Dell Computer** used a SWOT analysis to create a business strategy that helped it become a strong competitor in its industry value chain. Dell identified its strengths in selling directly to customers and in designing its computers and other products to reduce manufacturing costs. It acknowledged the weakness of having no relationships with local computer dealers. Dell faced threats from competitors such as Compaq (now a part of Hewlett-Packard) and IBM, both of which had much stronger brand names and reputations for quality at that time. Dell identified an opportunity by noting that its customers were becoming more knowledgeable about computers and could specify exactly what they wanted without having Dell salespeople answer questions or develop configurations for them. It also saw the Internet as a potential marketing tool. Dell carefully considered and answered the SWOT analysis questions shown in Figure 1-11. The results of Dell's SWOT analysis appear in Figure 1-12.

Strengths	**Weaknesses**
• Sell directly to consumers • Keep costs below competitors' costs	• No strong relationships with computer retailers
Opportunities	**Threats**
• Consumer desire for one-stop shopping • Consumers know what they want to buy • Internet could be a powerful marketing tool	• Competitors have stronger brand names • Competitors have strong relationships with computer retailers

FIGURE 1-12 Results of Dell's SWOT analysis

The strategy that Dell followed after doing the analysis took all four of the SWOT elements into consideration. Dell decided to offer customized computers built to order and sold over the phone, and eventually, over the Internet. Dell's strategy capitalized on its strengths and avoided relying on a dealer network. The brand and quality threats posed by Compaq and IBM were lessened by Dell's ability to deliver higher perceived quality because each computer was custom made for each buyer. Ten years later, Dell observed that the environment of personal computer sales had changed and did start selling computers through dealers.

INTERNATIONAL NATURE OF ELECTRONIC COMMERCE

Because the Internet connects computers all over the world, any business that engages in electronic commerce instantly becomes an international business. When companies use the Web to improve a business process, they are automatically operating in a global environment. The key issues that any company faces when it conducts international commerce include trust, culture, language, government, and infrastructure. These topics are covered in the following sections. The related issues of international law and currency are covered in Chapter 7.

Trust Issues on the Web

It is important for all businesses to establish trusting relationships with their customers. Companies with established reputations in the physical world often create trust by ensuring that customers know who they are. These businesses can rely on their established brand names to create trust on the Web. New companies that want to establish online businesses face a more difficult challenge because a kind of anonymity exists for companies trying to establish a Web presence. A now-famous cartoon that appeared in *The New Yorker* magazine is shown in Figure 1-13. The figure illustrates the inherent anonymity of the Web in a humorous way.

"On the Internet, nobody knows you're a dog."

FIGURE 1-13 This classic cartoon from *The New Yorker* illustrates anonymity on the Web

For example, a U.S. bank can establish a Web site that offers services throughout the world. No potential customer visiting the site can determine just how large or well established the bank is simply by browsing through the site's pages. Because Web site visitors will not become customers unless they trust the company behind the site, a plan for establishing credibility is essential. Sellers on the Web cannot assume that visitors will know that the site is operated by a trustworthy business.

Customers' inherent lack of trust in "strangers" on the Web is logical and to be expected; after all, people have been doing business with their neighbors—not strangers—for thousands of years. When a company grows to become a large corporation with multinational operations, its reputation grows commensurately. Before a company can do business in dozens of countries, it must prove its trustworthiness by satisfying customers for many years as it grows. Businesses on the Web must find ways to overcome this well-founded tradition of distrusting strangers, because today a company can incorporate one day and, through the Web, be doing business the next day with people all over the world. For businesses to succeed on the Web, they must find ways to quickly generate the trust that traditional businesses take years to develop.

Language Issues

Most companies realize that the only way to do business effectively in other cultures is to adapt to those cultures. The phrase "think globally, act locally" is often used to describe this approach. The first step that a Web business usually takes to reach potential customers in other countries, and thus in other cultures, is to provide local language versions of its Web site. This may mean translating the Web site into another language or regional dialect. Researchers have found that customers are far more likely to buy products and services from Web sites in their own language, even if they can read English well. Only about 400 million of the world's 6 billion people learned English as their native language.

Researchers estimate that about 50 percent of the content available on the Internet today is in English, but more than half of current Internet users do not read English. Industry analysts estimate that by 2015, more than 90 percent of Internet users will be outside the United States, and 70 percent of electronic commerce transactions will involve at least one party located outside the United States.

Some languages require multiple translations for separate dialects. For example, the Spanish spoken in Spain is different from that spoken in Mexico, which is different from that spoken elsewhere in Latin America. People in parts of Argentina and Uruguay use yet a fourth dialect of Spanish. Many of these dialect differences are spoken inflections, which are not important for Web site designers (unless, of course, their sites include audio or video elements); however, a significant number of differences occur in word meanings and spellings. You might be familiar with these types of differences, because they occur in the U.S. and British dialects of English. The U.S. spelling of *gray* becomes *grey* in Great Britain, and the meaning of *bonnet* changes from a type of hat in the United States to an automobile hood in Great Britain. Chinese has two main systems of writing: simplified Chinese, which is used in mainland China, and traditional Chinese, which is used in Hong Kong and Taiwan.

Most companies that translate their Web sites translate all of their pages. However, as Web sites grow larger, companies are becoming more selective in their translation efforts. Some sites have thousands of pages with much targeted content; the businesses operating those sites can find the cost of translating all pages to be prohibitive.

The decision whether to translate a particular page should be made by the corporate department responsible for each page's content. The home page should have versions in all supported languages, as should all first-level links to the home page. Beyond that, pages that are devoted to marketing, product information, and establishing brand should be given a high translation priority. Some pages, especially those devoted to local interests, might be maintained only in the relevant language. For example, a weekly update on local news and employment opportunities at a company's plant in Frankfurt probably needs to be maintained only in German.

Links to the Web sites of firms that provide Web page translation services and translation software for companies are included in the Additional Resources section of the Online Companion under the heading **Language Translation Services**. These firms translate Web pages and maintain them for a fee that is usually between 25 and 90 cents per word for translations done by skilled human translators. Languages that are complex or that are spoken by relatively few people are generally more expensive to translate than other languages.

Different approaches can be appropriate for translating the different types of text that appear on an electronic commerce site. For key marketing messages, the touch of a human translator can be essential to capture subtle meanings. For more routine transaction-processing functions, automated software translation may be an acceptable alternative. Software translation, also called **machine translation**, can reach speeds of 400,000 words per hour, so even if the translation is not perfect, businesses might find it preferable to a human who can translate only about 500 words per hour. Many of the companies in this field are working to develop software and databases of previously translated material that can help human translators work more efficiently and accurately.

The translation services and software manufacturers that work with electronic commerce sites do not generally use the term "translation" to describe what they do. They prefer the term **localization**, which means a translation that considers multiple elements of the local environment, such as business and cultural practices, in addition to local dialect variations in the language. The cultural element is very important because it can affect—and sometimes completely change—the user's interpretation of text.

Cultural Issues

An important element of business trust is anticipating how the other party to a transaction will act in specific circumstances. A company's brand conveys expectations about how the company will behave, therefore companies with established brands can build online businesses more quickly and easily than a new company without a reputation. For example, a potential buyer might like to know how the seller would react to a claim by the buyer that the seller misrepresented the quality of the goods sold. Part of this knowledge derives from the buyer and seller sharing a common language and common customs. Buyers are, for example, more comfortable doing business with sellers they know are trustworthy.

The combination of language and customs is often called **culture**. Most researchers agree that culture varies across national boundaries and, in many cases, varies across regions within nations. For example, the concept of private property is an important cultural value and underlies laws in many European and North American countries. Asian cultures do not value private property in the same way, so laws and business practices in those countries can be quite different. All companies must be aware of the differences in language and customs that make up the culture of any region in which they intend to do business. The Additional Resources section of the Online Companion includes links to Web sites that provide detailed information on cultural issues for specific countries under the heading **Global Trust and Culture**.

Managers at Virtual Vineyards (now a part of Wine.com), a company that sells wine and specialty food items on the Web, were perplexed. The company was getting an unusually high number of complaints from customers in Japan about short shipments. Virtual Vineyards sold most of its wine in case (12 bottles) or half-case quantities. Thus, to save on operating costs, it stocked shipping materials only in case, half-case, and two-bottle sizes. After an investigation, the company determined that many of its Japanese customers ordered only one bottle of wine, which was shipped in a two-bottle container. To these Japanese customers, who consider packaging to be an important element of a high-quality product such as wine, it was inconceivable that anyone would ship one bottle of wine in a two-bottle container. They were e-mailing to ask where the other bottle was, notwithstanding the fact that they had ordered only one bottle.

Some errors stemming from subtle language and cultural standards have become classic examples that are regularly cited in international business courses and training sessions. For example, General Motors' choice of name for its Chevrolet Nova automobile amused people in Latin America—*no va* means "it will not go" in Spanish. Pepsi's "Come Alive" advertising campaign fizzled in China because its message came across as "Pepsi brings your ancestors back from their graves."

Another story that is widely used in international business training sessions is about a company that sold baby food in jars adorned with the picture of a very cute baby. The jars sold well everywhere they had been introduced except in parts of Africa. The mystery was solved when the manufacturer learned that food containers in those parts of Africa always carry a picture of their contents. This story is particularly interesting because it never happened. However, it illustrates a potential cultural issue so dramatically that it continues to appear in marketing textbooks and international business training materials.

Designers of Web sites for international commerce must be very careful when they choose icons to represent common actions. For example, in the United States, a shopping cart is a good symbol to use when building an electronic commerce site. However, many Europeans use shopping *baskets* when they go to a store and may never have seen a shopping *cart*. In Australia, people would recognize a shopping cart image but would be confused by the text "shopping cart" if it were used with the image. Australians call them shopping *trolleys*. In the United States, people often form a hand signal (the index finger touching the thumb to create a circle) that indicates "OK" or "everything is just fine." A Web designer might be tempted to use this hand signal as an icon to indicate that the transaction is completed or the credit card is approved, unaware that in countries such as Brazil, this hand signal is an obscene gesture.

The cultural overtones of simple design decisions can be dramatic. In India, for example, it is inappropriate to use the image of a cow in a cartoon or other comical setting. Potential customers in Muslim countries can be offended by an image that shows human arms or legs uncovered. Even colors or Web page design elements can be troublesome. For example, white, which denotes purity in Europe and the Americas, is associated with death and mourning in China and many other Asian countries. A Web page that is divided into four segments can be offensive to a Japanese visitor because the number four is a symbol of death in that culture.

Japanese shoppers have resisted the U.S. version of electronic commerce because they generally prefer to pay in cash or by cash transfer instead of by credit card, and they have a high level of apprehension about doing business online. Softbank, a major Japanese firm that invests in Internet companies, devised a way to introduce electronic commerce to a reluctant Japanese population. Softbank created a joint venture with 7-Eleven, Yahoo! Japan, and Tohan (a major Japanese book distributor) to sell books and CDs on the Web. This venture, called eS-Books, allows customers to order items on the Internet, and then pick them up and pay for them in cash at the local 7-Eleven convenience store. By adding an intermediary that satisfies the needs of the Japanese customer, Softbank has been highly successful in bringing business-to-consumer electronic commerce to Japan.

Culture and Government

Some parts of the world have cultural environments that are extremely inhospitable to the type of online discussion that occurs on the Internet. These cultural conditions, in some cases, lead to government controls that can limit electronic commerce development. The Internet is a very open form of communication. This type of unfettered communication is not desired or even considered acceptable in some cultures. For example, a **Human Rights Watch** report stated that many countries in the Middle East and North Africa do not allow their citizens unrestricted access to the Internet. The report notes that many governments in this part of the world regularly prevent free expression by their citizens and have taken specific steps to prevent the exchange of information outside of state controls. For instance, Saudi Arabia, Yemen, and the United Arab Emirates all filter the Web content that is available in their countries. An organization devoted to the international promotion of democracy and civil liberties, **Freedom House**, offers a number of downloadable publications on its site, including in-depth reports on Internet censorship activities of governments throughout the world.

In most North African and Middle Eastern countries, officials have publicly denounced the Internet for carrying materials that are sexually explicit, anti-Islam, or that cast doubts on the traditional role of women in their societies. In many of these countries, uncontrolled use of Internet technologies is so at odds with existing traditions, cultures, and laws that electronic commerce is unlikely to exist locally at any significant level in the near future. In contrast, other Islamic countries in that part of the world, including Algeria, Morocco, and the Palestinian Authority, do not limit online access or content.

The censorship of Internet content and communications restricts electronic commerce because it prevents certain types of products and services from being sold or advertised. Further, it reduces the interest level of many potential participants in online activities. If large numbers of people in a country are not interested in being online, businesses that use the Internet as an information and product delivery channel will not develop in those countries.

Other countries, such as the People's Republic of China and Singapore, are wrestling with the issues presented by the growth of the Internet as a vehicle for doing business. These countries have a tradition of controlling their citizens' access to information from outside the country, but they want their economies to reap the benefits of electronic commerce. China created a complex set of registration requirements and regulations that govern any business that engages in electronic commerce. These regulations are enforced by the Public Security Bureau, which is a branch of the state police, not an independent administrative agency. For example, companies in China that sell Internet services must register all of their customers with the Public Security Bureau and must retain copies of all e-mail messages and chat room conversations for 60 days. Chinese citizens entering a chat room at Sohu.com, one of China's leading portal sites ("sohu" means "search fox" in Chinese), are greeted with a Web page containing the following text (translated here from the original Chinese):

> Warning! Please take note that the following issues are prohibited according to Chinese law: 1) Criticism of the People's Republic of China Constitution. 2) Revealing State secrets, and discussion about overthrowing the Communist government. 3) Topics which damage the reputation of the State.

The Chinese government regularly conducts reviews of ISPs and their records. Every year, the Chinese Public Security Bureau shuts down thousands of Internet cafes for failing to keep adequate records and requires many others to suspend operations while they implement required electronic record-keeping procedures. Operators of Web sites in China are required to monitor all content that appears on their sites. Blogbus, a Chinese site that allowed visitors to post essays, was shut down in 2004 because one posting (out of 15,000) contained an essay that included what the government deemed to be "forbidden content." Hundreds of people have been jailed in China for posting "subversive" content on Web pages. North Korea, Singapore, and a number of Middle Eastern countries have also adopted rules and policies that restrict their citizens' use of the Internet. These countries will continue to face difficult policy choices as they maintain their attempts to control individuals' use of the Internet while at the same time trying to encourage increases in online business transactions.

Some countries, although they do not ban electronic commerce entirely, have strong cultural requirements that have found their way into the legal codes that govern business conduct. In France, an advertisement for a product or service must be in French. Thus, a business in the United States that advertises its products on the Web and is willing to ship goods to France must provide a French version of its pages if it intends to comply with French law. Many U.S. electronic commerce sites include in their Web pages a list of the countries from which they will accept orders through their Web sites.

The official language of the Canadian province of Quebec is French. Quebec provincial law requires street signs, billboards, directories, and advertising created by Quebec businesses to be in French. In 1999, the government of Quebec fined Quebec photographer Michael Calomiris and ordered him either to remove his English-language Web site or add a French translation of the pages to the site. Calomiris had been advertising his photographs for sale on his Quebec-based Web site and had targeted his ads to the U.S. market. He saw no reason to create a second Web site in French. The controversy generated considerable media attention and Calomiris paid the fine of about $500 (U.S.) and continues to operate his English-language Web site at Michaels Photography Studio.

Infrastructure Issues

Businesses that successfully meet the challenges posed by trust, language, and culture issues still face the challenges posed by variations and inadequacies in the infrastructure that supports the Internet throughout the world. Internet infrastructure includes the computers and software connected to the Internet and the communications networks over which the message packets travel. In many countries other than the United States, the telecommunications industry is either government owned or heavily regulated by the government. In many cases, regulations in these countries have inhibited the development of the telecommunications infrastructure or limited the expansion of that infrastructure to a size that cannot reliably support Internet traffic.

Local connection costs through the existing telephone networks in many developing countries are very high compared to U.S. costs for similar access. This can have a profound effect on the behavior of electronic commerce participants. For example, in countries where Internet connection costs are high, few businesspeople would spend time surfing the Web to shop for a product. They would use a Web browser only to navigate to a specific site that they know offers the product they want to buy. Thus, to be successful in selling to businesses in such countries, a company would need to advertise its Web presence in traditional media instead of relying on Web search engines to deliver customers to their Web sites.

More than half of all businesses on the Web turn away international orders because they do not have the processes in place to handle such orders. Some of these companies are losing millions of dollars' worth of international business each year. This problem is global; not only are U.S. businesses having difficulty reaching their international markets, but businesses in other countries are having similar difficulties reaching the U.S. market.

The paperwork and often convoluted processes that accompany international transactions are targets for technological solutions. Most firms that conduct business internationally rely on a complex array of freight-forwarding companies, customs brokers, international freight carriers, bonded warehouses, and importers to navigate the maze of paperwork that must be completed at every step of the transaction to satisfy government and insurance requirements. A **freight forwarder** is a company that arranges shipping and insurance for international transactions. A **customs broker** is a company that arranges the payment of tariffs and compliance with customs laws for international shipments. A number of companies combine these two functions and offer a full range of export management services. A **bonded warehouse** is a secure location where incoming international shipments can be held until customs requirements are satisfied or until payment arrangements are completed. The multiple flows of information and transfers of physical objects that occur in a typical international trade transaction are illustrated in Figure 1-14.

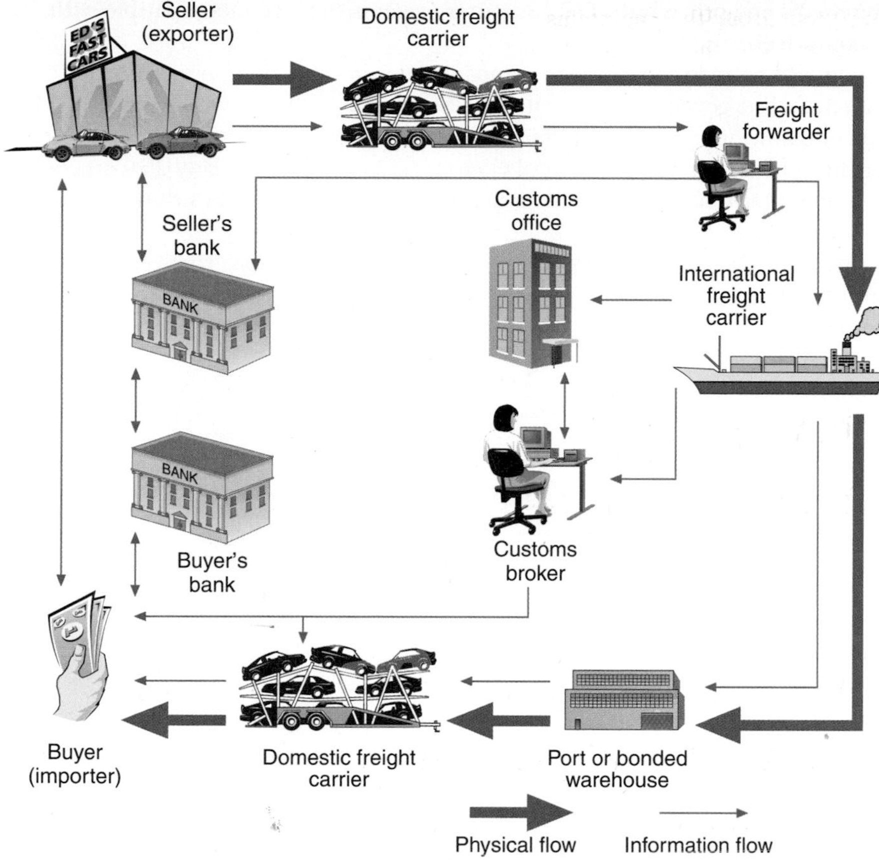

FIGURE 1-14 Parties involved in a typical international trade transaction

As you can see in Figure 1-14, the information flows can be complex. Domestic transactions usually include only the seller, the buyer, their respective banks, and one freight carrier. International transactions almost always require physical handling of goods by several freight carriers, storage in a freight forwarder's facility before international shipment, and storage in a port or bonded warehouse facility in the destination country. This handling and storage require monitoring by government customs offices in addition to the monitoring by seller and buyer that occurs in domestic transactions. International transactions usually require the coordinated efforts of customs brokers and freight forwarding agencies because the regulations and procedures governing international transactions are so complex. You will learn more about how businesses transfer money in international transactions in Chapter 11.

Industry experts estimate that the annual cost of handling paperwork for international transactions is $800 billion. Companies sell software that can automate some of the paperwork; however, many countries have their own paper-based forms and procedures with which international shippers must comply. To further complicate matters, some countries that have automated some procedures use computer systems that are incompatible with those of other countries.

Some governments provide assistance to companies that want to do international business on the Web. The Argentine government operates the **Fundación Invertir** Web site to provide information to companies that want to do business in Argentina. The **U.S. Commercial Service** (an agency of the U.S. Department of Commerce) operates the **BuyUSA** site, a portal for U.S. companies that want to sell abroad and non-U.S. companies that want to buy from U.S. companies.

Infrastructure issues will continue to prevent international business from reaching its full potential until technology is adapted to overcome barriers instead of being a part of those barriers.

Summary

In this chapter, you learned that commerce, the negotiated exchange of goods or services, has been practiced in traditional ways for thousands of years. Electronic commerce is the application of new technologies, particularly Internet and Web technologies, to help individuals, businesses, and other organizations conduct business more effectively. Electronic commerce is being adopted in waves of change. The first wave of electronic commerce ended in 2000. Today, a second wave with new approaches to integrating Internet technologies into business processes is under way. In this second wave, businesses are focusing less on overall business models and more on improving specific business processes.

Not all activities lend themselves to improvement with these technologies, but many do. Using electronic commerce, some businesses have been able to create new products and services, and others have improved the promotion, marketing, and delivery of existing offerings. Firms have also found many ways to use electronic commerce to improve purchasing and supply activities; identify new customers; and operate their finance, administration, and human resource management activities more efficiently. You learned that electronic commerce can help businesses reduce transaction costs or create network economic effects that can lead to greater revenue opportunities.

You examined an overview of markets, hierarchies, and networks—the economic structures in which businesses operate—and learned how electronic commerce fits into those structures. Porter's ideas about value chains at the business unit and industry levels were presented, and you learned how to use value chains and SWOT analysis as ways to understand business processes and analyze their suitability for electronic commerce implementation.

The inherently global nature of electronic commerce leads to many opportunities and a few challenges. You learned that companies engaged in international electronic commerce must understand the trust, cultural, language, and legal issues that arise when doing business across national borders.

Key Terms

Activity
Bonded warehouse
Business model
Business processes
Business unit
Business-to-business (B2B)
Business-to-consumer (B2C)
Business-to-government (B2G)
Commodity item
Company
Consumer-to-consumer (C2C)
Culture
Customs broker
Dot-com
E-procurement
Electronic business (e-business)
Electronic commerce (e-commerce)
Electronic data interchange (EDI)
Electronic funds transfer (EFT)
Firm
First-mover advantage
Freight forwarder
Hierarchical business organization
Industry
Industry value chain
Law of diminishing returns
Localization
Machine translation

Market
Merchandising
Mobile commerce (m-commerce)
Network economic structure
Network effect
Primary activities
Procurement
Pure dot-com
Revenue model
Shipping profile
Smart phone
Social networking site
Strategic alliance
Strategic business unit (SBU)
Strategic partner
Strategic partnership
Supply management
Supporting activities
SWOT analysis
Telecommuting
Telework
Trading partners
Transaction
Transaction costs
Value-added network (VAN)
Value chain
Value system
Vertical integration
Virtual community
Virtual company
Web 2.0
Wire transfer

Review Questions

RQ1. Describe three factors that would cause a company to continue doing business in traditional ways and avoid electronic commerce.

RQ2. Figure 1-5 lists roommate-matching services as a type of business that is well-suited to a combination of electronic and traditional commerce. In one paragraph, describe the elements of this service that would be best handled using traditional commerce and explain why.

RQ3. Choose one major difference between the first wave and the second wave of electronic commerce. Write a paragraph that describes this difference to a person who is not familiar with either business or Internet technologies.

RQ4. What are transaction costs and why are they important?

RQ5. Provide one example of how electronic commerce could help change an industry's economic structure from a hierarchy to a network.

RQ6. How might managers use SWOT analysis to identify new applications for electronic commerce in their strategic business units?

RQ7. In about 200 words, explain the difference between language translation and language localization.

Exercises

E1. You have decided to buy a new color laser printer for your home office. List specific activities that you must undertake as you gather information about printer capabilities and features. Use the **HPshopping.com**, **Office Depot**, **OfficeMax**, and **Staples** Web sites to gather information. Write a short summary of the process you undertook so that others who plan to undertake a similar task can use your information.

E2. Choose one of the Web sites listed in the previous question and identify three ways in which the company has reduced its transaction costs by using a Web site to provide information about printers. List these three transaction cost-reduction elements and write a paragraph in which you discuss one transaction cost–reduction opportunity that you believe the company missed.

E3. Read the following business messages and come up with a list of words or phrases in each message that you believe might be troublesome for automated translation software. Then use either the AltaVista Translation Web site or the FreeTranslation Web site to translate the messages from English to one of the foreign languages available on that site. Translate each message back into English. Write a short memo that compares the problems you anticipated with those that occurred in the automated translation. The business messages are:

a. The flight has been delayed for several hours and your shipment of components will not arrive as scheduled.

b. We would be happy to bid on your proposal; however, we will need the drawings of subassembly #24 and the supervising mechanical engineer's quality control report by next Thursday.

c. Our company offers the latest and greatest hot deals on wheels. We would love to send you a brochure that explains why our brakes, wheels, and suspension components will do the job for you effectively and economically.

E4. Create a diagram (similar to the diagram in Figure 1-10) that describes the industry value chain for the retail book business. You can use the Online Companion links for this exercise to examine the Web sites for Amazon.com, Barnes & Noble, Books-A-Million, eCampus, Internet Bookshop, and Powell's Books.

Cases

C1. Amazon.com

In 1994, a 29-year-old financial analyst and fund manager named Jeff Bezos became intrigued by the rapid growth of the Internet. Looking for a way to capitalize on this hot new marketing tool, he made a list of 20 products that might sell well on the Internet. After some intense analysis, he determined that books were at the top of that list. Although Bezos liked the name Abracadabra, he decided to call his online bookshop Amazon.com. Today, Amazon.com has more than 60 million customers and sells billions of dollars worth of all types of merchandise.

When he started, Bezos had no experience in the book-selling business, but he realized that books had an ideal shipping profile for online sales. He believed that many customers would be willing to buy books without inspecting them in person and that books could be impulse purchase items if properly promoted on a Web site. By accepting orders on its Web site, Bezos believed that Amazon.com could reduce transaction costs in the sale to the customer.

Several million book titles are in print at any one time throughout the world, and more than a million of those are in English. However, the largest physical bookstore cannot stock more than 200,000 books and carries even fewer titles because bookstores stock more than one copy of each title. Having a wide selection was important because Bezos believed it would help create a network economic effect. People would visit Amazon.com whenever they wanted to buy a book because it would be the most likely store (physical or online) to have a particular title. After becoming satisfied customers, people would return to Amazon.com to buy more books and would eventually stop looking elsewhere.

The structure of the supply side of the book business was equally important to Amazon.com's success. Music CDs, which were second on Bezos' list, were produced by a few major recording companies who could easily control Amazon.com's supply. In contrast, there were a large number of book publishers, none of which held a dominant position in the book-selling marketplace. Thus, it was unlikely that a single supplier could restrict Bezos' supply of books or enter his market as a competitor. He decided to locate his firm in Seattle, close to a large pool of programming talent and near one of the largest book distribution warehouses in the world. These supply factors were important because Bezos wanted to develop efficiencies that would allow Amazon.com to reduce transaction costs for its purchases as well as its sales transactions.

Bezos encouraged early customers to submit reviews and ratings of books, which he posted with the publisher's information about the book and with reviews written by Amazon.com employees. This customer participation served as a substitute for the corner bookshop staff's friendly advice and recommendations. Bezos saw the power of the Internet in reaching small, highly focused market segments, but he realized that his comprehensive bookstore could not be all things to all people. Therefore, he created a sales associate program in which Web sites devoted to a particular topic, such as model railroading, could provide links to Amazon.com books that related to that topic. In return, Amazon.com remits a percentage of the referred sales to the owner of the referring site.

Although Bezos' original vision was to create an online bookstore with the world's best selection, Amazon has moved into other product lines where opportunities for network economic effects and transaction cost reductions looked promising. In 1998, Amazon.com began selling music CDs and videos, first on VHS tape, then later on DVD. More recently, Amazon added MP3 music downloads. Today, Amazon offers thousands of products in more than a dozen categories.

By paying attention to every process involved in buying, promoting, selling, and shipping consumer goods, and by working to improve each process continually, Bezos and Amazon.com became one of the first highly visible success stories in electronic commerce. In fact, Amazon.com now generates significant revenue by supplying other sellers of consumer goods with the technology to sell those goods online. One of its first partnerships was with Toys R Us, a company that had experienced difficulties in selling online and making deliveries on time in the 1999 holiday shopping season. Toys R Us signed an agreement with Amazon.com in 2000 that placed Toys R Us products on the Amazon.com Web site. Amazon.com would accept the orders on its Web site and would ship products to customers for Toys R Us in exchange for a percentage of each sale. Amazon.com also agreed not to sell toys itself or on behalf of other partners for whom it might provide online sales services in the future. For example, when Amazon agreed to sell Target products online, it could not sell Target's toy lines on its Web site. (Target is the third-largest toy retailer in the world, behind Wal-Mart and Toys R Us.)

In addition to the online sales services Amazon.com provides to Toys R Us, Target, Borders, CDNow, and other large companies, it provides similar services to many smaller companies with its Amazon Marketplace offering. In Amazon Marketplace, small retailers become members of an online shopping mall on Amazon's site.

Toys R Us sales exceeded $300 million by 2004 on the Amazon.com site. Both Toys R Us and Amazon.com benefited from the network economics effect they obtained by having toys available for sale on Amazon.com's well-known electronic commerce site. Many small toy retailers in the Amazon Marketplace program also benefited because shoppers visited the Amazon.com site looking for toys. When a site visitor searched for a toy, the Amazon Marketplace retailers' offerings were presented on the search results page along with results from Toys R Us and Amazon.com.

Required:

1. In 2004, Toys R Us sued Amazon.com for violating terms of the agreement between the companies; specifically, Toys R Us objected to Amazon.com's permitting Amazon Marketplace retailers to sell toys (Note: when the lawsuit was filed, Amazon Marketplace was called "zShops"). Amazon.com responded by filing a countersuit. After more than two years of litigation, a New Jersey Superior Court judge ruled that the agreement had been violated by both parties. The judge ordered that the agreement be terminated and denied both companies' claims for monetary damages. Amazon.com appealed the ruling. In 2009, an appellate court affirmed the lower court ruling but reversed the ruling on damages, which had awarded Toys R Us $93 million plus interest. In June 2009, the two companies finally agreed in an out of court settlement that Amazon.com would pay damages of $51 million. Use your favorite search engine and the links in the Online Companion for Case C1 to review the courts' findings and rulings. Prepare a report of about 200 words in which you summarize each company's arguments and the rationale given by the judges for their decisions. Conclude the report by stating what you believe the outcome of the dispute should have been and why.
2. Outline the advantages and disadvantages that Amazon.com would have considered before it made the agreement with Toys R Us to limit competing toy sales. In about 200 words, summarize these advantages and disadvantages, then evaluate Amazon.com's decision to enter such an agreement.
3. In about 200 words, outline specific recommendations you would have made to Amazon.com in 2004 for negotiating a settlement with Toys R Us that would have benefited both companies and avoided litigation.
4. In 2009, Amazon.com purchased **Zappos**, a highly successful shoe retailer that was started in 1999. Many industry observers believe that the design and layout of the Zappos Web site has been an important element in the company's success. Visit the Zappos site and compare its layout and operation to the Amazon.com site. Determine whether Amazon.com should fold Zappos into its Web site or keep it operating in its current form. State and justify your position in the form of a memo to Amazon.com top management of about 300 words.

Note: Your instructor might assign you to a group to complete this case and might ask you to prepare a formal presentation of your results to your class.

C2. Hal's Hardware, Inc.

Hal Donovan is the president of Hal's Hardware, Inc. (HHI), a regional chain of 14 hardware stores located in Michigan, Ohio, and western Pennsylvania. HHI currently has a Web site that includes information about the company and some store information, such as locations and hours. Hal is thinking about expanding the HHI Web site to include online shopping. He believes that HHI customers might find the Web site to be a useful way to order items, see whether items are in stock at the nearest store, and comparison shop among different brands of a particular item. Hal is also hopeful that the Web site can reach customers who are not located near an HHI store. Many of the items sold at HHI are small and have high value-to-weight ratios, so they have good delivery service shipping profiles. Hal has decided that not all of HHI's inventory items should be available for sale on the Web site. Items such as wheelbarrows and live plants would probably be among the types of products that should be excluded. Hal does want customers to be able to research and order these items on the Web and pick them up in the store, however.

HHI enjoys an excellent reputation as a chain of friendly neighborhood stores. The store managers are all active in their communities and the stores regularly sponsor youth sports teams and support local charities. When hired, salespeople go through a comprehensive training program that includes skill training in the areas of the store in which they will work (plumbing, electrical, power tools, flooring, garden, and so on), and they are trained in customer service skills. As a result of HHI's focus on service, most of the stores have become community gathering places.

On Saturday afternoons, the stores are full of woodworking hobbyists, gardeners, and customers planning weekend projects of various kinds. On weekday mornings, electricians, plumbers, remodelers, and construction contractors stop by for the free coffee that the HHI stores offer when they open at 6:00 a.m. Each HHI store maintains a bulletin board next to the coffee urn in the contractors' area. Contractors can place help wanted or job wanted notices on the bulletin board. They can also place ads to buy and sell used equipment there. Many of HHI's regular customers obtained their current jobs through those bulletin boards.

HHI stores offer classes and workshops for the homeowner and hobbyist three evenings each month and regularly schedule seminars for professional customers on weekday mornings. Many of these workshops and seminars are underwritten and taught by manufacturers to promote their products, but an increasing number are being created by HHI staff members.

HHI's stores all face serious competition from national hardware chains such as **Home Depot** and **Lowe's**. These national chains have opened many new stores during the past few years, and they are larger, carry more items, and offer lower prices on some items. The competition is fierce; for example, all HHI stores have closed their lumber departments because of this competition. The national chains buy lumber in such large quantities that they can offer far lower prices. HHI was unable to earn a profit when matching the large competitors' prices, and the lumber operations consumed a large amount of store space. Hal is worried that this sort of problem could develop in other departments, so he is always looking for ways to add value to the HHI customer experience, especially in ways that the national chains are not willing or able to do. For example, Hal believes that most people want to try out a new power tool in person before they spend hundreds of dollars on a purchase. Thus, every HHI store has a tool demonstration area that is always staffed with salespeople who are experts in power tool operation. For each major type of power tool (drills, power saws, joiners, grinding tools, and so on), HHI has created a small booklet of hints for using that type of tool. HHI gives these booklets to customers as free handouts. HHI also sells its own low-cost instructional videotapes and DVDs.

Hal is also concerned about competition from other sources as well. Some of the tool manufacturing companies are talking about selling directly to customers on their Web sites. None of HHI's major suppliers has done this yet, but Hal is worried that it could occur in the future. HHI also faces competition from companies such as **Harbor Freight Tools**, **My Tool Store**, **Outlet Tool Supply**, and **Tool Crib**, which sells through the Amazon.com Web site.

HHI buys most of its inventory directly from the manufacturers, but it does buy some items from distributors. Most items are shipped to one of HHI's three warehouses, but some items are shipped directly to the store locations. HHI has a new companywide inventory control system that was just installed last year at a cost of about $200,000. This information system monitors inventory in real time. When a new shipment arrives at an HHI store, it is entered into the system on the receiving dock. Each item is bar coded so it can be tracked as it moves from the receiving dock to the warehouse to the store shelf and, finally, out the door past a point-of-sale terminal (which Hal still calls a cash register). This inventory-tracking system is accessible through a Web browser and can be connected to a Web site, so HHI could sell inventory from its existing warehouses and stores through the Web. The cost for the software is $42,000, including installation and configuration.

Required:

1. Conduct a SWOT analysis for HHI's proposed electronic commerce Web site. You can use the information in the case narrative, your personal knowledge of the retail hardware industry, and information you obtain by following links in the Online Companion or doing independent searches of the Web as you conduct your analysis. You should create a diagram similar to Figure 1-12 to summarize your SWOT analysis results.
2. Based on your SWOT analysis, write a report of about 400 words that includes a summary of your assumptions and a list of recommendations for HHI. The recommendations should be specific and should address the content that HHI's Web site should include, the features that HHI should make available on the site, and how HHI might overcome any of the weaknesses or threats you identified in the SWOT analysis.

Note: Your instructor might assign you to a group to complete this case and might ask you to prepare a formal presentation of your results to your class.

For Further Study and Research

Agrawal, V., L. Arjona, and R. Lemmens. 2001. "E-Performance: The Path to Rational Exuberance," *The McKinsey Quarterly,* January, 31–43.

Arthur, W. 2002. "Is the Information Revolution Dead? If History Is a Guide, It Is Not," *Business 2.0,* 3(3), March, 65–72.

Asdemir, K., V. Jacob, and R. Krishnan. 2009. "Dynamic Pricing of Multiple Home Delivery Options." *European Journal of Operational Research,* 196(1), July, 246–257.

Athitakis, M. 2003. "How to Make Money on the Net: The Second Internet Boom Is Quietly Taking Shape," *Business 2.0,* 4(4), May, 83–90.

Bannan, K. 2006. "Lost in Translation," *B to B,* June, 91(7), 21–23.

Berthon, P., L. Pitt, D. Cyr, and C. Campbell. 2008. "E-readiness and Trust: Macro and Micro Dualities for E-commerce in a Global Environment," *International Marketing Review,* 25(6), 700–714.

Betts, M. 2005. "Global Home Pages Receive Abysmal Report Cards," *Computerworld,* 39(27), July 4, 30.

Bodeen, C. 2004. "China Shuts Down Internet Blogs," *Salon.com,* March 19. (http://www.salon.com/news/wire/2004/03/19/blogs2/index.html)

Boles, C. and S. Morrison. 2007. "Yahoo Settles Suit Over Jailed Chinese Dissidents," *The Wall Street Journal,* November 14, A2.

Brown, J., S. Durchslag, and J. Hagel. 2002. "Loosening Up: How Process Networks Unlock the Power of Specialization," *The McKinsey Quarterly,* Special Edition, 59–69.

Castells, M. 1996. *The Rise of the Network Society.* Cambridge, MA: Blackwell.

Coase, R. 1937. "The Nature of the Firm," *Economica,* 4(4), November, 386–405.

Cohn, M. 2001. "China Seeks to Build the Great Firewall," *The Toronto Star,* July 21, A1.

Collett, S. 1999. "SWOT Analysis," *Computerworld,* 33(29), July 19, 58.

Computerworld. 2001. "Autopsy of a Dot Com," January 19. (http://www.computerworld.com/cwi/story/0,1199,NAV47_STO56616,00.html)

Drickhamer, D. 2003. "EDI Is Dead! Long Live EDI!" *Industry Week,* 252(4), April, 31–35.

Einhorn, B. and H. Green. 2005. "Blogs Under Its Thumb; How Beijing Keeps the Blogosphere From Spinning Out of Control," *Business Week,* August 8, 42.

Freeman, C. and F. Louçã. 2001. *As Time Goes By.* Oxford: Oxford University Press.

Friedman, M. 1999. "Photographer Fights Quebec Language Law," *Computing Canada,* 25(24), June 18, 1, 4.

Gold, J. 2004. "Amazon Countersues Toys R Us," *The Washington Post,* June 29, E5.

Goldstein, E. 1999. *The Internet in the Mideast and North Africa: Free Expression and Censorship.* Washington: Human Rights Watch.

Gosh, S. 1998. "Making Business Sense of the Internet," *Harvard Business Review,* 76(2), March–April, 126–135.

Hammer, M. and J. Champy. 1993. *Reengineering the Corporation: A Manifesto for Business Revolution.* New York: HarperBusiness.

Harrington, H., E. Esseling, and H. van Nimwegen. 1997. *Business Process Improvement Workbook: Documentation, Analysis, Design, and Management of Business Process Improvement.* New York: McGraw-Hill.

Harsany, J. 2004. "Web Grocer Hits Refresh: Online Grocer FreshDirect Takes the Hassle Out of City Shopping," *PC Magazine,* May 18, 76.

Hill, C., G. Zhang, and G. Scudder. 2009. "An Empirical Investigation of EDI Usage and Performance Improvement in Food Supply Chains," *IEEE Transactions on Engineering Management,* 56(1), February, 61–75.

Hof, R. 2003. "Reprogramming Amazon," *Business Week,* December 22, 82.

Holahan, C. 2007. "Yahoo! Agrees to Pay Prisoners' Families," *BusinessWeek,* November 14. (http://www.businessweek.com/technology/content/nov2007/tc20071113_712283.htm)

Horrigan, J. and L. Rainie. 2002. *Getting Serious Online.* Washington: Pew Internet & American Life Project.

Jackson, T. 2005. "New Car Buyers Flocking to Internet," *Bankrate.com,* February 15. (http://biz.yahoo.com/brn/050215/14987_1.html)

Jensen, M. 2002. *The African Internet: A Status Report.* Port St. Johns, South Africa: International Development Research Center. (http://www3.sn.apc.org/africa/afstat.htm)

Kristof, N. 2005. "Death by a Thousand Blogs," *The New York Times,* May 24, A21.

Lapres, D. 2000. "Legal Do's and Don'ts of Web Use in China," *China Business Review,* 27(2), March–April, 26–28.

Levaux, J. 2001. "Adapting Products and Services for Global E-Commerce: The Next Frontier is Beyond Localization," *World Trade,* 14(1), January, 52–54.

Lewis, S. 2002. "Online Lessons for Asia's SMEs," *Asian Business,* 38(1), January, 41.

Lightman, S. 2007. "Web Globalization," *B to B,* October, 92(13), 11.

Lunce, S., L. Lunce, Y. Kawai, and B. Maniam. 2006 "Success and Failure of Pure-Play Organizations: Webvan Versus Peapod, a Comparative Analysis," *Industrial Management & Data Systems,* 106(9), 1344–1358.

Mackey, C. 2003. "The Evolution of E-business," *Darwin,* May 1. (http://www.darwinmag.com/read/050103/ebiz.html)

MacLaggan, C. 2004. "Global Grocer," *Latin Trade,* 12(4), April, 51–54.

Mangalindan, M. 2006. "Court Rules Against Amazon In Toys Dispute," *The Wall Street Journal,* March 3, B1.

Martinez, A. 2009. "Amazon Will Pay Toys R Us $51 Million to Settle Lawsuit," *Seattle Times,* June 13, B1.

McConnon, A. 2008. "Salad Days For Web Grocers," *BusinessWeek,* September 15, 16.

Mearian, L. 2002. "Insurers Use IT to Fight Brokerage, Bank Rivals," *Computerworld,* 36(16), April 15, 12.

Moon, J., D. Chadee, and S. Tikoo. 2008. "Culture, Product Type, and Price Influences on Consumer Purchase Intention to Buy Personalized Products Online," *Journal of Business Research,* January, 61(1), 31–39.

Murphy, C. 2003. "Five Internet Myths: An Interview with Jeff Bezos," *Information Week,* June 11. (http://www.informationweek.com/story/showArticle.jhtml?articleID=10300770)

Music Business International. 2001. "Losing the Golden Egg-Laying Goose," 11(6), December 1, 11.

Mydans, S. 2007. "Agreeing to Block Some Videos, YouTube Returns to Thailand," *The New York Times,* September 1. (http://www.nytimes.com/2007/09/01/world/asia/01thai.html)

Narayanan, S., A. Marucheck, and R. Handfield. 2009. "Electronic Data Interchange: Research Review and Future Directions," *Decision Sciences,* 40(1), February, 121–163.

Ouchi, M. 2004. "Dual Suits: Amazon.com, Toysrus.com cry 'Foul,'" *The Seattle Times,* July 11, E1.

Perdue, L. 2001. "A Bright Future: After the Train Wreck," *Inc,* 23(4), March 15, 51–53.

Petzinger, T. 1999. *The New Pioneers: The Men and Women Who Are Transforming the Workplace and Marketplace.* New York: Simon & Schuster.

Porter, M. 1985. *Competitive Advantage.* New York: Free Press.

Porter, M. 1998. "Clusters and the New Economics of Competition," *Harvard Business Review,* 76(6), November–December, 77–90.

Porter, M. 2001. "Strategy and the Internet," *Harvard Business Review,* 79(3), March, 63–78.

Powell, W. 1990. "Neither Market nor Hierarchy: Network Forms of Organization," *Research in Organizational Behavior,* 12(3), 295–336.

Ramdeen, C., J. Santos, and H. Chatfield. 2009. "EDI and the Internet in the E-Business Era," *International Journal of Hospitality & Tourism Administration,* 10(3), 270–282.

Ramirez, C. 2001. "Disco Virtual Bills Four Times That of Offline Branch," *Business News Americas,* November 8. (http://www.bnamericas.com/story.xsql?id_noticia=78448&Tx_idioma=I&id_sector=1)

Rayport, J. and B. Jaworski. 2001. *E-Commerce.* New York: McGraw-Hill/Irwin.

Ring, R. and A. Van de Ven. 1992. "Structuring Cooperative Relationships Between Organizations," *Strategic Management Journal,* 13(4), 483–498.

Schneider, G. 2005. "Digital Products on the Web: Pricing Issues and Revenue Models," 154–174. In Kehal, H. and V. Singh, eds., *Digital Economy: Impacts, Influences, and Challenges.* Hershey, PA: Idea Group.

Shapiro, A. 1999. *The Control Revolution: How the Internet Is Putting Individuals in Charge and Changing the World We Know.* New York: The Century Foundation.

Shapiro, C. and H. Varian. 1999. *Information Rules: A Strategic Guide to the Network Economy.* Boston: Harvard Business School Press.

Shari, M. 2000. "Cutting Red Tape in Singapore," *Business Week,* September 18, 92.

Suarez, F. and G. Lanzolla. 2005. "The Half-Truth of First-Mover Advantage," *Harvard Business Review,* 83(4), April, 121–127.

Tapscott, D. 2001. "Rethinking Strategy in a Networked World: Or Why Michael Porter is Wrong About the Internet," *strategy+business,* 21(3), 1–8.

Taylor, D. and A. Terhune. 2001. *Doing E-Business: Strategies for Thriving in an Electronic Marketplace.* New York: John Wiley & Sons.

Thynne, J. 2008. "The E-revolution," *Bookseller,* October, 20–21.

Totty, M. and A. Grimes. 2002. "If at First You Don't Succeed . . . Some Retailers Are Finding Success in Industries Long Thought Off-Limits to E-Commerce," *The Wall Street Journal,* February 11, R6.

U.S. Census Bureau. 2008. *Statistical Abstract of the United States.* Washington: U.S. Census Bureau.

Vazdauskas, D. 2006. "To Stay Relevant, Large Brands Must Embrace Localization on Internet," *Advertising Age,* April 10, 77(15), 34.

Vascellaro, J. 2009. "Google to Tie Ads to Surfers' Habits," *The Wall Street Journal,* March 12, B8.

Wallraff, B. 2000. "What Global Language?" *The Atlantic Monthly,* 286(5), 52–66.

Watts, J. 2005. "Microsoft Helps China to Censor Bloggers," *The Guardian,* June 15, 14.

Williamson, O. 1975. *Markets and Hierarchies: Analysis and Antitrust Implications.* New York: Free Press.

Williamson, O. 1985. *The Economic Institutions of Capitalism.* New York: Free Press.

Willis, C. and S. Donahue. 1998. "Does Amazon.com Really Matter?" *Forbes,* 161(7), April 6, 55–58.

Yao, Y., M. Dresner, and J. Palmer. 2009. "Private Network EDI vs. Internet Electronic Markets: A Direct Comparison of Fulfillment Performance," *Management Science,* 55(5), 843–852.

CHAPTER 2

TECHNOLOGY INFRASTRUCTURE: THE INTERNET AND THE WORLD WIDE WEB

LEARNING OBJECTIVES

In this chapter, you will learn about:

- The origin, growth, and current structure of the Internet
- How packet-switched networks are combined to form the Internet
- How Internet protocols and Internet addressing work
- The history and use of markup languages on the Web, including SGML, HTML, and XML
- How HTML tags and links work on the World Wide Web
- The differences among internets, intranets, and extranets
- Options for connecting to the Internet, including cost and bandwidth factors
- Internet2 and the Semantic Web

INTRODUCTION

Most people who use the Internet and the Web today do so using a computer. As you will learn in this chapter, the ability to access the Internet generally costs money. The cost of Internet access combined with the cost of owning a computer puts the Web beyond the reach of many people around the world. In 2009, about 70 percent of the U.S. population had regular access to the Internet, but in China (with 1.4 billion residents, it is the most populous country on Earth), fewer than 25 percent of the population did. In the United States, most people access the Internet through a computer. In China, fully half of all Internet access is now through mobile phones or smart phones (nearly 200 million of them), and the proportion is increasing rapidly. Another 500 million people in China use mobile phones without Internet access, indicating great growth potential for China both in total mobile phone use and Internet access through mobile and smart phones.

In India (with a population of 1.2 billion), fewer than 250 million people have mobile phones and fewer than 1 percent of those have reliable Internet access through their phones. Fewer than 5 percent of the Indian population has any Internet access at all. But in 2009, India's telecom companies began a rapid expansion of the infrastructure that will allow them to offer better Internet access to their phone customers. Industry analysts expect that India mobile and smart phone use will soon be growing at annual rates of 15 percent to 20 percent, similar to the recent growth observed in China.

Although the first Internet-capable mobile phones were developed in the late 1990s, a number of technological issues prevented them from being very useful as a way to browse the Internet. Their screens were small and lacked color, they did not have alphanumeric keyboards, their ability to store information was limited, and the networks through which they connected to the Internet were slow and unreliable.

In 2001, Handspring introduced its Treo phones and Research in Motion (RIM) introduced its BlackBerry phones. These mobile phones included small alphanumeric keyboards, significantly larger memory capacities than other phones of the time, and were designed for quick access to e-mail. Nokia was quick to follow with smart phones that had similar features. By 2009, every major phone manufacturer offered a range of smart phones and Internet-capable mobile phones. Although many of these offerings were too expensive for markets in developing countries, some were not. Nokia has been especially effective in developing lower-cost phones specifically for these markets.

Although some Web sites have created pages for their mobile users that are designed to be used without a mouse and that are readable on the relatively small screens of phones, most have not. This can limit the usefulness of mobile phones as tools of electronic commerce. As more online businesses realize that mobile phone users are potential customers, more Web sites will be redesigned to give mobile users a better experience.

In the developed industrial countries, Internet-capable phones are tools of convenience; they provide continual access to e-mail and the Web for busy people who work from multiple locations. In the rest of the world, they are often the only affordable way to access the Internet. The rapid growth expected in the use of Internet-capable phones in parts of the world that have never had reliable access to the Internet and the Web offers the potential for vast increases in international electronic commerce.

THE INTERNET AND THE WORLD WIDE WEB

A **computer network** is any technology that allows people to connect computers to each other. An **internet** (small "i") is a group of computer networks that have been interconnected. In fact, "internet" is short for "interconnected network." One particular internet, which uses a specific set of rules and connects networks all over the world to each other, is called the **Internet** (capital "i"). Networks of computers and the Internet that connects them to each other form the basic technological structure that underlies virtually all electronic commerce. This chapter introduces you to many of the hardware and software technologies that make electronic commerce possible. First, you will learn how the Internet and the World Wide Web work. Then, you will learn about other technologies that support the Internet, the Web, and electronic commerce. In this chapter, you will be introduced to several complex networking technologies. If you are interested in learning more about how computer networks operate, you can consult one of the computer networking books cited in the For Further Study and Research section at the end of this chapter, or you can take courses in data communications and networking.

The part of the Internet known as the **World Wide Web**, or, more simply, the **Web**, is a subset of the computers on the Internet that are connected to one another in a specific way that makes them and their contents easily accessible to each other. The most important thing about the Web is that it includes an easy-to-use standard interface. This interface makes it possible for people who are not computer experts to use the Web to access a variety of Internet resources.

Origins of the Internet

In the early 1960s, the U.S. Department of Defense became concerned about the possible effects of nuclear attack on its computing facilities. The Defense Department realized that the weapons of the future would require powerful computers for coordination and control. The powerful computers of that time were all large mainframe computers.

Defense Department began examining ways to connect these computers to each other and also to connect them to weapons installations distributed all over the world. Employing many of the best communications technology researchers, the Defense Department funded research at leading universities and institutes. The goal of this research was to design a worldwide network that could remain operational, even if parts of the network were destroyed by enemy military action or sabotage. These researchers determined that the best path to accomplishing their goals was to create networks that did not require a central computer to control network operations.

The computer networks that existed at that time used leased telephone company lines for their connections. These telephone company systems established a single connection between sender and receiver for each telephone call, then that connection carried all data along a single path. When a company wanted to connect computers it owned at two different locations, the company placed a telephone call to establish the connection, and then connected one computer to each end of that single connection.

The Defense Department was concerned about the inherent risk of this single-channel method for connecting computers, and its researchers developed a different method of sending information through multiple channels. In this method, files and messages are broken into packets that are labeled electronically with codes for their origins, sequences, and destinations. You will learn more about how packet networks operate later in this chapter.

In 1969, Defense Department researchers in the Advanced Research Projects Agency (ARPA) used this direct connnection network model to connect four computers—one each at the University of California at Los Angeles, SRI International, the University of California at Santa Barbara, and the University of Utah—into a network called the ARPANET. The ARPANET was the earliest of the networks that eventually combined to become what we now call the Internet. Throughout the 1970s and 1980s, many researchers in the academic community connected to the ARPANET and contributed to the technological developments that increased its speed and efficiency. At the same time, researchers at other universities were creating their own networks using similar technologies.

New Uses for the Internet

Although the goals of the Defense Department network were to control weapons systems and transfer research files, other uses for this vast network began to appear in the early 1970s. E-mail was born in 1972 when Ray Tomlinson, a researcher who used the network, wrote a program that could send and receive messages over the network. This new method of communicating became widely used very quickly. The number of network users in the military and education research communities continued to grow. Many of these new participants used the networking technology to transfer files and access computers remotely.

The first e-mail mailing lists also appeared on these military and education research networks. A **mailing list** is an e-mail address that forwards any message it receives to any user who has subscribed to the list. In 1979, a group of students and programmers at Duke

University and the University of North Carolina started **Usenet**, an abbreviation for **User's News Network**. Usenet allows anyone who connects to the network to read and post articles on a variety of subjects. Usenet survives on the Internet today, with more than 1000 different topic areas that are called **newsgroups**. Other researchers even created game-playing software for use on these interconnected networks.

Although the people using these networks were developing many creative applications, use of the networks was limited to those members of the research and academic communities who could access them. Between 1979 and 1989, these network applications were improved and tested by an increasing number of users. The Defense Department's networking software became more widely used in academic and research institutions as these organizations recognized the benefits of having a common communications network. As the number of people in different organizations using these networks increased, security problems were recognized. These problems have continued to become more important, and you will learn more about network security issues in Chapter 10. The explosion of personal computer use during the 1980s also helped more people become comfortable with computers. During the 1980s, other independent networks were developed by academics worldwide (such as Bitnet) and researchers in specific countries other than the United States (such as the United Kingdom's academic research network, Janet). In the late 1980s, these independent academic and research networks from all over the world merged into what we now call the Internet.

Commercial Use of the Internet

As personal computers became more powerful, affordable, and available during the 1980s, companies increasingly used them to construct their own internal networks. Although these networks included e-mail software that employees could use to send messages to each other, businesses wanted their employees to be able to communicate with people outside their corporate networks. The Defense Department network and most of the academic networks that had teamed up with it were receiving funding from the **National Science Foundation (NSF)**. The NSF prohibited commercial network traffic on its networks, so businesses turned to commercial e-mail service providers to handle their e-mail needs. Larger firms built their own networks that used leased telephone lines to connect field offices to corporate headquarters.

In 1989, the NSF permitted two commercial e-mail services, MCI Mail and CompuServe, to establish limited connections to the Internet for the sole purpose of exchanging e-mail transmissions with users of the Internet. These connections allowed commercial enterprises to send e-mail directly to Internet addresses, and allowed members of the research and education communities on the Internet to send e-mail directly to MCI Mail and CompuServe addresses. The NSF justified this limited commercial use of the Internet as a service that would primarily benefit the Internet's noncommercial users. As the 1990s began, people from all walks of life—not just scientists or academic researchers—started thinking of these networks as the global resource that we now know as the Internet. Although this network of networks had grown from four Defense Department computers in 1969 to more than 300,000 computers on many interconnected networks by 1990, the greatest growth of the Internet was yet to come.

Growth of the Internet

In 1991, the NSF further eased its restrictions on commercial Internet activity and began implementing plans to privatize the Internet. The privatization of the Internet was substantially completed in 1995, when the NSF turned over the operation of the main Internet connections to a group of privately owned companies. The new structure of the Internet was based on four **network access points (NAPs)** located in San Francisco, New York, Chicago, and Washington, D.C., each operated by a separate telecommunications company. As the Internet grew, more companies opened more NAPs in more locations. These companies, known as **network access providers**, sell Internet access rights directly to larger customers and indirectly to smaller firms and individuals through other companies, called **Internet service providers (ISPs)**.

The Internet was a phenomenon that had truly sneaked up on an unsuspecting world. The researchers who had been so involved in the creation and growth of the Internet just accepted it as part of their working environment. However, people outside the research community were largely unaware of the potential offered by a large interconnected set of computer networks. Figure 2-1 shows the consistent and dramatic growth in the number of **Internet hosts**, which are computers directly connected to the Internet.

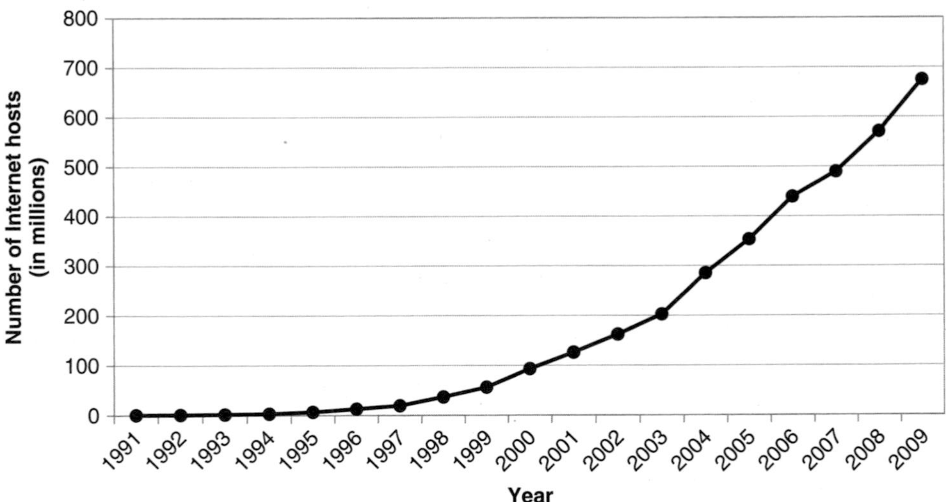

Source: Internet Software Consortium (http://www.isc.org/) and author's estimates

FIGURE 2-1 Growth of the Internet

In 40 years, the Internet has grown to become one of the most amazing technological and social accomplishments of the last millennium. Millions of people, from elementary schoolers to research scientists, now use this complex, interconnected network of computers. These computers run thousands of different software packages. The computers are located in almost every country of the world. Every year, billions of dollars change hands over the Internet in exchange for all kinds of products and services. All of this activity occurs with no central coordination point or control, which is especially ironic given that the Internet began as a way for the military to maintain control while under attack.

The opening of the Internet to business activity helped to dramatically increase its growth; however, there was another development that worked hand in hand with the commercialization of the Internet to spur its growth. That development was the World Wide Web.

Emergence of the World Wide Web

At a technological level, the Web is nothing more than software that runs on computers that are connected to the Internet. The network traffic generated by Web software is the largest single category of traffic on the Internet today, outpacing e-mail, file transfers, and other data transmission traffic. But the ideas behind the Web developed from innovative ways of thinking about and organizing information storage and retrieval. These ideas go back many years. Two important ideas that became key technological elements of the Web are hypertext and graphical user interfaces.

The Development of Hypertext

In 1945, **Vannevar Bush**, who was director of the U.S. Office of Scientific Research and Development, wrote an article in *The Atlantic Monthly* about ways that scientists could apply the skills they learned during World War II to peacetime activities. The article included a number of visionary ideas about future uses of technology to organize and facilitate efficient access to information. Bush speculated that engineers would eventually build a machine that he called the Memex, a memory extension device that would store all of a person's books, records, letters, and research results on microfilm. Bush's Memex would include mechanical aids, such as microfilm readers and indexes, that would help users quickly and flexibly consult their collected knowledge.

In the 1960s, Ted Nelson described a similar system in which text on one page links to text on other pages. Nelson called his page-linking system **hypertext**. Douglas Engelbart, who also invented the computer mouse, created the first experimental hypertext system on one of the large computers of the 1960s. In 1987, Nelson published *Literary Machines*, a book in which he outlined project Xanadu, a global system for online hypertext publishing and commerce. Nelson used the term *hypertext* to describe a page-linking system that would interconnect related pages of information, regardless of where in the world they were stored.

In 1989, Tim Berners-Lee was trying to improve the laboratory research document-handling procedures for his employer, CERN: European Laboratory for Particle Physics. CERN had been connected to the Internet for two years, but its scientists wanted to find better ways to circulate their scientific papers and data among the high-energy physics research community throughout the world. Berners-Lee proposed a hypertext development project intended to provide this data-sharing functionality.

Over the next two years, Berners-Lee developed the code for a hypertext server program and made it available on the Internet. A **hypertext server** is a computer that stores files written in **Hypertext Markup Language (HTML)**, the language used for the creation of Web pages. The hypertext server is connected through the Internet to other computers that can connect to the hypertext server and read those HTML files. Hypertext servers used on the Web today are usually called **Web servers**. HTML, which Berners-Lee developed from his original hypertext server program, is a language that includes a set of codes (or tags) attached to text. These codes describe the relationships among text elements. For example,

HTML includes tags that indicate which text is part of a header element, which text is part of a paragraph element, and which text is part of a numbered list element. One important type of tag is the hypertext link tag. A **hypertext link**, or **hyperlink**, points to another location in the same or another HTML document. The details of HTML and other markup languages are covered later in this chapter.

Graphical Interfaces for Hypertext

Several different types of software are available to read HTML documents, but most people use a Web browser such as Mozilla Firefox or Microsoft Internet Explorer. A **Web browser** is a software interface that lets users read (or browse) HTML documents and move from one HTML document to another through text formatted with hypertext link tags in each file. If the HTML documents are on computers connected to the Internet, you can use a Web browser to move from an HTML document on one computer to an HTML document on any other computer on the Internet.

An HTML document differs from a word-processing document in that it does not specify how a particular text element will appear. For example, you might use word-processing software to create a document heading by setting the heading text font to Arial, its font size to 14 points, and its position to centered. The document displays and prints these exact settings whenever you open the document in that word processor. In contrast, an HTML document simply includes a heading tag with the heading text. Many different browser programs can read an HTML document. Each program recognizes the heading tag and displays the text in whatever manner each program normally displays headings. Different Web browser programs might each display the text differently, but all of them display the text with the characteristics of a heading.

A Web browser presents an HTML document in an easy-to-read format in the browser's graphical user interface. A **graphical user interface (GUI)** is a way of presenting program control functions and program output to users and accepting their input. It uses pictures, icons, and other graphical elements instead of displaying just text. Almost all personal computers today use a GUI such as Microsoft Windows or the Macintosh user interface.

The World Wide Web

Berners-Lee called his system of hyperlinked HTML documents the World Wide Web. The Web caught on quickly in the scientific research community, but few people outside that community had software that could read the HTML documents. In 1993, a group of students led by Marc Andreessen at the University of Illinois wrote Mosaic, the first GUI program that could read HTML and use HTML hyperlinks to navigate from page to page on computers anywhere on the Internet. Mosaic was the first Web browser that became widely available for personal computers, and some Web surfers still use it today.

Programmers quickly realized that a system of pages connected by hypertext links would provide many new Internet users with an easy way to access information on the Internet. Businesses recognized the profit-making potential offered by a worldwide network of easy-to-use computers. In 1994, Andreessen and other members of the University of Illinois Mosaic team joined with James Clark of Silicon Graphics to found Netscape Communications (which is now owned by Time Warner). Its first product, the Netscape Navigator Web browser program based on Mosaic, was an instant success. Netscape became one of the fastest-growing software companies ever. Microsoft created its

Internet Explorer Web browser and entered the market soon after Netscape's success became apparent. Today, Internet Explorer is the most widely used Web browser in the world. Its main competitor, Mozilla Firefox, is a descendant of Netscape Navigator.

The number of Web sites has grown even more rapidly than the Internet itself. The number of Web sites is currently estimated at more than 250 million, and individual Web pages number more than 50 billion because each Web site might include hundreds or even thousands of individual Web pages. Therefore, nobody really knows how many Web pages exist. Figure 2-2 shows the overall rapid growth rate of the Web. Other than a brief consolidation period during the 2001–2002 economic downturn, the Web has grown at a consistently rapid rate.

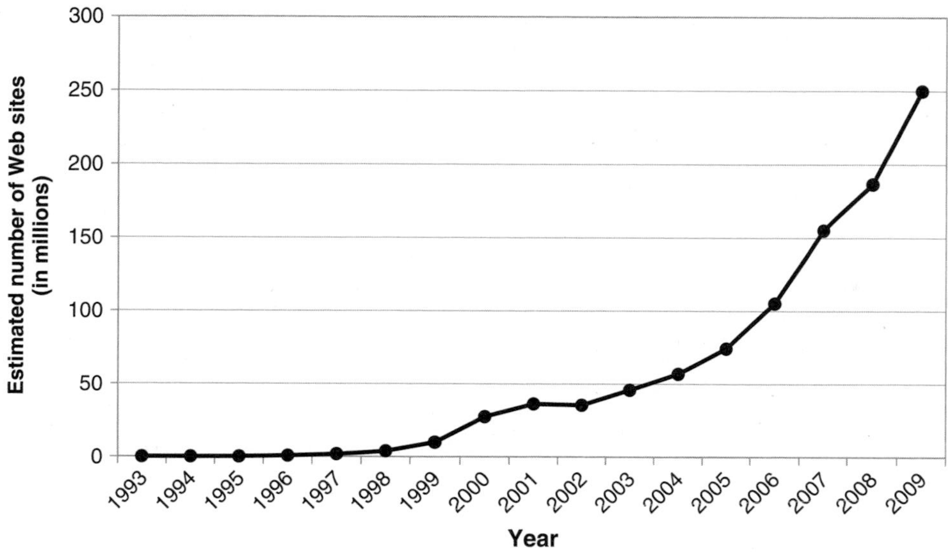

Adapted from Netcraft Computer Surveys (http://www.netcraft.com) and author's estimates

FIGURE 2-2 Growth of the World Wide Web

In addition to Web pages that are specifically programmed to exist in a permanent form, the Web provides access to customized Web pages that are created in response to a particular user's query. Such Web pages pull their content from databases. For example, if you visit Amazon.com and search for a book about "online business," computers at Amazon.com query their databases of information about books and create a Web page that is a customized response to your search. The Web page that lists your search results never existed before your visit. This store of information that is available though the Web is called the **deep Web**. Researchers, such as those at **Bright Planet**, estimate the number of possible pages in the deep Web to be in the trillions.

As more people gain access to the Web, commercial interest in using the Web to conduct business will continue to increase, and the variety of nonbusiness uses will become even greater. In the rest of this chapter, you will learn how Internet and Web technologies work to enable electronic commerce.

A network of computers that are located close together—for example, in the same building—is called a **local area network (LAN)**. Networks of computers that are connected over greater distances are called **wide area networks (WANs)**.

The early models (dating back to the 1950s) for WANs were the circuits of the local and long-distance telephone companies of the time, because the first early WANs used leased telephone company lines for their connections. A telephone call establishes a single connection path between the caller and receiver. Once that connection is established, data travels along that single path. Telephone company equipment (originally mechanical, now electronic) selects specific telephone lines to connect to one another by closing switches. These switches work like the switches you use to turn lights on and off in your home, except that they open and close much faster, and are controlled by mechanical or electronic devices instead of human hands.

The combination of telephone lines and the closed switches that connect them to each other is called a **circuit**. This circuit forms a single electrical path between caller and receiver. This single path of connected circuits switched into each other is maintained for the entire length of the call. This type of centrally controlled, single-connection model is known as **circuit switching**.

Although circuit switching works well for telephone calls, it does not work as well for sending data across a large WAN or an interconnected network like the Internet. The Internet was designed to be resistant to failure. In a circuit-switched network, a failure in any one of the connected circuits causes the connection to be interrupted and data to be lost. Instead, the Internet uses packet switching to move data between two points. On a **packet-switched** network, files and e-mail messages are broken down into small pieces, called **packets**, that are labeled electronically with their origins, sequences, and destination addresses. Packets travel from computer to computer along the interconnected networks until they reach their destinations. Each packet can take a different path through the interconnected networks, and the packets may arrive out of order. The destination computer collects the packets and reassembles the original file or e-mail message from the pieces in each packet.

Routing Packets

As an individual packet travels from one network to another, the computers through which the packet travels determine the most efficient route for getting the packet to its destination. The most efficient route changes from second to second, depending on how much traffic each computer on the Internet is handling at each moment. The computers that decide how best to forward each packet are called **routing computers**, **router computers**, **routers**, **gateway computers** (because they act as the gateway from a LAN or WAN to the Internet), or **border routers** (because they are located at the border between the organization and the Internet). The programs on router computers that determine the best path on which to send each packet contain rules called **routing algorithms**. The programs apply their routing algorithms to information they have stored in **routing tables** or **configuration tables**. This information includes lists of connections that lead to particular groups of other routers, rules that specify which connections to use first, and rules for handling instances of heavy packet traffic and network congestion.

Individual LANs and WANs can use a variety of different rules and standards for creating packets within their networks. The network devices that move packets from one part of a network to another are called hubs, switches, and bridges. Routers are used to connect networks to other networks. You can take a data communications and networking class to learn more about these network devices and how they work.

When packets leave a network to travel on the Internet, they must be translated into a standard format. Routers usually perform this translation function. As you can see, routers are an important part of the infrastructure of the Internet. When a company or organization becomes part of the Internet, it must connect at least one router to the other routers (owned by other companies or organizations) that make up the Internet. Figure 2-3 is a diagram of a small portion of the Internet that shows its router-based architecture. The figure shows only the routers that connect each organization's WANs and LANs to the Internet, not the other routers that are inside the WANs and LANs or that connect them to each other within the organization.

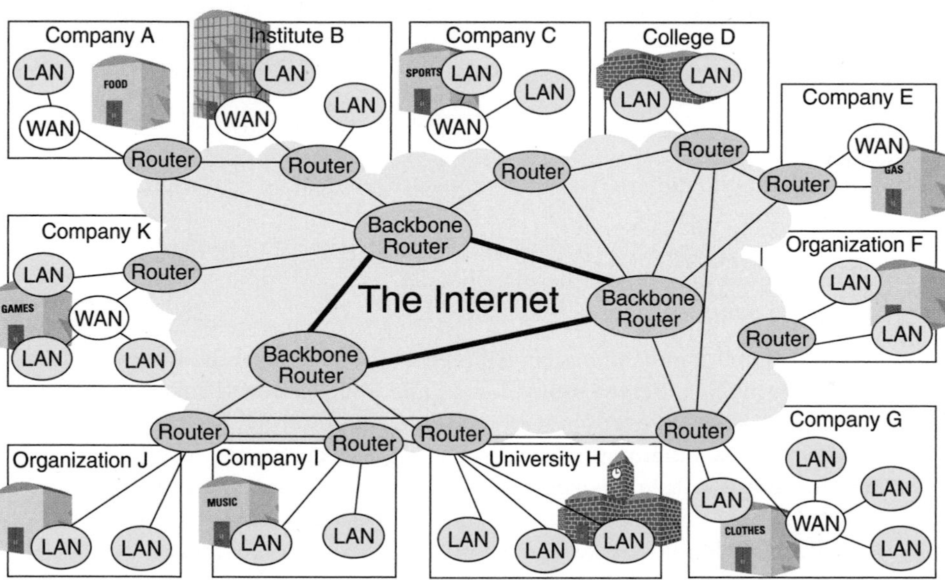

FIGURE 2-3 Router-based architecture of the Internet

The Internet also has routers that handle packet traffic along the Internet's main connecting points. These routers and the telecommunications lines connecting them are collectively referred to as the **Internet backbone**. These routers, sometimes called **backbone routers**, are very large computers that can each handle more than 3 billion packets per second! You can see in Figure 2-3 that a router connected to the Internet always has more than one path to which it can direct a packet. By building in multiple packet paths, the designers of the Internet created a degree of redundancy in the system that allows it to keep moving packets, even if one or more of the routers or connecting lines fails.

INTERNET PROTOCOLS

A **protocol** is a collection of rules for formatting, ordering, and error checking data sent across a network. For example, protocols determine how the sending device indicates that it has finished sending a message and how the receiving device indicates that it has received (or not received) the message. A protocol also includes rules about what is allowed in a transmission and how it is formatted. Computers that communicate with each other must use the same protocol for data transmission. As you learned earlier in this chapter, the first packet-switched network, the ARPANET, connected only a few universities and research centers. Following its inception in 1969, this experimental network grew during the next few years and began using the **Network Control Protocol (NCP)**. In the early days of computing, each computer manufacturer created its own protocol, so computers made by different manufacturers could not be connected to each other. This practice was called **proprietary architecture** or **closed architecture**. NCP was designed so it could be used by any computer manufacturer and was made available to any company that wanted it. This **open architecture** philosophy developed for the evolving ARPANET, which later became the core of the Internet, included the use of a common protocol for all computers connected to the Internet and four key rules for message handling:

- Independent networks should not require any internal changes to be connected to the network.
- Packets that do not arrive at their destinations must be retransmitted from their source network.
- Router computers act as receive-and-forward devices; they do not retain information about the packets that they handle.
- No global control exists over the network.

The open architecture approach has contributed to the success of the Internet because computers manufactured by different companies (Apple, Dell, Hewlett-Packard, Sun, etc.) can be interconnected. The ARPANET and its successor, the Internet, use routers to isolate each LAN or WAN from the other networks to which they are connected. Each LAN or WAN can use its own set of protocols for packet traffic within the LAN or WAN, but must use a router (or similar device) to move packets onto the Internet in its standard format (or protocol). Following these simple rules makes the connections between the interconnected networks operate effectively.

TCP/IP

The Internet uses two main protocols: the **Transmission Control Protocol (TCP)** and the **Internet Protocol (IP)**. Developed by Internet pioneers Vinton Cerf and Robert Kahn, these protocols are the rules that govern how data moves through the Internet and how network connections are established and terminated. The acronym **TCP/IP** is commonly used to refer to the two protocols.

The TCP controls the disassembly of a message or a file into packets before it is transmitted over the Internet, and it controls the reassembly of those packets into their original formats when they reach their destinations. The IP specifies the addressing details for each packet, labeling each with the packet's origination and destination addresses. Soon after the new TCP/IP protocol set was developed, it replaced the NCP that ARPANET originally used.

In addition to its Internet function, TCP/IP is used today in many LANs. The TCP/IP protocol is provided in most personal computer operating systems commonly used today, including Linux, Macintosh, Microsoft Windows, and UNIX.

IP Addressing

The version of IP that has been in use for the past 20 years on the Internet is **Internet Protocol version 4 (IPv4)**. It uses a 32-bit number to identify the computers connected to the Internet. This address is called an **IP address**. Computers do all of their internal calculations using a **base 2** (or **binary**) number system in which each digit is either a 0 or a 1, corresponding to a condition of either off or on. IPv4 uses a 32-bit binary number that allows for more than 4 billion different addresses ($2^{32} = 4,294,967,296$).

When a router breaks a message into packets before sending it onto the Internet, the router marks each packet with both the source IP address and the destination IP address of the message. To make them easier to read, IP numbers (addresses) appear as four numbers separated by periods. This notation system is called **dotted decimal** notation. An IPv4 address is a 32-bit number, so each of the four numbers is an 8-bit number ($4 \times 8 = 32$). In most computer applications, an 8-bit number is called a **byte**; however, in networking applications, an 8-bit number is often called an **octet**. In binary, an octet can have values from 00000000 to 11111111; the decimal equivalents of these binary numbers are 0 and 255, respectively.

Because each of the four parts of a dotted decimal number can range from 0 to 255, IP addresses range from 0.0.0.0 (written in binary as 32 zeros) to 255.255.255.255 (written in binary as 32 ones). Although some people find dotted decimal notation to be confusing at first, most do agree that writing, reading, and remembering a computer's address as 216.115.108.245 is easier than 11011000011100110110110011110101, or its full decimal equivalent, which is 3,631,433,189.

Today, IP addresses are assigned by three not-for-profit organizations: the **American Registry for Internet Numbers (ARIN)**, the **Reséaux IP Européens (RIPE)**, and the **Asia-Pacific Network Information Center (APNIC)**. These registries assign and manage IP addresses for various parts of the world: ARIN for North America, South America, the Caribbean, and sub-Saharan Africa; RIPE for Europe, the Middle East, and the rest of Africa; and APNIC for countries in the Asia-Pacific area. These organizations took over IP address management tasks from the Internet Assigned Numbers Authority (IANA), which performed them under contract with the U.S. government when the Internet was an experimental research project.

You can use the **ARIN Whois** page at the ARIN Web site to search the IP addresses owned by organizations in North America. You can enter an organization name into the search box on the page, then click the Search WHOIS button, and the Whois server returns a list of the IP addresses owned by that organization. For example, performing a search on the word *Carnegie* displays the IP address blocks owned by Carnegie Bank, Carnegie Mellon University, and a number of other organizations whose names begin with Carnegie. You can also enter an IP address and find out who owns that IP address. If you enter "3.0.0.0" (without the quotation marks), you will find that General Electric owns the entire block of IP addresses from 3.0.0.0 to 3.255.255.255. General Electric can use these addresses, which number approximately 16.7 million, for its own computers, or it can lease them to other companies or individuals to whom it provides Internet access services.

In the early days of the Internet, the 4 billion addresses provided by the IPv4 rules certainly seemed to be more addresses than an experimental research network would ever need. However, about 2 billion of those addresses today are either in use or unavailable for use because of the way blocks of addresses were assigned to organizations. The new kinds of devices on the Internet's many networks, such as wireless personal digital assistants and smart phones, promise to keep demand high for IP addresses.

Network engineers have devised a number of stopgap techniques to stretch the supply of IP addresses. One of the most popular techniques is **subnetting**, which is the use of reserved private IP addresses within LANs and WANs to provide additional address space. **Private IP addresses** are a series of IP numbers that are not permitted on packets that travel on the Internet. In subnetting, a computer called a **Network Address Translation (NAT) device** converts those private IP addresses into normal IP addresses when it forwards packets from those computers to the Internet.

The **Internet Engineering Task Force (IETF)** worked on several new protocols that could solve the limited addressing capacity of IPv4, and in 1997, approved **Internet Protocol version 6 (IPv6)** as the protocol that will replace IPv4. The new IP is being implemented gradually because the two protocols are not directly compatible. The process of switching over to IPv6 will take at least another 10 years; however, network engineers have devised ways to run both protocols together on interconnected networks. The major advantage of IPv6 is that it uses a 128-bit number for addresses instead of the 32-bit number used in IPv4. The number of available addresses in IPv6 (2^{128}) is 34 followed by 37 zeros—billions of times larger than the address space of IPv4. The new IP also changes the format of the packet itself. Improvements in networking technologies over the past 20 years have made many of the fields in the IPv4 packet unnecessary. IPv6 eliminates those fields and adds fields for security and other optional information.

IPv6 has a shorthand notation system for expressing addresses, similar to the IPv4 dotted decimal notation system. However, because the IPv6 address space is much larger, its notation system is more complex. The IPv6 notation uses eight groups of 16 bits ($8 \times 16 = 128$). Each group is expressed as four hexadecimal digits and the groups are separated by colons; thus, the notation system is called **colon hexadecimal** or **colon hex**. A **hexadecimal (base 16)** numbering system uses 16 characters (0, 1, 2, 3, 4, 5, 6, 7, 8, 9, a, b, c, d, e, and f). An example of an IPv6 address expressed in this notation is: CD18:0000:0000:AF23:0000:FF9E:61B2:884D. To save space, the zeros can be omitted, which reduces this address to: CD18:::AF23::FF9E:61B2:884D.

Domain Names

The founders of the Internet were concerned that users might find the dotted decimal notation difficult to remember. To make the numbering system easier to use, they created an alternative addressing method that uses words. In this system, an address such as www.course.com is called a domain name. **Domain names** are sets of words that are assigned to specific IP addresses. Domain names can contain two or more word groups separated by periods. The rightmost part of a domain name is the most general. Each part of the domain name becomes more specific as you move to the left.

For example, the domain name www.sandiego.edu contains three parts separated by periods. Beginning at the right, the name "edu" indicates that the computer belongs to an educational institution. The institution, University of San Diego, is identified by the name "sandiego." The "www" indicates that the computer is running software that makes it a part of the World Wide Web. Most, but not all, Web addresses follow this "www" naming convention. For example, the group of computers that operate the **Yahoo! Games** service is named games.yahoo.com.

The rightmost part of a domain name is called a **top-level domain (TLD)**. For many years, these domains have included a group of generic domains—such as .edu, .com, and .org—and a set of country domains. Since 1998, the **Internet Corporation for Assigned Names and Numbers (ICANN)** has had the responsibility of managing domain names and coordinating them with the IP address registrars. ICANN is also responsible for setting standards for the router computers that make up the Internet. Since taking over these responsibilities, ICANN has added a number of new TLDs. Some of these TLDs are **generic top-level domains (gTLDs)**, which are available to specified categories of users. ICANN is itself responsible for the maintenance of gTLDs.Other new domains are **sponsored top-level domains (sTLDs)** which are TLDs for which an organization other than ICANN is responsible. The sponsor of a specific sTLD must be a recognized institution that has expertise regarding and is familiar with the community that uses the sTLD. For example, the .aero sTLD is sponsored by SITA, an air transport industry association that has expertise in and is familiar with airlines, airports, and the aerospace industry. Individual countries are permitted to maintain their own TLDs, which their residents can use alone or in combination with other TLDs. For example, the URL of the University of Queensland in Brisbane, Australia is www.uq.edu.au, which combines .edu with .au to indicate that it is an educational institution in Australia. Figure 2-4 presents a list of some commonly used TLDs, the general TLDs added since 2000, and some of the more frequently used country TLDs.

TLD	Use
.com	U.S. commercial
.edu	Four-year educational institution
.gov	U.S. federal government
.mil	U.S. military
.net	U.S. general use
.org	U.S. not-for-profit organization
.us	U.S. general use
.asia	Companies, individuals, and organizations based in Asian–Pacific regions
.biz	Businesses
.info	General use
.name	Individual persons
.pro	Licensed professionals (such as accountants, lawyers, physicians)
.au	Australia
.ca	Canada
.de	Germany
.fi	Finland
.fr	France
.jp	Japan
.se	Sweden
.uk	United Kingdom

Source: Internet Assigned Numbers Authority Root Zone Database, http://www.iana.org/domains/root/db/

FIGURE 2-4 Commonly used domain names

Although these new domain names were chosen after much deliberation and consideration of more than 100 possible new names, many people were highly critical of the selections (see, for example, the **ICANNWatch** Web site). ICANN came under additional fire for acting in ways that many people thought violated the democratic principles on which the organization was founded. You can learn more about these issues on the Web sites of the **Internet Governance Project** and the **Convergence Center**, both at Syracuse University. Increases in the number of TLDs can make it more difficult for companies to protect their corporate and product brand names. You will learn more about these issues in Chapter 7.

Web Page Request and Delivery Protocols

The Web is software that runs on computers that are connected to each other through the Internet. **Web client computers** run software called **Web client software** or **Web browser software**. Examples of popular Web browser software include Google Chrome, Microsoft Internet Explorer, and Mozilla Firefox. Web browser software sends requests for Web page files to other computers, which are called Web servers. A Web server computer runs software called **Web server software**. Web server software receives requests from many different Web clients and responds by sending files back to those Web client computers. Each Web client computer's Web client software renders those files into a Web page. Thus, the purpose of a Web server is to respond to requests for Web pages from Web clients. This combination of client computers running Web client software and server computers running Web server software is an example of a **client/server architecture.**

The set of rules for delivering Web page files over the Internet is in a protocol called the **Hypertext Transfer Protocol (HTTP)**, which was developed by Tim Berners-Lee in 1991. When a user types a domain name (for example, www.yahoo.com) into a Web browser's address bar, the browser sends an HTTP-formatted message to a Web server computer at Yahoo! that stores Web page files. The Web server computer at Yahoo! then responds by sending a set of files (one for the Web page and one for each graphic object, sound, or video clip included on the page) back to the client computer. These files are sent within a message that is HTTP formatted.

To initiate a Web page request using a Web browser, the user types the name of the protocol, followed by the characters "//:" before the domain name. Thus, a user would type http://www.yahoo.com to go to the Yahoo! Web site. Most Web browsers today automatically insert the http:// if the user does not include it. The combination of the protocol name and the domain name is called a **Uniform Resource Locator (URL)** because it lets the user locate a resource (the Web page) on another computer (the Web server).

Electronic Mail Protocols

Electronic mail, or **e-mail**, that is sent across the Internet must also be formatted according to a common set of rules. Most organizations use a client/server structure to handle e-mail. The organization has a computer called an **e-mail server** that is devoted to handling e-mail. Software running on the e-mail server stores and forwards e-mail messages. People in the organization might use a variety of programs, called **e-mail client software**, to read and send e-mail. These programs include Microsoft Outlook, MozillaThunderbird, Pegasus Mail, and many others. The e-mail client software communicates with the e-mail server software on the e-mail server computer to send and receive e-mail messages.

Many people also use e-mail on their computers at home. In most cases, the e-mail servers that handle their messages are operated by the companies that provide their connections to the Internet. An increasing number of people use e-mail services that are offered by Web sites such as Yahoo! Mail, Microsoft's Hotmail, or Google's Gmail. In these cases, the e-mail servers and the e-mail clients are operated by the owners of the Web sites. The individual users only see the e-mail client software (and not the e-mail server software) in their Web browsers when they log on to the Web mail service.

With so many different e-mail client and server software choices, standardization and rules are very important. If e-mail messages did not follow standard rules, an e-mail message created by a person using one e-mail client program could not be read by a person using a different e-mail client program. As you have already learned in this chapter, rules for computer data transmission are called protocols.

SMTP and POP are two common protocols used for sending and retrieving e-mail. **Simple Mail Transfer Protocol (SMTP)** specifies the format of a mail message and describes how mail is to be administered on the e-mail server and transmitted on the Internet. An e-mail client program running on a user's computer can request mail from the organization's e-mail server using the **Post Office Protocol (POP)**. A POP message can tell the e-mail server to send mail to the user's computer and delete it from the e-mail server; send mail to the user's computer and not delete it; or simply ask whether new mail has arrived. The POP provides support for **Multipurpose Internet Mail Extensions (MIME)**, which is a set of rules for handling binary files, such as word-processing documents, spreadsheets, photos, or sound clips that are attached to e-mail messages.

The **Interactive Mail Access Protocol (IMAP)** is a newer e-mail protocol that performs the same basic functions as POP, but includes additional features. For example, IMAP can instruct the e-mail server to send only selected e-mail messages to the client instead of all messages. IMAP also allows the user to view only the header and the e-mail sender's name before deciding to download the entire message. POP requires users to download e-mail messages to their computers before they can search, read, forward, delete, or reply to those messages. IMAP lets users create and manipulate e-mail folders (also called mailboxes) and individual e-mail messages while the messages are still on the e-mail server; that is, the user does not need to download e-mail before working with it.

The tools that IMAP provides are important to the large number of people who access their e-mail from different computers at different times. IMAP lets users manipulate and store their e-mail on the e-mail server and access it from any computer. The main drawback to IMAP is that users' e-mail messages are stored on the e-mail server. As the number of users increases, the size of the e-mail server's disk drives must also increase. In general, server computers use faster (and thus, more expensive) disk drives than desktop computers. Therefore, it is more expensive to provide disk storage space for large quantities of e-mail on a server computer than to provide that same disk space on users' desktop computers. As the price of all disk storage continues to decrease, these cost concerns become less important. You can learn more about IMAP at the University of Washington's **IMAP Connection** Web site.

Unsolicited Commercial E-Mail (UCE, Spam)

Spam, also known as **unsolicited commercial e-mail (UCE)** or **bulk mail**, is electronic junk mail and can include solicitations, advertisements, or e-mail chain letters. The origin of the term spam is generally believed to have come from a song performed by the British comedy troupe, Monty Python, about Hormel's canned meat product, SPAM. In the song, an increasing number of people join in repeating the song's chorus: "Spam spam spam spam, spam spam spam spam, lovely spam, wonderful spam . . ." Just as in the song, e-mail spam is a tiresome repetition of meaningless text that eventually drowns out any other attempt at communication.

Besides wasting people's time and their computer disk space, spam can consume large amounts of Internet capacity. If one person sends a useless e-mail to a million people, that unsolicited mail consumes Internet resources for a few moments that would otherwise be available to other users. Once merely an annoyance, spam has become a major problem for companies. In addition to consuming bandwidth on company networks and space on e-mail servers, spam distracts employees who are trying to do their jobs and requires them to spend time deleting the unwanted messages. A considerable number of spam messages include content that can be offensive to recipients. Some employers worry that their employees might sue them, arguing that the offensive spam they receive while working contributes to a hostile work environment, which can be grounds for harassment allegations. Spam costs businesses more than $40 billion per year in lost productivity and the expenses of dealing with it. You will learn more about spam and how to deal with it in Chapter 8.

MARKUP LANGUAGES AND THE WEB

Web pages can include many elements, such as graphics, photographs, sound clips, and even small programs that run in the Web browser. Each of these elements is stored on the Web server as a separate file. The most important parts of a Web page, however, are the structure of the page and the text that makes up the main part of the page. The page structure and text are stored in a text file that is formatted, or marked up, using a text markup language. A **text markup language** specifies a set of tags that are inserted into the text. These **markup tags**, also called **tags**, provide formatting instructions that Web client software can understand. The Web client software uses those instructions as it renders the text and page elements contained in the other files into the Web page that appears on the screen of the client computer.

The markup language most commonly used on the Web is HTML, which is a subset of a much older and far more complex text markup language called **Standard Generalized Markup Language (SGML)**. Figure 2-5 shows how HTML, XML, and XHTML have descended from the original SGML specification. SGML was used for many years by the publishing industry to create documents that needed to be printed in various formats and that were revised frequently. In addition to its role as a markup language, SGML is a **metalanguage**, which is a language that can be used to define other languages. Another markup language that was derived from SGML for use on the Web is **Extensible Markup Language (XML)**, which is increasingly used to mark up information that companies share with each other over the Internet. The X in XML comes from the word extensible; you might see the word extensible shown as eXtensible. XML is also a meta language because users can create their own markup elements that extend the usefulness of XML (which is why it is called an "extensible" language).

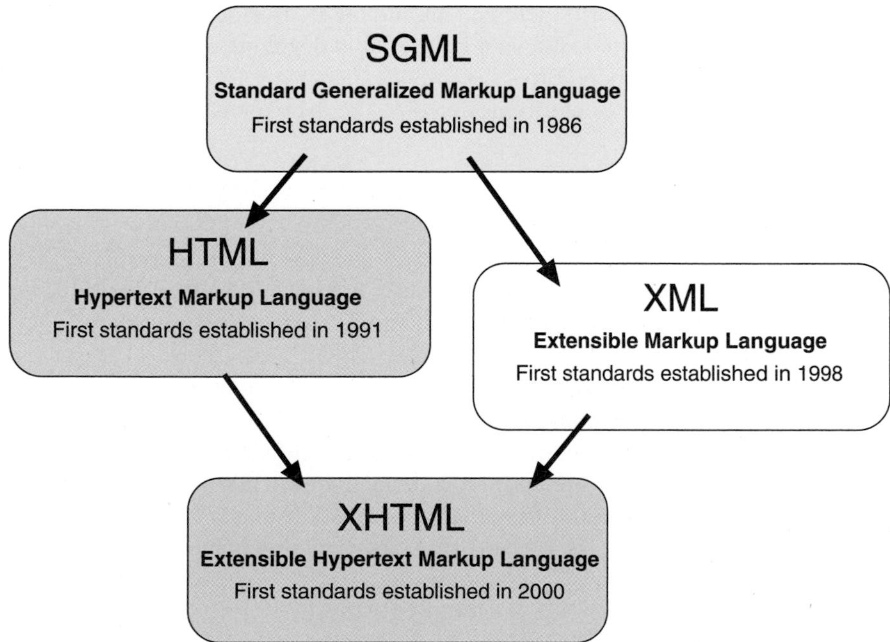

FIGURE 2-5 Development of markup languages

The **World Wide Web Consortium (W3C)**, a not-for-profit group that maintains standards for the Web, presented its first draft form of XML in 1996; the **W3C** issued its first formal version recommendation in 1998. Thus, it is a much newer markup language than HTML. In 2000, the W3C released the first version of a recommendation for a new markup language called **Extensible Hypertext Markup Language (XHTML)**, which is a reformulation of HTML version 4.0 as an XML application. The Online Companion includes a link to the **W3C XHTML Version 1.0 Specification**.

Markup Languages

Since the 1960s, publishers have used markup languages to create documents that can be formatted once, stored electronically, and then printed many times in various layouts that each interpret the formatting differently. U.S. Department of Defense contractors also used early markup languages to create manuals and parts lists for weapons systems. These documents contained many information elements that were often reprinted in different versions and formats. Using electronic document storage and programs that could interpret the formats to produce different layouts saved a tremendous amount of retyping time and cost.

A **Generalized Markup Language (GML)** emerged from these early efforts to create standard formatting styles for electronic documents. In 1986, after many elements of the standard had been in use for years, the **International Organization for Standardization (ISO)** adopted a version of GML called SGML. SGML offers a system of marking up documents that is independent of any software application. Many organizations, such as the Association of American Publishers, Hewlett-Packard, and Kodak, use SGML because they have complex document-management requirements.

SGML is nonproprietary and platform independent and offers user-defined tags. However, it is not well suited to certain tasks, such as the rapid development of Web pages. SGML is costly to set up and maintain, requires the use of expensive software tools, and is hard to learn. Creating document-type definitions in SGML can be expensive and time consuming.

Hypertext Markup Language

HTML includes tags that define the format and style of text elements in an electronic document. HTML also has tags that can create relationships among text elements within one document or among several documents. The text elements that are related to each other are called **hypertext elements**.

HTML is easier to learn and use than SGML. HTML is the prevalent markup language used to create documents on the Web today. The early versions of HTML let Web page designers create text-based electronic documents with headings, title bar titles, bullets, lines, and ordered lists. As the use of HTML and the Web itself grew, HTML creator Berners-Lee turned over the job of maintaining versions of HTML to the W3C. Later versions of HTML included tags for tables, frames, and other features that helped Web designers create more complex page layouts. The W3C maintains detailed information about HTML versions and related topics on its **W3C HTML Working Group** page.

The process for approval of new HTML features takes a long time, so Web browser software developers created some features, called **HTML extensions**, that would only work in their browsers. At various times during the history of HTML, both Microsoft and Netscape enabled their Web browsers to use these HTML extension tags before those tags were approved by the W3C. In some cases, these tags were enabled in one browser and not the other. In other cases, the tags used were never approved by the W3C or were approved in a different form than the one implemented in the Web browser software. Web page designers who wanted to use the latest available tags were often frustrated by this inconsistency. Many of these Web designers had to create separate sets of Web pages for the different types of browsers, which was inefficient and expensive. Most of these tag difference issues were resolved when the W3C issued the specification for HTML version 4.0 in 1997, although enough of them remained to cause regular problems for Web designers.

After HTML 4.0 was finalized in 1999, development on new versions of HTML slowed to a snail's pace. Browser developers worked on adding new features to their software and the W3C directed its efforts to other matters. In 2007, three browser developers (Apple, Opera, and the Mozilla Foundation) began working on an updated version of HTML that would include features such as audio and video within the markup language itself. Audio and video in Web pages have always required the use of add-on software. You can learn more about the current working draft of HTML version 5.0 by visiting the **W3C HTML 5** page.

HTML Tags

An HTML document contains document text and elements. The tags in an HTML document are interpreted by the Web browser and used by it to format the display of the text enclosed by the tags. In HTML, the tags are enclosed in angle brackets (<>). Most HTML tags have an **opening tag** and a **closing tag** that format the text between them. The closing tag is preceded by a slash within the angle brackets (</>). The general form of an HTML element is:

```
<tagname properties>Displayed information affected by tag</tagname>
```

Two good examples of HTML tag pairs are the strong character-formatting tags and the emphasis character-formatting tags. For example, a Web browser reading the following line of text:

```
<strong>A Review of the Book <em>HTML Is Fun!</em></strong>
```

would recognize the <strong> and </strong> tags as instructions to display the entire line of text in bold and the <em> and </em> tags as instructions to display the text enclosed by those tags in italics. The Web browser would display the text as:

A Review of the Book *HTML Is Fun!*

Some Web browsers allow the user to customize the interpretations of the tags, so that different Web browsers might display the tagged text differently. For example, one Web browser might display text enclosed by strong tags in a blue color instead of displaying the text as bold. Tags are generally written in lowercase letters, however older versions of HTML allowed the use of either case and you might still see Web pages that include uppercase (or mixed case) HTML tags. Although most tags are two-sided (they use both an opening and a closing tag), some are not. Tags that only require opening tags are known as one-sided tags. The tag that creates a line break (</br>) is a common one-sided tag. Some tags, such as the paragraph tag (<p>...</p>), are two-sided tags for which the closing tag is optional. Designers sometimes omit the optional closing tags, but this practice is poor markup style.

In a two-sided tag set, the closing tag position is very important. For example, if you were to omit the closing bold tag in the preceding example, any text that followed the line would be bolded. Sometimes an opening tag contains one or more property modifiers that further refine how the tag operates. A tag's property may modify a text display, or it may designate where to find a graphic element. Figure 2-6 (on the next page) shows some sample text marked up with HTML tags and Figure 2-7 (on page 76) shows this text as it appears in a Web browser. The tags in these two figures are among the most common HTML tags in use today on the Web.

```
<html>

    <head>

        <title>HTML Tag Examples</title>

    </head>

    <body>

    <h1>This text is set in Heading one tags</h1>
    <h2>This text is set in Heading two tags</h2>
    <h3>This text is set in Heading three tags</h1>

    <p>
    This text is set within Paragraph tags. It will appear as one paragraph: the
    text will wrap at the end of each line that is rendered in the Web browser no
    matter where the typed text ends. The text inside Paragraph tags is rendered
    without regard to extra spaces typed in the text, such as these:
    Character formatting can also be applied within Paragraph tags. For
    example, <strong>the Strong tags will cause this text to appear bolded in
    most Web browsers</strong> and <em>the emphasis tags will cause this to
    appear italicized in most Web browsers</em>.
    </p>

    <pre>
    HTML includes tags that instruct the Web browser to render the text
    Exactly     the     way      it      is       typed,
    as in this example.
    </pre>

    <p>
    HTML includes tags that instruct the Web browser to place text in bulleted or
    numbered lists:
    </p>

    <ul>
        <li>Bulleted list item one</li>
        <li>Bulleted list item two</li>
        <li>Bulleted list item three</li>
    </ul>

    <ol>
        <li>Numbered list item one</li>
        <li>Numbered list item two</li>
        <li>Numbered list item three</li>
    </ol>

    <p>
    The most important tag in HTML is the Anchor Hypertext Reference tag,
    which is the tag that provides a link to another Web page (or another location
    in the same Web page). For example, the underlined text
    <a href="http://www.w3c.org/">World Wide Web Consortium</a>
    is a link to the not-for-profit organization that develops Web technologies.
    </p>

    </body>

</html>
```

FIGURE 2-6 Text marked up with HTML tags

This text is set in Heading one tags

This text is set in Heading two tags

This text is set in Heading three tags

This text is set within Paragraph tags. It will appear as one paragraph: the text will wrap at the end of each line that is rendered in the Web browser no matter where the typed text ends. The text inside Paragraph tags is rendered without regard to extra spaces typed in the text, such as these: Character formatting can also be applied within Paragraph tags. For example, **the Strong tags will cause this text to appear bolded in most Web browsers** and *the emphasis tags will cause this to appear italicized in most Web browsers.*

```
HTML includes tags that instruct the Web browser to render the text
Exactly        the       way        it       is         typed,
as in this example.
```

HTML includes tags that instruct the Web browser to place text in bulleted or numbered lists:

- Bulleted list item one
- Bulleted list item two
- Bulleted list item three

1. Numbered list item one
2. Numbered list item two
3. Numbered list item three

The most important tag in HTML is the Anchor Hypertext Reference tag, which is the tag that provides a link to another Web page (or another location in the same Web page). For example, the underlined text World Wide Web Consortium is a link to the not-for-profit organization that develops Web technologies.

FIGURE 2-7 Text marked up with HTML tags as it appears in a Web browser

Other frequently used HTML tags (not shown in the figures) let Web designers include graphics on Web pages and format text in the form of tables. The text and HTML tags that form a Web page can be viewed when the page is open in a Web browser by clicking the Page button and selecting View Source in Internet Explorer or by selecting View, Page Source from the command menu in Firefox. A number of good Web sources (such as the **W3C Getting Started with HTML** page) and textbooks are available that describe HTML tags and their uses, and you may wish to consult them for an in-depth look at HTML.

HTML Links

The Web organizes interlinked pages of information residing on sites around the world. Hyperlinks on Web pages form a "web" of those pages. A user can traverse the interwoven pages by clicking hyperlinked text on one page to move to another page in the web of pages. Users can read Web pages in serial order or in whatever order they prefer by following hyperlinks. Figure 2-8 illustrates the differences between reading a paper catalog in a linear way and reading a hypertext catalog in a nonlinear way.

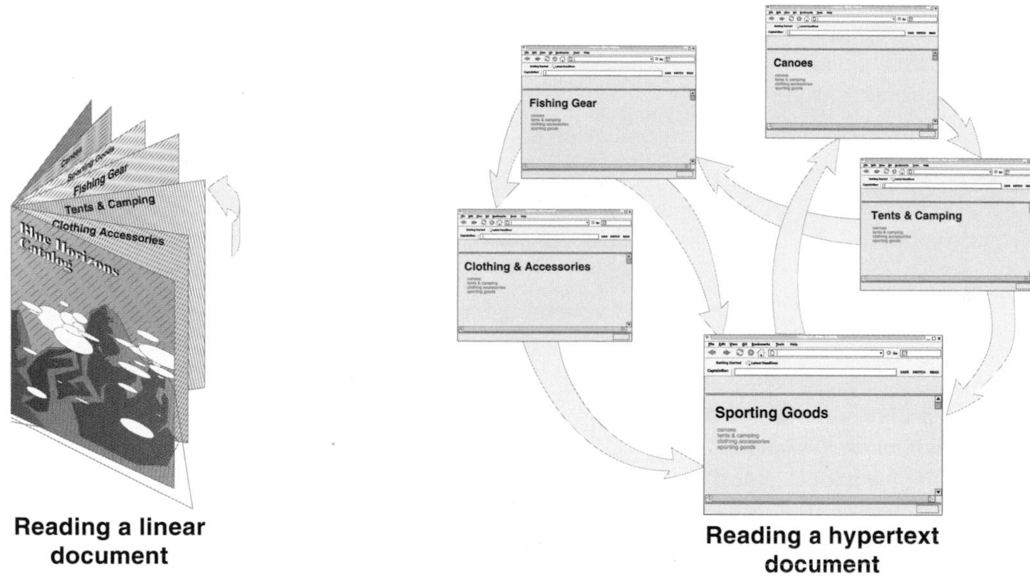

FIGURE 2-8 Linear vs. nonlinear paths through documents

Web sites can use links to direct customers to pages on the company's Web server. The way links lead customers through pages can affect the usefulness of the site and can play a major role in shaping customers' impressions of the company. Two commonly used link structures are linear and hierarchical. A **linear hyperlink structure** resembles conventional paper documents in that the reader begins on the first page and clicks the Next button to move to the next page in a serial fashion. This structure works well when customers fill out forms prior to a purchase or other agreement. In this case, the customer reads and responds to page one, and then moves on to the next page. This process continues until the entire form is completed. The only Web page navigation choices the user typically has are Back and Continue.

Another link arrangement is called a hierarchical structure. In a **hierarchical hyperlink structure**, the Web user opens an introductory page called a **home page** or **start page**. This page contains one or more links to other pages, and those pages, in turn, link to other pages. This hierarchical arrangement resembles an inverted tree in which the root is at the top and the branches are below it. Hierarchical structures are good for leading customers from general topics or products to specific product models and quantities. A company's home page might contain links to help, company history, company officers, order processing, frequently asked questions, and product catalogs. Many sites that use a hierarchical structure include a page on the Web site that contains a map or outline listing of the Web pages in their hierarchical order. This page is called a **site map**. Of course, hybrid designs that combine linear and hierarchical structures are also possible. Figure 2-9 illustrates these three common Web page organization structures.

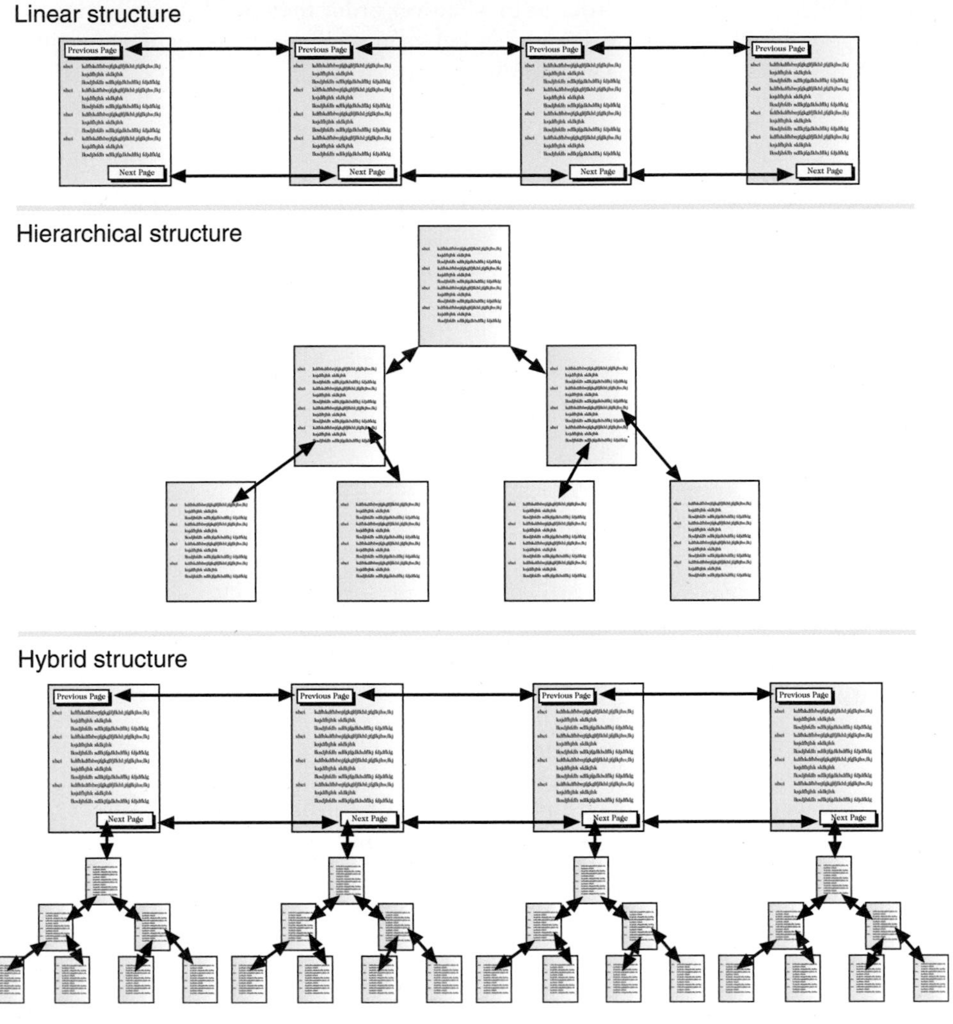

FIGURE 2-9 Three common Web page organization structures

In HTML, hyperlinks are created using the HTML **anchor tag**. Whether you are linking to text within the same document or to a document on a distant computer, the anchor tag has the same basic form:

```
<a href="address">Visible link text</a>
```

Anchor tags have opening and closing tags. The opening tag has a hypertext reference (HREF) property, which specifies the remote or local document's address. Clicking the text following the opening link transfers control to the HREF address, wherever that happens to be. A person creating an electronic résumé on the Web might want to make a university's name and address under the Education heading a hyperlink instead of plain text. Anyone viewing the résumé can click the link, which leads the reader to the university's home page. The following example shows the HTML code to create a hyperlink to another Web server:

```
<a href="http://www.gsu.edu">Georgia State University </a>
```

Similarly, the résumé could include a local link to another part of the same document with the following marked up text:

```
<a href="#references">References are found here</a>
```

In both of these examples, the text between the anchors appears on the Web page as a hyperlink. Most browsers display the link in blue and underline it. In most browser software, the action of moving the mouse pointer over a hyperlink causes the mouse pointer to change from an arrow to a pointing hand.

Scripting Languages and Style Sheets

Versions of HTML released by the W3C after 1997 include an HTML tag called the object tag and include support for **Cascading Style Sheets (CSS)**. Web designers can use the object tag to embed scripting language code on HTML pages. You will learn more about Web page scripting techniques in Chapter 8.

CSS are sets of instructions that give Web developers more control over the format of displayed pages. Similar to document styles in word-processing programs, CSS lets designers define formatting styles that can be applied to multiple Web pages. The set of instructions, called a **style sheet**, is usually stored in a separate file and is referenced using the HTML style tag; however, it can be included as part of a Web page's HTML file. The term *cascading* is used because designers can apply many style sheets to the same Web page, one on top of the other, and the styles from each style sheet flow (or cascade) into the next. For example, a three-stage cascade might include one style sheet with formatting instructions for text within heading 1 tags, a second style sheet with formatting instructions for text within heading 2 tags, and a third style sheet with formatting instructions for text within paragraph tags. A designer who later decides to change the formatting of heading 2 text can just replace the second style sheet with a different one. Those changes would cascade into the third style sheet.

Extensible Markup Language (XML)

As the Web grew, HTML continued to provide a useful tool for Web designers who wanted to create attractive layouts of text and graphics on their pages. However, as companies began to conduct electronic commerce on the Web, the need to present large amounts of data on Web pages also became important. Companies created Web sites that contained lists of inventory items, sales invoices, purchase orders, and other business data. The need to keep these lists updated was also important and posed a new challenge for many Web designers. The tool that had helped these Web designers create useful Web pages, HTML, was not such a good tool for presenting or maintaining information lists.

In the late 1990s, companies began turning to XML to help them maintain Web pages that contained large amounts of data. XML uses paired start and stop tags in much the same way as database software defines a record structure. For example, a company that sells products on the Web might have Web pages that contain descriptions and photos of the products it sells. The Web pages are marked up with HTML tags, but the product information elements themselves, such as prices, identification numbers, and quantities on hand, are marked up with XML tags. The XML document is embedded within the HTML document.

XML includes data-management capabilities that HTML cannot provide. To better understand the strengths of XML and weaknesses of HTML in data-management tasks, consider the simple example of a Web page that includes a list of countries and some basic facts about each country. A Web designer might decide to use HTML tags to show each fact the same way for each country. Each fact would use a different tag. Assume that the Web designer in this case decided to use the HTML heading tags to present the data. Figure 2-10 shows the data and the HTML heading tags for four countries (this is only an example; the actual list would include more than 150 countries). The first item in the list provides the definitions for each tag. Figure 2-11 (on the next page) shows this HTML document as it appears in a Web browser.

```
<html>
   <head>
      <title>Countries</title>
   </head>
   <body>
      <h1>Countries</h1>

      <h2>CountryName</h2>
      <h3>CapitalCity</h3>
      <h4>AreaInSquareKilometers</h4>
      <h5>OfficialLanguage</h5>
      <h6>VotingAge</h6>

      <h2>Argentina</h2>
      <h3>Buenos Aires</h3>
      <h4>2,766,890</h4>
      <h5>Spanish</h5>
      <h6>18</h6>

      <h2>Austria</h2>
      <h3>Vienna</h3>
      <h4>83,858</h4>
      <h5>German</h5>
      <h6>19</h6>

      <h2>Barbados</h2>
      <h3>Bridgetown</h3>
      <h4>430</h4>
      <h5>English</h5>
      <h6>18</h6>

      <h2>Belarus</h2>
      <h3>Minsk</h3>
      <h4>207,600</h4>
      <h5>Byelorussian</h5>
      <h6>18</h6>
   </body>
</html>
```

FIGURE 2-10 Country list data marked up with HTML tags

Countries

CountryName

CapitalCity

AreaInSquareKilometers

OfficialLanguage

VotingAge

Argentina

Buenos Aires

2,766,890

Spanish

18

Austria

Vienna

83,858

German

19

Barbados

Bridgetown

430

English

18

Belarus

Minsk

207,600

Byelorussian

18

FIGURE 2-11 Country list data as it appears in a Web browser

These figures reveal some of the shortcomings of using HTML to present a list of items when the meaning of each item in the list is important. The Web designer in this case used HTML heading tags. HTML has only six levels of heading tags; thus, if the individual items had additional information elements than shown in this example (such as population and continent), this approach would not work at all. The Web designer could use various combinations of text attributes such as size, font, color, bold, or italics to distinguish among items, but none of these tags would convey the meaning of the individual data elements. The only information about the meaning of each country's listing appears in the first list item, which includes the definitions for each element. In the late 1990s, Web professionals began to consider XML as a list-formatting alternative to HTML that would more effectively communicate the meaning of data.

XML differs from HTML in two important respects. First, XML is not a markup language with defined tags. It is a framework within which individuals, companies, and other organizations can create their own sets of tags. Second, XML tags do not specify how text appears on a Web page; the tags convey the meaning (the semantics) of the information included within them. To understand this distinction between appearance and semantics, consider the list of countries example again. In XML, tags can be created for each fact that define the meaning of the fact. Figure 2-12 shows the countries data marked up with XML tags. Some browsers, such as Internet Explorer, can render XML files directly without additional instructions. Figure 2-13 (on the next page) shows the country list XML file as it would appear in an Internet Explorer browser window.

FIGURE 2-12 Country list data marked up with XML tags

```
<?xml version="1.0" ?>
<CountriesList>
- <Country Name="Argentina">
    <CapitalCity>Buenos Aires</CapitalCity>
    <AreaInSquareKilometers>2,766,890</AreaInSquareKilometers>
    <OfficialLanguage>Spanish</OfficialLanguage>
    <VotingAge>18</VotingAge>
  </Country>
- <Country Name="Austria">
    <CapitalCity>Vienna</CapitalCity>
    <AreaInSquareKilometers>83,858</AreaInSquareKilometers>
    <OfficialLanguage>German</OfficialLanguage>
    <VotingAge>19</VotingAge>
  </Country>
- <Country Name="Barbados">
    <CapitalCity>Bridgetown</CapitalCity>
    <AreaInSquareKilometers>430</AreaInSquareKilometers>
    <OfficialLanguage>English</OfficialLanguage>
    <VotingAge>18</VotingAge>
  </Country>
- <Country Name="Belarus">
    <CapitalCity>Minsk</CapitalCity>
    <AreaInSquareKilometers>207,600</AreaInSquareKilometers>
    <OfficialLanguage>Byelorussian</OfficialLanguage>
    <VotingAge>18</VotingAge>
  </Country>
</CountriesList>
```

FIGURE 2-13 Country list data marked up with XML tags as it would appear in Internet Explorer

The first line in the XML file shown in Figures 2-12 and 2-13 is the declaration, which indicates that the file uses version 1.0 of XML. XML markup tags are similar in appearance to SGML markup tags, thus the declaration can help avoid confusion in organizations that use both. The second line and the last line are the root element tags. The root element of an XML file contains all of the other elements in that file and is usually assigned a name that describes the purpose or meaning of the file.

The other elements are called child elements; for example, Country is a child element of CountriesList. Each of the other attributes is, in turn, a child element of the Country element. Unlike an HTML file, when an XML file is displayed in a browser, the tags are visible. The names of these child elements were created specifically for use in this file. If programmers in another organization were to create a file with country information, they might use different names for these elements (for example, "Capital" instead of "CapitalCity"), which would make it difficult for the two organizations to share information. Thus, the greatest strength of XML, that it allows users to define their own tags, is also its greatest weakness.

To overcome that weakness, many companies have agreed to follow common standards for XML tags. These standards, in the form of data-type definitions (DTDs) or XML schemas, are available for a number of industries, including the **ebXML** initiative for electronic commerce standards, the **Extensible Business Reporting Language (XBRL)** for accounting and financial information standards, **LegalXML** for information in the legal profession, and **MathML** for mathematical and scientific information. A number of industry groups have formed to create standard XML tag definitions that can be used by all companies in that industry. **RosettaNet** is an example of such an industry group. In 2001, the W3C released a set of rules for XML document interoperability that many researchers believe will help resolve incompatibilities between different sets of XML tag definitions. A set of XML tag definitions is sometimes called an **XML vocabulary**. Hundreds of publicly defined XML vocabularies have been developed or are currently circulating. You can find links to many of them on the Oasis **Cover Pages: XML Applications and Initiatives** Web page. You can learn more about XML by reading the **W3C XML Pages**.

Although it is possible to display XML files in some Web browsers, XML files are not intended to be displayed in a Web browser. XML files are intended to be translated using another file that contains formatting instructions or to be read by a program. Formatting instructions are often written in the **Extensible Stylesheet Language (XSL)**, and the programs that read or transform XML files are usually written in the Java programming language. These programs, sometimes called **XML parsers**, can format an XML file so it can appear on the screen of a computer, a smart phone, an Internet-capable mobile phone, or some other device. A diagram showing one way that a Web server might process HTTP requests for Web pages generated from an XML database in different formats for different Web browsing devices appears in Figure 2-14.

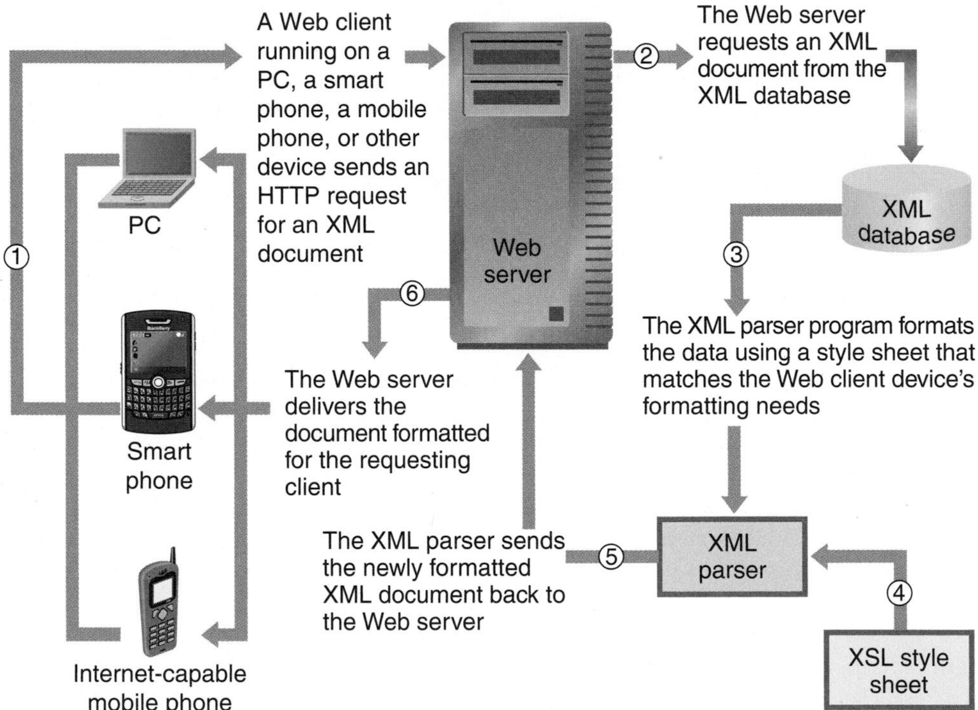

FIGURE 2-14 Processing requests for Web pages from an XML database

HTML and XML Editors

Web designers can create HTML documents in any general-purpose text editor or word processor. However, a special-purpose HTML editor can help Web designers create Web pages much more easily. HTML editors are also included as part of more sophisticated programs that are sometimes called Web site design tools. With these programs, Web designers can create and manage complete Web sites, including features for database access, graphics, and fill-in forms. These programs display the Web page as it will appear in a Web browser in one window and display the HTML-tagged text in another window. The designer can edit in either window and changes are reflected in the other window. For example, the designer can drag and drop objects such as graphics onto the Web browser view page and the program automatically generates the HTML tags to position the graphics.

Web site design programs also include features that allow the designer to create a Web site on a PC and then upload the entire site (HTML documents, graphics files, and so on) to a Web server computer. When the site needs to be edited later, the designer can edit the copy of the site on the PC, then instruct the program to synchronize those changes on the copy of the site that resides on the Web server. The most widely used Web site design tool is **Adobe Dreamweaver**. The Additional Resources section of the Online Companion for this chapter includes links to Web sites that offer downloads of these **HTML Editing and Web Page Design Programs**.

XML files, like HTML files, can be created in any text editor. However, programs designed to make the task of designing and managing XML files easier are also available. These programs provide tag validation and XML creation capabilities in addition to making the job of marking up text with XML tags more efficient. You can find links to these programs' Web sites in the Additional Resources section of the Online Companion under the heading **XML Editing Programs**.

INTRANETS AND EXTRANETS

Not all TCP/IP networks connect to the Internet. Many companies build internets (small "i"), or interconnected networks, that do not extend beyond their organizational boundaries. An **intranet** is an interconnected network (or internet), usually one that uses the TCP/IP protocol set, and does not extend beyond the organization that created it. An **extranet** is an intranet that has been extended to include specific entities outside the boundaries of the organization, such as business partners, customers, or suppliers. Although fax, telephone, e-mail, and overnight express carriers have been the main communications tools for business for many years, extranets can replace many of them at a lower cost.

Public and Private Networks

A **public network** is any computer network or telecommunications network that is available to the public. The Internet is one example of a public network. Although a company can operate its extranet using a public network, very few do because of the high level of security risks. The Internet, as you will learn in later chapters, does not provide a high degree of security in its basic structure.

A **private network** is a private, leased-line connection between two companies that physically connects their intranets to one another. A **leased line** is a permanent telephone connection between two points. Unlike the normal telephone connection you create when you dial a telephone number, a leased line is always active. The advantage of a leased line is security. Only the two parties that lease the line to create the private network have access to the connection. The largest drawback to a private network is cost. Leased lines are expensive. Every pair of companies wanting a private network between them requires a separate line connecting them. For instance, if a company wants to set up an extranet connection over a private network with seven other companies, the company must pay the cost of seven leased lines, one for each company. If the extranet expands to 20 other companies, the extranet-sponsoring company must rent another 13 leased lines. As each new company is added, costs increase by the same amount and soon become prohibitive. Vendors refer to this as a **scaling problem**; that is, increasing the number of leased lines in private networks is difficult, costly, and time consuming. As the number of companies that need to join the extranet increases, other networking options become appealing.

Virtual Private Network (VPN)

A **virtual private network (VPN)** is an extranet that uses public networks and their protocols to send sensitive data to partners, customers, suppliers, and employees using a system called IP tunneling or encapsulation. **IP tunneling** effectively creates a private passageway through the public Internet that provides secure transmission from one computer to another. The virtual passageway is created by VPN software that encrypts the packet content and then places the encrypted packets inside another packet in a process called **encapsulation**. The outer packet is called an **IP wrapper**. The Web server sends the encapsulated packets to their destinations over the Internet. The computer that receives the packet unwraps it and decrypts the message using VPN software that is the same as, or compatible with, the VPN software used to encrypt and encapsulate the packet at the sending end. The "virtual" part of VPN means that the connection seems to be a permanent, internal network connection, but the connection is actually temporary. Each transaction between two intranets using a VPN is created, carries out its work over the Internet, and is then terminated.

VPN software must be installed on the computers at both ends of the transmission. A VPN provides security shells, with the most sensitive data under the tightest control. The VPN is like a separate, covered commuter lane on a highway (the Internet) in which the passengers are protected from being seen by the vehicles traveling in the other lanes. Company employees in remote locations can send sensitive information to company computers using the VPN private tunnels established on the Internet.

Unlike private networks using leased lines, VPNs establish short-term logical connections in real time that are broken once the communication session ends. Establishing VPNs does not require leased lines. The only infrastructure required outside each company's intranet is the Internet.

Extranets are sometimes confused with VPNs. Although a VPN is an extranet, not every extranet is a VPN. You will learn more about VPNs, firewalls, and other network security devices in Chapter 10.

INTERNET CONNECTION OPTIONS

The Internet is a set of interconnected networks. Most organizations have their computers connected to each other using a network. Many families have their home computers connected to each other in a network. Mobile phones are connected to the wireless phone service provider's network. These networks can be connected to the Internet in a number of ways. You will learn about Internet connection options in this section. Companies that provide Internet access to individuals, businesses, and other organizations, called **Internet access providers (IAPs)** or ISPs, usually offer several connection options. Links to the Web sites of companies that offer the various types of Internet connections described in this section appear in the Online Companion under the heading **Internet Service Providers**. This section briefly describes current connection choices and presents their advantages and disadvantages.

Connectivity Overview

ISPs offer several ways to connect to the Internet. The most common connection options are voice-grade telephone lines, various types of broadband connections, leased lines, and wireless. One of the major distinguishing factors between various ISPs and their connection options is the bandwidth they offer. **Bandwidth** is the amount of data that can travel through a communication medium per unit of time. The higher the bandwidth, the faster data files travel and the faster Web pages appear on your screen. Each connection option offers different bandwidths, and each ISP offers varying bandwidths for each connection option. Traffic on the Internet and at your local service provider greatly affects **net bandwidth**, which is the actual speed that information travels. When few people are competing for service from an ISP, net bandwidth approaches the carrier's upper limit. On the other hand, users experience slowdowns during high-traffic periods.

Bandwidth can differ for data traveling to or from the ISP depending on the user's connection type. Connection types include:

- **Symmetric connections** that provide the same bandwidth in both directions.
- **Asymmetric connections** that provide different bandwidths for each direction.

Bandwidth refers to the amount of data that travels and the rate at which it travels. The two bandwidth types in an asymmetric connection are as follows:

- **Upstream bandwidth**, also called **upload bandwidth**, is a measure of the amount of information that can travel from the user to the Internet in a given amount of time.
- **Downstream bandwidth**, also called **download** or **downlink bandwidth**, is a measure of the amount of information that can travel from the Internet to a user in a given amount of time (for example, when a user receives a Web page from a Web server).

Voice-Grade Telephone Connections

The most common way for an individual to connect to an ISP is through a modem connected to your local telephone service provider. **Plain old telephone service (POTS)** uses existing telephone lines and an analog modem to provide a bandwidth of between 28 and 56 Kbps. Some telephone companies offer a higher grade of service called **Digital Subscriber Line (DSL)** protocol. DSL connection methods do not use a modem. They use a piece of networking equipment that is similar to a network switch, but most people call this piece of equipment (incorrectly) a "DSL modem." **Integrated Services Digital Network (ISDN)** was the first technology developed to use the DSL protocol suite and has been available in parts of the United States since 1984. ISDN is more expensive than regular telephone service and offers bandwidths of between 128 and 256 Kbps.

Broadband Connections

Connections that operate at speeds of greater than about 200 Kbps are called **broadband** services. One of the newest technologies that uses the DSL protocol to provide service in the broadband range is **asymmetric digital subscriber line (ADSL**, usually abbreviated **DSL)**. It provides transmission bandwidths from 100 to 640 Kbps upstream and from 1.5 to 9 Mbps (million bits per second) downstream. For businesses, a **high-speed DSL (HDSL)** connection service can provide more than 768 Kbps of symmetric bandwidth.

Cable modems—connected to the same broadband coaxial cable that serves a television—typically provide transmission speeds between 300 Kbps and 1 Mbps from the client to the server. The downstream transmission rate can be as high as 10 Mbps. In the United States alone, more than 160 million homes have broadband cable service available, and more than 110 million homes subscribe to cable television. The latest estimates indicate that there are more than 11 million cable modem subscribers in the United States. In recent years, DSL monthly fees have been slightly lower than those of cable companies in markets where they compete. Today, about 13 million households have broadband DSL connections. Virtually all companies and organizations of any size have some type of broadband Internet connection.

DSL is a private line with no competing traffic. Unlike DSL, cable modem connection bandwidths vary with the number of other subscribers competing for the shared resource. Transmission speeds can decrease dramatically in heavily subscribed neighborhoods at prime times—in neighborhoods where many people are using cable modems simultaneously.

Connection options based on cable or telephone line connections are wonderful for urban and suburban Web users, but those living in rural areas often have limited telephone service and no cable access at all. The telephone lines used to cover the vast distances between rural customers are usually **voice-grade lines**, which cost less than telephone lines designed to carry data, are made of lower-grade copper, and were never intended to carry data. These lines can carry only limited bandwidth—usually less than 14 Kbps. Telephone companies have wired most urban and suburban areas with **data-grade lines** (made more carefully and of higher-grade copper than voice-grade lines) because the short length of the lines in these areas makes it less expensive to install than in rural areas where connection distances are much longer.

LEARNING FROM FAILURES

NorthPoint Communications

In 1997, Michael Malaga was a successful telecommunications executive with an idea. He wanted to sell broadband Internet access to small businesses in urban areas. DSL technology was just gaining acceptance, and leased telephone lines were available from telephone companies. He wanted to avoid residential customers because they would soon have inexpensive cable modem access to meet their broadband needs. He also wanted to avoid suburban and rural businesses to keep the telephone line leasing costs low (lease charges are higher for longer distances). He and five friends started NorthPoint Communications with $500,000 of their combined savings and raised another $11 million within a few months.

Continued

After six months, the company had raised more money from investors and had acquired 1500 customers, but it was posting a net loss of $30 million. On the strength of its number of customers, the company began the task of raising the $100 million that Malaga estimated it would need to create the network infrastructure.

Independent DSL providers such as NorthPoint were pressed by customers to install service rapidly, but had to rely on local telephone companies to ensure that their lines would support DSL. In many cases, the telephone companies had to install switches and other equipment to make DSL work on a particular line. The telephone companies often were in no rush to do this because they also sold DSL service, and speedy service would be helping a competitor. The delays led to unpredictable installation holdups and many unhappy NorthPoint customers. Customers with problems after the service was installed were often bounced from the telephone company to NorthPoint, without obtaining satisfactory or timely resolutions of their problems.

Although NorthPoint was unable to make its relationship with each customer profitable, Malaga and his team were rapidly raising money in the hot capital markets of the time. The company raised $162 million before its first stock offering in 1999, which brought in an additional $387 million. At that time, the company had 13,000 customers, which means that NorthPoint had raised more than $42,000 from outside investors for each customer. Considering that each customer would generate revenue of about $1,000 per year, the economics of the business did not look good. By the end of 1999, NorthPoint had spent $300 million of the cash it had raised to build its network infrastructure and reported an operating loss of $184 million. At this point, NorthPoint was operating in 28 cities.

During the next year, the company continued to raise additional funds, gain more customers, and lose money on each customer. In August 2000, the telephone company Verizon agreed to purchase 55 percent of the company for $800 million paid in installments. The total funding that NorthPoint had obtained by the end of 2000, including the partial payments received from Verizon, added up to $1.2 billion. By the end of the year, NorthPoint was in 109 cities and needed to spend $66 million in cash per month just to stay in business. Verizon withdrew from the purchase agreement, the stock plunged, and the layoffs began.

NorthPoint filed for bankruptcy in January 2001 and sold its networking hardware to AT&T in March for $135 million. AT&T was not interested in continuing the DSL business (it just wanted the hardware), so NorthPoint's 87,000 small business customers lost their Internet service overnight. In many of the cities that NorthPoint had served, there were no competitors to pick up the service. Because the capital markets of the late 1990s were so eager to invest in anything that appeared to be connected with the Internet, NorthPoint was able to raise incredible amounts of money. However, NorthPoint sold Internet access to customers for less than it cost to provide the service. No amount of investor money could overcome that basic business mistake.

Leased-Line Connections

Large firms with large amounts of Internet traffic can connect to an ISP using higher bandwidth connections that they can lease from telecommunications carriers. These connections use a variety of technologies and are usually classified by the equivalent number of telephone lines they include. (The connection technologies they use were originally developed to carry large numbers of telephone calls.)

A telephone line designed to carry one digital signal is called DS0 (digital signal zero, the name of the signaling format used on those lines) and has a bandwidth of 56 Kbps.

A **T1** line (also called a DS1) carries 24 DS0 lines and operates at 1.544 Mbps. Some telecommunications companies offer **fractional T1**, which provides service speeds of 128 Kbps and upward in 128-Kbps increments. **T3** service (also called DS3) offers 44.736 Mbps (the equivalent of 30 T1 lines or 760 DS0 lines). All of these leased telephone line connections are much more expensive than POTS, ISDN, or DSL connections.

Large organizations that need to connect hundreds or thousands of individual users to the Internet require very high bandwidth. NAPs use T1 and T3 lines. NAPs and the computers that perform routing functions on the Internet backbone also use technologies such as **frame relay** and **asynchronous transfer mode (ATM)** connections and **optical fiber** (instead of copper wire) connections with bandwidths determined by the class of fiber-optic cable used. An OC3 (optical carrier 3) connection provides 156 Mbps, an OC12 provides 622 Mbps, an OC48 provides 2.5 Gbps (gigabits, or 1 billion bits per second), and an OC192 provides 10 Gbps.

Wireless Connections

For many people in rural areas, satellite microwave transmissions have made connections to the Internet possible for the first time. In the first satellite technologies, the customer placed a receiving dish antenna on the roof or in the yard and pointed it at the satellite. The satellite sent microwave transmissions to handle Internet downloads at speeds of around 500 Kbps. Uploads were handled by a POTS modem connection. For Web browsing, this was not too bad, since most of the uploaded messages were small text messages (e-mails and Web page requests). People who wanted to send large e-mail attachments or transfer files over the Internet found the slow upload speeds unsatisfactory.

Today, companies offer satellite Internet connections that do not require a POTS modem connection for uploads. These connections use a microwave transmitter for Internet uploads. This transmitter provides upload speeds as high as 150 Kbps. Initially, the installation charges were much higher than for other residential Internet connection services because a professional installer was needed to carefully aim the transmitter's dish antenna at the satellite. Recently, the accuracy of the antennas improved, and some of these companies now offer a self-installation option that drastically reduces the initial cost. For installations in North America, the antennas must have a clear line of sight into the southwestern sky. This requirement can make these services unusable for many people living in large cities or on the wrong side of an apartment building. In the United States, about 2 million homes are connected to the Internet through a satellite broadband service.

Although satellite connections were the only wireless Internet access media for many years, many types of wireless networks are available now. People today use Internet-capable mobile phones, smart phones, game consoles, and notebook computers equipped with wireless network cards to connect to a variety of wireless networks that, in turn, are connected to the Internet. More than half of U.S. Internet users have used a wireless device to access the Internet.

Bluetooth and Ultra Wideband (UWB)

One of the first wireless protocols, designed for personal use over short distances, is called **Bluetooth**. (The protocol was developed in Norway and is named for Harald Bluetooth, a 10th century Scandinavian king.) Bluetooth operates reliably over distances of up to 35 feet and can be a part of up to 10 networks of eight devices each. It is a low-bandwidth technology, with speeds of up to 722 Kbps. Bluetooth is useful for tasks such as wireless synchronization of laptop computers with desktop computers and wireless printing from laptops or mobile phones. These small Bluetooth networks are called **personal area networks (PANs)** or **piconets**.

One major advantage of Bluetooth technology is that it consumes very little power, which is an important consideration for mobile devices. Another advantage is that Bluetooth devices can discover one another and exchange information automatically. For example, a person using a laptop computer in a temporary office can print to a local Bluetooth-enabled printer without logging in to the network or installing software on either device. The printer and the laptop computer electronically recognize each other as Bluetooth devices and can immediately begin exchanging information.

Another wireless communication technology, **Ultra Wideband (UWB)**, provides wide bandwidth (up to about 480 Mbps in current versions) connections over short distances (30 to 100 feet). UWB was developed for short-range secure communications in military applications during the 1960s. Many observers believe that UWB and other similar technologies will be used in future personal area networking applications such as home media centers (for example, a PC could beam stored video files to a nearby television) and in linking mobile phones to the Internet.

Wireless Ethernet (Wi-Fi)

The most common wireless connection technology for use on LANs is called **Wi-Fi**, **wireless Ethernet**, or **802.11b** (802.11 is the number of the technology's **network specification**, which is the set of rules that equipment connected to the network must follow). Wireless networking specifications are created by the **IEEE** (originally an acronym for an organization named the Institute of Electrical and Electronic Engineers, the letters are now used as the title of the organization and are pronounced eye-triple-E). A computer equipped with a Wi-Fi network card can communicate through a wireless access point connected to a LAN to become a part of that LAN. A **wireless access point (WAP)** is a device that transmits network packets between Wi-Fi-equipped computers and other devices that are within its range. The user must have authorization to connect to the LAN and might be required to perform a login procedure before the laptop can access the LAN through the WAP.

Wi-Fi that uses the 802.11b specification has a potential bandwidth of 11 Mbps and a range of about 300 feet. In actual installations, the achieved bandwidth and range can be dramatically affected by the construction material of the objects (such as walls, floors, doors, and windows) through which the signals must pass. For example, reinforced concrete walls and certain types of tinted glass windows greatly reduce the effective range of Wi-Fi. Despite these limitations, organizations can make Wi-Fi a key element of their LAN structures by installing a number of WAPs throughout their premises.

In 2002, an improved version of Wi-Fi, called **802.11a** (the 802.11b protocol was easier to implement, thus it was introduced first) was introduced. The 802.11a protocol is capable of transmitting data at speeds up to 54 Mbps, but it is not compatible with 802.11b devices. Later in 2002, the **802.11g** protocol, which has the 54-Mbps speed of 802.11a and is compatible with 802.11b devices, was introduced. Because of its compatibility with the many 802.11b devices that were in use, 802.11g was an immediate success.

In 2003, work began on the **802.11n** standard, which was originally planned to be completed in 2006. The expected completion dates were extended to 2007, then 2008, and finally 2010. Although the IEEE continues its work on this standard, drafts of the specification have been published and vendors currently sell Wi-Fi equipment built to the draft standard. The IEEE has promised that any further changes to the specification will not affect the ability of existing "Draft-N" products. The 802.11n wireless networking products provide significantly higher actual bandwidths (80–130 Mbps) than any earlier Wi-Fi standard products. When the 802.11n specification is finalized, the technology should provide bandwidths in the 300–450-Mbps range.

Wi-Fi devices are capable of **roaming**, that is, shifting from one WAP to another, without requiring intervention by the user. Some organizations, including airports, convention centers, and hotels, operate WAPs that are open to the public. These access points are called **hot spots**. Some organizations allow free access to their hot spots, others charge an access fee. A growing number of retail establishments, such as McDonald's, Panera, and Starbucks, offer hot spots. Hotels and office buildings have found that installing a WAP can be cheaper and easier than running network cable, especially in older buildings. Some hotels offer wireless access free, others charge a small fee. Users of fee-based networks authorize a connection charge when they log in. There are Web sites that offer hot spot directories that show hot spots by location, but these sites tend to open and close frequently, so these directories become out of date rather quickly. The best way to find hot spots (or a hot spot directory) is to use your favorite search engine.

Some communities have installed wireless networks that can be accessed from anywhere in the area. For example, the city of Grand Haven, Michigan, installed a metropolitan area Wi-Fi network. Grand Haven is a growing town on the shores of Lake Michigan. The company that built the network, Ottawa Wireless, sells network access to residents and businesses throughout the area. The company offers access not only on land, but on boats up to 15 miles out on Lake Michigan. Several small company owners use this network to conduct their online business while sailing!

Fixed-Point Wireless

In a growing number of rural areas that do not have cable TV service or telephone lines with the high-grade wires necessary to provide Internet bandwidths, some small companies have begun to offer fixed-point wireless service as an inexpensive alternative to satellite service. One version of **fixed-point wireless** uses a system of repeaters to forward a radio signal from the ISP to customers. The **repeaters** are transmitter–receiver devices (also called **transceivers**) that receive the signal and then retransmit it toward users' roof-mounted antennas and to the next repeater, which receives the signal and passes it on to the next repeater, which can be up to 20 miles away. The users' antennas are connected to a device that converts the radio signals into Wi-Fi packets that are sent to the users' computers or wireless LANs. Another version of fixed-point wireless directly transmits Wi-Fi packets through hundreds, or even thousands, of short-range transceivers that are located close to each other. This approach is called **mesh routing**. As Wi-Fi technologies improve, the number and variety of options for wireless connections to the Internet should continue to increase.

Cellular Telephone Networks

By the end of 2010, industry experts estimate that about 6 billion mobile phones will be in use around the world. These phones are sometimes called cellular (or cell) phones because they broadcast signals to (and receive signals from) antennas that are placed about 3 miles apart in a grid, and the hexagonal area that each antenna covers within this grid is called a cell.

Although mobile phones were originally designed to handle voice communications, they have always been able to transmit data. However, their data transmission speeds were very low, ranging from 10 to 384 Kbps. Several changes in mobile phone technology have increased the speeds in today's most capable mobile phones to 2 Mbps. The devices that combine the latest technologies available today are called **third-generation (3G) mobile phones**. Many mobile phones have a small screen and can be used to send and receive short text messages using a protocol called **short message service (SMS)**. As you learned at the beginning of this chapter, Internet-enabled mobile phones and smart phones are very popular in highly developed countries as convenient ways to stay connected while traveling. But more importantly, mobile phones are giving large numbers of people in developing countries their first access to the online world.

Many companies have seen great business potential for these wireless networks and the devices connected to them. They use the term **mobile commerce** or **m-commerce** to describe the kinds of resources people might want to access (and pay for) using wireless devices. You will learn more about revenue models that use wireless technologies in Chapter 3 and cost-reduction strategies that use wireless technologies in Chapter 5. Chapter 6 includes an overview of the development of mobile commerce to date and an outline of future directions. In Chapter 11, you will learn how some companies are using these technologies to process online payments for goods and services. Figure 2-15 summarizes speed and cost information for the most commonly available wired and wireless options for connecting a home or business to the Internet.

Service	Upstream Speed (Kbps)	Downstream Speed (Kbps)	Capacity (Number of Simultaneous Users)	One-time Startup Costs	Continuing Monthly Costs
Residential-Small Business Services					
POTS	28–56	28–56	1	\$0–\$20	\$9–\$20
Cellular 3G network	10–800	10–2000	1	\$50–120	\$50–150
ISDN	128–256	128–256	1–3	\$60–\$300	\$50–\$90
ADSL	100–640	500–9000	4–20	\$50–\$100	\$200–\$500
Cable	300–1500	500–10,000	4–10	\$0–\$100	\$100–\$300
Satellite	125–150	400–500	1–3	\$0–\$800	\$40–\$100
Fixed-point wireless	250–1500	500–3000	1–4	\$0–\$350	\$50–\$150
Business Services					
Leased digital line (DS0)	64	64	1–10	\$50–\$200	\$40–\$150
Fractional T1 leased line	128–1544	128–1544	5–180	\$50–\$800	\$100–\$1000
Fixed-point wireless	500–10,000	500–10,000	5–1000	\$0–\$500	\$300–\$5000
T1 leased line	1544	1544	100–200	\$100–\$2000	\$600–\$1600
T3 leased line	44,700	44,700	1000–10,000	\$1000–\$9000	\$5000–\$12,000
Large Organization					
OC3 leased line	156,000	156,000	1000–50,000	\$3000–\$12,000	\$9000–\$22,000
OC12 leased line	622,000	622,000	Backbone	Negotiated	\$25,000–\$100,000
OC48 leased line	2,500,000	2,500,000	Backbone	Negotiated	Negotiated
OC192 leased line	10,000,000	10,000,000	Backbone	Negotiated	Negotiated

FIGURE 2-15 Internet connection options

INTERNET2 AND THE SEMANTIC WEB

At the high end of the bandwidth spectrum, a group of network research scientists from nearly 200 universities and a number of major corporations joined together in 1996 to recapture the original enthusiasm of the ARPANET with an advanced research network called **Internet2**. When the National Science Foundation turned over the Internet backbone to commercial interests in 1995, many scientists felt that they had lost a large, living laboratory. **Internet2** is the replacement for that laboratory. An experimental test bed for new networking technologies that is separate from the original Internet, Internet2 has achieved bandwidths of 10 Gbps and more on parts of its network.

Internet2 is also used by universities to conduct large collaborative research projects that require several supercomputers connected at very fast speeds, or that use multiple video feeds—things that would be impossible on the Internet given its lower bandwidth limits. For example, doctors at medical schools that are members of Internet2 regularly use its technology to do live videoconference consultations during complex surgeries. Internet2 serves as a proving ground for new technologies and applications of those technologies that will eventually find their way to the Internet. In 2008, CERN (the birthplace of the original Web in Switzerland) began using Internet2 to share data generated by its new particle accelerator with a research network of 70 U.S. universities. Every few weeks, each university downloads about two terabytes (a terabyte is one thousand gigabytes) of data within a four-hour time period.

The Internet2 project is focused mainly on technology development. In contrast, Tim Berners-Lee began a project in 2001 that has a goal of blending technologies and information into a next-generation Web. This **Semantic Web** project envisions words on Web pages being tagged (using XML) with their meanings. The Web would become a huge machine-readable database. People could use intelligent programs called **software agents** to read the XML tags to determine the meaning of the words in their contexts. For example, a software agent given the instruction to find an airline ticket with certain terms (date, cities, cost limit) would launch a search on the Web and return with an electronic ticket that meets the criteria. Instead of a user having to visit several Web sites to gather information, compare prices and itineraries, and make a decision, the software agent would automatically do the searching, comparing, and purchasing.

The key elements that must be added to Web standards so that software agents can perform these functions include XML, a resource description framework, and an ontology. You have already seen how XML tags can describe the semantics of data elements. A **resource description framework (RDF)** is a set of standards for XML syntax. It would function as a dictionary for all XML tags used on the Web. An **ontology** is a set of standards that defines, in detail, the relationships among RDF standards and specific XML tags within a particular knowledge domain. For example, the ontology for cooking would include concepts such as ingredients, utensils, and ovens; however, it would also include rules and behavioral expectations, such as that ingredients can be mixed using utensils, that the resulting product can be eaten by people, and that ovens generate heat within a confined area. Ontologies and the RDF would provide the intelligence about the knowledge domain so that software agents could make decisions as humans would.

The development of the Semantic Web is expected to take many years. The first step in this project is to develop ontologies for specific subjects. Thus far, several areas of scientific inquiry have begun developing ontologies that will become the building blocks of the Semantic Web in their areas. Biology, genomics, and medicine have all made progress toward specific ontologies. These fields can benefit greatly from a tool like the Semantic Web, which can increase the speed with which research results, experimental data, and new procedures can be made available to all researchers in the field. Thus, these fields have a high incentive to collaborate on the hard work involved in creating ontologies. Other sciences, such as climatology, hydrology, and oceanography have similar incentives (as many researchers around the world work on common problems such as global warming) and are working on ontologies for their disciplines. The government of the United Kingdom is also developing an ontology for data it collects with the hope that it will be useful to a wide range of researchers.

Although many researchers involved in the Semantic Web project have expressed frustration at its slow progress, a number of important users of the Semantic Web have developed important ontologies that will allow the project to continue moving forward. You can learn more about the current status of this project by following the link in the Online Companion to the **W3C Semantic Web** pages.

Summary

In this chapter, you learned about the history of the Internet and the Web, including how these technologies emerged from research projects and grew to be the supporting infrastructure for electronic commerce today. You also learned about the protocols, programs, languages, and architectures that support the Internet and the World Wide Web. TCP/IP is the protocol suite used to create and transport information packets across the Internet. IP addresses identify computers on the Internet. Domain names such as www.amazon.com also identify computers on the Internet, but those names are translated into IP addresses by the routing computers on the Internet. HTTP is the set of rules for transferring Web pages and requests for those Web pages on the Internet. POP, SMTP, and IMAP are protocols that help manage e-mail. Unsolicited commercial e-mail (or spam) has become a major irritation for Internet users.

Hypertext Markup Language (HTML), was derived from the more generic meta language SGML. HTML defines the structure and content of Web pages using markup symbols called tags. Over time, HTML has evolved to include a large number of tags that accommodate graphics, Cascading Style Sheets, and other Web page elements. Hyperlinks are HTML tags that contain a URL. The URL can be a local or remote computer. HTML editors facilitate Web page construction with helpful tools and drag-and-drop capabilities.

Extensible Markup Language (XML) is also derived from SGML. However, unlike HTML, XML uses markup tags to describe the meaning, or semantics, of the text, rather than its display characteristics. XML offers businesses hope for a common language that they will be able to use to describe products, services, and even business processes to each other in common, shared databases. XML could help companies dramatically reduce the costs of handling intercompany information flows.

Intranets are private internal networks that use the same protocols as the Internet. Employees can access the intranet and find, view, or print information just as they would Internet-based material. When companies want to collaborate with suppliers, partners, or customers, they can connect their intranets to each other and form an extranet. There are three types of extranets: public network, private network, and virtual private network. Virtual private networks, or VPNs, provide security at a low cost, whereas public network extranets have no security at all.

Internet service providers offer many different types of connections to the Internet. Basic telephone connections are the most economical and easiest to install, but they are the slowest. Broadband cable, satellite microwave transmission, and DSL services provide Internet access at relatively high speeds. Other, more expensive options provide the bandwidth that larger businesses need. A variety of wireless connection options are becoming available, including fixed-point wireless. The wireless connection options available through mobile phones show promise in creating new opportunities for revenue generation, cost reduction, and payment-processing applications.

Internet2 is an experimental network built by a consortium of research universities and businesses that provides a test bed for creating and perfecting the high-speed networking technologies of tomorrow. The Semantic Web project, although still in an early developmental stage, has spurred scientists in various fields to contribute to the basic structure it will need to achieve its goal of making research data widely available. The project could also enable many user interactions with the Web to be handled by intelligent software agents.

Key Terms

802.11a, 802.11b, 802.11g, 802.11n
Anchor tag
Asymmetric connection
Asymmetric digital subscriber line (ADSL or DSL)
Asynchronous transfer mode (ATM)
Backbone router
Bandwidth
Base 2 (binary)
Bluetooth
Border router
Broadband
Bulk mail
Byte
Cascading Style Sheets (CSS)
Circuit
Circuit switching
Client/server architecture
Closed architecture
Closing tag
Colon hexadecimal (colon hex)
Computer network
Configuration table
Data-grade lines
Deep Web
Digital Subscriber Line (DSL)
Domain name
Dotted decimal
Download
Downstream bandwidth (downlink bandwidth)
Electronic mail (e-mail)
E-mail client software
E-mail server
Encapsulation
Extensible Hypertext Markup Language (XHTML)
Extensible Markup Language (XML)
Extensible Stylesheet Language (XSL)
Extranet
Fixed-point wireless
Fractional T1
Frame relay
Gateway computer
Generalized Markup Language (GML)
Generic top-level domain (gTLD)
Graphical user interface (GUI)
Hexadecimal (base 16)
Hierarchical hyperlink structure
High-speed DSL (HDSL)
Home page
Hot spot
HTML extensions
Hypertext
Hypertext element
Hypertext link (hyperlink)
Hypertext Markup Language (HTML)
Hypertext server
Hypertext Transfer Protocol (HTTP)
IEEE
Integrated Services Digital Network (ISDN)
Interactive Mail Access Protocol (IMAP)
Internet, internet (small "i")
Internet access providers (IAP)
Internet backbone
Internet host
Internet Protocol (IP)
Internet Protocol version 4 (IPv4)
Internet Protocol version 6 (IPv6)
Internet service provider (ISP)
Internet2
Intranet
IP address
IP tunneling
IP wrapper
Leased line
Linear hyperlink structure

Local area network (LAN)
Mailing list
Markup tags (tags)
Mesh routing
Metalanguage
Mobile commerce (m-commerce)
Multipurpose Internet Mail Extensions (MIME)
Net bandwidth
Network access points (NAPs)
Network access provider
Network Address Translation (NAT) device
Network Control Protocol (NCP)
Network specification
Newsgroup
Octet
Ontology
Open architecture
Opening tag
Optical fiber
Packet
Packet-switched
Personal area network (PAN)
Piconet
Plain old telephone service (POTS)
Post Office Protocol (POP)
Private IP address
Private network
Proprietary architecture
Protocol
Public network
Repeater
Resource description framework (RDF)
Roaming
Router
Router computer (routing computer)
Routing algorithm
Routing table
Scaling problem
Semantic Web
Short message service (SMS)
Simple Mail Transfer Protocol (SMTP)
Site map
Software agents
Spam
Sponsored top-level domains (STLD)
Standard Generalized Markup Language (SGML)
Start page
Style sheet
Subnetting
Symmetric connection
T1
T3
TCP/IP
Text markup language
Third-generation (3G) mobile phones
Top-level domain (TLD)
Transceiver
Transmission Control Protocol (TCP)
Ultra Wideband (UWB)
Uniform Resource Locator (URL)
Unsolicited commercial e-mail (UCE)
Upload bandwidth
Upstream bandwidth
Usenet (User's News Network)
Virtual private network (VPN)
Voice-grade lines
Web
Web browser
Web browser software
Web client computer
Web client software
Web server
Web server software
Wi-Fi (wireless Ethernet, 802.11b, 802.11a, 802.11g, 802.11n)
Wide area network (WAN)
Wireless access point (WAP)
World Wide Web (Web)
World Wide Web Consortium (W3C)
XML parser
XML vocabulary

Review Questions

RQ1. In one or two paragraphs, explain the difference between a network access provider and an Internet service provider.

RQ2. Describe in two paragraphs the origins of HTML. Explain how markup tags work in HTML, and describe the role of at least one person involved with HTML's development.

RQ3. In about 200 words, compare the POP e-mail protocol to the IMAP e-mail protocol. Describe situations in which you would prefer to use one protocol over the other and explain the reasons for your preference.

RQ4. In about 400 words, describe the similarities and differences between XML and HTML. Provide examples of at least two situations in which you would use XML and two situations in which you would use HTML.

RQ5. In about 200 words, outline the issues that a user might encounter when using a Web browser on a smart phone to view a Web page. Explain what a Web designer might do to address those issues.

RQ6. In about 100 words, explain the differences between a private network and a virtual private network.

Exercises

E1. You are the assistant to Julie Davidson, the sales manager of Old Reliable Life Insurance Company. Julie is interested in equipping her sales force with the technology they need to sell Old Reliable's insurance products. Most of her salespeople visit customers in their homes or offices. Today, the salespeople carry a notebook computer to present value projections and cash flow summaries for various policies. These types of presentations can run to several pages, each full of numbers and charts (when showing these projections and summaries to customers on a notebook computer, a salesperson can flip through the presentation a page at a time). Many of them also carry a smart phone to stay in touch with customers and to keep track of their appointments and contacts. Julie would like to ensure that salespeople have access to the home office server computers while they are making their sales presentations to customers. This access will let salespeople download the latest product information and obtain online assistance from office staff and in-house experts when the salespeople get a question from a customer that they are not able to answer. A correct and quick answer to a customer's question can often help close a difficult sale. Julie asks you to investigate various options for giving salespeople wireless remote access to the home office server computers. She wants you to consider options that use the sales force members' notebook computers or that use their smart phones. Prepare a report for Julie in which you discuss the advantages and disadvantages of using notebook computers and smart phones to access the home office servers. Then, briefly review at least three options for connecting the notebook computers (the smart phones are connected through a corporate wireless phone plan that provides unlimited data transfers each month), writing no more than two paragraphs for each option. Then choose the best option and write a one-page evaluation of your choice's strengths and weaknesses. Use the Online Companion links and your favorite Web search engines to do your research.

E2. In 2003, ICANN and the major domain name registries began offering a five-day grace period for new domain registrations. The idea was to give registrants time to correct typographical errors and misspellings in the names they registered. If a registrant found an error in that five-day period, they could cancel their registration and, presumably, re-register a corrected domain name. This policy led to a problem called "domain tasting" that required considerable effort and cooperation to resolve nearly six years after the policy was implemented. Using your library or your favorite search engine, learn more about domain tasting. Prepare a report of about 300 words that defines domain tasting, outlines its negative effects on Web users, and describes how the problem of domain tasting was resolved.

E3. Bridgewater Engineering Company (BECO), a privately held machine shop, makes industrial-quality, heavy-duty machinery for assembly lines in other factories. It sells its presses, grinders, and milling equipment using a few inside salespeople and telephones. This traditional approach worked well during the company's start-up years in the early 1990s, but BECO is getting a lot of competition from abroad. Because you worked for the company during the summers of your college years, BECO's president, Tom Dalton, knows you and realizes that you are Web savvy. He wants to form close relationships with the steel companies and small-parts manufacturers that are BECO's suppliers so that he can tap into their ordering systems and request supplies when he needs them. Tom wants you to investigate how he can use the Internet to set up such electronic relationships. Use the Web and the links in the Online Companion to locate information about extranets and VPNs. Write a report that briefly describes how companies use extranets to link their systems with those of their suppliers, then write an evaluation of at least two companies (using information you have gathered in your Web searches) that could help develop an extranet that would work for Tom. Close the report with an overview of how BECO could use VPN technologies in this type of extranet. The three parts of your report should total about 500 words.

E4. Frieda Bannister is the IT manager for the state of Iowa's Department of Transportation (DOT). She is interested in finding ways to reduce the costs of operating the DOT's vehicle repair facilities. These facilities purchase replacement parts and repair supplies for all of the state's cars, trucks, construction machinery, and road maintenance equipment. Frieda has read about XML and thinks that it might help the DOT send orders to its many suppliers throughout the country more efficiently. Use the Online Companion links, the Web, and your library to conduct research on the use of XML in state, local, and federal government operations. Provide Frieda with a report of about 500 words that includes sections that discuss what XML is and explain why XML shows promise for the ordering application Frieda envisions. Your report should also identify other DOT business processes or activities that might benefit from using XML. The report should also include a summary of the main disadvantages of using XML today for integrating business transactions. End the report with a brief statement regarding how the W3C Semantic Web project results might help the DOT operate more efficiently in the future.

E5. As you learned in this chapter, XML allows users to define their own markup tags. You also learned that this flexibility can lead to problems when IT professionals who have developed tag sets for their own organizations are asked to share information with other organizations that are using other tag sets. One way organizations can avoid this problem is to agree to follow common standards. A common standard for financial information is XBRL.

Accountants and financial analysts around the world have agreed to use XBRL to format financial statements and other reports. In about 300 words, outline the advantages that companies and financial analysts can obtain by using the XBRL standard. You can research this subject in your school library or online using your favorite search engine and the links provided for this exercise in the Online Companion.

Cases

C1. Covad

In 1996, three enterprising executives decided to leave their jobs at Intel and form a company that would take advantage of an opportunity provided by the recently enacted Telecommunications Act of 1996. The law eliminated the monopoly that local telephone companies had held and allowed other companies to offer telecommunications services to businesses and individuals in what had been the local telephone companies' protected service areas. Because the goal of the company was to offer converged voice and data services, the founders named the company Covad. During its first two years, Covad became a solid regional company in the San Francisco Bay and Silicon Valley areas that sold Internet access to businesses and ISPs. Its ISP customers provided DSL access to smaller businesses and residential customers. But the Internet boom was in full swing, and in 1998, Covad hired U.S. West Senior Vice President Robert Knowling to take the company to the next level. Over the next two years, Covad raised more than $2 billion from stock and bond offerings and expanded into 98 metropolitan areas throughout the country. By the end of 1999, it had more than 200,000 customers, including AOL, MCI, and some of the fastest-growing regional ISPs in the country. It was following the lead of its main competitor, NorthPoint Communications (featured in this chapter's Learning from Failures feature), and pursuing a strategy that included rapid expansion using external funds.

In 2000, Covad's largest customers, the ISPs that sold Internet access to smaller companies and residential users, stopped paying their Covad bills because their customers were disappearing. The Internet bubble had burst. Covad had expanded too fast and was in serious trouble. It had put all of its investors' money into equipment and infrastructure during its rapid growth and had no cash reserves to take it through a period of slower growth. In 2001, the company brought in a new manager, Charlie Hoffman, to take the company through a Chapter 11 bankruptcy reorganization. Covad's bondholders received 19 cents on each dollar after the reorganization. This gave the company a much lower debt payment load and allowed it to focus on rebuilding its business. Hoffman changed the basic strategy of the company by decreasing its emphasis on sales to ISPs who would resell Internet DSL access to small businesses and residential customers. Instead, Covad began selling these access services directly to those customers. Covad's sales continued to increase and, in 2008, the company was acquired by Platinum Equity for about $300 million.

Although the company's original plans were to sell both voice and data services, Covad grew rapidly selling only data services. In 2004, Covad began selling a service (called voice-over-IP, or VoIP) that allows organizations to transmit telephone traffic over its data lines. Today, the company continues to sell data and voice services (using VoIP), but it has gained many small and mid-sized business customers in recent years by bundling phone service with Internet access in an integrated package.

In the direct market for Internet access and VoIP services, Covad faces serious competition from cable companies, who have offered Internet access for many years and who are now also offering VoIP services. Covad's Internet access services also face competition from independent DSL ISPs (including many of Covad's former customers) and from satellite and fixed-point wireless access providers.

Required:

1. Use the links in the Online Companion for this chapter, your favorite search engine, and resources in your library to learn more about Covad and identify some of its current competitors. Choose two of the competitors you have identified and, in about 400 words, present a comparison of their VoIP service offerings with those of Covad.
2. Use your favorite search engine and resources in your library to learn more about Covad's wireless Internet access business and its current competitors in that market. Choose two of the competitors you have identified and, in about 400 words, present a comparison of their business wireless Internet access offerings with those of Covad.

Note: Your instructor might assign you to a group to complete this case, and might ask you to prepare a formal presentation of your results to your class.

C2. Portable Fun Instruments

Yash Gupta is the founder and president of Portable Fun Instruments (PFI), a company that has had great success in the handheld game market. Its first products were dedicated handheld devices that each offered a specific game, such as backgammon, checkers, or chess. As the power of microprocessors for handheld devices grew, and the size and cost of those microprocessors shrank, PFI was able to build better and more complex games into its devices.

Today, PFI offers a wide variety of dedicated handheld devices on which users can play card games, adventure games, and sports simulations, and solve various kinds of puzzles. Most of the elements in the game displays are graphics, not words. This helps PFI sell the devices in many different markets around the world without having to build separate interfaces for each language. PFI's game devices have retail prices that range between $20 and $40, but the retailers and distributors buy them from PFI for prices that range between $4 and $18.

PFI is profitable because Yash has worked hard to keep development and production costs low. Most of the programming is done in Bangalore, India, and the devices are built in production facilities located in Xixiang, China, and Penang, Malaysia. Although Yash has been successful in controlling production costs, he worries about continuing to operate the company with a long-term strategy that requires PFI to build a new physical device for each sale. The large retail chains that have become PFI's main customers are always asking for discounts and reduced prices on new orders, and production costs are creeping upward even though the facilities are located in some of the lowest-cost areas in the world.

Yash wants to explore the potential PFI has for moving its games to other platforms. PFI has translated some of its games to run on smart phones, but the results have been disappointing. Until recently, most smart phone users have been businesspeople who use their smart phones for e-mail, appointments, address books, travel expenses, and other data-management functions. These users are not avid game players, and sales of PFI's games for these platforms have not been strong.

Some of PFI's marketing team members have been telling Yash about the success of Apple's iPhone and the online store for software that runs on that phone (called Applications for iPhone). Apple shares the revenue earned from software sales on its site with the developers of that software. Other team members have mentioned Japan's DoCoMo, which has offered a variety of entertainment products that users download from the Internet to use on their mobile phones. DoCoMo also shares revenue with software providers.

Yash has hired you as a consultant to investigate the Apple iPhone, DoCoMo, and any other delivery systems (such as Google's Android or the Palm Pre) for selling online access to PFI's games to smart phone users.

Required:

1. Use the links in the Online Companion for this case, your favorite search engine, and resources in your library to learn more about Android, Apple, DoCoMo, Palm, and similar content delivery systems for smart phones. Prepare a 400-word executive summary for Yash that describes each delivery system you identify and outlines the current or likely near-term availability of each system for content providers such as PFI.
2. Prepare a report for Yash and the PFI executive team in which you outline and analyze the strengths and weaknesses of each content delivery system you have identified. Your report should conclude with a specific recommendation regarding the suitability of each content delivery system for PFI's games. This report should be about 500 words in length.

Note: Your instructor might assign you to a group to complete this case, and might ask you to prepare a formal presentation of your results to your class.

For Further Study and Research

Alschuler, L. 2001. "Getting the Tags In: Vendors Grapple with XML-Authoring, Editing and Cleanup," *Seybold Report on Internet Publishing,* 5(6), February, 5–10.

Angwin, J. 2002. "ICANN Leader Seeks Big Changes in How Internet Is Governed," *The Wall Street Journal,* February 26, B6.

Arthur, C. 2009. "China's Internet Users Surpass U.S. Population," *The Guardian,* July 16. (http://www.guardian.co.uk/technology/2009/jul/16/china-internet-more-users-us-population)

Bellman, E. 2009. "Rural India Snaps Up Mobile Phones," *The Wall Street Journal,* February 9, B1, B5.

Belson, K. 2007. "Unlike U.S., Japanese Push Fiber Over Profit," *The New York Times,* October 3. (http://www.nytimes.com/2007/10/03/business/worldbusiness/03broadband.html)

Bergman, M. 2001. *The Deep Web: Surfacing Hidden Value.* Sioux Falls, SD: BrightPlanet.com. (http://brightplanet.com/technology/deepweb.asp)

Boles, C. 2007. "States Step In to Close Broadband Gap," *The Wall Street Journal,* November 1, B3.

Bonner, P. 2002. "The Semantic Web," *PC Magazine,* 21(13), July, IP01–IP02.

Bonson, E., V. Cortijo, and T. Escobar. 2009. "Toward the Global Adoption of XBRL Using International Financial Reporting Standards (IFRS)," *International Journal of Accounting Information Systems,* 10(1), March, 46–60.

Bosak, J. and T. Bray. 1999. "How XML Will Fix the Web: Tags Categorizing Facts, Not Formats, Speed Up Transactions," *Scientific American,* 280(5), May, 89.

Brewin, B. 2004. "Michigan City Turns on Citywide Wi-Fi," *Computerworld,* July 30. (http://www.computerworld.com/mobiletopics/mobile/wifi/story/0,10801,94928,00.html)

Bruno, A. 2009. "Call of the iPhone," *Billboard,* April 4, 24–28.

Campbell, T. 1998. "The First E-Mail," *Pretext Magazine,* March. (http://www.pretext.com/mar98/features/story2.htm)

Chao, L., J. Ye, and Y. Kane. 2009. "Apple, Facing Competition, Readies iPhone for Launch in Giant China Market," *The Wall Street Journal,* August 27, B1–B2.

Chester, J. 2006. "The End of the Internet?" *The Nation,* February 1. (http://www.thenation.com/doc/20060213/chester)

Computergram Weekly. 2003. "Cisco Sees Flat Sales But Chambers More Cheerful," May 7, 7–8.

Cramer, J. 2009. "The Biggest Thing Since E-mail: Why the Smart Phone Market Is Only Just Beginning to Take Off," *New York,* August 24, 36–38.

Davis, K. and E. Burt. 2001. "Mad as Hell about DSL," *Kiplinger's Personal Finance Magazine,* 55(7), July 2001, 84–85.

Dipert, B. 2009. "802.11n: Complicated and About to Become Even Messier," *EDN,* May 28. (http://www.edn.com/article/CA6659414.html)

Dornan, A. 2003. "Unwiring the Last Mile," *Network Magazine*, 18(1), January, 34–37.

Duffy, J. 2003. "RBOCs and Cable Wage Turf War," *Network World*, August 18, 11–14.

Dyck, T. 2002. "Going Native: XML Databases," *PC Magazine,* 21(12), June 30, 136–139.

The Economist. 2002. "ICANNOT," March 2, 59.

The Economist, 2008. "India: 3G at Last," *The Economist Intelligence Unit Country Monitor,* 16(28), July 28, 1.

EContent. 2009. "XML for the Masses," 32(3), April, 45.

Einhorn, B. 2009. "Will China Pick Up the oPhone?" *BusinessWeek,* September 7, 20.

Ely, A. 2008. "Where in the World is IPv6?" *InformationWeek,* December 22, 43–44.

Fensel, D., J. Hendler, H. Lieberman, and W. Wahlster. 2002. *Spinning the Semantic Web: Bringing the World Wide Web to Its Full Potential.* Cambridge, MA: MIT Press.

Fitchard, K. 2004. "Covad's Quiet Authority," *Telephony,* 245(12), June 7, 34–39.

Garbellotto, G. 2009. "XBRL Implementation Strategies: The Built-in Approach," *Strategic Finance,* 91(2), August, 56–57.

Goldfarb, C. 1981. "A Generalized Approach to Document Markup," *ACM Sigplan Notices,* (16)6, June, 68–73.

Hannon, N. and M. Willis. 2005. "Combating Everyday Data Problems with XBRL," *Strategic Finance,* 87(1), July, 57–59.

Hannon, N. and M. Willis. 2005. "Combating Everyday Data Problems with XBRL, Part 2," *Strategic Finance,* 87(2), August, 59–61.

Hawn, C. 2001. "Management By Stock Market: NorthPoint Rode the Web Wave," *Forbes,* 167(10), April 30, 52–53.

Henschen, D. 2005. "XBRL Offers a Faster Route to Intelligence," *Intelligent Enterprise,* 8(8), August, 12.

Horrigan, J. 2009. *Wireless Internet Use.* Washington, DC: Pew Internet & American Life Project. (http://pewinternet.org/Reports/2009/12-Wireless-Internet-Use.aspx)

Horrigan, J. 2009. *Home Broadband Adoption 2009.* Washington, DC: Pew Internet & American Life Project. (http://pewinternet.org/Reports/2009/10-Home-Broadband-Adoption-2009.aspx)

International Telecommunications Union (ITU). 2009. *Measuring the Information Society - The ICT Development Index, 2009 Edition.* Geneva: ITU.

Kim, H., W. Kim, and M. Lee. 2009. "Semantic Web Constraint Language and its Application to an Intelligent Shopping Agent," *Decision Support Systems,* 46(4), March, 882–894.

Kim, W. 2009. "Mobile WiMAX: The Leader of the Mobile Internet Era," *IEEE Communications Magazine,* 47(6), June, 10–12.

Kisiel, R. 2009. "Dealership Web sites shrink to fit on phones," *Automotive News,* March 16, 30.

Kristof, N. 2005. "When Pigs Wi-Fi," *The New York Times,* August 7, 13.

LaBarba, L. 2001. "DSL Pains Reach End Users," *Telephony,* 240(15), April 9, 14–15.

Lawson, S., K. Miyake, and J. Evers. 2002. "IPv6 Enters the Real World," *InfoWorld,* 24(7), February 18, 35–36.

Lawton, C. 2009. "Making the Connection," *The Wall Street Journal,* April 20, R4.

Lawton, C. and S. Silver. 2009. "Smart Phones are Edging Out Other Gadgets," *The Wall Street Journal,* March 24, D1–D3.

Lee, M. 2008. "HTML 5 Comes to Fruition," *InformationWeek,* March 31, 48–49.

Liebman, L. 2001. "XML's Tower Of Babel," *InternetWeek,* April 30, 25–26.

Lowry, T. 2004. "Satellite's Hot Pursuit of Cable," *Business Week,* May 24, 46.

Luk, L. and J. Scheck. 2009. "Dell Developing Phones for China," *The Wall Street Journal,* August 18, B4.

Malnig, A. 2005. "XBRL: Deep Drilling for Financials," *Seybold Report: Analyzing Publishing Technologies,* 5(4), May 18, 11–14.

Marriot, M. 2006. "Hey Neighbor, Stop Piggybacking on My Wireless," *The New York Times,* March 5. (http://www.nytimes.com/2006/03/05/technology/05wireless.html)

Marsan, C. 2004. "It's a New Domain-Name Game," *Network World,* March 1, 1, 14.

McCracken, H. 2009. "Smart Phone OS Smackdown," *PC World,* 27(2), February, 54–58.

Nelson, T. 1987. *Literary Machines.* Swarthmore, PA: Nelson.

Nielsen, J. 2003. "Mobile Devices: One Generation From Useful," *Alertbox,* August 18. (http://www.useit.com/alertbox/20030818.html)

Nielsen, J. 2009. "Mobile Usability," *Alertbox,* July 20. (http://www.useit.com/alertbox/mobile-usability.html)

Nolle, T. 2002. "Why Is Cisco Making Money?" *Network World,* 19(22), June 3, 51.

O'Connor, R. 2000. "Under Construction: Two Research Groups Work to Build a Better Internet," *Interactive Week,* 7(46), November 13, 44–48.

Olivia, R. 2001. "The Promise of XML," *Marketing Management,* 10(1), Spring, 46–49.

Panko, R. 2008. *Business Data Networks and Telecommunications*. Seventh Edition. Upper Saddle River, NJ: Prentice Hall.

Pimm, F. 2001. "Boeing Shows How XML Can Help Business," *Computerworld,* 35(11), March 12, 28–29.

Poppcuviu, C. 2009. "Implementing IPv6," *Broadcast Engineering,* 51(7), July, 38–40.

Pringle, D. 2005. "Wi-Fi Woes: Wireless Networks Are Great—If You Can Figure Out How to Set Them Up," *The Wall Street Journal,* July 18, R11.

Rendleman, J. 2002. "Cisco Positioned to Profit From Changing Market," *InformationWeek,* May 13, 32.

Rodenbaugh, M. 2009. "Abusive Domain Registrations: ICANN Policy Developments (or Lack Thereof?), *Computer & Internet Lawyer,* 26(5), May, 17–22.

Rupley, S. 2005. "I'm Drowning in Cables," *PC Magazine,* 24(14), August 23, 100.

Saint-Andre, P. 2009. "XMPP: Lessons Learned from Ten Years of XML Messaging," *IEEE Communications Magazine,* 47(4), April, 92–96.

Shadbolt, N., T. Berners-Lee, and W. Hall. 2006. "The Semantic Web Revisited," *IEEE Intelligent Systems,* 21(3), 96–101.

Simon, B. 2003. "Some Bet the Future of Broadband Belongs to Regional Bells, Not Cable," *The New York Times,* July 21. (http://www.nytimes.com/2003/07/21/technology/21BROA.html)

Strategic Finance. 2009. "XBRL Reporting Is Now Mandatory," 90(7), January, 61.

Tie, R. 2005. "XBRL: It's Unstoppable: Interview With Charles Hoffman," *Journal of Accountancy,* August, 32–35.

Thurm, S. 2002. "Cisco Profit Exceeds Expectations," *The Wall Street Journal,* May 8, A3.

Vogelstein, F. 2004. "The Cisco Kid Rides Again," *Fortune,* 150(2), July 26, 132–137.

Weber, T. 2002. "Wanted: A Peace Envoy to End Net's Bickering Over Address System," *The Wall Street Journal,* March 25, B1.

Weinberg, N. 2008. "802.11n: It's MIMO Time-O," *Network World,* January 14, 36.

Weinberger, D. 2009. "The Dream of the Semantic Web," *KM World,* 18(3), March, 1–3.

White, C. 2002. *Data Communications and Computer Networks: A Business User's Approach.* 2nd edition. Boston: Course Technology.

Witte, G. 2003. "Bringing Broadband Over the Mountain: Roadstar Puts Wireless Technology to the Test," *The Washington Post,* September 15, E1.

Wylie, I. 2005. "Bluetooth Killers," *Fast Company,* July, 30.

Zhang, M. and R. Wolff. 2004. "Crossing the Digital Divide: Cost-Effective Broadband Wireless Access for Rural and Remote Areas," *IEEE Communications Magazine,* 42(2), February, 99–105.

PART 2

BUSINESS STRATEGIES FOR ELECTRONIC COMMERCE

CHAPTER 3

SELLING ON THE WEB: REVENUE MODELS AND BUILDING A WEB PRESENCE

LEARNING OBJECTIVES

In this chapter, you will learn about:

- Revenue models
- How some companies move from one revenue model to another to achieve success
- Revenue strategy issues that companies face when selling on the Web
- Creating an effective business presence on the Web
- Web site usability
- Communicating effectively with customers on the Web

INTRODUCTION

In the 1980s, **Progressive** was a relatively small auto insurance company that specialized in writing policies for people who could not qualify for regular policies with other insurers. Progressive was able to charge higher premiums for these policies, which the insurance industry calls substandard policies. Often, other insurers who could not write standard polices for customers would refer those customers to Progressive. The combination of high premiums and the lower cost of a smaller sales force allowed

Progressive to earn good profits on the substandard business. Eventually, other insurers noticed Progressive's success and began to offer their own substandard policies.

To respond to the increased competition, Progressive improved its claim service and was one of the first insurance companies to offer 24/7 service every day of the year. Through the 1990s, Progressive developed a full line of auto insurance products for all types of drivers and worked hard to make sure that it offered the lowest prices in every market.

Like most other companies selling auto insurance, Progressive offers policy quotes and service on its Web site. Progressive's marketing mentions the quality of its service, but it always emphasizes its low prices. In 2002, Progressive began comparing its prices to those of other insurers on its Web site. Progressive's Web site offers quotes that include its price along with prices of similar policies offered by its competitors, even when one or more of the competitors offers a lower price.

People shopping for auto insurance often visit the Web sites of various insurers. By offering to provide quotes from other companies in addition to its own price, Progressive hopes to convince shoppers to include its site in their list of Web sites to visit. By offering several quotes, Progressive can save shoppers time. The practice of displaying competitors' quotes also creates an impression of openness and honesty. Progressive believes that people prefer to buy insurance from honest companies who offer the best prices. In recent years, Progressive has used television advertising that emphasizes the price comparison feature of its Web site. The comparison shopping feature on its Web site is an important element in Progressive's overall marketing efforts to convince potential customers that the company is both honest and able to offer the lowest prices on auto insurance.

REVENUE MODELS

As you learned in Chapter 1, a useful way to think about electronic commerce implementations is to consider how they can generate revenue. Not all electronic commerce initiatives have the goal of providing revenue; some are undertaken to reduce costs or improve customer service. You will learn about those types of initiatives in Chapter 5. In this chapter, you will learn about various models that online businesses currently use to generate revenue, including Web catalog, digital content, advertising-supported, advertising-subscription mixed, and fee-based models. These approaches can work for both business-to-consumer (B2C) and business-to-business (B2B) electronic commerce. Many companies create one Web site to handle both B2C and B2B sales. Even when companies create separate sites (or separate pages within one site), they often use the same revenue model for both types of sales.

Web Catalog Revenue Models

Many companies sell goods and services on the Web using an adaptation of a mail-order catalog revenue model that is more than 100 years old. In 1872, a traveling salesman named Aaron Montgomery Ward started selling dry goods to farmers through a one-page list. Richard Sears and Alvah Roebuck began mailing catalogs to farmers and small-town residents in 1895. Both Montgomery Ward (which closed in 2001) and Sears, Roebuck & Company grew to become dominant retailers in the United States by the 1950s, with retail stores serving urban markets in addition to the catalog business that served their rural and small-town markets.

In this traditional catalog-based retail revenue model, the seller establishes a brand image, and then uses the strength of that image to sell through printed information mailed to prospective buyers. Buyers place orders by mail or by calling the seller's toll-free telephone number. This revenue model, which is often called the **mail-order** or **catalog model**, has proven to be successful for a wide variety of consumer items, including apparel, computers, electronics, housewares, and gifts.

Companies can take this catalog model online by replacing or supplementing their print catalogs with information on their Web sites. When the catalog model is expanded this way, it is often called the **Web catalog revenue model**. Customers can place orders through the Web site or by telephone. This flexibility is important because many consumers are still reluctant to buy on the Web. In the first few years of consumer electronic commerce, most shoppers used the Web to obtain information about products and compare prices and features, but then made their purchases by telephone. These shoppers found early Web sites hard to use and were often afraid to send their credit card numbers over the Internet. Although these fears are less prevalent today, most companies that use the Web catalog revenue model successfully do give customers a way to complete the payment part of the transaction by telephone or by mail.

Many of the most successful Web catalog sales businesses are firms that were already operating in the mail-order business and simply expanded their operations to the Web. Other companies that use the Web catalog revenue model adopted it after realizing that the products they sold in their physical stores could also be sold on the Web. This additional sales outlet did not require them to build additional stores, yet provided access to customers throughout the world. Types of businesses using the Web catalog revenue model include sellers of computers and consumer electronics; books, music, and videos; luxury goods; clothing; flowers and gifts; and general discount merchandise. In the next sections, you will learn how these types of businesses have applied the Web catalog revenue model to their operations.

Computers and Consumer Electronics

The leading computer manufacturers, including **Apple**, **Dell**, **Gateway**, **Hewlett-Packard**, and **Sun Microsystems**, have had great success selling on the Web. All of these companies sell a full range of products—from small notebook computers to large server computers—to individuals, businesses, and other organizations through their Web sites.

Dell has been a leader in allowing customers to specify exactly the configuration of computers they order on the Web. Dell created value by designing its entire business around offering this high degree of configuration flexibility to its customers. Other personal computer manufacturers that sell directly to customers on the Web have followed Dell's lead by offering visitors different ways to access product information. These sites often offer links to specific products and pages designed for specific categories of customers, such as home, small business, education, or government users.

Retailers of consumer electronics products have also been active in undertaking electronic commerce using the Web catalog revenue model. Companies such as **Crutchfield** expanded their successful mail-order catalog operations to include Web sites. Other companies that had strong retail presences in their physical stores, such as **Best Buy**, **J&R Music World**, and **Radio Shack**, also created Web sites to sell the same products that they had been selling in their stores.

Having more than one way to reach customers is often a good idea for companies. Each different pathway to customers is called a **marketing channel**. Companies find that having several marketing channels lets them reach more customers at less cost. For example, it is expensive to stock a large number of different items in a physical store, so a company such as Best Buy will stock the most popular items in its stores but will sell a wider variety of items (including those that are not in high demand at every one of its retail locations) on its

Web site. Customers who want to have physical contact with a product (putting fingers on a laptop computer's keyboard, for example) before buying can visit the retail location. A customer who wants a high-end and expensive home theater system can find it on the Web site. By having two marketing channels (retail store and Web site), Best Buy reaches more customers and offers more products than it could using either channel alone.

Some retailers combine the benefits of these two marketing channels by offering in-store online ordering. This allows customers to examine a product in the store, and then specify exactly the features they want by placing an order on the retailer's Web site from the store. For example, customers wanting a computer similar to one on display in the retail store could examine the product, talk with a salesperson about the product, then enter the exact specifications of the computer they want on the in-store computer, which is logged in to the retailer's Web site. The computer is custom built for that customer and shipped either to the store or to the customer's home or office.

Similarly, a retailer that mails out print catalogs might include a product's general description and photo in the catalog, but refer customers to the retailer's Web site for detailed specifications or more information about the product. Mailed catalogs (or newspaper advertising inserts) continue to be an effective marketing tool because they inform customers of products they might not otherwise know about. The catalog arrives in the mail (or the newspaper insert arrives with the newspaper) to inform them. A Web site only delivers the marketing message if the customer visits the Web site.

Using multiple marketing channels to reach the same set of customers can be an effective strategy for retailers. Retailers can use a variety of possible channels, many of which you will learn about later in this book. Figure 3-1 shows two examples of how retailers might combine two marketing channels.

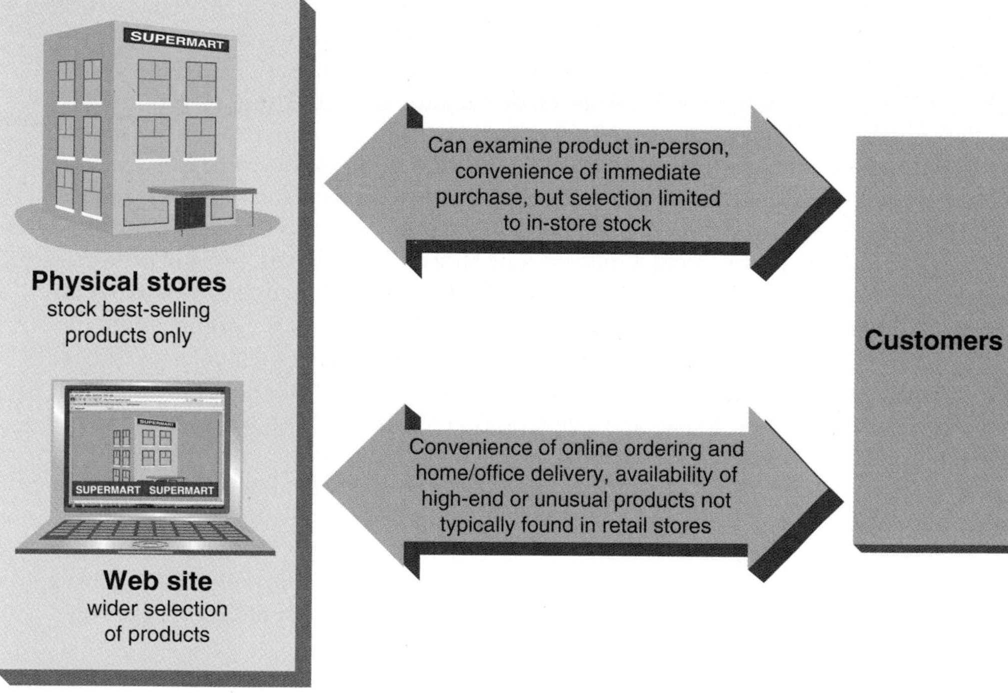
Retailer with physical stores and Web site
SUPERMART
Physical stores
stock best-selling products only
SUPERMART SUPERMART
Web site
wider selection of products
Can examine product in-person, convenience of immediate purchase, but selection limited to in-store stock
Convenience of online ordering and home/office delivery, availability of high-end or unusual products not typically found in retail stores
Customers

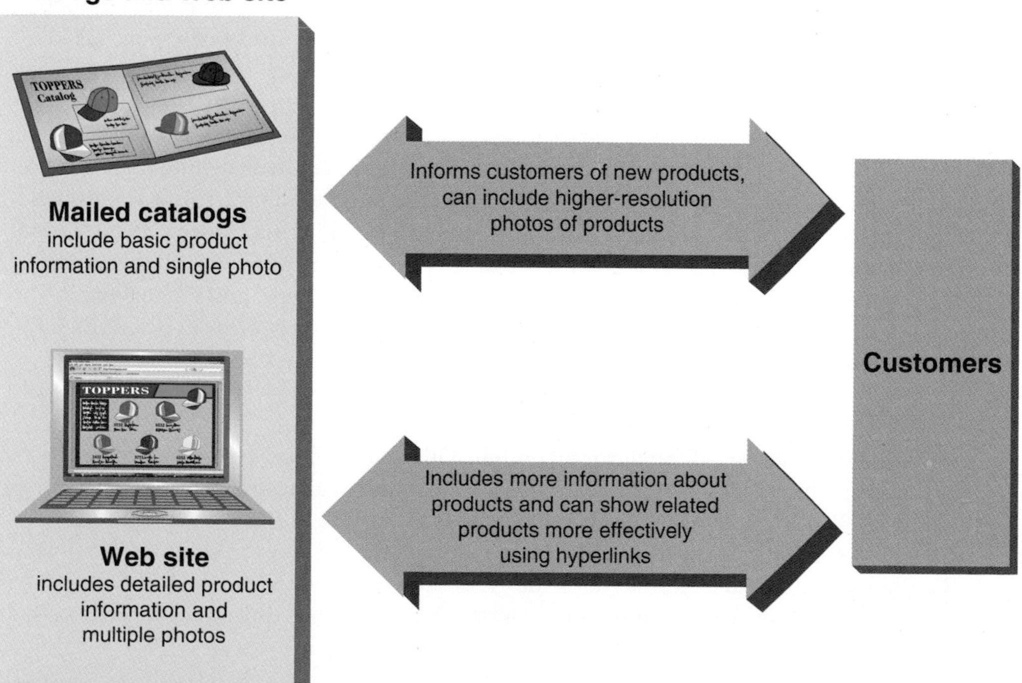
Retailer with mailed catalogs and Web site
TOPPERS Catalog
Mailed catalogs
include basic product information and single photo
TOPPERS
Web site
includes detailed product information and multiple photos
Informs customers of new products, can include higher-resolution photos of products
Includes more information about products and can show related products more effectively using hyperlinks
Customers

FIGURE 3-1 Combining marketing channels: Two retailer examples

Books, Music, and Videos

Retailers using the Web catalog revenue model to sell books, music, and videos have been among the most visible examples of electronic commerce. In 1994, a 29-year-old Wall Street financial analyst named Jeff Bezos became intrigued by the rapid growth of the Internet. Looking for a way to capitalize on this new marketing tool, he made a list of 20 products that he thought would sell well on the Internet. After some intense analysis, he determined that books were at the top of that list. Bezos had no experience in the book-selling business, but he realized that books were small-ticket commodity items and were easy and inexpensive to ship. He knew many customers would be willing to buy books without inspecting them in person and that books could be impulse purchase items if properly promoted. More than 4 million book titles are in print at any one time throughout the world; however, even the largest physical bookstore cannot stock more than 200,000 books. Bezos had identified a strategic opportunity for selling online. Fifteen years later, **Amazon.com**, the company Bezos formed to sell books on the Internet, has annual sales of more than $22 billion and more than 100 million customers. Amazon.com has evolved to become a general retailer that sells books, music, videos, consumer electronics, housewares, tools, and many other items.

The rapid growth of Amazon.com inspired many booksellers to undertake electronic commerce. A number of well-established companies that operated physical bookstores, such as **Barnes & Noble**, **Blackwell's**, **Books-A-Million**, **Borders**, and **Powell's Books**, all adopted the Web catalog revenue model in their online sales endeavors. In 2001, Borders closed its site and had Amazon.com handle its online business, but ended the strategic alliance after seven years and reopened its site in 2008.

In 1994, the same year that Jeff Bezos started his online bookstore, 24-year-old twin brothers Jason and Matthew Olim began an online music store they called **CDnow** that used the Web catalog revenue model. Other online retailers such as **CD Universe** followed CDnow's approach and also used the Web catalog revenue model. Despite many competitors, by 1997 CDnow had one-third of the online music business. After being purchased by German music conglomerate Bertelsmann AG, CDnow entered a strategic alliance to have its online store operated by Amazon.com.

The success of these online CD sellers forced traditional music retailers such as Camelot, Musicland, Sam Goody, and Tower Records, which had been selling music in their retail stores for decades, to create Web sites that could compete online. These traditional retailers struggled for years, gradually closing most or all of their retail stores, as they tried to compete against online CD retailers (and against online sellers of downloadable music, described later in this chapter). With their physical stores shuttered, and having gone through a series of buyouts and mergers, these traditional music retailers exist online today as the **f.y.e.** and **Tower Records** Web sites.

Luxury Goods

Some types of products are difficult to sell online. This is particularly true for expensive luxury goods and high-fashion clothing items that customers generally want to see in person or touch. The Web sites of couturiers **Vera Wang** and **Versace**, for example, were not constructed to generate revenue directly, but to provide information to shoppers who would visit the physical stores to examine items they had seen on the sites. Such sites tend to make heavy use of graphics and animation. **Evian**, the purveyor of premium-priced bottled water, created a Web site that presents information about its product and company in what it hopes is a visually stunning way. This presentation is intended to convey a feeling of exclusivity to those who choose to drink the water.

Clothing Retailers

A number of apparel sellers have adapted their catalog sales model to the Web, including **bebe, Gap, Lands' End, L.L. Bean, Talbots**, and **Wet Seal**. Unlike sellers in the high-fashion clothing category previously discussed, these Web stores display photos of casual and business clothing categorized by style and described with prices, sizes, colors, and tailoring details. Their intent is to have customers examine the clothing and place orders through the Web site. Lands' End pioneered the idea of online Web shopping assistance with its Lands' End Live feature in 1999. A Web customer with a question can initiate a text chat with a customer service representative or click a button on the Web page to have the representative call. In addition to answering questions, the representative can offer suggestions by pushing Web pages to the customer's browser.

Lands' End also has personal shopper and virtual model features on its site. The **personal shopper** is an intelligent agent program that learns the customer's preferences and makes suggestions. The **virtual model** is a graphic image built from customer measurements and descriptions on which customers can try clothes. About 15 percent of visitors to the site use the virtual model and, on average, dress the model 40 times during a visit. Lands' End has found that the dollar amount of orders placed by customers who use the virtual model is about 10 percent higher than other orders. The Canadian company that developed this Web site feature, **My Virtual Model**, has sold the technology to a number of other clothing retailers. The My Virtual Model Web site stores an individual's virtual model details and makes that information available through any other clothing retailer site that offers the service.

Other online general apparel retailers have added online chat, personal shopper, and virtual model features to their sites. Some of these sites include a feature that lets two shoppers browse the Web site together from different computers. Only one of the shoppers can purchase items, but either shopper can select items to view. The selected items appear in both Web browsers. Web sites can buy this technology from vendors such as **DecisionStep** (its product is called ShopTogether).

In the fast-changing clothing business, retailers have always had to deal with the problem of overstocks—products that did not sell as well as hoped. Many retailers use outlet stores to sell their overstocks. Lands' End found that its overstocks Web page worked so well that it has closed some of its physical outlet stores. An online overstocks store works well because it reaches more people than a physical store and it can be updated more frequently than a printed overstocks catalog. Overstocks and clearance sale pages have become a standard element of clothing retailers' Web sites.

In addition to general apparel retailers, a number of specialty retailers opened stores on the Web. For example, women's shoe retailers such as **Steve Madden** and **Nine West** use the Web catalog model to sell directly to consumers online.

One problem that the Web presents for clothing retailers of all types is that the color settings on computer monitors vary widely. It is difficult for customers to get an accurate idea of what the product's color will look like when it arrives. Most online clothing stores will send a fabric swatch on request. The swatch also gives the customer a sense of the fabric's texture—an added benefit not provided by catalogs. Most Web catalog retailers also have generous return policies that allow customers to return unused merchandise for any reason.

Flowers and Gifts

Gift retailers also use the Web catalog revenue model. The florist **1-800-Flowers** created an online extension to its highly successful telephone order business to compete with online-only florists such as **Proflowers.com**. Chocolatier **Godiva** offers business gift plans on its site. For gift shoppers who want a familiar brand name, shopping mall mainstays **Hickory Farms** and **Mrs. Fields Cookies** both have Web catalog sites. When **Harry and David**, famous for its trademarked "Fruit-of-the-Month" club, opened an informational Web site to promote its catalog business, they were surprised by the volume of sales leads that the site generated and quickly added online ordering features.

General Discounters

A number of companies began their first retail operations online. Some of these businesses, such as **Buy.com** and **Overstock.com**, operate as Web-based deep discounters. Borrowing a concept from the physical world's Wal-Marts and discount club stores, these discounters sell merchandise such as computer equipment, software, consumer electronics, books, and sports equipment at extremely low prices.

Traditional discount retailers, such as **Costco**, **Kmart**, **Target**, and **Wal-Mart**, were slow to implement online sales on their Web sites, which were originally used for general information distribution. They had huge investments in their physical stores, were making large amounts of sales in those stores, and did not really understand the world of online retailing. However, after some false starts and learning challenges, all of these major retailers now use the Web catalog revenue model in their successful online sales operations.

LEARNING FROM FAILURES

WALMART.COM

Wal-Mart is the world's largest retailer, with more than 7000 stores and annual sales exceeding $400 billion. Founded in 1962 by retailing legend Sam Walton, the company has won numerous awards for business innovation. However, Wal-Mart's move into online retailing was troubled, to say the least.

Wal-Mart launched its first Web site in July 1996. Like most company sites of that time, it contained some information about the company, but did not offer any products for sale. Wal-Mart did little to develop the Web site over the next three years, but it did add a Web store—just in time to participate in the disastrous 1999 holiday shopping season.

Wal-Mart was not the only Web retailer to have trouble in 1999. Many companies found that they were ill-prepared for the large number of customers who decided to try electronic commerce in that year's holiday season. Lost orders, unfilled orders, and shipments that failed to arrive until January 2000 were common for many Web retailers that year. Wal-Mart was noted as an industry leader in shipping and logistics management; however, the announcement on its Web site that it could not promise Christmas delivery for items ordered after December 14 was particularly embarrassing.

Continued

To make matters worse, Wal-Mart was in the middle of developing a new Web site that it had hoped to launch before the holiday season. The project, which industry analysts estimate cost more than $100 million, ran months late and did not operate until January 2000.

After eight months of operating the new Web site, Wal-Mart found itself with low levels of customer traffic (well below those of its major rivals J.C. Penney, Sears, Kmart, and Target) and high levels of criticism from Web site design experts who found the site slow, difficult to use, and lacking customer service features.

In October 2000, Wal-Mart closed the site completely for four weeks. Earlier in the year, it had created Walmart.com, a joint venture with Accel Partners to develop a new Web site, but the new site was not ready to launch until November. Industry analysts widely criticized Wal-Mart's decision to completely shut down its Web operations for such a long time period at the beginning of the holiday shopping season.

The new Web site is a vast improvement over the old site. It is much better organized and offers improved browsing and search functions. The new site offers about the same number of items as the old site did (about 500,000—several times more than what the physical stores carry); however, the new site has more offerings of consumer electronics, toys, photo services, and sporting goods, and fewer offerings of consumable products. Behind the scenes is a new distribution center that serves Walmart.com exclusively.

Wal-Mart's experience is a testament to how difficult it can be to get Web retailing right. Success eluded the largest retailer in the world for years. Wal-Mart is estimated to have spent more than $150 million on its various Web implementations over five years before it was able to present a truly usable site to its customers.

Digital Content Subscription Revenue Models

Firms that own written information (words or numbers) or rights to that information have embraced the Web as a highly efficient distribution mechanism. Most of these companies use a **digital content revenue model;** that is, they sell subscriptions for access to the information they own. Although many types of information are now sold by subscription online, most of these digital content providers specialize in legal, academic research, business, or technical material.

Legal Content

LexisNexis began as a legal research tool, and it has been available as an online product for years. Today, LexisNexis offers a variety of information services, including legal information, corporate information, government information, news, and resources for academic libraries. The original legal information product exists on the Web today as **Lexis.com** and provides full-text search of court cases, laws, patent databases, and tax regulations. In the past, law firms had to subscribe to and install expensive dedicated computer systems to obtain access to this information, but the Web has given LexisNexis customers much more flexibility in how they purchase information. Through the Lexis.com Web site, law firms can subscribe to several versions of the service, which are customized for different firm sizes and usage patterns. The Web site even offers a credit card charge option for infrequent users who do not want a subscription. LexisNexis has used the Web to improve the delivery and variety of its existing product line and has been able to devise new products that take advantage of the Web's features.

Academic Research Content

ProQuest, a Web site that sells digital copies of published documents, has its roots in two businesses: the former Bell and Howell learning materials business and University Microfilms International (UMI). These firms acquired reproduction rights to a variety of published and unpublished materials. For example, UMI had contracts with most North American universities to publish all doctoral dissertations and masters theses on demand. ProQuest offers digital versions of these documents for sale, along with a number of newspapers, journals, and other specialized academic publications. Many schools and libraries have subscriptions to ProQuest. **Ovid** and **EBSCO Information Services** also sell subscriptions to digital versions of journals to corporate and university libraries. These companies sell access to bibliographic databases and electronic journals to schools, companies, and libraries as well.

Business Content

Dow Jones, a business-focused publisher of newspapers such as *The Wall Street Journal* and *Barron's*, was one of the first publishers to create a Web site for selling subscriptions to digitized newspaper, magazine, and journal content. The Dow Jones Interactive site offered a customized digital clipping service that provided subscribers with a daily e-mail message of news on topics of interest to them. In 2002, Dow Jones launched an online content management and integration service called **Factiva**. Today, Factiva gives companies the ability to manage internal information and integrate it with external information to track company and industry news, perform analysis of acquisition candidates, and manage the company's risk in a dynamic business environment.

Technical Content

One of the first academic organizations to make the transition to electronic distribution on the Web was (not surprisingly) the Association for Computer Machinery (ACM). The **ACM Digital Library** offers subscriptions to electronic versions of its journals to its members and to library and institutional subscribers. Academic publishing has always been a difficult business in which to make a profit because the base of potential subscribers is so small. Even the most highly regarded academic journals often have fewer than 2000 subscribers. To break even, academic journals must often charge each subscriber hundreds or even thousands of dollars per year. Electronic publishing eliminates the high costs of paper, printing, and delivery, and makes dissemination of research results less expensive and more timely.

Advertising-Supported Revenue Models

The **advertising-supported revenue model** is the one used by broadcast network television in the United States. Broadcasters provide free programming to an audience along with advertising messages. The advertising revenue is sufficient to support the operations of the network and the creation or purchase of the programs. Web advertising grew from essentially zero in 1994 to $2 billion in 1998. However, Web advertising was flat or declining in the years 2000 to 2002. Since then, Web advertising has once again resumed its growth and, as you will learn in Chapter 4, is well established as an important component of the advertising mix for businesses of all types.

Online advertising has been challenged by two major problems. First, no consensus has emerged on how to measure and charge for site visitor views. Because Web sites can take multiple measurements, such as number of visitors, number of unique visitors, number of click-throughs, and can measure other attributes of visitor behavior, Web advertisers have struggled to develop a standard for advertising charges. In addition to the number of visitors or page views, stickiness is a critical element in creating a presence that attracts advertisers. The **stickiness** of a Web site is its ability to keep visitors at the site and attract repeat visitors. People spend more time at a **sticky** Web site and are thus exposed to more advertising.

The second problem is that very few Web sites have sufficient numbers of visitors to interest large advertisers. Although a few Web sites have succeeded by appealing to a large general audience that advertisers want to reach, most successful advertising on the Web is targeted at specific groups. The set of characteristics that marketers use to group visitors is called **demographic information**, which includes things such as address, age, gender, income level, type of job held, hobbies, and religion. It can be difficult to determine whether a given Web site is attracting a specific market segment unless that site collects demographic information from its visitors—information that visitors often are reluctant to provide because of privacy concerns.

One solution to this second problem has been found by an increasing number of specialized information Web sites. These sites are successful in using an advertising-supported revenue model because they draw a specialized audience that certain advertisers want to reach. These sites do not need to gather demographic information from their visitors because anyone drawn to the site will have the specific set of interests that makes them a prized target for certain advertisers. In most cases, advertisers will pay high enough rates to support the operation of the site and in some cases, the advertising revenue is large enough to make these sites quite profitable.

Two examples of successful advertising-supported sites that appeal to audiences with specific interests are **The Huffington Post** and the **Drudge Report**. Each of these Web sites appeals to people who are interested in politics (liberal and conservative, respectively). Advertisers that want to target an audience with a specific political interest are willing to pay rates that are high enough to make these sites profitable enterprises. Online news sites that focus their coverage on a particular town or metropolitan area can use the advertising-supported revenue model successfully. Companies that want to reach potential customers in that area would find such sites to be useful for targeted marketing, since the Web sites would draw visitors with a specific interest in the geographic area.

Similarly, **HowStuffWorks** is a Web site that explains, as the name suggests, how things work. Each set of Web pages in the site attracts visitors with highly focused interests. For example, a visitor looking for an explanation of how heating stoves work would be a good prospect for advertisers that sell heating stoves. HowStuffWorks does not need to obtain any specific information from its visitors; the fact that visitors are viewing the heating stoves information page is enough justification for charging heating stove companies a higher rate for ads on those pages. HowStuffWorks is an attractive online advertising option for a wide variety of companies because the site has pages on a large range of very specific products and processes.

These three strategies—general interest, specific interest, and collection of specific interests—for implementing an advertising-supported revenue model are summarized in Figure 3-2.

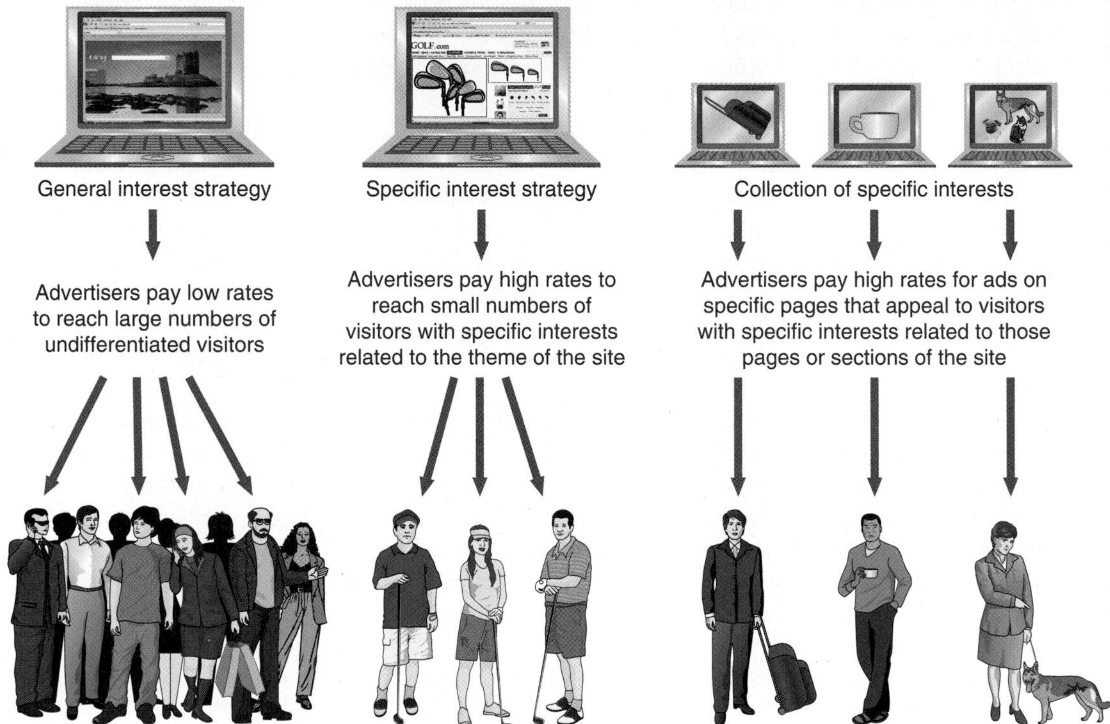

FIGURE 3-2 Three strategies for an advertising-supported revenue model

Web Portals

Some companies have been successful using the general interest strategy shown in Figure 3-2 by operating a Web portal. A **portal** or **Web portal** is a site that people use as a launching point to enter the Web (the word "portal" means "doorway"). A portal almost always includes a Web directory or search engine, but it also includes other features that help visitors find what they are looking for on the Web and thus make the Web more useful. Most portals include features such as shopping directories, white pages and yellow pages searchable databases, free e-mail, chat rooms, file storage services, games, and personal and group calendar tools.

One of the leading Web portal sites is Yahoo!, which was one of the first Web directories. A **Web directory** is a listing of hyperlinks to Web pages. Because the Yahoo! portal's search engine presents visitors' search results on separate pages, it can include advertising on each results page that is triggered by the terms in the search. For example, when the Yahoo! search engine detects that a visitor has searched on the term *new car deals*, it can place a Ford ad at the top of the search results page. Ford is willing to pay more for this ad because it is directed only at visitors who have expressed interest in new cars.

Besides Yahoo!, portal sites that use the general interest strategy today are AOL, Excite, Google, and Bing. Smaller general interest sites, such as the Web directory refdesk.com, have had more difficulty attracting advertisers than the larger sites.

Not all portals use a general interest strategy, however. Some portals are designed to help visitors find information within a specific knowledge domain. The technology portal C-NET is one example of this type of site. C-NET uses the collection of specific interest strategy. The entire site is devoted to technology products and the site includes many reviews of specific technologies and related products. Advertisers pay more to have their ad appear near a discussion of a technology related to their product or on a page that reviews the product.

Travel portals such as Kayak have also been successful as advertising-supported online businesses. The Kayak site allows visitors to specify travel dates and destinations, and then searches multiple sites to find the best airfares, car rentals, and hotel rooms. It searches provider sites such as those of the airlines, hotels, and car rental companies, but it also searches sites that consolidate travel products and sell them at reduced prices. Kayak benefits its visitors by saving them the trouble of visiting multiple sites to find the best travel deals. And it sells targeted advertising space to companies that want to reach travelers with near-term travel plans.

Newspaper and Magazine Publishers

Many newspapers and magazines publish all or part of their print content on the Web. They sell advertising to cover the costs of converting their print content to an online format and operating the Web site. The Internet Public Library Newspapers Collection page includes links to hundreds of newspaper sites around the world.

Some publications, such as local shopping news and alternative press newspapers, have always been fully supported by advertising revenues and are distributed at retail locations and newsstands without charge. Many of these publications have made an easy transition to an advertising-supported revenue model. Most newspapers and magazines, however, have relied on subscription and newsstand revenue to supplement their advertising revenue. These publications have had a more difficult time in making their online editions generate sufficient revenue.

It remains unclear whether an online presence helps or hurts the business operations of these publishers. Although a Web site can provide greater exposure for the publication's name and a larger audience for advertising that it carries, an online edition also can divert sales from the print edition. Like retailers or distributors whose online sales lead to the loss of their brick-and-mortar sales, publishers also experience sales losses as a result of online distribution. Newspapers and other publishers worry about these sales losses because they are very difficult to measure.

In addition to the concern about lost sales of print editions, most newspaper and magazine publishers have found that the cost of operating their Web sites cannot be covered by the revenue they generate from selling advertising on the sites. Many publishers continue to experiment with various other ways of generating revenue from their Web sites. You will learn about these other revenue models later in this chapter.

Targeted Classified Advertising Sites

In the past, newspapers generated a significant percentage of their revenue from their classified advertising pages. You have already learned that targeted advertising can command higher rates than general advertising. Newspaper classified advertising was the original version of targeted advertising. Each ad is placed in a specific classification and only readers interested in that type of ad will read that classification. For example, a person looking for an apartment to rent would look in the Rentals classification. The growth of classified advertising Web sites has been very bad for newspapers. Sites such as **craigslist** now carry many free classified ads that would once have produced substantial classified advertising revenue for local newspapers. Craigslist and similar sites run most ads for free, only charging for a small proportion of the ads they carry (craigslist charges for job ads, brokered rental ads in New York City, and a few other categories). Craigslist generates enough revenue to continue operating, but many other classified advertising sites generate substantial revenue, replacing newspapers' historical role as the primary carrier of classified ads.

The most successful targeted classified advertising category has been Web employment sites. Companies such as **CareerBuilder.com** offer international distribution of employment ads. These sites offer advertisers access to targeted markets. When a visitor specifies an interest in, for example, engineering jobs in Dallas, the results page can include a targeted ad for which an advertiser will pay more because it is directed at a specific market segment. Other employment ad sites, such as **The Ladders** and **Guru.com**, charge both job seekers and employers for ads and access to those ads.

Employment ad sites such as **Monster.com** also target specific categories of job seekers by including short articles on topics of interest. These articles increase the site's stickiness and attract people who are not necessarily looking for a job. This is a good tactic because people who are not looking for a job are often the candidates most highly sought by employers.

Another type of online classified advertising business is the used vehicle site. Trader Publishing has printed advertising newspapers for many years and now operates the **AutoTrader.com** site. **CycleTrader.com** and **BoatTrader.com** are similar sites that accept paid advertising from individuals and companies that want to sell cars, motorcycles, and boats. If the product has a dedicated following, this type of site can be successful by catering to small audiences. For example, the **VetteFinders** site sells classified ads for Corvette automobiles only.

Any product that is likely to be useful after the original buyer uses it provides the potential for a classified advertising site. People who want to sell used musical instruments can place ads on the **Musicians Buy-Line** site. Comic book collectors will find classified ads directed to them at **ComicLink.com**. Golfers who have given up the game or moved on to better clubs can place classified ads for their old equipment on **The Golf Classifieds**.

Advertising-Subscription Mixed Revenue Models

In an **advertising-subscription mixed revenue model**, which has been used for many years by traditional print newspapers and magazines, subscribers pay a fee, but also accept some level of advertising. On Web sites that use the advertising-subscription revenue model, subscribers are typically subjected to much less advertising than they are on sites supported completely by advertising. Firms have had varying levels of success in applying this mixed revenue model and a number of companies have moved to or from this model as they try to find the best way to generate revenue online.

Two of the world's most distinguished newspapers, ***The New York Times*** and ***The Wall Street Journal***, have each used a mixed advertising-subscription model since they first took their publications online. *The New York Times* Web site today derives the bulk of its revenue from advertising, but the newspaper has experimented in recent years with charging fees for access to various parts of its site. In 2005, *The New York Times* began charging a fee for access to its Op Ed and news columns. By 2007, the newspaper decided that it could earn more advertising revenue by providing free access to those pages than it was earning in subscription fees, so it went back to relying on an advertising-supported revenue stream. Today, the newspaper charges only for access to its premium crossword puzzle pages and for older articles retrieved from its archives. *The Wall Street Journal's* mixed model is weighted more heavily to subscription revenue. The site allows nonsubscriber visitors to view the classified ads and certain stories from the newspaper, but most of the content is reserved for subscribers who pay an annual fee for access to the site. Visitors who already subscribe to the print edition are offered a reduced rate on subscriptions to the online edition.

Most newspapers and magazines that use the mixed advertising-subscription revenue model for their online publications follow *The New York Times* approach of making most content available online, but a number of them do limit free content as *The Wall Street Journal* does. Figure 3-3 shows the revenue models used by a number of newspapers and magazines, including the advertising-supported model, the mixed advertising-subscription model with most content freely available, and the mixed advertising-subscription model with most content available only to subscribers.

	Mixed Advertising-Subscription Supported	
Advertising-Supported	**Most Content Free to All Visitors**	**Most Content Available Only to Subscribers**
The Boston Globe	BusinessWeek	The Economist
Cleveland Plain Dealer	Forbes	Foreign Affairs
Financial Times	Inc. Magazine	Harvard Business Review
Newsweek	The Los Angeles Times	National Geographic
InStyle	The New York Times	Nature
PC Magazine	The Washington Post	People
San Francisco Chronicle	Salon.com	Scientific American
Smithsonian	Technology Review	Sports Illustrated
Time		The Wall Street Journal

FIGURE 3-3 Revenue models used by online editions of newspapers and magazines

Sports fans visit the **ESPN** site for all types of sports-related information. Leveraging its brand name from its cable television businesses, ESPN is one of the most-visited sports sites on the Web. It sells advertising and offers a vast amount of free information, but die-hard fans can subscribe to its Insider service to obtain access to even more sports information. Thus, ESPN uses a mixed model that includes advertising and subscription revenue, but it only collects the subscription revenue from Insider subscribers, who make up a small portion of site visitors.

Consumers Union, the publisher of product evaluations and ratings monthly magazine *Consumer Reports*, operates a Web site, **ConsumerReports.org**, that relies exclusively on subscriptions (that is, it is a purely subscription-supported site). Consumers Union is a not-for-profit organization that does not accept advertising as a matter of policy because it might appear to influence its research results. Thus, the site is supported by a combination of subscriptions and a small amount of charitable donations. The Web site does offer some free information as a way to attract subscribers and fulfill its organizational mission of encouraging improvements in product safety.

Fee-for-Transaction Revenue Models

In the **fee-for-transaction revenue model**, businesses offer services for which they charge a fee that is based on the number or size of transactions they process. Some of these services lend themselves well to operating on the Web. To the extent that companies can offer Web site visitors the information they need about the transaction, companies can offer much of the personal service formerly provided by human agents. If customers are willing to enter transaction information into Web site forms, these sites can provide options and execute transactions much less expensively than traditional transaction service providers. The removal of an intermediary, such as a human agent, from a value chain is called **disintermediation**. The introduction of a new intermediary, such as a fee-for-transaction Web site, into a value chain is called **reintermediation**.

Travel

Travel agents earn commissions on each airplane ticket, hotel reservation, auto rental, or vacation that they book. These commissions are paid to the travel agent by the transportation or lodging provider. The travel agency revenue model involves receiving a fee for facilitating a transaction. The value added by a travel agent is that of information consolidation and filtering. A good travel agent knows many things about the traveler's destination and knows enough about the traveler to select the information elements that are useful and valuable to the traveler. Computers, particularly computers networked to large databases, are very good at information consolidation and filtering. In fact, travel agents have used networked computers, such as the **Sabre Travel Network**, for many years to make reservations for their customers.

When the Internet emerged as a new way to network computers and then became available to commercial users, a number of online travel agencies began doing business on the Web. Existing travel agencies did not, in general, rush to the new medium. They believed that the key value they added, personal customer service, could not be replaced with a Web site. Therefore, the first Web-based travel agencies were new entrants. One of these sites, **Travelocity**, is based on the same Sabre system that traditional travel agents use. (Travelocity is also owned by Sabre.)

Microsoft was an early participant in the online travel agency business with its **Expedia** subsidiary. **Travelocity**, **Expedia**, **Hotels.com**, and **Hotel Discount Reservations** are regularly listed among the top electronic commerce sites in surveys and industry analyst rankings. All four are profitable. In 2001, a consortium of five major U.S. airlines (American, Continental, Delta, Northwest, and United) launched **Orbitz**, which quickly became one of the most visited travel sites on the Web. The Orbitz home page appears in Figure 3-4.

FIGURE 3-4 Orbitz home page

In addition to earning commissions from the transportation and lodging providers, these sites generate advertising revenue from ads placed on travel information pages. These ads are similar to those on search engine results pages because advertisers can target them without obtaining demographic details about the site visitor. For example, if you are booking a flight to Chicago, the page that lists airline ticket options may also carry a banner ad for a hotel in Chicago or a car rental company that is running a promotion in the Chicago area.

Many traditional travel agents were squeezed out of the business as larger online operations took their most lucrative business. Airlines reduced or eliminated the commissions they once paid to travel agents on each ticket. Many travel agents (including the online travel sites) now charge their customers a flat fee for processing an airline ticket, and most passengers today buy their own tickets from online travel sites or from the airlines' Web sites directly.

The smaller travel agencies that have survived often specialize in cruise vacations. Cruise lines still view travel agents as an important part of their selling strategy and continue to pay reasonable commissions to travel agents on the sales that they make. Web sites that make discounted cruise packages easy to search, such as **VacationsToGo.com**, or that provide detailed information about cruises, such as **Cruise Specialists**, have been successful in this travel industry niche.

Other small travel agencies have been successful by following a reintermediation strategy with a focus on specific groups of travelers. These travel agents identify a group of travelers with specific needs and create travel packages designed for that group. For example, surf vacations have become increasingly popular. The stereotypical surfer of years gone by (a young unemployed male) has been replaced by a much broader demographic. Today's surfers often have significant financial resources and enjoy surfing in exotic locations. Web sites such as **WaveHunters.com** have followed a reintermediation strategy and cater to this highly specialized market in ways that generalist travel agents have not. Travel agencies that specialize in unusual or exotic destinations, such as Antarctica, have also been successful as intermediaries if they have particular expertise, knowledge, or local contacts that help them create custom itineraries.

Automobile Sales

Auto dealers buy cars from the manufacturer and sell them to consumers. They provide showrooms and salespeople to help customers learn about product features, arrange financing, and make a purchase decision. Most auto dealers negotiate the prices at which they sell their cars; thus, the salesperson's job also includes extracting the highest possible price from the consumer. Many people do not like negotiating car prices, especially if they have taken the time to learn about car features, arrange financing, and are ready to purchase a car without further assistance from a salesperson.

Autobytel and similar firms, such as **MSN Autos** and **CarsDirect.com**, provide an information service to car buyers. Each of these firms implements the fee-for-transaction revenue model in a slightly different way. For example, CarsDirect.com offers customers the ability to select a specific car (model, color, options) at a price it determines. CarsDirect.com then finds a local dealer that has such a car and is willing to sell it for the CarsDirect.com price. Alternatively, **Autoweb.com** and Autobytel locate dealers in the buyer's area that are willing to sell the car specified by the buyer (including make, model, options, and color) for a small premium over the dealer's nominal cost. The buyer can purchase the car from the dealer without negotiating with a salesperson. Autobytel and Autoweb.com charge participating dealers a fee for this service. In effect, firms such as Autobytel, Autoweb.com, CarsDirect.com, and MSN Autos are taking the salesperson out of the value chain. To the extent that the salesperson provides little or no value to the consumer, these firms are reducing the transaction costs in the process. The car salesperson is disintermediated and the Web site becomes the new intermediary in the transaction, which is an example of reintermediation.

Stockbrokers

Stock brokerage firms also use a fee-for-transaction model. They charge their customers a commission for each trade executed. In the past, stockbrokers offered investment advice and made specific buy and sell recommendations to customers in addition to their transaction execution services. They did not charge for this advice, but they did charge relatively high commissions on the trades they executed. After the U.S. government deregulated the securities trading business in the early 1970s, a number of discount brokers opened. These discount brokers distinguished themselves from the established "full-line" brokerage houses by not offering any investment advice and charging very low commissions. Because the full-line brokers had failed to provide value to some of their customers (those who had no need for investment advice or buy/sell recommendations), those customers were very happy to move their business to the discount brokers who provided nothing more than fast, inexpensive trade execution.

The Web made it possible for firms such as **E*TRADE** and Datek (later purchased by **TD Ameritrade**) to offer investment advice (posted on Web pages or sent in e-mailed newsletters) similar to that offered by a full-line broker, without incurring many of the costs of distributing the advice (such as stockbroker salaries, overhead, and the costs of printing and mailing newsletters). Web-based brokerage firms could also offer fast execution of trades that customers entered into Web page forms. Thus, in the 1990s, discount brokers who had taken business away from full-line brokers for 15 years faced new competition from online firms. Of course, the full-line brokers found that they were losing business to both the discount brokers and the online brokers. In response, both discount brokers (such as **Charles Schwab** and TD Ameritrade) and full-line brokers (such as **Merrill Lynch** and **MorganStanley SmithBarney**) opened new stock trading and information Web sites.

Online brokers offer customers the same kind of transaction cost reductions as the online auto-buying sites offer car shoppers. Traditional stockbrokers were disintermediated just as car salespeople were. And the financial crisis of 2008 took its toll on the remaining full-service brokerage firms. Today, most individuals who buy and sell stocks regularly use online brokers.

Insurance Brokers

Other sales agency businesses are moving to the Web. Although insurance companies themselves were slow to offer policies and investments for sale on the Web, a number of intermediaries that sell insurance policies from a variety of companies have been online since the early days of the Web. Quotesmith, which began business in 1984 as a policy-quoting service for independent insurance brokers, decided in 1996 to offer its policy price quotes directly to the public over the Internet. By quoting policies and accepting applications directly, Quotesmith is disintermediating the independent insurance agents with whom it formerly worked.

Other Web sites that offer insurance policy information, comparisons, and sales include **InsWeb**, **Answer Financial**, and **Insurance.com**. As you learned in the case at the beginning of this chapter, **Progressive** provides quotes on its Web site for both its insurance products and for its competitors' products. **The General** (General Automobile Insurance Services) uses its Web site to reach auto insurance buyers who might have had trouble getting insurance from other companies. It advertises its online insurance quotes as being "fast and anonymous." By offering a comfortable environment to potential customers who have been rejected by other companies because of credit problems or a record with traffic tickets, The General has been successful in this specific niche of the insurance market. Today, many major insurance companies, such as **Allstate**, **GEICO**, and **State Farm Insurance**, offer information and policies for sale on their Web sites.

Event Tickets

Before the Web made online sales possible, obtaining tickets for concerts, shows, and sporting events could be a challenge. Some venues only offered tickets for sale at their own box offices, and others sold tickets through ticket agencies that were difficult for patrons to find or impossible to reach by telephone. The Web gave event promoters the ability to sell tickets from one virtual location to customers practically anywhere in the world. Established ticket agencies such as Ticketmaster were early participants in online ticket sales. Other companies, such as Tickets.com and TicketWeb, also offer a wide variety of tickets for events in many different locations. These ticket brokers earn a fee on every ticket they sell.

In addition to the original sale of tickets, the Web created opportunities for those who deal in secondary market tickets (tickets that have already been sold by the event's producer and that are being offered for resale to other persons). Companies such as StubHub and TicketsNow operate as brokers to connect owners of tickets with buyers in this market. These ticket resellers earn fees on tickets they resell for others, but they can also profit by buying blocks of tickets and reselling them at a higher price. Both ticket brokers and ticket resellers reduce transaction costs for both buyers and sellers of tickets by creating a central marketplace that is easy to find and that facilitates buyer-seller negotiation.

Real Estate and Mortgage Loans

Other fee-for-transaction businesses are also starting to open electronic commerce Web sites, including real estate brokers and mortgage loan brokers. Online real estate brokers provide all of the services that a traditional broker might provide—except that online brokers provide these services through their Web sites. Most traditional real estate brokers have created Web sites, such as Coldwell Banker and Prudential. The industry's trade association, the National Association of Realtors, sponsors a Web site, Realtor.com, that carries ads for houses listed by its member firms.

Although the financial crisis of 2008 dramatically reduced the number of mortgage brokers in business, a number of them continue to do business online. Both Ditech and E-LOAN still provide information and take mortgage loan applications online.

Online Banking and Financial Services

Because financial services do not involve a physical product, they are easy to offer on the Web. The greatest concerns that most people have when they consider moving their financial transactions to the Web are security and the reliability of the financial institution—the same concerns that exist in the physical world. However, on the Web, it is much more difficult for a firm to establish its reputation for security and trust than it is in the physical world, where massive buildings and clearly visible room-sized safes can help create the necessary image. Many people who are willing to buy products and services online are unwilling to trust a Web site for their banking services, but the number who do is growing. Researchers estimate that more than 25 percent of all people who have made a purchase online also conduct their banking business online. In Chapter 11, you will learn more about how online payments and other financial transactions are processed.

Most banks that entered the Web banking business did so by opening online "branches" that carried the identification and reputation of the bank's brand as it existed in the physical world. Other firms started online banks that were not affiliated with an existing bank (such as the **First Internet Bank of Indiana**). Bank One opened an online bank under the name Wingspan in 1999. Bank One decided to present Wingspan as a new and separate entity, in the spirit of the dot-com boom that was then under way. After operating Wingspan separately for about two years, Bank One decided to close Wingspan and merge it with its main Web site (Bank One has since been acquired by Chase). Today, most banks understand that their online operations can benefit from using their established name and reputation to provide customers with a sense of trustworthiness.

Online bank operations handle only a small portion of the world's financial transactions today, but more customers accept them every year as a good way to conduct their banking business. Banks benefit from serving their customers online because it costs the bank less to provide services online than to provide those same services through personal interactions with bank employees in a branch office.

In addition to customers' concerns about trust and security online, two other significant barriers are preventing a more rapid rate of growth in the online banking business: a lack of bill presentment features and a lack of account aggregation tools.

Although online banks let customers pay their bills electronically, most customers still receive their bills in the mail. Unfortunately, most people must visit a different Web site to view each online bill. As online banks add bill presentment services that allow their customers to view all of their bills on the bank's Web site (and pay each of them with a single click), those banks will find more customers willing to do their banking on the Web. A **bill presentment** service provides an electronic version of an invoice or billing statement (such as a credit card bill or a mobile phone services statement) with all of the details that would appear in the printed document.

Another important feature that few online banks currently offer is **account aggregation**, which is the ability to obtain bank, investment, loan, and other financial account information from multiple Web sites and display it all in one location at the bank's Web site. Many of a bank's best customers have credit card, loan, investment, and brokerage accounts with several different financial institutions. Having all of this information aggregated in one place is very useful for these customers. Although some banks have created their own account aggregation and bill presentment software, companies such as **Yodlee** sell these services to banks and other financial institutions. The number of banks that offer aggregation is growing rapidly. Industry analysts expect that most banks (online and traditional) will offer aggregation services by 2012.

Online Music

The recording industry was slow to embrace online distribution of music because audio files are digital products that can be easily copied once purchased. The digital copies are perfect and thus can seriously impair future sales of the original audio file. Music files are in great demand and are easily copied, which is why in the early days of online music, many otherwise law-abiding persons illegally copied and shared music files. As you will learn in Chapter 7, recording companies fought this illegal sharing of music files by suing some of the people who shared files and the Web sites that facilitated their sharing activity. Although the recording companies still file lawsuits, they have also finally decided that they should capture some of the market for music files by selling their audio tracks online.

The largest online music stores include Amazon MP3, Apple's iTunes, eMusic, Microsoft's MSN Music, Napster, Rhapsody, Yahoo! Music, and Walmart.com Music Downloads. These sites sell single songs (tracks) for less than a dollar each and sell albums at various prices (most are between $5 and $12). Although some sites offer subscription plans, most of the sales revenue on these sites is generated using the fee-for-transaction model.

The online music market has been complicated because each store does not offer all of the music that is available in digital format and because each store tries to promote its own music file format. Artists and recording companies sometimes only offer their music through one store and some refuse to offer their music online at all. By promoting its own file format, each store is trying to force music consumers to use their store exclusively. Some online music sellers require buyers to download and install software, called **Digital Rights Management (DRM)** software, which limits the number of copies that can be made of each audio file. This does not prevent illegal copying, but it does make it somewhat more difficult and the sellers hope that the extra effort required will discourage some of this copying. However, each store has different rules about how many copies are permitted and on which devices the files can be played. Consumers, especially those who buy music from more than one store, have found these varying restrictions confusing.

The online music market has been an example of an industry that has failed to embrace the network effect it could gain by adopting one standard file format (or a set of compatible file formats). By trying to gain an advantage in the market, each company inadvertently limited the growth of the overall market.

Some stores (such as Mondomix MP3 and Smithsonian Folkways) have always sold audio files in a generally compatible file format with no copying restrictions. However, the music sold on these sites is not produced by the major recording companies.

In 2007, the Amazon MP3 store was the first major online retailer to offer music tracks from several major recording companies in DRM-free MP3 format. Since then, the other major retailers have followed Amazon's lead and most of them now offer some or all of their music in DRM-free, compatible file formats. Also, without DRM, it is now easier to convert files from one format to another.

With the problems of the complexity of DRM and incompatible formats nearing resolution, online music sales are increasing rapidly. Industry experts estimate that 80 percent of all music sold in 2012 will be sold online.

Online Video

Digital video can be sold or rented online as either a file download or as a streaming video. DRM software provides control over the number of copies that can be made of the downloaded video, the devices on which the video can be installed, and restrictions on how long the video remains available for watching. Videos offered for sale online include previously released movies, television shows, and programming that is developed specifically for the online market.

Until recently, video sales have been hampered by three main issues: the large size of video files (which can make download times long and streaming feeds uneven), concern that such sales might impair other sales of the video, and technological barriers that prevent downloaded videos from being played on a variety of devices. Online businesses are working continually on these issues and are having some success in overcoming all three of them.

First, videos are still the largest types of files that are regularly transmitted on the Internet, but companies are continually experimenting with technologies that improve the delivery of large files and video streams. You will learn more about these content delivery technologies, pioneered by companies such as Akamai, in Chapter 8.

Second, the companies that produce media are learning more about how online distribution fits into their overall revenue strategy. Movies traditionally have been released by the major Hollywood studios (20th Century Fox, Paramount, Sony, Walt Disney, Warner Brothers, and Universal) into different markets in a well-defined serial pattern. Movies were first distributed to theaters, which paid a high price for the right to show the movie first. After its initial theater run, the movie might then have been sold to airlines for in-flight showings and to premium cable channels such as HBO or Starz. Next, the movie was released on DVD and became available for purchase or rental through retail video stores. Eventually, the movie was sold to broadcast television stations and basic cable channels. This serial release pattern was designed to provide the movie's creators with the highest revenue obtainable at each point in the life of the product. Media producers released movies in this pattern for years, out of fear that any online distribution might steal sales away from one of their traditional outlets. These media producers now are experimenting with alternative distribution strategies. Some are now releasing movies online and on DVD simultaneously. As the number of online content distributors that charge either a subscription or a per-view fee for movies increases, media producers will be more amenable to releasing their product online because they can get paid for it.

Finally, the delivery of movies through a standard Web browser (and the appearance of Web browsers on devices other than computers; for example, mobile phones and video game appliances) is mitigating concern about technology barriers on multiple devices.

Amazon.com and Wal-Mart both offer video on their Web sites. Video rental giant **Blockbuster** sells and rents access to video downloads, as does **Netflix**, which includes online access to movies on its Web site as part of its DVD rental subscription plans. Apple's **iTunes** service includes video offerings for rent or purchase in addition to its many free video downloads.

Television programs are also available online. Three of the major U.S. broadcast networks (ABC, Fox, and NBC) formed a joint venture to operate **Hulu**, which offers video clips of popular television programs and movies. Hulu offers some programs and movies in their entirety. The other major U.S. broadcast network, CBS, operates **TV.com**, which operates in a similar manner. Unlike the movie distribution sites mentioned above, which charge a fee or use a subscription for service revenue model, both Hulu and TV.com use an advertising-supported revenue model.

Electronic Books

Another type of digital product sold online is the electronic book. **Audible** has sold digital audio editions of books for many years, first in the form of CDs, then later as various types of digital files. Today, Audible sells subscriptions that allow customers to download a certain number of books each month. Since the pricing is per book, rather than a subscription fee for unlimited access to books, the service is included in this section of the chapter as a fee-for-transaction revenue model. Audible also sells spoken-word audio of magazines, newspapers, and other information and entertainment digital products.

For electronic books that can be read, Amazon.com offers books, newspapers, magazines, and other digital format items that are delivered directly to its line of Kindle readers, which are portable electronic book storage and display devices. Kindle books can be purchased using a Web browser on a user's computer or through the Kindle device itself. The items purchased are downloaded to the Kindle, but are also stored on Amazon.com's servers (in case the Kindle reader is lost or stolen).

Most industry analysts believe that the relatively high initial cost of the Kindle reader (between $300 and $500) and its lack of a color display are the two most important reasons that sales of the device and its related digital media have not been higher.

Fee-for-Service Revenue Models

Companies are offering an increasing variety of services on the Web for which they charge a fee. These are neither broker services nor services for which the charge is based on the number or size of transactions processed. The fee is based on the value of the service provided. These **fee-for-service revenue models** range from games and entertainment to financial advice and the professional services of accountants, lawyers, and physicians.

Online Games

Computer and video games are a huge industry. In the United States alone, more than $11 billion per year is spent on these types of games. An increasing portion of that revenue is generated online. Although many sites that offer games relied on advertising revenue in the past (and some, such as GSN.com, still do), a growing number now include premium games in their offerings. Site visitors must pay to play these premium games, either by buying and downloading software to install on their computers, or by paying a subscription fee to enter the premium games area on the site. MSN Games, Station.com, RealArcade, and Electronic Arts are among the leading game sites that include subscription game services. The Entertainment Software Association is an industry group that tracks computer and video game use. Its Web site includes a number of interesting statistics about computer game sales and demographics of game players. For example, the average game player is 35 years old and has been playing computer or video games for 12 years.

Professional Services

State laws have been one of the main forces preventing U.S. professionals (such as physicians, lawyers, accountants, and engineers) from extending their practices to the Web. Since most professionals are licensed by individual states, state laws can prevent them from practicing their professions on the Web because online patients or clients would likely be located in other states. If they were to offer their services online to persons in other states, professionals could be charged with unlicensed practice in those other states. State laws concerning the imputed location of service delivery are vague; it can be difficult to determine exactly where a service provided online actually occurs. This uncertainty arises because most state professional practice laws were written long before the Internet existed.

Although some medical, legal, and other professional practices allow patients to make appointments online, and a few professionals do online consultations, most are reluctant to do any element of their practices on the Web. Many professionals are worried about protecting the privacy of their patients or clients online.

The **Law on the Web** site offers legal consultations on a variety of matters for residents of the United Kingdom. Accounting professionals in the United States can be located through the **CPA Directory**, and a number of legal referral sites can direct site visitors to local attorneys. The online version of the well-known Martindale-Hubbell lawyer directory is also available online at **Martindale.com**. Although a large number of Web sites, such as **RealAge**, **Dr. Andrew Weil's Self Healing**, and **WebMD**, offer general health information, physicians and other health care professionals have been reluctant to sell specific advice to specific patients online. The difficulty of diagnosing medical problems without a physical examination of the patient is a significant barrier to providing most types of health care services online, but some physicians are beginning to offer online consultations to patients with whom they have an ongoing, established relationship.

Free for Many, Fee for a Few

Chris Anderson, the editor of *Wired Magazine*, proposed in 2004 that the economics of producing and selling digital products is substantially different from the economics of producing and selling physical products. In his books (see references to his work in the For Further Study and Research section at the end of this chapter), he explains that physical products benefit from the production of standardized versions that generate economies of scale. Because each product requires materials and labor, using the same materials allows large producers to buy those materials at lower costs by ordering in bulk. Labor costs can be reduced by training workers to do specific production tasks efficiently. Since most of the cost of a physical product is in the manufacture of each unit (as opposed to the design of the prototype), the key to making a profit is to reduce the cost of manufacturing. Digital products work differently. They tend to have large up-front costs. Once those costs are incurred, additional units can be made at very low additional cost. For example, a software program can cost thousands of dollars to create. It can take many hours of expensive programmer time to design, code, and test. But once it is in production, creating additional units (especially if those units are distributed in digital form, online) costs very little. Making minor changes in the program so it works better for different types of customers can be inexpensive, too. Thus, the economics of digital products are quite different from the economics of physical products.

The result of Anderson's logic is that it can be profitable to offer a digital product to a large number of customers for free, then charge a small number of customers for an enhanced, specialized, or otherwise differentiated version of the product. If you can charge the small number of customers enough to cover the cost of developing the digital product and yield a profit, you can give away many copies of the product, especially if those free copies entice more paying customers for the enhanced product. For example, Yahoo! offers free e-mail accounts to site visitors. This draws visitors to the Yahoo! site and allows the company to sell some advertising on the pages that display the e-mail service. But some e-mail users will want an enhanced version of the service. Perhaps they want pages with no advertising, the ability to send large attachments with their e-mails, or more storage space for their e-mails. Yahoo! charges for a premium version of its service that offers these features. It costs the company very little to offer this service, but it generates considerable revenue.

Companies selling physical products have often used a mixture of free and not-free products. For example, a bakery might have a plate of cookies available for customers to taste. The bakery hopes that enough customers will be impressed with the taste of the free cookies that they will buy cookies or other baked goods. They give away a small number of physical products to boost sales.

Anderson argues that this logic works for digital products distributed online, but in reverse. Companies can afford to give away large numbers of digital products at no cost to lure a few paying customers into buying similar, but enhanced, digital products. This principle underlies many of the mixed advertising-subscription revenue models you learned about earlier in this chapter.

REVENUE MODELS IN TRANSITION

Many companies have gone through transitions in their revenue models as they learn how to do business successfully on the Web. As more people use the Web to buy goods and services, and as the behavior of those Web users changes, companies often find that they must change their revenue models to meet the needs of those new and changing Web users. Some companies created electronic commerce Web sites that needed many years to grow large enough to become profitable. This is not unusual; both CNN and ESPN took more than 10 years to become profitable and they had both created new businesses in television, which was an existing and well-established medium. Many Web companies found that their unprofitable growth phases were lasting longer than they had anticipated and were forced either to change their revenue models or go out of business.

This section describes the revenue model transitions undertaken by five different companies as they gained experience in the online world and faced the changes that occurred in that world. In the second wave of electronic commerce, these and other companies might well face the need to make further adjustments to their revenue models.

Subscription to Advertising-Supported Model

Microsoft founded its ***Slate*** magazine Web site as an upscale news and current events publication. Because *Slate* included experienced writers and editors on its staff, many people expected the online magazine to be a success. Microsoft believed that the magazine had a high value, too. At a time when most online magazines were using an advertising-supported revenue model, *Slate* began charging an annual subscription fee after a limited free introductory period.

Although *Slate* drew a wide readership and received acclaim for its incisive reporting and excellent writing, it was unable to draw a sufficient number of paid subscribers. At its peak, *Slate* had about 27,000 subscribers generating annual revenue of $500,000, which was far less than the cost of creating the content and maintaining the Web site. *Slate* is now operated as an advertising-supported site. Because it is a part of Microsoft, *Slate* does not report its own profit numbers, but most industry observers believe that the site does not earn a profit. Microsoft maintains the *Slate* site as part of its Bing portal, so it is likely that the value of the publication to Microsoft is to increase the portal's stickiness.

Advertising-Supported to Advertising-Subscription Mixed Model

Another upscale online magazine, ***Salon.com***, which has also received acclaim for its innovative content, has moved its revenue model in the direction opposite of *Slate*'s transition. After operating for several years as an advertising-supported site, *Salon.com* now offers an optional subscription version of its site. The subscription offering was motivated by the company's inability to raise the additional money from investors that it needed to continue operations.

Subscribers pay an annual fee to view a version of the magazine called *Salon Premium*, which is free of advertising and can be downloaded for storage and later offline reading on the subscriber's computer. Premium subscribers also gain access to additional content such as downloadable music, e-books, audio books, and other extras such as free magazine subscriptions.

Advertising-Supported to Fee-for-Services Model

XdriveTechnologies opened its original advertising-supported Web site in 1999. Xdrive offered free disk storage space online to users. The users saw advertising on each page and had to provide personal information that allowed Xdrive to send targeted e-mail advertising to them. Its offering was very attractive to Web users who had begun to accumulate large files, such as MP3 music files, and wanted to access those files from several computers in different locations.

After two years of offering free disk storage space, Xdrive found that it was unable to pay the costs of providing the service with the advertising revenue it had been able to generate. After being bought by AOL in 2005, Xdrive switched to a subscription-supported model (AOL-registered users were eligible for a small free storage service) and began selling the service to business users as well as individuals. In recent years, disk drive costs have dropped and Xdrive frequently adjusted its monthly fee downward. AOL finally closed the service in 2009. Companies that are successful in the online storage business today generally charge a fee for their services that is based on the amount of storage used.

Advertising-Supported to Subscription Model

Northern Light was founded in August 1997 as a search engine, but a search engine that did more than search the Web. It also searched its own database of journal articles and other publications to which it had acquired reproduction rights. When a user ran a search, Northern Light returned a results page that included links to Web sites and abstracts of the items in its own database. Users could then follow the links to Web sites, which were free, or purchase access to the database items.

Thus, Northern Light's revenue model was a combination of the advertising-supported model used by most other Web search engines plus a fee-based information access service, similar to the subscription services offered by ProQuest and EBSCO that you learned about earlier in this chapter. The difference in the Northern Light model was that users could pay for just one or two articles (the cost was typically \$1–\$5 per article) instead of paying a large amount of money for unlimited access to its database on an annual subscription basis. Northern Light also offered subscription access to most of its database to companies, schools, and libraries.

In January 2002, Northern Light decided that the advertising revenue it was earning from the ads it sold on search results pages was insufficient to justify continuing to offer that service. It stopped offering public access to its search engine and converted to a new revenue model that was primarily subscription supported. Northern Light's new model generates revenue from annual subscriptions to large corporate clients. It still offers an individual account option, however. A person who wants to search the Northern Light database can open an account, supply a credit card number, and be billed monthly for the articles accessed.

Multiple Transitions

Encyclopædia Britannica is an excellent example of a company that transferred its existing reputation for high quality to the Web. Over its 240-year publishing history, Encyclopædia Britannica has developed one of the most respected brand names in research and education. It is particularly interesting that Encyclopædia Britannica began in 1768 as a sort of precomputer-age frequently asked questions (FAQ) list. A group of academics collected notes they had made while conducting research and decided to publish them as a series of articles.

When Encyclopædia Britannica first moved onto the Web in 1994, it began with two Web-based offerings. The Britannica Internet Guide was a free Web navigation aid that classified and rated information-laden Web sites. It featured reviews written by Britannica editors who also selected and indexed the sites. The company's other Web site, Encyclopædia Britannica Online, was available for a subscription fee or as part of the Encyclopædia Britannica CD package. Britannica used the free site to attract users to the paid subscription site.

In 1999, disappointed by low subscription sales of Encyclopædia Britannica Online, Britannica converted to a free, advertising-supported site. The first day the new site, **Britannica.com**, became available at no cost to the public, it had more than 15 million visitors, forcing Britannica to shut down for two weeks to upgrade its servers.

The Britannica.com site then offered the full content of the encyclopedia's print edition in searchable form, plus access to the *Merriam-Webster's Collegiate Dictionary* and the *Britannica Book of the Year*. One of the most successful aspects of the site was the way it integrated the Britannica Internet Guide Web-rating service with its print content. The Britannica Store sold the CD version of the encyclopedia along with other educational and scientific products to help generate revenue.

After two years of trying to generate a profit using this advertising-supported model, Britannica faced declining advertising revenues. In 2001, Britannica returned to a mixed model in which it offered free summaries of encyclopedia articles and free access to the *Merriam-Webster's Collegiate Dictionary* on the Web, with the full text of the encyclopedia available through an annual subscription plan.

Britannica went from being a print publisher to a seller of information on the Web to an advertising-supported Web site to a mixed advertising subscription model—three major revenue model transitions—in just a few short years. The main value that Britannica has to sell is its reputation and the expertise of its editors, contributors, and advisors. For now, Britannica has decided that the best way to capitalize on that reputation and expertise is through a mixed revenue model of subscriptions and advertising support, with the bulk of its revenue coming from subscriptions.

REVENUE STRATEGY ISSUES

In the first part of this chapter, you learned about the revenue models that companies are using on the Web today. In this section, you will learn about some issues that arise when companies implement those models. You will also learn how companies deal with those issues.

Channel Conflict and Cannibalization

Companies that have existing sales outlets and distribution networks often worry that their Web sites will take away sales from those outlets and networks. For example, **Levi Strauss & Company** sells its Levi's jeans and other clothing products through department stores and other retail outlets. The company began selling jeans to consumers on its Web site in mid-1998. Many of the department stores and retail outlets that had been selling Levi's products for many years complained to the company that the Web site was now competing with them. In January 2000, Levi Strauss decided to stop selling products on its own Web site.

Such a **channel conflict** can occur whenever sales activities on a company's Web site interfere with its existing sales outlets. The problem is also called **cannibalization** because the Web site's sales consume sales that would be made in the company's other sales channels. The **Levi's** Web site now provides product information, but directs customers who want to buy its products to online stores that carry those products. Levi's product pages also include links that lead to a store finder page, so that customers who want to shop for Levi's products in a physical store can find stores near them.

Maytag, the manufacturer of home appliances, found itself in the same position as Levi Strauss. It created a Web site that allowed customers to order directly from Maytag. After less than two years of operating its direct sales outlet and receiving many complaints from its authorized distributors and resellers, Maytag decided to incorporate online partners into its Web site store design. Now, after searching and gathering information about specific products from the Maytag Web site, a customer can select a retailer who will deliver and install the appliance. These retail store partners are authorized Maytag distributors. The customer can complete the transaction on the Maytag site or can choose to complete the transaction on the retailer's site.

Both Levi's and Maytag faced channel conflict and cannibalization issues with their retail distribution partners. Their established retailers sold many times the dollar volume than either company could ever hope to sell on their own Web sites. Thus, to avoid angering their retailers, who could always sell competing products, both Levi's and Maytag decided that it would be best to work with their retail partners. Similar issues can also arise within a company if that company has established sales channels that would compete with direct sales on the company's own Web site.

Eddie Bauer, a retailer of clothing and outdoor gear, was selling through a catalog and retail stores located primarily in major shopping malls when it decided to begin selling products on its Web site. The company believed that it could make online sales more attractive by allowing customers to return unwanted products that they had purchased online at the retail store locations. The managers of these stores were concerned about the time it would take for their sales associates to process these returns and about having to add the items to their stores' inventories. In a retail store operation, managing labor costs and inventory are very important in achieving store profitability. The managers at the company's catalog division were also worried. They feared that sales through the Web site would cannibalize sales through the catalog.

By making adjustments in the managers' compensation and bonus plans, Eddie Bauer was able to convince all of the managers to support the Web site. The retail store managers were credited with an inventory and labor cost allowance for each Web site return they handled. The catalog division managers were given a credit for existing catalog customers who purchased goods from the Web site. By giving their customers access to the company's products through a coordinated presence in all three distribution channels, Eddie Bauer was able to increase overall sales to those customers. This type of solution is called **channel cooperation**.

Strategic Alliances

As you learned in Chapter 1, when two or more companies join forces to undertake an activity over a long period of time, they are said to create a strategic alliance. When companies form a strategic alliance, they are operating in the network form of organization that you learned about in Chapter 1. Companies form strategic alliances for many purposes. An increasing number of businesses are forming strategic alliances to sell on the Web. For example, the relationships that Levi's created with its retail partners by giving them space on the Levi's Web site to sell Levi's products is an example of a strategic alliance.

Earlier in this chapter you learned about Yodlee, the account aggregation services provider, and the online bank sites that offer these services to consumers. The relationship between Yodlee and its bank clients is another example of a strategic alliance. Yodlee can concentrate on developing the technology and services while the banks provide the customers. Account aggregation services decrease the likelihood that customers will consider moving to another bank, which helps the bank hold on to its customers. Thus, both parties benefit from the strategic alliance.

As you learned earlier in this chapter, Amazon.com has added many product lines to its original offering of books. In some cases, Amazon.com built these businesses from the ground up. In other cases, it forged strategic alliances with existing firms. Amazon joined with Target to sell that discount retailer's products on a Web site devoted to Target products. The Target site is housed within the Amazon.com site. Amazon.com has teamed up with CDnow to sell music and video products on the Amazon.com Web site. Most of these alliances have worked well for both parties, but not all have been fully satisfactory relationships. ToysRUs was one of Amazon.com's earliest strategic partners, but the two companies have sued each other, alleging violations of their strategic alliance agreement. Now-defunct electronics retailer Circuit City also had a strategic alliance with Amazon.com, but decided to end the arrangement after several years and sell through its own site.

CREATING AN EFFECTIVE WEB PRESENCE

Businesses have always created a presence in the physical world by building stores, factories, warehouses, and office buildings. An organization's **presence** is the public image it conveys to its stakeholders. The **stakeholders** of a firm include its customers, suppliers, employees, stockholders, neighbors, and the general public. Most companies tend not to worry much about the image they project until they grow to a significant size—until then, they are too focused on just surviving to spare the effort. On the Web, presence can be much more important. Many customers and other stakeholders of a Web business know the company only through its Web presence. Creating an effective Web presence can be critical even for the smallest and newest firms operating on the Web.

Identifying Web Presence Goals

When a business creates a physical space in which to conduct its activities, its managers focus on very specific objectives. Few of these objectives are image driven. The new company must find a location that will be convenient for its customers, with sufficient floor space and features to allow the selling activity to occur. A new business must balance its needs for inventory storage space and employee work space with the costs of obtaining that space. The presence of a physical business location results from satisfying these many other objectives and is rarely a main goal of designing the space.

On the Web, businesses and other organizations have the luxury of building their Web sites intentionally to create distinctive presences. A firm's physical location must satisfy so many other business needs that it often fails to convey a good presence. A good Web site design can provide many image-creation and image-enhancing features very effectively—it can serve as a sales brochure, a product showroom, a financial report, an employment ad, and a customer contact point. Each entity that establishes a Web presence should decide which features the Web site can provide and which of those features are the most important to include.

An effective site is one that creates an attractive presence that meets the objectives of the business or organization. These objectives include:

- Attracting visitors to the Web site
- Making the site interesting enough that visitors stay and explore
- Convincing visitors to follow the site's links to obtain information
- Creating an impression consistent with the organization's desired image
- Building a trusting relationship with visitors
- Reinforcing positive images that the visitor might already have about the organization
- Encouraging visitors to return to the site

Making Web Presence Consistent with Brand Image

Different firms, even those in the same industry, might establish different Web presence goals. For example, **Coca Cola** and **Pepsi** are two companies that have established powerful brand images in the same business, but they have developed significantly different Web presences. These two companies frequently change their Web pages, but the Coca Cola page usually includes a trusted corporate image such as the Coke bottle. Alternatively, the Pepsi page is usually filled with links to a variety of activities and product-related promotions.

These Web presences convey the images each company wishes to project. Each presence is consistent with other elements of the marketing efforts of these companies—Coca Cola's traditional position as a trusted classic, and Pepsi's position as the upstart product favored by a younger generation.

Matching Site Design to Function

The **Volkswagen of America** site that appears in Figure 3-5 is a good example of Web site design that accomplishes important functions for the company. The site provides links to detailed information about all of Volkswagen's models, links to a dealer locator page, links to information about the company, and a link to a set of shopping tools.

Volkswagen's home page gives visitors access to a large number of resources on the page, which means that they do not need to wade through multiple pages to find things in which they are interested. At the same time, the page design is consistent with Volkswagen's corporate goal of providing cars that meet the needs of a wide variety of customers. The home page conveys a Web presence that meets the needs of most visitors quickly and effectively.

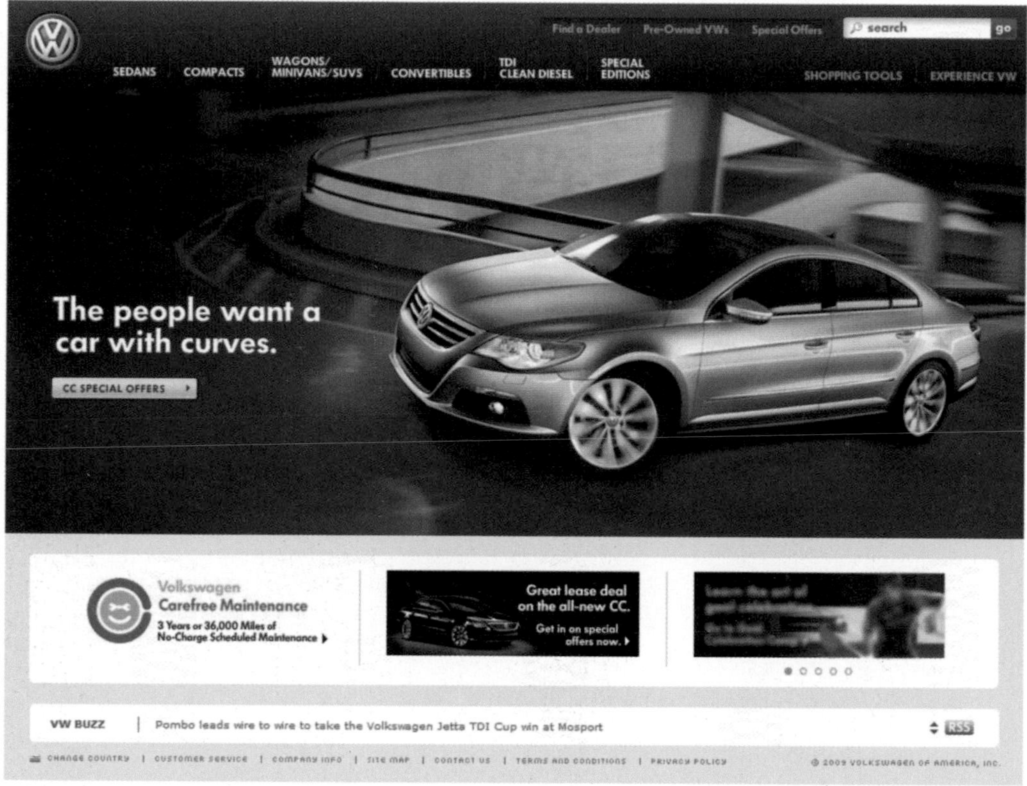

FIGURE 3-5 Volkswagen of America home page

Not-for-Profit Organizations

The Volkswagen Web page example shows how a company can enhance its image by providing useful information to customers online. For some organizations, this image-enhancement capability is a key goal of their Web presence efforts. Not-for-profit organizations are an excellent example of this. They can use their Web sites as a central resource for communications with their varied and often geographically dispersed constituencies.

A key goal for the Web sites of many not-for-profit organizations is information dissemination. The Web allows these groups to integrate information dissemination with fund-raising in one location. Visitors who become engaged in the issues presented are usually just one or two clicks away from a page offering memberships or other opportunities to donate using a credit card. Web pages also provide a two-way contact channel for people who are engaged in the organization's efforts but who do not work directly for the organization—for example, many not-for-profits rely on volunteers and coordination with other organizations to accomplish their goals. This combination of information dissemination and a two-way contact channel is a key element on any successful electronic commerce Web site. For example, the **American Civil Liberties Union (ACLU)**, which is devoted to the advocacy of individual rights in the United States, includes many communication opportunities on its Web site.

The ACLU home page, shown in Figure 3-6, gives visitors an opportunity to learn about the organization and contribute money or join if their interests are piqued by what they see. The ACLU home page includes links to information about each major issue on which the ACLU has taken a position. The ACLU's Web site is especially valuable to it because the organization serves many different constituencies, not all of whom agree with the ACLU or with each other on all issues. If the ACLU were to create a print newsletter that contained interesting information for some of its supporters, that same information might offend other supporters. The Web site allows visitors to select the issues in which they are interested—and only those issues.

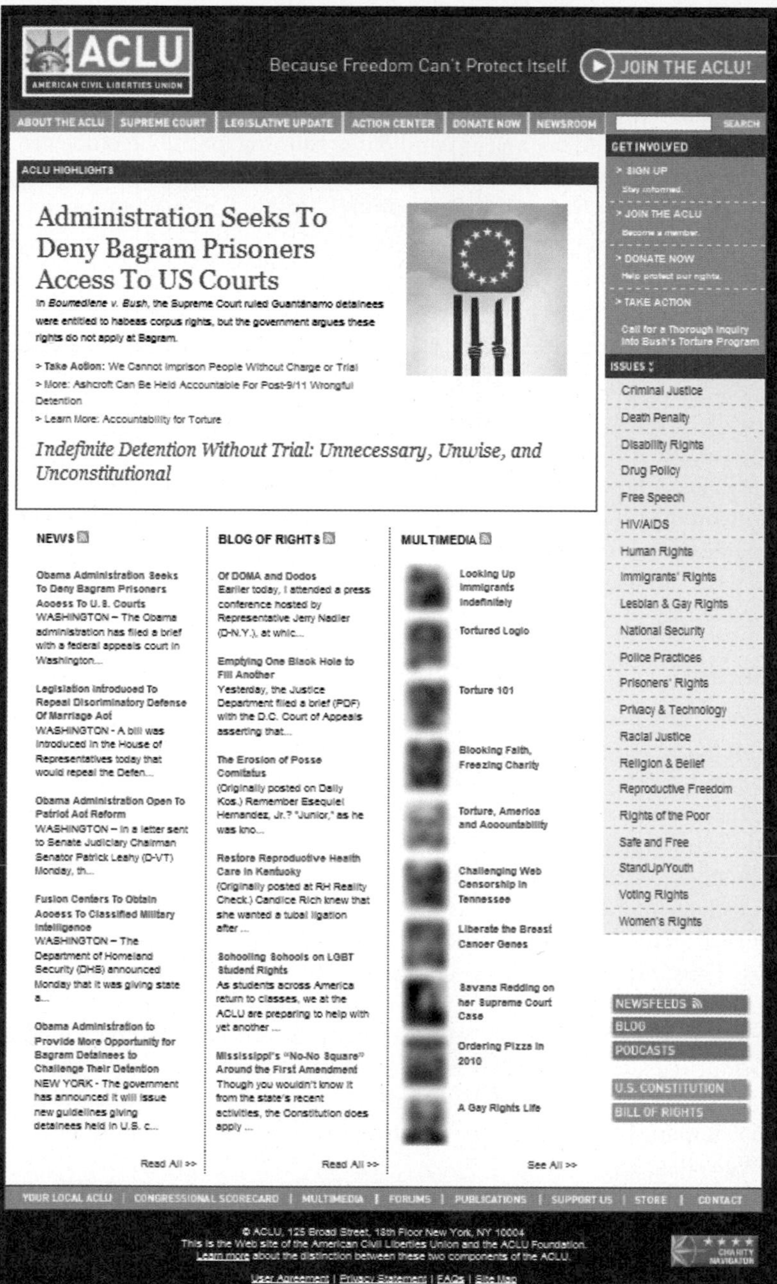

FIGURE 3-6 ACLU home page

Not-for-profit organizations can use the Web to stay in touch with existing stakeholders and identify new opportunities for serving them. Political parties want to offer information about party positions on issues, recruit members, keep existing members informed, and provide communication links to visitors who have questions about the party. All the major U.S. political parties have Web sites, and each year candidates running for public office set up their own Web sites. In addition, political organizations that are not affiliated with a specific party, such as the nonpartisan **Center for Responsive Politics**, also accomplish similar goals with their Web presences.

WEB SITE USABILITY

Research indicates that few businesses accomplish all of their goals for their Web sites in their current Web presences. Even sites that succeed in achieving most of these goals often fail to provide sufficient interactive contact opportunities for site visitors.

In this section, you will learn how the Web is different from other ways in which companies have communicated with their customers, suppliers, and employees in the past. You will learn how companies can improve their Web presences by making their sites accessible to more people and easier to use, and by making sure that their sites encourage visitors to trust and even develop feelings of loyalty toward the organization behind the Web site.

How the Web Is Different

Through years of trial, error, and research, firms have come to realize that doing business online differs greatly from doing business in the physical world. When firms first started creating Web sites in the mid-1990s, they often built simple sites that conveyed basic information about their businesses. Few firms conducted any market research to see what kinds of things potential visitors might want to obtain from these Web sites, and even fewer considered what business infrastructure adjustments would be needed to service the site. For example, few firms had e-mail address links on their sites. Those firms that did include an e-mail link often understaffed the department responsible for answering visitors' e-mail messages. Thus, many site visitors sent e-mail messages that were never answered.

This failure to understand how the Web is different from other presence-building media continues to be an important reason that so many businesses do not achieve their Web objectives. To learn more about this issue, see Jakob Nielsen's **Failure of Corporate Web sites** page in the Online Companion; the article was written in 1998, but still accurately describes far too many Web sites.

Most Web sites that are designed to create an organization's presence in the Web medium include links to a fairly standard information set. The site should give the visitor easy access to the organization's history, a statement of objectives or mission statement, information about products or services, financial information, and a way to communicate with the organization. Sites achieve varying levels of success based largely on how they offer this information. Presentation is important, but so is realizing that the Web is an interactive medium. The Web gives even large companies the ability to engage in two-way, meaningful communication with their customers. Companies that do not make effective use of this ability will lose customers to competitors that do.

Meeting the Needs of Web Site Visitors

Businesses that are successful on the Web realize that every visitor to their Web site is a potential customer or partner. Thus, an important concern for businesses crafting Web presences is the variation in visitor characteristics. People who visit a Web site seldom arrive by accident; they are there for a reason.

Varied Motivations of Web Site Visitors

Unfortunately for the Web designer trying to make a site that is useful for everyone, visitors arrive for many different reasons, including these:

- Learning about products or services that the company offers
- Buying products or services that the company offers
- Obtaining information about warranty, service, or repair policies for products they purchased
- Obtaining general information about the company or organization
- Obtaining financial information for making an investment or credit-granting decision
- Identifying the people who manage the company or organization
- Obtaining contact information for a person or department in the organization
- Following a link into the site while searching for information about a related product, service, or topic

Creating a Web site that meets the needs of visitors with such a wide range of motivations can be challenging. Not only do Web site visitors arrive with different needs, they arrive with different experience and expectation levels. In addition to the problems posed by the diversity of visitor characteristics, technology issues can also arise. These Web site visitors are connected to the Internet through a variety of communication channels that provide different bandwidths and data transmission speeds. They will also be using different Web browsers running on different devices (including computers, mobile phones, smart phones, television sets, and even game consoles). Even those using the same browser can be running different versions or have it configured in various ways. Different browser add-in and plug-in software can add yet another dimension to visitor variability. Considering and addressing the implications of these many variations in visitor characteristics when building a Web site can help convert these visitors into customers.

Making Web Sites Accessible

One of the best ways to accommodate a broad range of visitor needs, including the needs of visitors with disabilities, is to build flexibility into the Web site's interface. Many sites offer separate versions with and without frames and give visitors the option of choosing either one. Some sites offer a text-only version. As researchers at the **Trace Center** note, this can be an especially important feature for visually impaired visitors who use special browser software to access Web site content. Approximately 10 percent of all Web users have some kind of disability. The **W3C Web Accessibility Initiative** site includes a number of useful links to information regarding these issues.

A site can give the visitor the option to select smaller versions of graphic images so that the page loads on a low-bandwidth connection in a reasonable amount of time. If the site includes streaming audio or video clips, it can give the visitor the option to specify a connection type so that the streaming media adjusts itself to the bandwidth for that connection.

A good site design lets visitors choose among information attributes, such as level of detail, forms of aggregation, viewing format, and downloading format. Many online stores give visitors a selectable level of detail by presenting product information by product line. The site presents one page for each line of products. A product line page contains pictures of each item in that product line accompanied by a brief description. By using hyperlinked graphics for the product pictures, the site offers visitors the option of clicking on the product picture, which opens a page of detailed specifications for that product.

The use of **Adobe Flash** to create animated graphic elements on Web pages has been controversial for years. These pages (or large portions of the pages) are not rendered in HTML and can be very large files that take considerable time to download. Web pages built with Flash do not provide the same navigation tools or visual hints that Web pages created in HTML offer.

Some Web site designers love Flash because it is an exciting creative design tool, but many electronic commerce sites are reluctant to use it because of the non-standard interface it can present to customers. For interesting discussions of the disadvantages of Flash and similar tools, see WebWord.com's **Flash Usability Challenge** pages or Jakob Nielsen's commentaries **Flash: 99% Bad**, **Ephemeral Web-Based Applications**, and **Top Ten Web Design Mistakes of 2005**. A number of sites address the issue by giving visitors an option to select a Flash or non-Flash version of the site on its home page.

Some specific tasks that customers want to perform do lend themselves to animated Web pages. For example, the **Lee®** Jeans **FitFinder** is a series of Flash animation pages that can help customers find the right size and style of jeans. One of the Lee® Jeans FitFinder animation pages is shown in Figure 3-7.

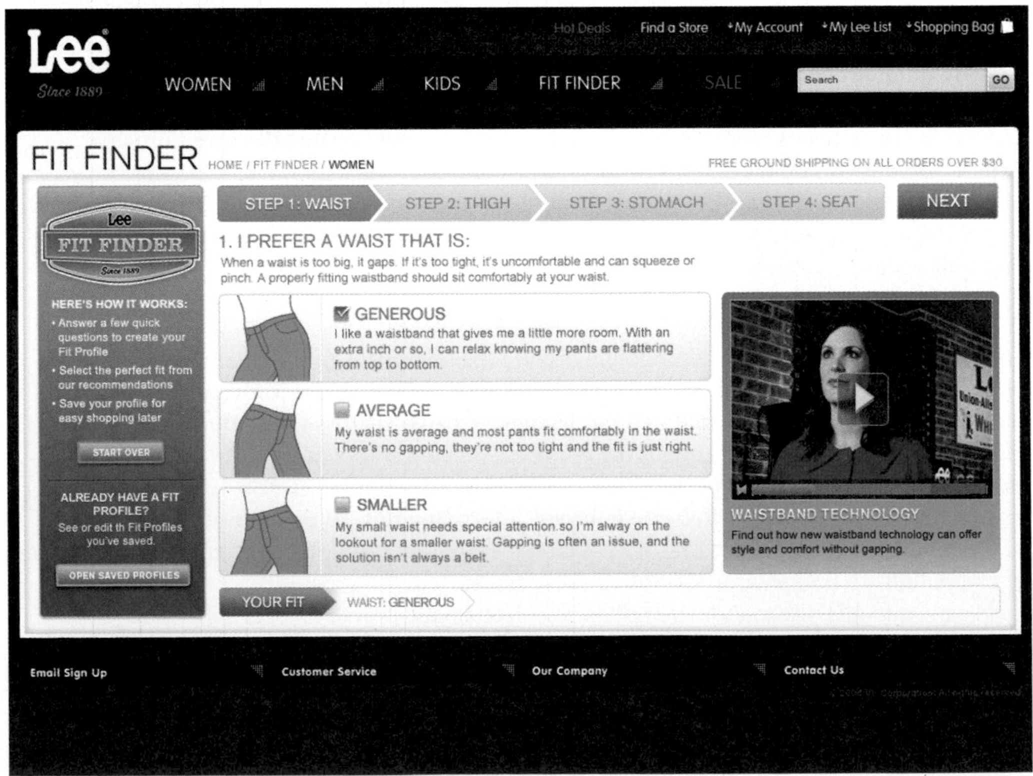

FIGURE 3-7 Lee® Jeans FitFinder Flash animation

Web sites can also offer visitors multiple information formats by including links to files in those formats. For example, a page offering financial information could include links to an HTML file, an Adobe PDF file, and an Excel spreadsheet file. Each of these files would contain the same financial information in different formats; visitors can then choose the format that best suits their immediate needs. Visitors looking for a specific financial fact might choose the HTML file so that the information appears in their Web browsers. Other visitors who want a copy of the entire annual report as it was printed would select the PDF file and either view it in their browsers or download and print the file. Visitors who want to conduct analyses on the financial data would download the spreadsheet file and perform calculations using the data in their own spreadsheet software.

To be successful in conveying an integrated image and offering information to potential customers, businesses should try to meet the goals shown in Figure 3-8 when constructing their Web sites.

Business Web sites need to:

- Offer easily accessible facts about the organization
- Allow visitors to experience the site in different ways and at different levels
- Provide visitors with a meaningful, two-way (interactive) communication link with the organization
- Sustain visitor attention and encourage return visits
- Offer easily accessible information about products and services and how to use them

FIGURE 3-8 Goals for business Web sites

Trust and Loyalty

When companies first started selling on the Web, many of them believed that their customers would use the abundance of information to find the best prices and disregard other aspects of the buying experience. For some products, this may be true; however, most products include an element of service. When customers buy a product, they are also buying that service element. A seller can create value in a relationship with a customer by nurturing the customer's trust and developing it into loyalty. Business researchers have found that a 5 percent increase in customer loyalty (measured as the proportion of returning customers) can yield profit increases of 25 to 80 percent.

Even when products are commodity items, the service element can be a powerful differentiating factor for which customers will pay extra. These services include such things as delivery, order handling, help with selecting a product, and after-sale support. Because many of these services are things that a potential customer cannot evaluate before purchasing a product, the customer must trust the seller to provide an acceptable level of service.

When a customer has an experience with a seller who provides good service, that customer begins to trust the seller. When a customer has multiple good experiences with a seller, that customer feels loyal to the seller. Thus, the repetition of satisfactory service can build customer loyalty, which can prevent a customer from seeking alternative sellers who offer lower prices.

Many companies doing business on the Web spend large amounts of money to obtain customers. If they do not provide levels of customer service that lead customers to develop trust in and loyalty to the firm, the companies are unlikely to recover the money they spend to attract the customers in the first place, much less earn a profit.

Customer service is a problem for many electronic commerce sites. Recent research indicates that customers rate most retail electronic commerce sites to be average or low in customer service. A common weak spot for many sites is the lack of integration between the companies' call centers and their Web sites. As a result, when a customer calls with a complaint or problem with a Web purchase, the customer service representative does not have information about Web transactions and is unable to resolve the caller's problem.

Even in the second wave of electronic commerce, e-mail responsiveness of electronic commerce sites is disappointing. Many major companies are slow to respond to e-mail inquiries about product information, order status, or after-sale problems. A significant number of companies in these studies never acknowledged or responded to the e-mail queries.

Rating Electronic Commerce Web Sites

Several companies routinely review electronic commerce Web sites for usability, customer service, and other factors. Most of these sites sell the information they gather directly to the companies that operate the Web sites and include suggestions for improvements. BizRate.com posts ratings on its Web site and provides a comparison shopping service with links to sites with low prices and good service ratings for specific products. BizRate.com compiles its ratings by conducting surveys of sites' customers. When the customer places an order, a pop-up window appears asking for a rating of various aspects of his or her experience with the site. The customer is offered a chance at a prize in exchange for providing this information.

Usability Testing

Most companies do not perform any **usability testing** on their Web sites; however, an increasing number are realizing its importance and are doing some usability testing. As the practice of usability testing becomes more common, more Web sites will meet the goals outlined previously in this chapter.

Experts estimate that average electronic commerce Web sites frustrate as many as half of their potential customers to the point that they leave without buying anything. Even the best sites lose many customers because the sites are confusing or difficult to use. Simple changes in site usability can increase customer satisfaction and sales. For example, some Web sites do not include telephone contact information in the belief that not staffing a call center will save the business money. However, if your customers cannot reach you, they will not continue to do business with you. Most customers will give up when they cannot communicate with you when they need to, using the medium they prefer for that communication.

Companies that have done usability tests, such as Eastman Kodak, T. Rowe Price, and Maytag, have found that they can learn a great deal about meeting visitor needs by conducting focus groups and watching how different customers navigate through a series of Web site test designs. Industry analysts agree that the cost of usability testing is so low compared to the total cost of a Web site design or overhaul that it should almost always be included in such projects. Two pioneers of usability testing are Ben Shneiderman and Jakob Nielsen. Dr. Shneiderman founded the **University of Maryland Human-Computer Interaction Lab** and has published a number of books on interface design. Dr. Nielsen's **Alertbox** Web site includes information about how to conduct usability testing and how to use its results to improve Web site design and operation.

Customer-Centric Web Site Design

An important part of a successful electronic business operation is a Web site that meets the needs of potential customers. In the list of goals for constructing Web sites that you learned about earlier in the chapter, the focus was on meeting the needs of all site visitors. Putting the customer at the center of all site designs is called a **customer-centric** approach to Web site design. A customer-centric approach leads to some guidelines that Web designers can follow when creating a Web site that is intended to meet the specific needs of *customers*, as opposed to all Web site visitors. These guidelines include the following:

- Design the site around how visitors will navigate the links, not around the company's organizational structure.
- Allow visitors to access information quickly.
- Avoid using inflated marketing statements in product or service descriptions.
- Avoid using business jargon and terms that visitors might not understand.

Build the site to work for visitors who are using the oldest browser software on the oldest computer connected through the lowest bandwidth connection—even if this means creating multiple versions of Web pages.

- Be consistent in use of design features and colors.
- Make sure that navigation controls are clearly labeled or otherwise recognizable.
- Test text visibility on a range of monitor sizes; text can become too small to read on a small monitor and so large it shows jagged edges on a large monitor.
- Check to make sure that color combinations do not impair viewing clarity for color-blind visitors.
- Conduct usability tests by having potential site users navigate through several versions of the site.

Web marketing consultant Kristin Zhivago of **Zhivago Marketing Partners** has a number of recommendations for Web sites that are designed specifically to meet the needs of online customers. She encourages Web designers to create sites focused on the customer's buying process rather than the company's perspective and organization. For example, she suggests that companies examine how much information their Web sites provide and how useful that information is for customers. If the site does not provide substantial "content for your click" to visitors, they will not become customers.

Using these guidelines when you create your site can help make visitors' Web experiences more efficient, effective, and memorable. Usability is an important element of creating an effective Web presence. For an interesting look at Web design issues, you can visit the **Webby Awards** site. The Webby Awards are given to sites that "exemplify the kinds of sites that Internet users should visit every day for information and entertainment," as judged by a panel of Web designers, journalists, and industry leaders.

CONNECTING WITH CUSTOMERS

An important element of a corporate Web presence is communicating with site visitors who are customers or potential customers. In this section, you will learn how Web sites can help firms identify and reach out to customers.

The Nature of Communication on the Web

Most businesses are familiar with two general ways of identifying and reaching customers: personal contact and mass media. These two approaches are often called **communication modes** because they each involve a characteristic way (or mode) of conveying information from one person to another (or communicating). In the **personal contact** model, the firm's employees individually search for, qualify, and contact potential customers. This personal contact approach to identifying and reaching customers is sometimes called **prospecting**. In the **mass media** approach, firms prepare advertising and promotional materials about the firm and its products or services. They then deliver these messages to potential customers by broadcasting them on television or radio, printing them in newspapers or magazines, posting them on highway billboards, or mailing them.

Some experts distinguish between broadcast media and addressable media. **Addressable media** are advertising efforts directed to a known addressee and include direct mail, telephone calls, and e-mail. Since few users of addressable media actually use address information in their advertising strategies, in this book, we consider addressable media to be mass media. Many businesses use a combination of mass media and personal contact to identify and reach customers. For example, Prudential uses mass media to create and maintain the public's general awareness of its insurance products and reputation, whereas its salespeople use prospecting techniques to identify potential customers. Once an individual becomes a customer, Prudential maintains contact through a combination of personal contact and mailings.

The Internet is a medium with unique qualities. It occupies a central space in the continuum of media choices. It is not a mass medium, even though a large number of people now use it and many companies seem to view their Web sites as billboards or broadcasts. Nor is the Internet a personal contact tool, although it can provide individuals the convenience of making personal contacts through e-mail and newsgroups. Jeff Bezos, founder of Amazon.com, described the Web as the ideal tool for reaching what he calls "the hard middle"—markets that are too small to justify a mass media campaign, yet too large to cover using personal contact. Figure 3-9 illustrates the position of the Web as a customer contact medium, located between the large markets addressed by mass media and the highly focused markets addressed by personal contact selling and promotion techniques.

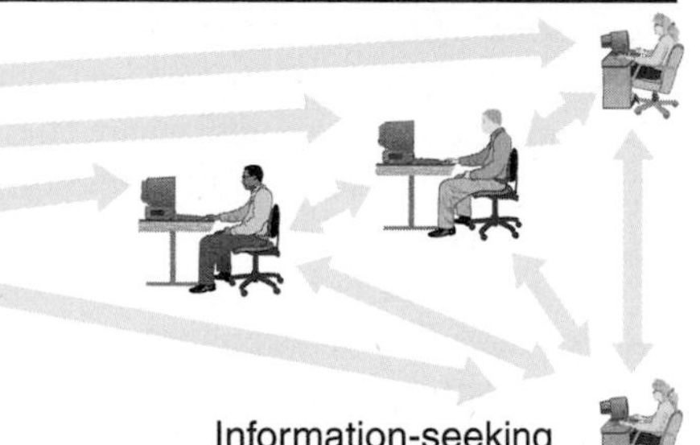

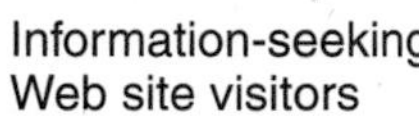

FIGURE 3-9 Business communication modes

To help you better understand the differences shown in Figure 3-9, read the following scenario. The scenario assumes that you have heard about a new book, but would like to learn more about it before buying it. Consider how your information acquisition process would vary, depending on the medium you used to gather the information.

- *Mass media*: You might have been exposed to general promotional messages from book publishers that have created impressions about quality associated with particular book brands. If your existing knowledge includes a brand identity for the book's publisher, these messages might influence your perceptions of the book. You might have been exposed to an ad for the title on television, radio, or in print. You might have heard the book's author interviewed on a radio program or read a review of the book in a publication such as *The New York Times Book Review* or *Booklist* magazine. Notice that most of these process elements involve you as a passive recipient of information. This communication channel is labeled "Mass media" and appears at the top of Figure 3-9. Communication in this model flows from one advertiser to many potential buyers and thus is called a **one-to-many communication model**. The defining characteristic of the mass media promotion process is that the seller is active and the buyer is passive.

- *Personal contact*: Small-value items are not frequently sold through this medium because the costs of devoting a salesperson's efforts to a small sale are prohibitive. However, in the case of books, local bookshop owners and employees often devote considerable time and resources to developing close relationships with their customers. Although each individual book sale is a small-value transaction, people who frequent local bookshops tend to buy large numbers of books over time. Thus, the bookseller's investment in developing personal contacts is often rewarded. In this scenario, you may visit your local bookshop and strike up a conversation with a knowledgeable bookseller. In the personal contact model, this would most likely be a bookseller with whom you have already established a relationship. The bookseller would offer an opinion on the book based on having read that book, books by the same author, or reviews of the book. This opinion would be expressed as part of a two-way conversational interchange. This interchange usually includes a number of conversational elements (small talk, such as discussions about the weather, local sports, or politics) that are not directly related to the transaction you are considering. These other interchanges are part of the trust-building and trust-maintaining activities that businesses undertake to develop the relationship element of the personal contact model. The underlying **one-to-one communication** model appears at the bottom of Figure 3-9 and is labeled "Personal contact." The defining characteristic of information gathering in the personal contact model is the wide-ranging interchange that occurs within the framework of an existing trust relationship. Both the buyer and the seller (or the seller's representative) actively participate in this exchange of information.
- *The Web*: To obtain information about a book on the Web, you could search for Web site references to the book, the author, or the subject of the book. You would likely identify a number of Web sites that offer such information. These sites might include those of the book's publisher, firms that sell books on the Web, independent book reviews, or discussion groups focused on the book's author or genre. *The New York Review of Books* and *Booklist* magazine, both staples of mass media book promotion, are available online. Book review sites that did not originate in a print edition, such as *BookBrowse*, also appear on the Web. Most online booksellers maintain searchable space on their sites for readers to post reviews and comments about specific titles. If the author of the book is famous, there might even be independent Web fan sites devoted to him or her. If the book is about a notable person, incident, or time period, you might find Web sites devoted to those notable topics that include reviews of books related to the topic. You could examine any number of these resources to any extent you desired. You might encounter some advertising material created by the publisher while searching the Web. However, if you choose not to view the publisher's ads, you will find it as easy to click the Back button on your Web browser as it is to surf television channels with your remote control. The Web affords you many communication channels. Figure 3-9 shows

only one of the communication models that can occur when using the Web to search for product information. The model labeled "The Web" in Figure 3-9 is the **many-to-one communication model**. The Web gives you the flexibility to use a one-to-one model (as in the personal contact model) in which you communicate over the Web with an individual working for the seller, or engage in **many-to-many communications** with other potential buyers. The defining characteristic of a product information search on the Web is that the buyer actively participates in the search and controls the length, depth, and scope of the search.

Summary

In this chapter, you learned that businesses are using six main approaches to generate revenue on the Web: the Web catalog, digital content sales, advertising-supported, advertising-subscription mixed, fee-for-transaction, and fee-for-service models. You learned how these models work and what kinds of businesses use which models. You also learned that some companies have changed models as they learned more about their customers and the business environment in which their Web sites operate.

Companies sometimes face the challenges of channel conflict and cannibalization either within their own organizations or with the companies that have traditionally provided sales distribution to consumers for them. In accordance with the network model of organization that you learned about in Chapter 1, companies undertaking electronic commerce initiatives sometimes form strategic alliances with other companies to obtain their skills in Web site operation.

By understanding how the Web differs from other media and by designing a Web site to capitalize on those differences, companies can create an effective Web presence that delivers value to visitors. Every organization must expect that visitors to its Web site arrive with a variety of expectations, prior knowledge, and skill levels, and are connected to the Internet through different technologies. Knowing how these factors can affect the visitor's ability to navigate the site and extract information from the site can help organizations design better, more usable Web sites. Enlisting the help of users when building test versions of the Web site is also a good way to create a Web site that represents the organization well.

Firms must understand the nature of communication on the Web so they can use it to identify and reach the largest possible number of customers and qualified prospects. Using a many-to-one communication model enables Web sites to effectively reach potential customers.

Key Terms

Account aggregation
Addressable media
Advertising-subscription mixed revenue model
Advertising-supported revenue model
Bill presentment
Cannibalization
Catalog model
Channel conflict
Channel cooperation
Communication modes
Customer-centric
Demographic information
Digital content revenue model
Digital Rights Management (DRM)
Disintermediation
Fee-for-service revenue model
Fee-for-transaction revenue model
Mail-order model
Many-to-many communications
Many-to-one communication model
Marketing channel
Mass media
One-to-many communication model
One-to-one communication model
Personal contact
Personal shopper
Portal (Web portal)
Presence
Prospecting
Reintermediation
Stakeholders
Stickiness

Sticky
Usability testing
Virtual model
Web catalog revenue model
Web directory
Web portal

Review Questions

RQ1. Write a paragraph in which you describe the conditions under which a Web site could become profitable by relying exclusively on advertising revenue. In a second paragraph, provide an example of a company not mentioned in the chapter that is using the advertising-supported model and that is likely to be successful in the long run. Explain why you think it will succeed.

RQ2. In two paragraphs, outline ways in which not-for-profit organizations can design their Web sites to increase the number and amount of donations they receive from supporters.

RQ3. In two paragraphs, explain why a customer-centric Web site design is so important, yet is so difficult to accomplish.

RQ4. In one paragraph, define the term "presence." Write an additional paragraph in which you explain why companies that do business on the Web should be more concerned about presence than firms that operate only in the physical world.

RQ5. Many real estate agents today have Web sites that list the properties they have for sale. These agents also advertise the properties on Realtor.com and sometimes in television ads. However, most real estate agents would tell you that personal contact provides their most important connections with clients, potential clients, and client referral sources. Write three paragraphs in which you briefly describe the things that real estate agents can best accomplish through (1) their Web sites, (2) mass media advertising, and (3) personal contact.

Exercises

E1. Page 149 lists things that Web sites can do to meet the needs of visitors. Create a table in which the first column is a list of at least five needs of Web site visitors. Find three Web sites that meet three or more of the needs. Create a column for each Web site next to the first column (columns two through four) and rate how well each site meets each need in the first column. You may want to use the **Webby Awards** site as a starting point in your search, but do not use any of the award nominees or winners in your table.

E2. Evaluate the usability of two Web sites that sell large-screen LCD high-definition televisions. A list of links to companies that sell this type of product is included in the Online Companion for this exercise, but you may use other sites if you wish. In your evaluation, compare the sites on how easy it is to learn about the product and purchase the product. Your report should include a section of about 200 words in which you describe the criteria you used in your evaluation, a section of about 300 words that summarizes your findings, and a section of about 100 words in which you present your conclusion.

E3. You are a Web business consultant and have been retained by Bob Drudge, the owner of **refdesk.com**, to explore revenue-generating alternatives. Currently, the site is using an advertising-supported revenue model. Bob wants you to consider each of the other revenue models and the potential of strategic alliances that might make sense for his site.

Write a report of about 400 words in which you summarize your research and state your recommendations.

Note: Your instructor might assign you to a group to complete this exercise and might also ask you to present your recommendations in class.

E4. High-end jewelry retailers such as **Cartier**, **Harry Winston**, and **Tiffany** often use Adobe's Flash software to create their Web sites. Present three arguments for and three arguments against the use of Flash animations in sites such as these. Consider the retailers' objectives, the characteristics of the products being sold, and the type of customers who visit these sites. Limit your answer to 400 words.

E5. Many local newspapers are ending their business of printing daily newspapers. Some are going out of business entirely; others are continuing in existence by publishing local news stories on a Web site. Assume you are a consultant to a local newspaper that is converting to online publication. List the links that you believe would be essential to include on the newspaper Web site's home page. For each link, provide a one- or two-sentence statement about why it is important to include it on the home page.

E6. Describe two possible service-for-fee offerings that could be introduced on smart phones in the near future. These would be services delivered to the phone by the wireless carrier, which would charge a monthly subscription fee for the service. Write one paragraph for each service in which you outline the profit potential and risk of losses for each.

Cases

C1. Lonely Planet

In 1972, Tony and Maureen Wheeler were newlyweds who decided to have one last adventurous travel experience before settling down. Their trip was an overland trek from London to Australia through Asia. So many other travelers asked them about their experiences that they sat down at their kitchen table and wrote a book titled *Across Asia on the Cheap*. They published the book themselves and were surprised by how many copies they sold. More than three decades and 60 million books later, their publishing enterprise has turned out to be one of the most successful in history.

The Wheelers' publishing company, Lonely Planet, has grown rapidly, with typical annual sales increases of 20 percent or more. In 2007, BBC Worldwide purchased a 75 percent ownership interest in the company. Lonely Planet TV now produces a variety of travel and documentary programs that appear on cable networks throughout the world. The company is privately held and does not release sales figures, but industry analysts estimate current annual revenues to be about $85 million. Lonely Planet publishes more than 600 titles and holds a 16 percent share of the travel guide market. The company has more than 400 employees in its UK, U.S., French, and Australian offices performing editorial, production, graphic design, and marketing tasks. Travel guide content is written by a network of more than 300 contract authors in 22 countries. These authors are knowledgeable about everything from visa regulations to hotel prices to the names of the hottest new entertainment spots. The combined expertise of the in-house staff and the in-country authors has kept Lonely Planet ahead of its competitors for many years.

Lonely Planet also offers travel services that include a phone card, hotel and hostel room-booking, airplane tickets, European rail travel reservations and tickets, package tours, and travel insurance. These services are sold by telephone and on the Lonely Planet Web site.

The Web site has won numerous awards, including the Society of American Travel Writers Silver Award and a spot on *Time* magazine's "Fifty Best Web Sites" list. It has also won the best travel site Webby multiple times. The site was launched in 1994 and includes an online store in which Lonely Planet publications are sold. However, the site's main draws are its comprehensive collection of information about travel destinations and its online discussion area, the Thorn Tree, which has nearly a half million registered users.

Lonely Planet is always looking for ways to expand its market and brand image through new technologies. For example, it offers audio phrasebooks and city guides that can be downloaded to several brands of smart phones.

Despite its excellent Web site and its use of new technologies, most of Lonely Planet's revenues are still generated by book sales. The typical production cycle of a travel guide is about eight months long. This is the time it takes to commission authors, conduct research, work through several drafts of writing and editing, select photos, create the physical book, and print it. This production cycle causes new books to be almost a year out of date by the time they are published. Only the most popular titles are revised annually. Other titles are on two-, three-, or four-year revision cycles. The time delay in publication means that many details in the guides are outdated or wrong; restaurants and hotels close (or move), exchange rates and visa regulations change, and once-hot night spots are abandoned by fickle clientele.

Lonely Planet publications are well researched and of high quality, but the writers do not work continually because the books are not published continually. The Web site often has information that is more current than the published travel guides. The site's online shop does offer some custom guides, which are parts of its existing travel guides packaged in different ways, and it does let customers buy specific chapters from its books, but it still is largely focused on selling books. Lonely Planet has adopted new technologies, but has not used them to change its revenue model in any major way or to make basic changes in the production of its main product, the travel guides.

Required:

1. Prepare a report in which you analyze the marketing channel conflicts and cannibalization issues that Lonely Planet faces as it is currently operating. Suggest solutions that might reduce the revenue losses or operational frictions that result from these issues.
2. Prepare a list of new products or services that Lonely Planet might introduce to take advantage of Internet technologies (including wireless technologies for mobile devices) and address customers' concerns about the timeliness and currency of information in the printed travel guides. Briefly describe any problems that Lonely Planet will face as it introduces these new products.
3. Many loyal Lonely Planet customers carry their travel guides (which can be several hundred pages thick) with them as they travel around the world. In many cases, these customers do not use large portions of the travel guides. Also, Internet access can be a problem for many of these customers while they are traveling. Describe a product (or products) that might address this customer concern and also yield additional revenue for Lonely Planet. Your answer here could build on ideas that you developed in your solution to part 2.

Note: Your instructor might assign you to a group to complete this case and might ask you to prepare a formal presentation of your results to your class.

C2. Association for the Study of International Business

The Association for the Study of International Business (ASIB) is an organization of researchers, professors, and business executives interested in the study, analysis, and promotion of business activities beyond domestic borders. Mario DiPonetti, ASIB's executive director, has hired you as a consultant to help him map out a future Web revenue strategy for the association.

The ASIB has about 3000 members located in countries throughout the world; however, about half of its members are in the United States. Each member pays an annual membership fee of $100, so ASIB's dues revenue totals about $300,000 per year. ASIB sponsors several conferences each year; it also publishes a monthly newsletter and two journals. The conferences break even; that is, the conference and exhibitor fees cover the costs of running the conference, but they do not yield any profit that can be applied to other ASIB operating costs.

One of the journals, *Annals of International Business*, has an academic focus and is read by researchers interested in international business topics. All ASIB members receive a copy of this journal and ASIB sells about 600 subscriptions to the journal at $300 per year. Most of the subscribers are university libraries. This journal is published four times each year. The second journal, *International Business Today*, is written for business executives. It includes articles and features that report on current trends in international business. All ASIB members receive a copy of this journal and ASIB sells about 1000 subscriptions to the journal at $60 per year. Most of the subscribers are business executives. This journal is published 12 times each year. The total subscription revenue from the two journals is $240,000 per year. The business journal also sells advertising that yields about $20,000 per year. ASIB uses that total revenue of $260,000 to cover the costs of producing and mailing both journals. The cost of producing one issue of either journal, which includes proofreading, editing, and typesetting costs, is about $5000. The printing and mailing costs, which have been increasing rapidly over the past several years, average about $2 per journal (the mailing costs to some members are much higher than others because they are located in distant countries). Each year, ASIB produces 16 issues (four of the academic journal and 12 of the business journal) and mails 62,400 journals (14,400 of the academic journal and 48,000 of the business journal) to members and subscribers at a total cost of $204,800 (16 × $5000 plus 62,400 × $2). Thus, ASIB's current journal operations yield a net profit of $55,200 ($260,000 – $204,800) that can help support other ASIB activities.

ASIB has a Web site that it constructed at a cost of $56,000 three years ago. One of ASIB's staff members spends approximately half of her time managing the site. One-half of her salary along with other recurring expenses, such as software licenses and computer upgrades for the Web site, total about $35,000 per year. Mario explains to you that one of the ASIB's greatest cost reduction successes was last year's decision to offer the newsletter by e-mail. About half of the members chose to receive the newsletter by e-mail. The paper newsletters cost 50 cents each to print and mail, but creating and sending the e-mails took less than $50 worth of staff members' time. Thus, ASIB realized an immediate savings of about $700 each month. The newsletters are also placed on the Web site so that members can check there if they happen to miss the e-mailed newsletter. This success prompted Mario to think about ways to reduce the cost of distributing the journals. He wants to make sure, however, that ASIB continues to receive as much of the journal revenue as possible under any new revenue model.

One of the companies you learned about in the chapter, EBSCO, approached Mario with an offer to handle electronic distribution of the academic journal. EBSCO will take a copy of the journal when it is published, convert each article into Adobe Portable Document Format (PDF) and into HTML format, index the articles, and place them into several of EBSCO's databases. Many university and research libraries subscribe to EBSCO databases. The EBSCO representative explained to Mario that most of the libraries would continue their print subscriptions to the journal, but that about 30 percent of the libraries would stop subscribing and rely on their electronic access to the journal through the EBSCO database. Mario called some of his friends who are executive directors of other associations and confirmed that this percentage was correct in their experience. EBSCO would pay ASIB $10,000 per year for access to the journal plus $50 per year for every library that subscribed to an EBSCO database that included the journal. The EBSCO representative estimated that the number of subscribing libraries would be about 1000.

Mario outlined an alternative to the EBSCO contract. In this alternative, ASIB would itself scan the journals into PDF files and make them available on the ASIB Web site for a subscription fee. Mario estimated that it would cost about $1000 to create the PDF files for one issue and place them on the Web site. He also estimated that managing the accounts and passwords would consume about $500 per month of staff time and costs.

EBSCO was not interested in purchasing access to the business journal, but Mario is considering ways to make some or all of the content from that journal available on the ASIB Web site. He is considering offering reduced-rate "Web access only" subscriptions to business executives. He is also thinking about offering some of the best stories from the print edition on the Web and including ads offering full subscriptions on each page. He is even considering placing the first part of the best stories on the Web site and offering readers a chance to subscribe so they can read the rest of the story.

Several companies that sell products and services to international businesses currently run ads in the business journal. These companies expressed an interest in placing ads on ASIB Web pages that contain content (such as stories from the business journal). Mario estimates that ASIB could earn between $3000 and $9000 per month from these ads, but he is concerned that having the best content from the business journal on the Web site might convince some business executives to drop their subscriptions to the print edition.

Required:

Prepare a comprehensive report for Mario in which you outline and analyze the possible revenue models that ASIB might use for its Web site. You should address the two journals as separate issues. Your report should provide the basis for a presentation to the ASIB executive board and should include specific recommendations where possible.

Note: Your instructor might assign you to a group to complete this case and might ask you to prepare a formal presentation of your results to your class.

For Further Study and Research

Anderson, C. 2008. *The Long Tail Revised and Updated Edition: Why the Future of Business is Selling Less of More.* New York: Hyperion.

Anderson, C. 2009. *Free: The Future of a Radical Price.* New York: Hyperion.

Carr, D. 2003. "Slate Sets a Web Magazine First: Making Money," *The New York Times,* April 28, C1.

Christensen, C. and M. Overdorf. 2000. "Meeting the Challenge of Disruptive Change," *Harvard Business Review,* 78(2), March–April, 66–75.

Costa, D. 2007. "The Music Wants to Be Free," *PC Magazine,* December 4, 81.

Crawford, W. 2004. "Keeping the Faith: Playing Fair with Your Visitors," *EContent,* 27(4), September, 42–43.

Cyr, D., M. Head, H. Larios, and B. Pan. 2009. "Exploring Human Images in Website Design: A Multi-method Approach," *MIS Quarterly,* 33(3), 539–575.

Daly, J. 2000. "Sage Advice: Interview with Peter Drucker," *Business 2.0,* August 22, 134–144.

Davidson, B. 2003. *Breakthrough: How Great Companies Set Outrageous Objectives and Achieve Them.* New York: Wiley.

Doonar, J. 2004. "It's Not Such a Lonely Planet," *Brand Strategy,* January, 24–25.

Duff, A. 2003. "Lonely at the Top," *Director;* 57(3), October, 78–82.

Egol, M., H. Hawkes, and G. Springs. 2009. "Reinventing Print Media," *strategy+business,* 56, Autumn, *80–83.*

Eisenmann, T. 2002. *Internet Business Models.* New York: McGraw-Hill.

Evans, P. and T. Wurster. 1997. "Strategy and the New Economics of Information," *Harvard Business Review,* 75(5), September–October, 71–83.

Gentzkow, M. 2005. "Valuing New Goods in a Model with Complementarities: Online Newspapers," University of Chicago Unpublished Working Paper, May 5. (http://gsbwww.uchicago.edu/fac/matthew.gentzkow/research/)

Greenstein, S. and M. Devereux. 2006. *The Crisis at Encyclopaedia Britannica.* Kellogg School of Management Case 5-306-504. Evanston, IL: Northwestern University.

Gupta, S. and C. Mela. 2009. "What Is a Free Customer Worth?" *Harvard Business Review,* 86(11), 102–109.

Hill, A. 2001. "Stop Shopping Cart Abandonment: Top Five Reasons Customers Abandon Shopping Carts," *Smart Business,* February 13. (http://www.zdnet.com/smartbusinessmag/stories/all/0,6605,2677306,00.html)

Holmes, E. 2009. "CBS's TV.com Boosts Offerings in Bid to Secure Foothold," *The Wall Street Journal,* January 12, B3.

Jones, K., L. Leonard, and C. Riemenschneider. 2009. "Trust Influencers on the Web," *Journal of Organizational Computing & Electronic Commerce,* 19(3), 196–213.

Keighley, G. 2003. "The Secrets of Drudge, Inc." *Business 2.0,* April. (http://www.business2.com/articles/mag/0,1640,47762,00.html)

Kemp, T. 2000. "Wal-Mart No Web Mart," *InternetWeek,* October 9, 1–2.

Kotha, S., S. Rajgopal, and M. Venkatachalam. 2004. "The Role of Online Buying Experience as a Competitive Advantage: Evidence from Third-Party Ratings for E-Commerce Firms," *Journal of Business,* 77 (Supplement), April, S109–S134.

McCoy, A. 2008. "Reel Estate: Downloads Are Changing the Movie Rental Landscape," *Pittsburgh Post-Gazette,* February 6. (http://www.post-gazette.com/pg/08037/854979-42.stm)

Medical Economics. 2009. "Website to Offer Online Visits Nationwide," August 7, 18.

Netherby, J. 2009. "Zucker has Hulu Profit in Sight," *Video Business,* June 1, 3, 21.

Neuborne, E. 2001. "Bridging the Loyalty Gap," *Business Week,* January 22, EB10.

Nielsen, J. 1999. *Designing Websites With Authority: Secrets of an Information Architect.* Indianapolis, IN: New Riders.

Nielsen, J. 2000. "End of Web Design," *Alertbox,* July 23. (http://www.useit.com/alertbox/20000723.html)

Nielsen, J. 2000. "Flash: 99% Bad," *Alertbox,* October 29. (http://www.useit.com/alertbox/20001029.html)

Nielsen, J. 2001. "Usability Metrics," *Alertbox,* January 21. (http://www.useit.com/alertbox/20010121.html)

Nielsen, J. and M. Tahir. 2002. *Homepage Usability: 50 Websites Deconstructed.* Indianapolis, IN: New Riders.

Nielsen, J., K. Coyne, and M. Tahir. 2001. "Make It Usable," *PC Magazine,* 20(3), February 6, IPO1–IPO6.

Palvia, P. 2009. "The Role of Trust in E-commerce Relational Exchange: A Unified Model," *Information & Management,* 46(4), 213–220.

Pegoraro, R. 2005. "Priorities for the Store-Shopping List," *The Washington Post,* August 28, F1.

Pérez-Peña, R. 2007. "Times to End Charges on Web Site," *The New York Times,* September 18. (http://www.nytimes.com/2007/09/18/business/media/18times.html)

Rayport, J. and J. Sviokla. 1995. "Exploiting the Virtual Value Chain," *Harvard Business Review,* 73(6), November–December, 75–85.

Sanderfoot, A. and C. Jenkins. 2001. "Content Sites Pursue Fee-Based Model," *Folio: The Magazine for Magazine Management,* 30(6), 15–16.

Schwartz, E. 1997. *Webonomics.* New York: Broadway Books.

Schwartz, E. 1999. *Digital Darwinism.* New York: Broadway Books.

Seelye, K. 2005. "Why Newspapers Are Betting on Audience Participation," *The New York Times,* July 4, C2.

Shneiderman, B. 1997. *Designing the User Interface: Strategies for Effective Human-Computer Interaction.* Reading, MA: Addison-Wesley.

Sklar, J. 2009. *Principles of Web Design*, Fourth Edition. Boston, MA: Course Technology.

Smith, E. 2008. "Napster to Sell Downloads for Most Music Players," *The Wall Street Journal,* January 7, B2.

Steel, E. 2007. "Job-Search Sites Face a Nimble Threat; Online Boards Become Specialized, Challenging Web-Print Partnerships," *The Wall Street Journal,* October 9, B10.

Stone, B. 2008. "Netflix Partners With LG to Bring Movies Straight to TV," *The New York Times,* January 3. (http://www.nytimes.com/2008/01/03/technology/03netflix.html)

Tedeschi, B. 2005. "New Era of Ticket Resales: Online and Aboveboard," *The New York Times,* August 29, C4.

Trachtenberg, J. 2007. "Borders Business Plan Gets a Rewrite," *The Wall Street Journal,* March 22, B1–B2.

Weingarten, M. 2001. "Flash Backlash," *The Industry Standard,* March 5. (http://www.thestandard.com/article/0,1902,22330,00.html)

Weiss, T. 2000. "Walmart.com Back Online After Four-Week Overhaul," *Computerworld,* 34(45), November 6, 24.

Williams, T. 2005. "NYTimes.com to Offer Subscription Service," *The New York Times,* May 17, C5.

Zeitchik, S. 2003. "New Worlds at Lonely Planet," *Publishers Weekly,* 250(25), June 23, 12.

Zimmerman, A. 2000. "Wal-Mart Launches Web Site for a Third Time, This Time Emphasizing Speed and Ease," *The Wall Street Journal,* October 31, B12.

CHAPTER **4**

MARKETING ON THE WEB

LEARNING OBJECTIVES

In this chapter, you will learn about:

- When to use product-based and customer-based marketing strategies
- Communicating with different market segments
- Customer relationship intensity and the customer relationship life cycle
- Using advertising on the Web
- E-mail marketing
- Technology-enabled customer relationship management
- Creating and maintaining brands on the Web
- Search engine positioning and domain name selection

INTRODUCTION

In September 1997, a new gift shop opened for business on the Web. There were already many gift shops on the Web at that time; however, this store, named 911Gifts.com, carried items that were chosen specifically to meet the needs of last-minute gift shoppers. Including 911—the emergency telephone number used in most parts of the United States—in the store's name was intended to convey the impression of crisis-solving urgency. The company's two major strengths were its promise of next-day delivery on all items and its site layout, in which gift selections were organized by holiday rather than by product type. Thus, a harried shopper could simply click the Mother's Day gifts link and view a set of gift choices appropriate for that holiday that were ready for immediate delivery. The site also included a reminder service, called GiftAlert, to help its customers avoid another emergency gift situation on the next holiday.

By 1999, the company had 90,000 customers signed up for GiftAlert and was doing about $1 million in annual sales. It carried about 500 products, and each of the products was chosen to yield a gross margin of at least 40 percent. 911Gifts.com was a successful business, but the company's founders realized they would need to build wider awareness of their brand. They also realized that building a brand would require a substantial investment of funds. The company hired Hilary Billings, a retail marketing executive whose experience included building the Pottery Barn catalog business at Williams-Sonoma, to create a brand-building strategy and obtain financing to implement that strategy. Billings undertook a complete reevaluation of the 911Gifts.com marketing plan and, after revising it, took it to investors, who committed more than $30 million for a rebranding and complete overhaul of the company's Web site. In October 1999, the new brand was born as **RedEnvelope**. In many Asian countries, gifts of money are enclosed in a simple red envelope. The new brand was designed to create a sense of elegant simplicity to replace the sense of panic and emergency solutions conveyed by the old brand name.

The product line was revamped to fit the new image as well. About 300 products were dropped and replaced with different products that focus groups had judged to be more appealing. The new product line had an even higher average gross margin than the old line. Billings launched a massive brand-awareness campaign that included online advertising, buses in seven major cities painted red and festooned with large red bows, and print advertising in upscale publications. The most important change in advertising strategy was the launch of a print catalog. RedEnvelope catalogs are mailed to customers to coincide with major gift-giving holidays and serve as additional reminders. Because RedEnvelope sells a small set of products that are chosen for their visual appeal and for the status they are intended to convey, the full-color, lushly illustrated print catalogs are a powerful selling tool.

One year later, the results of this extensive makeover and substantial monetary investment were clear. RedEnvelope had tripled its number of customers and had increased sales by more than 400 percent. The company chose a specific part of the gifts market and targeted its offerings to meet the needs and desires of those customers. The company created a brand, a marketing plan, and a set of advertising and promotion strategies that would expose the company to the largest portion of that market it could afford to reach. The most important point is that RedEnvelope matched its inventory selection, delivery methods, and marketing efforts to each other and to the needs of its customers. Since 2008, RedEnvelope has been part of Provide Commerce, a company that operates online gift businesses such as Proflowers and Shari's Berries. The company continues to use print catalogs and a focus on upscale product lines to keep its sales increasing each year. Marketing an online business often requires the use of a combination of marketing techniques that sometimes include traditional approaches such as print catalogs.

WEB MARKETING STRATEGIES

In this chapter, you will learn how companies are using the Web in their marketing strategies to advertise their products and services and promote their reputations. Increasingly, companies are classifying customers into groups and creating targeted messages for each group. The sizes of these targeted groups can be smaller when companies are using the Web—in some cases, just one customer at a time can be targeted. New research into the behavior of Web site visitors has even suggested ways in which Web sites can respond to visitors who arrive at a site with different needs at different times. This chapter will also introduce you to some of the ways companies are making money by selling advertising on their Web sites.

Most companies use the term **marketing mix** to describe the combination of elements that they use to achieve their goals for selling and promoting their products and services. When a company decides which elements it will use, it calls that particular marketing mix its **marketing strategy**. As you learned in Chapter 3, companies—even those in the same industry—try to create unique presences in their markets. A company's marketing strategy is an important tool that works with its Web presence to get the company's message across to both its current and prospective customers.

Most marketing classes organize the essential issues of marketing into the **four Ps of marketing**: product, price, promotion, and place. **Product** is the physical item or service that a company is selling. The intrinsic characteristics of the product are important, but customers' perceptions of the product, called the product's **brand**, can be as important as the actual characteristics of the product.

The **price** element of the marketing mix is the amount the customer pays for the product. In recent years, marketing experts have argued that companies should think of price in a broader sense, that is, the total of all financial costs that the customer pays (including transaction costs) to obtain the product. This total cost is subtracted from the benefits that a customer derives from the product to yield an estimate of the **customer value** obtained in the transaction. Later in this book, you will learn how the Web can create new opportunities for creative pricing and price negotiations through online auctions, reverse auctions, and group buying strategies. These Web-based opportunities are helping companies find new ways to create increased customer value.

Promotion includes any means of spreading the word about the product. On the Internet, new possibilities abound for communicating with existing and potential customers. In Chapter 2, you learned how companies are using the Internet to engage in meaningful dialogues with their customers using e-mail and other means. In this chapter, you will learn even more communication techniques that companies are using to promote their products.

For years, marketing managers dreamed of a world in which instant deliveries would give all customers exactly what they wanted when they wanted it. The issue of **place** (also called **distribution**) is the need to have products or services available in many different locations. The problem of getting the right products to the right places at the best time to sell them has plagued companies since commerce began. Although the Internet does not solve all of these logistics and distribution problems, it can certainly help. For example, digital products (such as information, news, software, music, video, and e-books) can be delivered almost instantly through the Internet. Companies that sell products that must be shipped have found that the Internet gives them much better shipment tracking and control than did previous information technologies.

Product-Based Marketing Strategies

In Chapter 3, you learned about the importance of a company's Web presence and how this presence must integrate with the brand or other established images the company uses in its promotional activities. Most companies offer a variety of products that appeal to different groups. When creating a marketing strategy, managers must consider both the nature of their products and the nature of their potential customers.

Managers at many companies think of their businesses in terms of the products and services they sell. This is a logical way to think of a business because companies spend a great deal of effort, time, and money to design and create those products and services. If you ask managers to describe what their companies are selling, they usually provide you with a detailed list of the physical objects they sell or use to create a service. When customers are likely to buy items from particular product categories, or are likely to think of their needs in terms of product categories, this type of product-based organization makes sense. Most office supplies stores on the Web believe their customers think of their needs using a product category structure. For example, both The Home Depot and Staples use product categories as a very strong organizing theme in the design of their Web sites.

Many other online businesses use a similar product-based marketing strategy. Sears, a company that sold its products through catalogs and later in physical stores for many years before opening online, uses a product-based structure on its Web site. Most companies that used print catalogs in the past organized them by product category, and this design theme has carried over into many of their Web sites.

Many of these former catalog retailers organize their Web sites from an internal viewpoint, that is, according to the way that they arranged their product design and manufacturing processes. If customers arrive at these Web sites looking for a specific type of product, this approach works well. Alternatively, customers who are looking to fulfill a specific need, such as outfitting a new sales office or choosing a graduation gift, rather than find a specific product, might not find these Web sites as useful. Many marketing researchers and consultants advise companies to think as if they were their own customers and to design their Web sites so that customers find them to be enabling experiences that can help customers meet their individual needs. Sometimes this requires the Web site to offer alternative shopping paths. For example, an online florist's Web site could allow customers to specify an arrangement that includes specific flowers (satisfying customers with a desire for a specific product), yet provide a separate shopping path for customers who want to buy an arrangement for a specific occasion (birthday, anniversary, Mother's Day, and so on).

Customer-Based Marketing Strategies

In Chapter 3, you learned that the Web creates an environment that allows buyers and sellers to engage in complex communications modes. The communication structures on the Web can become much more complex than those in traditional mass media outlets such as broadcast and print advertising. When a company takes its business to the Web, it can create a Web site that is flexible enough to meet the needs of many different users. Instead of thinking of their Web sites as collections of products, companies can build their sites to meet the specific needs of various types of customers.

A good first step in building a customer-based marketing strategy is to identify groups of customers who share common characteristics. **Sabre Holdings** is a company that sells marketing services and technology to support those services to the travel industry. Its customers can be categorized into three groups: airlines, travel agencies and large companies' in-house travel departments, and consumers who would be interested in the Travelocity Web site. The Sabre Holdings home page, which appears in Figure 4-1, includes links to separate sections of its site that are designed to meet the needs of each of these customer groups, airlines, consumers, and travel agencies (including corporate travel departments). By following these links, Sabre's different categories of customers can find specific products and services targeted to each of their needs.

Although Sabre's approach of breaking customers into three main groups is a good first step, subgroups probably exist within each of those groups. Marketers can use their experience with selling in their industries to identify those subgroups and then develop marketing strategies and tactics that will effectively reach customers in each subgroup. The use of customer-based marketing approaches was pioneered on B2B sites. B2B sellers were more aware of the need to customize product and service offerings to match their customers' needs than were the operators of B2C Web sites. In recent years, B2C sites have increasingly added customer-based marketing elements to their Web sites. One of the most noticeable trends in this direction is in university Web sites.

FIGURE 4-1 Sabre home page

In the early days of the Web, university sites were usually organized around the internal elements of the school (such as departments, colleges, and programs). Today, most university home pages include links to separate sections of the Web site designed for specific stakeholders, such as current students, prospective students, parents of students, potential donors, and faculty.

COMMUNICATING WITH DIFFERENT MARKET SEGMENTS

Identifying groups of potential customers is just the first step in selling to those customers. An equally important component of any marketing strategy is the selection of communication media to carry the marketing message.

In the physical world, companies can convey large parts of their messages by the way they construct buildings and design their floor spaces. For example, banks have traditionally been housed in large, solid-looking buildings that provide passersby an ample view of the main safe and its thick, sturdy door. Banks use these physical manifestations of reliability and strength to communicate an important part of their service offerings—that a customer's money is safe and secure with the bank.

Media selection can be critical for an online firm because it does not have a physical presence. The only contact a potential customer might have with an online firm could well be the image it projects through the media and through its Web site. The challenge for online businesses is to convince customers to trust them even though they do not have an immediate physical presence.

Trust, Complexity, and Media Choice

The Web is an intermediate step between mass media and personal contact, but it is a very broad step. Using the Web to communicate with potential customers offers many of the advantages of personal contact selling and many of the cost savings of mass media. Figure 4-2 shows how these three information dissemination modes compare on the important dimensions of trust and product (or service) complexity.

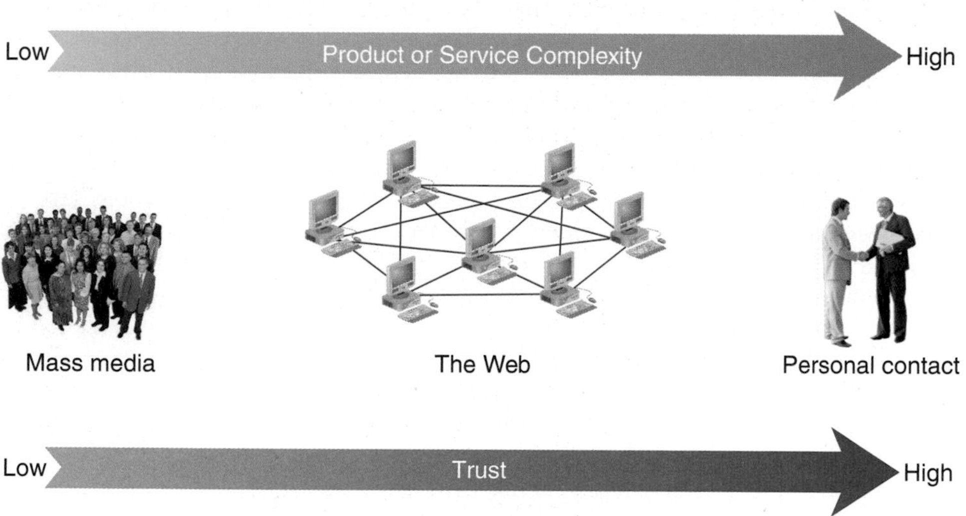

FIGURE 4-2 Trust in three information dissemination models

Although mass media offers the lowest level of trust, many companies continue to use it successfully. The cost of mass media advertising can be spread over the many people in its large audiences. For example, the cost of creating and running a television ad can be millions of dollars, but that ad will be viewed by millions of people. Thus, the cost of advertising per viewer is very low. Its low cost per viewer makes mass media advertising attractive to many companies. In 2009, Ford Motor Company shifted a significant portion of its advertising budget from traditional car ads that focused on new vehicle features to ads that told stories about how Ford managers are running the company more intelligently than its competitors. Ford's two major U.S.-based competitors, Chrysler and General Motors, both needed taxpayer bailout money to survive the global economic recession. Ford was able to use mass media advertising to draw a sharp contrast between it and its competitors in the minds of millions of potential customers. The message was straightforward and could be delivered to all of Ford's customers (and potential customers) using the same language and images. Thus, mass media advertising was an ideal choice for delivering this message.

The level of complexity inherent in the product or service is also an important factor in media choice. Products that have few characteristics or that are easy to understand can be promoted well using mass media. Because mass media is expensive to produce, most companies use it to deliver short messages (although there are exceptions, such as infomercials). Highly complex products and services are best promoted through personal contact, which allows the potential customer to ask clarifying questions during the promotional presentation.

The Web occupies a wide middle ground and can be used for delivering short but focused messages that promote, but can also be used to deliver longer and more complex messages. The Web can even be used to engage the potential customer in a back and forth dialogue similar to that used in personal contact selling. Most importantly, a properly designed Web site can give potential customers the ability to choose their level of interaction. A company can present a mass media type of message that a site visitor can click to access a more detailed message. If the visitor still wants more information, the site can offer the opportunity for interactive communication (such as an online chat) with a customer service representative. Thus, the Web can offer elements of mass media messaging, personal contact interaction, and anything in between.

After years of being barraged by television and radio commercials, many people have developed a resistance to the messages conveyed in mass media. The impact on an audience of the shouted expression "New and improved!" is very low. The overuse of superlatives has caused many people to distrust or ignore much mass media. Television remote controls have mute buttons and make channel surfing easy for a reason. Attempts to recreate mass media advertising on the Web are likely to fail for the same reasons—many people ignore or resist messages that lack content of any specific personal interest to them.

Mass media advertising campaigns that are successful often rely on the passive nature of the media consumption experience. People watching television or listening to radio are usually in a passive and receptive state of mind. Thus, advertisers can include messages in mass media advertising that recipients might not consider valid or convincing if they were actively evaluating those statements. The messages are accepted by recipients because they are in a nonquestioning and passive state of mind. In contrast, Web users are actively engaged in the medium, with hands on the keyboard and mouse, as they view Web pages. This active state of mind makes Web users far more likely to actively evaluate advertising messages they see and less likely to accept the content of those messages in the same passive way that television viewers accept the content of television commercials.

Companies can use the Web to capture some of the benefits of personal contact, yet avoid some of the costs inherent in that approach. Most experts agree that it is better to make the trust-based model of personal contact selling work on the Web than to adopt the mass marketing approach. When companies started to sell online in the mid-1990s, rising consumer expectations and reduced product differentiation led to increased competition and a splintering of mass markets. Both of these results were reducing the effectiveness of mass media advertising. Thus, the Internet provided a new vehicle for achieving high levels of customer-focused marketing strategies.

The Internet has created new communications modalities for individuals and companies. People can post their thoughts on a Web site and invite others to add commentary. This type of Web site, known as a **Web log** or **blog**, has provided an outlet for political, religious, and other statements of strongly felt beliefs. In recent years, some retailers have experimented with blogs as an adjunct communication device. These retailers hope that blogs will give their online stores a personality and provide customers with a reason to visit their Web sites even if they are not shopping. For example, clothing retailer **Bluefly** operates a blog called **Flypaper** that is written and edited by employees in their spare time. Customers and other Web site visitors are invited to add commentary, ask questions, and state opinions, but Bluefly edits and controls what gets posted to the site. Bluefly hopes that the Flypaper blog will reinforce the company's image as a place to shop for customers who care more about current fashion than about getting a good price on clothing that might no longer be fashionable.

Blogs are examples of how companies can use the Web to engage in two-way communications that more closely resemble the high-trust personal contact mode of communication than the low-trust mass media mode. And they allow companies to achieve some of these benefits without incurring the high cost of traditional personal contact techniques.

Market Segmentation

Companies' response to the decrease in advertising effectiveness was to identify specific portions of their markets and target them with specific advertising messages. This practice, called **market segmentation**, divides the pool of potential customers into groups, or **segments**. Segments are usually defined in terms of customer characteristics such as age, gender, marital status, income level, and geographic location. Thus, for example, unmarried men between the ages of 19 and 25 might be one market segment.

In the early 1990s, firms began identifying smaller and smaller market segments for specific advertising and promotion efforts. This practice of targeting very small market segments is called **micromarketing**. However, the low cost per viewer of traditional mass media advertising campaigns becomes much higher when mass media methods are used to target very small market segments. This cost increase hampered the success of micromarketing strategies. Even though micromarketing was an improvement over mass media advertising, it still used the same basic approach and suffered from the weaknesses of that approach.

Marketers have traditionally used three categories of variables to identify market segments. One variable is location. Firms divide their customers into groups by where they live or work. In this type of segmentation, called **geographic segmentation**, companies create different combinations of marketing efforts for each geographical group of customers. The grouping can be by nation, state (or province), city, or even by neighborhood. Alternatively, companies can develop one marketing strategy for urban customers, another for suburban customers, and yet a third for rural customers.

The second category uses information about age, gender, family size, income, education, religion, or ethnicity to group customers. This type of segmentation is called **demographic segmentation**. Demographic variables are frequently used by traditional marketers because research has shown that customers' need for and usage of products are strongly related to these types of variables. Demographic segmentation also exists on the Web. For example, a number of sites are devoted to women's issues or directed at specific age groups (such as teenagers) whose members tend to purchase music CDs and trendy clothing. Often, demographic and geographic segmenting strategies are combined. For example, an airline might target middle-income families living in Wisconsin and Michigan with midwinter advertising for vacation trips to Florida.

In **psychographic segmentation**, marketers try to group customers by variables such as social class, personality, or their approach to life. For example, an auto company might direct advertising for a sports car to customers who are gregarious and have a high need for achievement. The use of psychographic segmentation has increased dramatically in recent years as marketers attempt to identify characteristic lifestyles and then design advertising to reach people who see themselves as having a particular lifestyle.

Companies that advertise on television often create messages designed to reach the likely audiences of various types of programs. These audiences represent one or more market segments. The market segments can be geographic, demographic, psychographic, or a combination of these. Figure 4-3 presents some examples from the television medium that show how companies do this.

Type of television program	Type of advertising
Children's cartoons	Children's toys and games
Daytime dramas	Household and laundry goods, pet foods
Late-night talk shows	Snack foods and nonprescription sleep aids
Golf tournaments	Golf equipment, investment services, and life insurance
Baseball and football games	Snack foods, beer, autos
Documentary films	Books, CDs, educational videotapes

FIGURE 4-3 Television advertising messages tailored to program audience

Children's television shows are likely to feature advertising for products that appeal to children. Ads on daytime dramas are directed at people who are home during the day and who thus might be interested in household and laundry care products. These people are more likely than others to own pets, so they also will see ads for pet foods. Advertisers on late-night talk shows often direct their ads at people who might have trouble falling asleep. Advertisers also believe that this late-night audience is receptive to promotions for snack foods to eat while watching these programs or for nonprescription medications for ailments that might be keeping them up so late.

Advertisers use sports programming as a vehicle for two different market segments. Some sports shows, such as golf tournaments or tennis matches, appeal to higher-income viewers. Other sports shows, such as baseball or football game broadcasts, appeal to viewers with more moderate incomes. As a result, programs that cover golf or tennis are more likely to include ads for investment and insurance products and luxury automobiles than are baseball or football programs. Also, because viewers of golf tournaments and tennis matches are likely to play the sport, these programs often include ads for game equipment. Baseball or football games rarely include ads for game equipment because few viewers of these games are participants in the sport themselves.

Programs that feature documentaries (such as those on the History Channel or the Discovery Channel) often carry ads for books, book clubs, CDs, and educational videos. Advertisers have found that these types of products appeal to the intellectual, arts-loving audiences of these programs.

Companies do much more than just match advertising messages to market segments. They also build a sales environment for their product or service that corresponds to the market segment they are trying to reach. In the physical world, store design and layout are often directed at specific market segments. If you walk through a shopping mall, you can observe that colors, displays, lighting, background music, and even the clothes worn by sales clerks vary with the targeted segment. For example, a clothing store for teenagers presents a completely different experience to its customers than a clothing store that sells expensive, conservative attire targeted toward more mature women with larger incomes.

Market Segmentation on the Web

The Web gives companies an opportunity to present different store environments online. For example, if you visit the home pages of **Juicy Couture** and **Talbots**, you will find that both pages are well designed and functional. However, they are each directed to different market segments. The Juicy Couture site is targeted at young, fashion-conscious buyers. The site uses a wide variety of typefaces, bold graphics, and photos of brightly colored products to convey its tone. The emphasis is to make a bold fashion statement and, presumably, become the envy of your friends. In contrast, the Talbots site is rendered in a more muted, conservative style. The site is designed for older, more established buyers. The messages emphasized are stability, home life, and the trademark Talbots red doors. These images appeal to a market segment of people looking for classics instead of the latest trends.

In the physical world, retail stores have limited floor and display space. These limitations often force physical stores to decide on one particular message to convey. Exceptions do exist, such as a music store that has a separate room for classical recordings (with background music that differs from the rest of the store) or a large department store that can use lighting and display space differently in each department; however, smaller retail stores usually choose the one image that appeals to most of their customers. On the Web, retailers can provide separate virtual spaces for different market segments. For example, Dell's home page includes links to separate sections of its site for home users, small and medium businesses, public sector organizations, and large enterprises. Some Web retailers provide the ultimate in targeted marketing—they allow their customers to create their own stores, as you will learn in the next section.

Offering Customers a Choice on the Web

Dell has done many things well in its online business. Its Web site offers customers a number of different ways to do business with the company. Its U.S. home page includes links for each major group of customers it has identified, including home, small business, medium and large business, government, education, and health care. Once the site visitor has selected a customer category, specific products and product categories are available as links.

Dell Premier accounts give users a high level of customer-based market segmentation. In these accounts, Dell offers each customer its own Dell Web site. Dell can customize a company's Premier account pages to show product selections for which price and terms have already been negotiated. Dell even allows individual employees of its customers to create their own personalized pages within their companies' Premier pages. This highly customized approach to offering products and services that match the needs of a particular customer is called **one-to-one marketing**. The Internet gives marketers the best opportunity for highly customized interactions with customers that they have had since the heyday of the door-to-door salesperson in the 1940s and 1950s.

BEYOND MARKET SEGMENTATION: CUSTOMER BEHAVIOR AND RELATIONSHIP INTENSITY

In the previous sections, you learned how companies can target as market segments groups of customers that share common characteristics. You also learned how one-to-one marketing gives companies a chance to create Web experiences that are unique to each individual customer. The next step—beyond market segmentation, even beyond one-to-one marketing—is when companies use the Web to target specific customers in different ways at different times.

Segmentation Using Customer Behavior

In the physical world, businesses can sometimes create different experiences for customers in response to their needs. For example, a company might decide that its mission is to sell prepared meals to hungry customers. A given potential customer responds to hunger in different ways at different times. If a person is hungry in the morning, but late for work, that person might drive through a fast food restaurant or grab a quick cup of coffee at the train station. Lunch might be a sandwich ordered and delivered to the office, or it could require a nice restaurant if a client needs to be entertained. Dinner could be at a restaurant with friends, take-out food from a neighborhood Chinese restaurant, or a delivered pizza.

The point is that the same person requires different combinations of products and services depending on the occasion. In general, the creation of separate experiences for customers based on their behavior is called **behavioral segmentation**. When based on things that happen at a specific time or occasion, behavioral segmentation is sometimes called **occasion segmentation**.

Usually, businesses that operate in the physical world can meet only one or a few of a customer's differing behavioral needs. For example, the Chinese restaurant mentioned earlier might offer dining room service and take-out service, but it probably would not offer a drive-through window or a morning coffee kiosk. Very few restaurants are able to offer everything from fast food through a five-course dinner. In the online world, it is much easier to design a single Web site that meets the needs of visitors who arrive in different behavioral modes. Thus, a Web site design can include elements that appeal to different behavioral segments.

Marketing researchers study how and why people prefer different combinations of products, services, and Web site features and how these preferences are affected by their modes of interaction with the site. Market researchers know that people want Web sites that offer a range of interaction possibilities. Remember that a particular person might visit a particular Web site at different times with different needs and will want an interaction that meets those needs on each visit. Customizing visitor experiences to match the site usage behavior patterns of each visitor or type of visitor is called **usage-based market segmentation**. Researchers have identified common patterns of online behavior and grouped patterns into categories. One set of categories that marketers use today includes browsers, buyers, and shoppers.

Browsers

Some visitors to a company's Web site are just surfing or browsing. Web sites intended to appeal to potential customers in this mode must offer them something that piques their interest. The site should include words that are likely to jog the memories of visitors and remind them of something they want to buy on the site.

These key words are often called **trigger words** because they prompt a visitor to stay and investigate the products or services offered on the site. Links to explanations about the site or instructions for using the site can be particularly helpful to this type of customer. A site should include extra content related to the product or service the site sells. For example, a Web site that sells camping gear might offer reviews of popular camping destinations with photos and online maps. Such content can keep a visitor who is in browser mode interested long enough to stay at the site and develop a favorable impression of the company. Once visitors have developed this favorable impression, they are more likely to buy on this visit or bookmark the site for a return visit.

Buyers

Visitors who arrive in buyer mode are ready to make a purchase right away. The best thing a site can offer a buyer is a direct route into the purchase transaction. For visitors who first choose a product from a printed catalog, many Web sites include a text box on their home pages that allows visitors to enter the catalog item number. This places that item in the site's shopping cart and takes the buyer directly to the shopping cart page. A **shopping cart** is the part of a Web site that keeps track of selected items for purchase and automates the purchasing process.

The shopping cart page should offer a link that takes the visitor back into the shopping area of the site, but the primary goal is to get the buyer to the shopping cart as quickly as possible, even if the buyer is at the site for the first time. The shopping cart should allow the buyer to create an account and log in after placing the item into the cart. To avoid placing barriers in the way of customers who want to buy, the site should not require visitors to log in until they near the end of the shopping cart procedure. You will learn more about shopping carts in Chapter 9.

Perhaps the ultimate in shopping cart convenience is the 1-Click feature offered by **Amazon.com**, which allows customers to purchase an item with a single click. Any items that a customer purchases using the 1-Click feature within a 90-minute time period are aggregated into one shipment. Amazon.com has a patent on the 1-Click feature. You will learn more about such business process patents and other legal issues in Chapter 7.

Shoppers

Some customers arrive at a Web site knowing that it offers items they are interested in buying. These visitors are motivated to buy, but they are looking for more information before they make a purchase decision. For the visitor who is in shopper mode, a site should offer comparison tools, product reviews, and lists of features. Sites such as **Crutchfield** and **Best Buy** allow customers to specify the level of detail presented for each product, sort products by brand, or price, and compare products with each other side by side.

Remember that a person might visit a Web site one day as a browser, and then return later as a shopper or a buyer. People do not retain behavioral categories from one visit to the next—even for the same Web site.

Alternative Models

Although many companies work with these three visitor categories, other researchers are exploring alternative models. Much of Web site visitor behavior is not yet well understood. One study conducted by major consulting firm McKinsey & Company examined the online behavior of 50,000 active Internet users and identified six different groups. Following are the six behavior-based categories and their characteristic traits:

- *Simplifiers* are users who like convenience. They are attracted by sites that make doing business easier, faster, or otherwise more efficient than is possible in the physical world.
- *Surfers* use the Web to find information, explore new ideas, and shop. They like to be entertained, and they spend far more time on the Web than other people. To attract surfers, sites must offer a wide variety of content that is attractive, well displayed, and constantly updated.
- *Bargainers* are in search of a good deal. Although they make up less than 10 percent of the online population, they make up more than half of all visitors to the eBay auction site. They enjoy searching for the best price or shipping terms and are willing to visit many sites to do that.
- *Connectors* use the Web to stay in touch with other people. They are intensive users of chat rooms, instant messaging services, social networking sites, electronic greeting card sites, and Web-based e-mail. Connectors tend to be new to the Web, less likely than other people to purchase on the Web, and actively trying to learn what the Web has to offer them.
- *Routiners* return to the same sites over and over again. They use the Web to obtain news, stock quotes, and other financial information. Routiners like the comfort of working with a user interface that they know well.
- *Sportsters* are similar to routiners, but they tend to spend time on sports and entertainment sites rather than news and financial information sites. Since they view the Web as an entertainment vehicle, sportsters are attracted by sites that are interactive and attractive.

Other research studies have identified similar sets of characteristics and categories. Companies in different industries or lines of business identify somewhat different sets of characteristics and group their Web site visitors using different names. The challenge for Web businesses is to identify which groups are visiting their sites and formulate ways of generating revenue from each segment. For example, some of these groups (such as simplifiers and bargainers) are ready to buy and would be interested in seeing specific product or service offerings. Other groups (such as surfers, routiners, and sportsters) would be good targets for specific types of advertising messages. As more researchers study Web site visitor behavior, perhaps the industry will learn how to recognize the various modes in which visitors arrive and then channel them into the appropriate sections of the site. Until then, many Web sites use Dell's approach, in which visitors are asked to identify themselves as belonging to a particular category of customer when they enter the sites.

Customer Relationship Intensity and Life-Cycle Segmentation

One goal of marketing is to create strong relationships between a company and its customers. The reason that one-to-one marketing and usage-based segmentation are so valuable is that they help to strengthen companies' relationships with their customers. Good customer experiences can help create an intense feeling of loyalty toward the company and its products or services. Researchers have identified several stages of loyalty as customer relationships develop over time. A five-stage model of customer loyalty that is typical of these models appears in Figure 4-4.

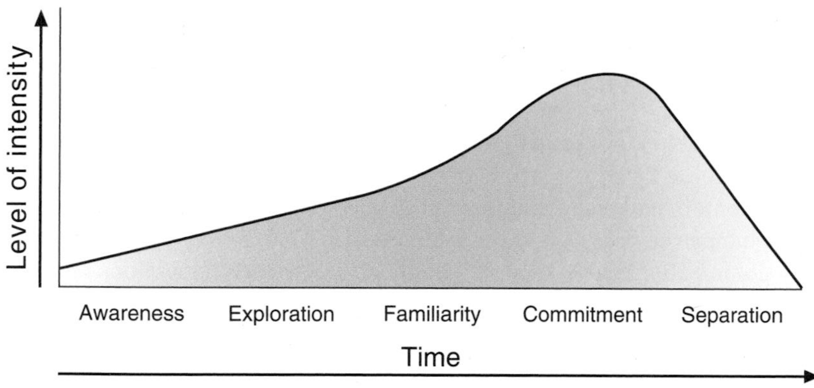

FIGURE 4-4 Five stages of customer loyalty

This model shows the increase in intensity of the relationship as the customer moves through the first four stages: awareness, exploration, familiarity, and commitment. In the fifth stage, separation, a decline occurs and the relationship terminates. Not all customers go through the full five stages; some stop at a stage and continue the relationship at that level of intensity or terminate the relationship at that point. Some customers in a particular stage might have contact with the company online while other customers in the same stage encounter the company offline. Companies should strive for a consistent customer experience at a particular life-cycle stage. That is, customers should experience the same level and quality of service whether they encounter the company online or offline. Online and offline customer contact points are often called **touchpoints**, and the goal of providing similar levels and quality of service at all touchpoints is called **touchpoint consistency**.

As the figure shows, changes in the nature of the relationship do not occur suddenly as a customer moves from one stage to the next. Within each stage, the level of intensity changes gradually as the customer moves through that stage. The characteristics of the five stages are outlined in the next sections.

Awareness

Customers who recognize the name of the company or one of its products are in the awareness stage of customer loyalty. They know that the company or product exists, but have not had any interaction with the company. Advertising a brand or a company name is a common way for companies to achieve this level of relationship with potential customers.

Exploration

In the exploration stage, potential customers learn more about the company or its products. The potential customer might visit the company's Web site to learn more, and the two parties will often communicate by telephone or e-mail. A large amount of information interchange can occur between the parties at this stage.

Familiarity

Customers who have completed several transactions and are aware of the company's policies regarding returns, credits, and pricing flexibility are in the familiarity stage of their relationship with the company. In this stage, they are as likely to shop and buy from competitors as they are from the company.

Commitment

After experiencing a considerable number of highly satisfactory encounters with a company, some customers develop a fierce loyalty or strong preference for the products or brands of that company. These customers have reached the commitment stage and are often willing to tell others about how happy they are with their interactions. To lure customers from the familiarity stage to the commitment stage, companies sometimes make concessions on prices or terms. Usually, the value of the strong relationship is worth more to the company than the costs of these concessions.

Separation

Over time, the conditions that made the relationship valuable might change. The customer might be severely disappointed by changes in the level of service (either as provided by the company or as perceived by the customer) or product quality. The company can also evaluate the relationship and conclude that the loyal, committed customer is costing too much to maintain. As the intensity of the relationship fades, the parties enter a separation stage.

An important goal of any marketing strategy should be to move customers into the commitment stage as rapidly as possible and keep them there as long as possible. Companies want to see customers move into the separation stage only if they are costing more to serve than they are worth.

Life-Cycle Segmentation

Analyzing how customers' behavior changes as they move through the five stages can yield information about how they interact with the company and its products in each stage. The five stages are sometimes called the **customer life cycle**, and using these stages to create groups of customers that are in each stage is called **life-cycle segmentation**. Two companies that undertake continuing research into market segmentation and how companies can use segment information to develop better relationships with their customers are **Claritas** and **Donnelley Marketing**.

Claritas created one of the first segment marketing databases, named PRIZM, in the early 1970s. Claritas built PRIZM to take advantage of people's tendency to live near other people with similar tastes and preferences. Thus, PRIZM identifies the demographic characteristics of people by neighborhood. Claritas developed a number of other products that offer marketers databases with specific demographic, financial, and psychographic characteristics. Donnelley Marketing offers similar products, such as its Buyer Behavior Indicator and Affluence Models databases. Both Donnelley and Claritas extended their research from traditional direct marketing to help firms sell online. You can learn more about these companies and their products by following their links in the Online Companion for this chapter.

Acquisition, Conversion, and Retention of Customers

One goal of the strategies and tactics you will learn about in the rest of this chapter is to attract new visitors to a Web site. The benefits of acquiring new visitors are different for Web businesses with different revenue models. For example, an advertising-supported site is interested in attracting as many visitors as possible to the site and then keeping those visitors at the site as long as possible. That way, the site can display more advertising messages to more visitors, which is how the site earns a profit. For sites that operate a Web catalog, charge a fee for services, or are supported by subscriptions, attracting visitors to the site is only the first step in the process of turning those visitors into customers. The total amount of money that a site spends, on average, to draw one visitor to the site is called the **acquisition cost**.

The second step that a Web business wants to take is to convert the first-time visitor into a customer. This is called a **conversion**. For advertising-supported sites, the conversion is usually considered to happen when the visitor registers at the site, or, in some cases, when a registered visitor returns to a site several times. For sites with other revenue models, the conversion occurs when the site visitor buys a good or service or subscribes to the site's content. The total amount of money that a site spends, on average, to induce one visitor to make a purchase, sign up for a subscription, or (on an advertising-supported site) register, is called the **conversion cost**. Most managers use a cumulative definition for conversion cost; that is, conversion cost includes acquisition cost.

For many Web businesses, the conversion cost is greater than the profit earned on the average sale (or the average first sale). In such cases, the Web business must induce the customer to return to the site and buy again (or renew the subscription, or view more advertising). Customers who return to the site one or more times after making their first purchases are called **retained customers**. Different businesses use different measures for determining when a customer is a retained customer. Some companies consider a customer retained if he or she returns just once and purchases again. Others use some number of subsequent purchases or some number of subsequent purchases within a specific time frame. The costs of inducing customers to return to a Web site and buy again are called **retention costs**.

Companies have found that measuring acquisition, conversion, and retention costs is important because it gives them an idea of which advertising and promotion strategies are successful. These measurements are more precise than classifying customers into the five stages of loyalty in the customer life-cycle model. It is much easier to determine, for example, whether a customer has been converted or retained than it is to determine whether that customer is in the familiarity stage or the commitment stage. A company that is evaluating its promotion campaign can measure the conversion costs and compare them to the profit generated by the average first-time sale. Most companies are very interested in retaining customers, because the cost of acquiring a new customer is between 3 and 15 times (depending on the type of business) the cost of retaining an existing customer.

In the rest of this chapter, you will learn some specific techniques that can be elements of successful Web marketing strategies. Remember that each of these techniques makes sense only when used in concert with another. Not all techniques work well in all situations.

For example, in the chapter's opening case, RedEnvelope found that a print catalog could be an integral part of promoting its online sales. RedEnvelope's success does not mean that printing catalogs is a good idea for all Web businesses (see the Kozmo Learning from Failures feature below). It is only a good idea if it provides customers with recognizable value and augments the rest of the company's marketing strategy.

LEARNING FROM FAILURES

Kozmo

Throughout New York City, people in their homes late at night crave entertainment and snack foods. Kozmo was launched in 1998 to meet the needs of those New Yorkers. With its orange-jacketed delivery people riding bicycles or motor scooters, Kozmo promised delivery of most items within an hour of ordering. Kozmo did not offer as wide a range of items as most convenience stores, so its main competitive advantage was its delivery service. Kozmo attempted to become profitable by adding high-margin items, such as DVD players and Sony PlayStations, and expanding its delivery areas to include higher-income neighborhoods. In addition to Manhattan, Kozmo operated for a short time in Houston and San Diego. In these cities, the higher average distances between deliveries made it even more difficult to cover costs.

Despite its best efforts, Kozmo was unable to create an image that was much different from that of a convenience store on wheels. Kozmo found it difficult to convince customers that delivered snack food items and videos were significantly more valuable than snack food items and videos on the shelves of nearby convenience stores. Most of Kozmo's product line consisted of items for which most people were accustomed to paying low prices.

In March 2001, just one month before closing operations, Kozmo announced a marketing plan that included spending $2.5 million to print and circulate 400,000 catalogs. The plan was a last-ditch attempt to increase brand awareness, gain new customers, and convince people who did not have an Internet connection to use Kozmo's phone order service. Unlike RedEnvelope, however, the Kozmo catalog was not a part of an integrated business plan and did not provide the same kind of added value that RedEnvelope's catalog provides—a bag of potato chips does not gain much appeal by appearing in a full-color catalog photo.

The lesson from Kozmo's experience is that using one element from a marketing strategy that worked for one company is no guarantee that it will work for every company. Marketing techniques are effective only when implemented as part of an integrated strategy that fits the company's products and gives customers a compelling reason to buy.

Customer Acquisition, Conversion, and Retention: The Funnel Model

Marketing managers need to have a good sense of how their companies acquire and retain customers. They often must evaluate competing marketing strategies to determine which are the most effective ways to attract and retain customers. The funnel model is used as a conceptual tool to understand the overall nature of a marketing strategy, but it also provides a clear structure for evaluating specific strategy elements.

The funnel model is very similar to the customer life-cycle model you learned about earlier in this chapter; however, the funnel model is less abstract and does a better job of showing the effectiveness of two or more specific strategies. The funnel is a good analogy for the operation of a marketing strategy because almost every marketing strategy starts with a large number of prospects and converts fewer and fewer of those prospects into serious prospects, customers, and finally, loyal customers. One example of a funnel model appears in Figure 4-5.

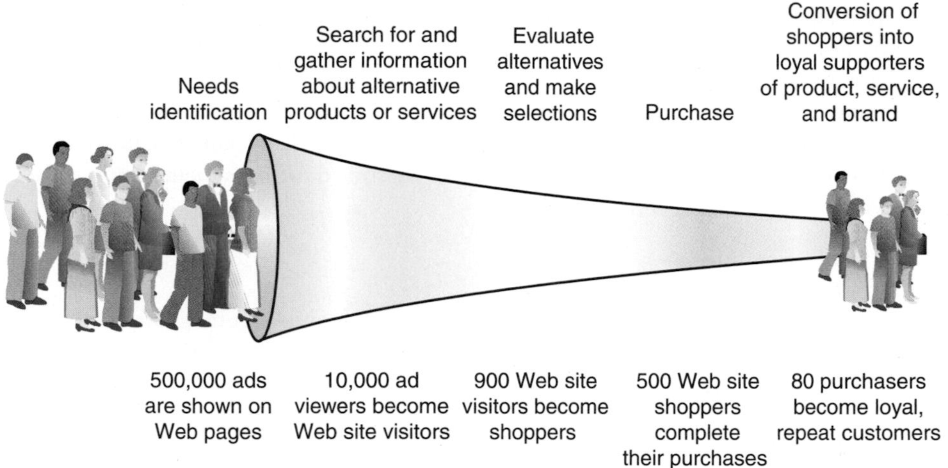

FIGURE 4-5 Funnel model of customer acquisition, conversion, and retention

In this funnel model of the steps that potential customers take as they become loyal, repeat customers are on the right side of the figure. The top of the figure explains the increasing level of commitment that occurs in each step. Using market research and past history as a guide, the marketing manager develops the numbers that show the effectiveness of the planned strategy. The wider the right end of the funnel, the better the strategy; that is, the more prospects are converted into loyal customers. The funnel model can be used in planning marketing strategies by comparing the projected results shown in the diagram with the results for alternative strategies shown in separate diagrams. The funnel model can also be used to show results that can then be compared with the costs of running the marketing campaign. Either way, the model gives marketing managers a tool for conceptualizing and evaluating alternative strategies.

ADVERTISING ON THE WEB

Advertising is all about communication. The communication might be between a company and its current customers, potential customers, or even former customers that the company would like to regain. To be effective, firms should send different messages to each of these audiences.

The five-stage customer loyalty model shown in Figure 4-4 (in the previous section) can be helpful in creating the messages to convey to each of these audiences. In the awareness stage, the advertising message should inform. The message could describe a new product, suggest new uses for existing products, or describe specific improvements to a product. Audiences in the exploration stage should receive messages that explain how a product or service works and encourage switching to that brand. In the familiarity stage, the advertising message should be persuasive—convincing customers to purchase specific products or request that a salesperson call. Customers in the commitment stage should be sent reminder messages. These ads should reinforce customers' good feelings about the brand and remind them to buy products or services. Companies generally do not target ads at customers who are in the separation stage.

Most companies that launch electronic commerce initiatives already have advertising programs in place. Online advertising should always be coordinated with existing advertising efforts. For example, print ads should include the company's URL. Banner ads are the dominant advertising format in use on the Web. Other online ad formats include pop-up ads, pop-behind ads, interstitial ads, and active ads.

Banner Ads

Most advertising on the Web uses banner ads. A **banner ad** is a small rectangular object on a Web page that displays a stationary or moving graphic and includes a hyperlink to the advertiser's Web site. Banner ads are versatile advertising vehicles—their graphic images can help increase awareness, and users can click them to open the advertiser's Web site and learn more about the product. Thus, banner ads can serve both informative and persuasive functions.

Early banner ads used a simple graphic, usually in GIF format, that loaded with the Web page and remained on the page until the user moved to another page or closed the browser. Today, a variety of **animated GIFs** and **rich media objects** created using Shockwave, Java, or Flash are used to make attention-grabbing banner ads. These ads can be rotated so that each time the Web page is loaded into a browser, the ad changes.

Although Web sites can create banner ads in any dimensions, advertisers decided early in the life of electronic commerce that it would be easier to standardize the sizes. The standard banner sizes that most Web sites have voluntarily agreed to use are called **interactive marketing unit (IMU) ad formats**. The Interactive Advertising Bureau (IAB) is a not-for-profit organization that promotes the use of Internet advertising and encourages effective Internet advertising. The IAB has established voluntary standards for IMUs. As the Web grew, so did the creativity of Web advertisers. They were using an increasing number of IMU ad formats. By 2003, advertisers were using more than 15 different IMU ad formats. The IAB decided to encourage its members to agree to use only four standard formats. However, as ad designers became more creative by using pop-up ads, buttons, and ads that filled entire page borders, the IAB created standards for each new type of online format. The result is a large number of standard ad formats, but many advertisers continue to use the four standard formats because they know that almost every Web site will be able to display ads in those formats properly. The four standard formats (and their IAB specifications) are medium rectangle (300 × 250 pixels), rectangle (180 × 150), leaderboard (728 × 90), and wide skyscraper (160 × 600). A **leaderboard ad** is a banner ad that is designed to span the top or bottom of a Web page. A **skyscraper ad** is a banner ad that is designed to be placed on the side of a Web page and remain visible as the user scrolls down through the page. You can learn more about banner ads, including examples of the latest IAB-approved sizes, by following the Online Companion link to the IAB Web site.

Most advertising agencies that work with online clients can create banner ads as part of their services. Web site design firms can also create banner ads. Charges for creating banner ads range from about $100 to more than $5000, depending on the complexity of the ad. Companies can make their own banner ads by using a graphics program or the tools provided by some Web sites. **AdDesigner.com** is an advertising-supported Web site that lets visitors design their own banner ads and download them for free. **AdReady** offers free "do-it-yourself" ad creation service alongside its professional creative services.

Banner Ad Placement

Companies have three different ways to arrange for other Web sites to display their banner ads. The first is to use a banner exchange network. A **banner exchange network** coordinates ad sharing so that other sites run one company's ad while that company's site runs other exchange members' ads. Usually, the exchange requires each member site to accept two ads on its site for every one of its ads that appears on another member's site. The exchange then makes its profit by selling the extra ad space to other businesses. Companies in the banner exchange business include **HitExchange** and **LinkReferral**.

Because banner exchanges are free, many smaller online businesses use them; however, it is often difficult to find a group of other Web sites that have formed an exchange or that belong to an exchange that are not direct competitors. This limitation prevents many businesses from using banner exchange networks.

The second way that businesses can place their banner advertising is to find Web sites that appeal to one of the company's market segments and then pay those sites to carry the ads. This can take considerable time and effort. Smaller sites may not have an established pricing policy for advertising. Larger sites usually have high standard rates that they discount for larger customers. Smaller customers generally pay the standard rates. A company can hire an advertising agency to negotiate lower rates and help with ad placement. A full-service advertising agency can help design the ads, create the banners, and identify appropriate Web sites on which to display them. Agencies that do a lot of Internet work can often negotiate lower advertising rates with sites because the agencies can consolidate their clients' budgets and buy large blocks of advertising space at one time.

A third way to place banner advertising is to use a banner advertising network. A **banner advertising network** acts as a broker between advertisers and Web sites that carry ads. The larger banner advertising networks, such as **DoubleClick** and **ValueClick**, offer many of the same services as comprehensive ad agencies and often broker space primarily on larger Web sites (such as Yahoo!) that have high traffic rates and are, thus, more expensive. The smaller firms, on the other hand, often sell only leftover discounted space.

New Strategies for Banner Ads

When banner ads first appeared on the Web in the mid-1990s, they were a novelty for Web surfers. As users saw more ads, however, the ads lost their ability to attract attention. Click-through rates, which had been as high as 2 percent when banner ads were first introduced, have steadily dropped and now range from .3 percent to .5 percent, depending on the site's content. Although some recent research suggest that Web site visitors see and are influenced by banner ads that they do not click, advertisers are reluctant to pay for ads that do not produce directly measurable results.

To battle the decrease in click-through rates, banner ad designers first introduced animated GIFs with moving elements in the hopes that they might be more attractive to the user's eye than stationary graphics. When animated GIFs failed to halt the decline, designers created ads that included rich media effects, such as movie clips. They also added interactive effects by writing Java programs that could respond to a user's click with some action (other than simply loading the advertiser's page into the browser). Some of these interactive ads even act like miniature video games.

Some designers created banner ads that appear to be dialog boxes in the hope that confused users would click them. Several examples of this type of banner ad are shown in Figure 4-6. These ads are designed to induce users to click a button in the ad to fix the "error," but the banners actually link to Web sites or begin installing a program on the user's computer.

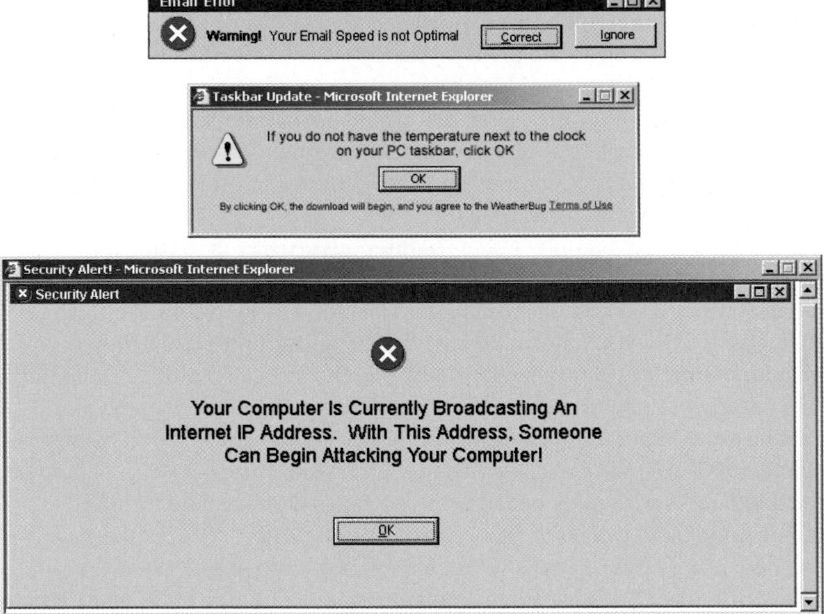

FIGURE 4-6 Disguised banner ads

Text Ads

An ad format that is deceptively simple but very effective is the text ad. A **text ad** is a short promotional message that does not use any graphic elements and is usually placed along the top or right side of a Web page. Google was the first company to use text ads successfully on the Web. Google places text ads on its search results pages. When you visit Google and use it to search for information, the page that provides the links relevant to your search query includes short text ads for products or services related to your search query. Google found that these ads were less obtrusive than banner ads and that they were very effective because they reached people who were interested in learning more about something (as reflected in the search query they had entered) related to the advertisers' products or services.

Text ads were so unobtrusive that Google was criticized when it first included them on its pages. Observers noted that site visitors might not be able to distinguish the paid ads from the search results. In response to this criticism, Google and most other search sites that use text ads now clearly label the ads to prevent users from being confused.

The use of text ads was one of the innovations that helped Google become one of the leading search sites on the Web. It gave Google an effective way to earn money while providing users with a useful search experience.

A number of sites that provide information use text ads in another way by turning some of the text in the stories they display into hyperlinks that lead to advertisers' sites. This type of advertising is called an **inline text ad**. Newspaper, magazine, and other sites that users visit to learn more about a topic can use this technique. For example, a newspaper site might have a story about local banks. Banks that are mentioned in the story could have their names presented in the story as links to ads for the banks' services. The newspaper would charge the advertising banks a fee for placing the link in the story. Another way information sites use text ads is to include them in the middle of the running text of a story as a separate, blocked off paragraph. These paragraphs are often labeled "sponsored links" or something similar so that readers understand that they are looking at a link to an ad. This use of inline text ads is common in online magazines devoted to specific industries and in general information sites such as About.com.

Other Web Ad Formats

The steady decline in the effectiveness of banner ads has prompted advertisers to explore other formats for Web ads. One of these formats is the pop-up ad. A **pop-up ad** is an ad that appears in its own window when the user opens or closes a Web page. The window in which the ad appears does not include the usual browser controls. The only way to dismiss the ad is to click the small close button in the upper-right corner of the window's frame. Many users find pop-up ads extremely annoying. A particularly irritating variation on the pop-up ad technique occurs at Web sites that open more than one pop-up ad when a user leaves the site or closes the browser. If the user does not act quickly enough, the browser spawns multiple windows and can even crash the computer.

Another type of pop-up ad is called the pop-behind ad. A **pop-behind ad** is a pop-up ad that is followed very quickly by a command that returns the focus to the original browser window. The result is an ad that is parked behind the user's browser, waiting to appear when the browser is closed.

Despite user objections to pop-up ads (in all their variations), an increasing number of Web sites are using them as a way of delivering a larger advertising image in a more forceful way. Some users have responded by using **ad-blocking software** that prevents banner ads and pop-up ads from loading. An increasing number of Web browsers can be configured not to display many of these ads; however, any site that uses methods for navigation that are similar to those used to deliver ads (such as pop-up information windows) cannot operate as intended in the reconfigured browser. Some researchers have found that pop-up ads not only annoy users, they actually create lasting bad will among users toward the company whose products are depicted in the ads. Despite these findings, many advertisers find pop-up ads to be effective tools for drawing customers to their sites and continue to use them.

Another intrusive ad format is the **interstitial ad**. When a user clicks a link to load a page, the interstitial ad opens in its own browser window, instead of the page that the user intended to load (the general meaning of the word "interstitial" is something that comes between two other things). Many interstitial ads close automatically, allowing the intended page to open in the existing browser window. Other interstitials require the user to click a button before they close. Because they open in a full-size browser window, interstitial ads offer the advertiser even more space than the pop-up ad format. These ads also completely cover the Web page that the user was trying to see. Many users find interstitials even more annoying than pop-up ads because they are larger and a more forceful interruption of the Web-browsing experience.

A fourth ad format is the rich media ad. **Rich media ads**, also called **active ads**, generate graphical activity that "floats" over the Web page itself instead of opening in a separate window. These ads always contain moving graphics and usually include audio and video elements. One of the first rich media ads featured the figure of a little man who walked into the displayed Web page, unrolled a movie poster, and then pasted the poster onto the Web page (covering up part of the Web page content—content that a user might have been reading!). After about 10 seconds, the figure walked off the page and the poster disappeared. While it was open on the page, the poster was an active link to the movie's Web site.

Another early rich media ad showed a Ford Explorer driving into the Web page. The Web page appeared to shake with the vibrations of the Explorer as it drove through. Rich media ads are certainly attention grabbers and are even more intrusive than pop-ups or interstitials because they occur on the Web page itself and offer users no obvious way to dismiss them. Many industry observers believe that advertisers will create new ad formats as users become accustomed to seeing active ads and they lose their effectiveness.

Rich media ads are also used on Web sites that deliver video clips. For example, a Web site that provides television shows will often include a rich media ad inside the video clip. A visitor opens the television show and must view a 30-second ad before the video content begins.

Site Sponsorships

Some Web sites offer advertisers the opportunity to sponsor all or parts of their sites. These **site sponsorships** give advertisers a chance to promote their products, services, or brands in a more subtle way than by placing banner or pop-up ads on the sites (although some sponsorship packages include a certain number of banner and pop-up ads).

Companies that buy Web site sponsorships have goals that are similar to those of sporting event sponsors or television program sponsors; that is, they want to tie the company or product name to an event or a set of information. The idea is that the quality of the event or information set will carry over to the company's products, services, or brands. In general, sponsorships are used to build brand images and develop reputations rather than to generate immediate sales. A site sponsorship can be exclusive, which prevents any other companies from sponsoring the site, or it can be shared, which means that other companies can be co-sponsors of the site. In general, an exclusive site sponsorship will cost more than a shared site sponsorship.

In some cases, the sponsor is given the right to create content for the site or to weave its advertising message into the site's content. This practice can raise ethical concerns if not done carefully. Sites that offer content spots to sponsors should always identify the content as an advertisement or as provided by the sponsor. Unfortunately, many sites do not use clear labels for sponsored content. This can confuse site visitors who are unable to distinguish between editorial content and advertising. Sites that offer medical information, for example, should be especially careful to distinguish between information that is generated by the site's reporters or editorial staff and information that is provided by pharmaceutical companies or medical device manufacturers.

Online Advertising Cost and Effectiveness

As more companies rely on their Web sites to make a favorable impression on potential customers, the issue of measuring Web site effectiveness has become important. Mass media efforts are measured by estimates of audience size, circulation, or number of addressees. When a company purchases mass media advertising, it pays a dollar amount for every thousand people in the estimated audience. This pricing metric is called **cost per thousand** (**CPM**; the "M" is from the Roman numeral for "thousand").

Measuring Web audiences is more complicated because of the Web's interactivity and because the value of a visitor to an advertiser depends on how much information the site gathers from the visitor (for example, name, address, e-mail address, telephone number, and other demographic data). Because each visitor voluntarily chooses whether to provide these bits of information, all visitors are not of equal value. Internet advertisers have developed some Web-specific metrics for site activity, but these are not generally accepted and are currently the subject of considerable debate.

A **visit** occurs when a visitor requests a page from the Web site. Further page loads from the same site are counted as part of the visit for a specified period of time. This period of time is chosen by the administrators of the site and depends on the type of site. A site that features stock quotes might use a short time period because visitors may load the page to check the price of one stock and reload the page 15 minutes later to check another stock's price. A museum site would expect a visitor to load multiple pages over a longer time period during a visit and would use a longer visit time window. The first time that a particular visitor loads a Web site page is called a **trial visit**; subsequent page loads are called **repeat visits**. Each page loaded by a visitor counts as a **page view**. If the page contains an ad, the page load is called an **ad view**.

Some Web pages have banner ads that continue to load and reload as long as the page is open in the visitor's Web browser. Each time the banner ad loads is an **impression**. If the visitor clicks the banner ad to open the advertiser's page, that action is called a **click** or **click-through**. Banner ads are often sold on a CPM basis where the "thousand" is 1000 impressions. Rates vary greatly and depend on how much demographic information the Web site obtains about its visitors and what kinds of visitors the site attracts, but most rates range between $1 and $50 CPM. Exclusive site sponsorships can be more expensive, sometimes hitting $100 CPM. And context-related text ads on sites with demographics that are very good for the particular targeted text ad can reach $200 CPM.

Rates have varied throughout the history of the Web. As the online advertising market grew, rates slowly climbed, peaking in the late 1990s, when they ranged from $5 to $100. After that time, they gradually drifted downward to their current levels. Figure 4-7 shows a comparison of CPM rates for banner ads and other Web advertising media to CPM rates for advertising placed in traditional media outlets.

Medium	Description	Total cost	Audience size	Cost per thousand (CPM)
Network television	30-second commercial	$80,000–$600,000	10 million–20 million	$5–$30
Local television station	30-second commercial	$1000–$50,000	50,000–2 million	$3–$25
Cable television	30-second commercial	$3000–$10,000	100,000–500,000	$8–$20
Radio	60-second commercial	$200–$1000	50,000–2 million	$1–$18
Major metro newspaper	Full-page ad	$20,000–$80,000	100,000–600,000	$80–$130
Regional edition of a national magazine	Full-page ad	$5000–$50,000	50,000–900,000	$40–$80
Local magazine	Full-page ad	$2000–$10,000	3000–80,000	$100–$140
Direct mail coupon pack	Mailed in letter-sized envelope	$100–$3000	10,000–200,000	$15–$20
Billboard	Highway billboard	$5000–$25,000	100,000–3 million	$2–$5
World Wide Web	Banner ad	$100–$2000	10,000–50 million	$1–$50
World Wide Web	Rich media ad	$200–$1 million	10,000–50 million	$18–$50
World Wide Web	Text ad	$100–$2000	10,000–50 million	$1–$200
World Wide Web	Site sponsorship (exclusive)	$600–$5 million	10,000–50 million	$60–$100
World Wide Web	Site sponsorship (shared)	$200–$2 million	10,000–50 million	$20–$50
Targeted e-mail	Single mailing	$50–$150,000	10,000–10 million	$5–$15

FIGURE 4-7 CPM rates for advertising in various media

One of the most difficult things for companies to do as they move onto the Web is gauge the costs and benefits of advertising on the Web. Many companies have developed new metrics to evaluate the number of desired outcomes their advertising yields. For example, instead of comparing the number of click-throughs that companies obtain per dollar of advertising, they measure the number of new visitors to their site who buy for the first time after arriving at the site by way of a click-through. They can then calculate the advertising cost of acquiring one customer on the Web and compare that to how much it costs them to acquire one customer through traditional channels.

Effectiveness of Online Advertising

After years of experimenting with a variety of online advertising formats, the effectiveness of online advertising remains difficult to measure. One major problem has been the lack of a single industry standard measuring service, such as the service that the Nielsen ratings provide for television broadcasting or the Audit Bureau of Circulations procedures provide for the print media. In 2004, a joint task force of the Interactive Advertising Bureau (IAB) and the Institute of Practitioners in Advertising (IPA) created a set of media measurement guidelines that all online advertisers can use to produce comparable ad view numbers.

Although the task force guidelines have helped to establish measures of ad views, difficulties remain in assessing the effectiveness of online advertising because site visitors change their Web surfing behaviors and habits as they gain experience using the Web. For example, an experienced Web user is far less likely than a new Web user to click a banner ad. Declining click-through rates might not be a good indicator of the success of online advertising, however. Many companies are finding that online advertising can be an important element in a comprehensive marketing strategy that uses several different media to deliver messages to potential customers. Recent survey results show that more potential car purchasers would be influenced by an online ad than by a television ad. Very few people would buy a car based solely on information contained in an online ad, but online ads might prove to be an effective way of building brand recognition and conveying information about cars to potential buyers. You can learn more about current developments in online advertising effectiveness by visiting the **AdAge.com**, **eMarketer**, and **Online Publishers Association** Web sites.

Most marketing analysts do agree that online advertising is much more effective if it is properly targeted. Online ads that reach site visitors who are looking for something specific that is related to the ad's message are much more successful than ads viewed by a general population. Thus, market segmentation is an important element in online advertising success. One useful marketing tool that uses market segmentation successfully is e-mail marketing, the subject of the next section.

E-MAIL MARKETING

Sociologists and cultural anthropologists have proclaimed e-mail to be one of the greatest tools for human communication to be developed in the 20th century. Because advertising is a process of communication, it is easy to see that e-mail can be a very powerful element in any company's advertising strategy. Many businesses would like to send e-mail messages to their customers and potential customers to announce new products, new product features, or sales on existing products. However, industry analysts have severely criticized some companies for sending e-mail messages to customers or potential customers. Some companies have even faced legal action after sending out mass e-mailings. You will learn more about the legal issues surrounding unsolicited commercial e-mail (also called "spam," as you learned in Chapter 2) in Chapter 7. However, sending e-mail messages to Web site visitors who expressly request the e-mail messages is a completely different story. A key element in any e-mail marketing strategy is to obtain customers' approvals before sending them any e-mail that includes a marketing or promotional message.

Permission Marketing

Many businesses are finding that they can maintain an effective dialogue with their customers by using automated e-mail communications. Sending one e-mail message to a customer can cost less than 1 cent if the company already has the customer's e-mail address. Purchasing the e-mail addresses of people who ask to receive specific kinds of e-mail messages adds between a few cents and a dollar to the cost of each message sent. Another factor to consider is the conversion rate. The **conversion rate** of an advertising method is the percentage of recipients who respond to an ad or promotion. Conversion rates on requested e-mail messages range from 10 percent to more than 30 percent. These are much higher than the click-through rates on banner ads, which are currently under .5 percent and decreasing.

The practice of sending e-mail messages to people who request information on a particular topic or about a specific product is called **opt-in e-mail** and is part of a marketing strategy called **permission marketing**. Seth Godin, the founder of YoYoDyne and later the vice president for direct marketing at Yahoo!, developed this marketing strategy and publicized it in a book he wrote with Don Peppers titled *Permission Marketing*. Godin argues that, as the pace of modern life quickens, time becomes a valuable commodity. Most marketing efforts that traditional businesses use to promote their products or services depend on potential customers having enough time to listen to sales pitches and pay attention to the best ones. As time becomes more precious to everyone, people no longer wish to hear and evaluate advertising and promotional appeals for products and services in which they have no interest. **ConstantContact** and **Yesmail** are two companies that offer permission-based e-mail and related services.

Thus, a marketing strategy that sends specific information only to people who have indicated an interest in receiving information about the product or service being promoted should be more successful than a marketing strategy that sends general promotional messages through the mass media. Companies such as **Return Path** offer opt-in e-mail services. These services provide the e-mail addresses to advertisers at rates that vary depending on the type and price of the product being promoted, but range from a minimum of about $1 to a maximum of 25–30 percent of the selling price of the product.

Combining Content and Advertising

One strategy for getting e-mail accepted by customers and prospects that many companies have found successful is to combine useful content with an advertising e-mail message. Articles and news stories that would interest specific market segments are good ways to increase acceptance of e-mail.

E-mail messages that include large articles or large attachments (such as graphics, audio, or video files) can fill up recipients' in boxes very quickly, so many advertisers send content by inserting hyperlinks into e-mail messages. The hyperlinks should take customers to the content, which is stored on the company's Web site. Once customers are viewing pages on the Web site, it is easier to induce them to stay on the site and consider making purchases. Using hyperlinks that lead to a Web page instead of embedding content in e-mail messages is especially important if the content requires a browser plug-in to play (as many audio and video files do). The Web page can provide a link to the needed plug-in software.

An important element in any marketing strategy is coordination across media outlets. If a company is using e-mail to promote its products or services, it should make sure that any other marketing efforts it is undertaking at the same time, such as press releases, print media ads, or broadcast media ads, are delivering a message that is consistent with the e-mail campaign's message.

Outsourcing E-Mail Processing

Many companies find that the number of customers who opt-in to information-laden e-mails can grow rapidly. The job of handling e-mail lists and mass mailing software can quickly outgrow the capacity of the company's information technology staff. A number of companies offer e-mail management services, and most small to midsized companies outsource their e-mail processing operations to an e-mail processing service provider.

The Additional Information section of the Online Companion pages for this chapter includes links to several companies that offer e-mail processing and management services. These companies will manage an e-mail campaign for a cost of between 1 and 5 cents per valid e-mail address. Many of these companies will also help their clients purchase lists of e-mail addresses from companies that compile such lists.

TECHNOLOGY-ENABLED CUSTOMER RELATIONSHIP MANAGEMENT

The nature of the Web, with its two-way communication features and traceable connection technology, allows firms to gather much more information about customer behavior and preferences than they can gather using micromarketing approaches. Now, companies can measure a large number of things that are happening as customers and potential customers gather information and make purchasing decisions. The information that a Web site can gather about its visitors (which pages were viewed, how long each page was viewed, the sequence, and similar data) is called a **clickstream**.

Technology-enabled relationship management is important when promoting and selling on the Web. **Technology-enabled relationship management** occurs when a firm obtains detailed information about a customer's behavior, preferences, needs, and buying patterns, *and* uses that information to set prices, negotiate terms, tailor promotions, add product features, and otherwise customize its entire relationship with that customer.

Although companies can use technology-enabled relationship management concepts to help manage relationships with vendors, employees, and other stakeholders, most companies currently use these concepts to manage customer relationships. Thus, technology-enabled relationship management is often called **customer relationship management (CRM)**, **technology-enabled customer relationship management**, or **electronic customer relationship management (eCRM)**. Figure 4-8 lists seven dimensions of the customer interaction experience and shows how technology-enabled customer relationship management differs from traditional seller–customer interactions in each of those dimensions.

Dimensions	Technology-enabled customer relationship management	Traditional relationships with customers
Advertising	Provide information in response to specific customer inquiries	"Push and sell" a uniform message to all customers
Targeting	Identify and respond to specific customer behaviors and preferences	Market segmentation
Promotions and discounts offered	Individually tailor to customer	Same for all customers
Distribution channels	Direct or through intermediaries; customer's choice	Through intermediaries chosen by the seller
Pricing of products or services	Negotiated with each customer	Set by the seller for all customers
New product features	Created in response to customer demands	Determined by the seller based on research and development
Measurements used to manage the customer relationship	Customer retention; total value of the individual customer relationship	Market share; profit

FIGURE 4-8 Technology-enabled relationship management and traditional customer relationships

CRM as a Source of Value in the Marketspace

Harvard Business School researchers Jeffrey Rayport and John Sviokla observed that firms today do business in both a physical world and a virtual, information world. Rayport and Sviolka distinguish between commerce in the physical world, or marketplace, and commerce in the information world, which they term the **marketspace**. In the information world's marketspace, digital products and services can be delivered through electronic communication channels, such as the Internet.

In Chapter 1, you learned that the value chain model described the primary and support activities that firms use to create value. This value chain model is valid for activities in the physical world and in the marketspace. However, value creation requires different processes in the marketspace. By understanding that value creation in the marketspace is different, firms can identify value opportunities effectively in both the physical and information worlds.

For years, businesses have viewed information as a part of the value chain's supporting activities, but they have not considered how information itself might be a source of value. In the marketspace, firms can use information to create new value for customers. Many electronic commerce Web sites today offer customers the convenience of an online order history, recommendations based on previous purchases, and show current information about products in which the customer might be interested.

Successful Web-marketing approaches all involve enabling the potential customer to find information easily and customizing the depth and nature of that information; such approaches should encourage the customer to buy. Firms should track and examine the behaviors of their Web site visitors, and then use that information to provide customized, value-added digital products and services in the marketspace. Companies that use these technology-enabled relationship management tools to improve their contact with customers are more successful on the Web than firms that adapt advertising and promotion strategies that were successful in the physical world, but are less effective in the virtual world.

In the early days of the Web, many companies attempted to create comprehensive CRM systems that captured every bit of information about every customer. Many of these systems failed because they were overly complex and required company staff to spend too much time entering data. In recent years, companies have had more success with CRM systems that are less ambitious in scope. By limiting data collection to key facts that matter to salespeople and customers, these systems provide valuable information, yet they do not overly burden sales and administrative staff with data entry work. More companies are getting better at automating the collection of data, which also increases the likelihood that a CRM implementation will be successful.

Today's CRM systems use information gathered from customer interactions on the company's Web site and combine them with information gathered from other customer interactions, such as calls to customer service departments. As you learned earlier in this chapter, the occurrence of contact between the customer and any part of the company is called a **customer touchpoint**. A good CRM system will gather information from every customer touchpoint and combine it with information from other sources about industry trends, general economic conditions, and market research about changes in general preference levels that might affect demand for the company's products or services.

In a CRM system, the multiple sources of information about customers, their preferences, and their behavior is entered into a large database called a **data warehouse**. On a regular basis, analysts query the data warehouse using sophisticated software tools to perform data mining and statistical modeling. **Data mining** (also called **analytical processing**) is a technique that examines stored information and looks for patterns in the data that are not yet known or suspected. In CRM, analysts might apply data mining techniques to the data warehouse and find that customers often buy two specific products at the same time. By offering both products together at a reduced price whenever a customer views either product page, the company could increase sales of both products. **Statistical modeling** is a technique that tests theories that CRM analysts have about relationships among elements of customer and sales data. For example, a statistical model could be used to test whether free shipping increases sales enough to cover the cost of offering the free shipping. Figure 4-9 shows the elements in a typical CRM system.

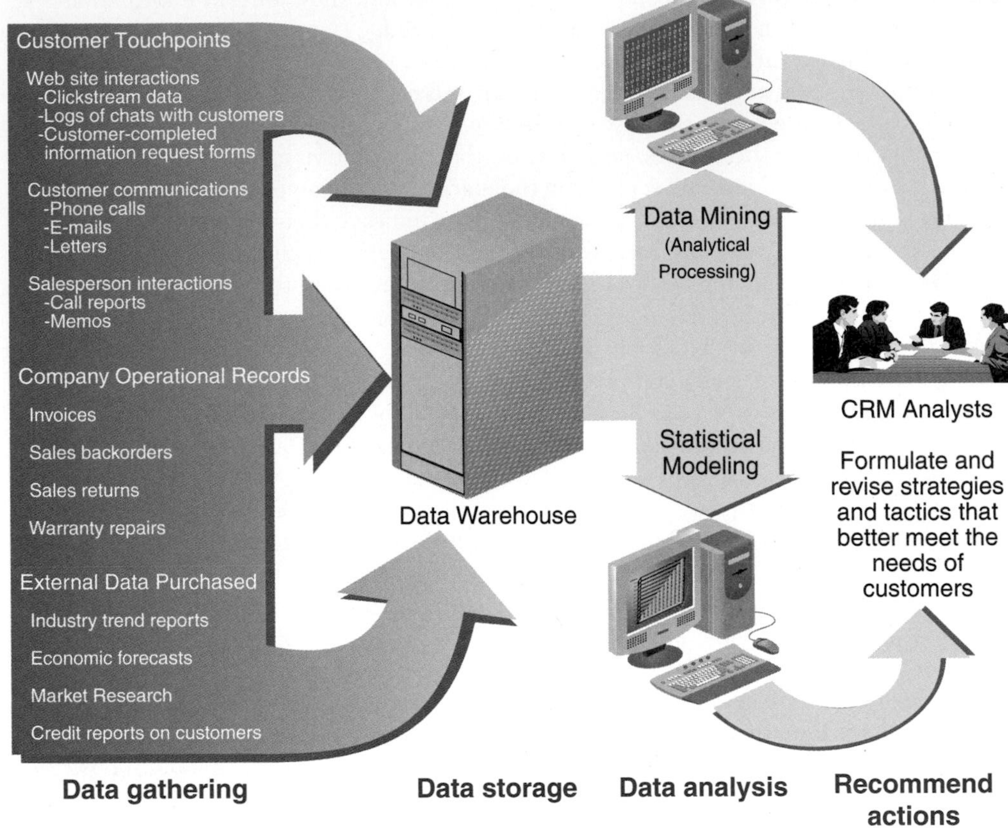

FIGURE 4-9 Elements of a typical CRM system

You can obtain updates on current developments in CRM at the **destinationCRM.com** Web site. You can learn more about data warehousing at the **Data Warehousing Information Center** and about data mining at **The Data Mine**. In Chapter 9, you will learn more about software tools and other technologies that companies are using to implement CRM.

CREATING AND MAINTAINING BRANDS ON THE WEB

A known and respected brand name can present to potential customers a powerful statement of quality, value, and other desirable characteristics in one recognizable element. Branded products are easier to advertise and promote, because each product carries the reputation of the brand name. Companies have developed and nurtured their branding programs in the physical marketplace for many years. Consumer brands such as Ivory soap, Walt Disney entertainment, Maytag appliances, and Ford automobiles have been developed over many years with the expenditure of tremendous amounts of money. However, the value of these and other trusted major brands far exceeds the cost of creating them.

Elements of Branding

The key elements of a brand, according to researchers at the advertising agency Young & Rubicam, are differentiation, relevance, and perceived value. Product differentiation is the first condition that must be met to create a product or service brand. The company must clearly distinguish its product from all others in the market. This makes branding difficult for commodity products such as salt, nails, or plywood—difficult, but not impossible.

A classic example of branding a near-commodity product is Procter & Gamble's creation of the Ivory brand more than 100 years ago. The company was experimenting with manufacturing processes and had accidentally created a bar soap that contained a high percentage of air. When one of the workers noted that the soap floated in water, the company decided to sell the soap using this differentiating characteristic in packaging and advertising by claiming "it floats." Thus was the Ivory soap brand born. **Procter & Gamble** maintains this brand differentiation on its Web site even today by listing the link to its **Ivory Soap** site under the heading "Beauty and Skin Care Products."

The second element of branding—relevance—is the degree to which the product offers utility to a potential customer. The brand only has meaning to customers if they can visualize its place in their lives. Many people understand that **Tiffany & Co.** creates a highly differentiated line of jewelry and gift products, but very few people can see themselves purchasing and using such goods.

The third branding component—perceived value—is a key element in creating a brand that has value. Even if your product is different from others on the market and potential customers can see themselves using this product, they will not buy it unless they perceive value. Some large fast food outlets have well-established brands that actually work against them. People recognize these brands and avoid eating at these restaurants because of negative associations—such as low overall quality and high-fat-content menu items. Figure 4-10 summarizes the elements of a brand.

Element	Meaning to customer
Differentiation	In what significant ways is this product or service unlike its competitors?
Relevance	How does this product or service fit into my life?
Perceived value	Is this product or service good?

FIGURE 4-10 Elements of a brand

If a brand has established that it is different from competing brands and that it is relevant and inspires a perception of value to potential purchasers, those purchasers will buy the product and become familiar with how it provides value. Brands become established only when they reach this level of purchaser understanding and acceptance.

Unfortunately, brands can lose their value if the environment in which they have become successful changes. A dramatic example is Digital Equipment Corporation (DEC). For years, DEC was a leading manufacturer of midrange computers. When the market for computing shifted to personal computers, DEC found that its branding did not transfer to the personal computers that it produced. The consumers in that market did not see the same perceived value or differentiation in DEC's personal computers that the buyers of midrange systems had seen for years. This is an important element of branding for Web-based firms to remember, because the Web is still evolving and changing at a rapid pace.

Emotional Branding vs. Rational Branding

Companies have traditionally used emotional appeals in their advertising and promotion efforts to establish and maintain brands. One branding expert, Ted Leonhardt, has described "brand" as "an emotional shortcut between a company and its customer." These emotional appeals work well on television, radio, billboards, and in print media, because the ad targets are in a passive mode of information acceptance. However, emotional appeals are difficult to convey on the Web because it is an active medium controlled to a great extent by the customer. Many Web users are actively engaged in such activities as finding information, buying airline tickets, making hotel reservations, and obtaining weather forecasts. These users are busy people who will rapidly click away from emotional appeals.

Marketers are attempting to create and maintain brands on the Web by using **rational branding**. Companies that use rational branding offer to help Web users in some way in exchange for their viewing an ad. Rational branding relies on the cognitive appeal of the specific help offered, not on a broad emotional appeal. For example, Web e-mail services such as Excite Mail, Windows Live HotMail, or Yahoo! Mail give users a valuable service—an e-mail account and storage space for messages. In exchange for this service, users see an ad on each page that provides this e-mail service.

Brand Leveraging Strategies

Rational branding is not the only way to build brands on the Web. One method that is working for well-established Web sites is to extend their dominant positions to other products and services, a strategy called **brand leveraging**. Yahoo! is an excellent example of a company that has used brand-leveraging strategies. Yahoo! was one of the first directories on the Web. It added a search engine function early in its development and has continued to parlay its leading position by acquiring other Web businesses and expanding its existing offerings. Yahoo! acquired GeoCities and Broadcast.com, and entered into an extensive cross-promotion partnership with a number of Fox entertainment and media companies. Yahoo! continues to lead its two nearest competitors, Excite and Go.com, in ad revenue by adding features that Web users find useful and that increase the site's value to advertisers. Amazon.com's expansion from its original book business into CDs, videos, and auctions is another example of a Web site leveraging its dominant position by adding features that are useful to existing customers.

Brand Consolidation Strategies

Another way to leverage the established brands of existing Web sites was pioneered by Della & James, an online bridal registry that is now doing business as part of WeddingChannel.com. Although a number of national department store chains, such as Macy's, have established online registries for their own stores, Della & James created a single registry that connects to several local and national department and gift stores, including Crate&Barrel, Gump's, Neiman Marcus, Tiffany & Co., and Williams-Sonoma. The logo and branding of each participating store are featured prominently on the WeddingChannel.com site.

The founders identified an opening for a market intermediary because the average engaged couple registers at three stores. Thus, WeddingChannel.com provides a valuable consolidating activity for registering couples and their wedding guests that no store operating alone could provide. WeddingChannel.com also provides wedding planning services and access to every item that a bride and groom might need—from the bridal gown to the cake—all in one convenient Web location.

Costs of Branding

Transferring existing brands to the Web or using the Web to maintain an existing brand is much easier and less expensive than creating an entirely new brand on the Web. In 1998, a large number of companies began spending significant amounts of money to build new brands on the Web. According to studies by the Intermarket Group, the top 100 electronic commerce sites each spent an average of $8 million that year to create and build their online brands. Two of the top spenders included the battling Web sites **Amazon.com**, which spent $133 million, and **BarnesandNoble.com**, which spent $70 million. Most of this spending was for television, radio, and print media—not for online advertising. Online brokerages E*TRADE and Ameritrade Holding were also among the top five in that first year of major brand building on the Web, spending $71 million and $44 million, respectively.

Brand-building activity continued on the Web through 1999 and into the first months of 2000. In March 2000, the supply of money from lenders and venture capitalists began drying up, which resulted in smaller advertising expenditures for most firms. By 2001, the peak of brand-building spending was over for new companies on the Web. Traditional firms realized that an opportunity had opened for them to move their offline brands to the Web.

Promoting any company's Web presence should be an integral part of brand development and maintenance. The company's URL should always be included on product packaging and in mass media advertising on radio, television, and in print. Integrating the URL with the company logo on brochures can also be helpful in getting the word out about the Web site. Ensuring that the site appears in search engine listings is also very important, as you will learn in the next section.

Affiliate Marketing Strategies

Of course, this leveraging approach works only for firms that already have Web sites that dominate a particular market. As the Web matures, it will be increasingly difficult for new entrants to identify unserved market segments and attain dominance. A tool that many new, low-budget Web sites are using to generate revenue is affiliate marketing. In **affiliate marketing**, one firm's Web site—the affiliate firm's—includes descriptions, reviews, ratings, or other information about a product that is linked to another firm's site that offers the item for sale. For every visitor who follows a link from the affiliate's site to the seller's site, the affiliate site receives a commission. The affiliate site also obtains the benefit of the selling site's brand in exchange for the referral.

The affiliate saves the expense of handling inventory, advertising and promoting the product, and processing the transaction. In fact, the affiliate risks no funds whatsoever. CDnow and Amazon.com were two of the first companies to create successful affiliate programs on the Web. CDnow's Web Buy program, which included more than 250,000 affiliates before the company entered into its joint marketing agreement with Amazon.com, was one of CDnow's main sources for new customers. The Amazon.com program (which now includes the CDnow program) has more than 1 million affiliate sites. Most of these affiliate sites are devoted to a specific issue, hobby, or other interest. Affiliate sites choose books or other items that are related to their visitors' interests and include links to the seller's site on their Web pages. Books and CDs are a natural for this type of shared promotional activity, but sellers of other products and services also use affiliate marketing programs to attract new customers to their Web sites.

One of the more interesting marketing tactics made possible by the Web is **cause marketing**, which is an affiliate marketing program that benefits a charitable organization (and, thus, supports a "cause"). In cause marketing, the affiliate site is created to benefit the charitable organization. When visitors click a link on the affiliate's Web page, a donation is made by a sponsoring company. The page that loads after the visitor clicks the donation link carries advertising for the sponsoring companies. Many companies have found that the click-through rates on these ads are much higher than the typical banner ad click-through rates.

Affiliate Commissions

Affiliate commissions can be based on several variables. In the **pay-per-click model**, the affiliate earns a commission each time a site visitor clicks the link and loads the seller's page. This is similar to the click-through model of charging for banner advertising, and the rates paid per thousand click-throughs are similar to those paid for banner ads.

In the **pay-per-conversion model**, the affiliate earns a commission each time a site visitor is converted from a visitor into either a qualified prospect or a customer. An example of a seller that might use the qualified prospect definition is a credit card–issuing bank. The bank might decide that its best strategy is to pay affiliates only when the visitor turns out to be a good credit risk. Alternatively, the bank might decide it wants to pay the affiliate only if the visitor is approved for the card and then accepts the card (completes the sale). A site that pays its affiliates on completed sales usually pays a percentage of the sale amount rather than a fixed amount per conversion. Some sites use a combination of these methods to pay their affiliates. Commissions on completed sales range from 5 to 20 percent of the sale amount, depending on variables such as the type of product, the strength of the product's brand, how profitable the product is, and the size of an average order.

You can learn more about affiliate programs by visiting an affiliate program broker site that offers affiliate program opportunities for a number of Web sites. An **affiliate program broker** is a company that serves as a clearinghouse or marketplace for sites that run affiliate programs and sites that want to become affiliates. These brokers also often provide software, management consulting, and brokerage services to affiliate program operators. For example, Proflowers uses affiliate program broker LinkShare to manage its affiliate program. LinkShare tracks affiliates' sales, calculates and pays affiliates' commissions, and handles any problems that arise. Commission Junction and DirectTrack are two other popular affiliate program brokers. Other companies, such as Performics, offer affiliate program brokering along with other marketing services.

Viral Marketing Strategies

Traditional marketing strategies have always been developed with an assumption that the company would communicate with potential customers directly or through an intermediary acting on behalf of the company, such as a distributor, retailer, or independent sales organization. Because the Web expands the types of communication channels available, including customer-to-customer communication, another marketing approach, viral marketing, has become popular on the Web. **Viral marketing** relies on existing customers to tell other people—the company's prospective customers—about the products or services they have enjoyed using. Much as affiliate marketing uses Web sites to spread the word about a company, viral marketing approaches use word of mouth through individual customers to do the same thing. The number of customers increases the way a virus multiplies, thus the name.

BlueMountainArts, an electronic greeting card company, purchased very little advertising but grew rapidly. Electronic greeting cards are e-mail messages that include a link to the greeting card site. When people received Blue Mountain Arts electronic greeting cards in their e-mail, they clicked a link in the e-mail message that opened the Blue Mountain Arts Web site in their browser. Once at the Blue Mountain Arts site, they were likely to search for cards that they might like to send to other friends. A greeting card recipient might send electronic greeting cards to several friends, who could then send greetings to their friends. Each new visitor to the site could spread the "virus," which in this case was the knowledge of Blue Mountain Arts. By late 1999, when the company was sold to At Home Corporation for $780 million, Blue Mountain had more than 10 million people visiting its site each month. Blue Mountain Arts built a large following using its approach to viral marketing. Today, the site requires visitors to pay for a subscription before they can send electronic greeting cards. However, the site's original strategy of offering free greetings combined with a viral marketing strategy helped it build a large customer base very quickly.

SEARCH ENGINE POSITIONING AND DOMAIN NAMES

Potential customers find Web sites in many different ways. Some site visitors are referred by a friend or click a link on a referring Web site. Others are referred by an affiliate marketing partner of the site. Some see the site's URL in a print advertisement or on television. Others arrive unintentionally after typing a URL that is similar to the company's name. But many site visitors are directed to the site by a search engine or directory Web site.

Search Engines and Web Directories

A **search engine** is a Web site that helps people find things on the Web. Search engines contain three major parts. The first part, called a **spider**, a **crawler**, or a **robot** (or simply **bot**), is a program that automatically searches the Web to find Web pages that might be interesting to people. When the spider finds Web pages that might interest search engine site visitors, it collects the URL of the page and information contained on the page. This information might include the page's title, key words included in the page's text, and information about other pages on that Web site. In addition to words that appear on the Web page, Web site designers can specify additional key words in the page that are hidden from the view of Web site visitors, but that are visible to spiders. These key words are enclosed in an HTML tag set called meta tags. The word "meta" is used for this tag set to indicate that the key words describe the content of a Web page and are not themselves part of the content.

The spider returns this information to the second part of the search engine to be stored. The storage element of a search engine is called its **index** or **database**. The index checks to see if information about the Web page is already stored. If it is, it compares the stored information to the new information and determines whether to update the page information. The index is designed to allow fast searches of its very large amount of stored information.

The third part of the search engine is the search utility. Visitors to the search engine site provide search terms, and the **search utility** takes those terms and finds entries for Web pages in its index that match those search terms. The search utility is a program that creates a Web page that is a list of links to URLs that the search engine has found in its index that match the site visitor's search terms. The visitor can then click the links to visit those sites. You will learn more about the technologies used in search engines in later chapters of this book.

Some search engine sites also provide classified hierarchical lists of categories into which they have organized commonly searched URLs. Although these sites are technically called Web directories, most people refer to them as search engines. The most popular of these sites, such as Yahoo!, include a Web directory and a search engine. They give users the option of using the search engine to find categories of URLs as well as the URLs themselves. This combination of Web directory and search engine can be a powerful tool for finding things on the Web. Nielsen//NetRatings, the online audience measurement and analytics consulting firm, issues press releases that list the most frequently visited Web sites. The search engine and Web directory sites AltaVista, AOL, Excite, Google, Lycos, MSN, and Yahoo! regularly appear on these lists.

Marketers want to make sure that when a potential customer enters search terms that relate to their products or services, their companies' Web site URLs appear among the first 10 returned listings. The weighting of the factors that search engines use to decide which URLs appear first on searches for a particular search term is called a **search engine ranking**. For example, if a site is near the top of the list of links returned for the search term "auto," that site is said to have a high search engine ranking for "auto." The combined art and science of having a particular URL listed near the top of search engine results is called **search engine positioning**, **search engine optimization**, or **search engine placement**. For sites that obtain most of their visitors from search engines, a high ranking that places their URL near the top of the list of links returned by the search engine is extremely important.

Paid Search Engine Inclusion and Placement

Today, a number of search engine sites make it easier to obtain good ad placement on search results pages—but for a price. These search engine sites offer companies a **paid placement** (also called a **sponsorship** or a **search term sponsorship**; however, note that these search term sponsorships are not the same thing as the general site sponsorships you learned about earlier in this chapter), which is the option of purchasing a top listing on results pages for a particular set of search terms. The rates charged vary tremendously depending on the desirability of the search terms to potential sponsors.

Another option for companies is to buy banner ad space at the top of search results pages that include certain terms. For example, Chevrolet might want to buy banner ad space at the top of all search results pages that are generated by queries containing the words "new" and "car." Most search engine sites sell banner ad space on this basis. An increasing number sell space on results pages for the most desirable terms only to companies that agree to package deals that include paid placement and banner ad purchases.

Search engine positioning is a complex subject. A number of consulting firms do nothing but advise companies on positioning strategy. Entire books have been written on the subject (one of the best currently available is Frederick Marckini's book, which is referenced in the For Further Study and Research section at the end of this chapter), and several major conferences are devoted to the subject each year.

Spending on online advertising grew rapidly in the early days of the Web. The amount spent in the United States went from virtually zero in 1995 to about $8 billion in 2000. The Internet slump of 2001-2002 did result in a drop to about $6 billion, but since then, the growth has been remarkable, both in absolute terms and as a percentage of total advertising. Figure 4-11 shows the amount of online advertising sold and projected to be sold in the United States from 2007 through 2014.

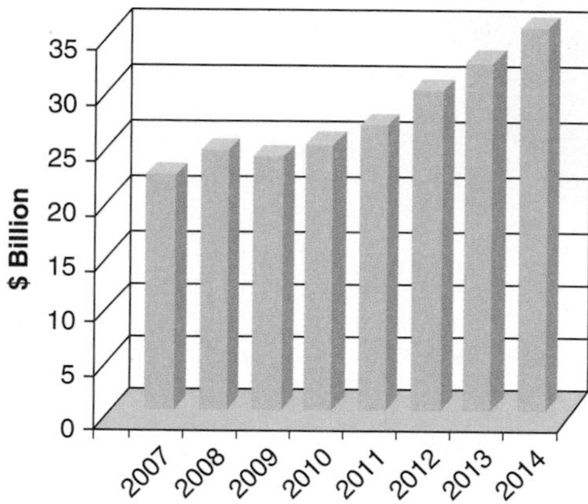

Source: Adapted from reports by eMarketer, Forrester Research, Nielsen NetRatings, and from industry sources.

FIGURE 4-11 U.S. online advertising expenditures, actual and projected

Online advertising is growing much faster than any other type of advertising or advertising spending in general. Thus, online advertising is becoming a larger proportion of all advertising. Figure 4-12 shows how online advertising compares to other U.S. advertising. Online advertising in the rest of the world is expanding rapidly as well, but it is a smaller proportion of total advertising outside the United States.

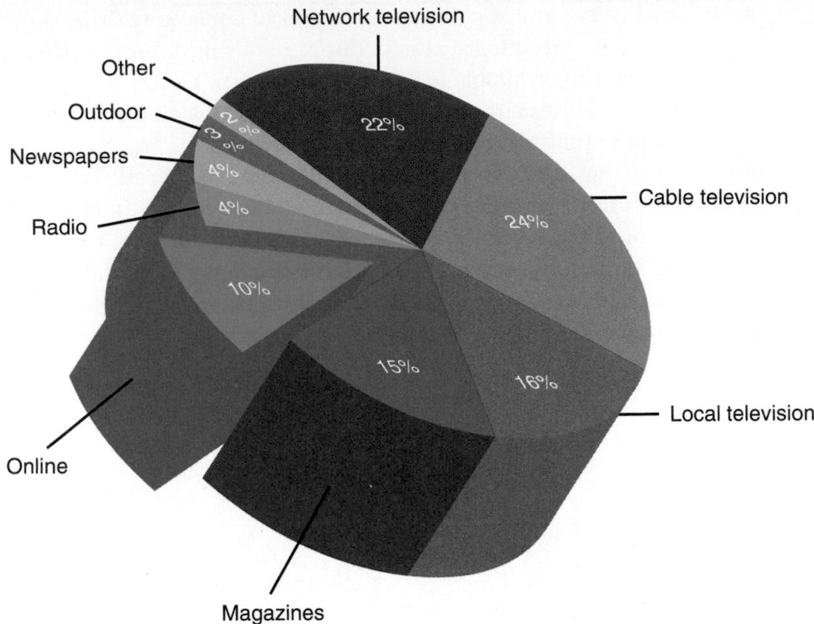

Source: Adapted from reports by eMarketer, Nielsen NetRatings, and from industry sources.

FIGURE 4-12 U.S. advertising expenditures by medium, 2010 estimates

The business of selling search engine inclusions and placements is complex because many search engines do not sell inclusion and placement rights on their pages directly to advertisers. They use **search engine placement brokers**, which are companies that aggregate inclusion and placement rights on multiple search engines and then sell those combination packages to advertisers. **LookSmart** is an example of a large search engine placement broker. Another reason for the complexity in this business is that recent years have brought a flurry of mergers and acquisitions. For example, in 2003, Yahoo! purchased Overture, a search engine placement broker. This put Yahoo! in the business of selling advertising for several of its major competitors (who had been using Overture as their search engine placement broker). An excellent resource for keeping up with the rapid changes in this business is Danny Sullivan's **Search Engine Watch** Web site. Although some of the content on the site is limited to paid subscribers, the site does include many free resources and explanations that are useful for learning about search engines, placement brokers, and search engine optimization in general.

The most popular search engine, Google, does not use a placement broker to sell search term inclusion and placement for its site. Google sells these services directly through its **Google AdWords** program. The home page for Google's AdWords program appears in Figure 4-13.

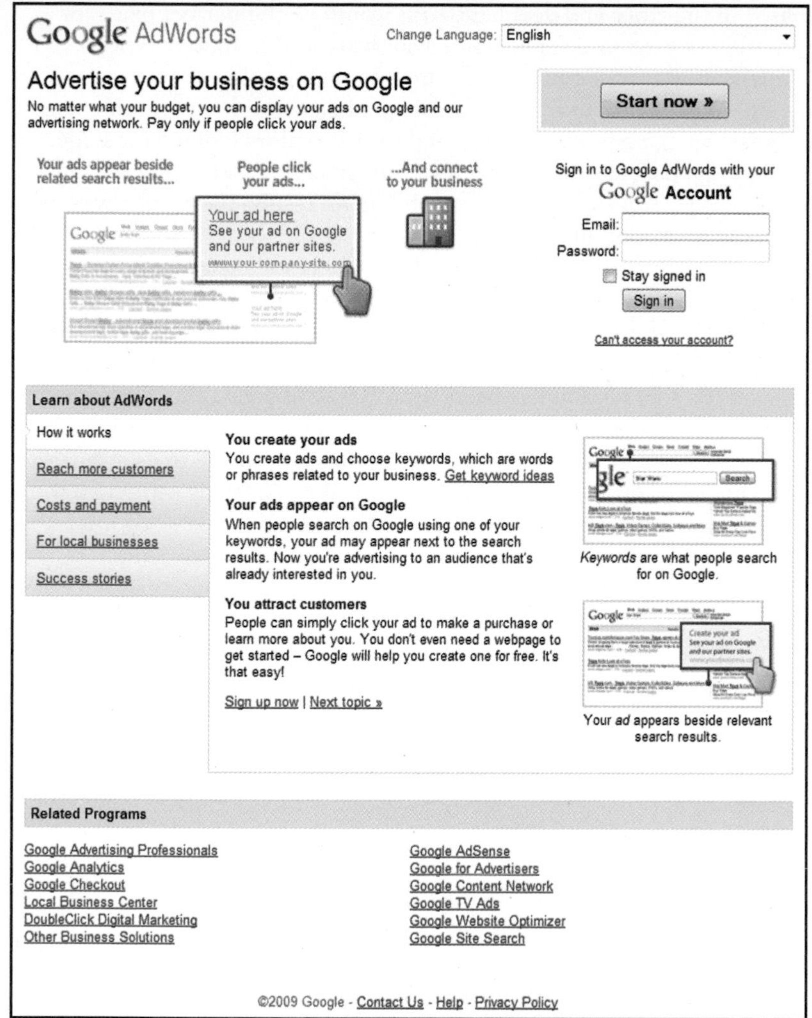

FIGURE 4-13 Google's AdWords program home page

Web sites that offer content can also participate in paid placement. Google offers its **AdSense** program to sites that want to carry ads that match the content offered on the site. Other companies, such as **Kanoodle** and Yahoo!'s **Overture** division, offer similar ad brokerage services, but Google is the leader in this market. The content site receives a placement fee from the broker in exchange for the ad placement and the broker sells the placement slots to interested advertisers. These techniques in which ads are placed in proximity to related content is sometimes called **contextual advertising**.

Of course, this approach is not without its flaws. In 2003, the *New York Post* ran a sensational story that described a gruesome murder. The murder victim's body had been cut into pieces, which the murderer hid in a suitcase. When the newspaper's Web site ran the story, it appeared with a paid placement ad for luggage. The ad broker's software had noted the word "suitcase" in the story and decided that it would be the perfect place for a luggage ad. Today, ad brokers use more sophisticated software and human reviewers to prevent this type of error; however, some industry analysts believe that contextual advertising on content sites will never be as successful as paid placement on search engine pages. They argue that search engine pages are provided to site visitors looking for something specific, often as part of a purchasing process. Content sites are used to explore and learn about more general things. Thus, an ad on a search engine results page will always be more effective than an ad on a content site page.

Another variation of paid placement ads uses search engine results pages that are generated in response to a search for products or services in a specific geographical area. This technique, called **localized advertising**, places ads related to the location on the search results page. Localized advertising came about as a result of local search services. In 2004, Google launched a local search service that lets users search by ZIP code or local address. All of the other major search engine and Web directory sites followed Google's lead and now offer some form of localized search, either as part of their main search page or as a separate service. The local advertising market (in outlets such as the Yellow Pages) is estimated to be more than $25 billion, a very attractive market for online advertisers.

Web Site Naming Issues

Companies that have a well-established brand name or reputation in a particular line of business usually want the URLs for their Web sites to reflect that name or reputation. Obtaining identifiable names to use on the Web can be an important part of establishing a Web presence that is consistent with the company's existing image in the physical world.

Two airlines that started their online businesses with troublesome domain names have both purchased more suitable domain names. Southwest Airlines' domain name was www.iflyswa.com until it purchased www.southwest.com. Delta Air Lines' original domain name was www.delta-air.com. After several years of complaints from confused customers who could never remember to include the hyphen, the company purchased the domain name www.delta.com.

Companies often buy more than one domain name. Some companies buy additional domain names to ensure that potential site visitors who misspell the URL will still be redirected (through the misspelled URL) to the intended site. For example, Yahoo! owns the name Yahow.com. Other companies own many URLs because they have many different names or forms of names associated with them. For example, General Motors' main URL is GM.com, but the company also owns GeneralMotors.com, Chevrolet.com, Chevy.com, GMC.com, and many others. In 1995, Procter & Gamble purchased hundreds of domain names that included the names of its products, such as Crisco.com, Folgers.com, Jif.com, and Pampers.com. It also bought names related to its products such as Flu.com, BadBreath.com, Disinfect.com, and Stains.com. Procter & Gamble hoped that people searching the Web for information about stains, for example, would find the Stains.com site, which featured links to the company's cleaning products. Procter & Gamble even purchased Pimples.com and Underarms.com.

Buying, Selling, and Leasing Domain Names

In 1998, a poster art and framing company named Artuframe opened for business on the Web. With quality products and an appealing site design, the company was doing well, but it was concerned about its domain name, which was www.artuframe.com. After searching for a more appropriate domain name, the company's president found the Web site of Advanced Rotocraft Technology, an aerospace firm, at the URL www.art.com. After finding out that Advanced Rotocraft Technology's site was drawing 150,000 visitors each month who were looking for something art related, Artuframe offered to buy the URL. The aerospace firm agreed to sell the URL to Artuframe for $450,000. Artuframe immediately relaunched as **Art.com** and experienced a 30 percent increase in site traffic the day after implementing the name change.

The newly named site did not rely on the name change alone, however. It entered a joint marketing agreement with Yahoo! that placed ads for Art.com on art-related search results pages. Art.com also created an affiliate program with businesses that sell art-related products and not-for-profit art organizations. Although Art.com was ultimately unsuccessful in building a profitable business on the Web and liquidated in mid-2001, the domain name was snapped up immediately by already profitable Allwall.com for an undisclosed amount. The new Allwall.com site, relaunched with the Art.com domain name, experienced a 100 percent increase in site visitors within the first month.

Another company that invested in an appropriate domain name was **Cars.com**. The firm paid $100,000 to the speculator who had originally purchased the rights to the name. Cars.com is a themed portal site that displays ads for new cars, used cars, financing, leasing, and other car-related products and services. The major investors in this firm are newspaper publishers that wanted to retain an interest in automobile-related advertising as it moved online. As you learned in Chapter 3, classified ads are an important revenue source for many newspapers.

More recently, higher prices have prevailed in the market for domain names. Names such as Fruits.com, Question.com, Speaker.com, Tower.com, and Wisdom.com have each sold for more than $100,000. Other names, including Cinema.com, Drugs.com, and ForSaleByOwner.com, have sold for more than $500,000 each. Not long ago, eCompanies paid $7.5 million for the domain name Business.com. Although most domains that have high value are in the .com TLD, the name engineering.org sold at auction to the American Society of Mechanical Engineers, a not-for-profit organization, for just under $200,000. Figure 4-14 lists domain names that sold for more than $1 million each.

Domain name	Price
Business.com	$7.5 million
Altavista.com	$3.3 million
Loans.com	$3.0 million
Wine.com	$3.0 million
Autos.com	$2.2 million
Express.com	$2.0 million
WallStreet.com	$1.0 million

FIGURE 4-14 Domain names that sold for more than $1 million

Some companies and individuals invested their money in the purchase of highly desirable domain names. Instead of selling these names to the highest bidder, some of these domain name owners decided to retain ownership of the domain names and lease the rights to the names to companies for a fixed time period. Usually, these domain name lessors rent their domain names through URL brokers.

URL Brokers and Registrars

Several legitimate online businesses, known as **URL brokers**, are in the business of selling, leasing, or auctioning domain names that they believe others will find valuable. Companies selling "good" (short and easily remembered) domain names include **BuyDomains.com** and **GreatDomains**.

Companies can also obtain domain names that have never been issued, or that are currently unused, from a domain name registrar. The Internet Corporation for Assigned Names and Numbers (**ICANN**; about which you learned in Chapter 2) maintains a list of accredited registrars. Many of these registrars offer domain name search tools on their Web sites. A company can use these tools to search for available domain names that might meet their needs. Another service offered by domain name registrars is domain name parking. **Domain name parking**, also called **domain name hosting**, is a service that permits the purchaser of a domain name to maintain a simple Web site (usually one page) so that the domain name remains in use. The fees charged for this service are usually much lower than those for hosting an active Web site.

Summary

In this chapter, you learned how companies can use the principles of marketing strategy and the four Ps of marketing to achieve their goals for selling products and offering services on the Web. Some companies use a product-based marketing strategy and some use a customer-based strategy. The Web enables companies to mix these strategies and give customers a choice about which approach they prefer.

Market segmentation using geographic, demographic, and psychographic information can work as well on the Web as it does in the physical world. The Web gives companies the powerful added ability to segment markets by customer behavior and life-cycle stage, even when the same customer exhibits different behavior during different visits to the company's site.

Online advertising has become more intrusive since it was introduced in the mid-1990s, even though research has shown that users find such ads to be irritating. You learned how companies are using various types of online ads, including banners, pop-ups, pop-behinds, text, inline text, and interstitials to promote their sites to potential customers. Permission marketing and opt-in e-mail offer alternatives that can be used with or instead of Web page ads.

Many companies are using the Web to manage their relationships with customers in new and interesting ways. By understanding the nature of communication on the Web, companies can use it to identify and reach the largest possible number of qualified customers. Technology-enabled customer relationship management can provide better returns for businesses on the Web than the traditional unaided approaches of market segmentation and micromarketing. After many companies experienced CRM system failures in the early years of the Web, companies began to limit the scope of these implementations. These focused CRM efforts have been more successful than the earlier comprehensive attempts to manage customer relationships with technology.

Firms on the Web can use rational branding instead of the emotional branding techniques that work well in mass media advertising. Some businesses on the Web are sharing and transferring brand benefits through affiliate marketing and cooperative efforts among brand owners. Others are using brand leveraging and viral marketing to increase their appeal and their customer bases.

Successful search engine positioning and domain name selection can be critical for many businesses in their quests for new online customers. A growing number of advertisers are paying for inclusion and placement services to guarantee that their sites' URLs appear among the top results provided to potential customers by search engines. They are also paying for placement of advertising messages in those pages and on other sites, such as content sites and local information sites. The most important theme in this chapter is that companies must integrate the Web marketing tools they use into a cohesive and customer-sensitive overall marketing strategy.

Key Terms

Acquisition cost
Active ad
Ad-blocking software
Ad view
Affiliate marketing
Affiliate program broker
Analytical processing
Animated GIF
Banner ad
Banner advertising network
Banner exchange network
Behavioral segmentation

Blog
Brand
Brand leveraging
Cause marketing
Click
Clickstream
Click-through
Contextual advertising
Conversion
Conversion cost
Conversion rate
Cost per thousand (CPM)
Crawler
Customer life cycle
Customer relationship management (CRM)
Customer touchpoint
Customer value
Database
Data mining
Data warehouse
Demographic segmentation
Domain name hosting
Domain name parking
Electronic customer relationship management (eCRM)
Four Ps of marketing
Geographic segmentation
Impression
Index
Inline text ad
Interactive marketing unit (IMU) ad format
Interstitial ad
Leaderboard ad
Life-cycle segmentation
Localized advertising
Market segmentation
Marketing mix
Marketing strategy
Marketspace
Micromarketing
Occasion segmentation
One-to-one marketing
Opt-in e-mail
Page view
Paid placement (sponsorship)
Pay-per-click model
Pay-per-conversion model
Permission marketing
Place (distribution)
Pop-behind ad
Pop-up ad
Price
Product
Promotion
Psychographic segmentation
Rational branding
Repeat visit
Retained customer
Retention cost
Rich media ad
Rich media object
Robot (bot)
Search engine
Search engine optimization
Search engine placement
Search engine placement broker
Search engine positioning
Search engine ranking
Search term sponsorship
Search utility
Segments
Shopping cart
Site sponsorship
Skyscraper ad
Spider
Statistical modeling
Technology-enabled customer relationship management
Technology-enabled relationship management
Text ad

- Touchpoints
- Touchpoint consistency
- Trial visit
- Trigger words
- URL brokers
- Usage-based market segmentation
- Viral marketing
- Visit
- Web log (blog)

Review Questions

RQ1. Assume you are a consultant to Fred's Sticks, a golf club manufacturer that sells its clubs directly to customers on the Web. Review Figure 4-3, which describes what types of television programs would be good hosts for various types of advertising. Applying the logic presented in Figure 4-3, create a list of four Web sites (other than Web sites with information about golf or golf equipment) in which Fred's Sticks should consider placing online advertising to support its Web sales effort. For each Web site, write one paragraph in which you explain why that Web site would be a good advertising outlet to reach potential customers of an online golf club store.

RQ2. In about 200 words, outline a marketing strategy that could help an online shoe store improve its customer retention. Present facts and logical arguments that support the strategy you outline.

RQ3. Select a retail store with which you are familiar that has a Web site on which it sells products or services similar to those it sells in its physical retail stores. Explore the Web site and examine it carefully for features that indicate the level of service it provides. Using your experience in the physical store and your review of the Web site, write a 200-word evaluation of the company's touchpoint consistency.

RQ4. Many people have strong negative reactions to pop-up, pop-behind, interstitial, and rich media ads. Assume you are the director of an advertising agency that specializes in creating and placing these ads. You see an opinion article in your local online newspaper that harshly criticizes these ads as intrusive and unnecessary. Write a 200-word rejoinder to post in the comments section of this article in which you explain, from the advertiser's viewpoint, why these ads can be more effective advertising media than text ads.

RQ5. In one or two paragraphs, explain how CRM analysts might use the information contained in a data warehouse to increase their company's online sales.

RQ6. Briefly state the three elements of a brand. Then, assume you are the marketing director for PerfectSeasons, a new line of cookware sponsored by a famous celebrity chef. In about 300 words, describe how you would promote each of the three brand elements for this new product line on the celebrity chef's Web site.

Exercises

E1. Visit **FTD.com** to examine how that company implements occasion segmentation. Write a report of approximately 200 words in which you describe two clear examples of occasion segmentation on the site and explain why an online florist would mix occasion segmentation with product segmentation rather than use one or the other separately.

E2. You are the new online advertising manager for the *Midland Daily Courier*, a local newspaper. The newspaper wants to sell advertising on its Web site in a variety of formats to meet the needs of its advertisers. Examine the **IAB** Web site and other online resources of your choosing, then prepare a memo of about 300 words to the newspaper's advertising manager that recommends specific types of ads (banner, text, interstitial, and so on) that the newspaper should offer to its advertisers. If you decide that specific types of ads might work better on specific pages or sections (Sports, Entertainment, Local News, and so on) of the online newspaper, include that information in your recommendation. Be sure to support your recommendation with facts and logical arguments.

E3. You have been employed by **HGTV** to sell space on its site to advertisers. Create a memo of approximately 300 words in which you describe the advantages of advertising on HGTV in a form that the HGTV sales team can use as a resource when they are making presentations to potential advertisers. You may choose to promote space on the main page, other specific pages, or all pages. You may also choose to include the advantages of HGTV's permission-based e-mail marketing system as part of the promotional package. Be prepared to explain why your promotional strategy should work.

E4. Marti Baron operates a small Web business, The Cannonball, that sells parts, repair kits, books, and accessories to hobbyists who restore antique model trains. Many model train hobbyists and collectors have created Web sites on which they share photos and other information about model trains. Marti is interested in creating an affiliate marketing program that would allow those hobbyists to place links on their sites to The Cannonball and be rewarded with commissions on sales that result from visitors following those links. Examine the services offered by **Commission Junction**, **LinkShare**, and any other affiliate program brokers you can find on the Web. Recommend at least one affiliate program broker that would be a good fit for Marti's business. In about 500 words, explain your recommendation. Be sure to consider the characteristics of Marti's business in your analysis.

E5. Choose a business that you would like to own and write a short description of that business, including the business name, the products or services it would sell, and the types of customers the business would have. Use **BuyDomains.com** or a similar online service to search for suitable domain names for the Web site for your business and to get an idea of the cost of those names. Evaluate at least five specific names to determine whether the cost of the name would be worth its benefits for your business. Summarize the results of your search and analysis in about 200 words.

Cases

C1. Oxfam

For more than 60 years, Oxfam has worked through and with its donors, staff, project partners, and project participants to overcome poverty and injustice around the world. Early in World War II, Greece was occupied by the Nazis. Allied forces created a naval blockade around Greece to prevent further German expansion; however, the blockade created severe shortages of food and medicine among Greek civilian communities. In 1942, a number of Famine Relief Committees were established in Great Britain to ship emergency supplies through the Allied blockade. Although most of these committees ceased operations after the war ended, the Oxford Committee for Famine Relief saw a continuing need and enlarged its operations to provide aid throughout post-war Europe, and in later years, the rest of the world. The Committee eventually became known by its abbreviated telegraph address, Oxfam, and the name was formally adopted in 1965.

Oxfam's success and growth was due to many dedicated volunteers and donors who continued and expanded their financial support of the organization. In the 1960s, Oxfam began to generate significant revenues from its retail stores. These shops, located throughout Great Britain, accept donations of goods and handcrafted items from overseas for resale. Today, those stores number more than 800 and are staffed by more than 20,000 volunteers.

Oxfam often deals with humanitarian disasters that are beyond the scope of its resources. In these cases, the organization provides aid by mobilizing an international lobbying staff that has contacts with key aid agencies based in other countries, governments in the affected area, and the United Nations.

In 1996, Oxfam opened a Web site to provide information about its efforts to supporters and potential donors. The Web site included detailed reports on Oxfam's work, past and present, and allows site visitors to make donations to the organization. Although Oxfam gladly accepts any donations, it encourages supporters to commit to a continuing relationship by making regular donations. In exchange, it provides regular updates about its activities on the Web site and through an e-mailed monthly newsletter. The Web site includes a sign-up page for the e-mail newsletter, which goes out to several hundred thousand supporters.

Oxfam has been involved in relief work in Sudan since the 1970s, when it provided help to Ugandan refugees in the southern part of the country. More recently, Oxfam was an early responder to the 2004 crisis in that country. Oxfam set up sanitary facilities and provided clean drinking water in camps set up for thousands of displaced people fleeing pro-government Arab militias. The need in Sudan rapidly exceeded Oxfam's capacity and it decided to use e-mail to mobilize support for the project.

Oxfam planned an e-mail campaign that would send three e-mails in HTML format to supporters on its existing e-mail list over a six-week period. The first e-mail included a photo of children in one of the camps. The text of the e-mail message described Oxfam's efforts to provide clean water to the displaced people living in the Sudanese camps. The e-mail included links in two places that took recipients to a Web page that had been created specifically to receive visitors responding to that e-mail message. The Web page allowed visitors to make a donation and asked them to provide their e-mail addresses, which would be used to send updates on the Sudan project. A second e-mail was sent two weeks later to addresses on the list that had not yet responded. This second e-mail included a video file that played automatically when the e-mail was opened. The video conveyed the message that Oxfam had delivered $300,000 in aid to the camps but that more help was urgently needed in the region. This second e-mail included three links that led to the Web page created for the first e-mail. Two weeks later, a final e-mail was sent to addresses on the list that had not responded to either of the first two e-mails. This third e-mail included an audio recording in which Oxfam's executive director made a plea for the cause. The e-mail also included text that provided examples of which aid items could be provided for specific donation amounts.

Oxfam's three-part e-mail campaign was considered a success by direct marketing standards. The first e-mail was opened by 32 percent of recipients and had a click-through rate of 8 percent. The second e-mail had similar, but somewhat higher, results (33 percent opened, 10 percent clicked-through). Ninety percent of those who opened the e-mail watched the video. The third e-mail continued the slightly increasing trends for opening and attention (34 percent opened, and 94 percent listened to the audio), but the click-through rate was much higher than the previous two e-mails (14 percent). Also, the dollar amount of donations increased with each subsequent e-mailing. The e-mail campaign raised more than $450,000 in its six-week period.

Oxfam coordinated this e-mail effort with other awareness activities it was conducting in the same time period. The organization sent letters to supporters who had not provided e-mail addresses and ran ads in two newspapers (*The Independent* and *The Guardian*) that carried messages similar to those in the e-mails.

Required:

1. Oxfam chose not to use online banner ads this campaign. In about 100 words, explain the advantages and disadvantages that Oxfam would have experienced by using banner ads to achieve the objectives of this campaign.
2. Oxfam used only its existing e-mail list for this campaign; it did not purchase (or borrow from other charitable organizations) any additional e-mail addresses. Evaluate this decision. In about 300 words explain the advantages and disadvantages of acquiring other e-mail addresses for a campaign of this nature.
3. For this campaign, Oxfam chose to use e-mails that contained HTML, audio, and video elements rather than using plain-text e-mails. In about 100 words, describe the advantages and disadvantages of using formats other than plain-text in this type of e-mail campaign. Be sure to identify any specific trade-offs that Oxfam faced in deciding not to use plain-text e-mail.
4. Oxfam used HTML in the first e-mail, video in the second, and audio in the third. Evaluate the use of different e-mail formats for this type of message and consider the sequencing of the formats that Oxfam used in this campaign. In about 300 words, summarize the considerations that would affect a decision to use a particular sequence of e-mail formats in a campaign such as this and evaluate the sequence that Oxfam used.
5. A manager at Oxfam might be tempted to conclude that the sequence of formats used in the e-mail messages was related to the increase in donations over the six weeks of the campaign. In about 100 words, present at least two reasons why this would be an incorrect conclusion.

Note: Your instructor might assign you to a group to complete this case, and might ask you to prepare a formal presentation of your results to your class.

C2. Montana Mountain Biking

Jerry Singleton founded Montana Mountain Biking (MMB) 18 years ago. MMB offers one-week guided mountain biking expeditions based in four Montana locations. Most of MMB's new customers hear about the company and its tours from existing customers. Many of MMB's customers come back every year for a mountain biking expedition; about 80 percent of the riders on any given expedition are repeat customers.

Jerry is happy with this high repeat percentage, but he is worried that MMB is missing a large potential market. He has been reluctant to spend a lot of money on advertising. About 10 years ago, he spent $80,000 on a print advertising campaign that included ads in several outdoor interest and sports magazines, but the ads did not generate enough additional customers to cover the cost of the advertising. Five years ago, a marketing consultant advised Jerry that the ads had not been placed well. The magazines did not reach the serious mountain bike enthusiast, which is

MMB's true target market. After all, a casual mountain bike rider would probably not be drawn to a week-long expedition.

Another concern of Jerry's is that more than 90 percent of MMB's customers come from neighboring states. Jerry has always thought that MMB was not reaching the sizable market of serious mountain bike enthusiasts in California. He talked to the marketing consultant about buying an address list and sending out a promotional mailing, but producing and mailing the letters seemed too expensive. The cost of renting the list was $0.10 per name, but the printing and mailing were $4 per letter. There were 60,000 addresses on the list, and the consultant told him to expect a conversion rate of between 1 and 3 percent. At best, the mailing would yield 1800 new customers and MMB's profit on the one-week expedition was only about $100 per customer. It looked like the conversion cost would be about $246,000 (60,000 × $4.10) to obtain a profit of $180,000 (1800 × $100). The consultant explained that it was an investment; because MMB had such a high customer retention rate, the profit from the new customers in the second or third years would exceed the one-time cost of the mailing in the first year. Jerry was not convinced.

Nine years ago, MMB launched its first Web site. It included information about the company and its tours, but Jerry did not see any need to include an expedition-booking function on the site. He did think about selling caps and jackets with the MMB logo, but that idea never was implemented. The MMB logo is well known in the mountain biking community in the upper Midwest.

The MMB Web site includes an e-mail address so that visitors to the site can send an e-mail requesting more information about the expeditions. Robin Davis, one of MMB's expedition leaders, is an amateur photographer who has taken many photos while on the trails over the years. Last year, she had those photos digitized and put them on the MMB Web site. The number of e-mail inquiries increased dramatically within a month. Many of the inquiries were about MMB's expeditions, but a surprising number asked for permission to use the photos, or asked if MMB had more photos like those for sale. Jerry is not quite sure what to make of the popularity of those photos. He is, after all, in the mountain bike expedition business.

Required:

1. Review the five stages of customer loyalty shown in Figure 4-4 and prepare a report of about 200 words in which you classify MMB's customers. Estimate the percentage of MMB customers who fall into each of the five categories. Support your classification with logic and evidence from the case narrative.
2. In a report of about 200 words, recommend an e-mail marketing strategy for MMB. In your recommendation, consider the results of MMB's earlier print mail advertising campaign, your answer to the first requirement, and the potential offered by permission marketing.
3. In about 300 words, explain how MMB could use viral marketing to gain new customers and cement its relationships with existing customers. In your answer, be sure to discuss features that MMB should include on its Web site to support the viral marketing initiative.
4. Prepare a report of about 500 words in which you outline an affiliate marketing strategy for MMB. Include a description of the types of Web sites that MMB should attempt to recruit as affiliates, and present at least five examples of specific sites that would be good referral sources.

Note: Your instructor might assign you to a group to complete this case, and might ask you to prepare a formal presentation of your results to your class.

For Further Study and Research

Agarwal, A., D. Harding, and J. Schumacher. 2004. "Organizing for CRM," *The McKinsey Quarterly,* June, 80–91.

Andrews, R. and I. Currim. 2004. "Behavioral Differences Between Consumers Attracted to Shopping Online Vs. Traditional Supermarkets: Implications for Enterprise Design and Marketing," *International Journal of Internet Marketing and Advertising,* 1(1), January–March, 38–61.

Armitt, C. 2004. "Case Study: Crisis in Sudan Email Campaign," *New Media Age,* September 2, 22.

Bergert, S. and K. Kazimer-Shockley. 2001. "The Customer Rules," *Intelligent Enterprise,* 4(11), July 23, 31–34.

Blair, J. 2001. "Behind Kozmo's Demise: Thin Profit Margins," *The New York Times,* April 13. (http://www.nytimes.com/2001/04/13/technology/13KOZM.html)

Bruton, C. and G. Schneider. 2003. "Multiple Channels for Online Branding," *Academy of Marketing Studies Journal,* 7(1) 109–114.

Chan, A., J. Dodd, and R. Stevens. 2004. *The Efficacy of Pop-ups and the Resulting Effect on Brands.* Oxfordshire, UK: Bunnyfoot Universality.

Chan, Y. 2009. "Effects Beyond Click-through: Incidental Exposure to Web Advertising. *Journal of Marketing Communications,* 15(4), September, 227–246.

Clifford, S. 2009. "Put Ad on Web. Count Clicks. Revise." *The New York Times,* May 31, BU1, BU5.

Delio, M. 2001. "Kozmo Kills the Messenger," *Wired News,* April 13. (http://www.wired.com/news/business/0,1367,43025,00.html)

Fallows, J. 2004. "How Google Took the Work Out of Selling Advertising," *The New York Times,* June 13, C5.

Gardner, E. 1999. "Art.com," *Internet World,* March 15, 13. (http://www.iw.com/print/1999/03/15/)

Godin, S. 2005. *All Marketers Are Liars: The Power of Telling Authentic Stories in a Low-Trust World.* New York: Portfolio.

Godin, S. and D. Peppers. 1999. *Permission Marketing: Turning Strangers into Friends, and Friends into Customers.* New York: Simon & Schuster.

Hanlon, P. and J. Hawkins. 2008. "Expand Your Brand Community Online," *Advertising Age,* January 7, 14–15.

Harvard Business Review. 2003. "How to Measure the Profitability of Your Customers," 81(6), June, 74.

Hilzenrath, D. 2001. "Saylor Firm Spent Millions Investing in Web Addresses," *Washington Post,* April 10, E1.

Hoffman, D. and T. Novak. 2000. "How to Acquire Customers on the Web," *Harvard Business Review,* 78(3), May–June, 179–188.

Interactive Advertising Bureau (IAB). 2008. *IAB Ad Campaign Measurement Process Guidelines.* New York: IAB. (http://www.iab.net/media/file/ad_campaign_measurement_2008.pdf)

Interactive Advertising Bureau (IAB). 2009. *IAB Audience Reach Measurement Guidelines.* New York: IAB. (http://www.iab.net/media/file/audience_reach_022009.pdf)

Ives, N. 2007. "Forecast for '08 is OK, But Only Online Shines," *Advertising Age,* December 3, 3–4.

Jiang, T. and A. Tuzhilin. 2009. "Improving Personalization Solutions through Optimal Segmentation of Customer Bases," *IEEE Transactions on Knowledge & Data Engineering,* 21(3), March, 305–320.

Jukic, B., D. Dravitz, N. Jukic, A. Tekleab, L. Meamber, and L. Dashnaw. 2009. "Multilevel Information Presentation Strategy and Customer Reaction: An Empirical Investigation in an Online Setting," *Journal of Organizational Computing & Electronic Commerce,* 19(3), July-September, 173–195.

Kilby, N. 2007. "Doubling Your Search Efforts," *Marketing Week,* May 17, 31–34.

Kiley, D. and B. Helm. 2009. "The Great Trust Offensive," *BusinessWeek,* September 28, 38–42.

King, D. 2008. "Waiting for the Day that Search Becomes Four-Dimensional," *New Media Age,* January 17, 13.

Koprowski, G. 1998. "The (New) Hidden Persuaders: What Marketers Have Learned About How Consumers Buy on the Web," *The Wall Street Journal,* December 7, R10.

Livingston, B. 2002. "How an Ad-Based Online Company Grew in 2001," *InfoWorld,* April 2. (http://www.infoworld.com/articles/op/xml/02/04/04/020404opsecrets.xml)

Lytel, J. 2000. "Domain-Name Disputes Get Personal," *BizReport,* September 22. (http://www.bizreport.com/marketing/2000/09/2000922-1.htm)

Maddox, K. 2004. "The Return of the Boom," *B to B,* 89(7), 23.

Marckini, F. 2001. *Search Engine Positioning.* San Antonio, TX: Republic of Texas Press.

Masters, D. 2007. "Inline Text Ads," *Success on the Web,* September 5. (http://successontheweb.blogspot.com/2007/09/inline-text-ads.html)

McKay, L. 2009. "Microsites to Serve Microsegments," *CRM Magazine,* 13(8), August, 21–22.

McWilliams, B. 2002. "Dot-Com Noir: When Internet Marketing Goes Sour," *Salon.com,* July 1. (http://www.salon.com/tech/feature/2002/07/01/spyware_inc/index.html)

Meyer, M. and L. Kolbe. 2005. "Integration of Customer Relationship Management: Status Quo and Implications for Research and Practice," *Journal of Strategic Marketing,* 13(3), September, 175–198.

New Media Age. 2004. "Has Branding Got Lost Amid Search?" September 2, 21–22.

Overholt, A. 2004. "Search for Tomorrow," *Fast Company,* August, 69–71.

Payne, A. and P. Frow. 2005. "A Strategic Framework for Customer Relationship Management," *Journal of Marketing,* 69(4), October, 167–176.

Plosker, G. 2004. "What Does Paid Search Mean to You?" *Online,* 28(5), September–October, 49–51.

Rapoza, J. 2004. "Annoying Web Ads Redux," *eWeek,* 21(15), April 12, 70.

Rayport, J. and J. Sviokla. 1994. "Managing in the Marketspace," *Harvard Business Review,* 72(6), November–December, 141–150.

Rayport, J. and J. Sviokla. 1995. "Exploiting the Virtual Value Chain," *Harvard Business Review,* 73(6), November–December, 75–85.

Rigby, D. and D. Ledingham. 2004. "CRM Done Right," *Harvard Business Review,* 82(11), November, 118–127.

Ryals, L. 2005. "Making Customer Relationship Management Work: The Measurement and Profitable Management of Customer Relationships," *Journal of Marketing,* 69(4), October, 252–261.

Sandoval, G. 2001. "Kozmo to Shut Down, Lay Off 1,100," *News.com,* April 11. (http://www.zdnet.com/ecommerce/stories/main/0,10475,5081050,00.html)

Schneider, G. and C. Bruton. 2003. "Communication Modalities for Commercial Speech on the Internet," *Journal of Organizational Culture, Communication, & Conflict,* 7(2) 89–94.

Seda, C. 2004. *Search Engine Advertising.* Indianapolis, IN: New Riders.

Tedeschi, B. 2005. "Blogging While Browsing, But Not Buying," *The New York Times,* July 4. (http://www.nytimes.com/2005/07/04/technology/04ecom.html)

The Wall Street Journal, 2008. "Online Ad Revenues Topped $21 Billion in '07," February 26, B4.

Weber, T. 2001. "Can You Say 'Cheese'? Intrusive Web Ads Could Drive Us Nuts," *The Wall Street Journal,* May 21, B1.

CHAPTER 5

BUSINESS-TO-BUSINESS ACTIVITIES: IMPROVING EFFICIENCY AND REDUCING COSTS

LEARNING OBJECTIVES

In this chapter, you will learn about:

- How businesses use the Internet to improve purchasing, logistics, and other support activities
- Electronic data interchange and how it works
- How businesses have moved some of their electronic data interchange operations to the Internet
- Supply chain management and how businesses are using Internet technologies to improve it
- Electronic marketplaces and portals that make purchase–sale negotiations easier and more efficient

INTRODUCTION

General Electric (GE) is one of the largest and most successful companies in the world. It engages in a wide range of businesses around the world, including the production of appliances and electrical and electronic products, broadcasting, and a variety of financial and insurance activities. One of its oldest lines of business is GE Lighting, which produces more than 30,000 different kinds of light bulbs in its 28 North American plants and other locations around the world. The raw materials used in making light bulbs are fairly standard items: glass, aluminum, various insulating plastics, and filament materials. However, a major portion of each light bulb's cost is the money that GE Lighting spends on indirect materials and parts for the machines used to fabricate and assemble the bulbs. These indirect materials and parts must conform to detailed specifications that GE stores on more than 3 million blueprints and other design drawings.

Because the technologies for making light bulbs are mature and well known, GE Lighting can solicit bids from a variety of suppliers for indirect materials and machinery replacement parts without worrying about the possible disclosure of trade secrets. Unfortunately, the bidding process at GE Lighting had become very slow and inefficient. Each transaction required the Purchasing Department to request the relevant blueprints, photocopy them, attach them to other material specification documents, and mail the whole package to suppliers that might be interested in bidding on the item. It would often take Purchasing personnel more than four weeks to gather the information, send it to potential suppliers, obtain and evaluate suppliers' bids, negotiate with the chosen suppliers, and place an order. These long delays were limiting GE Lighting's flexibility and ability to respond to requests from its customers.

By applying the tools of electronic commerce to these purchase transactions, GE Lighting was able to make major improvements to the entire parts acquisition process. Today, Purchasing personnel have access to a procurement system through their desktop computers. When they need to buy replacement parts for a machine, they create a new purchase file that includes basic quantity, delivery date, and delivery location information. Then, from a list generated by a continually updated supplier database, they select suppliers from which they request quotes. Finally, they attach electronic copies of all necessary blueprints and engineering drawings, which are now digitized and stored in another database; with a mouse click, they send the entire bid package off in an encrypted format to all the selected suppliers.

Assembling the bid package now takes hours instead of a week or more. Suppliers are asked to respond within a short time period—usually a week—through the Internet. The Purchasing staff member can evaluate the returned bids and award a contract online, completing the entire process in about 10 days.

The most significant savings for GE Lighting were in process-time reduction—from four weeks or more to 10 days—and in the elimination of paper and the costs of handling paper. However, the company also realized other benefits. Because the online system made it easier to send out bid packages, the Purchasing Department could send out more bids to a wider range of suppliers. In particular, many overseas suppliers that had been difficult to reach with mailed bid packages could be included in the solicitation for quotes. Having more suppliers has driven down prices for GE Lighting and suppliers appreciate the reduced time lag between submitting the bid and learning whether GE Lighting will award them the contract because it increases the efficiency of their production planning, allowing them to make more money even with the lower prices.

PURCHASING, LOGISTICS, AND SUPPORT ACTIVITIES

In the previous two chapters, you learned about strategy issues that arise when businesses and other organizations provide information to potential customers. In terms of the value chain model described in Chapter 1, you learned about the primary activities: identify customers, market and sell, and deliver. You also became familiar with a number of business models for selling on the Web. Although many of these business models are used in business-to-business electronic commerce, the emphasis in Chapters 3 and 4 was on business-to-consumer advertising, promotion, and sales activities.

In this chapter, you will learn how companies use electronic commerce to improve their purchasing and logistics primary activities, and all of their support activities (which include finance and administration, human resources, and technology development). You can refer to Figure 1-9 in Chapter 1 for a review of primary activities and support activities. Although the work might not be as glamorous as designing a Web site or creating an advertising campaign, the potential for cost reductions and business process improvements in purchasing, logistics and support activities is tremendous.

Governments seldom sell products or services to customers, but they perform many functions for the individual citizens, businesses, and other organizations that they serve.

Governments are increasingly using electronic commerce to improve the efficiency with which they undertake their own support activities and serve their stakeholders better. These electronic commerce activities are collectively referred to as **e-government**.

As Internet technologies become commonplace in businesses, the potential for synergies increases. Many of these synergies are forming the basis for second-wave electronic commerce opportunities. You will learn about a number of these second-wave opportunities in this chapter.

An important characteristic of purchasing, logistics, and support activities is flexibility. A purchasing or logistics strategy that works this year may not work next year. Fortunately, economic organizations are evolving from the hierarchical structures used since the Industrial Revolution to new, more flexible network structures. These network structures are, in many cases, made possible by the transaction cost reductions that companies realize when they use Internet and Web technologies to carry out business processes.

Purchasing Activities

Purchasing activities include identifying and evaluating vendors, selecting specific products, placing orders, and resolving any issues that arise after receiving the ordered goods or services. These issues might include late deliveries, incorrect quantities, incorrect items, and defective items. By monitoring all relevant elements of purchase transactions, purchasing managers can play an important role in maintaining and improving product quality and reducing costs. In Chapter 1, you learned how companies can organize their strategic business unit activities using an industry value chain. The part of an industry value chain that precedes a particular strategic business unit called that business unit's **supply chain**. A company's supply chain for a particular product or service includes all the activities undertaken by every predecessor in the value chain to design, produce, promote, market, deliver, and support each individual component of that product or service. For example, the supply chain of an automobile manufacturer includes every activity undertaken by each individual component supplier, including engine manufacturers, steel fabricators, glass manufacturers, wiring harness assemblers, and thousands of others.

The Purchasing Department within most companies traditionally has been charged with buying all of these components at the lowest price possible. Usually, Purchasing staff did this by identifying qualified vendors and asking them to prepare bids that described what they would supply and how much they would charge. The Purchasing staff would then select the lowest bid that still met the quality standards for the component. This bidding process led to a very competitive environment with a large number of suppliers; this process focused excessively on the cost of individual components and ignored the total supply chain costs, including the cost to the manufacturing organization of dealing with such a large number of suppliers. As you learned in Chapter 1, many managers call this function "procurement" instead of "purchasing" to distinguish the broader range of responsibilities. Procurement generally includes all purchasing activities, plus the monitoring of all elements of purchase transactions. It also includes managing and developing relationships with key suppliers. Another term that is used to describe procurement activities is supply management.

In many companies, procurement staff must have high levels of product knowledge to identify and evaluate appropriate suppliers. The part of procurement activity devoted to identifying suppliers and determining the qualifications of those suppliers is called **sourcing**.

In Chapter 1, you learned that the use of Internet technologies in procurement activities is called e-procurement. Similarly, the use of Internet technologies in sourcing activities is called **e-sourcing**. Specialized Web-purchasing sites can be particularly useful to procurement professionals responsible for sourcing. The business purchasing process is usually much more complex than most consumer purchasing processes. Figure 5-1 shows the steps in a typical business purchasing process.

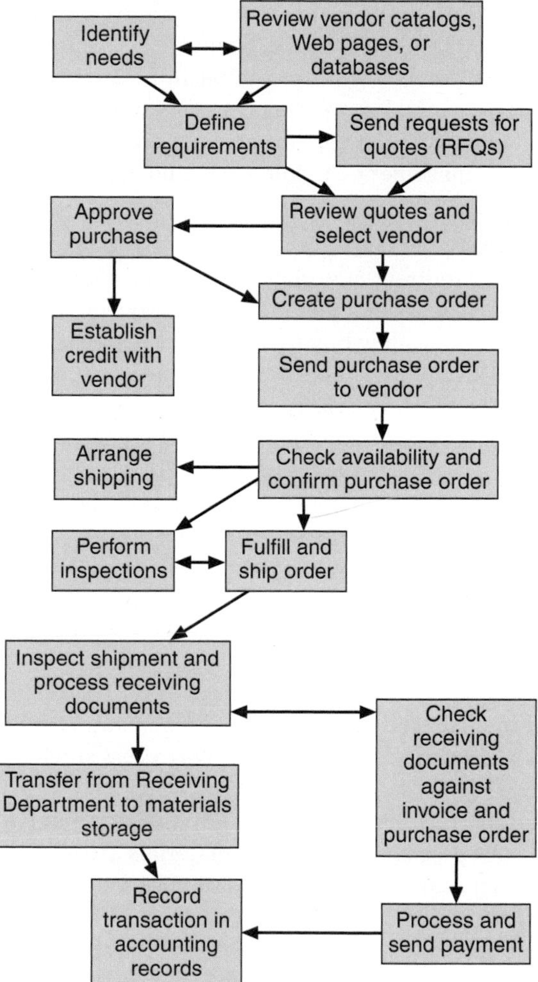

FIGURE 5-1 Steps in a typical business purchasing process

As you can see, the business purchasing process includes many steps. The business purchasing process also requires a number of people to coordinate their individual activities as part of the process. In large companies, the Procurement Department that supervises the purchasing process might include hundreds of employees who supervise the purchasing of materials, inventory for resale, supplies, and all of the other items that the company needs to buy. The total dollar amount of the goods and services that a company buys during a year is called its **spend**. In large companies, the spend can be many billions of dollars. Managing the spend in those companies is an important function and can be a key element in a company's overall profitability. For example, Motorola has a spend of about $60 billion. In its worldwide operations, it issues more than a million purchase orders and records inventory receipts more than six million times each year. In 2002, when it implemented a set of Internet technologies in its procurement operation, it saved $2.5 billion.

For many years, the National Association of Purchasing Management has been the main organization for procurement professionals. In 2002, the association changed its name to the **Institute for Supply Management (ISM)**. ISM runs conferences, publishes a monthly journal (*Inside Supply Management*), and offers helpful information on its Web site. Many of the articles in recent issues of the journal have dealt with electronic commerce. Full-time students who want to learn more about supply management can join ISM at no cost.

Direct vs. Indirect Materials Purchasing

Businesses make a distinction between direct and indirect materials. **Direct materials** are those materials that become part of the finished product in a manufacturing process. Steel manufacturers, for example, consider the iron ore that they buy to be a direct material. The procurement process for direct materials is an important part of any manufacturing business because the cost of direct materials is usually a very large part of the cost of the finished product. Large manufacturing companies, such as auto manufacturers, engage in two types of direct materials purchasing. In the first type, called **replenishment purchasing** (or **contract purchasing**), the company negotiates long-term contracts for most of the materials that it will need. For example, an auto manufacturer estimates how many cars it will make during a year and contracts with two or three steel mills to supply most of the steel it will need to build those cars. By negotiating the contracts in advance and guaranteeing the purchase, the auto manufacturer obtains low prices and good delivery terms. Of course, actual demand never matches expected demand perfectly. If demand is higher than the auto company's estimate, it must buy additional steel during the year. These purchases are made in a loosely organized market that includes steel mills, warehouses, speculators (who buy and sell contracts for future delivery of steel), and companies that have excess steel that they purchased on contract (demand for their products was lower than they had anticipated). This market is called a **spot market**, and buying in this market, the second type of direct materials purchasing, is called **spot purchasing**. **Indirect materials** are all other materials that the company purchases, including factory supplies such as sandpaper, hand tools, and replacement parts for manufacturing machinery.

Large companies usually assign responsibility for purchasing direct and indirect materials to separate departments. Most companies include the purchase of nonmanufacturing goods and services—such as office supplies, computer hardware and software, and travel expenses—in the responsibilities of the indirect materials Procurement Department. Many vendors that manufacture general industrial merchandise and standard machine tools for a variety of industries have created Web sites through which their customers can purchase materials. A number of customers buy these indirect material products on a recurring basis, and many of them are commodities, that is, standard items that buyers usually select using price as their main criterion. These indirect materials items are often called **maintenance, repair, and operating (MRO)** supplies. Procurement professionals generally use the terms "indirect materials" and "MRO supplies" interchangeably. Most companies have a difficult time controlling MRO spending from a centralized procurement office because many MRO purchases are numerous and small in dollar value. One way that Procurement Departments control MRO spending is by issuing **purchasing cards** (usually called **p-cards**). These cards, which resemble credit cards, give individual managers the ability to make multiple small purchases at their discretion while providing cost-tracking information to the procurement office.

By using a Web site to process orders, the vendors in this market can save the costs of printing and shipping catalogs and handling telephone orders. They can also keep price and quantity information continually updated, which would be impossible to do in a printed catalog. Some industry analysts estimate that the cost to process an MRO order through a Web site can be less than one-tenth of the cost of handling the same order by telephone.

Two of the largest MRO suppliers in the world are **McMaster-Carr** and **W.W. Grainger**. The Grainger Web site offers more than 475,000 different products for sale. Grainger's Web store, which appears in Figure 5-2, offers visitors a variety of ways to access information about and order Grainger products.

FIGURE 5-2 Grainger.com Web store

A visitor to the Grainger site can enter the online catalog, use the product search box at the top of the page, or search by clicking a hyperlink to one of the categories listed in the middle of the page.

Office equipment and supplies are also items that are used by a wide variety of businesses. Market leaders **Office Depot** and **Staples** each have well-designed Web sites devoted to helping business Purchasing Departments buy these routine items as easily as possible. On their business-to-business Web sites, **Digi-Key** and **Newark.com** sell electronic parts.

Logistics Activities

The classic objective of logistics is to provide the right goods in the right quantities in the right place at the right time. Logistics management is an important support activity for both the sales and the purchasing activities in a company. Businesses need to ensure that the products they sell to customers are delivered on time and that the raw materials they buy from vendors and use to create their products arrive when needed. The management of materials as they go from the raw materials storage area through production processes to become finished goods is also an important part of logistics.

Logistics activities include managing the inbound movements of materials and supplies and the outbound movements of finished goods and services. Thus, receiving, warehousing, controlling inventory, scheduling and controlling vehicles, and distributing finished goods are all logistics activities. The Web and the Internet are providing an increasing number of opportunities to manage these activities better as they lower transaction costs and provide constant connectivity between firms engaged in logistics management. Web-enabled automated warehousing operations are saving companies millions of dollars each year. Major transportation companies such as **Schneider National**, **Ryder System**, and **J.B. Hunt** now want to be seen by their customers as information management firms as well as freight carriers.

For example, the Schneider Track and Trace system delivers real-time shipment information to Web browsers on its customers' computers. This system shows the customer which freight carrier is transporting a shipment, where the shipment is, and when it should arrive at its destination. J.B. Hunt, which operates more than 100,000 trucks, trailers, and containers, implemented a Web site that lets its customers track their shipments themselves. With customers doing their own tracking, J.B. Hunt needs far fewer customer service representatives. Also, J.B. Hunt found that its customers could monitor their own shipments more effectively than the company, saving J. B. Hunt more than $12,000 per week in labor and lost shipment costs. When transportation and freight companies engage in the business of operating all or a large portion of a customer's materials movement activities, the company is called a **third-party logistics (3PL) provider**. For example, Ryder has a multiyear contract to design, manage, and operate all of Whirlpool's inbound freight activities and is considered a 3PL provider to Whirlpool.

FedEx has freight-tracking Web pages available to its customers, as does UPS. Firms that run their own trucking operations have implemented tracking systems that use global positioning satellite (GPS) technology to monitor vehicle movements. These freight-handling companies are also moving into the 3PL provider business as a way to generate additional revenue from the investment they made in information technology to support their core businesses. The marriage of GPS and portable computing technologies with the Internet is an excellent example of second-wave electronic commerce.

Support Activities

Support activities include the general categories of finance and administration, human resources, and technology development. Finance and administration includes activities such as making payments, processing payments received from customers, planning capital expenditures, and budgeting and planning to ensure that sufficient funds will be available to meet the organization's obligations as they come due. The operation of the computing infrastructure of the organization is also an administration activity. Human resources activities include hiring, training, and evaluating employees; administering benefits; and complying with government record-keeping regulations. Technology development can include a wide variety of activities, depending on the nature of the business or organization. It can include networking research scientists into virtual collaborative workgroups, posting research results, publishing research papers online, and providing connections to outside sources of research and development services. Figure 5-3 shows these categories of support activities.

Finance and Administration	Human Resources	Technology Development
Making payments to suppliers Processing payments from customers Planning capital expenditures Budgeting Planning operations Operating computing infrastructure	Hiring employees Training employees Evaluating employees Administering benefit programs Compliance with government record-keeping regulations	Creating and maintaining virtual collaborative research workgroups Posting research results Publishing research reports online Connecting researchers to outside sources of research and development services

FIGURE 5-3 Categories of support activities

A few years ago Allegiance was growing rapidly and hiring more than 100 people each month to staff its sales offices throughout the United States. Each new hire had to receive a full briefing on medical, dental, and retirement benefits plans, and then he or she had to select from among several options for each. Because Allegiance was growing so rapidly, its human resources staff was spread thin and could not be in every sales office for every hire. The company turned to **A.D.A.M.**, a firm that duplicates its clients' human resources functions on a password-protected Web site that is accessible to clients' employees. The employees can then access their employers' benefits information, find the answers to frequently asked questions, and even perform complex benefit option calculations. **CompuPay** offers payroll processing services online. Larger firms are building these types of functions into their intranets. These larger firms are also including Web-enabled sales support and sales force automation functions in their extranets.

One common support activity that underlies multiple primary activities is training. In many companies, the Human Resources Department handles training. Other companies may decentralize this function and have individual departments administer it. For example, insurance firms expend large amounts of resources on sales training. In most insurance companies, the Sales and Marketing Department administers this training. By putting training materials on the company intranet, insurance companies can distribute the training materials to many different sales offices, yet coordinate the use of those materials in the corporate headquarters sales office.

The Swedish telecommunications giant Ericsson runs an extranet for current and former employees, families of those employees, and employees of approved business partners. Ericsson has more than 100,000 employees scattered across the globe. One part of this extranet includes a Web site that enables current employees, retirees, and other recipients of payments from the company's medical and retirement plans to efficiently track their benefits. Another part of the extranet includes a Web site designed to facilitate knowledge management. **Knowledge management** is the intentional collection, classification, and dissemination of information about a company, its products, and its processes. This type of knowledge is developed over time by individuals working for or with a company and is often difficult to gather and distill. You will learn more about knowledge management and the software tools used to facilitate it in Chapter 9.

Ericsson managers hope that their knowledge network will generate new ideas, help solve problems, and improve business processes throughout the international organization. Designers of the system have identified their biggest challenge: to direct the information they collect in the extranet to projects and product development activities that will benefit from that information.

BroadVision, a software development and consulting firm, installed an internal system called K-Net, or Knowledge Network, that organizes all information sources used regularly by its employees. It found that many of its employees were visiting between 10 and 20 Web sites each day in the course of doing their jobs. K-Net brings together all of the information that each employee needs and combines it into one dashboard-style interface presented on a Web browser. Much of the interface is customized for individual employees, although some parts of the interface—such as health insurance, vacation days, and other human resources information—are standardized for all employees. BroadVision has found the K-Net system to be so useful that it is partnering with Bank of America, Hewlett-Packard, and Amadeus (a European travel services company) to develop a version of K-Net to sell to other companies. You can learn more about knowledge management in general at the **KMWorld** Web site. In Chapter 9, you will learn about software that companies can use to build knowledge management systems.

E-Government

Although governments do not typically sell products or services to customers, they perform many functions for their stakeholders. Many of these functions can be enhanced by the use of electronic commerce. Governments also operate businesslike activities; for example, they employ people, buy supplies from vendors, and distribute benefit payments of many kinds. They also collect a variety of taxes and fees from their constituents (you will learn more about how governments use the Web in administering their tax laws in Chapter 7). The use of electronic commerce by governments and government agencies to perform these functions is often called e-government.

In 2000, the U.S. government's Financial Management Service (FMS) opened its **Pay.gov** Web site. The FMS is the agency responsible for receiving the government's tax, license, and other fee revenue (more than $2 trillion per year). It is also responsible for paying out more than $1.5 trillion per year in Social Security benefits, veterans' benefits, tax refunds, and other disbursements. Federal agencies can link their Web sites to Pay.gov, which lets site visitors pay taxes and fees they owe to these agencies using their credit cards, debit cards, or various forms of electronic funds transfer. The U.S. government's Bureau of Public Debt operates the **TreasuryDirect** site, which allows individuals to buy savings bonds and financial institutions to buy treasury bills, bonds, and notes.

Following the terrorist attacks of September 11, 2001, the U.S. government became aware of a lack of activity coordination and information sharing among several of its agencies, including the Federal Bureau of Investigation (FBI), the Central Intelligence Agency (CIA), and the Bureau of Customs and Border Protection. A number of initiatives that use Internet technologies are under way to increase the availability of information within and among these agencies under the auspices of the **Department of Homeland Security (DHS)**.

Other countries' national governments are finding that e-government can reduce administrative costs and provide better service to stakeholders. In the United Kingdom, the **Department for Work and Pensions** Web site provides information on unemployment, pension, and social security benefits. Smaller countries are also launching Web sites, such as **Singapore Government Online**, that provide information to stakeholders and ways for citizens to interact with their governments online.

State governments are also creating Web sites for conducting business and interacting with their stakeholders. In 2001, the state of California opened its one-stop portal site, **my.ca.gov**, which appears in Figure 5-4.

FIGURE 5-4 State of California portal site my.ca.gov

This site gives visitors access to virtually every California government agency and state operation. Site visitors can transact a wide array of business with the state from renewing a driver's license to reserving a camp site. The goal of the site is to give constituents one site through which they can conduct all of their business with the state of California. For businesses, the site offers the full text of all California business laws and regulations. It also provides information about how to sell to and buy from the state and its agencies.

Most other U.S. state governments (and, in other countries, provincial or regional governments) have similar Web sites. States can reduce the cost of providing services while providing those services more efficiently by using Web technologies to serve their stakeholders. The most common services offered by states and similar regional governments are the following: access to the text of state laws and regulations, renewal of licenses, promotion of the state to businesses considering new locations, job listings, promotion of tourism in the state, tax forms and filing information, and information for companies that want to do business with the state. The State of New York's **New York State Citizen Guide** is a good example of a comprehensive site that offers information for both individuals and businesses that are located in New York or that might be considering relocating to the state.

Many local governments now have Web sites that offer residents a variety of information. The Web sites of larger cities (such as **Minneapolis** or **New Orleans**) include transcripts of city council meetings, local laws and regulations, business license and tax administration functions, and promotional information about the city for new residents or businesses seeking new locations. Smaller cities, towns, and villages are also using the Web to communicate with residents (see the **Cheviot, Ohio** Web site for one example). These local government Web sites have been proven to be useful general communication tools. In the aftermath of Hurricane Katrina in 2005, the New Orleans Web site carried a daily message from the mayor and continually updated information about which parts of the city were open to returning evacuees. You can learn more about applications of Internet technologies in state and local governments by reviewing articles on e.Republic's **Government Technology** Web site.

Network Model of Economic Organization in Purchasing

In Chapter 1, you learned about the three different forms of economic organization: markets, hierarchies, and networks. One trend that is becoming clear in purchasing, logistics, and support activities is the shift away from hierarchical structures toward network structures. The traditional purchasing model had one hierarchically structured firm negotiating purchase terms with several similarly structured supplier firms, playing each supplier against the others. As is typical in a network organization, more businesses are now giving their Procurement Departments new tools to negotiate with suppliers, including the possibility of forming strategic alliances. For example, a buying firm might enter into an alliance with a supplier to develop new technology that will reduce overall product costs. The technology development might be done by a third firm using research conducted by a fourth firm. Such alliances and outsourcing contracts are examples of the move toward network economic structures that you learned about in Chapter 1.

While reading the previous sections in this chapter, you might have noticed that companies can have other firms perform various support activities for them. Again, these are examples of firms moving toward a network model of economic organization. Imagine a business that uses one supplier to manage its payroll, another to administer its employee benefits plans, and a third to handle its document storage needs. The document storage service supplier might store the documents of the payroll service supplier and the benefits administration firm. The payroll service supplier might handle the payroll for the benefits administration firm. A fourth firm might provide online backup storage for the files of the other three companies. Of course, the payroll firm and the employee benefits firm might form a marketing partnership to sell both of their services to particular market segments. The document storage firm and the online backup storage firm might form a similar strategic alliance. Some researchers who study the interaction of firms within an industry value chain are beginning to use the term **supply web** instead of "supply chain" because many industry value chains no longer consist of a single sequence of companies linked in a single line, but include many parallel lines that are interconnected in a web or network configuration.

Highly specialized firms can now exist and trade services very efficiently on the Web. The Web is enabling this shift from hierarchical to network forms of economic organization. These emerging networks of firms are more flexible and can respond to changes in the economic environment much more quickly than hierarchically structured businesses. You can learn more about the economics of networked organizations at the **Network Economics** Web site maintained by the University of California, Berkeley. The roots of Web technology for business-to-business transactions, however, lie in a hierarchically structured approach to interfirm information transfer: electronic data interchange.

ELECTRONIC DATA INTERCHANGE

In Chapter 1 you learned that electronic data interchange (EDI) is a computer-to-computer transfer of business information between two businesses that uses a standard format of some kind. The two businesses that are exchanging information are trading partners. Firms that exchange data in specific standard formats are said to be **EDI compatible**. The business information exchanged is often transaction data; however, it can also include other information related to transactions, such as price quotes and order status inquiries. Transaction data in business-to-business (B2B) transactions includes the information traditionally included on paper invoices, purchase orders, requests for quotations, bills of lading, and receiving reports. The data on these five types of forms accounts for more than 75 percent of all information exchanged by trading partners in the United States. Thus, EDI was the first form of electronic commerce to be widely used in business—some 20 years before anyone used the term "electronic commerce" to describe anything!

It is very important that you understand what EDI is designed to accomplish and how it came to be the preferred way for businesses to exchange information, because most B2B electronic commerce is an adaptation of EDI or is based on EDI principles. Another important reason for being familiar with EDI is that EDI is still the method used for most electronic B2B transactions. According to industry analysts, the dollar amount of EDI transactions is about equal to the total amount of all other B2B electronic transactions combined. This section provides you with a brief history of EDI and explains how it works. It also explains why conducting EDI is better than processing mountains of paper transactions.

Early Business Information Interchange Efforts

The emergence of large business organizations in the late 1800s and early 1900s brought with it the need to create formal records of business transactions. In the 1950s, companies began to use computers to store and process internal transaction records, but the information flows between businesses continued to be printed on paper; purchase orders, invoices, bills of lading, checks, remittance advices, and other standard forms were used to document transactions.

The process of using a person or computer to generate a paper form, mailing that form, and then having another person enter the data into the trading partner's computer was slow, inefficient, expensive, redundant, and unreliable. By the 1960s, businesses that engaged in large volumes of transactions with each other had begun exchanging transaction information on punched cards or magnetic tape. Advances in data communications technology during the 1960s and 1970s allowed trading partners to transfer data over telephone lines instead of shipping punched cards or magnetic tapes to each other.

Although these information transfer agreements between trading partners increased efficiency and reduced errors, they were not an ideal solution. Because the data translation programs that one trading partner wrote usually would not work for other trading partners, each company participating in this information exchange had to make a substantial investment in computing infrastructure. Only large trading partners could afford this investment, and even those companies had to perform a significant number of transactions to justify the cost. Smaller or lower-volume trading partners could not afford to participate in the benefits of these paper-free exchanges.

In 1968, a number of freight and shipping companies joined together to reduce their combined paperwork burden They created a standardized information set that included all the data elements that shippers commonly included on bills of lading, freight invoices, shipping manifests, and other paper forms. Instead of printing a paper form, shippers could convert information about shipments into a computer file, which could be transmitted to any freight company that had adopted the standard. The freight company could then use the data its own information systems. The savings from not printing and handling forms, not entering the data twice, and not having to worry about error-correction procedures were significant for most shippers and freight carriers.

Although these early industry-specific data interchange efforts were very helpful, their benefits were limited to members of the industries that created standard-setting groups. In addition, most businesses that are in a particular industry buy goods and services from businesses that are in other industries. For example, a machinery manufacturer might buy materials from steel mills, paint distributors, electrical assembly contractors, and container manufacturers. Also, almost every business needs to buy office supplies and the services of freight and transportation companies. Thus, full realization of EDI's economies and efficiencies required standards that could be used by companies in all industries.

Emergence of Broader EDI Standards

After spending most of the 1970s engaging in fragmented attempts to set broader EDI standards, a number of industry groups and several large companies decided to mount a major effort to create a set of cross-industry standards for electronic components, mechanical equipment, and other widely used items. The **American National Standards Institute (ANSI)** has been the coordinating body for standards in the United States since 1918. ANSI does not set standards itself, but it has created a set of procedures for the development of national standards and it accredits committees that follow those procedures.

In 1979, ANSI chartered a new committee to develop uniform EDI standards. This committee is called the **Accredited Standards Committee X12 (ASC X12)**. The **ASC X12** committee meets three times each year to develop and maintain EDI standards. The committee and its subcommittees include information systems professionals from more than 800 businesses and other organizations. Membership is open to organizations and individuals who have an interest in the standards. The administrative body that coordinates ASC X12 activities is the **Data Interchange Standards Association (DISA)**.

The ASC X12 standard has benefited from the participation of members from a wide variety of industries. The standard currently includes specifications for several hundred **transaction sets**, which are the names of the formats for specific business data interchanges. Figure 5-5 lists some of the more commonly used ASC X12 transaction sets.

104 - Air Shipment Information
110 - Air Freight Details and Invoice
125 - Multilevel Railcar Load Details
151 - Electronic Filing of Tax Return Data Acknowledgement
170 - Revenue Receipts Statement
180 - Return Merchandise Authorization and Notification
204 - Motor Carrier Shipment Information
210 - Motor Carrier Freight Details and Invoice
211 - Electronic Bill of Lading
213 - Motor Carrier Shipment Status Inquiry
214 - Transportation Carrier Shipment Status Message
304 - Shipping Instructions
317 - Delivery/Pickup Order
325 - Consolidation of Goods in Container
350 - U.S. Customs Release Information
404 - Rail Carrier Shipment Information
410 - Rail Carrier Freight Details and Invoice
421 - Estimated Time of Arrival and Car Scheduling
440 - Shipment Weights
466 - Rate Request
511 - Requisition
810 - Invoice
812 - Credit/Debit Adjustment
813 - Electronic Filing of Tax Return Data
820 - Payment Order/Remittance Advice
828 - Debit Authorization
829 - Payment Cancellation Request
840 - Request for Quotation
841 - Specifications/Technical Information
842 - Nonconformance Report
843 - Response to Request for Quotation
846 - Inventory Inquiry/Advice
847 - Material Claim
850 - Purchase Order
853 - Routing and Carrier Instruction
854 - Shipment Delivery Discrepancy Information
855 - Purchase Order Acknowledgment
856 - Advance Ship Notification
857 - Shipment and Billing Notice
859 - Freight Invoice
860 - Purchase Order Change Request–Buyer Initiated
861 - Receiving Advice/Acceptance Certificate
865 - Purchase Order Change Acknowledgment/Request–Seller-Initiated
867 - Product Transfer and Resale Report
869 - Order Status Inquiry
870 - Order Status Report
879 - Price Change
893 - Item Information Request
920 - Loss or Damage Claim–General Commodities
924 - Loss or Damage Claim–Motor Vehicle
997 - Functional Acknowledgment
998 - Set Cancellation

FIGURE 5-5 Commonly used ASC X12 transaction sets

Although the X12 standards were quickly adopted by major firms in the United States, in many cases, businesses in other countries continued to use their own national standards. In the mid-1980s, the United Nations Economic Commission for Europe invited North American and European EDI experts to work together on designing a common set of EDI standards based on the successful experiences of U.S. firms in using the ASC X12 standards. In 1987, the United Nations published its first standards under the title **EDI for Administration, Commerce, and Transport (EDIFACT**, or **UN/EDIFACT)**. As you can see from Figure 5-6, a number of the commonly used UN/EDIFACT standard transaction sets are similar to those in the ASC X12 standard.

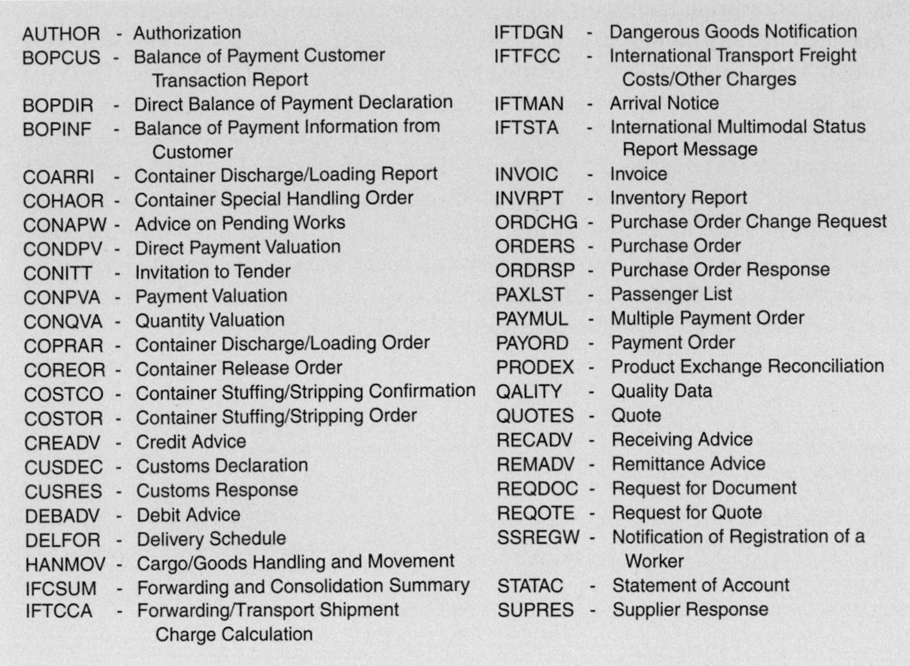

Code	Transaction set
AUTHOR	Authorization
BOPCUS	Balance of Payment Customer Transaction Report
BOPDIR	Direct Balance of Payment Declaration
BOPINF	Balance of Payment Information from Customer
COARRI	Container Discharge/Loading Report
COHAOR	Container Special Handling Order
CONAPW	Advice on Pending Works
CONDPV	Direct Payment Valuation
CONITT	Invitation to Tender
CONPVA	Payment Valuation
CONQVA	Quantity Valuation
COPRAR	Container Discharge/Loading Order
COREOR	Container Release Order
COSTCO	Container Stuffing/Stripping Confirmation
COSTOR	Container Stuffing/Stripping Order
CREADV	Credit Advice
CUSDEC	Customs Declaration
CUSRES	Customs Response
DEBADV	Debit Advice
DELFOR	Delivery Schedule
HANMOV	Cargo/Goods Handling and Movement
IFCSUM	Forwarding and Consolidation Summary
IFTCCA	Forwarding/Transport Shipment Charge Calculation
IFTDGN	Dangerous Goods Notification
IFTFCC	International Transport Freight Costs/Other Charges
IFTMAN	Arrival Notice
IFTSTA	International Multimodal Status Report Message
INVOIC	Invoice
INVRPT	Inventory Report
ORDCHG	Purchase Order Change Request
ORDERS	Purchase Order
ORDRSP	Purchase Order Response
PAXLST	Passenger List
PAYMUL	Multiple Payment Order
PAYORD	Payment Order
PRODEX	Product Exchange Reconciliation
QALITY	Quality Data
QUOTES	Quote
RECADV	Receiving Advice
REMADV	Remittance Advice
REQDOC	Request for Document
REQOTE	Request for Quote
SSREGW	Notification of Registration of a Worker
STATAC	Statement of Account
SUPRES	Supplier Response

FIGURE 5-6 Commonly used UN/EDIFACT transaction sets

The ASC X12 organization and the UN/EDIFACT group agreed in 2000 to develop one common set of international standards; however, this undertaking was never successful. Today, both standards survive and the software that companies use to implement EDI must work with both standards.

How EDI Works

Although the basic idea behind EDI is straightforward, its implementation can be complicated, even in fairly simple business situations. For example, consider a company that needs a replacement for one of its metal-cutting machines. This section describes the steps involved in making this purchase using a paper-based system, and then explains how the process would change using EDI. In both of these examples, assume that the vendor uses its own vehicles instead of a common carrier to deliver the purchased machine.

Paper-Based Purchasing Process

The buyer and the vendor in this example are not using any integrated software for business processes internally; thus, each information processing step results in the production of a paper document that must be delivered to the department handling the next step. Information transfer between the buyer and vendor is also paper based and can be delivered by mail, courier, or fax. The information flows that occur in the paper-based version of the purchasing process example are shown in Figure 5-7.

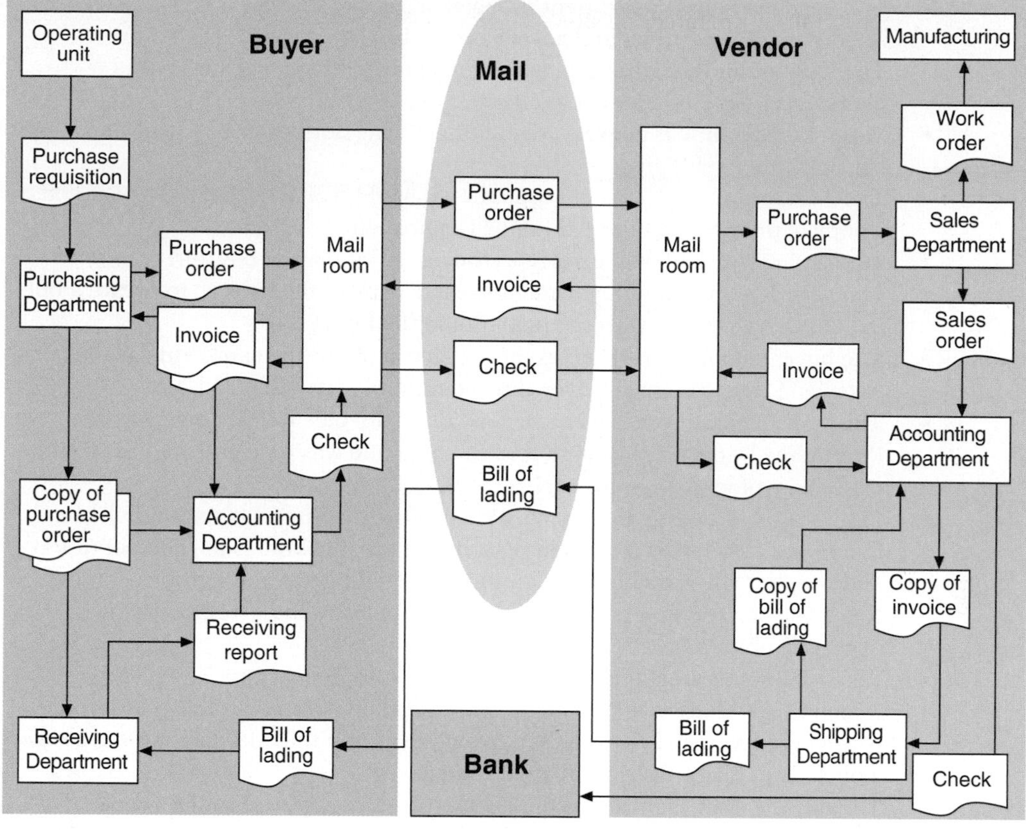

FIGURE 5-7 Information flows in a paper-based purchasing process

Once the production manager in the operating unit decides that the metal-cutting machine needs to be replaced, the following process begins:

- The production manager completes a purchase requisition form and sends it to Purchasing. This requisition describes the machine that is needed to perform the metal-cutting operation.
- Purchasing contacts vendors to negotiate price and terms of delivery. When Purchasing has selected a vendor, it prepares a purchase order and forwards it to the mail room.
- Purchasing also sends one copy of the purchase order to the Receiving Department so that Receiving can plan to accept delivery when scheduled; Purchasing sends another copy to Accounting to advise it of the financial implications of the order.
- The mail room sends the purchase order it received from Purchasing to the selected vendor by mail or courier.
- The vendor's mail room receives the purchase order and forwards it to its Sales Department.

- The vendor's Sales Department prepares a sales order that it sends to its Accounting Department and a work order that it sends to Manufacturing. The work order describes the machine's specifications and authorizes Manufacturing to begin work on it.
- When the machine is completed, Manufacturing notifies Accounting and sends the machine to shipping.
- The Accounting Department sends the original invoice to the mail room and a copy of the invoice to the Shipping Department.
- The mail room sends the invoice to the buyer by mail or courier.
- The vendor's Shipping Department uses its copy of the invoice to create a bill of lading and sends it with the machine to the buyer.
- The buyer's mail room receives the invoice at about the same time as its Receiving Department receives the machine with its bill of lading.
- The buyer's mail room sends one copy of the invoice to Purchasing so the Purchasing Department knows that the machine was received, and sends the original invoice to Accounting.
- The buyer's Receiving Department checks the machine against the bill of lading and its copy of the purchase order. If the machine is in good condition and matches the specifications on the bill of lading and the purchase order, Receiving completes a receiving report and delivers the machine to the operating unit.
- Receiving sends a completed receiving report to Accounting.
- Accounting makes sure that all details on its copy of the purchase order, the receiving report, and the original invoice match. If they do, Accounting issues a check and forwards it to the mail room.
- The buyer's mail room sends the check by mail or courier to the vendor.
- The vendor's mail room receives the check and sends it to Accounting.
- Accounting compares the check to its copies of the invoice, bill of lading, and sales order. If all details match, Accounting deposits the check in the vendor's bank and records the payment received.

EDI Purchasing Process

The information flows that occur in the EDI version of this sample purchasing process are shown in Figure 5-8. The mail service has been replaced with the data communications of an EDI network, and the flows of paper within the buyer's and vendor's organizations have been replaced with computers running EDI translation software.

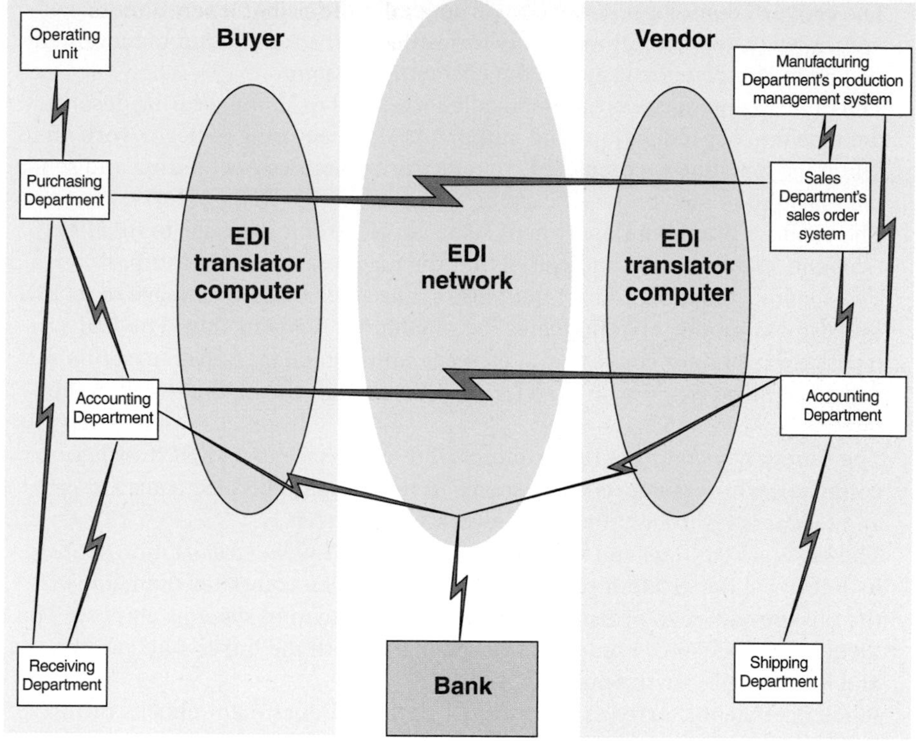

FIGURE 5-8 Information flows in an EDI purchasing process

In the EDI purchasing process, when the operating unit manager decides that the metal-cutting machine needs to be replaced, the following process begins:

- The operating unit manager sends an electronic message to its Purchasing Department. This message describes the machine that is needed to perform the metal-cutting operation.
- Purchasing contacts vendors by telephone, e-mail, or through their Web sites to negotiate price and terms of delivery. After selecting a vendor, Purchasing sends a message to the Sales Department announcing the selection.
- The buyer's EDI translator computer converts this message to a standard format purchase order transaction set, and then forwards the message through an EDI network to the vendor.
- Purchasing also sends one electronic message to the buyer's Receiving Department so it can plan to accept delivery when it is scheduled; Purchasing sends another electronic message to the buyer's Accounting Department that includes details such as the agreed purchase price.
- The vendor's EDI translator computer receives the purchase order transaction set message and converts it to the file format used by the vendor's information systems.

- The converted purchase order details appear in the Sales Department's sales order system and are automatically forwarded to the production management system in Manufacturing and to the accounting system.
- The information that was automatically forwarded to Manufacturing describes the machine's specifications and authorizes Manufacturing to begin work on it.
- When the machine is completed, Manufacturing notifies Accounting and sends the machine to the vendor's Shipping Department.
- The vendor's Shipping Department sends an electronic message to its Accounting Department indicating that the machine is ready to ship.
- The vendor's Shipping Department also sends an electronic message to its EDI translator computer that indicates the machine is ready to ship. The EDI translator computer converts the message into a standard 856 transaction set (Advance Ship Notification) and forwards it through the EDI network to the buyer.
- The vendor's Accounting Department sends a message to its EDI translator computer, which converts the message to the standard invoice transaction set and forwards it through the EDI network to the buyer.
- The buyer's EDI translator computer receives the invoice transaction set before its Receiving Department receives the machine. The computer then converts the invoice data to a format that the buyer's information systems can use. The invoice data becomes immediately available to both the buyer's Accounting and Receiving Departments.
- When the machine arrives, the buyer's Receiving Department checks the machine against the invoice information on its computer system. If the machine is in good condition and matches the specifications shown in the buyer's system, Receiving sends a message to Accounting confirming that the machine has been received in good order. It then delivers the machine to the operating unit.
- The buyer's Accounting Department system compares all details in the purchase order data, receiving data, and decoded invoice transaction set from the vendor. If all the details match, the accounting system notifies its bank to reduce the buyer's account and increase the vendor's account by the amount of the invoice. The EDI network may provide services that perform this task.

Value-Added Networks

As you can see by comparing the paper-based purchasing process in Figure 5-7 to the EDI purchasing process in Figure 5-8, the departments are exchanging the same messages among themselves, but EDI reduces paper flow and streamlines the interchange of information among departments within a company and between companies. These efficiencies were responsible for the benefits described in the GE Lighting example presented in the introduction to this chapter. The three key elements shown in Figure 5-8 that alter the process so dramatically are the EDI network (instead of the mail service) that connects the two companies and the two EDI translator computers that handle the conversion of data from the formats used internally by the buyer and the vendor to standard EDI transaction sets. Trading partners can implement the EDI network and EDI translation processes in several ways. Each of these ways uses one of two basic approaches: direct connection or indirect connection.

The first approach, called **direct connection EDI**, requires each business in the network to operate its own on-site EDI translator computer (as shown in Figure 5-8). These EDI translator computers are then connected directly to each other using modems and dial-up telephone lines or dedicated leased lines. Because dedicated leased-lines are expensive and modems and dial-up telephone lines are slow and not very reliable, only a few companies still use direct connection EDI, which is illustrated in Figure 5-9.

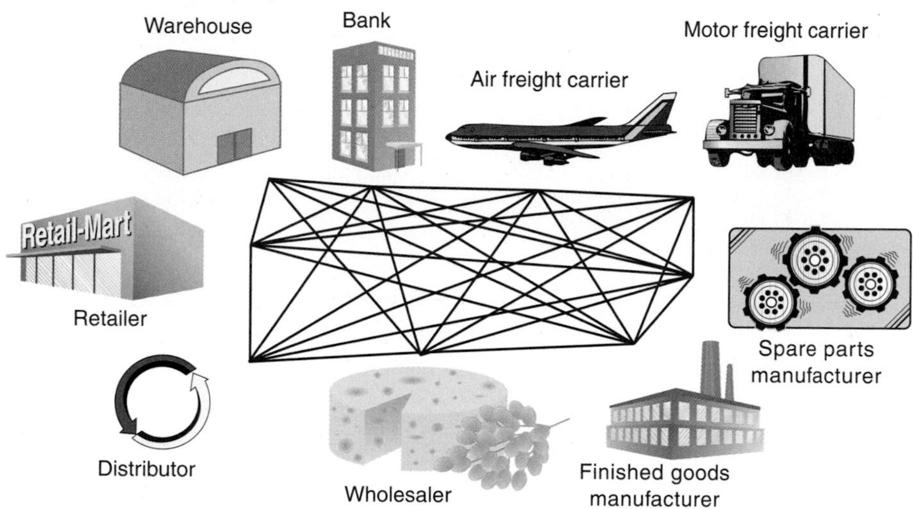

FIGURE 5-9 Direct connection EDI

Instead of connecting directly to each of its trading partners, a company might decide to use the services of a value-added network. As you learned in Chapter 1, a value-added network (VAN) is a company that provides communications equipment, software, and skills needed to receive, store, and forward electronic messages that contain EDI transaction sets. To use the services of a VAN, a company must install EDI translator software that is compatible with the VAN. Often, the VAN supplies this software as part of its operating agreement.

To send an EDI transaction set to a trading partner, the VAN customer connects to the VAN using a dedicated or dial-up telephone line and then forwards the EDI-formatted message to the VAN. The VAN logs the message and delivers it to the trading partner's mailbox on the VAN computer. The trading partner then dials in to the VAN and retrieves its EDI-formatted messages from that mailbox. This approach is called **indirect connection EDI** because the trading partners pass messages through the VAN instead of connecting their computers directly to each other. Figure 5-10 illustrates indirect connection EDI using a VAN.

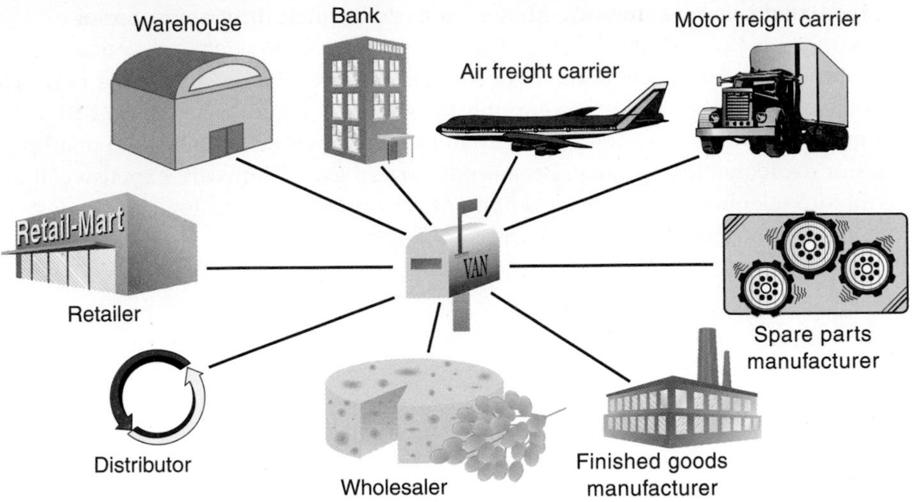

FIGURE 5-10 Indirect connection EDI through a VAN

Companies that provide VAN services include **Advanced Data Exchange**, **Behr Technologies**, **GXS**, **Inovis**, **Kleinschmidt**, **Promethean Software Services**, **SPS Commerce**, and **Sterling Commerce**. Advantages of using a VAN are as follows:

- Users need to support only the VAN's one communications protocol instead of many possible protocols used by trading partners.
- The VAN records message activity in an audit log. This VAN audit log becomes an independent record of transactions; this record can be helpful in resolving disputes between trading partners.
- The VAN can provide translation between different transaction sets used by trading partners (for example, the VAN can translate an ASC X12 set into a UN/EDIFACT set).
- The VAN can perform automatic compliance checking to ensure that the transaction set is in the specified EDI format.

VANs do have some disadvantages, however. One major issue is cost. Most VANs require an enrollment fee, a monthly maintenance fee, and a transaction fee. The transaction fee can be based on transaction volume, transaction length, or both. Fees based on transaction length range between two and ten cents per thousand characters; transaction volume fees range between a few cents and a dollar per transaction. Trading partners with few transactions often find it difficult to justify the high fixed costs of the enrollment and monthly maintenance fees. For example, the up-front cost of implementing indirect connection EDI, including software, VAN enrollment fee, and hardware, can exceed $20,000. Other trading partners with high transaction volumes find the VAN's ongoing transaction-based fees prohibitive.

In the past, many vendors were forced into bearing the high costs of participating in EDI to satisfy the needs of one or two large customers. This happened frequently to suppliers of the auto industry and the retail merchandising industry. Using VANs can become cumbersome and expensive for companies that want to do business with a number of trading partners, each using different VANs. Although some VANs do offer the service of exchanging messages with other VANs, the cost of this service can be unpredictable. Also, inter-VAN transfers do not always provide a clear audit trail for use in dispute resolution. Firms precluded from adopting EDI because of its high cost welcomed the Internet as a low-cost communications medium that could help them overcome some of the disadvantages of traditional EDI.

EDI Payments

Some EDI transaction sets provide instructions to a trading partner's bank. These transaction sets are negotiable instruments; that is, they are the electronic equivalent of checks. All banks have the ability to perform electronic funds transfers (EFTs), which are the movement of money from one bank account to another. You learned about EFTs in Chapter 1. The bank accounts involved in EFTs may be customer accounts or the accounts that banks keep on their own behalf with each other. When EFTs involve two banks, they are executed using an **automated clearing house (ACH)** system, which is a service that banks use to manage their accounts with each other. In the United States, banks can use the ACH operated by the U.S. Federal Reserve Banks or one of the private ACHs operated by a group of banks or a separate company. You will learn more about how banks process ACH payments in Chapter 11.

EDI on the Internet

As the Internet gained prominence as a tool for conducting business, trading partners using EDI began to view the Internet as a potential replacement for the expensive leased lines and dial-up connections required to support both direct and VAN-aided EDI. Companies that had been unable to afford EDI began to look at the Internet as an enabling technology that might help them sell to large customers that demanded EDI capabilities from their suppliers.

The major roadblocks to conducting EDI over the Internet initially were concerns about security and the Internet's general inability to provide audit logs and third-party verification of message transmission and delivery. As the basic TCP/IP structure of the Internet was enhanced with secure protocols and other encryption schemes (you will learn about these in Chapter 10), businesses worried less about security issues; however, concerns still existed. Because EDI transactions are business contracts and often involve large amounts of money, the issue of nonrepudiation is significant. **Nonrepudiation** is the ability to establish that a particular transaction actually occurred. It prevents either party from repudiating, or denying, the transaction's validity or existence. In the past, the nonrepudiation function was provided either by a VAN's audit logs for indirect connection EDI or a comparison of the trading partners' message logs for direct connection EDI. Recently developed EDI protocols now address the nonrepudiation issue.

In the mid-1990s, a number of firms began providing EDI services on the Internet. Companies that originally provided traditional VAN services now offer EDI on the Internet, along with a number of new companies that entered the market with their Internet EDI services. EDI on the Internet is called **Internet EDI** or **Web EDI**. It is also called **open EDI** because the Internet is an open architecture network, as you learned in Chapter 2. Today, most

EDI exchanges occur over the Internet using **EDIINT (Electronic Data Interchange-Internet Integration**, also abbreviated **EDI-INT**), which is a set of protocols for the exchange of data (EDI, XML, and other formats) over the Internet. Most EDIINT exchanges today are encoded using the **AS2 (Applicability Statement 2)** specification, which is based on the HTTP rules for Web page transfers, although some companies are using a more secure specification, **AS3 (Applicability Statement 3)**. Wal-Mart, for example, currently requires all of its vendors to use EDI following the EDIINT protocol transmitted using AS2. EDIINT using AS2 or AS3 provides secure transmission, which resolves concerns most companies had about using EDI on the Internet. Also, AS2 and AS3 return a secure electronic receipt for each transmission to the sender, which resolves the issue of nonrepudiation.

EDI was the original form of electronic commerce, and it appears that it will continue to evolve and be a part of ongoing electronic commerce growth on the Internet. In the late 1990s, many industry analysts announced the impending death of EDI as communication using the Internet became available to most businesses. However, large companies have a huge investment in EDI systems and trained personnel. They were reluctant to change their business processes and move to alternative transaction processing technologies. Fortunately, EDIINT emerged and allowed companies to preserve their EDI investments while affording a more efficient and secure data transmission path.

SUPPLY CHAIN MANAGEMENT USING INTERNET TECHNOLOGIES

You learned earlier in this chapter that the part of an industry value chain that precedes a particular strategic business unit is called a supply chain. Many companies use strategic alliances, partnerships, and long-term contracts to create relationships with other companies in the supply chains for the products that they manufacture or sell. These relationships can be quite complex, with suppliers helping their customers develop new products, specify product features, refine product specifications, and identify needed product improvements. In many cases, companies are able to reduce costs by developing close relationships with a few suppliers rather than negotiating with a large number of suppliers each time they need to buy materials or supplies. When companies integrate their supply management and logistics activities across multiple participants in a particular product's supply chain, the job of managing that integration is called **supply chain management**. The ultimate goal of supply chain management is to achieve a higher-quality or lower-cost product at the end of the chain.

Value Creation in the Supply Chain

In recent years, businesses have realized that they can save money and increase product quality by taking a more active role in negotiations with suppliers. By engaging suppliers in cooperative, long-term relationships, companies have found that they can work together with these suppliers to identify new ways to provide their own customers with faster, cheaper, and better service. By coordinating the efforts of supply chain participants, firms that engage in supply chain management are reaching beyond the limits of their own organization's hierarchical structure and creating a new network form of organization among the members of the supply chain.

Supply chain management was originally developed as a way to reduce costs. It focused on very specific elements in the supply chain and tried to identify opportunities for process efficiency. Today, supply chain management is used to add value in the form of benefits to the ultimate consumer at the end of the supply chain. This requires a more holistic view of the entire supply chain than had been common in the early days of supply chain management.

Businesses that engage in supply chain management work to establish long-term relationships with a small number of very capable suppliers. These suppliers, called **tier-one suppliers**, in turn develop long-term relationships with a larger number of suppliers that provide components and raw materials to them. These **tier-two suppliers** manage relationships with the next level of suppliers, called **tier-three suppliers**, that provide them with components and raw materials. A key element of these relationships is trust between the parties. The long-term relationships created among participants in the supply chain are called **supply alliances**. The level of information sharing that must take place among the supply chain participants can be a major barrier to entering into these alliances. Firms are not accustomed to disclosing detailed operating information and often perceive that information disclosure might hurt the firm by placing it at a competitive disadvantage.

Dell Computer is one company that has been able to reduce supply chain costs by sharing information with its suppliers. The moment Dell receives an order from a customer, it makes that information available to its tier-one suppliers, who can then better plan their production based on Dell's exact demand trends. For example, a supplier of disk drives can change its production plans immediately when it sees a shift in Dell's customer orders from computers with one size disk drive to another, usually larger, size disk drive. This prevents the supplier from overproducing the smaller drive, which reduces the supplier's costs (for unsold drives) and costs in the supply chain overall (the supplier does not need to charge more for the disk drives it does sell to Dell to recover the cost of the unsold drives).

In exchange for the stability of the closer, long-term relationships, buyers expect annual price reductions and quality improvements from suppliers at each stage of the supply chain. However, all supply chain participants share information and work together to create value. Ideally, the supply chain coordination creates enough value that each level of supplier can share the benefits of reduced cost and more efficient operations. Supply chain management has been gaining momentum during the past decade and is supported by major purchasing groups such as the Supply Chain Council. By working together, supply chain members can reduce costs and increase the value of the product or service to the ultimate consumer.

One area in which differences in organizational goals often arise is described by Marshall Fisher in his 1997 *Harvard Business Review* article. He explains that firms often organize themselves to achieve either efficient process goals or market-responsive flexibility goals. Some companies structure themselves to be efficient producers, whereas others structure themselves to be flexible producers. The kinds of things that allow a firm to be an efficient, low-cost producer are exactly the things that prevent a firm from being flexible enough to respond to market changes. For example, the efficient producer invests in expensive machines that can stamp out large numbers of low-cost items. This investment drives down the cost of production, but makes it difficult for the producer to be flexible. A large investment in specialized machinery prevents that producer from reconfiguring the plant layout. If even one member of the supply chain for a product that requires flexible production operates as an efficient producer (instead of as a flexible producer), every other firm in the supply chain suffers. The efficient producer creates bottlenecks that hamper the best efforts of all other supply chain members. Clear communication up and down the supply chain can keep each participant informed of what the ultimate consumer demands. The participants can then plot a strategy to meet those demands.

Clear communications, and quick responses to those communications, are key elements of successful supply chain management. Technologies, and especially the technologies of the Internet and the Web, can be very effective communications enhancers. For the first time, firms can effectively manage the details of their own internal processes and the processes of other members of their supply chains. Software that uses the Internet can help all members of the supply chain review past performance, monitor current performance, and predict when and how much of certain products need to be produced. Figure 5-11 lists the advantages of using Internet technologies in supply chain management. The only major disadvantage of using Internet technologies in supply chain management is the cost of the technologies. In most cases, however, the advantages provide value that greatly exceeds the cost of implementing and maintaining the technologies.

Suppliers can:

- Share information about changes in customer demand
- Receive rapid notification of product design changes and adjustments
- Provide specifications and drawings more efficiently
- Increase the speed of processing transactions
- Reduce the cost of handling transactions
- Reduce errors in entering transaction data
- Share information about defect rates and types

FIGURE 5-11 Advantages of using Internet technologies in supply chain management

Increasing Supply Chain Efficiencies

Many companies are using Internet and Web technologies to manage supply chains in ways that yield increases in efficiency throughout the chain. These companies have found ways to increase process speed, reduce costs, and increase manufacturing flexibility so that they can respond to changes in the quantity and nature of ultimate consumer demand.

For example, **Boeing**, the largest producer of commercial aircraft in the world, faces a huge task in keeping its production on schedule. Each airplane requires more than 1 million individual parts and assemblies, and each airplane is custom configured to meet the purchasing airline's exact specifications. These parts and assemblies must be completed and delivered on schedule or the production process comes to a halt.

In 1997, production and scheduling errors required Boeing to shut down two entire assembly operations for several weeks, costing the company more than $1.5 billion. To prevent this from ever happening again, Boeing invested in a number of new information systems that increase production efficiency by providing planning and control over logistics in every element of its supply chain. Using EDI and Internet links, Boeing works with suppliers so that they can provide exactly the right part or assembly at exactly the right time. Even before an airplane enters into production, Boeing makes the engineering specifications and drawings available to its suppliers through secure Internet connections. As work on the airplane progresses, Boeing keeps every member of the supply chain continually informed of completion milestones achieved and necessary schedule changes.

By its second year using these new systems, Boeing had cut in half the time needed to complete individual assembly processes. It has realized similar reductions in part defect costs. The combined effects of these increased efficiencies have helped Boeing do a much better job of meeting its customers' needs. Instead of waiting 36 months for delivery, customers can now have their new airplanes in 10 months or less.

To further benefit its customers, Boeing launched a spare parts Web site, **Boeing PART** (part analysis and requirements tracking). More than 500 airlines that are Boeing customers do not use EDI to order replacement parts. Boeing PART lets these customers register and then order parts using their Web browsers. The site processes thousands of transactions each day at a significantly lower cost to Boeing than if it were handling faxes, telephone calls, and mailed purchase orders. Boeing can deliver most parts ordered through Boeing PART on the same or next day.

Although Dell Computer is famous for its use of the Web to sell custom-configured computers to individuals and businesses, it has also used technology-enabled supply chain management to give customers exactly what they want. Dell reduced the amount of inventory it keeps on hand from three weeks' sales to two hours' sales. Ultimately, Dell wants to see inventory levels measured in minutes. By increasing the amount of information it has about its customers, Dell has been able to dramatically reduce the amount of inventory it must hold. Dell has also shared this information with members of its supply chain.

Dell's top suppliers have access to a secure Web site that shows them Dell's latest sales forecasts, along with other information about planned product changes, defect rates, and warranty claims. In addition, the Web site tells suppliers who Dell's customers are and what they are buying. All of this information helps these tier-one suppliers plan their production much better than they could otherwise. The information sharing goes in both directions in Dell's supply chain: tier-one suppliers are required to provide Dell with current information on their defect rates and production problems. As a result, all members of the supply chain work together to reduce inventories, increase quality, and provide high value to the ultimate consumer. Much of this cooperative work requires a high level of trust. To enhance this trust and develop a sense of community, Dell maintains bulletin boards as an open forum in which its supply chain members can share their experiences in dealing with Dell and with each other.

For Boeing, Dell, and other firms, the use of Internet and Web technologies in managing supply chains has yielded significantly increased process speed, reduced costs, and increased flexibility. All of these attributes combine to allow a coordinated supply chain to produce products and services that better meet the needs of the ultimate consumer.

Using Materials-Tracking Technologies with EDI and Electronic Commerce

Tracking materials as they move from one company to another and as they move within the company has always been a troublesome task. Companies have been using optical scanners and bar codes for many years to help track the movement of materials. In many industries, the integration of bar coding and EDI has become prevalent. Figure 5-12 shows a typical bar-coded shipping label that is used in the auto industry. Each bar-coded element is a representation of an element of the ASC X12 transaction set number 856, Ship Advance Notification. If you examine the figure carefully, you can see that five of the 856 transaction set's elements have been bar coded (including Part Number, Quantity Shipped, Purchase Order Number, Serial Number, and Packing List Number).

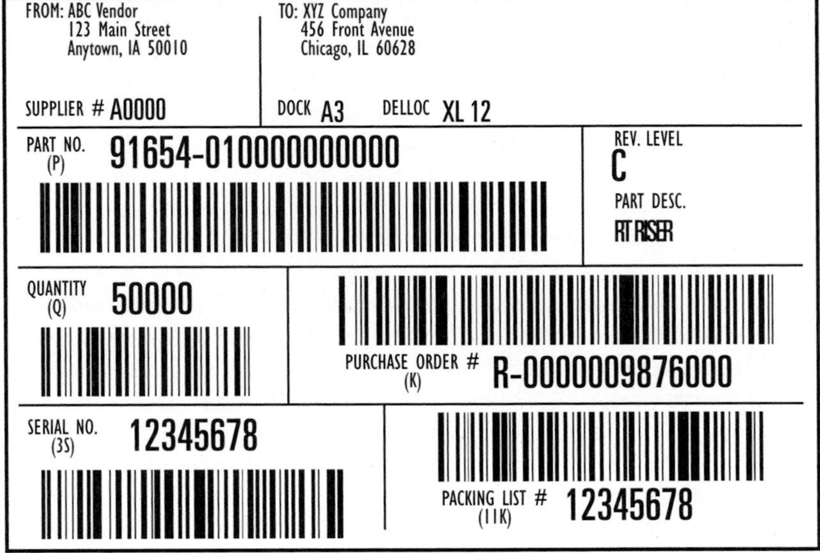

FIGURE 5-12 Shipping label with bar-coded elements from EDI transaction set 856, Advance Ship Notification

These bar codes allow companies to scan materials as they are received and to track them as they move from the materials warehouse into production. Companies can use this bar-coded information along with information from their EDI systems to manage inventory flows and forecast materials needs across their supply chains.

In the second wave of electronic commerce, companies are integrating new types of tracking into their Internet-based materials-tracking systems. The most promising technology now being used is **Radio Frequency Identification Devices (RFIDs)**, which are small chips that use radio transmissions to track inventory. RFID technology has existed for many years, but until recently, it required each RFID to have its own power supply (usually a battery). RFIDs can be read much more quickly and with a higher degree of accuracy than bar codes. Bar codes must be visible to be scanned. RFID tags can be placed anywhere on or in most items and are readable even when covered with packing materials, dirt, or plastic bands. A bar-code scanner must be placed within a few inches of the bar code. Most RFID readers have a range of about six feet.

An important development in RFID technology is the passive RFID tag, which can be made cheaply and in very small sizes. A passive RFID tag does not need a power source.

It receives a radio signal from a nearby transmitter and extracts a tiny amount of power from that signal. It uses the power it extracts to send a signal back to the transmitter. That signal includes information about the inventory item to which the RFID tag has been affixed. RFID tags are small enough to be installed on the face of credit cards or sewn into clothing items.

In 2003, Wal-Mart began testing the use of RFID tags on its merchandise for inventory tracking and control. Wal-Mart initiated a plan to have all of its suppliers install RFID tags in the goods they shipped to the retailer. Wal-Mart wanted suppliers to do this within three years. Having all incoming inventory RFID tagged would allow Wal-Mart to manage its inventory better and reduce the incidence of stockouts. A **stockout** occurs when a retailer loses sales because it does not have specific goods on its shelves that customers want to buy. Many of Wal-Mart's suppliers found the RFID tags, readers, and the computer systems needed to manage tagged inventory to be quite expensive. These suppliers pushed Wal-Mart to slow down the implementation of its plan. Wal-Mart responded by encouraging suppliers to use RFID tags, but focused its energies on developing pilot projects within Wal-Mart to test RFID-based inventory management systems.

Many industry observers have concluded that general acceptance of RFID tagging will not occur in most industries until 2014. Although the cost of a passive RFID tag is now below ten cents, the cost can be prohibitive for companies that ship large volumes of low-priced goods. The cost of RFID tags is expected to continue dropping, and as it does, more and more companies will find them to be useful in an increasingly wide range of situations. You can learn more about current developments in this technology by visiting the ***RFID Journal*** online. Figure 5-13 shows a typical passive RFID tag.

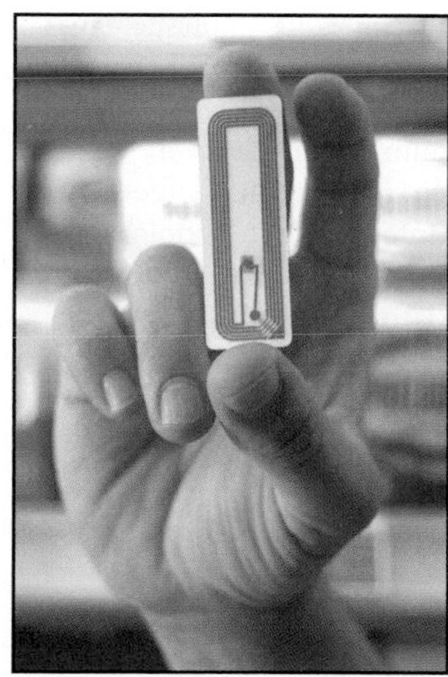

Courtesy, Moeller-Horcher. Source: Metro

FIGURE 5-13 Passive RFID tag

Creating an Ultimate Consumer Orientation in the Supply Chain

One of the main goals of supply chain management is to help each company in the chain focus on meeting the needs of the consumer at the end of the supply chain. Companies in industries with long supply chains have, in the past, often found it difficult to maintain this customer focus, which is often called an **ultimate consumer orientation**. Instead, companies have directed their efforts toward meeting the needs of the next member in the supply chain. This short-sighted approach can cause companies to miss opportunities to add value in subsequent steps of the chain.

One company that pioneered the use of Internet technology to go beyond the next step in its value chain is Michelin North America. Michelin has a highly respected brand name and reputation in the tire business. However, most consumers rely on local tire dealers to make specific recommendations when they need replacement tires for their vehicles. Michelin spends a great deal of money on direct advertising to its ultimate consumers. This advertising is directed at maintaining Michelin's powerful brand and convincing the consumer of the value of Michelin tires. The advertising and brand building effort can be wasted, however, if the consumer goes to a local tire dealer who recommends another brand.

Michelin launched an online business initiative in 1995 called BIB NET (after the company's famous Michelin Man mascot, whose name is Bibendum). The goal of this initiative was to sell more Michelin tires to consumers, but the initiative was directed at Michelin's tire dealers, not the ultimate consumers. BIB NET was an extranet that allowed tire dealers to access tire specifications, inventory status, and promotional information about Michelin products through a simple-to-use Web browser interface. Before BIB NET, dealers calling Michelin for product information were sometimes placed on hold. A dealer who is talking to a customer cannot afford to wait on hold. By giving dealers the power to access Michelin product information directly and immediately, Michelin saved money (maintaining a Web page is much less expensive than answering thousands of phone calls) and gave dealers better service. Dealers using BIB NET are much less likely to recommend a competitor's tires to their customers.

Because Internet technologies are tools that improve communications at a very low cost, they are ideal aids for enhancing the creation of a highly coordinated and effective supply chain. A number of polls and studies confirm that most information technology and purchasing managers believe that information technology is helping to improve their firms' relationships with suppliers and supply chain management initiatives.

Building and Maintaining Trust in the Supply Chain

The major issue that most companies must deal with in forming supply chain alliances is developing trust. Continual communication and information sharing are key elements in building trust. Because the Internet and the Web provide excellent ways to communicate and share information, they offer new avenues for building trust. Most procurement professionals have built trust on years of doing business with the same vendors. In many industries, vendors send sales representatives to call on buyers regularly. Vendors also participate actively in trade shows and conferences. By giving buyers frequent opportunities to interact with vendor representatives, vendors help build trust.

Vendors are finding that the Web gives them an opportunity to stay in contact with their customers more easily and less expensively. Although most buyers still see sales representatives regularly, e-mail and the Web give them nearly instant access to their sales representative and other vendor personnel. By providing comprehensive information at a moment's notice, vendors can build buyers' trust in the vendor's ability to deliver products and provide the personalized service that buyers need. Many supply chain management researchers are working on new ways to accumulate information about supplier performance and report that information to supply chain partners. This type of monitoring and reporting could help companies establish trust more quickly. Many issues, such as the objectivity and validity of performance measurements, must still be resolved before these information networks become generally accepted and used by the supply chain community. The task of developing information exchange resources that can provide supplier performance summaries is one of the great challenges that B2B electronic commerce faces as it moves into its second wave.

ELECTRONIC MARKETPLACES AND PORTALS

In the late1990s a number of industry-focused hubs opened and began offering marketplaces and auctions in which companies in the industry could contact each other and transact business. The idea was that these hubs would offer a doorway (or portal) to the Internet for industry members. Because these hubs were vertically integrated (that is, each hub would offer services to just one industry), they were called **vertical portals**, or **vortals**. In this section, you will learn how these B2B electronic marketplaces were conceived, developed, and operated as this sector of electronic commerce matured from 1997 through the present.

Independent Industry Marketplaces

The first vertical portals were trading exchanges focused on a particular industry. These vertical portals became known by various names that highlighted different elements of their collective nature, including **industry marketplaces** (focused on a single industry), **independent exchanges** (not controlled by a company that was an established buyer or seller in the industry), or **public marketplaces** (open to new buyers and sellers just entering the industry). These portals are also known collectively as **independent industry marketplaces**. Ventro opened its first industry marketplace, Chemdex, in early 1997 to trade in bulk chemicals. To leverage the high investment it had made in trading exchange technology, Ventro followed Chemdex with other Web marketplaces, including Promedix in specialty medical supplies, Amphire Solutions in food service, MarketMile in general business products and services, and a number of others. Other companies were quick to follow in Ventro's chosen markets as well as many others. SciQuest founded an industry marketplace in life science chemicals.

The number of new entrants into these businesses grew rapidly. By mid-2000, there were more than 2200 independent exchanges in a wide variety of industries. As venture capital funding became scarce for companies that were not earning profits—and virtually none of these marketplaces were earning profits—many of them closed. By 2010, there were fewer than 70 industry marketplaces still operating. Ventro, for example, has closed all of the dozens of marketplaces it had opened during the boom years. It turned out that no more than one or two independent marketplaces in any particular industry could survive.

Some of the industry pioneers who closed their industry marketplace operations, such as Ventro, were able to build successful businesses selling the software and technology that they developed to run their marketplaces. Today, leading software vendors such as IBM, Microsoft, Oracle, and SAP also offer products that can be used to build B2B marketplaces. In the mid-2000s, B2B marketplace models gradually replaced independent marketplaces as the dominant form of operation in this type of electronic commerce. You will learn about four of these B2B marketplace models—private stores, customer portals, private company marketplaces, and industry consortia-sponsored marketplaces—in the remainder of this section.

LEARNING FROM FAILURES

MetalSite

Although a number of small steel manufacturing plants (called minimills) have opened in the past 20 years, most of the world's steel is still produced in very large steel mills. In these steel mills, it is economical to produce steel only in large batches. Because of the high cost of reconfiguring machinery, a steel mill set up to create one type of steel (for example, rolled sheets) requires significant time and money to change over to produce another type of steel (for example, bar steel). To minimize these changeover costs, steel mills produce steel products in large batches to meet estimated demand rather than actual orders. Because production quantities are designed to meet estimated demand instead of actual demand, steel mills often have overproduction of some items.

Companies such as Bethlehem Steel, with annual revenues of more than $4 billion and 14,000 employees, solved this problem in the past by sending faxes to potential buyers of their excess production. Buyers would respond with a bid on the product in which they were interested, and Bethlehem would negotiate with them to determine price and delivery terms.

In 1998, MetalSite was one of the first metal trading exchanges to begin doing business on the Web. These exchanges offered manufacturers such as Bethlehem an efficient way to reach a larger market for their excess production. By mid-2000, there were more than 200 metal exchanges operating on the Web. These exchanges were following a reintermediation strategy; that is, they were entering the supply chain of the steel industry to provide some added value that had not existed in the supply chain before. However, most industry analysts agreed that there was no need for more than one or two exchanges in the steel industry. In 2001, metal trading exchange sites began to fail.

MetalSite had grown rapidly. With more than $35 million of investors' money, MetalSite was able to sign up 24,000 registered users and by mid-2001, was trading about $30 million worth of steel each month. However, its commissions of between 1 percent and 2 percent on each trade did not yield enough money to cover operating costs. The steel business was in a downturn along with the rest of the U.S. economy, and the downward pressure on commissions from competing exchanges was increasing rapidly. The major steel companies were discussing ways to form alliances to operate their own exchanges. After three years of operation and a desperate last-minute search for new investors, MetalSite closed in August 2001.

MetalSite had entered a business that could not support more than a few companies, and it was unable to become one of the survivors. The lesson from MetalSite's experience is that a reintermediation strategy must add significant value to the supply chain, and the company pursuing that strategy must be able to construct significant barriers that competitors must overcome to enter the business. MetalSite was unable to do either and thus failed. Many other B2B exchange sites that found themselves in similar competitive situations have also failed.

Private Stores and Customer Portals

As established companies in various industries watched new businesses open marketplaces, they became concerned that these independent operators would take control of transactions from them in supply chains—control that the established companies had spent years developing. Large companies that sell to many relatively small customers can exert great power in negotiating price, quality, and delivery terms with those customers. These sellers feared that industry marketplaces would dilute that power.

Many of these large sellers had already invested heavily in Web sites that they believed would meet the needs of their customers better than any industry marketplace would. For example, Cisco and Dell offer private stores for each of their major customers within their selling Web sites. A **private store** has a password-protected entrance and offers negotiated price reductions on a limited selection of products—usually those that the customer has agreed to purchase in certain minimum quantities. Other companies, such as Grainger, provide additional services for customers on their selling Web sites. These **customer portal** sites offer private stores along with services such as part number cross referencing, product usage guidelines, safety information, and other services that would be needlessly duplicated if the sellers were to participate in an industry marketplace.

Private Company Marketplaces

Similarly, large companies that purchase from relatively small vendors can exert comparable power over those vendors in purchasing negotiations. The Procurement Departments of these companies can invest in procurement software from companies such as Ariba and CommerceOne (you will learn more about all types of electronic commerce software in Chapter 9). This software, generally referred to as **e-procurement software**, allows a company to manage its purchasing function through a Web interface. It automates many of the authorizations and other steps, described in Figure 5-1, that are part of business procurement operations. Although e-procurement software was originally designed to help manage the MRO procurement process, today it includes other marketplace functions, such as requests for quote posting areas, auctions, and integrated support for purchasing direct materials. E-procurement software for large companies can cost millions of dollars for licensing fees, installation, and customization; however, a growing number of companies are offering e-procurement software for smaller businesses. For example, **Coupa** lets small companies log in to their Web site and use e-procurement software for a few thousand dollars a year.

Companies that implement e-procurement software usually require their suppliers to bid on their business. For example, an office supplies provider would create a schedule of prices at which it would sell to the company. The company would then compare that pricing to bids from other suppliers. The selected supplier would provide product price and description information to the company, which would insert that information into its e-procurement software. This permits authorized employees to order office supplies at the negotiated prices through a Web interface.

When industry marketplaces opened for business, these larger companies were reluctant to abandon their investments in e-procurement software or to make the software work with industry marketplaces' software—especially in the early years of industry marketplaces when there were many of them in each industry. These companies use their power in the supply chain to force suppliers to deal with them on their own terms rather than negotiate with suppliers in an industry marketplace.

As marketplace software became more reliable, many of these companies purchased software and technology consulting services from companies, such as Ventro and e-Steel, that had abandoned their industry marketplace businesses and were offering the software they had developed to companies that wanted to develop private marketplaces. A **private company marketplace** is a marketplace that provides auctions, request for quote postings, and other features (many of which are similar to those of e-procurement software) to companies that want to operate their own marketplaces. United Technologies, which annually sells more than $35 billion of high-technology products and services to the aerospace and building systems industries, was one of the first major companies to open a private company marketplace, launching its site in 1996. Since then, United Technologies has saved billions of dollars through lower prices and transaction cost savings on those purchases.

Industry Consortia-Sponsored Marketplaces

Some companies had relatively strong negotiating positions in their industry supply chains, but did not have enough power to force suppliers to deal with them through a private company marketplace. These companies began to form consortia to sponsor marketplaces. An **industry consortia-sponsored marketplace** is a marketplace formed by several large buyers in a particular industry.

One of the first such marketplaces was Covisint, which was created in 2000 by a consortium of DaimlerChrysler, Ford, and General Motors. Several thousand auto industry suppliers belong to **Covisint** (and Covisint is expanding into other industries, such as health care). In the hotel industry, Marriott, Hyatt, and three other major hotel chains formed a consortium to create the **Avendra** marketplace. Boeing led a group of companies in the aerospace industry to create the **Exostar** marketplace.

These consortia-based marketplaces—along with private company marketplaces, private Web stores, and customer portals—have taken a large part of the market from the industry marketplaces that appeared to be so promising in the early days of B2B electronic commerce. One concern that suppliers have when using an industry marketplace is its ownership structure. For example, Covisint was created by a consortium of buyers in the auto industry. In 2004, the consortium decided to sell Covisint to an independent operator, Compuware, that had no ties to the founding companies. Covisint was sold, at least in part, to convince suppliers that the marketplace would not be operated to keep them at a bargaining disadvantage with the large buyers in that industry. Today, Covisint operates successful online marketplaces in several manufacturing industries and has developed marketplaces and electronic records management systems for the health care industry. Covisint counts more than 45,000 companies as participants in its various marketplaces and users of its related procurement software products.

On the other hand, some marketplaces have found that including industry participants in their ownership is helpful. ChemConnect, the independent industry marketplace you learned about earlier in this chapter, sold ownership interests to about 40 companies in the chemicals industry.

Figure 5-14 summarizes the characteristics of five general forms of marketplaces that exist in B2B electronic commerce today. The information in the figure comes from several sources, but the structure of the figure is adapted from one presented by Warren Raisch, a Web marketplace consultant, in his book *The eMarketplace*.

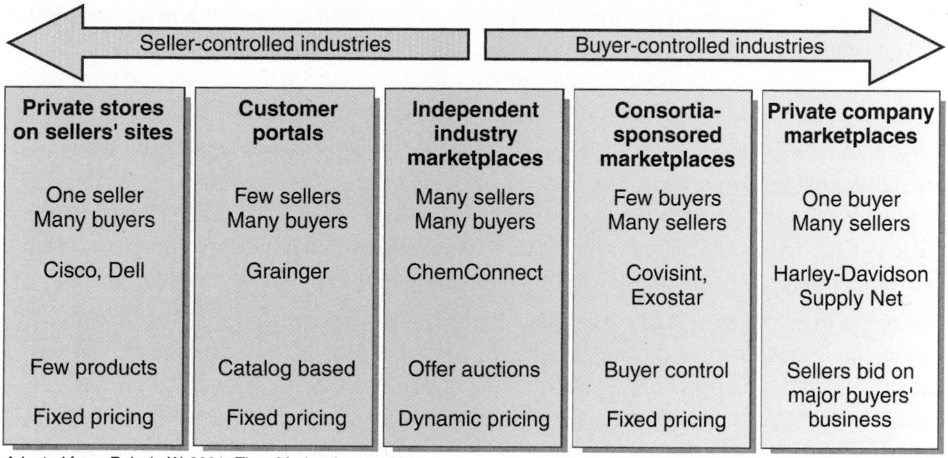

← Seller-controlled industries | Buyer-controlled industries →

Private stores on sellers' sites	Customer portals	Independent industry marketplaces	Consortia-sponsored marketplaces	Private company marketplaces
One seller Many buyers	Few sellers Many buyers	Many sellers Many buyers	Few buyers Many sellers	One buyer Many sellers
Cisco, Dell	Grainger	ChemConnect	Covisint, Exostar	Harley-Davidson Supply Net
Few products	Catalog based	Offer auctions	Buyer control	Sellers bid on major buyers' business
Fixed pricing	Fixed pricing	Dynamic pricing	Fixed pricing	

Adapted from: Raisch, W. 2001. *The eMarketplace, p. 225.*

FIGURE 5-14 Characteristics of B2B marketplaces

Although the figure shows five distinct B2B marketplace categories, the lines between them are not always clear. For example, Dell has from time to time sold other companies' products on its private store site, which would make it more like a customer portal than a private store. As the B2B marketplace industry matures, it is unlikely that one type of marketplace will become dominant. Most B2B experts believe that a variety of marketplaces with the characteristics of these five general categories will continue to exist for some time.

Summary

In this chapter, you learned that companies are using Internet and Web technologies in a variety of ways to improve their purchasing and logistics primary activities. Businesses are also making similar improvements in a wide range of support activities such as human resources, accounting, and technology development. Companies and other large organizations, such as government agencies, are finding it more important than ever to extend the reach of their enterprise planning and control activities beyond their organizations' legal definitions to include parts of other organizations. This emerging network model of organization was introduced in Chapter 1 and is used in this chapter to describe the growth in interorganizational communications and coordination.

EDI, the first example of electronic commerce, was first developed by freight companies to reduce the paperwork burden of processing repetitive transactions. The spread of EDI to virtually all large companies over the past 30 years has led smaller businesses to seek an affordable way to participate in EDI. The Internet is now providing the inexpensive communications channel that EDI lacked for so many years and is allowing smaller companies to participate in Internet EDI.

The increase in communications capabilities offered by the Internet and the Web is, and will continue to be, an important force driving the adoption of supply chain management techniques in a variety of industries. Supply chain management incorporates several elements that can be implemented and enhanced through the use of the Internet and the Web. Increasingly, firms are connecting with their supply chain alliance partners and other companies, such as 3PL providers, to become more efficient and provide more value to the ultimate consumer of their value chains' products and services.

The emergence of industry electronic marketplaces in the mid-1990s gave way to the development of several different models for B2B electronic commerce, including private stores, customer portals, private marketplaces, and industry consortia-sponsored marketplaces. Today, all four of these models continue to coexist with the original industry marketplace model. Although industry consortia-sponsored marketplaces appear to be the most successful today, most B2B experts believe that all five models will continue to exist in one industry or another for the foreseeable future.

Key Terms

Accredited Standards Committee X12 (ASC X12)
American National Standards Institute (ANSI)
AS2 (Applicability Statement 2), AS3 (Applicability Statement 3)
Automated clearing house (ACH)
Contract purchasing
Customer portal
Direct connection EDI
Direct materials
EDI compatible
EDI for Administration, Commerce, and Transport (EDIFACT, or UN/EDIFACT)
EDIINT (Electronic Data Interchange-Internet Integration, EDI-INT)
E-government
E-procurement software
E-sourcing
Independent exchange
Independent industry marketplace
Indirect connection EDI
Indirect materials

Industry consortia-sponsored marketplace
Industry marketplace
Internet EDI
Knowledge management
Maintenance, repair, and operating (MRO)
Nonrepudiation
Open EDI
Private company marketplace
Private store
Public marketplace
Purchasing card (p-card)
Radio Frequency Identification Device (RFID)
Replenishment purchasing
Sourcing
Spend
Spot market
Spot purchasing
Stockout
Supply alliances
Supply chain
Supply chain management
Supply web
Third-party logistics (3PL) provider
Tier-one suppliers
Tier-three suppliers
Tier-two suppliers
Transaction sets
Ultimate consumer orientation
Vertical portal (vortal)
Web EDI

Review Questions

RQ1. Define "direct materials" and "indirect materials." List reasons that a large company would have two separate departments to manage the purchasing activities for each.

RQ2. Define "knowledge management." In one paragraph, describe three advantages that a management consulting firm could gain over its competitors by creating an internal knowledge management system.

RQ3. Many towns and small cities have Web sites that they use to interact with their citizens. In 100 words, describe three departments that should be included on the home page of a small town's Web site and describe the citizen interactions that should be facilitated by the site for each department.

RQ4. Companies in a particular supply chain can work together to eliminate costs from the supply chain. In many cases, these cost savings are not shared evenly among the companies in the supply chain. Using research resources on the Web or in your library, identify an industry in which savings are not shared equally. In two or three paragraphs, explain why some supply chain participants in your chosen industry can obtain more benefit than others from cost reductions in the supply chain.

RQ5. In about 300 words, describe the reasons a buyer might have for wanting to participate in an industry consortium marketplace instead of setting up its own private company marketplace.

Exercises

E1. Use the ThomasNet Web site to locate an industrial product with which you are completely unfamiliar. Note how many companies offer that product, have catalogs or Web sites, offer online ordering, and offer literature by fax or e-mail. Summarize what you learn about the product and its availability on the Web in a report of approximately 400 words.

Note: Your instructor might ask you to prepare a formal presentation of your findings in class.

E2. You work for Andrew Wheeler, who is the president of Fabro-Max, a small plastic parts fabricator. He wants you to look into improving customer interactions through Internet EDI. Select two of the EDI service providers from the list provided in the Online Companion that would be suitable for a small manufacturing firm and examine their Web sites. For the two EDI service providers that you choose, determine whether they are offering Internet EDI services, such as EDIINT. In a memo to Andrew of approximately 150 words, explain why the two providers you chose would be suitable for his business.

E3. A number of standard-setting organizations offer memberships to business firms. You are working for Grace Henry, chief information officer (CIO) of Flex-Electric, a mid-sized company that manufactures components for electronic medical and laboratory instruments. Grace asks you to investigate the benefits of joining an industry standard-setting organization, **RosettaNet**. Prepare a memo to Grace in which you outline the purposes of the organization and the costs and benefits of becoming a member. Close your memo with a recommendation regarding whether your company should join the organization.

Cases

C1. Harley-Davidson

Harley-Davidson manufactures high-end motorcycles and sells them worldwide. The company sells more than $6 billion in motorcycles and related products each year, and has one of the most recognized brands in the world. However, business was not always so good for the company. In the 1980s, the company was on the brink of bankruptcy. Facing increasing competition from Japanese and German manufacturers, Harley-Davidson had allowed its quality standards and cost controls to slip. In a legendary business turnaround, the company rebuilt itself. Harley-Davidson completely changed its supply chain to fulfill the expectations of its brand-aware customers.

Over a period of several years, Harley-Davidson reduced its number of suppliers from 4000 to fewer than 350. More importantly, it began to work with those suppliers to reduce costs throughout the supply chain. Each supplier is expected to find ways (with the help and cooperation of Harley-Davidson) to reduce manufacturing costs and improve quality every year. This was the only way Harley-Davidson believed it could avoid moving its factories to lower-cost locations in other countries. The efforts paid off and the company still manufactures its motorcycles only in the United States.

In 2000, the company decided to focus its cost reduction and quality improvement efforts on its information technology infrastructure. Since it had been so successful in working with its suppliers to reduce manufacturing costs and improve quality, Harley-Davidson wanted to do the same thing with information technology. By using Internet technologies to share information throughout the supply chain, the company hoped to find opportunities for efficiencies and cost reductions at all stages of the process of creating motorcycles.

When the company first talked with its suppliers about its information technology initiative, those suppliers noted that each of Harley-Davidson's main factories used different invoices, production schedules, and purchasing procedures. The suppliers explained that this created difficulties for them when they dealt with more than one factory and increased their cost of doing business with Harley-Davidson. Thus, one of the first things the company did was to standardize forms and procedures. Then it moved to require all suppliers to use EDI. For smaller suppliers, the company set up a Web site that had Internet EDI capabilities. The smaller suppliers could simply log in to the Web site and conduct EDI transactions through their Web browsers.

This Web browser interface grew to become a complete extranet portal called Harley-Davidson Supply Net. All suppliers now use the portal to consolidate orders, track production schedule changes, obtain inventory forecasts in real time, and obtain payments for materials shipped. The portal also allows suppliers to obtain product testing information, part specifications, and product design drawings.

Key elements in both EDI and the Web portal systems have been bar codes and scanners. Most individual parts and all shipments are bar coded. The bar-code information is integrated with the materials tracking, invoicing, and payment information in the systems and is made available, as appropriate, to suppliers. Harley-Davidson uses bar-code standards developed by the Automotive Industry Action Group.

Required:

1. Become familiar with RFID technology and its potential uses in Harley-Davidson's supply chain using the information presented in this chapter and information you obtain through the Online Companion links, your favorite search engine, and your library. In about 400 words, evaluate the advantages and disadvantages for Harley-Davidson of replacing its bar codes and scanners technology with RFID.
2. Compare and contrast the issues that Wal-Mart and other large retailers faced when they tried to implement RFID in their supply chains with those that Harley-Davidson will likely face as it moves into RFID implementations with its suppliers and customers.
3. Develop and present a timetable for the adoption of RFID technology with specific recommendations on where Harley-Davidson should first implement it. For example, RFID tags could be installed in motorcycles as they leave final assembly, in various parts before they are shipped from suppliers, or in subassemblies as they are created at various Harley-Davidson manufacturing operations. Justify the time delays you propose in the adoption of RFID at each stage of the supply chain.

Note: Your instructor might assign you to a group to complete this case, and might ask you to prepare a formal presentation of your results to your class.

C2. American Packaging Machinery

American Packaging Machinery (APM) is a company that provides repair and maintenance services to companies that operate large packaging systems. Packaging systems are arrangements of machinery that place items in containers such as boxes or bags and apply plastic shrink wrap to the containers. These machines must be adjusted regularly, and they have hundreds of parts that can wear out or fail. APM offers service contracts on most major packaging systems. A typical service contract provides for an APM technician to make regular visits to the customer site to perform preventive maintenance. The service contract also includes a certain number of emergency repair visits per year. APM also sends technicians to perform repairs for companies that do not have service contracts.

APM technicians are paid by the hour, with additional pay for overtime hours and time they work outside of standard working hours, such as weekends and holidays. APM technicians are members of a labor union, the International Brotherhood of Electrical Workers (IBEW), which negotiates pay rates and working conditions for the technicians. APM subtracts union dues from each technician's weekly paycheck and submits the total dues collected each week to the IBEW regional office. The union contract currently provides that APM technicians are covered by a medical insurance plan underwritten by the Prudential Trust Insurance Company. Although APM pays most of the insurance premium, technicians do pay a part of the premium cost. This contribution to the premium is withheld from their paychecks each week.

You are the director of electronic commerce for APM and you report to Laura Adams, APM's CIO. Laura asks for your help in outlining a new automated system she wants to install, which would use EDI and EFTs to handle APM's technician payroll and related transactions. She has provided the following narrative that describes how the system will work:

1. Technicians will record their time worked by entering the start and stop times for each job into a program that runs on their handheld computers (the technicians already use these handheld computers to look up wiring and mechanical diagrams for the machinery on which they work and to receive their job assignments). The time worked information will be transmitted from the handheld computer to APM's Payroll Department.
2. The Payroll Department will summarize the time worked information and send it to supervisors' desktop computers. Each supervisor will indicate an authorization for each technician's time worked, overtime, and holiday/weekend hours. That authorization will be returned by the system each day to the Payroll Department.
3. The Payroll Department will summarize the time worked information each week and calculate gross pay, deductions, and net pay for each employee. The deductions include the federal and state taxes that must be withheld by law, the contribution to the medical insurance premium, and the union dues that are withheld under the IBEW union contract.
4. The Payroll Department will send an electronic summary of the payroll information, including deductions, to the Accounting Department, which will prepare payroll tax returns and make the necessary entries in the APM accounting system to record payroll and the related tax expenses.
5. The Payroll Department will send electronic authorizations to APM's bank to make the necessary EFTs to deposit: the amount of each technician's net pay to that technician's bank account; the amount of each tax withheld to the account of the appropriate government agency; the amount of the total contributions to the medical insurance premium to the insurance company's account; and the amount of the union dues withheld to the IBEW's account. Most of these accounts are at other banks.
6. The Payroll Department will send electronic notifications to Prudential Trust and the IBEW regional office, notifying them of the transferred amounts each week.
7. The Payroll Department will send an electronic summary of the hours worked by each technician and the amount of gross pay, including overtime and holiday/weekend pay, to the APM union steward's desktop computer. The union steward is an APM technician who is elected by the technicians to monitor the terms of the union contract and handle any grievances that arise between the technicians and APM management.

Required:

1. Draw a diagram of the proposed payroll EDI and EFT system (you can use Figure 5-8 as a guide).
2. List and briefly describe any problems or issues that you think might arise in the implementation of this system.
3. Provide a rationale and recommendation as to which elements of this system—if any—you think APM should hire an outside company to implement.

Note: Your instructor might assign you to a group to complete this case, and might ask you to prepare a formal presentation of your results to your class.

For Further Study and Research

Abid-Ali, A. 2009. "Driving Efficiency with RFID," *Electronics Weekly,* May 13, 11–12

Albrecht, C., D. Dean, and J. Hansen. 2005. "Marketplace and Technology Standards for B2B E-commerce: Progress, Challenges, and the State of the Art," *Information & Management,* 42(6), September, 865–875.

Anwin, J. 2004. "Top Online Chemical Exchange Is an Unlikely Success Story," *The Wall Street Journal,* January 8, A15.

Asher, A. 2007. "Developing a B2B E-Commerce Implementation Framework: A Study of EDI Implementation for Procurement," *Information Systems Management,* 24(4), Fall, 373–390.

Ayers, J. 1999. "Supply Chain Strategies," *Information Systems Management,* 16(2), Spring, 72–80.

Bacheldor, B., L. Sullivan, C. Murphy, and R. Whiting. 2004. "RFID Kick-start," *Information Week,* May 24, 20–22.

Bills, S. 2009. "Fed EDI Service for Small-Bank Clients," *American Banker,* June 15, 10.

Binns, S. 2004. "Businesses Miss Benefits of High-Tech Radio Tagging," *Supply Management,* 9(2), January 22, 13.

Bovel, D. and M. Joseph. 2000. "From Supply Chain to Value Net," *Journal of Business Strategy,* 21(4), July–August, 24–28.

Boye, J. 2008. "Enterprise Portal Market Overview 2008," *KM World,* 17(5), May, 8–10.

Clark, L. 2003. "Covisint Leads Drive to Move Motor Industry From EDI to XML," *Computer Weekly,* May 20, 16.

Clark, P. 2001. "MetalSite Kills Exchange, Seeks Funding," *B to B,* 86(13), June 25, 3.

Cleary, M. 2001. "Metal Meltdown Doesn't Deter New Ventures," *Interactive Week,* 8(27), July 9, 29.

Colberg, T., N. Gardner, K. Horan, D. McGinnis, P. McLauchlin, and Y.-H. So. 1995. *The Price Waterhouse EDI Handbook.* New York: John Wiley & Sons.

Commercial Carrier Journal. 2008. "EDI's a Habit Hard to Break," January, 58–59.

DiSera, M. 2009. "How to Improve ROI with RFID," *Control Engineering,* 56(4), April, 48–51.

Dobbs, J. 1999. *Competition's New Battleground: The Integrated Value Chain.* Cambridge, MA: Cambridge Technology Partners.

Drickhamer, D. 2003. "EDI is Dead! Long Live EDI!" *Industry Week/IW,* 252(4), April, 31–35.

Duvall, M. 2007. "Wal-Mart Changes its Faltering RFID Strategy to Lure More Suppliers, But Insists it's not Turning Back," *Baseline,* October, 43–55.

Financial Executive. 2008. "E-procurement," 24(1), February, 61.

Fisher, M. 1997. "What Is the Right Supply Chain for Your Product?" *Harvard Business Review,* 75(2), March–April, 105–116.

Fox, P. 2001. "Boeing Shows How XML Can Help Business," *Computerworld,* 35(11), March 12, 28–29.

Fraser, J. 2007. "Commercial Tools Boost Partner Connection in the Value Network," *Manufacturing Business Technology,* 25(11), November, 43.

Fulcher, J. 2007. "Internet-based EDI May be Reliable and Less Expensive, but not Necessarily Easier," *Manufacturing Business Technology,* 25(6), June, 40–42.

Garcia-Dastugue, S. and D. Lambert. 2003. "Internet-Enabled Coordination in the Supply Chain," *Industrial Marketing Management,* 32(2), June, 251–263.

Huang, Z., B. Janz, and M. Frolick. 2008. "A Comprehensive Examination of Internet-EDI Adoption," *Information Systems Management,* 25(3), Summer, 273–286.

Kaplan, S. and M. Sawhney. 2000. "E-Hubs: The New B2B Marketplaces," *Harvard Business Review,* 78(3), May–June, 97–103.

Karpinski, R. 2002. "Wal-Mart Mandates Secure, Internet-Based EDI for Suppliers," *InternetWeek,* September 12. (http://www.internetwk.com/security02/INW20020912S0011)

Kenney, B. 2008. "Ten Reasons to Adopt RFID," *Industry Week/IW,* February, 63.

Kim, K. and N. Umanath. 2005. "Information Transfer in B2B Procurement: an Empirical Analysis and Measurement," *Information & Management,* 42(6), September, 813–828.

Lekakos, G. 2007. "Exploiting RFID Digital Information in Enterprise Collaboration," *Industrial Management & Data Systems,* 107(8), 1110–1122.

Marcella, A. and S. Chan. 1993. *EDI Security, Control, and Audit.* Norwood, MA: Artech House.

McCartney, L. and A. Virzi. 2007. "GlobalSpec: The Little Engine that Could," *Baseline,* October, 57–58.

Messmer, E. 2007. "Dot-com Survivor Stays the Course: Covisint Remains a Valuable Player in Auto Industry E-commerce," *Network World,* 24(43), November 5, 18.

Moozakis, C. and D. Joachim. 2001. "Auto Hub Revamps," *InternetWeek,* August 20, 9.

Morgan, J. and R. Monczka. 2003. "Why Supply Chains Must Be Strategic," *Purchasing,* April 17, 42–45.

Ngai, E. and F. Riggins. 2008. "RFID: Technology, Applications, and Impact on Business Operations," *International Journal of Production Economics,* 112(2), April, 507–509.

Purchasing. 2001. "MetalSite Shuts Operations While Seeking New Owner," July 5, 32.

Purchasing. 2004. "Easing into E-procurement with Indirect Spend," February 19, 35–36.

Raisch, W. 2001. *The eMarketplace: Strategies for Success in B2B Ecommerce.* New York: McGraw-Hill.

Rinat, Z. 2001. "Beyond Private Exchanges: The Private Business Network," *E-Business Advisor,* July–August, 20.

Roberts, B. 1998. "Portals, You Say? This One's Private: Ericsson's Intranet Is a Give-and-Take Affair with Employees," *Intranet Design Magazine,* December 14. (http://idm.internet.com/articles/200003/pt_03_15_00f.html)

Senn, J. 1992. "Electronic Data Interchange," *Information Systems Management,* 9(1), Winter, 45–53.

Silver, B. 2005. "Content in the Age of XML," *Intelligent Enterprise,* June 1, 24–26.

Songini, M. 2004. "Supply Chain System Failures Hampered Army Units in Iraq," *Computerworld,* 38(30), July 26, 1–2.

Stockdale, R. and C. Standing. 2002. "A Framework for the Selection of Electronic Marketplaces: A Content Analysis Approach," *Internet Research: Electronic Networking Applications and Policy,* 12(3), 221–234.

Sullivan, L. 2004. "Ready to Roll," *Information Week,* March 8, 45–47.

Sullivan, M. 2001. "High-Octane Hog," *Forbes,* 168(6), September 10, 8–10.

Supplier Selection & Management Report. 2003. "How Harley-Davidson Teamed With 16 Major Suppliers To Cut Costs," 3(1), January, 1–3.

Tanner, C., R. Wölfle, P. Schubert, and M. Quade. 2008. "Current Trends and Challenges in Electronic Procurement: An Empirical Study," *Electronic Markets,* 18(1), January, 6–18.

Taylor, D. 2004. "No Time to Spare: A Guide to Supply Chain Performance Management," *Intelligent Enterprise,* 7(10), June 12, 20–24.

Taylor, D. and A. Terhune. 2001. *Doing E-Business: Strategies for Thriving in an Electronic Marketplace.* New York: John Wiley & Sons.

Teschler, L. 2000. "New Role for B-to-B Exchanges: Helping Developers Collaborate," *Machine Design,* 72(19), October 5, 52–58.

Tillett, S. 2001. "Medical Companies Track E-Learning," *InternetWeek,* August 20, 13.

Ufelder, S. 2004. "B2B Survivors: Why Did Some Online Exchanges Survive While Many Others Failed?" *Computerworld,* February 2, 27–29.

Ustundag, A. and M. Tanyas. 2009. "The Impact of Radio Frequency Identification (RFID) Technology on Supply Chain Costs," *Transportation Research,* 45(1), January, 29–38.

Waugh, R. and S. Elliff. 1998. "Using the Internet to Achieve Purchasing Improvements at General Electric," *Hospital Material Management Quarterly,* 20(2), November, 81–83.

Yao, Y., M. Dresner, and J. Palmer. 2009. "Private Network EDI vs. Internet Electronic Markets: A Direct Comparison of Fulfillment Performance," *Management Science,* 55(5), May, 843–852.

Young, E. 2002. "Web Marketplaces That Really Work," *Fortune/CNET Tech Review,* Winter, 78–86.

CHAPTER **6**

SOCIAL NETWORKING, MOBILE COMMERCE, AND ONLINE AUCTIONS

LEARNING OBJECTIVES

In this chapter, you will learn about:

- Social networking and online business activities
- Using mobile devices to do business online
- Online auctions and auction-related businesses

INTRODUCTION

In 2003, Mark Zuckerberg and several other students at Harvard University were working independently on ways to create online information spaces that would network Harvard students with each other. Zuckerberg's Web site rapidly became successful, attracting more than half of Harvard's undergraduate student body as participants. These students posted photos and information about themselves and their activities.

Although Zuckerberg ran into some resistance from the school's administration and was forced to take down his site, he believed the concept had merit. So, he continued working on the idea and, after dropping out of school and moving to California, he and two fellow students launched TheFacebook.com, a networking site for college and university students, in 2004. One of PayPal's founders,

Peter Theil, invested $500,000 in the fledgling enterprise and helped the company raise an additional $38 million over the next two years.

By 2006, the company had purchased the domain name Facebook.com for $200,000 and had signed major advertising deals, including a three-year agreement with Microsoft. Facebook had gradually expanded the range of users it allowed to set up pages on the site, and by 2006, it was open to everyone. As other Web sites that offered similar functions became less popular, **Facebook** continued to grow.

In 2009, Facebook reported having more than 300 million regular users (70 percent of whom were located outside the United States) and was valued at $10 billion in an investment transaction. The privately held company expects to break even in 2010. In this chapter, you will learn about Facebook and other Web sites that earn profits by facilitating visitors' connections to each other.

FROM VIRTUAL COMMUNITIES TO SOCIAL NETWORKS

In Chapters 3 and 4, you learned how businesses use the Web to create online identities, reach customers, and sell to them. In Chapter 5, you learned how businesses are using the Web to purchase goods and work with their suppliers more effectively. In all three of these chapters, the focus was on how companies can use the Web to improve the things that they have been doing for years; primarily buying and selling. In this chapter, you will learn how companies are using the Web to do things that they have never done before. The Web makes it possible for people to form online communities that are not limited by geography. Individuals and companies with common interests can meet online and discuss issues, share information, generate ideas, and develop valuable relationships.

As you learned in earlier chapters, the Internet reduces transaction costs in value chains and offers an efficient means of communication to anyone with an Internet connection. Combining the Internet's transaction cost-reduction potential with its role as a facilitator of communication among people has led companies to develop new ways of making money on the Web by serving as relationship facilitators.

This section begins with a brief history of online communities, then outlines how companies today operate Web sites that promote relationships among site visitors and companies that advertise or otherwise participate on the sites.

Virtual Communities

A **virtual community**, also called a **Web community** or an **online community**, is a gathering place for people and businesses that does not have a physical existence. Howard Rheingold described the characteristics of these communities in his 1993 book, *The Virtual Community*, which is widely recognized as the definitive book on the subject. Virtual communities began online even before the Internet was in general use. **Bulletin board systems (BBSs)** were computers that allowed users to connect through modems (using dial-up connections through telephone lines) to read and post messages in a common area, or electronic bulletin board. BBSs often hosted discussions on specific topics or issues related to specific geographic regions. Many BBSs were free, but some charged a monthly membership fee. Other discussion board services followed, provided by commercial enterprises such as Compuserv, Prodigy, and GEnie. These companies generated revenue by charging a monthly fee and selling advertising. Usenet newsgroups were another early form of virtual community. Started at Duke University in 1979, **Usenet** was a set of interconnected computers devoted to storing information on specific topics. **Usenet newsgroups** were message posting areas on those computers in which interested persons (primarily from the education and research communities) could discuss those topics.

Today, Web chat rooms and sites devoted to specific topics or the general exchange of information, photos, or videos can constitute virtual communities. These communities offer people a way to connect with each other and discuss common issues and interests. The social interaction in these communities can be considerable and many sociologists believe that the communication and relationship-forming activities that occur online are similar to those that occur in physical communities. The rest of this section describes the development of these communities into the Web sites that are used by people to form and maintain relationships online today.

Early Web Communities

One of the first Web communities was the **WELL**. The WELL, which is an acronym for "whole earth 'lectronic link," predates the Web. It began as a series of dialogues among the authors and readers of the *Whole Earth Review* in 1985. Most WELL members were originally from the San Francisco Bay area, and the influence of that area's counterculture heritage is a significant part of the WELL's ambiance. Members of the WELL pay a monthly fee to participate in its forums and conferences. The WELL has been home to many important researchers who participated in the creation of the Internet and the Web. Its membership also includes noted writers and artists. In 1999, Salon.com bought the WELL and continues to operate it as a monthly subscription service.

As the Web emerged in the mid-1990s, its potential for creating new virtual communities was quickly exploited. In 1995, Beverly Hills Internet opened a virtual community site that featured two Webcams aimed down Hollywood streets; the site also had links to entertainment information Web sites. The theme of this community was the formation of digital cities around the focus of the Webcams. Members were given free space on the Web site to create pages within these virtual cities on which to add their contributions. The Webcams never did attract much traffic, but the offer of free Web space did. As the site grew, it changed its name to GeoCities and earned revenue by selling advertising on members' Web pages and pop-up pages that appeared whenever a visitor accessed a member's site. GeoCities grew rapidly and was purchased in 1999 by Yahoo! for $5 billion. Yahoo! operated the site for ten years before closing it in 2009.

Other similar sites became virtual communities. Tripod was founded in 1995 in Massachusetts and offered its participants free Web page space, chat rooms, news and weather updates, and health information pages. Like GeoCities, Tripod sold advertising on its main pages and on participants' Web pages. Theglobe.com, also started in 1995, was the outgrowth of a class project at Cornell University. The students who created the site included bulletin boards, chat rooms, discussion areas, and personal ads. They then sold advertising to support the site's operation. Later additions included news feeds, an online art gallery, and shopping pages. Theglobe.com received several buyout offers during its lifetime, but refused them all. The company fell victim to the Web slowdown of 2000 and closed in 2001 after suffering serious declines in its advertising revenue.

Although most of these early Web community businesses have closed, the idea behind them has continued to inspire investors and online businesspersons. Virtual communities live on today in a form that emerged with the second wave of electronic commerce, as you will learn in the next section.

Social Networking in the Second Wave of Online Communities

In the early days of the Internet, virtual communities provided an important service to the small number of people who regularly used the medium. As the Internet and Web grew, some of these communities grew, but others found that their purpose as a place for sharing the new experiences of online communication began to fade. In the second wave of electronic commerce, a new phenomenon in online communication began. People who were using the Internet no longer found a common bond only in the fact that they were using the Internet; multiple common bonds joined people with all types of common interests. Later Internet communities were formed on these common interests and the Internet was no longer the focal point of the community, but was simply a tool that enabled communication among community members. This new focus on the social interactions among community members that are made possible by the Web has led to a new category of Web sites. Because these sites are designed to facilitate interactions among people, they are called social networking sites. A **social networking site** is a Web site that allows individuals to create and publish a profile, create a list of other users with whom they share a connection (or connections), control that list, and monitor similar lists made by other users. In this section, you will learn about several types of social networking sites that are emerging as important parts of electronic commerce.

The second wave of electronic commerce saw the introduction of a number of social networking sites. One of the first sites, Six Degrees, started in 1997. Six Degrees was based on the idea that no more than six persons separated anyone in the world from any other person. The site was unable to generate sufficient revenue to continue operations and closed in 2000.

More successful social networking sites followed several years later. Friendster was founded by Jonathan Abrams in 2002. Friendster was the first Web site to include most of the features found today in all social networking sites. After growing rapidly, its U.S. user base remained steady; however, it continued its rapid growth in Asia and today is one of the leading social networking sites in that part of the world. Similarly, **Orkut** (named for the Google employee who developed the site in 2004) found its U.S. user base leveling off after a period of rapid growth, but is today one of the most-visited Web sites in India and South America. In 2008, Google moved Orkut's headquarters to Brazil.

LinkedIn, a site devoted to facilitating business contacts, was founded in 2003. It has more than 50 million users, about 50 percent of whom are in the United States. The site allows users to create a list of trusted business contacts. Users then invite others to participate in several forms of relationships on the site, each of which is designed to help them either find jobs, find employees, or develop connections to business opportunities. The site has been profitable since 2006 and is the most popular social networking site devoted to business connections.

Other social networking sites, such as **Tribe.net**, have met with varying degrees of success. Some sites have developed a following by offering specific features; for example, **YouTube** (now owned by Google) popularized the inclusion of videos in social networking sites, and **MySpace** has become a popular social networking site for younger Web users. **Twitter** offers users a way to send short messages to other uses who sign up to follow their messages (called **tweets**).

The general idea behind all of these sites is that people are invited to join by existing members who think they would be valuable additions to the community. The site provides a directory that lists members' locations, interests, and qualities; however, the directory does not disclose the name or contact information of members. A member can offer to communicate with any other member, but the communication does not occur until the intended recipient approves the contact (usually after reviewing the sender's directory information).

In addition to searching the directory of the community, new members can work through friends they have established in the community (perhaps starting with the person who invited them to join). By gradually building up a set of connections, members can develop contacts within the community that might prove valuable later. Figure 6-1 shows the launch year for some of the more successful social networking sites.

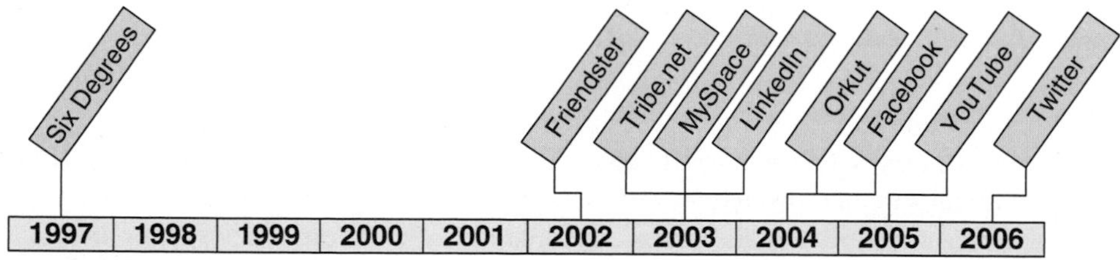

FIGURE 6-1 Social networking Web sites

Web Logs (Blogs)

As you learned in Chapter 4, Web logs, or blogs, are Web sites that contain commentary on current events or specific issues written by individuals. Many blogs invite visitors to add comments, which the blog owner may or may not edit. The result is a continuing discussion of the topic with the possibility that many interested persons will contribute to that discussion. Because blog sites encourage interaction among people interested in a particular topic, they are a form of a social networking site.

Most of the early blogs were focused on technology topics or on topics about which people have strong beliefs (for example, political or religious issues). The 2004 U.S. elections saw the first major use of blogs as a political networking tool. In previous elections, candidates had Web sites and political parties send out e-mail messages to supporters and potential donors, but in the 2004 elections, these activities were coordinated in a new way. Individuals working alone or with established political organizations set up Web sites that provided a place for people interested in a candidate or an issue to communicate with each other. These sites allowed people to discuss issues, plan strategies, and even arrange in-person meetings called **meetups**. By the 2008 U.S. elections, all of the major candidates were including blogs in the Web sites as essential tools for communicating their messages, organizing volunteers, and raising money.

After seeing the success of blogs and virtual communities as political networking tools, some retailers embraced blogs as a way to engage Web site visitors who were not ready to buy from the site, but who were interested in the products or services offered. Bluefly.com, the online discount apparel retailer, credits its blog Flypaper with drawing new customers to the store. The Flypaper blog invites visitors to discuss anything related to fashion. Bluefly.com is trying to appeal more to women who want to buy clothes and accessories that are currently fashionable rather than their current customer base of women who are looking for discounted items that might no longer be the latest trend. Online jeweler Ice.com operates several blogs, including one focused on celebrity jewelry. The company believes that the blogs encourage potential customers to visit their online store.

As blogs become more common, many businesses are likely to work them into their operating plans. CNN regularly includes information from blogs on its television newscasts and a number of newspapers are experimenting with blogs and virtual community spaces on their Web sites. Some small town newspapers now depend on readers to contribute information about community issues and events. Even larger newspapers would rather run a blog or Web site with reader contributions than pay reporters to write stories about events or issues that would interest only a small segment of their readership. By inviting information and opinion contributions, newspapers hope to reach members of the 18–35-year-old demographic group, a group that reads newspapers far less than their parents did. This trend toward having readers help write the online newspaper is called **participatory journalism**.

In addition to running a blog that is part of an existing activity (such as a political campaign, retail business, or newspaper), blogs can become a business in themselves if they can generate financial support through fees or advertising. Jake Dobkins writes about New York City on the blog site Gothamist. Instead of drawing a salary from a newspaper as a food and entertainment reporter, he blogs about the latest in New York nightlife. Advertising revenue has been sufficient to support Dobkins and the site's cofounder, Jen Chung. Now with a staff of bloggers, editors, and ad salespeople, these entrepreneurs are expanding into other cities. Michael Arrington began blogging in 2005 about new online business startups.

Again, instead of writing a column for a business magazine, he decided to put his research and reporting talents into his own business, which today is operating as TechCrunch, a successful advertising-supported Web site. Some industry observers consider Twitter to be a micro-blog, because it functions as a very informal blog site with entries (messages, or tweets) that are limited to 140 characters in length.

Social Networking Web Sites for Shoppers

The practice of bringing buyers and sellers together in a social network to facilitate retail sales is called **social shopping**. One of the first of these was craigslist, an information resource for San Francisco area residents that was created in 1995 by WELL member Craig Newmark. That community has grown to include information for most major cities in the United States and in several other countries. The site is operated by a not-for-profit foundation, and all postings other than help-wanted ads are free. The Etsy Web site provides a marketplace for people who want to sell handmade items. The social network here includes buyers and sellers interested in crafts of all types. In fact, the sense of community is so strong that a separate site, We Love Etsy, exists to provide a place for Etsy buyers and sellers to share information.

Social networking sites form communities based on connections among people. Other Web sites create communities based on the connections between ideas. These more abstract communities are called **idea-based virtual communities** and the people who participate in them are said to be engaging in **idea-based networking**. The del.icio.us site calls itself a "social bookmarks manager." Individuals place Web page bookmarks with one-word tags that describe the Web page in a community-accessible location on the site. The bookmark–tag combinations are focused on ideas and the contributions of all community members build a shared base of knowledge about those ideas. Among the most active tag names on the site are words such as design, reference, tools, music, news, howto, and photography. Another idea-based virtual community that uses shared tags is 43 Things. Although most of these virtual community sites are still fairly new, they show great promise for re-creating (on a much larger scale) the essence of the original Internet communities.

Virtual Learning Networks

One form of social network you might have used is the **virtual learning network**. Many colleges and universities now offer courses that use distance learning platforms such as Blackboard for student–instructor interaction. These distance learning platforms include tools such as bulletin boards, chat rooms, and drawing boards that allow students to interact with their instructors and each other in ways that are similar to the interactions that might occur in a physical classroom setting. Some open-source software projects are devoted to the development of virtual learning communities, including Moodle and uPortal. **Open source software** is developed by a community of programmers who make the software available for download at no cost. Other programmers then use the software, work with it, and improve it. Those programmers can submit their improved versions of the software back to the community. Open source software is an early and successful example of a virtual community. You can learn more about open-source software at the Open Source Initiative Web site.

Web Portals

Another example of a Web site that includes social networking features are the Web portal sites you learned about in Chapter 3. Sites such as Yahoo!, AOL, and MSN combine typical portal offerings such as search engines, directories, free e-mail, news stories, and weather reports with social networking elements such as games and chat rooms that allow site visitors to interact with each other. The combination of portal and social networking features keep visitors on the Web site (and viewing advertising) as long as possible.

Revenue Models for Social Networking Sites

By the late 1990s, virtual communities were selling advertising to generate revenue. Search engine sites and Web directories were also selling advertising to generate revenue. Beginning in 1998, a wave of purchases and mergers occurred among these sites. The new sites that emerged still used an advertising-only revenue-generation model and included all the features offered by virtual community sites, search engine sites, Web directories, and other information-providing and entertainment sites. These portals, which you first learned about in Chapter 3, are so named because their goal is to be every Web surfer's doorway to the Web.

Advertising-Supported Social Networking Sites

Visitors spend a greater amount of time at portal sites than they do at most other types of Web sites, which is attractive to advertisers. Other types of social networking sites can also draw large numbers of visitors that spend considerable time on the sites. This section describes how these characteristics make social networking sites appealing to advertisers.

Smaller social networking sites that have a more specialized appeal can draw enough visitors to generate significant amounts of advertising revenue, especially compared to the costs of running such a site. For example, software developer Eric Nakagawa posted a picture of a grinning fat cat on his Web site in 2007 with the caption "I can has cheezburger?" as a joke. He followed that with several more cat photos and funny captions over the next few weeks and added a blog so that people could post comments about the pictures. Within a few months, the site was getting more than 100,000 visitors a day. Nakagawa found that a site with that kind of traffic could charge between $100 and $600 per day for a single ad. Today, he spends his time fine-tuning the site to make it more attractive to visitors, who now submit their own photos and captions. **I Can Has Cheezburger** now generates a respectable income. Nakagawa has no illusions about expanding the site, hiring thousands of people, or selling stock to the public, but he is earning a comfortable living generated by a highly specialized social networking site.

As you learned in Chapter 3, sites that have higher numbers of visitors can charge more for advertising on the site. You also learned that stickiness (a Web site's ability to keep visitors on the site and attract repeat visitors) is also an important element of a site's attractiveness to advertisers. One rough measure of stickiness is how long each user spends at the site. Figure 6-2 lists the most popular Web sites in the world based on the number of users who accessed the sites during the month of October 2009. The leading sites often have more than 200 million unique visitors per month. The figure also shows the average amount of time each visitor spends on the site each month (an estimate of stickiness). The information in both figures is adapted from **Nielsen Online** reports and shows sites grouped by owner (for example, the Google listing includes YouTube; the Microsoft listing includes Microsoft software and technical support sites, MSN, and the Bing search engine; and News Corp includes MySpace). Web sites that are social networking sites (such as AOL and Facebook) or that include social networking elements (such as eBay, Google, NewsCorp, Microsoft, and Yahoo!) regularly appear on these Nielsen Online lists.

Owner	Millions of unique visitors	Average time per unique visitor per month (H:MM)
Google	354	2:53
Microsoft	318	3:13
Yahoo!	237	2:20
Facebook	200	5:47
eBay	159	1:51
Wikimedia Foundation	148	0:15
AOL Media Network	135	2:23
News Corp	121	1:07
Amazon.com	117	:24

Adapted from reports for October 2009 published by Nielsen NetView at http://www.nielsen.com/

FIGURE 6-2 Popularity and stickiness of leading Web sites

Because social networking sites often ask their members to provide demographic information about themselves, the potential for targeted marketing on these types of sites is very high. High visitor counts can yield high advertising rates for these sites. In the boom years of the first wave of electronic commerce, Web sites with high degrees of stickiness (which were usually Web portals) could obtain up-front cash payments from advertisers, which is very unusual for any kind of advertising sale. In recent years, all types of social networking sites have negotiated advertising deals that include a percentage of sales generated from sales leads on their sites. Second-wave advertising fees are based less on up-front site sponsorship payments and more on the generation of revenues from continuing relationships with people who use the social networking sites.

Mixed-Revenue and Fee-for-Service Social Networking Sites

Although most social networking sites use advertising to support their operations, some do charge a fee for some services. For example, the Yahoo! Web portal offers most of its services free (supported by advertising), but it does sell some of its social networking features, such as its All-Star Games package. Yahoo! also sells other features, such as more space to store messages and attached files, as part of its premium e-mail service. These fees help support the operation of the social networking elements of the site.

Some advertising-supported social networking sites have followed the lead of Yahoo! in a strategy called monetizing eyeballs or monetizing visitors. **Monetizing** refers to the conversion of existing regular site visitors seeking free information or services into fee-paying subscribers or purchasers of services. Sites that monetize visitors by charging them always worry about visitor backlash. They can never be sure how many existing visitors will pay for services that have been offered in some form at no cost.

Other social networking sites that use a mixed-revenue model are the financial information sites **The Motley Fool** and **TheStreet.com**. These sites offer investment advice, stock quotes, and financial planning help. Some of the information is provided at no cost, additional information is available to subscribers who pay no fee but who are required to provide personal information, and even more information is available to subscribers who agree to pay a fee.

Fee-Based Social Networking

An early attempt to monetize social networking by charging a fee for a specific service was the **Google Answers** site. Google Answers gave people a place to ask questions that were then answered by an expert (called a Google Answers Researcher) for a fee. Google administered a test to determine which members of the community qualified to become Google Answers Researchers. Google operated this service from 2002 to 2006 (questions and answers posted during that time period are still available on the Web site). Similar services operated by Yahoo! (**Yahoo! Answers**) and Amazon (**Askville**) allow volunteers to answer questions, but provide no opportunity for researchers to earn fees. These services do generate advertising revenue for the sites, however.

After Google closed its service, a number of the people who had been Google Researchers joined together and started a similar service on the site **Uclue**. Researchers earn 75 percent of the total fee paid to Uclue. Advocates of using paid researchers argue that the quality of the answers is higher than on free sites and that the questions tend to be more serious and better formulated. Both approaches are examples of how Web sites can generate revenue by providing a place in which virtual communities can interact.

Microlending Sites

One of the most interesting uses of social networking on the Web has been the emergence of sites that function as clearinghouses for microlending activity. **Microlending** is the practice of lending very small amounts of money to people who are starting or operating small businesses, especially in developing countries. Microlending became famous in 2006 when Muhammad Yunus and the Grameen Bank won the Nobel Peace Prize for their work in developing microlending initiatives in Bangladesh.

A key element of microlending is working within a social network of borrowers. The borrowers provide support for each other and an element of pressure to ensure the loans are repaid by each member of the group. **Kiva** and **MicroPlace** are examples of social networking sites that bring together many small investors who lend money to groups and individuals all over the world who need loans to start or continue their small business ventures. Kiva partners with microfinance institutions that are knowledgeable about business conditions in their parts of the world. These institutions select local individuals they believe are good credit risks and help them post a loan request on the Kiva site. Lenders can review the loan requests and agree to fund part (or all) of the loan amount using the Kiva Web site. The loans, which typically range from a few hundred to a few thousand dollars, are scheduled to be repaid within short time periods ranging from a few months to a year.

Internal Virtual Communities

A growing number of large organizations have built internal Web sites that provide opportunities for social interaction among their employees. These sites also include important information for employees. These sites run on the intranets you learned about in Chapter 2. Organizations can save significant amounts of money by replacing the printing and distribution of paper memos, newsletters, and other correspondence with a Web site. Internal social networking and community sites also provide easy access to employee handbooks, newsletters, and employee benefits information.

These organizations are also finding that an internal social networking Web site can become a good way of creating a virtual community among employees who are dispersed over a wide geographic area. For example, a global company could create a question and answer page for all of its networking technicians. Such a page would provide mentoring and informal help functions for the networking technician community within the company.

Many companies are adding wireless connectivity to their internal community sites and are using this technology to extend the reach of the site to employees who are traveling, meeting with customers or suppliers, or telecommuting. These extended community sites are yet another example of a second-wave combination of technology (wireless communications) with a business strategy from the first wave (internal Web portals).

The use of mobile technology is becoming an important part of almost every social networking business strategy as people use their mobile phones to do everything from take photos they will post on Facebook to send tweets to their followers on Twitter. In the next section you will learn about the potential for combining mobile phone technologies with the idea of social networking to create new online business opportunities.

MOBILE COMMERCE

An increasing number of mobile phones include Web browsers. Almost all phones sold today include **short messaging service (SMS)**, which allows mobile phone users to send short text messages to each other. Mobile phones such as the BlackBerry have had the ability to send and receive e-mail for years, but until recently, many owners of these phones used them only for phone calls. However, two developments coincided in the United States in 2008 that made these phones more viable as devices for browsing the Web. First, high-speed mobile telephone networks grew dramatically in availability, and second, manufacturers began offering a huge range of smart phones that include a Web browser (and a screen large enough to make it usable), an operating system, and the ability to run applications on that operating system. In this section, you will learn about the impact of this confluence of technologies on the potential for online business using these devices, called **mobile commerce (m-commerce)**.

Mobile Operating Systems and Applications

In Japan and parts of Southeast Asia, mobile commerce has been a much larger part of online business activity than it has elsewhere in the world (including in the United States). One reason is that these countries introduced high-capacity mobile phone networks long before U.S. network providers did. NTT DoCoMo, which is the largest phone company in Japan, pioneered mobile commerce in 2000 with its i-mode service. Starting with the sale of games and other programs that run on the phones, NTT DoCoMo has been a leader in expanding mobile commerce, including online shopping and payments. Since 2004, it has been selling mobile phones, called **mobile wallets** (*osaifu-ketai*, in Japanese), that function as credit cards. Although the individual applications on DoCoMo phones are not overwhelming (for example, one application lets you use a mobile phone to pay for a vending machine purchase in Japan), their combined capabilities generate a significant amount of business.

In the United States, the introduction of smart phones and the high-capacity networks that make them able to support mobile commerce did not begin until 2008. These smart phones, such as the Apple iPhone, the Palm Pre, several BlackBerry models, and phones that use the Android operating system, opened the door for serious U.S. mobile commerce for the first time. Figure 6-3 shows several examples of designs used in smart phones today.

FIGURE 6-3 Smart phones come in a range of different styles

Some smart phones and wireless PDAs display Web pages using the **Wireless Application Protocol (WAP)**. WAP allows Web pages formatted in HTML to be displayed on devices with small screens, such as mobile phones. Another approach, made possible by increased screen resolution, is to display a normal Web page on the device. The Apple iPhone was one of the first devices to include touch screen controls that make viewing and navigating a normal Web page easy to do on a small handheld device. A third approach is to design Web sites to match specific smart phones. This is much more difficult to accomplish, because there can be many different phones that use the same operating system, and each phone has a different interface (the buttons, touches, or gestures that perform specific functions often vary).

Apple, BlackBerry, and Palm each use their own proprietary operating systems. Other phone makers, such as HTC, Motorola, and Nokia have, in the past, created their own operating systems and software applications (for common tasks such as maintaining an appointments calendar, managing contacts, and retrieving e-mail). Today, these phone manufacturers often use a standard operating system provided by a third party when building their smart phones. The most common third party operating systems are Android, Windows Mobile, and Symbian. Android is an open source operating system created by Google. Windows Mobile is a proprietary operating system sold by Microsoft. Symbian, which is the most widely used smart phone operating system, started as a proprietary system but became open source in 2008 when Nokia purchased the software from its developer and joined with a number of other mobile phone manufacturers and service providers to form the Symbian Foundation. Nokia donated the software to the foundation, which manages continued open source development of the operating system.

The emergence of common operating systems (instead of each phone manufacturer using its own operating system) occurred because the way software applications are developed and sold has changed. In the past, U.S. mobile phone companies generated revenue by controlling the application software (usually called **apps**) that could run on their phones. Companies would license the apps from software developers and then charge subscribers a monthly usage fee for each app. Apple turned this revenue strategy on its head when AT&T agreed to be its sole outlet for the iPhone and agreed to allow Apple to sell apps for the phone directly. The **Apple Apps for iPhone** online store became an instant success, making a wide variety of software available for the phone. Since Apple allowed independent developers to create apps and sell them (on a revenue sharing basis) through their Apps for iPhone store, a number of software developers made hundreds of thousands of dollars for their creations. Zynga, a company that develops games for mobile phones has earned more than $100 million in revenues by selling its game apps for the iPhone and other phones.

BlackBerry and Palm have followed Apple's lead and now have apps stores of their own (**BlackBerry App World** and **Palm Pre Applications**), and the open source Android and Symbian phones also have software developers creating apps for them (see **Android Market** and **SymbianGear**, for example). A number of companies now develop apps for multiple platforms.

The Future of Mobile Commerce

Companies that want to participate in mobile commerce should first review their Web sites to determine how well the site works when viewed on a mobile device. Many companies that are serious about connecting with mobile users are creating separate Web sites for mobile users. For example, the **Scottrade Mobile** Web site is optimized for display on the small screens used in smart phones. The site gives Scottrade customers quick access to financial markets information and to their trading accounts. **Yahoo! Mobile** provides a version of its Web portal that is similarly optimized for the small screen and limited controls of most smart phones.

Although the use of mobile phones for online banking is still in its early stages in the United States, forward-looking financial institutions such as **Wescorp** are working on ways to draw in younger customers by offering complete banking services through a Web site that is optimized for specific smart phones.

The Veterans Affairs Medical Center in Washington, D.C. has issued BlackBerry smart phones to its physicians. They use the phones to send and receive messages, but in addition, they can use the phones to read detailed information needed for treating patients. For example, a cardiologist can read electrocardiograms (EKGs) on their smart phones, saving time and often a trip to the hospital. Other hospitals are using smart phones in equally creative ways. For example, diabetic patients can track what they eat, insulin injections, blood sugar readings, and their level of physical activities on their phones. Doctors treating these patients can access the data using their own smart phones and can better help patients manage their diabetes. The University of Louisville Medical School provides a suite of smart phone apps to their students, including Epocrates (a drug information database), and apps that let them look up information about diseases and access reference works.

Most smart phones have global positioning satellite (GPS) service capabilities, which means that apps that combine the phone user's location with the availability of retail stores and services can be interwoven into creative mobile business opportunities. For example, an app such as Flixter's iPhone Movies can direct the user to specific business locations (such as restaurants, movie theaters, or auto repair facilities) based on the user's current location. In the next section, you will learn how online business pioneers adapted auctions, a very old business practice, to a new online business opportunity.

ONLINE AUCTIONS

In many ways, online auctions provide a business opportunity that is perfect for the Web. An auction site can charge both buyers and sellers to participate, and it can sell advertising on its pages. People interested in trading specific items can form a market segment that advertisers will pay extra to reach. Thus, the same kind of targeted advertising opportunities that search engine sites generate with their results pages are available to advertisers on auction sites. This combination of revenue-generating characteristics makes it relatively easy to develop online auctions that yield profits early in the life of the project.

One of the Internet's strengths is that it can bring together people who share narrow interests but are geographically dispersed. Online auctions can capitalize on that ability by either catering to a narrow interest or providing a general auction site that has sections devoted to specific interests. Before you learn more about online auctions, the next section introduces some basic auction terminology and principles.

Auction Basics

The earliest written records of auctions are from Babylon and date from 500 BC. In those auctions, men bid against each other for the women they wished to marry. Roman soldiers used auctions to liquidate the property they took from their vanquished foes. In AD 193, the Praetorian Guard auctioned off the entire Roman Empire after killing the Emperor Pertinax. In later years, Buddhist temples held auctions to sell off the possessions of deceased monks. Auctions became common activities in 17th-century England, where taverns held regular auctions of art and furniture. The 18th century saw the birth of two British auction houses—**Sotheby's** in 1744 and **Christie's** in 1766—that continue to be major auction firms today. The British settlers of the colonies that would become the United States brought auctions with them. Colonial auctions were used to sell farm equipment, animals, tobacco and, sad to say, human beings.

In an auction, a seller offers an item or items for sale, but does not establish a price. This is called "putting an item up for bid" or "putting an item on the (auction) block." Potential buyers are given information about the item or some opportunity to examine it; they then offer **bids**, which are the prices they are willing to pay for the item. The potential buyers, or **bidders**, each have developed **private valuations**, or amounts they are willing to pay for the item. The whole auction process is managed by an **auctioneer**. In some auctions, people employed by the seller or the auctioneer can make bids on behalf of the seller. These people are called **shill bidders**. Shill bidders can artificially inflate the price of an item and may be prohibited from bidding by the rules of a particular auction.

English Auctions

Many different kinds of auctions exist. Most people who have attended or seen an auction on television have experienced only one type of auction, the **English auction**, in which bidders publicly announce their successive higher bids until no higher bid is forthcoming. At that point, the auctioneer pronounces the item sold to the highest bidder at that bidder's price. This type of auction is also called an **ascending-price auction**. An English auction is sometimes called an **open auction** (or **open-outcry auction**) because the bids are publicly announced; however, there are other types of auctions that use publicly announced bids that are also called open auctions.

In some cases, an English auction has a minimum bid, or reserve price. A **minimum bid** is the price at which an auction begins. If no bidders are willing to pay that price, the item is removed from the auction and not sold. In some auctions, a minimum bid is not announced, but sellers can establish a minimum acceptable price, called a **reserve price**, or simply **reserve**. If the reserve price is not exceeded, the item is withdrawn from the auction and not sold.

English auctions that offer multiple units of an item for sale and allow bidders to specify the quantity they want to buy are called **Yankee auctions**. When the bidding concludes in a Yankee auction, the highest bidder is allotted the quantity he or she bid. If items remain after satisfying the highest bidder, those remaining items are allocated to successive lower (next highest) bidders until all items are distributed. Although all successful bidders (except possibly the lowest successful bidder) receive the quantity of items on which they bid, they only pay the price bid by the *lowest* successful bidder.

To understand Yankee auctions better, consider this example. A seller places nine items up for bid. When the bidders stop increasing their bids, the successful bidders include the following: the highest bidder, who bid $85, quantity five; the second-highest bidder, who bid $83, quantity three; and the third-highest bidder, who bid $81, quantity four. All three of the successful bidders pay $81 per item, but the highest bidder receives five items, the second-highest bidder receives three items, and the third-highest bidder receives the one remaining item, despite having bid for a quantity of four, because only one is left after satisfying the quantity bids of the higher bidders.

English auctions have drawbacks for both sellers and bidders. Because the winning bidder is only required to bid a small amount more than the next-highest bidder, winning bidders tend not to bid their full private valuations, which prevents sellers from obtaining the maximum possible price. Bidders risk becoming caught up in the excitement of competitive bidding and then bidding more than their private valuations. This psychological phenomenon, called the **winner's curse**, has been extensively documented by William Thaler (see the

Thaler reference in the "For Further Study and Research" section at the end of this chapter) and other behavioral economists.

Dutch Auctions

The **Dutch auction** is a form of open auction in which bidding starts at a high price and drops until a bidder accepts the price. Because the price drops until a bidder claims the item, Dutch auctions are also called **descending-price auctions**. Farmers' cooperatives in the Netherlands use this type of auction to sell perishable goods such as produce and flowers, which is how it came to be known as a "Dutch" auction. In most Dutch auctions, the seller offers a number of similar items for sale. One common implementation of a Dutch auction uses a clock that drops the price with each tick. The first bidder to call out "stop," which stops the clock, becomes the winning bidder. The winning bidder can take all or any part of the auctioned items at that price. If any items remain, the clock is restarted and continues to run until all the items are taken by successive lower bidders. A Dutch auction is often better for the seller because the bidder with the highest private valuation will not let the bid drop much below that valuation for fear of losing the item to another bidder. Dutch auctions are particularly good for moving large numbers of commodity items quickly. A few online stores have offered Dutch auctions from time to time. For several years, women's clothing retailer Coldwater Creek used Dutch auctions to sell closeout items on its site.

In 2004, Google used a Dutch auction to sell its stock to investors in its initial public offering. The financial community considered this use of a Dutch auction to be highly innovative and very successful. Google used the Dutch auction to obtain the highest price possible for its shares. In a similar financial transaction, online advertising and technology company LookSmart used a Dutch auction to buy back some of its stock. Usually, when a company announces a share buyback, the price of the stock moves upward and the company must pay an increasing price as it buys the shares on the open market. LookSmart announced a price range and let shareholders place bids that specified the number of shares and the price within that range at which they would be willing to sell. When the auction was over, LookSmart had repurchased exactly the number of shares it had wanted to buy at the lowest price it had specified, which meant that the Dutch auction worked very well for it.

First-Price Sealed-Bid Auctions

In **sealed-bid auctions**, bidders submit their bids independently and are usually prohibited from sharing information with each other. In a **first-price sealed-bid auction**, the highest bidder wins. If multiple items are auctioned, successive lower (next highest) bidders are awarded the remaining items at the prices they bid.

Second-Price Sealed-Bid Auctions

The **second-price sealed-bid auction** is the same as the first-price sealed-bid auction except that the highest bidder is awarded the item at the price bid by the *second*-highest bidder. At first glance, one might wonder why a seller would even consider such an auction because it gives the item to the winning bidder at a lower price. William Vickrey won the

1996 Nobel Prize in Economics for his studies of the properties of this auction type. He concluded that it yields higher returns for the seller, encourages all bidders to bid the amounts of their private valuations, and reduces the tendency for bidders to collude. Because the winning bidder is protected from an erroneously high bid, all bidders tend to bid higher than they would in a first-price sealed-bid auction. Second-price sealed-bid auctions are commonly called **Vickrey auctions**.

Open-Outcry Double Auctions

The **Chicago Board of Trade** conducts **open-outcry double auctions** of commodity futures and stock options. The buy and sell offers are shouted by traders standing in a small area on the exchange floor called a trading pit. Each commodity or stock option is traded in its own pit. The action in a trading pit can become quite frenzied as 20 or 30 traders shout offers aloud. Double auctions, either sealed bid or open outcry, work well only for items of known quality, such as securities or graded agricultural products, which are regularly traded in large quantities. Such items can be auctioned without bidders inspecting the items before placing their bids.

Double Auctions

In a **double auction**, buyers and sellers each submit combined price–quantity bids to an auctioneer. The auctioneer matches the sellers' offers (starting with the lowest price and then going up) to the buyers' offers (starting with the highest price and then going down) until all the quantities offered for sale are sold to buyers. Double auctions can be operated in either sealed-bid or open-outcry formats. The **New York Stock Exchange** conducts sealed-bid double auctions of stocks and bonds in which the auctioneer, called a specialist, manages the market for a particular stock or bond issue. The specialist company must use its own funds, when necessary, to maintain a stable market in the specific security it manages. Although the specialist system has been in use for more than a century, critics have charged that specialists can and do use their knowledge to enrich themselves at the expense of investors. In 2007, the New York Stock Exchange added an electronic trading system that automatically matches buyer and seller offers. Today the automated system, which bypasses specialists, handles most of the trading volume on the exchange.

Reverse (Seller-Bid) Auctions

In a **reverse auction** (also called a **seller-bid auction**), multiple sellers submit price bids to an auctioneer who represents a single buyer. The bids are for a given amount of a specific item that the buyer wants to purchase. The prices go down as the bidding continues until no seller is willing to bid lower. Reverse auctions have been operated for consumers from time to time, but most reverse auctions involve businesses as buyers and sellers. In many business reverse auctions, the buyer acts as auctioneer and screens sellers before they can participate. You will learn more about specific implementations of reverse auctions later in this chapter.

The seven auction types described in this section are the most commonly used in business today. Figure 6-4 summarizes the key characteristics of each of these seven major auction types.

Auction type	Key characteristics
English auction	Starting from a low price, bidding increases until no bidder is willing to bid higher.
Dutch auction	Starting from a high price, bidding automatically decreases until the bidder accepts the price.
First-price sealed-bid auction	Secret bidding process; the highest bidder pays the amount of the highest bid.
Second-price sealed-bid auction (Vickrey auction)	Secret bidding process; the highest bidder pays the amount of the *second*-highest bid.
Double auction (open-outcry)	Buyers and sellers declare combined price–quantity bids. The auctioneer matches seller offers (lowest to highest) with buyer offers (highest to lowest). Buyers and sellers can modify bids based on knowledge gained from other bids.
Double auction (sealed-bid)	Buyers and sellers declare combined price–quantity bids. The auctioneer (specialist) matches seller offers (lowest to highest) with buyer offers (highest to lowest). Buyers and sellers cannot modify their bids.
Reverse auction (seller-bid)	Multiple sellers submit price bids to an auctioneer that represents a single buyer. The bids are for a given amount of a specific item that the buyer wants to purchase. Prices go down as the bidding continues until no seller is willing to bid lower.

FIGURE 6-4 Key characteristics of seven major auction types

Online Auctions and Related Businesses

Millions of people buy and sell all types of goods on consumer auction sites each year. Although the online auction business is changing rapidly as it grows, three broad categories of auction Web sites have emerged: general consumer auctions, specialty consumer auctions, and business-to-business auctions. Some industry analysts consider the two types of consumer auctions to be business-to-consumer electronic commerce. Other analysts believe that a more appropriate term for the electronic commerce that occurs in general consumer auctions is consumer-to-consumer or even **consumer-to-business** (because the bidders at a general consumer auction might be businesses). Their argument is that many sellers who participate in general consumer auctions are not really businesses; they are ordinary people who use these auctions to sell personal items instead of holding a garage sale, for example. Whether you prefer to think of online auctions as business-to-consumer, consumer-to-consumer, or consumer-to-business, the largest number of auction transactions occurs on general consumer auction sites.

General Consumer Auctions

The most successful consumer auction Web site today is **eBay**. Sellers and buyers must register with eBay and agree to the site's basic terms of doing business. Sellers pay eBay a listing fee and a sliding percentage of the final selling price. Buyers pay nothing to eBay. In addition to paying the basic fees, sellers can choose from a variety of enhanced and extra-cost services, including having their auctions listed in boldface type and featured in lists of preferred auctions.

In an attempt to address buyer concerns about seller reliability, eBay instituted a rating system. Buyers can submit ratings of sellers after doing business with them. These ratings are converted into graphics that appear with the seller's nickname in each auction in which the seller participates. Although this system is not perfect, many eBay bidders feel that it affords them some protection from unscrupulous sellers. eBay also uses buyer ratings of sellers to place restrictions on sellers (such as withholding funds for three weeks) or, if the ratings are low enough, prohibit them from selling on eBay at all. The converse is true also; sellers rate buyers, which provides sellers some protection from unscrupulous buyers.

Although eBay does not release any statistics about buyer and seller frauds, most industry observers agree that sellers face larger potential losses than buyers. Sellers' greatest risks are from buyers who use stolen credit card numbers or who place the winning bid but never contact the seller to conclude the transaction. Buyers' risks include sellers who never deliver or who misrepresent their merchandise. You will learn about ways that sellers and buyers can protect themselves later in this chapter.

The most common format used on eBay is a computerized version of the English auction. The eBay English auction allows the seller to set a reserve price. In eBay English auctions, the bidders are listed, but the bid amounts are not disclosed until after the auction is over. This is a slight variation on the in-person English auction, but because eBay always shows a continually updated high bid amount, a bidder who monitors the auction can see the bidding pattern as it occurs. The main difference between eBay and a live English auction is that bidders do not see the details of the bidding history (which bidders placed which bids when) until the auction is over. The eBay English auction also allows sellers to specify that an auction be made private. In an eBay private auction, the site never discloses bidders' identities and the prices they bid. At the conclusion of the auction, eBay notifies only the seller and the highest bidder. Another auction type offered by eBay is an increasing-price format for multiple-item auctions that eBay calls a Dutch auction. However, these auctions are actually the Yankee auction variant of an English auction.

In either type of eBay auction, bidders must constantly monitor the bidding activity if they intend to win the auction. All eBay auctions have a **minimum bid increment**, the amount by which one bid must exceed the previous bid, which is about 3 percent of the bid amount. To make bidding easier, eBay allows bidders to make a proxy bid. In a **proxy bid**, the bidder specifies a maximum bid. If that maximum bid exceeds the current bid, the eBay site automatically enters a bid that is one minimum bid increment higher than the current bid. As new bidders enter the auction, the eBay site software continually enters higher bids for all bidders who placed proxy bids. Although this feature is designed to make bidding require less bidder attention, if a number of bidders enter proxy bids on one item, the bidding rises rapidly to the highest proxy bid offered. This rapid rise in the current bid often occurs in the closing hours of an eBay auction, usually as the result of bidders raising their proxy bid levels.

To attract sellers who frequently offer items or who continually offer large numbers of items, eBay offers a platform called eBay stores within its auction site. At a very low cost, sellers can establish eBay stores that show items for sale as well as items being auctioned. This can help sellers generate additional profits from sales of items related to those offered in their auctions. These eBay stores are integrated into the auction site; that is, when a bidder searches for an item, the results page includes auctions and listings from sellers' eBay stores.

eBay has been so successful because it was the first major Web auction site for consumers that did not cater to a specific audience and because it advertises widely. eBay spends about $1 billion each year to market and promote its Web site. A significant portion of this promotional budget is devoted to traditional mass media outlets, such as television advertising. For eBay, such advertising has proven to be the best way to reach its main market: people who have a hobby or a very specific interest in items that are not locally available. Whether those items are jewelry, antique furniture, coins, first-edition books, or stuffed animals, eBay has created a place where people can become collectors, dispose of their collections, or trade out of their collections.

Because one of the major determinants of Web auction site success is attracting enough buyers and sellers to create markets in many different items, some Web sites that already have a large number of visitors entered the general consumer auction business. **Yahoo!** created an auction site patterned after eBay. Yahoo! believed that it could leverage its brand name and capitalize on its large number of site visitors to compete with eBay.

Yahoo! had some early success in attracting large numbers of auction participants, in part because it offered its auction service to sellers at no charge. Yahoo! was less successful in attracting buyers, resulting in less bidding action in each auction than generally occurs on eBay. In January 2001, Yahoo! began charging sellers in the face of dropping ad revenues in its other Web operations. Within one month, Yahoo! lost about 80 percent of its auction listings; however, the percentage of listed items that ended in a sale increased six-fold, and the dollar amount of completed auctions remained constant. Because Yahoo! draws a large number of visitors every month, the company hoped that it would be able to further increase participation in its auctions and attract some of the sellers who left in reaction to the fees. However, in 2005, Yahoo! reverted to its original policy of not charging fees to sellers. Despite its efforts, Yahoo! was unable to draw enough buyers or sellers to its U.S. auction site and closed the operation in 2007.

Amazon.com also added a general consumer auction to its list of products and services. Unlike eBay, which was profitable from the start, Amazon took seven years to earn its first small profits from all of its businesses.

One way that Amazon attempted to compete with eBay was through its "Auctions Guarantee." This guarantee directly addressed concerns raised in the media by eBay customers about being cheated by sellers. When Amazon opened its Auctions site, it agreed to reimburse any buyer for merchandise purchased in an auction that was not delivered or that was "materially different" from the seller's representations up to $250.

In response to Amazon's guarantee, eBay immediately offered its customers a similar guarantee, but not before Amazon gained free publicity from the media coverage of its guarantee. In 2003, eBay increased its guarantee to $500 in the hopes that it would induce new customers to buy at eBay auctions. The experiment worked well; in fact, eBay increased its guarantee again in 2004 to $1000. In 2005, eBay reduced its guarantee to $200 with a $25 deductible, but continued to offer a $1000 guarantee through its payment processing subsidiary PayPal. This change encourages bidders to use PayPal, yet still provides some protection for bidders who do not. Some eBay users have complained that the company does not act quickly on claims under the guarantee and does its best to avoid paying claims; however, the guarantee remains a powerful marketing tool. Buyers of more expensive items can protect themselves by using a third-party **escrow service**, which holds the buyer's payment until he or she receives and is satisfied with the purchased item. Escrow services are available through most auction sites. You will learn more about escrow services later in this chapter.

Amazon also used other strategies to compete with eBay. For example, Amazon established an online joint venture with Sotheby's, the famous British auction house, to hold online auctions of fine art, antiques, jewelry, and other high-value collectibles. Despite its years of effort, Amazon was unable to draw sellers and buyers in sufficient numbers and closed its general consumer auction site in 2006.

The success of eBay has inspired competition from a number of powerful and well-financed companies. Most of these competitors have met the same fate as Yahoo! and Amazon, failing after spending large amounts of money in their efforts. The strongest competitor to eBay that is currently operating in the U.S. market is **Overstock.com**, an online retailer that specializes in closeout sales of brand-name merchandise. The company launched an online auction site in 2004. **Overstock Auctions** started out strong, with more than 600,000 registered users and 10 million items listed in its first year in business. Since then, the company has reported mixed results on its auction business. The listing fees that Overstock Auctions charges sellers are substantially less than eBay's. Despite this competition, the premier general consumer U.S. Web auction site today is still eBay. Any competitors, even large and well-financed companies, must overcome the strong advantage built by eBay. Future challengers to eBay will find that the economic structure of markets is biased against new entrants. Because markets become more efficient (yielding fairer prices to both buyers and sellers) as the number of buyers and sellers increases, new auction participants are inclined to patronize established marketplaces. Thus, existing auction sites, such as eBay, are inherently more valuable to customers than new auction sites. This basic economic fact, which economists call a **lock-in effect**, will make the task of creating other successful general consumer Web auction sites even more difficult in the future.

A somewhat ironic example of the lock-in effect exists in the Japanese general consumer auction market. In this market, unlike in the United States, Yahoo! was the first major company to offer online auctions. At the time (early 1999), Yahoo! did not charge fees to sellers. When eBay entered the Japanese market five months later, it charged fees and found few people interested in its services. Even when Yahoo! began charging fees in 2001 for its auctions, the lock-in effect preserved its strong lead in Japan. Today, Yahoo! Auctions holds more than 90 percent of the Japanese online auction market, while eBay's market share is less than 3 percent.

LEARNING FROM FAILURES

Auction Universe

One of the most promising new entrants into the general consumer auction business was Auction Universe. Times Mirror, the parent company of the *Los Angeles Times* newspaper, started Auction Universe in 1997 and then sold it in 1998 to a partnership of eight major newspaper companies (including Times Mirror itself) called **Classified Ventures**. These companies were concerned that classified advertising on the Web posed a threat to their newspapers' classified advertising, which is one of the most profitable elements in the newspaper business. Through their Classified Ventures partnership, these newspaper companies started their own Web sites for classified ads such as Apartments.com, Cars.com, and NewHomeNetwork.com.These sites earn revenue by charging for running ads, selling advertising on their pages, or both. Classified Ventures believed that the Auction Universe site could become an important and profitable part of its Web presence.

Unfortunately, Auction Universe closed in August 2000, but Classified Ventures' classified ad sites continue to operate. The Auction Universe site was modeled on eBay and offered similar types of auctions and services for buyers and sellers. Some critics believed that the Auction Universe interface was more intuitive than eBay's and included a better search engine; however, the site failed to mount a sustained challenge to eBay's dominance. Even with major corporate sponsorship and a $10 million advertising campaign behind it, Auction Universe was unable to displace the advantage eBay obtained from the lock-in effect it has created for a large number of auction bidders and sellers.

Specialty Consumer Auctions

Rather than struggle to compete with a well-established rival such as eBay in the general consumer auction market, a number of firms have decided to identify special-interest market targets and create specialized Web auction sites that meet the needs of those market segments.

JustBeads.com is one example of an auction site that caters to buyers and sellers who are geographically dispersed but share highly focused interests. Other specialty consumer auction sites include **Cigarbid.com** and **Winebid**. These sites gain an advantage by identifying a strong market segment with readily identifiable products that are desired by people with relatively high levels of disposable income. Cigars and wine meet those requirements. These specialized consumer auctions occupy profitable niches, which allows them to coexist successfully with large general consumer sites, such as eBay.

Consumer Reverse Auctions

In the past, a number of companies have created sites that allow site visitors to describe items or services they wish to buy. The site then routes the visitor's request to a group of participating merchants who reply to the visitor by e-mail with offers to supply the item at a particular price. This type of offer is often called a **reverse bid**. The buyer can then accept the lowest offer or the offer that best matches the buyer's criteria. None of these sites were successful in developing a large enough following to interest merchants, so they have all closed.

Many people think of **Priceline.com** as a seller-bid auction site. Priceline.com allows site visitors to state a price they are willing to pay for airline tickets, car rentals, hotel rooms, and a few other services. If the price is sufficiently high, the transaction is completed. However, Priceline.com completes many of its transactions from an inventory that it has purchased from airlines, car rental agencies, and hotels. To the extent that Priceline sells out of its inventory, it operates more as a liquidation broker (you will learn more about liquidation brokers in the next section) than as a true reverse auction site.

Group Shopping Sites

Another type of business that the Internet made possible is the **group purchasing site**, or **group shopping site**. On these sites, the seller posts an item with a tentative price. As individual buyers enter bids on the item (these bids are agreements to buy one unit of that item, but no price is specified), the site operators negotiate with the seller to obtain a lower price. The posted price will decrease as the number of bids increases, but only if the number of bids increases. Thus, a group shopping site builds up the number of buyers sufficiently to encourage the seller to offer a quantity discount. The effect is similar to the outcome achieved by a reverse auction.

The types of products that work well for group shopping sites are branded products with well-established reputations. This allows buyers to feel confident that they are getting a good bargain and are not just getting a lower price for a low quality product. Ideal products also have a high value-to-size ratio and are not perishable.

Two companies, Mercata and LetsBuyIt.com, operated major group shopping sites for several years, however, both closed their doors after failing to find consistent sources of products that sold well on their sites. They found that few sellers of products that are well suited to group shopping efforts—such as computers, consumer electronics, and small appliances—were willing to work with them. These sellers did not see any compelling advantage in offering reduced prices on their merchandise to Web sites that were probably cannibalizing sales in their existing marketing channels. They also worried about offending the regular distributors of their products by selling through group shopping sites.

Business-to-Business Auctions

Unlike consumer online auctions, business-to-business online auctions evolved to meet a specific existing need. Many manufacturing companies periodically need to dispose of unusable or excess inventory. Despite the best efforts of procurement and production management, businesses occasionally buy more raw materials than they need. Many times, unforeseen changes in customer demand for a product can saddle manufacturers with excess finished goods or spare parts.

Depending on its size, a firm typically uses one of two methods to distribute excess inventory. Large companies sometimes have liquidation specialists who find buyers for these unusable inventory items. Smaller businesses often sell their unusable and excess inventory to **liquidation brokers**, which are firms that find buyers for these items. Online auctions are the logical extension of these inventory liquidation activities to a new and more efficient channel, the Internet.

Two of the three emerging business-to-business Web auction models are direct descendants of these two traditional methods for handling excess inventory. In the large-company model, the business creates its own auction site that sells excess inventory. In the small-company model, a third-party Web auction site takes the place of the liquidation broker and auctions excess inventory listed on the site by a number of smaller sellers. The third business-to-business Web auction model resembles consumer online auctions. In this model, a new business entity enters a market that lacked efficiency and creates a site at which buyers and sellers who have not historically done business with each other can participate in auctions. An alternative implementation of this model occurs when a Web auction replaces an existing sales channel.

In the second business-to-business auction model, smaller firms sell their obsolete inventory through an independent third-party auction site. In some cases, these online auctions are conducted by the same liquidation brokers that have always handled the disposition of obsolete inventory. These brokers adapted to the changed environment and implemented electronic commerce to stay in business. One example is the **GoIndustry Dove Bid** site, established by the Ross-Dove Company, a traditional liquidation broker for many years. **Gordon Brothers Group**, another liquidation broker, has been selling the inventory of failed retailers since 1903. The company has used its expertise to launch or help others launch Web sites that liquidate retailer inventories.

A number of hospitals and other organizations are using online auctions to fill temporary employment openings. Health care workers, such as nurses, perform similar duties in specific health care settings in most hospitals. For example, the duties performed by an intensive care unit nurse are almost identical across hospitals. State regulations on nurse licensing require that nurses have similar levels of knowledge, skills, and abilities. Having similar job functions in workplaces and having similarly qualified persons working in those jobs allows both nurses and employers to treat the nursing function as a commodity. Therefore, nurses can easily work for a variety of employers and do not require long periods of training or learning procedures specific to a particular hospital. In the past, nurse agencies would coordinate placement, matching nurses who wanted to work particular days or shifts with hospitals and other health care organizations who had shifts to fill. The agency would earn a commission on each placement. Today, employers operate their own shift auctions. Nurses bid on the shifts they would prefer to work and the software manages the auctions. In an efficient matching of supply and demand, employers meet their staffing needs efficiently, nurses get to work when they want, and the agency fee is avoided.

Business-to-Business Reverse Auctions

In Chapter 5, you learned how businesses are creating various types of electronic marketplaces to conduct business-to-business (B2B) transactions. Many of these marketplaces include auctions and reverse auctions. Glass and building materials producer Owens Corning uses reverse auctions for items ranging from chemicals (direct materials) to conveyors (fixed assets) to pipe fittings (MRO). Owens Corning even held a reverse auction to buy bottled water. Asking its suppliers to bid has reduced the cost of those items by an average of 10 percent should all be on one line. Because Owens Corning buys billions of dollars worth of materials, fixed assets, and MRO items each year, the potential for cost savings is significant. Both the U.S. Navy and the federal government's General Services Administration use reverse auctions to acquire some of the billions of dollars worth of materials and supplies they purchase each year. Other companies that use reverse auctions include Agilent, Bechtel, Boeing, Raytheon, and Sony.

Not all companies are enthusiastic about reverse auctions, however. Some purchasing executives argue that reverse auctions cause suppliers to compete on price alone, which can lead suppliers to cut corners on quality or miss scheduled delivery dates. Others argue that reverse auctions can be useful for nonstrategic commodity items with established quality standards. Companies that have considered reverse auctions and decided not to use them include Cisco, Cubic, IBM, and Solar Turbines.

With compelling arguments on both sides, the advisability of using reverse auctions can depend on specific conditions that exist in a given company. A company can also determine whether to use reverse auctions based on guidelines that have emerged. For example, in some industry supply chains, the need for trust and long-term strategic relationships with suppliers makes reverse auctions less attractive. In fact, the trend in purchasing management over the last 30 years has been to build trust-based relationships that can endure for many years. Using reverse auctions replaces trusting relationships with a bidding activity that pits suppliers against each other and is seen by many purchasing managers as a step backward.

In some industries, suppliers are larger and more powerful than the buyers. In those industries, suppliers simply will not agree to participate in reverse auctions. If enough important suppliers refuse to participate, it is impossible to conduct reverse auctions. In industries where a high degree of competition exists among suppliers, however, reverse auctions can be an efficient way to conduct and manage the price bidding that would naturally occur in that market. Figure 6-5 lists the supply chain characteristics that support or discourage reverse auctions identified in research conducted by Dima Ghawi and the author of this book.

Supply Chain Characteristics that Support Reverse Auctions:

- Suppliers are highly competitive.
- Product features can be clearly specified.
- Suppliers are willing to reduce the margin they earn on this product.
- Suppliers are willing to participate in reverse auctions.

Supply Chain Characteristics that Discourage Reverse Auctions:

- Product is highly complex or requires regular changes in design.
- Product has customized features.
- Long-term strategic relationships are important to buyers and suppliers.
- Switching costs are high.

FIGURE 6-5 Supply chain characteristics and reverse auctions

Auction-Related Services

The growth of eBay and other auction sites has encouraged entrepreneurs to create businesses that provide auction-related services of various kinds. These include escrow services, auction directory and information services, auction software (for both sellers and buyers), and auction consignment services. This section describes each of these new industries that have arisen to meet the needs of auction participants. You will learn about yet another auction-related business, payment-processing services, in Chapter 11.

Auction Escrow Services

A common concern among people bidding in online auctions is the reliability of the sellers. Surveys indicate that as many as 18 percent of all Web auction buyers either do not receive the items they purchased, or find the items to be different from the seller's representation in some significant way. About half of those buyers are unable to resolve their disputes to their satisfaction. When purchasing high-value items, buyers can use an escrow service to protect their interests.

You learned earlier in this chapter that an escrow service is an independent party that holds a buyer's payment until the buyer receives the purchased item and is satisfied that the item is what the seller represented it to be. Some escrow services take delivery of the item from the seller and perform the inspection for the buyer. In such situations, buyers give the escrow service authority to examine. Usually, escrow agents that perform this service are art appraisers, antique appraisers, and the like who are qualified to judge quality, usually with better judgment than the buyer. Escrow services do, however, charge fees ranging from 1 to 10 percent of the item's cost, subject to a minimum fee, typically between $5 and $50. The minimum fee provision can make escrow services too expensive for small purchases. Escrow services that handle Web auction transactions include **Escrow.com**, **eDeposit**, and **Square Trade**. Some of these escrow firms also sell auction buyer's insurance, which can protect buyers from nondelivery and some quality risks. There have been cases of escrow fraud, especially in auctions of high value items. The Better Business Bureau recommends that consumers determine whether an escrow service is licensed and bonded before using it. Consumers can do this by contacting the appropriate licensing agency in the state in which the escrow service is located. The Better Business Bureau recommends avoiding offshore escrow companies entirely.

Wary bidders in low-price auctions (for which the minimum escrow charges would be excessive) do have some other ways to protect themselves. One way is to check the seller's record on the auction site to see how the seller is rated. Also, some Web sites offer lists of auction sellers who have failed to deliver merchandise or who have otherwise cheated bidders in the past. These sites are operated as free services (often by bidders who have been cheated), so they sometimes contain unreliable information and they open and close periodically, but you can use your favorite search engine to locate sites that currently carry such lists.

Auction Directory and Information Services

Another service offered by some firms on the Web is a directory of auctions. Sites such as Auctionguide.com offer guidance for new auction participants and helpful hints and tips for more experienced buyers and sellers along with directories of online auction sites. AuctionBytes is an auction information site that publishes an e-mail newsletter with articles about developments in the online auction industry.

Price Watch is an advertiser-supported site on which those advertisers post their current selling prices for computer hardware, software, and consumer electronics items. Although this monitoring is a retail pricing service designed to help shoppers find the best price on new items, Web auction participants find it can help them with their bidding strategies. PriceSCAN is a similar price-monitoring service that also includes prices on books, movies, music, and sporting goods, in addition to the types of items monitored by Price Watch.

Auction Software

Both auction buyers and sellers can purchase software to help them manage their online auctions. Sellers often run many auctions at the same time. Companies such as AuctionHawk and Vendio sell auction management software and services for both buyers and sellers. For sellers, these companies offer software and services that can help with or automate tasks such as image hosting, advertising, page design, bulk repeatable listings, feedback tracking and management, report tracking, and e-mail management. Using these tools, sellers can create attractive layouts for their pages and manage hundreds of auctions.

For buyers, a number of companies sell auction sniping software. **Sniping software** observes auction progress until the last second or two of the auction clock. Just as the auction is about to expire, the sniping software places a bid high enough to win the auction (unless that bid exceeds a limit set by the sniping software's owner). The act of placing a winning bid at the last second is called a **snipe**. Because sniping software synchronizes its internal clock to the auction site clock and executes its bid with a computer's precision, the software almost always wins out over a human bidder. The first sniping software, named Cricket Jr., was written by David Eccles in 1997. He sells the software on his Cricket Sniping Software site. A number of other sniping software sellers have entered the market—each claiming that its software will outbid other sniping software. Some sites offer sniping services; that is, the sniping software runs on their Web site and customers enter their sniping instructions on that site. Some of these companies offer subscriptions; others use a mixed-revenue model in which they offer some free snipes supported by advertising, but require payment for additional snipes. A good source for current information about the sniping software and services business is the AuctionBytes Web site. The home page of AuctionBytes is shown in Figure 6-6.

auction BYTES The Independent Trade Publication for Online Merchants

Subscribe to our 2 FREE Newsletters!

Google Web AuctionBytes Search

November 23, 2009

Home
Subscribe
Blog
Letters to Editor
EcommerceBytes
Podcasts
Forums
Merchant Directory
PR Service NEW!
AuctionBytes TV
ABU Back Issues

Sponsor

COOL TOOLS

Calendar
eBay Fee Calculator
Collectors' Links
eBay Promo History
Bookshelf
Fraud Resources
Auction Site Fees
Auction Management
Payment Services
Storefronts Chart
Sniping Chart
Email List Hosting
Consignment Services
Drop-Off Store Laws
Ecommerce Resources
Photo Tips
Marketing Inserts
Yellow Pages
Classifieds

AUCTIONBYTES

Our Writers

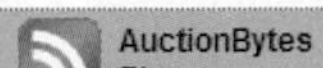

AuctionBytes $100 Best Buy Card Recipient is...Still 7 Left!

Letters to the Editor

eBay Cross Promotion Settings Do Work

Ecommerce Podcasts

Entrepreneur Haralee Weintraub on Getting a Good Night's Sleep

AuctionBytes NewsFlash Headlines

- eBay Search Outage Brings Site to Standstill on Saturday
- Etsy Hires Flickr's John Allspaw to Head Technical Operations
- Online Bidding a Major Factor in Auction of Bernie Madoff Assets
- Interview with eBay on New Cross Merchandising Feature

Industry Press Releases

- Truition Inc. the leading SaaS e-Commerce Software Provider announces acquisition by CDC Software
- Lottay Wish List Survey Forecasts Holiday Shopping Trends for Black Friday and Cyber Monday
- Webstore Free Online Marketplace Aims to Attract Craiglist Followers with Competing Product

Check out the Current Issue of AB-Update Below!

NEW! From the Editor

Read about the AuctionBytes $100 Best Buy gift card giveaway, a new portal for ecommerce industry news, a podcast interview with Greg Fant on eBay's holiday marketing campaign, and Google's brand new Product Listing Ads.

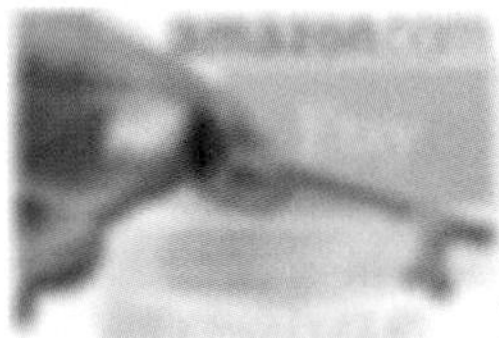

NEW! Survey Shows Sellers' Views on Customer Ownership Vary by Marketplace

AuctionBytes conducted a poll to see what online sellers felt about the issue of customer acquisition on marketplaces such as eBay (Whose Customer Is It, Anyway?). As we suspected, many merchants feel that if a shopper buys from them, the customer belongs to them. However, there was one exception to this rule. Find out what readers think - and what the marketplaces had to say about their policies.

NEW! Going Out of Business Part 1: Shutting Down When There's No Choice

If you've been selling online for over a decade like many individuals and businesses, there may come a time when you decide to close your retail activities. Whether the decision is planned or forced upon you, there are things you need to know in order to close down your business correctly. In today's installment of "Going out of Business," Barbara Weltman tackles, "Shutting Down When There's No Choice."

NEW! Tips on Optimizing Marketplace Listings for Google

News is coming fast and furious about Google's programs for online merchants. Read the latest information on what you can do to optimize your marketplace listings for Google to ensure you are doing everything

Stop Sharing Your Profits!

KEEP 100% OF THE SALE PRICE

Webstore

JOIN TODAY!

FREE REGISTRATION

NO FEES FOR LISTING / END OF SALE

NO FEES FOR BIDDING / BUYING

NO FEES AT ALL!

YOU HAVE NOTHING TO LOSE AND ALL THE PROFIT TO GAIN.

Classifieds

Cool Free Widget For eBay Sellers

98

Watchers

AuctionBytes Hotline

1-877-222-0856

TOLL-FREE

FIGURE 6-6 AuctionBytes home page

Auction Consignment Services

Several entrepreneurs have identified yet another auction-related business that meets the needs of people and small businesses who want to use an online auction, but do not have the skills or the time to become a seller. These companies, called **auction consignment services**, take an item and create an online auction for that item, handle the transaction, and remit the balance of the proceeds after deducting a fee that ranges from 25 to 50 percent of the selling price obtained. Items that do not sell are returned or donated to charity. The main auction consignment businesses include ePowerSellers, iSold It, and USA Auction Drop. Because one key to success in this business is having convenient locations at which customers can drop off their items, all of these companies are planning to open their own stores and franchise stores as rapidly as possible.

All of these auction-related businesses are excellent examples of the second wave of electronic commerce. In the first wave, the online auction business was made possible by the Web. In the second wave, the online auction business has itself created opportunities for even more entirely new types of business.

Summary

In this chapter, you learned how companies are now using the Web to do things that they have never done before, such as creating social networks, using mobile technologies to make sales and increase operational efficiency, operating auction sites, and conducting related businesses.

The Web's ability to bring together geographically dispersed people and organizations that share narrow interests has encouraged the development of virtual communities and social networks. Businesses are creating online communities using social networking features that connect them to their customers and suppliers. A growing number of businesses are exploiting the mobile commerce opportunities presented by smart phones with large screens and high-bandwidth access to the Internet. In the second wave of electronic commerce, individuals are increasingly using social networking sites for personal and business-related interactions. Companies are using internal social networking sites to communicate with employees and coordinate work across various organizational units.

You learned about the key characteristics of the seven major auction types, and learned how firms are using online auctions to sell goods to their customers and buy from their suppliers. Although some specialty sites do conduct significant auction activities, the consumer online auction business is dominated by eBay, at least in the United States. B2B auctions give companies a new and efficient way to dispose of excess inventory, and B2B reverse auctions provide an effective procurement tool under some conditions. A number of businesses offer ancillary services to Web users who participate in online auctions. These businesses include escrow services, auction directories and information sites, auction management software for both sellers and bidders, and auction consignment sites.

Key Terms

Apps
Ascending-price auction
Auction consignment services
Auctioneer
Bid
Bidder
Bulletin board system (BBS)
Consumer-to-business
Descending-price auction
Double auction
Dutch auction
English auction
Escrow service
First-price sealed-bid auction
Group purchasing site (group shopping site)
Idea-based networking
Idea-based virtual communities
Liquidation broker
Lock-in effect
Meetup
Microlending
Minimum bid
Minimum bid increment
Mobile commerce (m-commerce)
Mobile wallet
Monetizing
Online community
Open auction (open-outcry auction)

Open-outcry double auction
Open source software
Participatory journalism
Private valuation
Proxy bid
Reserve price (reserve)
Reverse auction (seller-bid action)
Reverse bid
Sealed-bid auction
Second-price sealed-bid auction
Shill bidder
Short messaging service (SMS)
Snipe
Sniping software
Social networking site
Social shopping
Tweets
Usenet
Usenet newsgroup
Vickrey auction
Virtual community
Virtual learning network
Web community
Winner's curse
Wireless Application Protocol (WAP)
Yankee auction

Review Questions

RQ1. In about 100 words, explain the differences between a social networking Web site and a blog.

RQ2. Identify a product that could be promoted using a social networking site such as Facebook. In about 100 words, explain why your chosen product would be a good candidate for a social networking-based promotion strategy.

RQ3. Successful Web portals have a high degree of stickiness. In about 200 words, explain how a Web portal would increase its stickiness and explain why it would want to do so.

RQ4. In about 100 words, outline the advantages and disadvantages a physician would see in being required to use a smart phone rather than a laptop computer to look up prescription drug information and review patient information.

RQ5. Explain in two or three paragraphs why you think mobile commerce has developed more rapidly in Asia than in the United States.

RQ6. In approximately 100 words, define the term "reserve price" and explain how the use of a reserve price can affect the progress and outcome of an auction.

RQ7. Assume you work in the procurement department of a small aerospace parts manufacturer. Your company builds switches used to control heating and ventilation systems in large buildings. The parts your company buys must meet precise specifications and the parts are not generally interchangeable; that is, your company's engineers must work with your suppliers to design specific parts for particular systems. Your director of purchasing is interested in using online reverse auctions to buy these parts. In approximately 200 words, outline arguments for and against using online reverse auctions in this situation and conclude with a specific recommendation.

RQ8. Some eBay users believe that the use of sniping software is unfair and that eBay should prohibit its use. In an essay of about 200 words, present facts and logical arguments that would convince eBay to prohibit the use of sniping software.

Exercises

E1. Review both the Etsy and the We Love Etsy Web sites. In about 300 words, outline the elements of Etsy's Web site and business philosophy that make it a social networking site in addition to being an online business that sells goods.

E2. Compare the software offered in the Apple Apps for iPhone online store to that offered in one of the other apps stores listed in the Online Companion under Smart Phone App Stores. In about 200 words, present a comparison of the software applications offered in each store. You may also comment on the usability of the online store.

E3. Follow the links in the Online Companion for Auction Consignment Sites to at least two of the sites and become familiar with the services they offer. Prepare a chart that compares the services offered by two of the sites you visit. Include any important factors that a customer would evaluate when deciding which site to use, but be sure to include a comparison of prices, specific services offered, exclusions and limitations on the services, and guarantees, if any. Summarize your findings in a paragraph or two in which you indicate which site you would recommend to a friend.

E4. Midland University, like most metropolitan universities, faces a chronic shortage of parking spaces on campus. Each stakeholder group in the typical university community (these groups include students, faculty, administrators, staff, and visitors) believes its members should have the top priority for parking spaces. You have been assigned to a university task force to study the problem. You decide that an annual online auction of parking spaces conducted on the university's intranet could provide a solution. In about 300 words, describe the elements of an annual online auction for parking spaces at Midland University. Be sure to include provisions for disabled persons and for those university employees who do not have regular access to computers in their typical work environment (such as janitors, physical plant maintenance workers, or gardeners).

Cases

C1. Alibaba.com

In 1995, Jack Ma taught English in Hangzhou, China, a city near the economic center of Shanghai. Ma wanted to get into the business world, so he raised $2000 from relatives and friends to start Chinapage.com, one of the first Chinese online businesses. He followed that experience with a job at the Ministry of Foreign Trade and Economic Cooperation. He grew frustrated with the slow pace of the government bureaucracy and left after a year to start his own company again. He placed an ad on the Internet advertising a language translation service for companies that wanted to do business in China. Within two hours, he had received six e-mailed inquiries. About 60 percent of the Chinese economy is manufacturing, and 90 percent of manufacturing companies are small or medium-sized businesses. Ma began collecting information from Chinese manufacturing companies that wanted to do business internationally. He translated and organized the information, then posted it on a B2B Web portal site he named Alibaba.com.

Alibaba.com has always concentrated on small and midsized businesses (SMBs). Ma believed that global companies spend most of their efforts on doing business with large companies. He sees China (and the rest of Asia) as having a different economic structure than the United States or Europe, where the economies are dominated by large companies. Ma believes that Alibaba.com's true opportunities lie in connecting SMBs around the world with SMBs in China.

He argues that SMBs seldom have any sales channels outside of their own country. To compensate, SMBs must travel extensively to meet suppliers and customers at exhibitions or trade fairs. Ma believes that Alibaba.com offers SMBs a reasonably priced alternative.

Foreign companies interested in buying from Chinese suppliers must register on Alibaba.com (buyer registration is free) before they can access the site's supplier database. Alibaba.com charges Chinese companies a membership fee of several thousand dollars for translating and listing their information. The site also lists foreign suppliers. These suppliers can list a small number of items at no charge, however, most choose to pay a small fee that pays for a credit check and allows them to be listed as TrustPass members on the site. The TrustPass designation provides assurance to Chinese companies that want to buy from these suppliers. By 2001, more than 1 million companies had registered with Alibaba.com. In 2003, the company reported its first profitable year, with a net income of $12 million. Since then, the company has grown steadily and continues to be profitable. Many of Alibaba.com's registered members are happy with the results they obtain, as indicated by the annual membership renewal rate, which exceeds 70 percent.

Alibaba.com, like all portal sites, suffered a setback during the 2001–2002 time period, but its fee-based revenue model allowed it to recover more quickly than portals that were dependent on advertising revenue. The company sees future growth in the continued expansion of trade between Chinese manufacturers and the rest of the world. Ma is also optimistic about the portal's potential for helping Chinese businesses connect with other Chinese businesses.

Required:

1. Alibaba.com was an early entrant into the B2B portal market in China. In about 100 words, explain how this might have created a lock-in effect, especially given the types of businesses the site attracts.
2. Alibaba.com currently charges foreign sellers an annual fee of about $400 for a TrustPass membership, but Chinese companies pay $8000 or more for their annual listings as China Gold Suppliers. In about 200 words, explain why the site has different listing charges for the two types of members and critically evaluate this practice.
3. You learned in Chapter 5 that large companies, such as General Electric and Sears, often require suppliers to follow specific rules if they want to do business (such as using EDI or even a specific EDI VAN). Alibaba.com currently focuses on connecting SMBs with each other. In about 200 words, discuss opportunities that might exist for Alibaba.com to become an intermediary in relationships between Chinese SMBs and large global companies such as General Electric and Sears.
4. In 2003, Alibaba.com launched Taobao.com to compete in the general consumer online auction market against eBay in China. After four years of an intensive and expensive battle, eBay withdrew from China completely. In about 200 words, describe the advantages Alibaba.com might have had over eBay in this new market, then describe the advantages eBay might have had over Alibaba.com. Be sure to include a discussion of lock-in effects where appropriate.
5. In 2005, Yahoo! paid $1 billion for a 40 percent interest in Alibaba.com. Yahoo! was interested in the company's Taobao.com auction site because Yahoo! had not been as successful as it would have liked in developing its own Chinese auction site. However, Yahoo! was also interested in using Alibaba.com's strong reputation in China to help it compete with Baidu.com, the top Chinese search engine site. In about 200 words, describe the ways in

which Alibaba.com's reputation could help Yahoo! compete more effectively as a search engine and Web portal in China.

Note: Your instructor might assign you to a group to complete this case and might ask you to prepare a formal presentation of your results to your class.

C2. Old Metamora

Betty Shriver is the owner of Betty's Crystal, a small shop that sells collectible glass figurines. Betty's shop carries many items that she purchased from estate sales and regional auctions, but the shop also sells new crystal figurines from manufacturers such as Baccarat, Lalique, Orrefors, and Swarovski. The shop is located in Metamora, Indiana, which is a popular tourist destination for weekend travelers in the Midwest. The town of Old Metamora is a small historic area in a rural setting that is less than a day's drive from seven major metropolitan areas: Chicago, Cincinnati, Columbus, Detroit, Indianapolis, Louisville, and St. Louis.

The shop is very busy on weekends and during the spring and summer months when tourists flock to Old Metamora. In the early fall, the tourist traffic slows considerably, and in the winter months, the town becomes almost deserted. Two years ago, Betty began to pick up extra business during the off season by auctioning items on eBay. Not only did the auctions help keep inventory moving during the slow months, but Betty found that she was able to carry a wider selection of items in the store. In the past, she would see unusual items at estate sales and auctions that she feared would not sell quickly in the shop. Now Betty knows that any item that does not sell in the shop can be auctioned online quite easily. Another unexpected benefit of participating in online auctions is that Betty developed relationships with regular buyers of crystal figurines and with people who run collectibles stores in other parts of the country. Every auction involves at least two e-mails (one to confirm the final bid and another to confirm the payment). Many successful bidders also send e-mail messages to Betty when they receive the item with questions about the item, or just to thank Betty for sending the item so quickly. Some of these e-mail exchanges continue with discussions related to crystal figurines and other collectible items.

Betty's online auction experiences prompted her to consider expanding the online portion of her business. She has heard (from other shop owners) that eBay allows people to create online stores within the eBay site and that Amazon.com offers a similar service that lists seller's items on Amazon.com's regular product pages. She is also interested in creating a Web site that contains photos and descriptions of popular crystal figurines with additional information about how they are made. Betty also wants to include a list of figurines that are no longer manufactured (which makes them more valuable) and a guide to buying collectible crystal figurines that could help her customers and bidders on her auctions make more informed decisions as they add to their collections. She believes that such a site could attract a large number of people interested in crystal figurines. She wants to find ways to direct these site visitors to her auctions and her proposed Web store. Betty has hired you as a consultant to build on her ideas and to help her develop an expansion strategy for her online business activities.

Required:

1. Search for information about Amazon Marketplace and eBay Stores on the Web and in your library that will help you make a recommendation to Betty regarding which alternative would provide the best avenue for her online business expansion. Support your recommendation with relevant facts, including specific costs of operating each type of store and specific benefits that Betty could gain by using one or the other. Summarize your recommendation and supporting facts in a report to Betty of 400 words.

2. Outline a strategy that Betty could implement using a social networking site such as Facebook that might direct traffic to her Web site, to her auctions on eBay, and to her products for sale on Amazon.com. For each element in the strategy, provide an explanation of how it would help achieve Betty's goals. Summarize the social networking promotion strategy in a report to Betty of about 500 words.

Note: Your instructor might assign you to a group to complete this case and might ask you to prepare a formal presentation of your results to your class.

For Further Study and Research

Ankeny, J. 2009. "NTT DoCoMo Rolling Out Mobile Payments Program," *Fierce Mobile Content,* July 2. (http://www.fiercemobilecontent.com/story/ntt-docomo-rolling-out-mobile-payments-program/2009-07-02)

Belson, K., R. Hof, and B. Elgin. 2001. "How Yahoo! Japan Beat eBay at Its Own Game," *Business Week,* June 4, 58.

boyd, d. and N. Ellison. (2007). "Social Network Sites: Definition, History, and Scholarship," *Journal of Computer-Mediated Communication,* 13(1). (http://jcmc.indiana.edu/vol13/issue1/boyd.ellison.html)

Borzo, J. 2004. "Using Online Networking, Job Seekers Turn Friendship into Employment," *The Wall Street Journal,* September 13, R14.

Brandel, M. 2009. "Start Connecting With Mobile Customers," *Computerworld,* October 5, 19–22.

Breckenridge, M. 2008. "Old Meets New at Etsy," *Akron Beacon Journal,* March 6, D1.

Burnham, K. 2009. "Scottrade: The Social Enterprise," *CIO,* November 1, 18.

Business Wire. 2008. "LookSmart Announces Final Results of Tender Offer for its Common Stock," February 21.

Cassady, R. 1967. *Auctions and Auctioneering.* Berkeley, CA: University of California Press.

Chang, A. 2003. "Hospitals Auction Nursing Shifts Online," *The Boston Globe,* December 28, A28.

Chen, B. 2009. "Verizon Drafts Developers into Mobile Software War on Apple," *Wired News,* July 14. (http://www.wired.com/gadgetlab/2009/07/smartphone-war/)

Chen, K. and K. Qiu Haixu. 2004. "Chinese E-Commerce Sites Allow Small Firms to Reach Wider Base," *The Wall Street Journal,* February 25, A12.

Cheng, A. and J. Thaw. 2005. "Yahoo! Raises Stakes Higher in China With Alibaba Deal," *The Seattle Times,* August 22, C4.

Clark, N. 2009. "Facebook Heads Towards Profit," *The Independent,* September 16. (http://www.independent.co.uk/news/business/news/facebook-heads-towards-profit-1788430.html)

Cohen, A. 2001. "The Sniper King," *On Magazine,* May.

ContactlessNews. 2008. "StarHub to Pilot Mobile Wallet Based on Japan's Osaifu-Keitai Service," June 18. (http://www.contactlessnews.com/2008/06/18/starhub-to-pilot-mobile-wallet-based-on-japans-osaifu-keitai-service)

Covel, S. 2008. "Online Video Contest Gets People Talking," *The Wall Street Journal,* March 6, B5.

Credit Union Management. 2007. "Focus on Microlending: Kiva is People Helping People," May, 12.

Dobrzynski, J. 2000. "F.B.I. Opens Investigation of eBay Bids," *The New York Times,* June 7, 1.

Doebele, J. 2005. "Alibaba.com: Standing Up to eBay," *Forbes.com,* April 18. (http://www.forbes.com/business/forbes/2005/0418/050.html)

The Economist. 1997. "Going, Going..." May 31, 61.

The Economist. 2001. "We Have Lift-Off." February 3, 69–71.

Ferraro, N. 2008. "Lending & Philanthropy 2.0," *InformationWeek,* February 4, 40.

Flandez, R. 2008. "Building an Online Community of Loyal and Vocal Users," *The Wall Street Journal,* March 6, B5.

Ghawi, D. and G. Schneider. 2004. "New Approaches to Online Procurement," *Proceedings of the Academy of Information and Management Sciences,* 8(2), October, 25–28.

Gilbert, J. and A. Kerwin. 1999. "Newspapers Carve Slice of Auction Pie," *Advertising Age,* 70(26), June 21, 32–34.

Gross, N. 1999. "Building Global Communities: How Business Is Partnering with Sites that Draw Together Like-Minded Consumers," *Business Week,* March 22, EB42.

Hafner, K. 2004. "With Internet Fraud Up Sharply, eBay Attracts Vigilantes," *The New York Times,* March 20, A1.

Hanlon, P. and J. Hawkins. 2008. "Expand Your Brand Community Online," *Advertising Age,* January 7, 14–15.

Intrator, Y. 2005. "The Trouble With Portals," *CIO Magazine Online,* May 9.

Kawakami, S. 2003. "China's Visionary B2B," *J@pan Inc.,* May, 14–16.

Keegan, V. 2008. "Entrepreneurs Come Out of the Webwork," *The Guardian,* February 28, 4.

Kennedy, J. 1998. "Radio Daze," *Technology Review,* 101(6), November–December, 68–71.

Kesmodel, D. 2005. "Beyond eBay: Small E-tailers Discover Life Outside the Big Online Marketplaces," *The Wall Street Journal,* July 18, R8.

Konrad, R. 2005. "eBay Losing Allure for Some Entrepreneurs," *Associated Press Financial Wire,* June 26.

Lee, J. 2003. "U.S. and States Join to Fight Internet Auction Fraud," *The New York Times,* May 1. (http://www.nytimes.com/2003/05/01/technology/01ONLI.html)

MacMillan, D., P. Burrows, and S. Ante. 2009. "The App Economy," *Businessweek,* November 2, 44–49.

Mello, J. 2006. "Social Networking Goes E-Commerce," *E-Commerce Times,* February 22. (http://www.ecommercetimes.com/story/48989.html)

Metz, C. 2004. "Social Networking: Make Contact," *PC Magazine,* 23(1), January 20, 131–136.

Mieszkowski, K. 2005. "Steal This Bookmark! Tagging Lets You See What Other People Are Reading and Thinking," *Salon.com,* February 8. (http://www.salon.com/tech/feature/2005/02/08/tagging/index.html)

Miller, K. 2007. "An eBay for the Arts and Crafts Set," *Business Week,* July 23, 70.

Norris, F. 2004. "Google's Offering Proves Stock Auctions Can Really Work," *The New York Times,* August 23, C6.

Petersen, A. 1999. "Some Places to Go When You Want to Feel Right at Home: Communities Focus on People Who Need People," *The Wall Street Journal,* January 6, B6.

Petrecca, L. and B. Snyder. 1998. "Auction Universe Puts in $10 Mil Bid for Customers," *Advertising Age,* 43(8), October 26, 8.

Purchasing. 2001. "What Top Supply Execs Say About Auctions," 130(12), June 21, S2–S3.

Quan, J. 1999. "Risky Business," *Rolling Stone,* March 4, 91–92.

Rheingold, H. 1993. *The Virtual Community: Homesteading on the Electronic Frontier.* New York: HarperCollins.

Rheingold, H. 2002. *Smart Mobs.* Cambridge, MA: Basic.

Robins, W. 2000. "Auctions.com Now a Dot-Goner," *Editor & Publisher,* August 28, 6.

Sacco, A. 2009. "Paging Dr. BlackBerry: Smartphones Deliver EKGs for Faster Diagnoses," *CIO,* November 1, 15–16.

Schonfeld, E. 2002. "eBay's Secret Ingredient," *Business 2.0,* 3(3), March, 52–58.

Schuyler, N. 2000. "Going ... Going ... Gotcha!" *PC World,* October 1, 181.

Seelye, K. 2005. "Why Newspapers Are Betting on Audience Participation," *The New York Times,* July 4, C2.

Spanbauer, S. 2008. "The Right Social Network for You," *PC World,* April, 105–110.

Stefano, T. 2007. "Social Networking: A Web 2.0 Revolution," *E-Commerce Times,* March 30. (http://www.ecommercetimes.com/story/56576.html)

Steiner, I. 2003. "Auction Drop-Off Stores Offer Consignment Services to Non-eBayers," *Auction-bytes Update,* November 2. (http://www.auctionbytes.com/cab/abu/y203/m11/abu0106/s02)

Tedeschi, B. 2000. "Creating Marketplaces for Business-to-Business Transactions," *The New York Times,* January 24, C10.

Tedeschi, B. 2005. "Blogging While Browsing, But Not Buying," *The New York Times,* July 4, C3.

Tedeschi, B. 2006. "Like Shopping? Social Networking? Try Social Shopping," *The New York Times,* September 11. (http://www.nytimes.com/2006/09/11/11ecom.html)

Thaler, R. 1994. *The Winner's Curse: Paradoxes and Anomalies of Economic Life.* Princeton, NJ: Princeton University Press.

Todras-Whitehall, E. 2005. "'Folksonomy' Carries Classifieds Beyond SWF and 'For Sale,'" *The New York Times,* October 5. (http://www.nytimes.com/2005/10/05/technology/techspecial/05ethan.html)

Tomchin, E. 2009. : "EBay Alternatives Review: EBid, OnlineAuction and Overstock Auctions," *AuctionBytes,* March 1. (http://www.auctionbytes.com/cab/abu/y209/m03/abu0234/s03)

Tugend, A. 2009. "Losing Out After Winning an Online Auction," *The New York Times,* October 24. (http://www.nytimes.com/2009/10/24/technology/24shortcuts.html)

Vara, V. 2007. "Facebook Gets Help From Its Friends," *The Wall Street Journal,* June 22, B1–2.

Vickrey, W. 1961. "Counterspeculation, Auctions, and Competitive Sealed Tenders," *Journal of Finance,* 16(1), March, 8–37.

Wagner, M. 2009. *Smartphone App: What the Doctor Ordered.* Manhasset, NY: InformationWeek.

Wang, S. 1999. "Analyzing Agents for Electronic Commerce," *Information Systems Management,* 16(1), Winter, 40–48.

Wingfield, N. 2004. "Taking on eBay," *The Wall Street Journal,* September 13, R10.

Wireless Federation. 2009. "NTT DoCoMo's Credit Payment Subscriptions Reach 10 Million Mark," August 26. (http://wirelessfederation.com/news/17894-ntt-docomos-credit-payment-subscriptions-reach-10mn-mark/)

Zimmerman, E. 2007. "Investing in the Women of Ghana," *FSB: Fortune Small Business,* 17(4), May, 101–102.

CHAPTER 7

THE ENVIRONMENT OF ELECTRONIC COMMERCE: LEGAL, ETHICAL, AND TAX ISSUES

LEARNING OBJECTIVES

In this chapter, you will learn about:

- Laws that govern electronic commerce activities
- Laws that govern the use of intellectual property by online businesses
- Online crime, terrorism, and warfare
- Ethics issues that arise for companies conducting electronic commerce
- Conflicts between companies' desire to collect and use data about their customers and the privacy rights of those customers
- Taxes that are levied on electronic commerce activities

INTRODUCTION

In 1999, Dell Computer and Micron Electronics (now doing business as Micron Technology), two companies that sold personal computers through their Web sites, agreed to settle U.S. Federal Trade Commission (FTC) charges that they had disseminated misleading advertising to their existing and potential customers. The advertising in question was for computer leasing plans that both companies had offered on their Web sites. The ads stated the price of the computer along with a monthly payment. Unfortunately for Dell and

Micron, stating the monthly payment without disclosing full details of the lease plan is a violation of the Consumer Leasing Act of 1976. This law is implemented through a federal regulation that was written and is updated periodically by the Federal Reserve Board. This regulation, called Regulation M, was designed to require banks and other lenders to fully disclose the terms of leases so that consumers would have enough information to make informed financing choices when leasing cars, boats, furniture, and other goods.

Both Dell and Micron had included the required information on their Web pages, but FTC investigators noted that important details of the leasing plans, such as the number of payments and the fees due at the signing of the lease, were placed in a small typeface at the bottom of a long Web page. A consumer who wanted to determine the full cost of leasing a computer would need to scroll through a number of densely filled screens to obtain enough information to make the necessary calculations.

In the settlement, both companies agreed to provide consumers with clear, readable, and understandable information in their lease advertising. The companies also agreed to record-keeping and federal monitoring activities designed to ensure their compliance with the terms of the settlement.

Dell and Micron are computer manufacturers. It apparently did not occur to them that they needed to become experts in Regulation M, generally considered to be a banking regulation. Companies that do business on the Web expose themselves, often unwittingly, to liabilities that arise from today's business environment. That environment includes laws and ethical considerations that may be different from those with which the business is familiar. In the case of Dell and Micron, they were unfamiliar with the laws and ethics of the banking industry. The banking industry has a different culture than that of the computer industry—it is unlikely that a bank advertising manager would have made such a mistake.

As you will learn in this chapter, Dell and Micron are by no means the only Web businesses that have run afoul of laws and regulations. As new and existing companies open online operations, they become subject to unfamiliar laws and different ethical frameworks much more rapidly than in the physical world.

THE LEGAL ENVIRONMENT OF ELECTRONIC COMMERCE

Businesses that operate on the Web must comply with the same laws and regulations that govern the operations of all businesses. If they do not, they face the same penalties—including fines, reparation payments, court-imposed dissolution, and even jail time for officers and owners—that any business faces.

Businesses operating on the Web face two additional complicating factors as they try to comply with the law. First, the Web extends a company's reach beyond traditional boundaries. As you learned in Chapter 1, a business that uses the Web immediately becomes an international business. Thus, a company can become subject to many more laws more quickly than a traditional brick-and-mortar business based in one specific physical location. Second, the Web increases the speed and efficiency of business communications. As you learned in Chapters 3 and 4, customers often have much more interactive and complex relationships with online merchants than they do with traditional merchants. Further, the Web creates a network of customers who often have significant levels of interaction with each other. Web businesses that violate the law or breach ethical standards can face rapid and intense reactions from many customers and other stakeholders who become aware of the businesses' activities.

In this section, you will learn about the issues of borders, jurisdiction, and Web site content and how these factors affect a company's ability to conduct electronic commerce. You will also learn about legal issues that arise when the Web is used in the commission of crimes, terrorist acts, and even the conduct of war.

Borders and Jurisdiction

Territorial borders in the physical world serve a useful purpose in traditional commerce: They mark the range of culture and reach of applicable laws very clearly. When people travel across international borders, they are made aware of the transition in many ways. For example, exiting one country and entering another usually requires a formal examination of documents, such as passports and visas. In addition, both the language and the currency usually change upon entry into a new country. Each of these experiences, and countless others, are manifestations of the differences in legal rules and cultural customs in the two countries. In the physical world, geographic boundaries almost always coincide with legal and cultural boundaries. The limits of acceptable ethical behavior and the laws that are adopted in a geographic area are the result of the influences of the area's dominant culture. The relationships among a society's culture, laws, and ethical standards appear in Figure 7-1, which shows that culture affects laws directly and indirectly through its effect on ethical standards. The figure also shows that laws and ethical standards affect each other.

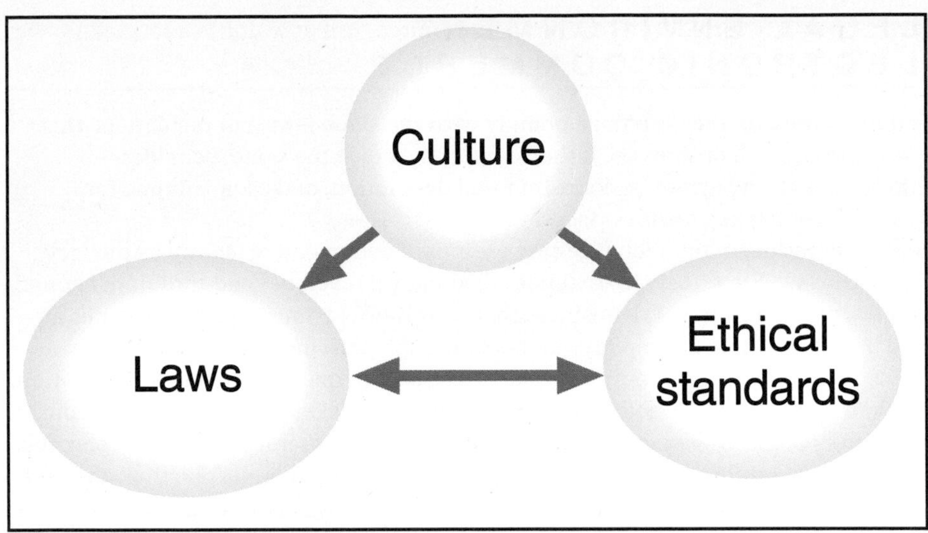

FIGURE 7-1 Culture helps determine laws and ethical standards

The geographic boundaries on culture are logical; for most of our history, slow methods of transportation and conflicts among various nations have prevented people from travelling great distances to learn about other cultures. Both restrictions have changed in recent years, however, and now people can travel easily from one country to another within many geographic regions. One example is the European Union (EU), which allows free movement within the EU for citizens of member countries. Most of the EU countries (Great Britain being a notable exception) now use a common currency (the euro) instead of their former individual currencies (for example, French francs, German marks, and Italian lire). Legal scholars define the relationship between geographic boundaries and legal boundaries in terms of four elements: power, effects, legitimacy, and notice.

Power

Power is a form of control over physical space and the people and objects that reside in that space, and is a defining characteristic of statehood. For laws to be effective, a government must be able to enforce them. Effective enforcement requires the power both to exercise physical control over residents, if necessary, and to impose sanctions on those who violate the law. The ability of a government to exert control over a person or corporation is called **jurisdiction**.

Laws in the physical world do not apply to people who are not located in or do not own assets in the geographic area that created those particular laws. For example, the United States cannot enforce its copyright laws on a citizen of Japan who is doing business in Japan and owns no assets in the United States. Any assertion of power by the United States over such a Japanese citizen would conflict with the Japanese government's recognized authority over its citizens. Japanese citizens who bring goods into the United States to sell, however, are subject to applicable U.S. copyright laws. A Japanese Web site that offers delivery of goods into the United States is, similarly, subject to applicable U.S. laws.

The level of power asserted by a government is limited to that which is accepted by the culture that exists within its geographic boundaries. Ideally, geographic boundaries, cultural groupings, and legal structures all coincide. When they do not, internal strife and civil wars can erupt.

Effects

Laws in the physical world are grounded in the relationship between physical proximity and the **effects**, or impact, of a person's behavior. Personal or corporate actions have stronger effects on people and things that are nearby than on those that are far away. Government-provided trademark protection is a good example of this. For instance, the Italian government can provide and enforce trademark protection for a business named Casa di Baffi located in Rome. The effects of another restaurant using the same name are strongest in Rome, somewhat less in geographic areas close to Rome, and even less in other parts of Italy. That is, the effects diminish as geographic distance increases. If someone were to open a restaurant in Kansas City and call it Casa di Baffi, the restaurant in Rome would experience few, if any, negative effects from the use of its trademarked name in Kansas City because it would be so far away and because so few people would be potential customers of both restaurants. Thus, the effects of the trademark infringement would be controlled by Italian law because of the limited range within which such an infringement has an effect.

The characteristics of laws are determined by the local culture's acceptance or rejection of various kinds of effects. For example, certain communities in the United States require that houses be built on lots that are at least 5 acres. Other communities prohibit outdoor advertising of various kinds. The local cultures in these communities make the effects of such restrictions acceptable.

Once businesses begin operating online, they found that traditional effects-based measures did not apply as well and that the laws based on these measures did not work well either. For example, France has a law that prohibits the sale of Nazi memorabilia. The effects of this law were limited to people in France and they considered it reasonable. U.S. laws do not include a similar prohibition because U.S. culture makes a different tradeoff between the value of memorabilia (in general) and the negative cultural memory of Nazism. When U.S.-based online auction sites began hosting auctions of Nazi memorabilia, those sites were in compliance with U.S. laws. However, because of the international nature of the Web, these auctions were available to people around the world, including residents of France. In other words, the effects of U.S. culture and law were being felt in France. The French government ordered Yahoo! Auctions to stop these auctions. Yahoo! argued that it was in compliance with U.S. law, but the French government insisted that the effects of those Yahoo! auctions extended to France and thus violated French law. To avoid protracted legal actions over the jurisdiction issue, Yahoo! decided that it would no longer carry such auctions.

Legitimacy

Most people agree that the legitimate right to create and enforce laws derives from the mandate of those who are subject to those laws. In 1970, the **United Nations** passed a resolution that affirmed this idea of governmental legitimacy. The resolution made clear that the people residing within a set of recognized geographic boundaries are the ultimate source of legitimate legal authority for people and actions within those boundaries. Thus, **legitimacy** is the idea that those subject to laws should have some role in formulating them.

Some cultures allow their governments to operate with a high degree of autonomy and unquestioned authority. China and Singapore are countries in which national culture permits the government to exert high levels of unchecked authority. Other cultures, such as those of the Scandinavian countries, place strict limits on governmental authority.

The levels of authority and autonomy with which governments of various countries operate varies significantly from one country to another. Online businesses must be ready to deal with a wide variety of regulations and levels of enforcement of those regulations as they expand their businesses to other countries. This can be difficult for smaller businesses that operate on the Web.

Notice

Physical boundaries are a convenient and effective way to announce the ending of one legal or cultural system and the beginning of another. The physical boundary, when crossed, provides **notice** that one set of rules has been replaced by a different set of rules. Notice is the expression of such a change in rules. People can obey and perceive a law or cultural norm as fair only if they are notified of its existence. Borders provide this notice in the physical world. The legal systems of most countries include a concept called constructive notice. People receive **constructive notice** that they have become subject to new laws and cultural norms when they cross an international border, even if they are not specifically warned of the changed laws and norms by a sign or a border guard's statement. Thus, ignorance of the law is not a sustainable defense, even in a new and unfamiliar jurisdiction.

This concept presents particular problems for online businesses, because they may not know that customers from another country are accessing their Web sites. Thus, the concept of notice—even constructive notice—does not translate very well to online business. The relationship between physical geographic boundaries and legal boundaries in terms of these four elements is summarized in Figure 7-2.

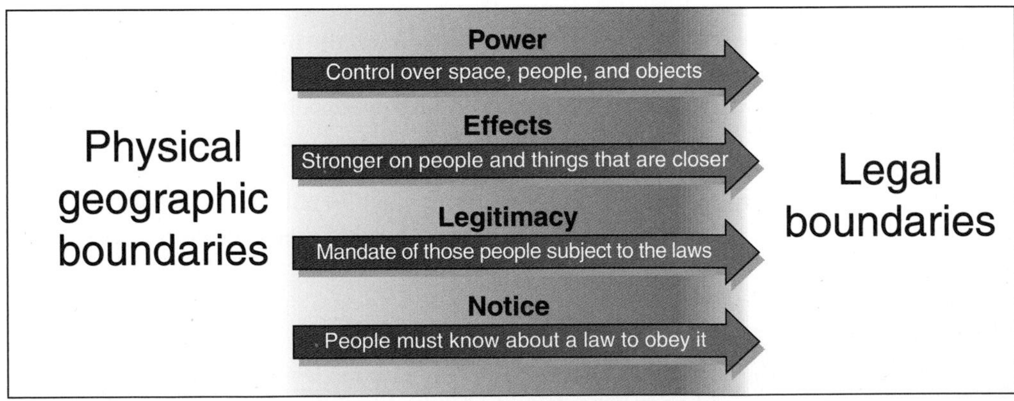

FIGURE 7-2 Physical geographic boundaries lead to legal boundaries

Jurisdiction on the Internet

The tasks of defining, establishing, and asserting jurisdiction are much more difficult on the Internet than they are in the physical world, mainly because traditional geographic boundaries do not exist. For example, a Swedish company that engages in electronic commerce could have a Web site that is entirely in English and a URL that ends in ".com," thus not indicating to customers that it is a Swedish firm. The server that hosts this company's Web page could be in Canada, and the people who maintain the Web site might work from their homes in Australia. If a Mexican citizen buys a product from the Swedish firm and is unhappy with the goods received, that person might want to file a lawsuit against the seller firm. However, the world's physical border-based systems of law and jurisdiction do not help this Mexican citizen determine where to file the lawsuit. The Internet does not provide anything like the obvious international boundary lines in the physical world. Thus, the four considerations that work so well in the physical world—power, effects, legitimacy, and notice—do not translate very well to the virtual world of electronic commerce.

Governments that want to enforce laws regarding business conduct on the Internet must establish jurisdiction over that conduct. A **contract** is a promise or set of promises between two or more legal entities—people or corporations—that provides for an exchange of value (goods, services, or money) between or among them. If either party to a contract does not comply with the terms of the contract, the other party can sue for failure to comply, which is called **breach of contract**. Persons and corporations that engage in business are also expected to exercise due care and not violate laws that prohibit specific actions (such as trespassing, libel, or professional malpractice). A **tort** is an intentional or negligent action (other than breach of contract) taken by a legal entity that causes harm to another legal entity. People or corporations that wish to enforce their rights based on either contract or tort law must file their claims in courts with jurisdiction to hear their cases. A court has **sufficient jurisdiction** to hear a matter if it has both subject-matter jurisdiction and personal jurisdiction.

Subject-Matter Jurisdiction

Subject-matter jurisdiction is a court's authority to decide a particular type of dispute. For example, in the United States, federal courts have subject-matter jurisdiction over issues governed by federal law (such as bankruptcy, copyright, patent, and federal tax matters), and state courts have subject-matter jurisdiction over issues governed by state laws (such as professional licensing and state tax matters). If the parties to a contract are both located in the same state, a state court has subject-matter jurisdiction over disputes that arise from the terms of that contract. The rules for determining whether a court has subject-matter jurisdiction are clear and easy to apply. Few disputes arise over subject-matter jurisdiction.

Personal Jurisdiction

Personal jurisdiction is, in general, determined by the residence of the parties. A court has personal jurisdiction over a case if the defendant is a resident of the state in which the court is located. In such cases, the determination of personal jurisdiction is straightforward. However, an out-of-state person or corporation can also voluntarily submit to the jurisdiction of a particular state court by agreeing to do so in writing or by taking certain actions in the state.

One of the most common ways that people voluntarily submit to a jurisdiction is by signing a contract that includes a statement, known as a **forum selection clause**, that the contract will be enforced according to the laws of a particular state. That state then has personal jurisdiction over the parties who signed the contract regarding any enforcement issue that arises from the terms of that contract. Figure 7-3 shows a typical forum selection clause that might be used on a Web site.

> These terms of use shall be governed by and construed in accordance with the laws of the State of Washington, without regard to its conflict of laws rules. Any legal action arising out of this Agreement shall be litigated and enforced under the laws of the State of Washington. In addition, you agree to submit to the jurisdiction of the courts of the State of Washington, and that any legal action pursued by you shall be within the exclusive jurisdiction of the courts of King County in the State of Washington.

FIGURE 7-3 A typical forum selection clause

In the United States, individual states have laws that can create personal jurisdiction for their courts. The details of these laws, called **long-arm statutes**, vary from state to state, but generally create personal jurisdiction over nonresidents who transact business or commit tortious acts in the state. For example, suppose that an Arizona resident drives recklessly while in California and, as a result, causes a collision with another vehicle that is driven by a California resident. Due to the driver's tortious behavior in the state of California, the Arizona resident can expect to be called into a California court. In other words, California's long-arm statute gives its courts personal jurisdiction over the matter.

Businesses should be aware of jurisdictional considerations when conducting electronic commerce over state and international lines. In most states, the extent to which these laws apply to companies doing business over the Internet is unclear. Because these procedural laws were written before electronic commerce existed, their application to Internet transactions continues to evolve as more and more disputes arise from online commercial transactions. The trend in this evolving law is that the more business activities a company conducts in a state, the more likely it is that a court will assert personal jurisdiction over that company through the application of a long-arm statute.

One exception to the general rule for determining personal jurisdiction occurs in the case of tortious acts. A business can commit a tortious act by selling a product that causes harm to a buyer. The tortious act can be a **negligent tort**, in which the seller unintentionally provides a harmful product, or it can be an **intentional tort**, in which the seller knowingly or recklessly causes injury to the buyer. The most common business-related intentional torts involve defamation, misrepresentation, fraud, and theft of trade secrets. Although case law is rapidly developing in this area also, courts tend to invoke their respective states' long-arm statutes much more readily in the case of tortious acts than in breach of contract cases. If the matter involves an intentional tort or a criminal act, courts will assert jurisdiction more liberally.

Jurisdiction in International Commerce

Jurisdiction issues that arise in international business are even more complex than the rules governing personal jurisdiction across state lines within the United States. The exercise of jurisdiction across international borders is governed by treaties between the countries engaged in the dispute. Some of the treaties that the United States has signed with other countries provide specific determinations of jurisdiction for disputes that might arise. However, in most matters, U.S. courts determine personal jurisdiction for foreign companies and people in much the same way that these courts interpret the long-arm statutes in domestic matters. Non-U.S. corporations and individuals can be sued in U.S. courts if they conduct business or commit tortious acts in the United States. Similarly, foreign courts can enforce decisions against U.S. corporations or individuals through the U.S. court system if those courts can establish jurisdiction over the matter.

Courts asked to enforce the laws of other nations sometimes follow a principle called **judicial comity**, which means that they voluntarily enforce other countries' laws or judgments out of a sense of comity, or friendly civility. However, most courts are reluctant to serve as forums for international disputes. Also, courts are designed to deal with weighing evidence and making findings of right and wrong. International disputes often require diplomacy and the weighing of costs and benefits. Courts are not designed to do cost–benefit evaluations and cannot engage in negotiation and diplomacy. Thus, courts (especially U.S. courts) prefer to have the executive branch of the government (primarily the State Department) negotiate international agreements and resolve international disputes.

The difficulties of operating in multiple countries are faced by many large companies that do business online. For example, eBay, which had struggled to compete in China for many years, finally closed its operations in the country in 2006. eBay entered China in 2003 with a $30 million investment. In subsequent years, it poured another $250 million into acquisitions and advertising in China. But the effort to compete effectively against Alibaba.com's TaoBao consumer auction unit failed. Some observers believe that a Chinese cultural tendency to favor home-grown online services was primarily to blame for eBay's failure. But many others noted that the Chinese government made it difficult for eBay to operate in China by passing laws that favored companies that were majority-owned by Chinese entities and that blocked eBay's PayPal unit from operating in China. Some have even accused the Chinese government of intentionally blocking access to eBay's site for a few minutes each day so that Chinese competitors (some of which are owned, in part or completely, by the Chinese government) would appear to be more reliable. Because eBay was a foreign company, it was at a considerable disadvantage regarding government regulation and many have argued that this disadvantage was a larger factor in its failure than cultural issues.

Jurisdictional issues are complex and change rapidly. Any business that intends to conduct business online with customers or vendors in other countries should consult an attorney who is well versed in issues of international jurisdiction. However, there are a number of resources online that can be useful to nonlawyers who want to do preliminary investigation of a legal topic such as jurisdiction. The Harvard Law School's **Berkman Center for Internet & Society** Web site includes links to many current Internet-related legal issues. The **UCLA Online Institute for Cyberspace Law and Policy** contains an archive of legal reference materials published between 1995 and 2002, important years in the development of online law.

Conflict of Laws

In the United States, business is governed by federal laws, state laws, and local laws. Sometimes, these laws address the same issues in different ways. Lawyers call this situation a **conflict of laws**. Since online businesses usually serve broad markets that span many localities and many states, they generally look to federal laws for guidance. On occasion, this can lead to problems with state and local laws.

One online business that faced a serious conflict of laws problem was the direct wine sales industry. Most U.S. states have heavily regulated all types of alcoholic beverage sales since the repeal of Prohibition in 1933. The U.S. Constitution's Commerce Clause prohibits the states from passing laws that interfere with interstate commerce. However, the states do have the right to regulate matters pertaining to the health and welfare of their citizens. Under this right, most states have laws that require alcoholic beverages be sold through a regulated system of producers, wholesalers, and retailers. Some states allowed producers (such as wineries) to sell directly to the public, but only within that state. When online wine stores wanted to sell their products across state lines, they encountered these laws. Some states allowed the sales, others allowed the sales if the online store delivered to a licensed retailer in the destination state, and some states prohibited all direct sales. This situation resulted in a classic conflict of laws. State laws regulated the sale of alcoholic beverages in the interest of the health and welfare of the state's citizens, yet those same laws gave in-state producers an advantage over out-of-state producers (in some states, in-state producers could sell direct without adding the markup of a retailer; in other states, out-of-state producers could not compete at all). When a state law gives an in-state business an advantage over an out-of-state business, the free flow of interstate commerce is impeded and, in general, the U.S. Constitution's Commerce Clause is violated.

For years, the online wine industry worked to find a way to resolve these issues with the states, but did not have much success. Finally, wineries filed suit on the Commerce Clause violation issue. In 2005, the U.S. Supreme Court voted 5–4 to strike down Michigan and New York laws that barred out-of-state wineries from selling directly to consumers. The online wine industry was happy with the outcome, as were wine lovers throughout the country who could buy wine directly from the more than 3400 wineries and online wine shops. Since then, the enthusiasm has dampened somewhat. The Supreme Court decision prohibits states from establishing laws that discriminate against out-of-state sellers; however, each state still can enforce laws limiting direct sales by all sellers and can specify that shipments originate within the state. After several years of trying to develop an online wine store, Amazon.com put its plans on indefinite hold in 2009, citing the difficulty of complying with the maze of state laws that govern online sales of alcoholic beverages.

Contracting and Contract Enforcement in Electronic Commerce

Any contract includes three essential elements: an offer, an acceptance, and consideration. The contract is formed when one party accepts the offer of another party. An **offer** is a commitment with certain terms made to another party, such as a declaration of willingness to buy or sell a product or service. An offer can be revoked as long as no payment, delivery of service, or other consideration has been accepted. An **acceptance** is the expression of willingness to take an offer, including all of its stated terms. **Consideration** is the agreed-upon exchange of something valuable, such as money, property, or future services. When a party accepts an offer based on the exchange of valuable goods or services, a contract has been created. An **implied contract** can also be formed by two or more parties that act as if a contract exists, even if no contract has been written and signed.

Creating Contracts: Offers and Acceptances

People enter into contracts on a daily, and often hourly, basis. Every kind of agreement or exchange between parties, no matter how simple, is a type of contract. Every time a consumer buys an item at the supermarket, the elements of a valid contract are met, for example, through the following actions:

- The store invites offers for an item at a stated price by placing it on a store shelf.
- The consumer makes an offer by indicating a willingness to buy the product for the stated price. For example, the consumer might take the item to a checkout station and present it to a clerk with an offer to pay.
- The store accepts the customer's offer and exchanges its product for the consumer's payment at the checkout station.

Contracts are a key element of traditional business practice, and they are equally important on the Internet. Offers and acceptances can occur when parties exchange e-mail messages, engage in electronic data interchange (EDI), or fill out forms on Web pages. These Internet communications can be combined with traditional methods of forming contracts, such as the exchange of paper documents, faxes, and verbal agreements made over the telephone or in person. The requirements for forming a valid contract in an electronic commerce transaction are met, for example, through the following actions:

- The Web site invites offers for an item at a stated price by serving a Web page that includes information about the item.
- The consumer makes an offer by indicating a willingness to buy the product for the stated price by, for example, clicking an "Add to Shopping Cart" button on the Web page that displays the item.
- The Web site accepts the customer's offer and exchanges its product for the consumer's credit card payment on its shopping cart checkout page.

As you can see, the basic elements of a consumer's contract to buy goods are the same whether the transaction is completed in person or online. Only the form of the offer and acceptance are different in the two environments. The substance of the offer, acceptance, and the completed contract are the same.

When a seller advertises goods for sale on a Web site, that seller is not making an offer, but is inviting offers from potential buyers. If a Web ad were considered to be a legal offer to form a contract, the seller could easily become liable for the delivery of more goods than it has available to ship. A summary of the contracting process that occurs in an online sale appears in Figure 7-4.

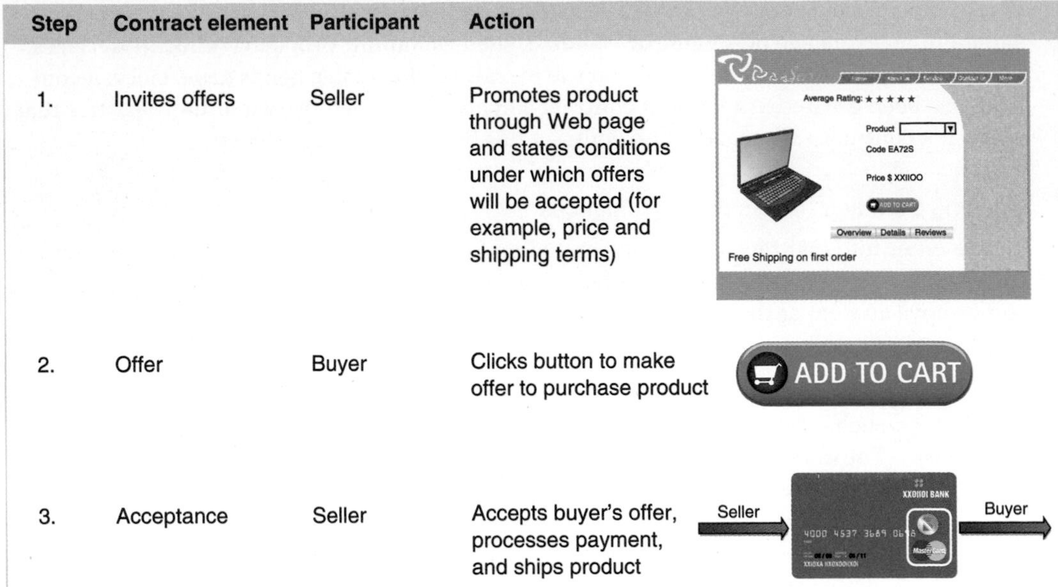

Step	Contract element	Participant	Action
1.	Invites offers	Seller	Promotes product through Web page and states conditions under which offers will be accepted (for example, price and shipping terms)
2.	Offer	Buyer	Clicks button to make offer to purchase product
3.	Acceptance	Seller	Accepts buyer's offer, processes payment, and ships product

FIGURE 7-4 Contracting process in an online sale

When a buyer submits an order, which is an offer, the seller can accept that offer and create a contract. If the seller does not have the ordered items in stock, the seller has the option of refusing the buyer's order outright or counteroffering with a decreased amount. The buyer then has the option to accept the seller's counteroffer.

Making a legal acceptance of an offer is quite easy to do in most cases. When enforcing contracts, courts tend to view offers and acceptances as actions that occur within a particular context. If the actions are reasonable under the circumstances, courts tend to interpret those actions as offers and acceptances. For example, courts have held that a number of different actions—including mailing a check, shipping goods, shaking hands, nodding one's head, taking an item off a shelf, or opening a wrapped package—are each, in some circumstances, legally binding acceptances of offers. An excellent resource for many of the laws concerning contracts, especially as they pertain to U.S. businesses, is the Cornell Law School Web site, which includes the full text of the **Uniform Commercial Code (UCC)**.

Click-Wrap and Web-Wrap Contract Acceptances

Most software sold today (either on CD or downloaded from the Internet) includes a contract that the user must accept before installing the software. These contracts, called **end-user license agreements (EULAs)**, often appear in a dialog box as part of the software installation process. When the user clicks the "Agree" button, the contract is deemed to be signed. Years ago, when most software was sold in boxes that were encased in plastic shrink wrap, EULAs were included on the box with a statement indicating that the buyer accepted the conditions of the EULA by removing the shrink wrap from the box. This action was called a **shrink-wrap acceptance**. Today, a Web site user can agree to that site's EULA or its terms and conditions by clicking a button on the Web site (called a **click-wrap acceptance**) or by simply using the Web site (called a **Web-wrap acceptance** or **browser-wrap acceptance**).

Creating Written Contracts on the Web

In general, contracts are valid even if they are not in writing or signed. However, certain categories of contracts are not enforceable unless the terms are put into writing and signed by both parties. In 1677, the British Parliament enacted a law that specified the types of contracts that had to be in writing and signed. Following this British precedent, every state in the United States today has a similar law, called a **Statute of Frauds**. Although these state laws vary slightly, each Statute of Frauds specifies that contracts for the sale of goods worth more than $500 and contracts that require actions that cannot be completed within one year must be created by a signed writing. Fortunately for businesses and people who want to form contracts using electronic commerce, a writing does not require either pen or paper.

Most courts will hold that a **writing** exists when the terms of a contract have been reduced to some tangible form. An early court decision in the 1800s held that a telegraph transmission was a writing. Later courts have held that tape recordings of spoken words, computer files on disks, and faxes are writings. Thus, the parties to an electronic commerce contract should find it relatively easy to satisfy the writing requirement. Courts have been similarly generous in determining what constitutes a signature. A **signature** is any symbol executed or adopted for the purpose of authenticating a writing. Courts have held names on telegrams, telexes, faxes, and Western Union Mailgrams to be signatures. Even typed names or names printed as part of a letterhead have served as signatures. It is reasonable to assume that a symbol or code included in an electronic file would constitute a signature. As you will learn in Chapter 10, the United States now has a law that explicitly makes digital signatures legally valid for contract purposes.

Firms conducting international electronic commerce do not need to worry about the signed writing requirement in most cases. The main treaty that governs international sales of goods, Article 11 of the United Nations Convention on Contracts for the International Sale of Goods (CISG), requires neither a writing nor a signature to create a legally binding acceptance. You can learn more about the CISG and related topics in international commercial law at the **Pace Law School CISG Database** Web site.

Implied Warranties and Warranty Disclaimers on the Web

Most firms conducting electronic commerce have little trouble fulfilling the requirements needed to create enforceable, legally binding contracts on the Web. One area that deserves attention, however, is the issue of warranties. Any contract for the sale of goods includes implied warranties. An **implied warranty** is a promise to which the seller can be held even though the seller did not make an explicit statement of that promise. The law establishes these basic elements of a transaction in any contract to sell goods or services. For example, a seller is deemed to implicitly warrant that the goods it offers for sale are fit for the purposes for which they are normally used. If the seller knows specific information about the buyer's requirements, acceptance of an offer from that buyer may result in an additional implied warranty of fitness, which suggests that the goods are suitable for the specific uses of that buyer. Sellers can also create explicit warranties by providing a specific description of the additional warranty terms. It is also possible for a seller to create explicit warranties, often unintentionally, by making general statements in brochures or other advertising materials about product performance or suitability for particular tasks.

Sellers can avoid some implied warranty liability by making a warranty disclaimer. A **warranty disclaimer** is a statement declaring that the seller will not honor some or all implied warranties. Any warranty disclaimer must be conspicuously made in writing, which means it must be easily noticed in the body of the written agreement. On a Web page, sellers can meet this requirement by putting the warranty disclaimer in larger type, a bold font, or a contrasting color. To be legally effective, the warranty disclaimer must be stated obviously and must be easy for a buyer to find on the Web site. Figure 7-5 shows a portion of a sample warranty disclaimer for a Web site. The warranty disclaimer is printed in uppercase letters to distinguish it from other text on the page. This helps satisfy the requirement that the warranty disclaimer be easily noticed.

warranty disclaimer text is capitalized for emphasis

Disclaimers

WE DO NOT PROMISE THAT THIS WEB SITE OR ANY CONTENT, ELEMENT, OR FEATURE OF THIS SITE WILL BE ERROR-FREE OR UNINTERRUPTED, OR THAT ANY DEFECTS WILL BE CORRECTED, OR THAT YOUR USE OF THE SITE WILL PROVIDE SPECIFIC RESULTS. THE SITE AND ITS CONTENT ARE DELIVERED ON AN "AS-IS" BASIS. INFORMATION PROVIDED ON THE SITE IS SUBJECT TO CHANGE WITHOUT NOTICE. WE CANNOT ENSURE THAT ANY PROGRAMS, FILES OR OTHER DATA YOU DOWNLOAD FROM THE SITE WILL BE FREE OF VIRUSES OR DESTRUCTIVE FEATURES.

WE DISCLAIM ALL WARRANTIES, EXPRESS OR IMPLIED, INCLUDING ANY WARRANTIES OF ACCURACY, NON-INFRINGEMENT, MERCHANTABILITY AND FITNESS FOR A PARTICULAR PURPOSE. WE DISCLAIM ANY AND ALL LIABILITY FOR THE ACTS, OMISSIONS AND CONDUCT OF ANY THIRD PARTIES IN CONNECTION WITH OR RELATED TO YOUR USE OF THE SITE AND/OR ANY APPLE SERVICES. YOU ASSUME TOTAL RESPONSIBILITY FOR YOUR USE OF THE SITE AND ANY LINKED SITES. YOUR SOLE REMEDY AGAINST US FOR DISSATISFACTION WITH THIS SITE OR ANY CONTENT CONTAINED ON THE SITE IS TO STOP USING THE SITE OR THE CONTENT. THIS LIMITATION OF RELIEF IS A PART OF THE BARGAIN BETWEEN THE PARTIES.

The above disclaimers apply to any damages, liability or injuries caused by any failure of performance, error, omission, interruption, defect of any kind, delay of operation or function, computer virus, communication failure, theft or destruction of or unauthorized access to, alteration of, or use, whether for breach of contract, tort, negligence or any other cause of action.

FIGURE 7-5 A Web site warranty disclaimer

Authority to Form Contracts

As explained previously in this section, a contract is formed when an offer is accepted for consideration. Problems can arise when the acceptance is issued by an imposter or someone who does not have the authority to bind the company to a contract. In electronic commerce, the online nature of acceptances can make it relatively easy for identity forgers to pose as others.

Fortunately, the Internet technology that makes forged identities so easy to create also provides the means to avoid being deceived by a forged identity. In Chapter 10, you will learn how companies and individuals can use digital signatures to establish identity in online transactions. If the contract is for any significant amount, the parties should require each other to use digital signatures to avoid identity problems. In general, courts will not hold a person or corporation whose identity has been forged to the terms of the contract; however, if negligence on the part of the person or corporation contributed to the forgery, a court may hold the negligent party to the terms of the contract. For example, if a company was careless about protecting passwords and allowed an imposter to enter the company's system and accept an offer, a court might hold that company responsible for fulfilling the terms of that contract.

Determining whether an individual has the authority to commit a company to an online contract is a greater problem than forged identities in electronic commerce. This issue, called **authority to bind**, can arise when an employee of a company accepts a contract and the company later asserts that the employee did not have authority to do so. For large transactions in the physical world, businesses check public information on file with the state of incorporation, or ask for copies of corporate certificates or resolutions, to establish the authority of persons to make contracts for their employers. These methods are available to parties engaged in online transactions; however, they can be time consuming and awkward. You will learn about some good electronic solutions, such as digital signatures and certificates from a certification authority, in Chapter 10.

Terms of Service Agreements

Many Web sites have stated rules that site visitors must follow, although most visitors are not aware of these rules. If you examine the home page of a Web site, you will often find a link to a page titled "Terms of Service," "Conditions of Use," "User Agreement," or something similar. If you follow that link, you find a page full of detailed rules and regulations, most of which are intended to limit the Web site owner's liability for what you might do with information you obtain from the site. These contracts are often called **terms of service (ToS)** agreements even when they appear under a different title. In most cases, a site visitor is held to the terms of service even if that visitor has not read the text or clicked a button to indicate agreement with the terms. The visitor is bound to the agreement by simply using the site, which is an example of the Web-wrap (or browser-wrap) acceptance you learned about earlier in this chapter. Figure 7-6 shows the page on which Yahoo! displays its Terms of Service agreement.

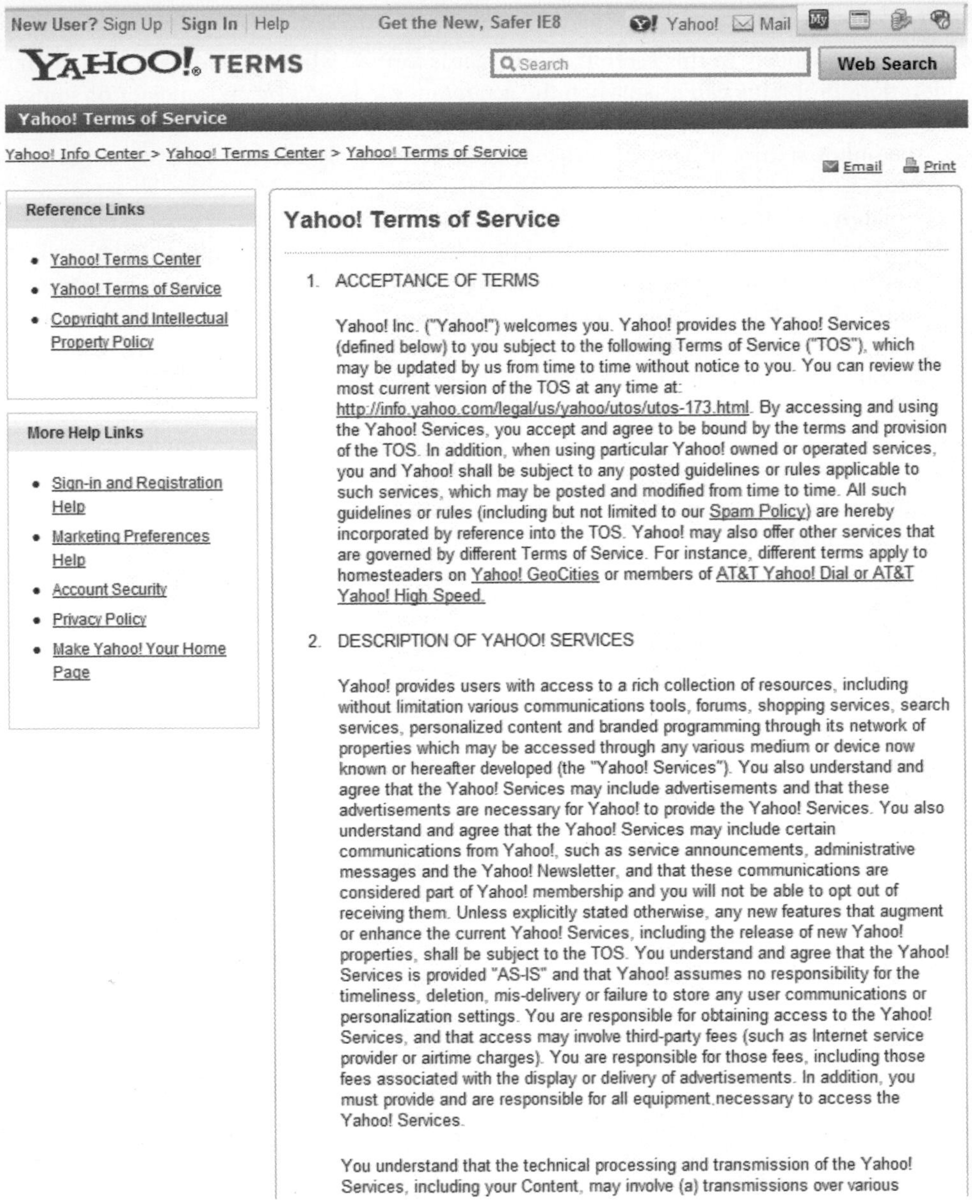

New User? Sign Up | Sign In | Help   Get the New, Safer IE8   Yahoo! Mail

YAHOO! TERMS   Search   Web Search

Yahoo! Terms of Service

Yahoo! Info Center > Yahoo! Terms Center > Yahoo! Terms of Service

Email Print

Reference Links

- Yahoo! Terms Center
- Yahoo! Terms of Service
- Copyright and Intellectual Property Policy

More Help Links

- Sign-in and Registration Help
- Marketing Preferences Help
- Account Security
- Privacy Policy
- Make Yahoo! Your Home Page

Yahoo! Terms of Service

1. ACCEPTANCE OF TERMS

   Yahoo! Inc. ("Yahoo!") welcomes you. Yahoo! provides the Yahoo! Services (defined below) to you subject to the following Terms of Service ("TOS"), which may be updated by us from time to time without notice to you. You can review the most current version of the TOS at any time at: http://info.yahoo.com/legal/us/yahoo/utos/utos-173.html. By accessing and using the Yahoo! Services, you accept and agree to be bound by the terms and provision of the TOS. In addition, when using particular Yahoo! owned or operated services, you and Yahoo! shall be subject to any posted guidelines or rules applicable to such services, which may be posted and modified from time to time. All such guidelines or rules (including but not limited to our Spam Policy) are hereby incorporated by reference into the TOS. Yahoo! may also offer other services that are governed by different Terms of Service. For instance, different terms apply to homesteaders on Yahoo! GeoCities or members of AT&T Yahoo! Dial or AT&T Yahoo! High Speed.

2. DESCRIPTION OF YAHOO! SERVICES

   Yahoo! provides users with access to a rich collection of resources, including without limitation various communications tools, forums, shopping services, search services, personalized content and branded programming through its network of properties which may be accessed through any various medium or device now known or hereafter developed (the "Yahoo! Services"). You also understand and agree that the Yahoo! Services may include advertisements and that these advertisements are necessary for Yahoo! to provide the Yahoo! Services. You also understand and agree that the Yahoo! Services may include certain communications from Yahoo!, such as service announcements, administrative messages and the Yahoo! Newsletter, and that these communications are considered part of Yahoo! membership and you will not be able to opt out of receiving them. Unless explicitly stated otherwise, any new features that augment or enhance the current Yahoo! Services, including the release of new Yahoo! properties, shall be subject to the TOS. You understand and agree that the Yahoo! Services is provided "AS-IS" and that Yahoo! assumes no responsibility for the timeliness, deletion, mis-delivery or failure to store any user communications or personalization settings. You are responsible for obtaining access to the Yahoo! Services, and that access may involve third-party fees (such as Internet service provider or airtime charges). You are responsible for those fees, including those fees associated with the display or delivery of advertisements. In addition, you must provide and are responsible for all equipment necessary to access the Yahoo! Services.

   You understand that the technical processing and transmission of the Yahoo! Services, including your Content, may involve (a) transmissions over various

FIGURE 7-6 Yahoo! Terms of Service agreement

USE AND PROTECTION OF INTELLECTUAL PROPERTY IN ONLINE BUSINESS

Online businesses must be careful with their use of intellectual property. **Intellectual property** is a general term that includes all products of the human mind. These products can be tangible or intangible. Intellectual property rights include the protections afforded to individuals and companies by governments through governments' granting of copyrights and patents, and through registration of trademarks and service marks. Depending on where they live, individuals may have a **right of publicity**, which is a limited right to control others' commercial use of an individual's name, image, likeness, or identifying aspect of identity. This right exists in most U.S. states but is limited by the provisions of the U.S. Constitution, specifically its First Amendment. Online businesses must take care to avoid deceptive trade practices, false advertising claims, defamation or product disparagement, and infringements of intellectual property rights by using unauthorized content on their Web sites or in their domain names. A number of legal issues can arise regarding the Web page content of electronic commerce sites. The most common concerns involve the use of intellectual property that is protected by other parties' copyrights, patents, trademarks, and service marks.

Copyright Issues

A **copyright** is a right granted by a government to the author or creator of a literary or artistic work. The right is for the specific length of time provided in the copyright law and gives the author or creator the sole and exclusive right to print, publish, or sell the work. Creations that can be copyrighted include virtually all forms of artistic or intellectual expression—books, music, artworks, recordings (audio and video), architectural drawings, choreographic works, product packaging, and computer software. In the United States, works created after 1977 are protected for the life of the author plus 70 years. Works copyrighted by corporations or not-for-profit organizations are protected for 95 years from the date of publication or 120 years from the date of creation, whichever is earlier.

The idea contained in an expression cannot be copyrighted. It is the particular form in which an idea is expressed that creates a work that can be copyrighted. If an idea cannot be separated from its expression in a work, that work cannot be copyrighted. For example, mathematical calculations cannot be copyrighted. A collection of facts can be copyrighted, but only if the collection is arranged, coordinated, or selected in a way that causes the resulting work to rise to the level of an original work. For example, the Yahoo! Web Directory is a collection of links to URLs. These facts existed before Yahoo! selected and arranged them into the form of its directory. However, most copyright lawyers would argue that the selection and arrangement of the links into categories probably makes the directory copyrightable.

In the past, many countries (including the United States) required the creator of a work to register that work to obtain copyright protection. U.S. law still allows registration, but registration is no longer required. A work that does not include the words "copyright" or "copyrighted," or the copyright symbol ©, but was created after 1989, is copyrighted automatically by virtue of the copyright law unless the creator specifically released the work into the public domain.

Most U.S. Web pages are protected by the automatic copyright provision of the law because they arrange the elements of words, graphics, and HTML tags in a way that creates an original work (in addition, many Web pages have been registered with the U.S. Copyright Office). This creates a potential problem because of the way the Web works. As you learned in Chapter 2, when a Web client requests a page, the Web server sends an HTML file to the client. Thus, a copy of the HTML file (along with any graphics or other files needed to render the page) resides on the Web client computer. Most legal experts agree that this copying is a fair use of the copyrighted Web page. The U.S. copyright law includes an exemption from infringement actions for fair use of copyrighted works. The **fair use** of a copyrighted work includes copying it for use in criticism, comment, news reporting, teaching, scholarship, or research. The law's definition of fair use is intentionally broad and can be difficult to interpret. Figure 7-7 shows the text of the U.S. law that creates the fair-use exception.

Title 17, Chapter 1, § 107 of the United States Code

Limitations on exclusive rights: Fair use

Notwithstanding the provisions of sections 106 and 106A, the fair use of a copyrighted work, including such use by reproduction in copies or phonorecords or by any other means specified by that section, for purposes such as criticism, comment, news reporting, teaching (including multiple copies for classroom use), scholarship, or research, is not an infringement of copyright. In determining whether the use made of a work in any particular case is a fair use the factors to be considered shall include

(1) the purpose and character of the use, including whether such use is of a commercial nature or is for nonprofit educational purposes;
(2) the nature of the copyrighted work;
(3) the amount and substantiality of the portion used in relation to the copyrighted work as a whole; and
(4) the effect of the use upon the potential market for or value of the copyrighted work.

The fact that a work is unpublished shall not itself bar a finding of fair use if such finding is made upon consideration of all the above factors.

FIGURE 7-7 U.S. law governing the fair-use exception

As you can see in the figure, the law includes four specific factors that a court will consider in determining whether a specific use qualifies as a fair use. The first factor gives nonprofit educational uses a better chance at qualifying than commercial uses. The second factor allows the court to consider a painting using different standards than a sound recording. The third factor is often used to allow small sections of a work to qualify as fair use when the use of the entire work (or a substantial part of the work) might not qualify. The fourth factor, which is a deciding factor in most fair-use cases, allows the court to consider the amount of damage the use might cause to the value of the copyrighted work. The **University of Texas Crash Course in Copyright** is a particularly helpful source of information on making fair-use determinations. If you make fair-use of a copyrighted work for a school assignment, you should provide a citation to the original work to avoid charges of plagiarism.

Copyright law has always included elements, such as the fair-use exemption, that make it difficult to apply. The Internet has made this situation worse because it allows the immediate transmission of exact digital copies of many materials. In the case of digital music, the original Napster site provided a network that millions of people used to trade music files that they had copied from their CDs and compressed into MPEG version 3 format, commonly referred to as MP3. This constituted copyright infringement on a grand scale, and a group of music recording companies sued Napster for facilitating the individual acts of infringement.

Napster argued that it had only provided the "machinery" used in the copyright infringements—much as electronics companies manufacture and sell VCRs that might be used to make illegal copies of videotapes—and had not itself infringed on any copyrights. Both the U.S. District Court and the Federal Appellate Court held that Napster was liable for vicarious copyright infringement, even though it did not directly infringe any music recording companies' copyrights. An entity becomes liable for **vicarious copyright infringement** if it is capable of supervising the infringing activity and obtains a financial benefit from the infringing activity. Because Napster failed to monitor its network and indirectly profited (by selling advertising on its Web site) from the infringement, the company was held liable even though it did not itself transfer any copies. The courts shut down Napster and the company agreed to pay $26 million in copyright infringement damages before filing for bankruptcy. Software maker **Roxio** bought Napster's intellectual property, including its name and Web site, from the bankruptcy trustee for about $5 million. Roxio now operates the **Napster** site, which offers legal music downloads to subscribers.

With the growth in popularity of portable music devices such as Apple's iPod, the demand for music in the MP3 (and similar) formats has continued to increase. The companies that sell music online today each have different rules and restrictions that come with the downloaded files. Some sites allow one copy to be installed on a portable music device. Others allow a limited number of copies to be installed. Still others allow unlimited copies, but only if the devices on which the copies are installed are owned by the person who downloaded the file.

The common practice of copying files from music CDs and placing those files on a portable music device (or onto another CD) raises some interesting legal issues. This type of copying is governed in the United States by the fair-use provisions of the copyright laws, which you learned about earlier in this chapter. The fair-use provisions as they relate to copying music tracks are, at best, unclear and difficult to interpret. Some lawyers would argue that a person has the right under the fair-use provisions to make a backup copy of a music CD track, but other lawyers would disagree. A person who makes one copy for a portable music device, a second copy for a computer, and a third copy on a CD for backup purposes would be less likely to be protected under the fair-use provisions, but some lawyers would argue that all three uses should be protected.

Patent Issues

A **patent** is an exclusive right granted by the government to an individual to make, use, and sell an invention. In the United States, patents on inventions protect the inventor's rights for 20 years. An inventor may decide to patent the design of an invention instead of the invention itself, in which case the patent protects the design for 14 years. To be patentable, an invention must be genuine, novel, useful, and not obvious given the current state of technology. In the early 1980s, companies began obtaining patents on software programs that met the terms of the U.S. patent law. However, most firms that develop software to use in Web sites and for related transaction processing have not found the patent law to be very useful. The process of obtaining a patent is expensive and can take several years. Most developers of Web-related software believe that the technology in the software could become obsolete before the patent protection is secured, so they rely on copyright protection.

One type of patent has been of interest to companies engaging in electronic commerce. A U.S. Court of Appeals ruled in 1998 that patents could be granted on "methods of doing business." The **business process patent**, which protects a specific set of procedures for conducting a particular business activity, is quite controversial. In addition to the Amazon.com patent on its 1-Click purchasing method (which you read about in Chapter 4), other Web businesses have obtained business process patents. The Priceline.com "name your own price" price-tendering system, About.com's approach to aggregating information from many different Web sites, and Cybergold's method of paying people to view its Web site have each received business process patents.

The ability of companies to enforce their rights under these patents is not yet clear. Many legal experts and business researchers believe that the issuance of business process patents grants the recipients unfair monopoly power and is an inappropriate extension of patent law. In 1999, Amazon.com sued Barnes & Noble for using a process on its Web site that was similar to the 1-Click method. The case was settled out of court in 2002, but the terms of the settlement were not disclosed.

The stakes in business process patent cases can be high. For example, a federal judge in 2007 entered a final judgment of $30 million against eBay in a business process patent case. MercExchange, a company that makes a business of buying patents and attempting to enforce them, had sued eBay for its use of a fixed price sales option that eBay calls "Buy It Now." MercExchange argued that several of its patents covered the business process of offering a fixed price option in an online auction. After winning the monetary damages, MercExchange continued to litigate the case, hoping to win an injunction that would prevent eBay from using the feature at all. In 2008, eBay agreed to buy three patents from MercExchange for an undisclosed sum to end the litigation.

Business process patents are common only in the United States. The intellectual property laws of most other countries do not permit patents to be issued for business processes. The appropriateness of business process patents is an issue that sparks intense debate among legal scholars and online business managers. To read an interesting discussion of both sides of the business process patent issue that includes exchanges between Jeff Bezos, founder of Amazon.com, and book publisher Tim O'Reilly, see the article posted at **My Conversation with Jeff Bezos**.

Trademark Issues

A **trademark** is a distinctive mark, device, motto, or implement that a company affixes to the goods it produces for identification purposes. A **service mark** is similar to a trademark, but it is used to identify services provided. In the United States, trademarks and service marks can be registered with state governments, the federal government, or both. The name (or a part of that name) that a business uses to identify itself is called a **trade name**. Trade names are not protected by trademark laws unless the business name is the same as the product (or service) name. They are protected, however, under common law. **Common law** is the part of British and U.S. law established by the history of court decisions that has accumulated over many years. The other main part of British and U.S. law, called **statutory law**, arises when elected legislative bodies pass laws, which are also called statutes.

The owners of registered trademarks have often invested a considerable amount of money in the development and promotion of their trademarks. Web site designers must be very careful not to use any trademarked name, logo, or other identifying mark without the express permission of the trademark owner. For example, a company Web site that includes a photograph of its president who happens to be holding a can of Pepsi could be held liable for infringing on Pepsi's trademark rights. Pepsi can argue that the appearance of its trademarked product on the Web site implies an endorsement of the president or the company by Pepsi.

Domain Names and Intellectual Property Issues

Considerable controversy has arisen about intellectual property rights and Internet domain names. **Cybersquatting** is the practice of registering a domain name that is the trademark of another person or company in the hopes that the owner will pay huge amounts of money to acquire the URL. In addition, successful cybersquatters can attract many site visitors and, consequently, charge high advertising rates.

A related problem, called **name changing** (also called **typosquatting**), occurs when someone registers purposely misspelled variations of well-known domain names. These variants sometimes lure consumers who make typographical errors when entering a URL. For example, a person might easily type LLBaen.com instead of LLBean.com.

Since 1999, the U.S. Anticybersquatting Consumer Protection Act has prevented businesses' trademarked names from being registered as domain names by other parties. The law provides for damages of up to $100,000 per trademark. If the unauthorized registration of the domain name is found to be "willful," damages can be as much as $300,000.

Registering a generic name such as Wine.com is not cybersquatting. Registering a generic name is speculation that the name might one day become valuable and is completely legal. Disputes that arise when one person has registered a domain name that is an existing trademark or company name are settled by the World Intellectual Property Organization (WIPO). WIPO began settling domain name disputes in 1999 under its Uniform Domain Name Dispute Resolution Policy (UDRP). The problems of international jurisdiction made enforcement by the courts of individual countries cumbersome and ineffective. As an international organization, WIPO can transcend borders and provide rulings that will be effective in a global online business environment. Figure 7-8 shows the WIPO Domain Name Dispute Resolution information page.

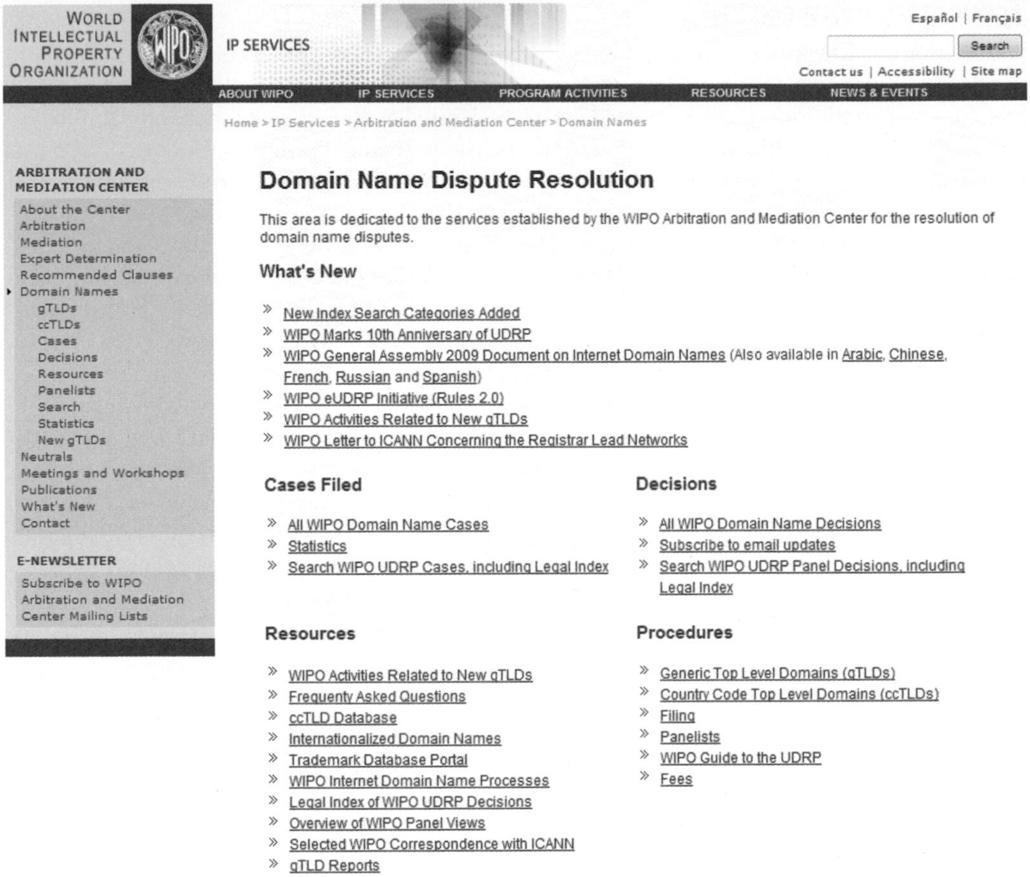

WORLD INTELLECTUAL PROPERTY ORGANIZATION

IP SERVICES

Español | Français

Search

Contact us | Accessibility | Site map

ABOUT WIPO IP SERVICES PROGRAM ACTIVITIES RESOURCES NEWS & EVENTS

Home > IP Services > Arbitration and Mediation Center > Domain Names

ARBITRATION AND MEDIATION CENTER

- About the Center
- Arbitration
- Mediation
- Expert Determination
- Recommended Clauses
- Domain Names
  - gTLDs
  - ccTLDs
  - Cases
  - Decisions
  - Resources
  - Panelists
  - Search
  - Statistics
  - New gTLDs
- Neutrals
- Meetings and Workshops
- Publications
- What's New
- Contact

E-NEWSLETTER

Subscribe to WIPO Arbitration and Mediation Center Mailing Lists

Domain Name Dispute Resolution

This area is dedicated to the services established by the WIPO Arbitration and Mediation Center for the resolution of domain name disputes.

What's New

» New Index Search Categories Added
» WIPO Marks 10th Anniversary of UDRP
» WIPO General Assembly 2009 Document on Internet Domain Names (Also available in Arabic, Chinese, French, Russian and Spanish)
» WIPO eUDRP Initiative (Rules 2.0)
» WIPO Activities Related to New gTLDs
» WIPO Letter to ICANN Concerning the Registrar Lead Networks

Cases Filed

» All WIPO Domain Name Cases
» Statistics
» Search WIPO UDRP Cases, including Legal Index

Decisions

» All WIPO Domain Name Decisions
» Subscribe to email updates
» Search WIPO UDRP Panel Decisions, including Legal Index

Resources

» WIPO Activities Related to New gTLDs
» Frequenty Asked Questions
» ccTLD Database
» Internationalized Domain Names
» Trademark Database Portal
» WIPO Internet Domain Name Processes
» Legal Index of WIPO UDRP Decisions
» Overview of WIPO Panel Views
» Selected WIPO Correspondence with ICANN
» gTLD Reports

Procedures

» Generic Top Level Domains (gTLDs)
» Country Code Top Level Domains (ccTLDs)
» Filing
» Panelists
» WIPO Guide to the UDRP
» Fees

FIGURE 7-8 WIPO Domain Name Dispute Resolution information page

Disputes can arise when a business has a trademark that is a common term. If a person obtains the domain name containing that common term, the owner of the trademark must seek resolution at WIPO. In more than 80 percent of its cases, WIPO rules in favor of the trademark owner, but a win is never guaranteed.

In one example, three cybersquatters made headlines when they tried to sell the URL barrydiller.com for $10 million. Barry Diller, then the CEO of USA Networks, won a WIPO decision (*Barry Diller v. INTERNTCO Corp.*) that ordered the domain name transferred to him. The ruling established that a famous person's own name is a common law service mark. The WIPO panel in the Barry Diller case found that the cybersquatters had no legitimate rights or interests in the domain name and that they had registered the name and were using it in bad faith.

In another example, Gordon Sumner, who has performed music for many years as Sting, filed a complaint with WIPO because a Georgia man obtained the domain name www.sting.com and offered to sell it to Sting for $25,000; however, in this case, WIPO noted that the word "sting" was in common and general use and had multiple meanings other than as an identifier for the musician. WIPO refused to award the domain to Sumner. After the WIPO decision, Sumner purchased the domain name for an undisclosed sum. The musician's official Web site is now at www.sting.com.

Many critics have argued that the WIPO UDRP has been enforced unevenly and that many of the decisions under the policy have been inconsistent. One problem faced by those who have used the WIPO resolution service is that the WIPO decisions are not appealed to a single authority. Instead, the party losing in the WIPO hearing must find a court with jurisdiction over the dispute and file suit there to overturn the WIPO decision.

No central authority maintains records of all WIPO decisions and appeals. You can learn more about WIPO UDRP decisions by reading the Harvard Law School's Berkman Center UDRP Opinion Guide. A complete list of all UDRP decisions with links to the text of each decision appears on the ICANN UDRP Proceedings Web pages.

Another example of domain name abuse is name stealing. **Name stealing** occurs when someone other than a domain name's owner changes the ownership of the domain name. A **domain name ownership change** occurs when owner information maintained by a public domain registrar is changed in the registrar's database to reflect a new owner's name and business address. Once the domain name ownership is changed, the name stealer can manipulate the site, post graffiti on it, or redirect online customers to other sites—perhaps to sites selling competing products. The main purpose of name stealing is to harass the site owner because the ownership change can be reversed quickly when the theft is discovered, however, name stealing can cut off a business from its Web site for several days.

Protecting Intellectual Property Online

Several methods can be used to protect copyrighted digital works online, but they only provide partial protection. One technique employs steganography to create a **digital watermark**. The watermark is a digital code or stream embedded undetectably in a digital image or audio file. It can be encrypted to protect its contents, or simply hidden among the bits—digital information—composing the image or recording. Verance is a company that provides, among other products, digital audio watermarking systems to protect audio files on the Internet. Its systems identify, authenticate, and protect intellectual property. Verance's ARIS MusiCode system enables recording artists to monitor, identify, and control the use of their digital recordings.

The audio watermarks do not alter the audio fidelity of the recordings in which they are embedded. The Verance SoniCode product provides verification and authentication tools. SoniCode was originally developed by ARIS Technologies, which is now owned by Verance Corporation. SoniCode can ensure that telephonic conversations have not been altered. The same is true for audiovisual transcripts and depositions. Blue Spike produces a watermarking system called Giovanni. Like the SoniCode system, the Giovanni watermark authenticates the copyright and provides copy control. **Copy control** is an electronic mechanism for limiting the number of copies that one can make of a digital work.

Digimarc is another company providing watermark protection systems and software. Its products embed a watermark that allows any works protected by its Digimarc system to be tracked across the Web. In addition, the watermark can link viewers to commerce sites and databases. It can also control software and playback devices. Finally, the imperceptible watermark contains copyright information and links to the image's creator, which enables nonrepudiation of a work's authorship and facilitates electronic purchase and licensing of the work.

Defamation

A **defamatory** statement is a statement that is false and that injures the reputation of another person or company. If the statement injures the reputation of a product or service instead of a person, it is called **product disparagement**. In some countries, even a true and honest comparison of products may give rise to product disparagement. Because the difference between justifiable criticism and defamation can be hard to determine, commercial Web sites should consider the specific laws in their jurisdiction (and consider consulting a lawyer) before making negative, evaluative statements about other persons or products.

Web site designers should be especially careful to avoid potential defamation liability by altering a photo or image of a person in a way that depicts the person unfavorably. In most cases, a person must establish that the defamatory statement caused injury. However, most states recognize a legal cause of action, called **per se defamation**, in which a court deems some types of statements to be so negative that injury is assumed. For example, the court will hold inaccurate statements alleging conduct potentially injurious to a person's business, trade, profession, or office as defamatory per se—the complaining party need not prove injury to recover damages. Thus, online statements about competitors should always be carefully reviewed before posting to determine whether they contain any elements of defamation.

An important exception in U.S. law exists for statements that are defamatory but that are about a public figure (such as a politician or a famous actor). The law allows considerable leeway for statements that are satirical or that are valid expressions of personal opinion. Other countries do not offer the same protections, so operators of Web sites with international audiences do need to be careful.

Also, recall that defaming or disparaging statements must be false. This protects Web sites that include unfavorable reviews of products or services if the statements made are not false. For example, if a person reads a book and believes it to be terrible, that person can safely post a review on Amazon.com that includes assessments of the book's lack of literary value. Such statements of personal opinion are true statements and thus neither defamatory nor disparaging. Finally, in many U.S. states, use of an individual's name, photo, or other elements of personal identity can violate that individual's right of publicity. A company that does business in a jurisdiction that recognizes this right must be careful to obtain permission for any use of individuals' identifying characteristics on their Web sites.

Deceptive Trade Practices

The ease with which Web site designers can edit graphics, audio, and video files allows them to do many creative and interesting things. Manipulations of existing pictures, sounds, and video clips can be very entertaining. If the objects being manipulated are trademarked, however, these manipulations can constitute infringement of the trademark holder's rights. Fictional characters can be trademarked or otherwise protected. Many personal Web pages include unauthorized use of cartoon characters and scanned photographs of celebrities; often, these images are altered in some way. A Web site that uses an altered image of Mickey Mouse speaking in a modified voice is likely to hear from the Disney legal team.

Web sites that include links to other sites must be careful not to imply a relationship with the companies sponsoring the other sites unless such a relationship actually exists. For example, a Web design studio's Web page may include links to company Web sites that show good design principles. If those company Web sites were not created by the design studio, the studio must be very careful to state that fact. Otherwise, it would be easy for a visitor to assume that the linked sites were the work of the design studio.

In general, trademark protection prevents another firm from using the same or a similar name, logo, or other identifying characteristic in a way that would cause confusion in the minds of potential buyers of the trademark holder's products or services. For example, the trademarked name "Visa" is used by one company for its credit card and another company for its synthetic fiber. This use is acceptable because the two products are significantly different and few consumers of credit cards or synthetic fibers would likely be confused by the identical names. However, the use of very well-known trademarks can be protected for all products if there is a danger that the trademark might be diluted. Various state laws define **trademark dilution** as the reduction of the distinctive quality of a trademark by alternative uses. Trademarked names such as "Hyatt," "Trivial Pursuit," and "Tiffany," and the shape of the Coca-Cola bottle have all been protected from dilution by court rulings. Thus, a Web site that sells gift-packaged seafood and claims to be the "Tiffany of the Sea" risks a lawsuit from the famous jeweler claiming trademark dilution.

Advertising Regulation

In the United States, advertising is regulated primarily by the **Federal Trade Commission (FTC)**. The FTC publishes regulations and investigates claims of false advertising. Its Web site includes a number of information releases that are useful to businesses and consumers. The FTC business education campaign publications are available on its Advertising Guidance page, shown in Figure 7-9. These publications include information to help businesses comply with the law.

FEDERAL TRADE COMMISSION
PROTECTING AMERICA'S CONSUMERS

Search >

Privacy Policy | Advanced Search | En Español

Home | News | Competition | Consumer Protection | Economics | General Counsel | Actions | Congressional | Policy | International

About BCP | Consumer Information | Business Information | Resources | File a Complaint | Protección del Consumidor en Español

Business Categories

- Advertising
- Automobiles
- Clothing & Textiles
- Credit
- E-Commerce
- Energy & the Environment
- Franchise & Business Opportunities
- Fraud Prevention
- Health
- Identity Theft, Privacy, & Security
- Resources for your Business
- Telemarketing & Direct Marketing
- Video Library
- En Español

Advertising

Microsites

Red Flag: Bogus Weight Loss Claims
Guide for media on detecting bogus weight loss claims in ads. How to spot false claims for weight loss, and help protect your customers, your bottom line, your reputation, and the good name of your legitimate advertisers.

Facts For Business

A Businessperson's Guide to Federal Warranty Law
Business guide to federal warranty law. Explains the Magnuson-Moss Act.

A Dealer's Guide to the Used Car Rule [PDF]
A compliance checklist for car dealers. 8.5"x11", 18 pages.

Ads for Business Opportunities: How to Detect Deception [PDF] [en español]
Provides advertising sales staff with claims that are tip-offs to fraudulent business opportunity offers. 8.5"x11", 2 pages.

Advertising Consumer Leases [PDF]
Answers frequently asked questions about the advertising requirements of the Consumer Leasing Act and Regulation M. 8.5"x11", 4 pages.

Advertising FAQ's: A Guide for Small Business [PDF]
Guide for small businesses explains the truth-in-advertising laws. 8.5"x 11", 36 pages, color.

Advertising and Marketing on the Internet: Rules of the Road [PDF]
Explains how businesses can comply with truth-in-advertising laws when marketing on the Internet. 8.5"x 11", 16 pages, color.

Advertising Retail Electricity and Natural Gas [PDF]
Advises utilities suppliers how to make truthful marketing claims. 8.5"x 11", 14 pages, color.

Big Print. Little Print. What's the Deal? How to Disclose Details [PDF]
Advertising and disclosure requirements for sellers of "free" or low-cost computers. 8.5"x11", 4 pages.

Business Guide to the Mail and Telephone Order Merchandise Rule [PDF]
Explains what the Rule covers, how to comply, questions and answers about the Rule, and where to go for more information. Includes a copy of the Rule. 8.5"x11", 20 pages, color.

Complying with the Appliance Labeling Rule: A Guide for Retailers [PDF]
Explains how sellers must use the EnergyGuide label on appliances and how they can comply with the disclosure requirements of the FTC's Appliance Labeling Rule. 8.5"x 11", 4 pages.

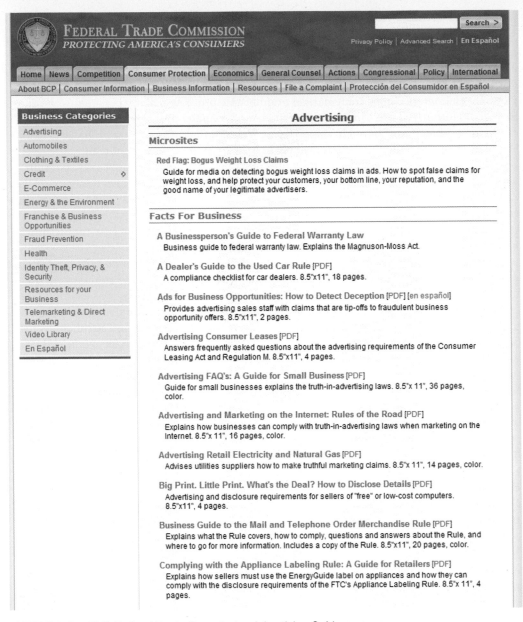

FIGURE 7-9 U.S. Federal Trade Commission Advertising Guidance page

Any advertising claim that can mislead a substantial number of consumers in a material way is illegal under U.S. law. In addition to conducting its own investigations, the FTC accepts referred investigations from organizations such as the Better Business Bureau. The FTC provides policy statements that can be helpful guides for designers creating electronic commerce Web sites. These policies include information on what is permitted in advertisements and cover specific areas such as these:

- Bait advertising
- Consumer lending and leasing
- Endorsements and testimonials
- Energy consumption statements for home appliances
- Guarantees and warranties
- Prices

Other federal agencies have the power to regulate online advertising in the United States. These agencies include the Food and Drug Administration (FDA), the Bureau of Alcohol, Tobacco, and Firearms (BATF), and the Department of Transportation (DOT). The FDA regulates information disclosures for food and drug products. In particular, any Web site that is planning to advertise pharmaceutical products will be subject to the FDA's drug labeling and advertising regulations. The BATF works with the FDA to monitor and enforce federal laws regarding advertising for alcoholic beverages and tobacco products. These laws require that every ad for such products includes statements that use very specific language. Many states also have laws that regulate advertising for alcoholic beverages and tobacco products. The state and federal laws governing advertising and the sale of firearms are even more restrictive. Any Web site that plans to deal in these products should consult with an attorney who is familiar with the relevant laws before posting any online advertising for such products. The DOT works with the FTC to monitor the advertising of companies over which it has jurisdiction, such as bus lines, freight companies, and airlines.

ONLINE CRIME, TERRORISM, AND WARFARE

The Internet has opened up many possibilities for people to communicate and get to know each other better—no matter where in the world they live. The Internet has also opened doors for businesses to reach new markets and create opportunities for economic growth. It is sad that some people in our world have found the Internet to be a useful tool for perpetrating crimes, conducting terrorism, and even waging war.

Online Crime

Crime on the Web includes online versions of crimes that have been undertaken for years in the physical world, including theft, stalking, distribution of pornography, and gambling. Other crimes, such as commandeering one computer to launch attacks on other computers, are new.

Law enforcement agencies have difficulty combating many types of online crime. The first obstacle they face is the issue of jurisdiction. As you learned earlier in this chapter, determining jurisdiction can be tricky on the Internet. Consider the case of a person living in Canada who uses the Internet to commit a crime against a person in Texas. It is unclear which elements of the crime could establish sufficient contact with Texas to allow police there to proceed against a citizen of a foreign country. It is possible that the actions that are considered criminal under Texas and U.S. law might not be considered so in Canada. If the crime is theft of intellectual property (such as computer software or computer files), the questions of jurisdiction become even more complex. You can learn more about online crime issues at the U.S. Department of Justice **Cybercrime.gov** Web site.

The difficulty of prosecuting fraud perpetrators across international boundaries has always been an issue for law enforcement officials. The Internet has given new life to old fraud scams that count on jurisdictional issues to slow investigations of crimes. The advance fee fraud has existed in various forms for many years, but e-mail has made it inexpensive for perpetrators to launch large numbers of attempts to ensnare victims. In an **advance fee fraud**, the perpetrator offers to share the proceeds of some large payoff with the victim if the victim will make a "good faith" deposit or provide some partial funding first. The perpetrator then disappears with the deposit. In some online versions of this fraud, the perpetrator asks for identity information (bank account number, Social Security number, credit card number, and so on) and uses that information to steal the advance fee.

The most common online version of these schemes is the **Nigerian scam** (also called the **419 scam**, after the number of the section of the Nigerian penal code that specifies penalties for fraud in that country), in which the victim receives an e-mail from a Nigerian government official requesting assistance in moving money to a foreign bank account. The Financial Crimes Division of the U.S. Secret Service receives more than 100 reports each day about this type of fraud attempt.

Enforcing laws against the distribution of pornographic material has also been difficult because of jurisdiction issues. The distinction between legal adult material and illegal pornographic material is, in many cases, subjective and often difficult to make. The U.S. Supreme Court has ruled that state and local courts can draw the line based on local community standards. This creates problems for Internet sales. For example, consider a case in which questionable adult content is sold on a Web site located in Oregon to a customer who downloads the material in Georgia. A difficult question arises regarding which community standards might apply to the sale.

A similar jurisdiction issue arises in the case of online gambling. Many gambling sites are located outside the United States. If people in California use their computers to connect to an offshore gambling site, it is unclear where the gambling activity occurs. Several states have passed laws that specifically outlaw Internet gambling, but the jurisdiction of those states to enforce laws that limit Internet activities is not clear. In 2008, the United States Department of the Treasury and the Federal Reserve Bank jointly issued regulations that implement the Unlawful Internet Gambling Enforcement Act (UIGEA) of 2006. As a federal law, the UIGEA gives clearer jurisdiction to law enforcement officers than any state law could. The law prohibits gambling businesses from knowingly accepting payments in connection with unlawful Internet gambling, including payments made through credit cards, electronic funds transfers, and checks. Under the UIGEA regulations, "unlawful Internet gambling" includes making bets using the Internet that are unlawful under any federal or state law in the jurisdiction where the bet or wager is initiated, received, or otherwise made. The first major enforcement action under the regulations occurred in 2009, when federal authorities seized the bank accounts of some 27,000 online poker players, which contained more than $34 million.

Similar laws that restrict online gambling have been passed in other countries. However, some of these laws have been challenged by the countries in which the online gambling companies operate as being discriminatory. If a country's laws permit gambling within the country, but exclude foreign companies from providing gambling services (over the Internet), a basis exists for a discrimination complaint under the World Trade Organization's General Agreement on Trade and Services. The governments of Antigua and Barbados have each filed such complaints against the United States, arguing that the United States engaged in discriminatory trade practices by enforcing the UIGEA.

Another problem facing law enforcement officers is the difficulty of applying laws that were written before the Internet became prevalent to criminal actions carried out on the Internet. For example, most states have stalking laws that provide criminal penalties to people who harass, annoy, or alarm another person in a way that presents a credible threat. Many of these laws are triggered by physical actions, such as physically following the person targeted. The Internet gives a stalker the opportunity to use e-mail or chat room discussions to create the threatening situation. Laws that require physical action on the part of the stalker are not effective against online stalkers. Only a few states have passed laws that specifically address the problem of online stalking.

The Internet can amplify the effects of acts that, in the physical world, can be dealt with locally. For example, school playgrounds have long been the realm of bullying. Students who engaged in bullying were dealt with by school officials; only in extreme cases were such cases referred to law enforcement officials. Today, young people can use technology to harass, humiliate, threaten, and embarrass each other. These acts are called **cyberbullying**. Cyberbullying can include threats, sexual remarks, or pejorative comments transmitted on the Internet or posted on Web sites (social networking sites are often used for such postings). The perpetrator might also pose as the victim and post statements or media, such as photos or videos (often edited to cast the victim in an unfavorable light), that are intended to damage the victim's reputation. Because the Internet increases both the intensity and reach of these attacks, they are much more likely to draw the attention of law enforcement officials than bullying activities in the physical world.

An increasing number of companies have reported attempts by competitors and others to infiltrate their computer systems with the intent of stealing data or creating disruptions in their operations. Smaller companies are easier targets because they generally do not have strong security in place (you will learn more about security in electronic commerce in Chapter 10), but larger organizations are not immune to these attacks. In 2004, lawyer and computer expert Myron Tereshchuk was convicted for criminal extortion. Over a period of two years, he threatened MicroPatent, a patent and trademark services company, with disclosure of confidential client information unless the company paid him $17 million. MicroPatent spent more than $500,000 on legal and technical consultants during the investigation and devoted significant internal resources to the effort. MicroPatent's sales managers also had to spend a tremendous amount of time with clients, reassuring them that their confidential information (details of their pending patent and trademark applications, for example) had not been compromised. MicroPatent's experience was not unusual. According to a recent Computer Security Institute survey of 634 companies, the average loss due to unauthorized data access was more than $300,000 and the average loss due to information theft was more than $350,000. Another survey by *InformationWeek*/Accenture found that 78 percent of surveyed companies believed that they were more vulnerable because attackers were getting more sophisticated.

Although the Internet has made the work of law enforcement more difficult in many cases, there are exceptions. As police agencies become more experienced in using the Web, they have found that it can help track down the perpetrators of crime in some cases. A number of cases have been solved because criminals have bragged about elements of their crimes on social networking sites. From the Pennsylvania graffiti artists that posted photos of their work on their MySpace profiles to the California teens who firebombed an airplane hangar and uploaded a video of themselves in action, criminals who use the Internet are making it easy for police to track them down. In other cases, criminals leave clues in their online profiles that police can use to corroborate other evidence, as in the case of the suspected murderer who described his favorite murder weapon in his online profile. Although privacy watchdog groups have expressed some concern about law enforcement officers randomly surfing the Web looking for leads, anything posted online is public information and is subject to their scrutiny.

Online Warfare and Terrorism

Many Internet security experts believe that we are at the dawn of a new age of terrorism and warfare that could be carried out or coordinated through the Internet. A considerable number of Web sites currently exist that openly support or are operated by hate groups and terrorist organizations. Web sites that contain detailed instructions for creating biological weapons and other poisons, discussion boards that help terrorist groups recruit new members online, and sites that offer downloadable terrorist training films now number in the thousands.

The U.S. Department of Homeland Security and international police agencies such as Interpol are devoting considerable resources to monitoring terrorist activities online. Historically, these agencies have not done a very good job of coordinating their activities around the world. The threat posed by global terrorist organizations that use the Internet to recruit members and to plan and organize terrorist attacks has motivated Interpol to update and expand its computer network monitoring skills and coordinate global antiterrorism efforts.

The Internet provides an effective communications network on which many people and businesses have become dependent. Although the Internet was designed from its inception to continue operating while under attack, a sustained effort by a well-financed terrorist group or rogue state could slow down the operation of major transaction-processing centers. As more business communications traffic moves to the Internet, the potential damage that could result from this type of attack increases. You will learn more about security threats and countermeasures for those threats in Chapter 10.

ETHICAL ISSUES

Companies using Web sites to conduct electronic commerce should adhere to the same ethical standards that other businesses follow. If they do not, they will suffer the same consequences that all companies suffer: the damaged reputation and long-term loss of trust that can result in loss of business. In general, advertising or promotion on the Web should include only true statements and should omit any information that could mislead potential customers or wrongly influence their impressions of a product or service. Even true statements have been held to be misleading when the ad omits important related facts. Any comparisons to other products should be supported by verifiable information. The next section explains the role of ethics in formulating Web business policies, such as those affecting visitors' privacy rights and companies' Internet communications with children.

Ethics and Online Business Practices

Online businesses are finding that ethical issues are important to consider when they are making policy decisions. Recall from Chapter 3 that buyers on the Web often communicate with each other. A report of an ethical lapse that is rapidly passed among customers can seriously affect a company's reputation. In 1999, *The New York Times* ran a story that disclosed Amazon.com's arrangements with publishers for book promotions. Amazon.com was accepting payments of up to $10,000 from publishers to give their books editorial reviews and placement on lists of recommended books as part of a cooperative advertising program. When this news broke, Amazon.com issued a statement that it had done nothing wrong and that such advertising programs were a standard part of publisher–bookstore relationships. The outcry on Internet newsgroups and mailing lists was overwhelming. Two days later—before most traditional media outlets had even reported the story—Amazon.com announced that it would end the practice and offer unconditional refunds to any customers who had purchased a promoted book. Amazon.com had done nothing illegal, but the practice appeared to be unethical to many of its existing and potential customers.

In early 1999, eBay faced a similar ethical dilemma. Several newspapers had begun running stories about sales of illegal items, such as assault weapons and drugs, on the eBay auction site. At this point in time, eBay was listing about 250,000 items each day. Although eBay would investigate claims that illegal items were up for auction on its site, eBay did not actively screen or filter listings before the auctions were placed on the site.

Even though eBay was not legally obligated to screen the items auctioned, and even though screening would be fairly expensive, eBay decided that screening for illegal and copyright-infringing items would be in the best long-run interest of eBay. The team decided that such a decision would send a signal about the character of the company to its customers and the public in general. EBay also decided to remove an entire category—firearms—from the site. Not all of eBay's users were happy about this decision—the sale of firearms on eBay, when done properly, is completely legal. However, eBay again decided that its overall image as an open and honest marketplace was so important to its future success that the company chose to ban all firearms sales.

In 2009, a number of software developers complained that the Apple Apps Store (which you learned about earlier in this book) was slow to approve software to be sold on its Web site. Apple responded that it had a responsibility to protect its customers (the owners of its iPhone product) from unscrupulous software vendors who might try to sell applications for the iPhone that do not function properly, crash the phone, or install malware. Apple argued that its testing and approval program was necessary to maintain customer confidence in its products, even though it had no legal obligation to perform such testing on software provided by third-party developers and sold on the Apps Store Web site.

An important ethical issue that organizations face when they collect e-mail addresses from site visitors is how the organization limits the use of the e-mail addresses and related information. In the early days of the Web, few organizations made any promises to visitors who provided such information. Today, most Web sites state the organization's policy on the protection of visitor information, but many do not. In the United States, organizations are not legally bound to limit their use of information collected through their Web sites. They may use the information for any purpose, including the sale of that information to other organizations. This lack of government regulation that might protect site visitor information is a source of concern for many individuals and privacy rights advocates. These concerns are discussed in the next section.

Privacy Rights and Obligations

The issue of online privacy is continuing to evolve as the Internet and the Web grow in importance as tools of communication and commerce. Many legal and privacy issues remain unsettled and are hotly debated in various forums. The **Electronic Communications Privacy Act of 1986** is the main law governing privacy on the Internet today. Of course, this law was enacted before the general public began its wide use of the Internet. The law was written to update an existing law that prevented the interception of audio signal transmissions so that any type of electronic transmissions (including, for example, fax or data transmissions) would be given the same protections. In 1986, the Internet was not used to transmit commercially valuable data in any significant amount, so the law was written to deal primarily with interceptions that might occur on leased telephone lines.

In the United States, a number of laws have been enacted that address online privacy issues, but none have survived constitutional challenges. In 1999, the FTC issued a report that examined how well Web sites were respecting visitors' privacy rights. Although the FTC found a significant number of sites without posted privacy policies, the report concluded that companies operating Web sites were developing privacy practices with sufficient speed and that no federal laws regarding privacy were required at that time. Privacy advocacy groups responded to the FTC report with outrage and calls for legislation. The Direct Marketing Association (DMA), a trade association of businesses that advertise their products and services directly to consumers using mail, telephone, Internet, and mass media outlets, has established a set of privacy standards for its members. Critics note that past efforts by the DMA to regulate its members' activities have been less than successful and continue to push for privacy laws. The DMA lobbies legislators on behalf of its members, who generally do not want any privacy laws that would interfere with their business activities.

Ethics issues are significant in the area of online privacy because laws have not kept pace with the growth of the Internet and the Web. The nature and degree of personal information that Web sites can record when collecting information about visitors' page-viewing habits, product selections, and demographic information can threaten the privacy rights of those visitors. This is especially true when companies lose control of the data they collect on their customers (and other people). In recent years, many companies have made news headlines because they allowed confidential information about individuals to be released without the permission of those individuals. Examples include incidents such as:

- ChoicePoint (a company that compiles information about consumers) sold the names, addresses, Social Security numbers, and credit reports of more than 145,000 people to thieves who posed as legitimate businesses. More than 1000 fraud cases have been documented as a result of that privacy violation.
- Hackers broke into customer databases at DSW Shoe Warehouse and stole the credit card numbers, checking account numbers, and driver's license numbers of more than 1.4 million customers.
- A computer at Boston College was penetrated and the addresses and Social Security numbers of 120,000 alumni were exposed.

Not all privacy compromises are the work of external agents. Sometimes, companies just lose things. Examples include incidents such as:

- In 2005, Ameritrade, Bank of America, and Time Warner each reported that they had lost track of shipments containing computer backup tapes that held confidential information for hundreds of thousands of customers or employees.
- In 2008, Horizon Blue Cross Blue Shield of New Jersey reported that an employee's laptop computer had been stolen. The laptop contained the personal information (including Social Security numbers) of more than 300,000 individuals.

The number of security breaches leading to the loss of personal information continues to increase. In 2008, the Identity Theft Resource Center reported 446 incidents that exposed private information contained in more than 127 million records and projected that the upward trend in incidents will continue.

The Internet has also changed traditional assumptions about privacy because it allows people anywhere in the world to gather data online in quantities that would have been impossible a few years ago. For example, real estate transactions are a matter of public record in the United States. These transactions have been registered in county records for many years and have been available to anyone who wanted to go to the county recorder's office and spend hours leafing through large books full of handwritten records. Many counties have made these records available on the Internet, so now a researcher can examine thousands of real estate transaction records in hours without traveling to a single county office. Many privacy experts see this change in the ease of data access to be an important shift that affects the privacy rights of those who participate in real estate transactions. Because the Internet makes such data more readily available to a wider range of people, the privacy previously afforded to the participants in those transactions has been reduced.

Differences in cultures throughout the world have resulted in different expectations about privacy in electronic commerce. In Europe, for example, most people expect that information they provide to a commercial Web site will be used only for the purpose for which it was collected. Many European countries have laws that prohibit companies from exchanging consumer data without the express consent of the consumer. In 1998, the European Union adopted a Directive on the Protection of Personal Data. This directive codifies the constitutional rights to privacy that exist in most European countries and applies them to all Internet activities. In addition, the directive prevents businesses from exporting personal data outside the European Union unless the data will continue to be protected in accordance with provisions of the directive. The European Union and its member countries have consistently exhibited a strong preference for using government regulations to protect privacy. The United States has exhibited an opposite preference. U.S. companies, especially those in the direct mail marketing industry, have consistently and successfully lobbied to avoid government regulation and allow the companies to police themselves. Companies that do business internationally must be aware of these differences. For example, a U.S. company that does business in the European Union is subject to its privacy laws.

One of the major privacy controversies in the United States today is the opt-in vs. opt-out issue. Most companies that gather personal information in the course of doing business on the Web would like to be able to use that information for any purpose of their own.

Some companies would also like to be able to sell or rent that information to other companies. No U.S. law currently places limits on companies' use of such information. Companies are, in general, also free to sell or rent customer information. An increasing number of U.S. companies do provide a way for customers who would like to restrict use of their personal information to do so. The most common policy used in U.S. companies today is an opt-out approach. In an **opt-out** approach, the company collecting the information assumes that the customer does not object to the company's use of the information unless the customer specifically chooses to deny permission (that is, to opt out of having their information used). In the less common **opt-in** approach, the company collecting the information does not use the information for any other purpose (or sell or rent the information) unless the customer specifically chooses to allow that use (that is, to opt in and grant permission for the use). Figure 7-10 shows an example Web page that presents a series of opt-in choices to site visitors. The Web site will not send any of these three items to a site visitor unless that visitor opts in by checking one or more boxes.

Many of our site visitors and customers enjoy receiving our newsletter, periodic notices of sales and special product offerings, and offers from other companies that we have chosen to ensure that they will be of interest to our site visitors. Please check the boxes below to add your e-mail address to our distribution list for any or all of these electronic mailings.

☐ Weekly e-mail newsletter

☐ Periodic notices of sales and special product offerings

☐ Offers from other companies

FIGURE 7-10 Example Web page showing opt-in choices

Figure 7-11 shows the opt-out approach. A Web site that uses the opt-out approach will send all three items to the site visitor unless the site visitor checks the boxes to indicate that the items are not wanted.

Many of our site visitors and customers enjoy receiving our newsletter, periodic notices of sales and special product offerings, and offers from other companies that we have chosen to ensure that they will be of interest to our site visitors. Please check the boxes below if you do not wish to be added to our distribution list for any or all of these electronic mailings.

☐ Weekly e-mail newsletter

☐ Periodic notices of sales and special product offerings

☐ Offers from other companies

FIGURE 7-11 Example Web page showing opt-out choices

As you can see, it is easy for site visitors to misread the text and make the wrong choice when deciding whether or not to check the boxes. Sites that use the opt-out approach are often criticized for requiring their visitors to take an affirmative action (checking the empty boxes) to prevent the site from sending items. Another approach to presenting opt-out choices is to use a page that includes checked boxes and instructs the visitor to "uncheck the boxes of the items you do not wish to receive." Most privacy advocates believe that the opt-in approach is preferable because it gives the customer privacy protection unless that customer specifically elects to give up those rights. Most U.S. businesses have traditionally taken the position that they have a right to use the information they collect unless the provider of the information explicitly objects. Some of these companies are changing to the opt-in approach, often at the prodding of privacy advocacy groups.

Until the legal requirements of privacy regulation becomes more clear, privacy advocates recommend that electronic commerce Web sites be conservative in their collection and use of customer data. Mark Van Name and Bill Catchings, writing in *PC Week* in 1998, outlined four principles for handling customer data that provide a good outline for Web site administrators even today. These principles are as follows:

- Use the data collected to provide improved customer service.
- Do not share customer data with others outside your company without the customer's permission.
- Tell customers what data you are collecting and what you are doing with it.
- Give customers the right to have you delete any of the data you have collected about them.

Today, this list should also include a recommendation that customer data, once collected, be kept as secure as possible. A number of organizations are active in promoting privacy rights. You can learn more about current developments in privacy legislation and practices throughout the world by following the links to these organizations' Web sites that appear under the heading **Privacy Rights Advocacy Groups** in the Online Companion.

LEARNING FROM FAILURES

DoubleClick

As you learned in Chapter 4, **DoubleClick** is one of the largest banner advertising networks in the world. DoubleClick arranges the placement of banner ads on Web sites. Like many other Web sites, DoubleClick uses **cookies**, which are small text files placed on Web client computers, to identify returning visitors.

Most visitors find the privacy risk posed by cookies to be acceptable. Visitors to Amazon.com, for example, have Amazon.com cookies placed on their computers so that the Web server at Amazon.com recognizes them when they return. This can be useful, for example, when a visitor who has placed several items in a shopping cart before being interrupted can return to Amazon.com later in the day and find the shopping cart intact—the Web server can read the client's Amazon.com cookie and find the shopping cart from the client's previous session. The Amazon.com server can read only its own cookies; it cannot read the cookies placed on the client computer by any other Web server.

There are two important differences between the Amazon.com scenario and what happens when DoubleClick serves a banner ad. First, the visitor usually does not know that the banner ad is coming from DoubleClick (and thus, does not know that the DoubleClick server could be writing a cookie to the client computer). Second, DoubleClick serves ads through Web sites owned by thousands of companies. As a visitor moves from one Web site to another, that visitor's computer can collect many DoubleClick cookies. The DoubleClick

Continued

server can read all of its own cookies, gathering information from each one about which ads were served and the sites through which they were served. Thus, DoubleClick can compile a tremendous amount of information about where a visitor has been on the Web.

Even this amount of information collection would not trouble most people. DoubleClick can use the cookies to track a particular computer's connections to Web sites, but it does not record any identity information about the owner of that computer. Therefore, DoubleClick accumulates a considerable record of Web activity, but cannot connect that activity with a person.

In 1999, DoubleClick arranged a $1.7 billion merger with Abacus Direct Corporation. Abacus had developed a way to link information about people's Web behavior (collected through cookies such as those placed by DoubleClick's banner ad servers) to the names, addresses, and other information about those people that had been collected in an offline consumer database.

The reaction from online privacy protection groups was immediate and substantial. The FTC launched an investigation, the Internet's privacy issues e-mail lists and chat rooms buzzed with furious conversation, and, in the end, DoubleClick abandoned its plans to integrate its cookie-generated data with the identity information in the Abacus database. Although DoubleClick is still one of the largest banner advertising networks, it had been counting on generating additional revenue by using the information in the combined database that it was unable to create.

When the FTC probe concluded two years later, DoubleClick was not charged with any violations of laws or regulations. The lesson here is that a company violates the Internet community's ethical standards at its own peril, even if the transgression does not break any laws.

Communications with Children

An additional set of privacy considerations arises when Web sites attract children and engage in some form of communication with those children. Adults who interact with Web sites can read privacy statements and make informed decisions about whether to communicate personal information to the site. The communication of private information (such as credit card numbers, shipping addresses, and so on) is a key element in the conduct of electronic commerce.

The laws of most countries and most sets of ethics consider children to be less capable than adults in evaluating information sharing and transaction risks. Thus, we have laws in the physical world that prevent or limit children's ability to sign contracts, get married, drive motor vehicles, and enter certain physical spaces (such as bars, casinos, tattoo parlors, and race tracks). Children are considered to be less able (or unable) to make informed decisions about the risks of certain activities. Similarly, many people are concerned about children's ability to read and evaluate privacy statements and then consent to providing personal information to Web sites. In 2006, MySpace hired a former federal prosecutor to serve as the site's security officer. MySpace was responding to concerns that participants in the social networking site, many of whom are under 18 and post personal information and photos, might be easy prey for sexual predators. MySpace regularly uses software that compares each registered participant against a database of known sex offenders and deletes the accounts of any it finds. However, most experts agree that no technology will ever protect as well as parental involvement in their children's online activities.

Under the laws of most countries, people under the age of 18 or 21 are not considered adults. However, those countries that have proposed or passed laws that specify differential treatment for the privacy rights of children often define "child" as a person below the age of 12 or 13. This approach complicates the issue because it creates two classes of nonadults.

In the United States, Congress enacted the Children's Online Protection Act (COPA) in 1998 to protect children from "material harmful to minors." This law was held to be unconstitutional because it unnecessarily restricted access to a substantial amount of material that is lawful, thus violating the First Amendment. Congress was more successful with the **Children's Online Privacy Protection Act of 1998 (COPPA)**, which provides restrictions on data collection that must be followed by electronic commerce sites aimed at children. This law does not regulate content, as COPA attempted to do, so it has not been successfully challenged on First Amendment grounds. In 2001, Congress enacted the Children's Internet Protection Act (CIPA). CIPA requires schools that receive federal funds to install filtering software on computers in their classrooms and libraries. Filtering software is used to block access to adult content Web sites. In 2003, the Supreme Court held that CIPA was constitutional.

Companies with Web sites that appeal to nonadults must be careful to comply with the laws governing their interactions with these young visitors. **Disney Online** is a site that appeals primarily to young children. The Disney Online registration page offers three choices to visitors who want to register with the site and receive regular communications and updates. The first registration choice is for adults, a second choice is for "teens," and a third choice is for "kids." The "kids" choice leads to a screen that asks for a parent's e-mail address so that Disney can invite the parent to set up a family account. The Disney.com registration page for "teens" asks for the visitor's name, birthday, and the e-mail address of a parent. Disney uses the birthday to calculate the visitor's age and, if the age is less than 13, Disney uses the parent's e-mail address to notify parents of their child's registration and to invite them to set up a family account. Family accounts are controlled by parents who can elect to allow family members who are under the age of 13 to use the site. By refusing to enroll any child under age 13 as a site subscriber, Disney Online meets the requirements of the COPPA law. Other sites that appeal to a young audience use similar techniques to limit unsupervised access to their Web pages. For example, Sanrio (the company that produces Hello Kitty and related products) asks for a birth date before allowing access to its English-language site that is directed at U.S. customers, **Sanriotown**. As shown in Figure 7-12, the site encourages visitors to notify the company that operates the site if they know a child who has gained access to the site in violation of COPPA.

Sanriotown.com does not collect personal information from persons under the age of 13. In order to ensure adherence to this policy, the opening page of our website asks for the date, month and year of birth of each visitor and denies further access to visitors whose birth date shows that they are under 13 years of age. If you believe that a child under 13 has gained access to the sanriotown.com site, or if you have any questions concerning sanriotown.com's privacy policy and practices, please contact us at:

Sanrio Digital (HK) Ltd
Unit 1109, Level 11, Cyberport 2
100 Cyberport Road
Hong Kong
Email: info@sanriotown.com

FIGURE 7-12 Sanrio's approach to COPPA compliance

TAXATION AND ELECTRONIC COMMERCE

Companies that do business on the Web are subject to the same taxes as any other company. However, even the smallest Web business can become instantly subject to taxes in many states and countries because of the Internet's worldwide scope. Traditional businesses may operate in one location and be subject to only one set of tax laws for years. By the time those businesses are operating in multiple states or countries, they have developed the internal staff and record-keeping infrastructure needed to comply with multiple tax laws. Firms that engage in electronic commerce must comply with these multiple tax laws from their first day of existence.

An online business can become subject to several types of taxes, including income taxes, transaction taxes, and property taxes. **Income taxes** are levied by national, state, and local governments on the net income generated by business activities. **Transaction taxes**, which include sales taxes, use taxes, excise taxes, and customs duties, are levied on the products or services that the company sells or uses. Customs duties are taxes levied by the United States and other countries on certain commodities when they are imported into the country. **Property taxes** are levied by states and local governments on the personal property and real estate used in the business. In general, the taxes that cause the greatest concern for Web businesses are income taxes and sales taxes.

Nexus

A government acquires the power to tax a business when that business establishes a connection with the area controlled by the government. For example, a business that is located in Kansas has a connection with the state of Kansas and is subject to Kansas taxes. If that company opens a branch office in Arizona, it forms a connection with Arizona and becomes subject to Arizona taxes on the portion of its business that occurs in Arizona. This connection between a tax-paying entity and a government is called **nexus**. The concept of nexus is similar in many ways to the concept of personal jurisdiction discussed earlier in this chapter. The activities that create nexus in the United States are determined by state law and thus vary from state to state. Nexus issues have been frequently litigated, and the resulting common law is fairly complex. Determining nexus can be difficult when a company conducts only a few activities in or has minimal contact with the state. In such cases, it is advisable for the company to obtain the services of a professional tax advisor.

Companies that do business in more than one country face national nexus issues. If a company undertakes sufficient activities in a particular country, it establishes nexus with that country and becomes liable for filing tax returns in that country. The laws and regulations that determine national nexus are different in each country. Again, companies will find the services of a professional tax lawyer or accountant who has experience in international taxation to be valuable.

U.S. Income Taxes

The **Internal Revenue Service (IRS)** is the U.S. government agency charged with administering the country's tax laws. A basic principle of the U.S. tax system is that any verifiable increase in a company's wealth is subject to federal taxation. Thus, any company whose U.S.-based Web site generates income is subject to U.S. federal income tax. Furthermore, a Web site maintained by a company in the United States must pay federal income tax on income generated outside of the United States. To reduce the incidence of double taxation of foreign earnings, U.S. tax law provides a credit for taxes paid to foreign countries. The IRS Web site's home page appears in Figure 7-13.

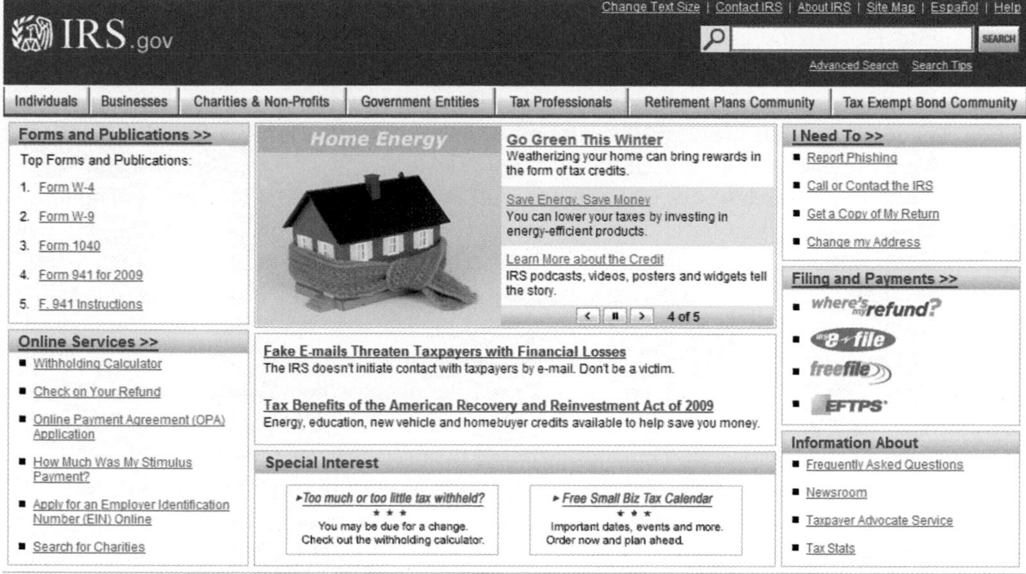

FIGURE 7-13 Internal Revenue Service home page

The IRS site includes links to downloadable tax forms, copies of IRS publications, current tax news, and other useful tax information. The home page offers links to sections of the Web site that are designed to help specific categories of site visitors.

Most states levy an income tax on business earnings. If a company conducts activities in several states, it must file tax returns in all of those states and apportion its earnings in accordance with each state's tax laws. In some states, the individual cities, counties, and other political subdivisions within the state also have the power to levy income taxes on business earnings. Companies that do business in multiple local jurisdictions must apportion their income and file tax returns in each locality that levies an income tax. The number of taxing authorities (which includes states, counties, cities, towns, school districts, water districts, and many other governmental units) in the United States exceeds 30,000.

Companies that sell through their Web sites do not, in general, establish nexus everywhere their goods are delivered to customers. Usually, a company can accept orders and ship from one state to many other states and avoid nexus by using a contract carrier such as FedEx or UPS to deliver goods to customers.

U.S. State Sales Taxes

Most U.S. states levy a transaction tax on goods sold to consumers. This tax is usually called a sales tax. Businesses that establish nexus with a state must file sales tax returns and remit the sales tax they collect from their customers. If a business ships goods to customers in other states, it is not required to collect sales tax from those customers unless the business has established nexus with the customer's state. However, the customer in this situation is liable for payment of a use tax in the amount that the business would have collected as sales tax if it had been a local business.

A **use tax** is a tax levied by a state on property used in that state that was not purchased in that state. Most states' use tax rates are identical to their sales tax rates. In addition to property purchased in another state, use taxes are assessed on property that is not "purchased" at all. For example, lease payments on vehicles are subject to use taxes in most states. The leased vehicle is not purchased (in any state) but when it is used in the lessee's state, it incurs that state's use tax. In the past, few consumers filed use tax returns and few states enforced their use tax laws with regularity. However, an increasing number of states are providing a line on their individual income tax returns that asks people to report and pay their use tax for the year along with their state income taxes. Some states allow taxpayers to estimate their use tax liability; others require an exact statement of the use tax amount.

Larger businesses use complex software to manage their sales tax obligations. Not only are the sales tax rates different in the 7500 U.S. sales tax jurisdictions (which include states, counties, cities, and other sales tax authorities), but the rules about which items are taxable differ. For example, New York's sales tax law provides that large marshmallows are taxable (because they are "snacks"), but small marshmallows are not taxable (because they are "food").

Some purchasers are exempt from sales tax, such as certain charitable organizations and businesses buying items for resale. Thus, to determine whether a particular item is subject to sales tax, a seller must know where the customer is located, what the laws of that jurisdiction say about taxability and tax rate, and the taxable status of the customer.

The sales tax collection process in the United States is largely regarded as a serious problem. Even the Supreme Court, in one of its sales tax decisions more than 10 years ago, stated that the situation is needlessly confusing and encouraged Congress to act. Although a number of bills have been introduced over the years, none has become law. Some large online retailers, such as Amazon.com, have announced that they will begin collecting and remitting sales tax on all sales, even when the sale is delivered into a state with which the company does not have nexus.

Many of the states have joined together through the **National Governor's Association** and the **National Conference of State Legislatures** to create the Streamlined Sales and Use Tax Agreement (SSUTA). The SSUTA simplifies state sales taxes by making the various state tax codes more congruent with each other while allowing each state to set its own rates. Each state must adopt the agreement, and once a state does adopt it, companies in the state can choose one of several simple procedures for collecting and remitting sales taxes nationwide.

Import Tariffs

All countries in the world regulate the import and export of goods across their borders. In many cases, goods can only be imported into a country if a tariff is paid. A **tariff**, also called a **customs duty** or **duty**, is a tax levied on products as they enter the country. Countries have many reasons for imposing tariffs, and a complete discussion of tariffs and the role they play in international economics and foreign trade policy is beyond the scope of this book. Goods that are ordered online are subject to tariffs when they cross international borders. Even products that are delivered online (such as downloaded software) can be subject to tariffs. Many online shoppers have been surprised when an item they ordered from another country arrives with a bill from their government for the tariff.

European Union Value Added Taxes

The United States raises most of its revenue through income taxes. Other countries, especially those in the European Union (EU), use transfer taxes to generate most of their revenues. The Value Added Tax (VAT) is the most common transfer tax used in these countries. A VAT is assessed on the amount of value added at each stage of production. For example, if a computer keyboard manufacturer purchased keyboard components for $20 and then sold finished keyboards for $50, the value added would be $30. VAT is collected by the seller at each stage of the transaction. A product that goes through five different companies on its way to the ultimate consumer would have VAT assessed on each of the five sales. In most countries, VAT is calculated at the time of each intermediate sale and remitted to the country in which that sale occurs.

The EU enacted legislation concerning the application of VAT to sales of digital goods that became effective in 2003. Companies based in EU countries must collect VAT on digital goods no matter where in the EU the products are sold. This legislation has attracted the attention of companies based outside of the EU that sell digital goods to consumers based in one or more EU countries. Under the law, non-EU companies that sell into the EU must now register with EU tax authorities and levy, collect, and remit VAT if their sales include digital goods delivered into the EU.

Summary

The legal concept of jurisdiction on the Internet is still unclear and ill defined. The relationship between geographic boundaries and legal boundaries is based on four elements: power, effects, legitimacy, and notice. These four elements have helped governments create the legal concept of jurisdiction in the physical world. Because the four elements exist in somewhat different forms on the Internet, the jurisdiction rules that work so well in the physical world do not always work well in the online world.

As in traditional commerce, contracts are a part of doing business on the Web and are established through various types of offers and acceptances. Any contract for the electronic sale of goods or services includes implied warranties. Many companies include contracts or rules on their Web sites in the form of terms of service agreements. Contracts can be invalidated when one of the parties to the transaction is an imposter; however, forged identities are becoming easier to detect through electronic security tools.

Seemingly innocent inclusion of photographs, whether manipulated or not, and other elements on a Web page can lead to infringement of trademarks, copyrights, or patents; defamation; and violation of publicity or privacy rights. An international administrative mechanism now exists for resolving domain name disputes that has reduced the need for lengthy and expensive litigation in many cases. Electronic commerce sites must be careful not to imply relationships that do not actually exist. Negative evaluative statements about entities, even when true, are best avoided given the subjective nature of defamation and product disparagement.

Unfortunately, some people use the Internet for perpetrating crimes, advocating terrorism, and even waging war. Law enforcement agencies have found it difficult to combat many types of online crime, and governments are working to create adequate defenses for online war and terrorism.

Web business practices such as collecting information and tracking consumer habits have led to questions of ethics regarding online privacy. Some countries are far more restrictive than others in terms of what type of information collection is acceptable and legal. Companies that collect personal information can use an opt-in policy, in which the customer must take an action to permit information collection, or an opt-out policy, in which the customer must take an action to prevent information collection. Opt-in policies are more protective of customers' privacy rights. Web businesses also must be careful when communicating with children. The laws of most countries require that parental consent be obtained before information is collected from children under the age of 13.

Companies that conduct electronic commerce are subject to the same laws and taxes as other companies, but the nature of doing business on the Web can expose companies to a large number of laws and taxes sooner than traditional companies usually face them. The international nature of all online business further complicates a firm's tax obligations. Although some legal issues are straightforward, others are difficult to interpret and follow because of the newness of electronic commerce and the unsettled nature of applicable law. The large number of government agencies that have jurisdiction and the power to tax makes it essential that companies doing business on the Web understand the potential liabilities of doing business with customers in those jurisdictions.

Key Terms

Acceptance
Advance fee fraud
Authority to bind
Breach of contract
Browser-wrap acceptance
Business process patent
Click-wrap acceptance
Common law
Conflict of laws
Consideration
Constructive notice
Contract
Cookies
Copy control
Copyright
Customs duty (duty)
Cyberbullying
Cybersquatting
Defamatory
Digital watermark
Domain name ownership change
Effects
End-user license agreement (EULA)
Fair use
Forum selection clause
Implied contract
Implied warranty
Income tax
Intellectual property
Intentional tort
Judicial comity
Jurisdiction
Legitimacy
Long-arm statute
Name changing (typosquatting)
Name stealing
Negligent tort
Nexus
Nigerian scam (419 scam)
Notice
Offer
Opt-in
Opt-out
Patent
Per se defamation
Personal jurisdiction
Power
Product disparagement
Property tax
Right of publicity
Service mark
Shrink-wrap acceptance
Signature
Statute of Frauds
Statutory law
Subject-matter jurisdiction
Sufficient jurisdiction
Tariff
Terms of service (ToS)
Tort
Trademark
Trademark dilution
Trade name
Transaction tax
Use tax
Vicarious copyright infringement
Warranty disclaimer
Web-wrap acceptance
Writing

Review Questions

RQ1. In the past, geographic borders have helped governments assert jurisdiction effectively. In about 200 words, explain how a government's power, and therefore its ability to enforce jurisdiction, is limited in matters relating to online business transactions.

RQ2. Assume you are working for a company that sells music online. The marketing department would like to send e-mails to customers who have purchased music from the Web site. These e-mails would use information about the genres of music customers have purchased in the past and would offer them discounts on new releases in those genres. Write the text of a memo (about 200 words) in which you make a case to the marketing manager for using an opt-in statement for permission to send such emails that would appear when customers make their first purchase.

RQ3. The advisability of allowing governments to issue patents on business processes has been vigorously debated by legal scholars and business researchers. A compromise proposal advanced by Jeff Bezos, founder of Amazon.com, would allow the issuance of business patents, but restrict the patent protection period to a short time, perhaps two or three years. In about 200 words, present logical and factual arguments that support the issuance of limited-term business process patents.

RQ4. In about 100 words, explain what a warranty disclaimer is and describe the circumstances under which a company that is doing business online might want to use one.

RQ5. In two or three paragraphs, explain how the WIPO's Domain Name Dispute Resolution process overcomes some of the jurisdictional issues that might arise if a United States court were to hear these types of disputes instead.

RQ6. In about 200 words, explain the idea of nexus. As part of your answer, explain why it is an important concept in state and international taxation and identify ways in which it is similar to jurisdiction.

Exercises

E1. Use your favorite Web search engine to obtain a list of Web pages that include the words "privacy statement." Visit the Web pages on the search results list until you find a page that includes the text of a privacy statement. Print the page and turn it in with a report of about 200 words in which you answer the following questions:

- Does the site follow an opt-in or opt-out policy (or is the policy not stated clearly in the privacy statement)?
- Does the privacy statement include a specific provision or provisions regarding the collection of information from children?
- Does the privacy statement describe what happens to the collected personal information if the company goes out of business or is sold to another company (list these provisions, if any)?

Close your report with one paragraph in which you evaluate the overall clarity of the privacy statement.

E2. Companies that do business online can find themselves in legal trouble if they commit a crime, breach a contract, or engage in a tortious action. In about 200 words, provide an online business example of each. As part of your answer, explain why you believe each action you describe is either a crime, a breach of contract, or a tort.

E3. Your friend Alex has developed an energy drink that she would like to sell online. Prepare a report of about 200 words in which you outline for Alex the rules and guidelines she should follow in presenting claims about this product on her Web site. Use the link to the **Federal Trade Commission: Advertising and Marketing on the Internet** and your favorite search engine to gather information for your report.

E4. Use your favorite search engine to find a Web site (other than Disney or Sanriotown) that is directed at young people. Examine the site to determine how it complies with COPPA. Test the site to ensure that it does not accept information from children under the age of 13. Evaluate the site's compliance with COPPA in a report of about 200 words.

E5. In the United States, a law called the Internet Tax Moratorium (ITM) has been enacted and renewed several times. The purpose of the ITM is to prevent federal, state, or local governments from enacting any new taxes on Internet business activities. Use Google or your favorite search engine to learn more about the ITM. In about 300 words, critically evaluate the rationale behind the law and take a position on whether the law should be renewed again when it expires.

Cases

C1. Nissan.com

The Nissan Motor Company of Japan had sold its cars in the United States under the brand name Datsun for many years. In the late 1980s, the company changed its branding policy and began selling cars in the U.S. market with the name of Nissan. However, the company did not realize that the Web would become an important marketing tool and did not register the name nissan.com as soon as it became available.

Nissan was not the only auto company to miss an opportunity to register its brand's domain name early. General Motors had registered the domain gm.com in 1992, but it had not registered generalmotors.com. The company had to purchase that name from Gil Vanorder, who had registered it in 1997. Vanorder's site featured a cigar-smoking, uniform-wearing cartoon character named "General John C. Motors." Volkswagen (which had registered vw.com when it first became available) successfully sued Virtual Works (an ISP) to obtain the domain name vw.net. Other auto companies have purchased or sued (with mixed results) to obtain domain names that included their product brand names. DaimlerChrysler was able to purchase dodge.com in 2001 from the London financial software company that had registered it originally. Ford had to sue National A-1 Advertising to obtain the right to use lincoln.com. However, Ford was unsuccessful in its attempts to obtain mercury.com. That name was owned by the New York City information technology services company, Mercury Technologies, which is now owned by Hewlett-Packard.

In 1991, Uzi Nissan formed a company named Nissan Computer Corp. in North Carolina to sell computer hardware and provide related repair and consulting services. Nissan's company also offered networking hardware for sale, along with related services. In 1994, the company registered the name nissan.com. In 1996, the company registered the domain name nissan.net and began offering ISP services to individuals and companies at that Web site.

In 1995, he received a letter from a lawyer representing Nissan Motor Co. The letter requested information about how Nissan was planning to use the domain name nissan.com. Since he was operating a computer company and Nissan Motor Co. was an auto company, Nissan decided there would be no potential confusion in customers' minds about the relationship (or lack thereof) between Nissan Computer and Nissan Motor Co. Nissan did not respond to the letter. The lawyer did not follow up with any other contact, so Nissan considered the issue closed.

In 2000, Nissan Motor Co. sued Nissan Computer under the U.S. Anticybersquatting Consumer Protection Act for $10 million and the exclusive right to use the names nissan.com and nissan.net. Uzi Nissan argued in court that he was just using his family name (which is a common name in the Middle East) to which he had a basic right, that he had no intent to profit from the name (he was unwilling to sell it to Nissan Motor Co. at any price), and that there was little likelihood that his computer store would be confused in the minds of the consumers with the international auto company of the same name. Nissan Motor Co. argued that its brand name was so well known that any alternative use of the name would be confusing to consumers.

In 2002, opinions issued by the California Superior Court and the U.S. Ninth Circuit District Court held that Nissan Computer had not acted in bad faith when it acquired the disputed domain names. However, the court ruled that Nissan Computer could no longer use the domain names for commercial purposes because of the potential confusion it could create in the minds of consumers. Nissan Computer would have to find a different domain name for its business. The court also ordered that Nissan could not place any advertising on his Web sites at nissan.com or nissan.net and prohibited him from placing disparaging remarks or negative commentary about Nissan Motor Co. (or links to such remarks or commentary) on the two sites. The court did not, however, order the transfer of the two domain names to Nissan Motor Co. The Online Companion includes links to the Web sites operated today by Nissan Computer and Nissan Motor Co. In 2005, the U.S. Supreme Court refused to hear Nissan Motor Co.'s appeal of the lower court rulings, which allows them to stand.

Required:

1. U.S. courts sometimes appoint advisors (often called Special Masters) to help them decide cases that involve complex business or technical issues. Assume you are a business advisor to a court that is hearing an appeal of the Nissan Motor Co. v. Nissan Computer Corp. case. In about 200 words, explain why Nissan Motor Co. is so concerned about the use of these two domain names and how a monetary damages judgment of $10 million could be justified (if you do not believe that the monetary damages are justified, explain why).
2. In about 200 words, provide an outline of the ethics of the position taken by Uzi Nissan in this dispute.
3. In about 200 words, provide an outline of the ethics of the position taken by Nissan Motor Co. in this dispute.
4. If you believe that the courts' decisions in this case are fair to the parties and the general public, explain why in about 200 words. If you believe that the courts' decisions are not fair, outline a decision (in about 200 words) that you believe would be fair.

Note: Your instructor might assign you to a group to complete this case, and might ask you to prepare a formal presentation of your results to your class.

C2. Ellasaurus Products Enterprises

Ellen Carson is the author and illustrator of a successful series of children's books that chronicle the adventures of Ellasaurus, a 4-year-old orange dinosaur. Ellen has done well with the books, but her business advisors have told her that she could earn considerably more money by creating a merchandising business around the Ellasaurus character. Following this advice, she has created Ellasaurus Products Enterprises (EPE), a company that has begun developing and marketing Ellasaurus toys, stuffed animals, coloring books, pajamas, and Halloween costumes.

EPE has had some success in its attempts to get major retailers to stock the Ellasaurus product line, but Ellen is concerned that retailers might not be willing to take on a new and unproven product. She would like to create a Web site through which EPE could sell its merchandise directly to customers. She also sees the Web site as a way to build customer loyalty. Ellen envisions a site with a number of portal features in addition to the product sales. For example, she would like to offer online games, chat rooms, e-mail accounts, and other activities that would promote EPE products and her books.

The Ellasaurus book series appeals to children who are between 4 and 6 years old. Ellen expects the EPE product line to appeal to children in about the same age range. Ellen has visited sites such as **Hello Kitty** and **Nick Jr.**, which appeal to similar age groups, to get ideas for the site. She would like the site to be appealing to her main audience, but she would like to obtain registration information from site visitors so EPE can send e-mails with information about new products and Web site features to them.

Ellen plans to limit the Web site's merchandise sales to U.S. residents at first, but she hopes to begin selling internationally within a few years. The site will allow visitors from any country to register and participate in the online portal features.

Required:

1. Ellen will use some copyrighted illustrations from her books on the Web site. She will also include themes from the story lines of her books in some of the games that will be available (free) on the site to registered visitors. Prepare a report of about 300 words in which you discuss at least two intellectual property issues that might arise in the operation of the Web site.
2. In about 200 words, describe the ethical issues that Ellen faces because of the ages of her intended audience members.
3. In about 300 words, outline the laws with which the site must comply when it registers site visitors under the age of 13. Include recommendations regarding how Ellen can best comply with those laws.
4. In about 300 words, describe the sales tax liabilities to which the Web site will be exposed. Assume that Ellen will operate the site from her home office in Michigan and that EPE will manufacture the merchandise in Texas. The merchandise will be warehoused at EPE distribution centers in New Jersey, Ohio, and California.

Note: Your instructor might assign you to a group to complete this case, and might ask you to prepare a formal presentation of your results to your class.

For Further Study and Research

Angwin, J. and D. Bank. 2005. "Time Warner Alerts Staff to Lost Data: Files for 600,000 Workers Vanish During Truck Ride," *The Wall Street Journal,* May 3, A3.

Bagby, J. and F. McCarty. 2003. *The Legal and Regulatory Environment of E-Business.* Cincinnati: Thomson South-Western.

Barry Diller v INTERNETCO Corp. 2001. WIPO Case No. D2000-1734, March 9. (http://www.wipo.int/amc/en/domains/decisions/html/2000/d2000-1734.html)

Barkacs, L., T. Dalton, G. Schneider, and C. Barkacs. 2004. "U.S. Sales Taxes on Internet Transactions: Historic Change is at the Door," *Journal of Accounting and Finance Research,* 12(5), 135–144.

Barnes, B. 2007. "Web Playgrounds of the Very Young," *The New York Times,* December 31. (http://www.nytimes.com/2007/12/31/business/31virtual.html)

Better Business Bureau. 2006. *Security & Privacy Made Simpler.* Arlington, VA: The Council of Better Business Bureaus.

Brilmayer, L. 1989. "Consent, Contract, and Territory," *Minnesota Law Review,* 74(1), 11–12.

Cass, S. 2002. "Nissan v. Nissan," *IEEE Spectrum,* 39(10), October, 53–54.

Cathcart, R. 2008. "MySpace Is Said to Draw Subpoena in Hoax Case," *The New York Times,* January 10. (http://www.nytimes.com/2008/01/10/us/10myspace.html)

Claburn, T., M. Garvey, and V. Koen. 2005. "The Threats Get Nastier," *InformationWeek,* August 29, 34–41.

Clark, P. 2001. "Doubts Cloud DoubleClick's Repositioning," *B to B,* 86(15), August 28, 1–2.

Coll, S. and S. Glasser. 2005. "Terrorists Turn to the Web as Base of Operations," *The Washington Post,* August 7, A1.

Crane, E. 2000. "Double Trouble," *Ziff Davis Smart Business,* 13(10), October, 62.

Digital Millennium Copyright Act. 1998. Public Law No. 105-304, 112 Statutes 2860.

Direct Marketing. 2001. "FTC Closes DoubleClick Investigation," 63(12), April, 18.

Federal Trade Commission (FTC). 1999. *Self-Regulation and Privacy Online: A Report to Congress.* Washington: FTC.

Fidler, S. 2007. "Terrorism Fight 'in Wrong Century,'" *Financial Times,* July 10, 4.

Foege, A. 2005. "Extortion.com," *Fortune Small Business,* September 1.

Foster, A. 2002. "Computer-Crime Incidents at 2 California Colleges Tied to Investigation Into Russian Mafia," *Chronicle of Higher Education,* June 24.

Granholm v.Heald 544 US 460 (2005).

Greene, S. 2001. "Reconciling Napster with the Sony Decision and Recent Amendments to Copyright Law," *American Business Law Journal,* 39(1), Fall, 57–98.

Hamblen, M. 2003. "Regulatory Requirements Place New Burdens on IT: U.S. Firms Scramble to Comply with EU Tax," *Computerworld,* June 30, 1.

Hardesty, D. 2004. *Sales Tax and Electronic Commerce.* Larkspur, CA: ClickBank.

Harmon, A. 2001. "As Public Records Go Online, Some Say They're Too Public," *The New York Times,* August 24, A1.

Hemphill, T. 2000. "DoubleClick and Consumer Online Privacy: An E-Commerce Lesson Learned," *Business & Society Review,* 105(3), Fall, 361–372.

Hulme, G. 2005. "Extortion Online," *InformationWeek,* September 13, 24–25.

Hwang, W. and J. Klosek. 2003. "Taxing the Sale of Digital Goods in Europe," *E-Commerce Law & Strategy,* 20(3), July 11, 1.

Ian, J. 2002. "The Internet Debacle: An Alternative View," *Performing Songwriter Magazine,* May. (http://www.janisian.com/)
Identity Theft Resource Center (ITRC). 2009. *2009 Breach List.* San Diego: ITRC.
Isenberg, D. 2000. "Many Trademarks, But Just One Domain Name," *Internet World,* July 1, 86.
Jones, K. 2007. "Sexual Predators: MySpace in the Middle," *Information Week,* May 21, 20.
Jordan, M. 2007. "Interpol Chief Calls U.K. Lax In Terror Fight; Failure to Share Data Also Cited," *Washington Post,* July 10, A11.
Journal of Internet Law. 2002. "Computer Firm's Use of Nissan.com Not Bad Faith Under Anticybersquatting Act," 6(1), July, 23.
Kaplan, C. 2002. "A Libel Suit May Decide E-Jurisdiction," *The New York Times,* May 27. (http://www.nytimes.com/2002/05/27/technology/27ELAW.html)
Kisiel, R. 2002. "Two Nissans Collide on Information Highway," *Automotive News,* December 16, 1IT–2IT.
Krim, J. 2004. "Justice Department to Announce Cyber-Crime Crackdown: Actions to Include Arrests, Subpoenas," *The Washington Post,* August 25, E5.
Lehman, P. and T. Lowry. 2007. "The Marshal of MySpace: How Hemanshu Nigam Is Trying to Keep the Site's 'Friends' Safe From Predators and Bullies," *Business Week,* April 23, 86.
Leonard, A. 2002. "Nissan vs. Nissan," *Salon.com,* June 3. (http://www.salon.com/tech/col/leon/2002/06/03/nissan/index.html)
Lessig, L. 2000. *Code and Other Laws of Cyberspace.* New York: Basic Books.
Liptak, A. 2003. "U.S. Courts' Role in Foreign Feuds Comes Under Fire," *The New York Times,* August 3, 1.
Mangalindan, M. 2007. "EBay Is Ordered to Pay $30 Million in Patent Rift," *The Wall Street Journal,* December 13, B4.
Manjoo, F. 2001. "Fine Print Not Necessarily in Ink," *Wired News,* April 6. (http://www.wired.com/news/business/0,1367,42858,00.html)
Maurer, H. and C. Lindblad. 2008. "Safer Networking," *Business Week,* January 28, 9.
Moran, J. and J. Kummer. 2003. "U.S. and International Taxation of the Internet: Part I," *Computer & Internet Lawyer,* 20(4), April, 1–18.
Moringiello, J. and W. Reynolds. 2008. "Survey of the Law of Cyberspace: Electronic Contracting Cases 2007-2008," *The Business Lawyer,* 64(1), November, 199–218.
Mueller, M. 2002. *Rough Justice: An–Analysis of ICANN's Uniform Dispute Resolution Policy.* Syracuse, NY: Syracuse University Convergence Center.
Murray, J. 2000. "E-Contracts Present Courts with Special Legal Challenges," *Purchasing,* 129(3), August 24, 119–120.
Nee, E. 2005. "Days of Wine and Roses," *CIO Insight,* July, 25–26.
Network Briefing Daily. 2002. "Amazon Settles 1-Click Patent Dispute," March 8, 3–4.
Newman, M. 2006. "MySpace.com Hires Official to Oversee Young Users' Safety," *International Herald Tribune,* April 13, 18.
Nigro, D. 2005. "Supreme Court Lifts Shipping Bans," *Wine Spectator,* 30(6), July 31, 12–12.
Nissan Motor Co. v. Nissan Computer Corp., 246 F.3d 675 (9th Cir. 2002).
Null, C. 2009. "Amazon Likely to Scrap Wine Sales Program," *Today in Tech,* October 24. (http://tech.yahoo.com/blogs/null/153950)
O'Brien, T. 2005. "The Rise of the Digital Thugs," *The New York Times,* August 7, C1.
Oder, N. 2002. "COPA Ruling Offers Mixed Message," *Library Journal,* 127(11), June 15, 15.

Oliva, R. and S. Prabakar. 1999. "Copyright Perils Can Lurk on the Business Web," *Marketing Management,* 8(1), Spring, 54–57.

Patchin, J. and S. Hinduja. 2008. "Offline Consequences of Online Victimization: School Violence and Delinquency," *Journal of School Violence,* 6(3), 89–112.

Phillips, D. 2003. "JetBlue Apologizes for Use of Passenger Records," *The Washington Post,* September 20, E1.

Porter, K. and S. Bradley. 1999. *eBay, Inc.* Case #9-700-007. Cambridge, MA: Harvard Business School.

Reagle, J. 1999. "The Platform for Privacy Preferences," *Communications of the ACM,* 42(2), February, 48–51.

Rewick, J. 2000. "DoubleClick Finds Its Abacus Unit Nettlesome," *The Wall Street Journal,* October 19, B6.

Richtel, M. 2004. "U.S. Steps Up Push Against Online Casinos by Seizing Cash," *The New York Times,* May 31, C1.

Romano, A. 2006. "Walking a New Beat: Surfing MySpace.com Helps Cops Crack the Case," *Newsweek,* April 24, 48.

Samborn, H. 2000. "Nibbling Away at Privacy," *ABA Journal,* 86(2), June, 26–27.

Samuelson, P. 1999. "Good News and Bad News on the Intellectual Property Front," *Communications of the ACM,* 42(3), March, 19–24.

Schneider, G., L. Barkacs, and C. Barkacs. 2006. "Software Errors: Recovery Rights Against Vendors," *Journal of Legal, Ethical and Regulatory Issues,* 9(2), 61–67.

Schwanhausser, M. 2008. "EBay Patent Case Settled: It Owns 'Buy It Now' After Six-Year Battle," *San Jose Mercury News.* February 29.

Shaller, D. 2000. "E-mail, the Internet, and Other Legal and Ethical Nightmares," *Strategic Finance,* August, 82(2), 48–52.

Smith, J. 2008. "New rules for Banks Target Online Gambling," *The Washington Post,* November 13. (http://www.washingtonpost.com/wp-dyn/content/article/2008/11/12/AR2008111202668.html)

Stellin, S. 2002. "In Fights Over .Com Names, Trademark Owners Usually Win," *The New York Times,* June 24, 4.

Stinson, J. 2007. "Interpol Chief Urges More Data Sharing, He Says Terrorism Information Should Flow Worldwide," *USA Today,* July 9, 9A.

Stone, M. 2001. "Court Dismisses Class Action Against eBay," *BizReport,* January 19. (http://www.bizreport.com/daily/2001/01/20010119-4.htm)

Surowiecki, J. 2003. "Patent Bending," *The New Yorker,* July 14, 36.

Tanford, J. 2005. "*Granholm v.Heald*: The Supreme Court Strikes Down Trade Barriers Against the Direct Sale of Wine," *Duke Law School: Supreme Court Online,* May. (http://www.law.duke.edu/publiclaw/supremecourtonline/commentary/gravhea.html)

Tynan, D. 2000. "Privacy 2000: In Web We Trust?" *PC World,* 18(6), June, 103–111.

United Nations. 1970. "Declaration on Principles of International Law Concerning Friendly Relations and Cooperation Among States in Accordance with the Charter of the United Nations," *General Assembly Resolution,* #2625, 35th Session.

Van Alstine, P. 2004. "Federal Common Law in an Age of Treaties," *Cornell Law Review,* 89(892), 917–927.

Van Name, M. and B. Catchings. 1998. "Practical Advice About Privacy and Customer Data," *PC Week,* 15(27), July 6, 38.

Vara, V. and L. Chao. 2006. "EBay Steps Back From Asia, Will Shutter China Site," *The Wall Street Journal,* December 19. (http://online.wsj.com/article/SB116647579560853680.html)

Venezia, P. 2009. "Are Apple's App Store Policies Ruining Everything?" *InfoWorld,* November 16. (http://www.infoworld.com/t/mobile-applications/are-apples-app-store-policies-ruining-everything-353)

Whitlock, C. 2005. "Briton Used Internet As His Bully Pulpit," *The Washington Post,* August 8, A1.

Wiley, L. 1999. "Proposed Revisions to European Copyright Laws Cause a Stir," *E Media Professional,* 12(4), April, 16–17.

Ybarra, M., K. Mitchell, J. Wolak, and D. Finkelhor. 2006. "Examining Characteristics and Associated Distress Related to Internet Harassment: Findings From the Second Youth Internet Safety Survey," *Pediatrics,* 118(4), 1169–1177.

PART 3

TECHNOLOGIES FOR ELECTRONIC COMMERCE

CHAPTER **8**

WEB SERVER HARDWARE AND SOFTWARE

LEARNING OBJECTIVES

In this chapter, you will learn about:

- Web server basics
- Software for Web servers
- E-mail management and spam control issues
- Internet and Web site utility programs
- Web server hardware

INTRODUCTION

As you learned in earlier chapters, **Lands' End** was one of the most successful clothing retailers on the Web before it was acquired by Sears in 2003. Now, as a division of Sears, Lands' End continues to be a leader in adding features that attract customers to its Web site and keep those customers coming back. Behind the scenes at Lands' End, a team of experienced technology professionals implements new Web page features and performs the many regular maintenance tasks that are necessary to keep the Lands' End Web site running smoothly.

Lands' End closely monitors the performance of its Web site to make sure that customers have a consistent experience each time they visit the site. The Web site's technical team works hard to make sure that site visitors do not notice the Web site's operating characteristics. This goal has not always been easy to attain because the site's traffic volume has increased each year since the site opened. Also, regular major improvements to the Lands' End site keep the Web team busy.

Lands' End's specific goals for performance change as Web technologies improve. For example, the site management team has a target for the time it takes one of the site's Web pages to load on a visitor's computer. In the early days of the site, that target was 15 seconds. Today, the target is under one second. The Web site's technical team has always taken a conservative approach to operating the site so that the site can meet its performance goals more easily. For example, the technical team specifies the maximum and average sizes of Web pages and graphics files that the content team can use. In addition, the technical team must complete all major changes to the site (including thorough testing) before November 1 each year, prior to the holiday selling season. Retailers such as Lands' End make more than half of their sales in November and December, so they rarely take the chance of making major Web site changes during that time period.

The server hardware at Lands' End is a mix of Sun and IBM computers that are managed by another computer that allocates incoming Web traffic. Some of the Web site's advanced features, such as the graphics-intensive My Virtual Model, are created on a separate set of computers. These computers are all located at the Lands' End division headquarters in a small town near Madison, Wisconsin. The computers run a UNIX-based operating system from Sun called Solaris and a version of the Apache Web server software, about which you will learn more in this chapter. Although the Lands' End technical team writes some of the software that it uses to monitor the Web site's performance, the company also uses the services of **Keynote Systems**. Keynote's software can measure how fast particular pages load or how rapidly transactions are completed at various times of the day and in various locations around the world. The Lands' End technical team uses this information to fine tune its hardware configuration.

By paying close attention to the details, the technical team at Lands' End keeps the Web site operating at or above expected levels. The technical team's goal is to prevent customers from being distracted from their shopping experiences by the operation of the site.

WEB SERVER BASICS

This chapter provides background information on the basic technologies used to build Web sites that can support online business operations. It includes a discussion of server software and hardware. It also includes an introduction to software that these sites use to perform utility functions such as site maintenance, diagnostics, and e-mail management. In later chapters, you will learn about software that accomplishes specific electronic commerce functions, such as order entry and processing, content management and delivery, user verification and security, and payment processing.

When people use their Internet connections to become part of the Web, their computers become Web client computers on a worldwide client/server network. Client/server architectures are used in LANs, WANs, and the Web. In a client/server architecture, the client computers typically request services, such as printing, information retrieval, and database access, from the server, which processes the clients' requests. The computers that perform the server function usually have more memory and larger, faster disk drives than the client computers they serve. Recall from Chapter 2 that Web browser software (for example, Microsoft Internet Explorer or Mozilla Firefox) is the software that makes computers work as Web clients. Thus, a Web browser is also called Web client software.

The Internet connects many different types of computers running different types of operating system software. Because Web software is platform neutral, it lets these computers communicate with each other easily and effectively. This platform neutrality was a critical ingredient in the rapid spread and widespread acceptance of the Web. Figure 8-1 shows how the Web's platform neutrality provides multiple interconnections among a wide variety of client and server computers.

The main job of a Web server computer is to respond to requests from Web client computers. The three main elements of a Web server are the hardware (computers and related components), operating system software, and Web server software. All three of these elements must work together to provide sufficient capacity in a given situation.

After most companies have decided on the goals they want to accomplish with their Web sites, they begin developing their sites by estimating the number of visitors they expect to have, how many pages those visitors will view during an average visit, how large those pages will be (including graphics and other page elements), and the likely maximum number of simultaneous visitors.

In the early days of electronic commerce, Web sites were collections of individual pages about the site's product or service offerings. Today, Web sites produce pages in response to customers' specific needs. You will learn how sites do that in the next section.

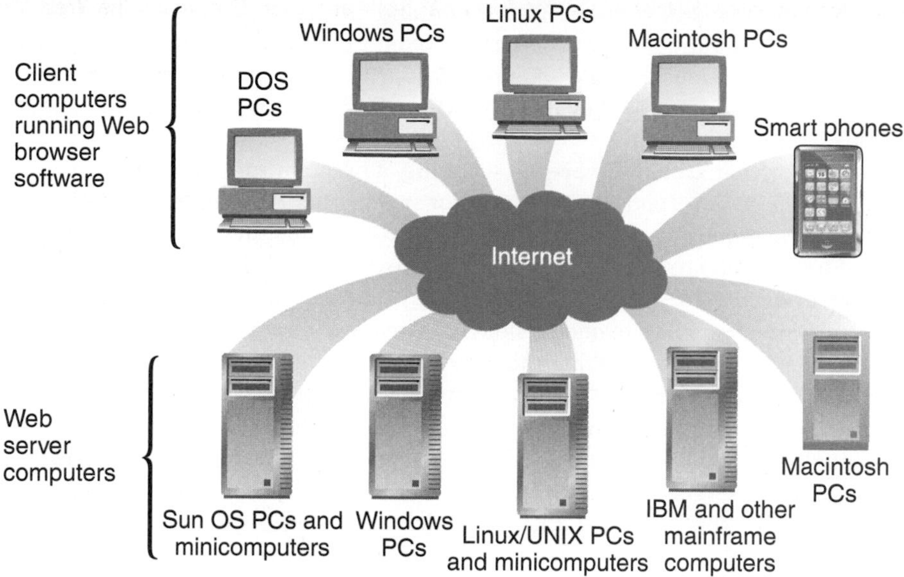

FIGURE 8-1 Platform neutrality of the Web

Dynamic Content Generation

A **dynamic page** is a Web page whose content is shaped by a program in response to user requests, whereas a **static page** is an unchanging page retrieved from a file (or, more typically, a set of files) on a Web server. On a Web site that is a collection of HTML pages, the content on the site can be changed only by editing the HTML in the pages. This is cumbersome and does not allow customized pages to be produced in response to specific queries from site visitors.

Dynamic content is nonstatic information constructed in response to a Web client's request. Dynamic content can give the user an interactive experience with the Web site. The text, graphics, form fields, and other Web page elements can change in response to user input or other variables. For example, if a Web client inquires about the status of an existing order by entering a customer number or order number into a form, the Web server generates a dynamic Web page based on the customer information stored in the company's database, thus fulfilling the client's request. A dynamic page is a specific response to the requester's query that is assembled from information stored in a company's back-end databases and internal data on the Web site.

Dynamic content can be created using two basic approaches. In the first approach, called **client-side scripting**, software operates on the Web client (the browser) to change what is displayed on the Web page in response to a user's actions (such as mouse clicks or keyboard text input). In client-side scripting, changes are generated within the browser using software such as JavaScript or Adobe Flash. The Web client retrieves a file from the Web server that includes code (JavaScript, for example). The code instructs the Web client to request specific page elements from the Web server and dictates how they will be displayed in the Web browser window. This approach is often used to manage the activity displayed on a Web page by various media elements (audio, video, changing graphics or text). Client-side scripting emerged on the Web in 1996, when the JavaScript language became widely available.

In the second approach, called **server-side scripting**, a program running on a Web server creates a Web page in response to a request for specific information from a Web client. The content of the request can be determined by several things, including text that a user has entered into a Web form in the browser, extra text added to the end of a URL, the type of Web browser making the request, or simply the passage of time. For example, if you are logged into an online banking site and do not enter any text or click anywhere on the page for a few minutes, you might find that the Web server ends your connection and sends a page to your browser indicating that "your session has expired."

A number of Web programming languages and frameworks have evolved that allow site designers to generate dynamic Web pages and make them interactive. In dynamic page-generation technologies, server-side scripts are mixed with HTML-tagged text to create the dynamic Web page. Microsoft developed the first widely used server-side dynamic page-generation technology, called **Active Server Pages (ASP)**. The current version of that technology is called **ASP.NET**. ASP allows Web programmers to use their choice of programming languages, such as VBScript, Jscript, or Perl. Sun Microsystems developed a similar technology called **JavaServerPages (JSP)**. Java, a programming language created by Sun, can also be used to produce dynamic pages. Such server-side programs are called **Java servlets**. The open-source Apache Software Foundation sponsored a third alternative called the **Hypertext Preprocessor (PHP)**. Yet another alternative is available from Adobe in its **ColdFusion** product. These server-side languages generally use the **Common Gateway Interface (CGI)**, which was introduced in 1993 as a standard way of interfacing external applications with Web servers. In its first applications, CGI was used to connect existing databases to Web servers, which allowed users all over the world to access those databases from their Web browsers. That is, CGI provided a gateway allowing users to enter remote databases.

Two dynamic page generation tools that have become popular in recent years include AJAX and Ruby on Rails. **AJAX** (asynchronous JavaScript and XML) is a development framework that can be used to create interactive Web sites that look like applications running in a Web browser. Most dynamic Web pages must reload in their entirety if any page content changes. AJAX lets programmers create Web pages that will update asynchronously by exchanging small amounts of data with the server while the remainder of the Web page continues to be displayed in the browser. Because the entire Web page does not reload with every change, the user experience is improved. Google Maps is an example of a dynamic page that is generated using Ajax. **Ruby on Rails** is another Web development framework that lets programmers create dynamic Web pages that present users with an interface that looks like application software running in a Web browser. **Python** is a scripting language that can also be used in dynamic Web page generation.

Various Meanings of "Server"

All computers that are connected to the Internet and contain documents that their owners have made publicly available through their Internet connections are called Web servers. Unfortunately, the term "server" is used in many different ways by information systems professionals. These multiple uses of the term can be confusing to people who do not have a strong background in computer technology. You are likely to encounter a number of different uses of the word "server."

A **server** is any computer used to provide (or "serve") files or make programs available to other computers connected to it through a network (such as a LAN or a WAN). The software that the server computer uses to make these files and programs available to the other computers is often called **server software**. Sometimes this server software is included as part of the operating system that is running on the server computer. Thus, some information systems professionals informally refer to the operating system software on a server computer as server software, a practice that adds considerable confusion to the use of the term "server."

Some servers are connected through a router to the Internet. As you learned in Chapter 2, these servers can run software, called Web server software, that makes files on those servers available to other computers on the Internet. When a server computer is connected to the Internet and is running Web server software (usually in addition to the server software it runs to serve files to client computers on its own network), it is called a Web server.

Similar terminology issues arise for server computers that perform e-mail processing and database management functions. Recall that the server computer that handles incoming and outgoing e-mail is usually called an e-mail server, and the software that manages e-mail activity on that server is frequently called e-mail server software. The server computer on which database management software runs is often called a **database server**.

Thus, the word "server" is used to describe several types of computer hardware and software, all of which might be found in a typical electronic commerce operation. The only way to determine which server people are talking about when they use the term is from the context or by asking a clarifying question. If you hear a computer technician say, "The server is down today," the problem might be in the hardware, the software, or a combination of the two!

Web Client/Server Architectures

In Chapter 2, you learned how the Web is software that runs on the Internet. In this section, you will learn more about how Web client and Web server software work. When a person uses a Web browser to visit a Web site, the Web browser (also known as a Web client) requests files from the Web server at the company or organization that operates the Web site. Using the Internet as the transportation medium, the request is formatted by the browser using HTTP and sent to the server computer. When the server receives the request, it retrieves the file containing the Web page or other information that the client requested, formats it using HTTP, and sends it back to the client over the Internet.

When the requested information—a file containing the text and markup tags of a Web page, in this instance—arrives at the client computer, the Web browser software determines that the information is an HTML page. It displays the page on the client machine according to the directions defined in the page's HTML code. This process repeats as the client requests, the server responds, and the client displays the result. Sometimes, a single client request results in dozens or even hundreds of separate server responses to locate and deliver information. A Web page containing many graphics and other objects can be slow to appear in the client's Web browser window because each page element (each graphic or multimedia file) requires a separate request and response.

The basic Web client/server model is a two-tier model because it has only one client and one server. All communication takes place on the Internet between the client and the server. Of course, other computers are involved in forwarding packets of information across the Internet, but the messages are created and read only by the client and the server computers in a **two-tier client/server architecture**. Figure 8-2 shows how a Web client and a Web server communicate with each other in a two-tier client/server architecture.

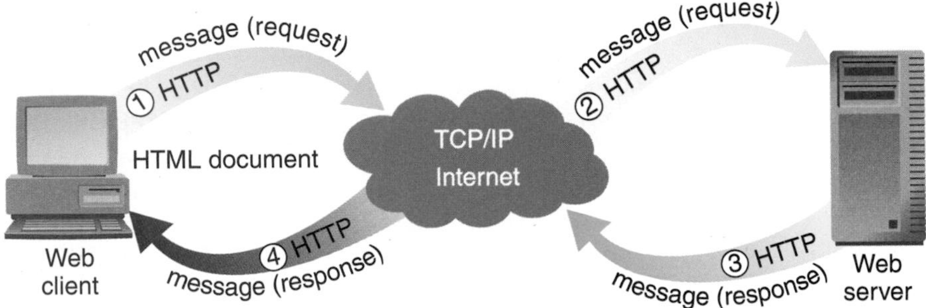

FIGURE 8-2 Message flows in a two-tier client/server network

The message that a Web client sends to request a file or files from a Web server is called a **request message**. A typical request message from a client to a server consists of three major parts:

- Request line
- Optional request headers
- Optional entity body

The **request line** contains a command, the name of the target resource (a file name and a description of the path to that file on the server), and the protocol name and version number. Optional **request headers** can contain information about the types of files that the client will accept in response to this request. Finally, an optional **entity body** is sometimes used to pass bulk information to the server.

When the server receives the request message, it executes the command included in the message (in this case, it sends a particular Web page file back to the client). The server does this by retrieving the Web page file from its disk (or another disk on a network to which it is connected) and then creating a properly formatted **response message** to send back to the client. A server's response consists of three parts that are identical in structure to a request message: a response header line, one or more response header fields, and an optional entity body. In the response, however, each part has a slightly different function than it does in the request. The **response header line** indicates the HTTP version used by the server, the status of the response (whether the server found the file that the client wanted), and an explanation of the status information. Response header fields follow the response header line. A **response header field** returns information describing the server's attributes. The entity body returns the HTML page requested by the client machine.

Although the two-tier client/server architecture works well for the delivery of Web pages, a Web site that delivers dynamic content and processes transactions must do more than respond to requests for Web pages. A **three-tier architecture** extends the two-tier architecture to allow additional processing (for example, collecting the information from a database needed to generate a dynamic Web page) to occur before the Web server responds to the Web client's request. The third tier often includes databases and related software applications that supply information to the Web server. The Web server can then use the output of these software applications when responding to client requests, instead of just delivering a Web page.

A good example of services supported by a database in a three-tier architecture is a catalog-style Web site with search, update, and display functions. Assume that a user requests a display of an online store's product selections. The client request is formulated into an HTTP message by the Web browser (tier 1), sent over the Internet to the Web server, and examined by the Web server. The Web server (tier 2) analyzes the request and determines that responding to the request requires the help of the server's database. The server sends a request to the database management software (tier 3) to search for, retrieve, and return all information about exotic fruit in the catalog database. The database information flows back through the database management software system to the server, which formats the response into an HTML document and sends that document inside an HTTP response message back to the client over the Internet. Figure 8-3 shows an overview of information flows in a three-tier architecture. Numbers on the flow arrows indicate the order in which the messages flow over the indicated paths.

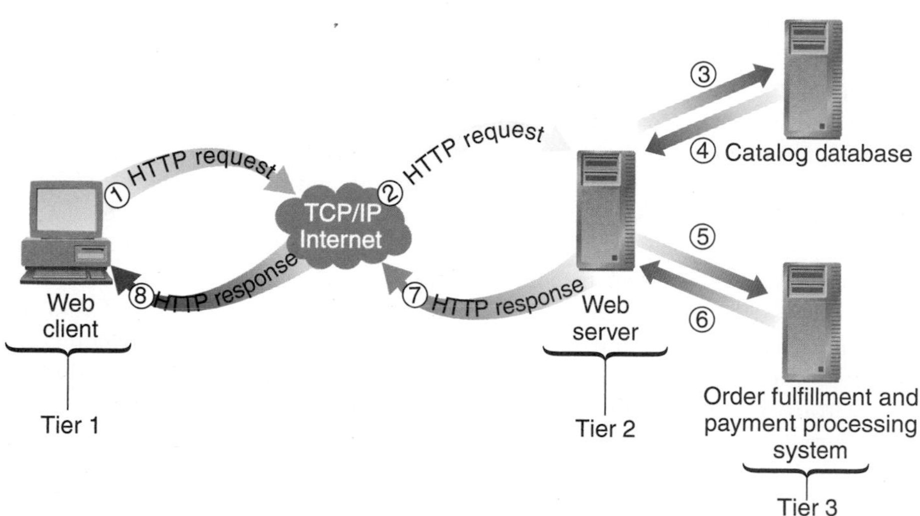

FIGURE 8-3 Message flows in a three-tier client/server network

Architectures that have four, five, or even more tiers divide into separate tiers the software applications and the databases and database management programs that work with those software applications. Also, some sites have software applications that generate information (a fourth tier) that feeds into other software applications or databases (in the third tier) that in turn generate information for the Web server to turn into Web pages (in the second tier), which then go to the requesting client (in the first tier). Architectures that have more than three tiers are often called **n-tier architectures**. N-tier systems can track customer purchases stored in shopping carts, look up sales tax rates, keep track of customer preferences, update in-stock inventory databases, and keep the company catalog current.

SOFTWARE FOR WEB SERVERS

Some Web server software can run on only one computer operating system, while some can run on several operating systems. In this section, you will learn about the operating system software used on most Web servers and the Web server software itself. You also will learn about other programs, such as Internet utilities and e-mail software, that companies often run on Web servers or other computers as part of electronic commerce operations.

Operating Systems for Web Servers

Operating system tasks include running programs and allocating computer resources such as memory and disk space to programs. Operating system software also provides input and output services to devices connected to the computer, including the keyboard, monitor, and printers. A computer must have an operating system to run programs. For large systems, the operating system has even more responsibilities, including keeping track of multiple users logged on to the system and ensuring that they do not interfere with one another.

Most Web server software runs on Microsoft Windows Server products, Linux, or UNIX-based operating systems such as FreeBSD or Sun's Solaris. Many companies believe that **Microsoft server products** are simpler for their information systems staff to learn and use than UNIX-based systems. Other companies worry about the security weaknesses caused by the tight integration between application software and the operating system in Microsoft products. UNIX-based Web servers are more popular, and many users believe that UNIX is a more secure operating system on which to run a Web server.

Linux is an open-source operating system that is fast, efficient, and easy to install. An increasing number of companies that sell computers intended to be used as Web servers include the Linux operating system in default configurations. Although Linux can be downloaded free from the Web, most companies buy it through a commercial distributor. These commercial distributions of Linux include useful additional software, such as installation utilities, and a support contract for the operating system. Commercial Linux distributors that sell versions of the operating system with utilities for Web servers include **Mandriva**, **Red Hat**, **SCO Group**, and **SuSE Linux Enterprise**. **Sun Microsystems** sells Web server hardware along with its UNIX-based operating system, **Solaris**.

Web Server Software

This section describes the most commonly used Web server programs today: Apache HTTP Server, Microsoft Internet Information Server (IIS), and Sun Java System Web Server (JSWS). These popularity rankings were accumulated through surveys done by **Netcraft**, a networking consulting company in Bath, England, known throughout the world for its Web server survey. Netcraft continually conducts surveys to tally the number of Web sites in existence and measure the relative popularity of Internet Web server software.

Figure 8-4 shows the use of Web server software by active sites in December 2009. You can click the **Netcraft Survey** link in the Online Companion to check out the latest Web survey results.

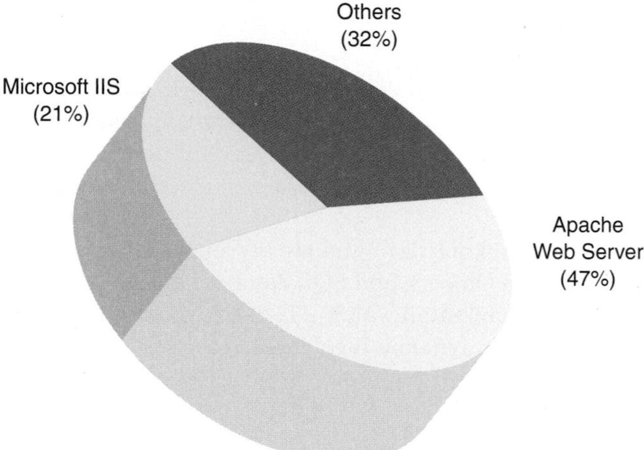

Source: Netcraft Web Surveys, http://www.netcraft.com

FIGURE 8-4 Percent of Web active sites that use major Web server software products

The Netcraft Web server surveys show that the market share of Web server software has stabilized in recent years. Apache generally holds about half of the market, and Microsoft's IIS usually holds between 20 and 35 percent of the market. A few other products account for the remainder of the market, including **QQ.com**, a Chinese Web server that began showing up on the Netcraft surveys in 2009.

The performance of one Web server differs from that of another based on workload, operating system, and the size and type of Web pages served. The sections that follow contain descriptions of the main Web server systems used in various electronic commerce applications.

Apache HTTP Server

Apache is an ongoing group software development effort. Rob McCool developed Apache while he was working at the University of Illinois at the National Center for Supercomputing Applications (NCSA) in 1994. Other Web site developers around the world created their own extensions to the server and formed an e-mail group so that they could coordinate their changes (known as "patches") to the system. The system consisted of the original core system with a lot of patches—thus, it became known as "a patchy" server, or simply, "Apache." The Apache Web server is currently available on the Web at no cost as open-source software.

Apache HTTP Server has dominated the Web since 1996 because it is free and performs very efficiently. Apache continues to be the most widely installed Web server software package. Apache runs on many operating systems (including FreeBSD-UNIX, HP-UX, Linux, Microsoft Windows, SCO-UNIX, and Solaris) and the hardware that supports them.

Microsoft Internet Information Server

Microsoft Internet Information Server (IIS) comes bundled with current versions of Microsoft Windows Server operating systems. IIS is used on many corporate intranets because many companies have adopted Microsoft products as their standard products. Small sites running personal Web pages use IIS, as do some of the largest electronic commerce sites on the Web.

IIS, as a Microsoft product, is designed to run only on Windows server operating systems. IIS supports the use of ASP, ActiveX Data Objects, and SQL database queries. IIS's inclusion of ASP provides an application environment in which HTML pages, ActiveX components, and scripts can be combined to produce dynamic Web pages.

Sun Java System Web Server

A descendant of the original NCSA Web server program, Sun Java System Web Server (JSWS) was formerly sold under the names Sun ONE, Netscape Enterprise Server, and iPlanet Enterprise Server. In 2009, Sun released key elements of the software as open source. Sun does sell support services for the software.

Sun JSWS runs on many operating systems, including HP-UX, Solaris, and Windows. According to recent estimates, Sun JSWS runs on about 1 percent of all Web servers. However, some of the busiest and best-known sites on the Internet, including BMW, Dilbert, E*TRADE, Excite, Lycos, and Schwab, run (or have run) some version of Sun JSWS.

Like most other server programs, Sun JSWS supports dynamic application development for server-side applications. Sun JSWS provides connectivity to a number of database products as well.

Finding Web Server Software Information

People who want to know the type of operating system and Web server software that a Web site is running can visit the **Netcraft** Web site. On Netcraft's home page is a link named "What's that site running?" that leads to a page with a search function. Visitors can use that search function to find out what operating system and what Web server software a specific site is now running and what the site ran in the past.

ELECTRONIC MAIL (E-MAIL)

Although the Web, with its interactions between Web servers and clients, is the most important technology used in electronic commerce today, many buyers and sellers also use e-mail to gather information, execute transactions, and perform other tasks related to electronic commerce. E-mail originated in the 1970s on the ARPANET. Although the goals of the ARPANET were to control weapons systems and transfer research files, general communications uses emerged on the network. As you learned in Chapter 2, in 1972, ARPANET researcher Ray Tomlinson wrote a program that could send and receive messages over the network. Today, e-mail is the most popular form of business communication—far surpassing the telephone, conventional mail, and fax in volume.

E-Mail Benefits

Not only was e-mail one of the first Internet applications, it was also one reason that many people were originally attracted to the Internet. E-mail conveys messages from one destination to another in a few seconds. Messages can contain simple ASCII text, or they can contain character formatting similar to word-processing programs.

One useful feature of e-mail is that documents, pictures, movies, worksheets, or other information can be sent along with the message itself. These **attachments** are frequently the most important part of the message. A business e-mail message attachment might contain an invoice, a 200-page wholesale catalog, or a set of Web pages that describe the company's products. Many electronic commerce sites use e-mail to confirm the receipt of customer orders and then the shipment of items ordered. Software vendors can also use e-mail to send information about a purchase to the buyer. As you learned in Chapter 3, many online stores use e-mail to announce specials, sales, or to keep in touch with customers.

E-Mail Drawbacks

Despite its many benefits, e-mail does have some drawbacks. One annoyance associated with e-mail is the amount of time that businesspeople spend answering their e-mail today. Researchers have found that most managers can deal with e-mail messages at an average rate of about five minutes per message. Some messages can be deleted within a few seconds, but those are balanced by the e-mails that require the manager to spend much more time finding facts, checking files, making phone calls, and doing other tasks as part of answering e-mail. Researchers have found that most people (not including those people who answer e-mails as a full-time job) begin to resent the time that e-mail consumes when they start getting more than 20 or 30 messages a day. At that point, the average person is spending about two hours a day answering e-mail.

A second major irritation brought by e-mail is the **computer virus**, more simply known as a **virus**, which is a program that attaches itself to another program and can cause damage when the host program is activated. Recall that e-mail messages can carry attachments. Although attached files usually carry useful information, they can contain viruses. Using virus protection software and dealing with e-mailed security threats is a cost that all must bear for the convenience of using e-mail. You will learn more about computer viruses and other threats that can be transmitted through e-mail (and how to control them) in Chapter 10.

As you learned in Chapter 2, the most frustrating and expensive problem associated with e-mail today is the issue of unsolicited commercial e-mail, also known as UCE or **spam**. This nagging problem is discussed in the next section.

Spam

Figure 8-5 shows the rapid increase in the proportion of all e-mail entering business e-mail servers that is spam. The sheer magnitude of the spam problem is hard to believe. During one recent 24-hour period, researchers estimated that 220 billion spam e-mail messages were sent. Many researchers who track the growth in spam believe that spam growth has leveled off, but that more than 90 percent of all e-mail messages (including messages transmitted to both business and personal users) will continue to be spam until effective technical solutions can be implemented. The growth of spam has leveled off (in part because it is approaching 100 percent) and appears to be declining slightly.

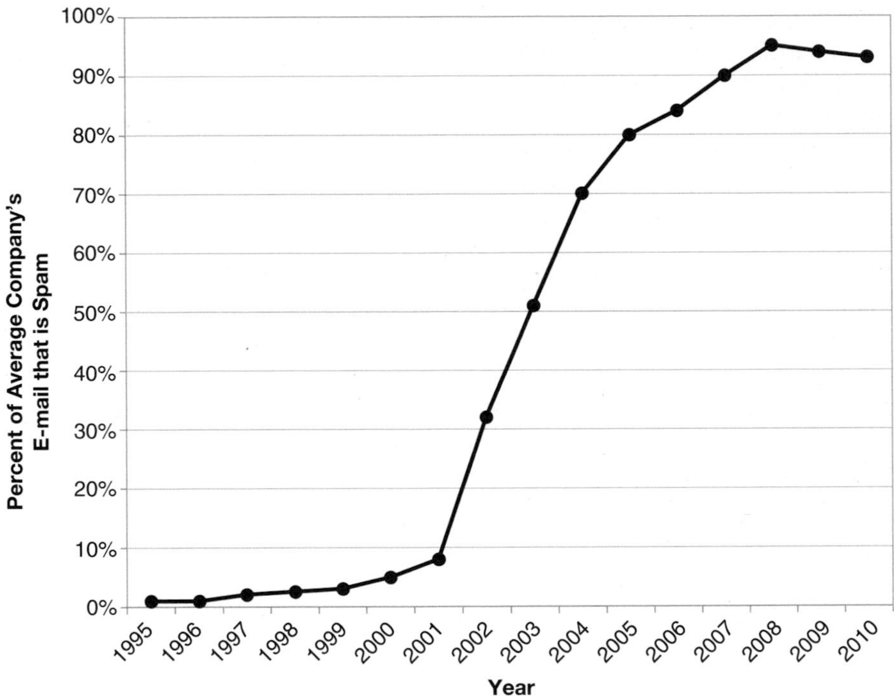

Various sources: Press, interviews, industry analysts

FIGURE 8-5 Growth of spam as a proportion of all business e-mail

A number of companies now offer software that organizations can run on their e-mail server computers to limit the amount of spam that gets through to their employees. Although individual users can install client-based spam-filtering programs on their computers or set filters that might be available within their e-mail client software, most companies find it more effective and less costly to eliminate spam before it is downloaded to user computers. These antispam efforts and software products can help limit the annoyance and cost of spam.

Solutions to the Spam Problem

As spam has grown to become a serious problem for all users of e-mail, the methods used to limit spam and its effects have taken various forms. Some of these approaches require the passing of laws, and some require technical changes in the mail-handling systems of the Internet. Other approaches can be implemented under existing laws and with current technologies, but only if large numbers of organizations and businesses cooperate. A few tactics that reduce spam can be undertaken by individual e-mail users. In the sections below you will learn more about each of these approaches to controlling the spam problem.

Individual User Antispam Tactics

One way individuals can limit spam is to reduce the likelihood that a spammer can automatically generate their e-mail addresses. Many organizations create e-mail addresses for their employees by combining elements of each employee's first and last names. For example, small companies often combine the first letter of an employee's first name with the entire last name to generate e-mail addresses for all employees. (Larger companies often must use more complex algorithms as they are likely to have both a Jane Smith and a Judy Smith working for them.) Any spam sender able to obtain an employee list can generate long lists of potential e-mail addresses using the names on the list. If no employee list is available, the spam sender can simply generate logical combinations of first initials and common names. The cost of sending e-mail is so low that a spammer can afford to send thousands of e-mails to randomly generated addresses in the hope that a few of them are valid. By using an e-mail address that is more complex, such as xq7yy23@mycompany.com, individuals can reduce the chances that a spammer can randomly generate his or her address. Of course, such an address is hard to remember, which somewhat defeats the purpose of e-mail as a convenient way to communicate.

A second way to reduce spam is to control the exposure of an e-mail address. Spammers use software robots to search the Internet for character strings that include the @ character (which appears in every e-mail address). These robots search Web pages, discussion boards, chat rooms, and any other online source that might contain e-mail addresses. Again, the spammer can afford to send thousands of messages to e-mail addresses gathered in this way. Even if only one or two people respond, the spammer can earn a profit because the cost of sending e-mail messages is so low.

Some individuals use multiple e-mail addresses to thwart spam. They use one address for display on a Web site, another to register for access to Web sites, another for shopping accounts, and so on. If a spammer starts using one of these addresses, the individual can stop using it and switch to another. Many Web hosting services include a large number (often 100 to 200) of e-mail addresses as part of their service, so this can be a useful tactic for people or small businesses with their own Web sites.

These three strategies focus on limiting spammer's access to or use of an e-mail address. Other approaches use one or more techniques that filter e-mail messages based on their contents.

Basic Content Filtering

All content-filtering solutions require software that identifies content elements in an incoming e-mail message that indicate the message is (or is not) spam. The content-filtering techniques differ in which content elements they examine, whether they look for indications that the message is (or is not) spam, and how strictly they apply the rules for classifying messages. Most basic content filters examine the e-mail headers (From, To, Subject) and look for indications that the message might be spam. The software that performs the filtering task can be placed on individual users' computers (called **client-level filtering**) or on mail server computers (called **server-level filtering**). Server-level filtering can be implemented on an ISP's mail server, an individual company's mail server, or both. Also, many individuals that have ISP and/or company mail servers that filter their e-mail also install client-level filters on their computers. Spam that gets through one filter can be trapped by another filter.

The most common basic content-filtering techniques are black lists and white lists. A **black list spam filter** looks for From addresses in incoming messages that are known to be spammers. The software can delete the message or put it into a separate mailbox for review. A black list spam filter can be implemented at the individual, organization, or ISP level. Several organizations, such as the Spam and Open Relay Blocking System collect black lists and make them available to ISPs and company e-mail administrators. Other groups, such as the Spamhaus Project, track known spammers and publish lists of the mail servers they use. Some of these are free services, others charge a fee. The biggest drawback to the black list approach is that spammers frequently change their e-mail servers, which means that a black list must be continually updated to be effective. This updating requires that many organizations cooperate and communicate information about known spammers. In addition to its black list, the Spamhaus Project maintains a list of known spammers on its site. These are individuals and companies who have had their services terminated by an ISP for spam-related violations of an acceptable use policy more than three times. The Spamhaus Project provides detailed information about those on this list to law enforcement agencies.

A **white list spam filter** examines From addresses and compares them to a list of known good sender addresses (for example, the addresses in an individual's address book). A white list filter is usually applied at the individual user level, although it is possible to do the filtering at the organization level if the e-mail administrator has access to all individuals' address books (some companies mandate such access for security purposes). The main drawback to this approach is that it filters out any messages sent by unknown parties, not just spam. Because the number of **false positives** (messages that are rejected but should not have been) can be very high for white list filters, the rejected e-mails are always placed into a review mailbox instead of being deleted.

White list and black list approaches can be used in client-level or server-level filters, but both have serious drawbacks. To overcome these drawbacks, the two approaches are often used together or with other content-filtering approaches to achieve an acceptable level of filtering without an excessive false positive rate.

Challenge-Response Content Filtering

One content-filtering technique uses a white list as the basis for a confirmation procedure. This technique, called **challenge-response**, compares all incoming messages to a white list. If the message is from a sender who is not on the white list, an automated e-mail response is sent to the sender. This message (the challenge) asks the sender to reply to the e-mail (the response). The reply must contain a response to a challenge presented in the e-mail.

These challenges are designed so that a human can respond easily, but a computer would have difficulty formulating the response. For example, a challenge might include a picture of a fruit bowl and would ask the sender to respond with the number of apples in the bowl. This prevents a spammer from setting up a computer that receives challenges and answers them (the program would have difficulty identifying and counting the number of apples). It would be inefficient for a spammer to hire a human to respond to thousands of challenges. To learn more about this technique, you can visit the **CAPTCHA Project** site at Carnegie Mellon University. An example of a challenge that uses distorted letters and numbers (in this case, 5BM6HW3F) is shown in Figure 8-6.

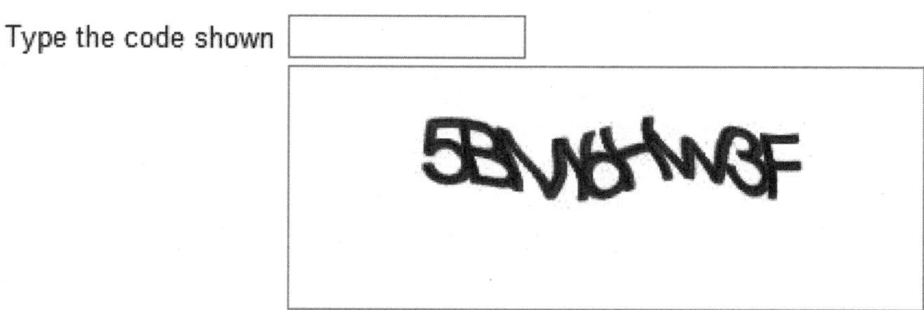

FIGURE 8-6 Example of a challenge that uses distorted letters and numbers

The major drawback to challenge-response systems is that they can be abused. For example, a perpetrator could send out thousands of e-mails to recipients that use challenge-response systems. If the perpetrator includes the victim's e-mail as the From address in those e-mails, the victim will be bombarded by the automated challenges sent out by the challenge-response systems of the recipients. What is worse, the potential damage of this tactic becomes greater as more e-mail servers install challenge-response systems.

Another issue with challenge-response systems could arise if they were to become widespread. Most mail that any individual receives from unknown senders is spam. A challenge-response system sends a challenge message to every unknown sender. That is, for every spam message received, a second e-mail is sent. A challenge-response system thus doubles the amount of useless e-mail messages that must be handled by the Internet's infrastructure. If everyone were to use a challenge-response system, the Internet capacity wasted by spam would approximately double. Because challenge-response systems require users to change their behavior, and because they do not provide an immediate and significant benefit (the benefit is spam reduction over time), these systems have not become very widely used.

Advanced Content Filtering

Advanced content filters that examine the entire e-mail message can be more effective than basic content filters that only examine the message headers or the IP address of the e-mail's sender. Creating effective content filters can be challenging. For example, a company might want to delete any e-mail message that includes the word "sex." If the company deletes all e-mails containing that character string, they will unintentionally delete all e-mailed orders from customers in the town of Essex.

Many advanced content filters operate by looking for spam indicators throughout the e-mail message. When the filter identifies an indicator in a message, it increases that message's spam "score." Some indicators increase the score more than others. Indicators can be words, word pairs, certain HTML codes (such as the code for the color white, which makes part of the message invisible in most e-mail clients), and information about where a word occurs in the message. Unfortunately, as soon as spam filter vendors identify a good set of indicators, spammers stop including those indicators in their messages.

One type of advanced content filter that is based on a branch of applied mathematics called Bayesian statistics shows some promise of staying one step ahead of the spammers. **Bayesian revision** is a statistical technique in which additional knowledge is used to revise earlier estimates of probabilities. In software that contains a **naïve Bayesian filter** (the most common type in use today), the software begins by not classifying any messages. The user reviews messages and indicates to the software which messages are spam and which are not. The software gradually learns (by revising its estimates of the probability that a message element appears in a spam message) to identify spam messages.

After seeing a few dozen messages classified, the naïve Bayesian filter can successfully classify spam messages about 80 percent of the time. As the filter continues to work, the user reviews its classifications and tells the software when it makes a mistake. After classifying a few hundred messages (and being corrected by the user when it errs), a naïve Bayesian filter typically reaches correct spam classification rates above 95 percent. Although these filters are highly effective and have low false positive rates, they must be trained, which takes time. The training is best done by each individual user because one person's spam can be another person's important message. Having users train their own filters provides the most rapid training and the best results. Most organizations do not currently use naïve Bayesian filters because they require attention by individual e-mail users. However, naïve Bayesian filters can be installed on some client computers (such as those used by people who receive large amounts of e-mail) in organizations that also use other techniques (such as white list or black list filters) at the server level. Most industry observers expect to see naïve Bayesian filtering used more widely in the future as the spam problem worsens and as more e-mail clients include such filters.

Research on naïve Bayesian filters began appearing in published research papers in 2002. An open-source software development project led by John Graham-Cumming released one of the first functional Bayesian filter products for individual users that year, named **POPFile**. POPFile is a program that runs on individual client computers and works with many different e-mail clients (including Microsoft Outlook, Mozilla Thunderbird,

Pegasus, and Eudora) to provide content filtering. Because it is open-source software, POPFile is free (although the project team welcomes donations). POPFile does require that e-mail be retrieved using a Post Office Protocol (POP) connection, so it cannot be used with most Web-based e-mail accounts such as Yahoo! or Hotmail. The latest releases of some e-mail client software, such as Qualcomm Eudora and Mozilla Thunderbird, now include naïve Bayesian filtering tools that work the same way POPFile does.

Figure 8-7 shows the training screen from an installation of POPFile. Each message is listed and classified into categories that the software calls buckets. These buckets are configurable by the user; in this case, the user has created two buckets, "spam" and "OK." The user reviews each message and changes the classification if necessary. Each time the user changes a classification, POPFile revises its internal database using a naïve Bayesian algorithm and uses the revised rules to classify new e-mail messages.

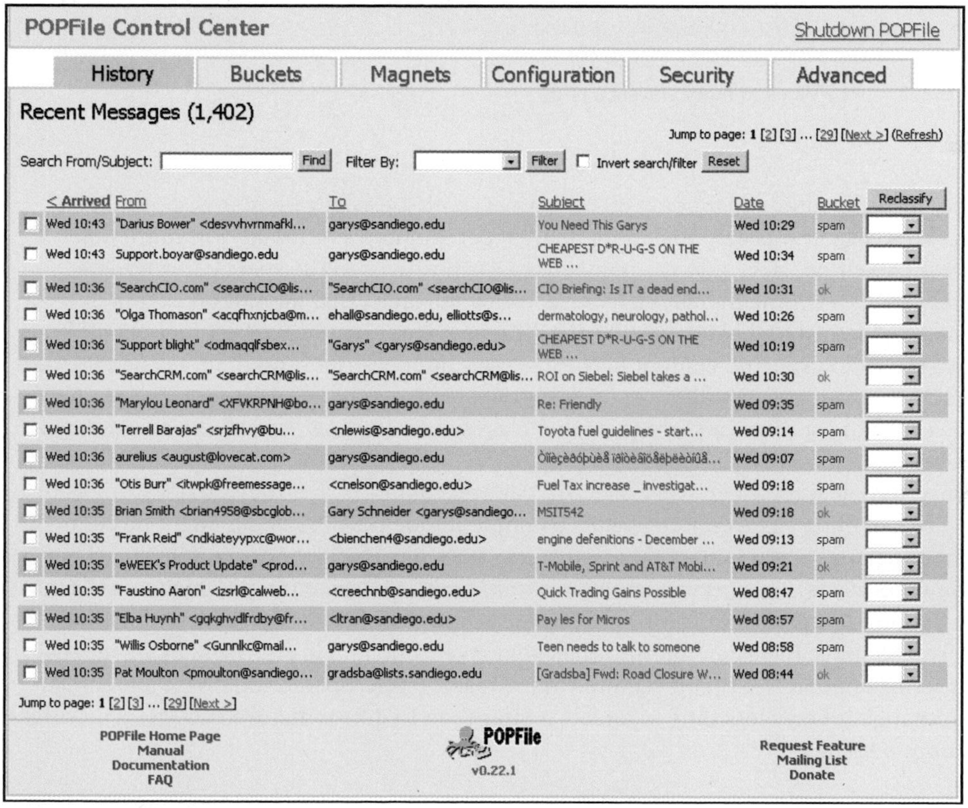

FIGURE 8-7 Training screen in the POPFile naïve Bayesian filter

Figure 8-8 shows the summary statistics page from a POPFile filter. This page reflects the filter's activity during a recent six-month period on one of the author's e-mail accounts.

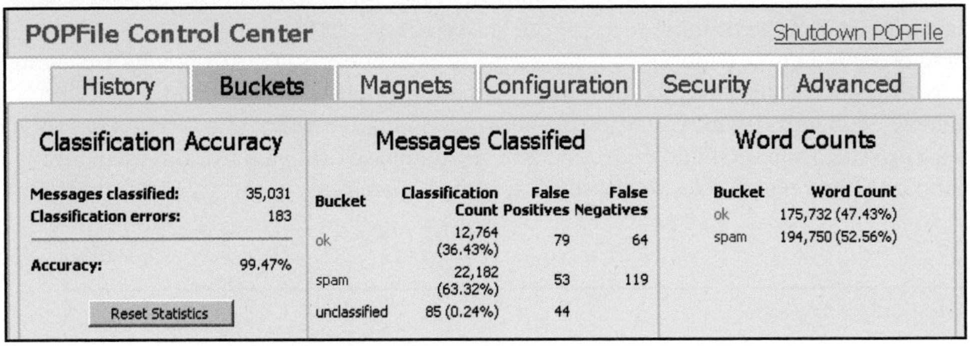

POPFile Control Center — Shutdown POPFile

History | Buckets | Magnets | Configuration | Security | Advanced

Classification Accuracy

Messages classified:	35,031
Classification errors:	183
Accuracy:	99.47%

Reset Statistics

Messages Classified

Bucket	Classification Count	False Positives	False Negatives
ok	12,764 (36.43%)	79	64
spam	22,182 (63.32%)	53	119
unclassified	85 (0.24%)	44	

Word Counts

Bucket	Word Count
ok	175,732 (47.43%)
spam	194,750 (52.56%)

FIGURE 8-8 POPFile summary statistics page

Although the filter caught only 30 percent of spam messages when it was installed, within two weeks, it was catching more than 90 percent and eventually was more than 99 percent accurate. Note that the number of false positives in the spam category is also quite small. POPFile includes a feature, called magnets, that allows the user to implement white list and black list filtering. The user can create a magnet that classifies messages based on specific content in the message and does not send the classified message through the naïve Bayesian filter. In this example, magnets that classify messages as "OK" operate as white list filters and magnets that classify messages as "spam" operate as black list filters.

Naïve Bayesian filters are very effective client-level filters, but they do not work well as server-level filters. The content that is common in one person's spam might be common in another person's valid e-mail; therefore, one user's reclassifications tend to cancel out those of other users. This prevents the filter from building its accuracy to high levels. One good solution for organizations is to use black list filters at the server level combined with white list and naïve Bayesian filters at the client level. The major drawback of any client-level filtering approach is that it requires individual users to update their own filters regularly. Although it takes less time to update a filter than to delete hundreds of spam messages, it still does take time.

Legal Solutions

A number of U.S. jurisdictions have passed laws that provide penalties for the sending of spam. In January 2004, the U.S. CAN-SPAM law (the law's name is an acronym for "Controlling the Assault of Non-Solicited Pornography and Marketing") went into effect. Researchers who track the amount of spam noted a drop in the percentage of all e-mail that was spam in February and March of that year. A **MessageLabs** study tracked the drop from 62 percent in January to 59 percent in February and 53 percent in March. However, by April, the rate was back up to a new high, 68 percent. It appears that spammers slowed down their activities immediately after the effective date of CAN-SPAM to see if a broad federal prosecution effort would occur. When the threat did not materialize, the spammers went right back to work.

The CAN-SPAM law is the first U.S. federal government effort to legislate controls on spam. It regulates all e-mail messages sent for the primary purpose of advertising or promoting a commercial product or service, including messages that promote the content displayed on a Web site. The law's main provisions include:

- *Misleading address header information*: E-mail headers and routing information, including the originating domain name and e-mail address, must be accurate and must identify the person who sent the e-mail.
- *Deceptive subject headers*: The e-mail's subject line cannot mislead the recipient about the contents or subject matter of the message.
- *Clear and conspicuous notice of message nature*: The e-mail must contain a clear and conspicuous notice that the message is an advertisement or solicitation and that the recipient can opt out of receiving further commercial e-mail from the sender.
- *Physical postal address*: The e-mail must include the sender's valid physical postal address.
- *Mandatory provision of an opt-out mechanism*: The e-mail must include a return e-mail address or another Internet-based response mechanism that allows a recipient to ask not to be sent future e-mail messages. These requests must be honored. The message may include a menu of choices that allows a recipient to opt out of certain types of messages, but one option on the menu must be an option to stop sending all commercial messages of any type.
- *Effectiveness of opt-out mechanism*: Opt-out requests must be honored within 10 business days. Any opt-out mechanism offered must be able to process opt-out requests for at least 30 days after the e-mail is sent. Once an opt-out request has been received, the sender is prohibited from helping any other entity send e-mail to the opt-out address or from having another entity send e-mail on the sender's behalf to that address.
- *Transfer of e-mail addresses*: Once a recipient has submitted an opt-out request, the sender is prohibited from selling or transferring that e-mail address to any other entity.

The law also prohibits misleading address header information in e-mail messages that facilitate an agreed-upon transaction or that update a customer in an existing business relationship. Each violation of a provision of the law is subject to a fine of up to $11,000. Additional fines are assessed for those who violate one of the above provisions and do one or more of the following:

- Harvest e-mail addresses from Web sites or Web services that have published a notice prohibiting the transfer of e-mail addresses for the purpose of sending e-mail.
- Send e-mail messages to addresses that have been generated by combining names, letters, or numbers into multiple combinations and permutations.
- Use scripts or other automated tools to register for multiple e-mail or user accounts that are then used to send commercial e-mail.
- Relay e-mails through a computer or network without the permission of the computer's or network's owner.

As you can see, a successful prosecution could cost the convicted spammer a great deal of money. The law further provides for criminal penalties, including imprisonment, for commercial senders of e-mail who do or conspire to do any of the following:

- Use another person's or entity's computer to send commercial e-mail from or through it without the computer owner's permission.
- Use a computer to relay or retransmit multiple commercial e-mail messages with the intent to deceive or mislead recipients or an Internet access service about the origin of the messages.
- Send multiple e-mail messages that contain false header information.
- Present false identification when registering for multiple e-mail accounts or domain names.
- Falsely represent themselves as owners of multiple IP addresses that are used to send commercial e-mail messages.

You can learn more about the law on the **U.S. Federal Trade Commission CAN-SPAM Law** information pages. The FTC issues new rules from time to time under the law. To obtain current updates on those rules, visit the **U.S. Federal Trade Commission Spam** information site. The home page of that site is shown in Figure 8-9.

The CAN-SPAM law has allowed U.S. prosecutors to bring a number of successful cases against spammers, including cases in which damages were assessed in the hundreds of millions of dollars. Some of the more notorious spammers have been sent to prison. Spammers' appeals of these decisions, usually based on the argument that spam is protected speech under the First Amendment, have been consistently rejected by the courts.

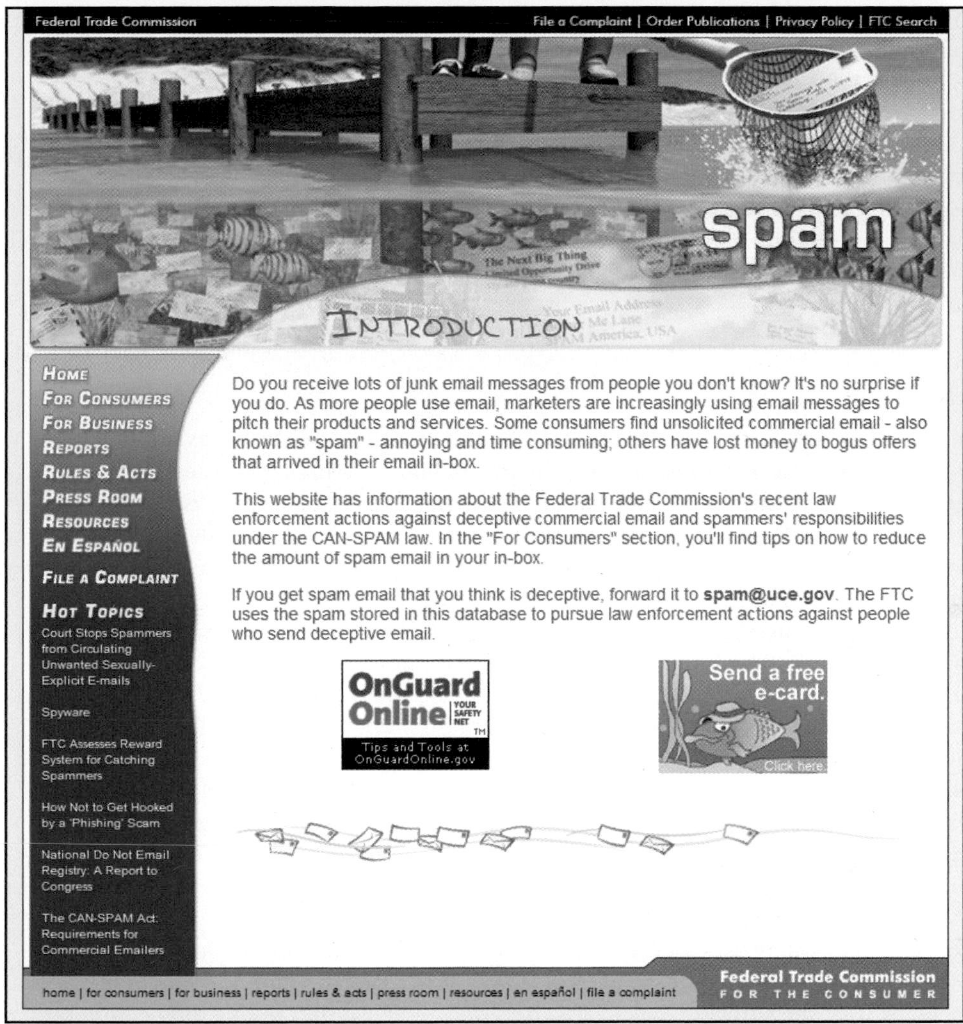

FIGURE 8-9 U.S. Federal Trade Commission Spam information site home page

Despite these successes, few industry experts expect CAN-SPAM or similar laws to be effective in stemming the tide of spam. After all, spammers have been violating existing deceptive advertising laws for years. Many spammers use mail servers located in countries that do not have (and that are unlikely to adopt) antispam laws. As you learned in Chapter 7, the issues of jurisdiction can be unclear for businesses that operate online. Even if a plaintiff is successful in court, enforcement of court-ordered fines or collection of damages can be difficult. Spammers can also evade cease-and-desist orders because they can move their operations from one server to another in minutes. Many spammers forward mail through servers that they have hijacked (you will learn more about threats to servers in Chapter 10).

In a decision that disappointed many in the information technology community, the FTC refused to create a do-not-spam list that would have been modeled after its do-not-call list, which has been reasonably successful in limiting marketers' phone calls.

Some critics argue that any legal solution to the spam problem is likely to fail until the prosecution of spammers becomes cost effective for governments. To become cost effective, prosecutors must be able to identify spammers easily (to reduce the cost of bringing an action against them) and must have a greater likelihood of winning the cases they file (or must see a greater social benefit to winning). The best way to make spammers easier to find is to make technical changes in the e-mail transport mechanism in the Internet's infrastructure.

Technical Solutions

The Internet was not designed to do many of the things it does today. It was not designed to be secure, to process transactions, or to handle billions of e-mail messages. As you learned in Chapter 2, Internet e-mail was an incidental afterthought in a system designed to transfer large files from one researcher to another. As it was originally designed, and as it operates today, the Internet did not include any mechanisms for ensuring that the identity of an e-mail sender would always be known to the e-mail's recipient.

At least one technical strategy for fighting spam exploits a weakness in the original design of the Internet. The Internet protocol that governs communication among servers on the Internet (including e-mail servers) was designed to be a polite set of rules. When one computer on the Internet sends a message to another computer, it will wait to receive an acknowledgment that the message has been received before sending more messages. In the ordinary course of Internet communications, the acknowledgment messages come back in far less than a second. If a computer is set to send the acknowledgment back more slowly, the originating computer will slow down because it must continue to scan for the acknowledgment (which consumes some of its processing power) and it will not send any more messages to that address until it does receive the acknowledgment.

To use this characteristic of the Internet messaging rules to counter spam, the defending company must develop a way to identify computers that are sending spam. Some vendors, such as IBM, sell software and access to a large database that tracks such computers continually. Other vendors sell software that identifies multiple e-mail messages coming from a single source in rapid succession (as would happen if a spammer were sending spam to everyone at a particular company). Once the spamming computer is identified, the software delays sending the message acknowledgments. It can also launch a return attack, sending e-mail messages back to the computer that originated the suspected spam. This practice is called **teergrubing**, which is from the German word for "tar pit." The objective is to ensnare the spam-sending computer in a trap that drags down its ability to send spam. Although many organizations use teergrubing as part of their spam defense strategy, some are concerned that launching a counterattack might violate laws that were enacted, ironically enough, to punish spammers.

Most industry observers agree that the ultimate solution to the spam problem will come when new e-mail protocols are adopted that provide absolute verification of the source of each e-mail message. This will require all mail servers on the Internet to be upgraded. The new protocols have not yet been written, so this solution is several years away.

Proposals for identification standards have been made by Time Warner's AOL division, Microsoft, Yahoo!, and other companies and organizations. The Internet Engineering Task Force (IETF) working group that is responsible for e-mail standards has rejected some of these proposals, but has stated its commitment to working out a set of standards that will accomplish sender authentication. You can learn more about current developments on this issue by following the links in the Online Companion in the Additional Information section under the heading **Spam Information Sites**.

WEB SITE UTILITY PROGRAMS

In addition to Web server software, people who develop Web sites work with a number of utility programs, or tools. TCP/IP supports a wide variety of these utility programs. Some of these programs run on the Web server itself, while others run on the client computers that Web developers use when they are creating Web sites. E-mail was one of the earliest Internet utility programs and it has become one of the most important. In earlier chapters, you learned how companies are using e-mail as a key element in their electronic commerce strategies. You will learn about several of these programs and see examples of how they work.

Finger and Ping Utilities

Finger is a program that runs on UNIX operating systems and allows a user to obtain some information about other network users. A Finger command yields a list of users who are logged on to a network, or reports the last time a user logged on to the network. Many organizations have disabled the Finger command on their systems for privacy and security reasons. For example, if you send a Finger command to a server at www.microsoft.com, you receive no response. Some e-mail programs have the Finger program built into them, so you can send the command while reading your e-mail.

A program called **Ping**, short for **Packet Internet Groper**, tests the connectivity between two computers connected to the Internet. Ping provides performance data about the connection between Internet computers, such as the number of computers (hops) between them. It sends two packets to the specified address and waits for a reply. Network technicians sometimes use Ping to troubleshoot Internet connections. Many freeware and shareware Ping programs are available on the Internet.

Tracert and Other Route-Tracing Programs

Tracert (TRACE RouTe) sends data packets to every computer on the path (Internet) between one computer and another computer and clocks the packets' round-trip times. This provides an indication of the time it takes a message to travel from one computer to another and back, ensures that the remote computer is online, and pinpoints any data traffic congestion. Route-tracing programs also calculate and display the number of hops between computers and the time it takes to traverse the entire one-way path between machines.

Route-tracing programs such as Tracert work by sending a series of packets to a particular destination. Each router along the Internet path between the originating computer and the destination computer reports its IP address and the time it took to reach it. After the program completes its packet transmissions, it displays the number of hops and how much time it took to reach each node and travel the entire path.

Graphical user interface route-tracing programs provide a plot of the packets' route on a map. Network engineers can use route-tracing programs to determine the location of the greatest delays on the Internet. Companies that provide Internet connections to customers often run route-tracing programs to monitor and improve services. Visualware offers its **VisualRoute** route-tracing program for download, trial, and purchase. The site also offers a demonstration of VisualRoute that runs on its Web site so potential customers can test the program without downloading any software. Figure 8-10 shows a route traced from a VisualRoute server in Ashburn, Virginia (USA), to a server at SingTel in Singapore, using the VisualRoute program.

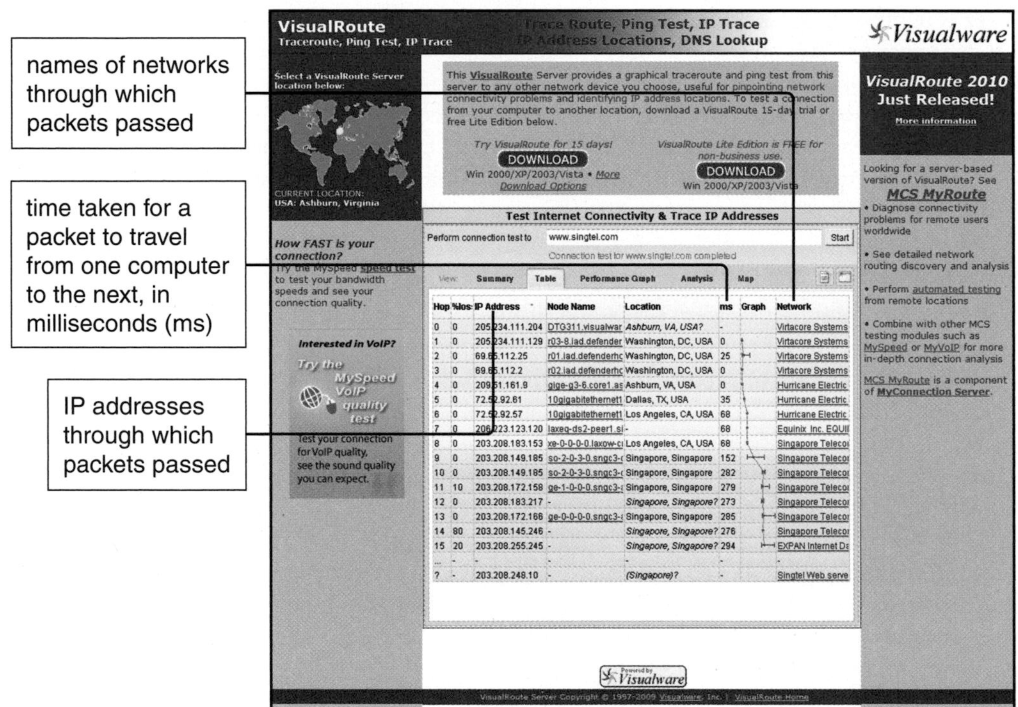

FIGURE 8-10 Tracing a path between two computers on the Internet

You can see that the packets traveled through 17 computers (that is, the path included 17 hops) and that the path went from Virginia to Washington, D.C., to Chicago, to San Jose, to Palo Alto, and then through a satellite or underwater cable, to Singapore. The test message took 248 milliseconds (ms), which is just under a quarter of a second, to travel more than halfway around the world.

Telnet and FTP Utilities

Telnet is a program that allows a person using one computer to access files and run programs on a second computer that is connected to the Internet. This remote login capability can be useful for running older software that does not have a Web interface. Several Telnet client programs are available as free downloads on the Internet, and Microsoft Windows systems include a Telnet client called Telnet.exe. Telnet lets a client computer give commands to programs running on a remote host, allowing for remote troubleshooting or system administration. Telnet programs use a set of rules called the **Telnet protocol**. Some Web browsers function as a Telnet client. A user can enter "telnet://" followed by the domain name of the remote host. As more companies place information on Web pages, which are accessible through any Web browser, the use of Telnet will continue to decrease.

The **File Transfer Protocol (FTP)** is the part of the TCP/IP rules that defines the formats used to transfer files between TCP/IP-connected computers. FTP can transfer files one at a time, or it can transfer many files at once. FTP also provides other useful services, such as displaying remote and local computers' directories, changing the current client's or server's active directory, and creating and removing local and remote directories. FTP uses TCP and its built-in error controls to copy files accurately from one computer to another.

Accessing a remote computer with FTP requires that the user log on to the remote computer. A number of FTP client programs exist; however, many people just use their Web browser software. Typing the protocol name, ftp://, before the domain name of the remote computer establishes an FTP connection. Users who have accounts on remote computers can log on to their accounts using the FTP client. FTP establishes contact with the remote computer and logs on to the account on that computer.

An FTP connection to a computer on which the user has an account is called **full-privilege FTP**. Another way to access a remote computer is called anonymous FTP. **Anonymous FTP** allows the user to log on as a guest. By entering the username "anonymous" and an e-mail address as a password, users can read and copy files that are stored on the remote computer.

Indexing and Searching Utility Programs

Search engines and indexing programs are important elements of many Web servers. Search engines or search tools search either a specific site or the entire Web for requested documents. An indexing program can provide full-text indexing that generates an index for all documents stored on the server. When a browser requests a Web site search, the search engine compares the index terms to the requester's search term to see which documents contain matches for the requested term or terms. More advanced search engine software (such as that used by the popular search engine site Google) uses complex relevance ranking rules that consider things such as how many other Web sites link to the target site. Many Web server software products also contain indexing software. Indexing software can often index documents stored in many different file formats.

Data Analysis Software

Web servers can capture visitor information, including data about who is visiting a Web site (the visitor's URL), how long the visitor's Web browser viewed the site, the date and time of each visit, and which pages the visitor viewed. This data is placed into a Web **log file**. As you can imagine, the file grows very quickly—especially for popular sites with thousands of visitors each day. Careful analysis of the log file can be fruitful and reveal many interesting facts about site visitors and their preferences. To make sense of a log file, you must run third-party Web log file analysis programs. These programs summarize log file information by querying the log file and either returning gross summary information, or accumulating details that reveal how many visitors came to the site per day, hour, or minute, or which hours of the day were peak loading times. Popular Web log file analysis programs include products by Adobe Omniture, Urchin from Google, and WebTrends.

Link-Checking Utilities

One function that is important to Web site managers is the ability to check the links on their sites. Over time, the Web sites that a given page links to can change their URLs or even disappear. A **dead link**, when clicked, displays an error message rather than a Web page. Maintaining a site that is free of dead links is vital because visitors who encounter too many dead links on a site might jump to another site. Web-browsing customers are just a click away from going to a competitor's site if they become annoyed with an errant Web link. The undesirable situation of a site that contains a number of links that no longer work is sometimes derisively called **link rot**.

A **link checker** utility program examines each page on the site and reports any URLs that are broken, seem broken, or are in some way incorrect. It can also identify orphan files. An **orphan file** is a file on the Web site that is not linked to any page. Other important site management features include script checking and HTML validation. Some management tools can locate error-prone pages and code, list broken links, and e-mail maintenance results to site managers.

Some Web site development and maintenance tools, such as Adobe's Dreamweaver, include link-checking features. Most link-checking programs, however, are separate utility programs. One of these link-checking programs, Elsop LinkScan, is available in a demo version as a free download. The results of the link checker either appear in a Web browser or are e-mailed to a recipient. Besides checking links, Web site validation programs sometimes check spelling and other structural components of Web pages.

LinxCop is one of several reverse link checkers available. A **reverse link checker** checks on sites with which a company has entered a link exchange program (which you learned about in Chapter 4) and ensures that link exchange partners are fulfilling their obligation to include a link back to the company's Web site.

Remote Server Administration

With **remote server administration** software, a Web site administrator can control a Web site from any Internet-connected computer. Although all Web sites provide administrative controls—most through a workstation computer on the same network as the server computer or through a Web browser—it is convenient for an administrator to be able to fix the server from wherever he or she happens to be. For example, an administrator can install Website Garage on any Internet-connected Windows computer and monitor and change anything on the Web site from that computer. NetMechanic offers a variety of link-checking, HTML troubleshooting, site-monitoring, and other programs that can be useful in managing the operation of a Web site.

WEB SERVER HARDWARE

Now that you have learned about Web server and Internet utility software, your next step is to learn about Web server hardware. Companies use a wide variety of computer brands, types, and sizes to host electronic commerce operations. Some small companies can run Web sites on desktop PCs. Most electronic commerce Web sites are operated on computers designed for site hosting, however.

Server Computers

Web server computers generally have more memory, larger (and faster) hard disk drives, and faster processors than the typical desktop or notebook PCs with which you are probably familiar. Many Web server computers use multiple processors; very few desktop PCs have more than one processor. Because Web server computers use faster and higher-capacity hardware elements (such as memory and hard disk drives) and use more of these elements, they are usually much more expensive than workstation PCs. Today, a high-end desktop PC with a good monitor costs between $800 and $1500. A company might be able to buy a low-end Web server computer for about the same amount of money, but most companies spend between $2000 and $200,000 on a Web server. Companies that sell Web server hardware, such as Dell, Gateway, Hewlett Packard, and Sun, all have configuration tools on their Web sites that allow visitors to design their own Web servers.

Although some Web server computers are housed in freestanding cases, most are installed in equipment racks. These racks are usually about 6 feet tall and 19 inches wide. They can each hold several midrange server computers. One popular server configuration involves putting small server computers on a single computer board and then installing many of those boards into a rack-mounted frame. These servers-on-a-card are called **blade servers**, and some manufacturers now make them so small that more than 300 of them can be installed in a single 6-foot rack.

Recall that the fundamental job of a Web server is to process and respond to Web client requests that are sent using HTTP. For a client request for a Web page, the server program finds and retrieves the page, creates an HTTP header, and appends the HTML document to it. For dynamic pages, the server uses an architecture with three or more tiers that uses other programs, receives the results from the back-end process, formats the response, and sends the pages and other objects to the requesting client program. IP-sharing, or a virtual server, is a feature that allows different groups to share a single Web server's IP address.

A **virtual server** or **virtual host** is a feature that maintains more than one server on one machine. This means that different groups can have separate domain names, but all domain names refer to the same physical Web server.

Web Server Performance Evaluation

Benchmarking Web server hardware and software combinations can help in making informed decisions for a system. **Benchmarking**, in this context, is testing that is used to compare the performance of hardware and software.

Elements affecting overall server performance include hardware, operating system software, server software, connection speed, user capacity, and type of Web pages being delivered. When evaluating Web server performance, a company should know exactly what factors are being measured and ensure that these are important factors relative to the expected use of the Web server. Another factor that can affect a Web server's performance is the speed of its connection. A server on a T3 connection can deliver Web pages to clients much faster than on a T1 connection.

The number of users the server can handle is also important. This can be difficult to measure because results are affected by the bandwidth of the Internet connection between the server and the client, and by the sizes of the Web pages delivered. Two factors to evaluate when measuring a server's Web page delivery capability are throughput and response time. **Throughput** is the number of HTTP requests that a particular hardware and software combination can process in a unit of time. **Response time** is the amount of time a server requires to process one request. These values should be well within the anticipated loads a server can experience, even during peak load times.

One way to choose Web server hardware configurations is to run tests on various combinations, remembering to consider the system's scalability. Of course, you need to have the hardware and software set up to do this, so it is difficult to evaluate potential configurations that you have not yet purchased. Independent testing labs such as **Mindcraft** test software, hardware systems, and network products for users. Its site contains reports and statistics comparing combinations of application server platforms, operating systems, and Web server software products, such as **WebStone**. Another company that offers these services is the **Standard Performance Evaluation Corporation**.

Anyone contemplating purchasing a server that will handle heavy traffic should compare standard benchmarks for a variety of hardware and software configurations. Customized benchmarks can give Web managers guidelines for modifying file sizes, cache sizes, and other parameters. Web managers should run benchmarks regularly.

Companies that operate more than one Web server must decide how to configure servers to provide site visitors with the best service possible. The various ways that servers can be connected to each other and to related hardware, such as routers and switches, are called **server architectures**.

Web Server Hardware Architectures

Earlier in this chapter, you learned that electronic commerce Web sites can use two-tier, three-tier, or n-tier architectures to divide the work of serving Web pages, administering databases, and processing transactions. Some electronic commerce sites are so large that more than one computer is required within each tier. For example, large electronic commerce Web sites must deliver millions of individual Web pages and process thousands of customer and vendor transactions each day.

Administrators of these large Web sites must plan carefully to configure their Web server computers, which can number in the hundreds or even thousands, to handle the daily Web traffic efficiently. These large collections of servers are called **server farms** because the servers are often lined up in large rooms, row after row, like crops in a field. One approach, sometimes called a **centralized architecture**, is to use a few very large and fast computers. A second approach is to use a large number of less-powerful computers and divide the workload among them. This is sometimes called a **distributed architecture** or, more commonly, a **decentralized architecture**. These two different approaches to Web site architecture are shown in Figure 8-11.

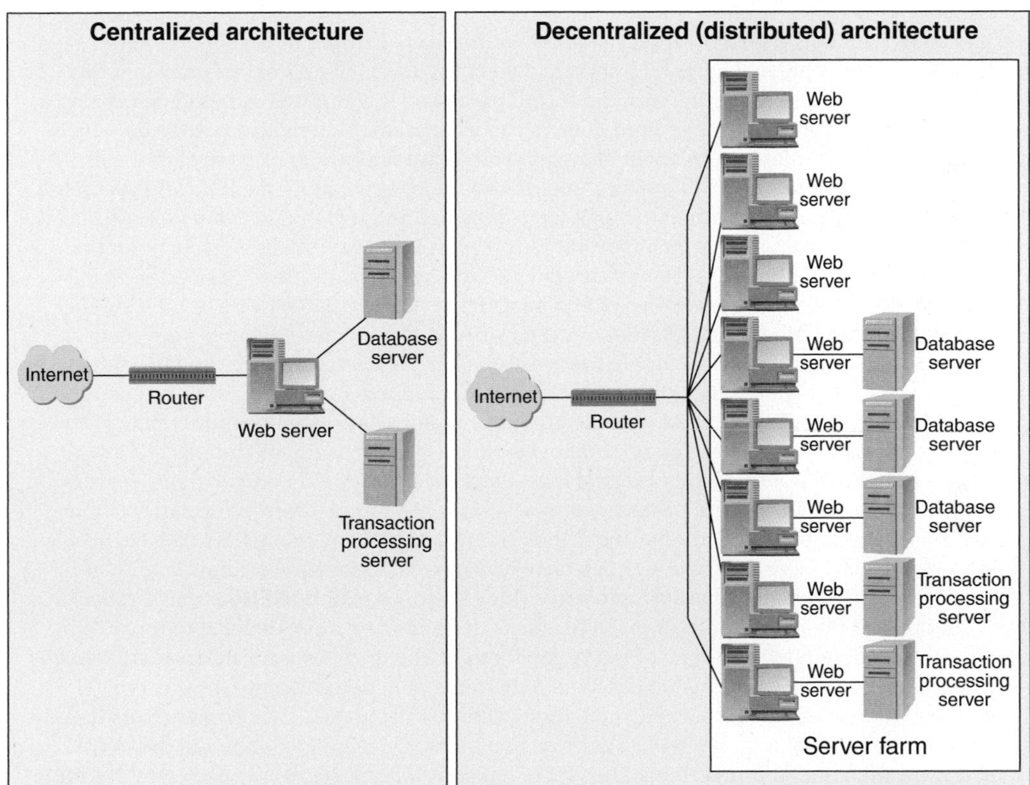

FIGURE 8-11 Centralized and decentralized Web site architectures

Each approach has benefits and drawbacks. The centralized approach requires expensive computers and is more sensitive to the effects of technical problems. If one of the few servers becomes inoperable, a large portion of the site's capability is lost. Thus, Web sites with centralized architectures must have adequate backup plans. Any server problem, no matter how small, can threaten the operation of the site. The decentralized architecture spreads that risk over a large number of servers. If one server becomes inoperable, the site can continue to operate without much degradation in capability. The smaller servers used in the decentralized architecture are less expensive than the large servers used in the centralized approach. That is, the total cost of 100 small servers is usually less than the cost of one large server with the same capacity as the 100 small servers. However, the decentralized architecture does require additional hubs or switches to connect the servers to each other and to the Internet. Most large decentralized sites use load-balancing systems, which cost additional money, to assign the workload efficiently.

LEARNING FROM FAILURES

Web Servers at Ebay

The online auction site **eBay** is very popular, as you have learned in earlier chapters. Indeed, it is so popular that its Web servers deliver hundreds of millions of pages per day. These pages are a combination of static HTML pages and dynamically generated Web pages. The dynamic pages are created from queries run against eBay's Oracle database, in which it keeps all of the information about all auctions that are under way or have closed within the most recent 30 days. With millions of auctions under way at any moment, this database is extremely large. The combination of a large database and high-transaction volume makes eBay's Web server operation an important part of the company's success and a potential contributor to its failure. The servers at eBay failed more than 15 times during the first five years (1995–2000) of the company's life. The worst series of failures occurred during May and June of 2000, when the site went down four times. One of these failures kept the site offline for more than a day—a failure that cost eBay an estimated $5 million. The company's stock fell 20 percent in the days following that failure.

At that point, eBay decided it needed to make major changes in its approach to Web server configuration. Many of eBay's original technology staff had backgrounds at Oracle, a company that has a tradition of selling large databases that run on equally large servers. Further, the nature of eBay's business—any visitor might want to view information about any auction at any time—led eBay management initially to implement a centralized architecture with one large database residing on a few large database server computers. It also made sense to use similar hardware to serve the Web pages generated from that database.

In mid-2000, following the worst site failure in its history, eBay decided to move to a decentralized architecture. This was a tremendous challenge because it meant that the single large auction information database had to be replicated across groups, or clusters, of Web and database servers. However, eBay realized that using just a few large servers had made it too vulnerable to the failure of those machines. Once eBay completed the move to decentralization, it found that adding more capacity was easier. Instead of installing and configuring a large server that might have represented 15 percent or more of the site's total capacity, clusters of six or seven smaller machines could be added that represented less than one percent of the site's capacity. Routine periodic maintenance on the servers also became easier to schedule.

The lesson from eBay's Web server troubles is that the architecture should be carefully chosen to meet the needs of the site. Web server architecture choices can have a significant effect on the stability, reliability, and, ultimately, the profitability of an electronic commerce Web site.

Load-Balancing Systems

A **load-balancing switch** is a piece of network hardware that monitors the workloads of servers attached to it and assigns incoming Web traffic to the server that has the most available capacity at that instant in time. In a simple load-balancing system, the traffic that enters the site from the Internet through the site's router encounters the load-balancing switch, which then directs the traffic to the Web server best able to handle the traffic. Figure 8-12 shows a basic load-balancing system.

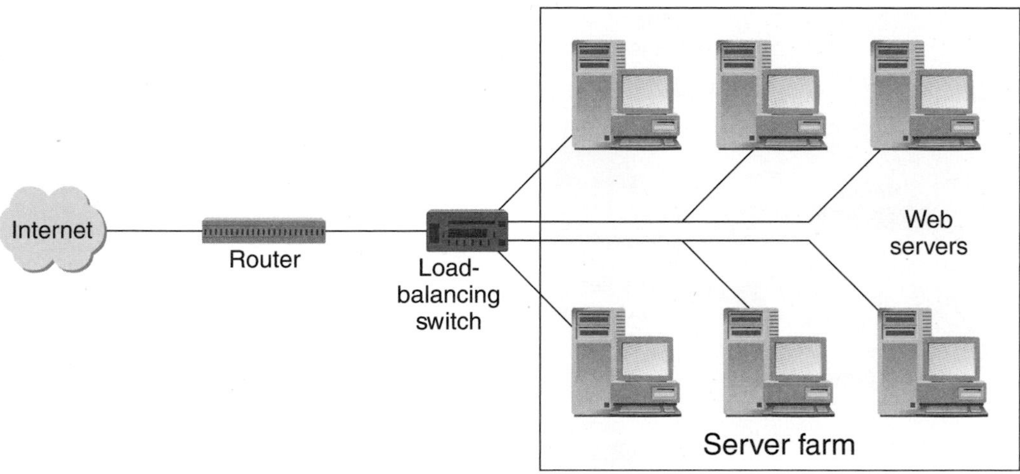

FIGURE 8-12 A load-balancing system in a decentralized architecture

In more complex load-balancing systems, the incoming Web traffic, which might enter from two or more routers on a larger Web site, is directed to groups of Web servers dedicated to specific tasks. In the sample complex load-balancing system that appears in Figure 8-13, the Web servers have been gathered into groups of servers that handle delivery of static HTML pages, servers that coordinate queries of an information database, servers that generate dynamic Web pages, and servers that handle transactions. Load-balancing switches and the software that helps them do their work cost roughly between $2000 and $30,000.

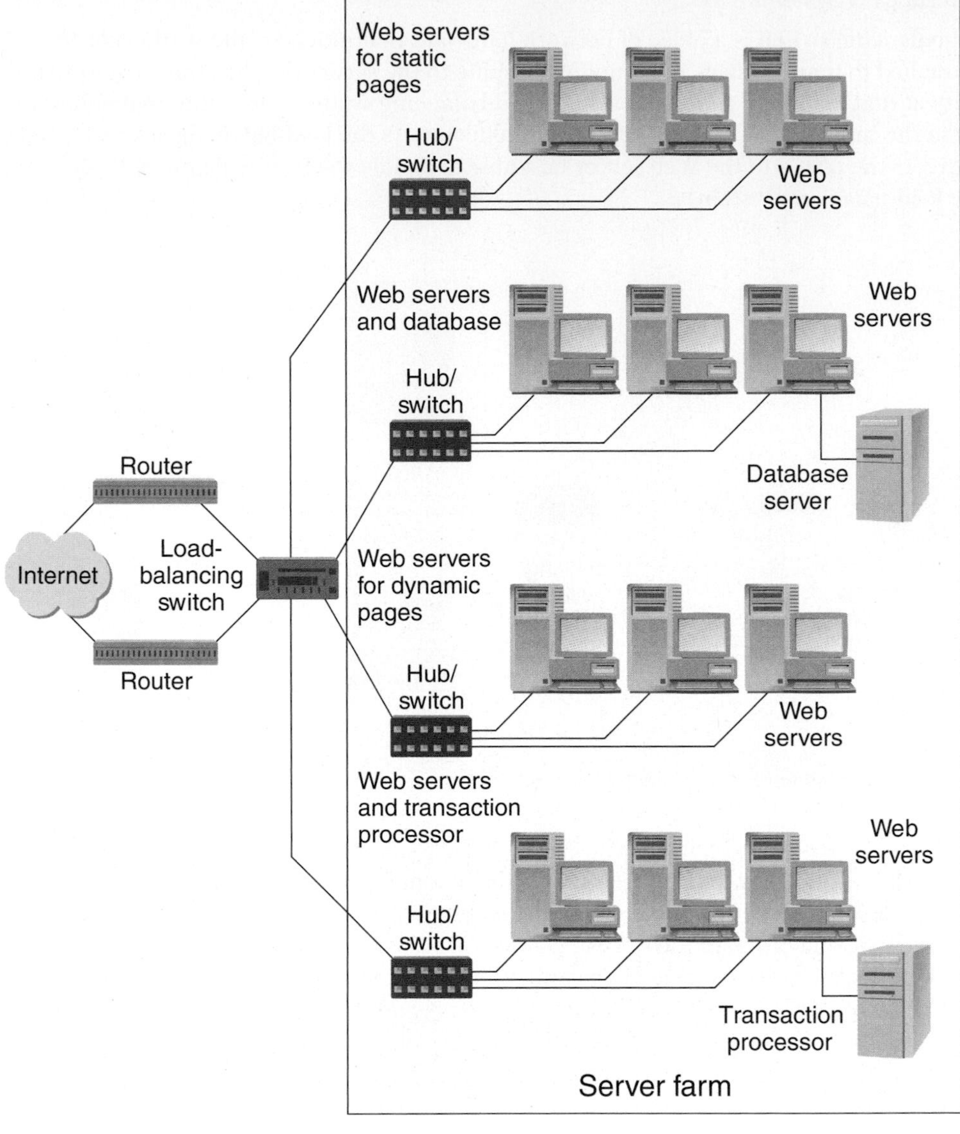

FIGURE 8-13 Complex load balancing

Summary

The Web uses a client/server architecture in which the client computer requests a Web page and a server computer that is hosting the requested page locates and sends a page back to the client. For simple HTTP requests, a two-tier architecture works well. The first tier is the client computer and the second tier is the server. More complicated Web interactions, such as electronic commerce, require the integration of databases and payment-processing software in a three-tier or higher (n-tier) architecture.

Operating systems commonly used on Web server computers include Microsoft server operating systems; UNIX-based operating systems, such as SunOS, FreeBSD; and Linux. The most popular Web server programs are Apache HTTP Server, Microsoft Internet Information Server, and Sun Java System Web Server. Web server computers also run a variety of utility programs such as Finger, Ping, Tracert, e-mail server software, Telnet, and FTP. Most Web servers also have software that helps with link checking and remote server administration tasks.

The problem of unsolicited commercial e-mail (spam) has grown dramatically in recent years. Content filters, particularly naïve Bayesian filters, can deal with the problem. Organizations are using a combination of server-level filters and client-level filters to reduce spam to tolerable levels. New laws designed to punish spammers have not stemmed the tide of spam. Some organizations are using counterattack strategies to impede spammers' ability to send large numbers of messages, but most industry experts believe spam will persist until new e-mail protocols are adopted that provide absolute authentication of e-mail senders' identities.

The operating system, connection speed, user capacity, and the type of pages that the site serves affect overall Web server performance. Benchmarking software and consulting firms that use it can help companies evaluate specific combinations of Web server hardware, software, and operating systems.

Web server hardware is also an important consideration in the design of an online business site. The server computer must have enough memory to serve Web pages to all site visitors and enough disk space to store the Web pages and the databases that store the elements of dynamically generated Web pages. Large Web sites that have many Web server computers use load-balancing hardware and software to manage their high-activity volumes.

Key Terms

Active Server Pages (ASP)
AJAX
Anonymous FTP
ASP.NET
Attachment
Bayesian revision
Benchmarking
Black list spam filter
Blade server
Centralized architecture
Challenge-response
Client-level filtering
Client-side scripting
ColdFusion
Common Gateway Interface (CGI)
Computer virus
Database server
Dead link
Decentralized architecture
Distributed architecture
Dynamic content
Dynamic page

Entity body
False positive
File Transfer Protocol (FTP)
Finger
Full-privilege FTP
Hypertext Preprocessor (PHP)
JavaServer Pages (JSP)
Java servlet
Link checker
Link rot
Load-balancing switch
Log file
Naïve Bayesian filter
N-tier architecture
Orphan file
Ping
Packet Internet Groper
Python
QQ.com
Remote server administration
Request header
Request line
Request message
Response header field
Response header line
Response message
Response time
Reverse link checker
Ruby on Rails
Server
Server architecture
Server farm
Server-level filtering
Server software
Server-side scripting
Spam
Static page
Teergrubing
Telnet
Telnet protocol
Three-tier architecture
Throughput
Tracert
Two-tier client/server architecture
Virtual host
Virtual server
Virus
White list spam filter

Review Questions

RQ1. Most electronic commerce Web sites use a three-tier client/server architecture. In about 100 words, explain why they do and briefly describe what happens in the third tier of most electronic commerce Web sites.

RQ2. Describe and briefly discuss two important measures of a Web site's performance.

RQ3. Beginning with the links provided in the Online Companion, locate more information about two of the three Web servers discussed in the chapter: Apache, Microsoft IIS, and Sun JSWS. Write approximately 100 words about each of the two servers you choose. Include descriptions of three features for each Web server and indicate the computer platforms and operating systems on which each runs.

RQ4. In one paragraph, outline the main differences between a typical desktop PC and a computer that would be suitable to use as a Web server for a small Web site.

RQ5. Using the Web or your school library, find articles that discuss the types of server hardware used by at least one electronic commerce site. Outline that site's architecture and approach to server hardware and software in an essay of about 200 words.

Exercises

E1. You are the information systems director for Abbon Laboratories, a biotechnology research firm with about 100 employees. Alice Stampler, Abbon's president, is aware that Abbon's incoming e-mail includes a great deal of spam and has always complained about the time it takes her to delete it. More importantly, she is concerned about the time wasted by the company's employees. Just thinking about those expensive Ph.D. researchers spending time deleting half of their e-mail drives her to distraction. Alice recently read a story in a business magazine about naïve Bayesian spam filters. Possessing a Ph.D. herself, she is fascinated by the prospect that sophisticated mathematics might solve the company's spam problem. Alice asks you to find out all you can about naïve Bayesian filters and present a short report (about 200 words) in which you evaluate the technique and whether it can work for Abbon. Alice envisions one filter installed on the e-mail server that would screen all e-mail as it enters the company's network. You can use your library, your favorite search engines, or the links in the Online Companion under the heading **Naïve Bayesian Filters** to do your research.

E2. You created a Web site for International Paper Products and Pulp, complete with links to other pages on your site and to pages on the Internet. Bob Pardee, your supervisor, wants you to check periodically that the links on the corporate site are still valid. Instead of purchasing and installing a link-checking program, you decide to investigate online link checkers (Web sites that allow you to enter a Web site's root or home address and then check all the links that emanate from that site). Use **W3C Link Check** or **Elsop LinkScan Quick Check** to check the links on any site of your choice. Print a few pages of the report and be prepared to turn them in to your instructor. Be patient. The program can take some time to complete its work—especially on a Web page that has a large number of links.

E3. In researching Web server computers, you find that many companies that sell these computers offer a configuration option for controlling computers' disk drives called "RAID." Using the Web and your library, investigate the purpose of RAID controllers. Learn what these controllers do and how they do it. Summarize your findings in a 600-word briefing report suitable for presentation to a nontechnical manager.

E4. Using the Web and your library, identify at least three different load balancing products. For each of those products write a paragraph in which you describe the product, its features, any limitations you can identify, and its price. Learn what these controllers do and how they do it. Summarize your findings in a 600-word briefing report suitable for presentation to a nontechnical manager.

Cases

C1. Microsoft and the People's Republic of China

Software piracy has been a major challenge for software makers such as Microsoft that want to sell software in the global marketplace. Laws that protect intellectual property vary from country to country, and the laws in many countries provide little or no protection. Governments in developing countries are reluctant to increase the protections afforded by their intellectual property laws because they see no point in passing laws that protect the profits of foreign corporations by imposing higher costs on their struggling local businesses and citizens. In the late 1990s, after years of holding firm on its global pricing, Microsoft began to offer significant discounts on its software to governments, small businesses, and individuals in developing countries. It also provided discounts on Windows operating systems software that was installed in new personal computers manufactured in developing countries. Microsoft donated software licenses to schools in developing countries. Just as these efforts were beginning to show some results, however, Microsoft faced a new threat to its global market position—open-source software.

Open-source operating system software, such as Linux, gives governments and businesses in developing countries a way to avoid paying any server software licensing fees to Microsoft. In 2000, the Brazilian state of Penambuco became the first governmental entity to pass a law that requires the use of open-source software on all computers used for state business. Shortly thereafter, the Brazilian state of Rio Grande do Sul passed a similar law that requires the use of open-source software in all of the state's offices and in all privately operated utilities. In 2003, IBM realized the potential for open-source consulting business in the country and opened several centers for the development of Linux-based application software in Brazil. Concerned about a Latin American open-source domino effect, Microsoft embarked on a public relations campaign in the region that included increased advertising spending and donations to public schools. In 2002, Peru was considering passing a law that would require public schools to use open-source software. Microsoft founder Bill Gates flew to Peru and, with great public fanfare, donated $550,000 to the schools that would have been affected by the legislation. The law was quietly dropped from consideration by the legislature shortly thereafter. In 2004, Microsoft announced that it would donate $1 billion in cash and software over five years through the United Nations Development Program to not-for-profit organizations in 45 countries.

Most industry observers believe that Microsoft's largest non-U.S. market today is the People's Republic of China (PRC). Although the PRC generates about $300 million in licensing revenue for Microsoft, more than 90 percent of all Microsoft products used in China today are pirated. Bootleg copies of the company's latest products can be purchased on the street for a few dollars. Thus, Microsoft believes that converting users to paid licenses could increase its PRC licensing revenues tremendously. As the PRC moves from being a less-developed country toward becoming a major economic power in the world, Microsoft sees an opportunity to increase its licensing revenue in the country. In the past, Microsoft has used a global anti-piracy strategy that relied on identifying users of pirated software and threatening those users with legal action, but the company is changing its approach in developing markets such as Latin America and Asia. In the PRC, Microsoft's near-term goal is to develop a market for full-price software licenses that includes large business and government customers. Its new approach focuses more on recruiting major PRC business organizations as customers and less on sending threatening letters to users of pirated Microsoft software.

In developing its business in the PRC, Microsoft faces a number of challenges. Juliet Wu, former general manager of Microsoft China, published a book in 2000 that was highly critical of the company. The book was widely read in the PRC and received many good reviews. PRC officials have often criticized Microsoft for many things ranging from high prices to the company's use of Taiwanese programmers (the PRC does not officially recognize Taiwan as an independent nation separate from the PRC). Government officials in the PRC are also concerned about security.

Microsoft has always maintained that the code to its software products is a trade secret and has refused to allow its publication or distribution. Companies that develop software that runs on Microsoft Windows, for example, must sign a nondisclosure agreement with Microsoft to obtain information they need about how Windows operates so they can make their software compatible with it. Many PRC officials believe that Microsoft, as a U.S.-based company, might include secret code in its software that would allow the U.S. government to enter PRC government computers undetected in a time of international conflict or war. At a very basic level, the ideology of the PRC's socialist government is a polar opposite to the highly competitive capitalist principles that have driven Microsoft to success. But the greatest challenge that Microsoft must overcome in the PRC is the attraction of open-source software.

Open-source programs' code is public; thus, it cannot include secret code. The PRC has established a record of preference for open-source software; for example, its growing personal computer manufacturing industry ships most of its domestic production with the Linux operating system. Also, the PRC's national lottery, post office, and social security systems all run on Linux operating systems. Since 2003, the Procurement Center of the State Council has required that any computer purchased by the government must be delivered with PRC-produced software only.

In the face of these challenges, Microsoft has worked hard to deliver its message that open-source software can result in higher total costs because even though it is free, it requires more effort to install, maintain, and update than Microsoft products. In large organizations, this effort results in extra hours worked and thus, extra costs. Microsoft also argues that open-source software's publicly available program code makes it a greater security risk. According to Microsoft, attackers can easily learn how any open-source program works and develop strategies for attacking the software when it is running on publicly accessible computers, such as Web servers.

Required:

1. Assume that you are on the staff of a PRC legislator. Outline the arguments that you would use to support a law that required all government agencies to use only open-source software on their Web servers.
2. Assume that you are working for the marketing department of Microsoft China. Develop a detailed list of briefing points that would help your salespeople convince top executives of large PRC companies to use Windows operating system software on their Web servers.
3. Assume that you are working for the business system's analysis department in IBM's PRC division, which offers both Microsoft Windows and Linux consulting services to PRC businesses and government offices. Develop a checklist that IBM analysts could use in consulting projects that could help advise clients as they make a choice between Windows or Linux operating system software for their Web servers.
4. Companies such as RedHat, Novell (with its SuSE distribution), and others offer Linux operating system software for sale. Although Linux is available at no cost from various sources, these companies charge a fee for installation and configuration help. They also offer service contracts to help users maintain and upgrade the software on a continuing

basis. Briefly outline the strategies that these companies might use to expand their market share in the PRC.

Note: Your instructor might assign you to a group to complete this case, and might ask you to prepare a formal presentation of your results to your class.

C2. Random Walk Shoes

Amy Lawrence, the owner of Random Walk Shoes, has asked you to help her as she launches her company's first Web site. In college, Amy was a business major with an artistic bent. She helped to pay her way through college by decorating sneakers with her hand-painted designs. Her business grew through word of mouth and through her participation in crafts fairs. By the time she earned her degree, Amy was running a successful business from her dorm room.

Amy expanded her sales efforts to include crafts fairs in nearby towns. She hired two college students to work for her, and she convinced several area gift shops to stock samples of her merchandise. The gift shops were not an ideal retail outlet for her products, however. Most people who want to buy decorated sneakers want to choose specific designs or have special designs created just for them. Customers also want to choose the specific shoes on which the design is placed. One of Amy's student workers suggested that she consider selling her products on the Web.

Realizing that the Web would give Random Walk Shoes a chance to reach a much wider audience and would allow customers to choose design–shoe combinations, Amy began gathering information and developing estimates about her planned Web activity. She bought a digital camera and took several hundred pictures of shoes, designs, and shoe–design combinations. She then hired a local Web designer to create sample pages for the Web site, including catalog pages that contained the digital images.

When the Web designer had completed a prototype of the site, Amy worked with the designer to calculate page sizes (including the images). The average page size was 85 KB. Amy and her employees then navigated the prototype site several hundred times to develop an estimate of how many pages an average visitor would download. They concluded that an average site visitor would visit 72 pages during each visit. Amy worked with the Web designer to develop estimates of the activity they expect to occur on the Web site during its first two years of operation. These estimates include:

- The database of Web page information (including the images) will require about 800 MB of disk space.
- The database management software itself will require about 500 MB of disk space.
- The shopping cart software will require about 100 MB of disk space.
- About 6000 customers will visit the site during the first month, and site traffic will grow about 20 percent each month during the first two years.
- The site should accommodate a peak traffic load of 1000 visitors at one time.

Amy wants to include features on the site that are similar to those found on competing sites (a list of links to businesses that sell customized shoes on the Web is included in the Online Companion for your reference). Amy wants the site to provide a good experience for visitors. If the site is successful, it will generate sufficient revenue to allow an upgrade after two years. However, she does not want to spend more money than is necessary to get the site up and keep it running for the next two years.

Required:

1. Determine the features and capacities (RAM, disk storage, processor speed) that Amy should include in the Web server computer she will need for her site. Summarize your purchase recommendation in a one-page memorandum to Amy. You may include information from vendors' sites (such as **Dell**, **Hewlett Packard**, or **Sun**) as an appendix to your memorandum.
2. Consider the advantages and disadvantages of each major operating system that Amy might use on the new Web server computer. In a one-page memorandum to Amy, make a specific recommendation and support it with facts and a logical argument. If you do not believe that one operating system is clearly superior for this application, explain why.
3. Consider the advantages and disadvantages of each major Web server software package for accomplishing the goals that Amy has for this site. In a one-page memorandum to Amy, make a specific recommendation regarding which Web server software package she should use. Provide an explanation that supports your recommendation.

Note: Your instructor might assign you to a group to complete this case, and might ask you to prepare a formal presentation of your results to your class.

For Further Study and Research

Abualsamid, A. 2001. "Dishing Up Dynamic Content," *Network Computing,* 12(8), April 16, 90–92.

Andrews, P. 2003. "Courting China," *U.S. News & World Report,* November 24, 44–45.

Ante, S. 2001. "Big Blue's Big Bet on Free Software," *Business Week,* December 10, 78–79.

Asay, M. 2007. "Study: 95 Percent of All E-mail Sent in 2007 Was Spam," December 12. (http://www.cnet.com/8301-13505_1-9831556-16.html)

Babcock, C. 2007. "Linux on Half of All New Servers? Red Hat's Got Plans," *Information Week,* November 12, 30.

Baran, N. 2001. "Load Testing Web Sites," *Dr. Dobb's Journal: Software Tools for the Professional Programmer,* 26(3), March, 112–116.

Bradner, S. 2008. "Irrelevant Victories in the War on Spam," *Network World,* March 24, 30.

Business Week Online. 2004. "China and Linux: Microsoft, Beware!" November 15.

Chabrow, E. 2005. "In The Fight Against Spam, A Few Knockouts: Microsoft Wins $7 Million Spam Settlement; Complaints From AOL Members Drop 85%," *InformationWeek,* August 15, 34.

Chen, L. 2008. "Four Tips on Load Balancing," *Communications News,* 45(5), May, 14.

Cheng, H. and I. Bose. 2004. "Performance Models of a Proxy Cache Server: The Impact of Multimedia Traffic," *European Journal of Operational Research,* 154(1), April, 218–229.

The Computer & Internet Lawyer. 2009. "Court Orders Spammers to Give Up $3.7 Million in US SAFE Web Case," 26(9), September, 26–27.

Epstein, J. 2004. "Standing Up to Redmond," *Latin Trade,* 12(6), June, 19.

Galli, P. 2004. "New IBM Unit to Target Emerging Markets," *eWeek,* 21(30), July 26, 9–10.

Gaudin, S. 2004. "Record Broken: 82% of U.S. E-mail Is Spam," *Internet News,* May 5. (http://www.internetnews.com/stats/article.php/3349921)

Glassman, M. 2003. "Fortifying the In Box as Spammers Lay Siege," *The New York Times,* July 31. (http://www.nytimes.com/2003/07/31/technology/circuits/31basi.html)

Graham, P. 2002. "A Plan for Spam," Paul Graham, July. (http://www.paulgraham.com/spam.html)

Graham, P. 2003. "Better Bayesian Filtering," Paul Graham, January. (http://www.paulgraham.com/better.html)

Gralla, P. 2002. "Making a List," *PC Magazine,* 21(10), May 21, 62–63.

Gross, G. 2004. "Judge Awards ISP $1 Billion in Spam Damages," *Computerworld,* December 20. (http://www.computerworld.com/governmenttopics/government/legalissues/story/0,10801,98421,00.html)

Hitchcock, J. 2009. "Is Spam Here to Stay?" *Information Today,* 26(3), March, 1, 44.

Hoover, J. 2008. "What Could Slow Down the Windows Server Juggernaut?" *Information Week,* March 3, 34.

Information Week. 2004. "AOL Reports Big Drop in Spam," December 27. (http://www.informationweek.com/story/showArticle.jhtml?articleID=56200528)

iTnews. 2007. "90 Percent of Email Will Be Spam by Year End," February 23.

Keizer, G. 2005. "CAN-SPAM Can't Slam Spam," *Information Week,* January 4. (http://www.informationweek.com/story/showArticle.jhtml?articleID=56900503)

Kopytoff, V. 2004. "Spam Mushrooms Despite a New Federal Law," *The San Francisco Chronicle,* September 2, C1.

Krim, J. 2004. "E-Mail Authentication Will Not End Spam, Panelists Say," *The Washington Post,* November 11, E01.

Lee, M. 2004. "Don't Give Up on E-mail," *Network Computing,* 15(12), June 24, 20.

Marsono, M., M. El-Kharashi, and F. Gebali. 2009. "Targeting Spam Control on Middleboxes: Spam Detection Based on Layer-3 E-mail Content Classification," *Computer Networks,* 53(6), April, 835–848.

Mears, J. and D. Dubie. 2003. "Users Banking on Blades," *Network World,* 20(40), October 6, 1–2.

Nelson, D. 2003. "Defending Your Site Against Spam," *O'Reilly Network,* June 26. (http://www.oreillynet.com/pub/a/linux/2003/06/26/blocklist.html)

Pavlov, O., N. Melville, and R. Plice. 2005. "Mitigating the Tragedy of the Digital Commons: The Problem of Unsolicited Commercial E-mail," *Communications of the AIS,* 2005(16), 73–90.

PC World, 2005. "Spam Law Test," 23(1), January, 20–22.

Roberts, P. 2004. "IETF Panel Deals Setback to Microsoft's Spam Proposal," *Computerworld,* 38(38), September 20, 14.

Schafer, S. 2004. "Microsoft's Cultural Revolution," *Newsweek,* June 28, E10–12.

Schonfeld, E. 2002. "To Preserve Social Capital Get Big Boxes and Some Really Mean Software," *Business* 2.0, 3(3), March, 57.

Schwartz, J. 2001. "Update: How the NYSE Crashed," *InternetWeek,* June 8.

Shen, X. 2005. "Intellectual Property and Open Source: A Case Study of Microsoft and Linux in China," *International Journal of IT Standards & Standardization Research,* 3(1), January–June, 21–43.

Ulfelder, S. 2004. "Spam-busters," *NetworkWorld,* 21(12), March 22, 69–71.

Vijayan, J. 2001. "Sun Attempts to Woo Users Away from IIS," *Computerworld,* 35(42), October 15, 28.

Wagner, M. and T. Kemp. 2001. "What's Wrong with eBay?" *InternetWeek,* January 15, 1–2.

White, B. 2008. "New Routers Catch the Eyes of IT Departments," *The Wall Street Journal,* March 25, B7.

Xiaobai, S. 2005. "Developing Country Perspectives on Software: Intellectual Property and Open Source, a Case Study of Microsoft and Linux in China," *International Journal of IT Standards & Standardization Research,* 3(1), January–June, 21–43.

Xinhua, 2004. "Microsoft Teams Up with China's Leading Server and Solutions Supplier," November 9.

CHAPTER 9

ELECTRONIC COMMERCE SOFTWARE

LEARNING OBJECTIVES

In this chapter, you will learn about:

- Finding and evaluating Web-hosting services
- Basic functions of electronic commerce software
- Advanced functions of electronic commerce software
- Electronic commerce software for small and midsize businesses
- Electronic commerce software for midsize to large businesses
- Electronic commerce software for large businesses that have an existing information technology infrastructure

INTRODUCTION

Many luxury clothing and jewelry items are sold online today. Some are sold directly through the manufacturers' Web sites, but most are sold through well-known retail merchandisers that have online stores. Of course, high-fashion brand goods sell for luxury prices in most cases. Shoppers who would like to buy these items, but cannot always afford them, might look for bargains at outlet stores. Gilt Groupe offers an interesting angle on the outlet store idea. At noon, its Web site lists a selection of designer clothes and other luxury brand items for sale at deep discounts. The store, which acquires the items through its network of high-end suppliers, sells only the listed items and only for 36 hours (or until an item sells out, which happens frequently). By midnight the next day, the sale is over and a new selection is listed the following noon.

This “limited time” element is designed to create a buying frenzy in which shoppers experience the excitement of a sale combined with the satisfaction of getting a true bargain. Shoppers must apply for a membership to be eligible to view and purchase the sale items, which adds to the feeling of exclusivity.

The operation of this Web site requires software that can display the items in an attractive way, process the sale transactions efficiently, and track information about customers and what they are buying. The tracking element is very important for Gilt because it helps the site negotiate purchases of highly desirable items from name-brand manufacturers. To get a sampling of the best new designs and innovative products, Gilt offers to share with its vendors information it gathers about how many of each item it sells and how rapidly the items sell.

Because Gilt compresses the lifetime of the sale event into 36 hours, it collects data about customer demand that a traditional retailer might not get for weeks, or even months. High-fashion product suppliers find this information to be valuable—so valuable, in fact, that they are willing to sell Gilt a sampling of their inventories at very low prices.

In this chapter, you will learn about the kinds of software that sites like Gilt uses to make its revenue model work, including software that enables catalog display of goods, shopping cart functions, and transaction processing activities. More importantly, Gilt uses software that can analyze sales and transmit that analysis to its buyers and to the suppliers of its luxury goods who use that information to adjust their production schedules so they are making more of the items that are likely to sell better in their regular sales outlets.

WEB HOSTING ALTERNATIVES

When companies need to incorporate electronic commerce components, they may opt to run servers in-house; this approach is called **self-hosting**. This is the option used most often by large companies. Other companies, especially midsize and smaller companies, often decide that a third-party Web-hosting service provider is a better choice than self-hosting. Many small Web stores use a third-party host provider for both Web services and electronic commerce functions, particularly when the Web site is small or the company sells a limited number of products.

As you learned in Chapter 2, a number of companies, called Internet service providers (ISPs), are in the business of providing Internet access to companies and individuals. Many of these companies offer Web-hosting services as well. To distinguish themselves from companies that provide only Internet access services, these hosting service firms sometimes call themselves something other than ISPs. Because the hosting services they offer are designed to help companies conduct electronic commerce, these hosting service firms sometimes call themselves **commerce service providers (CSPs)**. These firms often offer Web server management and rent application software (such as databases, shopping carts, and content management programs) to businesses; thus, these companies also sometimes call themselves **managed service providers (MSPs)** or **application service providers (ASPs)**. Despite the increasing variety of acronyms, many companies that provide some or all of these additional services still call themselves ISPs.

Service providers offer clients hosting arrangements that include shared hosting, dedicated hosting, and co-location. **Shared hosting** means that the client's Web site is on a server that hosts other Web sites simultaneously and is operated by the service provider at its location. With **dedicated hosting**, the service provider makes a Web server available to the client, but the client does not share the server with other clients of the service provider. In both shared hosting and dedicated hosting, the service provider owns the server hardware and leases it to the client. The service provider is responsible for maintaining the Web server hardware and software, and provides the connection to the Internet through its routers and other network hardware. In a **co-location** (also spelled **collocation** and **colocation**) service, the service provider rents a physical space to the client to install its own server hardware. The client installs its own software and maintains the server. The service provider is responsible only for providing a reliable power supply and a connection to the Internet through its routers and other networking hardware.

You can find service providers by looking in your local telephone directory or by using a Web directory such as The List, or a site listed in the Google Directory of Web Host Directories, which appears in Figure 9-1.

Google directory [Google Search] Directory Help

Search only in Directories Search the Web

Directories

Computers > Internet > Web Design and Development > Hosting > Directories

Go to Directory Home

Categories

ASP.NET (2)
Free Hosting (10)
United Kingdom (8)

Web Pages — Viewing in Google PageRank order — View in alphabetical order

Web Hosting Ratings - http://www.webhostingratings.com/
Searchable database of web hosting plans with user ratings and reviews, includes advanced search options and specialty directories.

Web Hosting Stuff - http://www.webhostingstuff.com/
Details of costs, diskspace and bandwidth for providers. Includes top ten rated lists.

HostVoice.net - http://www.hostvoice.com/
Find a web host by submitting a request and receiving custom offers.

HostingCatalog.com - http://www.hostingcatalog.com/
Large database to search by feature or option. Also articles and reviews.

HostChart - http://www.hostchart.com/
Compare hundreds of hosting companies and plans quickly and easily.

100 Best Free Web Space Providers - http://www.100best-free-web-space.com/
Contains prices and articles.

RateMyHost.com - http://www.ratemyhost.com
Rate your host, find a host by searching through features, pricing, ratings and reviews.

Web Host Magazine and Buyer's Guide - http://www.webhostmagazine.com/
Independent panel reviews on web hosts and host finders.

Compare web hosts - http://www.comparewebhosts.com/
Search and compare detailed web hosting services and pricing plans.

Hottest Hosts - http://www.thewhir.com/find/web-hosts/
A categorised directory of web hosting companies including virtual, dedicated and co-located servers.

Hosting Speeds - http://www.hostingspeeds.com
Lists web hosts based on their network speed and ranks them by performance.

Host Index - http://www.hostindex.com/
Categorical searching for web hosting companies by types and features.

All Cheap Hosting - http://www.allcheaphosting.com/
Directory of affordable web hosting providers.

Hosting Help - http://www.hostinghelp.com
Questions and answers about all things web hosting.

Collocation Facilities Directory - http://www.colosource.com
Provides service and contact information of colocation service providers.

HostSearch.com - http://www.hostsearch.com
News, articles, and a searchable database of web hosting providers.

WebHosters.com - http://webhosting.devshed.com
Web host search engine, customer reviews, news, and discussion.

TheWebHostingDir.com - http://www.thewebhostingdir.com
Companies by script type and country. Includes information on features offered and allows consumers to rate sites.

1Host.info - http://www.1host.info
Categorized directory of web hosting companies around the world. Includes multiple hosting categories and search tools.

Hostprofessor.com - http://www.hostprofessor.com
Categorized listing of web hosting companies complete with helpful articles.

http://www.adoloma.com/ - http://www.adoloma.com/
Offers host popularity rankings, ratings, reach and traffic graphs (powered by Alexa) and contact information.

HostSeek.com - http://www.hostseek.com
Simple host search.

Host Approval - http://www.hostapproval.com
Categorized, pay-per-click directory of web site hosting companies.

HostoHolic.com - http://www.hostoholic.com
Directory of Hosting companies with company details divided into specific categories.

Ask WebHost - http://www.askwebhost.com
A directory of web hosting offers.

iHostCafe.com - http://www.ihostcafe.com
User reviews and a help desk that matches prospective customers with a hosting company.

AngelicHosts.com - http://www.angelichosts.com
A Christian webhosting directory with Linux, Windows and free webhosts for individuals and organizations.

HostCheck - http://www.hostcheck.net/
Web hosting certification and review program site offering a searchable database of hosting companies. Allows users to compare web host features, and submit requests for hosting proposal quotes.

Host Byte Marketplace - http://www.hostbyte.com
Offers a searchable directory of web hosting providers, plans, articles, specials, and beginner guides.

Web Hosting Ratings.com - http://www.web-hosting-ratings.com
Rates web hosting plans and hosting providers.

100mostdynamic.com - http://www.100mostdynamic.com
A website awarding 100 hosting companies that demonstrate good web hosting services.

Host Record - http://www.hostrecord.com
Providing web hosting directory, search, reviews and discussion.

WebHostingSeeker.Com - http://www.webhostingseeker.com/
Links categorized by country and hosting type.

Webhost Knowledge Base - http://www.webhost-kb.com/
Search website hosting packages, compare prices and features.

Web Hosting Directory - http://www.webhostingdirectory.cc/
Searchable directory by cost, bandwidth and space. Includes news, reviews and articles.

Help build the largest human-edited directory on the web.
Submit a Site - Open Directory Project - Become an Editor

The content of the Google directory is based on the Open Directory and is enhanced using Google's own technology.
The following Open Directory editors contributed to this category:
tacke

Modified by Google - ©2009 Google
Advertise with Us - Jobs, Press, Cool Stuff...

FIGURE 9-1 The Google Web host directory

When making Web server–hosting decisions, a company should ask whether the hardware platform and software combination can be upgraded when the traffic on its Web site increases. A company's Web server requirements are directly related to its electronic commerce transaction volume and Web site traffic. The best hosting services provide Web server hardware and software combinations that are **scalable**, which means they can be adapted to meet changing requirements when their clients grow.

BASIC FUNCTIONS OF ELECTRONIC COMMERCE SOFTWARE

Because electronic commerce sites vary so greatly in terms of size, purpose, audience, and other factors, a vast range of software and hardware products are available for building electronic commerce sites. Sites with minimal needs can use externally hosted stores that provide software tools to build an online store on a host's site. At the other end of the range are sophisticated electronic commerce software suites that can handle high-transaction volumes and include a broad assortment of features and tools.

The type of electronic commerce software an organization needs depends on several factors, with size and budget being the primary drivers. One of the most important factors is the expected size of the enterprise and its projected traffic and sales. A high-traffic electronic commerce site with thousands of catalog inquiries each minute requires different software than a small online shop selling a dozen items. Another determining factor is budget. Creating an online store can be much less expensive than building a chain of retail stores. The start-up cost of an electronic commerce operation can be much lower than the cost of creating a brick-and-mortar sales and distribution channel that includes warehouses and multiple retail outlets. A traditional store requires a physical location with leases, employees, utility payments, and maintenance. The cost of creating the infrastructure for an online business can be much lower.

Another early decision is whether the company should use an external host or host the electronic commerce site in-house. Companies that have an existing information technology (IT) staff of programmers, Web designers, and network engineers are more likely to choose an in-house hosting approach. If a company does not have or cannot easily hire people with the skills required to set up and maintain an electronic commerce site, it can outsource all or part of the job to a service provider. Companies that are located outside of major metropolitan areas and want to host sites themselves must also consider whether their Internet connections are sufficient. In many cases, these companies find that they are not close enough to a major Internet access point or that their connections do not have sufficient bandwidth to handle large volumes of traffic efficiently. Even if these companies have employees with sufficient skills, they might decide to use a service provider to host their electronic commerce sites.

The specific duties that electronic commerce software performs range from a few fundamental operations to a complete solution—from catalog display to fulfillment notification. All electronic commerce software must provide:

- A catalog display
- Shopping cart capabilities
- Transaction processing

Larger and more complex electronic commerce sites also use software that adds other features and capabilities to the basic set of commerce tools. These additional software components can include:

- Middleware that integrates the electronic commerce system with existing company information systems that handle inventory control, order processing, and accounting
- Enterprise application integration
- Web services
- Integration with enterprise resource planning (ERP) software
- Supply chain management (SCM) software
- Customer relationship management (CRM) software
- Content management software
- Knowledge management software

Tools required by all electronic commerce sites are described in the following sections. The more advanced functions used by larger sites are covered later in this chapter.

Catalog Display

A catalog organizes the goods and services being sold. To further organize its offerings, a retailer may break them down into departments. As in a physical store, merchandise in an online store can be grouped within logical departments to make locating an item, such as a camping stove, simpler. Web stores often use the same department names as their physical counterparts. In most physical stores, each product is kept in only one place. A Web store has the advantage of being able to include a single product in multiple categories. For example, running shoes can be listed as both footwear and athletic gear.

A small commerce site can have a very simple static catalog. A **catalog** is a listing of goods and services. A **static catalog** is a simple list written in HTML that appears on a Web page or a series of Web pages. To add an item, delete an item, or change an item's listing, the company must edit the HTML of one or more pages. Larger commerce sites are more likely to use a dynamic catalog. A **dynamic catalog** stores the information about items in a database, usually on a separate computer that is accessible to the server that is running the Web site itself. A dynamic catalog can feature multiple photos of each item, detailed descriptions, and a search tool that allows customers to search for an item and determine its availability. The software that implements a dynamic catalog is often included in larger electronic commerce software packages; however, some companies write their own software to link their existing databases of product information to their Web sites. Both types of catalog (static and dynamic) are located in the third tier of the Web site architecture that you learned about in Chapter 8.

Many of the online businesses you read about in earlier chapters are large, well-known sites. These sites include many features and have a professional look. Figure 9-2 shows the Web page of a small electronic commerce site that sells patio furniture made from teak wood. This site uses simple, inexpensive electronic commerce software and has a clean look with few features beyond those necessary to make sales.

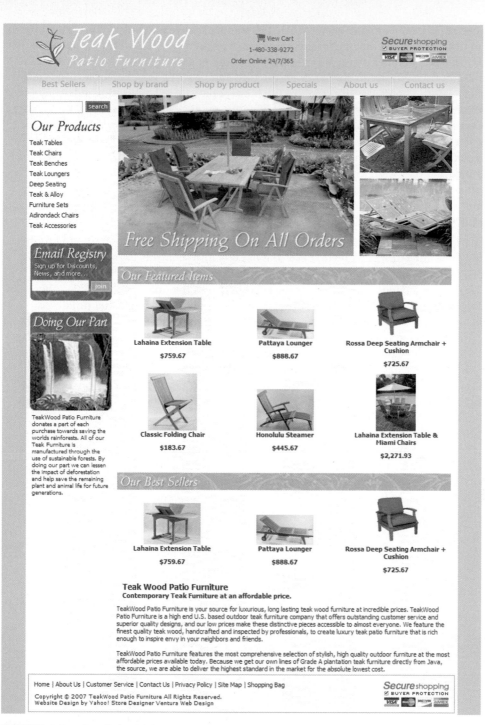

Teak Wood
Patio Furniture

View Cart
1-480-338-9272
Order Online 24/7/365

Secure shopping
BUYER PROTECTION

Best Sellers | Shop by brand | Shop by product | Specials | About us | Contact us

search

Our Products

Teak Tables
Teak Chairs
Teak Benches
Teak Loungers
Deep Seating
Teak & Alloy
Furniture Sets
Adirondack Chairs
Teak Accessories

Free Shipping On All Orders

Email Registry
Sign up for Discounts, News, and more...
join

Doing Our Part

TeakWood Patio Furniture donates a part of each purchase towards saving the worlds rainforests. All of our Teak Furniture is manufactured through the use of sustainable forests. By doing our part we can lessen the impact of deforestation and help save the remaining plant and animal life for future generations.

Our Featured Items

Lahaina Extension Table
$759.67

Pattaya Lounger
$888.67

Rossa Deep Seating Armchair + Cushion
$725.67

Classic Folding Chair
$183.67

Honolulu Steamer
$445.67

Lahaina Extension Table & Miami Chairs
$2,271.93

Our Best Sellers

Lahaina Extension Table
$759.67

Pattaya Lounger
$888.67

Rossa Deep Seating Armchair + Cushion
$725.67

Teak Wood Patio Furniture
Contemporary Teak Furniture at an affordable price.

TeakWood Patio Furniture is your source for luxurious, long lasting teak wood furniture at incredible prices. TeakWood Patio Furniture is a high end U.S. based outdoor teak furniture company that offers outstanding customer service and superior quality designs, and our low prices make these distinctive pieces accessible to almost everyone. We feature the finest quality teak wood, handcrafted and inspected by professionals, to create luxury teak patio furniture that is rich enough to inspire envy in your neighbors and friends.

TeakWood Patio Furniture features the most comprehensive selection of stylish, high quality outdoor furniture at the most affordable prices available today. Because we get our own lines of Grade A plantation teak furniture directly from Java, the source, we are able to deliver the highest standard in the market for the absolute lowest cost.

Home | About Us | Customer Service | Contact Us | Privacy Policy | Site Map | Shopping Bag

Copyright © 2007 TeakWood Patio Furniture All Rights Reserved.
Website Design by Yahoo! Store Designer Ventura Web Design

Secure shopping
BUYER PROTECTION

FIGURE 9-2 Small electronic commerce site

Small online stores that sell fewer than 100 items usually need only a simple list of products or categories. Organization of the items is not particularly important. Companies that offer only a small number of items can provide a photo of each item on the Web page that is a link to more information about the product. A static catalog is sufficient for their needs. Larger electronic commerce sites require the more sophisticated navigation aids and better product organization tools that are a part of dynamic catalogs.

Good sites give buyers alternative ways to find products. Besides offering a well-organized catalog, large sites with many products can provide a search engine that allows customers to enter descriptive search terms, such as "men's shirts," so they can quickly find the Web page containing what they want to purchase. Remember, the most important rule of all commerce is: Never stand in the way of a customer who wants to buy something.

Shopping Cart

In the early days of electronic commerce, shoppers selected items they wanted to purchase by filling out online forms. Using text box and list box form controls to indicate their choices, users entered the quantity of an item in the quantity text box, the SKU (stock-keeping unit) or product number in another text box, and the unit price in yet another text box. This system was awkward for ordering more than one or two items at a time.

One problem with forms-based shopping was that shoppers had to write down product codes, unit prices, and other information about the product before going to the order form, which was inevitably on another page. Another problem was that customers sometimes forgot whether they had clicked the submit button to send in their orders. As a result, they either sent the same order twice (pressing the submit button when they had already done so) or thought they had submitted the order when they really had not (consequently failing to submit the order). The forms-based method of shopping was confusing and error prone.

Figure 9-3 illustrates the problems that shoppers faced with forms-based ordering systems. First, many customers found it difficult to remember the exact descriptions of the products. Second, customers had to enter the item numbers, which were located on a different Web page, in the text boxes. Thus, the customers needed to either write down or memorize the numbers.

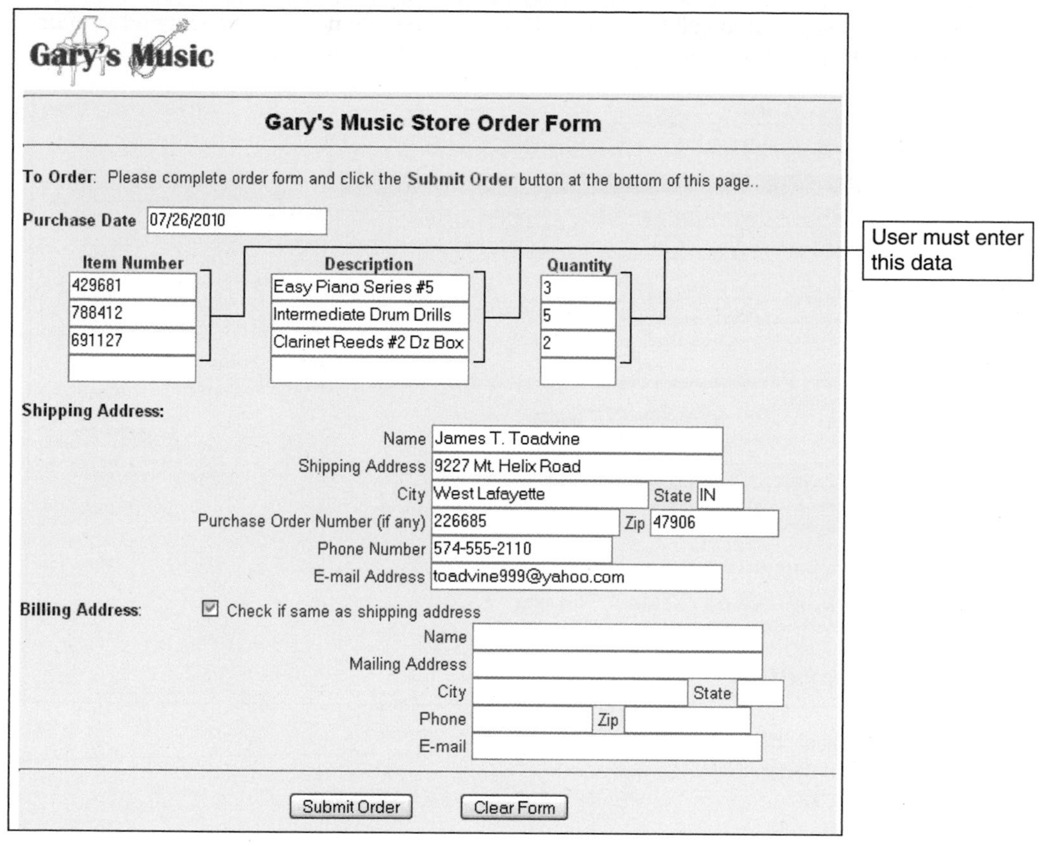

Gary's Music

Gary's Music Store Order Form

To Order: Please complete order form and click the **Submit Order** button at the bottom of this page..

Purchase Date 07/26/2010

Item Number	Description	Quantity
429681	Easy Piano Series #5	3
788412	Intermediate Drum Drills	5
691127	Clarinet Reeds #2 Dz Box	2

User must enter this data

Shipping Address:

Name: James T. Toadvine
Shipping Address: 9227 Mt. Helix Road
City: West Lafayette State: IN
Purchase Order Number (if any): 226685 Zip: 47906
Phone Number: 574-555-2110
E-mail Address: toadvine999@yahoo.com

Billing Address: ☑ Check if same as shipping address
Name
Mailing Address
City State
Phone Zip
E-mail

Submit Order Clear Form

FIGURE 9-3 Using a form to enter an order

Because forms-based ordering is cumbersome and error-prone, only a few of the smallest online stores still use it. Shopping carts are now the standard method for processing sales on most electronic commerce sites. As you learned in Chapter 4, a shopping cart, also sometimes called a shopping bag or shopping basket, keeps track of the items the customer has selected and allows customers to view the contents of their carts, add new items, or remove items. To order an item, the customer simply clicks that item. All of the details about the item, including its price, product number, and other identifying information, are stored automatically in the cart. If a customer later changes his or her mind about an item, he or she can view the cart's contents and remove the unwanted items. When the customer is ready to conclude the shopping session, the click of a button executes the purchase transaction. Figure 9-4 shows a typical shopping cart page at a site that sells computer equipment.

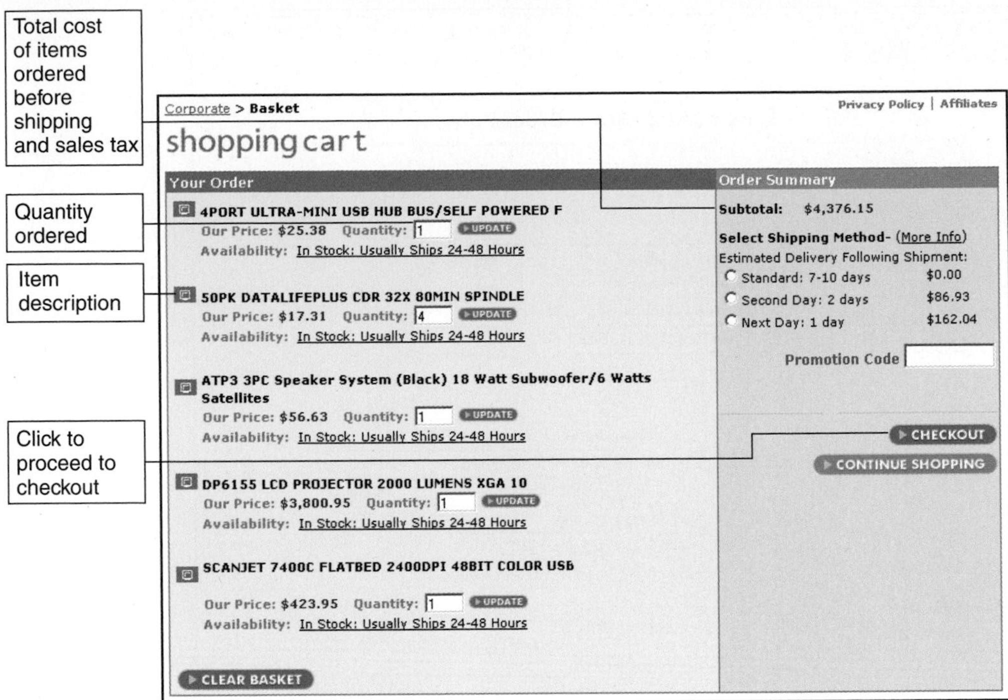

FIGURE 9-4 Typical shopping cart page

Clicking the Checkout button usually displays a screen that asks for billing and shipping information and that confirms the order. As you can see from the figure, the shopping cart software keeps a running total of each type of item. The shopping cart calculates a total as well as sales tax and shipping costs.

Some shopping cart software allows the customer to fill a shopping cart with purchases, put the cart in virtual storage, and come back days later to confirm and pay for the purchases. A number of companies, including **BIZNET Internet Services**, **SalesCart**, and **WebGenie Software**, sell shopping cart software that sellers can add to their Web sites. These software packages range in price from a few hundred dollars to several thousand dollars, plus an ongoing monthly fee. The shopping cart software sold by SalesCart works with several different Web site design tools, as shown in Figure 9-5.

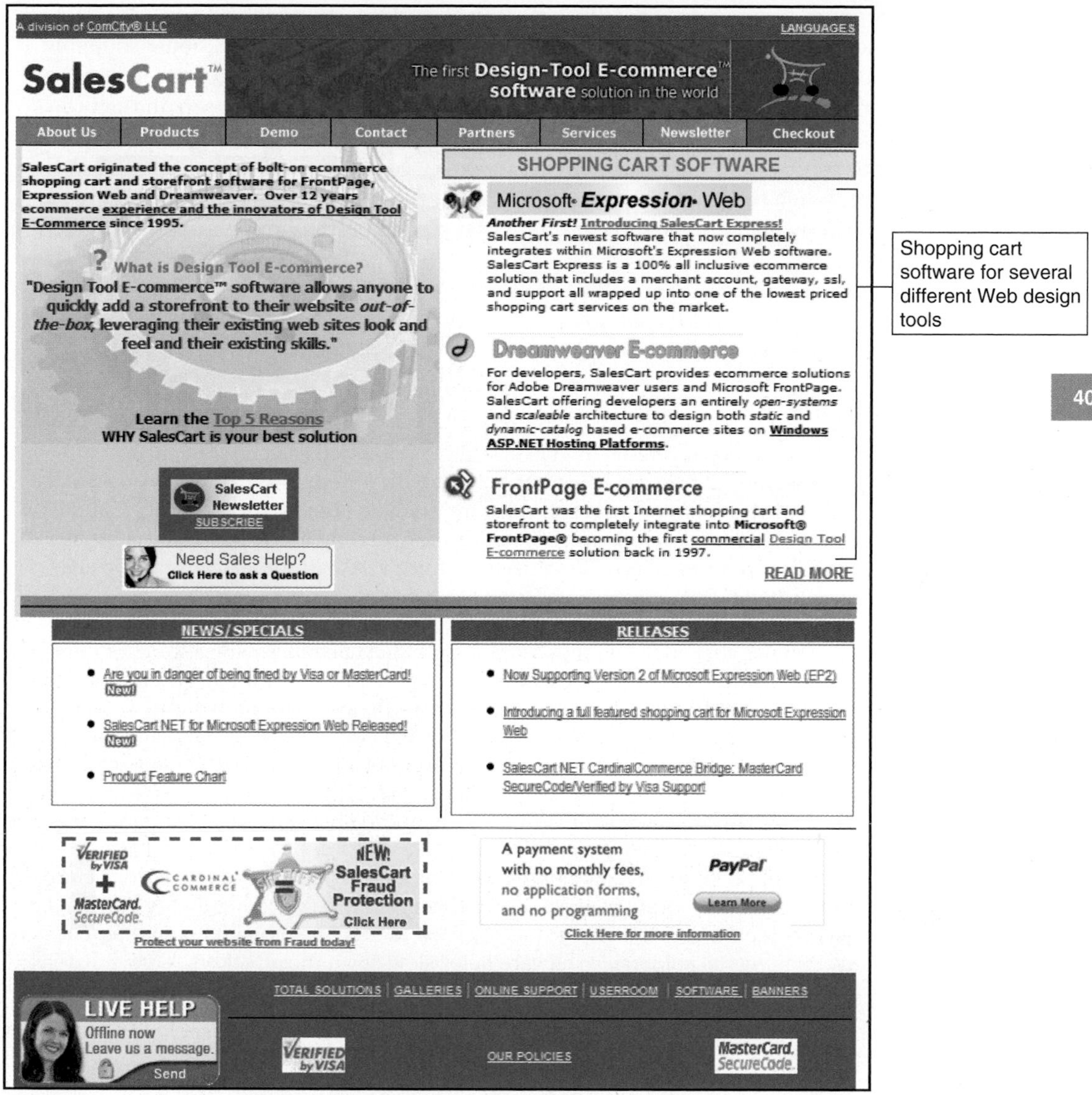

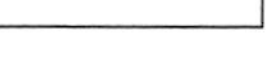

Shopping cart software for several different Web design tools

FIGURE 9-5 SalesCart shopping cart software page

Because the Web is a stateless system—unable to remember anything from one transmission or session to another—shopping cart information must be stored explicitly for the shopper to retrieve later. Furthermore, it must distinguish one shopper from another so that the purchases are not mixed up. One way to uniquely identify users and store information about their choices is to create and store cookies, which, as you learned in earlier chapters, are bits of information stored on a client computer. When a customer returns to a site that issued a particular cookie, the shopping software reads either the cookie from the customer's computer or the database record from the merchant's server.

If a shopper's browser does not allow storage of cookies, sites can use another way to preserve shopping cart information from one browser session to another. Some shopping cart software packages, such as **ShopSite**, do this by automatically assigning a shopper a temporary number. The number is added to the end of the URL that appears in the browser's address bar and persists as the shopper navigates from one Web site to another. When the customer returns, the URL still contains shopping cart information that the Web server can interpret. When the shopper closes the browser, the temporary number is discarded and is no longer available, even if the customer later reopens the browser and returns to the same Web site.

LEARNING FROM FAILURES

PDG Software

PDG Software is a company based in Tucker, Georgia, that sells electronic commerce software to companies that operate small and midsize electronic commerce Web sites. PDG sells shopping cart software, auction software, shopping mall software, and a number of other packages. Although it sells some of its software directly to the companies that use it, most of its sales are through resellers—firms that use PDG software as part of Web sites that they design, build, and deliver to customers as complete units.

An attacker discovered a vulnerability in the PDG software that allowed an intruder to enter the shopping cart and open the file that contained customer names, contact information, and credit card numbers. PDG developed a patch that would repair the software the same day it found out about the intrusions. PDG posted the patch on its Web site so that companies using the software could download and install the patch. Both PDG and the FBI issued press releases immediately to warn users of the problem with the shopping cart software and encourage them to obtain the patch. Unfortunately, the users of the software that had purchased it as part of a complete electronic commerce Web site were, in many cases, unaware that their sites included the PDG shopping cart software.

Because it took so long—several months, in some cases—to find and contact the companies using the software, online offenders were able to exploit this vulnerability and collect thousands of credit card numbers. In most cases such as this, the difficulty of finding the sites that are running the vulnerable software helps slow down the attackers. Unfortunately, in this case, the intruder who discovered the opening also found that entering a specific word in a search engine's search expression would instantly return a list of the thousands of sites running the PDG software.

Most of the Web sites found out about the problem when their customers called them, suspicious because their credit card information had been compromised. The lesson from this failure is that companies that operate electronic commerce Web sites must know the source of the software used in creating and maintaining their sites and must monitor news about the security of that software.

Transaction Processing

Transaction processing occurs when the shopper proceeds to the virtual checkout counter by clicking a checkout button. Then the electronic commerce software performs any necessary calculations, such as volume discounts, sales tax, and shipping costs. At checkout, the customer's Web browser software and the seller's Web server software both switch into a secure state of communication. You will learn more about how Web clients and servers establish these secure communication states in Chapter 10. Figure 9-6 shows how the three key functions of a basic electronic commerce Web site (catalog display, shopping cart, and transaction processing) are combined in the site's architecture.

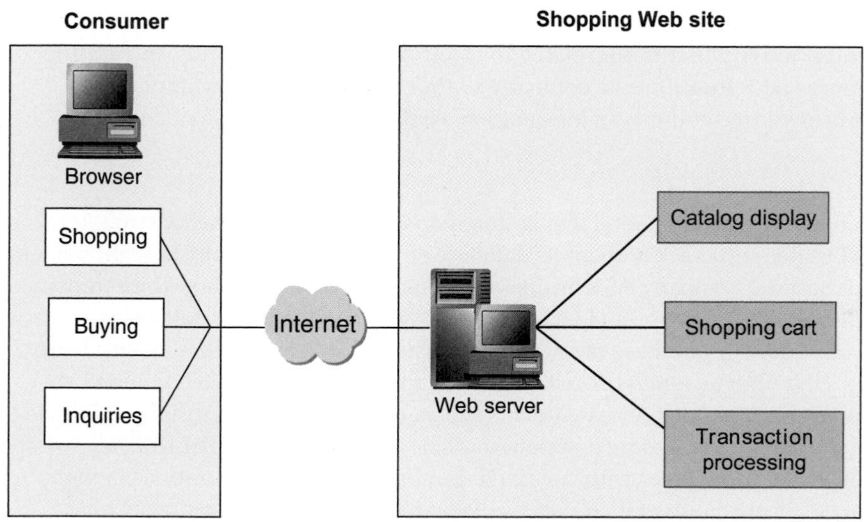

FIGURE 9-6 Basic electronic commerce Web site architecture

Although a basic online store's electronic commerce software can generate reports that summarize sales and inventory shipped, most midsize and larger companies use an accounting software package to record sales and inventory movements. To integrate effectively with accounting software, the electronic commerce software must communicate with that accounting software, which typically runs on other computers in the seller's network. When an item is sold online, the electronic commerce software must communicate that fact to both the sales and inventory management modules in the accounting software.

Computing sales taxes and shipping costs are also important parts of online sales. Sales tax rates and shipping rates can change often, so Web site managers must either monitor and update the rates continually or use software that updates the rates automatically. Shipping companies such as FedEx and UPS offer software to shippers that integrates with electronic commerce software to ensure that the rates they have are current. Other calculation complications include provisions for coupons, special promotions, and time-sensitive offers; for example, "purchase a round-trip ticket before the end of the month and receive a 50 percent discount."

In larger companies, the integration of the Web site's transaction processing into the accounting and operation-control systems of the company can be very complex. The next section discusses some of the advanced functions that larger companies look for in electronic commerce software.

ADVANCED FUNCTIONS OF ELECTRONIC COMMERCE SOFTWARE

In this section, you will learn about the features that larger companies need in their electronic commerce software. Although there are exceptions, such as Amazon.com and Buy.com, most large companies that have electronic commerce operations also have substantial business activity that is not related to electronic commerce. Thus, integrating electronic commerce activities into the company's other operations is very important. A basic element of any large company's information system is its collection of databases.

Databases

A **database** is a collection of information that is stored on a computer in a highly structured way. The rules a business establishes about its database structure are carefully thought out and take into account how the company does business (its **business rules**) and how the company can reduce the likelihood that errors and inconsistencies will develop in the database.

A **database manager** (or **database management software**) is software that makes it easy for users to enter, edit, update, and retrieve information in the database. One common low-end database manager is Microsoft Access. More complex database managers that can handle larger databases and can perform more functions at higher speeds include IBM DB2, Microsoft SQL Server, and Oracle. Companies with very large databases that have operations in many locations must make most (or all) of their data available to users in those locations. Large information systems that store the same data in many different physical locations are called **distributed information systems**, and the databases within those systems are called **distributed database systems**. The complexity of these systems leads to their high cost.

Most companies that can afford it do use commercial database products; however, an increasing number of companies and other organizations are using MySQL, which was developed and is maintained by a community of programmers on the Web. Similar to the Linux operating system you learned about in earlier chapters, **MySQL** is open-source software, even though it was developed by a Swedish company (MySQL AB), which has been owned since 2008 by Sun.

Except for small sites offering only a few products, companies should determine the level of database support provided by any electronic commerce software they are considering. Most online stores that sell many products use a database that stores product information, including size, color, type, and price details. Usually, the database that serves an online store is the same one that is used by the company's existing sales operations. It is usually better to have one database serving the two sales functions (online and in-store retail, for example) because it eliminates the errors that can occur when running parallel but distinct databases. If a company has existing inventory and product databases, then it should consider only electronic commerce software that supports these systems. The details of database design and operation are beyond the scope of this book, but you can learn more by taking courses in database design and database programming.

Middleware

Larger companies usually establish the connections between their electronic commerce software (that is, their catalog display, shopping cart, and transaction processing software) and their accounting and inventory management databases or applications by using middleware. **Middleware** is software that takes information about sales and inventory shipments from the electronic commerce software and transmits it to accounting and inventory management software in a form that these systems can read. For example, the sales module of an accounting system might be designed to accept the input of a telephone salesperson. The salesperson enters the product numbers, quantities, and shipping method into the sales module by using a keyboard while talking to the customer on the phone. Middleware would extract information about a sale from the Web site's shopping cart software and enter it directly into the accounting software's sales module without requiring that a person re-enter the information.

Some large companies that have sufficient IT staff write their own middleware; however, most companies purchase middleware that is customized for their businesses by the middleware vendor or a consulting firm. Thus, most of the cost of middleware is not the software itself, but the consulting fees needed to make the software work in a given company. Making a company's information systems work together is called **interoperability** and is an important goal of companies when they install middleware.

The total cost of a middleware implementation can range from $50,000 to several million dollars, depending on the complexity of the company's underlying operations and its existing information systems. Major middleware vendors include **BEA Systems**, **Broadvision**, **Digital River**, and **IBM Tivoli Systems**. As the market for this type of software has matured, the companies that provide this software have worked to build products that can integrate software throughout the enterprise with company Web sites.

Enterprise Application Integration

A program that performs a specific function, such as creating invoices, calculating payroll, or processing payments received from customers, is called an **application program**, **application software** or, more simply, an **application**. An **application server** is a computer that takes the request messages received by the Web server and runs application programs that perform some kind of action based on the contents of the request messages. The actions that the application server software performs are determined by the rules used in the business. These rules are called **business logic**. An example of a business rule is: When a customer logs in, check the password entered against the password file in the database.

In many organizations, the business logic is distributed among many different applications that are used in different parts of the organization. In recent years, many IT departments have devoted significant resources to the creation of links among these scattered applications so that the organization's business logic can be interconnected. The creation and management of these links is called **application integration** or **enterprise application integration**. The integration is accomplished by programs that transfer information from one application to another. For example, a program might transfer information from order entry systems in several different divisions to a single accounts receivable and sales system that integrates all enterprise-wide sales activity. In many cases, the data formats in the various programs are different and the transfer programs must edit and reformat the data before transferring it. Increasingly, programmers are using XML data feeds to move data from one application to another in enterprise integration implementations.

Application servers are usually grouped into two types: page-based and component-based systems. **Page-based application systems** return pages generated by scripts that include the rules for presenting data on the Web page with the business logic. Common page-based server systems include Adobe ColdFusion, JavaServer Pages (JSP), Microsoft Active Server Pages (ASP), and Hypertext Preprocessor (PHP). These page-based systems work quite well for small and midsize Web sites. Because they combine the page presentation logic with the business logic, however, they can be difficult to revise and update. Larger businesses often prefer to use a **component-based application system** that separates the presentation logic from the business logic. Each component of logic is created and maintained separately. This makes updating and changing elements of the system much easier—especially on large electronic commerce sites that are built and maintained by teams of programmers. The most common component-based systems used on the Web are Enterprise JavaBeans (EJBs), Microsoft Component Object Model (COM), and the Object Management Group Common Object Request Broker Architecture (CORBA).

Integration with ERP Systems

Many B2B Web sites must be able to connect to existing information systems such as enterprise resource planning software. **Enterprise resource planning (ERP)** software packages are business systems that integrate all facets of a business, including accounting, logistics, manufacturing, marketing, planning, project management, and treasury functions.

The two major ERP vendors are Oracle and SAP. A typical installation of ERP software costs between $2 million and $25 million; thus, companies that are already running these systems have made a significant investment in them and require that their electronic commerce and EDI operations to integrate with them.

Figure 9-7 shows a typical architecture for a B2B Web site that connects to several existing information systems, including the ERP system within the company and its trading partners' systems through EDI connections.

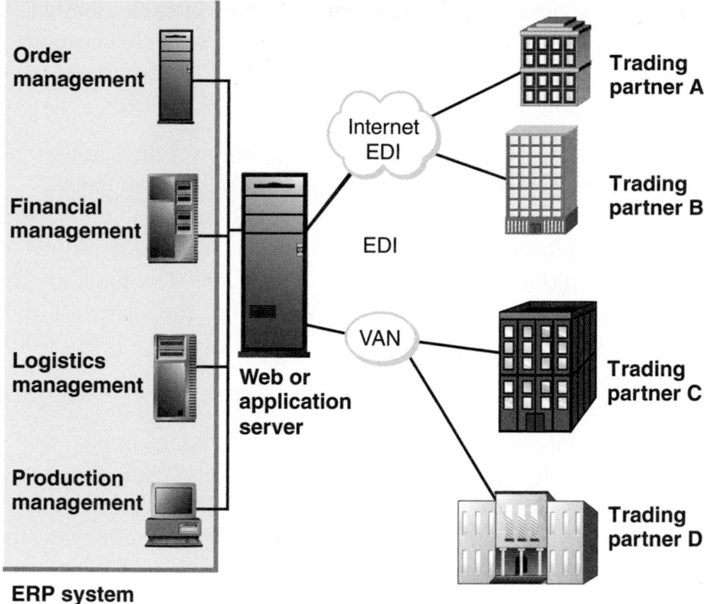

FIGURE 9-7 ERP system integration with EDI

Web Services

Companies are using the Internet to connect specific software applications at one organization directly to software applications at other organizations. The W3C defines **Web services** as software systems that support interoperable machine-to-machine interaction over a network. In other words, a Web service is a set of software and technologies that allow computers to use the Web to interact with each other directly, without human operators directing the specific interactions.

For example, a handbag manufacturer's computers can contact its customers' computers to learn which of its products are selling well. Once it obtains this information from a number of the company's customers, the computer can adjust manufacturing schedules, increasing the production of some handbags and reducing the production of others.

A general name for the ways programs interconnect with each other is **application program interface (API)**. When the interaction is done over the Web, the techniques are called **Web APIs**. Web services use Web APIs of various types, as you will learn later in this section. A number of major software vendors have embraced the idea of Web services in new technology initiatives such as Microsoft .NET and the Sun Java 2 Platform, Enterprise Edition.

What Web Services Can Do

Companies are using Web services to offer improved customer service and reduce costs. In some companies, Web services are used to transmit the XML-tagged data from one application to another in enterprise application integration efforts. In other applications, Web services provide data feeds between two different companies. Many companies that have used Web services to accomplish application integration have found it to be less expensive to implement than older approaches that required programmers to write or adapt multiple middleware software programs. Here are some examples of specific Web services implementations:

- J.P. Morgan Chase & Co., a major investment bank, uses Web services in its investment information portal. The Web services pull information, such as general economic forecasts, financial analyses of specific companies, industry forecasts, and financial markets results into continually updated online reports that customers can obtain on the J.P. Morgan Chase portal site. The bank's customers could obtain all of this information themselves, but the aggregation is a service that the bank provides. The information flow in this case is from the bank to its customers.
- Nationwide Building Society, a mortgage company in Swindon, England, uses a Web services tool to automate its communications with mortgage application service companies. These service companies obtain information from consumers who want mortgages and then forward the information in a prescribed XML format to Nationwide. The Nationwide Web services software reformats the submission and submits it to Nationwide's enterprise computer system. When a lending decision has been reached, the Web services tool conveys the decision back to the mortgage application service company. This Web services approach has reduced costs and decreased turnaround time for loan decisions at Nationwide.
- CUNA Mutual Group sells services to credit unions throughout the United States from its headquarters in Madison, Wisconsin. These services include everything from check clearing to construction management. CUNA provides many of its services by running programs on old computer systems that have been in operation for years. Instead of reprogramming everything so it could be accessible on the Web, CUNA created a Web services layer that takes information from the old computer systems and generates Web pages that its customers can use to obtain those services.
- The **MSN Money** site buys stock quotes from the Interactive Data Corporation, which delivers them, computer-to-computer, using Web services. If you view an MSN Money stock quote page, you can see the Interactive Data Real-Time Services acknowledgement for those stock quotes (along with those of other Web services providers that contributed to the page) near the bottom of the Web page under the heading "Data Providers."
- Merrill Lynch, which had more than 400 programs running on its old mainframe computers, wanted to combine the information managed by those programs into new reports to support the company's product management and sales efforts. The old programs had been refined over the years and were highly reliable, so Merrill Lynch did not want to rebuild them. Instead, it used Web services to create links into those programs and make their data available to software running in new environments (such as Sun's Java and Microsoft's .NET) on different computers. This integration project cost $30,000 instead of the estimated $800,000 it would have cost to use an older application integration approach.

How Web Services Work

A key element of the Web services approach is that programmers can write software that accesses these units of business application logic without knowing the details of how each unit is implemented. Web services can be mixed and matched with other Web services to execute a complex business transaction. Thus, Web services allow programs written in different languages on different platforms to communicate with each other and accomplish transaction processing and other business tasks.

The common format of this machine-to-machine communication was originally HTML; however, most Web services implementations now use XML. As you learned in Chapter 2, organizations can use XML to mark up content with agreed-upon sets of descriptive tags.

The first Web services were nothing more than sources of information. The Web services model allowed programmers to incorporate these information sources into software applications. For example, a company that wanted to collect all of its financial management information into one spreadsheet could use Web services to obtain information about bank account and loan balances, stock portfolio holdings, and current interest rates on financial instruments. Commonly available spreadsheet software can then be used to create a spreadsheet model that uses the information supplied by those Web services to update itself automatically. Some of the information might be available as a Web service at no cost; other information access might require a subscription. But Web services can make accessing the information much easier and more efficient.

A more advanced example would be a company that uses purchasing software to help manage that activity. The purchasing software can use Web services to obtain price information from a variety of vendors. After the purchasing agent reviews the price and delivery information and authorizes the purchase, the software can submit the order and track it until the shipment is received. On the other side of this transaction, the vendor's software can use Web services (in addition to providing price and delivery information) to check the buyer's credit and contract with a freight company to handle the shipment. As Web services become more sophisticated, they can make the decisions rather than simply providing information to people who then make decisions.

SOAP Specifications

The first widely used approach to Web services was **Simple Object Access Protocol (SOAP)**, which is a message-passing protocol that defines how to send marked-up data from one software application to another across a network. Implementing SOAP uses three rule sets (usually called protocols or specifications) that let programs work with the formatted (using XML or HTML) data flows to accomplish the communication that makes Web services work. The communication rules are included in the SOAP protocol. You can see the full SOAP specification and learn more about SOAP at the **W3C SOAP Page**. The other two rule sets are the **Web Services Description Language (WSDL)**, which is used to describe the characteristics of the logic units that make up specific Web services, and the **Universal Description, Discovery, and Integration Specification (UDDI)**, a set of protocols that identify the locations of Web services and their associated WSDL descriptions.

Programmers use the information in a WSDL description to modify an application program so it can connect to a Web service. WSDL descriptions also allow programs to configure themselves so they can connect to multiple Web services. You can learn more about WSDL and related topics at the **W3C Web Services Activity** pages.

Programmers (and the programs themselves) use UDDI to find the location of Web services before they can interpret their characteristics (described in WSDL) or communicate with them (using SOAP). The **UDDI** Web site is a good source of information about this specification and includes the current UDDI Business Registry, which provides a catalog of currently available Web services.

Much of the data in SOAP applications is stored and transmitted in XML format. Because there are so many variations of XML in use today, it is critical that data-providing and data-using partners agree on which XML implementation to use. SOAP-based Web services often include quality of service and service level specifications on which applications developers at each company can rely. In many cases, each Web services subscriber must work out a detailed agreement (specifying service levels, quality of service standards, and so on) with each Web services provider.

Although the SOAP set of protocols was the first approach to implementing Web services to be widely used (and continues to be widely used in large corporate information management applications), only about 20 percent of Web services today use SOAP, according to statistics compiled by ProgrammableWeb. An approach to Web services implementation that was developed later, but which uses a somewhat simpler structure, has become the leader in Web services implementations, as you will learn in the next section.

REST and RESTful Design

Roy Fielding, one of the authors of the original HTTP specification, wrote his doctoral dissertation in 2000 on the subject of network-based software architectures. In the dissertation, he outlined a principle called **Representational State Transfer (REST)**, that describes the way the Web uses networking architecture to identify and locate Web pages and the elements (graphics, audio clips, and so on) that make up those Web pages. Designers of Web services who found SOAP to be unnecessarily complex for the applications they were building turned to Fielding's REST idea and began using it as a structure for their work.

Web services that are built on the REST model are said to use **RESTful design** and are sometimes called **RESTful applications**. A RESTful application transfers structured information from one Web location to another. This structured information can be any type of media, but it is most often an XML-tagged data set. RESTful applications can also transfer HTML- or XHTML-tagged data. The Web service is made available at a specific address (much as a Web page is made available at its URL) and can be accessed by any other computer that has a Web browser function.

More than half of all Web services applications today are RESTful applications. Probably the most widely used is the **Atom Publishing Protocol**, a blogging application that simplifies the blog publishing process and makes its functions available as a Web service so other computers can interact with blog content. You can learn more about REST and RESTful applications by visiting the **RestWiki** and you can see examples of Web services that use RESTful design at **ProgrammableWeb**.

ELECTRONIC COMMERCE SOFTWARE FOR SMALL AND MIDSIZE COMPANIES

In this section you will learn about software that small and midsize businesses can use to implement online business Web sites. In most cases, these companies can create a Web site that stands alone in its business activities (primarily, promotion and sales activities) and does not need to be coordinated completely with the business' other activities, which would include human resources, purchasing, and so on.

Basic Commerce Service Providers

Using a service provider's shared or dedicated hosting services instead of building an in-house server or using a co-location service means that the staffing burden shifts from the company to the Web host. CSPs have the same advantages as ISP hosting services, including spreading the cost of a large Web site over several "renters" hosted by the service. The biggest single advantage—low cost—occurs because the host provider has already purchased the server and configured it. The host provider has to worry about keeping it working through lightning storms and power outages.

CSPs offer free or low-cost electronic commerce software for building electronic commerce sites that are then kept on the CSP's server. Services in this category usually cost less than $20 per month, and the software is built into the CSP's site, allowing companies to immediately begin building and storing a storefront using the Web interface of the software. These services are designed for small online businesses selling only a few items (usually no more than 50) and having relatively low transaction volumes (fewer than 20 transactions per day). **ValueWeb**, operating since 1996, is an example of a CSP. ValueWeb offers businesses comprehensive electronic commerce hosting services including shared hosting, dedicated hosting, and co-location services. **ProHosting.com** and **1&1 Internet** are other examples of Web-hosting companies serving the small and midsize company market. Because these companies offer a variety of services, they might be called ISPs, CSPs, MSPs, or ASPs by different users, depending on the service they are seeking.

Yahoo! offers a wide range of Web-hosting and electronic commerce services for companies of all sizes. Its commerce services are offered on its **Yahoo! Merchant Solutions** Web page, shown in Figure 9-8.

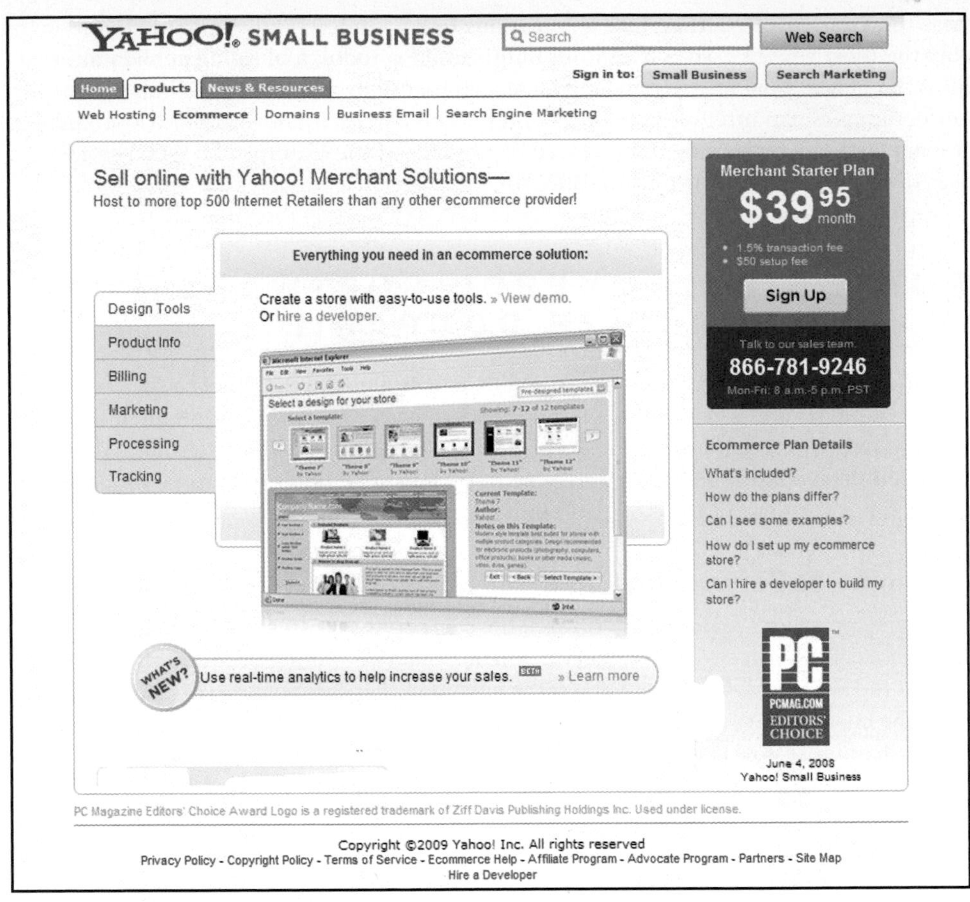

FIGURE 9-8 Yahoo! Merchant Services page

Mall-Style Commerce Service Providers

Mall-style CSPs provide small businesses with an Internet connection, Web site creation tools, and little or no banner advertising clutter. These service providers charge a low monthly fee and may also charge one-time setup fees. Some of these providers also charge a percentage of or fixed amount for each customer transaction. These Web hosts also provide online store design tools, storefront templates, an easy-to-use interface, and Web page-generation capabilities and page maintenance.

Mall-style CSPs provide shopping cart software or the ability to use another vendor's shopping cart software. They also provide payment processing services so the online store can accept credit cards.

In the early days of the Web, many mall-style CSPs were offering their services. Some even provided free Web site hosting in exchange for displaying ads on the sites. Today, the main mall-style CSP that remains in business is **eBay Stores**. You can open an eBay Store for a monthly fee that is less than $20. Another mall-style option for a beginning online merchant is to sell through Amazon.com, which allows an individual to sell certain used items (such as books) on the same page that Amazon.com lists the new product. Instead of the eBay Stores approach, in which each small merchant has its own store, Amazon.com lets merchants display their offerings product by product, mixed in with all of the other items Amazon.com offers for sale. For businesses that want to sell more than a few items, Amazon offers its Pro Merchant program.

Both basic and mall-style CSPs usually provide data-mining capabilities that search through site data collected in log files. Data mining, which you learned about in Chapter 4, can help businesses find customers with common interests and discover previously unknown relationships among the data. Reports can indicate problematic pages in a store's design where, for example, a large number of customers get stuck and then leave the Web site. Other facts that data-mining reports can reveal include the number of pages an average customer must load and display before locating the merchandise he or she wants. If customers have to load too many pages, they might become impatient and leave without making a purchase.

Estimating Operating Expenses for a Small Web Business

Figure 9-9 shows the approximate first-year expenses that a small business owner might incur to put a store on the Web using either a basic CSP or a mall-style CSP. The estimate assumes that the Web site will offer fewer than 100 items for sale and that the business owner already owns a computer and has Internet access for that computer. The total omits payment processing charges, which might average 50 cents per transaction and 2 percent of each sale's total. Most new merchants estimate that payment processing will cost between 3 percent and 5 percent of dollar sales. You will learn more about payment processing options for online businesses in Chapter 11. The costs shown are average low and high estimates for each item. Depending on which CSP and electronic commerce software options are chosen, the actual costs could be somewhat lower or considerably higher. For example, some CSPs include free registration for several domains when a store signs up for a one-year or longer contract for services.

	Cost estimates	
Operating costs	Low	High
Initial site setup fee	$ 0	$ 200
Annual CSP maintenance fee (12 x $20 to $150)	240	1800
Domain name registrations	0	200
Scanner for photo conversion or digital camera	300	900
Photo editing software	60	600
Occasional HTML and site design help	100	800
Merchant credit card setup fees	0	200
Total first-year costs	$700	$4700

FIGURE 9-9 Approximate costs to put a small store online

Contrast the preceding costs with comparable estimated costs for self-hosting a Web site. Setup and Web site maintenance costs include equipment, communications, physical location, and staff. Equipment—a server and networking gear—has a one-time cost ranging from $3000 to $20,000. A high-bandwidth Internet connection (see Chapter 2) costs between $600 and $12,000 per year. A server must be housed in a room that is both secure and convenient to communications access. The cost to secure a small room, properly air-condition it, and install a chemical fire extinguishing system could easily reach $5000 a year. A self-hosted system requires a staff of experts well versed in a variety of Web programming and scripting languages, electronic commerce packages, and database management systems. Technicians will likely be required to monitor and maintain equipment. Minimum staff costs range from $50,000 to $100,000 annually. In total, annual operating costs for self-hosting will generally run between $60,000 and $100,000. Companies should carefully compare their estimates of self-hosting costs with the fees charged by hosting services that provide similar capabilities.

The costs previously discussed are for a small online business site. Costs for larger sites are much more difficult to estimate. The cost of integrating the Web site with the existing systems of the company is often the largest element of the total cost. Midsized businesses typically incur start-up costs ranging from $100,000 to $500,000 and recurring annual costs of about half that amount. Large businesses typically spend between $1 million and $50 million to launch an electronic commerce site and then spend another 50 percent of the launch cost every year to operate, maintain, and improve the site. You will learn more about managing the costs of Web site implementation and operation for large organizations in Chapter 12.

Next, you will learn about midrange electronic commerce software packages that would be suitable for running larger businesses. These software packages have more features, are capable of handling more inventory items and types of transactions, and thus are more expensive than the template-driven CSP offerings described previously.

ELECTRONIC COMMERCE SOFTWARE FOR MIDSIZE TO LARGE BUSINESSES

This section includes a discussion of software that midsize and large companies can use to implement electronic commerce features on their Web sites. It also includes an outline of Web site development tools that can be used for that purpose and an overview of three specific midrange electronic commerce software products that are representative of the types of products available.

These midrange packages allow the merchant to have explicit control over merchandising choices, site layout, internal architecture, and remote and local management options. In addition, the midrange and basic electronic commerce packages differ on price, capability, database connectivity, software portability, software customization tools, and computer expertise required of the merchant.

Web Site Development Tools

Although they are more often used for creating small business sites, it is possible to construct the elements of a midrange electronic commerce Web site using the Web page creation and site management tools you learned about in Chapter 2.

After creating the Web site with these development tools, the designer can add purchased software elements, such as shopping carts and content management software, to the site. The final step is to create the middleware that connects the site to the company's existing product and transaction-processing databases.

Buying and using midrange electronic commerce software is significantly more expensive than using one of the CSPs described in the previous section, with annual costs ranging from $2000 to $50,000. Midrange software traditionally offers connectivity to database systems that store catalog information. Having the catalog stored in a database simplifies updates and changes. Several of the midrange systems provide connections into existing inventory and ERP systems. This can yield savings because there is no need to run duplicate inventory systems, and the cost of the existing systems is spread across several software systems.

Three midrange electronic commerce systems are described in this section. They are representative of the whole group, yet are different from one another in important ways. The systems are Intershop Enfinity, WebSphere Commerce Suite by IBM, and Commerce Server by Microsoft.

Intershop Enfinity

Intershop Enfinity provides search and catalog capabilities, electronic shopping carts, online credit card transaction processing, and the ability to connect to existing back-end business systems and databases. Intershop Enfinity has setup wizards and good catalog and data management tools. It provides many built-in storefront templates. Management and editing of a storefront are done through a Web browser—either locally at the server or remotely through any Internet connection. The products inventory management module tracks inventory levels and allows merchants to view the quantity of items available, create a list of inventory transactions, and enter new products into the inventory. Discount rules are also easy to enter. Merchants define the business rules for a discount and dates during which special discounts apply. Bundled with the software is a database management system. Alternatively, Enfinity can work with DB2 (IBM's relational database) or Oracle databases. The software includes an automated e-mail facility that can send order confirmations to customers. Enfinity includes support for secure transactions. A wide variety of site and customer reports are available to track Web page visits and customer activities.

IBM WebSphere Commerce Professional

IBM produces the **WebSphere Commerce Professional**, which is a family of electronic commerce packages. IBM WebSphere is a set of software components that provides software suitable for midsize to large businesses to sell goods and services on the Internet. It includes catalog templates, setup wizards, and advanced catalog tools to help companies create attractive and efficient electronic commerce sites. WebSphere Commerce Professional Edition can be used both for business-to-business and business-to-consumer applications and provides a smooth connection to existing corporate systems, such as inventory databases and procurement systems.

WebSphere Commerce products run on many different operating systems. Merchants can begin with a small store and then move up to a bigger, more capable store as necessary. A wizard leads the merchant through the process of creating a starter store. Once that is up and working, more functionality can be added by executing commands and writing code. With the basic pages built, the merchant can populate the catalog with products, prices, and product pictures. The WebSphere Commerce Professional Edition also accommodates electronic download products, such as audio tracks or software.

WebSphere offers a large collection of functions, utility programs, and commands that allow a merchant to create a customized online store experience. However, JavaScript, Java, or C++ expertise is required. Typical of commerce programs in this class, WebSphere can connect to existing databases and other legacy systems through DB2 or Oracle databases. A single store or several different stores can be administered from the same browser-based interface. A large number of midrange electronic commerce sites use WebSphere software. The system has all the standard electronic commerce features, including tools for a shopping cart, e-mail notifications upon sale completion, secure transaction support, promotions and discounting, shipment tracking, links to legacy accounting systems, and browser-based local and remote administration. A typical installation of WebSphere Commerce Professional Edition costs between $100,000 and $200,000, depending on how many servers will be running the product and which options are purchased with the software.

Microsoft Commerce Server

Microsoft **Commerce Server** allows businesses to sell products or services on the Web using tools such as user profiling and management, transaction processing, product and service management, and target audience marketing. Commerce Server has wizards that can help users build a site in several steps, but program code must be written to make the software meet specific user needs. The Microsoft Visual Studio .NET tools are bundled with the software and allow companies to customize the sites they build.

Like other midrange electronic commerce software, Commerce Server has tools that help companies engage the customer (through marketing and advertising), complete an order, and analyze the sales information after the sale. Commerce Server also includes tools for advertising, promotions, cross-selling, and customer targeting and personalization.

Commerce Server provides many predefined reports for analyzing site activities and product sales data. The system provides several storefront templates, wizards for setting up and initializing a store, and database connections. It also provides a shopping cart, confirms completed sales transactions by e-mail, and supports secure transactions. It can connect to existing accounting systems, and the administrator can oversee the site through a Web browser. The product only runs on systems that are running the Windows Server operating system and the SQL Server database system. Commerce Server licenses cost between $7100 and $21,000 per processor, but the required operating system and database software licenses add another $7000 per processor. Licensing a typical installation of Microsoft Commerce Server usually runs between $50,000 and $300,000.

ELECTRONIC COMMERCE SOFTWARE FOR LARGE BUSINESSES

Larger businesses require many of the same advanced capabilities as midsize firms, but the larger firms need to handle higher transaction loads. In addition, they need dedicated software applications to handle specific elements of their online business. In this section, you will learn about electronic commerce software that has higher transaction-load capability, and you will learn about software that accomplishes specific tasks in large businesses, such as customer relationship management, supply chain management, content management, and knowledge management.

The distinction between midrange and large-scale electronic commerce software is much clearer than the one between basic systems and midrange systems. The telltale sign is price. Other elements, such as extensive support for business-to-business commerce, also indicate that the software is in this category. Commerce software in this class is sometimes called **enterprise-class software**. The term "enterprise" is used in information systems to describe a system that serves multiple locations or divisions of one company and encompasses all areas of the business or enterprise. Enterprise-class electronic commerce software provides tools for both B2B and B2C commerce. In addition, this software interacts with a wide variety of existing systems, including database, accounting, and ERP systems. As electronic commerce has become more sophisticated, large companies have demanded that their Web sites and supporting information infrastructure do more things. The cost of these enterprise systems for large companies ranges from $100,000 for basic systems to $10 million and more for comprehensive solutions.

Enterprise-Class Electronic Commerce Software

Enterprise-class electronic commerce software running large online organizations usually requires several dedicated computers—in addition to the Web server system and any necessary firewalls. Examples of enterprise-class products that can be used to run a large online business with high transaction rates include **IBM WebSphere Commerce Enterprise**, **Oracle E-Business Suite**, and several products from **Broadvision**.

Enterprise-class software typically provides tools for linking to and supporting supply and purchasing activities. A large part of B2B commerce is ordering supplies from trading or business partners and issuing the appropriate documents (or EDI transaction sets), such as purchase orders. For a selling business, e-business software provides standard electronic commerce activities, such as secure transaction processing and fulfillment, but it can also do more. For instance, it can interact with the firm's inventory system and make the proper adjustments to stock, issue purchase orders for needed supplies when they reach a critically low point, and generate other accounting entries in ERP, legacy accounting, or file systems. In contrast, both basic and midrange electronic commerce packages usually require an administrator to check inventory manually and place orders explicitly for items that need to be replenished.

In B2C situations, customers use their Web browsers to locate and browse a company's catalog. For electronic goods (software, research papers, music tracks, and so on), customers can download the items directly from the site, or they can complete order forms and have the hard-copy versions of the products shipped to them. The Web server is linked to back-end systems, including a database management system, a merchant server, and an application server. The database usually contains millions of rows of information about products, prices, inventory, user profiles, and user purchasing history. The history provides a way to recommend to a user on a return visit related items that he or she might wish to purchase. A merchant server houses the e-business system and key back-end software. It processes payments, computes shipping and taxes, and sends a message to the fulfillment department when it must ship goods to a purchaser. Figure 9-10 shows a typical enterprise-class electronic commerce architecture.

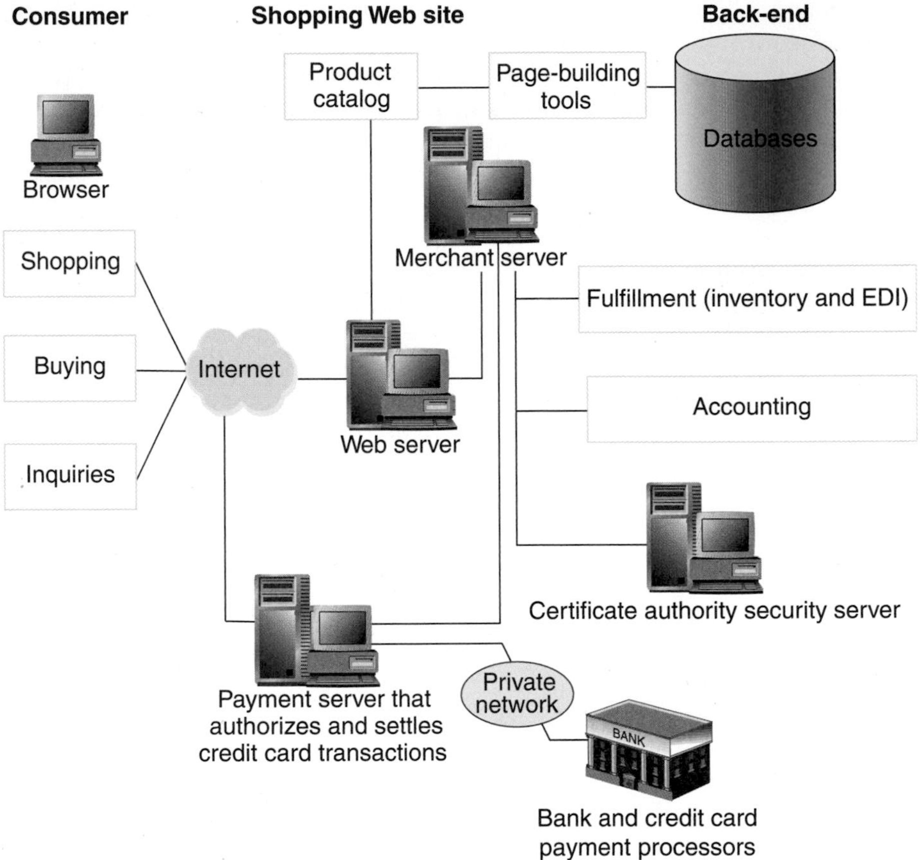

FIGURE 9-10 Typical enterprise-class electronic commerce architecture

Large companies also use additional specialized software to accomplish particular objectives that are not met by existing comprehensive electronic commerce software packages. For example, a company that wants to deliver entertainment (music or videos) directly to consumers' mobile devices might use **OpenMarket** software, a product designed to deliver and charge for that specific type of content in a mobile environment.

As you learned in Chapter 4, companies are storing data about site visitors in large databases and analyzing it to improve their relationships with those customers. These clickstreams track the path a visitor takes through a Web site, including which pages were viewed, the amount of time spent on each page, and the sequence in which pages were viewed. Thus, large electronic commerce sites must include customer relationship management software. In Chapter 5, you learned how companies are using the Web to integrate their supply chains. As a result, enterprise-class commerce Web sites must include or work with supply chain management software.

In Chapter 6, you learned about companies that were building business portal sites to engage their customers and suppliers. A significant part of that strategy is providing useful, fresh content to attract site visitors to the portal. This need has given rise to software that automatically manages and rotates content on Web sites. Some companies have even developed software that helps them manage the knowledge that exists in their businesses. An enterprise-class Web site often includes several of these types of software packages in its design. The next four sections discuss software that works with electronic commerce software in large companies to help those companies achieve all of their electronic commerce objectives.

Customer Relationship Management Software

You learned about the philosophy and techniques of customer relationship management (CRM) in Chapter 4. The goal of CRM is to understand each customer's specific needs and then customize a product or service to meet those needs. The idea is that a customer whose needs are being met exactly is willing to pay more for the goods or services that they need. Although companies of all sizes can practice CRM techniques, large companies can afford to buy and implement software products that automate many CRM functions.

Customer relationship management (CRM) software must obtain data from operations software that conducts activities such as sales automation, customer service center operations, and marketing campaigns. The software must also gather data about customer activities on the company's Web site and any other points of contact the company has with its existing and potential customers. CRM software uses this data to help managers conduct analytical activities, such as gathering business intelligence, planning marketing strategies, customer behavior modeling, and customizing the products and services to meet the needs of specific customers or categories of customers. In its most basic form, CRM uses information about customers to sell them more (or more profitable) goods or services. More advanced CRM is about delivering extremely attractive and positive experiences regularly to customers. CRM can be very important in maintaining customer loyalty in businesses where the purchase process is long and complex. Companies that design and install custom machinery, software products, or office workflow systems often find themselves involved in these types of long and complex processes. CRM software can help maintain positive and consistent contacts with multiple employees at the purchasing company.

Some companies create their own CRM software using outside consultants and their own IT staffs. In recent years, software vendors have increased the quality and variety of their offerings and today, most companies are likely to buy a CRM software package rather than create their own. Siebel Systems was the first company to specialize in CRM software and it had a large share of the market. In 2005, Oracle bought Siebel and merged its operations into its existing CRM business. The resulting division, called **Oracle Siebel CRM Applications**, continues to be the leading provider of CRM software to midsize and larger businesses. Other major software firms have created products in this market, including **SAP CRM**. Prices for these systems start at around $25,000 (on average, about $1500 per user); large implementations can cost millions of dollars. One of the most interesting new developments in the CRM software market has come from companies that offer the software for use on their Web site.

That is, the buyer does not have to install the CRM software on its own servers. The buyer's employees simply log in to the CRM vendor's Web site and use the software. The cost of this software is much lower; in fact, it can be under $200 per user per year. **Salesforce.com** is one of the leading vendors of this type of online CRM software. The Salesforce.com home page is shown in Figure 9-11.

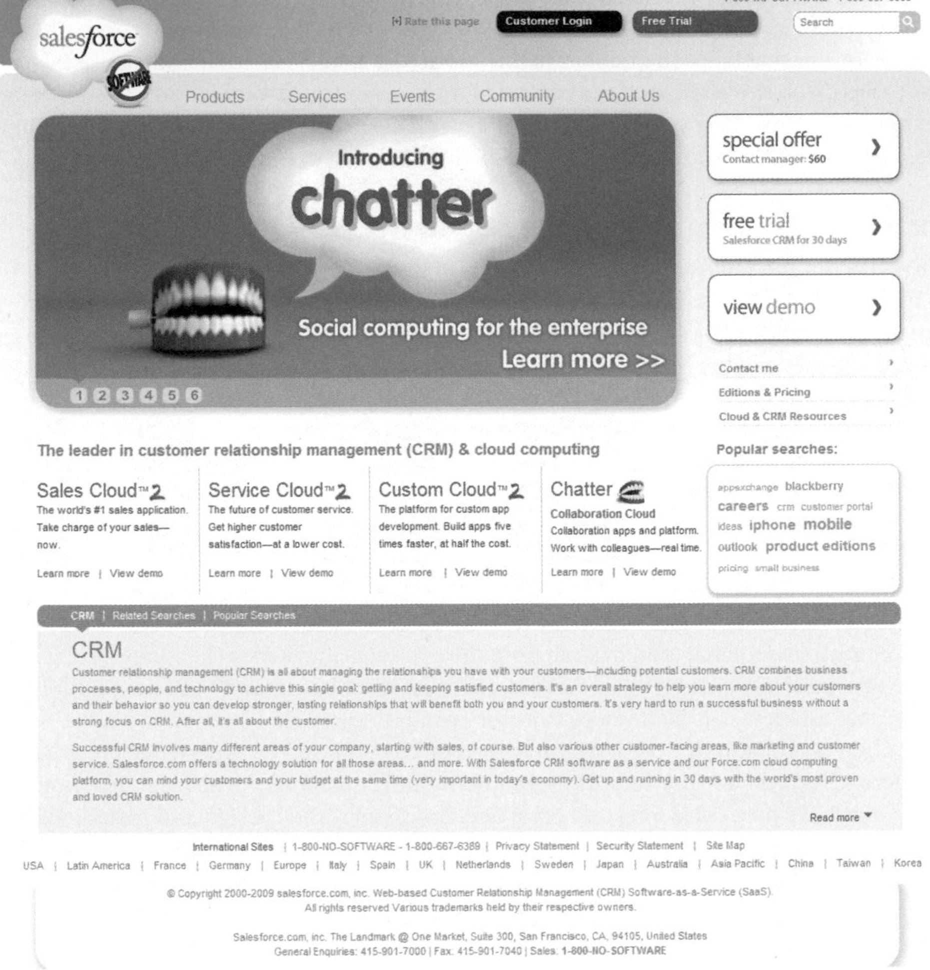

FIGURE 9-11 Salesforce.com home page

In the early days of CRM software implementation (approximately 1996–2000), companies spent many millions of dollars to buy CRM systems that promised to monitor and improve relationships with existing customers. Most of these systems were focused on giving companies the information they needed to identify changing customer preferences and respond very quickly to those changes. By responding quickly, companies hoped that they would be able to gain sales that might otherwise be lost to competitors that could respond better to the new customer preferences. In addition to gaining sales, the use of

CRM software was expected to help retain customers and reduce the need to spend money on marketing to find new customers. The goal was to instantly make available perfect information about all customer behaviors from all customer-interaction points throughout the company.

Most companies did not realize these benefits and CRM software sales dropped as a result. Many industry analysts dismissed CRM as just another business fad that would die as quickly as it had become fashionable

It turned out, however, that companies had learned from the bad experiences in which they invested large amounts of money to revamp their customer-interaction strategies completely. Companies became less likely to view CRM software as a tool for changing their overall customer strategy, and instead began using CRM software to solve smaller and more specific problems. For example, a cable company might use CRM to track service outages and repair team responses in real time, but would not expect the CRM system to calculate the profitability of on-demand video services on a continual basis.

One of the most popular targets for these focused CRM applications has been call center operations. By examining problems that arise in their call centers, many companies have identified specific applications where CRM software can improve response times, accuracy, and effectiveness.

In addition to general CRM software, many companies use small, precisely-focused software to address specific problems. For example, online clothing retailer Bluefly uses customer experience monitoring software from Tealeaf to identify specific issues in its operations. It identified a technical problem in its shopping cart software (the software was not displaying an error message it was supposed to present under a certain set of conditions) that was causing almost half of its customers who encountered the issue to abandon their shopping carts. By monitoring such metrics as shopping cart abandonments, product returns, product page views, and user session characteristics, these tools can help companies examine specific elements of the customer experience and make changes to their Web sites that can increase their effectiveness and profitability.

Supply Chain Management Software

Supply chain management (SCM) software helps companies to coordinate planning and operations with their partners in the industry supply chains of which they are members. SCM software performs two general types of functions: planning and execution. Most companies that sell SCM software offer products that include both components, but the functions are quite different. SCM planning software helps companies develop coordinated demand forecasts using information from each participant in the supply chain. SCM execution software helps with tasks such as warehouse and transportation management. The two major firms offering SCM software are i2 Technologies and JDA Software.

The i2 Technologies product, RHYTHM, includes components that manage demand planning, supply planning, and demand fulfillment. The demand planning module includes proprietary algorithms customized for specific industry markets that examine customers' buying patterns and generate continually updated forecasts. The supply planning module coordinates distribution logistics, inventory-level forecasting, collaborative procurement, and supply allocations. The demand fulfillment module handles the execution elements, including order management, customer verification, backlog control, and order fulfillment.

Most supply chain management software was developed for manufacturing firms that wanted to manage inventory purchases and manufacturing processes. JDA Software had a successful line of software products for managing retail order entry and the sales side of inventory control. In 2006, it decided to expand its product line to include supply chain management tools. Rather than develop its own software from the ground up, it purchased Manugistics, which had a full line of supply management, demand management, and transportation and logistics management software. JDA Software now offers software that companies can use to manage every operation in the supply chain, from raw materials purchase to the delivery of finished products to consumers.

The cost of SCM software implementations varies tremendously depending on how many locations (retail stores, wholesale warehouses, distribution centers, and manufacturing plants) are in the supply chain. For example, a retailer with 500 stores might pay between $3 million and $10 million for an SCM package that includes both planning and execution functions, but a wholesaler with only three or four distribution centers might be able to install an SCM product for under $1 million.

Content Management Software

Large companies are finding new ways to use the Web to share information among their employees, customers, suppliers, and partners. **Content management software** helps companies control the large amounts of text, graphics, and media files that have become crucial to doing business. Increased use of smart phones, netbook computers, and pad computing devices has made content management even more important.

Most electronic commerce software comes with wizards and other automated helpers that create template-driven pages, such as home pages, about pages, and contact pages. But most businesses want to customize Web pages with company and product pictures and text. Content management software should be tested before committing to it. The testing should ensure that company employees find the software's procedures for performing regular maintenance (for example, adding new categories of products and new items to existing product pages) to be straightforward. The software should also facilitate typical content creation tasks, such as adding sale-item specials.

Companies that need many different ways to access corporate information—for example, product specifications, drawings, photographs, or lab test results—often choose to manage the information and access to that information using content management software. The leading providers of content management software include IBM and Oracle, which provide the software as components in other enterprise software packages, and two companies, EMC and Open Text Corporation, that provide stand-alone content management software. Content management software generally costs between $100,000 and $500,000, but it can cost three or four times that much to customize, configure, and implement.

Knowledge Management Software

An increasing number of large companies have achieved cost savings by using content management software. Most content management software is designed to help companies manage information that, until recently, was stored in paper reports, schedules, analyses, and memos. Although the cost reductions that can be obtained by moving mountains of paper into an electronic format are significant, some companies have begun to understand that the true value of those documents is in the information contained in them. Thus, they began the search for systems that would help them manage the knowledge itself, rather than the documentary representations of that knowledge. The software that has been developed to meet that goal is called **knowledge management (KM) software**.

KM software helps companies do four main things: collect and organize information, share the information among users, enhance the ability of users to collaborate, and preserve the knowledge gained through the use of information so that future users can benefit from the learning of current users. KM software includes tools that read electronic documents (in formats such as Microsoft Word or Adobe PDF), scanned paper documents, e-mail messages, and Web pages. KM software often includes powerful search tools that use proprietary semantic and statistical algorithms to help users find the content, human experts, and other resources that can aid them in their research and decision-making tasks. Early KM systems often disrupted the flow of users' work. Today, KM systems collect knowledge elements by extracting them from the normal interactions users have with information.

The major software vendors have KM software offerings, including IBM and Microsoft SharePoint. Smaller companies, such as BMC Software and CustomerVision, also offer KM software and technologies. Total costs for a KM software implementation, including hardware, software licenses, and consultant fees, typically range from $10,000 to $1 million or more.

Summary

In this chapter, you learned about electronic commerce software for small, midsize, and large businesses and the functions provided by each software type. The electronic commerce software a company chooses depends on its size, objectives, and budget, and requires making major decisions. A company must first choose between paying a service provider to host the site and self-hosting. External hosting options include shared hosting, dedicated hosting, and co-location. Many hosting companies offer comprehensive services to merchants, such as databases, shopping carts, and content management, in addition to basic Web-hosting services.

Key elements of all electronic commerce software include catalogs, shopping carts, and transaction-processing capabilities. Companies can use Web services to get their information systems to work across organizational boundaries.

Small enterprises that are just starting an electronic commerce initiative might use a basic commerce service provider (CSP). Basic CSP and mall-style hosting services for small businesses provide a range of standard features, including tools for quickly creating storefronts, catalogs, and transaction processing. These packages are usually wizard and template driven.

If a company already has computing equipment and staff in place, purchasing a midrange electronic commerce software package provides more control over the site and allows for expansion. Midrange software can interact with database software to create dynamic catalogs and shopping carts and handle order processing.

Large enterprises that have high transaction rates, B2B partnerships, or a large investment in ERP and other existing information systems, need to invest in larger, more customizable systems that can provide needed features and flexibility. These packages can include customer relationship management, supply chain management, content management, and knowledge management capabilities, or they can work with dedicated software that performs these functions.

Key Terms

Application integration
Application program (application)
Application program interface (API)
Application server
Application service providers (ASPs)
Application software (application)
Atom Publishing Protocol
Business logic
Business rules
Catalog
Co-location (collocation, colocation)
Commerce service providers (CSPs)
Component-based application system
Content management software
Customer relationship management (CRM) software
Database
Database manager (database management software)
Dedicated hosting
Distributed database systems
Distributed information systems
Dynamic catalog
Enterprise application integration
Enterprise-class software
Enterprise resource planning (ERP)
Interoperability

Knowledge management (KM) software
Managed service providers (MSPs)
Middleware
Page-based application system
Representational State Transfer (REST)
RESTful applications
RESTful design
Scalable
Self-hosting
Shared hosting
Simple Object Access Protocol (SOAP)
Static catalog
Supply chain management (SCM) software
Transaction processing
Universal Description, Discovery, and Integration (UDDI) specification
Web APIs
Web services
Web Services Description Language (WSDL)

Review Questions

RQ1. Provide a brief definition of the term "middleware." In one or two paragraphs, explain why middleware can be difficult to write and test.

RQ2. Using your library or the Web, find an article that describes a successful application of Web services. In about 200 words, describe how the company implemented the Web services application and explain why using Web services was better than using an alternative approach to solve the problem.

RQ3. In a paragraph, outline how the REST approach to Web services differs from that used in protocols such as SOAP.

RQ4. In about 100 words, explain what kinds of features or characteristics a midsize business would seek in its electronic commerce software that would not matter to a smaller business.

RQ5. In about 100 words, summarize the advantages and disadvantages of using a mall-style CSP such as eBay Stores or Amazon.com's Pro Merchant program.

RQ6. Visit the product Web sites to learn more about two of the knowledge management software products discussed in the chapter. In a report of about 200 words addressed to the president of a local university, explain how that university could benefit from an implementation of knowledge management software.

Exercises

E1. Your friend Faye Borthick wants to set up a small Web site devoted to gardening. She believes her many years of experience in gardening give her an understanding of the kinds of gardening tools, fertilizers, soil amendment products, herbicides, pesticides, and plants that appeal to the serious gardener. Right now Faye does not want to sell anything, although she might change her mind in the future. She merely wants to display pages of plant photography, write and store short how-to papers for novice gardeners, and provide links to other gardening tips on the Web. She wants your advice on whether to self-host the Web site or use an ISP (or CSP) to start her endeavor. Use **The List** or the **TopHosts** sites to locate information on the cost of using a service provider to host a Web site. Then, estimate what a small Web site might cost in terms of the minimal configuration of hardware and software. Estimate the design and development costs and the annual maintenance costs. Then, select one of the Web server programs. Estimate the cost of a Web connection. Write a 200-word summary of everything you think Faye needs to know to use either of the two options (she builds it or she uses a service provider) for creating her site.

E2. Annette Jackson owns a small crafts store in central Missouri. She wants to expand her store's reach outside the region to increase her profits and simultaneously reduce her inventory. Annette's teenage daughter suggested that she consider selling online to expand her total sales. She asked you to help her estimate how much it might cost in the first year to create a simple store with a catalog of about 100 items. Annette wants you to investigate two CSP offerings and report back to her what you find. Because her store is small, limit your research to basic commerce and mall-style services. Annette would like to consider the following information for the two CSP offerings you examine:

- Costs: initial setup fee, monthly fee, and transaction fees
- Amount of disk space the CSP would provide for Annette's 100-item store
- Existence of a search engine within each store
- Promotion and marketing opportunities
- Customer communications capabilities, such as automated e-mail confirmation of orders
- Shopping cart or other order entry mechanism
- Storefront-building wizards for creating a new store
- Security provisions for transactions
- Nature of the domain names available (subdomain of the site or not)
- Upload capabilities for product names, descriptions, images, and costs (can they be uploaded from files or databases, or must the merchant enter each item individually?)
- Existence of an online user manual for the merchant

The Online Companion includes links to several CSP and mall-style hosting providers, but feel free to use your favorite search engine to find CSPs that might meet Annette's needs. Produce a report of about 500 words summarizing your findings.

E3. Write a 200-word report summarizing the costs and features of any enterprise-class commerce package for large businesses. You can review a product mentioned in the chapter or one of your own choosing. Pick seven characteristics of the software package and describe them in detail in your report. The Online Companion includes links to several vendors of these products under the Exercise 3 heading.

E4. Review the material in Chapter 4 on customer relationship management (CRM). Then visit the Web sites of Salesforce.com and at least one other provider of CRM software. In about 300 words, critically evaluate Salesforce.com and the other CRM software package by comparing what it accomplishes to the goals of CRM.

Cases

C1. Ingersoll-Rand Club Car Division

Ingersoll-Rand is a $9 billion diversified manufacturing company that sells its products worldwide. Its well-known brands include Ingersoll-Rand tools and portable power generators, Bobcat construction equipment, Thermo King refrigerated transport systems, Dexter and Schlage locks, and ARO industrial fluids equipment. The company's Club Car division manufactures and sells a variety of small electric cart vehicles to golf courses and industrial users. The division also sells a rough-terrain version designed for farmers, ranchers, construction workers, and recreational users.

In 2001, the Club Car division was experiencing a sales decline. The downturn in the general economy was affecting golf courses, which, in turn, were reducing the size and frequency of their golf cart orders. Club Car had a general sense that this major market segment was causing their revenues to decline, but their information systems were not providing enough data about exactly which sales were being most affected by the economic downturn.

Club Car sales managers relied on their sales representatives for information about likely future sales. Sales forecasting was a matter of judgment, guesswork, and a few spreadsheet software models scattered throughout the regional sales offices. The sales representatives had little influence on how the carts were customized for particular customer segments or for individual customers.

The company decided it needed better information about all of its sales and marketing activities, so it spent more than $2 million to install a comprehensive CRM system. This system was designed to automate the entire customer sales cycle: prospect evaluation, proposal writing, product configuration, and order entry. However, the users at Club Car division found the new system difficult to use and therefore were reluctant to spend much time learning how to use it. Thus, the promised benefits of improved productivity and more detailed reports were not forthcoming. Sales managers did not see the ultimate benefits that the system might provide. Salespeople found that the new system was requiring them to spend time entering data into the system rather than seeing customers. The order entry staff found the system to be cumbersome and unfamiliar.

When Club Car's president realized that the CRM system was not delivering on its promise, he had the management team go back and re-examine the key elements in the division's customer relationships and asked them to choose one or two issues that needed attention. The management team identified two major issues. First, the order entry process required the time of salespeople and order entry staff, but it did not include any interaction with customers. Second, the division was not producing accurate and timely sales forecasts.

In 2002, Club Car division re-launched its CRM efforts and focused on these two problem areas. The new effort included the sales representatives in redesigning the order entry process. The division was able to reduce the data entry time and effort required, especially the time of salespeople. Salespeople do have remote access to the system, so they can work on-site with customers to configure the carts to the customers' exact specifications. Salespeople can obtain pricing information and explore various alternatives with customers while they are at the customer's site. They can also examine manufacturing schedules and provide more accurate delivery date estimates. All of this remote, real-time information access helps salespeople close deals and increase sales volume and profitability.

Sales forecasts are more accurate now because the information about sales orders is automatically collected when the sales representatives close sales at the customers' sites. The CRM system combines this real-time sales order information with general industry information on cart demand, cart replacement cycles, and economic trends in their customers' industries. The increased accuracy of sales forecasts allows the company to create more stable production schedules, which means that more customers receive their carts on the delivery date they were promised.

Required:

1. List the types of information that Club Car division's CRM system makes available to sales representatives in the field. For each type of information, briefly explain how salespeople's remote access to that type of information can help them close sales on their customers' sites.
2. In the CRM re-launch, Club Car division focused on two CRM elements. In about 200 words, explain why this approach would work better, in general, than implementing a comprehensive CRM system that could track all of the division's sales activities and related information in real time.
3. In about 200 words, explain how Club Car division might use Web services in its CRM system.

Note: Your instructor might assign you to a group to complete this case, and might ask you to prepare a formal presentation of your results to your class.

C2. Web Services for State Government

You are a member of the Web site management team of a state government. You have worked on all of the state's Web sites from time to time and have managed the launch of four major sites and the redesign and relaunch of two others. Some of the Web sites on which you have worked include electronic commerce features such as order acceptance, payment processing, and purchasing.

You report to Anne Nelson, the state's CIO. Anne asked you to lead a project to explore the potential uses of Web services in carrying out state government activities. She scheduled a formal briefing at which you will present an overview of Web services technology. You will also outline specific applications of Web services technologies to specific tasks that the state either currently performs or that it might perform in the future.

Anne knows that the state has many current and potential applications that could use Web services technologies, so she asked you to focus on four specific areas of state government in your briefing. At the briefing, you will address the directors of four state departments: the Attorney General's Department of Corporation Records, the Tax Administration and Collection Department, the Department of Motor Vehicles, and the Department of Fish and Wildlife Management.

The Attorney General's Department of Corporation Records maintains the official records of corporations chartered by the state or holding licenses to do business in the state. In addition to the original charter or license, companies must file annual reports that include the names and addresses of corporate directors and officers, the amount of company stock issued or redeemed during the year, and the current address of the company.

The Tax Administration and Collection Department is responsible for accepting income tax, personal property tax, and sales tax return filings of companies and individuals. The department also processes payments of these taxes and authorizes the State Treasurer to issue refunds that are due to taxpayers who have overpaid their taxes. This department currently provides tax forms and instructions in Adobe PDF format on its Web site. It also maintains an extensive frequently asked questions (FAQs) list on the site.

The Department of Motor Vehicles issues driver's license renewals and vehicle registration renewals (for cars, trucks, and boats) and accepts auto dealerships' monthly reports of vehicles purchased or sold on its Web site. The site also includes extensive collections of information about motor vehicle laws and administrative rulings that visitors can review to ensure they are in compliance.

The Department of Fish and Wildlife Management provides downloadable applications for hunting and fishing licenses on its site. Current hunting and fishing license holders can renew their licenses and pay their annual fees on the Web site. Companies that have state-issued permits to undertake logging or mining operations can file their monthly activity reports on the department's Web site, too.

Anne suggests that you review current IT trade publications (both in print and on the Web) to learn more about Web services applications that have been implemented in government agencies. She also recommends that you examine a number of other state Web sites to see how they are performing these tasks.

Required:

1. Prepare a briefing report of about four double-spaced pages in which you describe Web services technology in a way that will be understandable to the four department directors. These directors are experienced administrators, but they are not technology experts.
2. Prepare a briefing report that outlines opportunities for the use of Web services in each department. Include about three double-spaced pages for each department.
3. Prepare an analysis of costs and benefits for each major application of Web services that you identify. In this setting, a benefit can arise from an increase in revenue, a reduction in expense, an improvement in the quality of service provided, or an increase in the speed with which a service is provided. This report should be directed to Anne and should include an implementation recommendation (whether the state should implement or should not implement) for each Web service application you identified.

Note: Your instructor might assign you to a group to complete this case, and might ask you to prepare a formal presentation of your results to your class.

For Further Study and Research

Abate, C. 2002. "Going Once, Going Twice... Sold!" *Smart Business,* 15(4), May, 72–76.

Bailor, C. 2004. "Ten Technologies That Are Reinventing the CRM Industry," *CRM Magazine,* 8(12), December, 44–48.

Benslimane, D., S. Dustdar, and A. Sheth. 2008. "Services Mashups: The New Generation of Web Applications," *IEEE Internet Computing,* 12(5), 13–15.

Berfield, S. 2009. "Susan Lyne on Gilt.com's Pleasures and Pressures," *BusinessWeek,* December 14, 17–18.

Booth, D., H. Haas, F. McCabe, E. Newcomer, M. Champion, C. Ferris, and D. Orchard. 2004. *Web Services Architecture: W3C Working Group Note.* Cambridge, MA: W3C (http://www.w3.org/TR/ws-arch/)

Boucher-Ferguson, R. 2007. "Salesforce Under Pressure," *eWeek,* November 26, 28.

Bruno, E. 2007. "SOA, Web Services, and RESTful Systems," *Dr. Dobb's Journal,* 32(7), July, 32–37.

Caton, M. 2005. "Lower-cost CRM Systems Deliver," *eWeek,* June 20, 43–50.

Cowley, S. 2005. "Salesforce.com Battles Rivals," *Network World,* 22(23), June 13, 31–32.

CRM Magazine. 2007. "Software AG Is Set to Acquire webMethods," 11(6), June, 16.

Duvall, M. 2007. "Merrill Lynch & Co.: Web Services, Millions of Transactions, All Good." *Baseline Magazine,* February 7. (http://www.baselinemag.com/c/a/Projects-Integration/Merrill-Lynch-Co-Web-Services-Millions-of-Transactions-All-Good/)

Ferguson, G. 2002. "Have Your Objects Call My Objects," *Harvard Business Review,* 80(6), June, 138–143.

Gartner, Inc. 2007. *Magic Quadrant for Enterprise Content Management.* Stamford, CT: Gartner, Inc.

Guernsey, L. 2003. "On the Web, Without Wasting Time," *The New York Times,* May 6, G10.

Hall, M. 2003. "Web Services' Sharp Edge," *Computerworld,* 37(20), May 19, 34.

Hoover, J. 2008. "Microsoft Extends SQL Server to the Web with Data Services," *Intelligent Enterprise,* 11(3), March, 1.

Ismail, A., S. Patil, and S. Saigal. 2002. "When Computers Learn to Talk: A Web Services Primer," *McKinsey Quarterly,* Special Edition (Issue 2), June, 70–78.

Jayachandran, S., S. Sharma, P. Kaufman, and P. Raman. 2005. "The Role of Relational Information Processes and Technology Use in Customer Relationship Management," *Journal of Marketing,* 69(4), October, 177–192.

Karpinski, R. 2008. "Web Services in Action," *Telephony,* 248(4), March 17, 6.

Kay, R. 2007. "Representational State Transfer (REST)," *Computerworld,* 41(32), August 6, 40.

Macvittie, L. 2004. "Choosing the Right Web Server," *Network Computing,* 15(17), September 2, 76–77.

Morochove, R. 2008. "Choosing a Host for Your E-commerce Site," *PC World,* 26(4), April, 36.

Morse, G. 2003. "Plumbing Web Connections," *Harvard Business Review,* 81(9), September, 18–19.

Nash, K. 2008. "How to Do CRM Online: Three Big Ideas for 2008," *CIO Magazine,* January 2. (http://www.cio.com/article/168353/How_To_Do_CRM_Online_Three_Big_Ideas_for_)

Payne, A. and P. Frow. 2005. "A Strategic Framework for Customer Relationship Management," *Journal of Marketing,* 69(4), October, 167–176.

RESTwiki. 2009. *REST in Plain English.* November 19. (http://rest.blueoxen.net/cgi-bin/wiki.pl?RestInPlainEnglish)

Rigby, D. and D. Ledingham. 2004. "CRM Done Right," *Harvard Business Review,* 82(11), November, 118–127.

Rosenberg, A. 2004. "Which CRM Is Right for You?" *Call Center Magazine,* 17(12), December, 28–35.

Schwartz, E. and T. Sullivan. 2005. "ASPs Clash Over Customization," *InfoWorld,* 27(12), March 21, 16–17.

Scribner, K. and S. Seely. 2009. *Effective REST Services via .NET.* Boston: Addison-Wesley.

Siebel Systems. 2004. *Ingersoll-Rand Maximizes Customer Focus.* San Mateo, CA: Siebel Systems. (http://www.siebel.com/downloads/case_studies/)

Tedeschi, B. 2005, "Small Internet Retailers Are Using Web Tools to Level the Selling Field," *The New York Times,* December 19. (http://www.nytimes.com/2005/12/19/technology/19ecom.html)

Wan, P., J. Zhi, L. Liu, and G. Cai. 2008. "Building Toward Capability Specifications of Web Services Based on an Environment Ontology," *IEEE Transactions on Knowledge and Data Engineering,* 20(4), April, 547–562.

Waxer, C. 2009. "Bluefly's Bug Zapper," *CIO Magazine,* December 1, 22.

CHAPTER **10**

ELECTRONIC COMMERCE SECURITY

LEARNING OBJECTIVES

In this chapter, you will learn about:

- Online security issues
- Security for client computers
- Security for the communication channels between computers
- Security for server computers
- Organizations that promote computer, network, and Internet security

INTRODUCTION

Large business and government Web sites are constantly under attack by a variety of potential intruders, ranging from computer-savvy high school students to highly trained espionage workers employed by competing businesses or other governments. For example, the U.S. Pentagon reports that its computers are scanned by potential attackers thousands of times every hour. These attackers are continually looking for a way to break through computer security defenses in the hopes of finding any information that could help their employers embarrass, disable, or hurt competitors or enemies. The software that potential attackers use to scan computers is widely available; therefore, government agencies, companies, organizations, and even individuals can expect that their computers are scanned frequently as well.

In 2009, several incidents provided examples of these issues. During the U.S. July 4 holiday and continuing for more than a week after, a series of attacks on U.S. and South Korean Web sites was launched from networks that included more than 200,000 computers located all over the world. These attacks, which targeted both government and business Web sites in both countries, shut down the sites for several hours and included attempts (none reported to be successful) to gather sensitive data. These attacks occurred just a few weeks after U.S. President Barack Obama had announced the creation of a new government agency devoted to defending the country against cyberterrorism, including attacks of exactly this nature. Although investigators believed that the attacks were the work of operatives of the North Korean government, they were not able to identify definitively those responsible for the attack.

Later in 2009, an attack was successful in obtaining an 11-page file that contained a briefing on defensive military operations that would be undertaken by the United States and South Korea if war were to break out with North Korea. A South Korean military officer had left a USB device containing the plans plugged into his computer when he switched the computer from a restricted-access military network to the Internet. Within minutes, an attacker accessed the document and stole a copy of the briefing. Investigators traced the attack to an IP address that is owned by the Chinese government, which had leased it to North Korea. Both governments denied any involvement in the theft.

In this chapter, you will learn how companies and governments protect themselves from attacks that are intended to shut down their Web sites or gain entry to data stored or transmitted in the course of their operational activities. Because the threats are constantly changing, and because the attackers are highly motivated and, in many cases, highly trained, the challenges are constant and dynamic.

ONLINE SECURITY ISSUES OVERVIEW

In the early days of the Internet, one of its most popular uses was electronic mail. Despite e-mail's popularity, business users of e-mail have been concerned about security issues. For example, a business rival might intercept e-mail messages for competitive gain. Another fear was that employees' nonbusiness correspondence might be read by their supervisors, with negative repercussions. These were significant and realistic concerns.

Today, the stakes are much higher. In addition to e-mail, people all over the world use the Internet and the Web for shopping and all types of financial transactions ranging from an individual buying an item on eBay using PayPal to a large company making a vendor payment through a VPN. These advances make security a concern for all users.

A common worry of Web shoppers is that their credit card numbers might be stolen as they travel across the Internet. Although online wiretapping does occur, it is far more likely that a credit card number will be stolen from a computer on which it is stored after being transmitted over the Internet. Recent surveys show that more than half of all Internet users have at least "some concern" about the security of their credit card numbers in electronic commerce transactions.

As you learned in Chapter 7, people are concerned about personal information they provide to companies over the Internet. Increasingly, people doubt that these companies have the willingness and the ability to keep customers' personal information confidential. This chapter examines security in the context of electronic commerce, presenting an introduction to important security problems and some solutions to those problems.

Computers and Security: A Brief History

When businesses began using computers more than 50 years ago, security was accomplished by using physical controls over access to the computers. Alarmed doors and windows, guards, security badges to admit people to sensitive areas, and surveillance cameras were the tools used to secure computers. Back then, interactions between people and computers were limited to the terminals of large mainframe computers. The terminals had no internal processing or data storage capabilities. There were no other connections to computers, and there were very few networks of computers (and those few networks did not extend outside the organization in which they existed). Computer security meant dealing with the few people who had access to terminals or physical access to the computer room.

For example, computer technicians ran programs by submitting decks of punched cards that were fed into card readers. The card readers translated the punched holes in the cards into electrical impulses that were processed by the computer. The computer printed out the results when it was finished running the program. When program users returned to the computer operations center (often the next day; computers were not very fast then), they would pick up the printouts and reclaim their punched card decks from the input/output clerk. Security was a pretty simple matter.

Both the population of computer users and the methods to access computing resources have increased tremendously since those early years of computing. Millions of people now have access to computing power over networks that connect millions of computers to each other. It is no longer a simple matter to determine who is using a computing resource. A user in South Africa could be using a computer in California. New security tools and methods have evolved and are used today to protect computers and the electronic assets they store. The transmission of valuable information, such as electronic receipts, purchase orders, payment data, and order confirmations, has drastically increased the need for security and new automatic methods to deal with security threats.

Data security measures date back to the time of the Roman Empire, when Julius Caesar coded information to prevent enemies from reading secret war and defense plans carried by his Roman legions. Many modern electronic security techniques were developed for wartime use. The U.S. Department of Defense was the main driving force behind early security requirements and more recent advances. In the late 1970s, the Defense Department formed a committee to develop computer security guidelines for handling classified information on computers. The result of that committee's work was *Trusted Computer System Evaluation Criteria*, known in defense circles as the "Orange Book" because its cover was orange. It spelled out rules for mandatory access control—the separation of confidential, secret, and top secret information—and established criteria for certification levels for computers ranging from D (not trusted to handle multiple levels of classified documents at once) to A1 (the most trustworthy level).

This early security work has been helpful because it provided a basis for electronic commerce security research. This research today provides commercial security products and practical security techniques. This early work also helped current security efforts by developing formal approaches to security analysis and evaluation, including the explicit evaluation and management of risk.

Computer Security and Risk Management

Computer security is the protection of assets from unauthorized access, use, alteration, or destruction. There are two general types of security: physical and logical. **Physical security** includes tangible protection devices, such as alarms, guards, fireproof doors, security fences, safes or vaults, and bombproof buildings. Protection of assets using nonphysical means is called **logical security**. Any act or object that poses a danger to computer assets is known as a **threat**.

Countermeasure is the general name for a procedure, either physical or logical, that recognizes, reduces, or eliminates a threat. The extent and expense of countermeasures can vary, depending on the importance of the asset at risk. Threats that are deemed low risk and unlikely to occur can be ignored when the cost to protect against the threat exceeds the value of the protected asset. For example, it would make sense to protect from tornadoes a computer network in Oklahoma, where there is significant and regular tornado activity. However, a similar network located in Maine would not require the same protection, because tornadoes are extremely rare in Maine. The risk management model shown in Figure 10-1 illustrates four general actions that an organization could take, depending on the impact (cost) and the probability of the physical threat. In this model, a tornado in Oklahoma would be in quadrant II, whereas a tornado in Maine would be in quadrant IV.

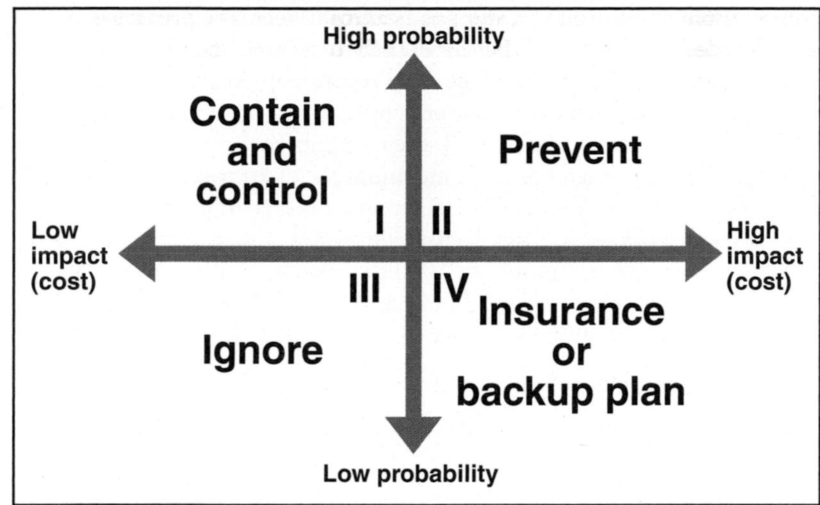

FIGURE 10-1 Risk management model

The same sort of risk management model applies to protecting Internet and electronic commerce assets from both physical and electronic threats. Examples of the latter include impostors, eavesdroppers, and thieves. An **eavesdropper**, in this context, is a person or device that can listen in on and copy Internet transmissions. People who write programs or manipulate technologies to obtain unauthorized access to computers and networks are called **crackers** or **hackers**.

A cracker is a technologically skilled person who uses their skills to obtain unauthorized entry into computers or network systems—usually with the intent of stealing information or damaging the information, the system's software, or even the system's hardware. Originally, the term hacker was used to describe a dedicated programmer who enjoyed writing complex code that tested the limits of technology. Although the term hacker is still used in a positive way—even as a compliment—by computer professionals (who make a strong distinction between the terms hacker and cracker), the media and the general public usually use the term to describe those who use their skills for ill purposes. Some IT people also use the terms **white hat hacker** and **black hat hacker** to make the distinction between good hackers and bad hackers.

To implement a good security scheme, organizations must identify risks, determine how to protect threatened assets, and calculate how much to spend to protect those assets. In this chapter, the primary focus in risk management protection is on the central issues of identifying the threats and determining the ways to protect assets from those threats, rather than on the protection costs or value of assets.

Elements of Computer Security

Computer security is generally considered to include three main elements: secrecy, integrity, and necessity (also known as denial of service). **Secrecy** refers to protecting against unauthorized data disclosure and ensuring the authenticity of the data source. **Integrity** refers to preventing unauthorized data modification. **Necessity** refers to preventing data delays or denials (removal). Secrecy is the best known of the computer security elements. Every month, news media report on break-ins to government computers or theft of stolen credit card numbers that are used to order goods and services. Integrity threats are reported less frequently and, thus, may be less familiar to the public. For example, an integrity violation occurs when an Internet e-mail message is intercepted and its contents are changed before it is forwarded to its original destination. In this type of integrity violation, which is called a **man-in-the-middle exploit**, the contents of the e-mail are often changed in a way that negates the message's original meaning. Necessity violations take several forms, and they occur relatively frequently. Delaying a message or completely destroying it can have grave consequences. Suppose that a message sent at 10:00 a.m. to an online stockbroker includes an order to purchase 1000 shares of IBM at market price. If the stockbroker does not receive the message (because an attacker delays it) until 2:30 p.m. and IBM's stock price has increased by $3, the buyer loses $3000.

Security Policy and Integrated Security

Any organization concerned about protecting its electronic commerce assets should have a **security policy** in place. A security policy is a written statement describing which assets to protect and why they are being protected, who is responsible for that protection, and which behaviors are acceptable and which are not. The policy primarily addresses physical security, network security, access authorizations, virus protection, and disaster recovery. The policy develops over time and is a living document that the company and security officer must review and update at regular intervals.

Both defense and commercial security guidelines state that organizations must protect assets from unauthorized disclosure, modification, or destruction. However, military security policy differs from commercial policy because military applications stress separation of multiple levels of security. Corporate information is usually classified as either "public" or "company confidential." The typical security policy concerning confidential company information is straightforward: Do not reveal company confidential information to anyone outside the company.

Most organizations follow a five-step process when creating a security policy. These steps include:

1. Determine which assets must be protected from which threats. For example, a company that stores customer credit card numbers might decide that those numbers are an asset that must be protected.
2. Determine who should have access to various parts of the system or specific information assets. In many cases, some of those users who need access to some parts of the system (such as suppliers, customers, and strategic partners) are located outside the organization.
3. Identify resources available or needed to protect the information assets while ensuring access by those who need it.
4. Using the information gathered in the first three steps, the organization develops a written security policy.
5. Following the written policy, the organization commits resources to building or buying software, hardware, and physical barriers that implement the security policy. For example, if a security policy disallows unauthorized access to customer information, (such as credit card numbers or credit history), then the organization must either create or purchase software that guarantees end-to-end secrecy for electronic commerce customers.

A comprehensive plan for security should protect a system's privacy, integrity, and availability (necessity), and authenticate users. When these goals are used to create a security policy for an electronic commerce operation, they should be selected to satisfy the list of requirements shown in Figure 10-2. These requirements provide a minimum level of acceptable security for most electronic commerce operations.

Requirement	Meaning
Secrecy	Prevent unauthorized persons from reading messages and business plans, obtaining credit card numbers, or deriving other confidential information.
Integrity	Enclose information in a digital envelope so that the computer can automatically detect messages that have been altered in transit.
Availability	Provide delivery assurance for each message segment so that messages or message segments cannot be lost undetectably.
Key management	Provide secure distribution and management of keys needed to provide secure communications.
Nonrepudiation	Provide undeniable, end-to-end proof of each message's origin and recipient.
Authentication	Securely identify clients and servers with digital signatures and certificates.

FIGURE 10-2 Requirements for secure electronic commerce

WindowSecurity.com is a good source of information about security policies. Its Network Security Library includes a number of white papers that provide guidance on how to craft a workable security policy. **Information Security Policy World** is another Web site that provides information about security policy matters.

Although absolute security is difficult to achieve, organizations can create enough barriers to deter most intentional violators. With good planning, organizations can also reduce the impact of natural disasters or terrorist acts. Integrated security means having all security measures working together to prevent unauthorized disclosure, destruction, or modification of assets. A security policy covers many security concerns that must be addressed by a comprehensive and integrated security plan. Specific elements of a security policy address the following points:

- *Authentication*: Who is trying to access the site?
- *Access control*: Who is allowed to log on to and access the site?
- *Secrecy*: Who is permitted to view selected information?
- *Data integrity*: Who is allowed to change data?
- *Audit*: Who or what causes specific events to occur, and when?

In this chapter, you will explore these security policy issues with a focus on how they apply to electronic commerce in particular. The electronic commerce security topics in this chapter are organized to follow the transaction-processing flow, beginning with the consumer and ending with the Web server (or servers) at the electronic commerce site. Each logical link in the process includes assets that must be protected to ensure security: client computers, the communication channel on which the messages travel, and the Web servers, including any other computers connected to the Web servers.

SECURITY FOR CLIENT COMPUTERS

Client computers, usually PCs, must be protected from threats that originate in software and data that are downloaded to the client computer from the Internet. In this section, you will learn that active content delivered over the Internet in dynamic Web pages can be harmful. Another threat to client computers can arise when a malevolent server site masquerades as a legitimate Web site. Users and their client computers can be duped into revealing information to those Web sites. This section explains these threats, describes how they work, and outlines some protection mechanisms that can prevent or reduce the threats they pose to client computers.

Cookies

The Internet provides a type of connection between Web clients and servers called a stateless connection. In a **stateless connection**, each transmission of information is independent; that is, no continuous connection (also called an **open session**) is maintained between any client and server on the Internet. Earlier in this book, you learned that cookies are small text files that Web servers place on Web client computers to identify returning visitors. Cookies also allow Web servers to maintain continuing open sessions with Web clients. An open session is necessary to do a number of things that are important in online business activity. For example, shopping cart and payment processing software both need an open session to work properly. Early in the history of the Web, cookies were devised as a way to maintain an open session despite the stateless nature of Internet connections. Thus, cookies were invented to solve the stateless connection problem by saving information about a Web user from one set of server–client message exchanges to another.

There are two ways of categorizing cookies: by time duration and by source. The two kinds of time duration cookie categories include **session cookies**, which exist until the Web client ends the connection (or "session"), and **persistent cookies**, which remain on the client computer indefinitely. Electronic commerce sites use both kinds of cookies. For example, a session cookie might contain information about a particular shopping visit and a persistent cookie might contain login information that can help the Web site recognize visitors when they return to the site on subsequent visits. Each time a browser moves to a different part of a merchant's Web site, the merchant's Web server asks the visitor's computer to send back any cookies that the Web server stored previously on the visitor's computer.

Another way of categorizing cookies is by their source. Cookies can be placed on the client computer by the Web server site, in which case they are called **first-party cookies**, or they can be placed by a different Web site, in which case they are called **third-party cookies**.

A third-party cookie originates on a Web site other than the site being visited. These third-party Web sites usually provide advertising or other content that appears on the Web site being viewed. The third-party Web site providing the advertising is often interested in tracking responses to their ads by visitors who have already seen the ads on other sites. If the advertising Web site places its ads on a large number of Web sites, it can use persistent third-party cookies to track visitors from one site to another. Earlier in this book, you learned about DoubleClick and similar online ad placement services that perform this function.

The most complete way for Web site visitors to protect themselves from revealing private information or being tracked by cookies is to disable cookies entirely. The problem with this approach is that useful cookies are blocked along with the others, requiring visitors to enter information each time they revisit a Web site. The full resources of some sites are not available to visitors unless their browsers are set to allow cookies. For example, most distance learning software used by schools to deliver online courses does not work properly in student Web browsers unless cookies are enabled.

Web users can accumulate large numbers of cookies as they browse the Internet. Most Web browsers have settings that allow the user to refuse only third-party cookies or to review each cookie before it is accepted. Browsers such as **Google Chrome**, **Microsoft Internet Explorer**, **Mozilla Firefox**, and **Opera** provide cookie management functions. Figure 10-3 shows the dialog box that can be used to manage stored cookies in the Mozilla Firefox Web browser.

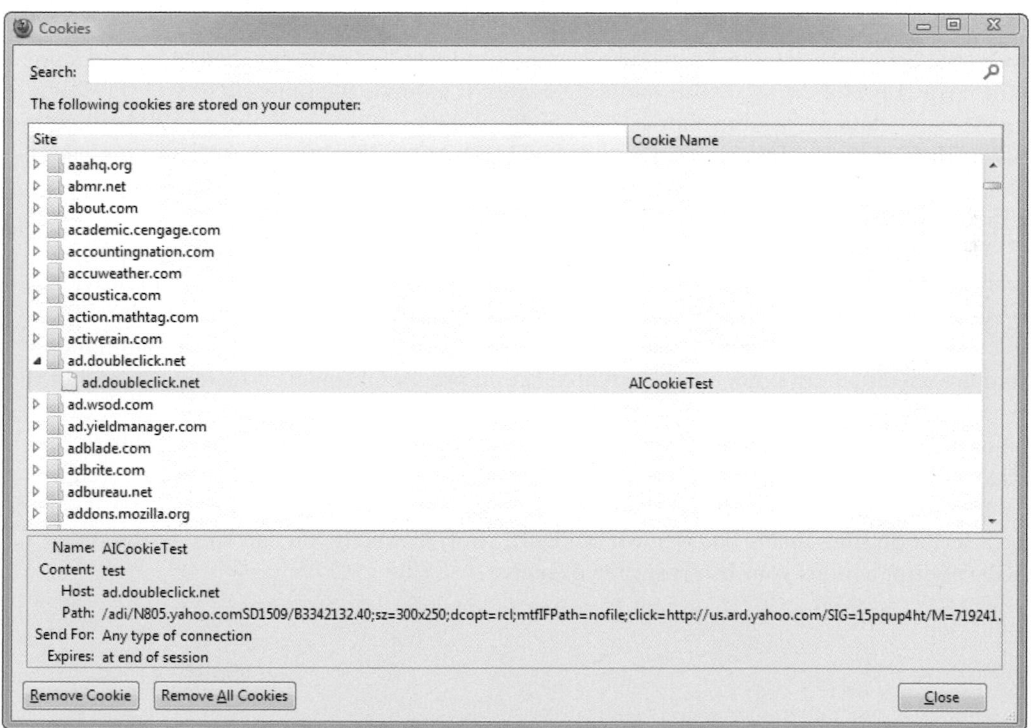

FIGURE 10-3 Mozilla Firefox dialog box for managing stored cookies

Companies such as **Omniture** provide software that Web site managers can use to analyze Internet traffic at their sites. These services also provide information to Web sites about who visits their sites and what sites the visitors came from.

Web Bugs

Some advertisers send images (from their third-party servers) that are included on Web pages, but are too small to be visible. A **Web bug** is a tiny graphic that a third-party Web site places on another site's Web page. When a site visitor loads the Web page, the Web bug is delivered by the third-party site, which can then place a cookie on the visitor's computer. A Web bug's only purpose is to provide a way for a third-party Web site (the identity of which is unknown to the visitor) to place cookies from that third-party site on the visitor's computer. The Internet advertising community sometimes calls Web bugs "clear GIFs" or "1-by-1 GIFs" because the graphics can be created in the GIF format with a color value of "transparent" and can be as small as 1 pixel by 1 pixel. You can learn more about Web bugs by visiting the Electronic Frontier Foundation's **Web Bug FAQ**.

Active Content

Until the debut of executable Web content, Web pages could do little more than display content and provide links to related pages with additional information. The widespread use of active content has changed the situation. **Active content** refers to programs that are embedded transparently in Web pages and that cause action to occur. For example, active content can display moving graphics, download and play audio, or implement Web-based spreadsheet programs. Active content is used in electronic commerce to place items into a shopping cart and compute a total invoice amount, including sales tax, handling, and shipping costs. Developers use active content because it extends the functionality of HTML and moves some data processing chores from the busy server machine to the user's client computer. Unfortunately, because active content elements are programs that run on the client computer, active content can damage the client computer. Thus, active content can pose a threat to the security of client computers.

Active content is provided in several forms. The best-known active content forms are cookies, Java applets, JavaScript, VBScript, and ActiveX controls. Other ways to provide Web active content include graphics, Web browser plug-ins, and e-mail attachments.

JavaScript and VBScript are **scripting languages**; they provide scripts, or commands, that are executed. An **applet** is a small application program. Applets typically run within the Web browser. Active content is launched in a Web browser automatically when that browser loads a Web page containing active content. The applet downloads automatically with the page and begins running. Some browsers include tools that can limit the actions taken by JavaScript applets. For example, the Options dialog box in Mozilla Firefox has an Advanced JavaScript Settings dialog box (shown in Figure 10-4) in which you can specify the types of JavaScript actions your browser may execute.

FIGURE 10-4 Advanced JavaScript settings in Mozilla Firefox

447

Because active content modules are embedded in Web pages, they can be completely invisible when you visit a page containing them. Crackers intent on doing mischief to client computers can embed malicious active content in these seemingly innocuous Web pages. This delivery technique is called a Trojan horse. A **Trojan horse** is a program hidden inside another program or Web page that masks its true purpose. The Trojan horse could snoop around a client computer and send back private information to a cooperating Web server—a secrecy violation. The program could alter or erase information on a client computer—an integrity violation. Zombies are equally threatening. A **zombie** is a Trojan horse that secretly takes over another computer for the purpose of launching attacks on other computers. The computers running the zombie are also sometimes called zombies. When a Trojan horse (or other type of virus) has taken over a large number of computers (and thus made them into zombies), the person who planted the virus can take control of all the computers and form a **botnet** (short for **robotic network**, also called a **zombie farm** when the computers in the network are zombies) that can act as an attacking unit, sending spam or launching denial-of-service attacks against specific Web sites.

Java Applets

Java is a programming language developed by Sun Microsystems that is used widely in Web pages to provide active content. The Web server sends the Java applets along with Web pages requested by the Web client. In most cases, the Java applet's operation will be visible to the site visitor; however, it is possible for a Java applet to perform functions that would not be noticed by the site visitor (such as reading, writing, or erasing files on the site visitor's computer). The client computer then runs the programs within its Web browser. Java can also run outside the confines of a Web browser. Java is platform independent; that is, it can run on many different computers. This "develop once, deploy everywhere" feature reduces development costs because only one program needs to be developed for all operating systems.

Java adds functionality to business applications and can handle transactions and a wide variety of actions on the client computer. That relieves an otherwise busy server-side program from handling thousands of transactions simultaneously. Once downloaded, embedded Java code can run on a client's computer and damage the computer, run a Trojan horse, or turn the computer into a zombie.

To counter this threat, the Java sandbox security model was developed. The **Java sandbox** confines Java applet actions to a set of rules defined by the security model. These rules apply to all untrusted Java applets. **Untrusted Java applets** are those that have not been established as secure. When Java applets are run within the constraints of the sandbox, they do not have full access to the client computer. For example, Java applets operating in the sandbox cannot perform file input, output, or delete operations. This prevents secrecy (disclosure) and integrity (deletion or modification) violations. You can follow the Online Companion link to the **Java Security Page** maintained by the Center for Education and Research in Information Assurance and Security (CERIAS) to learn more about Java applet security.

JavaScript

JavaScript is a scripting language developed by Netscape to enable Web page designers to build active content. Despite the similar-sounding names, JavaScript is based only loosely on Sun's Java programming language. Supported by popular Web browsers, JavaScript shares many of the structures of the full Java language. When a user downloads a Web page with embedded JavaScript code, it executes on the user's (client) computer.

Like other active content vehicles, JavaScript can be used for attacks by executing code that destroys the client's hard disk, discloses the e-mail stored in client mailboxes, or sends sensitive information to the attacker's Web server. JavaScript code can also record the URLs of Web pages a user visits and capture information entered into Web forms. For example, if a user enters credit card numbers while reserving a rental car, a JavaScript program could copy the credit card number. JavaScript programs, unlike Java applets, do not operate under the restrictions of the Java sandbox security model.

Unlike Java applets, a JavaScript program cannot commence execution on its own. To run an ill-intentioned JavaScript program, a user must start the program. For example, a site with a retirement income calculator might require a visitor to click a button to see a retirement income projection. Once the user clicks the button, the JavaScript program starts and does its work.

ActiveX Controls

An **ActiveX** control is an object that contains programs and properties that Web designers place on Web pages to perform particular tasks. ActiveX components can be constructed using many different programming languages, but the most common are C++ and Visual Basic. Unlike Java or JavaScript code, ActiveX controls run only on computers with Windows operating systems.

When a Windows-based Web browser downloads a Web page containing an embedded ActiveX control, the control is executed on the client computer. Other ActiveX controls include Web-enabled calendar controls and Web games. The **ActiveX page at Download.com** contains a comprehensive list of ActiveX controls.

The security danger with ActiveX controls is that once they are downloaded, they execute like any other program on a client computer. They have full access to all system resources, including operating system code. An ill-intentioned ActiveX control could reformat a user's hard disk, rename or delete files, send e-mails to all the people listed in the user's address book, or simply shut down the computer. Because ActiveX controls have full access to client computers, they can cause secrecy, integrity, or necessity violations. The actions of ActiveX controls cannot be halted once they begin execution. Most Web browsers can be configured to provide a notice when a Web site attempts to download and install an ActiveX control (or other software).

Graphics and Plug-Ins

Graphics, browser plug-ins, and e-mail attachments can harbor executable content. Some graphics file formats have been designed specifically to contain instructions on how to render a graphic. That means that any Web page containing such a graphic could be a threat because the code embedded in the graphic could cause harm to a client computer. Similarly, browser **plug-ins**, which are programs that enhance the capabilities of browsers, handle Web content that a browser cannot handle. Plug-ins are normally beneficial and perform tasks for a browser, such as playing audio clips, displaying movies, or animating graphics. Apple's QuickTime, for example, is a plug-in that downloads and plays movies stored in a special format.

Plug-ins can also pose security threats to a client computer. Users download these plug-in programs and install them so their browsers can display content that cannot be included in HTML tags. Popular plug-ins include Adobe's Macromedia's Flash Player, Apple's QuickTime Player, Microsoft's Silverlight, and RealNetworks' RealPlayer.

In 1999, *The New York Times* revealed that RealNetworks had been using its RealPlayer plug-in to gather information surreptitiously from users. Downloaded and installed easily from the Internet, RealPlayer was recording user information such as the RealPlayer user's name, e-mail address, country, ZIP code, computer operating system, and other details. RealPlayer used the Internet connection to send the information it had gathered back to RealNetworks. Soon after the discovery, and after considerable public embarrassment, RealNetworks issued a statement that a software patch was available that users could install to prevent the RealNetworks software from collecting and transmitting their information.

Many plug-ins execute commands buried within the media being manipulated. This opens the door to the possibility that someone intent on doing harm could embed commands within a seemingly innocuous video or audio clip. The ill-intentioned commands hidden within the object that the plug-in is interpreting could damage a client computer by erasing some (or all) of its files.

Viruses, Worms, and Antivirus Software

The potential dangers lurking in e-mail attachments get a lot of news coverage and are the most familiar to the general population. E-mail attachments provide a convenient way to send non-text information over a text-only system—electronic mail. Attachments can contain word-processing files, spreadsheets, databases, images, or virtually any other information you can imagine. Most programs, including Web browser e-mail programs, display attachments by automatically executing an associated program; for example, the recipient's Excel program reads an attached Excel workbook file and opens it, or Word opens and displays a Word document. Although this activity itself does not cause damage, Word and Excel macro viruses inside the loaded files can damage a client computer and reveal confidential information when those files are opened.

A virus is software that attaches itself to another program and can cause damage when the host program is activated. A **worm** is a type of virus that replicates itself on the computers that it infects. Worms can spread quickly through the Internet. A **macro virus** is a type of virus that is coded as a small program, called a macro, and is embedded in a file. You have probably read about or have personally experienced examples of e-mail attachment-borne virus attacks.

Although the history of e-mailed viruses dates back to the 1980s, the first virus to become major news in the mainstream media was the ILOVEYOU virus, also known as the "love bug," and its variants in 2000. The ILOVEYOU virus was eventually traced to a 23-year-old computer science student who lived in the Philippines. The virus spread through the Internet with amazing speed as an e-mail message. It infected the computer of anyone who opened the e-mail attachment and clogged e-mail systems with thousands of copies of the useless e-mail message. The virus spread quickly because it automatically sent itself to as many as 300 addresses stored in a computer's Microsoft Outlook address book. Besides replicating itself explosively through e-mail, the virus caused other harm, destroying digital music and photo files stored on the target computers. The ILOVEYOU virus also searched for other users' passwords and forwarded that information to the original perpetrator. Within days, the virus spread to 40 million computers in more than 20 countries and caused an estimated $9 billion in damages—most of it in lost worker productivity.

In 2001, the incidences of virus and worm attacks increased. With more than 40,000 reported security violations occurring that year, the parade of attacks included Code Red and Nimda virus–worm combinations, each affecting millions of computers and costing billions of dollars to clean up. Both Code Red and Nimda are examples of a **multivector virus**, so-called because they can enter a computer system in several different ways (vectors). Even though Microsoft issued security patches that should have stopped the Code Red virus–worm, it continued to propagate throughout the Internet in 2002. Both the original Code Red virus and a variant called Code Red 2 infected thousands of new computers during the year.

New virus–worm combinations also appeared in 2002 and 2003, including a version of the Code Red virus called Bugbear. Bugbear was spread through Microsoft Outlook e-mail clients. The person receiving the e-mail did not even have to click on an attachment to run the malicious code—Bugbear started itself through a security loophole in the connection between Outlook and the Internet Explorer browser. Of course, Microsoft issued a security patch for the browser, but many users did not install the patch (or, in many cases, did not even know about it). When launched, Bugbear first checked to see if the computer was running antivirus software. **Antivirus software** detects viruses and worms and either deletes them or isolates them on the client computer so they cannot run. If antivirus software existed on the system, Bugbear attempted to destroy it. Then it installed a Trojan horse program on the computer that let attackers access the computer through the Internet and upload or download files at will. Bugbear would then send out e-mail messages with attachments that would infect the recipients. It did not create its own e-mail messages, but took previously sent e-mail messages that were on the computer and resent them to different addresses. This often fooled recipients because the e-mail messages had subject headers that seemed normal and did not hint that the e-mail might contain a virus. Bugbear was difficult to eliminate from an infected computer because it gave its own files a randomly generated name; thus, the virus files had different names on every infected computer.

In 2005 and 2006, Zotob was unleashed on the world. One of a new breed of Trojan horse–worm combination threats, Zotob scans the ports of potential target computers and attacks those that have a specific security flaw. Zotob is designed to be helpful to identity thieves and perpetrators of corporate espionage. Once Zotob has infected a target computer, it logs keystrokes and captures screens with the goal of stealing logins, passwords, and even software keys that a user enters to register and activate newly installed programs. Zotob can make the target computer a zombie so it can be used to send spam or launch attacks on other computers.

In 2007, the Storm virus appeared. Storm appears as an e-mail message telling of an interesting news story with a related video clip included as an attachment. The attachment contains the virus, which allows a remote computer to take over the infected computers and form a botnet.

Beginning in 2008 and continuing into 2009, a similar virus named Conficker has been extremely successful. Conficker is believed to have infected nearly 10 million computers. Antivirus vendors and Microsoft have issued patches and updates that eradicate the virus, but it reinstalls itself and has proven to be quite resilient. The size of the ongoing infection has caused great concern, and a number of Internet service providers, computer security firms, and online businesses have formed the Conficker Working Group to monitor the virus. The large number of computers that remain infected provide a constant threat, since they could be activated remotely at any time to launch a major attack on any Web site in the world.

In 2009 and 2010, new viruses that are designed specifically to hijack users' online banking sessions were introduced or emerged. URLzone waits on the infected computer until a user logs into an account at one of the financial institutions that the virus is programmed to recognize. The virus accesses the bank account at the same time the unknowing victim does and transfers money from the victim's accounts to co-conspirators who take a cut and then use the money to buy goods shipped to a foreign address, where the perpetrator sells the goods and disappears. Clampi is a similar online banking virus that has been infecting computers for years, but only became active in 2009. Clampi is reported to recognize more than 4000 different bank, broker, and other financial institution logins. Figure 10-5 summarizes some of the major viruses, worms, and Trojan horses that have plagued Internet users over the years.

Year	Name	Type	Description
1986	Brain	Virus	Written in Pakistan, this virus infects floppy disks used in personal computers at that time. It consumes empty space on the disks, preventing them from being used to store data or programs.
1988	Internet Worm	Worm	Robert Morris, Jr., a graduate student at Cornell University, wrote this experimental, self-replicating, self-propagating program and released it onto the Internet. It replicated faster than he had anticipated, crashing computers at universities, military sites, and medical research facilities throughout the world.
1991	Tequila	Virus	Tequila writes itself to a computer's hard disk and runs any time the computer is started. It also infects programs when they are executed. Tequila originated in Switzerland and was mostly transmitted through Internet downloads.
1992	Michelangelo	Trojan horse	Set to activate on March 6 (Michelangelo's birthday), this Trojan horse overwrites large portions of the infected computer's hard disk.
1993	SatanBug	Virus	Infects programs when they run, causing them to fail or perform incorrectly. SatanBug was designed to interfere with antivirus programs so they cannot detect it.
1996	Concept	Virus, Worm	One of the first viruses to be written in Microsoft Word's macro language, Concept travels with infected Word document files. When an infected document is opened, Concept places macros in Word's default document template, which infects any new Word document created on that computer.
1999	Melissa	Virus, Worm	Melissa is a Microsoft Word macro virus that spreads by e-mailing itself automatically from one user to another. It inserts comments from "The Simpsons" television show and confidential information from the infected computer. Melissa spread throughout the world in a few hours. Many large companies were inundated by Melissa. For example, Microsoft closed down its e-mail servers to prevent the spread of this virus within the company.
2000	ILOVEYOU	Virus, Worm	Arrives attached to an e-mail message with the subject line "ILOVEYOU" and infects any computer on which the attachment is opened. It sends itself to addresses in any Microsoft Outlook address book it finds on the infected computer. The virus destroys music and photo files stored on the infected computers. When it was launched, it clogged e-mail servers in many large organizations and slowed down the operation of the entire Internet.
2001	Code Red	Virus, Worm, Trojan horse	Code Red can infect Web servers and personal computers. It defaces Web pages and can be transmitted from Web servers to personal computers. It can give hackers control over Web server computers. Code Red can reinstall itself from hidden files after it is removed.

FIGURE 10-5 Major viruses, worms, and Trojan horses

Year	Name	Type	Description
2001	Nimda	Virus, Worm	Nimda modifies Web documents and certain programs on the infected computer. It also creates multiple copies of itself using various file names. It can be transmitted by e-mail, a LAN, or from a Web server to a Web client.
2002	BugBear	Virus, Worm, Trojan horse	BugBear is spread through e-mail and through local area networks. It identifies antivirus software and attempts to disable it. BugBear can log keystrokes and store them for later transmission through a Trojan horse program that it installs on the infected computer. This program gives hackers access to the computer and allows file uploads and downloads.
2002	Klez	Virus, Worm	Klez is transmitted as an e-mail attachment and overwrites files, creates hidden copies of the original files, and attempts to disable antivirus software.
2003	Slammer	Worm	Slammer's primary purpose was to demonstrate how rapidly a worm could be transmitted on the Internet. It infected 75,000 computers in its first 10 minutes of propagation.
2003	Sobig	Trojan horse	Sobig turns infected computers into spam relay points. Sobig transmits mass e-mails with copies of itself to potential victims.
2004	MyDoom	Worm, Trojan horse	MyDoom turns the infected computer into a zombie that will participate in a denial of service attack on a specific company's Web site.
2004	Sasser	Virus, Worm	Written by a German high school student, Sasser finds computers with a specific security flaw and then infects them. The infected computers are slowed by the virus, often to the point that they must be rebooted.
2005	Zotob	Worm, Trojan horse	Zotob peforms port scans and infects computers that appear to have a specific security flaw. Once installed on a target computer, Zotob can log keystrokes, capture screens, and steal authentication credentials and CD software keys. Infected computers can also be used as zombies for mass mailing or attacking other computers.
2006	Nyxem	Worm, Trojan horse	Nyxem disables security and file sharing software. It destroys files created by Microsoft Office programs. Nyxem activates on the third of each month and spreads itself by mass mailing.
2006	Leap	Worm, Virus	Leap (also called Oompa-Loompa) infects programs that run on the Macintosh OS-X operating system. Delivered over the iChat instant messaging system, it can only spread within a specific network.
2007	Storm	Worm, Trojan horse	Storm gathers infected computers into a botnet from which it launches spam. It is spread as an e-mail containing phony news clips with an attachment that it alleges is a news film.

FIGURE 10-5 Major viruses, worms, and Trojan horses *(continued)*

Year	Name	Type	Description
2008	Conficker	Worm, Trojan horse	Conficker has not been used in any significant way, but it is able to reinstall itself and remains on more than 7 million computers. If activated, it could launch a devastating barrage of spam e-mail or a crippling denial-of-service attack on any Web site in the world.
2009	Clampi	Worm, Trojan horse	Activated in 2009 after lying dormant for years, Clampi captures username and password information for more than 4000 bank, broker, and other financial institution Web sites. It forwards information to perpetrators who can use it to purchase goods or transfer funds from victims' accounts.
2009	URLzone	Worm, Trojan horse	URLzone monitors user activity and hijacks session when victim logs into a financial institution Web site that it is programmed to recognize. It then transfers money from victim's accounts to confederates, who take their cut and then buy goods shipped to a foreign address used by the perpetrator. The perpetrator sells the goods and moves on.

FIGURE 10-5 Major viruses, worms, and Trojan horses *(continued)*

Symantec and McAfee, among other companies, keep track of viruses and sell antivirus software. You can follow the links in the Online Companion (**Symantec Security Response** and **McAfee Virus Information**) to find descriptions of thousands of viruses. Antivirus software is only effective if the antivirus data files are kept current. The data files contain virus-identifying information that is used to detect viruses on a client computer. Because people generate new viruses by the hundreds every month, users must be vigilant and update their antivirus data files regularly so that the newest viruses are recognized and eliminated. Some Web e-mail systems, such as Yahoo! Mail, let users scan attachments using antivirus software before downloading e-mail. In these cases, the antivirus software is run by the Web site and the user does not need to take any action to keep the software updated.

LEARNING FROM FAILURES

Microsoft Internet Information Server

As you learned in Chapter 8, Internet Information Server (IIS) is Microsoft's Web server software. Microsoft supplies IIS with the versions of its Windows server operating systems that are suitable for use in operating electronic commerce Web sites.

In August 2001, Microsoft faced an uncomfortable situation that many U.S. manufacturing companies have experienced with recalled, defective products—Microsoft executives stood by at a news conference while a U.S. government official announced to gathered reporters that there was a serious flaw in a Microsoft product. The director of the FBI's National Infrastructure Protection Center was warning reporters that the Code Red worm, which was spreading through the Internet for the third time in as many weeks, was a serious threat to the continued operation of the Internet.

The Code Red worm exploits a vulnerability in the Microsoft IIS Web server software. When the worm was first identified, Microsoft quickly made a patch available on its

Continued

Web site. Microsoft also announced that Web server installations that had kept current with all of the updates and patches that Microsoft had issued would not be subject to attack by the worm.

Many Microsoft customers were outraged by these statements, noting that Microsoft had issued more than 40 software patches in the first half of 2001 and 100 or more patches in each of several prior years. IIS users complained that keeping the software current was virtually impossible and called for Microsoft to deliver software that was more secure when first installed.

Many IIS users began to consider switching to other Web server software. Gartner, Inc., a major IT consulting firm, recommended to its clients that they seriously consider alternatives to IIS for their critical Web server installations. Many industry observers and software engineers agree that Microsoft was a victim of its own success. It had created a very popular and complex piece of software. It is extremely difficult to ensure that no bugs exist in complex software products, and the popularity of the software made it an attractive target for crackers—one worm could bring down many of the servers operating on the Internet. These two factors, plus the likelihood that many IIS servers would not have all of the available security upgrades installed, combined to make it an irresistible target for a worm creator.

Microsoft has struggled to gain the confidence of large corporate IT departments. The company has worked hard to convince users that its operating system software is reliable and trustworthy. For example, when Microsoft introduced version 7 of IIS in 2008, it announced that its architecture had been changed so that users could install only the modules they needed to reduce the software's "attack surface."

The Code Red worm attack on its Web server software was a major setback in its reputation-building effort. Since that attack, a number of security weaknesses have been identified in IIS and patched by Microsoft. The news reports that inevitably accompany these patches have created a continuing public relations issue for the company. You can review the **Microsoft Security Pages** through the link in the Online Companion to see how Microsoft deals with ongoing concerns that its software is secure in the face of continual attacks that are both regular and frequent.

Digital Certificates

One way to control threats from active content is to use digital certificates. A **digital certificate** or **digital ID** is an attachment to an e-mail message or a program embedded in a Web page that verifies that the sender or Web site is who or what it claims to be. In addition, the digital certificate contains a means to send an encrypted message—encoded so others cannot read it—to the entity that sent the original Web page or e-mail message. In the case of a downloaded program containing a digital certificate, the encrypted message identifies the software publisher (ensuring that the identity of the software publisher matches the certificate) and indicates whether the certificate has expired or is still valid. The digital certificate is a **signed** message or code. Signed code or messages serve the same function as a photo on a driver's license or passport. They provide proof that the holder is the person identified by the certificate. Just like a passport, a certificate does not imply anything about either the usefulness or quality of the downloaded program. The certificate only supplies a level of assurance that the software is genuine. The idea behind certificates is that if the user trusts the software developer, signed software can be trusted because, as proven by the certificate, it came from that trusted developer.

Digital certificates are used for many different types of online transactions, including electronic commerce, electronic mail, and electronic funds transfers. A digital ID verifies a Web site to a shopper and, optionally, identifies a shopper to a Web site. Web browsers or e-mail programs exchange digital certificates automatically and invisibly when requested to validate the identity of each party involved in a transaction.

Figure 10-6 displays the digital certificate owned by Delmar Cengage Learning. Whenever a browser indicates that it has established secure communication with a Web site; that is, when a padlock icon appears in the browser's status line or the name of the site appears in the browser's address bar with a colored background (the exact notification methods vary from browser to browser), the user can double-click the icon (or the site name that appears with a colored background) to display the Web site's security information and its digital certificate.

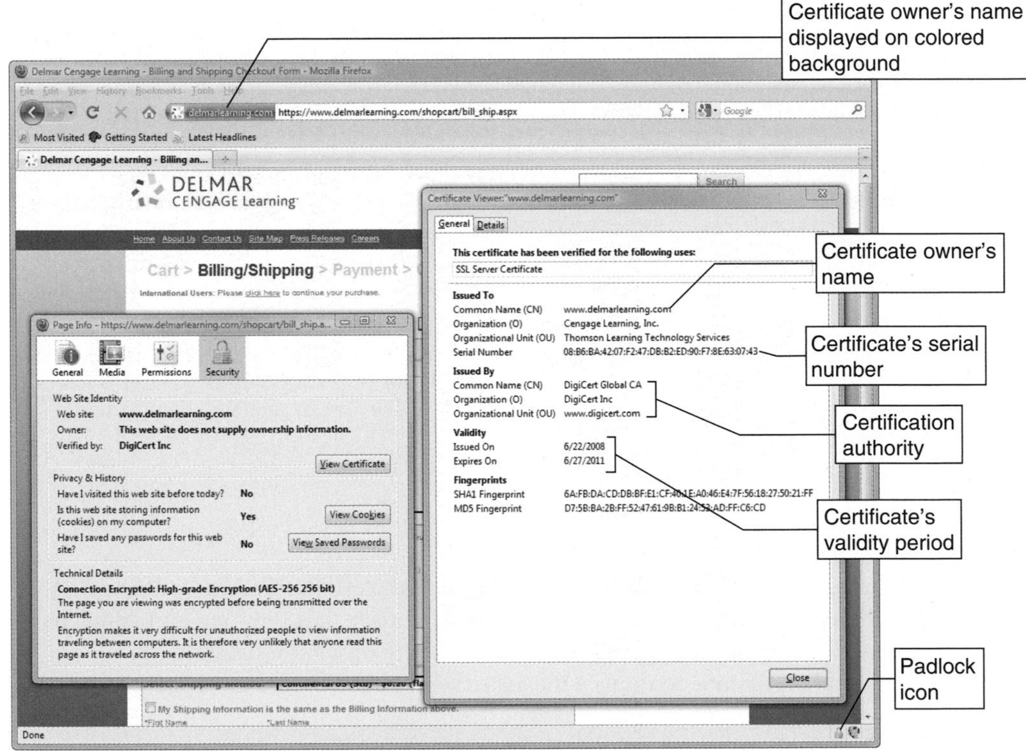

FIGURE 10-6 Delmar Cengage Learning's digital certificate information displayed in Firefox browser

A digital certificate for software is an assurance that the software was created by a specific company. The certificate does not attest to the quality of the software, just to the identity of the company that published it. Digital certificates are issued by a **certification authority (CA)**. A CA can issue digital certificates to organizations or individuals. A CA requires entities applying for digital certificates to supply appropriate proof of identity. Once the CA is satisfied, it issues a certificate. Then, the CA signs the certificate, and its stamp of approval is affixed in the form of a public encryption key (you will learn more about encryption keys later in this chapter), which "unlocks" the certificate for anyone who receives the certificate attached to the publisher's code. Digital certificates cannot be forged easily. A digital certificate includes six main elements, including:

- Certificate owner's identifying information, such as name, organization, address, and so on
- Certificate owner's public encryption key
- Dates between which the certificate is valid
- Serial number of the certificate
- Name of the certificate issuer
- Digital signature of the certificate issuer

A **key** is simply a number—usually a long binary number—that is used with the encryption algorithm to "lock" the characters of the message being protected so that they are undecipherable without the key. Longer keys usually provide significantly better protection than shorter keys. In effect, the CA is guaranteeing that the individual or organization that presents the certificate is who or what it claims to be.

Identification requirements vary from one CA to another. One CA might require a driver's license for individuals' certificates; others might require a notarized form or fingerprints. CAs usually publish identification requirements so that any Web user or site accepting certificates from each CA understands the stringency of that CA's validation procedures. Only a small number of CAs exist because the certificates issued are only as trustworthy as the CA itself, and only a few companies have decided to build the reputation needed to be a successful seller of digital certificates. Two of the most commonly used CAs are Thawte and VeriSign, but other companies such as DigiCert, Entrust, GeoTrust, Equifax Secure, and RapidSSL.com also offer CA services. The digital certificate for Delmar Learning (shown in Figure 10-6) was issued by DigiCert.

Although the use of digital certificates increased Web users' confidence in online shopping and banking sites, some CAs were performing just the minimum level of verification on certificate applicants before issuing the certificates. A growing concern that fraudulent Web sites might be obtaining digital certificates led a group of CAs to develop a more stringent set of verification steps.

In 2008, the higher standards for verification led to the establishment of stricter criteria and an assurance of consistent application of verification procedures. CAs that followed these more extensive verification procedures were permitted to issue a new type of certificate called a **Secure Sockets Layer-Extended Validation (SSL-EV) digital certificate**. To issue an SSL-EV certificate, a certification authority must confirm the legal existence of the organization by verifying the organization's registered legal name, registration number, registered address, and physical business address. The CA must also verify the organization's right to use the domain name and that the organization has authorized the request for an SSL-EV certificate.

You can tell if you are visiting a Web site that has an SSL-EV certificate by looking at the address window of your browser. In Firefox, the site's verified organization name appears in the address window to the left of the URL with a green background. In Internet Explorer, the background of the address window turns green and the verified name of the organization appears to the right of the URL and alternates with the name of the certification authority, as shown in Figure 10-7.

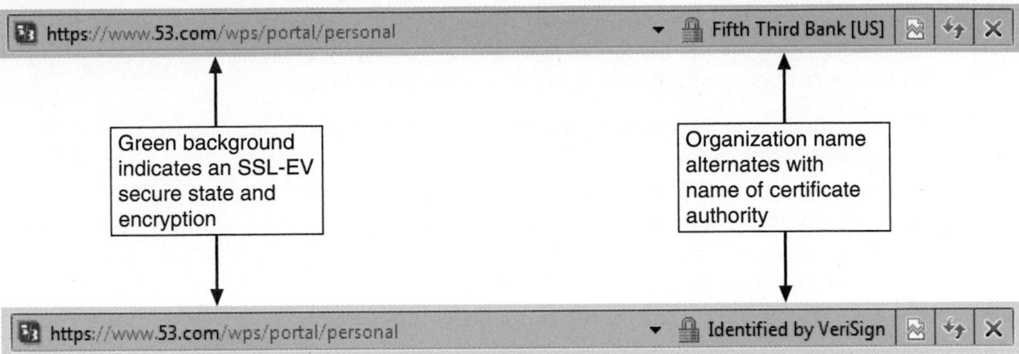

FIGURE 10-7 Internet Explorer address window display for an SSL-EV Web site

Annual fees for digital certificates range from about $200 to more than $1500, depending on the features they include (such as encryption strength, or the SSL-EV designation) and whether they are purchased alone or with certificates for other Web sites owned by the same company. Digital certificates expire after a period of time (often one year). This built-in limit provides protection for both users and businesses. Limited-duration certificates guarantee that businesses and individuals must submit their credentials for reevaluation periodically. The expiration date appears in the certificate itself and in the dialog boxes that browsers display when a Web page or applet that has a digital certificate is about to be opened. Certificates become invalid on their expiration dates or when they are revoked by the CA. If the CA determines that a Web site has delivered malicious code or has otherwise violated the terms to which it agreed, the CA will refuse to issue new certificates to that site and revoke existing certificates.

Steganography

The term **steganography** describes the process of hiding information (a command, for example) within another piece of information. This information can be used for malicious purposes. Frequently, computer files contain redundant or insignificant information that can be replaced with other information. This other information resides in the background and is undetectable by anyone without the correct decoding software. Steganography provides a way of hiding an encrypted file within another file so that a casual observer cannot detect that there is anything of importance in the container file. In this two-step process, encrypting the file protects it from being read, and steganography makes it invisible.

Many security analysts believe that the terrorist organization Al Qaeda used steganography to hide attack orders and other messages in images that its confederates posted on Web sites in preparation for the attacks of September 11, 2001. Messages hidden using steganography are extremely difficult to detect. This fact, combined with the fact that there are millions of images on the Web, makes the use of steganography by global terrorist organizations a deep concern of governments and security professionals. The Online Companion includes a link to a site with more information about **Steganography and Digital Watermarking**.

Physical Security for Clients

In the past, physical security was a major concern for large computers that ran important business functions such as payroll or billing; however, as networks (including intranets and the Internet) have made it possible to control important business functions from client computers, concerns about physical security for client computers have become greater. Many of the physical security measures used today are the same as those used in the early days of computing; however, some interesting new technologies have been implemented as well.

Devices that read fingerprints are now available for personal computers. These devices, which cost less than $100, provide a much stronger protection than traditional password approaches. In addition to fingerprint readers, companies can use other biometric security devices that are more accurate and, of course, cost more. A **biometric security device** is one that uses an element of a person's biological makeup to perform the identification. These devices include writing pads that detect the form and pressure of a person writing a signature, eye scanners that read the pattern of blood vessels in a person's retina or the color levels in a person's iris, and scanners that read the palm of a person's hand (rather than just one fingerprint) or that read the pattern of veins on the back of a person's hand.

COMMUNICATION CHANNEL SECURITY

The Internet serves as the electronic connection between buyers (in most cases, clients) and sellers (in most cases, servers). The most important thing to remember as you learn about communication channel security is that the Internet was not designed to be secure. Although the Internet has its roots in a military network, that network was not designed to include any significant security features. It was designed to provide redundancy in case one or more communications lines were cut. In other words, the goal of the Internet's packet-switching design was to provide multiple alternative paths on which critical military information could travel. The military always sends sensitive information in an encrypted form so that the content of messages traveling over any network—even if intercepted—remain secret. The security of messages traversing the military predecessors to the Internet was provided by software that operated independently of the network to encrypt messages. As the Internet developed, it did so without any significant security features that became a part of the network itself.

Today, the Internet remains largely unchanged from its original, insecure state. Message packets on the Internet travel an unplanned path from a source node to a destination node. A packet passes through a number of intermediate computers on the network before reaching its final destination. The path can vary each time a packet is sent between the same source and destination points. Because users cannot control the path and do not know where their packets have been, it is possible that an intermediary can read the packets, alter them, or even delete them. That is, any message traveling on the Internet is subject to secrecy, integrity, and necessity threats. This section describes these problems in more detail and outlines several solutions for those problems.

Secrecy Threats

Secrecy is the security threat that is most frequently mentioned in articles and the popular media. Closely linked to secrecy is privacy, which also receives a great deal of attention. Secrecy and privacy, though similar, are different issues. Secrecy is the prevention of unauthorized information disclosure. **Privacy** is the protection of individual rights to nondisclosure. The Privacy Council, which helps businesses implement smart privacy and data practices, created an extensive Web site surrounding privacy—covering both business and legal issues. Secrecy is a technical issue requiring sophisticated physical and logical mechanisms, whereas privacy protection is a legal matter. A classic example of the difference between secrecy and privacy is e-mail.

A company might protect its e-mail messages against secrecy violations by using encryption (you will learn more about encryption later in this chapter). In encryption, a message is encoded into an unintelligible form that only the proper recipient can convert back into the original message. Secrecy countermeasures protect outgoing messages. E-mail privacy issues address whether company supervisors should be permitted to read employees' messages randomly. Disputes in this area center around who owns the e-mail messages: the company or the employees who sent them. The focus in this section is on secrecy, preventing unauthorized persons from reading information they should not be reading.

One significant threat to electronic commerce is theft of sensitive or personal information, including credit card numbers, names, addresses, and personal preferences. This kind of theft can occur any time anyone submits information over the Internet because it is easy for an ill-intentioned person to record information packets (a secrecy violation) from the Internet for later examination. The same problems can occur in e-mail transmissions. Software applications called **sniffer programs** provide the means to record information that passes through a computer or router that is handling Internet traffic. Using a sniffer program is analogous to tapping a telephone line and recording a conversation. Sniffer programs can read e-mail messages and unencrypted Web client–server message traffic, such as user logins, passwords, and credit card numbers.

Periodically, security experts find electronic holes, called backdoors, in electronic commerce software. A **backdoor** is an element of a program (or a separate program) that allows users to run the program without going through the normal authentication procedure for access to the program. Programmers often build backdoors into programs while they are building and testing them to save the time it would take to enter a login and password every time they open the program. Sometimes programmers forget to remove backdoors when they are finished writing the program, other times, programmers intentionally leave a backdoor.

A backdoor allows anyone with knowledge of its existence to cause damage by observing transactions, deleting data, or stealing data. For example, a security consulting firm found that Cart32, a widely used shopping cart program, had a backdoor through which credit card numbers could be obtained by anyone with knowledge of the backdoor. This backdoor resulted from a programming error and not an intentional effort (and Cart32 provided a software patch that closed the backdoor immediately), but customers of the merchants who used Cart32 had their credit card numbers exposed to hackers around the world until those merchants applied the patch.

Credit card number theft is an obvious problem, but proprietary corporate product information or prerelease product data sheets mailed to corporate branches can be intercepted and passed along easily, too. Confidential information can be considerably more valuable than information about credit cards, which usually have spending limits. Stolen corporate information, such as blueprints, product formulas, or marketing plans, can be worth millions of dollars.

Here is an example of how an online eavesdropper might obtain confidential information. Suppose a user logs on to a Web site that contains a form with text boxes for name, address, and e-mail address. When the user fills out those text boxes and clicks the submit button, the information is sent to the Web server for processing. Some Web servers obtain and track that data by collecting the text box responses and placing them at the end of the server's URL (which appears in the address box of the user's Web browser). This long URL (with the text box responses appended) is included in all HTTP request and response messages that travel between the user's browser and the server.

So far, no violations have occurred. Suppose, however, that the user decides not to wait for a response from the server. Instead, the user visits another Web site. The server at this second Web site might be set up to collect Web demographics. If it is, it logs the URL from which the user just came by capturing it from the HTTP request message that the browser sends. Web sites use this URL logging technique for the completely legitimate purpose of identifying sources of customer traffic. However, any employee at the second site who has access to the server log can read the part of the URL that includes the information entered into those text boxes on the first site, thus obtaining that user's confidential information.

Web users continually reveal information about themselves when they use the Web. This information includes IP addresses and the type of browser being used. Such data exposure is a secrecy breach. Several Web sites offer an anonymous browser service that hides personal information from sites visited. These sites provide a measure of secrecy to Web surfers who use them by replacing the user's IP address with the IP address of the anonymous Web service on the front end of any URLs that the user visits. When the Web site logs the site visitor's IP address, it logs the IP address of the anonymous Web service rather than that of the visitor, which preserves the visitor's privacy.

Using such a service can make anonymous Web surfing possible, but tedious, because each URL that the user wants to visit must be typed into the text box on the anonymous Web service's home page. To make the process easier, companies such as **Anonymizer** provide browser plug-in software that users can download and install for an annual subscription fee. **ShadowSurf.com** provides a free anonymous browser service online.

Integrity Threats

An integrity threat, also known as **active wiretapping**, exists when an unauthorized party can alter a message stream of information. Unprotected banking transactions, such as deposit amounts transmitted over the Internet, are subject to integrity violations. Of course, an integrity violation implies a secrecy violation because an intruder who alters information can read and interpret that information. Unlike secrecy threats, where a viewer simply sees information he or she should not, integrity threats can cause a change in the actions a person or corporation takes because a mission-critical transmission has been altered.

Cybervandalism is an example of an integrity violation. **Cybervandalism** is the electronic defacing of an existing Web site's page. The electronic equivalent of destroying property or placing graffiti on objects, cybervandalism occurs whenever someone replaces a Web site's regular content with his or her own content. Recently, several cases of Web page defacing involved vandals replacing business content with pornographic material and other offensive content.

Masquerading or **spoofing**—pretending to be someone you are not, or representing a Web site as an original when it is a fake—is one means of disrupting Web sites. **Domain name servers (DNSs)** are the computers on the Internet that maintain directories that link domain names to IP addresses. Perpetrators can use a security hole in the software that runs on some of these computers to substitute the addresses of their Web sites in place of the real ones to spoof Web site visitors.

For example, a hacker could create a fictitious Web site masquerading as www.widgets.com by exploiting a DNS security hole that substitutes his or her fake IP address for Widgets.com's real IP address. All subsequent visits to Widgets.com would be redirected to the fictitious site. There, the hacker could alter any orders to change the number of widgets ordered and redirect shipment of those products to another address. The integrity attack consists of altering an order and passing it to the real company's Web server. The Web server is unaware of the integrity attack and simply verifies the consumer's credit card number and passes on the order for fulfillment.

Major electronic commerce sites that have been the victims of masquerading attacks in recent years include Amazon.com, AOL, eBay, and PayPal. Some of these schemes combine spam with spoofing. The perpetrator sends millions of spam e-mails that appear to be from a respectable company. The e-mails contain a link to a Web page that is designed to look exactly like the company's site. The victim is encouraged to enter username, password, and sometimes even credit card information. These exploits, which capture confidential customer information, are called **phishing expeditions**. The most common victims of phishing expeditions are users of online banking and payment system (such as PayPal) Web sites. You will learn more about the phishing problem and the measures banks and other companies are taking to combat it in Chapter 11.

Necessity Threats

The purpose of a **necessity threat**, which usually occurs as a **delay, denial,** or **denial-of-service (DoS) attack**, is to disrupt normal computer processing, or deny processing entirely. A computer that has experienced a necessity threat slows processing to an intolerably slow speed. For example, if the processing speed of a single ATM transaction slows from one or two seconds to 30 seconds, users will abandon ATMs entirely. Similarly, slowing any Internet service drives customers to competitors' Web or commerce sites—possibly discouraging them from ever returning to the original commerce site. In other words, slower processing can render a service unusable or unattractive. For example, an online newspaper that reports three-day-old news is worth very little. The Internet Worm attack of 1998, which disabled thousands of computer systems that were connected to the Internet, was the first recorded example of a DoS attack.

Attackers can use the botnets you learned about earlier in this chapter to launch a simultaneous attack on a Web site (or a number of Web sites) from all of the computers in the botnet. This form of attack is called a **distributed denial-of-service (DDoS) attack**. The attack on U.S. and South Korean government and business Web sites you learned about at the beginning of this chapter was a DDoS attack.

DoS attacks can remove information altogether, or delete information from a transmission or file. One denial attack caused some PCs that have Quicken (an accounting program) installed to divert money to the perpetrator's bank account. In another famous DoS attack against high-profile electronic commerce sites such as Amazon.com and Yahoo!, the attackers used a botnet to send a flood of data packets to the sites. This overwhelmed the sites' servers and choked off legitimate customers' access. Prior to the attack, perpetrators located vulnerable computers and loaded them with the software that attacked the commerce sites.

Threats to the Physical Security of Internet Communications Channels

The Internet was designed from its inception to withstand attacks on its physical communication links. Recall from Chapter 2 that the main purpose of the U.S. government research project that led to the development of the Internet was to provide an attack-resistant technology for coordinating military operations. Thus, the Internet's packet-based network design precludes it from being shut down by an attack on a single communications link on that network.

However, an individual user's Internet service can be interrupted by destruction of that user's link to the Internet. Few individual users have multiple connections to an ISP. However, larger companies and organizations (and ISPs themselves) often do have more than one link to the main backbone of the Internet. Typically, each link is purchased from a different network access provider. If one link becomes overloaded or unavailable, the service provider can switch traffic to another network access provider's link to keep the company, organization, or ISP (and its customers) connected to the Internet.

Threats to Wireless Networks

As you learned in Chapter 2, networks can use wireless access points (WAPs) to provide network connections to computers and other mobile devices within a range of several hundred feet. If not protected, a wireless network allows anyone within that range to log in and have access to any resources connected to that network. Such resources might include any data stored on any computer connected to the network, networked printers, messages sent on the network, and, if the network is connected to the Internet, free access to the Internet. The security of the connection depends on the **Wireless Encryption Protocol (WEP)**, which is a set of rules for encrypting transmissions from the wireless devices to the WAPs.

Companies that have large wireless networks are usually careful to turn on WEP in devices, but smaller companies and individuals who have installed wireless networks in their homes often do not turn on the WEP security feature. Many WAPs are shipped to buyers with a default login and password already set. Companies that install these WAPs sometimes fail to change that login and password. This has given rise to a new avenue of entry into networks.

In some cities that have large concentrations of wireless networks, attackers drive around in cars using their wireless-equipped laptop computers to search for accessible networks. These attackers are called **wardrivers**. When wardrivers find an open network (or a WAP that has a common default login and password), they sometimes place a chalk mark on the building so that other attackers will know that an easily entered wireless network is nearby. This practice is called **warchalking**. Some warchalkers have even created Web sites that include maps of wireless access locations in major cities around the world. Companies can avoid becoming targets by simply turning on WEP in their access points and changing the logins and passwords to something other than the manufacturers' default settings.

An early victim of a wireless attack, Best Buy was using wireless point-of-sale (POS) terminals in some of its stores. The wireless POS terminals could be moved easily from one area of the store to another, and they helped Best Buy handle large customer flows better than it could using only fixed POS terminals. Unfortunately, Best Buy had not enabled WEP on these terminals. A customer who had just purchased a wireless card for his laptop decided to launch a sniffer utility program on the laptop in his car in the parking lot. The customer was able to intercept data from the POS terminals, including transaction details and what he said looked like credit card numbers. Best Buy stopped using the wireless POS terminals when the story appeared on several Web sites and newswire services.

Encryption Solutions

Encryption is the coding of information by using a mathematically based program and a secret key to produce a string of characters that is unintelligible. The science that studies encryption is called **cryptography**, which comes from a combination of the two Greek words *krypto* and *grapho*, which mean "secret" and "writing," respectively. That is, cryptography is the science of creating messages that only the sender and receiver can read.

Cryptography is different from steganography, which makes text undetectable to the naked eye. Cryptography does not hide text; it converts it to other text that is visible, but does not appear to have any meaning. What an unauthorized reader sees is a string of random text characters, numbers, and punctuation.

Encryption Algorithms

The program that transforms normal text, called **plain text**, into **cipher text** (the unintelligible string of characters) is called an **encryption program**. The logic behind an encryption program that includes the mathematics used to do the transformation from plain text to cipher text is called an **encryption algorithm**. There are a number of different encryption algorithms in use today. Some have been developed by the U.S. government and others have been developed by IBM and other commercial enterprises. You can learn more about the development of encryption algorithms, including an evaluation of currently available algorithms, by consulting a Web security textbook (see, for example, the Mackey reference in the For Further Study and Research section at the end of this chapter).

Messages are encrypted just before they are sent over a network or the Internet. Upon arrival, each message is decoded, or **decrypted**, using a **decryption program**—a type of encryption-reversing procedure. Encryption algorithms are considered so vitally important to preserving security within the United States that the National Security Agency has control over their dissemination. Some encryption algorithms are considered so important that the U.S. government has banned publication of details about them. Currently, it is illegal for U.S. companies to export some of these encryption algorithms. The Freedom Forum Online contains a number of articles on lawsuits and legislation surrounding encryption export laws. Critics consider publication restrictions a freedom of speech issue. If you are interested in reading more about the latest arguments in the ongoing debates over freedom of speech and export law, search the Freedom Forum using the keyword "encryption" as the search term.

One property of encryption algorithms is that someone can know the details of the algorithm and still not be able to decipher the encrypted message without knowing the key that the algorithm used to encrypt the message. The resistance of an encrypted message to attack attempts depends on the size (in bits) of the key used in the encryption procedure. A 40-bit key is currently considered to provide a minimal level of security. Longer keys, such as 128-bit keys, provide much more secure encryption. A sufficiently long key can help make the security unbreakable.

The type of key and associated encryption program used to lock a message, or otherwise manipulate it, subdivides encryption into three functions:

1. Hash coding
2. Asymmetric encryption
3. Symmetric encryption

Hash Coding

Hash coding is a process that uses a **hash algorithm** to calculate a number, called a **hash value**, from a message of any length. It is a fingerprint for the message because it is almost certain to be unique for each message. Good hash algorithms are designed so that the probability of two different messages resulting in the same hash value, which would create a **collision**, is extremely small. Hash coding is a particularly convenient way to tell whether a message has been altered in transit because its original hash value and the hash value computed by the receiver will not match after a message is altered.

Asymmetric Encryption

Asymmetric encryption, or **public-key encryption**, encodes messages by using two mathematically related numeric keys. In 1977, Ronald Rivest, Adi Shamir, and Leonard Adleman invented the RSA Public Key Cryptosystem while they were professors at MIT. Their invention revolutionized the way sensitive information is exchanged. In their system, one key of the pair, called a **public key**, is freely distributed to the public at large—to anyone interested in communicating securely with the holder of both keys. The public key is used to encrypt messages using one of several different encryption algorithms. The second key—called a **private key**—belongs to the key owner, who keeps the key secret. The owner uses the private key to decrypt all messages received.

Here is an overview of how an asymmetric encryption system works: If Herb wants to send a message to Allison, he obtains Allison's public key from any of several well-known public places. Then, he encrypts his message to Allison using her public key. Once the message is encrypted, only Allison can read the message by decrypting it with her private key. Because the keys are unique, only one secret key can open the message encrypted with a corresponding public key, and vice versa. Reversing the process, Allison can send a private message to Herb using Herb's public key to encrypt the message. When he receives Allison's message, Herb uses his private key to decrypt the message and then read it. If they are sending e-mail to one another, the message is secret only while in transit. Once a message is downloaded from the mail server and decoded, it is stored in plain text on the recipient's machine for all to view.

One of the most popular technologies used to implement public-key encryption today is called **Pretty Good Privacy (PGP)**. PGP was invented in 1991 by Phil Zimmerman, who charged businesses for use of PGP, but allowed individuals to use PGP at no cost. PGP is a set of software tools that can use several different encryption algorithms to perform public-key encryption. The PGP business was purchased by Network Associates in 1997 and sold back to the product's developers, who formed the PGP Corporation in 2002. Today, individuals can download free versions of PGP for personal use from the **PGP Corporation** site and from the **PGP International** site. Individuals can use PGP to encrypt their e-mail messages to protect them from being read if they are intercepted on the Internet. The PGP Corporation site sells licenses to businesses that want to use the technology to protect business communication activities.

Symmetric Encryption

Symmetric encryption, also known as **private-key encryption**, encodes a message with an algorithm that uses a single numeric key, such as 456839420783, to encode and decode data. Because the same key is used, both the message sender and the message receiver must know the key. Encoding and decoding messages using symmetric encryption is very fast and efficient. However, the key must be guarded. If the key is made public, then all messages sent previously using that key become vulnerable, and the keys must be changed.

It can be difficult to distribute new keys to authorized parties while maintaining security and control over the keys. The catch is that to transmit anything privately (including a new secret key), it must be encrypted. Another problem with private keys is that they do not work well in large environments such as the Internet. Each pair of users on the Internet who wants to share information privately must have their own private key. That results in a huge number of key–pair combinations.

In secure environments such as the defense sector, using private-key encryption is simpler, and it is the prevalent method to encode sensitive data. Distribution of classified information and encryption keys is often used in military applications. It requires guards (two-person control) and secret transportation plans. The **Data Encryption Standard (DES)** is a set of encryption algorithms adopted by the U.S. government for encrypting sensitive or commercial information and is the most widely used private-key encryption system. The size of DES private keys must be increased regularly because researchers use increasingly fast computers to break them. For example, the Electronic Frontier Foundation's Deep Crack key breaker used a network of 100,000 PCs to break a DES-encrypted test message in under 23 hours.

As a result of these key-breaking experiments, the U.S. government began using a stronger version of the Data Encryption Standard, called **Triple Data Encryption Standard (Triple DES** or **3DES)**. Triple DES is still widely used in various applications; however, the U.S. government developed an alternative encryption standard called the **Advanced Encryption Standard (AES)**. Today, most U.S. government agencies and many private businesses use AES with various key bit lengths. AES uses longer bit lengths to increase the difficulty of cracking its keys, just as the DES methods do.

Comparing Asymmetric and Symmetric Encryption Systems

Public-key (asymmetric) systems provide several advantages over private-key (symmetric) encryption methods. First, the combination of keys required to provide private messages between enormous numbers of people is small. If *n* people want to share secret information with one another, then only *n* unique public-key pairs are required—far fewer than an equivalent private-key system. Second, key distribution is not a problem. Each person's public key can be posted anywhere and does not require any special handling to distribute. Third, public-key systems make implementation of digital signatures possible. This means that an electronic document can be signed and sent to any recipient with nonrepudiation. That is, with public-key techniques, it is not possible for anyone other than the signer to produce the signature electronically; in addition, the signer cannot later deny signing the electronic document.

Public-key systems have disadvantages. One disadvantage is that public-key encryption and decryption are significantly slower than private-key systems. This extra time can add up quickly as individuals and organizations conduct commerce on the Internet. Public-key systems do not replace private-key systems, but serve as a complement to them. Public-key systems are used to transmit private keys to Internet participants so that additional, more efficient communication can occur in a secure Internet session. Figure 10-8 shows a graphical comparison of the hashing, private-key, and public-key encryption methods: Figure 10-8a shows hash coding; Figure 10-8b depicts private-key encryption; and Figure 10-8c illustrates public-key encryption.

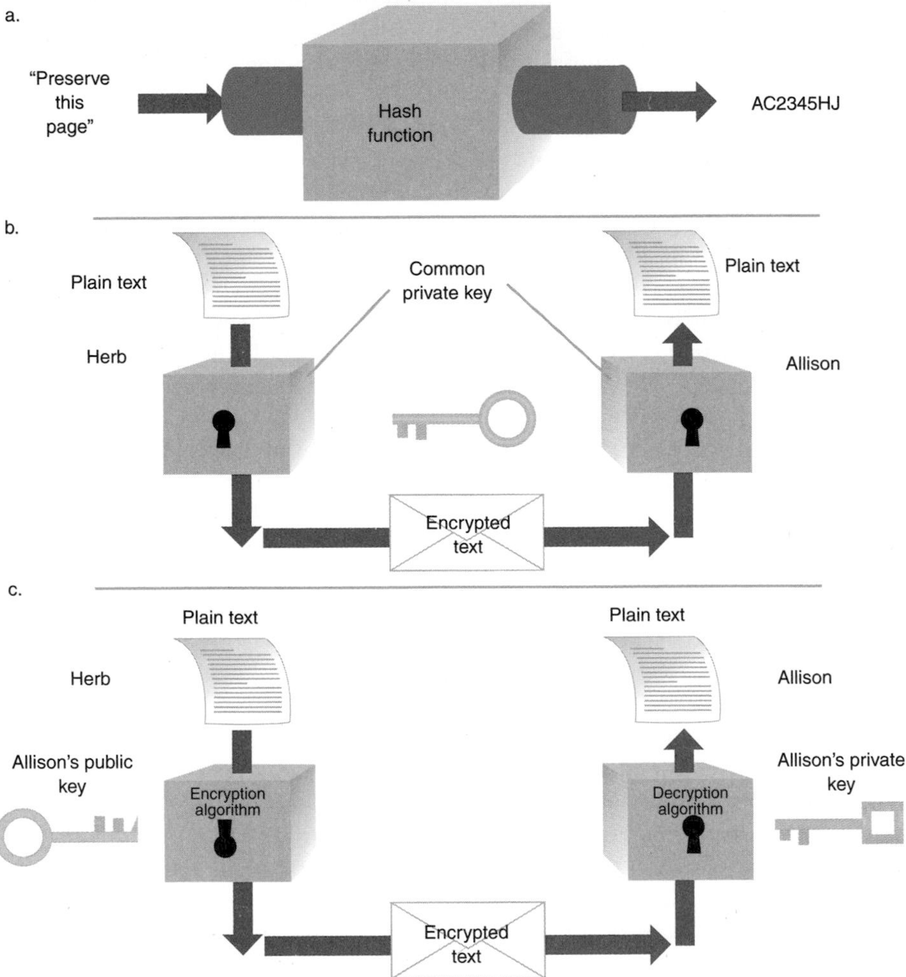

FIGURE 10-8 Comparison of (a) hash coding, (b) private-key, and (c) public-key encryption

Several encryption algorithms exist that can be used with secure Web servers. The U.S. government approves the use of several of these inside the United States. Electronic commerce Web servers can accommodate most of these algorithms because they must be able to communicate with a wide variety of Web browsers.

The **Secure Sockets Layer (SSL)** system developed by Netscape Communications and the Secure Hypertext Transfer Protocol (S-HTTP) developed by CommerceNet are two protocols that provide secure information transfer through the Internet. SSL and S-HTTP allow both the client and server computers to manage encryption and decryption activities between each other during a secure Web session.

SSL and S-HTTP have different goals. SSL secures connections between two computers, and S-HTTP sends *individual* messages securely. Encryption of outgoing messages and decryption of incoming messages happens automatically and transparently with both SSL and S-HTTP.

Secure Sockets Layer (SSL) Protocol

SSL provides a security "handshake" in which the client and server computers exchange a brief burst of messages. In those messages, the client and server agree on the level of security to be used for exchange of digital certificates and other tasks. Each computer identifies the other. After identification, SSL encrypts and decrypts information flowing between the two computers. This means that information in both the HTTP request and any HTTP response is encrypted. Encrypted information includes the URL the client is requesting, any forms containing information the user has completed (which might include sensitive information such as a login, a password, or a credit card number), and HTTP access authorization data, such as usernames and passwords. In short, *all* communication between SSL-enabled clients and servers is encoded. When SSL encodes everything flowing between the client and server, an eavesdropper receives only unintelligible information.

SSL can secure many different types of communication between computers in addition to HTTP. For example, SSL can secure FTP sessions, enabling private downloading and uploading of sensitive documents, spreadsheets, and other electronic data. SSL can secure Telnet sessions in which remote computer users can log on to corporate host machines and send their passwords and usernames. The protocol that implements SSL is HTTPS. By preceding the URL with the protocol name HTTPS, the client is signifying that it would like to establish a secure connection with the remote server.

Secure Sockets Layer allows the length of the private session key generated by every encrypted transaction to be set at a variety of bit lengths (such as 40-bit, 56-bit, 128-bit, or 168-bit). A **session key** is a key used by an encryption algorithm to create cipher text from plain text during a single secure session. The longer the key, the more resistant the encryption is to attack. A Web browser that has entered into an SSL session indicates that it is in an encrypted session (most browsers use an icon in the browser status bar). Once the session is ended, the session key is discarded permanently and not reused for subsequent secure sessions.

In an SSL session, the client and server agree that their exchanges should be kept secure because they involve transmitting credit card numbers, invoice numbers, or verification codes. To implement secrecy, SSL uses public-key (asymmetric) encryption and private-key (symmetric) encryption. Although public-key encryption is convenient, it is slow compared to private-key encryption. That is why SSL uses private-key encryption for nearly all its secure communications. Because it uses private-key encryption, SSL must have a way to get the key to both the client and server without exposing it to an eavesdropper. SSL accomplishes this by having the browser generate a private key for both to share. Then the browser encrypts the private key it has generated using the server's public key.

The server's public key is stored in the digital certificate that the server sent to the browser during the authentication step. Once the key is encrypted, the browser sends it to the server. The server, in turn, decrypts the message with its private key and exposes the shared private key.

Here is how SSL works with an exchange between a browser (SSL client) and a Web server (SSL server):

1. When a client browser sends a request message to a server's secure Web site, the server sends a hello request to the browser (client). The browser responds with a client hello. The exchange of these greetings, or the handshake, allows the two computers to determine the compression and encryption standards that they both support.
2. Next, the browser asks the server for a digital certificate as a proof of identity. In response, the server sends to the browser a certificate signed by a recognized certification authority.
3. The browser checks the serial number and certificate fingerprint on the server certificate against the public key of the CA stored within the browser. Once the CA's public key is verified, the endorsement is verified. That action authenticates the Web server. The browser responds by sending its client certificate and an encrypted private session key to be used. When the server receives this information, it initiates the session, which uses the private key now shared between the browser and the Web server.
4. With the session established as secure, request messages from the browser are accepted by the Web server, which sends the necessary responses. In this secure session, the browser user can make purchases, pay bills, or trade securities without worrying about threats to the security of the information passing between the two computers.

From this point on, public-key encryption is no longer used. Instead, only private-key encryption is used. All messages sent between the client and the server are encrypted with the shared private key, also known as the session key. When the session ends, the session key is discarded. A new connection between a client and a secure server starts the entire process all over again, beginning with the handshake between the client browser and the server. The client and server agree to use a specific bit level of encryption (for example, 40-bit encryption or 128-bit encryption) and also agree which specific encryption algorithm to use. Figure 10-9 illustrates the SSL handshake that occurs before a client and server exchange private-key-encoded business information for the remainder of the secure session.

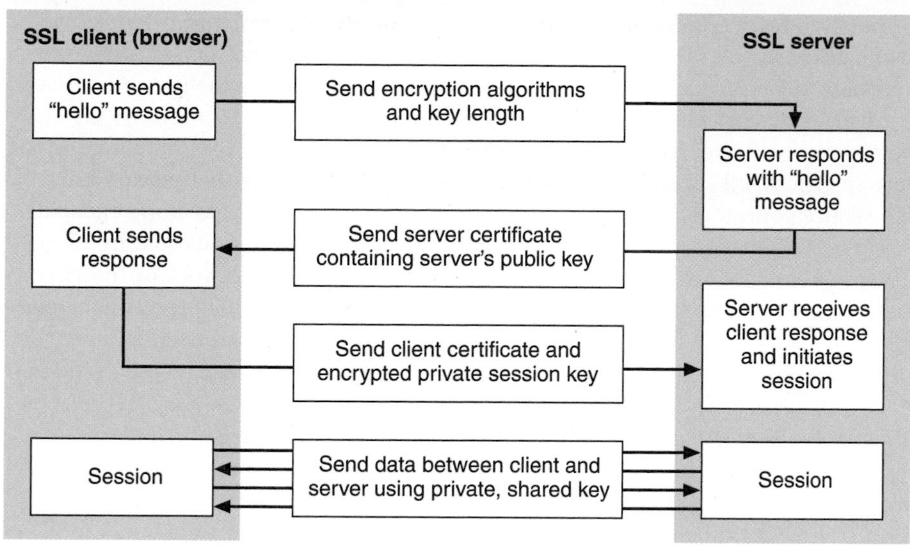

FIGURE 10-9 Establishing an SSL session

Secure HTTP (S-HTTP)

Secure HTTP (S-HTTP) is an extension to HTTP that provides a number of security features, including client and server authentication, spontaneous encryption, and request/response nonrepudiation. The protocol was developed by **CommerceNet**, a consortium of organizations interested in promoting electronic commerce. S-HTTP provides symmetric encryption for maintaining secret communications and public-key encryption to establish client/server authentication. Either the client or the server can use S-HTTP techniques separately. That is, a client browser may require security through the use of a private (symmetric) key, whereas the server may require client authentication by using public-key techniques.

The details of S-HTTP security are conducted during the initial negotiation session between the client and server. Either the client or the server can specify that a particular security feature be required, optional, or refused. When one party stipulates that a particular security feature be required, the client or server continues the connection only if the other party (client or server) agrees to enforce the specified security. Otherwise, no secure connection is established. Suppose the client browser specifies that encryption is required to render all communications secret. For example, in such a situation, the transactions of a high-fashion clothing designer purchasing silk from a Far East textile house will remain confidential. Eavesdropping competitors cannot learn which fabrics are featured next season. On the other hand, the textile mill may insist that integrity be enforced so that quantities and prices quoted to the purchaser remain intact. In addition, the textile mill may want assurances that the purchaser is who he or she claims to be, not an imposter. A form of nonrepudiation, this security property provides positive confirmation of an offer by a client and makes it impossible for the client to deny ever having made the offer.

S-HTTP differs from SSL in the way it establishes a secure session. SSL carries out a client–server handshake exchange to set up a secure communication, but S-HTTP sets up security details with special packet headers that are exchanged in S-HTTP. The headers define the type of security techniques, including the use of private-key encryption, server authentication, client authentication, and message integrity. Header exchanges also stipulate which specific algorithms each side supports, whether the client or the server (or both) supports the algorithm, and whether the security technique (for example, secrecy) is required, optional, or refused. Once the client and server agree to security implementations enforced between them, all subsequent messages between them during that session are wrapped in a secure container, sometimes called an envelope. A **secure envelope** encapsulates a message and provides secrecy, integrity, and client/server authentication. In other words, it is a complete package. With it, all messages traveling on the network or Internet are encrypted so that they cannot be read. Messages cannot be altered undetectably because integrity mechanisms provide a detection code that signals a message has been altered. Clients and servers are authenticated with digital certificates issued by a recognized certification authority. The secure envelope includes all of these security features. S-HTTP is no longer used by many Web sites. SSL has become a more generally accepted standard for establishing secure communication links between Web clients and Web servers.

You have learned how encryption provides message secrecy and confidentiality, and you have learned how digital certificates serve to authenticate a server to a client, and vice versa. In the next section, you will learn how to implement message integrity, which prevents an interloper from changing a message in transit.

Ensuring Transaction Integrity with Hash Functions

Electronic commerce ultimately involves a client browser sending payment information, order information, and payment instructions to the Web server and that server responding with a confirmation of the order details. If an Internet interloper alters any of the order information in transit, harmful consequences can result. For instance, the perpetrator could alter the shipment address so that he or she receives the merchandise instead of the original customer. This is an example of an **integrity violation**, which occurs whenever a message is altered while in transit between the sender and receiver.

Although it is difficult and expensive to *prevent* a perpetrator from altering a message, there are effective and efficient techniques that allow the receiver to *detect* when a message has been altered. When the receiver—a Web server, for example—receives a damaged message, the receiver simply asks the sender to retransmit the message. Apart from being annoying, a damaged message harms no one as long as both parties are aware of the alteration. Harm occurs when unauthorized message changes go undetected by the message's sender and receiver.

A combination of techniques creates messages that are both tamperproof and authenticated. Additionally, those techniques provide the property of nonrepudiation—making it impossible for message creators to claim that the message was not theirs or that they did not send it. To eliminate fraud and abuse caused by messages being altered, two separate algorithms are applied to a message. First, a hash algorithm is applied to the message. Hash algorithms are **one-way functions**, meaning that there is no way to transform the hash value back to the original message. This approach is acceptable because a hash value is compared only with another hash value to see if there is a match—the original, prehash values are never compared with one another.

All encryption programs convert text into a **message digest**, which is a small integer number that summarizes the encrypted information. A hash algorithm uses no secret key;

the message digest it produces cannot be inverted to produce the original information; the algorithm and information about how it works are publicly available; and finally, hash collisions are nearly impossible. Once the hash function computes a message's hash value, that value is appended to the message. Suppose the message is a purchase order containing the customer's address and payment information. When the merchant receives the purchase order and attached message digest, he or she calculates a message digest value for the message (exclusive of the original attached message digest). If the message digest value that the merchant calculates matches the message digest attached to the message, the merchant then knows the message is unaltered—that is, no interloper altered the amount or the shipping address information. Had someone altered the information, then the merchant's software would compute a message digest value different from the message digest that the client calculated and sent along with the purchase order. The discrepancy between the message digest values would alert both parties that the message was altered in transit.

Ensuring Transaction Integrity with Digital Signatures

Hash functions are not a complete solution. Because the hash algorithm is public and (by design) widely known, anyone could intercept a purchase order, alter the shipping address and quantity ordered, re-create the message digest, and send the message and new message digest on to the merchant. Upon receipt, the merchant would calculate the message digest value and confirm that the two message digest values match. The merchant is fooled into concluding that the message is unadulterated and genuine. To prevent this type of fraud, the sender encrypts the message digest using his or her private key.

An encrypted message digest (message hash value) is called a **digital signature**. A purchase order accompanied by a digital signature provides the merchant with positive identification of the sender and assures the merchant that the message was not altered. Because the message digest is encrypted using a public key, only the owner of the public/private key pair could have encrypted the message digest. Thus, when the merchant decrypts the message with the user's public key and subsequently calculates a matching message digest value, the result is proof that the sender is authentic. Furthermore, matching hash values prove that only the sender could have authored the message (nonrepudiation) because only his or her private key would yield an encrypted message that could be decrypted successfully by an associated public key. This solves the spoofing problem.

If necessary, both parties can agree to provide transaction secrecy in addition to the integrity, nonrepudiation, and authentication that the digital signature provides. Simply encrypting the entire string—digital signature and message—guarantees message secrecy. Used together, public-key encryption, message digests, and digital signatures provide a high level of security for Internet transactions. Figure 10-10 illustrates how a digital signature and a signed message are created and sent.

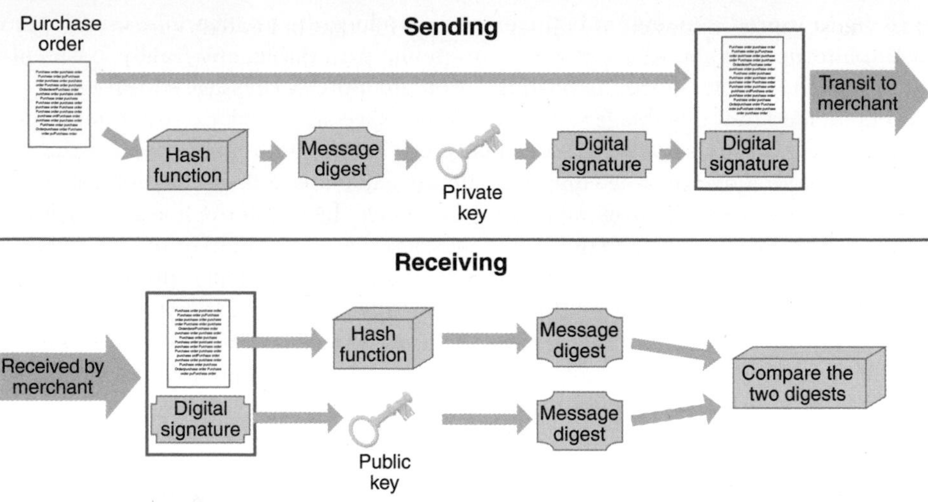

FIGURE 10-10 Sending and receiving a digitally signed message

Since 2000, digital signatures have had the same legal status as traditional signatures in the United States. The European Union and Canada followed closely on the heels of the U.S. legislation and enacted digital signature laws by the end of 2001. Today, most of the world's countries have laws that enable the use of digital signatures.

SECURITY FOR SERVER COMPUTERS

The server is the third link in the client–Internet–server electronic commerce path between the user and a Web server. Servers have vulnerabilities that can be exploited by anyone determined to cause destruction or acquire information illegally. One entry point is the Web server and its software. Other entry points include back-end programs containing data, such as a database and the server on which it runs. Although no system is completely safe, the Web server administrator's job is to make sure that security policies are documented and considered in every part of the electronic commerce operation.

Web Server Threats

Web server software, as you learned in Chapter 8, is designed to deliver Web pages by responding to HTTP requests. A Web server can compromise secrecy if it allows automatic directory listings. The secrecy violation occurs when the contents of a server's folder names are revealed to a Web browser. This can happen when a user enters a URL, such as http://www.somecompany.com/FAQ/, and expects to see the default page in the FAQ directory. The default Web page that the server normally displays is named index.htm or index.html. If that file is not in the directory, a Web server that allows automatic directory listings will display all of the file and folder names in that directory. Then, visitors can click folder names at random and open folders that might not be intended for public disclosure. Careful site administrators turn off this folder name display feature. If a user attempts to browse a folder where protections prevent browsing, the Web server issues a warning message stating that the directory is not available.

One of the most sensitive files on a Web server is the file that holds Web server username–password pairs. An intruder who can access and read that file can enter privileged areas masquerading as a legitimate user. To reduce this risk, most Web servers store user authentication information in encrypted files.

The passwords that users select can be the source of a threat. Users sometimes select passwords that are guessed easily, such as their mother's maiden name, the name of a child, or their telephone number. **Dictionary attack programs** cycle through an electronic dictionary, trying every word and common name as a password.

Users' passwords, once broken, may provide an opening for entry into a server that can remain undetected for a long time. To prevent dictionary attacks, some organizations require users to create passwords that contain a combination of letters, numbers, and special characters that are unlikely to appear in an attack program's dictionary. Other organizations use their own dictionary check as a preventive measure. When a user selects a new password, the password assignment software checks the password against its dictionary and, if it finds a match, refuses to allow the use of that password. Good password assignment software checks against common words, names (including common pet names), acronyms that are commonly used in the organization, and words or characters (including numbers) that have some meaning for the user requesting the password (for example, employees might be prohibited from using their employee numbers as passwords).

Database Threats

Electronic commerce systems store user data and retrieve product information from databases connected to the Web server. Besides storing product information, databases connected to the Web contain valuable and private information that could damage a company irreparably if disclosed or altered. Most database management systems include security features that rely on usernames and passwords. Once a user is authenticated, specific parts of the database become available to that user. However, some databases either store username/password pairs in an unencrypted table, or they fail to enforce security at all and rely on the Web server to enforce security. If unauthorized users obtain user authentication information, they can masquerade as legitimate database users and reveal or download confidential and potentially valuable information. Trojan horse programs hidden within the database system can also reveal information by changing the access rights of various user groups. A Trojan horse can even remove access controls within a database, giving all users complete access to the data—including intruders.

Other Programming Threats

Web server threats can arise from programs executed by the server. Java or C++ programs that are passed to Web servers by a client, or that reside on a server, frequently make use of a buffer. A **buffer** is an area of memory set aside to hold data read from a file or database. A buffer is necessary whenever any input or output operation takes place because a computer can process file information much faster than the information can be read from input devices or written to output devices. Programs filling buffers can malfunction and overfill the buffer, spilling the excess data outside the designated buffer memory area. This is called a **buffer overrun** or **buffer overflow** error. Usually, this occurs because the program contains an error or bug that causes the overflow. Sometimes, however, the buffer overflow is intentional. The Internet Worm of 1988 was such a program. It caused an overflow condition that eventually consumed all resources until the affected computer could no longer function.

A more insidious version of a buffer overflow attack writes instructions into critical memory locations so that when the intruder program has completed its work of overwriting buffers, the Web server resumes execution by loading internal registers with the address of the main attacking program's code. This type of attack can open the Web server to severe damage because the resumed program—which is now the attacker program—may regain control of the computer, exposing its files to disclosure and destruction by the attacking program. Good programming practices can reduce the potential damage from buffer overflows and some computers include hardware that works with the operating system to limit the effects of buffer overflows that are intentionally programmed to create damage.

A similar attack, one in which excessive data is sent to a server, can occur on mail servers. Called a **mail bomb**, the attack occurs when hundreds or even thousands of people each send a message to a particular address. The attack might be launched by a large team of well-organized hackers, but more likely the attack is launched by one or a few hackers who have gained control over others' computers using a Trojan horse virus or some other method of turning those computers into zombies. The accumulated mail received by the target of the mail bomb exceeds the allowed e-mail size limit and can cause e-mail systems to malfunction.

Threats to the Physical Security of Web Servers

Web servers and the computers that are networked closely to them, such as the database servers and application servers used to supply content and transaction-processing capabilities to electronic commerce Web sites, must be protected from physical harm. For many companies, these computers have become repositories of important data (information about customers, products, sales, purchases, and payments). They have also become important parts of the revenue-generating function in many businesses. As key physical resources, these computers and related equipment warrant high levels of protection against threats to their physical security.

As you learned in Chapter 9, many companies use commerce service providers (CSPs) to host their Web sites. The security that CSPs maintain over their physical premises is, in many cases, stronger than the security that a company could provide for computers maintained at its own location.

Companies can take specific steps to protect their Web servers. Many companies maintain backup copies of their servers' contents at a remote location. If the Web server operation is critical to the continuation of the business, a company can maintain a duplicate of the entire Web server physical facility at a remote location. In the case of a system failure, the company's Web operations can be switched over to the backup location in less than a second. Examples of mission-critical Web servers that would warrant such a comprehensive (and expensive) level of physical security include airline reservation systems, stock brokerage firm trading systems, and bank payment clearing systems.

Some companies rely on their service providers to help with Web server security. Major service providers that offer managed services, such as Cogent Communications, Level 3, and VerioSecurity Services, often include Web server security as an add-on service. Other companies hire smaller, specialized security service providers to handle security (see Learning From Failures—Pilot Network Services to learn more about one alternative to this approach). Having a service provider handle security usually adds an additional $1000 to $3000 per month to the bandwidth charges.

LEARNING FROM FAILURES

Pilot Network Services

Pilot Network Services began operations in 1993, at the dawn of commercial use of the Internet. Its goal was to build a network that would be secure for electronic commerce activities. The network it built included its own carefully monitored connections to the Internet and a database of attack signatures. Attack signatures are descriptions of the Internet traffic characteristics that indicate a cracker attack on a Web server. Pilot, as a firm specializing in security services, built an excellent collection of attack signatures and kept it updated much better than other firms that were not security specialists did at that time.

Pilot maintained the Web servers for many of its clients, and it used versions of the operating systems and Web server software that it had customized to be especially resistant to attacks. Pilot's engineers meticulously applied patches for all known points of access to the software and worked to identify new, as yet unknown, points of vulnerability—for which they immediately created and applied protective patches. For customers hosting their own servers, Pilot provided the Internet connection through its own secure network. The router between the client's network and Pilot's network and the operating system running the Pilot network were customized to eliminate any known security loopholes.

Pilot had 24/7 monitoring of its network by computer security experts, in addition to the network technicians that any other Web hosting company would provide as part of a managed services offering. Because it offered high-quality services, its fees were considerably higher than the service charges imposed by other service providers.

Even with their high prices, Pilot had many fans among the largest companies in the United States. Pilot never had more than 300 customers, but it monitored more than 70,000 individual networks for a customer list that included General Electric, PeopleSoft, Sovereign Bancorp, The Washington Post Company, and many other major accounts. By 1999, Pilot appeared to be doing well. Its revenue had increased more than 80 percent over 1998. News releases were issued regularly announcing new customers.

In late 2000, Pilot's stock price began to fall, along with the stock prices of many companies in Internet-related businesses. Although Pilot's sales were growing, its costs were escalating at an even more rapid rate. The company had never reported a profit, and its annual losses had increased to $21.7 million in 2000. Pilot executives assured customers that the company was financially sound, but the ability of companies in Internet-related businesses to survive on the promise of future earnings had disappeared. Pilot's ability to raise the cash it needed to continue operating had vanished.

In early 2001, some Pilot customers noticed that the service was failing. Phone calls and e-mails were not being returned quickly. On the afternoon of April 25, 2001, Pilot employees received four e-mails. The first explained that telephones would be disconnected that evening. The second asked all employees to turn in their mobile phones and pagers. The third announced that the chief financial officer had resigned. The last e-mail announced that all employees were out of a job as of 4:30 p.m.

Pilot's clients, many of which found out about the collapse from the Pilot employees who had been servicing their accounts, immediately faced serious problems. Connections

Continued

to the Internet vanished with no warning. The companies that had used Pilot to host their entire Web operations were in an even worse situation. A group of Pilot customers convinced AT&T (the provider of Pilot's Internet connections) to continue to carry traffic from Pilot, even though Pilot had not paid AT&T. Providian Financial, a major bank holding company and credit card processor, sent its own employees into Pilot operations centers to keep Providian's Web servers operating. Other Pilot customers that were Providian's competitors protested, concerned that their Web servers were suddenly open and vulnerable.

Several of Pilot's competitors tried to raise funding to take over the business, but all of those attempts failed, and on May 9, 2001—two weeks after the collapse—AT&T cut Internet service and Pilot was liquidated. Pilot's former customers scrambled to hire security staff, find alternative hosting firms, or find other ways to keep their Web sites operating. The lesson from this failure is that security is a critical part of an electronic commerce operation. It should be handled with the same care that a company would use to protect any physical asset. If any part of the security function is handed over to another company, that company's condition becomes an important concern and must be monitored carefully and continually.

Access Control and Authentication

Access control and authentication refers to controlling who and what has access to the Web server. Most people who work with Web servers in electronic commerce environments do not sit at a keyboard connected to the server. Instead, they access the server from a client computer. Recall that authentication is verification of the identity of the entity requesting access to the computer. Just as users can authenticate servers with which they are interacting, servers can authenticate individual users. When a server requires positive identification of a user, it requests that the client send a certificate.

The server can authenticate a user in several ways. First, the certificate represents the user's admittance voucher. If the server cannot decrypt the user's digital signature contained in the certificate using the user's public key, then the certificate did not come from the true owner. Otherwise, the server is certain that the certificate came from the owner. This procedure prevents the use of fraudulent certificates to gain entry to a secure server. Second, the server checks the timestamp on the certificate to ensure that the certificate has not expired. A server will reject an expired certificate and provide no further service. Third, a server can use a callback system in which the user's client computer name and address are checked against a list of usernames and assigned client computer addresses. Such a system works especially well in an intranet where usernames and client computers are controlled closely and assigned systematically. On the Internet, a callback system is more difficult to manage—particularly if client users are mobile and work from different locations. It is easy to see how certificates issued by trusted CAs play a central role in authenticating client computers and their users. Certificates provide attribution—irrefutable evidence of identity—if a security breach occurs.

Usernames and passwords can also provide some element of protection. To authenticate users using passwords and usernames, the server must acquire and store a database containing rightful users' passwords and usernames. Many Web server systems store usernames and passwords in a file. Large electronic commerce sites usually keep username/password combinations in a separate database with built-in security features.

The easiest way to store passwords is to maintain usernames in plain text and encrypt passwords using a one-way encryption algorithm. With the plain text username and encrypted password stored, the system can validate users when they log on by checking the usernames they enter against the list of usernames stored in the database. The password that a user enters when he or she logs on to a system is encrypted. Then the resulting encrypted password from the user is checked against the encrypted password stored in the database. If the two encrypted versions of the password match for the given user, the login is accepted. That is why even a system administrator cannot tell you what your forgotten password is on most systems. Instead, the administrator must assign a new temporary password that the user can change to another password. Passwords are not immune to discovery, and a person truly intent on stealing a password can often figure out a way to do so.

Note that the site visitor can save his or her username and password as a cookie on the client computer, which allows access to subscription areas of the site without entering the username and password on subsequent site visits. The trouble with that system of cookies is that the information might be stored on the client computer in plain text. If the cookie contains login and password information, then that information is visible to anyone who has access to the user's computer.

Web servers often provide access control list security to restrict file access to selected users. An **access control list (ACL)** is a list or database of files and other resources and the usernames of people who can access the files and other resources. Each file has its own access control list. When a client computer requests Web server access to a file or document that has been configured to require an access check, the Web server checks the resource's ACL file to determine if the user is allowed to access that file. This system is especially convenient to restrict access of files on an intranet server so that individuals can only access selected files on a need-to-know basis. The Web server can exercise fine control over resources by further subdividing file access into the activities of read, write, or execute. For example, some users may be permitted to read the corporate employee handbook, but not allowed to update or write to the file. Only the human resources (HR) manager would have write access to the employee handbook, and that access privilege is stored along with the HR manager's ID and password in an ACL.

Firewalls

A **firewall** is software or a hardware–software combination that is installed in a network to control the packet traffic moving through it. Most organizations place a firewall at the Internet entry point of their networks. The firewall provides a defense between a network and the Internet or between a network and any other network that could pose a threat. Firewalls all operate on the following principles:

- All traffic from inside to outside and from outside to inside the network must pass through it.
- Only authorized traffic, as defined by the local security policy, is allowed to pass through it.
- The firewall itself is immune to penetration.

Those networks inside the firewall are often called **trusted**, whereas networks outside the firewall are called **untrusted**. Acting as a filter, firewalls permit selected messages to flow into and out of the protected network. For example, one security policy a firewall might enforce is to allow all HTTP (Web) traffic to pass back and forth, but disallow FTP or Telnet requests either into or out of the protected network. Ideally, firewall protection should prevent access to networks inside the firewall by unauthorized users, and thus prevent access to sensitive information. Simultaneously, a firewall should not obstruct legitimate users. Authorized employees outside the firewall ought to have access to firewall-protected networks and data files. Firewalls can separate corporate networks from one another and prevent personnel in one division from accessing information from another division of the same company. Using firewalls to segment a corporate network into secure zones serves as a coarse need-to-know filter.

Large organizations that have multiple sites and many locations must install a firewall at each location that has an external connection to the Internet. Such a system ensures an unbroken security perimeter that is effective for the entire corporation. In addition, each firewall in the organization must follow the same security policy. Otherwise, one firewall might permit one type of transaction to flow into the corporate network that another excludes. Without a consistent policy, an unwanted access that occurs through a breach in one firewall can expose the information assets of the entire corporation to the threat.

Organizations should remove from their firewalls any unnecessary software. Having fewer software programs on the system should reduce the chances for malevolent software security breaches. Because the firewall computer is used only as a firewall and not as a general-purpose computing machine, only essential operating system software and firewall-specific protection software should remain on the computer. Access to a firewall should be restricted to a console physically connected directly to the firewall machine. Managers should forbid remote administration of the firewall to avoid the threat of an outside attacker gaining access to the firewall by posing as an administrator.

Firewalls are classified into the following categories: packet filter, gateway server, and proxy server. **Packet-filter firewalls** examine all data flowing back and forth between the trusted network (within the firewall) and the Internet. Packet filtering examines the source and destination addresses and ports of incoming packets and denies or permits entrance to the packets based on a preprogrammed set of rules.

Gateway servers are firewalls that filter traffic based on the application requested. Gateway servers limit access to specific applications such as Telnet, FTP, and HTTP. Application gateways arbitrate traffic between the inside network and the outside network. In contrast to a packet-filter technique, an application-level firewall filters requests and logs them at the application level, rather than at the lower IP level. A gateway firewall provides a central point where all requests can be classified, logged, and later analyzed. An example is a gateway-level policy that permits incoming FTP requests, but blocks outgoing FTP requests. That policy prevents employees inside a firewall from downloading potentially dangerous programs from the outside.

Proxy server firewalls are firewalls that communicate with the Internet on the private network's behalf. When a browser is configured to use a proxy server firewall, the firewall passes the browser request to the Internet. When the Internet sends back a response, the proxy server relays it back to the browser. Proxy servers are also used to serve as a huge cache for Web pages.

One problem faced by companies that have employees working from home is that the location of computers outside the traditional boundaries of the company's physical site expands the number of computers that must be protected by the firewall.

This **perimeter expansion** problem is particularly troublesome for companies that have salespeople using laptop computers to access confidential company information from all types of networks at customer locations, vendor locations, and even public locations, such as airports.

Another problem faced by organizations connected to the Internet is that their servers are under almost constant attack. Crackers spend a great deal of time and energy on attempts to enter the servers of organizations. Some of these crackers use automated programs to continually attempt to gain access to servers. Organizations often install intrusion detection systems as part of their firewalls. **Intrusion detection systems** are designed to monitor attempts to login to servers and analyze those attempts for patterns that might indicate a cracker's attack is underway.

Once the intrusion detection system identifies an attack, it can block further attempts that originate from the same IP address until the organization's security staff can examine and analyze the access attempts and determine whether they are an attack.

In addition to firewalls installed on organizations' networks, it is possible to install software-only firewalls on individual client computers. These firewalls are often called **personal firewalls**. The use of personal firewalls, such as **ZoneAlarm**, has become an important tool in the protection of expanded network perimeters for many companies. Many home computer users are installing personal firewalls on their home networks. You can learn more about firewall protection for your home computer at the **Gibson Research Shields Up!** Web site.

ORGANIZATIONS THAT PROMOTE COMPUTER SECURITY

Following the occurrence of the Internet Worm of 1988, a number of organizations were formed to share information about threats to computer systems. These organizations are devoted to the principle that sharing information about attacks and defenses for those attacks can help everyone create better computer security. Some of the organizations began at universities; others were launched by government agencies. In this section, you will learn about some of these organizations and their resources.

CERT

In 1988, a group of researchers met to study the infamous Internet Worm attack soon after it occurred. They wanted to understand how worms worked and how to prevent damage from future attacks of this type. The National Computer Security Center, part of the National Security Agency, initiated a series of meetings to figure out how to respond to future security breaks that might affect thousands of people. Soon after those meetings, the U.S. government created the Computer Emergency Response Team and housed it at Carnegie Mellon University in Pittsburgh.

The organization is now operated as part of the federally funded Software Engineering Institute at Carnegie Mellon, and it has changed its legal name from the Computer Emergency Response Team (which had been abbreviated to "CERT" by most people who wrote and talked about it) to **CERT**. CERT still maintains an effective and quick communications infrastructure among security experts so that security incidents can be avoided or handled quickly.

Today, CERT responds to thousands of security incidents each year and provides a wealth of information to help Internet users and companies become more knowledgeable about security risks. CERT posts alerts to inform the Internet community about security events, and it is regarded as a primary authoritative source for information about viruses, worms, and other types of attacks.

Other Organizations

CERT is the most prominent of these organizations and has formed relationships, such as the **Internet Security Alliance**, with other industry associations. However, CERT is not the only computer security resource. In 1989, one year after CERT was formed, a cooperative research and educational organization called the Systems Administrator, Audit, Network, and Security Institute was launched. Now known as the **SANS Institute**, this organization includes thousands of members who work in computer security consulting firms and information technology departments of companies as auditors, systems administrators, and network administrators.

Many SANS education and research efforts yield resources such as news releases, research reports, security alerts, and white papers that are available on the Web site at no cost. SANS also sells publications to generate funds that it uses for research and educational programs. The SANS Institute operates the **SANS Internet Storm Center**, a Web site that provides current information on the location and intensity of computer attacks throughout the world.

Purdue University's Center for Education and Research in Information Assurance and Security **(CERIAS)** is a center for multidisciplinary research and education in information security. The CERIAS Web site provides resources in computer, network, and communications security and includes a section on information assurance.

The **Center for Internet Security** is a not-for-profit cooperative organization devoted to helping companies that operate electronic commerce Web sites reduce the risk of disruptions from technical failures or deliberate attacks on their computer systems. It also provides information to auditors who review such systems and to insurance companies that provide coverage for companies who operate such systems.

For current information about computer security, you can visit **CSO Online**, which carries articles that have appeared in *CSO Magazine* along with other news items related to computer security. A British publication, **Infosecurity.com**, is available online and includes articles about all types of online security issues. The U.S. Department of Justice's **Cybercrime** site offers information about computer crimes and intellectual property violations.

Computer Forensics and Ethical Hacking

A small group of firms, endorsed by corporations and security organizations, have the unlikely job of breaking into client computers. Called **computer forensics experts** or **ethical hackers**, these computer sleuths are hired to probe PCs and locate information that can be used in legal proceedings. The field of **computer forensics** is responsible for the collection, preservation, and analysis of computer-related evidence. Ethical hackers are often hired by companies to test computer security safeguards. Links to the Web sites of several companies that offer computer forensics and ethical hacking services are included in the Additional Resources section of the Online Companion for this chapter.

Summary

Electronic commerce is vulnerable to a wide range of security threats. Attacks against electronic commerce systems can disclose or manipulate proprietary information. The three general assets that companies engaging in electronic commerce must protect are client computers, computer communication channels, and Web servers. Key security provisions in each of these parts of the Web client-Internet-Web server linkage are secrecy, integrity, and available service. Threats to commerce can occur anywhere in the commerce chain. More subtle threats are delivered as client-side applets. Java, JavaScript, and ActiveX controls can run on client machines and breach security. Cookies, if not controlled and used properly, can present threats to client computers. Antivirus software is an important element in the protection of client computers.

Communication channels, in general, and the Internet, in particular, are especially vulnerable to attacks. Encryption provides secrecy, and several forms of encryption are available that use hash functions or other more complex algorithms. They include private-key and public-key techniques. Integrity protections ensure that messages between clients and servers are not altered. Digital certificates provide both integrity controls and user authentication. Several Internet protocols, including Secure Sockets Layer and Secure HTTP, use encryption to provide secure Internet transmission capabilities. As wireless networks have grown to become important parts of the data communication infrastructure, security concerns have increased. Although many wireless networks (especially home networks) are installed without security features, wireless encryption methods that make them more secure are available. Most wireless networks installed in businesses today do have wireless encryption.

Web servers are susceptible to security threats. Programs that run on servers have the potential to damage databases, abnormally terminate server software, or make subtle changes in proprietary information. Attacks can come from within the server in the form of programs, or they can come from outside the server. Backup copies of servers provide redundancy in the case of a physical threat to a server. The Web server must be protected from both physical threats and Internet-based attacks on its software. Protections for the server include access control and authentication, provided by username and password login procedures and client certificates. Firewalls can be used to separate trusted inside computer networks and clients from untrusted outside networks, including other divisions of a company's enterprise network system and the Internet.

A number of organizations have been formed to share information about computer security threats and defenses. When large security outbreaks occur, the members of these organizations join together and discuss methods to locate and eliminate the threat. Computer forensics firms that undertake attacks against their clients' computers can play an important role in helping to identify security weaknesses.

Key Terms

Access control list (ACL)
Active content
Active wiretapping
ActiveX
Advanced Encryption Standard (AES)
Antivirus software
Applet
Asymmetric encryption
Backdoor
Biometric security device
Black hat hacker
Botnet
Buffer
Buffer overrun
Buffer overflow
Certification authority (CA)
Cipher text
Collision
Computer forensics
Computer forensics expert
Computer security
Countermeasure
Cracker
Cryptography
Cybervandalism
Data Encryption Standard (DES)
Decrypted
Decryption program
Delay attack
Denial attack
Denial-of-service (DoS) attack
Dictionary attack program
Digital certificate
Digital ID
Digital signature
Distributed denial-of-service (DDoS) attack
Domain name server (DNS)
Eavesdropper
Encryption
Encryption algorithm
Encryption program
Ethical hacker
Firewall
First-party cookies
Gateway servers
Hacker
Hash algorithm
Hash coding
Hash value
Integrity
Integrity violation
Intrusion detection system
Java sandbox
JavaScript
Key
Logical security
Macro virus
Mail bomb
Man-in-the-middle exploit
Masquerading
Message digest
Multivector virus
Necessity
Necessity threat
One-way function
Open session
Packet-filter firewall
Perimeter expansion
Persistent cookie
Personal firewall
Phishing expeditions
Physical security
Plain text
Plug-ins
Pretty Good Privacy (PGP)
Privacy

Private key
Private-key encryption
Proxy server firewall
Public key
Public-key encryption
Robotic network
Scripting language
Secrecy
Secure envelope
Secure Sockets Layer (SSL)
Secure Sockets Layer-Extended Validation (SSL-EV) digital certificate
Security policy
Session cookie
Session key
Signed (message or code)
Sniffer program
Spoofing
Stateless connection
Steganography
Symmetric encryption
Third-party cookies
Threat
Triple Data Encryption Standard (Triple DES or 3DES)
Trojan horse
Trusted (network)
Untrusted (network)
Untrusted Java applet
Warchalking
Wardrivers
Web bug
White hat hacker
Wireless Encryption Protocol (WEP)
Worm
Zombie
Zombie farm

Review Questions

RQ1. Refer to Figure 10-1. In about 100 words, discuss two threats that you would place in Quadrant II and explain why you would classify them as Quadrant II threats.

RQ2. In about 200 words, explain why Web sites use cookies. In your answer, discuss the reasons that cookies were first devised and explain where cookies are stored.

RQ3. Conficker (see Figure 10-5) is a multivector worm. In about 100 words, explain why the multivector nature of this worm has made it a more severe threat than it would otherwise be.

RQ4. Assume you are working for a medium-sized company that sells products on its Web site and that the company keeps the computers that run its Web server, database server, and transaction processing server in the office next to yours. In about 100 words, briefly describe what a biometric security device is and explain how your employer might use one or more of these devices to protect its servers.

RQ5. In about 200 words, describe the security threats that a company could face when it adds wireless access points (WAPs) to its network. Assume that the company occupies the six middle floors in a 12-story office building that is located in a downtown business area between two other buildings of similar height. Briefly explain how the company could reduce the risks it faces.

RQ6. Many organizations rely on a firewall to prevent or deter threats to information security that arise from outside the organization. In about 100 words, explain what the perimeter expansion problem is and why it can prevent a firewall from achieving its objective.

Exercises

E1. Wilderness Trailhead, Inc. (WTI) is a retailer that offers hiking, rock-climbing, and survival gear for sale on its Web site. WTI offers about 1200 different items for sale and has about 1000 visitors per day at its Web site. The company makes about 200 sales each day on its site, with an average transaction value of $372. WTI sells products primarily through its Web site to customers in the United States and Canada. WTI ships orders from its two warehouses; one in Vancouver, British Columbia, and another in Shoreline, Washington. WTI accepts four major credit cards and processes its own credit card transactions. It stores records of all transactions on a database server that shares a small room with the Web server computer at WTI's main offices in a small industrial park just outside of Bellingham, Washington. In about 500 words, outline a security policy for the WTI database server. Be sure to consider the threats that exist because that server stores customer credit card numbers. You can use the links included in the Online Companion for this exercise.

E2. You are on the information technology staff of a medium-sized life insurance company that sells policies online. Consider the reasons that programs such as Java applets that run on client machines are considered security threats. In about 200 words, explain how these programs could breach security and outline three specific things your company should include in its security policy that would minimize these threats. Consult sources on the Internet or in your library to help you complete this exercise.

E3. Third-party assurance providers such as **BBBOnline, Inc.**, and **Truste** sell their services to businesses that want to encourage Web site visitors to trust them with their personal information. Review the Web site of one or more of these third-party assurance providers and identify the security features the provider considers important in Web sites that it approves. Select two of the security features you identify and write a 200-word explanation of why the assurance provider considers these features to be important elements for preserving the privacy of site visitor information.

E4. Using your library or your favorite search engine, find three Web sites that have an SSL-EV digital certificate. Note that some sites that do have SSL-EV certificates will not show the green background until you log in to the site or place an item in the site's shopping cart. For each site, write a paragraph in which you identify the CA that provides the SSL-EV certificate and explain why that site decided to incur the additional expense of buying an SSL-EV certificate. The Online Companion entry for this exercise includes links to CAs that sell SSL-EV digital certificates, which you might find useful.

Cases

C1. Bibliofind

Bibliofind was one of the first Web sites to specialize in hard-to-find and collectible books. The site featured a powerful search engine for used and rare books. The search engine's database was populated with the results of Bibliofind's daily surveys of a worldwide network of suppliers. Registered site visitors could specify the title for which they were searching, a price range, and whether they were seeking a first edition. The site also allowed visitors to build a wish list that would trigger an e-mail when a specific book on the list became available.

Bibliofind had developed a large customer list, an excellent reputation, and a solid network of rare book dealers, all of which made the company an attractive acquisition for other online bookstores. In 1999, Amazon.com bought Bibliofind, but Bibliofind continued to operate its own Web site and conduct its business as it had before the acquisition.

In 2001, Bibliofind's Web site was hacked. The cracker had gained access to the company's Web server and replaced the company's Web pages with defaced versions. Bibliofind shut down its Web site for several days and undertook a complete review of its Web site's security. When the company's IT staff examined the server logs carefully, they found that the Web page hacking was only the tip of the iceberg. Entries in the logs showed that attackers had been accessing Bibliofind's computers for more than four months. Even worse, some of the crackers had been able to go through the Web servers to gain access to the computers that held Bibliofind customer information, including names, addresses, and credit card numbers. That information had been stored in plain text files on Bibliofind's transaction servers.

Bibliofind called in state and federal law enforcement officials to investigate the hacking incidents and sent an e-mail notification to the 98,000 customers whose private information might have been obtained by the crackers. The investigation did not result in any arrests, nor did it determine the identity of the intruders. Many of Bibliofind's customers were very upset when they learned what had happened.

A month after the hacking incident, Amazon.com moved Bibliofind into its zShops online mall (zShops was the original name of Amazon Marketplace). As an Amazon zShop, Bibliofind could process its transactions through Amazon's system and no longer needed to maintain private information about its customers on its computers. Eventually, Bibliofind was closed down. A successful business had been seriously damaged because it failed to maintain adequate security over the customer information it had gathered.

Required:

1. In about 300 words, explain how Bibliofind might have used firewalls to prevent the intruders from gaining access to its transaction servers. Be specific about where the firewalls should have been placed in the network and what kinds of rules they should have used to filter network traffic at each point.
2. In about 200 words, explain how encryption might have helped prevent or lessen the effects of Bibliofind's security breach.
3. California has a law that requires companies to inform customers whose private information might have been exposed during a security breach like the one that Bibliofind experienced. Before California enacted this law, businesses argued that the law would encourage nuisance lawsuits. In about 300 words, present arguments for and against this type of legislation.

Note: Your instructor might assign you to a group to complete this case, and might ask you to prepare a formal presentation of your results to your class.

C2. Materials Equipment

You are an information technology (IT) consultant to Materials Equipment, Inc. (MEI), a major industrial equipment distributor. Its products include materials-handling machinery for assembly lines and product-packaging areas, hydraulic equipment (for moving fluids), hoses, hose fittings, and similar items. MEI has been in business for more than 70 years and sells more than $200 million worth of parts and equipment each year to its 3000 customers. MEI's customers are located all over the world, but most are in the United States, Mexico, Malaysia, China, and Singapore.

Joe Everson, MEI's director of sales, has retained you to help him with a new marketing idea. He has read about other companies that have created Web portal sites for customers, and he is interested in developing a portal site that MEI could operate with three other companies that sell products (such as bearings, seals, hoses, and hose fittings) and services (design, layout, and installation of materials-handling equipment) that are complementary to MEI products. The portal would provide MEI customers with a Web site at which they could buy MEI products, buy the products and services of the three MEI strategic partners, and obtain information about current trends in industrial equipment technologies and the application of those technologies. The portal site would also include a used equipment area in which MEI customers could list equipment for sale. Joe believes that giving customers a convenient way to liquidate old equipment will make it easier for his sales representatives to sell new equipment to those customers.

Joe has put together an internal team to examine the feasibility of the portal site, including key employees from MEI's Sales, Finance, Product Engineering, and IT Services departments. The team has identified several security issues that they want to resolve before they take the portal idea much further. Joe would like you to help the team understand two security technologies—digital certificates and encryption—and how these techniques might be used in MEI's proposed portal site.

Required:

1. Prepare two briefing reports of about 700 words each for the MEI portal team—one about digital certificates and one about encryption. Each report should explain the technology and describe one or two common applications.
2. Assume that the MEI portal project is approved and implemented. Further assume that MEI has decided to require each customer that participates in the portal to obtain a digital certificate. Write a memo of about 500 words addressed to potential participants (MEI customers) in which you explain why they must obtain a digital certificate as a condition of participation.

Note: Your instructor might assign you to a group to complete this case, and might ask you to prepare a formal presentation of your results to your class.

For Further Study and Research

Anderson, R. and F. Petitcolas. 1998. "On the Limits of Steganography," *IEEE Journal of Selected Areas in Communications,* 16(4), May, 474–481.

Austin, R. and C. Darby. 2003. "The Myth of Secure Computing," *Harvard Business Review,* 81(6), June, 120–126.

Bank, D. and R. Richmond. 2005 "Where the Dangers Are: The Threats to Information Security That Keep the Experts Up at Night," *The Wall Street Journal,* July 18, R1.

Betts, M. 2000. "Digital Signatures Law to Speed Online B-to-B Deals," *Computerworld,* 34(26), June 26, 8.

Chickowski, E. 2009. "Is Your Information Really Safe?" *Baseline,* April, 18–23.

Connell, S. 2004. "Security Lapses, Lost Equipment Expose Students to Possible ID Theft Loss," *The Los Angeles Times,* August 29, B4.
Costanzo, C. 2003. "Dealing with Phishing and Spoofing," *American Banker,* 168(184), September 24, 10.
Creighton, D. 2004. "Chronology of Virus Attacks," *The Wall Street Journal,* May 13. (http://online.wsj.com/article/0,,SB108362410782000798,00.html)
DoD Directive 5215.1 CSC-STD-001-83. 1983. *Department of Defense Trusted Computer System Evaluation Criteria* (the "Orange Book"), Washington, D.C.
Dunleavey, M. 2005. "Don't Let Data Theft Happen to You," *The New York Times,* July 2, C7.
Erlanger, L. 2002. "Defensive Strategies," *PC Magazine,* 21(19), November 5, 70–72.
Evers, J. 2001. "Hackers Get Credit Card Data from Amazon's Bibliofind," *PC World,* March 6. (http://www.pcworld.com/news/article/0,aid,43582,00.asp)
Files, J. 2005. "For Fourth Time, Judge Seeks to Shield Indian Data," *The New York Times,* October 25, A17.
Gallagher, S. 2002. "Best Buy: May Day Mayday for Security," *Baseline,* June 7. (http://www.baselinemag.com/article2/0,3959,687,00.asp)
Garfinkel, S. and G. Spafford. 2002. *Web Security, Privacy, & Commerce.* Cambridge, MA: O'Reilly.
Glass, B. and D. Fisher. 2004. "Biometrics Security," *PC Magazine,* 23(1), January 20, 66.
Gonsalves, C. 2005. "Computing Insecurity," *eWeek,* May 23, 32.
Gorman, S. 2009. "FBI Suspects Terrorists Are Exploring Cyber Attacks," *The Wall Street Journal,* November 18, A4.
Gorman, S., E. Ramstad, J. Solomon, Y. Dreazen, R. Smith, and R. Sidel. 2009. "Cyber Blitz Hits U.S., Korea," *The Wall Street Journal,* July 9, A1, A4.
Grow, B., K. Epstein, and C. Tschang. 2008. "The New E-spionage Threat," *Business Week,* April 21, 33–41.
Gurley, J. 2001. "From Wired To Wiretapped," *Fortune,* 144(7), October 15, 214–215.
Hancock, B. 2001. "Terrorism and Steganography: Shaken, Not Stirred," *Computers & Security,* 20(2) 110–111.
Hayes, F. 2002. "Thanks, Warchalkers," *Computerworld,* 36(35), August 26, 56.
Hoover, J. 2008. "What Could Slow Down the Windows Server Juggernaut?" *Information Week,* March 3, 34.
Johnson, J. 2008. "Security Smarts: At Pacific Northwest National Laboratory, Network Defense Requires Layers of Strategic Thinking," *Information Week,* February 25, 43–46.
Katzenheisser, S. and F. Petitcolas (Eds.). 1999. *Information Hiding Techniques for Steganography and Digital Watermarking,* Norwood. MA: Artech House.
Krim, J. 2003. "WiFi Is Open, Free and Vulnerable to Hackers: Safeguarding Wireless Networks Too Much Trouble for Many Users," *The Washington Post,* July 27, A1.
Krim, J. 2003. "Microsoft Critic Forced Out, Firm Does Business With Software Giant," *The Washington Post,* September 26, E1.
Kuchinskas, S. 2003. "Lack of Trust Could Impact E-Commerce Sales," *E-Commerce Guide,* December 3.
Lee, C. 2008. "GAO Finds Data Protection Lagging," *The Washington Post,* February 26, A15.
Lohmeyer, D., J. McCrory, and S. Pogreb. 2002. "Managing Information Security," *The McKinsey Quarterly,* June, 12–15.

Mackey, D. 2003. *Web Security for Network and System Administrators.* Boston: Course Technology.

Manes, S. 2001. "Security, Microsoft Style: No Safety Net?" *PC World,* 19(11), November, 210.

McCracken, H. 2004. "Microsoft's Security Problem—and Ours," *PC World,* 22(1), January, 25.

McMillan, R. 2010. "After One Year, Seven Million Conficker Infections," *PC World,* January, 44.

Menn, J. 2009. "Crippling Cyber-attacks Relied on 200,000 Computers,"*Financial Times,* July 10, 6.

Nakashima, E. 2009. "Obama Set to Create A Cybersecurity Czar With Broad Mandate," *The Washington Post,* May 26, A4.

Nerney, C. 2003. "Get It Right, Redmond," *Internet News,* May 12. (http://www.internetnews.com/commentary/article.php/2205081)

The New York Times. 2009. "Hackers Steal South Korean, U.S. Military Secrets," December 18.

Nielsen, J. 2004. "User Education Is Not the Answer to Security Problems," *Alertbox,* October 25. (http://www.useit.com/alertbox/20041025.html)

Null, C. 2000. "Name Grab," *PC Computing,* 13(4), April, 40–42.

Palmer, C. 2001. "Ethical Hacking," *IBM Systems Journal,* 40(3), 769–780.

Pereira, J. 2008. "Data Theft Carried Out on Network Thought Secure," *The Wall Street Journal,* March 31, B4.

Petreley, N. 2001. "The Cost of Free IIS," *Computerworld,* 35(43), October 22, 49.

Piazza, P. 2003. "Phishing for Trouble," *Security Management,* 47(12), December, 32–33.

Powell, T. 2004. "Quick Tips for Web Application Security," *Network World,* 21(20), May 17, 50–51.

Regan, K. 2001. "Hack Victim Bibliofind to Move to Amazon," *E-Commerce Times,* April 6. (http://www.ecommercetimes.com/story/8768.html)

Rivest, R. 1992. *The MD5 Message-Digest Algorithm,* IETF RFC 1321.

Rosencrance, L. 2004. "Federal Audit Raises Doubts About IRS Security System," *Computerworld,* 38(36), September 6, 9.

Rutrell, Y. 2001. "So Many Patches, So Little Time," *InternetWeek,* October 8, 1–2.

Sang-Hun, C. and J. Markoff. 2009. "Cyberattacks Jam Government and Commercial Web Sites in U.S. and South Korea," *New York Times,* July 7, 4.

Sausner, R. 2009. "SSL Comes Under Fire," *Bank Technology News,* 22(9), September, 14.

Security Management, 2002. "Government Infosec Gets Failing Grade," 46(2), February, 34–35.

Shipley, G. 2001. "Growing Up with a Little Help from the Worm," *Network Computing,* 12(20), October 1, 39.

Shively, G. 2002. *Network InSecurity.* Newport Beach, CA: PivX Solutions.

Skoudis, E. 2005. "Five Malicious Code Myths and How To Protect Yourself in 2005," *SearchSecurity.com,* January 4. (http://searchsecurity.techtarget.com/tip/1,289483,sid14_gci1041736,00.html)

Steiner, I. 2008. "eBay Changes Criteria for Sellers 'Buyer Dissatisfaction' Rate," *AuctionBytes.com,* February 8. (http://www.auctionbytes.com/cab/abn/y08/m02/i08/s02)

Sterling, B. 2001. "Steganography Goes Digital," *The New York Times,* December 9, 102.

Strom, D. 2009. "Make E-mail Encryption Effortless," *Baseline,* December, 32–33.

Stuttard, D. and M. Pinto. 2007. *The Web Application Hacker's Handbook: Discovering and Exploiting Security Flaws.* New York: Wiley.

Thompson, H. and J. Whittaker. 2002. "Testing for Software Security," *Dr. Dobb's Journal,* November, 24–32.

U.S. National Institute of Standards and Technology. 1993. *Data Encryption Standard (DES): Federal Information Processing Standards Publication 46–2.* Gaithersburg, MD: U.S. Computer Systems Laboratory.

Vaidyanathan, G. and S. Mautone. 2009. "Security in Dynamic Web Content Management Systems Applications," *Communications of the ACM,* 52(12), December, 121–125.

Vamosi, R. 2010. "New Banking Trojan Horses Gain Polish," *PC World,* January, 41–42.

Verton, D. 2001. "Microsoft in Hot Seat After Code Red," *Computerworld,* 35(32), August 6, 1–2.

Verton, D. 2002. "Mapping of Wireless Networks Could Pose Enterprise Risk," *Computerworld,* August 14. (http://computerworld.com/securitytopics/security/story/0,10801,73479,00.html)

Vijayan, J. 2001. "Corporations Left Hanging as Security Outsourcer Shuts Doors," *Computerworld,* 35(18), April 30, 13.

Vijayan, J. 2005. "Companies Scramble to Bolster Online Security," *Computerworld,* 39(10), March 7, 1, 61.

Wilshusen, G. and D. Powner. 2009. "Cybersecurity: Continued Efforts Are Needed to Protect Information Systems from Evolving Threats," *GAO Reports,* November 17, 1–20.

Wilson, T. 2008. "Before Walls Go Up, Ask What You're Really Protecting," *Information Week,* April 14, 26.

Wolfe, D. 2009. "Online Perils," *American Banker,* December 9, 5.

Zhao, J. and S. Zhao. 2010. "Opportunities and Threats: A Security Assessment of State E-government Websites," *Government Information Quarterly,* 27(1), January, 49–56.

CHAPTER **11**

PAYMENT SYSTEMS FOR ELECTRONIC COMMERCE

LEARNING OBJECTIVES

In this chapter, you will learn about:

- The basic functions of online payment systems
- The use of payment cards in electronic commerce
- The history and future of electronic cash
- How electronic wallets work
- The use of stored-value cards in electronic commerce
- Internet technologies and the banking industry

INTRODUCTION

In 1991, a teenager named Max Levchin immigrated from the Ukraine to the United States. Settling in Chicago, Levchin had a burning interest in cryptography. Growing up in a Soviet police state convinced him that the ability to send coded messages that could not be read or intercepted was both important and useful. He majored in computer science at the University of Illinois and spent many hours at the school's **Center for Supercomputing**, pursuing his passion for making and breaking codes. When he graduated in 1998, he wanted to follow the American dream of turning his knowledge into money, so he headed for the heart of the computer industry in Palo Alto, California. Levchin's plan to build the ultimate transmission encryption scheme has not yet panned out, but he has managed to turn his knowledge into a successful business. As cofounder and chief technical officer of **PayPal**, an online payment processing company that you will learn about in this chapter, Levchin has used his expertise in cryptography and computer security to protect the firm from losses that could destroy it.

PayPal, founded in 1999, operates a service that lets people exchange money over the Internet. PayPal immediately carved itself a niche as the most popular payment system for processing auction payments on eBay. People can also use PayPal to send money to anyone who has an e-mail address, and a growing number of online stores accept PayPal in addition to (or instead of) credit cards. A number of charities accept donations through PayPal as well. These uses of PayPal, transferring money from one individual to another and as an alternative to paying by credit card at online stores, have grown rapidly in recent years. PayPal charges very small fees to business users and no fees at all to individuals, so its profit margins are small. However, it earns these small profit margins on a very large number of transactions.

One major concern for PayPal is that a single, well-organized, large-scale fraud attack could put the company out of business quickly. Levchin's contribution to the company's success was his development of payment surveillance software that continually monitors PayPal transactions. The software searches millions of transactions as they occur every day and looks for patterns that might indicate fraud. The software notifies PayPal managers immediately when it finds something suspicious.

The software has worked well. Companies that process credit card transactions have experienced much larger fraud occurrence rates on the Web (about 1.13 percent) than in physical stores (about .70 percent). PayPal has kept its fraud rate below .50 percent. As long as PayPal can keep its fraud rate low, it can continue to charge lower transaction fees than its competitors and still make a profit.

PayPal's largest customer group has always been the participants (buyers and sellers) on the auction Web site eBay. As you will learn in this chapter, eBay spent three years working to establish its own payments service that could compete effectively with PayPal but finally gave up and bought PayPal for $1.4 billion. Today, PayPal offers payment services under its own name as a division of eBay.

ONLINE PAYMENT BASICS

An important function of electronic commerce sites is the handling of payments over the Internet. Most electronic commerce involves the exchange of some form of money for goods or services. As you learned in Chapter 5, many transactions of payments between B2B companies are made using electronic funds transfers (EFTs). In this chapter, you will learn about a number of online payment alternatives that are available to businesses and individual consumers for B2C transactions.

Online payment systems for consumer electronic commerce are still evolving. A number of proposals and implementations of payment systems currently compete for dominance. Regardless of format, electronic payments are far cheaper than mailing paper checks. Electronic payments can be convenient for customers and can save companies money. Estimates of the cost of billing one person by mail range between $1 and $1.50. Sending bills and receiving payments over the Internet can drop the transaction cost to an average of 50 cents per bill. The total savings is huge when the unit cost is multiplied by the number of customers who could use electronic payment. For example, a telephone company in a major metropolitan area might have 5 million customers, each of whom receives a bill every month. In one year, a savings of 50 cents on each of those 60 million bills adds up to about $30 million. The environmental impact is also significant. Those 60 million paper bills weigh about 1.7 million pounds. It takes 2200 trees to make that much paper—in addition to the energy consumed and the wastes generated in the paper-making process.

Today, four basic ways to pay for purchases dominate both traditional and electronic business-to-consumer commerce. Cash, checks, credit cards, and debit cards account for more than 90 percent of all consumer payments in the United States today. A small but growing percentage of consumer payments are made by electronic transfer. The most popular consumer electronic transfers are automated payments of auto loans, insurance payments, and mortgage payments made from consumers' checking accounts. Figure 11-1 shows forecasted forms of payment for U.S. consumer transactions (both online and offline) for 2010 and 2020.

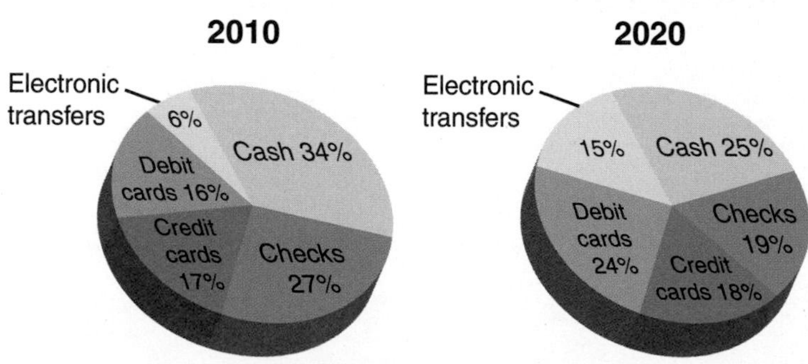

Adapted from forecasts compiled by ePaynews.com

FIGURE 11-1 Forecasted forms of payment for U.S. consumer transactions

Credit cards are by far the most popular method that consumers use to pay for online purchases. Recent surveys have found that more than 90 percent of worldwide consumer Internet purchases are paid for with credit cards. In the United States, the proportion is about 97 percent. Although credit and debit cards dominate online transactions today, industry analysts expect noncard payment alternatives (such as PayPal) to become increasingly popular, especially for smaller purchase denominations.

Another payment medium is limited-use scrip. **Scrip** is digital cash minted by a company instead of by a government. Most scrip cannot be exchanged for cash; it must be exchanged for goods or services by the company that issued the scrip. Scrip is like a gift certificate that is good at more than one store. In the early days of the Web, many experts predicted that scrip would become a popular way of making payments for consumer goods and services online. Unfortunately for many investors and companies, this turned out not to be true. Any online product or service must meet a real need of consumers, and it must not require those consumers to learn a new way to do something that they are already comfortable doing. The new product or service must also integrate well with existing systems and practices. Scrip did not do this. Most current scrip offerings, such as **eScrip**, focus on the not-for-profit fundraising market, which consists mainly of primary and secondary schools in the United States.

Online businesses must offer their customers payment options that are safe, convenient, and widely accepted. The key is to determine which choices work the best for the company and its customers. The information in this chapter will help you make those decisions. Companies such as **Payment Online**, shown in Figure 11-2, sell packages of payment processing services to Web merchants that allow those merchants to accept several different types of payments.

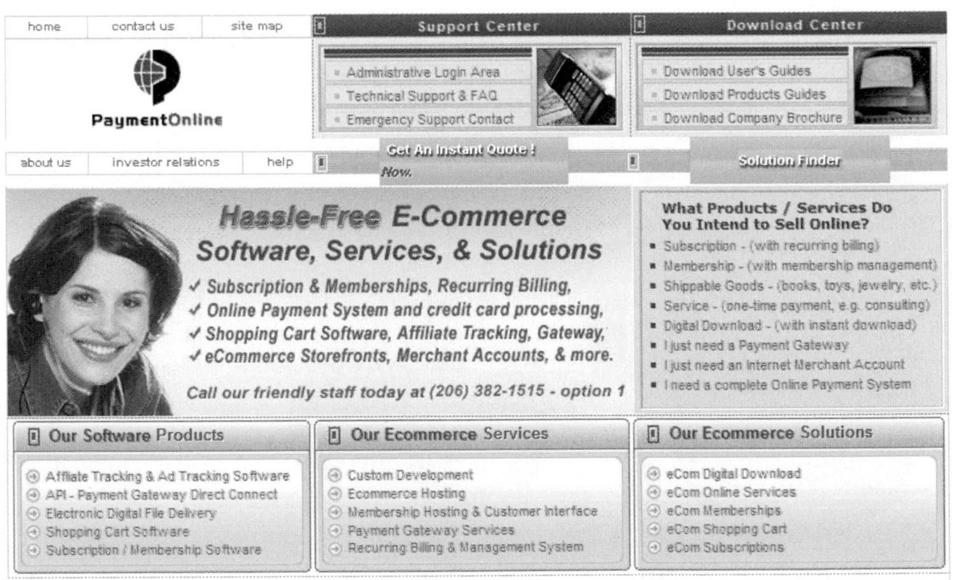

FIGURE 11-2 Payment processing service offerings of Payment Online

You will learn about four different payment technologies in this chapter: payment cards, electronic cash, software wallets, and smart cards (also called stored-value cards). Each technology has unique properties, costs, advantages, and disadvantages. Some are methods that are already popular and widely accepted; others are only beginning to catch on and have an unclear future. All of these electronic payment methods can work well for B2C Web commerce sites.

PAYMENT CARDS

Businesspeople often use the term **payment card** as a general term to describe all types of plastic cards that consumers (and some businesses) use to make purchases. The main categories of payment cards are credit cards, debit cards, and charge cards.

A **credit card**, such as a Visa or a MasterCard, has a spending limit based on the user's credit history; a user can pay off the entire credit card balance or pay a minimum amount each billing period. Credit card issuers charge interest on any unpaid balance. Many consumers already have credit cards, or are at least familiar with how they work. Credit cards are widely accepted by merchants around the world and provide assurances for both the consumer and the merchant. A consumer is protected by an automatic 30-day period in which he or she can dispute an online credit card purchase. Merchants that already accept credit cards in an offline store can accept them immediately for online payment because they already have established a mechanism for accepting credit card payments. Online credit card purchases are similar to telephone purchases in that the card holder is not present and cannot provide proof of identity as easily as he or she can when standing at the cash register. Online and telephone purchases are often called **card not present transactions** and both include an extra degree of risk for merchants and banks.

A debit card looks like a credit card, but it works quite differently. Instead of charging purchases against a credit line, a **debit card** removes the amount of the sale from the cardholder's bank account and transfers it to the seller's bank account. Debit cards are issued by the cardholder's bank and usually carry the name of a major credit card issuer, such as Visa or MasterCard, by agreement between the issuing bank and the credit card issuer. By branding their debit cards (with the Visa or MasterCard name), banks ensure that their debit cards will be accepted by merchants who recognize the credit card brand names.

A **charge card**, offered by companies such as American Express, carries no spending limit, and the entire amount charged to the card is due at the end of the billing period. Charge cards do not involve lines of credit and do not accumulate interest charges. (Note: In addition to its charge card products, American Express also offers credit cards, which do have credit limits and which do accumulate interest on unpaid balances.) In the United States, many retailers, such as department stores and oil companies that own gas stations, issue their own charge cards.

Many consumers have concerns about providing their payment card numbers to vendors online, especially when the vendor is unknown to them. To address this concern, several payment card companies began offering cards with disposable numbers. These cards, sometimes called **single-use cards**, gave consumers a unique card number that was valid for one transaction only. This prevented an unscrupulous vendor from using the card number to complete unauthorized transactions on the consumer's account or selling the card number to others. Despite a flurry of interest in single-use cards when they were first introduced in 2000, issuers found that consumers did not use them. After a few years, the companies that had introduced single-use cards withdrew them from the market. The problem with single-use cards was that they required consumers to behave differently. Not enough consumers saw a clear benefit to justify their learning how to use this new product.

Advantages and Disadvantages of Payment Cards

Payment cards have several features that make them an attractive and popular choice with both consumers and merchants in online and offline transactions. For merchants, payment cards provide fraud protection. When a merchant accepts payment cards for online payment or for orders placed over the telephone, the merchant can authenticate and authorize purchases using a payment card processing network (you will learn more about these networks later in this chapter). For U.S. consumers, payment cards are advantageous because the Consumer Credit Protection Act limits the cardholder's liability to $50 if the card is used fraudulently. Once the cardholder notifies the card's issuer of the card theft, the cardholder's liability ends. Frequently, the payment card's issuer waives the $50 consumer liability when a stolen card is used to purchase goods. Some other countries have similar laws, but this type of protection is not common for holders of credit cards issued outside the United States. The lack of this type of protection does limit the willingness of non-U.S. consumers to use payment cards for online purchases.

Perhaps the greatest advantage of using payment cards is their worldwide acceptance. Payment cards can be used anywhere in the world, and the currency conversion, if needed, is handled by the card issuer. For online transactions, payment cards are particularly advantageous. When a consumer reaches the electronic checkout, he or she enters the payment card number and his or her shipping and billing information in the appropriate fields to complete the transaction. The consumer does not need any special hardware or software to complete the transaction.

Payment cards have one significant disadvantage for merchants when compared to cash. Payment card service companies charge merchants per-transaction fees and monthly processing fees. These fees can add up, but merchants view them as a cost of doing business. Any merchant that does not accept payment cards for purchases risks losing a significant portion of sales to other merchants that do accept payment cards. The consumer pays no direct transaction-based fees for using payment cards, but the prices of goods and services are slightly higher than they would be in an environment free of payment cards. Most consumers also pay an annual fee for credit cards and charge cards. This annual fee is much less common on debit cards.

Payment cards provide built-in security for merchants because merchants have a higher assurance that they will be paid through the companies that issue payment cards than through the sometimes slow direct invoicing process. To process payment card transactions, a merchant must first set up a merchant account. The series of steps in a payment card transaction is usually transparent to the consumer. Several groups and individuals are involved: the merchant, the merchant's bank, the customer, the customer's bank, and the company that issued the customer's payment card. All of these entities must work together for customer charges to be credited to merchant accounts (and vice versa when a customer receives a payment card credit for returned goods).

Payment Acceptance and Processing

Most people are familiar with the use of payment cards: In a physical store, the customer or a sales clerk runs the card through the online payment card terminal and the card account is charged immediately. The process is slightly different on the Internet, although the purchase and charge processes follow the same rules. Payment card processing has been made easier over the past two decades because Visa and MasterCard, along with MasterCard's international affiliate, **MasterCard International** (formerly known as Europay), have implemented a single standard for the handling of payment card transactions called the **EMV standard** (EMV is derived from the names of the companies: Europay, MasterCard, and Visa).

In a brick-and-mortar store, customers walk out of the store with purchases in their possession, so charging and shipment occur nearly simultaneously. Online stores and mail order stores in the United States must ship merchandise within 30 days of charging a payment card. Because the penalties for violating this law can be significant, most online and mail order merchants do not charge payment card accounts until they ship merchandise. Payment card transactions follow these general steps once the merchant receives a consumer's payment card information, which is usually sent using the Secure Sockets Layer (SSL) encryption technique you learned about in Chapter 10:

1. The merchant authenticates the payment card to ensure it is valid and not stolen.
2. The merchant checks with the payment card issuer to ensure that credit or funds are available and puts a hold on the credit line or the funds needed to cover the charge.
3. Settlement occurs, usually a few days after the purchase, which means that funds travel between banks and are placed into the merchant's account.

Open and Closed Loop Systems

In some payment card systems, the card issuer pays the merchants that accept the card directly and does not use an intermediary, such as a bank or clearinghouse system. These types of arrangements are called **closed loop systems** because no other institution is involved in the transaction. American Express and Discover Card are examples of closed loop systems.

Open loop systems involve three or more parties. Suppose an Internet shopper uses his or her Visa card issued by the First Bank of Woodland to purchase an item from Web Wonders, whose bank account is at the Hackensack Commerce Bank. The banking system includes one or more intermediary banks that coordinate the transfer of funds from the First Bank of Woodland to the Hackensack Commerce Bank. Whenever a third party, such as the intermediary banks in this example, processes a transaction, the system is called an **open loop system**. Systems using Visa or MasterCard are the most visible examples of open loop systems. Many banks issue both cards. Unlike American Express or Discover, neither Visa nor MasterCard issues cards directly to consumers. Visa and MasterCard are **credit card associations** that are operated by the banks who are members in the associations. These member banks, which are also called **customer issuing banks**, issue credit cards to individual consumers and are responsible for establishing customer credit limits.

Merchant Accounts

A **merchant bank** or **acquiring bank** is a bank that does business with sellers (both Internet and non-Internet) that want to accept payment cards. In other words, to process payment cards for Internet transactions, an online merchant must set up a **merchant account**. When the merchant's bank collects credit card receipts on behalf of the merchant from the payment card issuer, it credits their value to the merchant's account.

A merchant must provide business information before the bank will provide an account through which the merchant can process payment card transactions. Typically, a new merchant must supply a business plan, details about existing bank accounts, and a business and personal credit history. The merchant bank wants to be sure that the merchant has a good prospect of staying in business and wants to minimize its risk. An online merchant that appears disorganized is less attractive to a merchant bank than a well-organized online merchant.

The type of business also influences the bank's likelihood of granting the account. In some industries, merchant banks will be reluctant to offer a merchant account because of the type of business; some businesses have a higher likelihood of customers repudiating payment card charges than others. For example, a business that sells a guaranteed weight loss scheme—a business in which many customers might want their money back—will find many merchant banks unwilling to provide an account. The bank assesses the level of risk in the business based on the type of business and the credit information that is provided. Merchant banks must estimate what percentage of sales are likely to be contested by cardholders. When a cardholder successfully contests a charge, the merchant bank must retrieve the money it placed in the merchant account in a process called a **chargeback**. To ensure that sufficient funds are available to cover chargebacks, a merchant bank might require a company to maintain funds on deposit in the merchant account. For example, a new or risky business that plans to make $100,000 in sales each month might be required to keep $50,000 or more on deposit in its merchant account.

One problem facing online businesses is that the level of fraud in online transactions is much higher than either in-person or telephone transactions of the same nature (that is, the same amount and the same type of good or service being purchased). Fewer than 10 percent of all credit card transactions are completed online, but those transactions are responsible for about 70 percent of the total dollar amount of credit card fraud.

The proportion of online transactions that are fraudulent increased steadily every year from the inception of electronic commerce through 2009. A CyberSource survey found that fraud losses dropped 18 percent from 2008 to 2009. Online fraud experts believe that the drop in fraud losses resulted from the accumulated effects of merchants' increased use of antifraud measures in recent years. These antifraud measures include the use of fraud scoring services that provide risk ratings for individual transactions in real time, shipping only to the card billing address, and requiring **card verification numbers (CVNs)** for card-not-present transactions. A CVN is a three- or four-digit number that is printed on the credit card, but is not encoded in the card's magnetic strip. Having a CVN establishes that the purchaser has the card (or has seen the card) and is likely not using a stolen card number.

A number of companies offer services that can handle all the details of processing online payment card transactions. The next section discusses payment card processing options for Internet stores.

Processing Payment Cards Online

Programs packaged with electronic commerce software can handle payment card processing automatically, or merchants can contract with a third party to handle payment card processing. Several companies, called **payment processing service providers**, offer these services. InternetSecure, for example, allows merchants to concentrate on business while it provides secure payment card services. InternetSecure supports payments with Visa and MasterCard for Canadian and U.S. accounts. The company provides risk management and fraud detection and handles transactions from online merchants using existing, bank-approved payment card processing infrastructure, secure links, and firewalls. InternetSecure notifies the merchant of all approved orders and also supplies authorization codes to buyers of digital content, who can download their purchases upon payment card approval. InternetSecure ensures that the transactions it processes are credited to the correct merchant's account. FirstData and Merchant Warehouse are two other companies that provide credit card processing software and services.

The products and services offered by these credit card processing software vendors connect to a network of banks called the **Automated Clearing House (ACH)** and to credit card authorization companies. You can learn more about ACHs by following the Online Companion links to the EPN, NACHA—The Electronic Payments Association, The Clearing House, and the U.S. Federal Reserve Bank's Federal Reserve Financial Services site. Banks connect to an ACH through highly secure, private leased telephone lines. The merchant sends the card information to a payment card authorization company, which reviews the customer account and, if it approves the transaction, sends the credit authorization to the issuing bank. Then the issuing bank deposits the money in the merchant's bank account through the ACH.

The merchant's Web site receives confirmation of the acceptance of the consumer transaction. After receiving notification of acceptance or rejection of the transaction, the merchant Web site confirms the sale to the customer over the Internet. In addition, the merchant site usually sends an e-mail confirmation of the sale to the consumer with details about the purchase price and shipping information. Figure 11-3 is a graphic representation of the process.

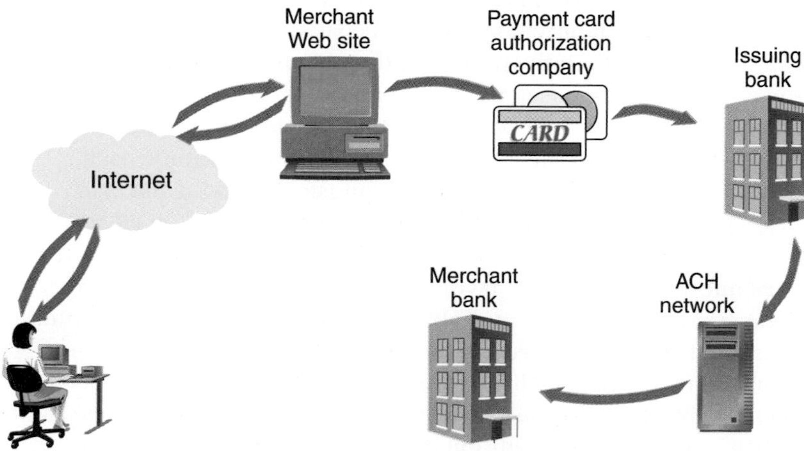

FIGURE 11-3 Processing a payment card transaction

Another credit card payment processing option is InfoSpace's **Authorize.Net**. Authorize.Net is an online, real-time payment card processing service that allows merchants to link their sites to the Authorize.Net system by inserting a small block of HTML code into their transaction page. With Authorize.Net, a customer's order is encrypted and transferred to the Authorize.Net server. The server, in turn, relays the transaction to a bank network through a private leased line. Merchants must have an Authorize.Net account to use the service. Customers are usually not aware that the transaction is being handled by a third-party supplier.

ELECTRONIC CASH

Although credit cards dominate online payments today, electronic cash shows promise for the future. **Electronic cash** (also called e-cash or digital cash) is a general term that describes any value storage and exchange system created by a private (nongovernmental) entity that does not use paper documents or coins and that can serve as a substitute for government-issued physical currency. A significant difference between electronic cash and scrip is that electronic cash can be readily exchanged for physical cash on demand. Because electronic cash is issued by private entities, there is a need for common standards among all electronic cash issuers so that one issuer's electronic cash can be accepted by another issuer. This need has not yet been met. Each issuer has its own standards and electronic cash is not universally accepted, as is government-issued physical currency.

As you learned in the previous section, banks that issue credit cards make money by charging merchants a processing fee on each transaction. This fee ranges from 1 percent to 4 percent of the value of the transaction. Often, banks impose a minimum fee of 20 cents or more per transaction. Many banks charge electronic commerce sites more than similar brick-and-mortar stores—up to $1 more per credit card transaction. The cost of an online transaction can be 50 percent higher than the cost to process the same transaction for a brick-and-mortar retailer.

Many stores that accept credit cards require a minimum purchase amount of $10 or $15. Merchants impose a minimum purchase amount because the bank fees for small purchase amounts would be greater than the profits on those transactions. The same is true for Internet purchases. Small purchases are not profitable for merchants that accept only credit cards for payment. There is a market for small purchases on the Internet—purchases below $10. This is one potentially significant market for electronic cash. With very low fixed costs, electronic cash provides the promise of allowing users to spend, for example, 50 cents for an online newspaper, or 80 cents to send an electronic greeting card.

Electronic cash has another factor in its favor: Most of the world's population does not have credit cards. Many adults cannot obtain credit cards due to minimum income requirements or past debt problems. Children and teens—eager purchasers representing a significant percentage of online buyers—are ineligible, simply because they are too young. People living in most countries other than the United States hold few credit cards because they have traditionally made their purchases in cash. For all of these people, electronic cash provides the solution to paying for online purchases.

Even though there have been many failures in electronic cash, the idea of electronic cash refuses to die. Electronic cash shows particular promise in two applications: the sale of goods and services priced less than $10—the lower threshold for credit card payments—and the sale of all goods and services to those persons without credit cards.

Micropayments and Small Payments

Internet payments for items costing from a few cents to approximately a dollar are called **micropayments**. Micropayment champions see many applications for such small transactions, such as paying 5 cents for an article reprint or 25 cents for a complicated literature search. However, micropayments have not been implemented very well on the Web yet. Another barrier to micropayments is a matter of human psychology. Researchers have found in a number of studies that many people prefer to buy small value items in fixed-price chunks rather than in individual small increments, even when buying the small increments would cost less money overall. A good example of this behavior is the preference most mobile telephone users have for fixed monthly payment plans over charges based on minutes used. The comfort of knowing the exact amount of the monthly bill is more important to many people than getting the lowest price on the minutes used.

Over the past 10 years, many companies have developed systems to process micropayments. Millicent, DigiCash, Yaga, and BitPass were among the companies that entered this business and failed. Industry observers see a need for a micropayments processing system on the Web, but no company has gained broad acceptance of its system. All of the companies who entered this market used systems that either accumulated micropayments and charged them periodically to a credit card or accepted a deposit and charged the micropayments against that deposit. Some companies that offer electronic cash and bill paying services do provide micropayment capabilities as part of their services, but no company is currently devoted solely to offering micropayment services.

The payments that are between $1 and $10 do not have a generally accepted name (some industry observers use the term micropayment to describe any payment of less than $10); in this book, the term **small payments** will be used to include all payments of less than $10.

Some companies have begun to offer small payment and micropayment services through mobile telephone carriers. Buyers make their purchases using their mobile phones and the charges appear on the buyers' monthly mobile phone bill. Although some industry observers see a bright future for such services, they have thus far been held back by the mobile carriers' substantial charges for providing the service, which can amount to 50 percent of each transaction. The company that offers the service typically takes another 10 percent, thus the buyer ends up paying more than double the cost of the purchase. For example, consider a mobile phone user that wants to buy a software application that would otherwise sell for $4, but buys it from the mobile carrier for $10 (so the carrier can take a $6 fee and the payments processor can take its $1 fee).

Privacy and Security of Electronic Cash

All electronic payment schemes have issues that must be resolved satisfactorily to allay consumers' fears and give them confidence in the technology. Concerns about electronic payment methods include privacy and security, independence, portability, and convenience. Privacy and security questions are probably the most important issues that have to be addressed with any payment system to be used by consumers. Consumers want to know whether transactions are vulnerable and whether the electronic currency can be copied, reused, or forged. Two characteristics of physical currency are important to have in any electronic cash implementation. First, it must be possible to spend electronic cash only once, just as with traditional currency. Second, electronic cash ought to be anonymous, just as hard currency is. That is, security procedures should be in place to guarantee that the entire electronic cash transaction occurs only between two parties, and that the recipient knows that the electronic currency being received is not counterfeit or being used in two different transactions. Ideally, consumers should be able to use electronic cash without revealing their identities—this prevents sellers from collecting information about individual or group spending habits.

Perhaps the most important characteristic of cash is convenience. If electronic cash requires special hardware or software, it is not convenient for people to use. Chances are good that people will not adopt an electronic cash system that is difficult to use. A company currently in the electronic cash business is Internet Cash.

Holding Electronic Cash: Online and Offline Cash

Two widely accepted approaches to holding cash exist today: online storage and offline storage. Online cash storage means that the consumer does not personally possess electronic cash. Instead, a trusted third party—an online bank—is involved in all transfers of electronic cash and holds the consumers' cash accounts. Online systems work by requiring merchants to contact the consumer's bank to receive payment for a consumer purchase, which helps prevent fraud by confirming that the consumer's cash is valid. This resembles the process of checking with a consumer's bank to ensure that a credit card is still valid and that the consumer's name matches the name on the credit card.

Offline cash storage is the virtual equivalent of money kept in a wallet. The customer holds it, and no third party is involved in the transaction. Protection against fraud is still a concern, so either hardware or software safeguards must be used to prevent fraudulent or double-spending. **Double-spending** is spending a particular piece of electronic cash twice by submitting the same electronic currency to two different vendors. By the time the same electronic currency clears the bank for a second time, it is too late to prevent the fraudulent act. The main deterrent to double-spending is the threat of detection and prosecution. Cryptographic algorithms are the keys to creating tamperproof electronic cash that can be traced back to its origins. A two-part lock provides anonymous security that also signals when someone is attempting to double-spend cash. When a second transaction occurs for the same electronic cash, a complicated process comes into play that reveals the attempted second use and the identity of the original electronic cash holder. Otherwise, electronic cash that is used correctly maintains a user's anonymity. This double-lock procedure protects the anonymity of electronic cash users and simultaneously provides built-in safeguards to prevent double-spending. Figure 11-4 shows a graphic representation of this double-spending detection process using a double-lock system.

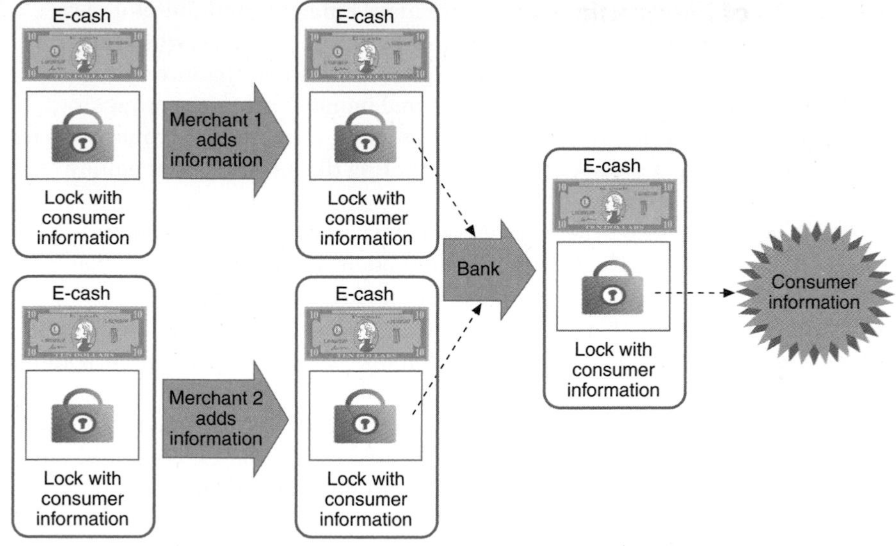

FIGURE 11-4 Detecting double-spending of electronic cash

Double-spending can neither be detected nor prevented with truly anonymous electronic cash. **Anonymous electronic cash** is electronic cash that, like bills and coins, cannot be traced back to the person who spent it. One way to be able to trace electronic cash is to attach a serial number to each electronic cash transaction. That way, cash can be positively associated with a particular consumer. That does not solve the double-spending problem, however. Although a single issuing bank could detect whether two deposits of the same electronic cash are about to occur, it is impossible to ascertain who is at fault in such a situation—the consumer or the merchant. Of course, electronic cash that contains serial numbers is no longer anonymous, and anonymity is one reason to acquire electronic cash in the first place. Electronic cash containing serial numbers also raises a number of privacy issues, because merchants could use the serial numbers to track spending habits of consumers.

Advantages and Disadvantages of Electronic Cash

Billing for goods and services that customers purchase is part of any business. Traditional billing methods in the brick-and-mortar paradigm are costly and involve generating invoices, stuffing envelopes, buying and affixing postage to the envelopes, and sending the invoices to the customers. Meanwhile, the Accounts Payable Department must keep track of incoming payments, post accounts in the database, and ensure that customer data is current.

Online stores have many of the same payment collection inefficiencies as their brick-and-mortar cousins. Most online customers use credit cards to pay for their purchases. Online auction customers also use conventional payment methods, including checks and money orders. Electronic cash systems, though less popular than other payment methods, provide advantages and disadvantages that are unique to electronic cash.

For the most part, electronic cash transactions are more efficient (and therefore less costly) than other methods, and that efficiency should foster more business, which eventually means lower prices for consumers. Transferring electronic cash on the Internet costs less than processing credit card transactions. Conventional money exchange systems require banks, bank branches, clerks, automated teller machines, and an electronic transaction system to manage, transfer, and dispense cash. Operating this conventional money exchange system is expensive.

Electronic cash transfers occur on the Internet, which is an existing infrastructure, and uses existing computer systems. No distribution method or human oversight is required. Thus, the additional costs that users of electronic cash must incur are nearly zero. Merchants can pay other merchants in a business-to-business relationship, and consumers can pay each other. Electronic cash does not require that one party obtain an authorization, as is required with credit card transactions.

Electronic cash does have disadvantages, and they are significant. Using electronic cash provides no audit trail. That is, electronic cash is just like real cash in that it cannot be easily traced. Because true electronic cash is not traceable, another problem arises: money laundering. **Money laundering** is a technique used by criminals to convert money that they have obtained illegally into cash that they can spend without having it identified as the proceeds of an illegal activity. Money laundering can be accomplished by purchasing goods or services with ill-gotten electronic cash. The goods are then sold for physical cash on the open market.

Electronic cash has been successful in some parts of the world, but it has not yet become a global commercial success. Making electronic cash a popular alternative payment system requires wide acceptance and a solution to the problems of multiple electronic cash standards. Customers do not want to have to carry a dozen different brands of electronic cash. Establishing electronic cash as a popular payment method requires that a standard be developed for electronic cash disbursement and acceptance.

Creating truly anonymous electronic cash requires a bank to issue electronic cash with embedded serial numbers such that the bank can digitally sign the electronic cash while removing any association of the cash with a particular customer. The process begins when a consumer creates a random serial number that he or she sends to the bank issuing the electronic cash. The bank uses the consumer's random serial number along with the bank's digital signature and sends the random number, electronic cash, and digital signature as one package back to the user. When the user receives the electronic cash bundle, the user extracts the original random serial number and keeps the bank's digital signature. The consumer can now spend the electronic cash, which is digitally signed by the bank. When the consumer spends the electronic cash and the merchant passes it along to the issuing bank, the bank validates the electronic cash because it contains the bank's digital signature. However, the bank cannot determine the identity of the spender. It only knows that the electronic cash is genuine.

Electronic Cash Systems

Electronic cash has not been nearly as successful in the United States as it has been in Europe and Japan. In the United States, most consumers have credit cards, debit cards, charge cards, and checking accounts. These payment alternatives work well for

U.S. consumers in both online and offline transactions. In most other countries of the world, consumers overwhelmingly prefer to use cash. Because cash does not work well for online transactions, electronic cash fills an important need for consumers in those countries as they conduct B2C electronic commerce. This type of need does not exist in the United States because U.S. consumers already use payment cards for traditional commerce, and these payment cards work well for electronic commerce.

KDD Communications (KCOM) is the Internet subsidiary of Kokusai Denshin Denwa, which is Japan's largest global phone company. KCOM has its own NetCoin electronic cash system and offers electronic cash online through its NetCoin Center Web site. Shoppers can visit the site and obtain electronic cash that can be stored on their computers. Then, they can shop online for recipes or travel directories, or download MP3s. Other content providers, such as Japanese newspapers, provide access to their newspaper archives and charge a small fee to retrieve articles. Japan also has a donation site where visitors can donate electronic coins to charitable organizations.

Specific reasons for the failures of electronic cash systems in the United States are not completely clear. Some industry observers blame the failure on the way that many electronic cash systems were implemented. Most of these systems required the user to download and install complicated client-side software that ran in conjunction with the browser. Also, there were a number of competing technologies; therefore, no standards were ever developed for the entire electronic cash system. The absence of electronic cash standards means that consumers are faced with choosing from an array of proprietary electronic cash alternatives—none of which are interoperable. **Interoperable software** runs transparently on a variety of hardware configurations and on different software systems.

PayPal is the electronic cash payment system that you read about in the opening case of this chapter. PayPal was founded in 1999, and in 2000 it merged with another payment processing service, X.com. PayPal provides payment processing services to businesses and to individuals. PayPal earns a profit on the **float**, which is money that is deposited in PayPal accounts and not used immediately. After two years in business, PayPal began charging a transaction fee to businesses that use the service to collect payments. Individuals who use PayPal to send money to other individuals do not pay a transaction fee. The free payment clearing service that PayPal provides to individuals is called a **peer-to-peer (P2P) payment system** because the payments are from one type of entity to another of the same type.

PayPal eliminates the need to pay for online purchases by writing and mailing checks or using payment cards. PayPal allows consumers to send money instantly and securely to anyone with an e-mail address, including an online merchant. PayPal is a convenient way for auction bidders to pay for their purchases, and sellers like it because it eliminates the risks posed by other types of online payments. PayPal transactions clear instantly so that the sender's account is reduced and the receiver's account is credited when the transaction occurs. Anyone with a PayPal account—online merchants or eBay auction participants alike—can withdraw cash from their PayPal accounts at any time by requesting that PayPal send them a check or make a direct deposit to their checking accounts.

To use PayPal, merchants and consumers must first register for a PayPal account. There is no minimum amount that a PayPal account must contain, and customers add money to their PayPal accounts by authorizing a transfer from their checking accounts or by using a credit card. Once members' payments are approved and deposited into their PayPal accounts, they can use their PayPal money to pay for purchases.

Merchants must have PayPal accounts to accept PayPal payments. Using PayPal to pay for auction purchases is very popular. A consumer can use PayPal to pay a seller for purchases even if the seller does not have a PayPal account. PayPal sends the seller an e-mail message indicating that a payment is waiting at the PayPal Web site. To collect PayPal cash, the seller or merchant that received the e-mail message must register and provide PayPal with payment instructions. PayPal then either sends the merchant a check or deposits funds directly into the merchant's checking account.

LEARNING FROM FAILURES

PayPal Challengers

PayPal grew rapidly by serving the needs of buyers and sellers on auction sites such as eBay. This success and the business niche's potential for profits were noticed by a number of other companies that were eager to challenge PayPal for a share of the online payments business.

Because PayPal's early success was driven largely by its use on the eBay auction site, eBay's management team decided to compete directly against PayPal with its own payment service. In 1999, eBay purchased a small electronic payments company and, one year later, sold a 35 percent stake in that company to Wells Fargo bank. This company, Billpoint, was operated as a joint venture by eBay and Wells Fargo. Billpoint grew rapidly, but PayPal maintained the advantage it had gained as the first company to offer payment services online. PayPal continued to be the most widely used payment processing system on eBay despite Billpoint's best efforts to promote itself as a part of eBay. After unsuccessfully battling PayPal for three years, eBay finally gave up and decided to buy PayPal, as you learned in this chapter's opening case.

The profit potential of online payments also attracted the interest of several banks, who thought they could use their years of experience in traditional payment processing to overcome PayPal's first-mover advantage. For example, Citibank operated its c2it payments service for several years before closing it in 2003, Other banks were similarly unsuccessful with their online payments operations.

Other financial services companies believed they could be successful in online payments, too. First Data Corporation, which owns Western Union, offered what it called electronic money orders that customers could use to settle auction transactions through its BidPay site. The company struggled to compete with PayPal for many years before closing in 2007.

PayPal performs its function very well and no other challengers have been able to find a way to do online payments any better. PayPal has prevailed not only because it was an early entrant, but because it performed as well as any of its challengers. PayPal users had no good reason to switch to any of the other providers.

ELECTRONIC WALLETS

As consumers are becoming more enthusiastic about online shopping, they have begun to tire of repeatedly entering detailed shipping and payment information each time they make online purchases. Filling out forms ranks high on online customers' lists of gripes about online shopping. To address these concerns, many electronic commerce sites include a feature that allows a customer to store their name, address, and credit card information on the site. However, consumers must enter their information at each site with which they want to do business. An **electronic wallet** (sometimes called an **e-wallet**), serving a function similar to a physical wallet, holds credit card numbers, electronic cash, owner identification, and owner contact information and provides that information at an electronic commerce site's checkout counter. Electronic wallets give consumers the benefit of entering their information just once, instead of having to enter their information at every site with which they want to do business.

Electronic wallets make shopping more efficient. When consumers select items to purchase, they can then click their electronic wallet to order the items quickly. In the future, wallets could serve their owners by tracking purchases and maintaining receipts for those purchases. Maintaining records of a consumer's purchasing habits is something that online giants such as Amazon.com have mastered, but an enhanced digital wallet could reverse that process and use a Web robot to suggest where the consumer might find a lower price on an item that he or she purchases regularly.

Electronic wallets fall into two categories based on where they are stored. A **server-side electronic wallet** stores a customer's information on a remote server belonging to a particular merchant or wallet publisher. For example, if you enter your information on a site such as Amazon.com and choose to store that information so you do not have to enter it when you next visit the site, Amazon.com stores your information in a server-side electronic wallet.

The main weakness of server-side electronic wallets is that a security breach could reveal thousands of users' personal information—including credit card numbers—to unauthorized parties. Typically, server-side electronic wallets employ strong security measures that minimize the possibility of unauthorized disclosure.

A **client-side electronic wallet** stores a consumer's information on his or her own computer. Many of the early electronic wallets were client-side wallets that required users to download the wallet software. This need to download software onto every computer used to make purchases is a chief disadvantage of client-side wallets. Server-side wallets, on the other hand, remain on a server and thus require no download time or installation on a user's computer. Before a consumer can use a server-side wallet on a particular merchant's site, the merchant must enable that specific wallet. Each wallet vendor must convince a large number of merchants to enable its wallet before it will be accepted by consumers. Thus, only a few server-side wallet vendors will be able to succeed in the market.

A disadvantage of client-side wallets is that they are not portable. For example, a client-side wallet is not available when a purchase is made from a computer other than the computer on which the wallet resides.

In a client-side electronic wallet, the sensitive information (such as credit card numbers) is stored on the user's computer instead of the wallet provider's central server. This removes the risk that an attack on a client-side electronic wallet vendor's server could reveal the sensitive information. However, an attack on the user's computer could yield that information. Most security analysts agree that storing sensitive information on client computers is safer than storing that information on the vendor server because it requires attackers to launch many attacks on user computers, which are more difficult to identify (even though the user computers are less likely than a vendor server to have strong security features installed). It also prevents the easily identified servers of the wallet vendors from being attractive targets for such attacks.

For a wallet to be useful at many online sites, it should be able to populate the data fields in any merchant's forms at any site that the consumer visits. This accessibility means that the electronic wallet manufacturer and merchants from many sites must coordinate their efforts so that a wallet can recognize what consumer information goes into each field of a given merchant's forms.

Electronic wallets store shipping and billing information, including a consumer's first and last names, street address, city, state, country, and postal code. Most electronic wallets also can hold many credit card names and numbers, affording the consumer a choice of credit cards at the online checkout. Some electronic wallets also hold electronic cash from various providers.

A number of companies entered the electronic wallet business, including major firms such as MasterCard. Most of these companies have abandoned their efforts because current versions of all major browsers now include a feature that remembers names, addresses, and other commonly requested information and provides a one-click completion of fields on Web forms that request that information. Two survivors in the e-wallet arena are Microsoft Windows Live ID and Yahoo! Wallet.

Microsoft Windows Live ID

Microsoft Windows Live ID (formerly called Passport or Microsoft .NET Passport) is a single sign-in service that includes a server-side electronic wallet operated by Microsoft. Windows Live ID functions in the same way as most other electronic wallets—by completing order forms automatically. All of the personal data entered into a Windows Live ID wallet is encrypted and password protected.

Windows Live ID consists of four integrated services: single sign-in service (SSI), Wallet service, Kids service, and public profiles. The sign-in service allows a user to sign in at a participating Web site using his or her username and password. The Wallet service provides electronic wallet functions such as secure storage and form completion of credit card and address information. When requested by a participating merchant, a consumer's secure information is released to the merchant so that the consumer does not need to enter data into a form. The Kids service helps parents protect and control their children's online privacy, and the public profiles service allows consumers to create a public page of information about themselves.

Yahoo! Wallet

Yahoo! Wallet is a server-side electronic wallet offered by the Web portal site Yahoo! The Yahoo! Wallet functions in the same way as most other electronic wallets—by completing order forms automatically with identifying information and credit card payment information. Yahoo! Wallet lets users store information about several major credit and charge cards, along with Visa and MasterCard debit cards.

Yahoo! Wallet is accepted by thousands of Yahoo! Store merchants (these are merchants on the Yahoo! Shopping section of the portal), and also can be used to pay for airplane tickets and hotel reservations booked through Yahoo! Travel. Yahoo! Wallet also works when users pay for services at Yahoo!, such as premium e-mail storage or Web hosting fees.

Yahoo! has the advantage of hosting a number of services and shops that it can be certain accommodate its own wallet; thus, it has a large number of merchants (including itself) that accept its wallet.

Some industry observers and privacy rights activist groups are concerned about electronic wallets because they give the company that issues the electronic wallet access to a great deal of information about the individual using the wallet.

STORED-VALUE CARDS

Today, most people carry a number of plastic cards—credit cards, debit cards, charge cards, driver's license, health insurance card, employee or student identification card, and others. One solution that could reduce all those cards to a single plastic card is called a stored-value card.

A **stored-value card** is an elaborate smart card with a microchip or a plastic card with a magnetic strip that records the currency balance. The microchip can store more information than a magnetic strip. More importantly, it can include a tiny computer processor that enables the smart card to do its own calculations and storage operations right on the card. The card readers needed for smart cards are different, too. Common stored-value cards include prepaid phone, copy, subway, and bus cards. Many people use the terms "stored-value card" and "smart card" interchangeably.

Magnetic Strip Cards

Most magnetic strip cards hold value that can be recharged by inserting them into the appropriate machines, inserting currency into the machine, and withdrawing the card; the card's strip stores the increased cash value. Magnetic strip cards are passive; that is, they cannot send or receive information, nor can they increment or decrement the value of cash stored on the card. The processing must be done on a device into which the card is inserted. Although both magnetic strip cards and smart cards can store electronic cash, a smart card is better suited for Internet payment transactions because it has some processing capability.

Smart Cards

A **smart card** is a stored-value card that is a plastic card with an embedded microchip that can store information. Credit, debit, and charge cards currently store limited information on a magnetic strip. A smart card can store about 100 times the amount of information that a magnetic strip plastic card can store. A smart card can hold private user data, such as financial facts, encryption keys, account information, credit card numbers, health insurance information, medical records, and so on.

Smart cards are safer than conventional credit cards because the information stored on a smart card is encrypted. For example, conventional credit cards show your account number on the face of the card and your signature on the back. The card number and a forged signature are all that a thief needs to purchase items and charge them against your card. With a smart card, credit theft is much more difficult because the key to unlock the encrypted information is a PIN; there is no visible number on the card that a thief can identify, nor is there a physical signature on the card that a thief can see and use as an example for a forgery.

Smart cards have been in use for more than a decade. Popular in Europe and parts of Asia, smart cards so far have not been as successful in the United States. In Europe and Japan, smart cards are being used for telephone calls at public phones and for television programs delivered by cable to people's homes. The cards are also very popular in Hong Kong, where many retail counters and restaurant cash registers have smart card readers. The city's transportation companies—subways, buses, railways, trams, and ferries—joined together and created a smart card called the **Octopus** that lets commuters use one card for all of their public transportation needs. The Octopus card, which is now owned by an independent company, can be reloaded at any transportation location or at 7-Eleven stores throughout Hong Kong.

Smart cards are beginning to appear in the United States. In San Francisco, the Bay Area Metropolitan Transportation Commission created a smart card system patterned after the Octopus Card. This system, **TransLink**, is the first integrated ticketing system for public transportation in the United States. The transportation smart card, implemented in a 2002 pilot program, allows commuters to ride most modes of public transit available in the city, including trains, buses, cabs, and ferries, by holding the smart card near a reader device for a moment in transit vehicles or in stations. TransLink users can reload their smart cards at several retail outlets or directly from their bank accounts. The pilot program was a success and TransLink is now available to all Bay Area transit customers.

In the United States, the **Smart Card Alliance** advances the benefits of smart cards. The organization promotes the widespread acceptance of multiple-application smart card technology. Its members include companies in banking, financial services, computer technology, healthcare, telecommunications, and a number of government agencies. The Alliance focuses on information exchange and member interaction. Every member of the Alliance recognizes that smart cards can succeed in the United States only if a critical mass of smart cards supports applications—both physical and Internet-based—of interest to consumers. The Alliance promotes compatibility among smart cards, card reader devices, and applications.

INTERNET TECHNOLOGIES AND THE BANKING INDUSTRY

As you learned earlier in this chapter, the largest dollar volume of payments today are still made using paper checks. These paper checks are processed through the world's banking system. The other major payment forms in use today also involve banks in one way or another. This section outlines how Internet technologies are providing new tools and creating new threats for the banking industry.

Check Processing

In the past, checks were processed physically by banks and clearinghouses. When a person wrote a check to pay for an item at a retail store, the retailer would deposit the check in its bank account. The retailer's bank would then send the paper check to a clearinghouse, which would manage the transfer of funds from the consumer's bank to the retailer's account. The paper check would then be transported to the consumer's bank, which might then send the cancelled check to the consumer. In recent years, many banks have stopped sending cancelled checks to their consumer account holders to save postage, instead providing access to PDF images of processed checks to account folders. Despite these savings, the cost of transporting tons of paper checks around the country has grown each year.

In addition to the transportation costs, another disadvantage of using paper checks is the delay that occurs between the time that a person writes a check and the time that check clears the person's bank. This delay (which is similar to the delay you learned about earlier in PayPal accounts, and which is also called float) makes it possible to write checks a few days before money is in the account to cover those checks. In effect, the bank's customer obtains the free use of funds for a few days and the bank loses the use of those funds for the same time period. Although the delay normally lasts only a few days, there are times when it can become significantly longer. Railroad and airline strikes, for example, have caused the float to be extended. The terrorist attacks of September 11, 2001 caused a significant increase in the float.

Banks have been working for years to develop technologies that will help them reduce the float. In 2004, a U.S. law went into effect that many bankers believe will eventually eliminate the float. This law, the Check Clearing for the 21st Century Act (usually referred to as **Check 21**), permits banks to eliminate the movement of physical checks entirely. In a Check 21-compliant world, the retailer can scan the customer's check. The scanned image is transmitted instantly through a clearing system and posts almost immediately to both accounts (that is, the withdrawal from the customer's account and the deposit to the retailer's account occur instantly), eliminating any float on the transaction.

You can learn more about the Check 21 law and its implementation by using the links in the Online Companion to the **Federal Reserve Financial Services - Check 21-Enabled Services** pages or the **American Bankers Association Check 21 Resource Center**.

LEARNING FROM FAILURES

NetBank

CompuBank and NetBank were two of the first Internet banks to open in the United States. They were both pure Internet banks; that is, neither was founded by an existing bank with a physical presence. After four years of operation, CompuBank had about 50,000 accounts and $64 million of deposits and was losing more than $20 million per year. NetBank had done considerably better, with 160,000 accounts and $1 billion of deposits and 10 consecutive quarters of profitability.

In early 2001, CompuBank decided to close its operations and found NetBank to be a willing purchaser of its accounts. When a bank buys accounts from another bank, it performs a series of procedures called due diligence. These **due diligence** procedures include checking the new customers' credit histories and banking records. Due diligence is usually performed before the transaction is completed and before the closing bank's customers look to the buying bank as the institution that will handle their accounts.

For a number of reasons, not all of which are clear, the due diligence process was still under way on the date that the transfer of accounts was to take place. NetBank placed holds on many accounts and sent letters to many account holders explaining that they were not acceptable customers by NetBank standards. For any bank, this would have been a difficult situation, but the nature of the two banks as Internet-only operations made things considerably worse for everyone.

Press accounts of the fiasco included stories of the problems that between 4000 and 8000 CompuBank depositors experienced. Some of the problems were small—online bill payments did not occur, debit and credit cards were rejected at stores and restaurants, and ATMs would not yield cash—while others were much larger. One couple who had kept the money to cover closing costs on a house purchase in a CompuBank account found that NetBank had placed a hold on the money. Because they could not pay the closing costs, they were forced to find another mortgage lender. In the suit they filed against NetBank, the couple asserted that the increased rate on the mortgage loan would cost them tens of thousands of dollars. Other CompuBank customers were irritated that they lost access to their money for weeks. Some customers could not determine whether the bills they had set up to be paid automatically had, in fact, been paid.

NetBank admitted failures in customer service related to the incident. Many customers who called to complain or ask for explanations experienced 45-minute waits on hold and then were transferred to the bank's Security Department, where a recording answered and asked callers to leave their Social Security numbers and wait to be called back. None of the customers reported being called back. The timing of NetBank's notification was problematic, too. Many customers reported receiving a letter from NetBank indicating that there were problems with their accounts. The letter, dated April 30, was received by the customers on or after May 14. The letter included a telephone number to call for assistance, but that number had been disconnected on May 12. Many of the unhappy customers found each other on Internet discussion boards and compared notes.

NetBank has never disclosed the number of customers it lost by its handling of this transition; indeed, it may not know. CompuBank's customers were largely experienced Internet users who chose to be part of the leading edge in handling their financial affairs. Many of them, after this experience, have sworn that they will never again do business with a bank that does not have a physical presence. The lesson from NetBank's experience is that customer service and the ability to communicate with customers become extremely important for companies that process electronic payments or are responsible for their customers' finances.

Mobile Banking

In Chapter 6, you learned about new opportunities that are emerging for businesses that want to reach customers who use smart phones and other mobile devices to connect to the Internet. In recent years, banks have begun to explore the potential of mobile commerce in their businesses, too.

In 2009, a number of banks launched sites that allow customers using smart phones to obtain their bank balance, view their account statement, or find a nearby ATM. These sites are designed for the smaller screen size of smart phones and make interacting with the bank easier than using a smart phone's Web browser to view the bank's regular site.

Many banks' future plans include offering downloadable applications that smart phone users can install and use to transact all types of banking business. These applications will allow smart phone users to copy and paste information from the bank's Web site into other applications on the phone more easily than if they were to access the bank's site using the smart phone's Web browser.

CRIMINAL ACTIVITY AND PAYMENT SYSTEMS: PHISHING AND IDENTITY THEFT

Online payment systems offer criminals and criminal enterprises an attractive arena in which to operate. The average consumers who engage in online payment transactions are easy prey for expert criminals. The large amounts of money involved make online payment systems tempting targets.

In Chapter 10, you learned about the phishing expedition, which is a technique for committing fraud against the customers of online businesses. Although phishing expeditions can be launched against all types of online businesses, they are of particular concern to financial institutions because their customers expect a high degree of security to be maintained over the personal information and resources that they entrust to their online financial institutions.

Phishing Attacks

The basic structure of a phishing attack is fairly simple. The attacker sends e-mail messages (such as the one shown in Figure 11-5) to a large number of recipients who might have an account at the targeted Web site (PayPal is the targeted site in the example shown in the figure).

The e-mail message tells the recipient that his or her account has been compromised and it is necessary for the recipient to log in to the account to correct the matter. The e-mail message includes a link that appears to be a link to the login page of the Web site. However, the link actually leads the recipient to the phishing attack perpetrator's Web site, which is disguised to look like the targeted Web site. The unsuspecting recipient enters his or her login name and password, which the perpetrator captures and then uses to access the recipient's account. Once inside the victim's account, the perpetrator can access personal information, make purchases, or withdraw funds at will.

Date: [Date removed] 08:05:42 +0600
From: "Services PayPal" <services@paypal.com>
Subject: PayPal Account sensitive features are access limited!
To: [E-mail addresses removed]

Dear valued **PayPal** member:

PayPal is committed to maintaining a safe environment for its community of buyers and sellers. To protect the security of your account, PayPal employs some of the most advanced security systems in the world and our anti-fraud teams regularly screen the PayPal system for unusual activity.

Recently, our Account Review Team identified some unusual activity in your account. In accordance with PayPal's User Agreement and to ensure that your account has not been compromised, access to your account was limited. Your account access will remain limited until this issue has been resolved. This is a fraud prevention measure meant to ensure that your account is not compromised.

In order to secure your account and quickly restore full access, we may require some specific information from you for the following reason:

We would like to ensure that your account was not accessed by an unauthorized third party. Because protecting the security of your account is our primary concern, we have limited access to sensitive PayPal account features. We understand that this may be an inconvenience but please understand that this temporary limitation is for your protection.

Case ID Number: PP-040-187-541

We encourage you to log in and restore full access as soon as possible. Should access to your account remain limited for an extended period of time, it may result in further limitations on the use of your account.

However, failure to restore your records will result in account suspension. Please update your records within 48 hours. Once you have updated your account records, your **PayPal** session will not be interrupted and will continue as normal.

To update your **Paypal** records click on the following link:
https://www.paypal.com/cgi-bin/webscr?cmd=_login-run

Thank you for your prompt attention to this matter. Please understand that this is a security measure meant to help protect you and your account. We apologize for any inconvenience.

Sincerely,
PayPal Account Review Department

PayPal Email ID PP522

Accounts Management As outlined in our User Agreement, **PayPal** will periodically send you information about site changes and enhancements.

Visit our Privacy Policy and User Agreement if you have any questions.
http://www.paypal.com/cgi-bin/webscr?cmd=p/gen/ua/policy_privacy-outside

FIGURE 11-5 Phishing e-mail message

When the e-mails used in a phishing expedition are carefully designed to target a particular person or organization, the exploit is called **spear phishing**. The spear phishing perpetrator must do considerable research on the intended recipient, but by obtaining detailed personal information and using it in the e-mail, the perpetrator can greatly increase the chances that the victim will open the e-mail and click the link to the phishing Web site. Spear phishers have launched attacks against employees of specific companies that include jargon and acronyms that are frequently used in the company or its industry. By using familiar language and terms, the spear phisher gains the victim's trust and is more likely to convince the victim to click the phishing link.

Phishing perpetrators are quick to capitalize on new opportunities to practice their fraud. In 2008, the U.S. government enacted an economic stimulus law that paid millions of its citizens a rebate check. Within a week of the law's passage, phishing e-mails began appearing in inboxes throughout the country. The e-mails appeared to be from the Internal Revenue Service and promised an early rebate to responders who clicked on the link (to the phishing Web site) and provided details such as bank account numbers, Social Security numbers, and passwords to online accounts.

The links in phishing e-mails are usually disguised. One common way to disguise the real URL is to use the @ sign, which causes the Web server to ignore all characters that precede the @ and only use the characters that follow it. For example, a link that displays:

https://www.paypal.com@218.36.41.188/fl/login.html

looks like it is an address at PayPal. However, the @ sign causes the Web server to ignore the "paypal.com" and instead takes the victim to a Web page at the IP address 218.36.41.188.

In the e-mail shown in the figure, the link appears in the victim's e-mail client software as:

https://paypal.com/cgi-bin/webscr?cmd=_login-run

but when the victim clicks the link, the browser opens a completely different URL:

http://leasurelandscapes.com/snow/webscr.dll

Instead of the URL it shows in the e-mail client, the link in the phishing e-mail actually includes the following JavaScript code:

```
<A onmouseover="window.status='https://www.paypal.com/cgi-bin/webscr?
cmd=_login-run'; return true" onmouseout="window.status= 'https://www.
paypal.com/cgi-bin/webscr?cmd=_login-run' "href ="http://
leasurelandscapes.com/snow/webscr.dll">https://www.paypal.com/cgi-bin/
webscr?cmd=_login-run</A>
```

This code is invisible in many e-mail clients, so the victim might never know that the Web browser has opened a phony site. Phishers use other tricks to hide URLs, including code that opens a pop-up window that displays the financial institution's URL and positions that window so it covers the browser's address bar. Phishing perpetrators often include graphics from the Web site of the victim's financial institution in the phishing e-mail to make it even more convincing. Figure 11-6 shows a phishing e-mail that includes graphics from the Bank of America Web site. You can learn more about the details of phishing techniques by visiting the Web sites of the **Conferences on Email and Anti-Spam** and the **Anti-Phishing Working Group (APWG)**.

From: Bank of America <BankofAmerica@service.com>
Subject: Bank of America Notices : Your Online Account Security Status
To: [Email address removed]
Date: [Date removed]

Online Banking Alert

Remember:
You are expected to complete this update not later than 2 working days from the receipt of this mail.

Verification of your current details.

Dear Valued Customer :
During our regular update and verification of the Bank of America Online Banking Service, we could not verify your current information. Either your information has been changed or incomplete, as a result your access to use our services has been limited. Please update your information.

To restore your online banking access, kindly update your information. You can update your online banking details by following the link below.

Click here to update your account!

Thank you for banking with Bank of America, the industry leader in safe and secure online banking

Sincerely,
Bank of America Customer Service

Our paperless statements securely store your statements online for you to view up to 18 months of activity. **Learn more**.

Important
Because E-Mail Is Not A Secure Form Of Communication, This E-Mail Box Is Not Equipped To Handle Replies.
If you are a Bank of America customer and have sensitive account-related questions, please call the phone number provided on your account statement or the appropriate phone number indicated in the following "Contact Us" link so we can properly verify your identity. For all other questions or comments, please use the Web forms available via Contact Us. We respect your privacy, and you can rest assured that we protect your information, including your email address, and will never sell or share it with marketers outside Bank of America.
To find out more, please read our Privacy Policy. Bank of America E-mail, 6th Floor, 101 North Tryon Street, Charlotte, NC 28255-0001

Bank of America, N.A. Member FDIC. Equal Housing Lender
? 2006 Bank of America Corporation. All Rights Reserved.

FIGURE 11-6 Phishing e-mail with graphics

Using Phishing Attacks for Identity Theft

Many perpetrators of phishing attacks are individuals working alone. However, the large amounts of illegal revenue that can be generated by combining phishing attacks with identity theft has drawn the attention of highly structured groups of criminals whose members possess a variety of specialized skills.

U.S. laws define **organized crime**, also called **racketeering**, as unlawful activities conducted by a highly organized, disciplined association for profit. The associations that engage in organized crime are often differentiated from less organized groups such as gangs and from organized groups that conduct unlawful activities for political purposes, such as terrorist organizations. Organized crime associations have traditionally engaged in criminal activities such as drug trafficking, gambling, money laundering, prostitution, pornography production and distribution, extortion, truck hijacking, fraud, theft, and insider trading. Often these activities are carried out simultaneously with legitimate business activities, which provide cover for the illegal activities.

The Internet has opened new opportunities for organized crime in their traditional types of criminal activities and in new areas such as generating spam (which you learned about in earlier chapters), phishing, and identity theft. **Identity theft** is a criminal act in which the perpetrator gathers personal information about a victim and then uses that information to obtain credit. After establishing credit accounts, the perpetrator runs up charges on the accounts and then disappears. Figure 11-7 includes a list of the types of personal information that identity thieves most want to obtain (listed in approximate order of usefulness to the criminal).

Social Security number
Driver's license number
Credit card numbers
Card verification numbers (CVNs)
Passwords (PINs)
Credit reports
Date of birth
ATM (or debit) card numbers
Telephone calling card numbers
Mortgage (or other loan) information
Telephone numbers
Home address
Employer address

FIGURE 11-7 Types of personal information most useful to identity thieves

Large criminal organizations can be highly efficient perpetrators of identity theft because they can exploit large amounts of personal information very quickly and efficiently. These organizations can use phishing attacks to gather personal information and then use it to perpetrate identity theft and other crimes. These criminal organizations often sell or trade information that they cannot use immediately to other organized crime entities around the world. Some of these criminal transactions are even conducted online. For example, a hacker who has planted zombie programs on a large number of computers (thus creating a **zombie farm**) might sell the right to use the zombie farm to an organized crime association that wants to launch a phishing attack (when a zombie farm is used this way, the attack is sometimes called a **pharming attack**). Individuals who commit these crimes have always posed a serious threat, but organized crime's entry into this activity increases the threat. There are two elements in phishing, the collection of the information (done by **collectors**) and the use of the information (done by **cashers**). The skills needed to perform these two activities are different. By facilitating transactions between collectors and cashers (and by participating as one or both), crime organizations have increased the efficiency and volume of phishing activity overall.

More than a million people fall victim to phishing attacks each year and as a group experience financial losses exceeding $500 million. Although the overall incidence of phishing attacks is decreasing as Internet users become aware of them, experts believe that the proportion of all phishing attacks committed by organized crime associations will continue to increase in the future because it is so profitable.

Phishing Attack Countermeasures

In Chapter 8, you learned that several groups are working on ways to improve the Internet's mail transport protocols so that spam senders can be identified. Since spam is a key element of phishing attacks, any protocol change that improves e-mail recipients' ability to identify the source of an e-mail message will also help to reduce the threat of phishing attacks.

The most important step that companies can take today, however, is to educate their Web site users. Most online banking sites continually warn their customers that the site never sends e-mails that ask for account information or that ask the recipient to log in to their Web site and make changes to his or her account information. PayPal occasionally interrupts its own login screen sequence to insert a page that provides information about phishing attacks.

Many companies, especially those that operate financial Web sites, have contracted with consulting firms that specialize in anti-phishing work. These consultants monitor the Web for new Web sites that use the company's name or logo and move quickly to shut down those sites. Most phishing perpetrators set up their entrapping Web sites a few days before they launch their e-mail campaign, so this technique can be effective. Another anti-phishing technique is to monitor online chat rooms that are used by criminals. By watching for offers of stolen credit card information and other phishing exploits, consultants can identify phishing schemes that are under way.

The incidence of phishing attacks has grown rapidly over the past two years and most industry analysts expect that phishing will be a problem that will plague online businesses for the near future. Phishing can be an extremely profitable criminal activity and as more companies increase their defenses, analysts expect phishing perpetrators to become even better at working around those defenses.

Summary

Online stores can accept a variety of forms of payment. Credit, debit, and charge cards (payment cards) are the most popular forms of payment on the Internet. They are ubiquitous, convenient, and easy to use.

Electronic cash, a form of online payment that is portable and anonymous, has been slow to catch on in the United States. A number of companies have failed as they attempted to introduce electronic cash to the online world. Electronic cash could be useful for making micropayments because the cost of processing payment cards for small transactions is greater than the profit on such transactions. Electronic cash can be stored online or offline. A third party, such as a bank, stores online electronic cash.

Electronic wallets provide convenience to online shoppers because they hold payment card information, electronic cash, and personal consumer identification. Electronic wallets eliminate the need for consumers to reenter payment card and shipping information at a site's electronic check-out counter. Instead, the electronic wallet automatically fills in form information at sites that recognize the particular wallet software's technology.

Stored-value cards, including smart cards and magnetic strip cards, are physical devices that hold information, including cash value, for the cardholder. Magnetic strip cards have limited capacity. Smart cards can store greater amounts of data on a microchip embedded in the card and are intended to replace the collection of plastic cards people now carry, including payment cards, driver's licenses, and insurance cards. Trials of smart cards in the United States have not been successful; however, smart cards are popular in other parts of the world.

Banks still process most monetary transactions, and a large part of the dollar volume of those transactions is still done by writing checks. Increasingly, banks are using Internet technologies to process those checks. Phishing expeditions and identity theft, especially when perpetrated by large criminal organizations, create a significant threat to online financial institutions and their customers. If not controlled, this threat could reduce the general level of confidence that consumers have in online business and hurt the growth of electronic commerce.

Key Terms

Acquiring bank
Anonymous electronic cash
Automated Clearing House (ACH)
Card not present transaction
Card verification number (CVN)
Casher
Chargeback
Charge card
Check 21
Client-side electronic wallet
Closed loop system
Collector
Credit card
Credit card association
Customer issuing bank
Debit card
Double-spending
Due diligence
Electronic cash
Electronic wallet (e-wallet)
EMV standard
Float
Identity theft
Interoperable software
Merchant account
Merchant bank

Micropayments
Money laundering
Open loop system
Organized crime
Payment card
Payment processing service provider
Peer-to-peer (P2P) payment system
Pharming attack
Racketeering
Scrip
Server-side electronic wallet
Single-use card
Small payments
Smart card
Spear phishing
Stored-value card
Zombie farm

Review Questions

RQ1. In about 100 words, describe the difficulties that can arise for merchants who want to process "card not present" credit card transactions.

RQ2. In about 200 words, outline the reasons that a consumer who owns a credit card might want to use an electronic payment system, such as PayPal, for an Internet transaction. In an additional 200 words, outline the reasons that a small merchant might want to use an electronic payment system in addition to, or instead of, accepting credit cards.

RQ3. In about 100 words, explain what electronic wallets are and how they can be useful to consumers.

RQ4. In about 200 words, outline the advantages and disadvantages of smart cards for online merchants.

RQ5. In Japan, consumers use their mobile phones to pay at vending machines and for small purchases such as subway fares and movie rentals. In about 100 words, outline reasons that you think mobile phone payment systems have not become widely used in the United States.

RQ6. Many banks have decided that the best way to combat the threat of phishing attacks is to educate their customers. In about 100 words, outline the contents of a letter that a bank could use to warn its customers about possible phishing attacks. Be sure to include tips for spotting a phishing e-mail and specific advice regarding what to do (or not do) with it.

Exercises

E1. Matt Remes has formed a small business and has just completed building an electronic commerce Web site that sells subscriptions to special-interest newsletters. The titles range from *Apple Growers Digest* to *Wilderness Backpacking Newsletter*. Many organizations and individuals produce the newsletters, and Matt's role is to raise the visibility of these somewhat obscure publications. The newsletters are published and available either biweekly or monthly. Unlike traditional subscription services, Matt's business has an agreement from all newsletter publishers that he can sell subscriptions for single issues or for periods of up to three years. He does not want to allow subscribers to use their payment cards to purchase a subscription that is less than two years in duration. But he finds that nearly 60 percent of the first-time customers on his site prefer to order a sample issue before committing to a subscription of a year or more. In about 200 words, describe existing systems that Matt could use to provide his subscribers with a system that does not depend on payment cards.

E2. Bonnie Carson has owned and managed her gift and card shop in the Central Shopping Mall for three years. Business has been good, but Bonnie wanted to expand her business. A year ago, she hired a Web designer and built a Web site hosted by a national Internet service provider. Part of the monthly ISP fee for her merchant site includes the software needed to process credit card purchases. She has obtained a merchant account with a national credit card processing company. Bonnie's Web-based business is beginning to pick up. She wants to provide more payment options to her customers and is considering a payment processing service such as PayPal as an additional option. Write a report of about 300 words in which you advise Bonnie on this. Identify at least three reasons that Bonnie should use such a service and at least three reasons why she should not.

E3. Evan Moskowitz has formed an Internet training company called Teach-U-Comp to market and sell computer programming courses online. Each course costs $95, and students receive continuing education units (CEUs) based on the duration of the course and its level of difficulty. Evan expects to sell about 50 courses each month during his first few years in operation. He would like the company to accept credit cards as payment for the courses. Evan is busy creating the online content and installing the course delivery software, so he hired you to investigate payment processing options for the site. Use your favorite search engine or the Open Directory Card Services page to identify three companies that process credit card payments for Web sites that sell services. Examine the processing services offered and fees charged by these three companies and choose one that you believe would be best for Teach-U-Comp. Write a 300-word report in which you summarize your findings. In the conclusion to your report, clearly state which company you would recommend to Evan and explain why.

E4. In about 200 words, outline the types of information bank customers might like to access using their smart phones. Briefly describe concerns that these customers might have because their smart phones have smaller screens than a typical computer's screen. You can use your library or your favorite search engine to conduct your research.

Cases

C1. First Internet Bank of Indiana

During the first wave of electronic commerce, many established banks opened online branches and a considerable number of new, completely online, banks were formed. Many of these online banking initiatives were closed, sold, or merged into other operations after the first wave of electronic commerce had subsided. By 2001, many notable names that had dominated the first wave were gone. For example, Bank One had closed its online subsidiary Wingspan Bank and merged its operations into its existing retail banking department. Royal Bank of Canada had done the same thing with its Security First Network Bank (generally believed to have been the first online bank). CompuBank and G&L Internet Bank were both sold to other banks, and USABancshares.com was closed in a flurry of fraud accusations and regulatory concerns.

Many early online-only banks faced similar challenges. They often bought loans instead of originating them. Purchased loans yield lower interest income because the originating bank always charges a fee or discount. They also tended to pay higher rates on customer deposits to attract new customers. These routes to rapid growth can significantly reduce profitability. Physical banks with many branches gain customers and market share because people walk or drive by a branch office and see the bank's name. New online-only banks must spend substantial sums on advertising that helps establish them as viable brands in a highly competitive market. And many well-established banks now operate online, offering customers a known brand name and the convenience of physical branches along with online banking services. Small businesses were reluctant to deal with online-only banks in the early years of their existence. Small businesses generate considerable profits for banks because they tend to borrow money at relatively high interest rates and also tend to keep large balances in their checking accounts. Thus, there were a number of challenges that made survival difficult for online-only banks.

In 2004, the U.S. Federal Deposit Insurance Corporation (FDIC) issued a report on "limited-purpose banks" (which included online-only banks) in its *Future of Banking Study* series. The FDIC report concluded that the economics of operating an online-only bank were not attractive and that very few such banks could ever expect to be successful in the long term. Despite the FDIC's gloomy outlook, a number of banks operate only online. One of those banks is the **First Internet Bank of Indiana** (often called First IB).

First IB was launched in early 1999. By 2001, the bank had become profitable and had more than $200 million in assets. By 2008, its assets had grown to nearly $600 million. Compared to the large international banks that dominate the financial world, $600 million is a relatively small amount (for example, the Bank of America has more than $500 billion in assets), but First IB was able to operate efficiently and with low costs because it had no physical branch offices and very few employees compared to traditional banks.

First IB invested its resources in building the best Web site it could design and then followed a process of continually adjusting the site's design and the services offered to respond to customer comments and requests. For example, First IB created a frequently asked questions (FAQ) feature that reduced customer inquiries dramatically. It was also one of the first banks to offer statements and check images online. In 2004, the bank began to make check images available online the day after the check cleared (the industry average delay at that time was four to seven days). The bank has consistently received excellent reviews of its services by online business rating agencies and in the press.

Required:

1. Create a list of 10 specific concerns that a consumer might have when considering an online-only bank. Write a paragraph for each concern that describes how First IB addresses or fails to address it.
2. Evaluate how well the design of the First IB Web site meets the needs of a potential small business customer. In about 300 words, discuss the elements of the site that work particularly well in meeting the needs of this type of site visitor. In about 300 words, outline specific changes you would make to the site to better meet the needs of a potential small business customer.
3. Assume you are a security consultant hired by First IB. The president of the bank has become concerned about the potential damage that a phishing expedition directed at First IB customers could do to the bank's reputation. In about 500 words, analyze the phishing threat that faces First IB and outline steps that First IB should take to counter the threat.

Note: Your instructor might assign you to a group to complete this case, and might ask you to prepare a formal presentation of your results to your class.

C2. The Moose Hut

Rod and Martha Nelson started The Moose Hut (TMH), a gift shop in Calgary, Alberta, more than 15 years ago. The Nelsons have capitalized on the tourist trade drawn by the Calgary Stampede, which is one of the largest rodeos in the world. The shop sells a wide range of Canadian-themed items to rodeo fans and other tourists who visit central Alberta throughout the year. TMH's offerings range from inexpensive food items, such as pure Canadian maple syrup and smoked salmon, to much more expensive handcrafted gifts, including Inuit and First Nations artwork. The company's trademark product, the Moose Mug, is one of its biggest-selling items.

Many of TMH's customers return to the store whenever they visit Calgary. TMH's line of Canada Day Party Favours is especially popular with homesick Canadians who have moved to other countries, and TMH has been selling those products by mail order for the past several years. After reviewing the sales numbers for these mail order items, Martha has decided that it might be a good idea to expand the mail order operation and begin accepting orders through a Web site. Many of the store's items have a high value-to-weight ratio and would be easy to ship to customers around the world.

TMH currently accepts only checks denominated in Canadian or U.S. currency in its mail order operation; however, taking orders on a Web site will probably require the company to be more flexible in accepting multiple payment methods. Rod and Martha asked you to help them examine payment processing alternatives for TMH's new Web business.

To be acceptable, a payment processing method needs to handle all major credit cards, perform currency conversions, and be available to a Canadian merchant. Most important is that the payment processing method must be reasonably priced. The margins on most gift items at TMH are between 10 percent and 30 percent of the selling price, but the extra costs of shipping and handling items sold through the Web site will reduce those margins. TMH would like to keep the payment processing costs below 4 percent of the selling price, if possible.

Required:

1. Using the links in the Online Companion for this case, identify at least three payment processing options that might be suitable for TMH. Write a report of about three double-spaced pages in which you describe each of the three payment processing options. Include specific advantages and disadvantages for each option.
2. Prepare a one-page memorandum in which you make a specific recommendation to Rod and Martha. Include an explanation of the reasons for your recommendation.

Note: Your instructor might assign you to a group to complete this case, and might ask you to prepare a formal presentation of your results to your class.

For Further Study and Research

Adams, J. 2009. "New Mobile Banking Tools Get One Step Closer to Payments," *American Banker,* November 3, 14.

AFP Exchange. 2007. "Electronic Payments More Prevalent Than Three Years Ago," November, 27(9), 34.

Albornoz, L. 2007. "Accounts Payable: The Final Frontier for IT," *Computerworld,* December 17, 30–31.

American Banker. 2002. "First Internet of Indiana Turns a Profit Again," 167(95), May 17, 13.

American Banker. 2009. "Online Merchants Cut Fraud Losses," December 1, 11.

Berney, L. 2008. "For Online Merchants, Fraud Prevention Can Be a Balancing Act," *Cards & Payments,* February, 21(2), 22.

Bills, S. 2009. "Consumer Demand for Mobile Banking Tools Growing Rapidly," *American Banker,* December 4. (http://www.americanbanker.com/issues/174_232/demand-mobile-tools-1004783-1.html)

Brandt, A. 2005. "Devious New Phishing Attack Outsmarts Typical Defenses," *PC World,* 23(3), March, 35.

Chang, R. 2009. "What Paying by Cellphone Will Mean for the Marketing World," *Advertising Age,* 80(33), October 5, 4, 29.

Credit Card Management, 2003. "A Dubious Honor for Online Payments," 15(13), March, 14.

Credit Management. 2007. "Electronic Billing Comes of Age," December, 26.

CyberSource Corporation. 2008. *Ninth Annual Online Fraud Report: Online Payment Fraud Trends and Merchants' Response.* Mountain View, CA: CyberSource.

DeCastro, M. 2009. "Mobile Takes a Breather," *American Banker,* October 29, 18–19.

Dragoon, A. 2004. "Fighting Phish, Fakes, and Frauds," *CIO Magazine,* 17(22), September 1, 33–38.

Drake, C., J. Oliver, and E. Koontz. 2004. "Anatomy of a Phishing Email," *Proceedings of the First Conference on Email and Anti-spam.* Mountain View, CA, July 30.

Fest, G. 2008. "How Will Payments Ride Rails?" *Bank Technology News,* 21(7), July, 1, 19.

Fitzgerald, K. 2009. "A Check Logjam For B2B Payments," *Cards & Payments,* 22(4), April, 20–22.

Galbraith, J. 1995. *Money: Whence it Came, Where it Went.* London: Penguin Books.

Gonsalves, A. 2009. "PayPal Unveils Plans to Open Payment Service," *InformationWeek,* November 4.

Grant, D. 2001. "Internet Banking Nightmare: Couple Sue After Access to Their Funds Was Cut Off for 10 Crucial Days," *EastSideJournal.com,* June 10.

Hernandez, W. 2009. "Noncard Payments Gaining Toehold in Bank Channel," *American Banker,* December 1, 6.

Keizer, G. 2005. "Phishing Economics 101 Reveals Collectors and Cashers," *InternetWeek,* July 29.

Kenneally, S. 2008. "Payments Cyber Roundtable: Who Moved the Payments System?" *Community Banker,* April, 17(4), 36–40.

Kingston, J. 2003. "E-Pay Overtaking Paper; Clients Want More Integration," *American Banker,* 168(81), April 29, 21.

Krim, J. 2005. "More ID May Be Required for Online Banking," *The Washington Post,* October 21, D5.

Kuykendall, L. 2003. "Citi to Pull the Plug on c2it Next Month," *American Banker,* October 1, 7.
Larkin, E. 2009. "Go Virtual for Safer Online Shopping," *PC World,* 27(11), November, 35–36.
Lewis, H. 2001. "NetBank, CompuBank Merge, Customers Get Squashed," *Bankrate.com,* May 22. (http://www.bankrate.com/bzrt/news/ob/20010521a.asp)
Markoff, J. 2002. "Vulnerability Is Discovered in Security for Smart Cards," *The New York Times,* May 13. (http://www.nytimes.com/2002/05/13/technology/13SMAR.html)
Marlin, S. 2003. "Who Needs Cash?" *Information Week,* December 29, 20–22.
Mearian, L. 2005. "Wells Fargo Buys into Check Image Sharing," *Computerworld,* January 14. (http://www.computerworld.com/databasetopics/data/story/0,10801,98966,00.html)
Mitchell, D. 2007. "In Online World, Pocket Change Is Not Easily Spent," *The New York Times,* August 27. (http://www.nytimes.com/2007/08/27/technology/27micro.html)
Musgrove, M. 2005. "'Phishing' Keeps Luring Victims," *The Washington Post,* October 22, D1.
Nevius, A. 2009. "IRS Expands Electronic Payment Options," *Journal of Accountancy,* 208(6), 78.
Oehlsen, N. 2009. "Smartphone Payment Apps: Are Developers Marking the Right Call?" *Cards & Payments,* 22(8), September, 26–31.
Orr, B. 2008. "A2A Payments: Next Generation of Online Banking?" *ABA Banking Journal,* April, 100(4), 53.

Ptacek, M. 2001. "CompuBank's Demise May Signal a New Era," *American Banker,* 166(63), April 2, 16.
Quain, J. 2003. "Can You Spare Some Change?" *PC Magazine,* 22(23), December 30, 25.
Ramsaran, C. 2004. "Catch of the Day: Banks Face New Phishing Scams," *Bank Systems & Technology,* December 1, 13.
Ramstad, E. 2004. "Hong Kong's Money Card Is a Hit," *The Wall Street Journal,* February 19, B3.
Rist, C. 2003. "Making Bank on Small Change," *Business 2.0,* 4(10), November, 56–57.
Rob, M. and E. Opara. 2003. "Online Credit Card Processing Models: Critical Issues to Consider by Small Merchants," *Human Systems Management,* 22(3), 133–142.
Roth, A. 2001. "CompuBank Merge Nettles NetBank," *American Banker,* 166(119), June 21, 1–2.
Stoneman, B. 2003. "FAQs Lighten Service Load at First Internet Bank of Indiana," *American Banker,* 168(2), January 13, 12.
Sturgeon, J. 2003. "Electronic Payments," *CFO Magazine,* 19(15), Winter, 52–53.
Tedeschi, B. 2004. "Protect Your Identity," *PC World,* 22(12), December, 107–112.
Torian, R., R. Schrader, O. Ireland, and R. Stinneford. 2008. "Current Developments in Electronic Banking and Payment Systems," *The Business Lawyer,* February, 63(2), 689–702.
Urban, M. 2005. "To Catch Phish, Banks Need Better Bait," *Bank Technology News,* 18(11), November, 57.
Wade, W. 2009. "With E-Transfers, Banks Target Gen-Y Payments," *American Banker,* December 18. (http://www.americanbanker.com/issues/174_242/e-transfers-1005381-1.html)
Wetherington, L. 2008. "The Electronic Payments Explosion," *Texas Banking,* February, 97(2), 14–17.
Wingfield, N. and J. Sapsford. 2002. "eBay to Buy PayPal for $1.4 Billion," *The Wall Street Journal,* July 9, A6.
Wolfe, D. 2008. "Mobile Micropayments to Target U.S. Teenagers," *American Banker,* December 22. (http://www.americanbanker.com/issues/173_258/-369264-1.html)
Yom, C. 2004. "Limited-purpose Banks: Their Specialties, Performance, and Prospects," *FDIC Future of Banking Study Series,* June, 1–45. Washington, D.C.: Federal Deposit Insurance Corporation (FDIC).

PART 4

INTEGRATION

CHAPTER 12

PLANNING FOR ELECTRONIC COMMERCE

LEARNING OBJECTIVES

In this chapter, you will learn about:

- Planning electronic commerce initiatives
- Strategies for developing electronic commerce Web sites
- Managing electronic commerce implementations

INTRODUCTION

AlliedSignal (now **Honeywell**) is a diversified manufacturing and technology business selling products in the aerospace, automotive, chemicals, fibers, and plastics industries. In 1999, the company had more than 70,000 employees and annual sales exceeding $15 billion. Although some of AlliedSignal's products used new technologies or helped other firms create new technologies, many of the products were commodity items that were manufactured and sold just as they had been for decades. In early 1999, AlliedSignal's CEO, Larry Bossidy, called together the heads of the company's business units for a one-day conference to develop strategic plans for electronic commerce at the company. He invited Michael Dell, chairman and CEO of **Dell Computers**, and John Chambers, CEO of **Cisco Systems**, to speak about their companies' electronic commerce implementation successes.

At the end of the day, Bossidy gave the business unit heads their marching orders. They were to take what they had learned and create a strategy for implementing electronic commerce in their business units—in two months. Bossidy told the room full of rather stunned managers that, although most of their business units were at or near the top of their industries, the Internet would change everything. He believed that the kinds of electronic commerce strategies that had worked so well for Dell and Cisco in the computer industry could also work in many of AlliedSignal's businesses. He wanted to make sure that AlliedSignal was the first to exploit those strategies and any other strategies that the business managers could devise. In two months, each manager reported back with a strategy that included multiple electronic commerce projects, such as Web sites for selling products, providing customer service, improving corporate infrastructure, managing supply chains, coordinating logistics, holding auctions, and creating virtual communities. These plans were evaluated in the company's regular annual budget process, and the best ones were chosen for funding and immediate implementation.

In a matter of months, one of the largest industrial enterprises in the world had drastically altered its course, setting sail for the uncharted waters of the first wave of electronic commerce. In the years since, AlliedSignal has gone through many changes, including a merger with Honeywell. The initiatives it undertook as a result of this first electronic commerce strategic planning session were important in making the company an attractive merger candidate. Today, as part of Honeywell, the businesses that were formerly AlliedSignal are using a wide range of Internet technologies in a variety of their supply chain management and purchasing functions.

IDENTIFYING BENEFITS AND ESTIMATING COSTS OF ELECTRONIC COMMERCE INITIATIVES

The ability of companies to plan, design, and implement cohesive electronic commerce strategies makes the difference between success and failure for the majority of them. The tremendous leverage that firms can gain by being the first to do business a new way on the Web has caught the attention of top executives in many industries. The keys to successful implementation of any information technology project are planning and execution. This chapter provides some useful guidelines for those readers who will manage the planning, implementation, and continuing operations of electronic commerce initiatives. A successful business plan for an electronic commerce initiative should include activities that identify the initiative's specific objectives and link those objectives to business strategies (strategies that you learned about in Chapters 3, 4, 5, and 6).

In setting the objectives for an electronic commerce initiative, managers should consider the strategic role of the project, its intended scope, and the resources available for executing it. In this section, you will learn how to identify objectives and link those business objectives to business strategies. In later sections of this chapter, you will learn about Web site development strategies and how to manage the implementation of an electronic commerce initiative.

Identifying Objectives

Businesses undertake electronic commerce initiatives for a wide variety of reasons. Objectives that businesses typically strive to accomplish through electronic commerce include: increasing sales in existing markets, opening new markets, serving existing customers better, identifying new vendors, coordinating more efficiently with existing vendors, or recruiting employees more effectively.

Organizations of different sizes will have different objectives for their electronic commerce initiatives. For example, small companies might want a Web site that encourages site visitors to do business using existing channels rather than through the Web site itself to reduce the cost of the site. A site that offers only product or service information is much less expensive to design, build, and maintain than a site that offers transaction handling, bidding, communications, or other capabilities. Decisions regarding resource allocations for electronic commerce initiatives should consider the expected benefits and costs of meeting the objectives. These decisions should also consider the risks inherent in the electronic commerce initiative and compare them to the risks of inaction—a failure to act could concede a strategic advantage to competitors.

Linking Objectives to Business Strategies

Businesses can use tactics called **downstream strategies** to improve the value that the business provides to its customers. Alternatively, businesses can pursue **upstream strategies** that focus on reducing costs or generating value by working with suppliers or inbound shipping and freight service providers.

In earlier chapters of this book, you learned about many of the things that companies are doing on the Web. The Web is a tremendously attractive sales channel for many firms; however, companies can use electronic commerce to do much more than sell. They can use the Web to complement their business strategies and improve their competitive positions. Electronic commerce opportunities can inspire businesses to undertake activities such as:

- Building brands
- Enhancing existing marketing programs
- Selling products and services
- Selling advertising
- Developing a better understanding of customer needs
- Improving after-sale service and support
- Purchasing products and services
- Managing supply chains
- Operating auctions
- Building virtual communities and Web portals

The success of these activities can be difficult to measure. In the first wave of electronic commerce, many companies engaged in these activities on the Web without setting specific, measurable goals. In the late 1990s, companies that had good ideas could find plenty of investors and start a business activity on the Web. These early activities were often highly speculative. Successes and failures were measured in broad strokes. A company would either become a leader in its industry (perhaps after being acquired by a larger company) or would disappear into bankruptcy—all within a few short years.

In the second wave of electronic commerce, companies are taking a closer look at the benefits and costs of their electronic commerce before committing resources to it. Today, a good online business implementation plan sets specific objectives for benefits to be achieved and costs to be incurred. Often, companies create pilot Web sites to test their online business ideas, then release production Web sites to handle full implementations. Companies must specify clear goals for their pilot tests so that they know when their sites are ready to go into full operation.

Identifying and Measuring Benefits

Some benefits of electronic commerce initiatives are obvious, tangible, and easy to measure. These include such things as increased sales or reduced costs. Other benefits are intangible and can be much more difficult to identify and measure, such as increased customer satisfaction. When identifying benefits, managers should try to set objectives that are measurable, even when those objectives are for intangible benefits. For example, success in achieving a goal of increased customer satisfaction might be measured by counting the number of first-time customers who return to the site and buy.

Many companies create Web sites to build brands or enhance their existing marketing programs. These companies can set goals in terms of increased brand awareness, as measured by market research surveys and opinion polls. Companies that sell goods or services online can measure sales volume in units or dollars. A complication that occurs in measuring either brand awareness or sales is that the increases can be caused by other things that the company is doing at the same time or by a general improvement in the economy. A good marketing research staff or outside consulting firm can help a company sort out the effects of marketing and sales programs. Firms might need these groups to help set and evaluate these kinds of goals for electronic commerce initiatives.

Companies that want to use Web sites to improve customer service or after-sale support might set goals of increased customer satisfaction or reduced costs of providing customer service or support. For example, **Philips Lighting** wanted to use the Web to provide an ordering system for its smaller customers that did not use EDI. The primary goal for this initiative was to reduce the cost of processing smaller orders. Philips had identified that responding to inventory availability and order status inquiries accounted for over half the cost of processing smaller orders. Customers who placed small orders often called or sent faxes asking for this information.

Philips built a pilot Web site and invited a number of its smaller customers to try it. The company found that customer service phone calls from the test group of customers dropped by 80 percent. Based on that measurable increase in efficiency, Philips decided to invest in additional hardware and personnel to staff a version of the Web site that could handle virtually all of its smaller customers. The reduction in the cost of handling small orders justified the additional investment.

Companies can use a variety of similar measurements to assess the benefits of other electronic commerce initiatives. Supply chain managers can measure supply cost reductions, quality improvements, or faster deliveries of ordered goods. Auction sites can set goals for the number of auctions, the number of bidders and sellers, the dollar volume of items sold, the number of items sold, or the number of registered participants. The ability to track such numbers is usually built into auction site software. Virtual communities and Web portals measure the number of visitors and try to measure the quality of their visitors' experiences.

Some sites use online surveys to gather this data; however, most settle for estimates based on the length of time each visitor remains on the site and how often visitors return. A summary of benefits and measurements that companies can make to assess the value of those benefits (these measurements are often called **metrics**) appears in Figure 12-1.

Electronic commerce initiatives	Common measurements of benefits provided
Build brands	Surveys or opinion polls that measure brand awareness, changes in market share
Enhance existing marketing programs and create new marketing programs	Change in per-unit sales volume, frequency of customer contact, conversion (to buyers) rate
Improve customer service	Customer satisfaction surveys, quantity of customer complaints, customer loyalty
Reduce cost of after-sale support	Quantity and type (telephone, fax, e-mail) of support activities, change in net support cost per customer
Improve supply chain operation	Cost, quality, and on-time delivery of materials or services purchased, overall reduction in cost of goods sold
Hold auctions	Quantity of auctions, bidders, sellers, items sold, registered participants; dollar volume of items sold; participation rate
Provide portals, social networks, and virtual communities	Number of visitors, number of return visits per visitor, duration of average visit, participation in online discussions

FIGURE 12-1 Measuring the benefits of electronic commerce initiatives

No matter how a company measures the benefits provided by its Web site, it usually tries to convert the raw activity measurements to dollars. Having the benefits measured in dollars lets the company compare benefits to costs and compare the net benefit (benefits minus costs) of a particular initiative to the net benefits provided by other projects. Although each activity provides some value to the company, it is often difficult to measure that value in dollars. Usually, even the best attempts to convert benefits to dollars yield only rough approximations.

Identifying and Estimating Costs

At first glance, the task of identifying and estimating costs may seem much easier than the task of setting benefits objectives. However, many managers have found that information technology project costs can be just as difficult to estimate and control as the benefits of those projects. Since Web development uses hardware and software technologies that change even more rapidly than those used in other information technology projects, managers often find that their experience does not help much when they are making estimates. Most changes in the cost of hardware are downward, but the increasing sophistication of software often requires more of the newer, less-expensive hardware. This often yields a net increase in overall hardware costs. The more sophisticated software often costs more than the amount originally budgeted, too. Even though electronic commerce initiatives are often completed within a shorter time frame than many other information technology projects, the rapid changes in Web technology can quickly destroy a manager's best-laid plans.

Total Cost of Ownership

In addition to hardware and software costs, the project budget must include the costs of hiring, training, and paying the personnel who will design the Web site, write or customize the software, create the content, and operate and maintain the site. Many organizations now track costs by activity and calculate a total cost for each activity. These cost numbers, called **total cost of ownership (TCO)**, include all costs related to the activity. Increasing some costs can reduce other costs, so most managers find the TCO of a project to be a more appropriate focus for their cost control efforts than the individual elements of the project's cost.

The TCO of an electronic commerce implementation includes the costs of hardware (server computers, routers, firewalls, and load balancing devices), software (licenses for operating systems, Web server software, database software, and application software), design work outsourced, salaries and benefits for employees involved in the project, and the costs of maintaining the site once it is operational. A good TCO calculation would, for example, include assumptions about how often the site would need to be redesigned in the future.

Opportunity Costs

For many companies, one of the largest and most significant costs associated with electronic commerce initiatives is the cost of not undertaking such an initiative. The foregone benefits that a company could have obtained from an electronic commerce initiative that they chose not to pursue are costs. Managers and accountants use the term **opportunity cost** to describe such lost benefits from an action not taken.

Web Site Costs

Over the past 15 years, information technology research firms (such as International Data Corporation and Gartner) and management consulting firms (such as Booz & Company and McKinsey & Company) have regularly estimated the costs of implementing various types of online business operations. Although the total dollar amounts required to create and operate a Web site have varied over the years (and with the specific types of businesses), the relative proportion of costs has remained quite stable. About 10 percent of the cost is for computer hardware, another 10 percent is for software, and about 80 percent of the cost is for labor (including both internal labor and the cost of outside consultants), Another ratio that has remained stable is the annual cost of operating an online business Web site, which ranges between 50 and 200 percent of the initial cost of the site.

As you learned in Chapter 9, a small online store can be placed in operation for under $5000, and a typical small to midsize online business operation with full transaction and payment processing capabilities usually requires an initial investment between $50,000 and $1 million. In fact, surveys of smaller companies showed that their expenditures on construction of new electronic commerce Web sites average $80,000.

Current estimates of the cost to launch electronic commerce sites for larger companies, especially those that must be integrated with existing business operations, are substantially higher. Figure 12-2 summarizes industry estimates for the cost of creating and operating online business Web sites.

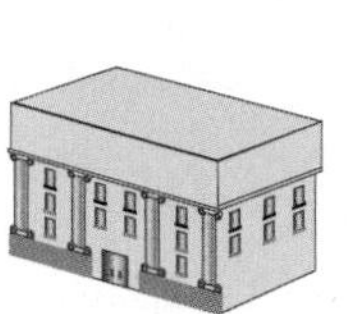

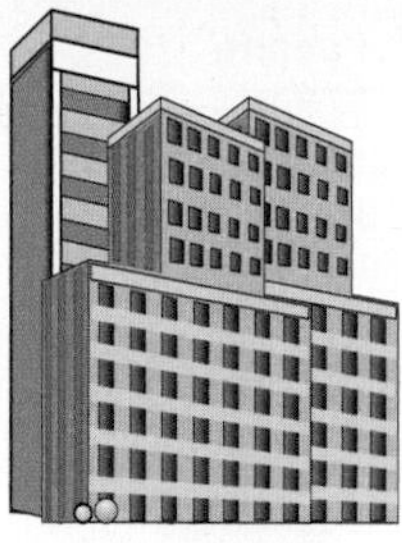

	Small online store	Midsize online business	Large online business	Large company's online business integrated with other business operations
Initial costs	$1000–$5000	$50,000–$1 million	$1 million–$5 million	$5 million–$100 million
Ongoing annual costs	$500–$10,000	$25,000–$2 million	$500,000–$10 million	$2.5 million–$200 million

FIGURE 12-2 Estimated costs for business Web sites

Although the ranges of costs shown in the figure are accurate, many industry observers have noted that costs are generally heading downward. Startup firms increasingly find they can get their operations launched for dollar amounts that are in the low end of the range in each category. Lower costs for broadband access and computer hardware play a major role, but the most significant trend is that the cost of developing and maintaining software to run an online business (a cost that includes a substantial labor component) is decreasing.

Sarah Lacy, a journalist who writes about high technology companies, compared one of the Internet's first successful startups, Netscape, with two more recent startup companies. She noted that Netscape needed more than $40 million to buy equipment, bandwidth, and to pay people to build the software it needed just to get started in the early 1990s. Kevin Rose started his online business, Digg, with an investment of under $500,000 in 2004.

An important element of the annual Web site operating cost (especially for smaller online business implementations) is determined by the choice of Web hosting service provider. Smaller sites can consult an ISP directory such as the directories you learned about in Chapter 9. These sites provide a search engine that helps visitors choose an ISP, Web hosting service, or ASP that meets their needs from the sites' thousands of listings.

For larger Web site implementations, the advice of consultants or other firms that rate service providers (ISPs, ASPs, and CSPs), such as **HostCompare.com** and **Keynote Systems** can be helpful. The most important factors to evaluate when selecting a hosting service are shown in Figure 12-3.

Feature	Typical measures
Functionality	Bandwidth, number of different operating systems and databases supported, disk space, number of e-mail accounts allowed, number and type of software provided (for Web site contruction, traffic analysis, and so on)
Reliability	Guaranteed uptime percentage, guaranteed speed of service reinstatement when it does fail
Scalability	Ease of expansion of bandwidth, disk space, additional software (database, traffic analysis, and so on) that can be added to an account as it grows
Security	Employee background checks, features that provide physical protection of the facilities (fences, alarms, guards, security cameras, and so on) and protection against online intrusions (firewalls, network security software and devices)
Backup and recovery	Frequency of backups, automation of backups, off-site storage of backup media
Cost	Initial and ongoing charges for setup and operation, additional charges for specific software and other features

FIGURE 12-3 Important Web hosting service features

Funding Online Business Startups

In the early days of the Web, many businesses were started by individuals who knew something about computers and technology and who had an idea for a business. Although most of those early businesses failed, some of them were successes. For example, both eBay and Yahoo! were started by computer enthusiasts who decided they might be able to make a little money with their hobbies.

As business interest in the Web grew in the late 1990s, many online startups were started by investors who wanted a chance to make some fast money in what had become the Internet boom. A person would come up with an idea for an online business and pitch it to a group of businesspersons who had money. These investors, often called **angel investors**, would fund the initial startup. In return for their capital, angel investors would become stockholders in the business and would often own more of the business than the founder. Typical funding by angel investors would be between a few hundred thousand dollars and a few million dollars. Angel investors hoped that the business would grow rapidly so that in a short time they could sell their interest in the company at a profit to the next round of investors, called venture capitalists.

Venture capitalists are very wealthy individuals, groups of wealthy individuals, or investment firms that look for small companies that are about to grow rapidly. They invest large amounts of money (between a million and a few hundred million dollars) hoping that in a few years the company will be large enough to sell stock to the public in an event called an **initial public offering (IPO)**. In the IPO, the venture capitalists take their profits and once again search for a new small company in which to invest.

This system of financing startup and initial growth of online businesses has both benefits (it provided access to large amounts of capital early in the life of the business) and costs (angel investors and venture capitalists got most of the profits and put great pressure on the business to grow rapidly) for the founders of those businesses. With the high costs of launching online business Web sites in the first wave of electronic commerce, business founders had few alternatives. Now that the costs of creating an online business have gone down, the number of founders who can avoid venture capitalists and even angel investors is increasing. By relieving the pressure to grow rapidly, online entrepreneurs can be more creative and have a chance to learn from their mistakes. Industry observers expect this trend toward more and smaller online ventures to continue as the cost of creating an online business continues to fall.

Comparing Benefits to Costs

Most companies have procedures that call for an evaluation of any major expenditure of funds. These major investments in equipment, personnel, and other assets are called **capital projects** or **capital investments**. The techniques that companies use to evaluate proposed capital projects range from very simple calculations to complex computer simulation models. However, no matter how complex the technique, it always reduces to a comparison of benefits and costs. If the benefits exceed the costs of a project by a comfortable margin, the company invests in the project.

A key part of creating a business plan for electronic commerce initiatives is the process of identifying potential benefits (including intangibles such as employee satisfaction and company reputation), identifying the total costs required to generate those benefits, and evaluating whether the value of the benefits exceeds the total of the costs. Companies should evaluate each element of their electronic commerce strategies using this cost/benefit approach. A representation of the cost/benefit approach appears in Figure 12-4.

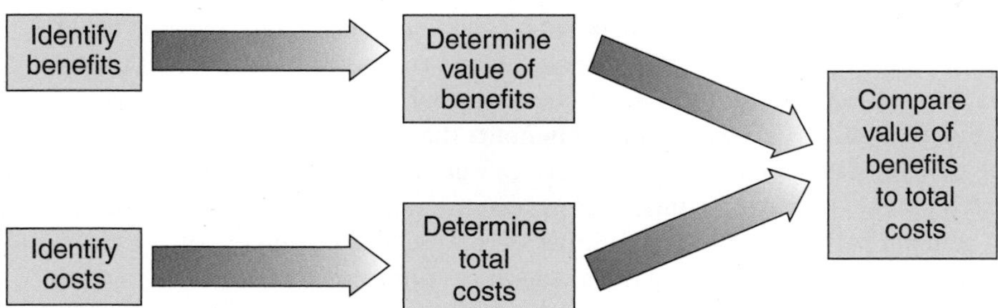

FIGURE 12-4 Cost/benefit evaluation of electronic commerce strategy elements

Return on Investment (ROI)

You might have learned techniques for capital project evaluation, such as the payback method, the net present value method, or the internal rate of return method, in your accounting or finance courses. These evaluation approaches are called **return on investment (ROI)** techniques because they measure the amount of income (return) that will be provided by a specific current expenditure (investment). ROI techniques provide a quantitative expression of whether the benefits of a particular investment exceed their costs (including opportunity costs). They can also mathematically adjust for the reduced value of benefits that the investment will return in future years (benefits received in future years are worth less than those received in the current year).

Although most companies evaluate the anticipated value of electronic commerce initiatives in some way before approving them, many companies see these projects as absolutely necessary investments. Thus, businesses might not subject these initiatives to the same close examination and rigid requirements as other capital projects. These companies fear being left behind as competitors stake their claims in the online marketspace. The value of early positioning in a new market is so great that many companies are willing to invest large amounts of money with few near-term profit prospects.

Newspaper Web sites are one example of an industry's willingness to incur losses to establish an online presence. In the first wave of electronic commerce, there were few profitable newspaper sites (such as Gannet's **USA Today** and *The Wall Street Journal's* **WSJ.com** sites). Most newspaper sites took many years to become profitable (and a significant number remain unprofitable today). As you learned earlier in this book, newspaper sites have experimented with various ways to generate revenue, such as charging for subscriptions, charging for access to certain content, or charging for access to archived articles. Despite their continuing losses, most newspaper companies believe that they cannot afford to ignore the long-term potential of the Web. These companies estimate that the opportunity costs of not being present on the Web (for example, the loss of future profits to be earned from the Web site or the risk of losing market share to competitors) are greater than the losses they are experiencing in their online operations.

In the second wave of electronic commerce, more companies began taking a harder look at Web-related expenditures. Many companies have turned to ROI as the measurement tool for evaluating new electronic commerce projects because that is what they used for other IT projects in the past. ROI is a simple-to-understand tool that is easily applied; however, managers should be careful when using it to evaluate online business initiatives. ROI has some built-in biases that can lead managers to make poor decisions.

First, ROI requires that all costs and benefits be stated in dollars. Because it is usually easier to quantify costs than benefits, ROI measurements can be biased in a way that gives undue weight to costs. Second, ROI focuses on benefits that can be predicted. Many electronic commerce initiatives have returned benefits that were not foreseen by their planners. The benefits developed after the initiatives were in place. For example, Cisco Systems created online customer forums to allow customers to discuss product issues with each other. The main benefits from this initiative were to reduce customer service costs and increase customer satisfaction regarding the availability of product information; however, the forums turned out to be a great way for Cisco engineers to get feedback from customers on new products that they were developing. This second use was not foreseen by the project's planners and has become the most important and beneficial outcome of the customer forums. An ROI analysis would have missed this benefit completely.

Yet another weakness of ROI is that it tends to emphasize short-run benefits over long-run benefits. The mathematics of ROI calculations do account for both correctly, but short-term benefits are easier to foresee, so they tend to get included in the ROI calculations. Long-term benefits are harder to imagine and harder to quantify, so they tend to be included less often and less accurately in the ROI calculation. This biases ROI calculations to weigh short-term costs and benefits more heavily than long-term costs and benefits. This can lead managers who rely on ROI measures to make incorrect decisions. You can learn more about this topic at the **CIO Budget** and the Computerworld **ROI Knowledge Center** Web pages.

STRATEGIES FOR DEVELOPING ELECTRONIC COMMERCE WEB SITES

When companies first established presences on the Web, the typical Web site was a static brochure that was not updated frequently with new information and seldom included any business transaction processing capabilities. Most Web sites today include transaction processing and a variety of other automated business processing capabilities. Web sites are important parts of companies' information systems infrastructures. This evolution of Web site functions is shown in Figure 12-5.

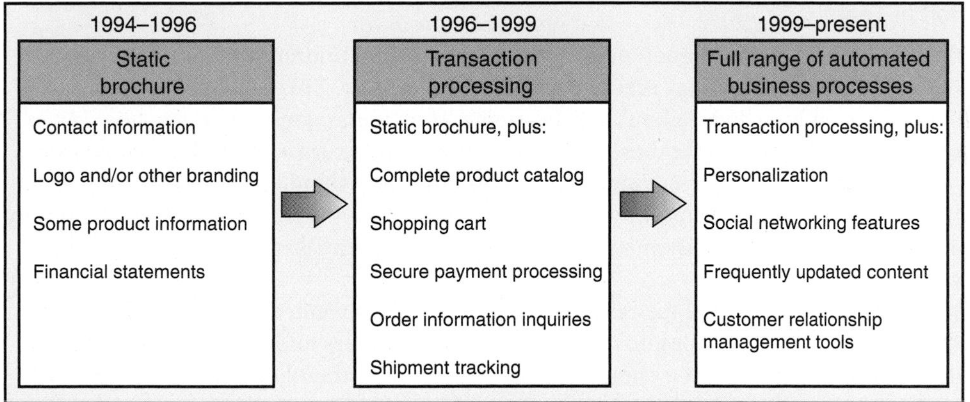

FIGURE 12-5 Evolution of Web site functions

This transformation occurred rapidly in most companies. Because the change in the focus of Web sites happened so fast, few businesses were able to change the way they developed and managed their Web sites to meet the demands of this new focus. Although the scope of business Web sites have expanded, few businesses manage their Web sites as the dynamic business applications they have become. Fortunately, large companies have developed tools that they use to manage their software development projects. As companies begin to see their Web sites as collections of software applications, they are beginning to use these tools to manage the development and maintenance of their Web sites.

Many larger companies have found it difficult to develop new information systems and Web sites that work with such systems to create new markets or reconfigure their supply chains. In the past, companies that have had success in exploring new ways of working with their customers and suppliers by reconfiguring supply chains have often had years to complete those reconfigurations. The Internet has changed markets and marketing channels throughout many industry value chains very quickly. Many companies have managed these changes by using alternatives to traditional systems development methods, including the incubator and fast venturing approaches that you will learn about later in this chapter.

Internal Development vs. Outsourcing

Although many companies would like to think that they can avoid electronic commerce site development problems by outsourcing the entire project, savvy leaders realize that they cannot. No matter what kind of electronic commerce initiative a company is contemplating, the initiative's success depends on how well it is integrated into and supports the activities in which the business is already engaged. Using internal people to lead all projects helps to ensure that the company's specific needs are addressed and that the initiative is congruent with the goals and the culture of the organization. Outside consultants are seldom able to learn enough about an organization's culture to accomplish these objectives. However, few companies are large enough or have sufficient in-house expertise to launch an electronic commerce project without some external help. Even Wal-Mart, the largest retailer in the world, did not undertake its 2000 Web site relaunch alone. The key to success is finding the right balance between outside and inside support for the project. Hiring another company to provide the outside support for all or part of the project is called **outsourcing**.

The Internal Team

The first step in determining which parts of an electronic commerce project to outsource is to create an internal team that is responsible for the project. This team should include people with enough knowledge about the Internet and its technologies to know what kinds of things are possible. Team members should be creative thinkers who are interested in taking the company beyond its current boundaries, and they should be people who have distinguished themselves in some way by doing something very well for the company. If they are not already recognized by their peers as successful individuals, the project may suffer from lack of credibility.

Some companies make the mistake of appointing as electronic commerce project leader a technical wizard who does not know much about the business and is not well-known throughout the company. Such a choice can greatly increase the likelihood of failure. Business knowledge, creativity, and the respect of the firm's operating function managers are all much more important than technical expertise in establishing successful electronic commerce. Project leaders need a good sense of the company's goals and culture to manage an implementation effectively.

Measuring the achievements of this internal team is very important. The measurements do not have to be monetary. Achievement can be expressed in whatever terms are appropriate to the objectives of the initiative. Customer satisfaction, number of sales leads generated, and reductions in order-processing time are examples of metrics that can provide a sense of the team's level of accomplishment. The measurements should show how the project is affecting the company's ability to provide value to the consumer. Many consultants advise companies to set aside between 5 percent and 10 percent of a project's budget for quantifying the project's value and measuring the achievement of that value.

Increasingly, companies are recognizing the value of the accumulated mass of employees' knowledge about the business and its processes. The value of an organization's pool of this type of knowledge is called **intellectual capital**. In the past, many companies ignored the value of intellectual capital because these human assets did not appear in the accounting records or financial statements.

Leif Edvinsson has pioneered the use of human capital measures at Skandia Group, a large financial services company in Sweden. In addition to acknowledging employees' competencies, Edvinsson's measures include the value of customer loyalty and business partnerships as part of a company's intellectual capital. This networking approach to evaluating intellectual capital shows promise as a tool for assessing and tracking the value of internal teams and their connections to external consultants. These measurements are now being adapted for use in measuring systems development efforts. You can learn more about the use of human capital measurements by reading the books by Edvinsson and Max Boisot, another proponent of human capital measurement, which are included in the For Further Study and Research section at the end of this chapter.

The internal team should hold ultimate and complete responsibility for the electronic commerce initiative, from the setting of objectives to the final implementation and operation of the site. The internal team decides which parts of the project to outsource, to whom those parts are outsourced, and what consultants or partners the company needs to hire for the project. Consultants, outsourcing providers, and partners can be extremely important early in the project because they often develop skills and expertise in new technologies before most information systems professionals.

Early Outsourcing

In many electronic commerce projects, the company outsources the initial site design and development to launch the project quickly. The outsourcing team then trains the company's information systems professionals in the new technology before handing the operation of the site over to them. This approach is called **early outsourcing**. Since operating an electronic commerce site can rapidly become a source of competitive advantage for a company, it is best to have the company's own information systems people working closely with the outsourcing team and developing ideas for improvements as early as possible in the life of the project.

Late Outsourcing

In the more traditional approach to information systems outsourcing, the company's information systems professionals do the initial design and development work, implement the system, and operate the system until it becomes a stable part of the business operation. Once the company has gained all the competitive advantage provided by the system, the maintenance of the electronic commerce system can be outsourced so that the company's information systems professionals can turn their attention and talents to developing new technologies that will provide further competitive advantage. This approach is called **late outsourcing**. Although for years late outsourcing has been the standard for allocating scarce information systems talent to projects, electronic commerce initiatives lend themselves more to the early outsourcing approach.

Partial Outsourcing

In both the early outsourcing and late outsourcing approaches, a single group is responsible for the entire design, development, and operation of a project—either inside or outside the company. This typical outsourcing pattern works well for many information systems projects. However, electronic commerce initiatives can benefit from a partial outsourcing approach, too. In **partial outsourcing**, which is also called **component outsourcing**, the company identifies specific portions of the project that can be completely designed, developed, implemented, and operated by another firm that specializes in a particular function.

Many smaller Web sites outsource their e-mail handling and response functions. Customers expect rapid and accurate responses to any e-mail inquiry they make of a Web site with which they are doing business. Many companies send the customer an automatic order confirmation by e-mail as soon as the order or credit card payment is accepted. A number of companies provide e-mail auto response functions on an outsourcing basis.

Another common example of partial outsourcing is an electronic payment system. Many vendors are willing to provide complete customer payment processing. These vendors provide a site that takes over when customers are ready to pay and returns the customers to the original site after processing the payment transaction.

One of the most common elements of electronic commerce initiatives that companies outsource using this approach is Web hosting activity. Web hosting service providers are usually willing to accommodate requests for a variety of service levels. Small businesses can rent space on an existing server at the ISP's location. Larger companies can purchase the server hardware and have the service provider install and maintain it at the service provider's location. The service provider has the continuous staffing and expertise needed to keep an electronic commerce site up and running 24 hours a day, seven days a week (this kind of service is often called **24/7 operation**).

A number of service providers offer services beyond basic Internet connectivity to companies that want to do business on the Web. Many of these services were described earlier as candidates for partial outsourcing strategies and include automated e-mail response, transaction processing, payment processing, security, customer service and support, order fulfillment, and product distribution.

LEARNING FROM FAILURES

Nordisk Aviation

Nordisk Aviation is a subsidiary of the Norwegian Norsk Hydro Group. It designs, manufactures, and repairs air cargo containers for both freight and passenger baggage for major airlines throughout the world and for freight carriers such as FedEx and UPS. It also designs and sells handling systems and pallets that work with the containers. The company has annual sales of more than $100 million and employs more than 150 people at its locations around the world.

Nordisk was a strong believer in using the outsourcing approach for its IT projects—its IT Department included only two people. These two IT staff members worked as the overseers of every IT design and implementation project for the company. They also managed the ongoing IT services provided to Nordisk by other companies.

In late 2000, Manfred Gollent, the president of Nordisk, decided it was time to upgrade the company's Web site—which had been operating as an information site for several years—to include portal features that would allow Nordisk customers to check order status and learn about current developments in container and container-handling systems design.

Continued

The logical approach for Nordisk was to find a company to which it could outsource the project.

The two members of Nordisk's IT staff went to work finding suitable Web developers. The previous Web developer had disappeared; they were unable to find any trace of the person who had created the existing Web site. The developer had created the Web site so that it used a number of programs to deliver dynamic pages. Unfortunately, the developer had given Nordisk only the executable code and not the actual programs. He also did not provide Nordisk with any documentation of the programs.

When the Web site was initially created, it was not an important strategic project for Nordisk. The IT staff members, who were busy with other important projects, did not ensure that the application code and documentation were received. Nordisk had to hire a company to rebuild the site completely to obtain the additional portal functions it wanted to add to the site. The lesson from the Nordisk case is that even when a company is outsourcing virtually all of its Web development, it must have procedures in place to ensure that the project is internally managed and documented.

New Methods for Implementing Partial Outsourcing

Although partial outsourcing has been used in IT management for many years, new ways of implementing it were developed specifically for Web businesses. The next two sections describe two of these new implementation approaches: incubators and fast venturing.

Incubators

An **incubator** is a company that offers start-up companies a physical location with offices, accounting and legal assistance, computers, and Internet connections at a very low monthly cost. Sometimes, the incubator offers seed money, management advice, and marketing assistance as well. In exchange, the incubator receives an ownership interest in the company, typically between 10 percent and 50 percent.

When the company grows to the point that it can obtain venture capital financing or launch a public offering of its stock, the incubator sells all or part of its interest and reinvests the money in a new incubator candidate. One of the first Internet incubators was **Idealab**, which helped companies such as CarsDirect.com, Overture, and Tickets.com get their starts. Today, Idealab focuses on its own internally generated ideas rather than soliciting ideas from outside entrepreneurs, but it still operates as an incubator.

Some companies have created internal incubators. A number of companies used internal incubators in the past to develop technologies that the companies planned to use in their main business operations. Most of these programs, such as the Kodak internal venturing program of the 1980s, were unsuccessful and, ultimately, were shut down. Employees in internal incubators found it difficult to maintain an entrepreneurial spirit when they knew that the technology they were developing would ultimately be taken away and controlled by the parent company.

More recently, companies such as Matsushita Electric's U.S. Panasonic division started internal incubators to help launch new companies that will grow to become important strategic partners. The companies launched in the incubator retain their individual management teams and the assets they develop. These strategic partner incubators have yielded much better results than old-style technology development incubators.

Fast Venturing

Often, large companies struggle to emulate the entrepreneurial spirit of smaller companies as they launch their Internet business initiatives. Many of these companies are trying to expand the internal incubator model and create an effective support system for new business and technology ideas, such as electronic commerce initiatives. One approach that is becoming popular is called fast venturing.

In **fast venturing**, an existing company that wants to launch an electronic commerce initiative joins external equity partners and operational partners that can offer the experience and skills needed to develop and scale up the project very rapidly. Equity partners are usually banks or venture capitalists that sometimes offer money, but are more likely to offer experience gained from guiding other start-ups that they have funded. Operational partners are firms, such as systems integrators and consultants, that have experience in moving projects along and scaling up prototypes. The roles of each participant in fast venturing are described in Figure 12-6.

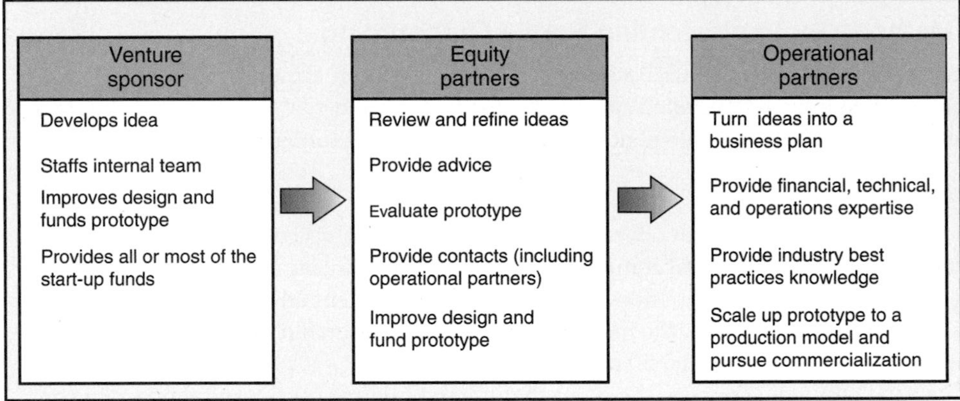

FIGURE 12-6 Elements of fast venturing

Fast venturing starts with the venture sponsor, an existing company that wants to launch the electronic commerce initiative, but that does not have experience in starting new businesses. Then, equity partners, which are entities that have provided start-up money to new ventures in the past and have developed knowledge about operating new ventures, provide advice to the venture sponsor. The operational partners are people and companies that previously have built Web business sites. Thus, they can provide expertise in the technologies and business practices needed to create a successful operating electronic commerce site. The figure shows the flow of information and activities over time, starting with the venture sponsor, whose activities lead to the work done by the equity partners, which then pass the project on to the operational partners for implementation.

MANAGING ELECTRONIC COMMERCE IMPLEMENTATIONS

The best way to manage any complex electronic commerce implementation is to use formal management techniques. Project management, project portfolio management, specific staffing, and postimplementation audits are methods businesses use to efficiently administer their electronic commerce projects.

Project Management

Project management is a collection of formal techniques for planning and controlling the activities undertaken to achieve a specific goal. Project management was developed by the U.S. military and the defense contractors that worked with the military in the 1950s and the 1960s to develop weapons and other large systems. Not only was defense spending increasing in those years, but individual projects were becoming so large that it became impossible for managers to maintain control over them without some kind of assistance.

The project plan includes criteria for cost, schedule, and performance—it helps project managers make intelligent trade-off decisions regarding these three criteria. For example, if it becomes necessary for a project to be completed early, the project manager can compress the schedule by either increasing the project's cost or decreasing its performance.

Today, project managers use specific application software called **project management software** to help them oversee projects. Commercial project management software products, such as Oracle Primavera P6 and Microsoft Project, give managers an array of built-in tools for managing resources and schedules. The software can generate charts and tables that show, for example, which parts of the project are critical to its timely completion, which parts can be rescheduled or delayed without changing the project completion date, and where additional resources might be most effective in speeding up the project. Open Workbench is an open-source project management software package that offers many of the same features as the leading commercial products. In addition to managing the people and tasks of the internal team, project management software can help the team manage the tasks assigned to consultants, technology partners, and outsourced service providers. By examining the costs and completion times of tasks as they are completed, project managers can learn how the project is progressing and continually revise the estimated costs and completion times of future tasks.

Information systems development projects have a well-deserved reputation for running out of control and ultimately failing. They are much more likely to fail than other types of projects, such as building construction projects. The main causes for information systems project failures are rapidly changing technologies, long development times, and changing customer expectations. Because of this vulnerability, many teams rely on project management software to help them achieve project goals.

Although electronic commerce certainly uses rapidly changing technologies, the development times for most electronic commerce projects are relatively short—often they are accomplished in under six months. This gives both the technologies and the expectations of users less time to change. Thus, electronic commerce initiatives are, in general, more successful than other types of information systems implementations.

You can learn more about project management by reading the references listed in the For Further Study and Research section at the end of this chapter, or by clicking the Online Companion link for the **Project Management Institute**, a not-for-profit organization devoted to the promotion of professional project management practices.

Project Portfolio Management

Larger organizations often have many IT implementation projects going on simultaneously—a number of which could be electronic commerce implementations or updates. Some chief information officers (CIOs) of larger companies now use a portfolio approach to managing these multiple projects. **Project portfolio management** is a technique in which each project is monitored as if it were an investment in a financial portfolio. The CIO records the projects in a list (usually using spreadsheet or database management software) and updates the list regularly with current information about each project's status. By managing each project as a portfolio element, project portfolio managers can make tradeoffs between cost, schedule, and quality across projects as well as within individual projects. This gives the organization more flexibility in allocating resources to achieve the best set of benefits from all of the projects in the most timely manner.

Project management software performs a function similar to this for the tasks within a project, but most project management software packages are designed to handle individual projects and do not do a very good job of consolidating activities across multiple projects. Also, the information used in project portfolio management differs somewhat from the information used to manage specific projects. Project management software tracks the details of how each project is accomplishing its specific goals. In project portfolio management, the CIO assigns a ranking for each project based on its importance to the strategic goals of the business and its level of risk (probability of failure).

To develop these rankings, the CIO can use any of the methods that financial managers use to evaluate the risk of making investments in business assets. Indeed, using the tools of financial management helps the CIO to explain electronic commerce projects as investments in assets—using the language that financial managers (and often the CEO) understand. You can learn more about project portfolio management by reading the Berinato article cited in the For Further Study and Research section at the end of this chapter.

Staffing for Electronic Commerce

Regardless of whether the internal team decides to outsource parts of the design and implementation activity, it must determine the staffing needs of the electronic commerce initiative. The general areas of staffing that are most important to the success of an electronic commerce initiative include:

- Chief information officer
- Business managers
- Project managers
- Project portfolio managers
- Account managers
- Applications specialists

- Web programmers
- Web graphics designers
- Content creators
- Content managers or editors
- Social networking administrators
- Online marketing managers
- Customer service reps
- Systems administrators
- Network operators
- Database administrators

The **chief information officer** (**CIO**) is an organization's top technology manager. As such, the CIO is responsible for overseeing all of the information systems and related technological elements required to undertake and operate online business activities. The CIO's perspective is strategic and the person holding this position often serves as an important advocate for online business initiatives. CIOs frequently have an undergraduate degree in computer information systems (or a similar field) and a graduate degree in business or information technology management. They must have many years of experience in increasingly responsible management positions.

The business management function should include internal staff. The **business manager** should be a member of the internal team that sets the objectives for the project. The business manager is responsible for implementing the elements of the business plan and reaching the objectives set by the internal team. If revisions to the plan are necessary as the project proceeds, the business manager develops specific proposals for plan modifications and additional funding and presents them to the internal team and top management for approval.

The business manager should have experience and knowledge related to the business activity that is being implemented on the electronic commerce site. For example, if business managers are assigned to a retail consumer site, they should have experience managing a retail sales operation.

In addition to including the business manager, the business management function in large electronic commerce initiatives may include other individuals who carry out specialized functions, such as project management or account management, that the business manager does not have time to handle personally. A **project manager** is a person with specific training or skills in tracking costs and the accomplishment of specific objectives in a project. Many project managers are certified by organizations such as the Project Management Institute (which you learned about earlier in this chapter) and have skills in the use of project management software.

The **project portfolio manager** is usually promoted from the ranks of the project managers and has the responsibility for tracking all ongoing projects and managing them as a portfolio. This is the person who makes the tradeoffs in cost, schedule and quality across projects and balances the needs of the organization with the resources devoted to all projects.

An **account manager** keeps track of multiple Web sites in use by a project or keeps track of the projects that will combine to create a larger Web site. Most larger projects will have a test version, a demonstration version, and a production version of the Web site located on different servers. The test version is the "under construction" version of a

Web site. Because most sites are frequently updated with new features and content, the test version gives the company a place to make sure that each new feature works before exposing it to customers. The demonstration version has features that have passed testing and must be demonstrated to an internal audience (for example, the Marketing Department) for approval. The production version is the full operating version of the site that is available to customers and other visitors. The account manager supervises the location of specific Web pages and related software installations as they are moved from test to demonstration to production. In smaller projects, the business manager handles the project and account management functions.

As more vendors provide packaged software solutions for electronic commerce, such as those you learned about in Chapter 9, companies need information systems staff that can install and maintain the software. Most large businesses have **applications specialists** who maintain accounting, human resources, and logistics software. Similarly, electronic commerce sites that buy software to handle catalogs, payment processing, and other features need applications specialists to maintain the software. Although the installation of these software packages can be outsourced, most companies prefer to train internal staff to serve in this function when the site becomes operational.

Web sites have evolved from static HTML to more complex designs built with dynamic Web page generation technologies and XML data integration. As Web sites have become more complicated, the need for **Web programmers**, who design and write the underlying code for dynamic database-driven Web pages, has increased. Good Web programmers are familiar with several different dynamic Web page generation technologies and are highly skilled in at least one of them. Many Web programmers also have database manipulation and query skills, such as the ability to write SQL or PHP code.

Because the Web is a visual medium, the role of graphic elements on individual Web pages is important. A company must either retain the services of a graphics design firm, a Web design firm that includes graphics designers, or must hire employees with graphics design skills. A **Web graphics designer** is a person trained in art, layout, and composition and who also understands how Web pages are constructed. The Web graphics designer, or design team for larger sites, must ensure that the Web pages on the site are visually appealing, easy to use, and make consistent use of graphics elements from page to page.

Most larger sites and many smaller sites include content created specifically for the Web site. Other sites adapt content from existing sources within the company for use on the Web site, or purchase content to use on the site. These activities require that the company hire **content creators** to write original content and **content managers** or **content editors** to purchase existing material and adapt it for use on the site.

A relatively new addition to the online business team, the position of **social networking administrator** is responsible for managing the virtual community elements of the Web operation. These administrators might have backgrounds in technology, sales, customer service, or in widely diverse fields such as sociology or anthropology. They must coordinate all of the technologies that make the site work as a social network in ways that create value for the organization.

Although many organizations operate their online marketing function out of their traditional marketing departments, employees with the position of **online marketing manager** specialize in the specific techniques used to build brands and increase market share using the Web site and other online tools, such as e-mail marketing. These managers often have an extensive background in marketing and combine that with knowledge of technologies that allow them to manage the organization's online marketing function.

The Web offers businesses a unique opportunity to reach out to their customers. Thus, business-to-consumer and business-to-business sites that want to capitalize on that opportunity must include a customer relationship management function. **Customer service** personnel help design and implement customer relationship management activities in the electronic commerce operation. They can, for example, issue and administer passwords, design customer interface features, handle customer e-mail and telephone requests for service or follow-up action, and conduct telemarketing for the site. Companies strive to provide the best possible service to satisfy the demands of their customers. The increasing power of customers to organize and express their expectations on the Web is a natural extension of the increase in consumerism that has occurred over the past two decades.

Some companies outsource parts of their customer relationship management operation to independent call centers. A **call center** is a company that handles incoming customer telephone calls and e-mails for other companies. Using a call center often makes sense for smaller companies that do not have the volume of customer inquiries to justify creating an internal call center operation. Some call centers work with a variety of businesses; others focus on one specialty area. For example, a specialized call center might contract with software manufacturers to provide installation help for their software products. Call center employees who are skilled in helping customers install one software package are often able to learn how to support other software packages very quickly.

A systems administrator who understands the server hardware and operating system is an essential part of a successful electronic commerce implementation. The **systems administrator** is responsible for the system's reliable and secure operation. If the site operation is outsourced to a service provider, the service provider supplies this function. If the site is hosted by the company, it needs to devote at least one person to this job. In addition, the internal system administrator needs sufficient staff to maintain full 24/7 operation and site security. These **network operations** staff functions include load estimation and load monitoring, resolving network problems as they arise, designing and implementing fault-resistant technologies, and managing any network operations that are outsourced to service providers or telephone companies.

Most electronic commerce sites require a **database administration** function to support activities such as transaction processing, order entry, inquiry management, or shipment logistics. These activities require either an existing database into which the site is being integrated, or a separate database established for the electronic commerce initiative. It is important to have a database administrator who can effectively manage the design and implementation of this function.

Postimplementation Audits

After an electronic commerce site is successfully launched, most of the project's resources are devoted to maintaining and improving the site's operations. However, an increasing number of businesses are realizing the value of a postimplementation audit. A **postimplementation audit** (also called a **postaudit review**) is a formal review of a project after it is up and running.

The postimplementation audit gives managers a chance to examine the objectives, performance specifications, cost estimates, and scheduled delivery dates that were established for the project in its planning stage and compare them to what actually happened. In the past, most project reviews focused on identifying individuals to blame for cost overruns or missed delivery dates. Because many external forces in technology projects can overwhelm the best efforts of managers, this blame identification approach was generally unproductive, as well as uncomfortable, for the managers on the project. Today, the postimplementation audit is used by most organizations to gather lessons learned from both successful and unsuccessful projects. These lessons can be accumulated and, over time, used to create and update a set of standard best practices for the organization.

A postimplementation audit allows the internal team, the business manager, and the project manager to raise questions about the project's objectives and provide their "in-the-trenches" feedback on strategies that were set in the project's initial design. By agreeing beforehand not to lay blame, the company obtains valuable information that it can use in planning future projects and gives the participants a meaningful learning experience.

The audit should result in a comprehensive report that analyzes the project's overall performance, how well the project was administered, whether the organizational structure was appropriate for the project, and the specific performance of the project team(s). Each section of the report should compare actual results to the project's objectives. Many companies modify their project management organization structure after completing each project based on the contents of postaudit review reports. Many companies also include a confidential section in the report that evaluates each team member's performance on the project. Summaries of member performance can help managers decide which employees should be included in future team projects.

Change Management

Any information system project involves change, and change can be upsetting to people. As employees of an organization become accustomed to their specific duties, many of them draw comfort from their knowledge and develop a sense of security because they know their jobs well and are good at doing them. When changes are introduced into a workplace, employees become concerned about their abilities to cope with the changes and with their ability to continue to do good work. They often become worried that they might lose their jobs. These concerns can lead to increased stress that can be damaging to morale and work performance.

Management researchers have developed strategies for **change management**, which is the process of helping employees cope with these changes. Change management techniques include communicating the need for change to employees, including employees in the decision processes leading up to the change, allowing employees to participate in the planning for the change, and other tactics designed to help employees feel that they are a part of the change. This helps employees overcome the feelings of powerlessness that can lead to stress and reduced work performance.

Summary

This chapter provided an overview of key elements that are typically included in business plans for electronic commerce implementations. The first step is setting objectives. Specific objectives derive from the initiative's overall goals and include planned benefits and planned costs. The benefit and cost objectives should be stated in measurable terms, such as dollars or quantities. Before undertaking an electronic commerce project, most companies will evaluate its estimated costs and benefits.

Businesses use a number of evaluation techniques; however, most businesses calculate projects' return on investment to gauge their value. In the early days of electronic commerce, many companies undertook electronic commerce projects without evaluating their costs and benefits in detail because they feared being left out of the Internet boom. In the second wave of electronic commerce, fewer companies are undertaking electronic commerce initiatives without subjecting them to the same quantitative analysis they use for other IT projects. However, the benefits of electronic commerce projects can be harder to define and quantify than the benefits expected from most other IT projects, so managers should be careful when using these quantitative measures to evaluate electronic commerce projects.

Companies must decide how much, if any, of an electronic commerce project to outsource. The first step in determining an outsourcing strategy is to form an internal team that includes knowledgeable individuals from within the company. The internal team develops the specific project objectives and is responsible for meeting those objectives. The internal team designs an outsourcing strategy, selects a hosting service (or decides to have the company host its own Web server), and supervises the staffing of the project.

Project management is a formal way to plan and control specific tasks and resources used in a project. It provides project managers with a tool they can use to make informed trade-offs among the project elements of schedule, cost, and performance. Large organizations are beginning to use project portfolio management techniques to track and make trade-offs among multiple ongoing projects. Electronic commerce initiatives are usually completed within a short time frame and thus are less likely to run out of control than other information systems development projects.

The company must staff the electronic commerce initiative regardless of whether portions of the project are outsourced. Critical staffing areas include business management, application specialists, customer service staff, systems administration, network operations staff, and database administration. A good way for all participants to learn from project experiences is to conduct a postimplementation audit that compares project objectives to the actual results.

Key Terms

24/7 operation
Account manager
Angel investor
Applications specialist
Business manager
Call center
Capital investment
Capital project
Change management
Chief information officer (CIO)
Component outsourcing
Content creator
Content editor
Content manager
Customer service
Database administration

Downstream strategies
Early outsourcing
Fast venturing
Incubator
Initial public offering (IPO)
Intellectual capital
Late outsourcing
Metrics
Network operations
Online marketing manager
Opportunity cost
Outsourcing
Partial outsourcing
Postimplementation audit (postaudit review)
Project management
Project management software
Project manager
Project portfolio management
Project portfolio manager
Return on investment (ROI)
Social networking administrator
Systems administrator
Total cost of ownership (TCO)
Upstream strategies
Venture capitalist
Web graphics designer
Web programmer

Review Questions

RQ1. Name three benefit objectives that a business might decide to measure in an electronic commerce initiative, then write one paragraph about each in which you explain how the business might measure its accomplishment of that objective.

RQ2. In one paragraph, outline the types of costs that would be included in the total cost of ownership of an electronic commerce implementation.

RQ3. In about 100 words, explain why more businesses are using measures such as return on investment in the second wave of electronic commerce than in the first wave.

RQ4. In about 100 words, describe the functions of angel investors and venture capitalists. Be sure to include an explanation of how they differ from each other.

RQ5. In one paragraph, explain why late outsourcing is seldom used in electronic commerce projects.

RQ6. In about 100 words, explain why the head of the business management function of an electronic commerce initiative should be an employee of the company implementing the project even if most of the work is outsourced.

RQ7. In about 100 words, explain why IT projects (such as Web site development or redesign) are less likely to be delivered on time and within budget than large building construction projects. Include a discussion of how project management software can help IT project managers achieve their goals.

Exercises

E1. The Grover Cams Company manufactures cams and other components for diesel engines. As Web site manager for Grover, you created an attractive Web site that includes information about the company's history, its financial statements, and digitized depictions of the company's main products. You have been talking with your manager, chief information officer Tom Buckles, for several months about adding electronic commerce features to the

Web site that will allow your smaller customers to order directly from Grover instead of through their local distributors. Tom finally created a capital budget proposal for the Web site expansion and submitted it to Grover's board of directors. The board always calculates and evaluates a capital project's return on investment before approving it. The board told Tom that the project did not provide a high enough financial return to approve it. However, the board realized that electronic commerce initiatives could be important to Grover's future strategic position in the business; thus, it is willing to consider nonmonetary factors as a basis for approving the project. Tom would like to take the project back to the board next month with a solid proposal that includes nonmonetary factors. He wants you to write a memo that outlines some of those nonmonetary factors and explains why they are important to Grover's future strategic position. In addition to considering the discussion in this chapter, you may want to use your library and the Online Companion section for this exercise as you prepare your memo.

E2. You are working for International Delicacies, which has become successful selling unusual food and gift items through its mail order catalog. Most customers call the toll-free telephone number on the catalog, but some still send in orders by mail. Your manager, Jagdish Singh, wants to add an online store that will complement the company's existing mail order and telephone sales channels. He wants you to lead the internal team for the project. Write a memo to Jagdish of about 500 words in which you outline the steps you will take to staff the internal team, make decisions about internal development vs. outsourcing, and choose a hosting service. Be sure to include an evaluation of whether an incubator or a fast venturing strategy might make sense for this project.

E3. As manager of networks and computing operations for Fashion Land, a retailer of women's clothing and accessories, you have seen the business grow from seven stores in Kansas City to over 100 stores located throughout the Midwest. Fashion Land's marketing research team realizes that the majority of its target customer group—females between the ages of 15 and 35—are regular users of the Web. The researchers have asked you for help in developing an electronic commerce initiative for Fashion Land. Alone, or in a team assigned by your instructor, do the following:

1. Outline a business strategy for Fashion Land's electronic commerce initiative. The outline should include a list of specific objectives and the costs and benefits of accomplishing each objective. The outline should also include recommendations regarding what to outsource and what staff should be hired.
2. Prepare a memo that lists and briefly describes the major hardware, software, security, payment processing, advertising, international, legal, and ethics issues that might arise in the development of this electronic commerce site.

Cases

C1. Idealab

Bill Gross started his first company (a solar-powered device manufacturer) when he was 15 years old. After graduating from Caltech, he started a software company, GNP, that he later sold to Lotus (the spreadsheet software pioneer that is now part of IBM). Gross had made a considerable amount of money and was interested in exploring better ways of getting ideas converted into profitable businesses. He became fascinated by the idea of business incubators about the same time he became fascinated with the business potential of the Internet. In 1996, he pooled some of his wealth with contributions from several partners to create Idealab.

Idealab was one of the first companies to provide an incubator that was open to individual entrepreneurs. Idealab provided venture capital and gave entrepreneurs a place to work and develop their business ideas alongside other entrepreneurs. In the first wave of electronic commerce, Idealab was very successful. Although many of its incubated companies eventually failed, enough of them succeeded that Idealab was able to fund several generations of new businesses through its operations. In its first year, it supported 10 new businesses, including the very successful CitySearch Web site. In its second year, Idealab helped create another 10 businesses, including the successful sites Shopping.com, Tickets.com, and WeddingChannel.com. In subsequent years, Idealab incubated companies such as NetZero, Cooking.com, CarsDirect.com, Picasa, and GoTo.com (which later became Overture and was eventually acquired by Yahoo!). Not all of Idealab's companies were successful, however. One of the most dramatic failures of the first wave of electronic commerce, eToys, had been an Idealab company. Idealab had more winners than losers, though; by early 2000, the company had more than $4 billion in assets.

In 2000, Gross devised a new strategy that would go beyond Idealab's original purpose as an incubator. He developed a plan to compete with Amazon.com using existing Idealab companies. His plan was to combine about 10 of the companies in the incubator (including specialty retailer Eve.com and online jewelry store Ice.com) and promote them (using large amounts of money that would be raised from outside investors) as a single marketplace under the name Big.com. However, just as Gross began raising money to support the launch of this new marketplace, the pool of dot-com investment funds dried up. The new combined company quickly failed. Eve.com and Big.com no longer exist. The founders of Ice.com bought their company back from Idealab and moved it to their home in Montreal (where the company is now operating profitably). Within a few months, the failure of Big.com and the lower stock market valuations of Idealab's holdings reduced the value of the company's assets from $4 billion to $200 million.

Idealab's investors were upset by Gross' change in strategy and by the drop in their company's value. In January 2002, 44 of them sued Gross and other Idealab managers for $750 million. The suit alleged mismanagement of the funds invested and further alleged that Gross had used Idealab funds to pay personal expenses. Eighteen months later, a court held that the allegations were without merit and the suit was dismissed. Gross was once again able to devote his time to operating Idealab as an incubator.

Gross laid off more than two-thirds of Idealab's employees and stopped accepting outside venture capital. Idealab no longer provides incubator space for entrepreneurs who have developed ideas on their own. The company only funds ideas generated by the Idealab management team. Idealab's asset value has rebounded somewhat and is now between $400 million and $800 million. Although Idealab still incubates a number of online businesses, its most recent start-ups have been in the areas of solar power generation and electric autos.

Required:

1. In its first three years of operation, Idealab recruited entrepreneurs to its incubator who had business experience, but who did not know much about the Internet. In about 300 words, explain what benefits Idealab was able to provide to these entrepreneurs and why the incubator environment was beneficial to them.

2. In about 200 words, analyze Idealab's 2000 decision to change its focus from being an incubator to merging its companies in an attempt to compete with Amazon.com. In your analysis, discuss whether the decision was a strategic error or just a case of bad timing.
3. In about 200 words, explain why you think Gross decided to devote Idealab's resources to the development of internally generated ideas in 2003. Be sure to consider whether this change will help Idealab succeed in the second wave of electronic commerce.

Note: Your instructor might assign you to a group to complete this case, and might ask you to prepare a formal presentation of your results to your class.

C2. Davis Humanics

Davis Humanics (DH) is a company founded in 1982 that provides human resources services to about 7000 companies with a total of nearly 100,000 employees. These services include payroll processing, tax filing, health insurance and claims management, and retirement plan management. DH has annual sales of $2 billion and about 1000 employees. DH has grown rapidly and has clients of all sizes, ranging from smaller companies with fewer than 50 employees to Fortune 500 companies.

As DH grows, it is having trouble maintaining a consistent quality of service. Account managers each must handle more clients, and it is becoming difficult for those account managers to maintain a high degree of personal contact with the human resources executives who control DH's contracts. In the past, account managers worked with a small set of client contact people, but now account managers must work with more people, many of whom they have never met. In addition to account managers, client personnel have regular contacts with DH operations staff (who handle input tasks), DH systems staff (who help customize the interfaces between DH systems and client systems), and DH professional staff (lawyers, actuaries, and human resources professionals who consult with DH clients and their legal counsel regarding the operation of their retirement and benefits plans).

Because DH's clients are so different in size and how they operate, DH has to be flexible in handling input data. For example, DH's payroll-processing service allows clients many different ways to send in time card data. The largest clients arrange for customized computer-to-computer transfer of information. Some large clients use EDI transfers. Most medium and smaller-sized clients e-mail or fax the time card information, but a significant number of them mail paper lists that DH must scan into its systems. The health insurance claims-handling operation is even more troublesome. In addition to having clients send information in various formats, the insurance companies demand that information be submitted in specific formats, each of which is different.

The complexity of DH's operations is growing as rapidly as the company adds new clients. Sandi Higbee, DH's director of Operations, asks for your help in outlining a Web-based customer relationship management (CRM) system that will help manage the account managers' ever-increasing levels of customer contact. Sandi reviewed the products offered by several leading CRM vendors and believes that one might work as a base product, but no matter which product is chosen, she believes that substantial customization will be necessary because DH's operations are so complex and different from most companies that sell products or simple services to customers. A good CRM system for DH would need to monitor all types of customer interactions with DH account managers, operations staff, systems staff, and professional staff. In addition, the system's Web interface should allow DH clients to access parts of the CRM system so they can track DH's follow-up on their work requests and pending inquiries.

DH evaluates all capital projects, including IT projects, using ROI. Sandi is worried about this because she believes that many of the benefits of this CRM project will be hard to quantify. On the other hand, the costs of the CRM project (software and hardware purchase and cost of consultants who will customize the CRM software to meet DH's specific needs) will be very easy to quantify and will be large. Sandi expects the vendor-consultant teams to submit bids of between $1 million and $2 million for this project.

Required:

1. Prepare an outline of the benefits that DH might expect to obtain from this CRM project. Use categories to organize your list of benefits; for example, you might identify benefits that will accrue to DH's account managers, operations staff, IT staff, and professional staff. Because DH's clients will also benefit, you might be able to identify benefits that will accrue to DH's Marketing and Sales departments or to DH's New Product Development department. Be sure to include any long-term benefits that you think might occur after the CRM system has been in place for several years.
2. Estimate the dollar value of each benefit you identified in the first part of your answer.
3. Prepare a one-page memorandum to the DH board of directors in which you argue against using ROI as the primary method for evaluating this project. Keep in mind that these directors have little time to review your arguments and are very much inclined to use ROI for all project evaluations.

Note: Your instructor might assign you to a group to complete this case, and might ask you to prepare a formal presentation of your results to your class.

For Further Study and Research

Abdel-Hamid, T. and S. Madnick. 1991. *Software Project Dynamics: An Integrated Approach.* Englewood Cliffs, NJ: Prentice Hall.

Abdel-Hamid, T., K. Sengopta, and C. Sweet. 1999. "The Impact of Goals on Software Project Management: An Experimental Investigation," *MIS Quarterly,* 23(4), December, 531–555.

Anthes, G. 2008. "What's Your Project Worth?" *Computerworld,* 42(11), March 10, 29–31.

Aragon, L. 2004. "Idealab: Bubble Fund Finds Itself Back at Square One," *Venture Capital Journal,* 44(6), June, 20.

Bannan, K. 2004. "Entrepreneur Learns Why It's Best to Optimize Site Before It Launches," *B to B,* 89(15), December 13, 19.

Barias, D. 2002. "Gevity HR," *Line56: The E-Business Executive Daily,* July 26.

Barsh, J., E. Kramer, D. Maue, and N. Zuckerman. 2001. "Magazine's Home Companion," *The McKinsey Quarterly,* June, 83–91.

Berry, J. 2001. "Sometimes It's OK to Skip ROI Model," *InternetWeek,* October 22, 41.

Berry, J. 2003. "Assume Nothing. Audit Instead," *Computerworld,* 37(14), April 7, 43.

Blazier, A. 2003. "Far from Dead, Idealab Continues to Build for Future," *San Gabriel Valley Tribune,* July 12, C1.

Brandel, M. 2008. "Xtreme ROI," *Computerworld,* 42(7), February 11, 30–33.

Brooks, F. 1995. *The Mythical Man-Month: Essays on Software Engineering, Anniversary Edition.* Reading, MA: Addison-Wesley.

Buderi, B. 2005. "Conquering the Digital Haystack: New Start-ups Are Changing the Way People Search the Web," *Inc.*, January, 34–35.

Canadian Business. 2003. "Dot-com Wonder Boys," 76(7), April 14, 30–36.

Canadian Business. 2003. "It Seemed Like a Good Idea," 76(7), April 14, 34.

Cerpa, N. and J. Verner. 2009. "Why Did Your Project Fail?" *Communications of the ACM,* 52(12), December, 130–134.

Edvinsson, L. and M. Malone. 1997. *Intellectual Capital: Realising Your Company's True Value by Finding its Hidden Brainpower.* New York: HarperCollins.

Fisher, T. 2009. "ROI in Social Media: A Look at the Arguments," *Journal of Database Marketing & Customer Strategy Management,* 16(3), September, 189–195.

Fleming, Q. and J. Koppelman. 2003. "What's Your Project's Real Price Tag?" *Harvard Business Review,* 81(9), September, 20–21.

Glass, R. 1997. *Software Runaways: Lessons Learned from Massive Software Project Failures.* Upper Saddle River, NJ: PTR Prentice Hall.

Goldratt, E. 1997. *Critical Chain.* Great Barrington, MA: North River Press.

Grimes, A. 2004. "Court Deals Blow to Investors' Suit Against Idealab," *The Wall Street Journal,* June 30, B6.

Havenstein, H. 2007. "IT Execs Seek New Ways to Justify Web 2.0," *Computerworld,* 41(33), August 13, 14–15.

Hellweg, E. and S. Donahue. 2000. "The Smart Way to Start an Internet Company," *Business 2.0,* March 1, 64–66.

Jepson, K. 2009. "How Two Credit Unions Are Achieving Banner ROI On Their Web Sites," *Credit Union Journal,* September 21, 1–15.

Kambil, A., E. Eselius, and K. Monteiro. 2000. "Fast Venturing: The Quick Way to Start a Web Business," *Sloan Management Review,* 41(4), Summer, 55–67.

Keefe, P. 2003. "Backing Up ROI," *Computerworld,* 37(12), March 24, 22.

Keen, P. 2000. "Six Months—or Else," *Computerworld,* 34(15), April 10, 48.

Keil, M. and D. Robey, 1999. "Turning Around Troubled Software Projects: An Exploratory Study of the De-Escalation of Commitment to Failing Courses of Action," *Journal of Management Information Systems,* 15(4), 63–87.

Keil, M., P. Cule, K. Lyytinen, and R. Schmidt. 1998. "A Framework for Identifying Software Project Risks," *Communications of the ACM,* 41(11), November, 76–83.

Kerzner, H. 2009. *Project Management: A Systems Approach to Planning, Scheduling, and Controlling.* Tenth Edition. New York: John Wiley & Sons.

Lacy, S. 2008. *Once You're Lucky, Twice You're Good: The Rebirth of Silicon Valley and the Rise of Web 2.0.* New York: Gotham Press.

Leung, L. 2003. "Managing Offshore Outsourcing," *Network World,* 20(49), December 8, 59.

Manjoo, F. 2008. "Oh, No, Not Silicon Valley Again," *Salon.com,* May 15.

McConnell, S. 1996. *Rapid Development: Taming Wild Software Schedules.* Redmond, WA: Microsoft Press.

Murthi, S. 2002. "Managing the Strategic IT Project," *Intelligent Enterprise,* 5(18), November 15, 49–52.

Nocera, J. and E. Florian. 2001. "Bill Gross Blew Through $800 Million in Eight Months (and He's Got Nothing to Show for It): Why Is He Still Smiling?" *Fortune,* 143(5), March 5, 70–77.

Pentina, I. and R. Hasty. 2009. "Effects of Multichannel Coordination and E-Commerce Outsourcing on Online Retail Performance," *Journal of Marketing Channels,* 16(4), 359–374.

Ramsey, C. 2000. "Managing Web Sites as Dynamic Business Applications," *Intranet Design Magazine,* June. (http://idm.internet.com/articles/200006/wm_index.html)

Rivard, S. and R. Dupré. 2009. "Information systems project management in PMJ: A brief history," *Project Management Journal,* 40(4), December, 20–30.

Sacks, D. 2005, "The Accidental Guru," *Fast Company,* January, 64–71.

Sawhney, M. 2002. "Damn the ROI, Full Speed Ahead: 'Show Me the Money' May Not Be the Right Demand for E-Business Projects," *CIO,* 15(19), July 15, 36–38.

Schonfeld, E. 2007. "The Startup King's New Gig," *Business 2.0,* 8(9), October, 68.

Schwalbe, K. 2009. *Information Technology Project Management.* Fifth Edition. Boston, MA: Course Technology.

Stewart, T. 1999. "Larry Bossidy's New Role Model: Michael Dell," *Fortune,* 139(7), April 12, 166–167.

Tan, B., N. Tang, and P. Forrester. 2004. "Application of Quality Function Deployment for e-Business Planning," *Production Planning & Control,* 15(8), December, 802–815.

Teo, T. and T. Koh. 2010. "Lessons From Multi-Agency Information Management Projects: Case of the Online Business Licensing Service Project, Singapore," *International Journal of Information Management,* 30(1), February, 85–93.

United States Department of Justice Inspector General. 2002. *Audit Report No. 03-09: Federal Bureau of Investigation's Management Of Information Technology Investments.* Washington, D.C.: U.S. Department of Justice.

United States General Accounting Office. 2002. *Desktop Outsourcing: Positive Results Reported, But Analyses Could Be Strengthened.* Washington, D.C.: U.S. General Accounting Office.

Wysocki, B. 2000. "U.S. Incubators Help Japan Hatch Ideas," *The Wall Street Journal,* June 12, A1.

Yourdon, E. and P. Becker. 1997. *Death March: The Complete Software Developer's Guide to Surviving "Mission Impossible" Projects.* Upper Saddle River, NJ: Prentice Hall.

GLOSSARY

24/7 operation The operation of a site or service 24 hours a day, seven days a week.

802.11a, 802.11b, 802.11g, 802.11n An improved version of Wi-Fi introduced in 2002; capable of transmitting data at speeds up to 54 Mbps.

Acceptance An expression of willingness to take an offer, including all of its stated terms.

Access control list (ACL) A list of resources and the usernames of people who are permitted access to those resources within a computer system.

Account aggregation A feature of online banks that allows a customer to obtain bank, investment, loan, and other financial account information from multiple Web sites and to display it all in one location at the bank's Web site.

Account manager A person who keeps track of multiple Web sites in use by a project or keeps track of the projects that combine to create a larger Web site.

Accredited Standards Committee X12 (ASC X12) A committee that develops and maintains uniform EDI standards in the United States.

Acquiring bank Synonymous with merchant bank, which is a bank that does business with merchants who want to accept credit cards.

Acquisition cost The total amount of money that a site spends, on average, to draw one visitor to the site.

Active ad A Web ad that generates graphical activity that "floats" over the Web page itself instead of opening in a separate window.

Active content Programs that are embedded transparently in Web pages that cause action to occur.

Active Server Pages (ASP) Applications that generate dynamic content within Web pages using either Jscript code or Visual Basic.

Active wiretapping An integrity threat that exists when an unauthorized party can alter a message stream of information.

ActiveX An object, or control, that contains programs and properties that are put in Web pages to perform particular tasks.

Activity A task performed by a worker in the course of doing his or her job.

Ad view A Web site visitor page request that contains an advertisement.

Ad-blocking software A program that prevents banner ads and pop-up ads from loading.

Addressable media Advertising efforts sent to a known addressee; these include direct mail, telephone calls, and e-mail.

Advance fee fraud A scam in which the perpetrator offers to share the proceeds of some large payoff with the victim if the victim will make a "good faith" deposit or provide some partial funding first. The perpetrator then disappears with the deposit.

Advanced Encryption Standard (AES) The encryption standard designed to keep government information secure using the Rijndael algorithm. Introduced in February 2001 by the National Institute of Standards and Technology (NIST).

Advertising-subscription mixed revenue model A revenue model in which subscribers pay a fee and accept some level of advertising.

Advertising-supported revenue model A revenue model in which Web sites provide free content along with advertising or messages provided by other companies that pay the Web site operator for delivering the advertising or messages.

Affiliate marketing An advertising technique in which one Web site (called an "affiliate") includes descriptions, reviews, ratings, or other information about products that are sold on another Web site. The affiliate site includes links to the selling site, which pays the affiliate site a commission on sales made to visitors who arrived from a link on the affiliate site.

Affiliate program broker A company that serves as a clearinghouse or marketplace for sites that run affiliate programs and sites that want to become affiliates.

AJAX (asynchronous JavaScript and XML) A development framework that can be used to create interactive Web sites that look like applications running in a Web browser.

American National Standards Institute (ANSI) The coordinating body for electrical, mechanical, and other technical standards in the United States.

Analytical processing A technique that examines stored information and looks for patterns in the data that are not yet known or suspected; also called data mining.

Anchor tag The HTML tag used to specify hyperlinks.

Angel investors Investors who fund the initial startup of an online business. In return for their capital, angel investors become stockholders in the business and often own more of the business than the founder. Typical funding by angel investors is between a few hundred thousand dollars and a few million dollars.

Animated GIF Animated Web ad graphics that grab a visitor's attention.

Anonymous electronic cash Electronic cash that cannot be traced back to the person who spent it.

Anonymous FTP A protocol that allows users to access limited parts of a remote computer using FTP without having an account on the remote computer.

Antivirus software Software that detects viruses and worms and either deletes them or isolates them on the client computer so they cannot run.

Applet A program that executes within another program; it cannot execute directly on a computer.

Application integration The coordination of all of a company's existing systems to each other and to the company's Web site.

Application program (application, application software) A program that performs a specific function, such as creating invoices, calculating payroll, or processing payments received from customers.

Application program interface (API) A general name for the ways programs interconnect with each other.

Application server A middle-tier software and hardware combination that lies between the Internet and a corporate back-end server.

Application service provider (ASP) A Web-based site that provides management of applications such as spreadsheets, human resources management, or e-mail to companies for a fee.

Application software Synonymous with application, which is a program that performs a specific function.

Applications specialist The member of an electronic commerce team who is responsible for maintenance of software that performs a specific function, such as catalog, payment processing, accounting, human resources, and logistics software.

Apps Application software that is sold for use on mobile phones.

AS2 (Applicability Statement 2) A specification based on the HTTP rules for Web page transfers.

AS3 (Applicability Statement 3). A more secure version of AS2.

Ascending-price auction A type of auction in which bidders publicly announce their successively higher bids until no higher bid is forthcoming; also called an English auction.

ASP.NET Microsoft-developed server-side dynamic Web page-generation technology.

Asymmetric connection An Internet connection that provides different bandwidths for each direction.

Asymmetric digital subscriber line (ADSL) Internet connections using the DSL protocol with bandwidths from 16 to 640 Kbps upstream and 1.5 to 9 Mbps downstream.

Asymmetric encryption Synonymous with public-key encryption, which is the encoding of messages using two mathematically related but distinct numeric keys.

Asynchronous transfer mode (ATM) Internet connections with bandwidths of up to 622 Gbps.

Atom Publishing Protocol A blogging application that simplifies the blog publishing process and makes its functions available as a Web service so other computers can interact with blog content.

Attachment A data file (document, spreadsheet, or other) that is appended to an e-mail message.

Auction consignment services Companies that take an item and create an online auction for that item, handle the transaction, and remit the balance of the proceeds after deducting a fee. These services are performed on behalf of people and small businesses who want to use an online auction but do not have the skills or the time to become a seller.

Auctioneer The person who manages an auction.

Authority to bind The ability of an individual to commit his or her company to a contract.

Automated clearing house (ACH) One of several systems set up by banks or government agencies, such as the U.S. Federal Reserve Board, that process high volumes of low dollar amount electronic fund transfers.

Backbone routers Computers that handle packet traffic along the Internet's main connecting points; they can each handle more than 50 million packets per second.

Backdoor An electronic hole in electronic commerce software left open by accident or intentionally that allows users to run the program without going through the normal authentication procedure for access to the program.

Bandwidth The amount of data that can be transmitted in a fixed amount of time. Also, the number of simultaneous site visitors that a Web site can accommodate without degrading service.

Banner ad A small rectangular object on a Web page that displays a stationary or moving graphic and includes a hyperlink to the advertiser's Web site.

Banner advertising network An organization that acts as a broker between advertisers and Web sites that carry ads.

Banner exchange network An organization that coordinates ad sharing so that other sites run your ad and your site runs other exchange members' ads.

Base 2 (binary) A number system in which each digit is either a 0 or a 1, corresponding to a condition of either "off" or "on." Also known as a binary system.

Bayesian revision A statistical technique in which additional knowledge is used to revise earlier estimates of probabilities.

Behavioral segmentation The creation of a separate experience for customers based on their behavior.

Benchmarking Testing that compares hardware and software performances.

Bid An offer of a certain price made on an item that is up for auction.

Bidder A potential buyer at an auction; one who places bids.

Bill presentment A Web site feature that allows customers to view and pay bills online.

Biometric security device A security device that uses an element of a person's biological makeup to confirm identification. These devices include writing pads that detect the form and pressure of a person writing a signature, eye scanners that read the pattern of blood vessels in a person's retina, and palm scanners that read the palm of a person's hand (rather than just one fingerprint).

Black hat hackers Hackers who use their skills for ill purposes.

Black list spam filter Software that looks for From addresses in incoming messages that are known to be spammers. The software can delete the message or put it into a separate mailbox for review.

Blade server A server configuration in which small server computers are each installed on a single computer board and then many of those boards are installed into a rack-mounted frame.

Blog Synonymous with Web log, which is a Web site on which people post their thoughts and invite others to add commentary.

Bluetooth A wireless standard that is used for short distances and lower bandwidth connections.

Bonded warehouse A secure location where incoming international shipments can be held until customs requirements are satisfied or until payment arrangements are completed.

Border router The computers located at the border between the organization and the Internet that decide how best to forward each packet of information as it travels on the Internet to its destination. Synonymous with gateway computer and gateway router.

Botnet A robotic network that can act as an attacking unit, sending spam or launching denial-of-service attacks against specific Web sites. Synonymous with zombie farm.

Brand Customers' perceptions of the attributes of a product or service, including name, history, and reputation.

Brand leveraging A strategy in which a well-established Web site extends its dominant positions to other products and services.

Breach of contract The failure of one party to comply with the terms of a contract.

Broadband Connections that operate at speeds of greater than about 200 Kbps.

Browser-wrap acceptance Synonymous with Web-wrap acceptance, which is the compliance with EULA conditions with which a user agrees through the act of using a Web site.

Buffer An area of a computer's memory that is set aside to hold data read from a file or database.

Buffer overrun An error that occurs when programs filling buffers malfunction and overfill the buffer, spilling the excess data outside the designated buffer memory area. Also called buffer overflow.

Bulk mail Electronic junk mail that can include solicitations, advertisements, or e-mail chain letters. Also called spam or unsolicited commercial e-mail.

Bulletin board system (BBS) Computers that allow users to connect through modems (using dial-up connections through telephone lines) to read and post messages in a common area.

Business logic Rules of a particular business.

Business manager The member of an electronic commerce team who is responsible for implementing the elements of the business plan and reaching the objectives set by the internal team. The business manager should have experience in and knowledge of the business activity being implemented in the site.

Business model A set of processes that combine to yield a profit.

Business process patent A patent that protects a specific set of procedures for conducting a particular business activity.

Business processes The activities in which businesses engage as they conduct commerce.

Business rules The way a company runs its business.

Business-to-business (B2B) Transactions conducted between businesses on the Web.

Business-to-consumer (B2C) Transactions conducted between shoppers and businesses on the Web.

Business-to-government (B2G) A category of electronic commerce that includes business transactions with government agencies, such as paying taxes and filing required reports.

Business unit A unit within a company that is organized around a specific combination of product, distribution channel, and customer type. Synonymous with strategic business unit.

Byte An 8-bit number (in most computer applications).

Call center A company that customer handles telephone calls and e-mails for other companies.

Cannibalization The loss of traditional sales of a product to its electronic counterpart.

Capital investment A major outlay of funds made by a company to purchase fixed assets such as property, a factory, or equipment.

Capital project Synonymous with capital investment.

Card not present transaction A credit card transaction in which the card holder is not at the merchant's location and the merchant does not see the card. Includes mail order, online, and telephone sales.

Card verification number (CVN) A three- or four-digit number that is printed on the credit card, but is not encoded in the card's magnetic strip, which establishes that the purchaser has the card (or has seen the card) and is likely not using a stolen card number.

Cascading Style Sheets (CSS) An HTML feature that allows designers to apply many predefined page display styles to Web pages.

Casher The participant in a phishing scam who uses the acquired information.

Catalog On electronic commerce sites, a listing of goods or services that may include photographs and descriptions, often stored in a database.

Catalog model A revenue model in which the seller establishes a brand image, then uses the strength of that image to sell through printed catalogs mailed to prospective buyers. Buyers place orders by mail or by calling the seller's toll-free telephone number.

Cause marketing An affiliate marketing program that benefits a charitable organization.

Centralized architecture A server structure that uses a few very large and fast computers.

Certification authority (CA) A company that issues digital certificates to organizations or individuals.

Challenge-response A content-filtering security technique that requires an unknown sender to reply to a challenge presented in an e-mail. These challenges are designed so that a human can respond easily, but a computer would have difficulty formulating the response.

Change management The process of helping employees cope with changes in the workplace.

Channel conflict The problem that arises when a company's sales in one sales outlet interfere with its sales in another sales outlet; for example, when sales through the company's Web site interfere with sales in that company's retail store.

Channel cooperation A strategy that coordinates sales and credit among various sales outlets, including online, catalog, and brick-and-mortar sales.

Charge card A payment card with no preset spending limit. The entire amount charged to the card must be paid in full each month.

Chargeback The process in which a merchant bank retrieves the money it placed in a merchant account as a result of a cardholder successfully contesting a charge.

Check 21 A U.S. law that permits banks to replace the physical movement of checks with transmission of scanned images.

Chief information officer (CIO) An organization's top technology manager; responsible for overseeing all of the business's information systems and related technological elements.

Cipher text Text that is composed of a seemingly random assemblage of bits. Cipher text is what messages become after they are encrypted.

Circuit A specific route between source and destination along which data travels.

Circuit switching A way of connecting computers or other devices that uses a centrally controlled single connection. In this method, which is used by telephone companies to provide voice telephone service, the connection is made, data is transferred, and the connection is terminated.

Click Synonymous with click-through.

Clickstream Data about site visitors.

Click-through The loading of an advertiser's Web page that results from a visitor clicking on an advertisement on another Web page.

Click-wrap acceptance A user's compliance with a site's EULA or its terms and conditions through the clicking a button on the Web site.

Client-level filtering An e-mail content filtering technique in which the filtering software is placed on the individual user's computer.

Client/server architecture A combination of client computers running Web client software and server computers running Web server software.

Client-side electronic wallet An electronic wallet that stores a consumer's information on the consumer's own computer.

Client-side scripting The generation of active content through software on the browser.

Closed architecture The use of proprietary communication protocols by computer manufacturers in the early days of computing, preventing computers made by different manufacturers from being connected to each other. Also called proprietary architecture.

Closed loop system A payment card arrangement involving a consumer, a merchant, and a payment card company (such as American Express or Discover) that processes transactions between the consumer and merchant without involving banks.

Closing tag The second half of a two-sided HTML tag; it is identified by a slash (/) that precedes the tag's name.

ColdFusion Adobe's server-side dynamic page-generation technology.

Collector In a phishing attack, the computer that collects data from the potential victim.

Collision The occurrence of two messages resulting in the same hash value; the probability of this happening is extremely small.

Co-location (collocation, colocation) An Internet service arrangement in which the service provider rents a physical space to the client to install its own server hardware.

Colon hexadecimal (colon hex) The shorthand notation system used for expressing IPv6 addresses that uses eight groups of 16 bits ($8 \times 16 = 128$). Each group is expressed as four hexadecimal digits and the groups are separated by colons.

Commerce service provider (CSP) A Web host service that also provides commerce hosting services on its computer.

Commodity item A product or service that has become so standardized and well-known that buyers cannot detect a difference in the offerings of various sellers; buyers usually base their purchase decisions for such products and services solely on price.

Common Gateway Interface (CGI) A standard way of interfacing external applications with Web servers.

Common law The part of English and U.S. law that is established by the history of law.

Communication modes Ways of identifying and reaching customers.

Company A business engaged in commerce; synonymous with firm.

Component outsourcing Synonymous with partial outsourcing; the outsourcing of the design, development, implementation, or operation of specific portions of an electronic commerce system.

Component-based application system A business logic approach that separates presentation logic from business logic.

Computer forensics The field responsible for the collection, preservation, and analysis of computer-related evidence to be used in legal proceedings.

Computer forensics expert An individual hired to access client computers to locate information that can be used in legal proceedings.

Computer network Any technology that allows people to connect computers to each other.

Computer security The protection of computer resources from various types of threats.

Computer virus Synonymous with virus, which is software that attaches itself to another program and can cause damage when the host program is activated.

Configuration table Information about connections that lead to particular groups of routers, specifications on which connections to use first, and rules for handling instances of heavy packet traffic and network congestion.

Conflict of laws A situation in which federal, state, and local laws address the same issues in different ways.

Consideration The bargained-for exchange of something valuable, such as money, property, or future services.

Constructive notice The idea that citizens should know that when they leave one area and enter another, they become subject to the laws of the new area.

Consumer-to-business An industry term for electronic commerce that occurs in general consumer auctions; bidders at a general consumer auction might be businesses.

Consumer-to-consumer (C2C) A category of electronic commerce that includes individuals who buy and sell items among themselves.

Content creator A person who writes original content for a Web site.

Content editor A person who purchases and adapts existing material for use on a Web site.

Content management software Software used by companies to control the large amounts of text, graphics, and media files used in business.

Content manager Synonymous with content editor.

Contextual advertising An advertising technique in which ads are placed in proximity to related content.

Contract An agreement between two or more legal entities that provides for an exchange of value between or among them.

Contract purchasing Direct materials purchasing in which the company negotiates long-term contracts for most of the materials that it will need. Also called replenishment purchasing.

Conversion The transition of a first-time visitor to a customer.

Conversion cost The total amount of money that a site spends, on average, to induce one visitor to make a purchase, sign up for a subscription, or (on an advertising-supported site) register.

Conversion rate Used in advertising to calculate the percentage of recipients that respond to an ad or promotion.

Cookies Bits of information about Web site visitors created by Web sites and stored on client computers.

Copy control An electronic mechanism for providing a fixed upper limit to the number of copies that one can make of a digital work.

Copyright A legal protection of intellectual property.

Cost per thousand (CPM) An advertising pricing metric that equals the dollar amount paid to reach 1000 people in an estimated audience.

Countermeasure A physical or logical procedure that recognizes, reduces, or eliminates a threat.

Cracker A technologically skilled person who uses his or her skills to obtain unauthorized entry into computers or network systems, usually with the intent of stealing information or damaging the information, the system's software, or the system's hardware.

Crawler Synonymous with spider, which is the first part of a search engine, which automatically and frequently searches the Web to find pages and updates its database of information about old Web sites.

Credit card A payment card that has a spending limit based on the cardholder's credit limit. A minimum monthly payment must be made against the balance on the card, and interest is charged on the unpaid balance.

Credit card associations Member-run organizations that issue credit cards to individual consumers. Also called customer issuing banks.

Cryptography The science that studies encryption, which is the hiding of messages so that only the sender and receiver can read them.

Culture The combination of language and customs that are unique to a particular population.

Customer-centric The Web site development approach of putting the customer at the center of all site designs.

Customer issuing banks Member-run organizations that issue credit cards to individual consumers. Also called credit card associations.

Customer life cycle The five stages of customer loyalty.

Customer portal A corporate Web site designed to meet the needs of customers by offering additional services such as private stores, part number cross-referencing, product-use guidelines, and safety information.

Customer relationship management Synonymous with technology-enabled relationship management, it is the obtaining and use of detailed customer information.

Customer relationship management (CRM) software Software that collects data on customer activities; this data is then used by managers to conduct analytical activities.

Customer service The people within an electronic commerce team who are responsible for managing customer relationships in the electronic commerce operation.

Customer touch point Any occurrence of contact between the customer and any part of the company.

Customer value The cost that a customer pays for a product, minus the benefits the customer gains from the product.

Customs broker A company that arranges the payment of tariffs and compliance with customs laws for international shipments.

Customs duty (duty) A tax levied on a product as it enters a country.

Cyberbullying Threats, sexual remarks, or pejorative comments transmitted on the Internet or posted on Web sites.

Cybersquatting The practice of registering a domain name that is the trademark of another person or company with the hope that the trademark owner will pay huge amounts of money for the domain rights.

Cybervandalism The electronic defacing of an existing Web site page.

Data Encryption Standard (DES) An encryption standard adopted by the U.S. government for encrypting sensitive information.

Data-grade lines The quality of telephone wiring in most urban and suburban areas; made more carefully of higher grade copper than voice-grade lines so they can better carry data.

Data mining A technique that examines stored information and looks for patterns in the data that are not yet known or suspected. Also called analytical processing.

Data warehouse In a CRM system, the database containing information about customers, their preferences, and their behavior.

Database The storage element of a search engine.

Database administration The person or team that is responsible for defining the data elements in an organization's database design and the operation of its database management software.

Database manager (database management software) Software that stores information in a highly structured way.

Database server The server computer on which database management software runs.

Dead link A Web link that when clicked displays an error message instead of a Web page.

Debit card A payment card that removes the amount of the charge from the cardholder's bank account and transfers it to the seller's bank account.

Decentralized architecture A server structure that uses a large number of less-powerful computers and divides the workload among them.

Decrypted Information that has been decoded. The opposite of encrypted.

Decryption program A procedure to reverse the encryption process, resulting in the decoding of an encrypted message.

Dedicated hosting A Web hosting option in which the hosting company provides exclusive use of a specific server computer that is owned and administered by the hosting company.

Deep Web Information that is stored in databases and is accessible to users through Web interfaces.

Defamatory statement A statement that is false and injures the reputation of a person or company.

Delay attack A computer attack that disrupts normal computer processing.

Demographic information Characteristics that marketers use to group visitors, including address, age, gender, income level, type of job held, hobbies, and religion.

Demographic segmentation The grouping of customers by characteristics such as age, gender, family size, income, education, religion, or ethnicity.

Denial-of-service (DoS) attack (denial attack) A computer attack that disrupts normal computer processing or denies processing entirely.

Descending-price auction Synonymous with Dutch auction, which is an open auction in which bidding starts at a high price and drops until a bidder accepts the price.

Dictionary attack program A program that cycles through an electronic dictionary, trying every word in the book as a password.

Digital certificate (digital ID) An attachment to an e-mail message or data embedded in a Web page that verifies the identity of a sender or Web site.

Digital content revenue model A revenue model in which a business sells subscriptions for access to the information it owns.

Digital content revenue model A revenue model in which a business sells subscriptions for access to the information it owns.

Digital ID See digital certificate.

Digital signature An encryption message digest.

Digital Subscriber Line (DSL) Telephone-line ISP connectivity that is a higher grade than standard 56K connectivity.

Digital watermark A digital code or stream embedded undetectably in a digital image or audio file.

Direct connection EDI The form of EDI in which EDI translator computers at each company are linked directly to each other through modems and dial-up telephone lines or leased lines.

Direct materials Materials that become part of the finished product in a manufacturing process.

Disintermediation The removal of an intermediary from a value chain.

Distributed architecture Synonymous with decentralized architecture, which is a server structure that uses a large number of less-powerful computers and divides the workload among them.

Distributed database system A database within a large information system that stores the same data in many different physical locations.

Distributed denial-of-service (DDoS) attack A simultaneous attack on a Web site (or a number of Web sites) from all of the computers in a botnet.

Distributed information system A large information system that stores the same data in many different physical locations.

Domain name The address of a Web page, it can contain two or more word groups separated by periods. Components of domain names become more specific from right to left.

Domain name hosting A service that permits the purchaser of a domain name to maintain a simple Web site so that the domain name remains in use.

Domain name ownership change The changing of owner information maintained by a public domain registrar in the registrar's database to reflect the new owner's name and business address.

Domain name parking Synonymous with domain name hosting, which is a service that permits the purchaser of a domain name to maintain a simple Web site so that the domain name remains in use.

Domain name server (DNS) A computer on the Internet that maintains directories that link domain names to IP addresses.

Dot-com A company that operates only online.

Dotted decimal The IP address notation in which addresses appear as four separate numbers separated by periods.

Double auction A type of auction in which buyers and sellers each submit combined price-quantity bids to an auctioneer. The auctioneer matches the sellers' offers (starting with the lowest price, then going up) to the buyers' offers (starting with the highest price, then going down) until all of the quantities are sold.

Double-spending The spending of the same unit of electronic cash twice by submitting the same electronic currency to two different vendors.

Download To receive a file from another computer.

Downstream bandwidth (downlink bandwidth) The connection that occurs when information travels to your computer from your ISP.

Downstream strategies Tactics that improve the value that a business provides to its customers.

Due diligence Background research procedures.

Dutch auction A form of open auction in which bidding starts at a high price and drops until a bidder accepts the price.

Dynamic catalog An area of a Web site that stores information about products in a database.

Dynamic content Nonstatic information constructed in response to a Web client's request.

Dynamic page A Web page whose content is shaped by a program in response to a user request.

Early outsourcing The hiring of an external company to do initial electronic commerce site design and development. The external team then trains the original company's information systems professionals in the new technology, eventually handing over complete responsibility of the site to the internal team.

Eavesdropper A person or device who is able to listen in on and copy Internet transmissions.

EDI compatible Firms that are able to exchange data in specific standard electronic formats with other firms.

EDI for Administration, Commerce, and Transport (EDIFACT) The 1987 publication that summarizes the United Nations' standard transaction sets for international EDI.

EDIINT (Electronic Data Interchange-Internet Integration or EDI-INT) A set of protocols for the exchange of data (EDI, XML, and other formats) over the Internet.

Effect The impact of an action.

E-government The use of electronic commerce by governments and government agencies to perform businesslike activities.

Electronic business (e-business) Another term for electronic commerce; sometimes used as a broader term for electronic commerce that includes all business processes, as distinguished from a narrow definition of electronic commerce that includes sales and purchase transactions only.

Electronic cash A form of electronic payment that is anonymous and can be spent only once.

Electronic commerce (e-commerce) Business activities conducted using electronic data transmission over the Internet and the World Wide Web.

Electronic customer relationship management (eCRM) Synonymous with technology-enabled relationship management, it is the obtaining and use of detailed customer information.

Electronic data interchange (EDI) Exchange between businesses of computer-readable data in a standard format.

Electronic funds transfer (EFT) Electronic transfer of account exchange information over secure private communications networks.

Electronic mail (e-mail) Messages that are exchanged among users using particular mail programs and protocols.

Electronic wallet (e-wallet) A software utility that holds credit card information, owner identification and address information, and provides this data automatically at electronic commerce sites; electronic wallets can also store electronic cash.

E-mail client software Programs used to read and send e-mail.

E-mail server A computer that is devoted to handling e-mail.

EMV standard A single standard for the handling of payment card transactions developed cooperatively by Visa, MasterCard, and MasterCard Europe.

Encapsulation The process that occurs when VPN software encrypts packet contents, then places the encrypted packets inside an IP wrapper in another packet.

Encryption The coding of information using a mathematical-based program and secret key; it makes a message illegible to casual observers or those without the decoding key.

Encryption algorithm The logic that implements an encryption program.

Encryption program A program that transforms plain text into cipher text.

End-user license agreement A contract that the user must accept before installing software.

English auction A type of auction in which bidders publicly announce their successively higher bids until no higher bid is forthcoming.

Enterprise application integration The coordination of all of a company's existing systems to each other and to the company's Web site.

Enterprise-class software Commerce software used by large-scale electronic commerce businesses.

Enterprise resource planning (ERP) Business software that integrates all facets of a business, including planning, manufacturing, sales, and marketing.

Entity body The part of a message from a client that contains the HTML page requested by the client and passes bulk information to the server.

E-procurement The use of Internet technologies in a company's purchasing and supply management functions.

E-procurement software Software that allows a company to manage its purchasing function through a Web interface.

Escrow service An independent third party who holds an auction buyer's payment until the buyer receives the purchased item and is satisfied that it is what the seller represented it to be.

E-sourcing The use of Internet technologies in the activities a company undertakes to identify vendors that offer materials, supplies, and services that the company needs.

Ethical hacker A computer security specialist hired to probe computers and computer networks to assess their security; can also be hired to locate information that can be used in legal proceedings.

Extensible Hypertext Markup Language (XHTML) A new markup language proposed by the WC3 that is a reformulation of HTML version 4.0 as an XML application.

Extensible Markup Language (XML) A language that describes the semantics of a page's contents and defines data records on a page.

Extensible Stylesheet Language (XSL) A language that formats XML code for viewing in a Web browser.

Extranet A network system that extends a company's intranet and allows it to connect with the networks of business partners or other designated associates.

Fair use The approved limited use of copyright material when certain conditions are met.

False positive An e-mail message that is incorrectly rejected by an e-mail filter as being spam when it is actually valid e-mail.

Fast venturing The joining of an existing company that wants to launch an electronic commerce initiative with external equity partners and operational partners who provide the experience and skills needed to develop and scale up the project very rapidly.

Fee-for-service revenue model A revenue model in which payment is based on the value of the service provided.

Fee-for-transaction revenue model A revenue model in which businesses charge a fee for services based on the number or size of the transactions they process.

File Transfer Protocol (FTP) A protocol that enables users to transfer files over the Internet.

Finger An Internet utility program that runs on UNIX computers and allows a user to obtain limited information about other network users.

Firewall A computer that provides a defense between one network (inside the firewall) and another network (outside the firewall, such as the Internet) that could pose a threat to the inside network. All traffic to and from the network must pass through the firewall. Only authorized traffic, as defined by the local security policy, is allowed to pass through the firewall. Also used to describe the software that performs these functions on the firewall computer.

Firm A business engaged in commerce.

First-mover advantage The benefit a company can gain by introducing a product or service before its competitors.

First-party cookie A cookie that is placed on the client computer by the Web server site.

First-price sealed-bid auction A type of auction in which bidders submit their bids independently and privately, with the highest bidder winning the auction.

Fixed-point wireless A data transmittal service that uses a system of repeaters to forward a radio signal from an ISP to customers.

Float Money deposited in a customer's account that earns interest for the merchant.

Forum selection clause A statement within a contract that dictates that the contract will be enforced according to the laws of a particular state; signing a contract with a forum selection clause constitutes voluntary submission to the jurisdiction named in the forum selection clause.

Four Ps of marketing The essential issues of marketing: product, price, promotion, and place.

Fractional T1 High bandwidth telephone company connections that operate at speeds between 128 Kbps and 1.5 Mbps in 128-Kbps increments.

Frame relay A routing technology.

Freight forwarder A company that arranges shipping and insurance for international transactions.

Full-privilege FTP A protocol that allows users to upload files to and download files from a remote computer using FTP.

Gateway computers Synonymous with routers, which are computers that determine the best way for data packets to move forward.

Gateway server A firewall that filters traffic based on applications requested by clients on the trusted network.

Generalized Markup Language (GML) An early markup language resulting from efforts to create standard formatting styles for electronic documents.

Generic top-level domain (gTLD) The main top-level domain names, including .com, .net, .edu, .gov, .mil, .us, and .org.

Geographic segmentation The grouping of customers by location of home or workplace.

Graphical user interface (GUI) Computer program control functions that are displayed using pictures, icons, and other easy-to-use graphical elements.

Group purchasing site (group shopping site) A type of auction Web site that negotiates with a seller to obtain lower prices on an item as individual buyers enter bids on that item.

Hacker A dedicated programmer who writes complex code that tests the limits of technology; usually meant in a positive way.

Hash algorithm A security utility that mathematically combines every character in a message to create a fixed-length number (usually 128 bits in length) that is a condensation, or fingerprint, of the original message.

Hash coding The process used to calculate a number from a message.

Hash value The number that results when a message is hash coded.

Hexadecimal (base 16) A number system that uses 16 digits.

Hierarchical business organization Firms that include a number of levels with cumulative responsibility. These organizations are typically headed by a top-level president or officer. A number of vice presidents report to the president. A larger number of middle managers report to the vice presidents.

Hierarchical hyperlink structure A hyperlink structure in which the user starts from a home page and follows links to other pages in whatever order they wish.

High-speed DSL (HDSL) An Internet connection service that provides 768 Kbps of symmetric bandwidth.

Home page In a hierarchical Web page structure, the introductory page of a Web site. Synonymous with start page.

Hot spot A wireless access point (WAP) that is open to the public.

HTML extensions Developer-created Web page features that only work in certain browsers.

Hyperlink A type of tag that points to another location within the same or another HTML document. Also called a hypertext link.

Hypertext A system of navigating between HTML pages using links.

Hypertext elements HTML text elements that are related to each other within one document or among several documents.

Hypertext link (hyperlink) A type of tag that points to another location within the same or another HTML document.

Hypertext Markup Language (HTML) The language of the Internet; it contains codes attached to text that describe text elements and their relation to one another.

Hypertext Preprocessor (PHP) A Web programming language that can be used to write server-side scripts that generate dynamic Web pages.

Hypertext server Synonymous with Web server, which is a computer that is connected to the Internet and that stores files written in HTML that are publicly available through an Internet connection.

Hypertext Transfer Protocol (HTTP) The Internet protocol responsible for transferring and displaying Web pages.

Idea-based networking The act of participating in Web communities that are based on the connections between ideas.

Idea-based virtual community A Web community based on the connections between ideas.

Identity theft A criminal act in which the perpetrator gathers personal information about a victim and then uses that information to obtain credit in the victim's name. After establishing credit accounts, the perpetrator runs up charges on the accounts and then disappears.

IEEE An organization that creates wireless networking specifications; originally named the Institute of Electrical and Electronic Engineers.

Implied contract An agreement between two or more parties to act as if a contract exists, even if no contract has been written and signed.

Implied warranty A promise to which the seller can be held even though the seller did not make an explicit statement of that promise.

Impression The loading of a banner ad on a Web page.

Income tax Taxes that are levied by national, state, and local governments on the net income generated by business activities.

Incubator A company that offers start-up businesses a physical location with offices, accounting and legal assistance, computers, and Internet connections at a very low monthly cost.

Independent exchange A vertical portal that is not controlled by a company that was an established buyer or seller in the industry.

Independent industry marketplace A vertical portal that is focused on a specific industry.

Index A list containing every Web page found by a spider, crawler, or bot.

Indirect connection EDI The form of EDI in which each company transmits and receives EDI messages through a value-added network.

Indirect materials Materials and supplies that are purchased by a company in support of the manufacturing of an item, but not directly used in the production of the product.

Industry Multiple firms selling similar products to similar customers.

Industry consortia-sponsored marketplace A marketplace formed by several large buyers in a particular industry.

Industry marketplace A vertical portal that is focused on a single industry.

Industry value chain The larger stream of activities in which a particular business unit's value chain is embedded.

Initial public offering (IPO) The original sale of a company's stock to the public.

Inline text ad A text ad consisting of text in an article or story that is displayed as a hyperlink and that leads to an advertiser's Web site.

Integrated Services Digital Network (ISDN) High-grade telephone service that uses the DSL protocol and offers bandwidths of up to 128 Kbps.

Integrity The category of computer security that addresses the validity of data; confirmation that data has not been modified.

Integrity violation A security violation that occurs whenever a message is altered while in transit between sender and receiver.

Intellectual capital The value of the accumulated mass of employees' knowledge about a business and its processes.

Intellectual property A general term that includes all products of the human mind, including tangible and intangible products.

Intentional tort A tortious act in which the seller knowingly or recklessly causes injury to the buyer.

Interactive Mail Access Protocol (IMAP) A newer e-mail protocol with improvements over POP.

Interactive marketing unit (IMU) ad format The standard banner sizes that most Web sites have voluntarily agreed to use.

Internet A global system of interconnected computer networks. An internet (small "i") is a group of computer networks that have been interconnected.

Internet access provider (IAP) Synonymous with Internet service provider.

Internet backbone Routers that handle packet traffic along the Internet's main connecting points.

Internet EDI EDI on the Internet.

Internet host A computer that is directly connected to the Internet.

Internet Protocol Within TCP/IP, the protocol that determines the routing of data packets. See TCP/IP.

Internet Protocol version 4 (IPv4) The version of IP that has been in use for the past 20 years on the Internet; it uses a 32-bit number to identify the computers connected to the Internet.

Internet Protocol version 6 (IPv6) The protocol that will replace IPv4.

Internet service provider (ISP) A company that sells Internet access rights directly to Internet users.

Internet2 A successor to the Internet used for conducting research; it offers bandwidths in excess of 1 Gbps.

Interoperability The coordination of a company's information systems so that they all work together.

Interoperable software Software that runs transparently on a variety of hardware and software configurations.

Interstitial ad An intrusive Web ad that opens in its own browser window, instead of the page that the user intended to load.

Intranet An interconnected network of computers operated within a single company or organization.

Intrusion detection system A part of a firewall that monitors attempts to log in to servers and analyzes those attempts for patterns that might indicate a cracker's attack is under way.

IP address The 32-bit number that represents the address of a particular location (computer) on the Internet.

IP tunneling The creation of a private passageway through the public Internet that provides secure transmission from one extranet partner to another.

IP wrapper The outer packet in the encapsulation process.

Java sandbox A Web browser security feature that limits the actions that can be performed by a Java applet that has been downloaded from the Web.

Java servlet An application that runs on a Web server and generates dynamic content.

JavaScript A scripting language developed by Netscape to enable Web page designers to build active content.

JavaServer pages (JSP) A server-side scripting program developed by Sun Microsystems.

Judicial comity An accommodation by a court in one country in which it voluntarily enforces another country's laws or court judgments when no strict requirement to do so exists.

Jurisdiction A government's ability to exert control over a person or corporation.

Key A number used to encode or decode messages.

Knowledge management The intentional collection, classification, and dissemination of information about a company, its products, and its processes.

Knowledge management (KM) software Software that helps companies collect and organize information, share the information among users, enhance the ability of users to collaborate, and preserve the knowledge gained for future use.

Late outsourcing The hiring of an external company to maintain an electronic commerce site that has been designed and developed by an internal information systems team.

Law of diminishing returns The characteristic of most activities to yield less value as the amount of consumption increases.

Leaderboard ad Web site banner ad that is designed to span the top or bottom of a Web page.

Leased line A permanent telephone connection between two points; it is always active.

Legitimacy The idea that those subject to laws should have some role in formulating them.

Life-cycle segmentation The use of customer life cycle stages to identify groups of customers that are in each stage.

Linear hyperlink structure A hyperlink structure that resembles conventional paper documents in which the user reads pages in serial order.

Link checker A site management tool that examines each page on the site and reports any URLs that are broken, that seem to be broken, or that are in some way incorrect.

Link rot The undesirable situation of a site that contains a number of links that no longer work.

Liquidation broker An agent that finds buyers for unusable and excess inventory.

Load-balancing switch A piece of network hardware that monitors the workloads of servers attached to it and assigns incoming Web traffic to the server that has the most available capacity at that instant in time.

Local area network (LAN) A network that connects workstations and PCs within a single physical location.

Localization A type of language translation that considers multiple elements of the local environment, such as business and cultural practices, in addition to local dialect variations in the language.

Localized advertising Online advertising in which ads are generated in response to a search for products or services in a specific geographic area.

Lock-in effect The inherent greater value to customers of existing companies than new sites.

Log file A collection of data that shows information about Web site visitors' access habits.

Logical security The protection of assets using nonphysical means.

Long-arm statute A state law that creates personal jurisdiction for courts.

Machine translation Language translation that is done by software; such translation can reach speeds of 400,000 words per hour.

Macro virus A virus that is transmitted or contained inside a downloaded file attachment; it can cause damage to a computer and reveal otherwise confidential information.

Mail bomb A security attack in which many computers (hundreds or thousands) each send a message to a particular address, exceeding the recipient's allowable mail limit and causing mail systems to malfunction; the computers are often under the surreptitious control of a third party.

Mail order model Synonymous with catalog model.

Mailing list An e-mail address that forwards messages to certain users who are subscribers.

Maintenance, repair, and operating (MRO) Commodity supplies, including general industrial merchandise and standard machine tools that are used in a variety of industries.

Managed service provider (MSP) A Web site hosting service firm; synonymous with ASP and CSP.

Man-in-the-middle exploit A message integrity violation in which the contents of the e-mail are changed in a way that negates the message's original meaning.

Many-to-many communications model A model of communications in which a number of entities communicate with a number of other entities.

Many-to-one communications model A model of communications in which a number of entities communicate with a single other entity.

Market A real or virtual space in which potential buyers and sellers come into contact with each other and agree on a medium of exchange (such as currency or barter).

Market segmentation The identification by advertisers of specific subsets of their markets that have common characteristics.

Marketing channel Each different pathway that a business uses to reach its customers.

Marketing mix The combination of elements that companies use to achieve their goals for selling and promoting their products and services.

Marketing strategy A particular marketing mix that is used to promote a company or product.

Marketspace A market that occurs in the virtual world instead of in the physical world.

Markup tags (tags) Web page code that provides formatting instructions that Web client software can understand.

Masquerading Pretending to be someone you are not (for example, by sending an e-mail that shows someone else as the sender) or representing a Web site as an original when it is an imposter. Synonymous with spoofing.

Mass media The method of contacting potential customers through the distribution of broadcast, printed, billboard, or mailed advertising materials.

Meetup An in-person meeting between people who are acquainted through a blog.

Merchandising The combination of store design, layout, and product display intended to create an environment that encourages customers to buy.

Merchant account An account that a merchant must hold with a bank that allows the merchant to process payment card transactions.

Merchant bank A bank that does business with merchants who want to accept credit cards.

Mesh routing A version of fixed-point wireless that directly transmits Wi-Fi packets through hundreds of short-range transceivers that are located close to each other.

Message digest The number that results from the application of an encryption algorithm to plain text information.

Metalanguage A language that comprises a set of language elements and can be used to define other languages.

Metrics Measurements that companies use to assess the value of site visitor activity.

Microlending The practice of lending very small amounts of money to people who are starting or operating small businesses, especially in developing countries.

Micromarketing The practice of targeting very small and well-defined market segments.

Micropayments Internet payments for items costing very little—usually $1 or less.

Middleware Software that handles connections between electronic commerce software and accounting systems.

Minimum bid In an English auction, the price for an item at which the auctioning begins.

Minimum bid increment The amount by which one bid must exceed the previous bid.

Mobile commerce (m-commerce) Resources accessed using devices that have wireless connections, such as stock quotes, directions, weather forecasts, and airline flight schedules.

Mobile wallet A mobile phone that operates as a credit card.

Monetizing The conversion of existing regular site visitors seeking free information or services into fee-paying subscribers or purchasers of services.

Money laundering A technique used by criminals to convert money that they have obtained illegally into cash that they can spend without having it identified as the proceeds of an illegal activity.

Multipurpose Internet Mail Extension (MIME) An e-mail protocol that allows users to attach binary files to e-mail messages.

Multivector virus A virus that can enter a computer system in several different ways.

Näive Bayesian filter E-mail filtering software that classifies messages based on learned patterns indicated by the e-mail user's categorization of incoming mail. The filter eventually learns to recognize spam and filter it out.

Name changing (typosquatting) A problem that occurs when someone registers purposely misspelled variations of well-known domain names. These variants sometimes lure consumers who make typographical errors when entering a URL.

Name stealing Theft of a Web site's name that occurs when someone, posing as a site's administrator, changes the ownership of the domain name assigned to the site to another site and owner.

Necessity The category of computer security that addresses data delay or data denial threats.

Necessity threat The disruption of normal computer processing or denial of processing. Also called delay, denial, or denial-of-service threat (DoS).

Negligent tort A tortious act in which the seller unintentionally provides a harmful product.

Net bandwidth The actual speed information travels, taking into account traffic on the communication channel at any given time.

Network access points (NAPs) The four primary connection points for access to the Internet backbone in the United States.

Network access providers The few large companies that are the primary providers of Internet access; they, in turn, sell Internet access to smaller Internet service providers.

Network Address Translation (NAT) device A computer that converts private IP addresses into normal IP addresses when they forward packets to the Internet.

Network Control Protocol (NCP) Used by ARPANET in the early 1970s to route messages in its experimental wide area network.

Network economic structure A business structure wherein firms coordinate their strategies, resources, and skill sets by forming a long-term, stable relationship based on a shared purpose.

Network effect An increase in the value of a network to its participants, which occurs as more people or organizations participate in the network.

Network operations Web site staff whose responsibilities include load estimation and monitoring, resolving network problems as they arise, designing and implementing fault-resistance technologies, and managing any network operations that are outsourced to ISPs, CSPs, or telephone companies.

Network specification The set of rules that equipment connected to a network must follow.

Newsgroup A topic area in Usenet where people read and post articles.

Nexus The association between a tax-paying entity and a governmental taxing authority.

Nigerian scam (419 scam) A scam in which the victim receives an e-mail from a Nigerian government official requesting assistance in moving money to a foreign bank account.

Nonrepudiation Verification that a particular transaction actually occurred; this prevents parties from denying a transaction's validity or its existence.

Notice The expression of a change in rules (usually, legal or cultural rules) typically represented by a physical boundary.

N-tier architecture Higher-order client-server architectures that have more than three tiers.

Occasion segmentation Behavioral segmentation that is based on things that happen at a specific time or occasion.

Octet An 8-bit number.

Offer A declaration of willingness to buy or sell a product or service; it includes sufficient details to be firm, precise, and unambiguous.

One-to-many communication model A model of communications in which one entity communicates with a number of other entities.

One-to-one communication model A model of communications in which one entity communicates with one other entity.

One-to-one marketing A highly customized approach to offering products and services that match the needs of a particular customer.

One-way function An algorithm that cannot be converted back to its original value.

Online community Synonymous with virtual community, which is an electronic gathering place for people with common interests.

Online marketing manager An employee who specializes in the specific techniques used to build brands and increase market share using the Web site and other online tools, such as e-mail marketing.

Ontology A set of standards that defines, in detail, the structure of a particular knowledge domain; in the Semantic Web, it defines the relationships among RDF standards and specific XML tags.

Open architecture The philosophy behind the Internet that dictates that independent networks should not require any internal changes to be connected to the network, packets that do not arrive at their destinations must be retransmitted from their source network, routers do not retain information about the packets they handle, and no global control exists over the network.

Open auction (open-outcry auction) An auction in which bids are publicly announced (such as an English auction).

Open EDI EDI conducted on the Internet instead of over private leased lines.

Open loop system A payment card arrangement involving a consumer and his or her bank, a merchant and its bank, and a third party (such as Visa or MasterCard) that processes transactions between the consumer and merchant.

Open-outcry double auction A double auction in which buy and sell offers are announced publicly. Typically conducted in exchange floor or trading pit environments for items of known quality, such as securities or graded agricultural products, that are regularly traded in large quantities.

Open session A continuous connection that is maintained between a client and server on the Internet.

Open-source software Software that is developed by a community of programmers who make the software available for download and use at no cost.

Opening tag An HTML tag that precedes the text that a tag affects.

Opportunity cost Lost benefits from an action not taken.

Optical fiber A data transmission cable that uses glass fibers to achieve bandwidths up to 10 Gbps.

Opt-in A personal information collection policy in which the company collecting the information does not use the information for any other purpose (or sell or rent the information) unless the customer specifically chooses to allow that use.

Opt-in e-mail The practice of sending e-mail messages to people who have requested information on a particular topic or about a specific product.

Opt-out A personal information collection policy in which the company collecting the information assumes that the customer does not object to the company's use of the information unless the customer specifically chooses to deny permission.

Organized crime Unlawful activities conducted by a highly organized, disciplined association for profit. Also called racketeering.

Orphan file A file on a Web site that is not linked to any page.

Outsourcing The hiring of another company to perform design, implementation, or operational tasks for an information systems project.

Packet-filter firewall A firewall that examines all data flowing back and forth between a trusted network and the Internet.

Packets The small pieces of files and e-mail messages that travel over the Internet.

Packet-switched A network in which packets are labeled electronically with their origin, sequence, and destination addresses. Packets travel from computer to computer along the interconnected networks until they reach their destination. Each packet can take a different path through the interconnected networks and the packets may arrive out of order. The destination computer collects the packets and reassembles the original file or e-mail message from the pieces in each packet.

Page view A page request made by a Web site visitor.

Page-based application system Application server software that returns pages generated by scripts that include the rules for presenting data on the Web page with the business logic.

Paid placement (sponsorship) The purchasing of a top listing in results listings for a particular set of search terms.

Partial outsourcing The outsourcing of the design, development, implementation, or operation of specific portions of an electronic commerce system.

Participatory journalism The practice of inviting readers to help write an online newspaper.

Patent An exclusive right to make, use, and sell an invention granted by a government to the inventor.

Payment card A general term for plastic cards used instead of cash to make purchases, including credit cards, debit cards, and charge cards.

Payment processing service provider A third-party company that handles payment card processing for online businesses.

Pay-per-click model A revenue model in which an affiliate earns payment each time a site visitor clicks a link to load the seller's page.

Pay-per-conversion model A revenue model in which an affiliate earns payment each time a site visitor is converted from a visitor into either a qualified prospect or a customer.

Peer-to-peer (P2P) payment system Payments from one type of entity to another of the same type.

Per se defamation A legal cause of action in which a court deems some types of statements to be so negative that injury is assumed.

Perimeter expansion The increase in firewall limits beyond traditional borders caused by telecommuting.

Permission marketing A marketing strategy that only sends specific information to people who have indicated an interest in receiving information about the product or service being promoted.

Persistent cookie A cookie that exists indefinitely.

Personal area network (PAN) A small, low-bandwidth Bluetooth network of up to 10 networks of eight devices each. It used for tasks such as wireless synchronization of laptop computers with desktop computers and wireless printing from laptops, PDAs, or mobile phones. Synonymous with piconet.

Personal contact A method of identifying and reaching customers that involves searching for, qualifying, and contacting potential customers.

Personal firewall A software-only firewall that is installed on an individual client computer.

Personal jurisdiction A court's authority to hear a case based on the residency of the defendant; a court has personal jurisdiction over a case if the defendant is a resident of the state in which the court is located.

Personal shopper An intelligent agent program that learns a customer's preferences and makes suggestions.

Pharming attack The use of a zombie farm, often by an organized crime association, to launch a massive phishing attack.

Phishing expedition A masquerading attack that combines spam with spoofing. The perpetrator sends millions of spam e-mails that appear to be from a respectable company. The e-mails contain a link to a Web page that is designed to look exactly like the company's site. The victim is encouraged to enter his or her username, password, and sometimes credit card information.

Physical security Tangible protection devices such as alarms, guards, fireproof doors, fences, and vaults.

Piconet A small, low-bandwidth Bluetooth network of up to 10 networks of eight devices each. It is used for tasks such as wireless synchronization of laptop computers with desktop computers and wireless printing from laptops, PDAs, or mobile phones. Synonymous with personal area network.

Ping (Packet Internet Groper) A program that tests the connectivity between two computers connected to the Internet.

Place (distribution) The need to have products or services available in many different locations.

Plain old telephone service (POTS) The network that connects telephones; it provides a reliable data transmission bandwidth of about 56 Kbps.

Plain text Normal, unencrypted text.

Plug-in An application that helps a browser to display information (such as video or animation) but is not part of the browser.

Pop-behind ad A pop-up ad that is followed very quickly by a command that returns the focus to the original browser window, resulting in an ad that is parked behind the user's browser waiting to appear when the browser is closed.

Pop-up ad An ad that appears in its own window when the user opens or closes a Web page.

Portal A Web site that serves as a customizable home base from which users do their searching, navigating, and other Web-based activity. Synonymous with Web portal.

Post Office Protocol (POP) The protocol responsible for retrieving e-mail from a mail server.

Postimplementation audit (postaudit review) A formal review of a project after it is up and running.

Power A form of control over physical space (such as a state) and the people and objects that reside in that space.

Presence The public image conveyed by an organization to its stakeholders.

Pretty Good Privacy (PGP) A popular technology used to implement public-key encryption to protect the privacy of e-mail messages.

Price The amount a customer pays for a product.

Primary activities Activities that are required to do business: design, production, promotion, marketing, delivery, and support of products or services.

Privacy The protection of individual rights to nondisclosure of information.

Private company marketplace A marketplace that provides auctions, requests for quotes postings, and other features to companies that want to operate their own marketplace.

Private IP addresses A series of IP numbers that have been set aside for subnet use and are not permitted on packets that travel on the Internet.

Private key A single key that is used to encrypt and decrypt messages. Synonymous with symmetric key.

Private network A private, leased-line connection between two companies that physically links their individual computers or intranets.

Private store A password-protected area of a Web site that offers individual customers negotiated price reductions on a limited selection of products and other customized features.

Private valuation The amount a bidder is willing to pay for an item that is up for auction.

Private-key encryption The encoding of a message using a single numeric key to encode and decode data, it requires both the sender and receiver of the message to know the key, which must be guarded from public disclosure.

Procurement The business activity that includes all purchasing activities plus the monitoring of all elements of purchase transactions.

Product The physical item or service that a company is selling.

Product disparagement A statement that is false and injures the reputation of a product or service.

Project management Formal techniques for planning and controlling activities undertaken to achieve a specific goal.

Project management software Application software that provides built-in tools for managing people, resources, and schedules.

Project manager A person with specific training or skills in tracking costs and the accomplishment of specific objectives in a project.

Project portfolio management A technique in which each project is monitored as if it were an investment in a financial portfolio.

Project portfolio manager An employee who is responsible for tracking all ongoing projects and managing them as a portfolio.

Promotion Any means of spreading the word about a product.

Property tax Taxes levied by states and local governments on the personal property and real estate used in a business.

Proprietary architecture The use of vendor-specific communication protocols by computer manufacturers in the early days of computing, preventing computers made by different manufacturers from being connected to each other. Also called closed architecture.

Prospecting The part of personal contact selling in which the salesperson identifies potential customers.

Protocol A collection of rules for formatting, ordering, and error-checking data sent across a network.

Proxy bid In an electronic auction, a predetermined maximum bid submitted by a bidder.

Proxy server firewall A firewall that communicates with the Internet on behalf of the trusted network.

Psychographic segmentation The grouping of customers by variables such as social class, personality, or their approach to life.

Public key One of a pair of mathematically related numeric keys, it is used to encrypt messages and is freely distributed to the public.

Public marketplace A vertical portal that is open to new buyers and sellers just entering an industry.

Public network An extranet that allows the public to access its intranet or when two or more companies link their intranets.

Public-key encryption The encoding of messages using two mathematically related but distinct numeric keys.

Purchasing card (p-card) Payment cards that give individual managers the ability to make multiple small purchases at their discretion while providing cost tracking information to the procurement office.

Pure dot-com A company that operates only online; also called dot-com.

Python A scripting language that can be used in dynamic Web page generation.

QQ.com Chinese Web server software.

Racketeering Unlawful activities conducted by a highly organized, disciplined association for profit. Also called organized crime.

Radio frequency identification device (RFID) Small chips that include radio transponders; they can be used to track inventory as it moves through an industry value chain.

Rational branding An advertising strategy that substitutes an offer to help Web users in some way in exchange for their viewing an ad.

Reintermediation The introduction of a new intermediary into a value chain.

Remote server administration Control of a Web site by an administrator from any Internet-connected computer.

Repeat visits Subsequent visits a Web site visitor makes to a particular page.

Repeater A transmitter-receiver device used in a fixed-point wireless network to forward a radio signal from the ISP to customers. Synonymous with transceiver.

Replenishment purchasing Direct materials purchasing in which the company negotiates long-term contracts for most of the materials that it will need. Also called contract purchasing.

Representational State Transfer (REST) A principle that describes the way the Web uses networking architecture to identify and locate Web pages and the elements (graphics) that make up those Web pages.

Request header The part of an HTTP message from a client to a server that contains additional information about the client and more information about the request.

Request line The part of an HTTP message from a client to a server that contains a command, the name of the target resource (without the protocol or domain name), and the protocol name and version.

Request message The HTTP message that a Web client sends to request a file or files from a Web server.

Reserve price (reserve) The minimum price a seller will accept for an item sold at auction.

Resource description framework (RDF) A set of standards for XML syntax.

Response header field In a client/server transmission, it follows the response header line and returns information describing the server's attributes.

Response header line The part of a message from a server to a client that indicates the HTTP version used by the server, status of the response, and an explanation of the status information.

Response message The reply that a Web server sends in response to a client request.

Response time The amount of time a server requires to process one request.

RESTful applications (REST) Web services that are built on the REST model.

RESTful design The use of the REST model in building Web services.

Retained customer A customer who returns to a site one or more times after making his or her first purchase.

Retention costs The costs of inducing customers to return to a Web site and buy again.

Return on investment (ROI) A method for evaluating the potential costs and benefits of a proposed capital investment.

Revenue model The combination of strategies and techniques that a company uses to generate cash flow into the business from customers.

Reverse auction (seller-bid auction) A type of auction in which sellers bid prices for which they are willing to sell items or services.

Reverse bid The process in which an auction customer seeks products by describing an item or service in which he or she is interested, and then entertains responses from merchants who offer to supply the item at a particular price.

Reverse link checker A Web site management program that checks on sites with which a company has entered a link exchange program and ensures that link exchange partners are fulfilling their obligation to include a link back to the company's Web site.

Rich media ad A Web ad that generates graphical activity that "floats" over the Web page itself instead of opening in a separate window. Also called an active ad.

Rich media objects Programming components of attention-grabbing Web banner ads.

Right of publicity A limited right to control others' commercial use of an individual's name, image, likeness, or identifying aspect of identity.

Roaming The shifting of Wi-Fi devices from one WAP to another without requiring intervention by the user.

Robot (bot) A program that automatically searches the Web to find Web pages that might be interesting to people.

Robotic network A network that can act as an attacking unit, sending spam or launching denial-of-service attacks against specific Web sites. Synonymous with botnet or zombie farm.

Router A computer that determines the best way for data packets to move forward to their destination.

Router computers (routing computers) The computers that decide how best to forward each packet of information as it travels on the Internet to its destination. Synonymous with gateway computers and routers.

Routing algorithm The program used by a router to determine the best path for data packets to travel.

Routing table Synonymous with configuration table, which is information about connections that lead to particular groups of routers, specifications on which connections to use first, and rules for handling instances of heavy packet traffic and network congestion.

Ruby on Rails A Web programming development framework for creating dynamic Web pages that present users with an interface similar in appearance to application software running in a Web browser.

Scalable A system's ability to be adapted to meet changing requirements.

Scaling problem The exponential increase in cost that results from the expansion of a private network.

Scrip A limited-use digital or paper value store issued by a private company rather than a government. It generally must be exchanged for goods or services with the company that issued it and usually cannot be exchanged for cash.

Scripting language A programming language that provides scripts, or commands, that are executed.

Sealed-bid auction An auction in which bidders submit their bids independently and are usually prohibited from sharing information with each other.

Search engine Web software that finds other pages based on key word matching.

Search engine optimization (search engine positioning, search engine placement) The combined art and science of having a particular URL listed near the top of search engine results.

Search engine placement broker A company that aggregates inclusion and placement rights on multiple search engines and then sells those combination packages to advertisers.

Search engine ranking The weighting of the factors that search engines use to decide which URLs will appear first on searches for a particular search term.

Search term sponsorship The option of purchasing a top listing on results pages for a particular set of search terms. Also called paid placement or sponsorship.

Search utility The part of a search engine that finds matching Web pages for search terms.

Second-price sealed-bid auction A type of auction in which bidders submit their bids independently and privately; the highest bidder wins the auction but pays only the amount bid by the second-highest bidder.

Secrecy The category of computer security that addresses the protection of data from unauthorized disclosure and confirmation of data source authenticity.

Secure envelope A security utility that encapsulates a message and provides secrecy, integrity, and client/server authentication.

Secure Sockets Layer (SSL) A protocol for transmitting private information securely over the Internet.

Secure Sockets Layer-Extended Validation (SSL-EV) digital certificate A more secure certificate for which a certification authority must confirm the legal existence of the organization by verifying the organization's registered legal name and other facts.

Security policy A written statement describing assets to be protected, the reasons for protecting the assets, the parties responsible for protection, and acceptable and unacceptable behaviors.

Segment Also called a market segment; a subset of a company's potential customer pool that has common demographic characteristics.

Self-hosting A system of Web hosting in which the online business owns and maintains the server and all its software.

Semantic Web A project initiated by Tim Berners-Lee intended to blend technologies and information to create a next-generation Web in which words on Web pages are tagged (using XML) with their meanings.

Server A powerful computer dedicated to managing disk drives, printers, or network traffic.

Server architecture The different ways that servers can be connected to each other and to related hardware such as routers and switches.

Server farm A large collection of electronic commerce Web site servers.

Server-level filtering An e-mail content filtering technique in which the filtering software resides on the mail server.

Server software The software that a server computer uses to make files and programs available to other computers on the same network.

Server-side electronic wallet An electronic wallet that stores a customer's information on a remote server that belongs to a particular merchant or to the wallet's publisher.

Server-side scripting A Web page response approach in which programs running on the Web server create Web pages before sending them back to the requesting Web clients as parts of response messages.

Service mark A distinctive mark, device, motto, or implement used to identify services provided by a company.

Session cookie A cookie that exists only until you shut down your browser.

Session key A key used by an encryption algorithm to create cipher text from plain text during a single secure session.

Shared hosting A Web hosting arrangement in which the hosting company provides Web space on a server computer that also hosts other Web sites.

Shill bidder An individual employed by a seller or auctioneer who makes bids on behalf of the seller, sometimes artificially inflating an item's price. Shill bidders may be prohibited by the rules of a particular auction.

Shipping profile The collection of attributes, including weight and size, that affect how easily a product can be packaged and delivered.

Shopping cart An electronic commerce utility that keeps track of items selected for purchase and automates the purchasing process.

Short message service (SMS) A protocol used to transmit short text messages to cell phones and other wireless devices.

Shrink-wrap acceptance A buyer's acceptance of the conditions of the EULA, demonstrated by removing the shrink wrap from the product box.

Signature Any symbol executed or adopted for the purpose of authenticating a writing.

Signed (message or code) The status of a message or Web page when it contains an attached digital certificate.

Simple Mail Transfer Protocol (SMTP) A standardized protocol used by a mail server to format and administer e-mail.

Simple Object Access Protocol (SOAP) A message-passing protocol that defines how to send marked up data from one software application to another across a network.

Single-use card A payment card with disposable numbers, which gives consumers a unique card number that is valid for one transaction only.

Site map On a hierarchically structured Web site, a page that contains a map or listing of the Web pages in their hierarchical order.

Site sponsorship The opportunity for an advertiser to sponsor part or all of a Web site to promote its products, services, or brands. Site sponsorships are more subtle than banner or pop-up ads.

Skyscraper ad A large banner ad on the side of a Web page that remains visible as the user scrolls down through the page.

Small payment Any payment of less than $10.

Smart card A plastic card with an embedded microchip that contains information about the card owner.

Smart phone A mobile phone that includes a functional Web browser and a full keyboard.

Sniffer program A program that taps into the Internet and records information that passes through a router from the data's source to its destination.

Snipe The act of placing a winning bid in an online auction at the last possible moment.

Sniping software Auction software that observes auction progress until the last second or two of the auction clock, then places a bid high enough to win the auction.

Social networking administrator An employee who is responsible for managing the virtual community elements of the Web operation.

Social networking site A Web site that individuals and businesses can use to conduct social interactions online.

Social shopping The practice of bringing buyers and sellers together in a social network to facilitate retail sales.

Software agent A program that performs information gathering, information filtering, and/or mediation on behalf of a person or entity. Synonymous with intelligent software agent.

Sourcing The part of procurement devoted to identifying suppliers and determining the qualifications of those suppliers.

Spam (unsolicited commercial e-mail or bulk mail) Electronic junk mail.

Spear phishing A phishing expedition in which the e-mails are carefully designed to target a particular person or organization.

Spend The total dollar amount of the goods and services that a company buys during a year.

Spider The first part of a search engine, it automatically and frequently searches the Web to find pages and updates its database of information about old Web sites.

Sponsored top-level domain (sTLD) A top-level domain for which an organization other than ICANN is responsible.

Spoofing Synonymous with masquerading, which is pretending to be someone you are not (for example, by sending an e-mail that shows someone else as the sender) or representing a Web site as an original when it is an imposter.

Spot market A loosely organized market within a specific industry.

Spot purchasing Direct materials purchasing that occurs within a spot market.

Stakeholders The various entities involved in a business; these include customers, suppliers, employees, stockholders, neighbors, and the general public.

Standard Generalized Markup Language (SGML) An old, complex text markup language used to create frequently revised documents that need to be printed in various formats.

Start page In a hierarchical Web page structure, the introductory page of a Web site. Synonymous with home page.

Stateless connection A connection between a client and server over the Internet in which each transmission of information is independent; no continuous connection is maintained.

Static catalog A simple list of products written in HTML and displayed on a Web page or a series of Web pages.

Static page A Web page that displays unchanging information retrieved from a disk.

Statistical modeling A technique that tests theories that CRM analysts have about relationships among elements of customer and sales data.

Statute of Frauds State law that specifies that contracts for the sale of goods worth more than $500 and contracts that require actions that cannot be completed within one year must be created by a signed writing.

Statutory law That part of British and U.S. law that comprises laws passed by elected legislative bodies.

Steganography The hiding of information (such as commands) within another piece of information.

Stickiness The ability of a Web site to keep visitors at its site and to attract repeat visitors.

Sticky The condition of having stickiness.

Stockout A loss of sales suffered by a retailer when it does not have specific goods on its shelves that customers want to buy.

Stored value card Either an elaborate smart card or a simple plastic card with a magnetic strip that records currency balance, such as a prepaid phone, copy, subway, or bus card.

Strategic alliance The coordination of strategies, resources, and skill sets by companies into long-term, stable relationships with other companies and individuals based on shared purposes.

Strategic business unit (SBU) A unit within a company that is organized around a specific combination of product, distribution channel, and customer type.

Strategic partners The entities taking part in a strategic alliance.

Strategic partnership Synonymous with strategic alliance.

Style sheet A set of instructions used for Web page formatting. It is stored in a separate file and lets designers apply specific formatting styles to a page.

Subject-matter jurisdiction A court's authority to decide a dispute between entities based on the issue of dispute.

Subnetting The use of reserved private IP addresses within LANs and WANs to provide additional address space.

Sufficient jurisdiction A court's ability to hear a matter if it has both subject-matter jurisdiction and personal jurisdiction.

Supply alliances Long-term relationships among participants in the supply chain.

Supply chain The part of an industry value chain that precedes a particular strategic business unit. It includes the network of suppliers, transportation firms, and brokers that combine to provide a material or service to the strategic business unit.

Supply chain management The process of taking an active role in working with suppliers and other participants in the supply chain to improve products and processes.

Supply chain management (SCM) software Software used by companies to coordinate planning and operations with their partners in the industry supply chains of which they are members.

Supply management Synonymous with procurement, which is the business activity that includes all purchasing activities plus the monitoring of all elements of purchase transactions.

Supply web An industry value chain that includes many participants that are interconnected in a web or network configuration.

Supporting activities Secondary activities that back up primary business activities. These include human resource management, purchasing, and technology development.

SWOT analysis Evaluation of the strengths and weaknesses of a business unit, and identification of the opportunities presented by the markets of the business unit and threats posed by competitors of the business unit.

Symmetric connection An Internet connection that provides the same bandwidth in both directions.

Symmetric encryption The encryption of a message using a single numeric key to encode and decode data. Synonymous with private-key encryption.

Systems administrator A member of an electronic commerce team who understands the server hardware and software and is responsible for the system's reliable and secure operation.

T1 High-bandwidth Internet connections that operate at 1.544 Mbps.

T3 High-bandwidth Internet connections that operate at 44.736 Mbps.

Tariff A tax levied on products as they enter the country; also called duty or customs duty.

TCP/IP The set of protocols that provide the basis for the operation of the Internet. The TCP protocol includes rules that computers on a network use to establish and break connections. The IP protocol determines routing of data packets.

Technology-enabled customer relationship management Synonymous with technology-enabled relationship management.

Technology-enabled relationship management The business practice of obtaining detailed information about a customer's behavior, preferences, needs, and buying patterns and using that information to set prices, negotiate terms, tailor promotions, add product features, and provide other customized interactions.

Teergrubing A antispamming approach in which the receiving computer launches a return attack against the spammer, sending e-mail messages back to the computer that originated the suspected spam.

Telecommuting An employment arrangement in which the employee logs in to the company computer from an off-site location through the Internet instead of traveling to an office.

Telework Synonymous with telecommuting.

Telnet A program that allows users to log on to a computer and access its contents from a remote location.

Telnet protocol The set of rules used by Telnet programs.

Terms of service (ToS) Rules and regulations intended to limit the Web site owner's liability for what a visitor might do with information obtained from the site.

Text ad A short promotional message that does not use any graphic elements and is usually placed along the top or right side of a Web page.

Text markup language A language that specifies a set of tags that are inserted into the text.

Third-generation (3G) mobile phone A cell phone that incorporates the latest transmission technologies to achieve data speeds of up to 2 Mbps and also uses the SMS protocol to send and receive text messages.

Third-party cookie A cookie that originates on a Web site other than the site being visited.

Third-party logistics (3PL) provider A transportation or freight company that operates all or most of a customer's material movement activities.

Threat An act or object that poses a danger to assets.

Three-tier architecture A client/server architecture that builds on the two-tier architecture by adding applications and their associated databases that supply non-HTML information to the Web server on request.

Throughput The number of HTTP requests that a particular hardware and software combination can process in a unit of time.

Tier-one suppliers The capable suppliers that work directly with and have long-term relationships with businesses.

Tier-three suppliers Suppliers that provide components and raw materials to tier-two suppliers.

Tier-two suppliers Suppliers that provide components and raw materials to tier-one suppliers.

Top-level domain (TLD) The last part of a domain name; the most general identifier in the name.

Tort An action taken by a legal entity that causes harm to another legal entity.

Total cost of ownership (TCO) Business activity costs including the costs of hiring, training, and paying the personnel who will design the Web site, write or customize the software, create the content, and operate and maintain the site. TCO also includes hardware and software costs.

Touchpoint Online and offline customer contact points.

Touchpoint consistency The provision of similar levels and quality of service in all of a company's interactions with its customers, whether those interactions occur in person, on the telephone, or online.

Tracert A route-tracing program that sends data packets to every computer on the path (Internet) between one computer and another computer and clocks the packets' round-trip times, providing an indication of the time it takes a message to travel from one computer to another and back, pinpointing any data traffic congestion, and ensuring that the remote computer is online.

Trade name The name (or a part of that name) that a business uses to identify itself.

Trademark A distinctive mark, device, motto, or implement that a company affixes to the goods it produces for identification purposes.

Trademark dilution The reduction of the distinctive quality of a trademark by alternative uses.

Trading partners Businesses that engage in EDI with one another.

Transaction An exchange of value.

Transaction costs The total of all costs incurred by a buyer and seller as they gather information and negotiate a transaction.

Transaction processing Processes that occur as part of completing a sale; these include calculation of any discounts, taxes, or shipping costs and transmission of payment data (such as a credit card number).

Transaction sets Formats for specific business data interchanges using EDI.

Transaction taxes Sales taxes, use taxes, excise taxes, and customs duties that are levied on the products or services that a company sells or uses.

Transceiver A transmitter-receiver device used in a fixed-point wireless network to forward a radio signal from the ISP to customers. Synonymous with repeater.

Transmission Control Protocol The protocol that includes rules that computers on a network use to establish and break connections. See TCP/IP.

Trial visit The first visit a Web site visitor makes to a particular page.

Trigger word A key word used to jog the memory of visitors and remind them of something they want to buy on the site.

Triple Data Encryption Standard (3DES) A robust version of the Data Encryption Standard used by the U.S. government that cannot be cracked even with today's supercomputers.

Trojan horse A program hidden inside another program or Web page that masks its true purpose (usually destructive).

Trusted (network) A network that is within a firewall.

Tweet A short message sent from one Twitter user to another.

Two-tier client/server architecture A client/server architecture in which only a client and server are involved in the requests and responses that flow between them over the Internet.

Ultimate consumer orientation A focus on the needs of the consumer who is at the end of an industry value chain.

Ultra Wideband (UWB) A wireless communication technology that provides wide bandwidth (up to about 480 Mbps in current versions) connections over short distances (30 to 100 feet).

Uniform Resource Locator (URL) Names and abbreviations representing the IP address of a particular Web page. Contains the protocol used to access the page and the page's location. Used in place of dotted quad notations.

Universal Description, Discovery and Integration (UDDI) specification The set of protocols that identify locations of Web services and their associated WSDL descriptions.

Unsolicited commercial e-mail (UCE) Electronic junk mail that can include solicitations, advertisements, or e-mail chain letters. Also called spam or bulk mail.

Untrusted (network) A network that is outside a firewall.

Untrusted Java applet A Java applet that is not known to be secure.

Upload bandwidth Synonymous with upstream bandwidth.

Upstream bandwidth The connection that occurs when you send information from your connection to your ISP.

Upstream strategies Tactics that focus on reducing costs or generating value by working with suppliers or inbound logistics.

URL broker A business that sells or auctions domain names that it believes others will find valuable.

Usability testing The testing and evaluation of a company's Web site for ease of use by visitors.

Usage-based market segmentation Customizing visitor experiences to match the site usage behavior patterns of each visitor or type of visitor.

Use tax A tax levied by a state on property used in that state that was not purchased in that state.

Usenet (User's News Network) One of the first mailing lists; it allows subscribers to read and post articles within topic areas.

Usenet newsgroup Message posting areas on Usenet computers in which interested persons (primarily from the education and research communities) can discuss those topic areas.

Value chain A way of organizing the activities that each strategic business unit undertakes to design, produce, promote, market, deliver, and support the products or services it sells.

Value system Synonymous with industry value chain.

Value-added network (VAN) An independent company that provides connection and EDI transaction forwarding services to businesses engaged in EDI.

Venture capitalist A very wealthy individual or investment firm that invests in small companies that are about to grow rapidly. By investing large amounts of money (between a million and a few hundred million dollars), venture capitalists attempt to help these growing companies become large enough to sell stock to the public.

Vertical integration The practice of an existing firm replacing one of its suppliers with its own strategic business unit that creates the supplied product.

Vertical portal (vortal) A vertically integrated Web information hub focusing on an individual industry.

Vicarious copyright infringement The violation of an organization's rights that occurs when a company capable of supervising the infringing activity fails to do so and obtains a financial benefit from the infringing activity.

Vickrey auction Synonymous with second-price sealed-bid auction. Named for William Vickrey, who won the 1996 Nobel Prize in Economics for his studies of the properties of this auction type.

Viral marketing Tactics that rely on existing customers to tell other persons—the company's prospective customers—about the products or services they have enjoyed using.

Virtual community An electronic gathering place for people with common interests.

Virtual company A strategic alliance occurring among companies that operate on the Internet.

Virtual host Multiple servers that exist on a single computer.

Virtual learning network A virtual community used for distance learning.

Virtual model A graphic image built from customer measurements and physical traits on which customers can try clothes. Typically found on sites selling clothing and accessories.

Virtual private network (VPN) A network that uses public networks and their protocols to transmit sensitive data using a system called "tunneling" or "encapsulation."

Virtual server Synonymous with virtual host.

Virus Software that attaches itself to another program and can cause damage when the host program is activated.

Visit The request of a Web site visitor for a page from a Web site.

Voice-grade line Telephone wiring that costs less than lines designed to carry data, is made of lower-grade copper, and was never intended to carry data. These lines can only carry limited bandwidth—usually less than 14 Kbps.

Warchalking The practice of placing a chalk mark on a building that has an easily entered wireless network.

Wardrivers Network attackers who drive around in cars using their wireless-equipped laptop computers to search for unprotected wireless network access points.

Warranty disclaimer A statement indicating that the seller will not honor some or all implied warranties.

Web See World Wide Web.

Web 2.0 Technologies that include software that allow users of Web sites to participate in the creation, editing, and distribution of content on a Web site owned and operated by a third party.

Web APIs Techniques for interconnection of programs with each other over the Web.

Web browser (Web browser software) Software that lets users read HTML documents and move from one HTML document to another using hyperlinks.

Web bug A tiny, invisible Web page graphic that provides a way for a Web site to place cookies.

Web catalog revenue model A revenue model of selling goods and services on the Web wherein the seller establishes a brand image that conveys quality and uses the strength of that image to sell through catalogs mailed to prospective buyers. Buyers place orders by mail or by calling the seller's toll-free telephone number.

Web client computer A computer that is connected to the Internet and is used to download Web pages.

Web client software Software that sends requests for Web page files to other computers.

Web community Synonymous with virtual community.

Web directory A listing of hyperlinks to Web pages that is organized into hierarchical categories.

Web EDI EDI on the Internet.

Web graphics designer A person trained in art, layout, and composition who also understands how Web pages are constructed and who ensures that the Web pages are visually appealing, are easy to use, and make consistent use of graphics elements from page to page.

Web log A Web site on which people post their thoughts and invite others to add commentary. Synonymous with blog.

Web portal Synonymous with portal, which is a Web site that serves as a customizable home base from which users do their searching, navigating, and other Web-based activity.

Web programmer A programmer who designs and writes the underlying code for dynamic database-driven Web pages.

Web server A computer that receives requests from many different Web clients and responds by sending HTML files back to those Web client computers.

Web server software Software that makes files available to other computers on the Internet.

Web services A combination of software tools that let application software in one organization communicate with other applications over a network using the SOAP, UDDI, and WSDL protocols.

Web Services Description Language (WSDL) A language that describes the characteristics of the logic units that make up specific Web services.

Web-wrap acceptance The compliance with EULA conditions with which a user agrees through the act of using a Web site.

White hat hackers Hackers who use their skills for positive purposes.

White list spam filter Software that looks for From addresses in incoming messages that are known to be good addresses.

Wide area network (WAN) A network of computers that are connected over large distances.

Wi-Fi (wireless Ethernet, 802.11b, 802.11a, 802.11g, 802.11n) The most common wireless connection technology for use on LANs; it can communicate through a wireless access point connected to a LAN to become a part of that LAN.

Winner's curse A psychological phenomenon that causes bidders to become caught up in the excitement of competitive bidding and bid more than their private valuation.

Wire transfer Synonymous with electronic funds transfer, which is the electronic transfer of account exchange information over secure private communications networks.

Wireless access point (WAP) A device that transmits network packets between Wi-Fi-equipped computers and other devices that are within its range.

Wireless Application Protocol (WAP) A protocol that allows Web pages formatted in HTML to be displayed on devices with small screens, such as PDAs and mobile phones.

Wireless Encryption Protocol (WEP) A set of rules for encrypting transmissions from wireless devices.

World Wide Web (Web) The subset of Internet computers that connects computers and their contents in a specific way, and that allows for easy sharing of data using a standard interface.

World Wide Web Consortium (W3C) A not-for-profit group that maintains standards for the Web.

Worm A virus that replicates itself on other machines.

Writing A tangible representation of the terms of a contract.

XML parser A program that can format an XML file so it can appear on the screen of a computer, a wireless PDA, a mobile phone, or other device.

XML vocabulary A set of XML tag definitions.

Yankee auction A type of English auction that offers multiple units of an item for sale and allows bidders to specify the quantity of items they want to buy.

Zombie A program that secretly takes over another computer for the purpose of launching attacks on other computers. Zombie attacks can be difficult to trace to their perpetrators.

Zombie farm A group of computers on which a hacker has planted zombie programs.

INDEX

Note: **Bold** page numbers indicate where a key term is defined in the text.

A

B

C

D

E

F

G

H

I

J

K

L

M

N

O

P

Q

R

S

T

U

V

W

X

Y

Z

CREDITS

CHAPTER 3

Figure 3-4 Reprinted with permission of Orbitz, LLC, Chicago, IL. © 2001–2009, Orbitz, LLC. All rights reserved

Figure 3-5 Courtesy of © 2009 Volkswagen of America, Inc.

Figure 3-6 Courtesy of © ACLU, 125 Broad Street, 18th Floor New York, NY 10004. 2009 American Civil Liberties Union. Reprinted with permission of the American Civil Liberties Union

Figures 3-7 Courtesy of © 2009 Lee Jeans, a division of VF Jeanswear Limited Partnership

CHAPTER 4

Figure 4-1 Courtesy of © 2003–2010 Sabre Inc. All rights reserved

Figure 4-13 Courtesy of © 2010 Google

CHAPTER 5

Figure 5-2 Courtesy of © 1994–2009 W. W. Grainger, Inc. All rights reserved

Figure 5-13 Courtesy of Moeller-Horcher. Source: Metro

CHAPTER 6

Figure 6-6 Courtesy of © 1999–2010. Steiner Associates LLC. All rights reserved

CHAPTER 7

Figure 7-6 Reproduced with permission of Yahoo! Inc. © 2010 Yahoo! Inc. YAHOO! and the YAHOO! logo are registered trademarks of Yahoo! Inc.

Figure 7-12 Courtesy of © Copyright 2009 SANRIO CO., LTD

CHAPTER 8

Figure 8-4 Courtesy of © Netcraft Ltd 2010. All Rights Reserved (http://www.netcraft.com)

Figure 8-10 Courtesy of © 1997–2009 Visualware Inc. All Rights Reserved

CHAPTER 9

Figure 9-1 Courtesy of © 2010 Google

Figure 9-2 Courtesy of Copyright © TeakWood Patio Furniture. All Rights Reserved

Figure 9-5 Courtesy of Copyright © 1995–2008 SalesCart™. All Rights Reserved

Figure 9-8 Reproduced with permission of Yahoo! Inc. © 2010 Yahoo! Inc. YAHOO! and the YAHOO! logo are registered trademarks of Yahoo! Inc.

Figure 9-11 © 2000–2010 salesforce.com, Inc. All rights reserved. Various trademarks held by their respective owners.

CHAPTER 10

Figure 10-3 and Figure 10-4 Courtesy of © 2010 Mozilla. All rights reserved

CHAPTER 11

Figure 11-2 Courtesy of © 1997–2010. Payment Online, Inc. All rights reserved